W9-CMN-222

DISCARDED

1751	Publication of the *Encyclopédie* begins: great vehicle of the Enlightenment
1756	The Diplomatic Revolution; outbreak of the Seven Years' War
1763	End of Seven Years' War: victory of Britain and Prussia; French losses in North America and India
1776	American Declaration of Independence
	The Wealth of Nations, by Adam Smith
1787	United States Constitution drawn up
1789	(June 20) Tennis-Court Oath: onset of the French Revolution
1799	(November 9-10) *Coup d'état* of Brumaire: Napoleon in power
1807	Tilsit settlement between Napoleon and Tsar Alexander I: Napoleon at height of power
1810	Revolution in Buenos Aires: Latin-American independence movement under way
1815	(June 18) Battle of Waterloo
	Vienna settlement reshaping Europe after Napoleonic Wars
1823	Monroe Doctrine: United States opposition to European intervention in New World
1830	Revolutions in France, Belgium, Poland
1832	First Reform Bill in Britain: victory of middle-class liberalism
1846	Repeal of British Corn Laws: another liberal victory
1848	Wave of liberal and nationalistic revolutions in Europe
	The Communist Manifesto, by Marx and Engels
1851	(December 2) *Coup d'état* by Louis Napoleon in France
1853	"Opening" of Japan by United States Commodore Perry
1859	*Origin of Species*, by Darwin
	On Liberty, by J. S. Mill
1861	Civil War in the United States
	Emancipation of serfs by Tsar Alexander II

901
B77h

121210

DATE DUE			

DISCARDED

Modern Civilization

Modern

Crane Brinton

McLean Professor of Ancient and Modern History, Harvard University

John B. Christopher

University of Rochester

Robert Lee Wolff

Archibald Cary Coolidge Professor of History, Harvard University

[library stamp, illegible]

Civilization

CARL A. RUDISILL LIBRARY
LENOIR RHYNE COLLEGE

A History of the Last Five Centuries

Second Edition

Prentice-Hall, Inc.   Englewood Cliffs, New Jersey

Modern Civilization

A History of the Last Five Centuries, Second Edition

Brinton, Christopher, and Wolff

© *Copyright 1957, 1967 by Prentice-Hall, Inc.,*
Englewood Cliffs, New Jersey
All rights reserved. No part of this book
may be reproduced in any form, by mimeograph or any other means,
without permission in writing from the publishers.
Library of Congress Catalog Card Number 67-13122
Printed in the United States of America

Maps by Vincent Kotschar

Picture Editor: Gabriele Wunderlich

Design by Walter Behnke

C

Current Printing (last digit):

15   14   13   12   11   10   9   8   7   6   5   4   3   2

Preface

In preparing this new edition of *Modern Civilization* we have had a double aim in view. We have sought to interpret the fast-moving and often bewildering events that have occurred since the publication of the first edition, ten years ago. And we have also rearranged the sequence of chapters, so that from the Renaissance (Chapter 3) on, each chapter is identical with its counterpart in the two-volume parent work, *A History of Civilization*. In addition, the maps and illustrations have been completely revamped. The result represents not a mere tinkering with the original book but a thorough revision and, we hope, a more attractive and more useful book.

In particular, the account of the ancient and medieval background of modern civilization in Chapter 1 has been strengthened. Chapter 2 brings together materials on western and eastern Europe at the close of the Middle Ages that were widely separated in the earlier edition. The chapters dealing with the eighteenth and early nineteenth centuries have been reorganized, so that the Russia of Peter the Great is considered together with the Old Régime and the international balance (Chapter 8), the American Revolution is now coupled with the Enlightenment (Chapter 9), the French Revolution with Napoleon (Chapter 10), and the Romantic movement with post-Napoleonic Europe (Chapter 11). The last three chapters have been entirely recast, so that Chapter 22 surveys the world scene following World War II, Chapter 23 continues the survey from the death of Stalin in 1953, and Chapter 24 assesses the main intellectual and cultural trends of the present century.

The reading suggestions have been greatly changed to take account both of the flow of new scholarly works and of the mounting tide of excellent paperbacks. New maps have been added, old ones redrawn, and all printed in two colors to make them more appealing and more instructive. The great majority of the illustrations are new and have been selected with an eye to their freshness and their appropriateness in reflecting the changing climates and "styles" of human culture.

A revision of these dimensions would scarcely have been possible without the help of many people. We thank all the teachers and students who have taken the trouble to write in, and express special appreciation to the experts who made detailed critiques of the parent volumes. We wish to record a particularly heavy debt to those with whom we have worked most closely: to the members of the Project Planning Department of Prentice-Hall, who have applied their skills and energies most generously and effectively; to Miss Gabriele Wunderlich, for her taste and resourcefulness in obtaining illustrative materials; to Vincent Kotschar, for his clear and painstaking revision of the maps; and to our colleagues and our families whose sympathy, understanding, and aid mean that the authors' salute is no mere gesture but a response from the heart.

CRANE BRINTON   JOHN B. CHRISTOPHER   ROBERT L. WOLFF

A Note on the Tables of Historical Dates

Some day psychologists may be able to tell us just what and how to remember. But at present we know little more than this: though a few exceptional people can absorb and tap at will large stores of systematically arranged facts—say, the list of popes from St. Peter on—most human beings cannot remember great systems of facts for very long unless they make fairly regular use of them. The average educated American does not remember such a relatively short list as that of the presidents of the United States. Indeed, if we never did any figuring at all, most of us would forget the multiplication table. Few of us make any regular use of history. Fortunately, the modern world is admirably supplied with works of ready reference that can free our minds for more useful work than just memorizing. The engineer, for example, does not need to keep in mind all the formulas and equations he might need; he has his engineer's handbook. So anyone using history has a host of reference books available in libraries, and on his desk he may have for immediate use such a storehouse of information as the one-volume *Encyclopaedia of World History* (Houghton Mifflin, 1948), edited by W. L. Langer.

Yet we do need something like a historian's equivalent of the multiplication table, if only to give us a frame of reference. The trouble with most historical tables, however, is that they are much too long and contain far too many facts for the average person. It is as if our multiplication table, instead of stopping with twelve times twelve, or even ten times ten, went on to fifty times fifty. The lists of dates to be found on the endpapers of the books are an attempt to construct the historian's equivalent of the multiplication table. It is a simple list of approximately a hundred dates, a kind of rough map of historic time. It is worth memorizing bit by bit and keeping in memory.

The list is not necessarily meant to include all the "hundred great dates." It is meant rather to assist the reader to keep his mind on the course of history by focusing on two threads that serve to put an order, a pattern, into a complex set of facts.

First, there is the concept of recorded history as a series of streams which have different sources on this earth, but which finally flow together in the One World of the present. Of course, some of the streams—the Chinese, the East Indian, the African, for example—have by no means wholly mingled, and are still present as separate currents. We take as the main stream in the endpapers, as we do in this book, our western civilization with its sources in the river valleys of the ancient Near East.

Second, there is the concept of a specific region or nation as a leader, a center, a focal point of historic change in our own western civilization at a given period. Periclean Athens, the Rome of the Caesars, and Victorian Britain are classic examples. Very broadly speaking, these centers of leadership have since 3000 B.C. swung westward and northward in a huge arc, from Egypt and Mesopotamia to Greece, Rome, western and central Europe, the United States. But the metaphor is imperfect. As we have taken pains to point out in this book, in the thousand years after the "fall" of the western Roman Empire, the Byzantines, the Slavs, and even perhaps the Moslems were in some ways quite as focal to western history as the medieval westerners. Moreover, leadership, especially in politics, may pass from one region to another, and former leaders like ancient Athens may fall almost to the status of ghost towns. Yet on the whole the area of western civilization constantly widens. Those parts left behind in the march of history do not lapse into an entirely separate existence; they remain a part, though only a subsidiary part, of the West.

A Note on the Reading Suggestions

A list of reading suggestions is appended to each chapter of this book. Almost all historical bibliographies nowadays begin with the statement that they are highly selective and do not, of course, aspire to be exhaustive. This apology is hardly necessary, for the fact is that in most fields of history we have outrun the possibility of bringing together in one list all the books and articles in all languages on a given topic. There are for the wide fields of this book, and in English alone, thousands of volumes and hundreds of thousands of articles in periodicals. The brief lists following each chapter are simply suggestions to the reader who wishes to explore a given topic further.

Each list attempts to give important and readable books, with special attention to paperbacks, which are often the editions most available in a college community. A useful guide is *Paperbound Books in Print*, a monthly review of new paperbacks, with encyclopaedic cumulative issues published three or four times a year. In addition, good readings in original sources, the contemporary documents and writings of an age, are sometimes listed, though the reader can supplement these listings from the text itself and from the footnotes. In addition, there are many good collections of sources for European history, notably the *Introduction to Contemporary Civilization in the West* (1954), prepared by faculty members at Columbia University; this begins with the Middle Ages and gives much longer selections from the sources than such compilations usually do.

Other good collections are to be found in the Portable Readers (published by Viking). There are also many source books and pamphlets on central or controversial problems in European history. A good example is K. M. Setton and H. R. Winkler, eds., *Great Problems in European Civilization*, rev. ed. (Prentice-Hall, 1965). Another is the series of pamphlets edited by R. W. Greenlaw under the general title "Problems in European Civilization" (D. C. Heath).

Our lists also include historical novels and, occasionally, dramas. Professional historians are likely to be somewhat severe in their standards for a historical novel. They naturally want its history to be sound, and at bottom they are likely to be somewhat prejudiced against the form. The historical novels listed here are all readable and all reasonably good as history. But note that historical novels, like historical films, though accurate on such material matters as authentic settings and appropriate costumes, often fail to capture the immaterial aspects—the psychology, the spirit—of the age they are written about. Many such novels motivate their characters, especially in love, as if they were modern Europeans and Americans. Exceptions to this rule are noted in the lists.

It is easy to assemble more material on a given topic than is furnished by our reading lists. American libraries, large and small, have catalogues with subject and title listings, as well as a section of reference books with encyclopaedias and bibliographies. Many libraries have open shelves where, once a single title is discovered, many others may be found in the immediate area. Perhaps the first printed list of books to be consulted is *A Guide to Historical Literature* (Macmillan, 1931) and its sequel, *The American Historical Association's Guide to Historical Literature* (Macmillan, 1961). For more recent books one can turn, for American history, to the *Harvard Guide to American History* (Belknap, 1954), edited by O. Handlin and others. And for the history of Europe and other areas there are many good bibliographies; see, for example, those in "The Rise of Modern Europe" series edited by W. L. Langer (Torch); in the multivolumed *Oxford History of England;* and in R. R. Palmer and J. Colton, *A History of the Modern World* (Knopf, 1965). For historical fiction, one may consult two older specialized guides: E. A. Baker, *A Guide to Historical Fiction* (Macmillan, 1914) and J. Nield, *A Guide to the Best Historical Novels and Tales* (Elkins, Mathews, and Marrot, 1929). The more recent *Fiction Catalogue* (Wilson, 1951) while covering much besides historical fiction, does furnish keys to books that cover particular countries and particular historical eras.

What is much more difficult than assembling titles is securing an evaluation of individual books. For older books the *Guide to Historical Literature*, already mentioned, gives the most useful references to critical reviews of the titles it discusses. *The Book Review Digest* gives capsule reviews and references to longer ones. For current books the weekly book section of *The New York Times* and *The Times Literary Supplement* (published in London) usually provide informative reviews of historical works soon after they are published. Later—sometimes as much as three years later—full scholarly appraisals are published in the *American Historical Review*, its British equivalent, the *English Historical Review*, and in more specialized reviews, such as the *Journal of Modern History, Speculum* (for medieval studies), *The Middle East Journal*, and many others. A new American scholarly journal, *History and Theory,* covers a field of great interest to historians today. By reading a few reviews of a book one can usually get a fair indication of its scope and quality. In our reading suggestions we have tried, within a very brief compass, to give comparable indications.

Contents

1

The Ancient and Medieval Background
of Modern Civilization   *1*

I THE NEW HISTORY AND THE OLD.   II THE FIRST MEN. *Prehistory. The Neolithic Revolution.*
III THE FIRST CIVILIZATIONS. *Our Own Beginnings: The Near East. Religious and Political Begin-*
nings.   IV GREECE AND ROME. *Some Greek "Firsts." The Style of Greco-Roman Culture. The Ro-*
mans. The Roman Empire. Early Christianity.   V THE MIDDLE AGES. *Early Middle Ages. Charle-*
magne, the Empire, the Northmen. Feudalism. Towns. The Church and Education. Medieval Learning.
Monarchy: France, England, Germany. Literature and the Arts. The Cathedral.

2

Europe at the Close of the Middle Ages   *33*

I INTRODUCTION.   II THE NEW MONARCHS IN THE WEST. *France: Louis XI. England: Henry*
VII. Spain: Ferdinand and Isabella.   III GERMANY AND ITALY. *Germany. The Italian States. The*
North Italian States. The "School of Europe."   IV ECONOMIC CHANGES IN THE WEST. *Trade. The*
Hanse. Venice, Industry. Banking. The Impact of Economic Change.   V TWO HEIRS OF OTHER
TRADITIONS: THE RUSSIANS AND THE OTTOMANS. *The Byzantine Heritage. The Ottoman Turks.*
VI MUSCOVITE RUSSIA TO 1682. *The Princes of Moscow. The Imperial Political Theory. Nobles and*
Serfs. The Reign of Ivan the Terrible. The Time of Troubles. The Role of the Zemski Sobor. *The Role*
of the Church. The Expansion of Russia. Russia and the West.   VII THE OTTOMAN SUCCESSOR-
STATE, 1453–1699. *The Ottoman System. Ottoman Expansion to 1566. Ottoman Decline, 1566–1699.*
The End of an Era.

The Renaissance 81

3

I INTRODUCTION. II LITERATURE AND THOUGHT. *The Rise of the Vernaculars. Humanism. Dante. Petrarch. Boccaccio. Preservation of the Classics. Chaucer and Rabelais. The Platonic Revival. Erasmus.* III THE ARTS. *Main Characteristics. Giotto. Patrons. Subjects, and Techniques. Leonardo. Michelangelo and Titian. Northern European Painting. Sculpture. Architecture. Music.* IV SCIENCE. *The Place of the Renaissance in the History of Science. Technology and Invention. Anatomy and Medicine. Astronomy.* V RELIGION. *The Relationship between the Renaissance and Religion. The Condition of the Church. Proposals for Reform and Renewal.* VI CONCLUSION: THE RENAISSANCE STYLE.

The Protestant Reformation 117

4

I PROTESTANT ORIGINS: LUTHER. *The End of Medieval Formal Religious Unity. Luther and the Ninety-Five Theses. Luther's Revolt. The Reasons for Luther's Success. The Opposition to Luther. The Lutheran Church. Knights' War and Peasants' Rebellion.* II PROTESTANT ORIGINS: ZWINGLI, CALVIN, AND OTHER FOUNDERS. *Zwingli. Calvin. The English Reformation. The Anabaptists. Unitarianism.* III PROTESTANT BELIEFS AND PRACTICES. *Common Denominators. Anglicanism. Lutheranism. Calvinism: Predestination. Calvinist Practice: Puritanism. The Left Wing.* IV THE CATHOLIC REFORMATION. *The Jesuits. The Inquisition. The Council of Trent.* V THE PLACE OF PROTESTANTISM IN HISTORY. *Protestantism and Progress. Protestantism and Capitalism. Protestantism and Nationalism.*

Dynastic and Religious Wars 151

5

I INTERNATIONAL POLITICS. *The Competitive State-System. Dynastic State and Nation State. Diplomacy. The Armed Forces.* II HABSBURG AND VALOIS. *The Italian Wars of Charles VIII and Louis XII. Charles V and Francis I: The First Round. Charles V and Francis I: The Second Round. The Peace of Augsburg. The Wars of Philip II. The Dutch Revolt. The End of Philip II.* III THE NEW STATES: SPAIN AND FRANCE. *The "Age of Absolutism." Power and Limits of Spanish Absolutism. The Spanish Economy. The Spanish Style. The French Monarchy. The French Wars of Religion, 1562–1598. The Victory of Henry of Navarre. The* Politiques. IV THE NEW STATES: ENGLAND AND HOLLAND. *Henry VIII. 1509–1547. Tudor Parliaments. Religious Difficulties. Elizabeth the Queen. The English Renaissance. The Dutch Republic.* V GERMANY AND THE THIRTY YEARS' WAR. *Nature and Causes. The Bohemian Period. 1618–1625. The Danish Period. 1625–1629. The Swedish Period. 1630–1635. The Swedish and French Period. 1635–1648. Effects on Germany. The Peace of Westphalia.*

6

The Expansion of Europe   *195*

Fifteenth Through Seventeenth Centuries

I INTRODUCTION. *Ancient and Modern Expansion Contrasted. The Motives and Nature of Modern Expansion.* II EAST BY SEA TO THE INDIES. *Prince Henry and the Portuguese. Africa. India. China. The Portuguese Empire.* III WEST BY SEA TO THE INDIES. *Columbus. Later Explorers. The Foundation of the Spanish Empire. The First True Colonial Empire. The Balance Sheet of Latin-American Empire.* IV THE LATECOMERS: FRANCE, HOLLAND, ENGLAND. *Early French and English Activity. The Thirteen Colonies: Settlement. The Thirteen Colonies: Institutions. New France. The Indies, West and East. Africa. The Far East* V THE BEGINNINGS OF ONE WORLD. *The Black Side of the Record. The Economic Record. Effects of Expansion on the West. The One World of the Eighteenth Century.*

7

Divine-Right Monarchy — and Revolution   *231*

I INTERNATIONAL POLITICS: FRANCE AS AGGRESSOR. *Before Louis XIV: Henry IV and Sully. Before Louis XIV: Richelieu and Mazarin. The Successes of Louis XIV. The Failures of Louis XIV. The Utrecht Settlement. French Agression in Review.* II THE FRANCE OF LOUIS XIV. *Divine-Right Monarchy. The Nobility. The Clergy. The Royal Administration. Mercantilism in Theory. Mercantilism in Practice: Colbert.* III ENGLAND IN REVOLUTION. *The Constitutional Tradition. The Role of the Crown. Issues between Crown and Parliament. The Reign of James I (1603–1625). The Troubles of Charles I. The Road to Civil War. 1638–1642. The Civil War, 1642–1649. Cromwell and the Interregnum, 1649–1660. The Revolution in Review. The Restoration, 1660–1668. The Glorious Revolution of 1688–1689* IV THE CENTURY OF GENIUS. *Natural Science. The Implications of Scientific Progress. The Classical Spirit. The Arts. Seventeenth-Century Culture in Review.*

8

The Old Régime and the International Balance, 1715–1789   *273*

I INTRODUCTION: THE PROSPECT IN *1715.* II THE WESTERN POWERS. *The Commercial Revolution. The Mississippi and South Sea Bubbles. The Agricultural Revolution. The Beginnings of the Industrial Revolution. The Assets of Britain. Cabinet Government. The Liabilities of France. The Other Western States.* III ITALY AND GERMANY. *Disunited Italy. Divided Germany: The Habsburg Dominions. The Rise of Prussia. Frederick William I.* IV THE EASTERN POWERS. *The Early Years of Peter the Great. The Western Trip. Peter's Wars. The Machinery of Peter's Government. Other Innovations of Peter the Great. Peter the Great: A Final Evaluation. Poland and Turkey.* V WAR AND DIPLOMACY, *1713–1789. Main Characteristics. The Turkish and Polish Questions. 1716–1739. The War of Jenkins' Ear. The War of the Austrian Succession, 1740–1748. The Uneasy Peace, 1748–1756. The Seven Years' War, 1756–1763. The International Balance in Review.*

9 The Enlightenment   *313*

I BASIC PRINCIPLES AND TRAITS. *The Inheritance from Locke and Newton. Eighteenth-Century Science. French Leadership.* II THE REFORM PROGRAM OF THE PHILOSOPHES. *Laissez-Faire Economics. Justice. Education. Attitudes toward Religion. Political Thought: Montesquieu. Political thought: Rousseau. Enlightened Despotism.* III THE ENLIGHTENED DESPOTS. *Prussia: Frederick the Great. Austria: Maria Theresa and Joseph II. Other Despots. Limitations of Enlightened Despotism.* IV RUSSIA, 1725–1825. *The Fate of the Autocracy. 1725–1762. Nobles and Serfs, 1730–1762. Catherine the Great (1762–1796). Paul (1796–1801). Alexander I (1801–1825). Russian Foreign Policy, 1725–1796.* V GEORGE III AND THE AMERICAN REVOLUTION. *George III. Background of the Revolution. Implications of the Revolution.* VI THE CULTURE OF THE EIGHTEENTH CENTURY. *The Limitations of Reason. The Evangelical Revival. Literature. Art. The Great Musicians.*

10 The French Revolution and Napoleon   *359*

I CAUSES OF THE REVOLUTION. *The Monarchy. The First and Second Estates. The Third Estate. The Financial Crisis. The Estates General.* II THE DISSOLUTION OF THE MONARCHY. *Popular Uprisings, July–October, 1789. The National Assembly, 1789–1791. The Constitution of 1791. The Legislative Assembly, October, 1791–September, 1792.* III THE FIRST REPUBLIC. *The September Massacres, 1792. Gironde and Mountain. The Reign of Terror, June, 1793–July, 1794. The Record of the Terror. The Thermidorean Reaction. The Directory, October, 1795–November, 1799.* IV NAPOLEON AND FRANCE. *The First Coalition, 1792–1795. Napoleon's Early Career. Brumaire. Napoleonic Government. Law and Justice. Religion. Education. Economics.* V NAPOLEON AND EUROPE. *The War, 1800–1807. The Empire at Its Height, 1807–1812. The Continental System. The Peninsular War. German Resistance. The Russian Campaign. The Downfall.* VI THE LEGACY OF THE REVOLUTION AND NAPOLEON.

11 Revolution and Counter-Revolution, 1815–1850   *405*

I INTRODUCTION. II THE ROMANTIC PROTEST. *The Revolt against Reason. The Return to the Past. Music. The Arts. Religion and Philosophy. The Romantic "Style."* III THE CONSERVATIVE OUTLOOK AND THE VIENNA SETTLEMENT. *Burke and Metternich. The Congress of Vienna. The Quarantine of France.* IV THE REVOLUTIONS OF THE 1820's. *The Revolutionary Credo. The Iberian States and Naples. The Greek War of Independence. The Decembrist Revolt in Russia.* V THE REVOLUTIONS OF 1830. *France: The July Revolution. Belgium. Poland. Italy and Germany. The Lessons of 1830.* VI THE REVOLUTIONS OF 1848. *Common Denominators. France. Italy. Germany. The Habsburg Domains. The Lessons of 1848.*

The Impact of the Economic Revolutions   *447*

12

I THE INDUSTRIAL REVOLUTION. *Preparation and Take-off. Coal and Iron. Transport and Communication. Banking and Capital. The Timetable of Industrialization.* II ECONOMIC AND SOCIAL CONSEQUENCES OF INDUSTRIALIZATION. *The Agricultural Revolution. Changes in Population. The Aspirations of the Middle Class. The Grievances of the Working Class.* III THE RESPONSES OF LIBERALISM. *The Classical Economists. Utilitarianism: Bentham. Democratic Liberalism: Mill.* IV THE SOCIALIST RESPONSE—THE UTOPIANS. *Saint-Simon and Fourier. Owen. The Early Utopians Appraised.* V THE SOCIALIST RESPONSE—MARX. *Basic Principles. The Communist Manifesto. The Later Career of Marx.* VI OTHER RESPONSES. *The Anarchists. Proudhon. The Christian Socialists. The Catholic Response.*

The Western Democracies in the Nineteenth Century   *481*

13

I BRITAIN, *1815–1914. The Process of Reform. Parliamentary Reform. The Two-Party System: Liberals and Conservatives. The Two-Party System: An Explanation. Reforms of the Utilitarians. Free Trade. Labor and Factory Legislation. Education. Chartism. Foreign Policy. Imperial Policy. The Irish Problem. The Threat to Free Trade. The Welfare State. The Labor Party.* II FRANCE—SECOND EMPIRE AND THIRD REPUBLIC. *The Coup d'Etat of 1851. The Second Empire, 1852–1870: Domestic Developments. The Second Empire: Foreign Policy. The "Liberal Empire." The Birth of the Third Republic. The Constitution of 1875. Boulanger and Panama. The Dreyfus Case. The Republic after Dreyfus.* III ITALY, *1848–1914. Cavour and the Completion of Unification. Assets and Liabilities of United Italy.* IV THE UNITED STATES. *The Federal Union. Civil War and Reconstruction. Economic and Social Development. The Myth of Isolation.*

Central and Eastern Europe   *523*

To the Outbreak of World War I

14

I INTRODUCTION. II GERMANY, *1850–1914. Prussia and the German Confederation, 1850– 1859. Bismarck Comes to Power. The Schleswig-Holstein Question, 1863–1865. War with Austria, 1866. The North German Confederation. Showdown with France. The German Empire. Domestic Developments, 1871–1878. Domestic Developments, 1878–1890. William II. Domestic Tensions, 1890–1914.* III THE HABSBURG MONARCHY, *1850–1914. Character of the Empire. Political Experiments, 1850– 1867. Dual Monarchy, 1867. The Czechs. Poles and Ruthenians. Other Minorities in Austria. Minorities in Hungary: Slovaks, Rumanians, South Slavs. Croatia. Bosnia-Herzegovina. Austrian Society and Politics, 1867–1914. Hungarian Society and Politics, 1867–1914.* IV RUSSIA, *1825–1914. Character of the Empire. Nicholas I (1825–1855). The Crimean War. Alexander II and Reform. Russian Intellectual Life. Nihilism, Populism, Terrorism. Foreign Policy under Alexander II. The Reaction, 1881– 1904. The Russo-Japanese War. The Revolution of 1905. The Dumas, 1906–1914.* V CONCLUSION.

The Intellectual Revolution 567

15

I DARWINISM. *The Origin of Species. Darwin's Theories. The Effect on Theology. The Effect on Social and Economic Attitudes. Eugenics. "Racism." The New Historical Determinism.* II LITERATURE AND THE ARTS. *The Victorian Age. The Realistic Novel. The Naturalistic Novel: Zola. The Literature of Pessimism and Protest. Poetry. Painting. The Other Arts. Music. The Arts in Review.* III PHILOSOPHY. *Idealism and Realism. Dynamism and the Cult of the Will. The Revolt against Reason. The Chastened Rationalists. The Extreme Anti-Rationalists.* IV POLITICAL AND SOCIAL THOUGHT. V THE CENTURY OF HOPE.

Nineteenth-Century Imperialism 597

16

I THE MOVEMENT IN GENERAL. *The Economic Aspect. The Powers Involved. The Areas Involved.* II THE BRITISH EMPIRE. *South Africa. The Boer War and After. Egypt. The Rest of British Africa. Other British Spheres. India: Political Organization. India: "The Meeting of East and West."* III THE OTHER EMPIRES. *The French: North Africa. The French: Tropical Africa. The French: Asia. The Germans. The Italians and Belgians. The Americans. The Japanese.* IV THE DEBATE OVER IMPERIALISM. *Pro: The Argument from Social Darwinism. Pro: The Argument of Duty. Pro: The Defensive Argument. Con: Anti-Imperialist Arguments.* V THE COLONIES OF WHITE SETTLEMENT. *Canada: Background of Revolt. Canada: Durham and a New Status. The Extension of Dominion Status. The Commonwealth in Review.* VI THE RESULTS OF IMPERIALISM.

The First World War 627

17

I INTRODUCTION. II CAUSES OF THE WAR. *The Shift in the Balance of Power. The Role of Public Opinion. German Aspirations. British Aspirations. The Other Belligerents. The Era of Bismarck, 1871– 1890. Formation of the Triple Entente, 1890–1907. A Decade of Crises, 1905–1914. The Final Crisis, July–August, 1914. The Entry of Other Powers.* III THE COURSE OF THE WAR. *Resources of the Belligerents. The Western Front: German Offensive. The Eastern Front. The Italian Front. The Dardanelles. The Balkan Fronts. The Near East and the Colonies. The War at Sea. The Western Front: Allied Victory. Morale on the Fighting Fronts. The Home Fronts. The Role of Propaganda. Political Repercussions.* IV THE PEACE SETTLEMENTS. *The Aftermath of World War. The Fourteen Points. Opposing Hopes and Promises. The Process of Peacemaking. The Territorial Settlement. The Mandates. The Punishment of Germany. The Settlement Evaluated.*

Communist Russia, 1917—1941   667

18

I INTRODUCTION   II THE RUSSIAN REVOLUTION OF 1917. *The Immediate Background. The March Revolution. The Provisional Government. Lenin and Bolshevism. The Coming of the November Revolution. The Constituent Assembly.*   III WAR COMMUNISM AND NEP, 1917–1928. *War Communism. Civil War. Why the Counter-Revolution Failed, NEP ("The New Economic Policy"). The Struggle for Power: Stalin versus Trotsky. The Struggle for Power: Stalin's Victory.* IV STALIN'S SUPREMACY: RUSSIAN INTERNAL AFFAIRS, 1928–1941. *Collectivized Agriculture. Industrialization. The Social Impact. The Purge Trials. The Authoritarian State. The Russian Thermidor?*   V SOVIET FOREIGN POLICY, 1918–1941. *Foreign Office and Comintern, 1918–1928. Stalin and the West, 1928–1939. Stalin and the Second World War.* VI CONCLUSION.

The Rise of Fascism, 1918—1939   707

19

I INTRODUCTION.   II ITALY AND FASCISM. *The Setting. Mussolini: Early Career. Mussolini: Rise to Power. The "March" on Rome. The Fascist Dictatorship. The Corporative State. Other Fascist Domestic Policies. Fascist Foreign Policy and its Consequences.*   III GERMANY AND THE WEIMAR REPUBLIC, 1918–1933. *The Impact of Defeat. Postwar Political Alignments and Activities. The Weimar Constitution, 1919. Right and Left Extremism, 1920–1922. Hitler: Early Career. The Inflation, 1922–1923. The Consequences of Inflation. The End of Inflation, 1923–1924. Recovery at Home, 1924–1929. "Fulfillment" Abroad, 1924–1930. The Impact of the Depression, 1929–1931. The Republic in Danger, 1931–1932. Hitler: Rise to Power, 1932–1933.*   IV GERMANY UNDER HITLER, 1933–1939. *The Nazi Dictatorship. Racism and Political Theory. The Bases of Foreign Policy. Legal and Economic Policies. Religion and Culture.*   V THE FAILURE OF PARLIAMENTARISM IN SPAIN AND EASTERN EUROPE, 1918–1939. *Spain: The Background. Birth of the Spanish Republic. Crisis of the Spanish Republic, 1933–1936. The Spanish Civil War, 1936–1939. Eastern Europe. Austria. Hungary. Yugoslavia. Other Authoritarian Régimes. Fascism in Review.*

The Democracies and the Colonial World   749
Domestic and Imperial Problems, 1919–1939

20

I INTRODUCTION.   II GREAT BRITAIN. *The Postwar Depression. The Conservative and Labor Programs. Postwar Politics. Settlement of the Irish Question. The Commonwealth of Nations.*   III FRANCE. *The Impact of the War. Social and Political Tensions. The Stavisky Case and the Popular Front. Divided France.*   IV THE UNITED STATES. *Isolationism. The Road to Internationalism. Boom—and Bust. The New Deal. Confident America.*   V THE LOOSENING OF IMPERIAL TIES. *Japan. China: The Revolution of 1911–1912. China between the World Wars. The Chinese Communists. Southeast Asia. India. The Middle East.*

The Second World War   *781*

21

I INTERNATIONAL POLITICS, *1919–1932. The "Era of Fulfillment." The Failure of "Fulfillment." The Aggressors.* II THE ROAD TO WAR, *1931–1939. The First Step: Manchuria, 1931. The Second Step: German Rearmament, 1935–1936. The Third Step: Ethiopia. 1935. The Fourth Step: The Spanish Civil War, 1936–1939. The Fifth Step: "Anschluss," 1938. The Sixth Step: Czechoslovakia Dismembered, 1938–1939. The Final Step: Poland, 1939. Democratic Policy in Review.* III THE NATURE OF THE WAR. IV EARLY SUCCESSES OF THE AXIS. *Polish and Finnish Campaigns. "Phony War" and Blitzkrieg in the West. "The Fall of France." The Battle of Britain. Mediterranean and Balkan Campaigns. The Invasion of Russia. American Policy. Pearl Harbor and After.* V THE VICTORY OF THE UNITED NATIONS. *The Turning Points. The Battle of Supply. The Axis on the Defensive. The Defeat of Germany. The Defeat of Japan. The Allied Coalition. Political Issues.*

The Post-War World, 1945–1953   *815*

22

I THE COLD WAR. *Atomic Weapons. A Divided World: Germany and China. The Two Coalitions. The United Nations.* II THE MAJOR FREE-WORLD STATES: *1945–1953. The United States. Canada. Western Europe. Great Britain. France. West Germany. The Other Western Countries.* III THE COMMUNIST BLOC, *1945 TO 1953. Soviet Government and the Economy. Soviet Intellectual Life. Soviet Foreign Policy: Europe. The Yugoslav Rebellion. Soviet Foreign Policy: Asia.* IV THE REVOLT AGAINST IMPERIALISM. *Causes of the Revolt. The Far East. Southeast Asia. India and Pakistan. The Middle East. Latin America.*

The Contemporary World since 1953   *851*

23

I THE COMMUNIST WORLD SINCE THE DEATH OF STALIN: THE U.S.S.R. AT HOME. *The Soviet Succession. The Denunciation of Stalin and its Consequences. The Khrushchev Era. The Bureaucratic Problems. The Khrushchev Era and Beyond: Industry and Agriculture. Education and the Art* II SOVIET CONFRONTATION WITH THE WEST. *Berlin. U-2, The Wall, Testing, Cuba. The Test-Ban Treaty. Rumania Disengages. The "Bloc" in 1966.* III THE U.S.S.R., CHINA, AND AMERICA IN ASIA. *The Soviet-Chinese Quarrel: Ideology. Southeast Asia: Vietnam and Laos. Khrushchev's Fall: Kosygin and Brezhnev.* IV THE EMERGING NATIONS. *East Asia. Southeast Asia. South Asia. The Middle East. Africa. Latin America and the West Indies.* V THE FREE WORLD SYSTEM. *NATO and the other American Alliance-Systems. The United Nations. The United States. Canada. Western Europe. Great Britain. West Germany. France. Italy.*

Man's Fate in the Twentieth Century   *911*

24

I   THE INTELLECTUAL REVOLUTION CONTINUES. *Psychology: Freud. The Implications of Freudianism. Psychology: Behaviorism. Socio-political Thought. Pareto. The Planners and Persuaders. Philosophy. The Sciences. Literature and the Arts. High Art: Literature. High Art: The Fine Arts.*   II   THE TEMPER OF OUR TIMES. *The Optimism of the Enlightenment. Repudiation or Revision of the Enlightenment.*

Illustrations   *939*

Index   *943*

Maps

Cradles of Civilization, 7

Ancient Greece, 9

Growth of Roman Dominions under the Empire, 44 B.C. *to 180* A.D., *15*

Carolingian Empire, 20

England and France during the Hundred Years' War, 36

Germany and the Baltic in the 15th Century, 41

Byzantine Empire, 55

Medieval and Early Modern Russia, 1190–1689, 67

Ottoman Empire to 1683, 75

Religious Situation about 1600, 143

Political Situation, mid-Sixteenth Century, 160–161

Europe in 1648, 190–191

Expansion of Europe 1529, 196

Expansion of Europe 1715, 196

Europe in 1715, 238–239

Growth of Prussia, 1740 to 1795, 289

Russian Expansion in Europe, 1689–1796, 295

North America and the Caribbean, 1763, 308

Partitions of Poland, 1772, 1795, 342

Napoleonic Europe, 1812, 394–395

Europe after 1815,   420 – 421

Centers of Revolution, 1820 – 1830, 1848 – 1849,   422

Latin America, 1828,   424

Industrial United States and Europe, 1860,   452 – 453

Europe in the mid-Nineteenth Century,   483

Unification of Italy, 1859 – 1870,   510

Growth of the United States and Southern Canada,   514

Unification of Germany, 1866 – 1871,   525

Nationalities in Central and Eastern Europe,   539

Africa and the Middle East, 1910,   599

Asia and the Pacific, 1910,   601

North America and the Caribbean, 1910,   614

Diplomatic Alignments before 1914,   634

Europe and the Near East, 1914 – 1918,   645

Territorial Settlements in Europe, 1919 – 1926,   659

The Balkans and the Middle East, 1878 – 1921,   662 – 663

Russia in Revolution, 1917 – 1921,   679

Europe on the Eve, August 1939,   792

European and Mediterranean Theaters, 1941 – 1945,   796

Asian and Pacific Theaters, 1941 – 1945,   809

The World, 1953,   820 – 821

Europe, 1953,   828 – 829

The Soviet Union, 1967,   834

Asia, 1967,   876

The Middle East, 1967,   882

Africa, 1967,   887

Caribbean America, 1967,   891

South America, 1967,   893

Modern Civilization

1

The Ancient
and Medieval Background
of Modern Civilization

I   The New History
and the Old

Only a generation or two ago,
the word "history" in American schools and
colleges meant either a study of our own history, or a traditional sequence of ancient,
medieval, modern, from the old states of the
Near East through Greece and Rome to the
origins and development of the states of modern Europe. "History" dealt almost wholly
with "past politics," kings and presidents, wars
and treaties.

In the twentieth century this old-fashioned
concept of what the study of history should
mean has come under attack. The newer historians regard the old concentration on our
modern European-American states and their
background in the Near East and the Mediterranean, as a form of narrowness and indeed
"self-worship." They propose the study of other

great civilizations with historical pasts: those of China and other lands of the Far East, of India, of Central and South America; and, insofar as anthropology and archaeology permit, the study of the past human groups all over the world. Some of the newer historians also argue that the old sequence of ancient, medieval, modern does violence to the real continuities of history, that it is a kind of hangover from the Age of Reason in the eighteenth century, with its shallow contempt for the so-called Middle Ages. Third, and most important, the newer historians insist that politics and war are only part of the record of history, perhaps a less important part than economic activity, art, literature, religion, even the routines of daily living of ordinary men and women. The study of history, in short, is to be not so much the study of past politics as the study of "past everything."

Now no sensible person will deny that these newer interpretations have greatly enriched and deepened the study of history. On the other hand, this new history is much more complex, difficult, and unwieldy than was the old. When you add the Chinese and the Incas, go back in time to the apes, and add to war and politics everything else that mankind has done, and *then* try to "introduce" the subject, the result too often becomes a mere gallop through the centuries. Instead of the old-fashioned arid list of emperors, popes, and generals, we get a new-fangled list of poets or inventors—often just as arid—since adding a hasty epithet or two: "ethereal" Shelley, "sweet-voiced" Keats, "ingenious and laborious" Edison—helps very little.

Here in this book we hope to retain the best of the old and add the best of the new. We shall concentrate on the history of one part of the world, the Europe sometimes scornfully called a "small peninsula of Asia." We shall trace the expansion of Europe as Europeans explored, settled, colonized, and traded in all parts of the globe. But we shall be concerned with non-European peoples only as they and their histories impinged on the development of European cultures. We are not motivated by any "self-worship," by any contempt for Asians or Africans, but simply by a desire to get our own record straight. As for time, we shall be concerned with the years since about 1450, the period we must still think of as "modern," if only as a matter of convenience and convention. Obviously, this is not all a good American citizen of the second half of the twentieth century needs to know about the past of *homo sapiens*. But it is an essential part of what he needs to know, probably the part he *most* needs to know, if he is to face the problems of human relations on this planet. Now for the first time, as a result of modern transportation and expanded communication, we are physically at least part of One World.

Finally, though we hope to do justice to the complexity and variety of man's activities during these centuries, we shall still find the center of our history in his political and military record. A general history must, it seems to us, focus on these activities, for without them "what really happened" cannot be understood. No doubt a general history must also give important clues to what are labeled economic, history, intellectual history, social history, history of science, history of religions, and so on. We shall do our best to give such clues. But all written history must omit vast amounts of information, facts, "coverage"; indeed, in these days the cluttered modern mind needs the kind of cleaning a general survey can afford.

II The First Men

One of the major changes that very "modern" times have brought is a shift in men's ideas of the length of time our species has lived on this earth. Not very many generations back, just about everyone accepted as an unquestioned fact that the first man appeared on earth about six thousand years ago in the Garden of Eden. Nowadays in the western world, all but a very small minority of fundamentalist Christians think of man as having "evolved" from some other primate form thousands and thousands of years ago. Indeed, the specialists have tended to push the antiquity of man further and further back, until the figure of about two million years for the existence of a manlike (anthropoid) creature is accepted. For man, *homo sapiens* as we know him, the figure is perhaps seven hundred thousand years. Of that long period, we have written historical records for only about five thousand years. In short, we have "history" for about one half of one per cent of the time man and his immediate ancestors have, we believe, lived on earth. The rest is "prehistory," for which our only direct evidence is archaeological—skeletal remains of men, their animal food, weapons, tools, and, toward the end of this vast period, such cultural artifacts as cave-painting and sepulchral monuments. We can get indirect evidence from observing existing "primitive" peoples like the Australian aborigines or the natives of New Guinea, who are fast disappearing or are being converted to the "modern" way of life. But such evidence must be used with care, and it rests on an unprovable, if plausible, assumption that these contemporary "primitives" are in fact much like "prehistoric" man.

Prehistory

The study of prehistory, and indeed the study of history, can always be justified by those who enjoy it as a form of enjoyment. And it can also be justified by a more dignified argument, that one of the great human attributes is to want to explore the unknown, to extend the boundaries of knowledge. But the utilitarian asks this question: "What *good* will it do me to learn about prehistory, about ancient history? Can I learn from the study of

Two polychrome reindeer from the Cavern of Font-de-Gaume, Dordogne, France.

the men of the Old Stone Age why I behave as I do, why others behave as they do?" Specialists in the study of human relations would by no means agree on answers to such questions. At one extreme are those who believe that social planning, or even social "engineering," can be based solely on the observation and analysis of current human behavior. A cultural engineer, they maintain, needs to know the nature of the human materials he works with, just as the construction engineer needs to know the nature of the steel, aluminum, and other materials he works with. But just as the construction engineer does not need to know about the geological history of his materials as ores, so the cultural engineer does not need to know human history, let alone prehistory.

On the other hand, there are those who believe that human beings behave as they do more because of what happened in the prehistoric millennia than because of what happened in those few centuries that produced our written history, our organized religion, our formal philosophies, our politics, our science. If you wish to change human behavior, they argue, you must find out how and why that behavior came to be what it is. To use a homely illustration: we have all seen a dog circle about, head apparently pursuing tail, before lying down. The generally accepted explanation of such behavior is that the dog's distant ancestors circled in the grass or low shrubs to make a comfortable place to lie down in. Our dog doesn't need to do this before lying down on our best rug, but he does. Suppose we human beings, with all our vaunted rationalism, do many things for no better reason than that our distant ancestors of the Stone Age did so? Wouldn't it be better, if we want to persuade people to do otherwise, to be able to show them the real and perhaps undignified reasons for doing certain things?

The mere historian can hardly pretend to answer such questions, which soon enter into high philosophic problems—determinism or free will, "nature" or "nurture," permanence or change—problems that our short historical record shows men have never agreed on. History supplies the materials for these grand debates, but it cannot settle them.

The historian can be reasonably sure, thanks to the hard labors of generations of archaeologists, of the outlines of human development in the long ages of prehistory. Roughly a million years ago, some higher primate apparently began to engage in an activity that no other animal on earth, so far as we know, has ever achieved: *talking in verbal symbols.* Other animals, as all who have pets know, can learn to recognize signs. Your dog Rex "knows" his name, of course; he has been conditioned to recognize the sound from your mouth as a *sign,* much as you have been conditioned to recognize a red light as a sign of danger. But don't try to teach him to recognize "rex"—the Latin for "king"—as an elaborate *symbol* of a complex human political achievement.

Language, the ability to express and communicate in symbols, enabled man to accumulate and transmit to his offspring ways of "coping" with his environment—that is, getting food, shelter, preserving himself against enemies, and so on. Rex's puppies—which, by the way, he will almost certainly not recognize as *his* puppies, for the recognition of paternity requires some pretty complicated symbolic thinking—will have to learn all over again, by trial and error, by means of what we call "conditioning," much of what Rex himself was conditioned to. Dogs simply do not have a "culture" in the sense of an accumulation of techniques and ideas preserved and transmitted in words, books, pictures, diagrams, and the like. Rex cannot, in the full human sense, "teach" his puppies.

Early men depended for their existence on hunting and food-gathering, and in this respect did not differ from their "wild animal" competitors. In terms of what we have come to call "progress," these early men were very slow in improving their competitive position. But over the ages they *did* improve it, most obviously by a gradual improvement in the tools they used—axes, spears, arrowheads, grindstones, needles, and other domestic implements. In fact, the principles on which the archaeologist divides prehistory into "periods" come from a close study of these tools. Almost all the time man or manlike creatures have been on earth is known as the Paleolithic period (Old Stone Age), and for the first part of this time it seems clear that man did not shape his tools at all. Indeed the earliest implements, which the archaeologist calls *eoliths* ("dawn stones"), are hard for the lay observer in a museum to recognize as tools. Toward the end of Paleolithic time, twenty thousand years ago or so, the chipped stone tools, including actual knives of flint or obsidian, became very good indeed. And finally, in Europe and the Near East there appeared about ten thousand years ago polished stone implements. The archaeologist now speaks of a Neolithic period (New Stone Age), which, however, very soon becomes the Age of Bronze and, again soon, of other metals, notably iron.

The Neolithic Revolution

The Neolithic Age marks one of the great turning points—one of the "revolutions"—in human development. We do not know exactly where or when it happened, but somehow men learned to *produce* rather than *gather* what they needed for food and shelter. This *domestication* of plants and animals was slow in comparison with our "Industrial Revolution" of the eighteenth and nineteenth centuries, but it was incredibly fast compared with the slow improvements in fist-hatchets made by men of the Old Stone Age. Domestication meant more and better food and shelter, and more human beings here on earth.

With the Neolithic, or agricultural and stock-raising revolution, then, a given area could support many more human beings. Moreover, instead of wandering about, men could—indeed had to—settle down in one place, first in villages, then in towns or cities. Man had become a political animal; his apparatus of culture, backed up by the power of symbolic thought, had become so complex that it had to be *recorded*. Writing (not at first alphabetical, but ideographic) was not the least of his inventions in the age that saw the domestication of plants and animals, the wheel, pottery, and much else. And with writing came written records, the basis for history as we know it, some five thousand years ago.

So far, we have limited ourselves to tracing culture in terms of its material remains. Toward the end of the Paleolithic, we find graves, little statuettes (perhaps used as charms or fetishes), the famous cave-paintings of animals, which may have had religious or magical functions, all of which indicate that their makers had a life of ideas. We find jewelry, an indication that some of these people could afford fairly complicated desires and satisfactions. But we cannot know what their religious or magical ideas were, what ethical ideas they cherished, what sort of social and political life they had. We can be sure they had "culture," in the sense that they depended on the communication of symbolic thinking; and we can guess that the improvement of their material implements was accompanied by political and social "invention."

III   The First Civilizations

In the later part of the "Neolithic revolution," this political and social invention made it possible for men to live in cities, to hold together larger political units than had been possible in a hunting and food-gathering culture. These were the first "civilizations:" human societies with some kind of writing, some "politics," and usually

with cities, division of labor, social classes or castes—and organized armed forces.

Recent archaeological discoveries in Palestine (Jericho, Jarmo) and in Asia Minor have pushed the date of these early urban societies back before 8000 B.C. Several millennia thereafter we find the celebrated river-valley civilizations arising independently in the valleys of the Tigris and Euphrates, of the Nile, and perhaps the Indus. A little later (fourth millennium B.C.) came the beginnings in China. By the third millennium B.C., the civilizations of the Tigris-Euphrates (Mesopotamia) and of the Nile (Egypt) had made contact with each other—commercial, diplomatic, and military. Until the beginnings of Europe's expansion only five hundred years ago, the Indian, Chinese, and (later) Peruvian and Mexican civilizations developed in relative isolation, although the Greeks and the Romans traded with India, and western Europeans knew a little about China after the famous travels of Marco Polo and others in the thirteenth century A.D. And from the steppes of Central Asia nomads raided east to China and west to Europe. But the isolation of civilizations tended to be the rule until Da Gama, Columbus, and the other great explorers started us all on the way to One World. This is especially true of the American civilizations that grew up with centers in Peru and in Central America. Even if Leif Ericson, the Viking leader, did reach North America about 1000 A.D., there was no real contact between the cultures of the "Red Indians" and those of Christian Europe until 1492.

Our Own Beginnings: The Near East

From the time when the civilizations of Mesopotamia and Egypt began, however, we can speak of the continuity of a "western" civilization. Continuity, note, not identity. There has been much change, even among the human stocks that shared this civilization. And the center of this civilization has moved generally northward and westward from the ancient Near East. The sequence of leadership is easiest to trace in politics and war, though usually it can be traced in art and thought as well. It runs from the Near East to Greece to Rome and Italy to Western and Central Europe, whence it seems to have passed to those diverse heirs of Europe, the United States and the Soviet Union.

During the five or six thousand years since the beginnings in the Near East, western man has always been aware—though sometimes only dimly—of a common past. The main written languages of Mesopotamia and Egypt were forgotten, and modern scientists had to relearn them before they could read the records, on clay tablets, stone, or papyrus. But two institutions kept this continuity alive: formal education, especially higher education, which until very recently was patterned after the civilization of the Greeks; and the Christian churches, which preserved much of Greco-Roman civilization, and that of the ancient Near East.

In these Near Eastern river valleys we find for the first time what we can recognize as a "state," and with it the famous law code of Hammurabi (about 1800 B.C.), the first known law code. Here first we encounter writing, and finally, from a people near or in Palestine, the first true alphabet, the direct ancestor of our own. Here first a number of "practical" techniques in building, engineering, farming, and business were devised, and, for the most part, never quite lost. Surveying will do as an example. The need to delimit farm fields, to apportion "property" among individual or corporate owners, and, in Mesopotamia, the complex demands of an irrigation system, forced men to turn their attention to the practical matter of surveying the land. But very soon men began to study such matters in other than a direct "practical" way. Some men became, not so much surveyors, as geometers, mathematicians, and astronomers. Here in the Near East—and *not* in Greece—we find the first scientists. And it seems likely that the origins of science were intertwined with age-old ideas and practices of magic.

With one exception, the arts and literature also first appear in the Near East. The exception is painting: in France and Spain Neolithic cave-paintings and drawings of animals have been found that are almost certainly at least ten or twelve thousand years old, far older than the pyramids of Egypt. The best of these paintings are striking not just as curiosities but as works of art. The reindeer of the cave-painters look more natural to us than the stiff and formal lions of the Assyrian sculptors, but

Cradles of Civilization

Areas of earliest civilization

—— Present-day boundaries

Present-day place names in color

we have nothing from the Stone Age that looks like a human being as the modern artist conceives him. In the bust of the Egyptian Queen Nefertiti, however, done more than three thousand years ago, we have one of the great works of our art. So our Neolithic exception for painting only proves the rule: it is the Near East that gave us our artistic inspiration

and our first written communications as well as our first recognizable political institutions.

Religious and Political Beginnings

Here in the Near East religions first take on forms that have been continuously alive in

7

the hearts and habits of men ever since. The completely orthodox "fundamentalist"—Jew, Christian, or Moslem—learns from his holy books just when God made known to man the true religion. But the historian knows that this monotheistic "higher' religion of the Near East developed from earlier more primitive beliefs, probably polytheistic.

Bust of Nefertiti (fourteenth century B.C.), the wife and sister of Ikhnaton.

Just how did polytheism develop into monotheism? Were the Jews the first monotheists, or was their Yahweh (in English traditional usage, Jehovah) just another private tribal god until very late—until, say, Egyptian and other

influences had begun to work on those Jewish intellectuals we call the prophets? Is the real transition from a primitive to a higher religion less a matter of the number of gods than of the relation of the believer to his god or gods? Is it a matter of *ethics* rather than *theology*, of recognition by the individual of a "force not himself making for righteousness"? Do such terms as "sin" and "conscience" first begin to have real meaning for western civilization in the ancient Near East? The answer to this last query is almost certainly yes, but all these questions are still debated.

Here too in the Nile and Mesopotamian valleys, and in the "fertile crescent" that links them, we find the first recorded contacts among organized human groups, the first "international relations." Here first is the *drama* of recorded history, the first rise and fall of men and empires, with intrigue, aspiration, success, and failure. Here too are what we may call the first case-histories for the modern social scientist. The tendency in international relations among many "sovereign states" is for one to hold precariously a hegemony or leadership in a rough "balance of power." Then over the long run one imperial power upsets the balance and tends to dominate all the other states; at the end of the great period of the ancient Near East this power was the Persian Empire, made famous by Cyrus, Darius, and Xerxes.

In sum, the long-dead Egyptians, Sumerians, Chaldaeans, Babylonians, Assyrians, Jews, Persians, and all the rest, though they lacked our modern command over power or energy—though they had only horses, oxen, and water-powered tools and no real machines—had almost everything else we have. They had cities, temples, armies, governments, schools, factories, stores, art, and all that these imply for men and women. Were they more like us than unlike us? It seems likely that they were very much like us, civilized men and women.

Ancient Greece

- Athenian Empire, 450 B.C.
- ■ Battle sites

Black Sea

Bosporus

THRACE

Byzantium

Propontis
(Sea of Marmora)

MACEDONIA

Hellespont

Troy

MT. OLYMPUS

PERSIAN

EPIRUS

LESBOS

ASIA MINOR

ITHACA

Thermopylae

CHIOS

Delphi

Thebes

Aegean Sea

SAMOS

Athens

EMPIRE

IONIA

Corinth

Miletus

Mycenae

Olympia

Argos

DELOS

Halicarnassus

Ionian Sea

PELOPONNESUS

see inset below

COS

Sparta

THERA

LACONIA

RHODES

Cretan Sea

Knossos

CRETE

0   50   100
Miles

Mediterranean Sea

MT. PARNASSUS

Delphi   ■ Chaeronea

BOEOTIA   Thebes

Gulf of Corinth   ■ Plataea   ATTICA   ■ Marathon

Eleusis

Megara   Athens

Salamis   Piraeus

Corinth   *Saronic*   *MT. LAURION*

Mycenae   *Gulf*

Epidaurus

Argos   Tiryns

0   25
Miles

Greek Colonial World

- Areas of Greek settlement

0   500
Miles

ALPS

Black Sea

PYRENEES

Massilia

ITALY

Byzantium

IBERIA

CORSICA

ASIA MINOR

SARDINIA

Paestum

Megara   Phocaea

Str. of   *Gibraltar*

"MAGNA   Croton   Corinth   Athens   IONIA

Segesta   GRAECIA"   GREECE   *RHODES*   PHOENICIA

Syracuse   SICILY   *CRETE*   CYPRUS   SYRIA

Carthage   Agrigento

Mediterranean Sea

Cyrene

AFRICA   EGYPT

IV   Greece and Rome

The heritage of the ancient Near East—with the great exception of monotheistic religion—has come to us via the Greeks and Romans, who made their own enormous contribution to it. We now know that the ancient Greeks were northern barbarians speaking a language akin to our own and to most of the others of modern Europe—the so-called Indo-European group of languages. They came into the Aegean area in various bands probably from about the fifteenth century B.C. to the eleventh. There they found a well-developed civilization with the island of Crete its most important center This civilization, called "Minoan" from Minos, the name the Cretans gave their kings, probably depended on sea power and sea-borne trade. It has left behind a vivid and sophisticated art in which the double axe, the bull, and the bare-breasted snake-goddess recur again and again. In the ruins of its palaces, archaeologists have found luxurious heating and plumbing systems. We also have many hundreds of tablets inscribed in two chief scripts, the older of which is still undeciphered. The younger we can now read: it is an early form of Greek, but unfortunately the tablets are mostly inventories of supplies, and tell us little about Minoan civilization. It seems probable that a great Mediterranean volcanic eruption and tidal wave about 1400 B.C. caused its ruin.

Some Greek "Firsts"

For the Greeks, however, besides the buildings, statues, inscriptions, and coins, we have many written materials of all kinds —epic, hymn, drama, and even history. The rugged mountainous terrain and jagged coastline of Greece and the Aegean area no doubt contributed to the Greek invention of the city-state, or *polis,* from which we take our word "politics." The city-state was a miniature nation. It had walls, a central fort, often a harbor, and a surrounding countryside with farms. But even the famous ones like Athens, Sparta, Thebes, or Corinth were no bigger than a smallish county in the eastern United States. Each city-state was independent. There was no political entity that could be called "Greece." A citizen of Athens had no higher political allegiance than to Athens. These independent city-states fought each other, made alliances, and in general created a pattern of "international" relations resembling that all too familiar to students of modern western history in the last four centuries. One after another Athens, Sparta, Thebes assumed the leadership of the Greek city-states, but none succeeded in uniting Greece. Still quarreling, the city-states fell easy victim in the fourth century B.C. to a people on the northern fringes of Greece, the Macedonians, whose king, Philip, had built a formidable military machine.

Philip and his son Alexander imposed their rule on Greece, and with Greek as well as Macedonian troops, Alexander in 334 B.C. set out to the east on an astonishing expedition. In eleven years he conquered Egypt and the entire Near East, and moved on into India, where his troops finally mutinied. Alexander had hoped to govern each region of his colossal empire according to its own traditions, with Greek culture as the cement to bind it together, but he died in 323 B.C. before he had had a chance to develop or try his system, and his empire fell apart into three major portions, each a "Great Power" of the Mediterranean: Egypt, Syria, and Macedonia-Greece.

But it would be deeply misleading to dismiss the Greek city-states as a failure just because they never succeeded in suppressing strife among themselves, and lost out in the end to Philip of Macedon. Unlike the Egyptian, the Assyrian, or even the Jew, the Greek

Archaic Greek sculpture: statue of a maiden, now in Acropolis Museum, Athens.

was a *citizen* of his *polis,* a voting, discussing, participating member of a commonwealth. Among the Greek cities, Athens in particular expected all citizens (slaves and resident aliens were excluded) to take a direct part in their democracy, which resembled a very large New England town meeting. The ancients did not achieve government by elected deputies or representatives.

In the world of ancient Greece we encounter for the first time just about all the human activities that we ourselves enjoy, from sport to formal philosophy. If we extend the cultural history of Greece to include that of imperial Rome down to the fifth century A.D., then its range is extraordinarily complete, so complete that in the arts, in literature, in philosophy, and in religious thought it is difficult to find anything since that seems entirely new. Even in science and technology, and in economic life, the Greco-Roman world produced at least a foreshadowing of what we have since achieved. There were capitalists, bankers, factories—operated by human power for the most part—and, by 300 B.C., large political units, bureaucracies, and professionals of all kinds, including professional soldiers. There were even machines; the word itself is Greek. And later Greek scientists made steam engines, which they exhibited as museum pieces, a kind of toy. One of the obvious differences between the Greco-Roman world and our own is that the ancients never really applied their technical knowledge to harness *power* and thus extend the labor force. *Why* they did not is still a subject for debate. The easiest explanation, though probably incomplete, is that since they had slaves they did not feel the need for labor-saving devices.

The Style
of Greco-Roman Culture

Any human group that gets at all established, even a family or a fraternity, comes to have what we shall here call its *style.* The style is a compound of many elements, tradition-cemented ways of going about the full round of living. The style of a great nation is complex, and is constantly changing and developing, or at least going through the cycle of youth, maturity, old age, and senility.

The Greeks, and even the more practical Romans, were at bottom *rationalists,* interested in trying to find out how things on this earth really ran, aware that immediate sense-impressions are often misleading, and also aware that they had inherited from their ancestors notions which, though sanctioned by religion, were in our own modern sense of the word, "myths." They freed their minds of these "myths" and "prejudices," and really tried to "reason things out." But they tended to rely too much on theory, on abstract speculation, and too little on detailed and undignified observation and experiment; and they tended to emphasize the finished, the com-

plete, even to the point of holding that change, development, and evolution are illusions. Their great mathematical achievement was Euclidean geometry, which deals with finished, unchanging forms and laws; they were not great algebraists, and they did not come near finding the infinitesimal calculus. There is in their mythology a strong sense of the harshness, the repetitiveness, the treadmill aspect, of human life on earth—Sisyphus who rolled a stone uphill, only to have it roll back; the Danaïdes, who had to pour water into sieves; Niobe, perpetually weeping; the Augean stables, which could never be cleaned. It is true that Hercules did clean these stables by channeling two rivers through them, a suggestion that the ancient Greeks had glimpses of technological progress. Still, not really be-

The Acropolis: the Erechtheum is to the left of the Parthenon, the little temple of Nike may be seen near the structures of the entrance, and the Roman theater of Herodus Atticus is below.

lieving in growth, they did not turn their attention to economic growth, to trying to change a planet—and its inhabitants—that they believed were at bottom unchanging, and unchangeable.

All these generalizations about the Greco-Roman "style" are suggestive, but they have numerous exceptions. For example, it is broadly true that the Greco-Roman intellectual did not get into a laboratory and dirty his hands—put more fairly, he was addicted to abstract "reasoning" after the Euclidean fashion from a few accepted postulates rather than from observation. Yet it is also true that the so-called Hippocratic school of medicine has left behind it concrete descriptions of symptoms of sick people, "case-histories" worthy of the best trained clinician of our own time.

Moreover, we owe our present possession of Greek and Roman writings largely to generations of schoolmasters and Christian monks, who preferred the tame to the wild, the decent to the indecent, the finished to the struggling and growing. So they probably selected for copying and preservation the works that suited their temperament and calling. Perhaps there were more heaven-stormers, more wild strivers among the Greeks, than we can ever know. Certainly the known political behavior of the Greek city-states suggests that the Greeks were often both unreasonable and irrational.

The Romans

Tradition says that Romulus and Remus, suckled by a she-wolf, founded Rome about 753 B.C. The date, at least, seems about right. The new city had a good strategic location in central Italy on a crossing of the Tiber River, although it lacked a harbor of its own. Its inhabitants seem to have been a mixture of various peoples already established in the peninsula. Partly under the influence of Greek city-states founded in southern Italy by emigrants from Greece itself, Rome too became a *polis,* and absorbed the surrounding villages and countryside in Latium (whence *Latin*). The Romans began a process of expansion that at first sight was not very different from that undertaken by Athens and Sparta. First the Italian peninsula was consolidated under Roman leadership, which the divided Greek city-states of the south were unable to resist. This expansion brought Rome squarely up against her first and most dangerous foe in large-scale international politics: Carthage, near what is now the North African city of Tunis. Carthage was originally a colony of Phoenicians from the Palestinian region, and a very successful merchant state that had expanded into Sicily and Spain. (Note, by the way, that our story is moving more and more into Europe.) In three wars, known from the Latin adjective for the Phoenicians as the "Punic Wars" (264–146 B.C.), the Romans broke Carthage and annexed her empire. Even before the victory over the Carthaginians was complete, the Romans had begun to challenge the heirs of Alexander in Greece. Next came Syria, and finally Egypt. By 30 B.C. Rome had overcome all the "Great Powers" of the western world, and had set the stage for the establishment of a universal western state.

The Roman Empire

How did the Romans do it? In part by superior strategy and tactics: they had the best armies and the biggest. In part by diplomacy: here, *divide et impera* (divide and rule) was their practice as they themselves described it. Moreover, the Romans, as they expanded, managed for the most part not to make irreconcilable enemies of the conquered peoples. No Ireland, no Poland, nursed eternal grievances against them; the Jews, who did nurse such grievances, were scattered by Roman power throughout the West, and were left without a political base. Not that the Romans were notably humane, nor even, so far as we know, intellectually interested in how to acquire and hold an empire. They could be tough indeed, as when they utterly destroyed the city of Carthage. Still, they did on the whole tend to leave to conquered peoples a good deal of autonomy; they respected local religion and local tradition; they brought a relief from local wars; and they brought a degree of law and order into all phases of international relations, including the economic.

Roman social practices also contributed to Roman success. From the early days of the Roman republic there developed a ruling class, an "élite." It was not a closed caste, but accessible to ambitious and able outsiders, even, later, to non-Romans. The Roman rulers were disciplined, "practical" rather than "intellectual," and above all, so secure in their own pride as Romans that they could let other peoples be themselves. In short, the Romans behaved toward other peoples in a way for which there was little precedent; they sought to *integrate* them into what in modern terms we call a "superstate."

It was in fact a super-city-state, for the Roman Empire never had any true representative institutions, nor any formal federal structure. The Empire itself is usually dated from the reign of the first emperor, Augustus, which began in 31 B.C. The old Roman republican institutions could not cope with the manifold problems of the new imperialism. It had taken nearly a century of civil strife, culminating in the victories of Julius Caesar, the great-uncle of Augustus, to establish the new imperial structure.

For a time, and especially in the second century A.D., the Roman Empire did bring law, order, and, above all, freedom from major wars. The Empire included the whole Mediterranean basin, modern France (known as Gallia to the Romans), England (known as Britannia), and the Teutonic lands up to the line of the Rhine and Danube. It was surrounded on the north and northeast by "barbarian" tribes eager to enjoy the spoils of civilization, and on the east by active and hostile successors to the old Persian state. "Frontier" wars were, therefore, frequent, but they were fought by professional soldiers and did not greatly disturb the peaceful inhabitants who lived in the interior parts of the Empire.

The Roman Empire has always appealed to the imagination of the West. In a sense, as we shall see when we come to medieval history in the final section of this chapter, the West Roman Empire lived on long after the deposition

in 476 A.D. of the last emperor in Rome itself. This old Roman One World has seemed especially successful to those who have lived through periods of grave international conflict like the present. Yet it had many serious weaknesses, and its full life was not long. There was always a large slave population, the bulk of which was never well off materially, and never seems to have felt itself part of the Empire. The imperial patriots were a small group, educated, and, as ruling classes go, conscientious and sometimes even kindly, but with no effective links with the masses. They formed the bureaucracy which along with the military leaders did the daily work of ruling, and they did hold the empire together. But they could not solve a whole series of political, social, and economic problems. The situation in Rome itself was typical. Here there was a population of perhaps a million, most of whom lived on a state dole and were entertained by the free shows in the Colosseum and the Circus Maximus, and in the game rooms, libraries, and pools of the public baths. Economically, Rome was a parasite on the Empire, which had to feed it and the far-flung armies as well. Fairly early, the ruling class began to bend under its burdens, to lose faith in itself, and actually to cease to reproduce itself. As the Germanic tribes pushed along into the Empire, the decline became obvious. There were rallies, in one of which, early in the fourth century A.D., the emperor Constantine made of old Byzantium a new captial called after himself Constantinople, and set up a nucleus that did hold off the barbarians and became the Eastern Roman or Byzantine Empire (see Chapter 2). But the empire in the Roman West was doomed.

Why did the Roman Empire in the West go down? Politically speaking, the emperors after 180 abandoned the practice of choosing a promising successor, and the throne soon afterward became a prize for which rival generals competed. Plagues and civil wars diminished the population, and crippled agriculture, already backward. Free farmers became serfs, and inflation diluted prosperity. Psychologically, the masses became alienated from their rulers, as mercenaries replaced the

Growth of Roman Dominions under the Empire

44 B.C. to 180 A.D.

At death of Caesar, 44 B.C.
To death of Augustus, 14 A.D.
To death of Marcus Aurelius, 180 A.D.
■ Battle sites

citizen-soldier. Perhaps the new and spreading faith of Christianity helped make its converts indifferent to life in this world, as they concentrated upon securing salvation in the next. Other cults fashionable among the Romans may also have contributed to otherworldliness. But all these factors, and many others that have been suggested and are now discounted—climatic change, racial mixture by Greeks and Orientals—would almost certainly not have led to collapse without the terrific pressures of the barbarian forces from outside the boundaries of the Empire.

In the arts, in literature, and in philosophy

the Romans were not innovators, but followed in the footsteps of the Greeks. But they made their great contribution in the fields of law and engineering. Though Roman law could be used to exalt the authority of the state over the individual, it recognized the rights of the citizen, afforded legal redress to slaves, and displayed an almost religious concern with equity. Through all the centuries since the fall of Rome, it has played a major role in keeping western man civilized. The Latin language remained for over a thousand years after the fall of the Empire the medium for all formal culture in the European West; above all, it

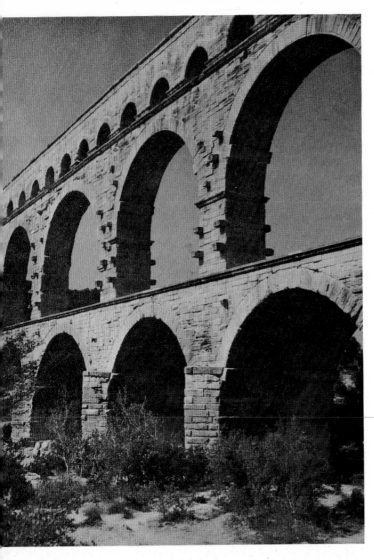

The Pont du Gard: Roman aqueduct built early in the first century A.D., near Nimes, France.

Early Christianity

Christianity began in the Greco-Roman world, with the preaching of Jesus in the Kingdom of Judea in Palestine, ruled over by a Hellenized Jewish dynasty loyal to Rome. Largely because Christians would not sacrifice before a statue of the emperor, and thus did not fulfill their civic duty as Romans, the Roman authorities often persecuted them, and at best treated them with a suspicious toleration. Yet, in the increasingly harsh conditions of the Empire, Christianity spread and won adherents until early in the fourth century the Emperor Constantine himself was converted. By the end of that century, Christianity had become the established religion of the imperial government, which now persecuted dying paganism.

During these centuries the Christians created an organized church: an apparatus of administration and government of the faithful necessary to the continued success of the faith on earth. Its bishops held power roughly corresponding to the rank and importance of their cities, and the Bishop of Rome, as chief cleric of the most important city of all, gradually became recognized as father—Papa—of the others. When the Emperor Constantine moved the capital to Constantinople (330 A.D.) the Pope of Rome became in many ways the successor of the Roman emperors in the West.

For all the centuries since the conversion of Constantine, men in the West—even though their conduct in their private lives might have been most "unChristian"—have accepted the Old and New Testaments as divinely revealed books of their faith. Not until the fifteenth and sixteenth centuries do we encounter doubters—at first only a few—who questioned the fundamentals of Christian beliefs. By the eighteenth century, skepticism was fashionable, and there were tens of thousands who openly said they were not Christians. But even today the vast majority of men and

remained the *lingua franca* of the Roman Catholic Church. Until only yesterday, Latin was an inescapable part of all higher education in the European West. Even now, it is embedded in all western tongues, even in German, and most certainly in English, as the carrier of most of our more general cultural ideas. We think as we do, in part at least, because of the way Caesar, Cicero, and thousands of forgotten Romans thought. Nor after all the religious and national wars of the past four centuries can we help wistfully reflecting on the Roman Peace.

16

women in our western world would list themselves as Christians. To the historian the Church and the specific content of its faith have had a history—that is, they have changed and developed in time and space, as part of this changing world. But it should not be forgotten that the Christian must believe that a history dealing with this world cannot possibly explain the *ultimates* of Christian belief, which do not depend on process, on history, but are beyond them, unchanging and absolute.

Yet Christianity has never, like many oriental religions, denied the reality of this changing world of the senses, the world of history. Despite its many individual mystics, it has never attempted to extinguish all normal sense-life to achieve a kind of perpetual trance or ecstasy. It has never been indifferent to the choices between "good" and "evil" met in daily life. For over two thousand years, Christianity has displayed an amazing range of belief and behavior. Yet its general tendency has been to preserve in fruitful tension its concepts of this imperfect world on earth and of the other perfect world in heaven. It has certainly never been "materialistic" in its cosmology; it has never countenanced the belief that "it's all chemistry, it's all physics." On the other hand, it has usually come to recognize that what the chemist is working with and on is real and important. To the absolutist temper, Christianity has compromised with this world of the senses. To most of us, it has rather accepted this shifting and unpredictable world of the senses as part of God's design, an indispensable complement of the unchanging and eternal.

Virgin and saints, from the chapel of a Coptic monastery in Egypt.

V   The Middle Ages

The thousand years from the fall of the West Roman Empire to the end of the fifteenth century A.D. are known as the "Middle Ages," or the *medieval* period. The term was invented by a seventeenth-century German named Keller, who was expressing the belief he shared with many of his contemporaries that the Ancient World represented one flowering of civilization, and the period in the West after about 1500 a second (the "Renaissance, or re-birth); but that all the ten centuries that separated the end of the first flowering from the beginning of the second were the "years between," the Middle Age. We still use the term, but, whereas Keller and other seventeenth- and eighteenth-century scholars believed that the thousand years of the Middle Ages represented a period when mankind pursued wrong ends, a period of ignorance and barbarism, of monkish superstition, of poverty and unchanging tradition, modern scholars have recognized the untruths, exaggerations, and distortions of these opinions. Yet traces of the older view still persist: in the term "Dark Ages," still often used for the first four or five of the medieval centuries (c. 400–800), and even in the term "Gothic," still used for the architecture of the great medieval churches of the twelfth century and later. "Gothic" originally meant "barbarous and crude" to its inventors, but we use it without its old connotations, since we have come to admire and appreciate the beauty of the buildings and the genius of their creators.

During the thousand years of the Middle Ages, the great cultural tradition, which began in the river valleys of the Near East and continues to the present day, split into three parts that can be distinguished as sub-cultures. Foreshadowed as early as the fourth century A.D. by the administrative changes of the emperors Diocletian (284–305) and Constantine (324–337), there came about a division between the eastern Orthodox culture centered in Constantinople, and the western Catholic culture centered in Rome. Then in the seventh century A.D. came Mohammed, the conquests of the Arab Moslems, adherents of his new religion, and the formation of the Moslem sub-culture including Arabia, Syria, Persia, North Africa, and parts of central Asia and of Spain. These three cultures were never out of touch with each other, and especially toward the end of the Middle Ages, came into very active contact. What we in the western European tradition call the Crusades (lasting from 1095 to the end of the thirteenth century) were a very thorough mixing up of all three. In the next chapter, when we consider the state of Europe at the end of the Middle Ages, we shall be dealing briefly with the earlier development of all three of these cultures, the western Christian, the eastern Christian, and the Moslem, and shall indicate some of the lasting effects of their mutual contacts.

Early Middle Ages

Although the overtones suggested by the old-fashioned phrase "Dark Ages" are not altogether misleading, we prefer the term "early middle ages" for the period down to about the year 1000. The breakdown of the West Roman Empire was a gradual process that lasted over several generations in any single region, such as Gaul. But there was nothing like a complete break with the past; had there been, you could hardly be reading a book of this sort in the twentieth century. The basic material discoveries of the Neolithic Revolution—agriculture, stock-raising, pottery, weaving, and many other arts and crafts—were maintained. There was even some improvement in techniques. The Anglo-Saxons in England devised a heavier plow that broke rich, wet clays that their predecessors, the Romano-Britons, had never tried to cultivate. The horse-collar, which gave the beast a better traction without shutting off his windpipe, came late in the period. At the higher levels of culture, the Christian religion, some essentials of Greco-Roman thought, some concept of imperial unity, survived.

What was lost during the long centuries of barbarian invasion, penetration, and settlement, was the political, economic, and intellectual techniques that had enabled the ancients to live together and govern themselves in an orderly way in large territorial units, with extensive trade carried on by good sea and land communications. By the seventh century, what had once been great cities, even imperial Rome itself, had shrunk to small towns at best, kept alive as administrative centers for the one great large-scale organization that did survive, the Roman Catholic Church. Most of the inhabitants of western and central Europe lived in the countryside in small local units, largely self-sufficient — producing all that they consumed. Trade was reduced to a minimum, though it never vanished. Warriors, for instance, always had weapons, and indeed armor; and iron and steel are not commodities that can always be locally produced. Little money circulated. The elaborate Roman bureaucracy to administer financial, judicial, and military affairs had been shattered and destroyed. Everything was more primitive, more rudimentary.

The Germanic peoples had long been filtering into the empire, sometimes as individuals or families who worked on the land or got jobs as soldiers. Individuals among them often rose to high position in the Roman armies, and helped defend the Empire against other barbarians, who by the third century were attacking in organized tribal war bands: Goths, Vandals, Franks, Angles, Saxons, Burgundians, Lombards. Although the Germans had rubbed up against the imperial frontier for several centuries, and had developed an envious admiration for Rome, their own political organization was at a far lower level, and they could not possibly take over and manage so elaborate a political and economic

structure. So while the basic unit of group life became the farming village with its peasants, craftsmen, village church, and local strong man or overlord, the memory remained of the former larger Roman provinces. And very gradually over long centuries the older territorial units would re-emerge, sometimes with new barbarian names. So Britannia became England, land of the Angles; Gallia became France, land of the Franks. Two other tribes gave their names to regions that might well have developed into separate modern states, Burgundy on the eastern borders of France, and Lombardy in the north Italian plain. Italy and Spain had retained their old Roman names, a sign that the Latin tradition was strong enough in these regions to assimilate the Germanic invaders, while the name Germany, of course, reflects the fact that all of the Germans had originated in its forests.

Charlemagne, the Empire, the Northmen

Toward the end of the eighth century the Franks provided a leader who briefly re-united large parts of western Europe. This was Charlemagne, who led his troops on expeditions eastward from his capital at Aachen across the Rhine against the still barbarian Saxons, and added to his holdings the region between the Rhine and the Elbe, thus bringing it for the first time within the boundaries of civilized Europe. His forces also challenged the Moslems, who had crossed from North Africa and seized Spain, and were threatening to spill north across the Pyrenees. All of northern and central Italy came under Charlemagne's control. Though Britain, most of Spain, southern Italy, Sicily, and North Africa lay outside his dominions, he did govern all the other former western Roman provinces and much German territory that Rome had never conquered. On Christmas day, 800, the pope crowned Charlemagne emperor in Rome. So mighty was the tradition of the Roman Empire, and so great its hold on men's minds, that more than three hundred years after the last emperor in the west had disappeared, the chief bishop of the

SCANDINAVIA

North Sea

SCOTLAND

IRELAND

NORTHUMBRIA

Whitby

ANGLO-
SAXON
KINGDOMS

WALES

MERCIA

EAST
ANGLIA

CORNWALL   WESSEX   London   Canterbury

ESSEX

SUSSEX   KENT

KINGDOM
OF
DENMARK

Baltic Sea

SAXONS

Cologne

Aachen

Rhine R.

Soissons

Verdun

Paris

Strasbourg

Seine R.

Danube R.

BOHEMIA

Elbe R.

Oder R.

MORAVIA

BAVARIA

PANNONIAN
MARCH

A   V   A   R   S

CARINTHIA

MARCH OF
FRIULI

Drava R.

BRITTANY

Fontenoy

Poitiers

Besançon

AQUITAINE

Geneva

Lyons

Loire R.

Rhône R.

BURGUNDY

LOMBARDY

Po R.

Pavia

Venice

CROATS

Danube R.

BULGARS

Ravenna

Spalato

SLAVIC PEOPLES

Roncesvalles

SPANISH MARCH

Ebro R.

Arles

Marseilles

DONATION

OF

PEPIN

Adriatic Sea

EMIRATE

OF

CORDOVA

Barcelona

CORSICA

Rome

Monte Cassino

DUCHY OF
BENEVENTO

Naples

THRACE

Constantinople

Thessalonica

SARDINIA

BALEARIC IS.

Carolingian Empire

SICILY

B Y Z A N T I N E   E M P I R E

Mediterranean Sea

CRETE

	Kingdom of Charlemagne, 768
	Acquired by Charlemagne to 814
	Areas tributary to Charlemagne's Empire
	Byzantine Empire
■	Battle sites

0   100   200   300   400
Miles

Partition of the Empire
Treaty of Verdun, 843

KINGDOM
OF CHARLES
THE BALD

KINGDOM
OF LOTHAIR

KINGDOM
OF LOUIS

Christian Church felt this to be the appropriate title for the victorious barbarian warlord.

Charlemagne was extremely intelligent, and a vigorous patron of the arts, which enjoyed a brilliant brief revival in his time. He knew Latin, and could read, but he could never learn to write. Naturally he could not re-create the old Roman imperial bureaucracy or invent a new and effective method for administering such a vast area: the trained manpower simply did not exist, and could not be summoned into existence. So Charlemagne's government was necessarily extremely simple: about 300 counts each governed a local county, sharing power and influence with the local bishops and other great landowners, checked only by occasional visits of investigation by officials of the emperor. Under Charlemagne's successors the old Frankish custom of dividing an inheritance evenly among the heirs reasserted itself. Though the title of emperor was passed down to a single heir in each generation, the territories were divided and re-divided; quarrels raged within the imperial family; and by the mid-ninth century the title had already become an empty honor. Yet the imperial idea remained alive, and in 962 another German ruler, this time a Saxon, Otto I, was crowned emperor by the pope. The institution thus launched—the Holy Roman Empire of the Germans—continued to exist down to 1806, when Napoleon abolished it, vivid testimony to the lasting power of the Roman imperial tradition over the European mind. Only a few decades after Charlemagne's death in 814 began the last and most savage of the barbarian attacks on Europe—the invasions of the Northmen from Scandinavia, who pillaged and ravaged along the coasts of England and France, penetrated into the Mediterranean through the Straits of Gibraltar, crossed the Baltic to what is now Russia, and sailed down its rivers to the Black Sea and beyond. Others in their Viking ships sailed westward to Iceland, Greenland, and, almost surely, to landings in the New World, probably in Canada and perhaps in New England. In Europe, these Vikings forced the Frankish king to cede to them a region along the lower Seine, still called Normandy (911). From

Normandy soon after the year 1000 expeditions went off to southern Italy, and founded a flourishing state there; and in 1066 the Norman Duke William crossed the English Channel and conquered England. Everywhere—in Normandy, south Italy, England, and even Russia—the Northmen when they ceased to be brigands, proved to be able administrators.

Feudalism

During the long centuries of the early Middle Ages, and especially during the disorderly period that followed the break-up of Charlemagne's empire, and saw the chaos wrought by

Ninth-century bronze statuette presumed to represent Charlemagne.

the Viking raids, human relations came to be governed by improvisations suitable for continued emergency. In order to survive, people had to make arrangements with each other — personal, territorial, and governmental — that would allocate responsibilities and privileges ordinarily associated with a central government. Local authority had somehow to perform the elementary duties of maintaining human life and — so far as possible — property. It was, of course, important people, people with land and money and power, not the masses of the population, who made the rules. For some of the arrangements they turned to traditional Roman practices, for others to barbarian practices, and for still others to practices current in the Church. The way of life that these rulers of society developed in these centuries we call by the name of feudalism.

The old German tribal war-band, organized for fighting and seizing booty, and the Roman practice of "patronage," whereby a rich man would take a poorer man as his "client," and offer him protection and rewards in exchange for service, provided ways in which a powerful man could rely on a less powerful man to render him service, perhaps military service, while the less powerful man could enjoy a measure of physical and economic security. Sometimes the patron would give the client the use of a piece of land for his lifetime. These practices developed and spread. The medieval word for the client was *vassal,* for the patron *suzerain,* for the land *benefice,* and later, if and when the benefice became hereditary in the family of the client, *fief,* in Latin: *feudum,* from which comes the word "feudal" that we use to describe all these practices. With the feudum or fief there passed to the heirs of the vassal the obligation to continue rendering service to the suzerain and *his* heirs. Often the grant of a fief to a vassal carried with it certain rights over the inhabitants of the piece of land in question, such as the right to judge cases arising between them, to impose fines, even to collect taxes. Feudal practices varied greatly from region to region. Some parts of Europe were thoroughly feudalized, such as France and the Low

Countries; others, like Germany, had more land that never became fiefs but remained private property.

Feudalism involved a contract between lord (suzerain) and vassal. When they entered upon their relationship, the vassal rendered homage to his lord, and promised him aid and counsel: he would appear fully armed and fight for the lord when needed (often at specified times of year), and would join with his fellow-vassals in the lord's court to render judgment. He usually had to assume certain financial obligations as well. For his part, the lord owed protection and justice to his vassal. If either broke the contract, the other could take recognized procedures against him. When either lord or vassal died, the contract had to be renewed with his successor. Within a feudal kingdom, the king occupied the top position in a theoretical pyramid of society. Immediately below him would be his vassals, men who held fiefs directly from the king, called tenants-in-chief. But they in turn would be feudal lords: that is, they would have given out various parts of their own property as fiefs to their own vassals. These men, the king's vassals' vassals, would be the king's "rear vassals," and so at the next lower level of the theoretical pyramid. But they too would often have vassals, and so on, for many more levels — a process called "subinfeudation."

Practice was even more complicated than theory. A tenant-in-chief might hold only a very small fief from the king, and not be a very important person at all, while a vassal's vassal's vassal might be rich and powerful. The Dukes of Normandy, who were vassals to the King of France, were for some centuries much stronger than their overlord. An individual might receive fiefs from more than one lord, and would so be vassal to more than one lord, owing homage and fealty to each. What was he to do if one of his lords quarreled with another and went to war? To which one would he owe priority? This kind of thing happened very often: one Bavarian count had 20 different fiefs held of 20 different lords. Gradually, there arose a new concept, that of a *liege* lord, the one to whom a vassal owed service ahead of any other; but in practice the difficulties often persisted. Even though feudal law became more and more subtle and complex, this was an era when armed might counted for more than legality.

All the complicated arrangements we have been discussing directly involved only the governing persons who fought on horseback as mounted knights, and whose fiefs consisted of landed property known as manors or estates. The total of such persons would hardly reach ten per cent of the population of Europe. The other ninety per cent mostly lived on the land as dependents of some property-holder, (or lord, in the sense of landlord) on such a manor, a farming estate with one or more villages to house the peasants. They were not slaves, but most of them were serfs. They could not leave the manor without the consent of the lord. Their children were serfs after them. The lord could not sell them or dispose of them unless he disposed of the land at the same time. If he did, they went with it. The lord of the manor had his own strips of land, perhaps a quarter to a third of the whole amount, reserved for the production of food for himself and his household. The serfs worked this land for him, often three days a week throughout the year, and full-time during the harvest season. Each serf-peasant family had its own strips of land, in theory designed to give him a bit of arable land, a bit of less fertile land, a bit of woodlot, and so on. In exchange for the right to pasture their beasts in the lord's fields, the serf might have to dig ditches or maintain the road. They paid fees to have their grain ground at the lord's mill and their bread baked in his oven.

As in feudalism, so on the manor, old traditions had combined: the Roman landlord's economic rights over his peasants, with the Germanic village headman's political control over the villagers. Custom alone prevailed in the lord's court when cases arose between peasants, and custom regulated the bargaining agreements reached between peasants for the use of scarce equipment. The serf had no rights, and could not appeal against an unjust lord. Only a deep sense of what was customary

often prevented a lord from being too extortionate or cruel.

Towns

The eleventh century proved to be a major turning point in the social and economic life of the West, although nobody alive at the time could have been fully conscious of what was happening. As the raids of the Northmen tapered off, most of western Europe found itself secure against outside attack. A major increase in the population of Europe occurred. The larger population led to greater demand for food and to pressure for the settlement of new farm lands, which pioneers were creating by felling trees or draining swamps.

As part of the same general development, trade slowly began to revive. Medieval farmers were helpless in the face of a bad harvest year, and plenty or scarcity varied widely from region to region. It was the natural thing to bring surpluses into areas of famine and sell them at high prices to the hungry. The first new commercial centers arose in places such as Venice and the Low Countries, where the local farms could not feed the increasing population. The people of Flanders, living in an area that was poor for growing grain but good for raising sheep, sold their raw wool, developed a woolen-manufacturing industry, and imported the food they needed.

The recovery of commerce and the beginnings of industries stimulated the growth of towns. Old Roman towns like London and Marseilles revived. New towns grew around a castle (*bourg* in France, *burgh* in England, *burg* in Germany), especially if it was strategically located for trade as well as for defense. And so the resident *bourgeois, burgesses,* or *burghers* enter the language as castle-dwellers, but soon become recognizable as residents of towns, engaged in commerce. Protected by the lord of the castle or sometimes by the abbot of a local monastery, the townsmen built walls and pursued their trade.

Mutual advantage soon led proprietors, including kings as well as lesser lords, to grant privileges to the townsmen by issuing a charter. Although the contents of such documents vary widely, most of them guaranteed free status to the townsmen; even an escaped serf within the town would acquire freedom if he could avoid capture for a year. The charter might also grant the townsmen the right to hold a perpetual market, to transfer property within the town walls, and to have their lawsuits tried in a town court by town custom.

Industry followed commerce into the town. The merchant, with his experience of distant markets, learned how to buy raw material, to have workmen do the manuacturing wherever it was cheapest, and to sell the finished products wherever he could get the best price. The workmen also soon began to organize themselves into craft guilds, which provided medical care and burial for the members, and often fixed minimum wages, the standards of quality of the product, and even the prices that were to be asked.

Enterprise was neither free nor private. It was highly regulated not only as an effort to reduce outside competition but also as a reflection of the ideas of the age. Men believed that a "just price" for a pair of shoes included the cost of the leather and the thread, the amount needed to sustain the shoemaker at his usual standard of life while he made the shoes, and a small addition to pay the seller for his time and trouble. To "make money" in the modern sense of charging all that the traffice would bear was in theory to cheat the customer. No doubt many medieval customers were in fact cheated in this sense, but the ethics of the time condemned the action. Finance capitalism—the use of money to make money, the investment of funds at interest—was condemned as usury.

The Church and Education

Towns and townsmen thus fitted awkwardly into the feudal way of life. So too in many ways with the Church and churchmen. The Church included not only the hierarchy of churchmen from priest on upward through bishop, archbishop and pope (all of them

called "secular" clergy because they lived in the world of affairs), but also the "regular" clergy (who lived by a *regula*) or rule: the monks and nuns in an ever increasing number of orders. Many a bishop or even abbot owned great properties, and was deeply involved in feudal society, exercising the powers of a great lord, judging purely worldly cases in his court, even at times wielding a mace on the battlefield. Certainly, at the level of the village, the priest owed his appointment to the lord of the manor, and was his useful servant. Yet no matter how enmeshed in the feudal-manorial network a cleric might be, great or humble, he also belonged to a great international organization with its own chain of command. Sometimes its interests conflicted directly with those of powerful laymen. More important, every churchman was for all mankind an agent of God upon earth, to be respected and heeded, and to be defied only at the greatest risk.

It was the clergy that alone directed and conducted education in the Europe of the Middle Ages. Unless destined for the priesthood, young men of the upper classes had little formal schooling, though the family chaplain often taught them to read and write. Their training was in war and hunting, and sometimes in the problems of managing their property. Monastic schools educated future monks and priests. Scholars of the time listed seven "liberal arts," the *trivium* (grammar, rhetoric, dialectic), and the *quadrivium* (arithmetic, geometry, astronomy, and music), the first three including much of what we might call the humanities today, the last four corresponding to the sciences. Only a few monastic schools in the eleventh century were prepared to offer instruction in all seven, and in general monks thought of their work as the preservation rather than the advancement of knowledge.

The cathedral schools, on the other hand, whose teachers were often less timid about studying pagan writings from the great classical past, fostered a more inquiring spirit. In France during the eleventh century at the cathedral schools of Paris, Chartres, Reims, and other towns, distinguished teachers now were often succeeded by men whom they had trained themselves, and distinguished pupils went on to join or found other schools. Scholarship no longer depended on the occasional advent of a single first-class mind. In Italy, where the connection with cathedrals was not so close, the medical school at Salerno had a tradition stretching back into the early Middle Ages; at Bologna law became the specialty, beginning as a branch of rhetoric, and so within the *trivium*. Students were attracted to Bologna from other regions of Italy, and even from northern Europe, and in the early twelfth century, as education became fashionable for young men ambitious for advancement in the Church or in royal service, the numbers of students grew rapidly.

The student body at Bologna organized itself into two associations: students from the near side of the Alps and students from the farther side of the Alps, and the two incorporated as the whole body, the *universitas,* or university. As a corporate body, they could protect themselves against being overcharged for food and lodging by threatening to leave town; they had no property, and could readily have moved. If the students did not like a professor, they simply stayed away from his lectures, and he starved or moved on, for he was dependent on tuition fees for his living. Soon the *universitas,* that is to say the students, fixed the price of room and board in town, and fined professors for absence or for lecturing too long. The professors organized too, and admitted to their number only those who had passed an examination, and so won a *license* to teach, remote ancestor of all our academic degrees.

In Paris and elsewhere in the north, the cathedral schools were the immediate forerunners of the universities; and it was the teachers, not the students, who organized first, as a gild of those who taught the seven liberal arts and who obtained their licenses from the cathedral authorities. By the thirteenth century pious citizens had founded in Paris the first residence halls for poor students, who might eat and sleep free in these "colleges." The practice crossed the Channel to Oxford and Cambridge. As in later times, the authorities of these medieval universities stoutly de-

fended themselves against encroachment by the secular power; there was often friction between "town" and "gown," as irrepressible high spirits among the students led to rioting and disorder.

Medieval Learning

Much of the learning taught and studied in the Middle Ages seems strange to us today, and it requires imagination to understand how exciting the exercise was to men discovering it for the first time.

It was only about the year 1100 that churchmen began to use logic learned from a few available fragments of ancient Greek philosophers as a means to approach the writings of the church fathers in a systematic way. Churchmen debated whether it was proper to use human reason in considering a particular theological question (for example, was Christ present in the sacramental wafer and wine?), and in all efforts to explain away inconsistencies in the Bible and the Fathers in general. Even those who attacked the use of reason used it themselves in making new definitions that enabled them to argue that bread and wine could indeed, in a certain way become flesh and blood.

Once the new method became available, the men of the late eleventh and early twelfth centuries employed it largely in a celebrated controversy over the philosophical problem of universals. A universal is a whole category of things; when we say "dog" or "table" or "man," we may mean not any specific individual dog or table or man, but the idea of all dogs, tables, or men: dogdom, tabledom, mankind. Now the question that exercised the medieval thinkers was whether universal categories have an existence: *is* there such a thing as dogdom, tabledom, or mankind?

If you said no, you were a nominalist; that is, you thought dogdom, tabledom, mankind were merely *nomina,* names that men give to a general category from their experience of individual members of it. We experience dogs, tables, men, and so we infer the existence of dogdom, tabledom, mankind because the individual members of the category have certain points of resemblance; but the category, the universal, has no existence in itself. If you said yes, you were a realist; that is, you thought that the general categories did exist. Many realists took this view a large step further, and said that the individual dog, table, or man was far less real than the generalizing category or universal, or even that the individual was a mere reflection of one aspect of the category, and existed by virtue of belonging to the category; a man exists only because he partakes of the nature of mankind, a dog because he partakes of the nature of dogdom.

If one transfers the problem to politics, and thinks of the state and the individual, one can see at once how great its practical importance may be. A nominalist would say that the state is simply a name, and exists only by virtue of the fact that the individuals who make it up are real; he would argue that the state must then serve its subjects, since after all it is only the sum of their individualities. A realist would say that the state is the only real thing, that the individual subjects exist only so far as they partake of its general character, and that the state by virtue of its existence properly dominates the individual. In religion, an extreme nominalist, arguing that what one can perceive through one's senses is alone real, might even have trouble believing in the existence of God. An extreme realist would tend to ignore or even to deny the existence of the physical world and its problems. Moderate realists have to start with faith, to believe so that they may know.

Peter Abelard (1079–1142), a popular lecturer in the University of Paris, tried to compromise the question. He argued that the universals were not merely names, as the nominalists held, nor did they have a real existence, as the realists held. They were, he said, concepts in men's minds, and as such had a real existence of a special kind in the mind, which had created them out of its experience of particulars: mankind from men, dogdom from dogs, and so on. Abelard insisted on the importance of understanding for true faith; he put reason first, and thus understood in order

that he might believe, instead of the other way around. His most famous work, *Sic et Non* (Yes and No), lists over 150 theological statements, and cites authorities both defending and attacking the truth of each. When Scripture and the Fathers were inconsistent, he seems to argue, how could a man make up his mind what to believe unless he used his head? A rationalist and lover of argument, Abelard was none the less a deeply pious believer. The mystical St. Bernard, however, suspicious of reason, believed him heretical, and had his views condemned and denounced repeatedly.

By the mid-twelfth century, the main body of Greek scientific writings chiefly by Aristotle—lost all these centuries to the West —was on its way to recovery, often through translations from Arabic into Latin. By using these instruments medieval thinkers were for the first time in a position to systematize and summarize their entire philosophical position. Yet the recovery of Aristotle also forced the Christian thinkers to try to reconcile the contradictions they found between the ancients—especially between Aristotle and fundamental Christian teaching. It was the Dominican Albertus Magnus (1193–1280), a German, and his pupil Thomas Aquinas (1225–1274), an Italian, who—in massive multi-volume works produced over a lifetime—achieved this reconciliation.

Aquinas' best-known writings were the *Summa Theologica* and the *Summa contra Gentiles.* He discussed God, man, and the universe, arranging his material in systematic, topical order, and in the form of an inquiry into and discussion of each open question. First he cited the evidence on each side, then he gave his own answer, and finally he demonstrated the falsity of the other position Though Aquinas always cited authority, he also never failed to provide his own logical analysis. For him reason was a most valuable instrument, but only when it recognized its own limitations. When reason unaided could not comprehend an apparent contradiction with faith, it must yield to faith, since reason by itself could not understand the entire universe. Certain fundamentals must be accepted as unprovable axioms of faith, although, once accepted, reason could show that they are probable.

If a man puts a series of arguments together and comes out with a conclusion contrary to what orthodox Christians believe, he is simply guilty of faulty logic, and the use of correct logic can readily show where he erred. Indeed, Aquinas delighted in the game of inventing arguments against accepted beliefs, matching them with a set of even more ingenious arguments, and then reconciling the two with an intellectual skill suggesting the trained athlete's ability in timing and co-ordination.

The Church, then, is central to all medieval history; if you could write a history of everything the Church touched, you would write a complete history of the Middle Ages. And the Church, like the towns, was a force that in the end acted to loosen feudal ties. Although in the realm of ideas, the Church usually defended and strengthened the established order, it was from the clergy that there came a whole series of reforming movements that questioned the relations of man to master, the distribution of wealth and power, and even, with Luther and Protestantism, the philosophic basis of the medieval outlook.

In the realm of institutions, the influence of the Church helped build the modern state. In a series of dramatic struggles that began in the latter half of the eleventh century, between popes and emperors, the popes successfully challenged the claims of the emperors to supreme power in Europe. Though within the embryonic nation-states the Church often resisted the centralizing work of the kings, over most of the West the Church helped the kings make the new states. The popes defeated the emperors, but they could not defeat the kings; therefore they sought to become allies of the kings.

Monarchy:
France, England, Germany

Indeed, as the last few sentences will have suggested, the struggle for power between the monarch and his vassals became the chief feature of political life in western Europe beginning with the eleventh century, and continued to hold the center of the stage until the fifteenth. The struggle took differing forms and had a different outcome in each of the different emerging nations. In France, during the Middle Ages the most feudal area in Europe, the monarch successfully asserted his supremacy over his vassals, who generally acted separately, and by the fourteen hundreds the king had established royal absolutism. In England, the monarch attained great power earlier than his French counterpart, but was then forced by his vassals, who got together and defended their corporate interests, to share power with them by allowing them to consult with him on certain key questions, so that by the fourteen hundreds we can clearly see in action the body that was the ancestor of our own representative institutions: parliament. In Germany, the prevalence of a non-feudal nobility, the great struggle with the popes, and the preoccupation of the ruler with the affairs of Italy —which, as Holy Roman Emperors, the German monarchs sought to rule—brought about a third result. Central authority was weakened, and each important noble became virtually sovereign over his own lands, even though their area might be small. Absolute monarchy in France, limited monarchy in England, princely particularism in Germany: these characteristic forms of government took shape during these later medieval centuries. What happened in these distant centuries largely determined the future character of the western European countries, and explains much about their attitudes and behavior in the modern world.

In France, the royal family of the Capetians (from Capet, family name of the first king, Hugh, chosen in 987) produced suitable male heirs for 350 years. In alliance with the Church, and soon with the new towns, the Capetians governed their compact small original domain, the Ile de France, including Paris and its environs. They successfully defeated the English threat to absorb French territory in the late twelfth and early thirteenth centuries, and added to their holdings by the conquest of Normandy (1204) and the south (1208–1249). They devised more efficient and more complicated forms of government: a new central and regional bureaucracy grew flexibly at their command. Gradually, trained lawyers helped render justice and trained accountants helped collect revenue. St. Louis (1226–1270) could issue decrees (*ordonnances*) for all of France without the previous assent of his vassals. Royal justice and royal money superseded feudal justice and baronial money.

When Philip IV (Philip the Fair, 1285–1304) needed money for his wars, he found new means of raising it, and despite his unpopularity, his feudal opponents did not unite to oppose his encroachments. So strongly had the Capetians built that the centralized French monarchy survived the dreadful strains of the Hundred Years' War with England (1338–1453), when at one moment (1420) the English ruled half of France and had

gained a promise of the other half for the future. The famous national revival begun by Joan of Arc (executed 1431) swept the invaders out of all of France by 1453 except for the seaport town of Calais, and Louis XI (1461–1483) consolidated both French territory and the royal grip on its government.

In England, the invading Duke of Normandy, William the Conqueror (1066), destroyed the Saxon kingdom, but kept its local government by sheriff and local court, continued to summon the militia (*fyrd*), and to collect the tax (Danegeld) originally levied to raise money for defense against the Danish northmen. He introduced knight-service, substituted his own council for that of the Anglo-Saxons, and, as conqueror, was able to take all of the land of England into absolute ownership before giving most of it to his vassals and the Church. Everybody swore primary obedience to him, and he ordered a massive survey of all landed property in England to assure the royal revenue. William was stronger at his death in 1087 than the French monarchy would be for more than two centuries. Under his successors the administration grew more elaborate and more effective, and the monarchs made royal justice cheap and attractive to their subjects by making available for purchase royal writs: orders that a royal official hear their cases. Travelling royal justices visited the provinces.

Despite occasional periods of civil war and quarrels with the papacy, the English monarchy stayed strong until John (1199–1216) persisted in punishing his vassals without trial and in raising money in ways they felt to be illegal. Banding together, the barons made him sign the famous Great Charter (Magna Carta, 1215) in which he promised to stop these irregularities. Though he and his successors often tried to break the promises and sometimes got away with it, the vassals, acting in their own selfish interests, had established the principle that the king was subject to the law, and if necessary might be forced to observe it. This is the chief reason why we are so often told that the Charter is the foundation-document of democratic liberties in the modern western world.

Plan of a medieval manor; the solid strips are the lord's demesne.

By the end of the thirteenth century, not only the great barons but lesser gentry and townsmen felt entitled to be consulted before the king levied taxes. More and more they attended the discussions (parliaments) of the large royal council. During the fourteenth century the great lords and higher clergy coalesced for these purposes into a body clearly the ancestor of the later House of Lords, while the lesser gentry and the townsmen coalesced into a body clearly the ancestor of the later House of Commons. These parliamentary foundations survived the upheavals of the Hundred Years' War with France and the subsequent decades (1455–1485) of terrible civil war among rival factions of the English nobility, known as the Wars of the Roses.

In Germany, out of the disintegration of the German portions of Charlemagne's empire there emerged five large duchies. The dukes, however, never could assert their feudal supremacy within the duchies, and many small and large estates continued to be owned by free men, vassals to nobody. By the tenth century one of the dukes was always elected king, but the kings experienced great difficulty in governing. To administer the royal domains the German kings early began to use the bishops, better educated than laymen and without children to whom they would wish to bequeath their properties and power. While the kings appointed the bishops, the Church in Germany furnished from its own lands much of the royal revenue and military manpower, and the papacy—weak and corrupt—raised no objections. But by the mid-eleventh century the German kings themselves by reforming the papacy had contributed to the downfall of their own system of government.

The reforming popes (notably Gregory VII, 1073–1085) challenged the imperial right to appoint bishops, and stirred up rebellions against the monarch at home. By the time the long struggle (Investiture Controversy) was over (1122), civil war in Germany made it impossible for the kings to reassemble their properties and put their government in order, and feudalizing tendencies increased just at the time the French kings were bringing them under control. The German kings, as Holy Roman Emperors after 962, also devoted much of their attention and resources to asserting their powers in Italy, where, by the late twelfth century they secured a large measure of control in the north, had made a dynastic alliance with the rich and powerful Norman kingdom in South Italy and Sicily, and threatened to catch the papal territories in a pincers. A new papal-imperial struggle began in the early thirteenth century, and by 1268 the popes had won: Germany was condemned to princely particularism—that is, to remain a collection of petty states, large and small, with no unifying central régime.

Literature and the Arts

The harshness of the Dark Ages and the early feudal world is reflected in the surviving literary works by laymen: for example, the Anglo-Saxon epic *Beowulf,* with its grim battles against monsters and its gloomy scenery. The eleventh century was a turning point in literature, too. The northern French *Chanson de Roland* (Song of Roland), though probably not written down in its present form until after 1100, is essentially an eleventh-century poem, telling of the exploits of Roland, a peer of Charlemagne, against the Moslems and in the face of treachery. Human beings replace monsters as the foe, the landscape brightens, Christian piety softens some of the worst horrors; Roland sees to it that his dead comrades receive a Christian blessing, and combines loyalty to his suzerain, Charlemagne, with love for "sweet France." Charlemagne himself, aged, troubled by the manifold problems of empire, weeping at the death of his loyal vassal, is a truly human figure.

In southern France, things were gentler still; no doubt the sunny climate, the greater leisure, and the proximity to the cultivated Moslems of Spain all played a part. Here lyric poetry became the preferred medium, and love the theme, but love with a curious code of its own, *courtoisie,* or courtly love. The lady was always the wife of somebody else; she was worshipped from afar, and the slightest kindness from her was celebrated in ecstasy, while her merest word was a command, and the knight gladly undertook the most arduous mission on her behalf without hope of reward. But a lady who failed to reward him was not playing quite according to the rules of this elaborate and artificial game. Southern French influence travelled as far as Germany. The code of courtly love formed part of a general code of behavior and manners for the lord and his vassal that we know as chivalry, from *chevalier*, a horseman or knight. Loyalty to the suzerain, like Roland's to Charlemagne, piety like Roland's, vigor and decency: real men as well as the heroes of romances regarded these as true virtues, and strove to live up to them.

Chivalric literature was written in the vernacular tongues—French, German, Provençal (the old language of southern France). But the larger portion of medieval writing was in Latin: the sermons and lives of the saints, which continued to enjoy great popularity, and the chronicles, which began in the eleventh century to be better written, more accurate, and more detailed. An occasional biography of a living man or even an autobiography made its appearance. In verse, the Latin hymn reached solemn heights in the twelfth and thirteenth centuries, while the dramatic character of the liturgy suggested that putting dialogue into the mouths of different persons would magnify the effect, and led to the actual writing of the earliest post-classical plays. Even popular literature—and only fragments survive—was mostly still in Latin, and often shows a shrewd earthy admiration for the cunning fellow and a scorn for fine words.

Unique in the period was the verse of the twelfth-century "Goliardic poets." These poets, usually renegade scholars or clerics, purported to serve Golias, a sort of Satan, who perhaps was derived from Goliath in the Old Testament. Their verses mocked both the form and the values of serious religious poetry, not sparing the clergy or the Bible itself in their satire, and singing the praises of wine, women, and song. Here is how the "Confession of Golias" (c. 1165) defined the highest good:

> My intention is to die
>   In the tavern drinking;
> Wine must be at hand, for I
>   Want it when I'm sinking.
> Angels when they come shall cry,
>   At my frailties winking:
> "Spare this drunkard, God, he's high,
>   Absolutely stinking!"*

The Cathedral

Admirers of the Middle Ages sometimes declare that the medieval craftsman worked in anonymity, content to carve or paint for the glory of God and the joy of creating beauty, and not for fame or money. Perhaps so, though we do not know the names of many medieval architects and sculptors simply because the records have been lost. Yet art and artists seem to have been closely tied to the community in the Middle Ages. The greatest of medieval arts, architecture, clearly shows this community stamp. In a medieval town the cathedral, parish churches, town hall, guild halls, and other *public* buildings dominate the scene.

The great medieval cathedrals were primarily places of worship, but they were also centers of community life where people came to stroll, to get out of the rain, to gossip, to do business, even to court. In the quiet side chapels the worshiper could pray in peace while the people thronged the nave. As long as reasonable decorum was observed, no one thought that these activities profaned God's house. Moreover, the statues, the paintings, the stained-glass windows, and the carvings served in effect as an illustrated Bible and as a history of the Church for a population that could not read. The wealth of detail served not only to decorate but also to teach.

During the early Middle Ages the Romanesque style of architecture prevailed in the West; it was derived largely from the classical Roman basilica, a great hall roofed with the

*George F. Whicher, *The Goliard Poets.* Copyright 1949 by George F. Whicher. Reprinted by permission of New Directions, Publishers.

round arch perfected by the Romans. The Gothic style developed from this—the arches became more and more lofty; pointed, not round; decoration became richer and richer, and tracery more and more delicate and elaborate.

Since the medieval builder had no structural steel to work with, he had to support the stone ceiling and the heavy roof with masonry. The round arch of the Romanesque produced barrel vaulting, in which the ceiling presses down evenly all along the walls with great weight. To withstand this weight, the walls had to be strong, with a minimum of openings, so that Romanesque buildings, while often having great dignity and solidity are usually poorly lighted. What freed the medieval Gothic builder to carry his buildings to soaring heights was the pointed arch. By means of this device, the builder could carry the weight of a vaulted ceiling along masonry ribs to fall on four great supports. These supports could be pillars rather than walls, thus freeing space for large windows. A subsidiary device, the flying buttress, supporting the walls from outside, gave the builder a chance to provide for even more light and height.

Gothic architecture is not wholly ecclesiastical. Yet its two other major manifestations—the great town halls and guild halls of medieval cities (at their best in the Low Countries), and the medieval castle—are both expressions of a commmunity need. The best of the town halls are comparatively late, profusely decorated, usually with splendid towers and with at least one great high room. Many of the massive castles were first of all designed for the purpose of keeping the enemy out. But even these great fortresses often have a chapel and a hall that bear the mark of the Gothic love of light, height, and decoration. Perhaps the most typical Gothic building is not the castle or town hall, nor even the cathedral, but the great monastic abbey, which combines elements of each. One of the best, though no longer a religious community, is the great abbey of St. Michel on the border of Brittany and Normandy. Mont-St.-Michel, a rocky islet tied to the mainland by a narrow causeway, is at once a fortress, a town, and a monastery.

All the fine arts contributed to these great community buildings; indeed up to the very last centuries of the Middle Ages they had hardly any other major outlet. Sculpture was subordinated to architecture. Statues and carvings were fitted into the design of the great churches, in niches on the fronts and porches, or on altars and shrines in the interior. The greatly admired statues on the early west front of Chartres are unnaturally elongated, but they fit all the better into the builder's purpose of framing the entrance arch. Later, the statues—like those at Rheims or Amiens, for example—are more "lifelike." But even this later Gothic sculpture, if only because it is

Nave of the Romanesque church of St. Sernin, Toulouse, from the early twelfth century.

bringing to life God, Christ, angels, saints —and devils—is never simply realistic in the way of the portrait bust, nor independently grand in the way of the equestrian statue. It is always part of the "stone Bible." It almost always tells a story, as in the many representations of the Last Judgment, which is a favorite subject of the medieval sculptor. The sculpture of the Middle Ages is fond of the grotesque. The capitals of the columns are carved in infinite variety, with motifs stemming from plant life but often interspersed with a variety of figures—human, animal, or purely fanciful.

Painting, too, was subordinated to the building. While the medieval church had no place for the canvas designed to be hung for exhibition, mosaics, wall painting, and above all stained glass contributed to the total design. Time has dealt harshly with most of the paintings on walls and pillars, which were apparently brightly colored, almost gay. The stained glass survives as the great medieval achievement in painting. The glass was not really painted of course; each separate bit of the design was stained in the making, and the whole was pieced together as a mosaic held in place by leaden tracery. The painting itself was at first stiff, whether in glass, murals, altar pieces, or in that characteristic medieval form, miniature painting on illuminated manuscripts. Like the sculpture, the painting owes a great debt to the Byzantines (see Chapter 2). Again, as with sculpture, design later grows freer, more "naturalistic."

Church music began in the sixth century with Gregorian chant or plain-song. Plain-song was simply a series of musical tones sung in unison, but with no set rhythmic interval between them. It was used in church services as a setting for the psalms and other prose. But apparently there were also hymns in metrical or verse form, which could be accommodated to a simple tune. By the eleventh century music, like the other arts, grew more and more complex. Our present method of musical notation—the staff—was invented, or at any rate developed and taught, by an eleventh-century Italian monk. Church music developed both melody and harmony—the sounding of two or more notes simultaneously—until the peak of balanced form and matter was reached in the thirteenth century. Later medieval church music sometimes became extremely complex musical puzzles.

To their immediate successors—and indeed to us—the men of the Middle Ages bequeathed a legacy that included a deep sense of the sanctity of a contract between men, and of the need for mutual personal and social responsibility. Here we encounter not only monarchs striving to be absolute, but rebellious subjects striving to tame their rulers and subject them to the rule of law. When the subjects meet to advise and consent and talk in parliaments, they are anticipating cherished aspects of our own political lives. Universities and the excitement of ideas, the theater and the dramatization of roles, praise of the delights of love, and the effort to reconcile reason with faith, the rational with the irrational: these things make the man of the medieval period less remote from us. Even the endless clashing of his weapons and the wretchedness of his lot on earth remind us that his problems remain our own.

Note: See *A History of Civilization,* 3rd edition, Volume I, Chapters 1–10, by Brinton, Christopher, Wolff for detailed reading lists on the subjects treated in this chapter.

Europe at the Close

of the Middle Ages

I   Introduction

Among the dates traditionally assigned for the close of the Middle Ages is 1453, the capture of Orthodox Byzantium by the Moslem Osmanli Turks. Yet in eastern Europe medieval institutions continued to flourish for two centuries and more after 1453. As later sections of this chapter will show, the tsars in Moscow and the sultans in Istanbul continued to act in their different ways as the successors of the Byzantine emperors. New "modern" ideas began to penetrate Russia only in the seventeenth century and the Ottoman Empire only in the eighteenth; by 1700, moreover, the characteristically medieval institution of serfdom was still growing in Russia. In the long perspective of history the Middle Ages ended yesterday in eastern Europe. In western Europe, on the other hand, the Middle

33

Ages ended five centuries ago, with the accession of realistic national monarchs to the thrones of England, France, and Spain. The first two sections of this chapter survey the political and economic forces that destroyed feudal society; succeeding chapters will examine the famous twin movements of Renaissance and Reformation that disrupted the Christian cultural synthesis and religious unity of the medieval West. Words like "destroyed" and "disrupted" should not suggest that the Middle Ages ended abruptly and that modern western civilization appeared with dramatic suddenness. The destruction and disruption did occur, but only as part of a complex process of transition that spanned the history of the West from the fourteenth century through the sixteenth.

The climax of the political transition in the West was the emergence of the "new" monarch, who was not at all interested in faded feudal glories but very much concerned with what the twentieth century knows as power politics. The "new" monarchs of the fifteenth century did not, of course, invent power politics. There had been hard-headed rulers in Antiquity and the Middle Ages. What distinguished the "new" monarchs of the fifteenth century from most of their predecessors was

their candor and their efficiency. They were outspoken in their pursuit of power, naked and unadorned with medieval trappings; they developed better instruments of governing, better soldiers, diplomats, bureaucrats. In short, they made politics more professional.

Outstanding representatives of this new-model monarchy, as we shall shortly see, occupied the thrones of the states along the Atlantic seaboard. In the late 1400's Louis XI of France, Henry VII of England, and Ferdinand and Isabella of Spain set to work putting their respective states in order and increasing their central authority. In these three instances state and nation tended to be identified, and the monarchs exploited the developing nationalism of their subjects to strengthen their own authority. Not all the "new" monarchs were actually kings or queens, however, nor were the new-model states always nations. Power politics flourished in late medieval Germany and Italy; its practitioners were usually to be found, however, not in the decadent office of Holy Roman Emperor but among the rulers of the particular German or Italian states. The German princes and, still more, the Italian despots accomplished on a sectional or regional basis what the Atlantic monarchs were achieving on the plane of the nation-state.

II   The New Monarchs in the West

France: Louis XI

In France Louis XI (1461–1483) was well qualified to reorganize France and revitalize the monarchy after the exhausting struggle of the Hundred Years' War. At his accession he was already a crafty and practiced politician, who despised the pageantry of kingship, liked a simple tavern meal better than elaborate royal fare, and preferred secret diplomacy to open war, soon earning the nickname of the "Universal Spider." Louis forced his protesting

subjects to pay higher taxes, then sweetened the dose, at least for the men of the middle class, by granting them favors and by giving them responsible posts in his administration. He enlarged the army yet used it only for the direst emergencies. And he countered the great threat posed by the Dukes of Burgundy, the rich and powerful vassals of the French kings.

The authority of the Burgundian dukes reached far beyond the Duchy of Burgundy in eastern France and the adjoining Free County (Franche Comté) and encompassed a large portion of the Low Countries. This sprawling Burgundian realm almost deserved to be called an emerging national state. But it was a divided state: the two main territorial blocs in eastern France and the Low Countries were separated by the non-Burgundian lands of Alsace and Lorraine. And it was a personal state, for Duke Philip the Good (1419–1467) had assembled it as much by good luck as by good management, inheriting some lands and acquiring others by conquest or negotiation. Yet it was also a menacing state, which might have interposed itself permanently as a middle kingdom between France and Germany. Philip had been allied with England in the Hundred Years' War. He could draw on the wealth of the Flemish and Dutch towns to support the most lavish court in Europe.

The decisive trial of strength between France and Burgundy took place under Philip's successor, Charles the Bold (1467–1477). Charles determined to build a true middle kingdom by bridging the territorial gap between Burgundy and the Low Countries and seizing Lorraine and Alsace. But since Alsace was a patchwork of feudal jurisdictions overlapping northern Switzerland, his designs threatened the largely independent Swiss confederation. Subsidized by Louis XI, who wanted allies to do his fighting for him, the Swiss defeated Charles three times in 1476 and 1477. In the last of the battles Charles was slain.

Since Charles left no son, his lands were partitioned. The Duchy of Burgundy passed permanently, and the Franche Comté temporarily, to France; the Low Countries went to Mary, the daughter of Charles. Mary married Maximilian of Habsburg, who later became Holy Roman Emperor; their son was to marry the daughter of Ferdinand and Isabella of Spain. The son of this latter union, the Emperor Charles V, was to rule Germany, the Low Countries, and Spain, and to threaten the kingdom of France with hostile encirclement (see Chapter 5). Although Louis XI did not keep all the Burgundian inheritance out of the hands of potential enemies, he did shatter the prospect of a middle kingdom. At his death

Portrait of King Louis XI of France, by Jean Fouquet.

the only major region of France still largely independent of the Crown was the Duchy of Brittany, which was to be brought under royal control during the reign of Louis' son.

The work of Louis XI was solid enough to survive the reigns of his mediocre successors and to give them a base for adventurous expeditions to Italy (see Chapter 5). The France of Louis XI was not yet a full-fledged national monarchy; the forging of the French people into a proud, cohesive, confident nation was to be the accomplishment of subsequent centuries. But he did lay the indispensable foundations for the later achievement by his consolidation of territorial unity and by his competent central administration.

England: Henry VII

In England the aftermath of the Hundred Years' War was the prolonged strife between

England and France during the Hundred Years' War

Areas under English influence, 1429

Boundary of France, 1453

Burgundian Dominions at the death of
Charles the Bold, 1477

■ Battle sites

0   50   100   150
Miles

IRELAND

Irish Sea

NORTHUMBERLAND

North Sea

YORK

Ouse R.

LANCASTER

Trent R.

WALES

Severn R.

ENGLAND

■ Bosworth

Gloucester

Oxford

London

Thames R.

Canterbury

Southampton

English Channel

HOLLAND

THE EMPIRE

Calais

Sluys ■

FLANDERS

Scheldt R.

BRABANT

LIMBURG

Brussels

Agincourt ■

HAINAULT

Meuse R.

Crécy ■

Arras

LUXEMBOURG

Moselle R.

Rhine R.

PICARDY

NORMANDY

Rouen

Seine R.

Rheims

Marne R.

Paris

Seine R.

LORRAINE

ALSACE

BRITTANY

Brétigny

Troyes

NEVERS

DUCHY OF
BURGUNDY

FRANCHE
COMTÉ

SWISS
CONFEDERATION

Orléans

Loire R.

F R A N C E

Bourges

Saône R.

Poitiers ■

DAUPHINY

Rhône R.

A Q U I T A I N E

Bordeaux

Garonne R.

Avignon

ARMAGNAC

Toulouse

Marseilles

NAVARRE

Mediterranean Sea

ARAGON

the rival royal houses of Lancaster and York which threatened grave impairment to the authority of both Crown and Parliament. The Wars of the Roses between the two houses finally ended in 1485 when the Lancastrian leader, Henry Tudor, defeated the Yorkist king, Richard III. The victorious Tudor, Henry VII (1485–1509), had only a tenuous hereditary claim to the throne. His right to be king really derived from his victory at Bosworth and from his subsequent confirmation by Parliament. The new king, however, had excellent qualifications for the job of tidying

King Henry VII of England, from a silver groat (c. 1500).

up after the dissipations of civil war. Shrewd and economical, able but far from heart-warming, Henry VII bore many resemblances to Louis XI of France.

Henry deprived the nobles of their private armies and also banned the nobles' old habit of interfering in the royal courts to intimidate the litigants. Measures like these had been tried by Henry's predecessors but had ultimately failed for lack of enforcement. Henry, however, enforced his measures most vigorously through an administrative court known as the Star Chamber, from the star-painted ceiling of the room in which it met. The Star

Chamber was a special committee of the King's Council, charged with the task of seeing that the apparatus of the law should not be used to back up local privileges, local abuses, local resistance to what Henry wanted. To make justice swift and implacable, the Star Chamber bypassed customary procedures, including trial by jury. It could trample on the rights of defendants and engage in the other arbitrary practices that have made "star-chamber proceedings" synonymous with the abuse of judicial authority. The court, however, did not fully acquire its bad reputation until the seventeenth century (see Chapter 7).

The men who did Henry's work for him were for the most part new men, men of the prosperous urban merchant class, or men who had worked their way up in the Church and who owed their careers to him, like the able lawyer Morton, who became Archbishop of Canterbury. Henry rewarded many of his advisers with lands confiscated from his opponents at the end of the Wars of the Roses. The King and his councilors more than doubled the revenues of the central government, yet they avoided a clash with Parliament, because they seldom had to raise taxes requiring parliamentary sanction. The King's obvious efficiency won him support in the increasingly significant business community. Since foreign vessels still carried the bulk of England's trade, Henry dared not revoke the special privileges of foreign merchants. But he used the threat of revocation to gain trading privileges for English merchants abroad, especially in Italy.

Henry VII left a well-filled treasury and a prosperous country; he had re-established law and order in an England weary of rebellion and civil war. His policies set the stage for the more dramatic reigns of his illustrious successors, Henry VIII and Elizabeth I (see Chapter 5). He restored the prestige of the monarchy, made it the rallying point of English nationalism, and fixed the pattern for the Tudor policy toward Parliament, a policy often given the misleading label of "Tudor absolutism." Henry VII and his successors were indeed strong monarchs but they were not absolute in the sense that they attempted to trample over Parliament. Henry, as we have just seen, asked Parliament for money as infrequently as possible; the later Tudors were to manage their parliaments but not to ignore them. Parliament, though somewhat eclipsed by the strong personalities of the Tudors, remained very much a going concern. Its vitality was to make the English monarchy fundamentally different from Continental monarchies, notably France, where the Estates General had faded into insignificance by the reign of Louis XI. At the death of Henry VII precedents for limiting a monarch's authority were not entirely forgotten; they lay at hand ready for use, if the time again should come when a tyrannical king needed to be curbed.

Spain:
Ferdinand and Isabella

The accomplishments of Henry VII and Louis XI, impressive though they were, were overshadowed by those of their great Spanish contemporaries, Ferdinand and Isabella. Henry and Louis ruled kingdoms which, however racked by internal dissensions, had long been well-defined states with established central institutions. Ferdinand and Isabella inherited a Spain that had never really been united; they had to build the structure of central government from the very foundations.

The decisive event in the early medieval history of Spain was the Moslem conquest, starting in the year 711, which engulfed the whole peninsula, with the exception of the extreme north. From the ninth century through the fifteenth, the Christian states of the north pressed southward until the Moslem remnant at Granada fell in 1492. This slow expansion by Catholic Spaniards has been likened to a crusade more than five hundred years long. It was indeed a crusade, and the proud, militant, intolerant spirit of the crusader left a permanent mark upon the style of Spanish civilization. The reconquest of Spain, like the great Crusades to the Holy Land, was a disjointed movement, undertaken in fits and starts by rival states that sometimes put more

energy into combating each other than into fighting the Moslem.

Three Christian kingdoms dominated the Iberian Peninsula in the middle of the fifteenth century. Castile, the largest and most populous, occupying the center of the peninsula, had assumed the leadership of the reconquest. The power of the Castilian kings, however, did not grow in proportion to their territory. The powerful organization of sheep-ranchers, the *Mesta,* controlled vast territories and constituted a virtual state within the state. Both the nobility and the towns, which played a semi-independent part in the reconquest, maintained many rights against the royal authority. Both were represented, together with the clergy, in the Cortes, the Castilian counterpart of the English Parliament. To the west of Castile, along the Atlantic coast, lay the second Christian kingdom, Portugal. Once a Castilian province, Portugal had won independence in the twelfth century; though still retaining close links with Castile, the Portuguese were gradually maturing their own particular national interests, especially in exploration and commerce overseas (see Chapter 6).

The third kingdom, located in northeastern Spain, was Aragon, which was as much a Mediterranean power as a Spanish one. Its kings controlled the Balearic Islands, ruled lands along the Mediterranean on the French side of the Pyrenees, and had an important stake in southern Italy. King Alfonso the Magnanimous of Aragon (1416–1458) ruled over Naples and the island of Sicily; at his death, Sicily and Aragon passed to his brother John, and Naples to his illegitimate son, Ferrante. In Aragon, as in Castile, the oldest established political institutions were those limiting the crown—the Cortes, the nobility, and the towns. Two of the territories of the Crown of Aragon on the Spanish mainland—Catalonia, with its great city of Barcelona, and Valencia—had Cortes of their own and so many other autonomous privileges that they were virtually separate states.

In 1469, Ferdinand, later King of Aragon (1479–1516), married Isabella, later Queen of Castile (1474–1504), and thus made the dynastic alliance that eventually consummated the political unification of Spain. The obstacles confronting them were immense. Not only was the royal power weak in both states; the inhabitants of Castile and Aragon did not always speak the same language, a difference still evident today in the distinction between the Castilian Spanish spoken in Madrid and the Catalan of Barcelona. Aragon looked toward the Mediterranean, Castile toward the Atlantic. Moreover, Ferdinand and Isabella themselves did not make a perfect political team. He was a wary realist of the stamp of Louis XI and an ardent promoter of Aragon's ambitions in Italy, where he successfully strove to regain Naples. Though given the honorific title of "The Catholic" by the Pope, he was skeptical and tolerant in religion. Isabella, on the other hand, adored the pomp and circumstance of the throne; in religion she was devout to the point of fanaticism, and in policy she was wholly absorbed in the task of consolidating her authority over Castile.

The welding of Castile and Aragon into a single Spanish nation was a formidable undertaking; even today it is incomplete, and regional feeling, in Catalonia, for example, remains strong. Ferdinand and Isabella, however, made an impressive beginning at the task of building a Spanish national monarchy. This they did, above all, by creating a strong central government in Isabella's Castile. The Queen summoned the Cortes as infrequently as she dared and entrusted much executive power to a potent new instrument of absolutism staffed by royal appointees, the Council of Castile. She allied herself with the middle class of the towns against the nobles and drew military support more from town militias than from feudal levies. Toward the *Mesta*, however, Isabella was indulgent, since payments made by the sheep interests were the mainstay of royal revenue until the wealth of the New World began to pour in.

While relying heavily on the Church in advancing the royal power, Isabella was also determined to bring the Church under royal discipline and prescribed a thorough purge of ecclesiastical corruption. The purified Spanish church was later to assume leadership of the Catholic Reformation (see Chapter 4). The Spanish monarchs also obtained from the papacy the right to make appointments to high offices in the Spanish church and to dispose of parts of its revenue. An individual and an institution cemented the alliance of Church and State in Spain. The individual was Cardinal Ximenes (or Jiménez, 1436–1517), the Archbishop of Toledo, and Isabella's chief minister. Ximenes executed her policies of purifying the Church, curbing the aristocracy, and making an alliance with the towns. The institution was the Inquisition, brought into Spain in 1478, which sought to promote Spanish nationalism by enforcing universal Catholicism, to create loyal subjects of the Crown by obliging men to be obedient children of the Church.

The chief targets of the new policy were the two important Spanish religious minorities — the Moslems and the Jews. Both groups had long enjoyed toleration; both owned some of the most productive farms and businesses in Spain. Their independence and wealth, together with their adherence to their traditional faiths, alarmed and offended the nationalism of Isabella and Ximenes. The introduction of the Inquisition set the stage for persecution, which began in earnest in 1492, when Jews were offered the alternatives of immediate baptism into the Christian faith, or immediate exile with loss of their property. Ten years later, it was the turn of the Moslems who were given no choice but baptism. Catholicism thereby won many apparent converts from Judaism and Islam, nominal Christians who conformed only because they feared the tortures and burnings which the Inquisition could prescribe if they wavered in their new faith. Isabella and Ximenes had secured religious uniformity but at the cost of alienating some of the most productive elements in Spain.

The year 1492, therefore, is the crucial date in the whole history of Spain. It was the year when Ferdinand and Isabella seized the last fragment of Moslem Spain and Columbus laid the first stones of the great Spanish Empire in the New World (see Chapter 6). But it was also the year when intolerance on a grand scale became national policy. The new Spanish monarchy already bore the stamp of the bigoted nationalism that was to be at once its strength and its weakness in generations to come.

III   Germany and Italy

Germany

In contrast to the new monarchies of western Europe, Germany had monarchs but no national monarchy. In the later Middle Ages power shifted steadily from the Holy Roman Emperor to the princes of the many particular states into which the Empire was divided. As the imperial crown passed from one family to another, each successive emperor used the imperial office to further his family's territorial ambitions, so that the position of the monarchy became simply that of another territorial princedom. The princes as a class secured a great victory in 1356 by obtaining from the Emperor Charles IV the famous Golden Bull, which confirmed the principle of elective monarchy. The seven electors, who would choose the emperor, were four secular princes—the Count Palatine of the Rhine, the Duke of Saxony, the Margrave of Brandenburg, and the King of Bohemia—and three ecclesiastical princes from the Rhineland, the Archbishops of Mainz, Trier, and Cologne. During the next century and a half, both the electors and the lesser German princes, who did not have electoral status, gradually consolidated their authority within their particular states.

With a host of sovereign princes firmly installed in their individual states, the Holy Roman Empire had become nearly meaningless. It had lost control over western lands, taken by France, and also over other frontier areas, notably Switzerland. In 1291 three forest cantons in the heart of the Alps had made a successful bid for effective self-rule. By the early sixteenth century the number of confederated cantons had quadrupled, and the Swiss, backed by France, had checked both Burgundian and German attempts to subjugate them. Another national state was emerging, but one distinguished by the absence of a strong central authority. The Swiss federal government was extremely weak, and the individual cantons enjoyed many prerogatives of the kind that Americans know as "states' rights."

As territorial losses and other visible signs of the Empire's weakness multiplied, the Germans themselves began to undergo a national awakening. The emperor would have been the natural rallying point of emerging national feeling, if the imperial office had not already become an instrument to advance the interests of particular dynasties. In 1438 the emperorship, though still elective, passed permanently to the house of Habsburg. Forty-five years later a most attractive scion of that house, Maximilian I (1493–1519), became emperor. He was a gentleman and a scholar, and an athlete and warrior as well, and he had acquired great riches by marrying Mary of Burgundy, the heiress of the Low Countries. Under his weak predecessors, the Habsburg position in central Europe had deteriorated; Maximilian re-established firm Habsburg power in Austria and its dependencies. He also arranged for his children and grandchildren marriages that promised to add vast new territories to the family possessions and that would make his grandson, Charles V, the ruler of half of Europe. On the other hand, Maximilian's projects for reforming the Empire came to little not only because of the vested interests of German particularism but also because of Maximilian's own dynastic concerns. German nationalism still awaited a leader.

Germany and the Baltic in the 15th Century

Habsburg Dominions
Lay electorates
Boundary of the Empire
Hanseatic League Centers

NORWAY

Bergen

SWEDEN

Stockholm

FINLAND

Gulf of Finland

Novgorod

ESTONIA

L. Peipus

RUSSIA

GOTLAND

Riga

COURLAND

Dvina R.

ÖLAND

Calmar

Baltic Sea

LITHUANIA

DOMAIN OF THE TEUTONIC KNIGTHS

Niemen R.

North Sea

Copenhagen

DENMARK

Danzig

Vistula R.

POLAND

Lübeck
Hamburg

Lüneburg
Bremen

Elbe R.

BRANDENBURG

Warthe R.

Brunswick

Magdeburg

GERMANY

Weser R.

Breslau

SILESIA

Cracow

Bruges

Cologne

Rhine R.

NASSAU

SAXONY

Prague

Meuse R.

Mainz

Bavaria

Nuremberg

BOHEMIA

LUXEMBOURG

Trier

PALATINATE

Moselle R.

Danube R.

Vienna

AUSTRIA

HUNGARY

Augsburg

STYRIA

FRANCE

SWISS
CONFEDERATION

TYROL

CARINTHIA

Sava R.

Danube R.

Rhône R.

SAVOY

MILAN

VENETIAN REPUBLIC

Venice

BOSNIA

SERBIA

Po R.

ITALY

Adriatic Sea

0   100   200
Miles

41

The Italian States

Italy, too, lacked an effective central authority, and had lacked even the shadow of control by the Holy Roman Emperor since the mid-thirteenth century. Italy, too, experienced the advance of particularism and the emergence of powerful local and regional rulers. In Germany the fifteenth century was the Age of the Princes; in Italy it was the Age of the Despots, power politicians *par excellence,* brilliant, ruthless, cultivated rulers who did much to set the style of the Renaissance.

Despots had not always ruled in Italy. The medieval struggle between popes and emperors had promoted the growth of independent towns, particularly in northern Italy. In the twelfth and thirteenth centuries, the towns were oligarchic republics, dominated by the nobility and by the newly rich businessmen. The ruling oligarchies, however, were torn by the factional strife between the pro-papal Guelfs and the pro-imperial Ghibellines; also, something close to class warfare arose between the wealthy, on the one hand, and the small businessmen and wage-earners, on the other. In town after town, from the thirteenth century on, social and political dissensions grew so bitter that arbitrary one-man government seemed to be the only remedy. Sometimes a despot seized power; sometimes he was invited in from outside by the contending factions. Often he was a *condottiere,* a captain of the mercenaries whom the states hired to fight their wars.

By the fifteenth century, the fortunes of politics and of war had worked significant changes in the map of Italy. Many towns that had been important in the Middle Ages were sinking into political obscurity, victims of their stronger neighbors. The states that now dominated Italy were the Two Sicilies in the south, the States of the Church in the center, and Milan, Florence, and Venice in the north.

The Two Sicilies comprised the island of Sicily and the Kingdom of Naples. In the twelfth and early thirteenth centuries they had been ruled by able Norman kings and German emperors and had become a great meeting point of the streams of eastern and western trade and culture. After the collapse of imperial power in the mid-thirteenth century, Naples went to the Angevin family from France, and Sicily went to the dynasty of Aragon in Spain. Naples remained Angevin until 1435, when it was taken by Alfonso the Magnanimous of Aragon. In 1458 it became an independent state again, ruled by Alfonso's illegitimate son Ferrante (Ferdinand, 1458–1494), a particularly ruthless despot. Under Angevin and Aragonese rule the Two Sicilies never fully recovered the vigor, the prosperity, and the cultural leadership they had enjoyed in their great medieval days. But their eclipse was by no means total; Alfonso the Magnanimous was a generous patron of art and learning, and Naples played at least a secondary role in the Renaissance.

The States of the Church had likewise suffered a material decline. At the opening of the fourteenth century, the papacy had lost a great struggle with the French monarchy; the result was the "Babylonian Captivity," 1305–1378, when the papal capital was removed from Rome to Avignon in southern France. The Babylonian Captivity was followed by the Great Schism, 1378–1417, when there were two rival popes, one at Avignon, the other at Rome, and by the Conciliar Movement of the early fifteenth century, a serious though ultimately unsuccessful attempt to make the papacy a kind of limited monarchy by enlarging the powers of councils of church dignitaries at the expense of papal authority. These successive blows not only weakened the prestige of the papacy in religious matters but also weakened the temporal authority of the pope over Rome and the Papal States, a band of territory across central Italy. The city of Rome came under the control of princely families, and the outlying papal lands fell to local feudal lords.

After 1450, the popes once more concentrated their attention on central Italy. Beginning with Nicholas V (1447–1455), and continuing with Pius II (1458–1464), and Sixtus IV (1471–1484), the papacy was held by a series of ambitious men, often highly cultivated, and often very secular as well, notorious for the favors lavished on their relatives. They restored Rome as a center of art and learning and began the reconquest of the papal dominions. The Borgia pope, Alexander VI (1492–1503), greatly aided by his aggressive and unscrupulous son, Cesare, made notable progress in subjugating the lords of central Italy and in breaking the power of the Roman princely families. Cesare Borgia employed almost any means — treachery, violence, assassination by poisoning — to gain his ends. The next pope, Julius II (1503–1513), a nephew of Sixtus IV, was a statesman and general who commanded his troops in person and who consolidated further the temporal, though hardly the spiritual, authority of the papacy. Soon, however, the double blow of the Reformation and the Habsburg-Valois Wars shattered the popes political ambitions (see Chapters 4 and 5).

The North Italian States

In the closing centuries of the Middle Ages, neither the States of the Church nor the Two Sicilies could effectively challenge the supremacy of the three chief north Italian states. Of these, the Duchy of Milan occupied a site of great strategic and economic value in the midst of the fertile Lombard plain, within sight of the Alps. Milan was the center of the bread-basket of Italy and the terminus of trade routes through the Alpine passes from northern Europe. It was also a textile and metallurgical center, famous for its velvets and brocades, its weapons and armor. Politically, medieval Milan had been a republic, run by the nobility in conjunction with a great council, in which all citizens of modest means could participate. This combination of aristocracy and democracy, however, proved unworkable, the more so since it was complicated by outbreaks of Guelf and Ghibelline factionalism. In 1277 power was seized by the noble Visconti family, henchmen of the powerful Archbishops of Milan, who soon secured recognition from the Emperor as Dukes of Milan. The age of despotism, begun by the

Visconti, continued when their direct line died out in 1447. Attempts to revive republican government were countered by Francesco Sforza, an energetic *condottiere,* who usurped the ducal office (1450–1466). He maintained the Visconti tradition of arbitrary rule but made it more tolerable by his soldierly efficiency and by his many public works. He founded a great hospital in the city, completed its elaborate Gothic cathedral and extended irrigation canals throughout the duchy.

The most famous of the Sforza dukes was a younger son of Francesco, Ludovico Il Moro, 1479–1500 (Lewis "the Moor"). A usurper, like his father, Il Moro seized the government from his sickly nephew. He assembled a retinue of outstanding artists and intellectuals, headed by Leonardo da Vinci, and made the court of Milan perhaps the most brilliant in all Europe. Il Moro had the reputation of being the craftiest diplomat of the age, but his craftiness did not suffice to defend him against the armies of France and Spain (see Chapter 5). Driven from his throne in 1500, Il Moro died in a French prison eight years later. The Duchy of Milan came under direct Spanish rule in 1535 and remained under the control of Spain for almost two hundred years. The Sforzas were true *condottieri,* soldiers of fortune who gained power — and lost it — almost overnight.

Not *condottieri* but bankers, merchants, and other entrepreneurs governed the Republic of Florence, on the banks of the Arno in Tuscany, midway between Milan and Rome. Class conflicts largely determined the course of politics in this pioneering center of industry and finance. By the thirteenth century the struggle between Guelfs and Ghibellines had become a contest for power between two noble factions, one ready to open its ranks to newly rich commoners, the other reluctant to do so. In the late 1200's, the more liberal Guelfs prevailed over the Ghibelline aristocrats, and proceeded to revise the constitution of the Republic so that a virtual monopoly of key government offices rested with the seven major guilds, which were controlled by the great woolen masters, bankers, and exporters. They denied any effective political voice to many nobles, to Ghibellines, common laborers, or the craftsmen and shopkeepers of the fourteen lesser guilds. Feuds soon split the dominant Guelfs, however, and factionalism continued to torment Florentine politics, though it did not prevent the remarkable cultural burgeoning of the city. The politically unprivileged sought to make the Republic more democratic; they failed, not only because of the power of the entrenched oligarchy, but also because of the hostility between the lesser guilds and the poor workmen, between what we would term the lower middle class and labor. Bank failures in the mid-fourteenth century aggravated social and political tensions, and early in the fifteenth a new rash of bankruptcies and a series of military reverses weakened the hold of the ruling clique. In 1434 some of its leaders were forced into exile, and power fell to a political champion of the poor, Cosimo de' Medici.

The Medici ran Florence for the next sixty years (1434–1494). Their championing of the poor had its ironic side, for they had large woolen and banking interests and were perhaps the wealthiest family in all Italy; yet they taxed the rich heavily and did a good deal to improve the status of the lower classes. The Medici were despots, but despots who operated quietly behind the façade of republican institutions. Cosimo kept himself in the background and seldom held public office. It was an old custom that the municipal executives should be chosen every two months by a sort of political lottery, by supposedly random selection from leather bags containing the names of eligible citizens. All Cosimo had to do to control the outcome of these "elections" was to arrange that only the names of his supporters get into the leather bags. Since, however, the incessant turnover of personnel hardly promoted political stability, Cosimo's grandson made a new Council of Seventy, with permanent membership, the real center of administration.

The grandson of Cosimo was Lorenzo, the most famous of the Medici, ruler of Florence from 1469 to 1492, and called *Il Magnifico* for want of any formal title. An admiring portrait of Lorenzo the Magnificent was drawn by another celebrated Florentine, Machiavelli:

It was throughout his aim to make the city prosperous, the people united, and the nobles honored. He loved exceedingly all who excelled in the arts, and he showered favors on the learned. . . . Lorenzo delighted in architecture, music, and poetry. . . . To give the youth of Florence an opportunity of studying letters he founded a college at Pisa, to which he had appointed the most excellent professors that Italy could produce. . . . His character, prudence, and good fortune were such that he was known and esteemed, not only by the princes of Italy, but by many others in distant lands. . . . In his conversation he was ready and eloquent, in his resolutions wise, in action swift and courageous. There was nothing in his conduct, although inclined to excessive gallantry, which in any way impaired his many virtues; it is possible he found more pleasure in the company of droll and witty men than became a man of his position; and he would often be found playing among his children as if he were still a child. To see him at one time in his grave moments and at another in his gay was to see in him two personalities, joined as it were with invisible bonds. . . . There had never died in Florence—nor yet in Italy—one for whom his country mourned so much, or who left behind him so wide a reputation for wisdom.[*]

Although Lorenzo possessed in abundance many of the qualities most admired in his time, neither his looks (he had a deformed nose) nor his policies were perfect. Lorenzo's neglect of military matters, his financial carelessness, and the failure of the Medici bank left Florence ill prepared for the wars that engulfed Italy at the turn of the century from the fifteenth to the sixteenth. Following the death of Lorenzo in 1492, the Florentines made two short-lived attempts to drive the Medici from power and to re-establish a genuine republic. In 1512 and again in 1530 the Medici returned. In 1569 they converted the Florentine Republic, which had now lost any claim to grandeur, into the Grand Duchy of Tuscany, with themselves as hereditary Grand Dukes.

[*]Machiavelli, *Florentine History*, W. K. Marriott, trans. (New York, 1909), 359–360.

Lorenzo de' Medici, terra cotta bust by Verrocchio.

The third great north Italian state, Venice, enjoyed a political stability that contrasted sharply with the turbulence of Florence and Milan. By the fifteenth century the Republic of St. Mark, as it was called, was in fact an empire. Its territories included the lower valley of the Po River (annexed to make secure its defenses and food supply), the Dalmatian shore of the Adriatic Sea, and part of the Greek islands and mainland. The Venetian Empire reflected the Republic's leadership in the eastern trade, which was unchallenged after it outdistanced the rival Genoese in the fourteenth century. The government also reflected the paramountcy of the Republic's commercial interests, since, unlike Florence or Milan, Venice had no traditional landed nobility.

The Venetian constitution assumed its definitive form in the early fourteenth century. Earlier, the chief executive had been the doge or duke, originally appointed by the Byzantine emperor, subsequently an elected official; the legislature had been a general assembly of all the citizens, somewhat resembling that of Milan. The Venetian merchants, however, feared that a powerful doge might establish a hereditary monarchy, and they found the assembly unwieldy. Accordingly, they relegated the doge to an ornamental role like that of a constitutional monarch today and made the assembly into the Great Council, a closed corporation whose membership of 240 men was limited to the families listed in a special "Golden Book." The Great Council, in turn, elected the Doge and the members of the smaller councils which really ran the government. Foremost among these was the Council of Ten, a powerful secret agency charged with maintaining the security of the Republic.

This system, therefore, vested a permanent monopoly of political power in the old merchant families, comprising about 2 per cent of the total population. It accounts for the label "Venetian oligarchy," often pinned on any government that seeks to perpetuate the privileges and profits of the few. The oligarchs of Venice, however, while denying the many a voice in politics and sternly repressing all opposition, did institute many projects for the general welfare, from neighborhood fountains on up to the great naval arsenal (see below, p. 51). They treated the subject cities of the empire with fairness and generosity, and they were pioneers—at least in the western world—in the development of a corps of diplomats to serve the far-reaching concerns of a great commercial power. Though they were unable to prevent the eventual decline of the city, they did pursue their business aims with single-minded efficiency for several hundred prosperous years. Seldom in history have political means been so perfectly adapted to economic ends.

The "School of Europe"

The Italian states of the fifteenth century have been called the "school of Europe," instructing the other European states in the new realistic ways of power politics. Despots like Il Moro, Cesare Borgia, Lorenzo the Magnificent, and the oligarchs of Venice might well have given lessons in statecraft to Henry VII of England or Louis XI of France. They were the most hard-boiled rulers in a hard-boiled age. In international affairs, the experiments with diplomatic missions made by Venice, by the Visconti of Milan, and by the Gonzaga

family in the small north Italian state of Mantua were soon copied by the national monarchies farther north and west. Italian reliance on *condottieri* foreshadowed the general use of mercenaries and the abandonment of the old feudal levies. The rival Italian states, though their mutual competition often led to open conflict, yet learned to co-exist in a precarious balance of power. This balance, served as a model or precedent for the European monarchies in later centuries.

This very example, however, reveals that Italy was the "school of Europe" in a negative sense, for she also furnished a compelling object lesson in how not to behave politically. By the close of the fifteenth century it was evident that the balance established among the Italian states was too precarious to preserve their independence. Beginning with the French invasion of 1494, Italy became a happy hunting ground for the new national and dynastic imperialists of France, Spain, and the Habsburg realm, and ended as a Spanish preserve. The national monarchy was the wave of the future, at least of a successful political future; the city-state was not, even when it ruled an empire, as Venice did, or when it was run by an efficient despot. The Italians of the Renaissance, like the ancient Greeks whom they resembled, were victimized by stronger neighbors and were penalized for their failure to form "one Italy."

These lessons from the "school of Europe" were first drawn by Niccolò Machiavelli (1469–1527), a diplomat who served the restored Florentine Republic in the early 1500's and was exiled when the Medici returned in 1512. Soon after, he wrote *The Prince* and dedicated it to the Medici ruler in the vain hope of regaining political favor. This essay on power politics, for all its notorious reputation, often makes rather dull reading; but in it may be found the statements that have given the word "Machiavellian" its sinister significance. Machiavelli has a low opinion of human nature:

For it may be said of men in general that they are ungrateful, voluble, dissemblers, anxious to avoid danger, and covetous of gain; as long as you benefit them, they are entirely yours; they offer you their blood, their goods, their life, and their children, . . . when necessity is remote; but when it approaches, they revolt.*

One might term this a secular adaptation of original sin, a transfer of Christian pessimism about mankind from the realm of religion to that of social and political psychology. The politics of *The Prince* follow directly from its estimate of human nature:

A prudent ruler ought not to keep faith when by so doing it would be against his interest, and when the reasons which made him bind himself no longer exist. If men were all good, the precept would not be a good one; but as they are bad, and would not observe their faith with you, so you are not bound to keep faith with them. . . .†

Accordingly, Machiavelli praises the vigorous and unscrupulous absolutism of Francesco Sforza, of Lorenzo the Magnificent, and, above all, of Cesare Borgia. After surveying the bad faith and deception practiced by Cesare Borgia to tighten his hold on the States of the Church, Machiavelli concludes:

I find nothing to blame, on the contrary, I feel bound . . . to hold him up as an example to be imitated by all who by fortune and with the arms of others have risen to power.**

The Prince was, first and last, a tract for the times, a drastic prescription against the severe political maladies afflicting Italy in the early 1500's. But what precisely was Machiavelli's diagnosis of Italy's ills, and what precisely his recommended prescription? Scholars do not entirely agree. A majority of them believe that *The Prince* is to be taken literally and that Italy's desperate plight in the face of foreign invasion—"without a head, without order, beaten, despoiled, lacerated, and overrun," as he wrote in the final chapter—required a desperate remedy. A minority, however, argue that Machiavelli's intention was satirical and that he was really warning his compatriots against relying on excessive despotism, even at the moment of national emergency.

Machiavelli wrote several longer works in addition to *The Prince—The Art of War, The History of Florence,* and, most important, *The Discourses on the First Ten Books of Titus Livius* (the Roman historian Livy). In the *Discourses* he addressed himself not to the immediate Italian crisis but to the problem of building a lasting government. To achieve stability, he argues, the state requires something more than a single prince endowed with power, more power, and yet more power. In a chapter entitled "The People Are Wiser and More Constant than Princes," Machiavelli writes:

I say that the people are more prudent and stable, and have better judgment than a prince. . . . We also see that in the election of their magistrates they make far better choice than princes; and no people will ever be persuaded to elect a man of infamous character and corrupt habits to any post of dignity, to which a prince is easily influenced in a thousand different ways. . . . We furthermore see the cities where the people are masters make the greatest progress in the least possible time, and much greater than such as have always been governed by princes. . . .*

In *The Discourses,* Machiavelli thus presents both an estimate of human nature and a political program seemingly in conflict with the statements of *The Prince.* But the conflict is perhaps more apparent than real. *The Discourses* concerned people, like the Athenians and Romans of old, who had great civic virtues and were capable of self-government. *The Prince* concerned people, Machiavelli's Italians, who in his view had lost their civic virtues and therefore (if we accept the interpretation of the majority of scholars) required the strongest kind of government from above.

Machiavelli blamed the Church for this loss of civic spirit. In the *Discourses* he attacked the papacy in particular for preventing Italian unity because of its temporal interests, and

---

The Prince, Ch. 17. This and succeeding quotations from Machiavelli are from the Modern Library edition of *The Prince and the Discourses* (New York, n.d.).
†*Ibid.,* Ch. 18.
**Ibid.,* Ch. 7.

The Discourses, Bk. I, Ch. 58.

then questioned the values of Christianity itself:

Reflecting now as to whence it came that in ancient times the people were more devoted to liberty than in the present, I believe that it resulted from this, that men were stronger in those days, which I believe to be attributable to the difference of education, founded upon the difference of their religion and ours. For, as our religion teaches us the truth and the true way of life, it causes us to attach less value to the honors and possessions of this world; whilst the Pagans, esteeming those things as the highest good, were more energetic and ferocious in their actions. . . . The Pagan religion deified only men who had achieved great glory, such as commanders of armies and chiefs of republics, whilst ours glorifies more the humble and contemplative men than the men of action. Our religion, moreover, places the supreme happiness in humility, lowliness, and a contempt for worldly objects, whilst the other, on the contrary, places the supreme good in grandeur of soul, strength of body, and all such other qualities as render men formidable. . . .*

Machiavelli evidently believed that the purpose of government was not to prepare men for the City of God but to make upstanding citizens of this world, ready to fight, work, and die for their earthly country.

In defending nationalism Machiavelli was exalting the doctrine that was to contribute so much to shaping the modern world. In defending secularism and power politics Machiavelli preached what others had already practiced. Henry VII, Louis XI, Ferdinand of Aragon, and the Italian despots, in their different ways, were all good Machiavellians. The businesslike character of their politics, in turn, was intermeshed with the increasingly businesslike character of economic life during these centuries of transition.

*The Discourses, Bk. II, Ch. 2.

IV   Economic Changes in the West

Trade

In the 1430's an unknown Englishman wrote a rhymed pamphlet, *The Libel of English Policy,* which may serve as an almanac of fifteenth-century commerce. *The Libel* notes that among English imports from Spain:

Bene fygues, raysns, wyne bastarde, and dates;
And lycorys, Syvyle ole [Seville oil], and grayne,
Whyte Castelle sope, and wax. . . .

And so on through "iren" and "wolle," "saffron" and "quiksilver."* The spelling is almost the only item of quaintness here; most of the wares mentioned still circulate in international trade today. Many of these items might also have appeared on a list for the twelfth century. To preserve food, the West had long imported

*Political Poems and Songs Relating to English History, Thomas Wright, ed. (London, 1861), II, 160.

salt from Spain, Italy, and Germany; to make food tasty if it had begun to spoil, the West had long sought the spices of the East. Since drafty medieval buildings made warm clothing essential, the furs of eastern Europe, the wool of England and Spain, and the woolen cloth of Flanders and Italy all commanded good markets. At the close of the Middle Ages supplies of palatable food and comfortable clothing were steadily increasing.

It is, then, essential to observe that the difference between the trade of the twelfth century and that of the fifteenth was one of degree, not of kind. It was the difference between some commerce and more commerce, rather than between no commerce and a reborn commerce. Nor did the expansion of trade proceed at a uniform rate. A prolonged economic depression set in during the mid-fourteenth century as a result of the Hundred Years' War and still more because of the Black Death, which is estimated to have killed a third of the population of western Europe. By the fifteenth century the West was beginning to recover, and its trade was for the first time beginning to compare in volume and variety with that of the Roman Empire and other prosperous eras of the past. Western merchants developed more elaborate commercial procedures and organizations, of which the Hanseatic towns of the Baltic and the trading cities of Italy provide useful illustrations.

The Hanse

The great *Hanse* (the German word means a league or confederation) of North German trading towns flourished in the fourteenth and fifteenth centuries. Among its leaders were Lübeck, Hamburg, Bremen, and Danzig; its membership included at one time or another almost a hundred towns. Hanseatic ships carried Baltic fish, timber, grain, furs, metals, and amber to western European markets and brought back cloth, wine, spices, and luxuries. Hanseatic merchants, traveling overland with carts and pack-trains, took their Baltic wares to Italy. The Hanse maintained especially large depots at Venice, London, Bruges (in Flanders), Novgorod (in northwestern Russia), and Bergen, in Norway, where the Hanseatic contingent was said to number 3,000 individuals. These establishments had so many special rights, and they were so largely ruled by their own German officials and their own German laws, that they were Hanseatic colonies on foreign soil.

Because the Empire was so weak, and also because many of the Hanseatic towns had originally been autonomous frontier outposts, the Hanse long exerted extensive political and military influence in addition to its economic power. Its policies were determined by meetings of representatives from the member towns, held usually in the guildhall at Lübeck. It had its own flag, its own diplomats, and its own legal code, the "Law of Lübeck." It made treaties, declared war, and sometimes used the weapon of undeclared war. In 1406, to teach a forceful lesson to English vessels fishing in

Fifteenth-century Hanseatic merchants.

the teeming waters off Norway, Hanseatic captains seized ninety-six English seamen, bound them hand and foot, and threw them overboard to drown.

The Hanseatic complex almost added up to an independent power of the first magnitude—almost, but not quite. It was weakened by the conservatism and rigidity of its merchants and by the rivalries between competing member towns and rival merchant families. Only a minority of the towns belonging to the Hanse usually sent representatives to the deliberations in Lübeck, and scarcely any of the members could be counted on for men and arms in an emergency. For all these reasons, the fortunes of the Hanse declined rapidly after 1500. The shifting of trade routes from the Baltic to the Atlantic also sapped the prosperity of the Hanseatic towns to the advantage of Holland and England. The loosely organized Hanse was no match for the stronger monarchical governments that were growing up along the rim of its old Baltic preserve in Sweden, in Russia, and even, with the development of Brandenburg-Prussia, in Germany itself.

Venice

The truly big business of the last medieval centuries was to be found in the cities of the Mediterranean world, especially Venice. Many of the Mediterranean cities were already thriving veterans of trade, toughened and enriched by the Crusades. In Italy, besides Venice, there were Genoa, Lucca, Pisa, Florence, Milan, and a dozen others; in southern France there were Narbonne, Montpellier, and Marseilles; and in Spain there was Barcelona. After settling accounts with her strongest rival, Genoa, in the 1300's, Venice was the undisputed mistress of Mediterranean trade. Her empire, as we have seen, was strung along the sea route from the northern Adriatic to Byzantium. The trade that enriched the merchants of Venice was the East-West traffic—spices, silks, cotton, and sugar from the East; wool, cloth, and other wares from the West. The area of Venetian business was enormous, stretching from Flanders and England in the West to the heart of Asia. In the thirteenth century the Venetian Marco Polo reached China after a great journey overland.

The main carrier of Venetian trade was the galley. The designers of the arsenal, the great government-operated shipyard, improved the traditional long, narrow, oar-propelled galley of the Mediterranean into a swifter and more capacious merchant vessel, relying mainly on sails and employing oarsmen chiefly for getting in and out of port. In the fifteenth century these merchant galleys had space for 250 tons of cargo. Although this figure is unimpressive in our day, when the capacity of freighters is computed in thousands and tens of thousands of tons, spices and luxuries were small in bulk and large in value. Records from the early fifteenth century show approximately forty-five galleys sailing annually, among them four to Flanders, four to Beirut on the Lebanon

coast, three to the Black Sea, three to Alexandria, two to southern France, and two or three transporting pilgrims to Jaffa in the Holy Land. The Flanders galleys touched both at Sluys, the harbor of Bruges, and at the English ports of London and Southampton. The Flanders fleet was a very important European economic institution, for it provided the first regular all-water service between Italy and northwestern Europe, and made shipments cheaper and more secure than they had been on the older overland route.

The state supervised the activities of these galleys from the cradle to the grave. Since the average life of galleys was ten years, government experts tested their seaworthiness periodically, and the arsenal undertook systematic replacements. The government provided for the defense of the galleys and their cargoes by requiring that at least twenty of the crew be bowmen. For the Flanders fleet the government determined the time of sailing (the spring), the number of galleys (usually four to six), and the policies of the captains (avoid "affrays and mischiefs" in English ports, even if the crew have to be denied shore leave, and, above all, get to Bruges before the Genoese do). To smooth the way for Venetian merchants, the Republic maintained an ambassador in England.

Industry

The expansion of trade stimulated the industries that furnished the textiles, metals, ships, and other requirements of the merchants. The towns of Flanders and Italy developed the weaving of woolen cloth into a big business, with a large production, large numbers of workmen, and large profits for a relatively few entrepreneurs. In the early fourteenth century, it is estimated, 200 masters controlled the wool guild of Florence, which produced nearly 100,000 pieces of cloth annually and employed 30,000 men. By and large, only the 200 had the capital—the saved-up funds—to finance the importation of fine raw wool from England and see it through all the processes that ended with the finished

A part of the city of Venice c. 1500; woodcut by Iacopo de Barbari.

cloth. The older medieval concept that all artisans were potential masters of a guild was giving way to the modern division into capital and labor.

Despite the growth of capitalism, Europe had not yet experienced a true industrial revolution. Manufacturing continued to be what the Latin roots of the word suggest—making by hand—though many hand tools were ingenious and efficient. Power-driven machines did not exist, except for an occasional experimental device operated by water or by draft animals. The modern aspects of late medieval industry, confined largely to a few advanced crafts, were the increase in output, the trend toward mass production of standardized articles, and the complementary trend toward the specialization of the labor force.

In Lübeck, Hanseatic capitalists promoted the mass output of rosaries by supplying ma-

terials and wages to bead-makers and by promoting a standard product. In the Habsburg lands of Central Europe, the silver mines anticipated modern practice by dividing their labor force into three parts, each working an eight-hour daily shift. Probably the largest industrial establishment in Europe was the aforementioned Venetian arsenal, which normally employed a thousand men, and many more in time of emergency. These workmen, called *Arsenalotti*, formed a pyramid of skills. At the bottom were the stevedores, helpers, and other unskilled laborers; then came the sawyers, who cut the timbers for the galleys, and the caulkers, who made the wooden hulls seaworthy; then the pulley-makers and mast-makers; and finally, at the top, the carpenters, who did the all-important work of shaping the lines of the hull. Supervisors, like modern foremen, disciplined the *Arsenalotti*, checking

51

on their presence at their posts during the working day; anyone who reported late, after the arsenal bell had ceased tolling its summons to work, forfeited a day's pay. By the sixteenth century the process of adding a superstructure to the hull and outfitting the vessel was so efficiently arranged that the *Arsenalotti* could complete and equip a hundred galleys for a campaign against the Turks in the space of two months.

Banking

The expansion of industry and trade promoted the rise of banking. New enterprises required new money, which in turn was supplied by merchants anxious to invest the excess capital they had accumulated. The risks of lending were great; kings in particular were likely to repudiate their debts. But the potential profits were also very large. Florentine bankers were known to charge 266 per cent annual interest on an especially risky loan, and in 1420 the Florentine government vainly tried to put a ceiling of 20 per cent on interest rates. The high rate of interest also reflected the demand for money. Kings, popes, and lesser rulers needed it for war and administration; businessmen needed it to finance trading voyages. Bankers were money-changers as well as money-lenders. Only an expert could establish the relative value of the hundreds upon hundreds of coins in circulation, varying wildly in reliability and metallic content, and minted by every kind of governmental unit from the big monarchy down to the small city and the tiny feudal principality.

Despite the widespread popular belief to the contrary, Jews did not play a leading part in banking activities except in Spain, and there only until 1492. The great European bankers were Italians, the so-called "Lombard" bankers, though many of them came not from Lombardy but from Florence, Siena, and other towns in Tuscany. Italian bankers became the fiscal agents of the pope, charged with the transfer of papal revenues from distant countries to Rome. The beautiful florins minted by the city of Florence were the first gold coins made outside Byzantium to gain international currency because of their reliability. In the fourteenth century Florentine bankers advanced large sums to the kings of England and France, but were subsequently ruined when the expenses of the Hundred Years' War led their royal clients to default on their debts. Florentine banking rallied in the fifteenth century under the dynamic Cosimo de' Medici, whose firm maintained branches in sixteen cities in Italy and abroad. By the close of the century, however, the Medici bank had failed because of the inefficiency of branch managers and the extravagance of Lorenzo the Magnificent.

Meantime, successful monetary institutions had appeared elsewhere. Barcelona and Genoa had important banks, and Venice minted ducats rivaling the florins in popularity. In Germany the little Bavarian cities of Augsburg and Nuremberg boasted a series of great banking families, of whom the most famous were the Fuggers of Augsburg. The founder of the family's prosperity was a linen-weaver and trader in the late fourteenth century. His sons and grandsons imported textiles and luxuries from Venice and began buying up mines, which were experiencing a prolonged boom. In the late 1400's they became bankers to the Habsburgs and, after the failure of the Medici bank, to the papacy as well. Through Habsburg favor they secured silver, iron, and copper mines in Hungary and the Tyrol. At the peak of their prosperity in the 1540's, the family fortune is estimated to have reached a figure worth about a quarter of a billion of our present-day dollars. Thereafter it dwindled, as the flood of gold and silver from America ended the central European mining boom, and as the Fuggers themselves extended repeated loans to the Habsburg Philip II of Spain (see Chapter 5), who went through repeated bankruptcies. In 1607 the family firm went bankrupt.

Two quotations will convey something of the personality of these German bankers. First, there is the prideful note of rugged individualism in the epitaph that Jacob Fugger, a grandson of the founder, composed for his own tomb in the early sixteenth century:

To the best, greatest God! Jacob Fugger of Augsburg, the ornament of his class and people, imperial councillor under Maximilian I and Charles V, who was behind no one in the attainment of extraordinary wealth, in generosity, purity of morals, and greatness of soul, is, as he was not comparable with anyone in his lifetime, even after death not to be counted among the mortals.*

But the haughty Fuggers were not just "robber barons," and so there is this note of philanthropy in the inscription at the entrance to the "Fuggerei," a charming garden village that they built for the poor of Augsburg:

Ulrich, George, and Jacob Fugger of Augsburg, blood brothers, being firmly convinced that they were born for the good of the city, and that for their great prosperity they have to thank chiefly an all-powerful and benevolent God, have out of piety, and as an example of special generosity founded, given, and dedicated 106 dwellings, both buildings and furnishings, to those of their fellow citizens who live righteously, but are beset by poverty.†

The Impact of Economic Change

Augsburg, with its special housing development for low-income families, begins to seem very much like a contemporary city. Yet we must not exaggerate its apparent modernity, for the total population of Augsburg at the zenith of Fugger power probably never exceeded 20,000. In fact, none of the centers of international economic life five or six hundred years ago was really a big city at all. One set of estimates for the fourteenth century puts the population of Venice, Florence, and Paris in the vicinity of 100,000 each; that of Genoa, Milan, Barcelona, and London at about 50,000; and that of the biggest Hanseatic and Flemish towns between 20,000 and 40,000. At the close of the Middle Ages, the great majority of Europeans still lived on the land.

*Quoted by Miriam Beard, *A History of the Business Man* (New York, 1938), 239– 240.
†J. Strieder, *Jacob Fugger the Rich* (New York, 1931), 176.

The urban minority, however, was beginning to bring important changes to the life of the rural majority. Ties between town and countryside tightened in those areas where towns were especially numerous — Lombardy, Tuscany, Flanders, the Rhine Valley, and northern Germany. Merchants often invested their wealth in farm properties, nobles who acquired interests in towns usually retained their country estates, and peasants often moved to town as workmen or became part-time artisans on the farm itself. Rural laborers made prayer beads for the capitalists of Lübeck and spun woolen yarn for the guild masters of Florence. Many manors, no longer largely self-sufficient, now specialized in a single commodity like grain or wool, olives or grapes; consequently, they had to purchase the necessities that they themselves no longer produced. The lords of these one-crop manors, depending increasingly on a monetary income, thus became capitalists, usually on a very modest scale. The more enterprising, however, wanted to sweep away what seemed to them inefficient medieval survivals. They demanded that their peasants pay their rent in money rather than in commodities or in labor. The sheep-raising capitalists of sixteenth-century England were to secure the right of enclosure, of fencing off for their own flocks common lands where the peasants had traditionally pastured their own livestock. In Spain, the great guild of sheep-raisers, the aforementioned *Mesta,* secured comparable exclusive rights to vast tracts of pasture.

Businessmen, too, attacked medieval economic customs. They wanted property in a form that they might readily buy and sell, free from the restrictions of feudal tenure. And they wanted laborers whom they could hire and fire, free from the restrictions of serfdom. All these forces, together with the labor shortage and peasant unrest created by the Black Death, precipitated the end of serfdom. Serfs had virtually disappeared in Italy, with its robust urban life, by 1300; two centuries later they had vanished in most areas of western Europe.

Thus, at the heart of economic and social

relationships, the cash nexus of the capitalist was beginning to replace the medieval complex of caste and service. These new developments blurred the old lines between classes. The ordinary individual very probably made a gain in real income by becoming a wage-earning laborer or rent-paying tenant farmer instead of a serf. Yet he also lost something — the security, the inherited job, the right to certain lands — which he had possessed in the days of manorialism. Hence the undercurrents of despair and discontent which came to the surface in peasant rebellions. Meantime, social tension increased in the towns and cities, as the guilds became more exclusive and the cleavage widened between the wealthy master and the ordinary workman.

The most immediate political result of the economic changes we have been surveying was the newly enlarged political role of the business class, the celebrated bourgeoisie. Sometimes the bourgeois themselves ruled, as did the Medici in Florence and the merchants in Venice and the Hanse. Sometimes the bourgeois provided monarchs with the money or the professional skills, or both, to further dynastic and national interests. Men of the middle class helped Henry VII bring law and order back to England; Fugger money supported the Habsburgs. The eventual bankruptcy of the Fuggers underscored the fact that, while the holders of political power were beholden to the wielders of economic power, the reverse was also true.

The economic leaders made their impact not only on politics but also on the whole "style" of the age. The medieval outlook on man was undergoing a significant change: witness the extreme of worldly pride asserted in the epitaph of Jacob Fugger. No medieval man would have been so presumptuous, so self-centered, so lacking in humility. The bourgeois were beginning to invade the Church's near-monopoly of the support of culture. The Fuggers, the Medici, and the well-to-do in general were undertaking the patronage of art and learning, and financing the building of public monuments. The palace or the library of the rich man challenged the monastery or the Church-dominated university as a center of scholarship. In the late 1400's, for example, the intellectual life of Florence revolved around the Platonic Academy, subsidized by Lorenzo the Magnificent.

The Church itself, the very keystone of medieval civilization, cracked and threatened to crumble under the impact of the new economic forces and the new secularism. There was little to distinguish the rich and cultivated prelate from the rich and cultivated layman. The popes of the later 1400's and early 1500's, like their contemporaries in the business world, were great admirers and amassers of material wealth, and great connoisseurs of art. Under popes like Sixtus IV, Alexander VI, and Julius II the Church participated to the hilt in the Age of Machiavelli and of the Renaissance.

V   Two Heirs of other Traditions: The Russians and the Ottomans

The nation-states of western Europe all emerged from the debris of the Roman Empire in the West, from the Latin or Germanic linguistic tradition, and from the uniting bond of the Roman Catholic Church. They resembled each other more closely than any of them resembled either Russia or the Ottoman Empire, successor-states to the East Roman or Byzantine Empire with its center at Constantinople (Byzantium or, as the Turks called it, Istanbul), which had dominated the eastern Mediterranean world for eleven hundred years, between the fourth and the fifteenth centuries.

Byzantine Empire

▨ Territory lost by Byzantine Empire between 565 (death of Justinian) and 1000

▤ Byzantine territory about 1000

■ Battle sites

The "Straits"

Black Sea
Constantinople (Byzantium)
Bosporus
Chalcedon
Sea of Marmora
Dardanelles (The Hellespont)
Aegean Sea

0   50   100
Miles

Although almost none of its vast territories, stretching thousands of miles from eastern Europe to the Pacific, had ever actually belonged to the Byzantine Empire, Russia, in its government, religion, and culture derived largely from Byzantium. As for the Ottoman Empire, it embraced not only most of the Balkan peninsula and other parts of eastern and southeastern Europe but also Anatolia (Asia Minor) and the Arab world, including Egypt, Syria, and North Africa. Moslem in religion and non-European in language, at first glance it appears entirely alien and strange to the European world. Yet in fact it occupied the territory and to a surprising degree inherited both the population and the institutions of Byzantium. Russia and the Ottoman Empire were thus the heirs of a different tradition: Byzantium was eastern not western, Greek not Latin, Orthodox not Catholic, yet it was both Roman and Christian, as was the West. With the Turks, moreover, we encounter a non-

Christian people, adherents to the faith of Islam. Russia and the Ottoman Empire both played a fundamental role in modern European history. Before we can understand their behavior, we must take a quick look at the traditions to which they had fallen heir.

The Byzantine Heritage

From the fourth century A.D. onward, the Byzantine emperor had ruled as a true autocrat—divinely ordained, the reflection here on earth of the single God in heaven, complete master of his subjects, who were called by a term meaning slaves. He lived in a "sacred palace," apart and mysterious, emerging to participate in a virtually constant round of formal ceremonies, regulated by a rigid code of etiquette. Not only did he promulgate the imperial law codes governing his subjects' behavior, but, "equal to the Apostles," he presided over the councils of the church, and pronounced on matters of doctrine. Very seldom was he challenged by the Bishop of Constantinople (the Patriarch). Unlike the Pope, the Patriarch was usually content to remain the head of a church that was rather a department of state. The Byzantines always maintained that theirs was the supreme power among all those on the inhabited globe. Often their power matched their pretensions: they won splendid victories, conducted skillful diplomacy, grew immensely rich, created a superb and opulent art, studied the Greek classics, and kept them alive during all the centuries when the West knew no Greek. So they exerted a powerful attraction upon the barbarians of eastern Europe (many of whom were Slavs), who looked upon the great city of Byzantium with an understandable mixture of admiration and envy.

First the Bulgarians, and then the Russians, and eventually the Serbs accepted Christianity, not from Rome (as did the Czechs and Poles and Croatians among their fellow-Slavs), but from Constantinople. Thus, the Russians inherited the tradition of ecclesiastical subordination to the state, and the immense emphasis on ritual, mystery, and magic in religion which was also characteristic of Byzantine Christianity. The quarrels between the churches of Rome and Constantinople, which culminated in a split (or schism) between the Roman Church and the Church of Byzantium in 1054, were therefore passed on by the Byzantines to their Russian pupils. Russian churchmen suspected and even hated Rome, and were thus cut off from most of the intellectual achievement of the West during the Middle Ages. The Roman Church required the use of Latin in the ritual, which gave a linguistic unity to its services wherever they might be conducted, and ensured the education of its priests. But the Byzantine Church did not require Greek; it permitted the use of the native tongue for the church services, and thus shut the Russian clergy away from education, and initiated a certain cultural lag in Russian life, later to be reinforced by other factors.

The medieval Russian state, centering on the city of Kiev, fell before the Mongolian Tartars in the early thirteenth century, and the next two centuries under Tartar domination accentuated this lag behind western Europe. When the native Russians freed themselves from the Tartars, beginning in the late fourteenth and fifteenth centuries, the newly emerging state of Moscow reverted to its Byzantine heritage when it created its own new institutions.

The Ottoman Turks

By that time, Byzantium itself had fallen, to the Ottoman Turks or Osmanlis (so-called after Osman, their first historic ruler), a tribe originally of central Asian origin, whose leaders began in the thirteenth century to move westward in the Anatolian plateau, and establish themselves in its northwest corner, immediately opposite Constantinople. In this region, the Greek population, discontented with harsh and ineffectual Byzantine rule, turned to the Osmanlis. The Osmanlis were Moslems, believers in the religion of Islam (submission), founded in the nomadic society of Arabia in the seventh century by the Prophet Mohammed; influenced to some degree by Judaism and Christianity, Mohammed wrote down the revelations that he believed came to him from the One God of the Jews and Christians. These were collected after his death in the Koran. Firmly monotheist, and believing that the trinitarian worship of the Christians was polytheism and therefore idolatry, he required his followers to pray five times daily facing Mecca, acknowledging God and Mohammed as his prophet, to fast one month in the year between sunrise and sunset, to give alms to the poor, and if possible to make a pilgrimage to Mecca. He believed in an afterlife, in which true Moslems were rewarded with fleshly delights. By the time of Mohammed's death in 632, he had converted only part of the population of Arabia itself, but the Moslem Arabs soon erupted from the peninsula, and carried their new faith by conquest into Syria and Persia, Egypt, North Africa, and Spain. From Persia it spread eastward into central Asia, home of the nomadic Turkish tribes.

Everywhere Islam brought the Arabic language as the language of the faith, but in Persia it encountered the traditions of an ancient civilization closely linked with the Greco-Roman world. Thus subsequent generations of Moslems were deeply indebted both to Persia and to classical antiquity. The early caliphs, rulers of Islam, the representatives of Mohammed on earth, were absolute autocrats like the Byzantine emperors. In theory, Moslems believed that all the world that was not yet theirs they must some day conquer. Though in theory they gave a conquered infidel the choice between conversion to Islam and death, in practice they ruled peacefully over millions of Christians, who merely paid a special tax, and suffered other minor disabilities. When the Moslems declared a holy war, however, they often adhered to the letter of the harsh law.

Though Moslems, the Osmanlis were not fanatical, and learned from the Greek population the arts of settled agricultural life. By the 1330's the nomad Osmanlis, rulers of northwest Anatolia, had settled down as farmers, and many of them had intermarried with the native Greeks. Too late, the Byzantine authorities realized the danger. Civil wars between rival claimants to the Byzantine throne gave the Turks new opportunities, as they were invited across the Straits to help one of the contestants. In 1356 they established a European capital at Adrianople; Constantinople itself became an island surrounded by Turkish territory.

The Byzantine Empire survived down to 1453, but only because the Turks decided to conquer the Balkan region first. Destroying independent Bulgarian and Serbian states, defeating the armies sent out by western Europe against them (1396), recovering from the temporary setback administered to them in 1402 by the savage Tartar Timur (Tamerlane), the Osmanlis finally and dramatically took Constantinople on May 29, 1453. The last Byzantine emperor perished bravely in the fight. The collapse of an empire that had ruled at the Straits for 1,100 years shocked and alarmed the Christian world.

One of the chief reasons for Turkish success was the mutual hatred between Greek Orthodox eastern Christians and Roman Catholic western Christians. The westerners felt that the Greeks were treacherous schismatics. Too preoccupied with their own concerns to send more than token forces to help the Byzantines, they demanded that the Greeks accept papal supremacy, and thus reunite the churches. For their part, the Greeks keenly remembered the outrages committed against them in the thirteenth century by the western crusaders who had occupied Constantinople for almost sixty years. Many Greeks openly preferred Turkish conquest to the acceptance of assistance from the West. Thus, though the Byzantine emperor had acknowledged papal supremacy at the council of Ferrara-Florence in 1439, and the churches had been re-united officially, the act did not command the support of the Byzantine population, and it gravely shocked the Russian Orthodox Church.

The "end" of the Byzantine Empire proved in fact to be more of an appearance than a reality. By 1453, the Osmanlis had become a largely European people. The sultan, deeply impressed by the prestige of the empire he had overthrown, and ruling from its capital, imitated many of its institutions. He vanished into a newly built palace, much like the "sacred palace" of his Byzantine predecessors. In all probability the Turks took over, at least in part, the late Byzantine system of military land-holdings and rendering of military service. Eventually, they granted to western trading powers the same valuable trading privileges and extra-territorial rights that the Byzantines had for several centuries been in the habit of granting to the mercantile cities of Italy.

Most important, perhaps, the Moslem Osmanlis placed the religious life of their Orthodox subjects in the control of the Greek Patriarch of Constantinople. He retained his religious authority. His taxes emptied the pockets of the Orthodox, and his courts judged their law-suits. Within the Ottoman Empire the Christians were members of a different community or *millet*. Only in cases of disputes with Moslems did the Ottoman government step in actively. Thus Byzantine ways of life and influences continued to remain strong throughout the Christian population of the Ottoman Empire, whether Greek or Slavic.

VI   Muscovite Russia to 1682

During the two centuries between the collapse of the Kievan Russian state and the rise of Moscow, Russia lay divided and subject to a variety of governmental and social systems. In the west, along the borders of Poland and Lithuania, a kind of feudalism reigned unchecked. In the north, the town commonwealth of Novgorod built up a prosperous mercantile existence supported by Baltic trade with the Germans, and explored and exploited a large, sparsely settled territory to the north and northeast. But the western feudal regions had fallen too greatly under the influence of the alien Roman Catholic Poles to act as the center of a new Russia; while Novgorod suffered from severe internal social conflicts and wide economic discrepancies between rich and poor, the sterile soil in the neighborhood rendered it dependent upon the Moscow region for its grain.

Moscow—then still only a primitive forest village—had other great assets. It lay near the watershed from which the Russian rivers flow north into the Baltic or south into the Black Sea. In Russia, the rivers always provided the routes for trade. When the Tartar grip relaxed, and commerce could resume, Moscow could take advantage of its geographical situation.

The Princes of Moscow

Moreover, the princes of Moscow proved extraordinarily able. First to arrive on the ground in the emigration from the southwest after the collapse of Kiev, they were able very early to establish the principle of seniority and primogeniture, so that the royal domain did not suffer a new division with the death of each prince—a practice that had proved the ruin of Kievan Russia. The early princes of Moscow married into rich families, steadily increased their territorial holdings, and consolidated their authority within the expanding borders of their own principality.

In addition, they developed useful relationships with their Tartar overlords, who had set up their own capital far to the east, at Sarai on the Volga, and who usually chose the princes of Moscow as their agents to collect the tribute from the other Russian princes, and to deliver it to Sarai. So the Muscovites could take the credit for excluding Tartar agents from Russia, and thus attract settlers to their lands. They also became familiar with conditions at the Tartar court. Thus, when the moment of Tartar weakness came, it was the princes of Moscow who took advantage of it, winning the first victories in 1378 and 1380. Though the Tartars exacted a fierce vengeance for the defeats, the very turn of the tide must have encouraged the Russians to realize that Tartar domination need not last forever.

The Muscovite princes could justly claim to be the agents of liberation and the champions of Russian resurgence. They could thus command the newly crystallizing Russian national sentiment. The Tartar state at Sarai did not disintegrate for several decades thereafter, and even when it did, the Tartars did not disappear from Russian life, but formed three new khanates or states from the debris of the old: one at Kazan, on the middle Volga, blocking the course of the river to Russian trade for another century and a half; one at Astrakhan at the mouth of the Volga on the Caspian Sea; and a third in the Crimea, which later became a vassal of the Ottoman sultan. Though the Tartars' influence on Russian society seems to have been largely negative, their relationships, both friendly and hostile, with the house of Moscow had clearly helped to launch their successors as the masters of Russia upon their long career.

Most important, the princes of Moscow secured the support of the Russian Church. In the early fourteenth century the Metropolitan Archbishop made Moscow the ecclesiastical capital of Russia. When the line of Muscovite princes faltered temporarily, it was the Metropolitan who administered the principality loyally and effectively until the royal house recovered. Thus the Russian Church, as it were, deliberately bet on Moscow.

The Imperial Political Theory

By the middle of the fifteenth century, Moscow was a self-conscious Russian national state able to undertake successful wars against both the Polish-Lithuanian state and the Tartars. Proclaiming himself heir to the princes of Kiev, and determined to regain the ancient Russian lands lost to the Poles and Tartars, Ivan III (1462–1505) made a national appeal, though a purely dynastic one. Many nobles living in the western lands came over to him with their estates and renounced their loyalties to the Lithuanian-Polish state. In 1492, the Prince of Lithuania was forced to recognize Ivan III as sovereign of "all the Russias." This new national appeal was fortified by a religious appeal as well, for Ivan acted as the champion of Orthodoxy against the Catholic Poles and the Moslem Tartars. His wars took on the character of a purely Russian crusade. But he felt himself to be much more than a mere Russian prince.

In 1472 Ivan married the niece of the last Byzantine emperor, Constantine XI. Ivan adopted the Byzantine title of autocrat, used the Byzantine double eagle as his seal, and began to behave as a Byzantine emperor. He occasionally used the title tsar (Caesar). He no longer consulted his nobles (the *boyars*), but reached decisions in solitude. Italian architects built him an enormous palace, the Kremlin, a building set apart, like the one at Byzantium. When the Holy Roman emperor in

the 1480's offered to confirm Ivan's princely titles, Ivan responded:

By God's grace we have been lords in our land since the beginning of time, since the days of our earliest ancestors. God has elevated us to the same position which they held, and we beg him to grant it to us and our children. We have never desired and do not now desire confirmation of this from any other source.*

This is the claim to unlimited power derived from God that the Byzantine emperor had been accustomed to make.

By the time of Ivan III's grandson, Tsar Ivan IV, the Terrible (1533–1584), we find the theory re-stated in even more emphatic terms. One of Ivan's trusted nobles, Prince Kurbsky, fled from Russia, perhaps in part because he had suffered a military defeat and feared punishment, but also because he felt increasingly uneasy over Ivan's autocratic behavior. From abroad, Kurbsky wrote to Ivan denouncing him for his failure to maintain the traditional privilege of the boyars to be consulted about important questions of policy. The Tsar replied that he was entirely free to bestow favors or to inflict punishment upon his slaves as he chose. To Ivan, all Russian boyars were simply the slaves of the autocrat.

Autocracy no doubt arose in part because the Russians lived in a constant state of war or preparation for war. A national emergency thus prolonged for centuries led naturally to a national dictatorship. Yet even more significant is the fact that in Muscovite territory feudalism had not, as it had, for example, in England, produced a united class of self-conscious nobles who would fight the rising monarchy for what they believed to be their traditional privileges. Kurbsky seems to have been an isolated voice, raised from outside Ivan's dominions. Inside, the nobles did not unite against the pretensions of the autocrat. Instead, they split into various factions, with which the Tsar could deal separately. Quite probably, the example of the Tartar Khans, who ruled despotically, and with whom the

*F. Adelung, *Kritisch-literarische Übersicht der Reisenden in Russland* (St. Petersburg and Leipzig, 1846), I, 153. Our translation.

Muscovites had been in intimate relationship for so long, helped furnish a model and a precedent.

But very important, too, was the ideology supplied by the Church and taken over largely from Byzantium. In the West, the Church itself was a part of feudal society, and jealous of its prerogatives. In Russia, as we have seen, it became the ally of the monarchy, and something like a department of state. Russian churchmen knew all about Rome's claim to world empire, and the age-long claim of Constantinople to be "new Rome," and therefore the successor of the old. Now that Constantinople had itself been conquered, Russian churchmen blamed the Byzantine defeat upon the emperors' concessions to the hated "heretical" papacy, and elaborated a famous new political theory that Moscow was the successor to the two former world capitals:

The Church of Old Rome fell because of its heresy; the gates of the Second Rome, Constantinople, have been hewn down by the axes of the infidel Turks; but the Church of Moscow, the Church of the new Rome, shines brighter than the Sun in the whole Universe. . . . Two Romes have fallen, but the Third stands fast; a fourth there cannot be.*

Russian churchmen also provided the imperial family with an imaginary ancestry going back to the Roman Emperor Augustus, and told the tale that the tsars had inherited certain insignia and regalia not only from the Byzantines but even from the Babylonians. At imperial coronations, right down to the last one in 1894, the tsars were crowned with a cap and clothed in a jacket that were actually of Byzantine manufacture. Thus imperial absolutism became one of the chief features of Russian life. Behind it lay the Byzantine tradition.

Nobles and Serfs

Between the accession of Ivan III in 1462 and the accession of Peter the Great in 1689,

*See R. L. Wolff, "The Three Romes," *Myth and Mythmaking,* ed., H. A. Murray (New York, 1960).

the autocracy succeeded in overcoming the opposition of the old nobility. This was done in part by virtually creating a new class of military-service gentry who owed everything to the tsar. Their estates (*pomestie*), at first granted only for life in exchange for service, eventually became hereditary. The estates (*vochina*) of the old nobility, which had always been hereditary but for which they had owed no service, gradually became service-estates. Thus, by the end of the period, the two types of noble and the two types of estate had by a gradual process become almost identical. The hereditary nobles often owed service. The military-service nobles often had hereditary land. During the eighteenth century this process was to be completed, and state service was to become universal. A central bureau in Moscow kept a census of the "service" men and of their obligations in time of war.

This tremendously important social process was accompanied by the growth of serfdom. In a fashion familiar in earlier times in the West and in Byzantium, economic factors and political unrest had forced more and more peasants to seek out large landowners for dependence. The peasants would accept contracts that required rent in produce and service on the landlord's own land. They would accept a money loan that had to be repaid over a period of years with interest or in the form of extra services. By the early seventeenth century it had become customary that the peasant could not leave his plot until he had paid off his debt. Since the debt was often too big for him to repay, he could in practice never leave.

The process was enormously speeded up when the tsars gave estates to the new military-service gentry. An estate was not much good unless there was farm labor to work it. In a period of bitter agrarian and political crisis such as the sixteenth and seventeenth centuries, it became advisable for the government to help the service gentry to keep their farmers where they were. Also since the peasants paid most of the taxes, it was easier for the government to collect its own revenues if the taxpayers stayed put. Gradually, it was made harder and harder for a tenant to leave his landlord, until by 1649 the avenues of escape were closed, and the serf was fixed to the soil. The landlord administered justice and had police rights on the estate. He collected the serfs' taxes. He himself could sell, exchange, or give away his serfs. And the serf status became hereditary; children of serfs were enrolled on the estate's census books as serfs like their fathers.

The Russian serfs were not emancipated until 1861. Together with the absolute autocracy, the institution of serfdom is the most characteristic feature of Russian society. It affected every Russian, whether landowner, serf, or neither, for all the centuries it existed. In a very real sense, the consequences of Russian serfdom are still with us today, posing a great problem not only for the rulers of the Soviet Union but for all the world that has to deal with Russia. Russian serfdom became a fixed custom far later in time than did western European serfdom. And it was widely extended during the eighteenth century, at a moment when the serfs in western Europe had long been on their way to complete liberation. This is another illustration of the fact that Russia went through many of the same processes as the West, but with greater intensity and at a later time.

The Reign of Ivan the Terrible

Most of the disorders that distinguish Russian history in the sixteenth and seventeenth centuries have their origin in the long reign of Ivan IV, the Terrible (1533–1584). Pathologically unbalanced, Ivan succeeded to the throne as a small child. He experienced helplessly the indignities inflicted on him by the various rival groups of boyars who were maneuvering and intriguing for power. Devoted to the rites of the Church, and fancying himself as a theologian, Ivan was none the less horribly cruel. He had perhaps as many as seven wives; he murdered his own son in a fit of lunatic rage. Soviet historians have at times tried to turn him into a hero by explaining that his wrath was directed against the selfish nobles who were conspiring to take over Russia. But, though the nobles were selfish enough, the danger of their intrigues was surely hugely exaggerated by the Tsar.

When Ivan finally was strong enough, in 1547, to assume the crown and throw off the tutelage of the boyars, he embarked upon a period (1547–1560) usually regarded as one of sound government and institutional reform. He regulated the rapacity of the imperial administrators in the provinces, who had oppressed the population. Several localities obtained the right to elect their own officials, both judicial and financial; yet, in the absence of any real sense of local initiative, we may question the effectiveness of the changes. Ivan also convoked the first *zemski sobor* (land assembly) a consultative body consisting of nobles, clerics, and representatives from the towns, to assist with the imperial business, particularly with important questions of war and peace. Though comparable in its social composition to the various assemblies of the medieval western European world, the *zemski sobor* under Ivan seems to have met only once,

Ivan the Terrible, a contemporary portrait now in the National Museum of Denmark.

and can in no sense be regarded as a parliamentary body.

When Ivan fell ill in 1553, the boyars refused to take an oath of allegiance to his son. This action apparently reawakened all his savagery, and upon his recovery he broke with his former moderate advisers, withdrew from Moscow, denounced the boyars and clergy, and soon afterward created a fantastic new institution: the *oprichnina,* or "separate realm." This was to belong to him personally, while the rest of Russia, called the *zemshchina,* continued to be administered as before. But the men whom Ivan now appointed to run the *oprichnina* (called *oprichniks*) were urged on to punish those who were prominent in the *zemshchina.* The *oprichniks,* grimly dressed in black and riding black horses, bore on their saddlebows a dog's head (for vigilance) and a broom (symbolizing a clean sweep). They waged a fierce, relentless war on the boyars, confiscating their estates, exiling them, killing them off. The Tsar, as was said, had divided his realm in two, and had set one part of it warring on the other. And in the diary of one *oprichnik* we find this revealing entry: "Today I did no harm to anyone: I was resting." The *oprichniks* took over the old estates of the men whom they were destroying. By the time of Ivan's death, many of the *oprichniks* themselves had been murdered at his orders, and Russian administration had degenereated to a state approximating chaos. Yet Ivan was able to extend Russian authority far to the East against the Kazan and Astrakhan Tartars, thus for the first time opening the whole Volga waterway to Russian commerce, and facilitating expansion further east, into Siberia.

The Time of Troubles

Though the territory was wide and the imperial rule absolute, ignorance, illiteracy, and inefficiency weakened the structure of Russian society. The few foreign observers who knew the Russia of Ivan could foresee chaos ahead. And the Tsar himself had his own dire forebodings: "The body is exhausted, the spirit is ailing, the spiritual and physical wounds multiply, and there is no doctor to cure me,"* he wrote in his last will. Though the old nobility had been dealt a series of blows, the new gentry had as yet no sense of corporate entity, and therefore was not firmly in control of the machinery. Ivan's son and heir, Fedor (1584–1598), was an imbecile, and with his death in 1598 the Moscow dynasty, descended from the rulers of the former Kievan state, died out. The cliques of rival nobles intrigued for power. Fedor's brother-in-law, Boris Godunov, emerged as the dominant figure in the state. During Fedor's reign he had managed to build up his own position of strength. When Fedor died, Boris summoned a *zemski sobor,* which duly elected him to be the new Tsar. One of his unsuccessful rivals for the throne was a certain Fedor Romanov, who, like Boris, came from the middle ranks of the nobility. After his election, Boris forced Romanov to become a monk, under the name of Filaret.

Though Boris Godunov was probably a man of talent, he could not overcome his handicaps: Ivan's legacy of disorder, the intrigues of the nobility, and the famine and plague that began in 1601. To the tens of thousands of peasants who had already fled from serfdom and the thousands of persons displaced from the cities and towns by the inequitable privileges accorded to the wealthier merchants, there were now added incalculable numbers of hungry refugees. Bands of brigands roamed the countryside, and when in 1603 a pretender arose under the protection of the King of Poland and declared that he was a son of Ivan the Terrible—who had in fact died long before—he was able to capture the support of many of the discontented. Russia was launched on the decade known as the Time of Troubles (1603–1613).

Boris Godunov died in 1605, and the Pretender, whoever he may really have been, ruled briefly as Tsar. But his Polish and Catholic leanings and the ambitions of the nobles led to an overturn within less than a year; he was murdered, and was succeeded by a certain Shuisky, a representative of the ancient aristocracy against which Ivan the Terrible had

*Quoted by M. T. Florinsky, *Russia, A History and an Interpretation* (New York, 1953), I, 208.

waged such implacable warfare. But Shuisky could not hold on to power; new pretenders arose; the mobs of peasants and brigands were rallied once again; civil war continued, as the Poles seized the opportunity to take advantage of Russian weakness. The Swedes also intervened. Shuisky fell in 1610, and was succeeded by no one tsar but by a small group of boyars, who planned that the heir to the Polish throne would become Tsar of Russia.

Polish forces took over in Moscow, and it soon appeared that the King of Poland himself intended not to turn over the power to his son but to reign in Russia himself. It was this specter of a foreign and Catholic domination that aroused the national sentiments of the Russians. In answer to a summons from the Patriarch, there assembled a kind of national militia, drawn largely from the prosperous free farmers of the middle Volga region, organized by a butcher named Kuzma Minin, and led by a nobleman named Dmitri Pozharsky. These two are the national heroes of the Time of Troubles. Under their command the militia won the support of other rebellious elements, and drove the Poles from Moscow in 1613.

The Role of the *Zemski Sobor*

A *zemski sobor* more widely representative than any previous one now was summoned to Moscow, where it elected as Tsar Michael Romanov, son of Filaret, who was only sixteen years old. From the election of Michael in 1613 to the Russian Revolution of 1917, the Romanov dynasty held the throne. Michael succeeded with no limitations placed upon his power by the *zemski sobor* or by any other body; he was that curious anomaly, an elected autocrat. For this reason the Time of Troubles has been called a turning-point in Russian history "at which history refused to turn." Yet amid the chaos left by the decade of civil war and foreign intervention, in the absence of any corporate body—baronage, townsmen, or clergy—with a program for limiting the power of the Tsar, we can hardly be surprised that the autocracy continued in

Russia quite unimpaired. The great boyars were weakened by the discreditable role many of them had played during the civil war. But the service gentry, coming into their own, imitated their noble predecessors. The rebellious serfs had to go back to their serfdom, which indeed became more onerous and difficult to escape than ever before.

For the first ten years of the reign of Michael Romanov, the *zemski sober* stayed in continual session. Since it had picked the new Tsar in the midst of crisis, it had indeed performed a constitutional function. It even included some representatives of the free peasantry. It assisted the uncertain new dynasty to get under way by endorsing the policies of the Tsar and his advisers, and thus lending them the semblance of popular support. One might have supposed that this would be the beginning of a new kind of partnership, and that, as had sometimes happened in the West, representatives of the various social classes would gain more and more political self-confidence and power, and might even transform the *zemski sobor* from a consultative to some sort of legislative assembly, a parliament.

But this was not to be. After 1623, for the remainder of the reign of Michael (down to 1645), and during the reign of his son and successor Tsar Alexis (1645–1676), the summons to the *zemski sobor* became more and more infrequent. It was still consulted on questions of the declaration of war or the making of peace, the approval of new taxation, and the sanctioning of important new legislation. It endorsed the accession of Alexis in 1645, and in 1649 confirmed the issuance of a new law code, summarizing and putting in order past statutes. After 1653 Alexis did not summon it again, nor did his son and successor, Fedor (1676–1682). Its last meetings were in 1682.

No law abolished the *zemski sobor*. None had created it. The dynasty was simply entrenched and no longer needed it. Tsardom, autocratic tsardom, was taken for granted. No tsar need consult with any of his subjects unless he felt the need to do so. No subject had the right to insist on being consulted, though all subjects had the duty to give advice when asked for it. As the Romanovs became entrenched, they no longer felt the need to consult anybody's wishes except their own and those of their court favorites.

Individually, the early Romanovs were neither distinguished nor talented. The central government consisted of a number of bureaus or ministries or departments (*prikazy*), often with ill-defined or overlapping areas of competence. Provincial governors continued to milk the long-suffering population, and local efforts at self-government were in practice limited to the choice of officials obliged to collect and hand over taxes to the central authorities. Opposition to the system there certainly was, but it came not from articulate or literate citizens leveling criticism or offering suggestions for improvement. It came from below, from the oppressed and hungry peasantry. And it expressed itself in the only form of action the serf knew: large-scale or small-scale revolt, the burning of the manor house, the slaughter of the landlord or the tax-collector, the ill-directed march about in the vast flat countryside. Such affairs were a matter of yearly occurrence, the largest and most famous being that of Stenka Razin (1676), the "Russian Robin Hood." Such Russian uprisings were almost never directed against the tsar but against the landlords and officials, of whose misdeeds the tsar was supposed not to know. Often indeed the peasant leaders would arouse their followers *in the name* of the tsar. Sometimes, as during the Time of Troubles, the leaders pretended to be tsars in order to obtain more followers.

The Role of the Church

During the sixteenth and seventeenth centuries the Church remained the partner of the autocracy. The tsar controlled the election of the Metropolitan of Moscow, and after 1589 that of the newly proclaimed Patriarch of Moscow, a rank to which the Metropolitan was elevated. In the seventeenth century, there were two striking instances when a patriarch actually shared power with the tsar. In 1619, the father of Tsar Michael Romanov,

Filaret, became patriarch and was granted the additional title of "great sovereign." He assisted his son in all the affairs of state, and indeed dominated Russia. In the next generation, Tsar Alexis appointed a cleric named Nikon to the patriarchal throne, and made him "great sovereign" too. Nikon proved so arrogant that he aroused protests from clergy as well as laity. He also argued that the authority of the Patriarch in spiritual affairs exceeded that of the tsar, while in temporal matters the two were equal: a claim like that of the more powerful medieval popes, but one that had almost never been advanced in Byzantium or in Russia. In 1666 a church council deposed Nikon, who died a mere monk. These two experiments with two-man government were never repeated. They are the exceptions that prove the rule in Russia: the Church depends upon the State.

As in the Byzantine Empire, so in Russia, monasteries became immensely rich. By 1500, it is estimated that they owned more than one-third of the land available for cultivation. Opposition to monastic worldliness arose within the Church itself, and one might have supposed that the government would have supported this movement. But those who favored monastic poverty also wished to enforce the non-interference of the State in monastic affairs. To preserve their right to control the monasteries in other respects, the government of the tsar was obliged to oppose this reforming movement with respect to monastic property.

The Church, almost alone, inspired the literature and art of the Muscovite period. History was written by monks, in the form of chronicles. Travel literature took the form of accounts of pilgrimages to the Holy Land, although we have one secular travel book, a report by a Novgorod merchant who went to India on business. A handbook of etiquette and domestic economy, called Household Management, advises its readers how to run a home and how to behave in company, revealing a conservative, well-ordered, and smug society. Theological tracts attack the Catholics, and also the Protestants, whose doctrines were known in the western regions. Almost all of this literature was written in Old Church Slavonic, the language of the liturgy and not the language of everyday speech. Though stately and impressive, Old Church Slavonic was not an appropriate vehicle for new ideas. There was no secular learning, no science, no flowering of vernacular literature, no lively debates on the philosophical level in the field of theology. In painting, the ikon, inherited from Byzantium, did flourish mightily, and various local schools produced works of great beauty and character.

The Expansion of Russia

The sixteenth and seventeenth centuries saw a tremendous physical expansion of the Russian domain. Russian pioneers, in search of furs to sell and new land to settle, led the way, and the government followed. Frontiersmen in Russia were known as Cossacks, or Kazakhs, a Tartar word meaning "free adven-

St. Basil Cathedral, Moscow (1554–1560).

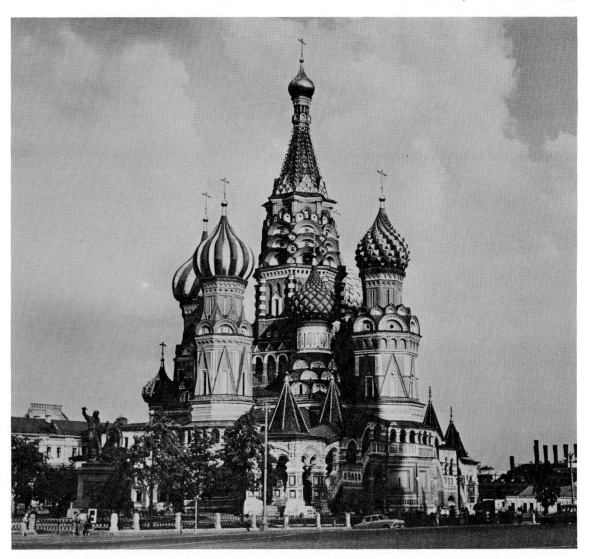

turer." The Cossacks were racially no different from the mass of Russians, but they lived on the frontiers and organized themselves for self-defense against the Tartars as our American pioneers did against the Indians. Two Cossack republics, one on the Dnieper, the other on the Don, lived in a kind of primitive democracy relatively independent of Moscow; other Cossack groups formed in the Volga, in the Urals, and elsewhere; they fought Tartars and Turks quite at their own free will. Cossacks could usually be counted upon to help the leader of any peasant uprising, and did so during the Time of Troubles. Also the Cossacks were deeply involved in the advancement of the Russian frontiers both in Europe and in Asia.

On the west, of course, Russia faced the Poles, who had inherited former Russian lands, which they were determined to keep. But in Poland the monarchy, instead of being hereditary, was elective. Each time the throne fell vacant, the diet, or assembly, of the nobility, would choose a successor, usually the man who had given the biggest bribes. Once elected, the kings were quite powerless, since they had already agreed to transfer royal prerogatives to the diet, which cherished its famous institution of the *liberum veto*: any one of its members, by opposing any proposal, could effectively block it. All the minority of one had to do was to shout "I do not wish it!" and then gallop off before his colleagues could catch up with him and make him change his mind. The diet was not a parliament in the western sense of the term, but an assembly of men each of whom thought of himself as a power unto himself, more like the Security Council of the United Nations. Thus unanimity was necessary for all decisions. Loosely knit, the Polish national state had no regular army or diplomatic corps. Its nobility had no concept of service to the Crown or indeed any sense of loyalty except to their own social class. They helped destroy a once-flourishing urban middle class by persecuting Jewish shopkeepers and foreign merchants. On their estates, the fate of their serfs was harsher if possible than in Russia.

By the 1650's, the Russo-Polish conflict was concentrated in the Ukrainian lands, where Pole and Russian competed for the assistance of the Cossacks. Here bitterness had been exacerbated by the Jesuit effort to convert the Orthodox peasants. In 1595, after a group of Orthodox clergy had accepted papal supremacy in the Union of Brest, the Catholics declared that all those who remained outside the Union must be persecuted. The Polish authorities also interfered with the traditional liberties of the Dnieper Cossacks, and in 1648 the Cossack leader Khmelnitsky revolted against the Poles, inviting Tsar Alexis to assist him in 1651. By 1654, the *zemski sobor* had approved the Tsar's acceptance of a protectorate over the Ukrainian lands, and a long war with Poland ensued, during which the Cossacks changed sides repeatedly, maneuvering desperately to preserve their independence. In 1667, by the Treaty of Andrussovo, the Russians obtained all the lands on the east bank of the Dnieper, as well as the privilege of occupying Kiev, on the west bank, for two years. They never left it.

The Cossacks, however, continued unruly, and in the next phase of the struggle, the Ottoman Turks, as suzerains over the Crimean Tartars, whose territories bordered on the Ukraine, took an active part in the fighting, which involved Poland and Russia once more. The general European anxiety over the Turkish menace (see p. 76) eventually brought the Poles reluctantly to grant Russia by a new treaty of eternal peace (1686) all the lands yielded at Andrussovo, plus Kiev. The continued decline of Poland meant that Sweden, guardian of the Baltic shore, would emerge as the chief rival on the west.

To the south and southeast, in the direction of the Black Sea and the Caucasus, Russia had to move more slowly. Not only did the Crimean Tartars block the path, but behind the Tartars loomed the figure of their overlord, the Ottoman sultan, whom the tsars could not yet challenge. Thus the Russian claim to be the successor to Byzantium in the Orthodox world was a spiritual and ideological claim only. Indeed, when a group of Cossacks seized the key Tartar seaport of Azov at the mouth of the Don, and offered it to Michael Romanov

1190

Before Tartar conquest

Arctic Ocean

N. Dvina R.
URAL MTS.
Ob R.
Irtysh R.
Tobol R.

Novgorod
L. Ilmen
Pskov
Polotsk
Tver
Suzdal
Vladimir
W. Dvina R.
Smolensk

Kiev
Dnieper R.
Dniester R.
Volga R.
Ural R.
Don R.

Danube R.
CRIMEA
Black Sea
Constantinople
CAUCASUS MTS.
Caspian Sea

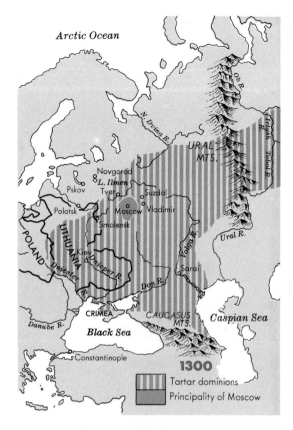

1300

Arctic Ocean

N. Dvina R.
URAL MTS.
Ob R.
Irtysh R.
Tobol R.

Novgorod
L. Ilmen
Pskov
Tver
Suzdal
Polotsk
Moscow
Vladimir
Smolensk
POLAND
LITHUANIA
Kiev
Dnieper R.
Dniester R.
Volga R.
Ural R.
Sarai
Don R.

Danube R.
CRIMEA
Black Sea
Constantinople
CAUCASUS MTS.
Caspian Sea

|||| Tartar dominions
▓ Principality of Moscow

Medieval and Early Modern Russia, 1190-1689

1505

At death of Ivan III

Arctic Ocean

N. Dvina R.
URAL MTS.
Ob R.
Irtysh R.
Tobol R.

Novgorod
L. Ilmen
Pskov
Kazan
W. Dvina R.
Polotsk
LITHUANIA
Smolensk
Moscow
POLAND
Kulikovo
Kiev
Dnieper R.
Dniester R.
Volga R.
Ural R.
Don R.
Astrakhan

Danube R.
CRIMEA
Black Sea
Constantinople
CAUCASUS MTS.
Caspian Sea

1689

At accession of Peter the Great

Arctic Ocean

N. Dvina R.
URAL MTS.
Ob R.
Irtysh R.
Tobol R.

Novgorod
L. Ilmen
Pskov
Kazan
W. Dvina R.
LITHUANIA
POLAND
Moscow
Kiev
Dnieper R.
Dniester R.
COSSACKS
Volga R.
Ural R.
Don R.
Astrakhan

Danube R.
CRIMEA
Black Sea
Constantinople
CAUCASUS MTS.
Caspian Sea

as a gift if he would only come and help hold on to it, the cautious tsar not only refused the offer, but wrote an apologetic letter to the sultan explaining that he had had no part in the aggression.

The most dramatic advance of Russia during this era came to the eastward, across the Urals, and the vast spaces of Siberia, all the way to the Pacific Ocean. This movement has often been likened to the American expansion from the Atlantic seaboard to the Pacific. Compared with the Russian advance to the Pacific, the American westward movement was relatively slow, however: the Russians covered some 5,000 miles in about forty years; we took longer to go a shorter distance. But the Russian advance left vast areas "behind the lines" unsettled and unabsorbed at each stage, whereas our own more gradual movement tended to consolidate each stage rather more than the Russians did.

Then too, the American pioneer faced formidable geographic barriers of mountain and desert, whereas the Russian had easier going on the enormous Siberian flatlands, where the river basins—the Ob, the Yenisei, the Lena, and their tributaries—facilitated rapid progress. For the Americans too, the native inhabitants—the American Indian—often posed serious military and political problems, whereas the Siberian tribesmen, widely scattered across the area, seem on the whole to have helped the Russians rather than to have opposed them. Though enormous in extent, Siberia continued to be very sparsely inhabited.

It was the victories of Ivan the Terrible over the Kazan Tartars that led to the first major advances in the sixteenth century. Private enterprise led the way: the Stroganov family obtained huge concessions in the Ural area, where they made great fortunes in the fur trade, and discovered and began to exploit the first iron mines known in Russia. The Stroganovs hired bands of Cossack explorers, who led the eastward movement. The government followed at some distance behind with administrators and tax-collectors, soldiers and priests, as each new area was opened up. At a suitable point on a river basin, the spearhead of the advance party would build a wooden palisade and begin to collect furs from the surrounding countryside. Almost before the defenses of each new position had been consolidated, the restless advance guard would have moved some hundreds of miles further eastward to repeat the process. The Daniel Boone of the Siberian adventure was surely the famous Cossack leader Yermak, whose exploits in his own lifetime took on legendary proportions.

Tobolsk, the first major Siberian center founded by the Russians, remained a major seat of administration; but Irkutsk and finally Okhotsk were reached by the 1640's. A Siberian *prikaz* in Moscow had nominal responsibility for the government of the huge area, but decisions had to be made on the spot because of the communications problem, although the Russians had an efficient postal service working quite early. Thus the Siberians always tended to have the independence traditionally associated with men of the "wide open spaces," and reinforced by the Cossack and outlaw traditions from which many of them sprang. Because Okhotsk and its neighborhood along the Pacific were intensely cold, and the ocean frozen for a good many months in the year, the Russians were soon looking enviously southward toward the valley of the Amur, which flowed into the Pacific at a point where the harbors were open all year round.

Explorations in this area brought the Russians into contact with the Chinese, whose lands they were now casually invading. But the Chinese government of the period did not care very much about these regions, which, from its own point of view, were far-northerly outposts. In 1689 the Chinese signed a treaty with Moscow, the first they had concluded with any European state. This treaty stabilized the frontier, demilitarized the Amur, and kept the Russians out of Manchuria, the home territory of the ruling Chinese dynasty. It also provided the two powers with a buffer region of Mongolian-inhabited territory, which acknowledged Chinese overlordship. Incidentally, it also recognized the Russian advances to the north. With almost incredible speed, the Russians had acquired an empire whose riches are even today by no means fully exploited. Russia's future as an Asian power with a vital interest in Pacific affairs was established at just about the time the English took New Amsterdam from the Dutch.

Russia and the West

During these two centuries foreigners and foreign ideas gradually penetrated Russia, a process warmly welcomed by some Russians, deeply deplored by others, and viewed in a mingled light by still others, who prized western technical advancement but feared western influence on Russian society. This ambivalent attitude toward westerners and western ideas became characteristic of later Russians: they loved what the West could give, but they often feared and even hated the giver.

The first foreigners to come to Russia in any significant numbers were the Italians, who helped build the Kremlin at the end of the fifteenth century. But the Italians were not encouraged to teach the Russians their knowledge, and they failed to influence even the court of Ivan III in any significant way. The English, who arrived in the mid-sixteenth century as traders to the White Sea (they had been looking for an Arctic route to China), were welcomed by Ivan the Terrible. He gave them valuable privileges, and encouraged them to trade their woolen cloth for Russian naval supplies, which helped build the great Elizabethan fleets. The English were the first to teach Russians western industrial techniques. They got along well with the Russians and supplied a large number of officers to the Tsar's armies, mostly Scotsmen. At one moment during the Time of Troubles, there was even a plan to make King James I Tsar of Russia; and in fact James was quite receptive to the idea. Toward the middle of the seventeenth century, the Dutch were able to displace the English as the most important foreign group engaged in commerce and manufacturing, and set up their own glass, paper, and textile plants in Russia.

After the accession of Michael Romanov in 1613, the foreign quarter of Moscow, always called the "German suburb," grew rapidly. Foreign technicians of all sorts—textile-weavers, bronze-founders, clock-makers—received enormous salaries from the state. Foreign merchants sold their goods, much to the distaste of the native Russians, who begged the tsars to prevent the foreigners from stealing the bread out of their mouths. Foreign physicians and druggists became fashionable, though always suspected of being wizards by the superstitious common people. By the end of the seventeenth century, western influence is apparent in the life of the court. The first play in Russia was performed in 1672—a solemn Biblical drama about Esther. A few nobles began to buy books and form libraries, and to learn Latin and French and German. Some of them were eating salad and taking snuff, and shyly beginning to try their skills at the social arts. A few Russians went abroad to travel, and, of these few, all who could refused to go back.

The people, meanwhile, distrusted the foreigners, looted their houses when they dared, and jeered at them in the street. As one intelligent writer of the seventeenth century put it:

Acceptance of foreigners is a plague. They live by the sweat and tears of the Russians. The foreigners are like bear-keepers who put rings in our noses and lead us around. They are Gods, we fools, they dwell with us as lords. Our Kings are their servants.

The most dramatic outbreak of anti-foreign feeling took place, as might have been expected, in the field of religion. Highly educated clerics from the western lands (the Ukraine) and Greek scholars recommended to Patriarch Nikon that the Holy Books be revised and corrected in certain places where the texts were not sound. Resentment against this reform took shape as a great schism in the Russian Church itself. Given the deep Russian regard for the externals of the faith, we must not be surprised at the horror that was aroused when the Russians were told that for centuries they had been spelling the name of Jesus incorrectly and had been crossing themselves with the wrong number of fingers. As at Byzantium, the religious protest reflected a deepseated hatred of change, particularly change proposed by foreigners. Declaring that the end of the world was at hand (since Moscow, the third Rome, had now itself become heretical), about 20,000 of the schismatics shut themselves up in their huts and burned themselves alive. When the world did not end, those schismatics who survived, always known as the "Old Believers," settled down and became sober, solid Russian citizens, many of them merchants and well-to-do peasants. Some later governments persecuted them, most did not; but the Russian Church was weakened as a result of the schism.

VII   The Ottoman Successor-State, 1453-1699

Part of the Ottomans' inheritance no doubt came from their far-distant past in Central Asia, when, like other Turks, they had almost surely come under the direct or indirect influence of China, and had lived like other nomads of the steppe. Their fondness and capacity for war and their rigid adherence to custom may go back to this early period, as did their native Turkish language. From the Persians and the Byzantines, who themselves had been influenced by Persia, the Turks seem to have derived their exaltation of the ruler, their tolerance of religious groups outside the state religion, and their practice of encouraging such groups to form independent communities inside their state. Persian was always the literary language and the source of Turkish literature, both in form and in content. From Islam, the Turks took the sacred law and their approach to legal problems, the Arabic alphabet in which they wrote their Turkish tongue, and the Arabic vocabulary of religious, philosophical, and other abstract terms. All the wellsprings of their inheritance—Asiatic, Persian-Byzantine, and Moslem—tended to make them an exceptionally conservative people.

The Ottoman System

Fortunate in finding their neighbors weak as they themselves grew in strength, and fortunate in their geographic position as near neighbors to the Byzantines, the Ottomans allowed the peoples that they conquered to pass through a stage of vassalage rather than insisting upon immediate annexation by force. Until the sixteenth century they showed tolerance to their infidel subjects, permitting Christians and Jews to serve the state, and allowing the Patriarch of Constantinople and the Grand Rabbi to act as leaders of their own religious communities. The religious leader not only represented his flock in its dealings with the Ottoman state but also had authority over them in civil, judicial, and financial matters that affected them alone. Non-Muslims paid the head-tax and lived in peace. The Patriarch of Constantinople exercised far more power than he ever had under the Byzantines.

From 1280 to 1566 ten successive able sultans ruled the Ottomans. They received early training in administration, and were expected on their accession to kill off all their brothers—on one occasion they numbered nineteen—in order to forestall civil strife. In theory, the sultan possessed the entire wealth of his dominions, and his object was to exploit it to the full. To do so the sultan maintained an elaborate system of administrators whose lives and property belonged absolutely to him, all of whom were slaves (*kullar*) and at the same time members of the ruling class (Ottomans). To belong to the ruling class a man had to be loyal to the sultan, a Moslem, and a true Ottoman: that is, he had to master the "Ottoman way" of speaking and behaving. All those who lacked one or more of these attributes were not members of the ruling class, but subjects (*raya*, literally, cattle). A *raya* could become an Ottoman by acquiring all three necessary attributes. Beyond the activities of collecting, spending, and increasing the imperial revenues, and defending and adding to the imperial possessions, the Ottomans had no duties, and the rayas could, in their own communities, take care of everything else.

The Ottoman ruling class included four sub-divisions, the "men of the Emperor," the "men of the sword," the "men of the pen," and the "sages." The "men of the Emperor" comprised an inner service, embracing the sultan himself and his wives, sons, servants, private purse, and palace attendants, including the entire harem; and an outer service, including the grand viziers and the other highest officers of the state, those who directed all the other branches of the service. In the early days of the Ottoman Empire, the Turkish princely families from Anatolia virtually monopolized both the inner and the outer services of this imperial class. But as early as the fourteenth century, and even more markedly in the fifteenth, the Sultans learned to balance their influence by recruiting new talent from among the newly acquired Christian subjects. Some entered the system as prisoners of war; some the Sultan bought or received as presents. But most he obtained through the regular levying of the *devshirme,* or tribute of children.

Every four years until sometime in the seventeenth century, specially trained officers, each with a quota of places to fill, visited the Balkan and Anatolian villages and selected and took away the strongest and ablest-

Mosque of Emperor Suleiman the Magnificent, Istanbul, sixteenth century.

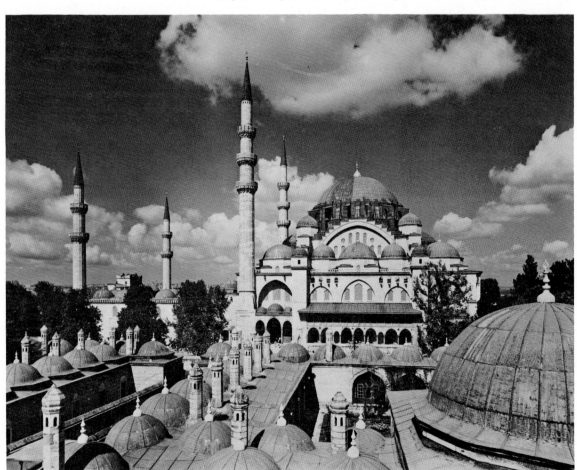

appearing unmarried Slavic or Albanian or Greek youths, between the ages of ten and twenty, especially those between fourteen and eighteen. Though many Christian families naturally hated and feared the practice, some may even have welcomed it, since it held out to the luckiest and most intelligent unlimited opportunities for advancement. The recruits had to accept Islam, and though we know of a few cases of resistance or escape, most seem to have become good Moslems, or at least indifferent to religious matters. All then received a systematic education, perhaps a tenth of the group every year going on to higher studies, and the very cream of the crop attending the sultan's own palace school as pages in his household. Here they studied languages, Moslem and Turkish law, ethics, and theology, as well as horsemanship and military science. Each year the state increased their allowance and reviewed their progress. If a man who had not at first been selected for one of the higher schools proved unexpectedly able, he would be transferred to one.

All left school at the age of twenty-five, and the top men received posts in the imperial class. One sixteenth-century Slav graduated from the page corps as a gatekeeper, advanced to chief taster to the Sultan, moved to the cavalry and became a general, then equerry, then commander of the picked infantry corps, governor of Egypt, and finally passed through the three grades of vizier, finishing his career as grand vizier, the very top officer of the state. So the *devshirme* recruits, all originally Christian, competed with the older Turkish aristocratic families for the honor of staffing the imperial class. A grand vizier presided over the council of state, and if the sultan trusted him might exercise great influence. If not the sultan would depose or kill him: as a slave, the vizier was completely subject to the sultan's whim.

The "men of the sword" included all those connected with the Ottoman armies. In addition to the usual irregular troops and the garrison forces, these were the cavalrymen, or *spahis,* who predominated in the early centuries of Ottoman history. They received fiefs of land (*timars,* or in the case of big fiefs, *ziamets*) in exchange for service, and could administer these fiefs as they wished, collecting taxes from their tenants, and keeping order and justice among them. The infantrymen, at first far less important, received fixed salaries from the treasury. But with the introduction of gunpowder and the development of artillery and rifles, the Ottomans founded a special new corps to use these weapons, the *yeni cheri* (new troops, janissaries). Most of the janissaries came from the *devshirme* recruits who were not selected for training for the imperial class. The janissaries lived in special barracks in the capital, and enjoyed special privileges. A source of strength, they also posed a constant potential danger to the state.

At the height of Turkish military successes, the sultans could put into the field formidable armies, sometimes amounting to more than a quarter of a million men on the march. They were absolutely fearless in battle and were the terror of all opponents. An ambassador from the Habsburgs who spent eight years in Constantinople between 1554 and 1562 compares their endurance favorably with that of European troops. The Turks, he says:

. . . take out a few spoonfuls of flour and put them into water, adding some butter, and seasoning the mess with salt and spices; these ingredients are boiled and a large bowl of gruel is thus obtained. Of this they eat once or twice a day. . . . it is the patience, self-denial, and thrift of the Turkish soldier that enable him to face the most trying circumstances and come safely out of the dangers that surround him. What a contrast to our men! Christian soldiers on a campaign refuse to put up with their ordinary food and call for thrushes, and other such like dainty dishes. . . . It makes me shudder to think what the result of a struggle between such different systems can be. . . .*

The "men of the pen" performed the other duties of government, striving to see that all land was tilled and all trade carried on as profitably as possible so that the sultan might obtain his share in taxes. Once the money

*O. G. Busbecq, *Turkish Letters,* C. T. Forster and F. H. B. Daniell, trans. (London, 1881), I, 220–221.

came in, these officials spent it on the necessary expenses of state, including all salaries for troops and other employees. To keep an official honest and zealous, the Ottoman system often rewarded him by giving him in lieu of salary a portion of the sultan's property to exploit for himself, a kind of fief, from which he might make as much money as he could by administering it. Sometimes he had to turn in a portion of his proceeds as revenue to the sultan, and more rarely he received a salary and had to turn in all the proceeds. In the countryside every farm and village, in town every business and trade, in the government every job, thus became a kind of fief. As the Ottoman system declined in the seventeenth and eighteenth centuries, the transformation of these fiefs in land or money into private possessions without obligations signalized the loss by the sultan's administration of its former power to extract wealth from all its resources.

The "sages" (ulema) included all those connected with religion: the judges who applied Moslem law in the courts, the teachers in the schools, and the scholars of the Koran and the holy law (Shariya), the muftis. The muftis, or jurists, answered questions that arose in the course of lawsuits and that were submitted to them by the judges. It was their function to apply the sacred law of Islam, and they usually gave short replies, without explanation. These replies settled the case. The grand mufti in Istanbul, whom the sultan himself consulted, was known as the Shiek-ul-Islam, the ancient or elder of Islam, and outranked everybody but the grand vizier. Since he could speak the final word on the sacred law, he may even be said to have exercised a kind of check on the absolute power of the sultan himself. He alone could proclaim the beginning of war, or denounce a sultan for transgression of the sacred law, and summon his subjects to depose him. The opinions of the muftis were collected as a body of interpretative law, lying between the changeless, age-old sacred law of Islam and the current enactments of the sultans. The general acceptance by all Moslems of the supremacy of the sacred law and the reluctance of the muftis to accept change were

two of the factors that accounted for the failure of the Ottoman system to develop with the times. There are no "reformations" in Turkish history until the twentieth century.

The effectiveness of this entire structure depended upon the character of the sultan himself. After the mid-sixteenth century, all were brought up in the stifling seclusion of the harem, with its constant quarrels and intrigues between rival concubines, and its often debilitating pleasures. After the first ten generations, the sultans mostly were weaklings, drunkards, debauchees, and men of little experience or political understanding. Harem intrigue played a great role in the state. But in its earlier centuries the Ottoman system flourished and its territories grew.

Ottoman Expansion to 1566

By the end of the 1460's most of the Balkan Peninsula had been consolidated under Ottoman rule, except for the tiny Slavic mountain region of Montenegro, which maintained a precarious independent existence. Thus the core of the new Ottoman state was Asia Minor and the Balkans, the same core around which the Byzantine Empire had been built. From this core before the death of Mohammed II in 1481, the Turks expanded across the Danube into modern Rumania, seized the Genoese outposts in the Crimea, and made this southern Russian region a vassal state under its Tartar rulers. They also fought against the Venetians and even landed forces in Italy. The limits of their expansion were marked by the great Hungarian fortress of Belgrade, key to a further advance into central Europe, and the island fortress of Rhodes in the Mediterranean, stronghold of the Hospitallers and key to a further naval advance westward.

Sultan Selim I (1512–1520) nearly doubled the territories of the Empire, but almost exclusively in Asia, at the expense of the Persians, and in Africa, where Egypt was annexed in 1517 and the rule of the slave-officers called Mamluks was ended. From them the

Sultan inherited the duty of protecting Mecca and Medina, the holy cities of Islam in Arabia. He also assumed the title of caliph, with the sacred insignia of office. It is doubtful whether this alone greatly enhanced his prestige, since the title had for centuries been much abused. At one moment in his reign, Selim contemplated a general massacre of all his Christian subjects. Only the refusal of the *Sheikh-ul-Islam* to grant his consent saved the Christians. This episode vividly illustrates the precariousness of Christian life under the Turks. It also demonstrates that the character of the Ottoman state was substantially altered by the acquisition of so much territory. It was now no longer necessary to appease the Christians by generous treatment, because the overwhelming majority of the population was Moslem. Moreover, most of the newly acquired Moslems were Arabs, more fanatical than the Ottoman Turks had hitherto been.

Suleiman the Magnificent (1520–1566), contemporary of the western Emperor Charles V and of Henry VIII of England, resumed the advance into Europe. Indeed, the Ottoman Empire now became deeply involved in western European affairs. It participated in the dynastic wars between the imperial house of Habsburg and the French royal house of Valois and affected the course of the Protestant Reformation in Germany by the threat of military invasion from the southeast. The newly consolidated national monarchies of the West had begun to outclass the old European enemies of the Turks, the Venetians and the Hungarians. Charles V had inherited Spain and now had to face the naval attacks of the Ottoman fleets. His younger brother, Ferdinand, as ruler of the Austrian and later the Hungarian territories, bore the brunt of the Turkish attacks on land. Cheering the Turks on were the French. Even though their king was the eldest son of the Church, their wars against the Habsburgs came first.

In 1521 Suleiman took Belgrade, and in 1522 Rhodes, thus removing the two chief obstacles to westward advance. In 1526, at Mohács in Hungary, he defeated the Christian armies, and the Turks entered Buda, the Hungarian capital on the middle Danube. In September, 1529, Suleiman besieged Vienna itself, posing a threat to Christendom greater than any since the original surge of Muslim expansion in the seventh and eighth centuries. But the Turkish lines of communication were greatly overextended; Suleiman had to abandon the siege after two weeks. Finally, in 1533, Ferdinand recognized Suleiman as overlord of Hungary. In the years that followed, Suleiman made good his claim to actual control over the south-central portion of Hungary, and added other lands north and east of the Danube. In North Africa he acquired Algeria, which remained an Ottoman vassal state in the western Mediterranean until the nineteenth century. In Asia he defeated the Persians, annexed modern Iraq, including Baghdad itself, and secured an outlet on the Persian Gulf. He even fought naval wars against the Portuguese in the Persian Gulf and the Indian Ocean.

In 1536 a formal treaty was concluded between France and the Ottoman Empire, the first of the famous "capitulations." It permitted the French to buy and sell throughout the Turkish dominions on the same basis as any Turk. They could maintain resident consuls with civil and criminal jurisdiction over Frenchmen in Turkey. In Turkish territory, Frenchmen were to enjoy complete religious liberty, and were also granted a protectorate over the Holy Places, the old aim of the Crusades. This was a great advance in prestige for the Roman Catholic Church. The Orthodox Church never accepted this settlement, and the same old dispute helped touch off the Crimean War in the nineteenth century. These "capitulations" gave the French a better position in the Ottoman Empire than that of any other European power and thus contributed to the wealth and prestige of France. They also brought the Turks into the diplomatic world of western Europe. And they are particularly interesting as parallels to the earlier Byzantine trade treaties with Venice and Genoa, who had received virtually the same privileges beginning at the end of the eleventh century. In this respect, as in so many others, the Ottoman sultans were behaving as the successors of the Byzantine emperors.

Ottoman Empire to 1683

RUSSIA

Caspian Sea

Volga R.

DAGHESTAN

GEORGIA

CIRCASSIA

P E R S I A

AZERBAIJAN

LURISTAN

SHAHRZUR

Baghdad

Euphrates R.

Don R.

KHANATE OF THE CRIMEA

Sea of Azov

CRIMEA

ARMENIA

Tigris R.

MESOPOTAMIA (IRAQ)

ARABIA

Dnieper R.

POLAND

PODOLIA

MOLDAVIA

Dniester R.

Pruth R.

TRANSYL-VANIA

Black Sea

İstanbul (Byzantium)

İznik (Nicaea)

Ankara

BITHYNIA

A N A T O L I A

Brusa

SYRIA

CYPRUS

Nile R.

Cairo

Sambor

Grosswardein

Danube R.

WALLACHIA

BULGARIA

Adrianople

GALLIPOLI PEN.

Aegean Sea

CHIOS

RHODES

EGYPT

POLAND

Tisza R.

Karlowitz

Belgrade

MACEDONIA

Athens

Monemvasia

CRETE

Buda

Pest

Mohacs

Sava R.

SERBIA

MONTE-NEGRO

BOSNIA

Lepanto

Lepanto

Butrinto

PELOPONNESUS (Morea)

Modon

THE EMPIRE

Danube R.

Vienna

HUNGARY

Agram (Zagreb)

Venice

Po R.

Ragusa

Antivari

Adriatic Sea

SICILY

Mediterranean Sea

Miles
0   100   200   300

Ottoman Empire, 1481
Territory Acquired, 1481-1520
Territory Acquired, 1520-1566
Territory Acquired, 1566-1683
States tributary to the Ottoman Empire
■ Battle sites

Ottoman Decline, 1566–1699

After Suleiman, the Ottoman system, already manifesting signs of weakness, deteriorated, despite occasional periods of Turkish success. The Ottoman capture of Cyprus in 1571 led to the formation of a western league against the Turk, headed by the pope, an enterprise as near to a crusade as the sixteenth century could produce. In 1571 the league won the great naval battle of Lepanto, off the Greek coast. It destroyed the Ottoman fleet but failed to follow up the victory, permitting the Turks to recover.

By the end of the century the sale of government offices had become a regular practice and the repeated rebellions of janissaries were jeopardizing the sultan's position. In 1606 a peace was signed that put an end to one of the perennial wars with the Habsburgs. Previously, all treaties with western states had been cast in the form of a truce granted as a divine favor from the sultan to a lesser potentate, and had been accompanied by a provision that the other party would pay tribute as part of the settlement. This time the Turks had to negotiate as equals. They gave the Habsburg emperor his proper title, and were unable to demand tribute.

Indeed, had it not been for the convulsion of the Thirty Years' War (1618–1648), which preoccupied the states of western Europe (see Chapter 5), the Ottoman Empire might have suffered even more severely in the first half of the seventeenth century than it did. As it was, internal anarchy rent the state; troops rioted and several sultans were deposed within a few years; the Persians recaptured Baghdad; and rebellion raged in the provinces. In 1622 the British ambassador wrote to his government:

The Empire has become, like an old body, crazed through many vices. All the territory of the Sultan is dispeopled for want of justice, or rather by reason of violent oppression: so much so that in his best parts of Greece and Anatolia a man may ride three, four, and sometimes six days, and not find a village to feed him and his horse. The revenue is so lessened that there is not wherewithal to pay the soldiers and maintain the court.[*]

Here we are already encountering what nineteenth-century statemen two hundred years later were still calling the "sick man of Europe."

Yet a firm sultan, Murad IV (1623–1640), temporarily restored order through the most brutal means. Despite a temporary retrogression after his death, what looked like a real revival began with the accession to power of a distinguished family of viziers, the Köprülüs. The first Köprülü ruthlessly executed 36,000 people in a five-year period (1656–1661), hanged the Greek patriarch for predicting in a private letter that Christianity would defeat Islam, rebuilt the army and navy, and suppressed revolt. Between 1661 and 1676 the second Köprülü led the Ottoman navies to a triumph in Crete, which they took from Venice. The Turks temporarily won large areas of the Ukraine from the Russians and Poles, only to lose them again in 1681. In 1683 the Turks again penetrated the heart of Europe, and for the last time Vienna was besieged, with all Europe anxiously awaiting the outcome. For the second time in two centuries, the Turkish wave was broken, and now Europe began a great counteroffensive against the Turks. Although the Köprülüs had galvanized the war like Ottoman armies into a last successful effort, they did not touch and could not touch the real evils of the Ottoman system.

The End of an Era

Now the Habsburgs drove the Turks out of Hungary, and the Venetians seized the Greek Peloponnesus. The Turks needed peace. In 1699, after an international congress at Karlovitz on the Danube, most of the gains of the European counteroffensive were recognized, including those of the Austrians, Poles, Venetians, and Russians. The Russians had appeared

[*]Quoted by E. S. Creasey, *History of the Ottoman Turks* (London, 1854), I, 392–393.

for the first time since the Tartar invasion on the shores of the Sea of Azov, which opens into the Black Sea. The extensive territorial losses suffered by the Turks, the strengthening of the Habsburgs to the east, and the appearance of Russia as an important enemy of the Turks all mark this settlement as a landmark. From now on the western European powers could stop worrying about the Ottoman menace, which had preoccupied them ever since the fourteenth century, and which had replaced the Crusades as a great cause for which Christendom could occasionally be united. From now on, the importance of Turkey is no longer its military potential, but its diplomatic position as a power in decline over whose possible disintegration and division the states of Europe might squabble and negotiate. With Karlovitz, what we call the "eastern question" may be said to have begun.

With this shift from the military offensive, which had been their only policy since their arrival in Anatolia in the thirteenth century, to a new enforced policy of defensive diplomacy, the Ottoman Turks were forced to go outside the slaves for administrators. Nobody trained in the old way had the proper equipment to act in the new. Thus it was that during the eighteenth century the Turks were forced, against their will, to rely more and more upon Christian Greeks to fill certain high offices of state. Born negotiators, with centuries of experience in commerce, and perhaps retaining the talents of their Byzantine ancestors, the Greeks now appear as the chief Ottoman diplomats. It is striking that the Turkish representative at Karlovitz should have been a Greek named Mavrocordato, from the island of Chios, who is said to have settled the disturbing question of protocol and precedence at the peace conference by inventing a round chamber with a door for each delegate, in the middle of which stood a round table. Each delegate could enter by his own door at the same moment, and sit in his own place at the round table with no question of higher and lower stations. This was a typically Greek idea, which no Turk could have had, and it signalized the opening of a new era.

Reading Suggestions on Europe at the Close of the Middle Ages

(Asterisk indicates paperbound edition.)

The West:
General Accounts

W. K. Ferguson, *Europe in Transition, 1300–1520* (Houghton, Mifflin, 1962). A comprehensive and up-to-date survey.

E. P. Cheyney, *The Dawn of a New Era, 1250–1453* (*Torch) and M. Gilmore, *The World of Humanism, 1453–1517* (*Torch). Good introductory accounts, with very full bibliographies; these books are in the important series, "Rise of Modern Europe," edited by W. L. Langer.

National Monarchies

E. Perroy, *The Hundreds Years' War* (*Capricorn). The standard treatment of the subject and the best introductory volume to French history in the fourteenth and fifteenth centuries.

A. R. Myers, *England in the Late Middle Ages, 1307–1536* (*Penguin). Brief survey.

C. W. S. Williams, *Henry VII* (Barker, 1937). A solid study of the first Tudor monarch.

S. B. Chrimes, *English Constitutional History,* 2nd ed. (Oxford Univ. Press, 1953). Reliable short guide to the subject.

J. H. Mariéjol, *The Spain of Ferdinand and Isabella,* B. Keen, ed. (Rutgers Univ. Press, 1961). Celebrated study by a late-nineteenth-century French scholar, translated and edited to bring it abreast of contemporary scholarship.

R. B. Merriman, *The Rise of the Spanish Empire in the Old World and the New,* Vol. II (Macmillan, 1918). Long the standard treatment of the reign of Ferdinand and Isabella in English.

Germany and Italy

G. Barraclough, *The Origins of Modern Germany* (*Capricorn). The best general treatment of late medieval Germany in English.

J. C. L. de Sismondi, *A History of the Italian Republics* (*Anchor). Famous account, from the early Middle Ages to the Renaissance, written in the early nineteenth century.

J. A. Symonds, *The Age of the Despots* (*Capricorn). First volume of an extended study of Renaissance Italy, first written almost a century ago.

J. Burckhardt, *The Civilization of the Renaissance in Italy,* 2 vols. (*Torch). Most celebrated study by a nineteenth-century scholar and a wellspring of interpretation; its contention that the modern state originated in Renaissance Italy is not any longer generally accepted.

H. Baron, *The Crisis of the Early Italian Renaissance,* revised ed. (*Princeton Univ. Press). A monograph fully abreast of recent scholarship, which affords many insights into Italian politics.

F. Schēvill, *Medieval and Renaissance Florence,* 2 vols. (*Torch) and *The Medici* (*Torch). Clear and useful detailed studies, first written a generation ago.

C. M. Ady, *Lorenzo de' Medici and Renaissance Italy* (*Collier). A brief, popular account.

D. L. Jensen, ed., *Machiavelli—Cynic, Patriot, or Political Scientist?* (*Heath). Helpful introduction to conflicting interpretations.

Economic
and
Social History

The Cambridge Economic History of Europe, Vol. II: *Trade and Industry in the Middle Ages* (Cambridge Univ. Press, 1954). An advanced scholarly study and a mine of information.

F. C. Lane, *Venetian Ships and Shipping of the Renaissance* (John Hopkins Univ. Press, 1934). An unusually interesting monograph.

A. W. O. von Martin, *Sociology of the Renaissance* (*Torch). Instructive study of Italian society in the 1300's and 1400's.

R. de Roover, *Rise and Decline of the Medici Bank, 1397–1494* (*Norton); R. Ehrenberg, *Capital and Finance in the Age of the Renaissance: A Study of the Fuggers and their Connections* (Harcourt, 1928). Two valuable accounts of high finance.

Russia
and the
Byzantine Heritage

G. Ostrogorsky, *History of the Byzantine State,* trans. J. Hussey (Rutgers Univ. Press, 1957). A brilliant historical synthesis.

J. Hussey, *The Byzantine World* (Hutchinson's University Library, 1957). Useful short sketch.

V. O. Kluchevsky, *A History of Russia,* 5 vols. (Dent, 1911–1931). The greatest single work on Russian history, its usefulness impaired by an uneven translation.

M. Florinsky, *Russia: A History and an Interpretation*, Vol. I (Macmillan, 1953). Solid and accurate textbook.

G. Vernadsky, *Kievan Russia*, and *The Mongols and Russia* (Yale Univ. Press, 1948, 1953). These two volumes in the "Yale History of Russia" are authoritative and complete.

Islam
and the
Ottoman Turks

H. A. R. Gibb, *Mohammedanism* (*Oxford). Scholarly introduction to Islam by a renowned authority.

C. Brockelmann, *History of the Islamic Peoples* (*Capricorn). Encyclopedic survey.

E. S. Creasy, *History of the Ottoman Turks,* 2 vols. (1854–1856, frequently reprinted). Despite its age, a good general account; based on a ten-volume German study.

H. A. R. Gibb and Harold Bowen, *Islamic Society and the West*, Vol. I, Parts 1 and 2 (Oxford Univ. Press, 1950, 1956). A detailed scholarly survey of Ottoman institutions.

H. A. Gibbons, *The Foundation of the Ottoman Empire* (Century, 1916). An older work whose conclusions are again finding favor.

P. Wittek, *The Rise of the Ottoman Empire* (The Royal Asiatic Society, 1938). A suggestive essay on the elements that helped to advance the Ottoman state.

Dorothy M. Vaughan, *Europe and the Turk: A Pattern of Alliances, 1350–1700* (Liverpool Univ. Press, 1954). Role of the Ottoman Empire in European diplomacy.

Sources

The History of Comines, T. Danett, trans. (D. Nutt, 1897). The famous account by Louis XI's contemporary.

Machiavelli, *The Prince and the Discourses*, Max Lerner, ed. (*Modern Library).

G. T. Matthews, ed., *News and Rumor in Renaissance Europe* (*Capricorn). Reports to the Fuggers by their agents.

Kritovulos, *History of Mehmed the Conqueror,* C. T. Riggs, trans. (Princeton Univ. Press, 1954). A Greek life of Mohammed the Conqueror.

The Life and Letters of Ogier Ghiselin de Busbecq, C. T. Forster and F. H. Blackburne Daniell, eds., 2 vols. (C. K. Paul, 1881). Perceptive and amusing reports of a Habsburg ambassador to Suleiman the Magnificent.

The Correspondence between Prince A. M. Kurbsky and Tsar Ivan IV of Russia, 1564–1579, ed. and trans. J. L. I. Fennell (Cambridge Univ. Press, 1955). A fundamental source for the political theories of the Tsar and his noble opponents.

Fiction

W. Scott, *Quentin Durward* (*Signet). Celebrated romantic novel set in the France of Louis XI.

V. Hugo, *The Hunchback of Notre Dame* (*Signet). Even more celebrated romantic novel, set in the Paris of Louis XI.

C. Reade, *The Cloister and the Hearth* (*Washington Square). Famous nineteenth-century novel set in late fifteenth-century Europe, based on scholarly research.

N. Balchin, *The Borgia Testament* (Houghton, Mifflin, 1949). A fictional autobiography as Cesare might have written it, by an accomplished writer of adventure tales.

3

The Renaissance

I Introduction

The Renaissance was one of the great periods of cultural and intellectual achievement in the West, a literary, artistic, and philosophical flowering that filled the centuries of transition from the medieval to the modern world. The Renaissance began in the 1300's and came to an end during the 1500's and early 1600's, as Europe passed into the ages of the Reformation and of dynastic and religious wars. The first writer to show some of the marks of the Renaissance "style," though he belonged primarily to the Middle Ages, was the Italian poet, Dante, who lived at the turn of the thirteenth century to the fourteenth. The last major figures of the Renaissance were Shakespeare, who lived three centuries after Dante, and John Milton, who lived still later, in the mid-seventeenth century

England of revolution and civil war. The homeland of the Renaissance was Italy, the Italy of aggressive and cultivated businessmen and politicians. As time went on, the movement reached France, Germany, and the Low Countries as well as England, but it did not flourish everywhere in the West. It scarcely touched the Scandinavian states, and it affected Portugal and Spain only mildly.

These chronological and geographical definitions, however, do not hint at the basic historical problem posed by the Renaissance. Like many simple labels attached to broad historical movements, as, for instance, the "Fall of Rome" or the "Dark Ages," the term Renaissance has aroused lively controversy among scholars, calling forth a bewildering variety of interpretations and reinterpretations. The word itself means "rebirth," the rebirth of the classical culture of ancient Greece and Rome. But what in actual fact was the Renaissance? Was Greco-Roman culture truly reborn? What accounted for the remarkable productivity of the writers, the sculptors, the painters, and all the other artists of the Renaissance?

Until the middle of the nineteenth century, most educated men would have offered simple answers to these questions. The chief reason for the classical revival appeared to be the capture of Constantinople by the Turks in 1453 and the subsequent flight of Greek scholars to Italy and other countries of western Europe, bringing the thousand years of medieval gloom to an end at long last. The eighteenth-century historian, Gibbon, saluted the event in his characteristically majestic prose:

Before the revival of classical literature, the barbarians in Europe were immersed in ignorance; and their vulgar tongues were marked with the rudeness and poverty of their manners. The students of the more perfect idioms of Rome and Greece were introduced to a new world of light and science; to the society of the free and polished nations of antiquity; and to a familiar converse with those immortal men who spoke the sublime language of eloquence and reason. Such an intercourse must tend to refine the taste, and to elevate the genius, of the moderns. . . .*

Today, however, these simple answers no longer suffice. We cannot attribute such exaggerated importance to the fall of Byzantium. Well before 1453, knowledge of Greek writings was filtering into the West from Moslem Spain, from Sicily, and from Byzantium itself. Moreover, Greek influence was by no means the only decisive factor in promoting the Renaissance. In an influential study, first published in 1860, Professor Jacob Burckhardt of the University of Basel in Switzerland insisted that much of the credit for Renaissance productivity must go also to the genius and individualism of Italians, from despots and *condottieri* to artists and writers. Burckhardt, however, accepted the traditional contrast between medieval darkness and Renaissance light that had first been drawn by the men of the Renaissance themselves. Today, of course, it is almost universally agreed that a great Christian civilization had in fact come to maturity during the Middle Ages, and that culture, even in the narrow sense of the heritage from classical antiquity, had never actually disappeared from the medieval West. It is both inaccurate and presumptuous to speak of a literal "rebirth" of culture at the close of the Middle Ages. Some historians have contended that the cultural rebirth occurred much earlier than the fourteenth century, perhaps as far back as the so-called "Carolingian Renaissance," which centered at the court of Charlemagne in Aachen about the beginning of the early ninth century.

But to find that the germ of the foundation of everything characteristic of the Renaissance had already existed long before 1300—to deny any originality to the Renaissance, as a few historians do—is to push the pendulum of reinterpretation too far. Unquestionably, the men of the Renaissance owed a large debt to the scholarship and art of their medieval predecessors, as we shall see. Unquestionably, the men of the Renaissance were often as re-

*Edward Gibbon, *The Decline and Fall of the Roman Empire,* Ch. LXVI.

ligious, as credulous, as caste-conscious, and as "feudal" as their forbears. But they were also materialistic, skeptical, and individualistic to a degree unknown in the Middle Ages. The Renaissance most decidedly had a "style" of its own, neither fully medieval nor fully modern but a transition between the two.

The examination of this transition will not be easy, since we are confronting an era swept by contradictory currents and cross-currents. In politics, the fifteenth century was torn between particularism or revived feudalism on the one hand and emerging national monarchies on the other. One scholar has suggested a comparable division in culture and thought, between "Renaissance" elements that incorporated the Christian values of the Middle Ages and "Counter-Renaissance" elements that denied or subverted those values. Although the two labels may seem somewhat illogical, the division they make is a useful one. The Italian historian, Professor Federico Chabod, has observed that the new secular elements may be summarized as follows: "art for art's sake, politics for politics' sake, science for science's sake."* That is, men were attempting to do things and study things as ends in themselves rather than as the means to the glorification of God and the salvation of humanity, much as Machiavelli divorced political thought from theology or as Machiavellian rulers cultivated power politics.

We shall now survey these attempts, first in literature and thought, then in art and science. The new secular elements will be found intermingling with the old, not neatly isolated or compartmentalized. The thinkers and the artists of the Renaissance expressed the nationalism and the materialism of the period; at the same time, they also continued the age-old examination into the mysteries of nature and the personality of man. Moreover, the world of culture, though never wholly separate from the workaday world of business and politics, is never wholly the same as that world. Parallels between the two exist, but they must not be pushed too far.

*F. Chabod, *Machiavelli and the Renaissance* (London, 1958), 184.

II   Literature and Thought

The Rise of the Vernaculars

Many writers in the Renaissance centuries employed the vernacular, a term meaning native or local and applying particularly to the languages of the western European countries. Everywhere the vernaculars developed slowly, arising deep in the Middle Ages as the spoken language of the people, then extending gradually to popular writing and later to formal and official works. Many of the vernaculars—Spanish, Portuguese, Italian, and French—developed from Latin; these were the Romance (Roman) languages. Castilian, the core of modern literary Spanish, attained official status early; the King of Castile ordered that it be used for government records in the thirteenth century. Italian, on the other hand, scarcely existed as a literary language until the very eve of the Renaissance, when Dante composed the *Divine Comedy*.

In medieval France, two families of vernaculars appeared. Southern Frenchmen spoke the *langue d'oc,* so called from their use of *oc* (the Latin *hoc*) for "yes"; their northern cousins spoke the *langue d'oïl,* in which "yes" was *oïl,* the ancestor of the modern *oui.* By 1400, the *langue d'oïl* of the Paris region was well on its way to replacing Latin as the official language of the whole kingdom.

Though Provençal eventually died out, another offshoot of the *langue d'oc* survives in Catalan, used on both the French and Spanish sides of the Pyrenees, and the name Languedoc is still applied to southern France west of the Rhône.

In Germany, by the thirteenth century, poetry was being written in Middle High German, the immediate ancestor of modern literary German. The minnesingers of thirteenth-century Germany also composed their poetry in Middle High German. The Anglo-Saxons of England had spoken a dialect of Low German which incorporated some words of Scandinavian or Celtic origin and later added many borrowings from Norman French and Latin to form the English vernacular. English achieved official recognition in the fourteenth century; meantime, it was also coming into its own as a literary language with such popular works as Chaucer's *Canterbury Tales.* Today the English of 1400 seems stranger and more difficult than the Shakespearean English of 1600, but it is still recognizable as English. Glance again at part of the passage quoted in Chapter 2 from the *Libel of English Policy,* which was almost contemporary with Chaucer; "Bene fyques, raysns, wyne bastarde, and dates; And lycorys, Syvyle ole [Seville oil], and grayne . . . ."

The rise of vernaculars often paralleled and assisted the growth of nationalism. Use of a common language undoubtedly heightened among Englishmen a common sense of national purpose and a common mistrust of foreigners who did not speak the King's English. The vernaculars quickened the emergence of distinctive national "styles" in England, in France, and in Spain. Yet the triumph of particularism in fifteenth-century Germany and Italy demonstrated that the vernaculars could not by themselves create national political units. Nor did the vernaculars divide western culture into water-tight national compartments. Translations kept ideas flowing across national frontiers, and some of the vernaculars themselves became international languages. In the Near East, for instance, the Italian that had been introduced by the Crusaders was the *lingua franca,* the western tongue most widely understood.

Humanism

In spite of the rise of the vernaculars, Latin remained the international language of the Church and the academic world. Scholars worked diligently to perfect their Latin and, in the later Renaissance, to learn at least the rudiments of Greek. They called themselves humanists — that is, followers of what Cicero had called *studia humanitatis,* or humane studies. These were rather more restricted than what the "humanities" or "liberal arts" connote today. They included rhetoric, grammar, history, poetry, and ethics, but they excluded logic and other philosophical disciplines and mathematics and the sciences. It may seem surprising that many avowed humanists both revered the classics and employed one of the vernaculars with great skill. This is an example of the Renaissance transition, the old and the new side by side. Indeed, generations of vernacular writers since the Renaissance have studied Cicero and other classical masters to improve their own style.

Humanism, however, was far more than a linguistic term. The humanist was more than a philologist, for he also studied the great men, the great ideas, and the great art of classical antiquity. He came to cherish the values of antiquity, pagan though they were, almost as much as the traditional Christian values; indeed, he sometimes cherished them even more. To cite an extreme example, Machiavelli found more virtues in pre-Christian Greece and Rome than he did in the Christian society of his own day. Other humanists, we shall find, sought a kind of common denominator in the best ancient moral teaching and in the highest Christian aspiration.

Altogether, humanism revolutionized men's attitudes toward the classical heritage. The medieval schoolmen had not disdained this heritage; they admired and copied its forms but transformed or adapted its ideas to fortify their own Christian views. They found in Vergil's *Aeneid,* for instance, not only the splendor of epic poetry but also an allegory of man's sojourn on earth. The humanists of the Renaissance, in turn, transformed their medieval heritage in the more secular spirit of their own age and in the light of their own more extensive knowledge of the classics. They revered both the style and the content of the classics and began to study them for their own sake, not to strengthen or enrich their faith. The two literary trends we have been sketching, the rise of the vernaculars and the evolution of humanism, may now be traced in more detail through the great writers of the later Middle Ages and early Renaissance, beginning with Dante Alighieri (1265–1321).

Dante

Much of Dante's writing, above all the *Divine Comedy*, was rooted in the Middle Ages. The chivalric concept of disembodied love inspired his poems to Beatrice, who was married to another and whom he seldom saw. No Ghibelline was more romantic, less realistic, about the unpromising Holy Roman emperors of the time. Though hostile to the political ambitions of the papacy—rather than of Pope Boniface VIII—Dante was no Machiavellian anticlerical but a good Christian who simply wanted the Pope to keep out of politics.

Dante also foreshadowed developments that were to characterize the Renaissance. He championed the vernacular, writing in Latin a plea for its toleration by pedants who refused to read Italian. For the *Divine Comedy* he deliberately chose the vernacular of his native Tuscany over the more respectable Latin, and he modeled his style on the popular poetry of the Provençal troubadours rather than on the loftier epic verse of the classics. In other respects, he gave the classics their full due. Among the characters of the *Comedy*, as Dante called it, are a host of classical figures, both real and mythological. Homer, Vergil's Aeneas, Vergil himself, Euclid, Plato, Socrates, Caesar, and other virtuous pagans dwell forever in Limbo on the edge of Hell, suffering only the hopelessness of the unbaptized who can never reach God's presence. Dante took from ancient mythology the tormentors of the

damned—the Minotaur, the Furies, and Cerberus, the three-headed hound of Hell and the symbol of gluttony.

Moreover, the concerns of this world are constantly with Dante in the other world. Thus, when he and Vergil board a boat to cross an infernal marsh, he observes that Vergil, being a shade, has no weight:

> So then my guide embarked, and at his call
> I followed him; and not till I was in
> Did the Boat seem to bear a load at all*

The lost souls are real people, from Judas through corrupt medieval clerics down to Dante's own fellow Florentines. Finally, Dante was not one of the medieval intellectuals who withdrew from society to the sanc-

The Divine Comedy: Hell, Canto, VIII, lines 25–27, D. L. Sayers, trans. (Penguin Classics, 1949).

Portrait of Dante attributed to the school of Giotto.

tuary of holy orders. Deeply involved in practical politics, he became a refugee from Florentine factionalism, and adopted the Renaissance expedient of obtaining the patronage of a minor despot, the ruler of Verona. As a man of letters, he achieved a remarkable popular success during his own lifetime. Half a century after his death, a group of Florentine citizens honored the memory of their exiled compatriot by founding a public lectureship for a person "well trained in the book of Dante."

Petrarch

Popular fame and classical enthusiasm positively obsessed the next important Italian literary figure, Francesco Petrarca (1304–1374), better known as Petrarch. His father, like Dante, was a political exile from Florence, and Petrarch himself spent much of his youth at the worldly court of the popes in Avignon. First and last a professional man of letters, Petrarch exhibited a remarkable zeal for collecting and copying the manuscripts of ancient authors. He assembled a splendid private library and found in an Italian cathedral some dusty and forgotten letters by Cicero which threw new light on that Roman's political career. Petrarch so admired the past that he addressed a series of affectionate letters to Cicero and other old masters. Although he never quite learned to read Greek, he could at least gaze reverently at his manuscripts of Homer and Plato. Aristotle, on the other hand, he disliked intensely because of his popularity with the medieval scholastic thinkers, whom Petrach believed hostile to the values of humanism.

Petrarch's attainments, even as young man, led the Senate of Rome (then a kind of municipal council) to revive the Greco-Roman custom of extending official recognition to excellence and crown him with a wreath of laurel in an elaborate ceremony. The new laureate reveled in the honor, for he wanted desperately to be ranked with the ancient Romans to whom he addressed his letters. Ironically, the writings of Petrarch most admired in

modern times are not those in his cherished Latin but those he esteemed the least, the vernacular love poems he addressed to his adored Laura, whom he courted in vain until she died during the Black Death. In these lyrics, Petrarch perfected the verse form known as the Italian sonnet, fourteen lines long, divided into one set of eight lines and another of six, each with its own rhyme scheme. The word "sonnet" literally means a little song, and Petrarch developed his from vernacular folk-songs. Almost despite himself, therefore, he proved to be one of the founders of modern vernacular literature.

Petrarch exemplified the emerging humanism of the Renaissance not only in his reverence for the classics but also in his deep feeling for the beauties of this world. He regarded Laura as a real woman, not a disembodied chivalric heroine, and he looked at nature with a fresh eye. Here is his account of reaching the summit of Mont Ventoux near Avignon:

At first I stood there almost benumbed, overwhelmed by a gale such as I had never felt before and by the unusually open and wide view. I looked around me: clouds were gathering below my feet, and Athos and Olympus grew less incredible, since I saw on a mountain of lesser fame what I had heard and read about them. From there I turned my eyes in the direction of Italy, for which my mind is so fervently yearning. The Alps were frozen stiff and covered with snow—those mountains through which that ferocious enemy of the Roman name once passed blasting his way through the rocks with vinegar if we may believe tradition.*

Then Petrarch's report takes a medieval turn:

I admired every detail, now relishing earthly enjoyment, now lifting up my mind to higher spheres after the example of my body, and I thought it fit to look into the volume of Augustine's *Confessions*. . . . I happened to hit upon the tenth book of the work. My brother stood beside me, intently expecting to hear something from Augustine on my mouth. I ask God to be my witness and my brother who was with me: Where I fixed my eyes first it was written: 'And men go to admire the high mountains, the vast floods of the sea, the huge

*Quoted in E. Cassirer, P. O. Kristeller, J. H. Randall, Jr., *The Renaissance Philosophy of Man* (Chicago, 1948), 41.

streams of the rivers, the circumference of the ocean, and the revolutions of the stars—and desert themselves.' I was stunned, I confess. I bade my brother, who wanted to hear more, not to molest me, and closed the book, angry with myself that I still admired earthly things.*

While the story may sound too pat, it is known that Petrarch owned a small manuscript of Augustine which could have fitted handily into a climber's kit.

In fact, Petrarch admired Augustine as much as he admired Cicero. From the religious teachings of the one and the Stoic philosophy of the other he hoped to make himself a better Christian. Petrarch found no conflict between his classical learning and Christian doctrine; both should make their contribution to enrich the human spirit. This was an attitude taken by many humanists, an excellent instance of the fusion of new and old in the Renaissance. Furthermore, Petrarch disliked the scholastic philosophers of the Middle Ages for their rationalism, their dependence on Aristotle, and their preoccupation with detail. In their concern with the letter of Christianity, he felt that they missed its spirit—they "desert themselves," as he read in Augustine on Mont Ventoux. This hostility to scholasticism and Aristotelianism was also an attitude characteristic of the humanists.

Boccaccio

Another humanist attitude, though one less frequently held, was taken by another famous Florentine, Petrarch's friend and pupil, Giovanni Boccaccio (1313–1375). This was the light-hearted and matter-of-fact view of human frailty which permeates the *Decameron,* the first major prose work in the Italian vernacular. The *Decameron* recounts the stories told by a company of gay young people to enliven their exile from Florence in a country villa where they have fled to escape the Black Death. Here is the gist of one of the stories:

You must know, then, that there was once in our city a very rich merchant called Arriguccio Ber-

Ibid., 44.

linghieri, who . . . took to wife a young gentlewoman ill sorting with himself, by name Madam Sismonda, who, for that he, merchant-like, was much abroad and sojourned little with her, fell in love with a young man called Ruberto.*

Arriguccio discovers his wife's infidelity and gives her the beating of her life—or so he thinks. The beating occurs in a darkened room, Sismonda has directed her maid to take her place, and it is actually the maid whom Arriguccio had thrashed. He, ignorant of the deception, plays the wronged husband to the hilt and summons Sismonda's brothers to witness her disgrace. "The brothers,—seeing her seated sewing with no sign of beating on her face, whereas Arriguccio avouched that he had beaten her to a mummy,—began to marvel." Sismonda immediately accuses her hapless husband of "fuddling himself about the taverns, foregathering now with this lewd woman and now with that and keeping me waiting for him . . . half the night." The result: the brothers give Arriguccio a thorough beating. And Boccaccio's moral:

Thus the lady, by her ready wit, not only escaped the imminent peril but opened herself a way to do her every pleasure in time to come, without evermore having any fear of her husband.

Boccaccio did not invent all the stories of the *Decameron;* he reworked some of the bawdy *fabliaux* of medieval France, particularly those exposing the sins of the clergy. But what he did do for the first time was to give these earthy tales a kind of literary respectability. He was reflecting the worldly, rather frivolous outlook of the court of the Angevin monarchs at Naples, where he spent part of his youth, and from then on this type of gay un-Christian story was to hold a small but acknowledged place in European literature.

Boccaccio himself, however, was no dilettante. He was a serious humanist, who aided Petrarch in tracking down ancient manuscripts and found a copy of Tacitus; he was more successful than his master in learning Greek;

*This and the following quotations are from the eighth story of the seventh day, as translated in the Modern Library edition of the *Decameron* (New York, n.d.).

he taught at the University in Florence, holding the Dante memorial lectureship. While anticlerical in the sense that he criticized the corruption of the clergy, he was not anti-Christian. The son of a Florentine banker, he turned to letters after an apprenticeship in banking left him disillusioned by the gap between the sharp business practices of wealthy Florentines and their professed Christian ideals. Note that the cuckolded husband in the tale above is a rich merchant.

Preservation of the Classics

The men of letters who followed Petrarch and Boccaccio may be divided into three groups. First, there were the conservers of classical culture, the bookworms, scholars, cultivated despots and businessmen, all the heirs of Petrarch's great humanistic enthusiasm for classical antiquity. Second were the vernacular writers who took the path marked out by the *Decameron,* from Chaucer at the close of the fourteenth century down to Rabelais and to Cervantes in the sixteenth. And third there were the synthesizers, headed by Pico della Mirandola and Erasmus, who endeavored to fuse Christianity, classicism, and other elements into a universal philosophy of man.

The devoted antiquarians of the fifteenth century uncovered a really remarkable number of ancient manuscripts. They ransacked monasteries and other likely places, in Italy and Germany, in France and Spain. They pieced together the works of Cicero, Tacitus, Lucretius, and other Latin authors. Collecting Greek manuscripts became a regular business, transacted for Italian scholars and patrons by agents who were active in Constantinople both before and after the city's fall in 1453. They did their work so thoroughly that almost all the Greek classics we now possess reached the West before 1500.

To preserve, catalogue, and study these literary treasures, the first modern libraries were created. Cosimo de' Medici supported three separate libraries in and near Florence and employed forty-five copyists. The humanist popes founded the library of the Vatican, to-

day one of the most important collections in the world. Even a minor state, like the Duchy of Urbino in northern Italy, had a major library, assembled by its cultivated duke.

Greek scholars as well as Greek manuscripts made the journey from Byzantium to Italy. One of the earliest of them, Manuel Chrysoloras, came to Italy in the closing years of the fourteenth century seeking help against the Ottomans, then turned from diplomacy to teach at Florence and Milan. The revival of Greek reached maturity in the 1460's with the emergence of the informal circle of Florentine humanists known as the Platonic Academy. Nevertheless, Greek did not attain the popularity of Latin. Many humanists found it easier to study Plato in a Latin translation than in the difficult original, and most of them neglected the Greek drama because they found the plays so hard to translate.

The classicists of the fifteenth century made a fetish of pure and polished Latin. The learned composed elaborate letters designed less for private reading than for the instruction of their colleagues. Papal secretaries began to make ecclesiastical correspondence conform to what we should call a manual of correct style. At their worst, these men were pedants, exalting manner over matter, draining vitality from the Latin language. At their best, they were keen and erudite scholars who sifted out the inaccuracies and forgeries in defective manuscripts to establish definitive texts of ancient writings.

Lorenzo Valla (c. 1405–1457) represented classical scholarship at its best. One of the few important figures of the Italian Renaissance not identified with Florence, Valla was reared in Rome and passed much of his adult life there and at Naples. Petty and quarrelsome, fond of exchanging insults with rival humanists, he also commanded both immense learning and the courage to use it against the most sacred targets. He translated into Latin the Greek historians Herodotus and Thucydides. He wrote a most popular study, *The Elegances of the Latin Language,* which went through sixty printings within a century and criticized the supposedly flawless prose of Cicero. He laid the foundation for humanist Biblical scholarship by a careful philological critique of the New Testament.

Valla's fame rests above all on his demonstration that the *Donation of Constantine*, long a basis for sweeping papal claims to temporal dominion, was actually a forgery. He proved his case by showing that both the Latin in which the *Donation of Constantine* was written and the events to which it referred dated from an era several centuries after Constantine, who had reigned in the early fourth century. For example, the *Donation* (here called the "privilege") mentioned Constantinople as the seat of a patriarch:

How in the world . . . could one speak of Constantinople as one of the patriarchal sees, when it was not yet a patriarchate, nor a see, nor a Christian city, nor named Constantinople, nor founded, nor planned! For the 'privilege' was granted, so it says, the third year after Constantine became a Christian; when as yet Byzantium, not Constantinople, occupied that site.*

When Valla published this exposure in 1440, he was secretary to Alfonso the Magnanimous (see p. 38), whose claim to Naples was being challenged by the papacy on the basis of the *Donation* itself. The Pope might well have been expected to condemn Valla as a heretic. Nothing of the kind occurred, and Valla soon accepted a commission to translate Thucydides under papal auspices, with no strings attached. The climate of opinion had indeed changed since the high Middle Ages.

Chaucer and Rabelais

The second group of literary men, the vernacular writers, illustrate once again the broad range of the Renaissance. The Englishman, Geoffrey Chaucer (c. 1340–1400), like Dante, belongs both to the Middle Ages and to the Renaissance. Chaucer's *Canterbury Tales* have a setting that is medieval; they are told by pilgrims on their way to the shrine of the martyred Becket, not by the gay young people of

*The Treatise of Lorenzo Valla on the Donation of Constantine, C. B. Coleman, ed. (New Haven, 1922), 95.

the *Decameron*. Yet Chaucer's tales are really not unlike Boccaccio's. He, too, uses the vernacular; he, too, borrows stories from the *fabliaux*. Although Chaucer apparently had not actually read the *Decameron*, he was familiar enough with other writings of Boccaccio to use the plot of one for his Knight's Tale and of another for *Troilus and Criseyde*, the long narrative poem about two lovers in the Trojan War. The Clerk's Tale, he reveals, "I Lerned at Padowe of a worthy clerk . . . , Fraunceys Petrark, the laureat poete," and the Wife of Bath mentions "the wyse poete of Florence That Highte Dant."

Chaucer came to know Italian literature in the course of several trips to Italy on official business for the English king. He led a busy and prosperous life in the thick of politics, domestic and international. Coming from a family of well-to-do London merchants, he was a justice of the peace in Kent, represented the county in the House of Commons, and filled the important posts of Controller of Customs and Clerk of the King's Works. The writings of Chaucer showed that the English vernacular was coming of age and that in England, as in Italy, the profession of letters was no longer a clerical monopoly.

The medieval values still evident in the writings of Chaucer had largely vanished a century and a half later in the works of the Frenchman, François Rabelais (c. 1494–1553). Rabelais contributed far more to literature than the salacious wit for which he is famous. He studied the classics, particularly Plato and the ancient physicians; practiced and taught medicine; and created two of the great comic figures of letters, Gargantua and his son Pantagruel. The two are giants, and everything they do is on the heroic scale. The abbey of Theleme, which Gargantua helps to found permits its residents a wildly unmonastic existence:

All their life was spent not in lawes, statutes or rules, but according to their own free will and pleasure. They rose out of their beds, when they thought good: they did eat, drink, labour, sleep, when they had a minde to it and were disposed for it. . . . In all their rule, and strictest tie of their order, there was but this one clause to be observed,

DO WHAT THOU WILT.*

But Rabelais recommends more than self-indulgence and Gargantua exhorts Pantagruel to learn everything. He is to master Arabic in addition to Latin, read the New Testament in Greek and the Old in Hebrew, and study history, geometry, architecture, music, and civil law. He must also know "the fishes, all the fowles of the aire, all the several kinds of shrubs and trees," "all the sorts of herbs and flowers that grow upon the ground: all the various metals that are hid within the bowels of the earth." "In brief," Gargantua concludes, "let me see thee an Abysse, and bottomless pit of knowledge."† Both his insatiable appetite for knowledge and the exuberant and ultimately exhausting way in which Rabelais wrote about it represent an important aspect of the Renaissance "style."

The Platonic Revival

Another facet of the Renaissance style was highlighted by the third group of writers, the philosophical humanists, who aspired not only to universal knowledge but also to a universal truth and faith. They were centered first at Florence, attracted by the Platonic Academy founded in 1462 when Cosimo de' Medici, who had become, in his later years, enthusiastic about Plato, decided to underwrite the translation of the master's works into Latin. He entrusted the commission to Marsilio Ficino (1433–1499), a medical student turned classicist, who translated not only the whole body of Plato's writings but some of the Neo-Platonists as well. These followers of Plato, who had lived several centuries after the master and emphasized the possibility of perceiving the divine through mystical experiences, exerted a powerful attraction on Ficino and his circle.

Platonism and Neoplatonism convinced Ficino that man achieved his highest potentiality by rising above the merely physical to awareness of the eternal. Man, Ficino wrote,

*Rabelais, *Gargantua and Pantagruel,* Urquhart trans. (New York, 1883), Bk. I, Ch. 57.
†*Ibid.,* Bk. I, Ch. 8.

has the unique faculty called intellect which he described as an "eye turned toward the intelligible light" or God. He coined the term "Platonic love" to describe the love that transcends the senses and may also lead man to mystical communion with God. He supported his arguments with appeals to a wide range of authorities—the wise men of the ancient Near East, the prophets of the Old Testament, the apostles of the New, and the Greek philosophers, including Pythagoras and Aristotle in addition to Plato. Ficino seemed to be attempting a mystic synthesis of all philosophy and religion.

The attempt was pressed further by Ficino's pupil, Pico della Mirandola (1463–1494), who died when he was thirty-one. Pico crowded much into his brief life and would have delighted Rabelais' Gargantua, for he knew Arabic and Hebrew in addition to Greek and Latin and studied Jewish allegory, Arab philosophy, and medieval scholasticism, which, almost alone among humanists, he respected. Pico's tolerance was as broad as his learning. In his short *Oration on the Dignity of Man,* he cited approvingly Chaldean and Persian theologians, the priests of Apollo, Socrates, Pythagoras, Cicero, Moses, St. Paul, St. Augustine, Mohammed, St. Francis, St. Thomas Aquinas, and many others.

In all the varied beliefs of this galaxy, Pico hoped to find the common denominator of a universal faith. This process of syncretism, of borrowing and assimilating from many sources, he was unable to complete, but he, together with Ficino, did help to found the great humane studies of comparative religion and comparative philosophy. And he reaffirmed and strengthened Ficino's idea that man was unique, the link between the mortal physical world and the immortal spiritual one, the hinge of the universe, so to speak. This concept of the uniqueness and centrality of man lay at the heart of the Renaissance style.

Erasmus

The man who gave the most mature expression of the humanist impulse to draw on all wisdom was not Italian but Dutch. Erasmus (1466–1536), the "Prince of Humanists," dominated the intellectual life of Europe as few other men have done. He was in fact a cosmopolitan, the foremost citizen of the Republic of Letters. He studied, taught, and lived at Oxford, Cambridge, and Paris, and in Italy, Switzerland, and Germany. Building on Valla's scholarship, he published a scholarly edition of the Greek New Testament. He carried on a prodigious correspondence in Latin and compiled a series of *Adages* and *Colloquies* to give students examples of good Latin composition. Because Erasmus never regarded elegance of style as an end in itself, he assailed the "knowledge-factories" of the grammarians in the satirical *Praise of Folly*:

As for those stilted, insipid verses they display on all occasions (and there are those to admire them), obviously the writer believes that the soul of Virgil has transmigrated into his own breast. But the funniest sight of all is to see them admiring and praising each other, trading compliment for compliment, thus mutually scratching each other's itch.*

*Erasmus, *Praise of Folly*. H. H. Hudson, trans. (Princeton, 1941), 71–72.

Erasmus, by Dürer.

In exposing human weaknesses, Erasmus played no favorites; he mocked any group or class inflated by a sense of its own importance—merchants, churchmen, scientists, philosophers, courtiers, and kings. He was one of the very first to detect the pretensions and hypocrisies of nationalism:

And now I see that it is not only in individual men that nature has implanted self-love. She implants a kind of it as a common possession in the various races, and even cities. By this token the English claim . . . good looks, music, and the best eating as their special properties. The Scots flatter themselves on the score of high birth and royal blood, not to mention their dialectical skill. Frenchmen have taken all politeness for their province. . . . The Italians usurp *belles lettres* and eloquence; and they all flatter themselves upon the fact that they alone, of all mortal men, are not barbarians. . . . The Greeks, as well as being the founders of the learned disciplines, vaunt themselves upon their titles to the famous heroes of old.*

In appraising human nature, however, Erasmus tempered criticism with geniality. In what proportions, asks an ironic passage in *Praise of Folly*, did Jupiter supply men with emotion and reason?

Well, the proportions run about one pound to half an ounce. Besides, he imprisoned reason in a cramped corner of the head, and turned over all the rest of the body to the emotions. After that he instated two most violent tyrants, as it were, in opposition to reason: anger, which holds the citadel of the breast, and consequently the very spring of life, the heart; and lust, which rules a broad empire lower down. . . .†

So, Erasmus concludes, we must cherish particularly the few outstanding individuals who have led great and good lives. Christ heads his list of great men; Cicero and Socrates rank very high. Plato's account of the death of Socrates moved Erasmus so deeply that he wanted to cry out, "Pray for us, Saint Socrates."

Erasmus possessed most of the main attributes of Renaissance humanism. He coupled a detached view of human nature with faith in

*Ibid., 61.
†Ibid, 23.

the dignity of man or at least of a few individuals. He joined love of the classics with respect for Christian values. While he was both testy and vain, he had little use for the finespun arguments of Scholasticism and was a tireless advocate of what he called his "philosophy of Christ," the application, in the most humane spirit, of the doctrines of charity and love taught by Jesus. Yet, though Erasmus always considered himself a loyal son of the Church, he nevertheless helped to destroy the universality of Catholicism. His edition of the Greek New Testament raised disquieting doubts about the accuracy of the Latin translation in the Vulgate and therefore of Catholic Biblical interpretations. His repeated insistence on elevating the spirit of piety above the letter of formal religious acts seemed to diminish the importance of the clergy, and his attacks on clerical laxity implied that the wide gap between the lofty ideals and the corrupt practices of the Church could not long endure. A famous sixteenth-century epigram states: "Where Erasmus merely nodded, Luther rushed in; where Erasmus laid the eggs, Luther hatched the chicks; where Erasmus merely doubted, Luther laid down the law." Erasmus was still in his prime when Luther "laid down the law" in 1517 and launched the Protestant revolt.

III   The Arts

Main Characteristics

During the centuries of the Renaissance the arts experienced both a reaction and a revolution. Under the influence of the humanists' enthusiasm for classical antiquity the artists, too, went back to Rome for their models. And under the influence of the growing secularism and individualism of the age, they experimented with new techniques and new forms. Painting and sculpture were emancipated from their medieval subservience to architecture, so long "queen of the arts." Whereas statues, carvings, altarpieces, and stained glass had done much to enhance the glory of Romanesque and Gothic cathedrals, they had not been entities in themselves but parts of a larger whole. In the Renaissance, architecture lost its old aesthetic predominance, and painting and sculpture came into their own, often still closely allied with architecture, but often functioning as "freestanding" arts. The picture or statue won importance as an independent work of art, an entity in itself and the artist gained increasing status as a professional man. The celebrated individualism of the Renaissance was replacing the stamp of the community found in the medieval West.

Reflecting the classical revival, the fashion in building changed from the soaring Gothic to adaptations of the ancient Roman temple, emphasizing symmetry, solidity, and the horizontal line. The contrast may be observed by comparing a Gothic cathedral like Chartres with a Renaissance monument like St. Peter's at Rome. Reflecting the increasing security, wealth, and materialism of the age, palaces and private residences began to rival cathedrals and churches in magnificence.

The arts as a whole, like society and culture in general, became less Christian and more secular than they had been in the Middle Ages. For patrons, artists turned increasingly to men of state and business; for subjects they chose their patrons and pagan gods as well as the traditional Virgin, Christ, and saints. Interest in the things of this world, however, did not exclude concern with the next world; the Renaissance was both worldly and otherworldly. The fame of Leonardo, for instance, rests both on the "Last Supper" and the "Mona Lisa."

The artists of the Renaissance, even more than its writers and thinkers, displayed an extraordinary range of talents and interests.

They produced both secular and sacred works; they imitated classical antiquity and launched bold new experiments in artistic expression; they took pride in their individual achievements, even boasted of them. Some of the very greatest were also the most versatile. Michelangelo executed heroic frescoes and heroic statues, and helped to plan St. Peter's on a truly heroic scale. Giotto designed buildings, painted, wrote verses, and did handsomely in business. Leonardo was a jack of all trades and a master of many—painter and sculptor, musician and physicist, anatomist and geologist, inventor and city-planner.

The Renaissance, in sum, was one of the great ages in the history of art. In sculpture, it rivaled the golden centuries of Greece. In painting, it was more than a rebirth; it transformed an old and rather limited medium of expression into a thrilling new aesthetic instrument. These wonders, of course, did not take place overnight. In the arts, as in literature, a distinctive Renaissance style began to emerge about 1300; after a long development the arts reached their fullest flowering two hundred years later. For example, the most celebrated names in painting—Leonardo, Raphael, Michelangelo, Titian, Dürer—belong to the "High Renaissance" of the late fifteenth and early sixteenth centuries. But the great forerunner of these masters was Giotto, a contemporary of Dante.

Giotto

Before 1300, Italian painters had generally followed the Byzantine tradition and done work that was both decorative and solemn but also flat and two-dimensional, lacking in depth. Giotto (c. 1270–1337), though not entirely forsaking Byzantine models, experimented to make painting more lifelike and less austere. He learned much from the realistic statues of Italian sculptors, who had been influenced by those striking sculptures decorating the portals of French Gothic cathedrals. We may take as examples the frescoes Giotto executed for the Arena Chapel at Padua near Venice. In the "Return of Joachim

to the Sheepfold," the dog greets his returned master with his right forepaw raised to scratch a welcome. In the "Entombment of Christ," the mood of grief is intensified by the lamentations of the mourners on the ground, and still more by the angels flying above the dead Christ. They did not glide placidly but seem to be beating their wings in a transport of distraction and sorrow.

Medieval artists had used the same tone of color throughout a picture, and this uniformity of tone intensified the flat quality of the painting. Giotto, on the other hand, varied the brightness of his colors and attempted contrasts of light and shade, the technique that goes by the Italian name of *chiaroscuro* ("bright-dark"). Through these experiments with highlights, Giotto achieved a three-dimensional quality, an illusion of depth.

As a person, Giotto anticipated the proud and versatile man of the Renaissance bent on worldly success. He was no anonymous craftsman, dedicated and withdrawn, content to work in obscurity, but a many-sided man, hungry for fame, and famous in his own day for his verses and his witty remarks as well as for his artistic accomplishments. His artistic commissions netted him a sizable fortune, which he augmented through a variety of business enterprises: lending money, running a debt-collection service, and renting looms (at stiff fees) to poor woolen-weavers. Giotto had many connections with the great and wealthy; he won the patronage of Roman cardinals, the King of Naples, and the guilds and millionaires of Florence. The richest man in Padua, Enrico Scrovegni, following a custom prevalent in the later Middle Ages, commissioned him to paint the frescoes in the Arena Chapel on behalf of his father's soul (the senior Scrovegni had been a notorious money-lender, and Dante's *Divine Comedy* has assigned his soul to Hell).

Patrons, Subjects, and Techniques

Thus, in the time of Giotto, art was beginning to attract the patronage of secular individuals in addition to that of the churchmen who had been its chief sponsors in the Middle Ages. During the next two centuries, more and more despots, kings, and merchant princes joined the ranks of patrons. This is one of the main strands in the history of Renaissance painting. A second strand is the introduction of humanistic and secular themes, and a third is technical: the advances in the use of *chiaroscuro,* perspective, color, oils, precise anatomical detail—all the techniques that expanded the potentialities of the medium.

By 1500, almost all the Italian states and many states outside Italy, had their court painters. In Florence, the government, the guilds, the wealthy magnates, and the churches and monasteries had all been patronizing artists since the time of Giotto, in a sustained campaign for civic beauty. Lorenzo the Magnificent subsidized a great painter like Botticelli as well as the humanists of the Platonic Academy. "Il Moro," the Sforza usurper in Milan, made Leonardo in effect his Minister of Fine Arts, Director of Public Works, and Master of the Revels. After the collapse of Il Moro's fortunes, Leonardo found new patrons in Cesare Borgia, the Pope, and the French kings, Louis XII and Francis I, ambitious rulers all. The popes employed Leonardo, Botticelli, Raphael, Michelangelo, and many other leading artists, for they had a keen appreciation of aesthetic values, and favored projects that would add to the luster of their rule. They intended to make St. Peter's the largest and the most resplendent church in Christendom, and to make Rome the artistic capital of the world.

"Joachim Returning to the Sheepfold," by Giotto, in Arena (Scrovegni) Chapel, Padua.

The mixture of secular and religious motives was evident in the subject matter of art. Time and again the painters of the Renaissance executed Madonnas, the Nativity, the Crucifixion, and all the rest of the grand Christian themes. But they interpreted them in their own individual ways, realistically or piously. And they applied equal skill to scenes from classical mythology, portraits of their secular contemporaries, and other subjects remote from the Christian tradition. Often the sacred and the secular could be found in the same picture. In a Florentine chapel, for instance, Giotto placed around a religious fresco a border of medallions portraying the sponsors, the banking family of the Peruzzi. Giotto's successors often introduced into a sacred painting the person who had commissioned it, and sometimes brought in the whole family; Botticelli's "Adoration of the Magi" includes Cosimo and Lorenzo de' Medici as well as the artist. While the patron usually assumed a reverent posture, the artist often revealed the acumen and ambition that had won him worldly success and permitted him to afford the luxury of commissioning a work of art. It is hard to tell whom such paintings were intended to honor, God or the donor.

Ambiguities also complicated the treatment of pagan and classical themes in Renaissance painting. At first, artists took figures like Jupiter and Venus out of their Olympian context and made them just another lord and lady of the chivalric class; the sense of historical appropriateness was conspicuously missing. Later painters attempted to depict the gods and goddesses in a proper classical setting, sometimes in a pagan state of undress, but not at all pagan in the sense of glorifying the flesh. For example, when Botticelli (1445–1510), another in the long file of talented Florentines, was commissioned by the Medici to paint the "Birth of Venus," he made Venus more ethereal than sensual and arranged the figures against a background of water in the fashion traditionally used to depict the baptism of Christ. In his "Primavera," a pagan allegory of spring, the chief figures—Mercury, the messenger of the gods; the Three Graces; Venus (again, rather ethereal); the goddess Flora, bedecked with blossoms; and Spring herself, blown in by the West Wind—are all youthful and delicate; all have tiny feet and the air of otherworldly serenity so characteristic of Botticelli.

It may be argued that Botticelli was to painting what the mystics of the Platonic Academy were to humanism. He seems to have moved in the circle of Pico della Mirandola at Florence, and his paintings often suggest an aspiration to some mystic Platonic realm. Yet Botticelli also knew the drive of raw religious emotion and rallied to the reforming friar, Savonarola, who briefly imposed a puritanical régime on Florence in the 1490's (see p. 112). When Savonarola prescribed the burning of all worldly "vanities," so the story has it, Botticelli threw some of his own paintings of nudes onto the flames.

The most significant contributor to the technique of painting after Giotto was Masaccio (1401– c.1428), yet another Florentine genius. Masaccio made bold experiments with *chiaroscuro* and perspective and learned from sculptors anatomical realism. In painting the expulsion from the Garden of Eden, he conveyed the shame and the sorrow of Adam and Eve both by their facial expressions and by the forlorn posture of their bodies. And he intensified the sense of tragedy by employing bold contrasts of light and shadow on the bodies. Masaccio had the rare gift of reducing a situation to its essentials.

Where Masaccio stressed fidelity to human nature, other artists strove for the more faithful representation of the natural environment. A botanist can identify the plants and flowers in Botticelli's "Primavera." Where Masaccio relied, as it were, on mass and perspective to achieve his artistic effects, others turned to line and to color. Botticelli was a superb colorist, and such a painstaking draughtsman that he seems to have brushed in every single hair on a human head.

A great step forward in the use of color came with the introduction of oil paints, developed first in Flanders and brought to Italy in the latter part of the fifteenth century. Until then, painters had generally worked in fresco

Masaccio: "Expulsion of Adam and Eve from Eden."

or tempera or a combination of the two. Fresco, the application of pigments to the wet plaster of a wall, required the artist to work swiftly before the surface dried and set and thus discouraged the showing of details. Tempera (or distemper) painting, in which the pigments were mixed with a sizing, often of eggs, permitted fuller details but tended to be muddy-looking. Oils overcame the disadvantages of fresco and tempera; they allowed the artist to work more slowly and delicately and assured him clearer and more lasting colors.

The major trends we have been following in patronage, subject matter, and technical proficiency reached a climax with the masters of the High Renaissance—Leonardo, Michelangelo, Titian, Raphael, Giorgione, Tintoretto, Veronese, and others. The first three may illustrate the scope and achievements of Italian painting.

Leonardo

Compared with other great masters Leonardo da Vinci (1452–1519) completed relatively few pictures. His scientific activities (see p. 107) and his innumerable services of every kind of his patrons demanded a large part of his time and energies. Some of his paintings deteriorated because of his unsuccessful experiments with new methods, and the "Last Supper" began to suffer during Leonardo's own lifetime because of the mold on the damp wall of the Milan monastery where he had painted it. Fortunately, Leonardo's talent and his extraordinary range of interests may be sampled in the voluminous collections of his drawings and notebooks. The drawings include every sort of sketch, from preliminary work for paintings through realistic human embryos and fanciful warmachines to mere "doodles." From the notebooks comes this characteristic advice of Leonardo:

. . . Since, as we know, painting embraces and contains within itself . . . whatever can be comprehended by the eyes, it would seem to me that he is but a poor master who makes only a single figure well.

96

For do you not see how many and how varied are the actions which are performed by men alone? Do you not see how many different kinds of animals there are, and also of trees and plants and flowers? What variety of hilly and level places, of springs, rivers, cities, public and private buildings; of instruments fitted for man's use; of divers costumes, ornaments and arts?—Things which should be rendered with equal facility and grace by whoever you wish to call a painter.

. . .

The painter will produce pictures of little merit if he takes the works of others as his standard; but if he will apply himself to learn from the objects of nature he will produce good results.*

*The Notebooks of Leonardo da Vinci, Edward MacCurdy, ed. (New York, n.d.), II, 256, 276.

Leonardo followed his own advice about studying nature afresh. He investigated plants, animals, and fossils. From his intensive study of human anatomy, he drew up rules for indicating the actions of human muscles and for establishing the proportions between the parts of the human body. He made many sketches of the deformed and of people suffering intense strain and anguish, combining a zeal for scientific precision with a concern for the grotesque that recalls the gargoyles of a Gothic cathedral.

Leonardo made the "Last Supper" in part an exercise in artistic geometry, arranging the apostles in four groups of three men each, around the central figure of Christ, and keeping the background deliberately simple to

Leonardo da Vinci: head of Christ.

accent the lines of perspective. Yet he did not make the picture superficially realistic; it would have been physically impossible for thirteen men to have eaten together at the relatively small table provided by Leonardo. Older painters had usually shown the group at the solemn yet peaceful moment of the final communion, and had suggested the coming treachery of Judas by placing him in isolation from the others. Not Leonardo. He chose the tense moment when Jesus announced the coming betrayal, and he placed Judas among the apostles, relying on facial and bodily expression to convey the guilt of the one and the consternation of the others.

Serenity, not tension, is found in Leonardo's head of Christ (illustrated on p. 97) and also in his "Madonna of the Rocks," where the plants and flowers have the accuracy of plates in a textbook. The arrangement of the figures in a pyramid—the Madonna flanked by the young St. John and by an angel supporting the Christ child—the foreshortening of the arms, and the careful painting of hair and draperies show Leonardo's geometrical sense and expert draughtsmanship. They also convey the religious tranquillity of the scene.

Michelangelo and Titian

Leonardo got on fairly amicably with his patrons; his strong-minded contemporary, Michelangelo Buonarotti (1475–1564), had a very different experience. He quarreled repeatedly with the imperious Pope Julius II (1503–1513); it took all the Pope's ingenuity to persuade Michelangelo to complete a vast fresco for the ceiling of the Sistine Chapel which Pope Sixtus IV had added to the Vatican. The Sistine ceiling is in every respect a prodigious piece of work. The area is approximately 54 by 134 feet, and Michelangelo covered it with 343 separate figures. He executed the whole in the space of four years, working almost single-handed, assisted only by a plasterer and a color-mixer, painting uncomfortably on his back atop a scaffolding, sometimes not bothering to descend for his night's rest, and arguing stormily with the im-

patient Pope, who dared to complain of the painter's slow rate of progress.

For this massive undertaking, Michelangelo boldly chose not a simple subject but a series of the grandest scenes from Genesis. They are arranged in a sequence that reflects Michelangelo's Neoplatonic convictions of the ascent from the very fleshly to the sublime, beginning over the entrance with the "Drunkenness of Noah" and culminating over the altar with the "Creation." Throughout, the recurring form is that most appropriate to a master sculptor-painter, the human figure. In this vast gallery of nudes in all types of poses, Michelangelo summed up all that Renaissance art had learned about perspective, anatomy, and motion. The Sistine ceiling also comes close to summarizing man's concepts of God; no medieval artist would have dared to represent the deity so directly. God appears repeatedly, draped in a mantle, an everchanging patriarch. Hovering over the waters, he is benign; giving life to the motionless Adam, or directing Eve to arise, he is gently commanding; creating the sun and moon, he is the all-powerful deity, formidable and urgent as a whirlwind.

Both Michelangelo and Leonardo had received their artistic training in Florence; Titian (1477–1576) was identified with Venice. In some respects Titian had the most remarkable career of any artist in that remarkable age, or any age. For eighty years he enjoyed almost unbroken professional success and produced an average of one picture a month. Even a partial listing of the commissions that he received underscores again the sweep of Renaissance painting and patronage. At the start of his career in Venice, Titian was hired to do frescoes for the headquarters of the German merchant colony. Then he undertook portraits for rich merchants, altarpieces and madonnas for churches and monasteries, and a great battle scene for the palace of the Doge. In the middle decades of the sixteenth century, Titian had become so famous that he received offers from half the despots of Italy and crowned heads of Europe. Pope Paul III, the Habsburg Emperor Charles V, and Charles' son, Philip II of Spain, became his patrons.

A gallery of Titians's portraits would make a splendid introduction to the high politics of the sixteenth century. There is Paul III, one of the last of the Renaissance popes, ambitious and authoritative; there is a *condottiere* at once handsome and worn, cultivated and shrewd, from the successful family of the della Rovere (which had produced Popes Sixtus IV and Julius II). Titian even accomplished the feat of making undistinguished-looking Charles V appear reasonably imperial. Rich, intense colors, especially purples and reds, are Titian's hallmark, and through them he transferred to paint the flamboyance and pageantry identified with Venice.

Northern European Painting

The fame and influence of Titian and many other Italians helped to stimulate the flowering of northern European painting in the sixteenth century. This northern Renaissance, however, also grew out of native traditions of Gothic art passed down from the Middle Ages. It centered chiefly in southern Germany and in the Low Countries. Among its leading artists were Albrecht Dürer (1471–1528) and Hans Holbein (c. 1497–1543), Bavarians both, and Pieter Breughel the Elder (c. 1520–1569), who was born near Brussels. These northerners, too, won the patronage of the mighty. Dürer received commissions from the Emperor Maximilian and Breughel had the support of businessmen in Antwerp and Brussels. Armed with an introduction from Erasmus, Holbein moved to England, where he soon won the custom of humanists, aristocrats, and the court of King Henry VIII. Holbein executed handsome portraits of his benefactors, including the very familiar representation of Henry VIII and a likeness of Erasmus, that seems to catch the great humanist's wit and intelligence.

Dürer was in many ways the Leonardo of Germany. His realistic yet compassionate

Michelangelo: "God separating water and earth," ceiling of the Sistine Chapel.

Breughel: Flemish proverbs.

portrait of his aged and homely mother might almost have been taken from da Vinci's sketch book. He collected monkeys and other tropical specimens, painted the Virgin in the unusual pose of a "Madonna with Many Animals," and, in the closing years of his career, wrote treatises on perspective and human proportions. By sensitive use of line and shading, Dürer revolutionized the hitherto primitive techniques of copper engraving and woodcuts. These innovations permitted the reproduction of drawings in many copies and enabled artists to illustrate whole editions of volumes prepared by the new process of printing. They brought Dürer closer than any Italian painter

to the rapidly expanding public of readers; they made him in effect the first artist in history to become a "best-seller."

Northern painters did not always share Italian tastes in subject matter; often they were more down-to-earth. Breughel, for example, delighted in scenes of peasant life—weddings, dances, and festivals, executed with Rabelaisian gusto. He also painted a series of lovely landscapes—another form neglected in Italy—showing the cycle of farming activities during the various months of the year. Apparently Breughel was not striving deliberately to be popular, as Dürer had sought popularity through the mass production of engravings

100

and woodcuts; wealthy individuals commissioned most of Breughel's plebeian subjects.

Lastly, northern art retained the old medieval fascination with the monstrous and the supernatural. Dürer showed this Gothic strain in a series of sixteen woodcuts depicting the Four Horsemen and the other grim marvels of the Apocalypse. In Breughel, the strain is almost obsessive. He made the "Tower of Babel" a nightmarish skyscraper, decayed, hideous, and unclean. His bizarre "Battle of the Angels and the Demons" is full of "things" whose nearest relatives populate the science fiction and the surrealist art of the twentieth century—coats-of-arms that actually fight, shellfish that fly, hybrids with insect wings, artichoke bodies, and flower heads. Most of these fantasies were designed to teach a moral lesson; they were sermons in paint or ink, almost as the Gothic cathedrals had been sermons in stone. The painting of northern Europe demonstrates once more the superficiality of the old notion that the men of the Renaissance had cast off all the traditions and values of the Middle Ages.

Sculpture

In the Renaissance, sculpture and painting maintained a close organic relationship; they were the two faces of a single artistic coin. Italian pictures owed their three-dimensional qualities partly to the painters' study of the sister art; some of the finest painters were also accomplished sculptors—Giotto, Leonardo, Michelangelo. Sculptors, too, turned to classical models and secular themes, studied human anatomy, and experimented with new techniques.

Many of these innovations are evident in Donatello (c. 1386–1466), a Florentine and the first great name in Renaissance sculpture. Donatello's equestrian statue of the *condottiere,* Gattemalata, in Padua is a landmark in artistic history. The subject is secular; the treatment is classical (Gattemalata looks like the commander of a Roman legion); and the material is bronze, not the stone that sculptors had been accustomed to use during the Middle Ages. In free-standing statues of religious figures, Donatello sometimes stressed physical realism and beauty to the exclusion of any spiritual quality. His bronze David, the first statue of a nude male since antiquity, is a handsome youth rather than the divinely inspired slayer of Goliath. In a masterpiece like the statue of Mary Magdalen, however, Donatello transcended literal realism. A critic has called her "an emaciated monster." Emaciated the figure certainly is, all skin and bone, lank hair, and tattered clothing; but everything about her accents the vertical line and contributes to the statue's extraordinary quality. Mary Magdalen is a saint who looks the part.

Half a century after Donatello, the genius of Michelangelo brought sculpture to the highest summit it had reached since the Age of Pericles, perhaps the highest in the whole record of the art. The man who painted the Sistine ceiling brought the same daring conceptions and concentrated energy to his sculptures. Early in his career, when the government of Florence offered him the exacting task of creating something beautiful from an enormous chunk of marble that another artist had already seemingly spoiled, Michelangelo produced the renowned colossal statue of David, more than sixteen feet tall. Late in his career, Michelangelo met another outstanding challenge to his skill when he made the four figures that adorn the tombs of the Medici family in Florence—Dawn, Day, Dusk, and Night. The figures recline on sloping cornices, and a lesser artist would have made them look precarious, about to slide off. Michelangelo gave them repose and yet suggested tremendous latent power, especially in the exuberantly muscled nudes of Day and Dusk. Even more than Donatello, Michelangelo gave his best work a realism surpassing the merely literal. His remarkable statue of Moses makes a good counterpart to his depictions of God on the Sistine ceiling: one side of the prophet's face shows compassion, the other reveals the stern and wrathful law-giver. In portraying the "Pietà," the Virgin grieving over the dead Christ, Michelangelo brilliantly solved the difficult technical problem of posing a seated woman with a full-grown corpse lying across

CARL A. RUDISILL LIBRARY
LENOIR RHYNE COLLEGE

her lap, and he triumphantly called attention to his feat by executing the work in highly polished marble. The face of Mary is sorrowful yet composed, and younger than that of the dead Christ. She is the eternal Virgin, Michelangelo explained, and so is always youthful and does not grieve as an earthly mother would.

Architecture

In 1546, at the age of seventy, Michelangelo shouldered one more artistic burden: he agreed to be the chief architect of St. Peter's. Though he died long before the great Roman basilica was finally completed in 1626, and his successors altered many of his details, the huge dome, the key feature of the whole structure, followed Michelangelo's basic design. St. Peter's shows most of the characteristics that separate the architectural style of the Renaissance from the Gothic of the High Middle Ages. Gone are the great spires and towers: in their place is Michelangelo's dome, which rises 435 feet above the floor below, yet is almost dwarfed in mass by the immense building underneath. While Gothic structures, with their great windows, pointed arches, and high-flung vaults, create an impression of strain and instability, St Peter's, with its round arches, heavier walls, and stout columns, seems to have been built for eternity.

St. Peter's also has the symmetry so admired by Renaissance builders; everything about it fits into a tidy geometrical pattern. Michelangelo cast that pattern in the shape of a Greek cross, which has four arms of equal length, whereas the Gothic cathedral had taken the form of a Latin cross, with the nave in the long arm. Though the Greek-cross design was later modified, St. Peter's still retains many traces of the original plan. The balanced character of the whole edifice is enhanced by the magnificent curving colonnades which were built in the early seventeenth century in the great square outside the basilica and which

Donatello: "Mary Magdalen."

carry the eye of the approaching visitor straight to the church of the pope.

The architects of the Renaissance studied ancient Roman remains and adapted many of their forms—domes, columns, round arches, geometrical symmetry. They also had some knowledge of humanistic learning, particularly the Platonic and Pythagorean concepts of perfect ideas and perfect geometric forms. Palladio, the foremost architectural theorist of the age, praised the Greek-cross plan for churches because of its symbolic values. If the apses (at the ends of the four arms) were rounded, and if the spaces between the arms were filled with rounded chapels, then the whole structure became an almost perfect circle. And the circle, according to Palladio, "demonstrates extremely well the unity, the infinite essence, the uniformity, and the justice of God."* Some scholars have taken the change in the plan of the church structure from the Latin cross to the circled Greek cross to symbolize a shift in religious emphasis. The Gothic stress on the sacrifice of Christ yields to the Renaissance celebration of the perfection of God.

The total architectural record of the Renaissance includes a large number of palaces, chateaux, villas, and other purely secular buildings. This conspicuous display of worldly wealth was partly an example of the decline of medieval values in the face of mounting materialism, political ambition, and other forms of secular pride. But it was also a simple question of economics and security. The expansion of business gave private individuals the money to finance the construction of lavish residences. The gradual growth of effective government meant that, even in country districts, a man's home could be a showplace and no longer had to be, quite literally, his castle.

Elaborately symmetrical villas now ornamented the countryside; in the cities the characteristic structure was the *palazzo* or palace, usually not a royal or official establishment but an imposing private town house combining business offices and residential

*Quoted by Rudolf Wittkower, *The Architectural Principles of the Age of Humanism* (London, 1949), 21.

Michelangelo: "Moses," in S. Pietro in Vincoli, Rome; commissioned by Pope Julius II for his tomb.

apartments. Palaces by the dozen went up in Rome and Florence; in Venice they lined the Grand Canal almost solidly from one end to the other. The usual *palazzo* was three-storied and rectangular, with its windows arranged in symmetrical rows. Architects relieved the effect of monotonous regularity by such decorative devices as pillars, pilasters, and cornices, and by using a different finish of stone for each story, with the roughest at the bottom. The largest of the *palazzi* in their dimensions even rivaled the monuments of ancient

Rome. The Pitti Palace, for example, which was erected in Florence by a millionaire rival of the Medici, was 475 feet long and 114 feet high.

The fame of Italian builders soon spread throughout Europe, even to distant Moscow, where Italian experts supervised the remodeling of the Kremlin for Ivan III. Most countries did not copy the Italian style straight-out, but grafted it onto the older native architecture. The resulting compound occasionally produced some strikingly elegant buildings, particularly the great chateaux of the Loire Valley in central France. The combination of elements taken from the feudal castle, the Gothic church, and the Italian palace gives these chateaux some of the magic and the unreality of a fairy tale.

Music

The structure of music is often called architectural. A musical composition, like a building, has its basic skeleton or form, its over-all line, and also its surface decorations and embellishments. The sacred music of the Middle Ages, had achieved very complex and elaborate combinations of form, line, and decoration. Piling voice upon voice in complicated harmony, a technique known as polyphony, fusing a multitude of parts

St. Peter's Basilica, Rome.

Palladio: Palazzo Chiericati, Vicenza.

into a single whole, these ecclesiastical compositions have sometimes been compared to Gothic cathedrals. In the late Middle Ages, the center of Gothic music was the Burgundian domain in northern France and the Low Countries. By the fifteenth century French and Flemish musicians were journeying to Italy, where a process of mutual influence developed. The northerners took up the simple tunes of folk songs and dances; the Italians, in turn, added a strain of Gothic complexity to the austere plain-song, which had long been the mainstay of their sacred music. The end-products of the interaction were the sacred and secular polyphonic compositions of the internationally renowned Flemish composer, Josquin des Prez (c. 1450–1521), and the hundred odd masses of the Italian, Palestrina (c. 1525–1594). Much of this music sounds quite otherworldly today, since it lacks the dissonances and the strong rhythms and climaxes to which we are accustomed.

Musicians, too, were affected by the secularism and individualism of the Renaissance and by its taste for experimentation. The Flemings sometimes based even their masses on rowdy popular tunes. Composers and performers began to lose the anonymity associated with the Middle Ages, although the era of prima donnas and other "stars" had not quite arrived. Paid professional singers staffed the famous choirs of Antwerp cathedral, in the fifteenth century, and of the Vatican, in the sixteenth. Josquin des Prez found patrons at the courts of Milan, Rome, and Paris, and both the Pope and various cardinals commissioned Palestrina to write masses. Musicians developed or imported a variety of new instruments—the violin, double-bass, and harpsichord; the organ, with its complement of keyboards, pedals, and stops; the kettle-drum, which was adopted from the Polish army; and the lute, which had originally been developed in medieval Persia and reached Italy by way of Moslem Spain.

Music was interwoven in the fabric of Renaissance society. A retinue of musicians became a fixture of court life, with the Dukes of Burgundy, Philip the Good and Charles the Bold, leading the way. Castiglione, an authority on etiquette, thought music proper for every social station:

We may see it used in the holy temples to render laud and thanks unto God, and it is a credible matter . . . that He hath given it unto us for a most sweet lightening of our travails and vexations. So that many times the boisterous laborers in the fields, in the heat of the sun, beguile their pain with rude and carterlike singing. With this the unmannerly countrywoman, that ariseth before day out of

105

sleep to spin and card, defendeth herself and maketh her labor pleasant. This is the most sweet pastime after rain, wind, and tempest unto the miserable mariners. With this do the weary pilgrims comfort themselves in their troublesome and long voyages.*

The "boisterous laborers," or more exactly, the artisans of German towns called themselves "mastersingers" and organized choral groups. The most famous of them, Hans Sachs, a cobbler in Nuremberg in the 1500's, was

*Castiglione, *The Courtier*, T. Hoby, trans., modernized (1907), 77.

later immortalized in Wagner's opera, *Die Meistersinger*.

The mastersingers followed directly in the tradition of the thirteenth-century minnesingers. And princely patronage of music went back at least to the court life of the twelfth century with its chivalric troubadours. The musicians as well as the poets, the troubadours and the minnesingers had sung of the great secular subjects, war and love. The history of music underlines once again the important fact that the Renaissance did not represent a sharp break with the past but instead built on the legacy it had received from the Middle Ages.

IV   Science

The Place of the Renaissance in the History of Science

Science is a field of human endeavor in which the term "Renaissance" must be used with great caution. A scientific revolution did occur in early modern times, but it came in the seventeenth century of Galileo and Newton after the Renaissance had run its course (see Chapter 7). In the history of science, the late medieval and Renaissance centuries—the fourteenth, fifteenth, and sixteenth—were a time of preparation. Men of science absorbed, enlarged, criticized, and modified the body of scientific knowledge handed down to them from the Middle Ages and from antiquity. The followers of the scholastic tradition of medieval rationalism, the new humanists, and artists and craftsmen of every kind, all contributed to this important work of preparation.

Medieval Scholasticism was by no means anti-scientific. The intellectual discipline of the Schoolmen, their habit of close work, and their enthusiasm for Aristotle made them, in a sense, precursors of the scientific revolution. These Scholastic traditions remained very

much alive after the eclipse of Scholasticism toward the close of the Middle Ages. Despite the bias of humanism against Aristotle, Aristotelian studies continued to be pursued vigorously at the universities of Paris and of Padua, in northern Italy. The humanists themselves steadily increased the amount of ancient scientific writing available to the scholarly world; Galen, Ptolemy, Archimedes, and others were for the first time translated from Greek into the more accessible Latin.

Humanism, however, also thwarted the advance of science; the worship of classical antiquity tended to put old authorities high on a pedestal, beyond the reach of criticism. Few men of the Renaissance believed it possible to improve on the astronomy taught by Ptolemy during the second century A.D., or on the medicine taught by Galen in the same century. Galen, for example, had advanced the erroneous theory that the blood moved from one side of the heart to the other by passing through invisible pores in the thick wall of tissue separating the two sides of the organ. Actually, as Harvey was to discover in the seventeenth century, the blood gets from the one side to the other by circulating through the body and lungs. Galen's theory of invisible pores, however, was enough to keep Leonardo from anticipating Harvey. Leonardo's anatomical studies led him up to the brink of discovery; then he backed away, for he was certain that Galen could not have been wrong.

Leonardo, in fact, illustrates both the shortcomings and the achievements of Renaissance science. On the one hand, he took notes in a hit-or-miss fashion, and in a secretive left-handed writing which must be held up to a mirror to be read. He exerted little direct influence, because he did not have the modern scientist's concern for the systematic cataloguing of observations and the frequent publication of findings and speculations. On the other hand, Leonardo also showed the real

Leonardo da Vinci: sketch for a parachute.

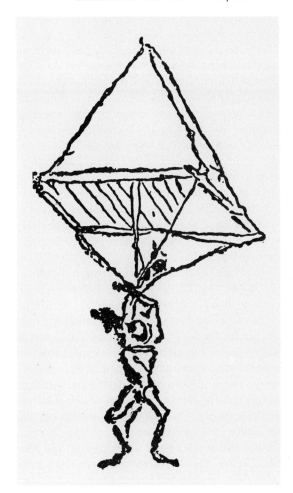

contribution that could be made by the inspired artist and craftsman. Witness his inventiveness: he projected lathes, pumps, war machines, flying machines, and many other contraptions, not all of them workable, to be sure, but all of them highly imaginative. Witness, too, his passionate curiosity for anatomy and proportions, and for almost everything about man and nature. His accurate drawings of human embryos differed radically from the older notion of the fetus as a perfectly formed miniature human being. Moreover, Leonardo did not always bow before established authority, as he did before Galen. His geological studies convinced him that the earth was far older than the men of his time thought it to be. The Po River, he estimated, must have been flowing for about 200,000 years to wash down the sediments forming its alluvial plain in northern Italy.

Technology and Invention

The best-known invention of the Renaissance — the printed book — furnishes an instructive case history of the way in which many technological advances contributed to the end result. The revolution in book production began when medieval Europeans imported paper from China and found it to be cheaper than the lambskin or sheepskin previously used by copyists. The next step came when engravers, pioneering in the methods later used by Dürer, made woodcuts or copper plates that could produce many copies of the same drawing. Then sentences were added to the cuts or plates to explain the sketches. Finally, movable type was devised. Each piece of type was simply a minute bit of engraving which could be combined with other pieces to form words, sentences, a whole page, and then salvaged to be used over and over again. This crucial invention occurred during the 1440's, almost certainly in the German Rhineland; Johann Gutenberg, who used to receive the credit for it, has been the focus of a scholarly controversy that has deflated his old heroic reputation.

This new invention was to gain wide popularity. By 1500, Italy alone had seventy-three presses employing movable type. The most famous of them was the Aldine Press in Venice, named for its founder, Aldus Manutius (1450–1515). The Aldine Press won its reputation by selling at reasonable prices scholarly editions of the classics printed in a beautiful type-face which, reportedly, was based on the handwriting of Petrarch. Everywhere the printing press suddenly made both classical and vernacular literature available to large numbers of people who could never have afforded hand-copied manuscripts. Without the perfection of printing, Erasmus might not have become the acknowledged arbiter of European letters. Without it, Luther could not have secured the rapid distribution of his antipapal tracts, and the Protestant Reformation might not have rent Christian Europe asunder.

Although no other single invention can be compared with printing on the score of quick and decisive effects, many innovations ultimately had comparable influence. Gunpowder, for example, brought from China to medieval Europe, was used in the fighting of the early 1400's, notably the later campaigns of the Hundred Years' War. Improved firearms and artillery were to doom both the feudal knight and the feudal castle, for both were vulnerable to the new weapons. In navigation, as we have seen, the Venetians made galleys swifter, more capacious, and more seaworthy. At the same time, important marine aids came into general use, particularly the magnetic compass and the sailing charts which, at least for the Mediterranean, established a high level of accuracy. By the close of the fifteenth century, Europeans possessed the equipment needed for the oncoming age of world discovery (see Chapter 6).

On land, the mining industry scored impressive technological advances. The engineers of the late medieval centuries solved some of the problems of extracting and smelting silver, iron, and other ores. Then, in 1556, a German physician and mining expert published a comprehensive treatise on the practices of the industry. Following the cus-

tom of the day, he called himself Agricola, a Latinized version of his German name, Bauer, which means peasant. His treatise, *De Re Metallica* ("all about metals"), was translated from Latin into English in 1912 by a famous American mining engineer and his wife, Mr. and Mrs. Herbert Hoover. Agricola's treatise was an early specimen of those handbooks that are indispensable to the engineer. And its detailed observations on soil structures also made it a pioneer study in geology.

Anatomy and Medicine

Medical knowledge advanced very unevenly during the Renaissance. Though anatomical studies moved ahead, aided by the wide dissemination of printed books with clear and reasonably accurate biological illustrations, the practical application of this knowledge to suffering humanity lagged, often very badly. Many so-called physicians were outright quacks; many teachers of medicine simply repeated for their classes the demonstrations that Galen had made more than a thousand years before, without attempting to test the validity of his findings. A striking exception to this rule was furnished by the physicians and scholars of the University of Padua. Protected against possible ecclesiastical censorship by the overlordship of Venice, which controlled the city, they maintained a lively tradition of scientific inquiry that presaged the seventeenth-century triumphs of the experimental method.

In 1537, a young Belgian named Vesalius (1514–1564), trained at Paris, took a teaching post at Padua. Vesalius repeated the dissections of Galen, but always with an open mind, always on the lookout for errors. Thus, he rejected Galen's notion of invisible pores in the wall of tissue within the heart, because he could not find such pores. In 1543, Vesalius published *De Humanis Corporis Fabrica* (Concerning the Structure of the Human Body). In the great anatomical study, he largely confirmed the teachings of older authorities, but he also pointed out some of their shortcomings. He prepared the work with admirable concern for accuracy and detail, and provided elaborate woodcuts for illustrations.

Astronomy

The year 1543 marked not only the appearance of Vesalius' treatise but also the launching of modern astronomical studies with the publication of Copernicus' *De Revolutionibus Orbium Coelestium* (Concerning the Revolutions of Heavenly Bodies). Born in Poland, of German extraction, Copernicus (1473–1543) studied law and medicine at Padua and other Italian universities, spent thirty years as canon of a cathedral near Danzig, and made his real career in mathematics and astronomy. His scientific work led him to attack the traditional hypothesis of the geocentric (earth-centered) universe derived from Ptolemy and other astronomers of antiquity. In its place, he advanced the revolutionary new hypothesis of the heliocentric (sun-centered) universe.

The concept of the geocentric universe generally accepted in the sixteenth century included an elaborate system of spheres. Around the stationary earth there revolved some eighty spheres, each, as it were, a separate sky containing some of the heavenly bodies, each moving on an invisible circular path, each transparent so that we mortals could see the spheres beyond it. This imaginative and symmetrical picture of the universe had already come under attack before the time of Copernicus, for observers had had trouble making it agree with the actual behavior of heavenly bodies. Copernicus used both these earlier criticisms and his own computations to arrive at the heliocentric concept. He prefaced this explanation to *De Revolutionibus:*

... What moved me to consider another way of reckoning the motions of the heavenly spheres was nothing else than my realisation that Mathematicians were not agreed about the matter of their research. ... In setting out the motions of the Sun and Moon and of the five other planets they did not in each case employ the same principles, assumptions and demonstrations of apparent revolutions and motions. For some used concentric circles only, others eccentrics and epicycles, by which, none the less, they were not able to fully arrive at what they sought. ...

And so after long consideration of the uncertainty of the mathematical traditions about the inferring of the motions of the spheres, it began to vex me that no more certain system of the motions of the machine of the world ... could be agreed upon by the philosophers. ...

I ... began to think about the mobility of the earth. And although it seemed an absurd opinion, ... I discovered by much and long observation, that if the motions of the rest of the planets are compared with the motion of the earth, ... not only do their appearances follow therefrom, but the system moreover so connects the orders and sizes both of the planets and of their orbits, and indeed the whole heaven, that in no part of it can anything be moved without bringing to confusion the rest of the parts and the whole universe.[*]

The Copernican hypothesis of a moving earth had quite radical implications. It destroyed the idea of the earth's uniqueness by suggesting that it acted like other heavenly bodies, and it opened the door to attacks on the uniqueness of the earth's human inhabitants. Nevertheless, once Copernicus had reversed the roles of the sun and the earth, his universe retained many Ptolemaic characteristics. Its heavens were still filled with spheres revolving along their invisible orbits. Only they now moved about a stationary sun, instead of the stationary earth, and Copernican astronomy required only thirty-four of them, not eighty. The revolution in astronomy begun by Copernicus did not reach its culmination for a hundred and fifty years. The circular orbits of Copernicus had to yield to elliptical orbits; the scheme of thirty-four spheres had to be modified; and a theory explaining the forces that kept the universe together had to be put forward. And all these developments had to await the genius of Galileo and Newton, and the detailed observations made possible by the invention of the telescope (see Chapter 7).

[*]Quoted in F. Sherwood Taylor, *A Short History of Science and Scientific Thought* (New York, 1949), 83–84.

V   Religion

The Relationship between the Renaissance and Religion

Although Copernicus dedicated his great book to the Pope himself, Christendom did not welcome a theory that challenged the orthodox belief in an earth-centered and man-centered universe. By the time Copernicus published, however, western Christendom was split into the warring factions of Catholic and Protestant. To what extent was the Renaissance responsible for the shattering religious crisis of the Reformation? There is no simple answer to this question. The next chapter examines in more detail the reasons for the Protestant revolt; here a few conclusions about the relationship between the Renaissance and religion may be suggested.

First, the Renaissance did not make the Reformation *inevitable*. It is an oversimplification to suppose that the religious individualism of Luther arose directly out of the more general individualism of the Renaissance. Looking back over the checkered culture of the age, one can find elements that are hard to reconcile with traditional Christian values. These are materialism, self-indulgence, power politics, and the other elements sometimes grouped under the label "Counter-Renaissance." If pushed to extremes, they could indeed become anti-Christian; but they were seldom pushed to extremes. Even the most ruthless *condottieri* of politics and business, men like Cesare Borgia and the Fuggers, remained nominal Christians. Also, a pronounced anticlerical like Machiavelli reserved his most stinging criticism for the Pope's claim to temporal authority, not his claim to ecclesiastical supremacy. And, in rebuking the Pope for political maneuvering, he was following the example of the profoundly Christian Dante.

Second, the most characteristic intellectual movement of the Renaissance — humanism — did not propose to replace the traditional Christian values of the Middle Ages with a whole new set of values. On a lower level, much of the fun in the *Decameron* derives from that time-honored object of satire, often lampooned in the Middle Ages, the misbehaving cleric. On a higher level, men like Pico and Erasmus proposed to enrich or purify Christianity; they did not intend to subvert it. As a matter of fact, the Neoplatonic doctrines cherished by Pico and the Platonic Academy had long been a mainstay of the mystical aspects of the Catholic faith. Erasmus, perhaps the most representative thinker of humanism, was too strongly attached to Catholicism and too moderate in temperament to be a revolutionary.

Third and finally, a religious crisis was indeed gathering during the Renaissance, but it was more internal than external. That is, the Church was only to a limited extent the victim of outside forces operating beyond its control, like the challenge presented to its old international dominion by the new national monarchies. If the Church of the 1400's had been strong and healthy, it might have met such external challenges successfully. Except in Spain, however, the Church was neither strong nor healthy.

The Condition of the Church

The Renaissance Church as a whole had a low moral tone, although many honorable exceptions to the prevailing laxity and backwardness could be found. Priests were often illiterate and immoral, ill prepared for the effective exercise of their parochial responsibilities. Many bishops—following good medieval precedent, it must be admitted—behaved as politicians, not as churchmen. Perhaps the worst shortcomings existed at the top, in the papacy itself. In the fourteenth and early fifteenth centuries, the papacy experienced a series of crises—the Babylonian Captivity, the Great Schism, and the Conciliar Movement (see Chapter 2). It emerged from the ordeal with its power reinvigorated, notably by its victory over the reformers who sought to make church councils a check against unlimited papal absolutism. The triple crisis, however, had gravely damaged the spiritual prestige of the office.

Sixtus IV, Alexander VI, Julius II, and the other popes of the High Renaissance did little to repair the damage. For three quarters of a century after 1450, the See of Peter was occupied by men who scored political and military successes or who were munificent patrons of art and learning. The modern world is indebted to them for the Vatican Library, the Sistine Chapel and its frescoes, and the beginning of the Basilica of St. Peter's. Yet their magnificence cost immense sums of money and increased the burden of ecclesiastical taxation, and with it increased the resentment that higher taxes usually arouse. Their indifference to their spiritual functions enfeebled the Church at a time when it needed firm and dedicated control. The Church was ruled by connoisseurs and *condottieri* when it needed reformers.

Intellectually, too, the clergy were losing the vitality they had possessed in the age of Abelard and Aquinas. Some of the monks and friars on university faculties hardly qualified as teachers; they blindly defended a decadent Scholasticism against the new humanist studies. These reactionary educators provoked the most blistering satire of the Renaissance, *The Letters of Obscure Men*. The story began when John Reuchlin (1455–1522), a German humanist, worked with Pico at Florence, caught his enthusiasm for comparative religious studies, and learned Hebrew in order to read the great books of Judaism. On returning to Germany, Reuchlin aroused the wrath of theological faculties by suggesting that a knowledge of Hebrew and of the sacred Jewish writings might enable a man to be a better-informed Christian. Arraigned in an ecclesiastical court, Reuchlin, who was a layman, assembled in his defense testimonials from leading humanists, *The Letters of Eminent Men.* Then, in 1516 and 1517, a couple of his friends published *The Letters of Obscure Men,* supposedly exchanged between Reuchlin's clerical opponents but actually a hoax designed to laugh the opposition out of court. One of the "obscure men," for instance, related the experience he had had in a Roman tavern:

> For you must know that we were lately sitting in an inn, having our supper, and were eating eggs, when on opening one, I saw that there was a young chicken within.
>
> This I showed to a comrade; whereupon quoth he to me, 'Eat it up speedily, before the taverner sees it, for if he mark it, you will have to pay for a fowl.'
>
> In a trice I gulped down the egg, chicken and all.
>
> And then I remembered that it was Friday!
>
> Whereupon I said to my crony, 'You have made me commit a mortal sin, in eating flesh on the sixth day of the week!'
>
> But he averred that it was not a mortal sin—nor even a venial one, seeing that such a chickling is accounted merely as an egg, until it is born.
>
> Then I departed, and thought the matter over.
>
> And by the Lord, I am in a mighty quandary, and know not what to do.
>
> It seemeth to me that these young fowls in eggs are flesh, because their substance is formed and fashioned into the limbs and body of an animal, and possesseth a vital principle.
>
> It is different in the case of grubs in cheese, and such-like, because grubs are accounted fish, as I learnt from a physician who is also skilled in Natural Philosophy.
>
> Most earnestly do I entreat you to resolve the question that I have propounded. For if you hold that the sin is mortal, then, I would fain get shrift here, ere I return to Germany.*

Never had the futility of theological hair-splitting come in for more scorn. While Reuch-

*Adapted from *Epistolae Obscurorum Virorum,* F. G. Stokes, ed. (New Haven. 1925), 445–447.

lin lost his case, he never paid the costs of the trial, as he was sentenced to do.

Proposals for Reform and Renewal

Dedicated Christians, both lay and clerical, were aware that the Church needed a thorough cleansing. Fresh attempts within the ecclesiastical hierarchy to increase the powers of representative church councils failed, however, in the face of papal opposition. And the great renovation of the Spanish Church fostered by Queen Isabella and Cardinal Ximenes was restricted to Spanish lands.

Meantime, a quiet kind of Catholic renewal was advanced by the activities of the association called the Brethren of the Common Life. Founded in the Low Countries about 1375, the Brethren followed a spiritual discipline resembling that of the monastic organizations. More than discipline, however, they emphasized service to one's fellow men as a means whereby individuals might attempt to realize in practice the high ideals of Christianity. Opposed to Scholasticism, they started their own schools. Erasmus, who was educated in one of them, reflected the goals of the Brethren in his "philosophy of Christ," with its belief that men should be guided in their daily lives by the example and the teaching of Jesus. This kind of appeal was essentially quietist, directed to the high-minded layman rather than to the Church. While it exerted a profound influence on such individuals as Erasmus, its total impact on the Christian community was limited.

Rather similar in ideal but utterly different in method was the reform movement centered on the Dominian friar, Savonarola (1452–1498). A puritanical fanatic, Savonarola won the favor of the Medici through the influence of Pico; his eloquent sermons and reputed gift of predicting the future soon made him the most popular preacher in Florence. Savonarola spared no one in his denunciations of unChristian conduct; here is a typical tirade:

You Christians should always have the Gospel with you, I do not mean the book, but the spirit, for if you do not possess the spirit of grace and yet carry with you the whole book, of what advantage is it to you? And again, all the more foolish are they who carry round their necks Breviaries, notes, tracts and writings, until they look like pedlars going to a fair. Charity does not consist in the writing of papers. The true books of Christ are the Apostles and saints, and true reading consists in imitating their lives. But in these days men are like books made by the Devil. They speak against pride and ambition and yet they are immersed in them up to their eyes. They preach chastity and maintain concubines. They enjoin fasting and partake of splendid feasts. . . . Only look to-day at the prelates. They are tied to earthly vanities. They love them. The cure of souls is no longer their chief concern. . . . In the Primitive Church the chalices were made of wood and the prelates of gold—to-day—chalices of gold, prelates of wood!*

He particularly abominated Pope Alexander VI, whom he cursed for "a devil" and "a monster" presiding over a "ribald" and "harlot" Church.

In the political confusion following the death of Lorenzo the Magnificent (1492), Savonarola rapidly gained power and prestige in Florence. He attracted many enthusiastic supporters, among them Botticelli and Michelangelo. By 1497, he was virtual dictator of the republic and organized troops of boys and girls to tour the city, collect all "vanities," from cosmetics to pagan books and paintings, and burn them on public bonfires. This hysterical pitch of zeal could not be sustained for long, however. Alexander VI excommunicated Savonarola, and his popular following began to disperse, especially after he had failed in his promise to bring a miracle to pass. He would demonstrate his divine inspiration by going unscathed through the ordeal by fire, but his political opponents secured the cancellation of the spectacle at the last moment. Within a short time, Savonarola was condemned for heresy; on May 23, 1498, he was hanged and his body was burnt.

Savonarola perished not only by the hands of his political and ecclesiastical enemies but also through his own fanaticism. Like most

*Quoted by Piero Misciatelli, *Savonarola* (New York, 1930), 60–61.

extreme puritans, he did not realize that morals could not be restored overnight; he was in a sense too unworldly to survive. But the Church that he sought to purge was too worldly to survive without undergoing the major crisis of the Reformation.

VI   Conclusion: The Renaissance Style

It is not easy to define the style of an era as complex as the Renaissance. No definition in fact can take in all its currents and cross-currents or encompass such extraordinarily different personalities as Erasmus and Savonarola. No single man of the time, no single masterpiece of art or literature, was fully typical of the Renaissance. And yet there is something about most of its great men and most of its great books, paintings, and sculpture that sets them apart from the great figures and works of other ages. Humanists like Petrarch, Pico, and Erasmus do differ from St. Thomas Aquinas; Cesare Borgia, Lorenzo the Magnificent, and Louis XI of France have very little in common with Louis IX; the sculpture of Michelangelo does not resemble that of Chartres, nor does a painting by Masaccio much resemble stained glass; St. Peter's belongs to an era unlike that of Mont-Saint-Michel or Notre Dame. The men of the Renaissance lived in a world no longer medieval but not yet fully modern. Their changing values and ideals were presented most sympathetically and disarmingly in a dialogue on manners published in 1528, *The Courtier* by Castiglione.

A solid book of etiquette may often reveal much about a way of life. Castiglione knew his subject inside out; himself an elegant aristocrat, he had spent years on diplomatic missions and at the highly civilized court of Urbino. He begins his delineation of the ideal courtier with a group of traits differing very little from those commended in the paladins of medieval chivalry:

I will have this our Courtier to be a gentleman born and of a good house. For it is a great deal less dispraise for him that is not born a gentleman to fail in the acts of virtue than for a gentleman.

I will have him by nature to have not only a wit and a comely shape of person and countenance, but also a certain grace, and, as they say, a hue, that shall make him at the first sight acceptable and loving unto who so beholdeth him.

I judge the principal and true profession of a Courtier ought to be in feats of arms, the which above all I will have him to practise lively.*

The chivalry of Castiglione has all the patronizing attitude of the patrician toward the plebeian, yet it never gets out of hand; it is restrained by the sense of balance and grasp of reality that we have already found in some of the humanists. In love, the perfect gentleman should adore in his lady "no less the beauty of the mind than of the body." In duels and private quarrels, he should be far more moderate than the medieval knight thought to be honorable. He should excel in sport, like the knight of old, should hunt, wrestle, swim, "play at tennis." Again, Castiglione sounds the note of balance:

Therefore will I have our Courtier to descend many times to more easy and pleasant exercises. And to avoid envy and to keep company pleasantly with every man, let him do whatsoever other men do.†

The courtier should also receive a good education

. . . in those studies which they call Humanity, and to have not only the understanding of the Latin tongue, but also of the Greek, because of the many and sundry things that with great excellency are written in it. Let him much exercise himself in

*Adapted from Castiglione, *The Courtier,* T. Hoby, trans., modernized (1907), 21, 23, 26.
†*Ibid.,* 35.

poets, and no less in orators and historiographers, and also in writing both rhyme and prose, and especially in this our vulgar tongue.*

Here in *The Courtier* we encounter once again the celebrated Renaissance concept of the universal man that we have already met in the writings of Pico and Rabelais and witnessed in the wide-ranging careers of Giotto, Leonardo, and Michelangelo.

Finally, when Castiglione praises the beauty of the world (which is, of course, Ptolemaic, not Copernican), he puts into words more eloquently than any of his contemporaries the style of the Renaissance:

Behold the state of this great engine of the world, which God created for the health and preservation of everything that was made: The heaven round beset with so many heavenly lights; and in the middle the Earth environed with the elements and upheld with the very weight of itself. . . . These things among themselves have such force by the knitting together of an order so necessarily framed that, with altering them any one jot, they should all be loosed and the world would decay. They have also such beauty and comeliness that all the wits men have can not imagine a more beautiful matter.

Ibid., 70.

Think now of the shape of man, which may be called a little world, in whom every parcel of his body is seen to be necessarily framed by art and not by hap, and then the form altogether most beautiful. . . . Leave Nature, and come to art. . . . Pillars and great beams uphold high buildings and palaces, and yet are they no less pleasureful unto the eyes of the beholders than profitable to the buildings. . . . Besides other things, therefore, it giveth a great praise to the world in saying that it is beautiful. It is praised in saying the beautiful heaven, beautiful earth, beautiful sea, beautiful rivers, beautiful woods, trees, gardens, beautiful cities, beautiful churches, houses, armies. In conclusion, this comely and holy beauty is a wondrous setting out of everything. And it may be said that good and beautiful be after a sort one self thing. . . .*

A medieval man might also have coupled the good and the beautiful, but he would have stressed the good, the mysterious ways in which God led man to righteousness. Medieval man had a vision of God's world. The age of Leonardo and of humanism, which Castiglione interpreted so faithfully, had a vision not only of God's world but also of nature's world and man's world.

Ibid., 348–349.

Reading Suggestions on the Renaissance

(Asterisk indicates paperbound edition.)

General Accounts

W. K. Ferguson, *Europe in Transition, 1300–1520* (Houghton, Mifflin, 1962). Comprehensive survey by a leading expert on the period.

E. P. Cheyney, *The Dawn of a New Era, 1250–1453* (*Torch), and M. Gilmore, *The World of Humanism, 1453–1517* (*Torch). Good introductory accounts, with very full bibliographies.

The New Cambridge Modern History, Vol. I: The Renaissance, 1493–1520 (Cambridge Univ. Press, 1957). A co-operative work by many hands; useful chiefly for reference.

J. H. Plumb, *The Italian Renaissance* (*Torch). Concise historical and cultural survey.

G. Mattingly *et al.*, *Renaissance Profiles* (*Torch). Lively sketches of nine representative Italians, including Petrarch, Machiavelli, Leonardo, and Michelangelo.

Interpretations

K. H. Dannenfeldt, ed., *Renaissance—Medieval or Modern?* (*Heath). Selections illustrating varying points of view.

G. C. Sellery, *The Renaissance: Its Nature & Origins* (*Univ. of Wisconsin Press). Clear and helpful survey.

W. K. Ferguson, *The Renaissance in Historical Thought: Five Centuries of Interpretation* (Houghton, Mifflin, 1948). A useful and stimulating monograph.

F. Chabod, *Machiavelli & the Renaissance* (*Torch). The chapter entitled "The Concept of the Renaissance" is most fruitful.

W. K. Ferguson, *et al., The Renaissance: Six Essays* (*Torch). Valuable papers on major aspects of the era by six experts; first presented at a symposium in 1953.

J. Burckhardt, *The Civilization of the Renaissance in Italy, 2 vols.* (*Torch). The classic statement of the hypothesis that the Renaissance was unique and revolutionary.

J. A. Symonds, *Renaissance in Italy,* 5 vols. (*Capricorn). A detailed study, often sharing Burckhardt's views, first written almost a century ago.

L. Olschki, *The Genius of Italy* (Cornell Univ. Press, 1954). Solid essays on many aspects of the Renaissance by a twentieth-century scholar.

Literature and Thought

W. H. Coates & H. V. White, *The Emergence of Liberal Humanism,* Vol. I (McGraw Hill, 1966). Informative survey of intellectual history from the Renaissance to the French Revolution.

R. R. Bolgar, *The Classical Heritage & Its Beneficiaries from the Carolingian Age to the End of the Renaissance* (*Torch). The last third of this scholarly study treats the Renaissance.

G. Highet, *The Classical Tradition: Greek & Roman Influences on Western Literature* (*Galaxy). A lively survey.

H. O. Taylor, *The Humanism of Italy* (*Collier) and *Erasmus & Luther* (*Collier). Selections from a highly-regarded two-volume study, *Thought & Expression in the Sixteenth Century.*

P. O. Kristeller, *Renaissance Thought,* 2 vols. (*Torch). Valuable study, stressing its diversity, by a ranking scholar.

N. A. Robb, *Neoplatonism of the Italian Renaissance* (Allen & Unwin, 1953). A good solid study of an intellectual common denominator of the age.

J. Huizinga, *Erasmus & the Age of the Reformation* (*Torch, 1957). Excellent analysis by a distinguished Dutch scholar.

A. Hyma, *The Christian Renaissance* (Shoe String, 1965). Reprint of an older study, stressing an aspect of the Renaissance often neglected.

P. Misciatelli, *Savonarola* (Appleton-Century-Crofts, 1930). A sound biography of the famous Florentine preacher.

The Fine Arts

H. Wolfflin, *The Art of the Italian Renaissance: A Handbook for Students and Travellers* (*Schocken). By a ranking expert of an earlier day.

B. Berenson, *The Italian Painters of the Renaissance* (*Meridian). Essays by a famous collector.

F. Antal, *Florentine Painting & Its Social Background* (Kegan, Paul, 1948). An attempt to relate art to economic and social currents.

E. Panofsky, *Studies in Iconology: Humanistic Themes in the Art of the Renaissance* (*Torch). By a distinguished and stimulating scholar.

K. M. Clark, *Leonardo da Vinci* (*Penguin). Lively study of his art.

E. MacCurdy, *The Mind of Leonardo da Vinci* (Dodd, Mead, 1928). Standard appraisal.

O. Benesch, *The Art of the Renaissance in Northern Europe* (Harvard Univ. Press, 1945). Examines the interrelations of artistic, religious, and intellectual history.

E. Panofsky, *The Life and Art of Albrecht Dürer* (Princeton Univ. Press, 1955). Standard work on the German artist.

R. Wittkower, *Architectural Principles in the Age of Humanism* (*Random House). A notable investigation of the connections between humanism and architecture.

Music

P. H. Láng, *Music in Western Civilization* (Norton, 1941). A detailed general history endeavoring to illuminate the relationship between music and other historical currents.

C. Gray, *The History of Music,* 2nd ed. (Knopf, 1947). Brief, trenchant survey.

E. J. Dent, *Music of the Renaissance in Italy* (British Academy, 1935). Informative lecture by a great authority.

Science

M. Boas, *The Scientific Revolution, 1450–1630* (*Torch). Helpful detailed account.

H. Butterfield, *The Origins of Modern Science, 1300–1800* (*Free Press). A controversial interpretation, minimizing the scientific contribution of the Renaissance.

G. Sarton, *Six Wings: Men of Science in the Renaissance* (*Univ. of Indiana Press, 1956) and *The Appreciation of Ancient & Medieval Science during the Renaissance* (*Perpetua). Clear and helpful studies by a distinguished historian of science.

A. C. Crombie, *Medieval & Early Modern Science,* Vol. II (Anchor). A good survey.

L. Thorndike, *Science and Thought in the Fifteenth Century* (Columbia Univ. Press, 1929). By a specialist on medieval science.

C. Singer *et al., A History of Technology* (Clarendon, 1954–58). Vol. III Standard work on the subject.

A. Castiglioni, *A History of Medicine,* 2nd ed. (Knopf, 1947). An excellent manual.

Sources

J. B. Ross and M. M. McLaughlin, *The Portable Renaissance Reader* (*Viking). An anthology.

W. L. Gundesheimer, ed., *The Italian Renaissance* (*Prentice-Hall). Selections from the writings of 11 representative figures, including Valla, Pico, Leonardo & Castiglione.

E. Cassirer *et al., The Renaissance Philosophy of Man* (*Phoenix). Excerpts from Petrarch, Pico, Valla, and other humanists, with helpful editorial comments.

Erasmus, *The Praise of Folly* (*Ann Arbor).

B. A. Milligan, ed. *Three Renaissance Classics: Machiavelli's Prince, Castiglione's Courtier, More's Utopia* (*Scribner's).

S. Putnam, ed., *The Portable Rabelais: Most of Gargantua & Pantagruel* (*Viking).

E. MacCurdy, ed., *The Notebooks of Leonardo da Vinci,* 2 vols. (Reynal & Hitchcock). An abbreviated sample in P. Taylor, ed., *The Notebooks of Leonardo: A New Selection* (*Mentor).

A. H. Popham, ed., *The Drawings of Leonardo da Vinci* (*Harvest).

Historical Fiction

D. Merezhkovsky, *The Romance of Leonardo* (*Washington Square). The best novel on the Renaissance, romanticized but based on Leonardo's notebooks.

4

The Protestant Reformation

Until we reach the subject of
this chapter, most of us westerners are not
fully committed by our birth and upbringing
to taking a strong stand on any historical issue.
With the issues between Protestantism and
Catholicism it is different. Complete detachment is impossible, even for the historian.
The conventional titles he must use commit
him. For the Protestant, the phrase "Protestant
Reformation" comes naturally; for the Catholic,
"Protestant *Revolt*." Nor can the modern secularist truly say he belongs to neither side and
feels the same way toward each. In the western
tradition, such non-Christians almost inevitably feel that Protestantism, if only because it
broke up medieval Catholic unity, is somehow
nearer to them, somehow prepared the way for
them. Inevitably, there are still alive the exag-

117

gerations, indeed the slanders, that emerged from the fierce partisan struggles of the times, notions such as that Luther led a revolt against the Church so that he, a monk, might marry; that the Catholic clergy actually *sold* salvation; that Henry VIII of England broke with the Pope so that he might marry Anne Boleyn; and many, many more.

The End of Medieval Formal Religious Unity

Protestant beginnings can be precisely dated, in the sense, for instance, that one can date the beginning of the American Revolution with the battles of Lexington and Concord, April 19, 1775. The great date is October 31, 1517, when the Augustinian monk Martin Luther nailed his Ninety-Five Theses to the door of the court church at Wittenberg in the German state of Saxony. The actual term "protestant" dates from April 19, 1529, when a group of German princes professing Lutheran doctrines lodged a formal "protest" at the Diet of Spires against the annulment of an earlier imperial decree. This decree had promised that a general council would consider the whole problem that Luther's activities had set. But of course the *origins* of the American Revolution go well back beyond the battle of Concord, and the origins of the Protestant movement go well back beyond Luther's Ninety-Five Theses. As we saw in Chapter 1, the medieval Catholic Church had faced many reform movements—the Cluniac, the Cistercian, the Franciscan, and, in the century or so before Luther, movements like those of Wiclif and Hus which had anticipated Protestant doctrines and had almost ended by setting up separate, or *schismatic,* religious bodies. The Conciliar Movement of the fifteenth century, though it failed to set general councils above the pope, brought into open discussion the question of papal authority.

The Protestant Reformation was, in fact, a major social, economic, and intellectual revolution. Leaders such as Luther and Calvin, let alone Henry VIII of England, can hardly have intended such a revolution; indeed, it is important for us to note that these leaders did not conceive themselves as initiators, as beginning *new* churches, but as going back to the true old Church.

The Reformation came in a time of great religious ferment, of economic change, of violence, uncertainty, even a sense of doom—in short, in times well described by the phrase of the distinguished Dutch historian Huizinga as "the autumn of the Middle Ages." Men everywhere were seeking something, characteristically not usually specific political or economic reforms, but something less readily definable or understandable by most of us today—spiritual salvation, renewal, the better world of Christian promise. Luther, notably, appealed from what he held to be existing evil to a potential—indeed, in men's souls already real—good. Hence the Lutheran appeal from *works,* from the conventions of established things, to *faith,* to something not evident to the outward eye, but there, inside us all, if we could but see it. Hence, too, much of the attractiveness to the religious temperament of many Protestant movements; the Protestants appealed from the spotted reality of the present to the promise of a better future, in heaven but also on earth.

Although Luther, when he posted his theses, had no clear intention of setting up a separate religious body, he did live to see a church, now called the Lutheran, organized outside the Catholic communion. The Lutheran was but the first of such Protestant churches or "denominations." Within the very generation that had seen the posting of the Ninety-Five Theses, there were organized dozens of them—Anglican, Calvinist, Anabaptist, and many others. The medieval unity of Catholic Christendom had given way to the multiplicity of churches we know so well that we often think such multiplicity "natural." In this country, churches, sometimes even Roman Catholic churches, have their denomination duly posted on signboards in front of them. In the Middle Ages this labeling would of course have been inconceivable, not so much because most people could not read as because no such labeling was necessary.

Luther
and the Ninety-Five Theses

Martin Luther (1483–1546) was a professor of divinity at the University of Wittenberg. When he posted his theses in 1517, he had recently experienced a great religious awakening, in effect a conversion, after a long period of spiritual despair. Luther's parents were peasants; his father, authoritarian in discipline as medieval fathers seemed to be, became a miner and in time a prosperous investor in a mining enterprise. He sent Martin to study law, but in 1505 the young man had a shattering experience. Caught in a severe thunderstorm, the terrified Luther prayed to Saint Anne for help and pledged himself to become a monk. Against his father's opposi-

Martin Luther, by Cranach (1525).

tion, he joined the order of Augustinian canons in fulfillment of his pledge and then soon found himself in a major personal crisis.

Luther was convinced that he was lost—literally lost, for as the distinguished psychologist Erik Erikson points out in his *Young*

Man Luther, modern depth psychology calls his an "identity crisis." None of Luther's good works, neither the monastic discipline of his order nor his pilgrimage in 1510 to Christian shrines in Rome, could free him of the gnawing feeling that he could not attain God's grace and was destined for the hell of lost souls. Finally, a wise confessor advised the desperate young man to study the Bible and to become a teacher of scripture. Through his reading in the Epistles of St. Paul and the writings of St. Augustine, Luther at last found a positive answer to his anxiety. The answer was that man should have faith in God, faith in the possibility of his own salvation. This answer had indeed long been the answer of the Roman Church; what later separated Luther doctrinally from this Church was his emphasis on *faith alone, to the exclusion of works.*

Fortified by his intense personal conviction of the great importance of faith, Luther questioned Catholic practices which in his view were abuses and tended to corrupt or weaken faith. He cast his questions in the form of the Ninety-Five Theses, written in Latin and in the manner of medieval Scholasticism as a challenge to academic debate. A casual observer who saw the manuscript on the door of the Wittenberg church might well have thought that here was another professor "sounding off." Yet this apparently academic exercise in Latin was the trigger-pull for revolution.

The specific abuse that Luther sought to prove un-Christian in the Ninety-Five Theses was what he called the "sale" of indulgences, and in particular, the activities of a talented ecclesiastical fund-raiser named Tetzel. In today's language, Tetzel was conducting a "campaign" or "drive" for voluntary contributions of money to help fill the treasury of a great institution, an institution which like the state possessed taxing powers, but which like many modern states could not in fact extend those taxing powers to keep up with the rising costs of an era of inflation and luxurious living. Tetzel was raising money to rebuild the great basilica of St. Peter's in Rome, and he had papal authorization for his campaign.

The theory of indulgences concerned the remission of the punishment of sins. Only

God can forgive a sin, but the repentant sinner also has to undergo punishment on earth in the form of penance and after death in purgatory, where sinners repentant on earth atone by temporary but painful punishment for their sins and are prepared for heaven. Indulgences could not assure the forgiveness of sins, according to the theory advanced by the medieval Schoolmen, but they could remit penance and part or all of the punishment in purgatory. The Church claimed authority to grant such remission by drawing on the Treasury of Merit, a storehouse of surplus good works accumulated by the holy activities of Christ, the Virgin, and the saints. Only the priest could secure for a layman a draft, as it were, on this heavenly treasury. The use of the word "sale" in connection with indulgences was a form of propaganda useful for the Protestants; the Catholics insist that indulgence was "granted" by the priest, and any monetary contribution thereupon made by the recipient was a free-will offering. The theory of indulgences, we may note, is of great theological subtlety. It is not a theory scientifically verifiable.

The doctrine of indulgences was thus a complex matter, too complex for the ordinary layman to grasp completely. To the man in the street in sympathy with the reformers, it must have looked as though a sinner could obtain not only remission of punishment but also forgiveness of sin if only he secured enough indulgences. Men like Tetzel, by making extravagant claims for the power of their indulgences, strengthened this popular feeling. Luther objected not only to Tetzel's perversion of indulgences but also to the whole doctrine behind them. He phrased his objections with great vehemence in the Ninety-Five Theses:

23. If any complete remission of penalties can be given to anyone it is sure that it can be given only to the most perfect; that is, to very few.
24. And therefore it follows that the greater part of the people is deceived by this indiscriminate and liberal promising of freedom from penalty.*

At the highest level of formal theological

*Documents of the Christian Church, Henry Bettenson, ed. (New York, 1947), 265.

thought, Luther's quarrel with his ecclesiastical superiors was over one of the oldest and most abiding tensions of Christian thought, the tension between faith and good works (see Chapter 1). Faith is inward and emotional belief, and good works are the *outward* demonstration of that belief expressed by doing good deeds, by partaking of the sacraments, and by submitting to the discipline of penances. Indulgences, certainly to the ordinary believer, permitted men to secure extra good works by drawing on those stored up in the Treasury of Merit. Now Christian practice usually insists on the need for *both* faith and good works. But at times of crisis some men pursue one extreme, others the other. In the years of crisis immediately after the posting of the Ninety-Five Theses, the challenged papal party stiffened into a resistance that in turn drove the Lutherans into further resistance. Moreover, Luther's own increasing hostility to things-as-they-were in his Germany drove him to emphasize things-as-they-ought-to-be—that is, drove him to minimize, and at his most excited moments to deny, the uses of the outward, the visible, the here-and-now which is works, earthly ecclesiastical organization, priestly ways of doing things; and to insist on the inward, the spiritual, the Church invisible which is faith.

Luther's Revolt

In Luther's personal spiritual struggle, as we have seen, faith had helped him immensely, and good works had helped him not at all. In the Ninety-Five Theses, he did not attack all works, but only those he felt to be wrong:

43. Christians are to be taught that to give to the poor or to lend to the needy is a better work than the purchase of pardons *i.e.,* indulgences.
44. And that because through a work of charity, charity is increased and a man advances in goodness; whereas through pardons there is no advance in goodness but merely an increased freedom from penalty.*

The theses, however, as our earlier quotation

*Ibid., 267.

from them shows, put great stress on the abuses, and Luther made some very harsh statements about the pope. Soon, under pressure of combat, Luther took a more extreme position on works: Men are saved by *faith alone*. Soon, he was driven to deny that the priest is at all necessary—that is, to the doctrine of the priesthood of all true believers, or, in our American phrase, the doctrine of "every man his own priest."

The Roman Church was quickly alerted to the high importance of the issues that Luther had raised. In 1518, at Augsburg, Luther was summoned before a papal legate, Cardinal Cajetan, and was directed to recant some of his propositions on indulgences; Luther defied the legate. In 1519, at Leipzig, a learned theologian, John Eck, taxed Luther in debate with disobeying the authoritative findings of popes and church councils. Luther denied that popes and councils were necessarily authoritative and, carrying his revolt further, explicitly declared adherence to some of Hus' teachings. These teachings had already been declared heretical by the Council of Constance. In 1520, Luther brought his defiance to its highest pitch by publishing a pamphlet, *The Appeal to the Christian Nobility of the German Nation,* which stated in part:

There has been a fiction by which the Pope, bishops, priests, and monks are called the 'spiritual estate'; princes, lords, artisans, and peasants are the 'temporal estate.' This is an artful lie and hypocritical invention, but let no one be made afraid by it, and that for this reason: that all Christians are truly of the spiritual estate, and there is no difference among them, save of office. As St. Paul says (1 Cor. xii), we are all one body, though each member does its own work so as to serve the others. This is because we have one baptism, one Gospel, one faith, and are all Christians alike; for baptism, Gospel, and faith, these alone make spiritual and Christian people.*

Luther's adherence to justification by faith alone had now led him to deny totally the central Catholic doctrine of works, that only the priest had the God-given power to secure for the layman remission of punishment for

*Documents, 274.

sin. In *The Appeal to the Christian Nobility* he swept aside the distinction between clergy and laity and declared the priesthood of all believers. The complete break between the rebel and the Church was now at hand. Late in 1520, Pope Leo X (1513–1521) issued a bull condemning Luther's teachings; Luther burnt the bull. In 1521, Luther was excommunicated and made an outlaw, the political equivalent, or rather, consequence, of being excommunicated. The Emperor Charles V and the imperial diet passed the sentence of outlawry in a most dramatic session at Worms. Luther was asked, once again, if he would recant. His reply contained his most famous words:

Your Imperial Majesty and Your Lordships demand a simple answer. Here it is, plain and unvarnished. Unless I am convicted of error by the testimony of Scripture or (since I put not trust in the unsupported authority of Pope or of councils, since it is plain that they have often erred and often contradicted themselves) by manifest reasoning I stand convicted by the Scriptures to which I have appealed, and my conscience is taken captive by God's word, I cannot and will not recant anything, for to act against our conscience is neither safe for us, nor open to us.

Hier stehe ich. Ich kann nicht anders. Gott helff mir. Amen. [On this I take my stand. I can do no other. God help me. Amen..*

The empire and the papacy took their drastic actions in vain. Luther was already gathering a substantial following and becoming a national hero. He had the protection of the ruler of his own German state, the Elector Frederick the Wise of Saxony (1463–1525), and was soon to secure the backing of other princes. In the next few years he translated the Bible into vigorous and effective German and remodeled the church in Saxony according to his own views. His revolt was a success.

The Reasons for Luther's Success

More than theology was at issue in Luther's revolt. The Catholic Church that Luther at-

*Ibid., 285.

tacked was, as many Catholic historians grant, at the time in one of its more worldly states. Especially in its center at Rome, it had come under the influence of the half-pagan Renaissance. New wealth had come to Italy, and new fashions of good living. The papacy, triumphant over the councils, had been drawn into Italian politics (see Chapter 2). The Rome Luther visited in his younger days was a shocking spectacle of intrigue, display, and corruption. Some part of Luther's success lies in the fact that he was attacking practices revolting to decent men.

There is a second great reason for his success: in the name of good Germans he was attacking the practices of Italians and Italianate Germans. Tetzel was in the eyes of Luther and his followers not only extending an abuse theologically and morally outrageous; the money he was raising was going to enrich Italy, and that was one more step in the exploitation of Germans by Italians.

> For Rome is the greatest thief and robber that has ever appeared on earth, or ever will. . . . Poor Germans that we are—we have been deceived! We were born to be masters, and we have been compelled to bow the head beneath the yoke of our tyrants. . . . It is time the glorious Teutonic people should cease to be the puppet of the Roman pontiff.*

In terms that come naturally to us today, the nationalistic and economic factors present in the Lutheran movement help explain its success. Notice especially Luther's statement that Germans were born to be masters. But a word of warning is necessary. These political and economic factors *help* explain Lutheran success; they do not in and of themselves wholly account for it. As always in human affairs, ideas and ideals worked together with material interests and powerful emotions such as patriotism to move the men of the Reformation.

The princes who supported Luther stood to gain financially, not only by the cessation of the flow of German money to Italy, but by the confiscation of Catholic property, especially monastic property, which was not needed for

Documents, 278–279.

the new Lutheran cult for it would not have monastic orders. Luther gave them a new weapon in the eternal struggle against their feudal overlord, the emperor. The princes were also moved by Luther's German patriotism. Some, like Frederick the Wise of Saxony, sympathized with many of his ideas. Philip of Hesse found Luther helpful in a very personal problem concerning his relations with women: he had decided on the somewhat un-Christian and indeed unpromising solution of trying bigamy. Though Luther did not precisely like this solution, he condoned it, much to the salving of Philip's conscience.

Nor must Luther's personality be left out of account. It is true enough that what he started was soon taken out of his hands by the German princes who joined the reform movement in part to strengthen their political power against the emperor, and to strengthen their treasuries by confiscating the possessions of the Catholic Church. Yet Lutheranism without Luther is inconceivable, save perhaps to single-minded devotees of the economic interpretation of history. He wrote the pamphlets that did for this revolution what Tom Paine and the Declaration of Independence did for ours. He put his *Appeal to the Christian Nobility of the German Nation* in the vernacular German, not the academic Latin, so that it became a "best-seller" overnight. Note that printing at this time first made possible wide popular dissemination of ideas. Luther's defiance of the papal legate Cajetan, of the papal champion Eck, and of the Pope himself—indeed all his actions—helped to focus German sentiments on what was, though not of course on our contemporary scale, already a mass movement influenced by mass media. Luther's translation of the Bible made that book a part of German life, and made Luther's language one of the bases of modern literary German. His marriage to a former nun and his raising of a large family dramatized the break with Rome. And back of all this was Luther's passionate conviction that he was doing what he had to do: *"Ich kann nicht anders."*

Moreover, Luther's doctrine of justification by faith alone has been, as we have noted, attractive to many religious dispositions. St.

Paul at the very beginnings of Christianity set up the contrast between the Spirit—invisible, in a sense private to the believer—and the Letter—only too visible, only too public. Established churches have always tended to balance spirit and letter, invisible and visible, internal and external, faith and works; but to the ardent, crusading Christian even a working successful balance of this sort seems a yielding to a gross materialism. He will have none of this compromise, but will imperiously assert the primacy of the spirit. In Luther's day, the established Roman Church had lost its medieval balance; the world was too much with it. The Lutheran felt the new church offered him something he could not get in the old.

The Opposition to Luther

A final reason for Luther's success—and this may well be true of revolutionary movements generally—lay in the relative weakness of the forces that opposed him. The opposition can be divided into the religious and the political, though the two were really inseparably connected. Religious opposition centered in the top levels of the Catholic bureaucracy; Pope Leo X did not so much head it as prove its willing instrument. Moderate Catholics, anxious to compromise and avert a schism, existed both within the Church and on its margin among the humanist scholars of the Renaissance. It is tempting to agree with the great liberal Catholic historian, Lord Acton, that had there been at the head of the Catholic Church a pope willing to reform in order to conserve, willing to make concessions that did not destroy the basic position of the Church as God's chosen instrument on earth, even Luther might have been reconciled. Luther's ablest associate, Melanchthon, was a moderate. Yet the historian can hardly avoid comparing this revolution with other great modern revolutions, the English, the French, the Russian, and noting that in all of them the moderates—gifted, numerous, and active though they were—could not hold up against the extremists. Once Leo X had excommunicated Luther in 1520, the way to compromise was

The Pope in Hell: anti-papal German woodcut, 1521.

probably blocked, for Luther's associates could have been won away from him only by concessions too great for a Catholic to make.

Politically, the opposition in these critical early years centered in the young Emperor Charles V, who came to the imperial throne in 1519. Charles of Habsburg was the fruit of a series of marriages that gave rise to the famous epigram: "Let others wage war; thou, happy Austria, marry." The combined inheritance of his Austrian father and Spanish mother made Charles ruler of the German Empire, the Low Countries, Spain, the Spanish Indies, Hungary, and parts of Italy. This looks on the map like the nearest thing to a real European superstate since Charlemagne, and Charles wanted very much to make it such a state in reality. The activities of Luther's princely German supporters seemed to him a threat to his hold over Germany, and might in themselves have sufficed to turn him against Luther. But Charles, though by no means a mere papal instrument, was by upbringing a good conventional Catholic, in no state of mind to throw his great influence on the side of the moderate group within the Catholic Church. He decided to fight—and had to fight the rest of his reign, thus gainsaying the famous epigram about his house.

Charles V entrusted the government of the Germans to his younger brother Ferdinand, who formed alliances with Bavaria and other Catholic German states to oppose the Lutheran states. Thus began a long series of alliances and combinations within the Germanies, the fruits of which were the religious wars of the next few generations, and the territorial divison of Germany into, roughly, a Protestant north and east and a Catholic south and west, which has endured to this day (see Chapter 5). The fact that Charles himself did not directly lead the fight in Germany gives another clue to the success of the Protestant movement in breaking down the unity of western Christendom. Charles had too many other fights on his hands to concentrate on Germany. His huge inheritance was a threat to the only remaining great power on the continent, France, which moreover was still committed to the Italian adventures Charles VIII had begun (see p. 157). Four general wars between Charles V and Francis I of France, really one great war, prevented anything like the forcible suppression of the German Protestants by imperial Habsburg power.

The Lutheran Church

Thus far, Luther has appeared in the role of the great revolutionary. But on some issues he also took a fundamentally conservative stand. He did not, for example, push his doctrines of justification by faith and the priesthood of all believers to their logical extreme, which is anarchy. If religion is wholly a matter between each man and his maker, an organized church becomes unneccesary if not impossible, or else there are as many churches as there are individuals. Reformers inspired by Luther, but more

radical, attempted to apply these anarchical concepts to the churches of Saxony; the consequences were immense confusion and popular unrest. Luther and his moderate followers who had no sympathy with such anarchistic experiments, intervened in Saxony. They organized a church that permitted its clergy to marry, but that did possess ordained clergymen, ritual, dogmas, even some sacraments—a whole apparatus of good works. To a skeptical outsider, even the Lutheran "faith alone, scripture alone, grace alone" is a formula, and can stand on the Letter side as well as on the Spirit side of Saint Paul's famous phrase.

And, most important for us to understand, the Lutherans did not found this church as an alternative choice to the Roman Catholic, but as the *one true church*. Where a Lutheran church was founded, a Catholic church ceased to be; indeed, the Lutherans commonly just took over the church building. Stimulated by Luther and his clerical and academic disciples, this process at first went on among the people of Germany almost spontaneously, without the intervention of political leaders.

But very soon the lay rulers of certain of the half-independent, or rather nine-tenths independent, German states took a hand. In Saxony, in Hesse, soon in most of northern Germany, princes and their ministers superintended and hastened the process of converting the willing to Lutheranism, and evicting the unwilling. A similar process went on in the Scandinavian countries. Here, as so often in any process of change, the formula "either . . . or" does not serve well for sensible interpretation. The Lutheran Church was not invented by Luther and the princes and foisted on the people; nor on the other hand was it solely the spontaneous work of the German and Scandinavian peoples. *Both* people and princes had a share in the complex process of the Protestant Reformation.

Knights' War
and Peasants' Rebellion

It was not only the great and near-great German princes who took advantage of the

Lutheran movement to assert themselves. Just beneath the princes, lay and ecclesiastical, in the German social pyramid and like them a legacy of the Middle Ages were the knights, the lesser nobility. Some of them held a castle and a few square miles direct from the emperor, and were in theory as "independent" as an Elector of Saxony; others were simply minor feudal lords. Many were younger sons, landless but still gentlemen, who could hardly have a career save that of arms. The class as a whole was caught in the squeeze of rising prices and the need for maintaining aristocratic standards of living. Luther's challenge to the established order, above all the chance it seemed to give for taking over ecclesiastical holdings, was too good an opportunity for many of these knights to miss. Under the leadership of Ulrich von Hutten and Franz von Sickingen, they rose in 1522 in what is called the "Knights' War." They were put down by the bigger lords, but only after a struggle, and their rising added to the confusion of the time.

The really bitter social struggle of the early German Reformation was the Peasants' Re-

Rebelling German peasants, 1525.

bellion of 1524–25. Now peasant risings were not unknown in the Middle Ages. In many ways, the German rising resembles the peasant revolts of the fourteenth century in England and France (see Chapter 2). Like them, it was directed against the burdens of the manorial system; like them, it lacked coordination and effective military organization and was cruelly put down by the possessing classes who did have command over military power. Like them, too, it was a rising, not of peasants who were in the very lowest state of oppression, but of peasants who were beginning to enjoy some gain from the slowly rising standards of living of medieval society, who had enough to know they wanted more. The German Peasants' Rebellion centered not in those eastern parts of the country where serfdom was most complete, where the status of the peasant was lowest, but in the southwestern parts where the peasant had at least the beginnings of the status of a landowning farmer.

Yet in one very important respect this sixteenth-century German rising looks more modern, more democratic, than its medieval counterparts in western Europe. Even more clearly than the English Peasants' Revolt, which had been influenced by Wiclif and the Lollards, it was led by educated men who were not themselves peasants and who had a program, a set of revolutionary ideas of what the new social structure should be. Their leaders drew up a set of demands known as the "Twelve Articles," which were given various regional forms. They are generally moderate enough, and are usually couched in Biblical language, which shows clearly their relation to the Reformation. Important articles demanded that each parish have the right to choose its own priest, that the tithes paid to the clergy and the dues paid to the lord be reduced, and that the peasants be allowed to take game and wood from the forests.

Luther's reaction to the Peasants' Rebellion was thoroughly conservative. He was horified at what the peasants' leaders had found in the Bible he had translated into German so that they might read it. He turned against them, directing at them impassioned abuse that sounds even stronger than his abuse of the Catholics. From this time on, he turned definitely to the princes, and the church he founded became itself an established church, respectful toward civil authority. Luther indeed is quoted in his *Table Talk* as saying: "The princes of the world are gods, the common people are Satan."

In fairness to Luther, it may be said that his conservatism in social, economic, and political matters is by no means inconsistent with his fundamental spiritual position. For if the visible, external world is really wholly subordinate to the invisible, spiritual world, the most one can hope for in this world of politics is that it be kept in as good orderliness, in as little imperfection as possible so that the spiritual may thrive. Authority, custom, law, existing institutions combine to provide this orderliness. Kings and princes are better for this wretched world than democratically chosen representatives of the people; obedience better than discussion.

Luther's conservative views on social and political questions had two important results. First, he won increasing support from kings and princes. By the mid-sixteenth century, Lutheranism had become the state religion in most of the principalities of northern Germany and in the Scandinavian kingdoms, Sweden and Denmark, together with the Danish dependency of Norway. The Scandinavian monarchs, in particular, appear to have been attracted to the Reformation for secular reasons, for the opportunities it presented to curb unruly bishops and confiscate monastic wealth. Second, it is hardly surprising that after the Peasants' Rebellion the initiative in the Protestant movement passed to other hands than those of the Lutherans.

II Protestant Origins: Zwingli, Calvin, and Other Founders

As we have seen (Chapter 2), there were in the fourteenth and fifteenth centuries movements like those of Wiclif in England and Hus in Bohemia, to say nothing of earlier revolts against the worldly success of the Church, which anticipate the Protestantism of the sixteenth century. Moreover, many of the things that had troubled Luther had long been troubling his contemporaries in Germany, France, England, and elsewhere. The great Dutch humanist Erasmus (see Chapter 3), the Englishman Thomas More (author of *Utopia*), the Frenchman Lefèvre d'Etaples, and many others condemned the worldliness and corruption of the Church and the over-subtleties of late Scholasticism. They had been seeking in their writing and preaching for a renewal of evangelical Christianity, for a return to what most of them held to be an earlier and better faith that had somehow gone wrong. Many of these reform-minded men wanted the Catholic Church to be reformed from within. They were shocked by Luther's intransigent revolt, and sought to tame the movement he had unloosed. Others, however, went on to a break more complete in many ways than Luther's. Of these other main founders of Protestantism the first in time was Zwingli and the first in importance was Calvin.

Zwingli

Almost contemporaneously with Luther's spectacular revolt, another German, Ulrich Zwingli (1484–1531), had begun in Switzerland a quieter reform, one that produced no great single organized church, but that nevertheless extended and deepened some of the fundamental theological and moral conceptions of Protestantism, and had a wide influence on the less "enthusiastic," less "fundamentalist," forms of Protestantism. Zwingli was a scholarly humanist trained in the tradition of Erasmus. Like Luther, he sought to combat what seemed to him the perversion of primitive Christianity that made the consecrated priest an agent, indeed a sharer, of a miraculous power not possessed by the layman. But, where the doctrine of the priesthood of the true believer drove the emotional Luther to the edge of anarchism, the humanistic Zwingli saw that individuals might achieve a common national discipline that would promote righteous living. This discipline would arise from the social conscience of enlightened and emancipated people led by their pastors.

Zwingli believed in a personal God and in the miraculous origin of the Christian religion. Indeed, his God was a highly transcendental one, so powerful, so real, and yet so far above this petty world of sense experience that to Zwingli he was not to be approached by mere sacraments. Hence Zwingli is fundamentally, basically, anti-sacramental in a way Luther was not. Hence Zwingli distrusted what many Protestants feel is the continuous appeal of the Catholics to "superstition," to belief in saints, to the use of images, to incense and candles, and of course to indulgences. Zwingli began the process of making the church building an almost undecorated hall, of making the service a sermon and responsive reading, of abolishing the Catholic liturgy. He thus started on the way toward the puritanical simplicity of the later Calvinists.

A good concrete example of Zwingli's attitude is his doctrine of the Eucharist. The Catholic doctrine of *transubstantiation* holds that by the miraculous power of the priest the elements, the bread and the wine, become in *substance* the body and blood of Christ, although their *accidents,* their make-up as far as chemistry or indeed common sense sees them, remain those of bread and wine. Luther stubbornly refused to eliminate the miraculous completely, and adhered to a difficult and confusing compromise doctrine called *consubstantiation.* Zwingli, however, went all the way to what is the usual Protestant doctrine that when we partake of the elements in communion we are indeed commemorating Christ's last supper with his disciples, but only in a symbolic way. We are not, in short, sharing through a sacrament in a miracle; we are merely sharing anew the eternal memory of Christ's stay on earth.

Calvin

Zwingli attracted adherents in the German-speaking parts of Switzerland. The independent French Swiss city of Geneva came under the domination of the French-born Jean Cauvin (1509–1564), better known in the Latin form of his name as Calvin. Under Calvin, the Protestant movement was shaped as a faith, a way of life, that gave it a European and not merely a German and Scandinavian basis. The historian finds it useful to take Calvinism as the middle—to borrow a political term, the center—of Protestant beliefs. In Germany and Scandinavia the Lutherans, and in England the Anglican Church, remained in doctrine what we may call to the right of Calvinism. In England, the Low Countries, and Germany there

Ulrich Zwingli (1484–1531).

grew up radical sects like the Anabaptists, to whom we shall shortly come, who were to the left of Calvinism.

With the moral and theological ideas of Calvin we shall deal in the next section of this chapter. Here we may note that in his *Institutes of the Christian Religion,* published in 1536, he laid a firm doctrinal basis for a Protestantism that, like Zwingli's, breaks completely with Catholic church organization and with Catholic ritual. Calvin had been trained as a lawyer. His system had a logical rigor and completeness that gave it great conviction. He had also a base from which to work, a town that was to become a Protestant Rome, Geneva, where after a temporary rejection in 1538 he returned in 1541 to organize his City of God. To Geneva came Protestant refugees from many parts of Europe, there to receive indoctrination in Calvin's faith, and to return, sometimes at the risk of their lives, to spread the word in their own countries. Within a generation or two, Calvinism had spread to Scotland, where it was led by a great preacher and organizer, John Knox; to England, whence it was brought to Plymouth in New England; to the Low Countries; and even to Hungary and Poland.

In the Low Countries, Calvinism had by the second half of the sixteenth century found a foothold, especially in cities like Antwerp. The Low Countries, both north and south, belonged to the Burgundian inheritance of Charles V, and passed to his heir, the austerely ardent Catholic Philip II. When Philip attempted to suppress the revolt of the Netherlands, the patriotism of the Dutch in the northern provinces was welded together with Calvinism into one of the firmest of spiritual alloys—a metal which resisted heavy Spanish pressures (see Chapter 5).

In France—where the intellectual classes have long been very serious-minded, and not at all as common opinion conceives Frenchmen, gay and irresponsible—concern over the worldliness of the Catholic Church was strong. From Jean Gerson, one of the leaders of the Conciliar Movement, to Lefèvre d'Etaples, Frenchmen had been seeking ways of reform. Calvin's ideas found ready acceptance among many Frenchmen, and soon there were organized Protestant churches especially in the southwest, called Huguenot (perhaps a corruption of a German word, *Eidgenossen,* "covenanted"). But France was a centralized monarchy. King Francis I (1515–1547) was not anxious, as so many of the German princes were, to stir up trouble with Rome. In 1516, he had signed with the Pope the Concordat of Bologna, an agreement that increased the royal authority over the Gallican Church. In the mid-sixteenth century, only a very few intellectuals could even conceive of the possibility of citizens or subjects of the *same* political unit professing and practicing *different* religious faiths. Protestantism in France had to fight, not for toleration, but to succeed Catholicism as the established religion of Frenchmen. The attempt failed, but only after the long hard struggle of the French wars of religion, only after Protestantism had left its mark on the French conscience (see Chapter 5).

The English Reformation

In strict chronology, the first great sixteenth-century religious overturn outside the Germanies was in England. The signal, the starting point, for the English Reformation was something very different from the Ninety-Five Theses of Luther. It was the desire of King Henry VIII (1509–1547) to put aside his wife, Catherine of Aragon, who had given him no male heir. The house of Tudor had only recently achieved the Crown, and Henry felt more strongly than was usual even in those days that a male heir was essential. He rested his case on the fact that Catherine had been married to his deceased brother Arthur, and that marriage with a deceased brother's widow is against canon law. Henry's case was hardly strengthened by the circumstance that he had taken nearly twenty years to discover the existence of this impediment. Moreover, Catherine was aunt to the Emperor Charles V, whom the Pope could scarcely risk offending by granting an annulment. Nevertheless Henry tried hard, through his minister Cardinal Wolsey, who was dismissed in disgrace for his failure. Henry then put his case to universities in England and on the Continent, and got a few favorable replies. Finally, he married Anne Boleyn, and Cranmer, the obliging Archbishop of Canterbury whom Henry had recently appointed, pronounced an annulment of the marriage with Catherine (it was not, as is frequently represented, a *divorce*). The Pope excommunicated Henry and declared the annulment invalid. Henry's answer was the Act of Supremacy in 1534, which set the king up as supreme head of the Church in England.

Much more than the private life of Henry VIII was involved in this English Reformation. Henry could not have secured the Act of Supremacy and other Protestant legislation from Parliament if there had not been a considerable body of English opinion favorable to the breach with Rome, particularly among the sizable and prosperous middle classes. Antipapal sentiment, which was an aspect of English nationalism, had long existed; it had motivated the fourteenth-century statutes of Edward III, which most certainly limited the right of the pope to intervene in the affairs of the English church. Anticlericalism went back to the days of Wiclif; in the days of Henry VIII it was aimed particularly at the monasteries, which were still wealthy landowners but had become corrupt since their great medieval days. In the eyes of many Englishmen, the monasteries had outlived their purpose and needed to be reformed or indeed abolished. Moreover, the ideas of Luther and other continental Protestants quickly won a sympathetic hearing in England. Many English scholars were in touch with continental reformers; one of them, Tindal, studied with Luther and published an English translation of the New Testament in 1526.

Henry VIII sponsored measures in addition to the Act of Supremacy which found favor with Protestant opinion in England. Most important, he closed the monasteries, confiscated their property, and distributed much of the loot among the nobility, the country gentry, and some of the rising merchant class. Historians seeking always a simple economic mo-

Henry VIII, by Holbein.

tivation have no doubt exaggerated the importance of the dissolution of monasteries. Still, there is no doubt that Tudor England enjoyed a high rate of economic growth, and the dislocations that often accompany growth. The dissolution of the monasteries was clearly one of the factors in this process. Henry gave influential subjects good reason to be grateful to him and to the Tudor dynasty. Moreover, this policy, by increasing the wealth of the landed aristocracy, amounted to a social and economic revolution. It is another illustration of how closely the religious and the secular threads were interwoven in the Reformation.

Yet Henry VIII did not really consider himself a Protestant. The church set up by the Act of Supremacy was in his eyes—and remains today in the eyes of some of its communicants—a Catholic body. Henry hoped to retain Catholic doctrines and ritual, doing no more than abolish monasteries and deny the pope's position as head of the Church in England. Inevitably, his policies aroused opposition. Part of that opposition was Roman Catholic, for some Englishmen greatly resented the break with Rome. And part, the more pressing and the larger part, was militantly Protestant. Hardly had Henry given the signal for the break with Rome when groups began even within the new Church of England to introduce such Protestant practices as marriage of the clergy, use of English instead of Latin in the ritual, abolition of auricular confession, abolition of the invocation of saints.

Henry used force against the Catholic opposition, and executed some of its leaders, notably Thomas More. He tried to stem the Protestant tide by appealing to a willing Parliament, many members of which were enriched by the spoliation of the Catholic Church. In 1539, Parliament passed the statute of the Six Articles, reaffirming transubstantiation, celibacy of the priesthood, confession, and other Catholic doctrines and ritual, and making their denial heresy. By this definition, indeed by almost any possible definition, there were far too many heretics to be repressed. The patriotic Englishman was against Rome and all its works. England from now on was to be a great center of religious variation and experimentation, much (though not all) of it peaceful. The Church of England, substantially more Protestant, less like the Roman Catholic, than Henry had intended, became a kind of central national core of precarious orthodoxy.

The Anabaptists

One major item is left to consider in this survey of Protestant origins. Socially and intellectually less "respectable" than the soon-established Lutheran and Anglican churches, or the rapidly sobered Calvinists, was a whole group of radical sects, the left wing of the Protestant revolution. In the sixteenth century, most of them were known loosely as Anabaptists, from the Greek for "baptizing again." Some of Zwingli's followers had come to hold that the Catholic sacrament of baptism of infants had no validity, since the infant could not possibly be said to "believe" or "understand." Here again the relation to Luther's basic doctrine of faith as a direct relation between the believer and God is clear — only for the Anabaptist it is a relation of rational understanding by the believer; here also can be seen one of the clearest elements of much Protestantism, an appeal to individual "reason" or "understanding." Yet note carefully that this appeal is not to "scientific" or "common-sense" reason, as it was to be with the eighteenth-century Enlightenment; and it is an appeal to reason that in these wilder sects is in fact quite congruous with very excited, "enthusiastic," evangelical practices, indeed, with what Americans know as "holy rolling."

The Anabaptists in these early years "baptized again" when the believer could hold that he was voluntarily joining the company of the elect. Later generations were never baptized until they came of age, so the prefix "ana" was dropped, and we have the familiar Baptists of our time. The Anabaptists split under the pressure of persecution and with the spread of private reading of the Bible. Indeed, for some Catholic observers, the proliferation of Protestant sects seems due inevitably to the Protestant practice of seeking in the Bible for an authority they refused to find in the established dogmas of Catholic authority. The Bible is — from the historian's point of view — a complex record of several thousand years of Jewish history, and it contains an extraordinary variety of religious experience from rigorous ritual to intense emotional commitment and mystical surrender. Especially the apocalyptic books of the Old Testament and the Revelation of St. John the Divine of the New can be made to yield almost anything a lively imagination wants to find. Many of the leaders of these new sects were uneducated men with a sense of grievance against the established order, proletarians in not quite the Marxist sense. They were seeking to bring heaven to earth, quickly.

Their best-known early manifestation in the Reformation gave the conservatives and moderates as great a shock as had the German Peasants' Rebellion, in which these same radical religious ideas had also played a large part. In the mid-1530's, a group of Anabaptists under the leadership of John of Leyden, a Dutch tailor, got control of the city of Münster in Germany, and set up a Biblical Utopia. They were put down by force, their leaders executed, and the faithful dispersed. We know about them chiefly from their opponents, who certainly exaggerated their doctrines and practices. Still, even if we allow for the distortions of propaganda, it seems clear that the Anabaptists of Münster were behaving in ways that western traditions do not permit large groups to adopt. For one thing, they preached, and apparently practiced, polygamy. They pushed the Lutheran doctrine of justification by faith to its logical extreme in anarchism, or in theological language, *antinomianism,* from the Greek "against law." Each man was to be his own law, or rather, to find God's universal law in his own conscience, not in *written* law and tradition. They did not believe in class distinctions or in the customary forms of private property. They were disturbers of an established order that was strong enough to put them down.

The great majority of Anabaptists were very far from being such wild fanatics as the men of Münster. Many Anabaptist groups sought to bring the Christian life to earth in quieter and more constructive ways. They established communities where they lived as they thought the primitive Christians had lived, in brotherhood, working, sharing, and praying together. These communities bore many resemblances to monasteries, though their members had taken no vows and did not observe celibacy. As we shall see in the next section of this chapter, some of the Anabaptist ideas—quietism, asceticism, the high sense of community—made a lasting contribution to the Protestant tradition. This sober majority of Anabaptists, too, met violent persecution in the sixteenth century. But something of their spirit lives on today in such diverse groups as the Baptists, the Quakers, the Hutterites of

How Anabaptists were reported to carry on: May-dance at Münster, 1535.

Canada, and the Mennonites and the Amish of the Pennsylvania "Dutch."

Unitarianism

A Protestant strain close to Anabaptism was that of Unitarianism, the denial of the Trinity and of the full divinity of Christ. Today, Unitarianism is usually identified with the rejection of the Trinity on the grounds that it is an irrational concept and with the view that Christ was simply a particularly inspired human being. But this version of Unitarianism derives largely from the rationalistic Enlightenment of the eighteenth century. Sixteenth-century Unitarianism was a very different matter and much more mystical in outlook. Its most famous advocate, the Spanish physician Servetus (1511–1553), believed that though Christ was not eternal, he was indeed the Son of God. His concept made Christ, as it were, less removed from man but not less removed from God. Thereby Servetus hoped to make it easier for humanity to acquire a mystic identification with Christ and thus to achieve salvation.

Even this mystic doctrine of Unitarianism greatly alarmed not only Catholics but also many Protestants. Servetus was finally prosecuted for heresy at Geneva by Calvin himself and burnt at the stake in 1553. The doctrines of Servetus, however, contributed to the teachings of another Unitarian, Socinus (in Italian, Sozzini, 1539–1604). This far-traveling Italian theologian gained a considerable following among the peoples of eastern Europe, particularly in Poland, Hungary, and Transylvania. The Socinians, too, suffered vigorous persecution at the hands of both Catholics and Protestants, but they were never to be fully stamped out.

III   Protestant Beliefs and Practices

Common Denominators

It is very difficult to establish a common denominator for Protestant beliefs. Henry VIII (who almost certainly never thought of himself as a Protestant), Luther, Zwingli, Calvin, John of Leyden, and Servetus make a most disparate group. Obviously they all, even the Anglican High Churchmen, repudiated the claim of the Roman Catholic Church to be the one true faith. They were all hostile to the Church of Rome.

One other generalization is almost as universally valid, if less obvious today. In these early days, each Protestant sect was convinced that it was the one true faith, that it and not Rome was the true successor of Christ and his apostles. Even the Antinomians, who believed that each man carried the truth in his own bosom, believed that if all the perversions that custom, education, and bad environment generally had set up as obstacles to the penetration of truth were swept away, each man would find the *same* truth in his bosom. Some early Protestants held that, though their own belief was the sole true belief, its ultimate prevailing on earth must be the slow process of educating men, of convincing them, of converting them. Others, however, could not wait for this slow process. Though they had once been persecuted themselves, they did not hesitate to persecute in their turn when they rose to power. Witness Calvin's condemnation of Servetus.

At this point, indeed, it must be emphasized that what we nowadays in the United States accept as normal—that is, the peaceful co-existence of many different churches, "freedom of religion," "separation of Church and State"—were certainly not normal, widespread concepts in the sixteenth-century, nor even in the seventeenth-century, western world. Religious toleration itself is a complex matter, based at one extreme on mere opportunism (the sheer impossibility of bringing the sects together) and at the other extreme on a belief that religious divergences are in themselves good, and toleration a positive benefit for all.

Only with the late seventeenth- and early eighteenth-century Enlightenment did the doctrine of religious toleration emerge into *full* prominence; and in that period many "enlightened" individuals were essentially nonbelievers in Christianity, for whom toleration was a way of letting Christianity wither on the vine. Nevertheless, the era of the Renaissance and Reformation saw the gradual emergence of a characteristic form of positive belief in religious toleration—that is, the belief that although there *is indeed* a single true religion which men may one day find, each man must find his own way to it freely, unforced by any external pressures. Therefore there must be no established church, no enforced conformity, no persecution. Many humanists held this view. One of them, Sebastian Castellio, or Châteillon, wrote in 1554 a book in Latin on "whether heretics are to be persecuted," attacking Calvin for the execution of Servetus in 1553. In this book one may discern clearly the positive doctrine of religious toleration: force must never be used to attempt to change a man's ideas about religion. But, as the experience of Roger Williams in seventeenth-century New England was to show, such ideas were only very slowly accepted in the western world. As denial of the wisdom and rightness of actual persecution, religious toleration is now firmly established in the West; there is still debate as to whether religious variation, and religious indifference, are in themselves good.

Finally, even the conservative established churches of the Reformation—the Anglican and the Lutheran—shared with the more radical Protestants certain reductions in ritual and other external manifestations of belief. All reduced somewhat the seven sacraments of the Catholic church; a general Protestant minimum was to retain baptism and communion. But the Protestant theological justification of these sacraments could range very widely, from Luther's consubstantiation to the symbolic view of the Eucharist, from an almost Roman *acceptance* of the miraculous to an almost secularist *denial* of the miraculous. Veneration of saints, pilgrimages, rosaries, amulets, and such "papist" practices disappeared even among the right-wing Protestants; the left wing also banished music, painting, indeed all the arts except the oratorical arts.

To these outward signs there corresponds an inner link that ties Protestantism together, loosely indeed, and often uncomfortably. All Protestants were rebels in origin. They had *protested* almost always in the name of an older, purer, primitive church, almost always maintaining that *Rome* was the real innovator, the wicked revolutionist. (This attempt of the rebel not to seem to be rebelling, his appeal to the past as legitimatizing his revolt, often recurs in western history.) The Protestants had appealed from an established order to a "higher law" not concretely established in the flesh, in institutions, on this earth. That is to say, all Protestantism has at least a tinge of the Lutheran appeal from works to faith, in the terms of St. Paul, from the "Letter" of the law to the "Spirit"; it has at least a tinge of *individualism*. This individualism is what early Protestantism bequeathed to the modern world.

The divergent beliefs of the separate Protestant churches may most conveniently be arranged in order of their theological distance from Roman Catholicism, beginning with those nearest Rome. But it must be noted that the political and social distance is not always the same as the theological.

Anglicanism

The Church of England, as we have already noted, contains communicants who think of themselves as Catholics; they represent the "High Church" point of view. But the Church of England also includes members who take a "Low Church" view; they are more Protestant in outlook, and some come very close to being Unitarians. The Church of England keeps a modified form of the Catholic hierarchy, with archbishops and bishops, though of course without acknowledging the authority of the pope. On the other hand, it permits its clergy to marry and, although it does nowadays have religious orders, it does not put anything like the Catholic emphasis on the regular clergy. Indeed, historically speaking, the Church of England has somehow managed to contain elements from almost the whole range of Protestant belief, though Anglicans have not been very cordial toward the more publicly demonstrative types of Protestantism, toward "holy rolling."

Perhaps the central core of Anglicanism has been a tempered ritualism, a tempered belief in hierarchy, in discipline from above, a tempered acceptance of this imperfect world—a moderate attitude really not very far from the Catholicism of St. Thomas Aquinas. Indeed, Richard Hooker, who wrote a great defense of the Anglican Church in the 1590's (*The Laws of Ecclesiastical Polity*), relied heavily on Aquinas. It is significant, too, that Hooker is usually called "the judicious Hooker," because of his efforts to reconcile divergent points of view and adjust them to Anglicanism.

On the other hand, there has also always been a strong puritanical or evangelical current in the broad stream of Anglicanism. The Puritans for the most part only reluctantly left the Anglican communion in the late sixteenth and early seventeenth century, and many of them stayed within it. This is not so much what later became the "Low Church" strain in Anglicanism or, in America, Episcopalianism, as it is a strain of earnest, evangelical piety, social service, plain living and high thinking—in short, Puritanism.

The Church of England assumed its definitive form during the reign of Henry VIII's daughter, Elizabeth I (1558–1603). The Thirty-Nine Articles enacted by Parliament in 1563 were a kind of constitution for the Church. They illustrate the essential conservatism of the Anglican Church and the compromises on which it is founded. The Thirty-Nine Articles rejected the more obvious forms of Romanism—the use of Latin, auricular confession, clerical celibacy, the allegiance to the pope. The thirtieth article took a firm Protestant stand on one of the great symbolic

points at issue. The Church of England gave communion in both kinds, both wine and bread, to the laymen, whereas the Catholic Church gave only the bread. Yet the articles also sought to compromise on some of the greater issues, and notably to avoid the anarchistic dangers of the doctrines of justification by faith and the priesthood of the believer. The article on the Lord's Supper was firm in its rejection of Catholic transubstantiation, but equally firm in its rejection of Zwinglian symbolism; the Anglican really was to receive the Eucharist as the body and blood of Christ.

The Church of England has always seemed to its enemies, and even to some of its friends, a bit too acquiescent in face of civil authority. In what was once a word of abuse, the Church of England has seemed *Erastian*. The term comes from the name of a sixteenth-century Swiss theologian and physician named Erastus (not to be confused with the Dutch humanist Erasmus), who by no means held the doctrine attributed to him. This doctrine in the abusive sense—and it has hardly any other—holds that the State is all-powerful against the Church, that the clergy are but the moral police force of the State; in short, that the government in power is always right. This extreme statement is indeed a caricature of Anglican practice. But a touch of subservience to political authority, a modified Erastianism, does remain in the Church of England. It is evident in the English civil and religious struggles of the seventeenth century (see Chapter 7).

Lutheranism

The first section of this chapter has already presented the main beliefs of the other great conservative Protestant church, the Lutheran. Once it had become established, Lutheranism preserved many practices which seem to outsiders Catholic in origin, but which to Luther represented a return to early Christianity before the corruption by Rome. Lutheranism preserved the Eucharist, now interpreted according to the mysterious doctrine of consub-

Title page of Luther's *To the Christian Nobility of the German Nation* (1520).

stantiation. It also preserved the notion of hierarchy, bishops, gowns, and something of the plastic arts. The tradition of good music in the church was not only preserved but greatly fortified.

Luther, like so many others upon whom character and fate have thrust rebellion, was at heart a conservative about things of this world, as we have seen. In his own lifetime he really wanted the forms of Lutheran worship to recall the forms he was used to. The Lutheran Church, like the Anglican, had its high or conservative party. Yet it also had a strong evangelical party and a tradition of Bible reading. To outsiders, the Lutheran Church has seemed even more Erastian than the Anglican. As the state church in much of North Germany and in Scandinavia, it was often a docile instrument of its political masters. And in its close association with the rise of Prussia—though Prussia's Hohenzollern rulers later became Calvinist—it was inevitably brought under the rule of the strongly bureaucratic Prussian state. Yet modern-day Lutherans often stood out more firmly against Hitler than did other Germans.

Calvinism: Predestination

The Protestant center is Calvinism, and the main theological problem of Calvinism is not so much Luther's problem of faith against good works as the related problem of predestination against free will. It is a problem that must seem tortured, unreal to many people, but the historian must record the fact that it keeps cropping up in western history—even in Marxism. The problem is an old one in Christianity, already evident in the fifth-century struggle over the heresy of Pelagius, a British monk. It is a problem on which the naturalistic-historical explanation which follows cannot help but offend the true believer, for whom conflict between God's goodness and man's sinfulness just does not exist. To the logical mind, the problem arises from the Christian concept that God is all-powerful, all-good, all-knowing. If this is so, he must will, must *determine*, everything that happens. He must will that the sinner shall sin. For if he did not so will, the individual would be doing something God did not want him to do, and God would not be all-powerful. But there is a grave moral difficulty here. If God wills that the sinner sin, the sinner cannot help himself, cannot be "blamed" for his sin. We seem to be at a dead end, where the individual can always say, no matter what he does, that he is doing what God makes him do. We seem, in short, to have cut the ground from individual moral responsibility. And—at least from their enemies' reports—that is just what John of Leyden and his Antinomians (see p. 130) did. When they took several wives at once, they argued that God must want them to, since they wanted to.

The dilemma is clear: If the individual can choose for himself between good and evil acts, if in theological terms he has *free will* to do what God does not want him to do—then it looks as if God were not all-powerful; if he has no such choice, if in theological terms he is subject to *predestination*—then it looks as if the individual were morally irresponsible. *Both* these conclusions are repugnant to the general nature of historical Christianity.

To an outsider, it looks as if most Christians most of the time solved the dilemma by embracing both horns at once—by holding that God determines every human act, and yet that human beings may do things God does not want them to do. Theologians do not of course put the matter this way. Most of their basic solutions preserve the moral responsibility of the individual by asserting the profound distance between God and man, a distance that the miracle—the grace—of faith alone can bridge. In terms of everyday life, this means that for the individual to claim that whatever he does is what God wants him to do is to make the incredibly presumptuous claim that he *knows* God's will, that his petty human understanding is on a par with God's. The individual can never be *certain* that what he wants to do is what God wants him to do. Therefore he should look about him and see what signs he can, limited though his vision be, of God's intentions. These he will find in Christian tradition and Christian history. To be concrete: If the individual is tempted to commit adultery, he will not follow the Antinomian and say that God wants him to do so; he will follow Christian tradition, and recognize the adulterous desire as an indication that he is being tempted to do wrong, and that if he does it he will not be saved, but damned.

Calvin himself, though he would certainly not have put it this way, would have reached the same conclusion. But he was, as we have noted, a logician. Both his temperament and his environment led him to reject *what he believed* to be the Catholic emphasis on easy salvation by indulgences and the like. He put his own emphasis on the hard path of true salvation, on the majesty of God and the littleness of man. He evolved therefore a very extreme form of the doctrine of predestination.

In Calvin's system, Adam's original sin was unforgivable. God, however, in his incomprehensible mercy, sent Jesus Christ to this earth to make salvation possible for some of Adam's progeny, stained though they were by original sin. Very few indeed, the elect, could attain this salvation, and that through no merit of their own, and certainly not on the wholesale scale the Roman Catholic Church of the sixteenth century was claiming. The elect were saved only through God's free and infinite grace, by means of which they were given the strength to gain salvation. Grace is not like anything else that touches human life on earth. It is not of a piece with law, morals, philosophy, and other human ways of relating man to his environment—to hold that it is, was to Calvin one of the errors of the Catholic. But it is not wholly divorced from these earthly relations—to hold that it is, is the error of the Antinomian. The elect actually tend to behave in a certain way, an identifiable way, a way not wholly misrepresented if it is called *puritanical.*

Classroom sketches of Calvin, by one of his students.

Our modern world has certainly exaggerated the gloom of Calvinist puritanism, and the spiritual pride and exclusiveness of its adherents. Yet to the rationalist, and certainly to the skeptic, there is the bite of reality behind Robert Burns' "Holy Willie's Prayer":

O Thou that in the heavens does dwell!
Wha, as it pleases best Thysel,
Sends one to heaven and ten to hell,
    A' for Thy glory;
And no for ony guid or ill
    They've done before Thee!

Yet I am here, a chosen sample,
To show Thy grace is great and ample.
I'm here, a pillar o' Thy temple.
    Strong as a rock;
A guide, a ruler, and example
    To a' Thy flock*

Calvinist Practice: Puritanism

Where the Calvinists were in complete control of an area (as in sixteenth-century Geneva) or in partial control of larger areas (as in England, Scotland, the Netherlands, or Puritan Massachusetts), they censored, forbade, banished, and punished behavior they thought sinful. They were sometimes petty tyrants and universal busybodies, denying the individual much of his privacy, pleasure, and individualism. They have, especially in our twentieth century, been attacked for the harshness, the inhumanity of their Puritanism. But in their own minds they were clearly God's agents, doing God's work. These firm believers in the inability of human efforts to change anything were among the most ardent of workers toward getting men to change their behavior. To an amazing extent, they succeeded. They helped make the industrial revolution and the modern world.

The note of Christianity the Calvinists most clearly emphasized is not so much asceticism or other-worldliness as austerity. The Calvinist did not seek to annihilate the senses but sought rather to select among his worldly desires

*Poetical Works of Robert Burns, ed. William Wallace (Chambers, 1958), 63.

those that would further his salvation, and to curb or suppress those that would not. The Calvinist thought the world a very serious place indeed, in which laughter was somewhat out of order. This world is for most of us, the Calvinist believed, an antechamber to hell and eternal suffering; if you really feel this, you are not likely to be much amused. The Calvinist thought that many pleasures to which the human race is addicted — music, dancing, gambling, fine clothes, drinking, and playgoing, among others — were the kind of thing Satan liked. Although the Calvinist did not hold that all sexual intercourse is sinful, he believed firmly that the purpose God had in mind in providing sexual intercourse was the continuation of the race, and not the sensuous pleasures of the participants. Those pleasures are all the more dangerous since they may lead to extramarital indulgence, which is a very great sin.

Calvinism also sounded very loudly the ethical note of Christianity. The Calvinist had a high moral code; he was always trying to live up to his code, and to see that other people did so too. Both inward and outward directions of this effort are important. The Calvinist certainly felt the "civil war in the breast," the struggle between what has become famous as the Puritan conscience and the temptations of this world. This notion of a higher part of human consciousness that can and should censor and suppress the promptings of a lower part has left a firm imprint on the West, an imprint especially strong where Calvinism has set the dominant tone.

In its outgoing direction, this Calvinist ethical concern has taken many forms other than that of the outright, police-enforced prohibition the critics of Puritanism single out for condemnation. The early Calvinists certainly prohibited dancing, the theater, and other pleasures — the more naturally because, as we shall see, they had no democratic worries about the freedom of the individual. But the Calvinist also believed in persuasion; he made the sermon a central part of his worship. He believed in hell-fire and in the moral uses of fear of hell-fire; he believed in emotional conversion, and was a good missionary, though not at his best among primitive peoples.

Calvinism appears in pure or diluted form in many sects, Presbyterian and Congregational in Britain, Reformed on the Continent. It influenced almost all the other sects, even the Anglican and the Lutheran. Theologically, its main opponent is a system of ideas in name almost as remote from us as the Erastian, but like Erastian a fighting word as late as the eighteenth-century beginnings of the United States. This is Arminianism, so-called from James Arminius, a late sixteenth-century Dutch divine. Arminianism may be classified among the free-will theologies, for Arminius held that election (and of course damnation) were conditional in God's mind — not absolute as Calvin had maintained — and that therefore what a man did on earth could change God's mind about the man's individual fate. Generally, Arminianism was more tolerant of the easy ways of this world than Calvinism, less "puritanical," more Erastian.

Calvinism can hardly be accused of being Erastian. Where it did become the established state church — in Geneva, in the England of the 1650's, in Massachusetts, for instance — the Calvinist Church ran or tried to run the state. This is *theocracy*, not Erastianism. Where Calvinism had to fight to exist, it preached and practiced an ardent denial of the omnipotence of the state over the individual, made affirmations of popular rights which later generations turned to the uses of their own struggle against kings — and churchmen. In this sense, Calvinism helped create modern democracy. Its basic original concepts are not, however, democratic, if democracy is based as we think it is, on equalitarian principles and on a generally kindly and optimistic view of ordinary human beings.

Finally, we must point out once more that in the world of the 1960's Calvinism is no longer the vigorous, in a sense, fundamentalist, and certainly fighting, creed it was in the sixteenth century. Its churches almost everywhere have gone part way along toward a kindlier view of human nature and human potential, toward optimism, a milder reforming zeal. Arminianism, with help from the Eighteenth-Century Enlightenment, has triumphed. But would Calvin recognize his twentieth-century children?

The Left Wing

The sects of the Protestant left were usually greatly influenced by Calvinist theology and by Calvinist example. The Anabaptists and the others generally arose among humble people, more often in cities or small towns than in open farming country. They broke sharply with Catholic forms of worship, in which the congregation, if not quite passive in the presence of age-old rites, was at least quiet and orderly. In the new sects, the congregation sometimes shouted and danced, and always sang hymns with great fervor. Preaching was even more important than in more conservative forms of Protestantism, and more emotionally charged with hopes of heaven and fears of hell. Many of the sects were vigorously chiliastic — that is, they expected an immediate second coming of Christ and the end of this world. Many were in aim, and among themselves in practice, economic equalitarians, communists of a sort. They did not share wealth, however, so much as the poverty that had seemed to St. Francis and now seemed to them an essential part of the Christian way.

Almost all of them had some beliefs, some goals, that alarmed many ordinary, conventional men and women. Many refused to take oaths on grounds of conscience. Most distrusted the state, regarding it as a necessary instrument operated by sinners to punish other sinners, an institution from which true Christians should hold aloof. What is most striking about these sects is the extraordinary range of their ideals and behavior. Some of them really behaved as badly — as insanely — as their conservative enemies have charged. John of Leyden, crowned at Münster as "King David" with two golden, jeweled crowns, one kingly, one imperial, with his "Queen Divara" and a whole harem in attendance, seems a mad parody of the Protestant appeal to the Bible. Yet the Anabaptists already scattered about northwestern Europe at the time were shocked by what went on in Münster; and if one examines their ideas and practices one finds, for the most part, pious and earnest pacifist Christians, living simply and productively as do their modern successors, Mennonites, Baptists, and Quakers.

These left-wing sects often display an illogical and magnificent combination of pacifist principles and ardent combativeness (as long as the weapons are not physical ones, conventional means of inflicting bodily harm). These men are fighting to end fighting. Here is Jacob Hutter, who founded the Hutterite sect of Moravian Anabaptists, addressing the Governor-General of Moravia, Ferdinand of Habsburg, a good Catholic who was ruling the Germanies for his brother Charles V:

Woe, woe! unto you, O ye Moravian rulers, who have sworn to that cruel tyrant and enemy of God's truth, Ferdinand, to drive away his pious and faithful servants. Woe! we say unto you, who fear that frail and mortal man more than the living, omnipotent, and eternal God, and chase from you, suddenly and inhumanly, the children of God, the afflicted widow, the desolate orphan, and scatter them abroad. . . . God, by the mouth of the prophet, proclaims that He will fearfully and terribly avenge the shedding of innocent blood, and will not pass by such as fear not to pollute and contaminate their hands therewith. Therefore, great slaughter, much misery and anguish, sorrow and adversity, yea, everlasting groaning, pain and torment are daily appointed you.*

Given the pacifist basis of most Anabaptist cults, the violence of this letter is extraordinary, even for the time. Yet these men did know how to die. They, too, were martyrs. And they were persecuted by the more moderate reformers with a violence as firm and principled as that which Protestant tradition attributes to the Catholic Inquisition.

It must not be concluded that all sectarians of the left were as violently nonviolent as Hutter. An even stronger and more long-lasting note is that sounded by a man like the English John Bunyan (1628–1688), whose *Pilgrim's Progress* has long been read far beyond the circles of the Baptist sect of which he was a lay preacher. This book is an allegory of life seen as a pilgrimage toward a happy end, and the joys of Beulahland, a pilgrimage full of trials, but not by any means a series of horrors. It is written in simple language, and its view of life is quite untortured.

*J. T. van Braght, *Martyrology*, I, 151–153, quoted in R. J. Smithson, *The Anabaptists* (London, 1935), 69–71.

IV   The Catholic Reformation

The dominant early Catholic response to the challenge of the Protestant Reformation was to stand pat and try to suppress the rebels. Such, basically, was the papal policy toward Luther. Yet the fact remains that the religious ferment out of which Protestantism emerged was originally a ferment *within* the Catholic Church. To that ferment many who remained within the Church had contributed. Erasmus and other Christian humanists (see p. 91) greatly influenced the early stages of what has come to be called the Catholic Reformation. Particularly in Spain, but spreading throughout the Catholic world, there was a revival of deep mystical impulses and a corresponding increase in popular participation in religion.

Within a long generation, the Catholic Church was to rally its spiritual and material forces, achieve a large measure of reform from within, and, by winning back areas in Germany, Bohemia, Hungary, and Poland, establish the territorial limits of Protestantism in the West substantially where they now are. This Catholic Reformation, in Protestant historical writing often called the Counter-

Reformation, was no mere negative defense, but a positive spiritual renewal in its own right. It did not restore the medieval unity of Christendom, but it did preserve and reinvigorate fundamental Catholic beliefs and practice.

They were not preserved without the aid of the secular arm. Both the Catholic and the Protestant Reformations were inseparably tied up with domestic and international politics, as we shall see in detail in the next chapter. The powerful House of Habsburg, both in its Spanish and its German branches, was the active head of political Catholicism in the next few generations. The French monarchs, though their support was perhaps rather more political than religious, none the less helped greatly to preserve France as a Catholic land. Moreover, in France itself the seventeenth century was to witness a firm Catholic revival, led by such great preachers as Massillon, Bossuet, and Fénelon. This religious revival, as is not uncommon, produced diverging strains as well as orthodox ones—the almost Calvinistic Jansenism of Port Royal, the quietism of Madame Guyon. In many parts of Germany and its Slavic borderlands, and in Italy, the reigning princes and their nobilities were powerful influences behind the old religion.

Nor were Catholic fundamentals preserved without special organization. Once more, as with the Cluniacs, the Cistercians, the mendicant orders, this renewal of Catholic strength, this need to achieve in the name of the old something quite new, produced a series of new orders of the regular clergy, a revival of the old monastic ideals of austere simplicity and social service. The reforming current was already gathering strength when the papacy was still in the lax hands of Leo X, Luther's opponent. During Leo's pontificate an earnest group formed at Rome the Oratory of Divine Love, dedicated to the deepening of spiritual experience through special services and religious exercises. In the 1520's, the Oratory inspired the foundation of the Theatines, an order aimed particularly at the education of the clergy. In the 1520's also, a new branch of the Franciscans appeared, the Capuchins, to lead the order back to Francis' own ideals of poverty and preaching to the poor. During the next decade or so, half a dozen other new orders were established.

The Jesuits

The greatest of these by far was the Society of Jesus, founded in 1540 by the Spaniard Ignatius Loyola (1491–1556). The founder, until he turned to religion after a painful wound received in battle, had been a soldier, and the Jesuit order was from the beginning the soldiery of the Catholic Church. Loyola set the rules for his order in his *Spiritual Exercises.* The following extracts bring out admirably two major characteristics of the Jesuits: first, the absolute (for once the word must be taken literally) obedience to higher authority, to the Catholic Church as embodied in its hierarchy; and second, the realistic, middle-of-the-road estimate of what can be expected of ordinary human beings in this world. Note the moderate position on predestination:

1. Always to be ready to obey with mind and heart, setting aside all judgment of one's own, the true spouse of Jesus Christ, our holy mother, our infallible and orthodox mistress, the Catholic Church, whose authority is exercised over us by the hierarchy.

13. That we may be altogether of the same mind and in conformity with the Church herself, if she shall have defined anything to be black which to our eyes appears to be white, we ought in like manner to pronounce it to be black. For we must undoubtedly believe, that the Spirit of our Lord Jesus Christ, and the Spirit of the Orthodox Church His Spouse, by which Spirit we are governed and directed to Salvation, is the same; . . . .

14. It must also be borne in mind, that although it be most true, that no one is saved but he that is predestinated, yet we must speak with circumspection concerning this matter, lest perchance, stressing too much the grace or predestination of God, we should seem to wish to shut out the force of free will and the merits of good works; or on the other hand, attributing to these latter more than belongs to them, we derogate meanwhile from the power of grace.*

Documents of the Christian Church, Henry Bettenson, ed. (New York, 1947), 363, 364–365.

Born in controversy, the Jesuits have always been a center of controversy. To their hostile critics, who have been numerous both within and without the Catholic Church, the Jesuits have seemed unscrupulous soldiers of the pope. Though they have rarely been accused of the simpler vices common gossip has long alleged against the regular clergy—fondness for food and drink, laziness, laxity with women—they have been accused of a subtler devotion to worldly power, to success in a quite unspiritual sense. They have been accused of preaching and practicing the doctrine that the end justifies the means, that as soldiers of the one true Church they may indulge in dirty fighting as long as such tactics seem likely to bring victory.

This is indeed a slander, for even at the purely worldly level, Jesuit devotion to Catholic tradition is too deep for them to make Machiavelli's mistake of underestimating the hold the moral decencies have on human beings. And the historical record leaves no doubt of Jesuit success in bolstering the spiritual as well as the material credit of Catholicism in these critical days of the sixteenth and seventeenth centuries. Jesuits were everywhere, in Hungary, in Poland, in England, in Holland, trying to win back lost lands and peoples from the Protestants. They were winning new lands and peoples on the expanding frontiers of the West, in India, in China, in Japan, in North America. They were martyrs, preachers, teachers, social workers, counselors of statesmen, always disciplined, never lapsing into the kind of fleshly worldliness that had been the fate of other monastic orders.

The Inquisition

The Jesuits were the chief new instruments of the Catholic Reformation. An old instrument of the Church was also employed—the Inquisition, a special ecclesiastical court which in its papal form was first established in the thirteenth century as part of the effort to put down the Albigensian heresy and in its Spanish form began in the fifteenth century as part of the effort of the new Spanish monarchy to enforce religious uniformity on its subjects (see Chapter 2). Both papal and Spanish inquisitions were medieval courts, which used medieval methods of torture. Both were employed against the Protestants in the sixteenth century.

Protestant tradition sometimes makes both the Inquisition and the Jesuits appear as the promoters of a widespread and veritable reign of terror. Certainly the Jesuits and their allies made full use of the many pressures and persuasions any highly organized society can bring to bear on nonconformists. And the Inquisition did perpetrate horrors against former Moslems in Spain and against Catholics-turned-Protestants in the Low Countries. But the Inquisition does not appear to have been a really major force in stemming the Protestant tide. It was most active in countries of southern Europe—Italy, Spain, Portugal—where Protestantism was never a real threat. And in

Ignatius Loyola: the only authentic portrait of the Saint, by Coello.

the regions where the Catholic Reformation was most successful in winning back large numbers to the Roman faith—the Germanies, the Slavic and Magyar marches of the East— sheer persecution was not a decisive factor.

The Council of Trent

The Catholic Reformation was not a change of dogma, not a change of spiritual direction. If anything, revulsion against the Protestant tendency toward some form of the "priesthood of the believer" hardened Catholic doctrines into a firmer insistence on the miraculous power of the priesthood. Protestant variation promoted Catholic uniformity. Not even on indulgences did the Church yield; interpreted as a spiritual return for spiritual effort, not as a money transaction, indulgences were reaffirmed by the Council of Trent. The work of this council ties together the various measures of reform and illustrates clearly the fact that what the Catholic Reformation reformed was not doctrine but practice.

The Council of Trent was called in 1545 by Paul III (1534–1549), the first of a line of popes devoted to the task of combatting real-

istically the inroads of Protestantism. To liberals—including liberal Catholics—it has seemed no true general council, but an instrument in the hands of the popes and the Jesuits, a mere rubber stamp. Certainly in conception it was meant to provide at least a chance for reconciliation with the Protestants. Leading figures in the more conservative Protestant groups were invited, but they never attended. The French clergy, with their Gallican tradition, did not co-operate freely, and indeed part of the work of the Council of Trent was not accepted in France for some fifty years. The Council was caught in the web of the religious wars and intrigues of high politics, and its work was several times interrupted. Nevertheless it continued to meet off and on for twenty years until it completed its work of re-affirming and codifying doctrine in 1564.

On matters of doctrine, the Council of Trent took a stand that ruled out all possibility of a compromise with the Protestants on the major issues separating them from Catholics. It reaffirmed the essential role of the priesthood, reaffirmed all seven sacraments, reaffirmed the great importance of *both* faith and works, reaffirmed that *both* the Scriptures and the spokesmen of the Church were au-

Execution of English Protestants under Mary Tudor.

Religious Situation about 1600

Legend:
- Roman Catholic
- Anglican (Church of England)
- Calvinist
- Lutheran
- Orthodox Christian
- Moslem

Note: Not all religious minority groups are shown

Map labels: NORWAY, SWEDEN, RUSSIA, Stockholm, Moscow, DENMARK, Copenhagen, Baltic Sea, PRUSSIA, Warsaw, POLAND, Edinburgh, SCOTLAND, IRELAND, ENGLAND, NETHER-LANDS, Amsterdam, Leyden, London, Canterbury, Münster, Berlin, Wittenberg, Leipzig, Wartburg, GERMANY, SAXONY, Prague, MORAVIA, Antwerp, HESSE, Spires, WURTEM-BERG, Paris, FRANCE, Basel, SWITZERLAND, Constance, Zurich, Augsburg, Vienna, AUSTRIA, HUNGARY, Trent, Geneva, La Rochelle, Avignon, Bologna, ITALY, Rome, Belgrade, OTTOMAN, Adriatic Sea, CRIMEA, Black Sea, Constantinople, EMPIRE, Athens, PORTUGAL, Madrid, SPAIN, Lisbon, Atlantic Ocean, Mediterranean Sea

Miles 0 — 500

thorities on theology. The uncompromisingly traditional stand taken by the Council is evident in the *Professio Fidei Tridentina* (the Trent Profession of Faith), which for long was subscribed to by converts to Catholicism. It runs in part:

I most firmly acknowledge and embrace the Apostolical and ecclesiastical traditions and other observances and constitutions of the same Church. I acknowledge the sacred Scripture according to that sense which Holy Mother Church has held and holds, to whom it belongs to decide upon the true

sense and interpretation of the holy Scriptures, nor will I ever receive and interpret the Scriptures except according to the unanimous consent of the Fathers.

. . .

I profess likewise that true God is offered in the Mass, a proper and propiatory sacrifice for the living and the dead, and that in the most Holy Eucharist there are truly, really and substantially the body and the blood, together with the soul and divinity of our Lord Jesus Christ, and that a conversion is made of the whole substance of bread into his body and of the whole substance of wine

143

into his blood, which conversion the Catholic Church calls transubstantiation.*

The Council of Trent and the reforming popes of the later sixteenth century effected in Catholic practice the kind of change that had been achieved under Cluniac auspices five hundred years earlier. The Council insisted on the strict observance of clerical vows and on the ending of abuses. It took measures against the sale of church offices and against non-residence of prelates. It called for the establishment of seminaries to give priests better training. To promote discipline among the laity, it imposed censorship on a large scale, issuing the *Index,* a list of books that Catholics were not to read because of the peril to their faith. The *Index* included not only the writings of heretics and Protestants but also the works of such anticlericals as Machiavelli and Boccaccio.

Under Pius V, Pope from 1566 to 1572, a standard catechism, breviary, and missal were drawn up to embody for purposes of instruction the codifying work of the Council of Trent. In short, the whole structure of the Church, both for the training of the priesthood and for the training of the layman, was tightened up, given a new spirit. The papal court was no longer just another Italian Renaissance court. It is true that, especially

*Bettenson, *Documents,* 374–375.

among the upper clergy a certain laxity had again crept in by the eighteenth century. That same century witnessed the inroads of excessive rationalism, especially in certain sections of the teaching clergy in France, Italy, and in the Hapsburg domains. But the widespread corruption against which Luther and his fellows inveighed never again prevailed in the West.

The strength of the Catholic Reformation is shown by the fact that, once it was well launched, the Protestants made few further territorial inroads. Within a century of Luther's revolt, the broad lines of the territorial division in the West between areas dominantly Catholic and areas dominantly Protestant were established much as they are today. England, Scotland, Holland, northern and eastern Germany (with a southward projection in Wurtemberg and Switzerland), and Scandinavia were predomiantly Protestant. Ireland, Belgium, France, southern Germany (with a northern projection in the valley of the Rhine), the Habsburg lands, Poland, Italy, and the Iberian Peninsula were predominantly Catholic. But only predominantly. There were Catholic minorities in England, Scotland, and Holland, and the two faiths interpenetrated most confusedly in a greatly divided Germany; there were Protestant minorities in Ireland, France, and even in some of the Habsburg lands the Jesuits had won back.

V   The Place of Protestantism in History

Protestantism and Progress

Protestants and free-thinking secularists sometimes interpret the Reformation as something peculiarly "modern," a decisive break with a "medieval" past, something forward-looking and even "democratic" as distinguished from the stagnant and status-ridden Middle Ages. This notion seems to gain support from the obvious fact that those parts of the West which in the last three centuries have been economically most prosperous, which have worked out most successfully democratic constitutional government, and which have made the most striking contributions to modern western culture, especially in the natural sciences, were predominantly Protestant. Moreover, the powers which, since the decline of Spanish power after 1600, have risen to a kind of preponderance of power and prestige in the West—namely France, the British Empire, Germany, and now the United States—have been with one exception predominantly Protestant. And the one exception, France, has had since the eighteenth century a strong, at times a leading, element among its people which, though not in the main Protestant, is strongly secularist and anticlerical. It looks as if the nations that went Protestant also went modern and progressive.

This notion that Protestantism is somehow a cause or at least an accompaniment of political and cultural leadership in the modern West needs to be examined carefully. It has, of course, the kind of truth certain modern philosophers have called the truth of the "myth." That is, for a good many years a good many Protestants and secularists in these prosperous countries have believed that their Protestantism was a major part of what made them prosperous. To the average Victorian Englishman, for instance, at the height of British power and wealth, the fact that his country had gone Protestant in the sixteenth century was at least as important as Magna Carta—and the existence of good deposits of coal and iron—in producing the prosperous England of which he was so proud. The historian must record the acceptance of the myth; he must also attempt to go back to the events that were used to construct the myth.

We find that Protestantism in the sixteenth century looks in many ways quite different from Protestantism seen from the nineteenth and twentieth centuries, just as Magna Carta in the thirteenth century looks quite different from Magna Carta looked back at from the nineteenth. First, as we have already noted, sixteenth-century Protestants were not rationalists. They were, to use an unfavorable word, almost as "superstitious" as the Catholics. Luther actually threw his ink bottle at the devil, or so they tell the tourists at the castle of the Wartburg where they point out the dark patch on the wall where the bottle struck; the Calvinists burned witches, or at any rate hanged them. To put the matter more favorably, the Protestants for the most part shared with their Catholic opponents very fundamental Christian conceptions of original sin, the direct divine governance of the universe, the reality of heaven and hell, and—most important—they had no more than did the Catholics a general conception of life on this earth as improving, as progressing systematically and regularly to an even better life for coming generations.

Second, these early Protestants were by no means tolerant, by no means believers in the separation of Church and State. When they were in a position to do so, they used governmental power to prevent public worship in any form other than their own. Many of them persecuted those who disagreed with them, both Protestants of other sects and Catholics —that is, they banished them or imprisoned them or even killed them. The classic instance is Calvin's condemnation and execution of Servetus, and there are many other instances.

Third, these early Protestants were hardly democratic, at least in most of the senses that loose (but indispensable) word has for twentieth-century Americans. *Logically,* the Protestant appeal from the authority of the pope backed by Catholic tradition to the conscience of the individual believer fits in with notions like "individualism," "rights of man," and "liberty." Some historians have even found a correlation between the Protestant appeal to the authority of the Bible and the later characteristic American appeal to the authority of a written constitution. But most of the early Protestant reformers certainly did not hold that all men are created equal; they were not social and economic equalitarians. Rather, they believed in an order of rank, in a society of status. Lutheranism and Anglicanism were clearly conservative in their political and social doctrines. Calvinism can be made to look very undemocratic indeed if we concentrate on its conception of an elect few chosen by God for salvation and an unregenerate majority condemned to eternal damnation. And in its early years in Geneva and in New England Calvinism was in fact a theocracy, a rule of the "saints."

In the long run, however, Calvinism favored the domination of a fairly numerous middle class. As we shall see shortly, the most persuasive argument for a causal relation between Protestantism and modern western democratic life does not proceed directly from the ideas of the early Protestants about men in society, but from the way Protestant moral ideals fitted in with the strengthening of a commercial and industrial middle class. Finally, among the Anabaptists and other radical sects, we do find even in the sixteenth century demands for political, social, and economic equality. But where these demands are made, they are cast in Biblical language and rest on concepts of direct divine intervention quite strange to us. Moreover, many of these sects tended not so much toward active social revolt to improve earthly standards of living as toward a peculiarly Protestant form of withdrawal from things of this earth, toward a pacifism and a mysticism quite compatible with leaving the unregenerate majority in possession of this unworthy sense-world.

The Protestant Reformation, then, did not create modern society single-handed. But it did challenge those in authority in many parts of Europe and did start all sorts of men, some of them in humble circumstances, thinking about fundamental problems of life in this world as well as in the next. Its educators and propagandists, using the new weapon of the printing press, began the drive toward universal literacy. It was one of the great destroyers of the medieval synthesis. Its most important positive action can best be traced through its part in forming the way of life of the middle classes who were to lay the foundations of modern western democracy. The relation between Protestant ethics and the "spirit of capitalism" has been admirably traced in the work of a modern German sociologist, Max Weber. His thesis, now a generation old, has always been controversial, and is now subject to what seems to be a uniformity of western intellectual history, that the new generation must attack, or at least revise, the work of its immediate predecessors. Even though Weber's ideas are nowadays sharply attacked, we believe that they are a permanent contribution and certainly deserve consideration.

Protestantism and Capitalism

In a simplified form, Weber's thesis runs as follows: Capital is the produced means of further production—not, in these early days, power-driven machines and factories, but tools, the division of labor, the production of specialized items for exchange and the complex instruments of that exchange. The accumulation of capital requires abstention from immediate consumption. A worker who has to grow all his own food can barely take time out to improve his tools. But if he can save or borrow enough to feed himself and keep warm while he is working on his tools, he can ultimately produce more than is needed to keep him alive. The surplus he can sell for money, which he can use to make further improvements, to increase his capital. As we have seen, not even in the early Middle Ages were manorial groups wholly reduced to living from hand to mouth. In a sense, there has always been in the historic West *some* "capitalism," some division of labor, some production for exchange. But toward the later Middle Ages, this process was greatly speeded up, and a class of men arose who traded on a fairly large scale, and who made large profits. The more they could "plough back" those profits into the business, especially if by so doing they could reduce the unit cost of the items they made or sold, the more capital they accumulated, and the bigger their business became.

Now this "ploughing back" of course meant not spending on immediate goods for their own consumption. It might also mean in part squeezing more work for the same or less pay from their workers. But at least this latter process could not go beyond the point where it ruined the effectiveness of the labor. It meant also that the capitalist, the businessman who worked very hard at his job, who spent all his time "making money," did in fact add to the total productiveness of the society. In very simple terms, hard work and no play, all along the line, but especially at the top, meant more actual production.

Protestantism, especially its Calvinist form, encouraged this sort of life. It encouraged hard work. The devil lies in wait for idle hands. Work keeps a man from temptation to run after women, or play silly games, or drink, or do many other things unpleasing to the Calvinist God. More, work is positively a good thing, a kind of tribute we pay to the Lord. Luther, too, glorified work of all kinds and preached the doctrine of the dignity of the vocation a man is called to, be it ever so humble. In almost all forms of Protestantism we find this feeling, so contrary to the contempt for work of the field and countinghouse evident in the tradition of chivalry.

It is for action that God maintaineth us and our activities; work is the moral as well as the natural end of power. . . . It is action that God is most served and honoured by. . . . The public welfare or the good of the many is to be valued above our own.*

So much for the work, for the positive side of the equation. But on the negative side, Protestanism, and in particular Calvinism, discouraged many kinds of consumption which took energies away from the large-scale production that is the essence of the modern economic system. The Calvinist, to put it mildly, discouraged the fine arts, the theater, the dance, expensive clothes, what the American economist Veblen has called "conspicuous consumption" generally. But he did not discourage—in fact he encouraged by his own way of living—the satisfaction of the simpler, commoner, needs of solid, substantial food, shelter, clothing, and the like, all needs most readily supplied by large-scale industry serving a mass demand. The Calvinist represents a new development of the perennial Christian ascetic tradition. This is not the asceticism of the hermits of the desert:

Question: But may I not cast off the world that I may only think of my salvation? Answer: You may cast off all such excess of worldly cares or business as unnecessarily hinder you in spiritual things. But

*Richard Baxter's Christian Directory, quoted in Max Weber, The Protestant Ethic and the Spirit of Capitalism, Talcott Parsons, trans. (London, 1930), 260.

you may not cast off all bodily employment and mental labour in which you may serve the common good. Everyone as a member of Church or Commonwealth must employ their parts to the utmost for the good of the Church and the Commonwealth. To neglect this and say: I will pray and meditate, is as if your servant should refuse his greatest work and tie himself to some lesser, easier part.*

A society with many Calvinists tended to produce much, to consume solidly but without "waste" (we are speaking here in terms of economics, not in terms of art or morals). Therefore, under competitive conditions, its business leaders accumulated the kind of surplus we call capital, which they could invest in the methods of production that have so enriched the West. All work and no play—well, not much—made the Calvinist society an economically prosperous one.

The Scots, the Dutch, the Swiss, the Yankees of New England—all of them markedly Calvinistic peoples—have long had a popular reputation for thrift, diligence, and driving a hard bargain. And it is surprising how many concrete bits of evidence reinforce the Weber thesis. The Protestant societies at once cut down the number of holy days—holidays without work. They kept Sunday very rigorously as a day without work, but the other six were all work days. The Calvinists even eliminated Christmas, and, since there were as yet no national lay equivalents of the old religious festivals, no Fourth of July or Labor Day, the early modern period in most Protestant countries had a maximum of work days per year. This is a marginal matter, but is in part by such margins that economic growth is won. Many Protestant theologians rejected the medieval Catholic doctrine that regarded interest on investments beyond a low, "just" rate as usury, an illegitimate and immoral thing. In general, they rejected most of the medieval doctrines suggested by the term "just price" (see p. 52) in favor of something much closer to our modern notions of free competition in the market. In the market, God would certainly take care of his own.

Moreover, it would appear that the Weber

*Ibid., 261–262.

thesis can be extended to include a certain rough parallel between the flourishing of Protestantism, especially of the Calvinist kind, and the flourishing of science-with-technology. This does not mean that Catholic countries produced no great scientists, or that there is anything in Catholic beliefs that inhibits the scientist in his work. It is rather, as with capitalism, that the Protestant ethic gave a slight extra push to the scientist and technologist in their pursuit of so this-wordly a concern as the detached study of natural phenomena.

Finally, the firm Calvinist retention of the other world as the supreme, but for the individual never *certain,* goal reinforced the class-consciousness of the middle class. It helped shield the individual wealthy Calvinist from the great temptation of the newly rich—that is, assimilation to the standards of life of a loose-living, spendthrift upper class. Family fortunes founded by hard work and inconspicuous consumption tended to hold together for several generations at least.

Weber's thesis must not be taken as the sole explanation of the rise of capitalism in early modern times. It is but one of many variables in a complex situation. In the first place, the stirrings of modern economic life far antedated Luther and Calvin, and were clearest and most important in many regions—Italy, southern Germany, Belgium—which were not actually won over to Protestantism. Banking began in northern Italy under Catholic rule—in Florence, for instance—when the theoretical official prohibition of usury still prevailed. Almost certainly relaxation of rules against usury would have received official Catholic theological sanction even had there been no Protestant Reformation. In the second place, there is no perfect co-ordination between Protestantism and industrial development on one hand and Catholicism and industrial backwardness (or notably slower development) on the other. Belgium, the German Rhineland, Piedmont, and Lombardy are striking examples of Catholic regions which on the whole have kept in modern times well up to the fore in general productiveness and prosperity. Protestant East Prussia, on the other hand, remained a basically rural region. In the third place, no sensible explanation of the rise of modern industrial economy can neglect the simple facts of geography and natural resources. Suppose, contrary to all likelihood, Italy had turned solidly Calvinistic; this still would not give Italy the coal and iron that Calvinist, or at least Protestant, England had.

Yet the "Protestant ethic" remains an important element in the economic transformation of modern Europe. It gave perhaps the extra fillip, the margin that started the West on its modern path—along with that opening up of Europe overseas which helped the Atlantic nations over the Mediterranean nations, along with the natural resources of northern and western Europe, along with the damp, temperate climate that made hard work easier than in the Mediterranean, along with free enterprise, freedom for science and invention, relatively orderly and law-abiding societies, and whatever else goes to produce that still not fully understood phenomenon, economic growth.

Protestantism and Nationalism

One final big generalization about the Protestant Reformation is much less disputable than attempts to tie that movement with modern individualism, democracy, and industrialism. After the great break of the sixteenth century, both Protestantism and Catholicism became important elements in the formation of modern nationalism. Here again we must not fall into the trap of one-way causation. The Protestants were not always patriots; French Huguenots sought help from the English enemy; French Catholics sought it from the Spanish enemy. Much besides the Reformation goes into the formation of the modern state-system of the West and its cementing patriotism. "French-ness" and modern "German-ness" perhaps began as far back as the Strasbourg oaths of the ninth century. *But where a specific form of religion became identified with a given political unit,* religious feeling and patriotic feeling each reinforced the other. This is most clear where a political unit had to struggle for its independence. Protestantism heightened Dutch resistance to the Spaniard; Catholicism heightened Irish resistance to the Englishman. But even in states already independent in the sixteenth century, religion came to strengthen patriotism. England from Elizabeth I on has, despite the existence of a Catholic minority, proudly held itself up as a Protestant nation. Spain has with at least equal pride identified itself as a Catholic nation. In the great wars to which we must now turn, religion and politics were inextricably mixed.

Reading Suggestions on the Protestant Reformation

(Asterisk indicates paperbound edition.)

General Accounts

L. von Ranke, *History of the Reformation in Germany* (many editions). A very famous work, more than a century old.

R. H. Bainton, *The Reformation of the Sixteenth Century* (*Beacon, 1952). By a sound Protestant historian, fully abreast of modern research.

E. H. Harbison, *The Age of Reformation* (Cornell Univ. Press). Admirable introduction.

H. J. Grimm, *The Reformation Era, 1500–1650* (Macmillan, 1954). A good American text book with a very thorough critical bibliography.

W. Durant, *The Reformation* (Simon & Schuster, 1957). The sixth part of the distinguished popularizer's "Story of Civilization," a by no means unsympathetic study made from a rationalist position. The bibliography marks works on the history of religious questions with C, P, J, and R after an author's name to indicate respectively Catholic, Protestant, Jewish, and Rationalist.

G. R. Elton, ed., *Reformation Europe 1517–1559* (*Collins, 1963). A recent general history, with a selection bibliography.

O. Chadwick, The Reformation (*Penguin). A very good popular account; Volume III of a current series, "The Pelican History of the Church," also available in hardcovers.

G. R. Elton, ed., *The Reformation, 1520–1559* (Cambridge Univ. Press, 1958). This is Vol. II of the *New Cambridge Modern History*. A collaborative work, the latest standard work of reference in the field. Unfortunately, the full bibliographies of the old *Cambridge Modern History* (1902–1912) are in this new one to be postponed to a later companion volume for the whole series.

L. W. Spitz, *The Reformation: Material or Spiritual?* (*Heath). One of a series of documents with a "problem" approach, with a useful critical bibliography.

H. Holborn, *A History of Modern Germany:* Vol. I, *The Reformation* (Knopf, 1959). Scholarly, readable, up-to-date.

Special Studies

R. H. Bainton, *Here I Stand: A Life of Martin Luther* (Abingdon-Cokesbury, 1950; *New American Library). Sympathetic, scholarly, and readable.

E. Erikson, *Young Man Luther* (*Norton, 1962). An important book by a distinguished psychoanalyst who is also an historian.

H. Grisar, *Martin Luther, His Life and Works* (Herder, 1930). From the Catholic point of view.

E. G. Schwiebert, *Luther and His Times* (Concordia, 1952). Particularly useful for the setting and the effects of Luther's revolt.

S. M. Jackson, *Ulrich Zwingli: The Reformer of German Switzerland* (Putnam's, 1900). An old work, but indispensable.

G. Harkness, *John Calvin, The Man and His Ethics* (Holt, 1931; *Apex). A good short introduction.

J. Huizinga, *Erasmus and the Age of Reformation* (*Harper Torchbook). A distinguished work by the great Dutch historian.

J. Mackinnon, *Calvin and the Reformation* (Longmans, Green, 1936); and W. Walker, *John Calvin, the Organizer of Protestantism* (Putman's, 1906). Solid, longer studies.

T. M. Parker, *The English Reformation to 1558* (Oxford Univ. Press, 1950. Home University Library). Excellent short account.

F. M. Powicke, *The Reformation in England* (Oxford Univ. Press, 1941). A scholarly study.

G. H. Williams, *The Radical Reformation* (Westminster Press, 1962). The indispensable book on the radical sects.

L. Pastor, *History of the Popes from the Close of the Middle Ages* (Herder, 1923–1953). The classic account; in many volumes.

B. J. Kidd, *The Counter-Reformation* (Society for Promoting Christian Knowledge, 1933) and P. Janelle, *The Catholic Reformation* (Bruce, 1951) are two modern scholarly accounts, the first by an Anglican, the second by a Catholic.

H. Daniel-Rops, *The Catholic Reformation* (Dutton, 1962). Translated from the admirable book of a French Catholic writer who has a long list of readable works on religious subjects.

H. Jedin, *History of the Council of Trent,* English trans. (Herder, 1957) A monumental and very detailed work in the course of publication. Two volumes so far have appeared.

T. J. Campbell, *The Jesuits, 1534–1921* (Encyclopaedia Press, 1921). Written from the Catholic standpoint.

H. Boehmer, *The Jesuits* (Castle, 1928). From the Protestant point of view.

M. Weber, *The Protestant Ethic and the Spirit of Capitalism,* T. Parsons, ed. (Scribner's, 1930; *paperback edition by same publisher). A famous and controversial work on the interrelationship of religion and economics.

E. Troeltsch, *Protestantism and Progress* (Putnam's, 1912; *Beacon). By one of the most important religious philosophers of modern times.

R. H. Tawney, *Religion and the Rise of Capitalism* (*Mentor). A modified English version of the Weber thesis, written by a leading intellectual associated with the Labor party.

R. H. Popkin, *A History of Skepticism from Erasmus to Descartes* (Humanities Press, 1964). A useful accompaniment to church history; good also for the study of the origins of the Enlightenment.

Sources

H. S. Bettenson, *Documents of the Christian Church* (Oxford Univ. Press, 1947). This admirably arranged compilation is particularly useful for the Reformation.

R. H. Bainton, *The Age of the Reformation* (Van Nostrand, 1956; *Anvil). A comprehensive selection from the great men and great works of the period.

H. J. Hillerbrand, *The Reformation in Its Own Words* (Harper and Row, 1964). A very useful collection of source materials.

Châteillon, *Concerning Heretics,* R. H. Bainton, ed. (Columbia Univ. Press, 1935). One of the earliest tracts urging religious freedom, not just toleration.

5

Dynastic and Religious Wars

I International Politics

Historians have chosen a number of different dates, usually in the last half of the fifteenth century, to mark the watershed between "medieval" and "modern." Americans, for understandable reasons, like to think of 1492 as the great date. In the kingdoms of western Europe, the historian singles out the appearance of strong and ambitious monarchs—1485, the first Tudor, Henry VII in England; 1461, Louis XI in France; 1469, the marriage of Ferdinand of Aragon and Isabella of Castile. Some historians feel that Luther's posting of the Ninety-Five Theses in 1517 is the real break with the Middle Ages. Others, focusing on what we now call international relations, choose a date obscure to most Americans—1494. In that year, Charles VIII of France led his army over the Alps toward the conquest of Italy, in what some consider the "first modern war."

All such dates are of course somewhat arbitrary. As we have seen (Chapter 1), the watershed between medieval and modern culture cannot be placed in a single country or a single year. Moreover, as we shall see later, it can be argued that what *really* makes the modern world modern—that is, new, different from preceding worlds—is the combination of rationalism, natural science, technology, and economic organization which has given men a new power over natural resources. If the standard of change is an economic and technological one, the great change comes as late as the eighteenth century, and the sixteenth and seventeenth centuries are but preparation.

The Competitive State-System

Still, for the historian of international relations, a difference between the medieval and the modern organization of the European state-system is noticeable as early as the late fifteenth century. First of all, there *was* a state-system, indeed in some senses a society of states. Some propagandists for world government in our own day like to insist that relations among states claiming to be "sovereign" or "independent" are really no relations at all, that the modern state-system is simply anarchic chaos. Actually, all political units, many of whose citizens have frequent relations of any kind—trade, travel, study, sport, war—with citizens of other units, are perforce members of the same state-system. Rome and China in 100 A.D. were not members of the same system, for though there are traces of some relations, some traffic across Asia between the two, these are slight indeed. But France, Spain, England, and indeed all the nations of Europe belonged to one system in the sixteenth century.

Western society in early modern times was a group of states, big, middle-sized, and little, each striving to grow, usually in a quite concrete way by annexing others in whole or in part, or at least by bringing them under some sort of control. In practice, at any given moment some states were on the offensive, trying to gain land, power, and wealth; others were on the defensive, trying to preserve what they had. Historically, some few of these units have been so small, so self-contained, that they have never tried to expand. Yet even the model small democracies of the twentieth century, like Sweden and Denmark, have taken the offensive at some time in the past five hundred years; and Sweden, briefly in the seventeenth century, was almost, if not quite, a "great power."

The constituent units of this system of competing states may be called "sovereign" or "independent." There is never a perfect achievement of sovereignty or independence; since by definition the states are in competitive relations, no one can ever be unaffected by the behavior of the others. But we may roughly call a state sovereign if its rulers have an armed force they can use against others. In this sense, there has been since the height of feudal disintegration, perhaps in the tenth century, a continuous though irregular process of reducing the number of sovereign states, until today the whole world contains no more than one hundred and twenty-odd.* If a feudal lord with his own armed retainers is called "sovereign," since he could and did make war on his own initiative, then the tenth-century West had thousands of such units. As we have seen in Chapter 2, the situation was never quite so bad as this. By the end of the Middle Ages, however, over large parts of the West the little feudal units had been absorbed into much bigger states and local wars had become impossible—or if they did occur, they were risings of barons against the big ruler, and were felt to be *civil wars*. The great but shadowy unity of western Christendom was destroyed at the end of the Middle Ages; but so too was the real disunity of numerous local units capable of organized war among themselves.

*Counting imperial knights, Germany alone before 1806 had three times as many. The number of these sovereign states was at a minimum in 1914. Since then, their number has actually increased.

As the modern state-system began to shape up in the fifteenth and sixteenth centuries, the three well-organized monarchies of Spain, France, and England dominated the western part of Europe. The smaller states of Scotland, Portugal, and Scandinavia generally played a subordinate role. In Central Europe, the Holy Roman Empire, with its many quasi-independent member states, did not have the kind of internal unity enjoyed by the Atlantic powers. Prussia, notably, was still a minor state. Yet, under the leadership of the Austrian Habsburgs, the Empire proved capable of taking a leading part in international competition. Between the French and Habsburg power centers lay the zone of fragmentation where the Burgundian dukes of the fifteenth century had tried to revive the middle kingdom (see Chapter 2). Out of this zone have come the modern small nations of Holland, Belgium, Luxembourg, Switzerland, and the larger (but never quite major) power, Italy. In the sixteenth century, Italy was divided into some dozen "sovereign" states, which among themselves formed a state system with wars, diplomacy, and "balance of power", which as early as the fourteenth century anticipated on a small scale the international politics of Europe as a whole in later centuries. Modern formal diplomacy, in particular, is of Italian origin. To the southeast was a new factor in international relations, Turkey, the Moslem successor to the old Byzantine Empire, with European lands right up to and beyond the Danube. To the east, the great state of Muscovite Russia was beginning to be formed, and Poland was already great at least in size. But save for Turkey, which sought to expand northwestward, and which was therefore actively anti-Habsburg, the eastern and southeastern states of Europe were not yet really integrated into high politics.

Save for the overseas expansion of Europe, we have here a picture that is not worlds apart from the present one. Italy is today one political nation instead of a dozen, the German power-unit was until 1945 one unified nation instead of the decentralized Holy Roman Empire, and on the east Russia is a very great

power indeed, Poland a lesser one. Still, on the whole, the European state-system has the broad lines it had five centuries ago. Its units are still "sovereign."

This comparative stability has not been maintained without threats to destroy it. In succession, certain states have attempted to break it down — sixteenth-century Spain, the France of Louis XIV of the seventeenth century and of the Revolution and Napoleon at the turn from the eighteenth to the nineteenth, the Germany of the Kaiser and Hitler in the twentieth. They have tried to absorb the other states, or at the very least to control them to a point where they were scarcely "sovereign," or in our contemporary terms, had become "satellites." Each time, the threatened units sooner or later joined together in a coalition that was able to beat the armies of the aggressive power and maintain the system. Each time, England, which after the late medieval venture of the Hundred Years' War never attempted to absorb lands on the Continent of Europe (save for the few square miles of Gibraltar), sooner or later intervened to bolster, often to lead, the coalition against the aggressor or in more neutral terms, the "disturber." To use a time-honored phrase, the system was maintained through the workings of the "balance of power." This principle is not primarily a moral one, though some writers have defended it as basically moral in the sense that it tends to preserve the independence of organized states. "Balance of power" is, rather, a descriptive principle, a thread through the intricacies of international politics in the modern West. We must take up this thread in 1494.

Dynastic State and Nation State

First, however, we must examine briefly the nature of the political units that make up the competitive state-system. It is the fashion to call them *dynastic* states up to about the end of the eighteenth century and *nation* states thereafter. The distinction is a good rough working one. In the early modern period, many states were loose agglomerations of formerly independent units that were sometimes separated from each other by foreign territory, that sometimes spoke separate languages, and that were tied together almost solely by the ruling dynasty. The Habsburg realm is a good example. In war and diplomacy the dynastic ruler and his circle of nobles and bureaucrats were a team imbued with team spirit, but the different peoples in the state had relatively little sense of patriotism, of common national effort and ambitions. Early modern wars were less than total wars. Except in their disastrous effects on government finances and on taxes, they scarcely touched the lives of common people who were not actually in the way of contending armies. In the peace settlements, no one talked about "national self-determination of peoples," or worried greatly about transferring areas and populations from one ruler to another.

The distinction between dynastic and nation states must not be exaggerated or oversimplified. Especially in the great monarchies of Spain, England, and France a degree of national patriotism existed as early as the sixteenth century. Many of the obvious signs of "national" feeling are clear, in spite of all the local variations common to these countries. The English had long known the French scornfully as "frogs," and the French had retaliated by calling the English *les godons,* the French mispronunciation of a familiar English blasphemy. In the great war between England and Spain which culminated in the defeat of the Spanish Armada, all the signs of intense popular patriotic feeling were clearly present in England. It is true that mingled with nationalist there were religious feelings; the Englishman hated and feared the Spaniard not only as a foreigner but as a Catholic. But this mingling of nationalism and religion was to last right down to our own time.

Even in divided Germany, Luther could count on Germans to dislike Italians. Hatred of the foreigner binds men together at least as effectively as love of one another. Nor does the custom, so strange to us, of transferring political units by marriage of ruling families really affect the basic similarity between the state-system of early modern times and our own. Perhaps the accidents of marriage account for the unusual combination of Germany and Spain under Charles V; but for the most part the alliances and alignments of the sixteenth century conform extremely well to conditions of geography, resources, tradition, and culture.

Indeed, the differences between our late modern and the early modern state are generally exaggerated by most of us today. The differences are real and they make these dynastic wars seem petty and confusing; but they are differences of degree of efficiency, centralization, ability to command vast numbers of men and great resources, rapidity of movement, not differences of kind. Possibly by mid-twentieth century such differences, embodied in the possibilities of total war, push-button execution, biological warfare, fusion bombs, and the like, did amount to differences in kind. But this does not hold of the past right up to the immediate present, including World War II, the Korean War, and the other struggles in Asia and Africa. Such a truth justifies the study in our next few chapters of these bewildering wars, big and little, the uncertain treaties of peace, the dubious diplomacy of early modern times. Such a study should at the very least give us some perspective on our present troubles. Politically and morally, if not technologically, they are much the same troubles that our forefathers have known for four centuries and that we know now.

By 1500, then, almost all these states possessed in at least a rudimentary form most of the social and political organs of a modern state. They lacked only a large literate population brought up in the ritual and faith of national patriotism. Notably they had two essential organs, a diplomatic service and an army, both professional, both usually controlled from a common governmental center.

Diplomacy

Some forms of diplomacy can be traced back into the Middle Ages, and indeed into ancient times. But the fifteenth and sixteenth centuries saw the full development of modern diplomatic agencies and methods. Governments established central foreign offices and sent diplomats on regular missions to foreign courts. Espionage and the secret services developed under the cover of open diplomacy. Formal peace conferences were held, and formal treaties were signed, to the accompaniment of the ceremony and protocol we now associate with such occasions. Finally, a set of rules governing all these formal relations began to take shape, a set of rules that can be called international law.

The apparatus of international politics developed most fully and soonest in Renaissance Italy, and found its classic expression in the admirably organized diplomatic service of the Republic of Venice. The detailed reports Venetian ambassadors sent back to the Senate from abroad are among the first documents of intelligence work we have. They are careful political and social studies of the personalities and lands involved rather than mere gossipy cloak-and-dagger reports. Here is an excerpt from the report of the Venetian ambassador to England in the reign of the Catholic Mary Tudor. If its estimate of English political psychology seems strange, remember that in less than twenty-five years the English had changed their religion officially three times.

But as for religion, speaking generally, your Highness may be sure that the example and the authority of the prince can here achieve everything. For as the English think highly of religion, and are moved by it, so they satisfy their sense of duty towards the prince, living as he lives, believing as he believes, and finally doing all he tells them to. In all this the English rather conform externally, in order not to be in disfavor with their ruler than follow any inner light, for they would conform in the same way to the Mohammedan or Jewish faith were the King to adopt such a faith and want them to, and indeed they would accommodate themselves to anything, but the more readily to something that seemed to promise them more freedom of living—or more utility.*

In those days, the diplomat abroad was a

*E. Alberi, *Relazione degli Ambasciatori veneti,* Series I (Florence, 1839 ff.)., II, 362. Our translation.

most important maker of policy in his own right. With rapid travel impossible, his government could not communicate with him in time to prescribe his acts minutely, and he had often to make important decisions on his own responsibility. Good or bad diplomacy, good or bad intelligence about foreign lands, made a vital difference in a state's success or failure in the struggle for power.

The Armed Forces

The armed forces made still more difference. These early modern centuries are the great days of the professional soldier, freed from the limitations of feudal warfare and not yet tied to the immense economic requirements and the inhuman scale of our modern warfare. The officer class in particular could plan, drill, and campaign on a fairly large but quite manageable scale; they could do more than the interminable jousting of late medieval times. They could, so to speak, handle warfare as an art and sometimes as a pleasure. The common soldiers had a less agreeable life. But they too, for the most part, were paid professionals; indeed the word "soldier" comes from *solidus,* the Latin for a "piece of money." Recruited usually from among the poor and dispossessed, sometimes by force, they became inured to many hardships and were on the whole rather more secure in food, clothing, and housing than their poorer civilian relatives. Certainly they rarely mutinied.

The armed forces were the ruler's forces, no longer mere feudal levies. They were paid professionals, often trained to parade, to dress ranks, to keep discipline. They were whipped if they broke discipline, although threats of punishment did not always prevent desertions when pay was late or rations inadequate. Each regiment, troop, or other unit commonly wore the same uniforms; whole armies, however, usually displayed such an extraordinary variety of costume that in battle recognition of friend and foe was not easy. Tactics and strategy in the field were under the control of a formal officer hierarchy that culminated in a general in command, who in turn was at least somewhat controlled by the central government through a ministry of war. In short, though these armies would look anarchic to a modern professional of the spit-and-polish school, they were far better organized and better disciplined than feudal levies had been.

Yet the early modern armies also show many feudal survivals, many forms of entrenched privilege, many ways of twisting away from centralized control. The officer class continued to preserve many of its old habits of chivalry, such as the duel, which often seriously menaced internal discipline. If the feudal lord no longer brought his own knights for the forty days of allotted time, his descendant as regimental colonel often raised his own regiment and financed it himself. Weapons were of an extraordinary variety. Reminders of the old hand-to-hand fighting survived in the sword and in the pike, the long shaft used by foot soldiers against the armored knight and his mount. Hand firearms—arquebus, musket, and many others—were slow-loading and slow-firing, and usually not even capable of being aimed with any accuracy. The cannon, quite unstandardized as to parts and caliber, and heavy and hard to move, fired solid balls, rather than exploding shells.

Armies on the march lived mostly off the land, even when they were in home territory.

But they were beginning to develop the elaborate modern organization of supply and the modern service of engineers. Both the growth of military technology and differences of national temperament were reflected in the shift of military predominance from Spain to France about 1600. Spain, the great fighting nation of the sixteenth century on land, excelled in infantry, where the pike was a major weapon. France, the great fighting nation of the seventeenth and early eighteenth centuries on land, excelled in artillery, engineering, and fortification, all services that were more plebeian, less suited to the former feudal nobility than infantry and cavalry.

Meanwhile, the first modern navies were also growing up. In the later Middle Ages, Venice, Genoa, and Pisa had all begun to assemble fleets of galleys disciplined both in the running of each ship and in maneuvers as a fleet. In the Renaissance, Venice took the lead with its arsenal and its detailed code of maritime regulations (see Chapter 2). Naval organization, naval supply, the dispatch and handling of ships, all required more orderly centralized methods than an army. They could not tolerate the survival of rugged feudal individualism, indiscipline, and lack of planning. The officer class, as in the armies, was predominantly aristocratic, but it came usually from the more adventurous, the less custom-

Hanging of thieves during the Thirty Years' War, from a contemporary engraving.

ridden part of that class. During the sixteenth century, naval supremacy passed out of the Mediterranean to the Atlantic, where it rested briefly with Spain, and thence passed in the seventeenth century to the northern maritime powers of England, Holland, and France.

II   Habsburg and Valois

The Italian Wars
of Charles VIII and Louis XII

Charles VIII of France (1483–1498) inherited from his parsimonious father Louis XI a well-filled treasury and a good army (see Chapter 2). He added to his kingdom by marrying the heiress to the Duchy of Brittany, which had long been largely independent of the French crown. Apparently secure on the home front, Charles decided to expand abroad. As the remote heir of the Angevins who had seized the throne of Naples in the thirteenth century, Charles disputed the right of the Aragonese Ferrante (see Chapter 2) to hold that throne. He chose to invade Italy, however, not only because he had this tenuous genealogical claim but also because Renaissance Italy was rich, held romantic attractions for the northerners, and was divided into small rival political units—it looked, in short, to be easy picking. So it was at first, for in the winter of 1494–95 Charles paraded his army through to Naples in triumph. But his acquisition of Brittany had already disturbed his neighbors, and his possession of Naples threatened the balance of power in Italy. The French intrusion provoked the first of the great modern coalitions, the so-called Holy League of the Papacy (which, remember, was also an Italian territorial state), composed of the Empire, Spain, Venice, Milan, and soon England. This coalition forced the French armies out of Italy without much trouble in 1495.

Charles was followed on the French throne by his cousin of the Orléans branch of the Valois family, Louis XII (1498–1515). Louis married Charles' widow to make sure of Brittany, and then tried again in Italy, reinforced by still another genealogical claim, this time to Milan. Since his grandmother came from the Visconti family, Louis regarded the Sforza dukes as simple usurpers; he proceeded to drive Il Moro from Milan in 1499 (see Chapter 2). In this second French invasion, the play of alliances was much subtler and more complicated, quite worthy of the age of Machiavelli. Louis tried to insure himself from the isolation that had ruined Charles by allying in 1500 with Ferdinand of Aragon, with whom he agreed to partition Naples. Then, in 1508, Louis helped form one of those cynical coalitions that look on paper as though they could break the balance-of-power principle, because they are the union of the strong against a much weaker victim. This was the League of Cambray, in which Louis, Ferdinand, Pope Julius II, and the Emperor Maximilian joined to divide up the lands held in the lower Po Valley by rich but—on land at least—militarily weak Republic of Venice.

The practical trouble with such combinations is that the combiners do not really trust one another, and usually fall to quarreling over the pickings. All went well for the despoilers at first, though the Venetians rallied and re-took their mainland stronghold of Padua. Then Ferdinand, having taken the Neapolitan towns he wanted, decided to desert Louis. The Pope, frightened at the prospect that France and the Empire might squeeze him out entirely, in 1511 formed another "Holy League" *with* Venice and Ferdinand, later joined by Henry VIII of England and the Emperor Maximilian, *against* France. Despite some early successes in the field, the French could not hold out against such a coalition, for they now had a war on two fronts.

Henry VIII attacked the north of France and won at Guinegate in 1513 a battle that has always been a sore spot with Frenchmen. It was called (by the English) the "battle of the spurs" from the speed with which the French cavalry spurred their flight from the battlefield. In Italy too the French were defeated, and Louis XII, like Charles VIII, was checkmated.

Charles V and Francis I: The First Round

These two French efforts were, however, merely preliminaries. The important phase of this first great modern test of the balance of power was to follow immediately, and to take a basically different form. For there were now really two aggressors: the French House of Valois, still bent on expansion, and the House of Habsburg. When the Habsburg Charles V succeeded his grandfather Maximilian as emperor in 1519, he was a disturber by the mere fact of his existence rather than by temperament or intent. As we have already seen in Chapter 4 he had inherited Spain, the Low Countries, Germany (that is, the imperial headship of the Holy Roman Empire), and the preponderance in Italy. He apparently had France squeezed in a perfect vise.

The vise almost closed. The French king, Francis I, was badly defeated by the imperial—mostly Spanish—forces at Pavia in 1525. Francis himself was taken prisoner and held in Madrid until he signed a treaty giving up all his Italian claims, and ceding the Duchy of Burgundy. This treaty he repudiated the moment he was safely back on French soil. It is probable that Charles V would not have "eliminated" France entirely even had he been able to. These early modern wars were in no sense "total" wars, and there were accepted limits to what might decently be done to the defeated. Certainly these people convey the impression of engaging in a kind of professional athleticism that was often bloody and unscrupulous but by no means without rules. The players sometimes changed sides. In fact, one of the imperial commanders at the battle

of Pavia in which the French were so badly beaten was the Constable de Bourbon, a great French noble at odds with his king.

Two years after Pavia, an incident occurred that burnt deeply into the minds of contemporaries—the horrible sack of Rome in 1527 by the Spanish and German mercenaries of the emperor, led by the Frenchman Bourbon. These mercenaries had become infuriated by delays in pay and supplies. In a sudden shift of alignment, Pope Clement VII, a Medici and a good Italian at heart, had turned against the foreign Charles, and had allied himself with Francis and the other main Italian powers in the League of Cognac in 1526. The siege of Rome was part of Charles' reply, but the sack was a horror that he had not planned, and that lay heavily on his conscience as a good Catholic. This was one of the horrors of war that outrage public opinion in all but the most hardened partisan circles.

Charles was now at the height of his power. By the end of the decade, he had made peace with the Pope and with Francis. In 1530, he was crowned by the Pope as Emperor and as King of Italy, the last ruler to receive this double crown, this inheritance of Charlemagne and the ages, with the full formality of tradition. But the western world over which he thus symbolically ruled was a very different world from Charlemagne's, and Charles was in fact no emperor, but a new dynast in a new conflict of power.

Charles V and Francis I: The Second Round

France was still in the vise between the Spanish and the German holdings of Charles, and Francis I, a proud, consciously virile Renaissance prince, was not one to accept for long so precarious a position—above all, a position in which he lost face. He used the death of the Sforza ruler of Milan in 1535 to reopen the old claim to Milan and to begin the struggle once more. Neither Francis nor Charles lived to see the end even of this particular phase of the Habsburg-Valois rivalry. Neither side secured decisive military victory.

In 1559, the important Treaty of Cateau-Cambrésis confirmed Habsburg control of Milan and Naples. It marked the failure of France to acquire a real foothold in Italy, but it also marked the failure of the Habsburgs to lessen the real strength of France. The vise had not been closed; the war had been stalemated.

It had not closed largely because France proved militarily, economically, and politically strong enough to resist the pressure. But the vise itself was a most imperfect instrument. Charles was not as strong as he looked on the map to be. His German arm was paralyzed by the political consequences of the Protestant Reformation (see Chapter 4). Even in the decade of the 1520's, when the power of Charles was at its height, the Protestant princes of Germany had formed the League of Torgau to resist him. All the rest of his life, Germany was to be in a state of civil war, marked by truces indeed, and by attempts to settle the religious question, but never permitting the Emperor to count on a united Germany against France.

The last phase of the personal duel between the aging rivals, Charles and Francis, is a concrete example of how many variables enter the play of balance of power. Francis, to gain allies, did not hesitate to turn to Charles' rebellious German subjects. Although head of a Catholic state, a "most Christian" king, he allied himself with the Protestant Duke of Cleves. He did not even stop with Protestants, but concluded an alliance with the Moslem Sultan Suleiman of Turkey (see Chapter 2), who attacked Charles in the rear in Hungary. At the death of Francis in 1547, his son Henry II continued the Protestant alliance.

One other participant in the complex struggles of the first half of the sixteenth century was England. Though not yet a great power, she was already a major element in international politics. The men who guided English policy were probably not moved by a consciously held theory of the balance of power which told them to intervene in Europe always on behalf of the group that was being beaten, that seemed weaker at the time; but they often behaved as though they had arrived intuitively at some such conclusion. Other

Francis I, by Clouet.

factors were also involved. For one thing, England after 1534 was deeply involved in her own religious troubles; moreover, she had on her northern border an independent Scotland, which tended to side with France. Finally, to English statesmen, with memories of the long medieval struggles with the French, the great hereditary enemy was always France. Yet in a pinch the English were quite capable of allying with the hereditary French enemy if they thought Charles was too strong. This happened in 1527, after Charles had won at Pavia and had taken Rome. The English minister, Cardinal Wolsey, in that year worked out an alliance with France.

But the English were quite capable of reversing themselves. In 1543, when Charles

Political Situation, mid-16th Century

Austrian
Spanish
⎫
⎬
⎭ Possessions of the House of Habsburg

········ Boundary of the Empire

■ Battle sites

NORWAY

SCOTLAND

North Sea

Edinburgh

IRELAND

DENMARK

Baltic

Dublin

ENGLAND
(TUDOR)

BRANDENBURG

Bremen

Elbe R.

Atlantic Ocean

Bosworth
Field

Torgau

SILESIA

London

Leipzig

SAXONY

Calais

NETHERLANDS

Cleves

Rhine R.

THE EMPIRE

BRITTANY

Seine R.

Vervins

LUXEMBOURG

45

Paris

Ivry

Verdun

Metz

Spires

BOHEMIA

Nantes

FRANCHE
COMTÉ

Toul

WÜRTTEM-
BERG

MORAVIA

Loire R.

Danube R.

Augsburg

AUSTRIA

15

FRANCE
(VALOIS)

BURGUNDY

Zurich

Vienna

Cognac

SWITZERLAND

BAVARIA

TYROL

STYRIA

AUVERGNE

Geneva

CARINTHIA

HU

Rhône R.

SAVOY

Trent

Milan

CARNIOLA

Avignon
(to the Papacy)

Pavia

Po R.

Padua

Venice

40

Valladolid

NAVARRE

BASQUE
PROV.

PROVENCE

Genoa

VENETIAN REPUBLIC

Tordesillas

Ebro R.

TUSCANY

PAPAL
STATES

Adriatic Sea

PORTUGAL

SPAIN

ARAGON

CORSICA
(to Genoa)

Madrid

NAPLES

Tagus R.

CASTILE

Rome

Toledo

BALEARIC IS.

SARDINIA

Naples

Guadalquivir R.

Palos

Seville

35

Cadiz

Mediterranean Sea

10

SICILY

(Tributary to Ottoman Empire)

B A R B A R Y   S T A T E S

MALTA

5

0

5

10

15

Inset map (top right)

0 — 100 — Miles

London
Armada sea fight
Utrecht
Calais
Bruges
Antwerp
FLANDERS
Boulogne
Guinegate
Scheldt R.
ARTOIS
NETHERLANDS
Cambray
Cateau-Cambrésis
FRANCE

60

55

50

Main map

25 30 35 40 45

TEUTONIC ORDER

Volga R.

55

R U S S I A

Moscow

Oka R.

W. Dvina R.

50

RUSSIA

L I T H U A N I A

Don R.

Volga R.

55

45

LAND

Kiev

UKRAINE

KHANATE

Ural R.

Dnieper R.

Dniester R.

OF THE

MOLDAVIA

CRIMEA

Caspian Sea

40

TRANSYLVANIA

50

Belgrade

WALLACHIA

Black Sea

Danube R.

ONTE-GRO

35

Constantinople

O T T O M A N   E M P I R E

Salonika

Tigris R.

Aegean Sea

Lepanto

Euphrates R.

PELOPONNESUS

(to Venice)

RHODES

CRETE

CYPRUS
(to Venice)

0 — 500

Miles

25 30 35 40 45

was beset by Protestants and Turks, Henry VIII came to his aid against Francis. But not too vigorously. In the campaign of 1544, something like a Christian revulsion against the French alliance with the heathen Turk had brought the Germans together for the moment, and a German army was actually on its way to Paris along the Marne Valley route. The English had landed on the Channel coast; had they really pressed matters in co-operation with the Germans, Paris itself might have fallen. But they rather deliberately besieged the Channel port of Boulogne, and Francis escaped with his capital city intact.

The Peace of Augsburg

Charles V, beset by Protestants, French, and Turks, allowed in 1555 the very important German religious settlement known as the Peace of Augsburg. By this peace, the Protestants were formally recognized as established in the regions over which they held power at the time. Augsburg marks the formal end of the first great effort to keep the Empire wholly Catholic. But it by no means established full toleration in the modern sense. Its guiding principle is in the Latin phrase *cuius regio eius religio,* freely translated as *whoever rules an area may establish the religion of that area.* The ruler of Saxony is Lutheran: Then all Saxons are practicing Lutherans. The ruler of Bavaria is Catholic: Then all Bavarians are practicing Catholics. To work, this settlement would have had to mean that all the many German states were self-sealed little blocks of one religion, which was quite impossible. Each had, in fact, religious minorities.

Two concrete failures of the Augsburg settlement made a renewal of religious strife almost certain. First, no solution was reached concerning "ecclesiastical reservation," the problem of what happened to the property of the Church in a given region if its ruler were a Catholic prelate who was converted to Protestantism. Second, by recognizing formally only the Catholic and Lutheran faiths, the settlement ignored the growing numbers

of militant Calvinists who were bound to press for equal treatment. Still, with all its weaknesses, Augsburg made possible the permanent establishment of Protestantism on a peaceful footing in Germany. Together with the Treaty of Cateau-Cambrésis, it brought to an end the first great Habsburg effort to dominate Europe.

The Wars of Philip II

The second effort at domination of Europe was less Habsburg than Spanish. In 1556, Charles V abdicated both his Spanish and imperial crowns and retired to a monastery, where he died two years later. His brother, Ferdinand I (1556–1564), secured the Austrian Habsburg complex of territories and, by election, the Empire. His son, Philip II (1556–1598), got Spain and the overseas colonies, the Burgundian inheritance of the Netherlands, and the Italian holdings of Milan and Naples. Philip's realm was no mere national state; even without the Germanies, it was a supranational state threatening France, England, and the whole balance of power. Its rich possessions in the New World helped provide it with resources for war.

Like his father, Philip II found Protestantism and the concept of many separate Christian political units intolerable. He sought, if not world conquest, at least the forced unity of the West. Philip's attempt to invade England and restore Catholicism there has left him as one of the villains of Anglo-Saxon tradition. He was indeed no bright, jovial Renaissance monarch, but he was hardly the cold-blooded "Devil of the south" he appeared to be to Protestants and moderate Catholics. He was a serious, hard-working administrator, and certainly no lover of war for its own sake. He saw Protestantism as an intolerable divisive force that must be wiped out by force if necessary. He was a doctrinaire chained to a past no one could restore, committed to a lost cause.

Philip's major points of involvement were: (1) Italy, which as long as it remained divided was to be a major source of difficulties in the play of balance of power or, put another way, a source of territory to be annexed by expansionist powers; (2) the Netherlands, where the revolt of his Dutch Protestant subjects was soon to involve Philip not only with them but with Protestant England; (3) France, where the second half of the century brought a series of civil wars of religion in which Philip was bound to appear as the Catholic champion, (4) the Mediterranean, where the Turks, now at the height of their naval power, threatened Spanish control; (5) finally, as we shall see in the next chapter, England and France were beginning to challenge the monopoly Spain and Portugal had tried to set up in the newly discovered Americas and in Asia. Since this New World as well as the Old World was at stake in Philip's wars, there is some justification for considering these as in fact the first "world wars."

The Dutch Revolt

The dramatic focal point of these struggles was the revolt of the Netherlands. When the Burgundian inheritance had come to the Habsburgs, Charles V had made no attempt to absorb these provinces into a unified superstate. They were simply parts of a great dynastic holding, parts that were essentially autonomous, with their own complex of feudal privileges confirmed by their new ruler. They had medieval estates or assemblies, representing privileged groups, which raised taxes and armies. Like most northern lands, the Low Countries had felt the full force of the Protestant Reformation. In mid-sixteenth century, the religious situation was still fluid. In resistance to Philip, the northern provinces which we often call "Holland" after the most important one, became firmly Calvinist.

Philip II was by nature and temperment bound to antagonize his subjects in the Low Countries. Charles V had liked the Low Countries and had made Brussels his favorite place of residence, but Philip was thoroughly Spanish in outlook. For all his medievalism,

he had up-to-date ideas about centralized, efficient rule and curtailed the political liberties of the Netherlands. And he hated all forms of Protestantism. Finally, the economic element was also present, for the Dutch were a seafaring commercial people, desirous of conducting a trade freed from the jealous restrictions of Spanish regulation of trade and industry.

This explosive mixture of religion, politics, and economic interests produced the revolt. Philip sent Spanish garrisons to the Netherlands, and attempted to enforce edicts against heretics. Opposition, which centered at first in the privileged classes who had been most affected by Philip's political restrictions, soon spread to the common people. In the riots that broke out, Catholic churches were destroyed; a league was formed against the Spaniards, proudly taking on the name of "Beggars," which had first been used by a scornful con-

Philip II of Spain.

servative; indeed all the apparatus of revolution made its appearance. When in 1567 Philip dispatched to the Netherlands an army of twenty thousand Spaniards headed by the unyielding, politically stupid Duke of Alba, the revolt had fully begun.

The Spanish infantry was in those days incomparably the best in Europe, and the Dutch were ill-armed and ill-prepared. The Dutch resistance, successful in the long run, was a heroic achievement against great odds, fully deserving the praise sympathetic historians have given it. It was, however, no extraordinary victory of weakness over strength, but rather a victory in full accord with what was until the twentieth century, and perhaps now is again, a fact of western political life—that no thoroughly disaffected population can be long held down by force alone. Alba had the force, and he set up a Council of Troubles, which applied executions, confiscations, and severe taxation on a large scale. The Council has received from history the significant title of the "Council of Blood." Yet all that this repression accomplished was to unite opposition against Alba, for the southern provinces of the Netherlands, which we know as Belgium, now joined the northern provinces. Both the ordinarily peaceful merchants and the great nobles like William the Silent, Prince of Orange, stood with the populace and with the adventurous "Beggars," who turned to a sort of naval guerrilla warfare. Alba gave up in despair in 1573, but it was not until the Duke of Parma was sent out in 1578 that Philip's policy showed signs of the essential element of statesmanship, a willingness to compromise in the face of facts.

Under Parma, the southern provinces at least were won back by political concessions to their old privileges of self-rule; they remained basically Catholic. But it was too late to win back the northern provinces, except perhaps by radical religious concessions which Philip was by temperament utterly unable to make. By the Union of Utrecht, the Dutch tightened their organization and in 1581 took the decisive step of declaring themselves independent of the Spanish Crown. They made

good that declaration by their courageous use of their now much better-organized land forces. But they were greatly helped by three facts. First, Philip, like most of the great aggressors, had been drawn into fighting on more than one land front. He had to cope with Turks, the French Protestants, and the anti-Spanish moderate French Catholics, as well as with grave internal economic problems. Second, fate gave the Dutch that invaluable spiritual aid, a martyr. And last and most important, they acquired the support from outside of a major ally.

The martyr was William the Silent, who was assassinated in 1584 by an individual moved either by religious hatred or by the reward Philip had set upon the outlawed Dutchman's head, or by both. William's death deprived the Dutch of the first great leader in their national history, but the assassination did not profit the Spanish cause. It made William, who was a western European nobleman without strong religious feeling, a Protestant and Dutch hero. The ally was England, now under Elizabeth I firmly Protestant and from the start sympathetic with the Dutch cause. Elizabeth, however, was no crusader, and her kingdom appeared to be no match for powerful Spain. She had been hesitant to come out openly on the Dutch side, especially since in the uncertain condition of French politics in the midst of internal religious wars, a Franco-Spanish alliance against England and Holland seemed by no means impossible. Here too Philip showed himself incapable of diplomacy. He permitted France to maneuver into neutrality, and provoked England by fomenting Catholic plots against Elizabeth. The English in turn, provoked Spain. For years they had been preying on Spanish commerce on the high seas, and Hawkins, Drake, and other English sailors had been raiding Spanish possessions in the New World. When an English army came to the aid of the Dutch in 1585, Philip decided to make formal war on England, though he still had the Dutch, the Turks, and other enemies on his hands. He, like all aggressors in the last few centuries, took on too many enemies at the same time, over-extended himself.

The End of Philip II

The great Spanish Armada of unwieldy men-of-war which he sent out to invade England was defeated in the English Channel in July, 1588, by a skillfully maneuvered lighter English fleet, and was utterly destroyed afterward by a great storm. The battle was the beginning of the end of Spanish preponderance, the beginning of English greatness in international politics, and the decisive step in the achievement of the independence of the Dutch Republic. These portentous results were not so evident in 1588 as they are now, but even at the time the defeat of the Armada was seen as a great event. Protestants everywhere were greatly heartened, and the great storm that finished the destruction of the Spanish fleet was christened the "Protestant wind."

Philip II died in 1598 after a long and painful illness, in the great, severe palace of the Escorial he had built near Madrid. He had ordered an open coffin put beside his bed, and a skull with a crown of gold. Save for the seven northern provinces of the Netherlands—and even these he had never officially given up—the great possessions with which he had begun to reign were still his. Indeed, he had added Portugal in 1580 at the death of the Portuguese Cardinal-King Henry and had made the whole Iberian Peninsula formally if briefly one. Yet he knew almost as clearly as we know that his life had been a failure. He left his kingdom, as we shall see, worn out, drained of men and money. And, whatever his

The battle between the English fleet and the Spanish Armada, 1588.

aims in international politics had been, whether a Spanish hegemony, a revived western Empire, or merely the extinction of the Protestant heresy, he had realized none of them. Under his illegitimate half-brother Don John of Austria, the Spanish fleet had indeed participated in the great naval victory over the Turkish fleet at Lepanto in 1571 (see p. 76). But Lepanto was at most a checking of Turkish expansion, not a great gain for the Spaniards. It was no balance for the loss of the great Armada.

III   The New States: Spain and France

The "Age of Absolutism"

We may now turn our attention to the domestic affairs of these "new" states, new by contrast with their medieval past. For the sixteenth and seventeenth centuries witnessed all over the West an uneven working out of the new political aims and methods of the Renaissance. The states that took part in the dynastic and religious wars we have just traced were all to a degree centralized states with paid professional armies and paid professional civilian bureaucrats. They had a central financial system with *some* control over even local taxation and the supply of money, a central legal system that made some attempt to apply the same kind of law to all individuals within the state, and a central authority— king, king and council, king and parliament, estates, Cortes, or other assembly—that could actually make new laws. Phrases like "Age of Absolutism" and "Divine Right of Kings" are frequently used of the early modern centuries, and not without reason. Over almost all of Europe, the control of central administration usually rested with a monarch who inherited his throne and claimed the right to make the kind of final decisions that modern democracies make by some sort of popular vote, or at least through legislatures.

But it is of major importance to note that everywhere in the sixteenth century there were strong survivals of the old medieval local privileges, of local ways of life quite different from the standards set by the court or the capital. The early modern governments were less "absolute," in at least one very significant sense of the term, than the government of a modern democracy like the United States. They could not possibly make *and enforce* the kind of regulation which federal and state agencies nowadays can make and enforce—public health regulations like pure food and drug acts, licensing the practice of medicine, setting of standards of measure, even the kind of standardization of higher education we have achieved in the training of teachers, for instance, by accreditation and other controls. This last instance suggests that standardization, the efficient application of general rules to large areas and large groups, is in the United States partly a matter of voluntary control from *below*. Generally speaking, such collaboration from below was not attained in these first modern centuries. The standardization came from *above*, from a small group that had been won over to these new methods of governing, which did increase their power. It is this active attempt of a minority to achieve "streamlining" that justifies our use of terms like absolutism for these centuries.

Power and Limits of Spanish Absolutism

Spain provides a clear-cut example of the difference between the concepts of absolutism with which this minority worked and the varied and often successfully recalcitrant groups on which this minority sought to impose its standardized rules. The reigns of the two hard-working Spanish monarchs, Charles V (technically, Charles I of Spain, 1516–1556, and Charles V as Holy Roman Emperor) and Philip II (1556–1598), span almost the whole sixteenth century. Charles was rather a medieval survival than a modern king. He did little to remodel the instruments of government he inherited from his grandparents, Ferdinand and Isabella (see Chapter 2). Brought up in the Low Countries, Charles came to Spain a stranger, with a Flemish following that already had the modern northern European contempt for "backward" Spain, and showed it. His election to the imperial throne made him further suspect in Spain. In 1520, a group of Spanish cities, led by Toledo, rose up in the revolt of the *comuneros*. This revolt, like most such uprisings, was compounded of many elements. The municipalities disliked the growth of central control; the aristocrats were restless in the face of the new monarchical dignity, no longer just like their own; the poor and the middling had class feelings and grievances.

The *comuneros* were put down in 1521, but Charles had been frightened out of what reforming zeal he may have had, and did his best not to offend his Spanish subjects. He son, at least, grew up a Spaniard first of all.

Philip II was much more willing and able to build a new-model centralized state in Spain. He did devise a system of consultative councils, topped by a council of state, and manned by great nobles; but these councils could do no more than advise. Philip made the final decisions, and the details were worked out by a series of private secretaries and local organs of government, not manned by nobles. Furthermore, Philip reduced the representative assemblies, the Cortes, to practical impotence, especially in Castile. Nobles and priests, because they did not pay direct taxes, no longer attended the sessions of the Cortes, and the delegates of the cities were left as a powerless rump. Above all, Philip had assured sources of income—his tax of a fifth of the value of the precious cargoes from America, direct taxes from the constituent states of his realm, revenues from the royal estates and

The Escorial, the combined palace, monastery, and mausoleum built by Philip II near Madrid.

from the sale of offices and patents of nobility, revenues from the authorized sale, at royal profit, of dispensations allowed by the pope (permission to eat meat on Fridays and in Lent, and even something very close to the very indulgences that had raised Germany against the pope). Philip, like most continental monarchs of his time, had no need to worry over representative bodies with control of the purse. Yet he was always heavily in debt, and at his death in 1598 left his government almost bankrupt.

Even in this matter of revenue, where Philip's power at first sight looks so complete and unchecked, the actual limitations of the absolute monarch of early modern times are clear. Except by borrowing and hand-to-mouth expedients like the sale of offices, he could not notably increase his income. He could not summon any representative group together and get them to vote new monies. In the first place, the constituent parts of his realm, Castile, Aragon, Navarre, the Basque Provinces, the Italian lands, the Low Countries, the Americas, and the newest Spanish lands, named after the monarch himself, the Philippine Islands, had no common organs of consultation. Each had to be dealt with as a separate problem. For the most part the nobility and clergy were tax-exempt, and could not be called upon for unusual financial sacrifices. Add to all this the difficulty of collection, the opportunities for graft, and the lack of a long accumulated administrative and financial experience, and one can see why Philip could not have introduced a more systematic general taxation.

Outside the financial sphere, the obstacles to really effective centralization were even more serious. The union of the crowns of Aragon and Castile, achieved by the marriage of Ferdinand and Isabella, had by no means made a unified Spain. To this day, regionalism—to call it by a mild name—is perhaps more acute in Spain than in any other large European state. In those days, some of the provinces did not even have extradition arrangements for the surrender of common criminals within the peninsula. Many of them could and did levy customs dues on goods from the others. The

old northern regions, which had never been well conquered by the Moslems, preserved all sorts of *fueros* or privileges. Aragon still preserved the office of *justicia mayor*, a judge nominated, it is true, by the Crown, but for life, and entrusted with an authority something remotely like that of the United States Supreme Court.

What the Habsburgs might have accomplished in Spain had they been able to expend their full energies on the task of uniting and developing their lands can never be known. What they did do was exhaust the peninsula and weaken the lands overseas in their effort to secure hegemony over Europe and to subdue the Protestant heresy. This was indeed the great age of Spain, the age when both on land and on sea the Spanish were admired and envied as the best fighters, the age when Spain seemed destined to be mistress of both the Americas, the age when Spain seemed the richest of states, the age of Loyola and Cervantes, the golden age of Spanish religion, literature, and art. But it was a brief flowering, and Spanish greatness largely vanished in the seventeenth century.

The Spanish Economy

Spain is a classical example of a great political unit that failed to maintain a sound economic underpinning for its greatness. The peninsula is mountainous, and its central tableland is subject to droughts, but its agricultural potentialities are greater, for example, than those of Italy as a whole and it has mineral resources, notably in iron. Moreover, Spain was the first of the great European states to attain lands overseas, and a navy and merchant marine to integrate the great resources of the New World with an Old World base. Yet all this wealth slipped through Spain's fingers in a few generations. Certainly a major factor in this decline was the immense cost of the wars of Charles V and Philip II. The Low Countries, which had brought in a large revenue to Charles, were a pure drain on Philip's finances. The famous Spanish infantry had to be paid everywhere it went, and the money thus spent went out of Spain forever, with nothing in the long run to show for it. Philip took over from his father a heavy debt, which grew heavier through his long reign.

Now governmental expenditure on armed forces, though in itself unproductive, is not necessarily fatal to a national economy. If such expenditure stimulates even greater productivity within the nation and its dependencies, then the nation may bear it, and even grow in wealth, as did imperial Germany after 1870. But this was not true of sixteenth-century Spain. She drew from the New World vast amounts of silver and many articles—sugar, indigo, tobacco, cocoa, hides—without which she could hardly have carried on her European wars at all. But it was not enough to pay for world dominion. The bullion passed through Spanish hands into those of bankers and merchants in other European countries, partly to pay for the Spanish armies and navies, partly to pay for the manufactured goods Spain had to send to the New World.

In accordance with an economic policy common to other colonial powers of the time, Spain forbade industrial production in her colonies and sought to supply them with manufactured goods. *But she could not, or did not, develop her own industrial production to take care of this need.* Her merchants had by royal decree a monopoly on trade with the Indies. But as the century wore on, they were more and more reduced to the role of mere middlemen, sending to the Indies goods increasingly imported from the rest of Europe—and paid for with the bullion of the Indies. The English, the Dutch, and other competitors smuggled goods into Spanish overseas territories on a large scale. To use a favorite modern term, Spain's governmental expenditures were not used to "prime the pump" for increased national productivity—or, more accurately, the pumps they primed were not Spanish, but foreign, pumps. By 1600, Spanish home industry was on the decline.

The free-trade economists of the nineteenth century offered a simple explanation for this failure of Spain to make good use of her economic opportunities—monopoly under government supervision. Sixteenth-century Spain was certainly moving toward that economic policy called *mercantilism*, which reached its fullest development in seventeenth-century France (see Chapter 7). Although Spain lacked the true mercantilist passion for building national wealth under government auspices, she used many mercantilist techniques, the endless regulation in general and the narrow channeling of colonial trade in particular. The Spanish system left little room for individual economic initiative. In Castile, a single institution, the famous *Casa de Contratación* (House of Trade), controlled every transaction with the Indies and licensed every export and import. The amount of sheer paper work, in an age unblessed by typewriters and mimeographs, was enormous.

Yet bureaucratic methods and monopolies were not the sole source of difficulty. The whole direction of Spanish civilization turned Spanish creative energies into other channels than the industrial. Warfare, politics, religion, art, traditional farming, or simply living like an *hidalgo* (*hijo de algo*, "son of somebody," hence nobleman, gentleman) were respectable activities. What Americans broadly understand by "business" was, if not disgraceful, certainly not an activity on which society set a premium. Not that as a nation the Spanish were lazy; the lower classes especially had to work very hard. That epitome of so much we think of as Spanish, Don Quixote, was hardly a lazy man, but his activity was not exactly productive of material wealth. If we take into consideration the numerous holidays, the habit of the siesta, the large numbers of beggars, soldiers, priests, monks, and *hidalgos*, as well as the lack of encouragement to new enterprises and techniques and the heavy hand of an inefficient bureaucracy—if we put all this together, it becomes clear that the total national effort was bound to be inadequate in competition with nations better organized for modern economic life. Spain, in short, presents almost the antithesis of the picture of what goes into the "capitalist spirit" drawn by Weber and his school (see Chapter 4).

The Spanish Style

Yet the Spanish supremacy, though short-lived, was real enough, and has helped make the world we live in. Half the Americas speak Spanish (or a rather similar tongue, Portuguese) and carry, however altered, a cultural inheritance from the Iberian Peninsula. French, Dutch, and English national unity and national spirit were hardened in resistance to Spanish aggression. The Spanish character, the Spanish "style," was set—some may say hardened—in this Golden Age, which has left to the West some magnificent paintings and one of the few really universal books, the *Don Quixote* of Cervantes (1547–1616). This Spanish style is not at all like those of France and Italy, so often tied with Spain as "Latin"—a term that is very misleading if used to contrast these nations with "Nordic" or "Germanic" nations. Perhaps the term is most misleading when it groups these lands and their peoples together as "sunny." For the Spanish spirit is among the most serious, most darkly passionate, most unsmiling, in the West. It is a striving spirit, carrying to the extreme the chivalric "point of honor," the religious pain of living in this flesh, the desire for something more.

The Spanish spirit stands out vividly in the paintings of an artist who was not a native Spaniard at all, but El Greco, "the Greek" (1541–1614). Born Domenico Theotokopouli on the island of Crete, trained both in the Byzantine tradition of the Aegean world and at the school of Titian in Venice, he settled at Toledo, the religious capital of Castile, when he was approaching the peak of his career. Despite his cosmopolitan background, El Greco belongs completely to the Spain of Philip II and the Catholic Reformation, not at all to the Renaissance.

The subject of one of El Greco's most famous paintings (see chapter opening) is a Spanish legend, the burial of the Count of Orgaz. This fourteenth-century Castilian nobleman had built a church at Toledo to honor

Saint Augustine and Saint Stephen. When he died, the two saints miraculously appeared to bury his body. In the painting, the two saints (Augustine is the bearded one) gently lift the Count, and the aristocratic mourners gravely witness the miracle as an angel conveys the Count's soul to the Virgin, to Christ, Saint Peter, and the host of the blessed waiting above. The whole effect is heightened by El Greco's characteristic distortion of human figures, with their long, thin heads, their great eyes turned upward. The painting stretches toward heaven like the pinnacles of a Gothic cathedral; it is a most extraordinary effort to record the mystic's unrecordable experience.

Spain is indeed the land of passionate religious will to overcome this world in mystical union with Christ. St. Theresa of Avila (1515–1582) and St. John of the Cross (1542–1591) bring back the tortured ecstasies of the early Christian ascetics, and add a dark, rebellious, note of their own. Theirs was no eastern attempt to withdraw from the world of sense and common sense, but a heroic effort to combat this world of the sense and thus transcend it. They were both familiar figures to the Spanish common people, who in their own way identified themselves with these saints in their struggle. Here is a portion of a modern writer's account of the funeral of St. John of the Cross:

Hardly had his breath ceased than, though it was an hour past midnight, cold and raining hard, crowds assembled in the street and poured into the convent. Pressing into the room where he lay, they knelt to kiss his feet and hands. They cut off pieces from his clothes and bandages and even pulled out the swabs that had been placed on his sores. Others took snippings from his hair and tore off his nails, and would have cut pieces from his flesh had it not been forbidden. At his funeral these scenes were repeated. Forcing their way past the friars who guarded his body, the mob tore off his habit and even took parts of his ulcered flesh.*

The creations of Cervantes, in their very different way, carry the mark of the Spanish

*Gerald Brenan, "A Short Life of St. John of the Cross," in *The Golden Horizon,* Cyril Connolly, ed. (London, 1953), 475–476.

style. Spain is Don Quixote tilting with the windmills, aflame for the Dulcinea he has invented, quite mad. But it is also the knight's servant, Sancho Panza, conventional, earthy, unheroic, and sane enough, though his sanity protects him not at all from sharing his master's misadventures. Cervantes almost certainly meant no more than an amusing satire of popular tales of chivalry. But his story has got caught up in the web of symbolism we live by, and the Don and his reluctant follower are for us Spain forever racked between ambitious heroism and reluctant common sense.

This tension runs all through *Don Quixote*. Chivalry is indeed silly, and worth satire —gentle satire:

'I would inform you, Sancho, that it is a point of honor with knights-errant to go for a month at a time without eating, and when they do eat, it is whatever may be at hand. You would certainly know that if you had read the histories as I have. There are many of them, and in none have I found any mention of knights eating unless it was by chance or at some sumptuous banquet that was tendered them; on other days they fasted. And even though it is well understood that, being men like us, they could not go without food entirely, any more than they could fail to satisfy the other necessities of nature, nevertheless, since they spent the greater part of their lives in forests and desert places without any cook to prepare their meals. . . .

'Pardon me, your Grace,' said Sancho, 'but seeing that, as I have told you, I do not know how to read or write, I am consequently not familiar with the rules of the knightly calling. Hereafter, I will stuff my saddlebags with all manner of dried fruit for your Grace, but inasmuch as I am not a knight, I shall lay in for myself a stock of fowls and other more substantial fare.'*

The extreme of pride—pride of race, of faith, of nation—has seemed to the outside world the mark of Spain. Perhaps there is little to choose among the triumphant prides of nations in triumph. Yet as the "shot heard round the world" sounds very American, so the Cid, the legendary hero of the reconquest, is very Spanish in these verses as he goes off to his crusade:

Don Quixote, Samuel Putnam, trans. (New York, 1949), I, 78–79.

Por necesidad batallo
Y una vez puesto en la silla
Se va ensanchando Castilla
Delante de mi caballo

[I fight by necessity: but once I am in the saddle, Castile goes widening out ahead of my horse.]

The French Monarchy

North of the Pyrenees another of the new monarchies had emerged in the fifteenth century. Perhaps no province of France—not even Brittany with its Celtic language and autonomous traditions, not even Provence with its language of the troubadours, its ties with Italy, its long history as a separate unit—shows the intense awareness of its own separateness that is to be found in Catalonia or the Basque Provinces of Spain. Moreover, unlike Greece, Italy, and the Iberian Peninsula, France for the most part is not cut up by mountain ranges into relatively isolated regions; the mountain barriers are mostly on her borders. Even so, France was but imperfectly tied together under Francis I (1515–1547), contemporary of Charles V and Henry VIII. Provinces like Brittany, which had only recently come under the Valois crown, retained their own local representative bodies (estates), their own local courts (*parlements*), and many other privileges. The nobility held on to feudal memories and attitudes, though it had lost most of its old governmental functions to royal appointees. The national bureaucracy was most rudimentary, a patchwork that could hardly fit into a modern administrative chart, with its little boxes showing who consults with whom, who obeys whom in a chain of authority.

As we have seen, however, the kingdom of Francis I possessed strength enough to counter the threat of encirclement by Charles V. The King himself was not another Louis XI. Self-indulgence weakened his health and distracted him from the business of government; his extravagant court and, far more, his frequent wars nearly wrecked the finances of the state. Yet in many respects Francis was a good Renaissance despot, thoroughly at home in the

The Chateau de Chambord, built by Francis I in the Loire Valley.

age of Machiavelli. In adversity he had courage: witness his successful recovery after the disaster at Pavia in 1525. In diplomacy he was unscrupulous and flexible: witness his alliance with the Turks and with the German Protestants. Good-looking (at least until his health broke down), amorous, courtly, lavish, Francis comported himself as many people expect royalty to behave. He did things on the grand scale; it is reported that it took 18,000 horses and pack animals to move the King and his court on their frequent journeys. Francis built the famous chateaux of Chambord and Fontainebleau, two of the masterpieces of French Renaissance architecture. In Paris he remodeled the great palace of the Louvre and founded the Collège de France, second only to the university (the Sorbonne) as an educational center. He patronized men of letters and artists, among them numerous Italians including Benvenuto Cellini and Leonardo da Vinci.

The artistic and humanist Renaissance spread gradually northward from Italy in the sixteenth century, taking on somewhat different characteristics in various countries. In France, the architecture of the Renaissance still bears the stamp of late Gothic, as at Chambord, or, as in the smaller chateaux like Chenonceaux, is classically French in its restraint and graceful ornamentation. French humanists are scholarly indeed, French poets conscious adapters of Latin and Greek concepts and language. Two very great sixteen-century French writers point up this national stamp, which is by no means without paradoxical contrasts, on a classic Renaissance ground: Rabelais (1494–1553), once a monk, exuberant, fleshly, optimistic, unreasonable, indecent, excited, undisciplined (but very learned), a perpetual reminder that not all French writers are logical, conventional adherents to literary standards of clarity and orderliness (see also pp. 89–90); and Montaigne (1533–1592), essayist, reasonable skeptic—very reasonable, a worried self-analyst, in his own way a seeker, and as a stylist one of the chief

172

makers of the rigorously disciplined, orderly, conventional French literary language (another, Blaise Pascal, we shall encounter in Chapter 7).

Francis was the last strong king of the House of Valois. After his death in 1547, his son Henry II and his grandsons, much under the control of Catherine de' Medici, their mother, were barely able to maintain the prestige of the Crown. Possibly not even a greatly gifted ruler could have prevented the disorders of the second half of the sixteenth century, disorders that seriously crippled France in the international rivalries of the day. These were the years of the French religious wars, the crisis that almost undid the centralizing work of Louis XI and his successors.

The French Wars of Religion, 1562–1598

Obvious parallels exist between the French religious wars and the German Thirty Years' War of the early seventeenth century (see p. 184). In both regions, important elements among the upper and middle classes welcomed the intellectual and spiritual concepts of Protestantism. In both regions, religious toleration at first found few supporters, and the result was endemic civil war. In both regions, the weakness of a land devoured by civil war involved it in the international strife between Catholic and Protestant and invited and secured foreign intervention. In both regions, exhaustion of the struggling parties brought with it in the end a perhaps reluctant official policy of religious toleration.

Yet the differences between the French and the German experience of wars of religion are striking and important. The French experience was briefer, and less crippling. Passions ran high, and the French wars laid one of the great blots on the historical record: the massacre of St. Bartholomew's Day (August 23–24, 1572). On that day, the Protestant leader Coligny was murdered in Paris and thousands of other Protestants in Paris and in the provinces were dragged from their beds and killed

according to a prearranged plan. Yet armies were small, and the great masses of the French people went on living not too badly. By the end of the sixteenth century, in spite of the recent chaos, France was on the threshold of its own era of preponderance.

In France, Protestantism scarcely touched the great peasant masses except for parts of the South, notably Languedoc. The Huguenots, as the French Protestants came to be known, were strong among the nobility and among the new classes of capitalists and artisans. The religious map of France also showed a territorial as well as a class division, an exception to the rule that in Europe the North tends to be Protestant and the South Catholic. The northernmost sections of France, up against the Low Countries, though affected by Lutheranism at first, remained ardently Catholic, as did Brittany, most of Normandy, and the region of Paris. By the later sixteenth century the Protestants were strongest in south-central France, above all in the lands where the Albigensian heresy had taken hold, and in the southwest. Even in these regions, however, the employer class was more likely to be Protestant, the workers to be Catholic. The French nobility took up with Protestantism in part for political reasons; the old tradition of local feudal independence among the nobles encouraged resistance to the centralized Catholic monarchy and its agents.

For the Valois kings remained firm, political Catholics. Francis I had extended the royal gains made the expense of the papacy in the Pragmatic Sanction of Bourges of 1438 under Charles VII. In the Concordat of Bologna, 1516, the pope allowed the king a very great increase in control over the Gallican Church, including the important right of choosing bishops and abbots. The German princes in revolt had everything to gain in a worldly way by confiscation of church property and establishment of an Erastian Lutheran Church (see Chapter 4). But the French kings after 1516 had everything to lose by a Protestant movement that strengthened their restive nobility and that in its Calvinist form was the very opposite of Erastian, was indeed anti-monarchical.

The most striking development to come out of the French religious wars was the establishment of the French Crown and its bureaucrats as a mediating power between the extreme Catholics and the Protestants. At the outbreak of the wars in 1562, the Queen-Mother, Catherine de' Medici, firmly opposed the growing Protestant party, if only because the great nobles who headed that party seemed to threaten the Crown itself. As the wars went on, however, the Huguenots, in spite of St. Bartholomew's Day and defeats in the field, remained strong. The Catholic nobles organized a threatening league headed by the powerful Guise family, and both sides took to negotiating with foreigners for help, the Catholics with Spain and the Protestants with England. Thus the French rulers found themselves pushed into opposition to *both* groups.

Henry IV (Henry of Navarre) (1553–1610).

The Victory of Henry of Navarre

The wars culminated in the "War of the Three Henries" (1585–1589)—named for Henry III, the actual King of France and the last of the grandsons of Francis I; Henry, Duke of Guise, head of the Catholic League; and Henry of Navarre, the Protestant cousin and heir-apparent of the childless king. The mere threat that a Protestant, Henry of Navarre, might succeed to the throne pushed the Catholic League to the extreme of proposing a deliberate violation of the rules of succession by making an uncle of Henry of Navarre, the Catholic Cardinal of Bourbon, king. But in an established monarchy rules of succession are in fact what we call "constitutional" laws and have behind them the full force of public opinion. Moderate French public opinion, already disturbed by the extremes of both Catholics and Protestants, now turned against the Catholic League.

Paris, however, was a strong Catholic city, and a popular insurrection there, the "Day of the Barricades" (May 12, 1588), frightened Henry III out of the city, which triumphantly acclaimed Guise as king. Henry III took the weak man's way out, and connived at—indeed almost certainly planned—the assassination of the two great men of the Catholic League, Henry of Guise and his brother Louis. Infuriated, the League rose in full revolt, and King Henry was forced to take refuge in the camp of his Protestant cousin, Henry of Navarre, where he in turn was assassinated by a monk.

Henry of Navarre was now by law King Henry IV (1589–1610), first of the House of Bourbon. The Catholics set up the aged Cardinal of Bourbon as "King Charles X," but in the decisive battle of Ivry in March, 1590, Henry won a great victory, and laid siege to Paris. Long negotiations now followed, and Henry was persuaded that if he would abjure his own Protestant faith he could rally the moderate Catholics and secure at least tolerated status for the Protestants. He turned

Catholic in 1593 and Paris was surrendered, giving rise to the perhaps apocryphal tale that he had remarked, "Paris is well worth a Mass." With the Edict of Nantes in 1598, the French religious wars were ended, but full religious freedom was not achieved. The Huguenots were allowed the exercise of their religion in certain areas, and their great nobles were permitted it in their own households; but notably at Paris and its environs, and in episcopal and archiepiscopal cities, the Huguenots were forbidden public worship. Nevertheless the Edict of Nantes was a major symbol of religious toleration. In the same year, 1598, the Treaty of Vervins with Spain put an end to Spanish intervention and restored to the French Crown all Spanish conquests in France.

The *Politiques*

Henry of Navarre was a gifted leader, a realist rather than a cynic—in spite of his alleged remark about Paris being worth a Mass—and, as we shall see in Chapter 7, the restorer of the French monarchy. He was fortunate in coming on the scene after the passions of civil war were nearing exhaustion; he could hardly have succeeded in his work of pacification had France not been ready for it. The intellectual preparation for the Edict of Nantes and the revived French monarchy had been in large part the work of a group of men known by the untranslatable French term, *politiques,* which is nearer to "political moralist" than it is to our "politician." The greatest of them, Jean Bodin, who died in 1596, has been rather unfairly labeled a proponent of absolute monarchy. He did indeed hold that the sole possibility of order in a divided France lay in obedience to a king above petty civil strife. We have already noted (see Chapter 4) that in the early modern world a pluralism of religious belief was not regarded as a good in itself. So too for the kind of political pluralism of parties, pressure-groups, and the like we accept in a democracy as a positive good, so long as public order is not violated. Bodin and his colleagues emphasized the need for political unity to maintain law and order.

But they were by no means what we now call "totalitarians." He was far from preaching that the king must be obeyed no matter what he did; he was a moderate who believed in acceptance of the limitations imposed by history and tradition on any practical program of politics. The *politiques* were convinced that under the supremacy of the French state Frenchmen could be allowed to practice different forms of the Christian religion.

Some of the *politiques* were unreligious persons; but the best of them, like Michel de l'Hospital, were Christians who held firmly to the belief that the basic aim of those who fought the religious wars—to put down by force those who disagreed with them in matters religious—was un-Christian. Here is l'Hospital addressing the Estates-General in 1560:

If they are Christians, those who try to spread Christianity with arms, swords, and pistols do indeed go contrary to their professed faith, which is to suffer force, not to inflict it. . . . Nor is their argument, that they take arms in the cause of God, a valid one, for the cause of God is not one that can be so defended with such arms. . . . Our religion did not take its beginnings from force of arms, and is not to be kept and strengthened by force of arms.

Yet l'Hospital is a good child of his age, and he cannot conceive that men can really hold and practice different religious faiths in the same political society:

It is folly to hope for peace, quiet and friendship, among persons of different religions. And there is no opinion so deeply planted in the hearts of men, as opinion in religion, and none which so separates one from another.

He can but hope that as good Frenchmen they will sink their quarrels in a common Frenchness and a common Christianity:

Let us pray God for the heretics, and do all we can to reduce and convert them; gentleness will do more than harshness. Let us get rid of those devilish names of seditious factions, Lutherans, Huguenots, Papists: let us not change the name of Christian.*

*P. J. S. Dufey, *Oeuvres complètes de Michel de l'Hospital* (Paris, 1824), I, 395–402. Our translation.

IV　The New States: England and Holland

Henry VIII, 1509–1547

In England, the first Tudor, Henry VII, had already established the new monarchy on a firm footing (see Chapter 2). He left his son, Henry VIII, a full treasury and a well-ordered kingdom. That Henry VIII did not run through his heritage and leave an exhausted treasury was not because he lacked the will to spend lavishly. Henry, unlike his father, loved display, and all the trappings of Renaissance monarchy. His summit conference (to use a modern term) with Francis I near Calais in 1520 has gone down in tradition as the "Field of the Cloth of Gold."

Henry did not, however, seriously weaken England's finances, and for many reasons. Basically, we must make a distinction between the finances of a government and the economy of a whole society. We may sometimes, as on the eve of the great French Revolution of 1789, find a poor, even bankrupt, government in a *relatively* prosperous society; we may even, as in eighteenth-century Prussia, find a prosperous, well-run government in a society *relatively* poor. Tudor England had the good fortune to enjoy *both* solvent government finances and a prosperous society. No doubt the great enclosures of land for sheep-farming and other factors helped create a new poor, but many Englishmen, and especially the new upper classes continued on the whole to thrive. Moreover, this national material wealth was not unduly expended in foreign wars, the really major cause of disastrous financial difficulties of modern governments. Good democrats have often accused European royalty of ruinous expenditures on palaces, retinues, pensions, mistresses, and high living of all sorts; yet the fact seems to be that such expenditures were usually a comparatively small part of the total outlay for purposes of government. Henry's wives—he had six—his court, his royal progresses, did not by any means beggar his country; the wars of Charles V and Philip II did beggar Spain.

Henry VIII made war in a gingerly manner, never really risking big English armies on the Continent, and contenting himself with playing a rather cautious game of balance of power. He made full use of the opportunities afforded him by the English Reformation (see Chapter 4) to add to royal revenues by confiscation of monastic property, and, even more important, by rewarding his loyal followers with lands so confiscated. Henry thus followed in the footsteps of his father in helping create a new upper class, which was soon actually a titled or noble class. In these critical years of English development, the new class was, in contrast to France, on the whole loyal to the Crown and yet, in contrast to some of the German states, by no means subservient to the Crown, by no means a mere ennobled bureaucracy. Henry continued the administrative policies of his father, strengthening his central administration and maintaining adequate supervision over the justices of the peace, who were the keystone of English local government.

Tudor Parliaments

Most important of all, Henry was able to get what he wanted from his Parliaments, including statutes that separated the English Church from Rome, and grants for his wars and conferences. Henry's Parliaments were very far from being elected legislatures based on wide suffrage. The Tudor House of Lords had a safe majority of men—titled nobles and, after 1534, bishops of the Anglican Church —who were in fact of Tudor creation or of Tudor allegiance. The membership of the companion body, the House of Commons, was composed of the knights of the shire, chosen by the freeholders of the shires, and of the burgesses, representatives of incorporated towns or boroughs (not by any means all towns). In most boroughs, a very narrow electorate chose these members of Parliament. Since the majority of the people of the shires were agricultural workers or tenants, rather than freeholders of land, the county franchise, too, was limited. In fact, the knights of the shire were chosen from among, and largely by, the squires and the lesser country gentlemen. Royal favor and royal patronage, as well as the patronage of the great lords, could pretty well mold the shape of a House of Commons.

Still, even the Tudor Parliaments are nearer a modern legislative assembly than the parallel assemblies, or estates, of the Continent. The great point of difference lies in the composition of the House of Commons, which had emerged from the Middle Ages not as a body representing an urban bourgeoisie but as a composite of the rural landed gentry and the ruling groups in the towns, meeting in one body. On the Continent, the assemblies corresponding to the English Parliament were *estates* (*Stände* in German, *états* in French). They usually sat in three distinct houses—one representing the clergy, another all the nobles, great and small, and a third the lay commoners. Some countries, as for instance Sweden, had four estates—clergy, nobles, townsmen, and peasants.

Historians today emphasize the fact that the political differences between England and the Continent rest on a somewhat, though by no means totally, different social structure. There was certainly an English nobility or aristocracy ranging from barons through viscounts, earls, and marquises to dukes at the top. These nobles, plus Anglican bishops, composed the House of Lords. For those just below the nobles the use of the term "gentry," or the status symbol "gentleman" is still much debated among social historians of early modern England. We may here content ourselves with noting, first, that younger sons of nobles in England were not themselves titled nobles, as they were on the Continent, but were members, usually top members, of a complex group for which there is no good single name, though Englishmen even today distinguish its members as "gentlemen"; and second, that this group, roughly divisible into the younger sons and descendents of nobles, the "squires" or "country gentlemen," the rich merchants and bankers (who almost always acquired landed estates and became "squires"), the leading lawyers, civil servants, Anglican clergy, "dons" at Oxford and Cambridge (who at first were usually in Anglican orders), officers in the army and navy, and a scattering of others in the liberal professions—this group was never a closed caste, but remained open to socially mobile individuals from the lower classes. The conventional term "middle class" certainly does not describe it in early modern times; the term "gentry" applies only to part of it; perhaps we can settle for "ruling class" or the recently popular British term "the establishment."

Finally, in England Parliament came out of the Middle Ages with the power to make laws or statutes, including money laws. These laws did indeed require royal consent. But at the end of the fifteenth century Parliament had already obtained much more than the merely advisory powers which were all that the French Estates-General, for instance, really had.

Purely in terms of constitutional structure, then, the Tudor Parliaments could have quarreled as violently with the Crown as did the Stuart Parliaments in the next century (see Chapter 7). Although the Tudor monarchs had their spats and difficulties with Parliament, on the whole they got what they wanted out of Parliament without serious constitutional crises. This was particularly true of Henry VIII and Elizabeth I. These monarchs succeeded in part, as we have noted, because their parliaments, if not precisely packed, were generally recruited from men favorable to the Crown, to which they owed so much. But the Tudor monarchs succeeded because they were skillful rulers, willing to use their prestige and gifts of persuasion to win the consent of Parliament, careful to observe the constitutional and human decencies. Moreover, both Henry and Elizabeth were good hearty persons, sure of themselves and their dignity, immensely popular with all classes of their subjects. Both were fortunate enough to be able to incorporate in their persons strong national feelings of patriotic resistance to the hated foreign foes, the Roman church and the Spanish monarchy.

The course of Tudor domestic history did not run with perfect smoothness. Henry VII had faced two pretenders; Henry VIII met opposition to his religious policy. A Catholic minority, strong in the north, continued throughout the sixteenth century to oppose the Protestant majority, sometimes in arms, sometimes in intrigues. The death of Henry VIII in 1547 marked the beginning of a period of really extraordinary religious oscillation.

Religious Difficulties

Henry was succeeded by his only son, the ten-year-old Edward VI. Led by his uncle, the Duke of Somerset, Edward's government pushed on into Protestant ways. The Six Articles (see p. 130), by which Henry had sought to preserve the essentials of Roman Catholic theology, worship, and even church organization, were repealed in 1547. The legal title of the statute commonly called the Six Articles had been "An Act for Abolishing Diversity in Opinion." The goal was still uniformity, and in the brief reign of Edward VI an effort was made to prescribe uniformity of religious worship through a prayer book and articles of faith duly imposed by Parliament. Cranmer, Archbishop of Canterbury, was a convinced Protestant and had committed himself by his marriage—as did Luther—to a clear, symbolic break with Roman Catholicism. Under his supervision, the patient bulk of the English people was pushed into Protestant worship.

Then, in 1553, the young king, Edward VI, always a frail boy, died. Protestant intriguers vainly attempted to secure the crown for a Protestant, Lady Jane Grey, a great-grandaughter of Henry VII and a quiet, scholarly young woman with no ambitions. But Edward VI was followed by his older sister Mary, daughter of the Catholic Catherine of Aragon whom Henry VIII had put aside. Mary had been brought up a Catholic, and at once began to restore the old ways. Of course there was a rebellion, which flared into the open when Mary announced a marriage treaty by which she was to wed Philip II of Spain. Yet Mary prevailed against the rebels, and Lady Jane Grey was executed for a plot she had never really shared in. The Catholic Cardinal Pole was made Archbishop of Canterbury, under Rome, and Cranmer was burned at the stake. Catholic forms of worship came back to the parishes, but significantly the church land settlement of Henry VIII remained undisturbed.

Mary, too, died after a short reign, in 1558. The last of Henry's children left was Elizabeth, daughter of Anne Boleyn. She had at her father's request been declared illegitimate by Parliament in 1536. Henry's last will, however, rehabilitated her, and she now succeeded as Elizabeth I (1558–1603). She had been brought up a Protestant, and once more the ordinary English churchgoer was required to switch religion. This time the Anglican Church was firmly established; the prayer book and Thirty-Nine Articles of 1563 issued under Elizabeth (see Chapter 4) have remained to this day essential documents of the Anglican faith.

The Elizabethan settlement, moderate and permanent though it was, did not fully settle the religious problem. England still had a Catholic party. Spain, especially after Elizabeth's repudiation of Catholicism, was a serious enemy; it seemed hardly likely that the heavy expenses of a real war could be long avoided. Moreover, independent Scotland could always be counted on in those days to take the anti-English side. The new Queen of Scotland was Mary Stuart, granddaughter of Henry VIII's sister, Margaret, and therefore the heir to the English throne should Elizabeth I die without issue. Mary did not wait for Elizabeth's death, but on the ground that Elizabeth was in fact illegitimate, herself assumed the title of "Queen of England and Scotland."

Finally, the English Catholics were by no means the most serious of Elizabeth's religious difficulties; numerous Protestant groups not satisfied with the Thirty-Nine Articles were coming to the fore. Broadly, these people are called "Puritans," since they wished to

Elizabeth I, portrayed on the silver medal commemorating the defeat of the Armada.

"purify" the Anglican Church of what they considered papist survivals in belief, ritual, and church government. Actually, the Puritans ranged from moderates to radicals. The moderates would be content with a simpler ritual but would retain bishops. The Presbyterians were Calvinists who would substitute councils (synods) of elders, or presbyters, for bishops, and would adopt the full Calvinist theology. The Brownists, named for their leader Robert Browne, were the radical wing of Puritanism; they were Calvinists who wanted to have each congregation an independent body.

Elizabeth the Queen

Thus Elizabeth faced a decidedly grim prospect during the early years of her reign. The troubles of the reigns of Edward and Mary had undone some of the work of the two Henries; dissension seemed all around her. Yet she was to reign for nearly fifty years and to give her name to one of the greatest times of flowering of English culture.

The personality of Elizabeth is hardly heartwarming. She was vain (or simply proud), not altogether proof against flattery, but too intelligent to be led astray by it in great matters. She was a good Renaissance realist (a better one than Machiavelli himself), somewhat too overpowering and impressive for a woman, but very effective in the pageantry and posing of public life. She was loved by her people if not by her intimates. She never married, a fact that has unleashed a good deal of quite unverifiable medical and psychological explanation. But in the early years of her reign she played off foreign and domestic suitors one against another with excellent results for her foreign policy, in which she was always trying to avoid the expenses and dangers of war, trying to get something for nothing. One may believe that her spinsterhood settled on her at first as no more than a policy of state, and later as a convenient habit. She had male favorites, but probably not lovers.

Under such able ministers as Burleigh and Walsingham, her government was put in excellent order. Thanks to skillful diplomacy, which made full use of the French and Dutch opposition to Spain, the showdown with Philip was postponed until 1588, when the kingdom was ready for it. Mary Queen of Scots proved no match at all for her gifted cousin, not merely because she was not a good politician, but even more because she had no sure Scottish base to work from. Mary was a Catholic, and Scotland under the leadership of John Knox was on its way to becoming one of the great centers of Calvinism. Mary managed everything wrong, including, and perhaps most important in a puritanical land, her love affairs. Her subjects revolted against her, and she was forced in 1568 to take refuge in England, where Elizabeth had her put in confinement. Mary alive was at the very least a constant temptation to all who wanted to overthrow Elizabeth. Letters, which Mary declared were forged, and over which historians still debate, involved her in what was certainly a very real conspiracy against Elizabeth, and she was tried, convicted, and executed in 1587, to become a romantic legend.

The dramatic crisis of the reign was the war with Spain, resolved in the defeat of the great Spanish Armada in 1588 (see p. 165). But Elizabeth's old age was not to be altogether quiet. In Ireland, the native masses were ruled by an Anglo-Irish landed class out of touch with the people. In 1542, the country had been made a kingdom, but by no means an independent one, since the crowns of England and Ireland were held by the same person. An earlier act, the Statute of Drogheda (Poynings'

Act), in 1495 had put the Irish Parliament firmly under English control and had made laws enacted in the English Parliament applicable to Ireland. The native Irish had remained firmly Catholic. The stage was set for the perennial Irish Problem, the long struggle for Irish national independence.

In 1597, the Irish rose under the leadership of Hugh O'Neill, Earl of Tyrone. The revolt was temporarily successful but was put down bloodily in 1601 after the favorite of Elizabeth's old age, the Earl of Essex, had failed dismally to cope with it. Essex, too, involved himself in a plot against his mistress, and was executed after its discovery and suppression. But the Elizabethan settlement of Ireland's troubles was no settlement, and we shall return in Chapter 7 to another phase of this running sore, closed only in the 1930's.

The Elizabethan Age, then, was no age of quiet, but rather one of wars, rebellions, personal and party strife, and intense competition. None the less, it never reached the fatal depths of destruction of a Thirty Years' War, though for a while it threatened to do so under Mary Tudor. There was a solid foundation under the state and society that produced the literature, music, architecture, science, and wealth and victories of the Elizabethan Age. That foundation was in part a good administrative system, itself based on a substantial degree of national unity, or, negatively, on the absence of the extreme local differences and conflicts of the Continent. It was in part general economic prosperity, based on individual enterprise in many fields—enterprise often unscrupulous and, as far as raids on the commerce of foreigners like the Spaniards went, piratical. It was certainly something not simply material, a common sentiment that kept Englishmen together and that traced for most of them limits beyond which they would not carry disagreement. Elizabeth herself played a large part in holding her subjects together; her religious policy, for example, was directed at stretching the already broad principles and practices of the Church of England so that they would cover near-Catholicism and near-Congregationalism. But there was a limit to this stretching, and Elizabeth "persecuted"

Mary Stuart, Queen of Scots, by Clouet.

—that is, did not grant to them the right to practice publicly their religion—Catholics on the Right and Brownists on the Left.

The English Renaissance

The Age of Elizabeth I was a flowering of English culture symbolized for all of us by Shakespeare (1564–1616). Elizabeth's actual reign, from 1558 to 1603, by no means measures the Age accurately. Much of her father's reign belongs to the flowering, as do the first ten or fifteen years of the reign of her successor, James I, the first Stuart king.

This is the English Renaissance, tardiest of the great classical Renaissances. It has the range and variety we have found in other lands and the same clear admiration for, the same dependence on, the old Greeks and Romans we have found elsewhere. It is hard to pick up a poem, an essay, a play, any piece of writing not purely religious, without coming very soon upon a classical allusion. Yet the English Renaissance did not imitate classical antiquity, so to speak, photographically. It holds on to much that could be grown only in the climate of the island. Tudor and early Stuart architecture is a clear case in point. The new palaces and manor houses are no longer much like the medieval castles; they are more open, more elegant. But they preserve all sorts of Gothic habits, mullioned windows, tracery and carving, traditional woodwork.

Painting, sculpture, the plastic arts in all their range—music itself—were for England in these years at a high level. Elizabethan ladies and gentlemen cultivated all the muses, sang madrigals, played the lute, appreciated modern paintings, had their houses built in the modern style, dressed as did ladies and gentlemen in the center of European culture of this sort, Italy. Yet the commonplace is unavoidable: England was not a land of great original creation in music and the plastic arts. The greatness of Elizabethan England, when it is not in the deeds of Drake, Hawkins, Wolsey, Burleigh, the Tudors themselves, lies in the words of St. Thomas More, Shakespeare, Francis Bacon, Spenser, Ben Jonson, and many others who are part of the formal higher education of English-speaking people all over the world.

They are a hard group to generalize about.

Tudor architecture: Hatfield House.

They are established "classics" and have suffered the popular admiration and neglect as well as the academic working-over that go with the status of classics in our culture. They belong to a culture now four hundred years past, and they wrote English before its structure and its word-order were tamed, partly by the influence of French prose, into their present straight-forward simplicity. For most of us, they are much easier to read about than to read. Finally, they have been targets for some debunking, but on the whole they have survived intact as classics. Shakespeare, notably, continues even outside the English-speaking world to be a kind of George Washington of letters, above reproach. He is the necessary great writer of a great people, as is Dante for the Italians, Goethe for the Germans, Pascal or Molière or Racine for the French, Cervantes for the Spanish, Tolstoy for the Russians.

These Elizabethans are overwhelmingly exuberant. They are exuberant even in refinement, full-blooded even in erudition. Above all, they are anxious to get in that something more, that transcending something that makes words more than words, and possibly more than sense. To a later generation, the tame, orderly admirers of measure and sense in the late seventeenth and eighteenth centuries, these Elizabethans were somewhat uncouth, undisciplined. To the nineteenth-century Romantics, they were brothers in romance, sharing the desire of the moth for the star. And indeed this exuberance, this love of the excessive, is obvious in much Elizabethan writing, in the interminable, allusion-packed, allegory-mad stanzas of Spenser's *Faerie Queene,* in the piling up of quotations from the ancient Greeks and Romans, in Shakespeare's love of puns and all kinds of rhetorical devices, in the extraordinarily bloody nature of their tragedies—remember the end of *Hamlet,* which finds the stage littered with corpses.

There is, however, a balancing quality in the Elizabethans. They had a good carnal appreciation of this earth; they seemed even to have enjoyed their gloom and depth when they left the world of the fleshly enjoyments for their brief trips into transcendence. The absurd notion that Shakespeare's works were written by Bacon—a notion apparently based on the assumption that Shakespeare was not formally and academically well enough trained to write the plays,—has at least some meaning in terms of the spirit of the age. Francis Bacon, lawyer and humanist, philosopher of inductive science (see Chapter 7), and rather bad practitioner of experimental science, was at bottom a heaven-stormer, intent on solving the problems of the ages. Yet he was at the same time an earth-bound Tudor gentleman, quite capable of enjoying himself in this harsh world. So, too, was Shakespeare, who has the dying Hamlet tell his friend Horatio:

If thou didst ever hold me in thy heart,
Absent thee from felicity a while
And in this harsh world draw thy breath in pain
To tell my story.

Bacon and Shakespeare have at least this in common: They are hearty of mind and spirit, wide-ranging, bound by no narrow formulas of literary or philosophic taste, willing to accept the world about them without drying up into conformity, willing to get beyond that world without indulging in complaint or rebellion.

However men may vary in their attempts to define the climate of Elizabethan opinion and the quality of its culture, there can be no doubt that the Elizabethans were good English patriots, lovers of their country in the first flush of its worldly success. Here is one of the most famous of quotations from Shakespeare, in itself an admirable sample of the English Renaissance, right down to the inevitable, and in this case rather flat, allusion to Greco-Roman mythology:

This royal throne of kings, this scepter'd isle,
This earth of majesty, this seat of Mars,
This other Eden, demi-paradise,
This fortress built by Nature for herself
Against infection and the hand of war,
This happy breed of men, this little world,
This precious stone set in the silver sea,
Which serves it in the office of a wall
Or as a moat defensive to a house,

Against the envy of less happier lands,
This blessed plot, this earth, this realm, this
England.*

The Dutch Republic

The late sixteenth and most of the seventeenth century is the great age of the Dutch, politically, economically, culturally. The northern provinces, as we have seen, succeeded in asserting their independence of Spain even before Philip's death in 1598, though the concert of Europe did not formally accept their independence until the Treaty of Westphalia in 1648 (see p. 189). The United Provinces, or United Netherlands, were a republic in the midst of great monarchical states; but they were an aristocratic merchant society, by no means a popular democracy. For a time, in spite of their relatively small territorial home base, they were a great power, colonizing in Asia, Africa and the Americas, trading everywhere, supporting an active and efficient navy. In religion, they practiced a wide toleration. Holland became a refuge for persecuted Jews from Portugal and Spain and even from Poland and Lithuania. In government the United Provinces were decentralized, preserving the local self-government that had long persisted. The central government was usually at the mercy of the provincial governments, though the office of stadhouder, held by a prince of the House of Orange, provided a symbol of national unity.

In economic life, above all, the Dutch were the pace-setters of seventeenth-century Europe. They managed government finances as adroitly and efficiently as they managed their private businesses; the state borrowed money at 2½ per cent interest, an amazingly low figure for the time. They made life insurance into a big business by putting it on a firm actuarial basis, and in the Bank of Amsterdam they fostered a great commercial institution that went far to make Amsterdam the financial capital of Europe. Highly successful specialized industries grew up in the cities and towns of Holland—diamond-cutting at Amsterdam, shipbuilding at Zaandam, the distilling of gin at Schiedam, and around Haarlem the growing of tulip bulbs, which set off a wild financial speculation. Abroad, Dutch ships played a large part in the international carrying trade; the Dutch got a foothold in North America at New Amsterdam, now New York, and the Dutch East India Company assembled and exploited a commercial empire (see Chapter 6).

The Dutch of the seventeenth century made major contributions to western culture. In painting, they produced in Rembrandt (1606–1669) one of the greatest of masters; and a whole school of artists painted technically admirable, "realistic" scenes of everyday life for the homes of prosperous businessmen. In science, Christian Huygens (1629–1695), son of a distinguished poet, was a major figure in the advance of mathematics and physics; in biological studies, Jan Swammerdam (1637–1680) pioneered in the use of the microscope and probably discovered the red corpuscles in the blood; and Anton van Leeuwenhoek (1632–1723), with a microscope of his own making, first described protozoa and bacteria. In philosophy, Baruch (or Benedict) Spinoza (1632–1677), a Jew rejected by his fellow religionists for his unorthodoxy, laid the basis for much modern philosophical thought by his self-conscious, high-minded, rigorous rationalism. Indeed, one of his books has the remarkable title: *Ethics Mathematically Demonstrated.*

The Dutch style at this flowering time is hard to define. It is solid, reasonable, sober, but far from colorless, and by no means puritanical in any ascetic sense. Perhaps the Dutch at their height are the best evidences for the Weber thesis of Protestant ethics (see Chapter 4). Certainly this little nation, through intelligence, hard work, adventurous exploration, and hard trading, and, as we shall see in the next chapter, some rather unscrupulous exploitation of non-European peoples, made for itself a great place in the world. But by 1700 the great days of Holland were coming to an end. The Dutch Republic declined, not

Richard II, Act II, Scene i.

absolutely, but relatively to the great powers around it—Britain, France, and Prussia. The Dutch, like the Swedes who reached a peak of power a bit later, simply did not have a home base extensive enough or populous enough to support the status of a great power.

V   Germany and the Thirty Years' War

Nature and Causes

We have now seen two of the great conflicts of early modern times—the Habsburg-Valois struggle between Charles V and Francis I, and the wars of Philip II. The third great conflict, the Thirty Years' War of 1618–1648, was fought largely in Germany. It was like the earlier wars we have discussed in this chapter, a war in part over religion, and like them, its focus was still a Habsburg focus. The Austrian Emperor, Ferdinand II (1619–1637), scarcely aspired to universal rule, but he did make the last serious political and military effort to unify Germany under Catholic rule. The Thirty Years' War began as a conflict between Catholics and Protestants; it ended as an almost purely political struggle to reduce the power of the Habsburgs in favor of France and a newcomer to high international politics, Sweden.

As we have already noted, the Augsburg Peace of 1555 (see p. 162) did not bring complete religious peach to Germany. It did not recognize Calvinism, to say nothing of the more radical Protestant sects, and it left unsettled the problem of ecclesiastical reservation. On this latter issue, an imperial decree provided that if a Catholic prelate were converted to Protestantism the property formerly under his control should remain in Catholic hands. But this was a one-sided proclamation; it had not been formally negotiated with the Protestants and it was naturally much resented by them.

By the opening of the seventeenth century, the religious situation in Germany was becoming increasingly unsettled. Incidents of vi-olence between Catholics and Protestants, especially Calvinists, were multiplying. In 1608, Calvinist elements formed a Protestant Union, which in turn prompted the creation of a Catholic League in 1609. Thus Germany was split into rival camps a decade before the outbreak of war. From the start, moreover, both the Protestant Union and the Catholic League had political as well as religious ambitions. Both really represented the interests of German particularism—that is, of the individual German states—against those of the Empire, even though the Catholic League and its leader, Maximilian of Bavaria, were to ally with the Emperor Ferdinand.

The Bohemian Period, 1618–1625

The war broke out in Bohemia, now part of Czechoslovakia, then a Habsburg crown land, with a strong Protestant minority known as the Utraquists. This name brings up one of the main quarrels between Protestants and Catholics, that of the actual administration of the Eucharist. In Catholic worship, the layman receives the bread but not the wine, the body but not the blood of Christ; only the officiating priest takes the wine. The Utraquist, from the Latin for "both," took both the wine and the bread in communion. As with the Hussite movement two centuries earlier, Utraquism was in part Czech nationalism. The Czech nationalists wanted local independence from the rule of Germans and of Vienna, and they caused the incident that actually provoked war, the "defenestration of Prague" in 1618. Rebels headed by Count Matthias of Thurn seized control of the Bohemian capital city and in an excited conference threw two royal governors out of a palace window. Though the victims fell seventy feet, they landed on a pile of dung and escaped with their lives.

The emperor-to-be, Ferdinand II of Habsburg (he was formally elected in 1619), was not prepared for civil war. The rebels, aided by Protestant forces from Germany, gained control in Bohemia and deposed Ferdinand as King of Bohemia. To fill his place, an assembly of the Bohemian estates chose the youthful Frederick V, Elector of the Palatinate in western Germany, and head of the Protestant Union. Although Frederick was the son-in-law of James I of England and as a Protestant was very popular there, England did not come to his aid, nor in effect did the Protestant Union. The Spaniards, however, did come in on the Catholic side and sent an army to the Palatinate, frightening the Protestant Union into a declaration of neutrality. In Bohemia, Frederick was defeated by the army of the Catholic League at the battle of the White Mountain (1620) and was forced to flee his new kingdom. The Protestant Union was dissolved, and small Protestant remnants were beaten by the imperial general Tilly.

The Danish Period, 1625–1629

At this low point in Protestant fortunes, a champion arose outside Germany proper in Denmark, where King Christian IV (1588–1648) took over the leadership of the Protestant forces. A vigorous and ambitious monarch, Christian had increased his royal power by taking full advantage of the increased authority that Lutheranism gave to the king. When he intervened in the war, he sought not only to defend his co-religionists but also to extend Danish political and economic hegemony over northern Germany.

Still another factor now entered the struggle, the famous — and infamous — private army of Wallenstein (1583–1634). This general, though born of a German Protestant family in Bohemia, was reared a Catholic and fought on the imperial side. His army was recruited and paid by himself, and lived off the land by requisitions and plunderings, sometimes at the expense of imperial and Catholic sympathizers. Wallenstein was in fact a German *condottiere*, a private citizen seeking to become a ruling prince, perhaps even dreaming of a united German empire, no longer the old medieval successor to Charlemagne's empire, but a fine, new-model monarchy. He never came close to success, but his army was a major factor in the war at its most critical period. Tilly's and Wallenstein's armies were enough to dispose of Christian IV. They overran Christian's North German lands and pushed into the Danish peninsula.

Then, at the height of the imperial and Catholic success, Ferdinand and his advisers overreached themselves. By the Edict of Restitution and the Treaty of Lübeck in 1629, they sought to take the fullest advantage of their victories. The Edict of Restitution not only reaffirmed the Augsburg exclusion of the Calvinists and Protestant radicals from toleration but also demanded the restoration of all ecclesiastical estates that had passed from Catholic to Lutheran hands since 1551, *three generations before.* The Treaty of Lübeck allowed Christian IV to recover his lands, but it exacted from him a promise not to intervene in Germany. This seemed to the outside world a sign that the Habsburg power was actually spreading to the Baltic, to a region thoroughly Protestant and hitherto only on the margin of imperial control. The old pattern was, then, repeated. The Habsburgs on the wave of success went outside the bounds of their customary spheres of influence; those upon whose spheres they thus encroached fought back against the trespass; the trespasser was finally forced to withdraw.

The Swedish Period, 1630–1635

For in 1630, at the height of Catholic Habsburg success, Gustavus Adolphus, Protestant King of Sweden (1611–1632), landed with a Swedish army on the North German coast. A new champion of the Protestants, a much stronger one than Christian of Denmark, had come out of the North. Once again, religious and secular motives were thoroughly intermixed. Gustavus was a strong Lutheran, who led an army of hymn-singing soldiers. In Sweden, as in Denmark, the coming of the Reformation had consolidated royal authority. Like Christian, Gustavus Adolphus had ambitions for political control in northern Germany, and he hoped, too, that Sweden might take over the old economic leadership of the Hanseatic League, hoped, indeed, to make the Baltic Sea a Swedish lake. He had already won territories along the eastern Baltic by waging successful wars against Russia and Poland. Significantly, his army, large and well equipped for so relatively poor a country as Sweden, was now in part paid for by subsidies received from the French monarchy through negotiations with its minister Richelieu, a cardinal of the Roman Catholic Church. For France, too, the great success of the old Habsburg enemy seemed a trespass, and those who guided French policy were eager to help Protestant Sweden beat Catholic Austria.

Gustavus Adolphus was a very skillful general whose intervention was to alter the whole course of the war—but not before a Catholic victory that probably did more to harm the Catholic cause than a defeat. The fall and sack of Magdeburg, the "Maiden City" of the Protestants and a great symbol of their cause, is one of those events that should warn the student of international politics that he must not leave moral forces out of his calculations. Magdeburg was taken by storm by the imperialists in May, 1631, and was almost wholly destroyed by fire and pillage. The imperial general Pappenheim, who commanded at the storming of the walls, estimated that twenty thousand people were killed. Each side sought to blame the sack on the other and to enlist in its cause public opinion all over Europe. A volume issued in 1931 on the three-hundredth anniversary of the sack of Magdeburg takes forty-six pages to list contemporary accounts in European newspapers (then in their infancy), pamphlets, broadsides, popular songs, and cartoons. The Protestants accused the imperial commander-in-chief, Tilly, of actually

planning the destruction of the city and the killing of its inhabitants, an accusation from which most historians absolve him, for the imperial troops clearly got out of hand. The Catholics countered by accusing the Protestants of setting the fires themselves as a deliberate "scorched-earth" policy. But the Protestants were the sufferers, and in the long run, as the outpourings of the press took effect, their cause was strengthened. In the field, the Swedes won two decisive victories at Leipzig in 1631 and at Lützen in 1632. Gustavus Adolphus was killed at Lützen, but his coming had turned the tide. Wallenstein withdrew

S. Michael. 2 Der Dom zu S. Maucitz. 3 S. Gongolf. 4 S. Sebaffia. 5 S. Nicola. 6 Vnf.liebe Frawen.
S. Anna. 8 zum h. Geift. 9 S. Vlrich. 10 S. Iohaanes. 11 das Rathaus. 12 Barfußer. 13 S. Catharina.
S. Maria Magdalena. 15 Hunenthurn. 16 S. Peter. 17 S. Iacob. 18 S. Auguftin. 19 Hohepfort.
Rathaus. 21 S. Laurentz. 22 S. Peter vnd Paul. 23 Sudenburg. 24 Newftatt. 25 Zollfchantz.

MAGDEBURG.

Die Elbe Flu:

The siege of Magdeburg during the Thirty Years' War, 1631.

into winter quarters and began negotiations that have baffled historians ever since. Certainly he was trying to set himself up as a mediator between the Protestants and the extremist wing of the imperial party, the Court at Vienna, the wing that had called in the Spaniards. Perhaps he was at heart a great patriot, striving to unite divided Germany. Whatever he was planning was cut short by his assassination in 1634, an assassination almost certainly not directly planned by the Emperor Ferdinand, but from which he cannot be dissociated, since he rewarded the assassins.

The Swedish and French Period, 1635–1648

Though the two great antagonists, Gustavus and Wallenstein, were now dead, the war went on. Swedish affairs were in the able hands of the chancellor Oxenstierna, aided by two able generals, Baner and Torstenson. In 1642, the Swedes won a second battle at Leipzig and threatened the core of Habsburg power, the hereditary lands of Bohemia and Austria. But these Swedish successes had begun to seem more Swedish than Protestant and drew from Christian IV of Denmark, the recent champion of Protestantism, a response not uncommon in the history of balance-of-power politics. Now more fearful of the nearby Swedes than of the distant Austrians, Christian went to war with Sweden, and saw his lands once more successfully invaded.

Meanwhile, however, the ultimately decisive force was entering the bewildering struggle. The French had decided that subsidies to German and Swedish opponents of the Habsburg power were not enough and that they would have to fight for themselves. French armies crossed the Rhine and struck at the imperialists through South Germany. Theirs was by no means a triumphal march, and bitter fighting took place in the last years of the war, from 1643 to 1648. Although the hard-pressed imperial armies gained an occasional victory, they lost on the whole. In 1645, the Danes gave up and made a separate peace. In 1648, a series of peace conferences met in the northwestern German region in Westphalia—the first of the great peace conferences of modern times. The Habsburgs were the vanquished; the French and Swedes were the victors.

In its last years the Thirty Years' War had in fact become a general war. On the seven seas the French and Spanish were at odds. In Italy, the French had tried to split communication between the Austrian and the Spanish Habsburgs by controlling the Alpine passes. This general war had, however, one striking difference from all others of modern times: The balance of power had to be achieved without one of its main factors, England. England kept out of the war for the obvious reason that in all these years she was facing domestic crisis and civil war (see Chapter 7).

Effects on Germany

The defeat of the Habsburgs in 1648, though it did not end in the sheer collapse of the defeated power, left the Germanies in a fearful state. Although the engines of destruction available to men in the seventeenth century were feeble in comparison with those available to us, it may well be that in terms of human suffering and material destruction the Thirty Years' War was quite as disastrous to Germany as the Second World War of the twentieth century. One obvious point: If we today can destroy more easily, we can also mend more easily. In the seventeenth century, the rebuilding of a destroyed town was a long process. On the human side, deaths from wounds, disease, and famine could not in the defective state of medicine and transport be effectively checked as they are today.

Religious and political passions combined to make each side unsparing of the other. Worse yet, much of the fighting was done by mercenaries hardened to the cruelties of war, badly disciplined, and forced by the inadequacies of military administration to live off the country of friend and foe alike. Here from a satirical novel, *Simplicissimus,* written by a man named Grimmelshausen, himself captured as a ten-year-old during the war, is a passage that gives the flavor of the times:

Now this same foraging is neither more nor less than attacking of villages (with great pains and labour: yea, often with danger to life and limb), and there threshing, grinding, baking, stealing, and taking all that can be found; harrying and spoiling the farmers, and shaming of their maids, their wives, and their daughters. And if the poor peasants did murmur, or were bold enough to rap a forager or two over the fingers, finding them at such work (and at that time were many such guests in Hesse), they were knocked on the head if they could be caught, or if not, their houses went up in smoke to heaven. Now my master had no wife (for campaigners of his kidney be not wont to take ladies with them), no page, no chamberlain, no cook, but on the other hand a whole troop of grooms and boys which waited both on him and his horse; nor was he himself ashamed to saddle his own horse or give him a feed; he slept ever on straw or on the bare ground, and covered himself with a fur coat. So it came about that one could often see great fleas or lice walk upon his clothes, of which he was not ashamed at all, but would laugh if any one picked one out.[*]

By the end of the war, men had got so used to constant warfare that armies were whole

*H. J. C. von Grimmelshausen, *Simplicissimus,* A. T. S. Goodrick, trans. (New York, 1912), 110.

little societies in themselves. It is estimated that although the imperial armies at the end of the war numbered about 40,000, the regular camp followers — wives, mistresses, children, servants, sutlers, and the like — numbered 140,000 and were kept in some kind of order by imperial officers known unofficially as "provosts of the harlots." Such details are more revealing than attempts at statistical estimates of the losses in men and things, which are not very trustworthy.

Some historians trace to this disastrous war aspects of modern Germany that have made her a disturbing influence in the modern world. They point to a national sense of inferiority heightened by her delayed achievement of national unity, a lack of the slow ripening in self-government that a more orderly growth in early modern times might have encouraged, a too strong need for authority and obedience brought out in response to the anarchic conditions of the seventeenth century. These are dangerously big generalizations that are at most suggestive; they can by no means be proved. And yet though modern revisionist scholarship tends to question the traditional view that Germany suffered unusual damage, both material and spiritual, there is little doubt that the Thirty Years' War was highly destructive, even if not so horrible as scholars used to think.

The Peace of Westphalia

The reality of 1648 was that Germany had reached a low point of political and cultural disintegration. In the great settlements of Westphalia, though some of the separate German states came out well, Germany herself was a major victim. The French got bits of land toward their northeast frontier, notably a foothold in Alsace. Sweden got lands south of the Baltic, on the German mainland, and a real start toward her ambitious goal of controlling the Baltic area. Due compensations and adjustments were made among the major German states. In particular, Brandenburg, though damaged by the cessions to Sweden on the mainland, got valuable compensations in

lands around Magdeburg, and in the next two centuries was to recover some of the cessions made to Sweden. Indeed, the beginning of the greatness of Brandenburg-Prussia is commonly dated from this Westphalian settlement of 1648.

Still more important, the Peace of Westphalia formally recognized the "independence" of the constituent elements of the German Empire. From now on, the German states could legally enter into alliances with one another and with foreign powers, as long as they were not directed against the emperor. This last was a face-saving for the Habsburgs, but the fact that the constituent states now had their own foreign services, their own armies, their own finances — three obvious earmarks of "independence" in our state-system — is clear evidence that the Holy Roman Empire of the German nation was no longer a viable political entity. The Westphalian settlement also formally recognized the independence of two smaller states, the Swiss Confederation, the nucleus of which had first broken away from Habsburg control during the later Middle Ages and the United Netherlands of the Dutch, already independent in fact for more than half a century.

We may note that the southern provinces of the old "Spanish Netherlands," mostly Catholic, were not part of the new United Netherlands, but remained Spanish until 1713, and then became the "Austrian Netherlands." After a brief and unsuccessful union with the Dutch in the Kingdom of the Netherlands in 1815–1830, they became independent Belgium. What in the early seventeenth century had been merely a truce line, which no one thought would be permanent, has lasted over 300 years as an international boundary.

Finally, the ecclesiastical provisions of the treaties really did settle matters, leaving German religious differences henceforth to take their relatively peaceful modern form of missionary and educational struggles. The Thirty Years' War was the last formal war between Protestants and Catholics, though by no means the last war in which their religious antagonism played a part. Calvinists now secured the same recognition as Catholics and Lutherans.

Europe in 1648

Legend:
- Brandenburg-Prussia
- Austrian Habsburg Lands
- Spanish Habsburg Lands
- Swedish possessions
- Venetian possessions
- Ottoman Empire
- ········· Boundary of the Holy Roman Empire
- ■ Battle sites

Approximate division line between Puritans and Cavaliers in England, May, 1643

SCOTLAND
Edinburgh
Dunbar   Berwick

North Sea

NORWAY
Oslo

S W E

Stoc

Balt

DENMARK
Copenhagen

Lübeck
Hamburg
Bremen

BRANDENBURG
Berlin

WEST-PHALIA
Magdeburg
Lützen

SAXONY

SILE

Oder R.
Elbe R.

ULSTER
Drogheda
IRELAND
Dublin
Wexford

Preston
Marston Moor

ENGLAND
Nottingham
Worcester
Naseby
London

Texel

UNITED NETHERLANDS

Osnabrück
Münster

THE

EMPIRE

Prague
BOHEMIA
MORA
AUSTRIA
Vienna
STYRIA

Atlantic Ocean

SPANISH NETHERLANDS
Verdun
Metz
Toul
PALATINATE
Heidelberg
Strasbourg
ALSACE

Rhône R.

Seine R.
Paris

FRANCE
Nantes
Orléans
Loire R.

FRANCHE COMTÉ

BAVARIA
Danube R.

CARINTHIA
CARNIOLA
TYROL
SWITZERLAND
VALTELLINE
Geneva

Venice

VENETIAN REPUBLIC

H

Bordeaux

Rhône R.

SAVOY
PIEDMONT
MILAN
Po R.
Genoa

Avignon
(to the Papacy)
Marseilles

Florence

PAPAL STATES
Rome

Ro

PORTUGAL
Lisbon

Burgos
SPAIN
Madrid
Ebro R.
Tagus R.

Barcelona
Valencia

Guadalquivir R.
Seville
Granada

BALEARIC IS.

CORSICA
(to Genoa)

NAPLES
Naples

SARDINIA

Mediterranean Sea

Palermo
SICILY

0   500
Miles

ALGIERS
(Tributary to Ottoman Empire)

TUNIS

MALTA

60

10

5

0

5

15

20

50

45

15

40

35

10

5

0

5

10

15

FINLAND

L. Onega

L. Ladoga

Gulf of Finland

INGRIA

ESTONIA

Novgorod

LIVONIA

Pskov

COURLAND

W. Dvina R.

LITHUANIA

Vilna

Smolensk

Moscow

R U S S I A

Volga R.

Volga R.

Oka R.

Ural R.

nigsberg

PRUSSIA

Volga R.

Warsaw

POLAND

Kiev

Vistula R.

Dnieper R.

Dniester R.

Caspian Sea

C R I M E A

Don R.

TRANSYLVANIA

MOLDAVIA

RY

Belgrade

WALLACHIA

Black Sea

Morava R.

Danube R.

ONTE-
NEGRO

O T T O M A N   E M P I R E

Vardar R.

Constantinople

Salonika

Tigris R.

Aegean Sea

Athens

Euphrates R.

RHODES

(to Venice)

CYPRUS

CRETE

Princes could still "determine" the faith of their territories, but the right of dissidents to emigrate was recognized. In most of Protestant Germany, multiplicity of sects was in fact accepted. The boundary between Protestant and Catholic regions recognized the Catholic gains made since the Catholic Reformation, and is today much as in 1648. On the vexed question of ecclesiastical reservation the year 1624 was taken as the *annus normalis,* the year from which ownership of ecclesiastical property was to be measured; as things were on January 1 of that year, so they were to be in the following years. After thirty years of trying to exterminate each other, Catholics and Protestants in Germany gave up the effort.

The simple "hard" explanation of this fact is that Protestants and Catholics were driven to mutual toleration by exhaustion and sheer despair of imposing their will on their opponents. The simple "soft" explanation is that at last men saw the light and came to believe in freedom of worship as an individual right. Neither explanation is fully true. By 1648, an intellectual minority had for some time been urging toleration as a good; men of peaceful disposition had been attacking the horrors of war and the futility of religious persecution. Another minority, thoroughly committed to the struggle, clearly accepted the peace as a mere truce. The majority, after all these years of war, were simply tired out. But once the settlement was made, once men grew used to the existence of Protestants and Catholics side by side, or at least in adjoining territories, such as arrangement came on the whole to seem entirely normal.

Reading Suggestions on the Dynastic and Religious Wars

(Asterisk indicates paperbound edition.)

General Accounts

D. Ogg, *Europe in the Seventeenth Century,* 6th ed. (Black, 1948); and G. N. Clark, *The Seventeenth Century,* 2nd ed. (Clarendon, 1947). Two good general histories, ranging in part well beyond the subject of this chapter.

C. J. Friedrich, *The Age of the Baroque, 1610–1660* (Harper, 1952). This volume, in the "Rise of Modern Europe" series, is unusually firm and provocative. Emphasizes culture and political theory. NOTE: The important bibliographies of these "Rise of Modern Europe" volumes were recently revised. All are available in paperbacks with the revised bibliographies.

C. Petrie, *Earlier Diplomatic History, 1492–1713* (Macmillan, 1949). A useful manual of the history of international relations.

C. H. Carter, *The Secret Diplomacy of the Hapsburgs, 1598–1625* (Columbia Univ. Press, 1964). Scholarly and interesting study based on archives, not actually a general survey.

Special Studies: England

C. Read, *The Tudors* (Holt, 1936). A most readable introduction by a sound historian.

J. D. Mackie, *The Earlier Tudors, 1485–1558* (Clarendon, 1952); and J. B. Black, *The Reign of Elizabeth, 1558–1603* (Clarendon, 1936). These two volumes in the "Oxford History of England" are scholarly and comprehensive.

G. R. Elton, *The Tudor Revolution in Government* (*Cambridge Univ. Press, 1953). An important study of the shift to the "new-model" bureaucratic state.

D. L. Keir, *The Constitutional History of Modern Britain, 1485–1937,* 4th ed. (Black 1950). A good introduction to an important and difficult subject.

J. E. Neale, *Queen Elizabeth* (Harcourt, Brace, 1934; *Anchor). Generally considered the best single volume on the famous queen. The author has also written several specialized works on aspects of political life under Elizabeth.

C. Read, *Mr. Secretary Walsingham and the Policy of Queen Elizabeth* (Harvard Univ. Press, 1925). A thorough study of a key figure in Tudor government.

A. L. Rowse, *The Expansion of Elizabethan England* (St. Martin's, 1955), and *The England of Elizabeth: The Structure of Society* (Macmillan, 1950). These complementary studies are the work of a "maverick" English scholar in rebellion against academic caution.

E. Jenkins, *Elizabeth the Great* (Coward-McCann, 1959). Deservedly a best-seller; focused on the queen as a person.

G. Mattingly, *The Armada* (Houghton Mifflin, 1959). Now a paperback. A truly great history.

W. K. Jordan, *Philanthropy in England 1480–1660; The Charities of London, 1480–1660; The Charities of Rural England, 1480–1660* (Allen and Unwin, 1959–1961). A monumental trilogy.

J. Ridley, *Thomas Cranmer* (Oxford Univ. Press, 1962). An excellent biography of an important figure.

L. B. Wright and V. A. LaMar, eds., *Life and Letters in Tudor and Stuart England* (Cornell Univ. Press, 1962). A miscellany addressed to the general reader, with much interesting material.

K. R. Andrews, *Elizabethan Privateering During the Spanish War, 1585–1603* (Cambridge Univ. Press, 1964). Scholarly yet most readable.

Special Studies: Primarily Spain, Sweden, Germany, the Netherlands

R. B. Merriman, *The Rise of the Spanish Empire in the Old World and the New* (Macmillan, 1918–1934). Volumes III and IV of this now classic work deal with Charles V and Philip II.

John Lynch, *Spain Under the Hapsburgs*, Vol. I, *Europe and Absolutism, 1516–1598*, (Oxford Univ. Press, 1964). Thorough and scholarly treatment to be followed by a second volume.

J. H. Elliot, *Imperial Spain 1469–1716* (St. Martin's Press, 1964). Recent, authoritative general study.

R. Trevor Davies, *The Golden Century of Spain* (Macmillan, reprinted 1954). A standard shorter study of sixteenth-century Spain.

K. Brandi, *The Emperor Charles V* (Jonathan Cape, 1939). A very complete study of the man who first tried to secure something like control over the European state-system.

C. Petrie, *Philip II of Spain* (Norton, 1963). Interesting and, for an Englishman, impartial.

J. H. Elliot, *The River of Catalans: A Study in the Decline of Spain, 1598–1640* (Cambridge Univ. Press, 1963). A significant monograph.

M. Roberts, *Gustavus Adolphus: A History of Sweden*, 1611–1632, 2 vols. (Longmans, Green, 1953–1958). Sympathetic biography which is also a full history of these important years for Sweden.

C. V. Wedgwood, *The Thirty Years' War* (Jonathan Cape, 1938; *Anchor). A full and generally well-balanced account.

H. Holborn, *A History of Modern Germany:* Vol. 1, *The Reformation;* Vol. 2, *1648–1820* (Knopf, 1959–1963). A third volume is promised in this authoritative study by a distinguished historian.

C. J. Cadoux, *Philip of Spain and the Netherlands* (Lutterworth Press, 1947). A modest restatement of the Protestant and liberal thesis with interesting reflections on moral judgments in history.

P. Geyl, *The Revolt of the Netherlands, 1555–1609* (*Barnes and Noble); *The Netherlands in the Seventeenth Century*, 2 vols. (Barnes and Noble, 1961–1964). Translation of a most important work by a Dutch historian. A single volume of lectures, *History of the Low Countries* (St. Martin's Press, 1964) is a fine summary of Geyl's life work.

C. V. Wedgwood, *William the Silent* (Yale Univ. Press, 1945). An excellent biography.

Special Studies: France

L. von Ranke, *Civil Wars and Monarchy in France in the Sixteenth and Seventeenth Century* (Harper, 1853). An old and famous work by one of the greatest nineteenth-century historians; may still be read with profit.

A. J. Grant, *The Huguenots* (Butterworth, 1934. Home University Library). A brief and reasonably dispassionate account.

J. E. Neale, *The Age of Catherine de' Medici* (Jonathan Cape, 1943). A solid study.

J. W. Thompson, *The Wars of Religion in France, 1559–1576* (Univ. of Chicago Press, 1909). A detailed narrative.

Pierre de L' Estoile, Selections from his *Mémoires-Journaux,* trans. and ed. by Nancy Lyman Roelker under the title, *The Paris of Henry of Navarre* (Harvard Univ. Press, 1958). A fine translation; a rich source of information on Henry IV.

Q. Hurst, *Henry of Navarre* (Appleton-Century-Crofts, 1938). A standard biography in English of King Henry IV of France.

W. J. Stankiewicz, *Politics and Religion in Seventeenth Century France* (Univ. of California Press, 1960). Goes back to the *politiques* of the sixteenth century.

J. R. Major, *The Estates General of 1560* (Princeton Univ. Press, 1951); *The Deputies to the Estates General in Renaissance France; Representative Institutions of Renaissance France* (Univ. of Wisconsin Press, 1960). An important series of related studies.

Special Studies: Other Topics

G. Mattingly, *Renaissance Diplomacy* (Houghton Mifflin, 1955). Indispensable for the topic.

H. Nicolson, *The Evolution of Diplomatic Method* (Macmillan, 1954). A brief survey, which goes back to the Greeks, and is especially good on the techniques and spirit of early modern diplomacy.

G. H. Sabine, *A History of Political Theory,* rev. ed. (Holt, 1950). This admirably sane and lucid treatment has very useful sections covering topics dealt with in this chapter.

J. W. Allen, *Political Thought in the Sixteenth Century,* 3rd ed. (Barnes and Noble, 1951). A more detailed and difficult account of the subject.

F. L. Nussbaum, *A History of the Economic Institutions of Modern Europe* (Appleton-Century-Crofts, 1933). Incorporates the views of the important German economic historian, Sombart.

G. Renard and G. Weulersse, *Life and Work in Modern Europe (Fifteenth through Eighteenth Centuries)* (Knopf, 1926). Useful for the general economic background.

(Note: For other useful works on economics and political theory, consult the titles listed at the close of Chapter 4.

C. W. C. Oman, *A History of the Art of War in the Sixteenth Century* (Dutton, 1937). A highly interesting study of an aspect of history often neglected.

J. F. C. Fuller, *A Military History of the Western World,* 3 vols. (Funk & Wagnalls, 1954–1956). By an informative and rather unorthodox general; Vols. I and II include material relating to this chapter.

L. Goldscheider, *El Greco* (Phaidon, 1954). An excellently illustrated book on the painter who expresses so well the Spanish "style."

Historical Fiction

Cervantes, *Don Quixote,* S. Putnam, trans., 2 vols. (Viking, 1949). Widely considered the best translation of this great classic.

H. J. C. von Grimmelshausen, *Simplicissimus* (Dutton, 1924). This novel of the Thirty Years' War, written in the seventeenth century, is an important document of social history. Good reading, despite its rather strange form.

W. Scott, *Kenilworth* (many editions). Elizabethan England is the scene of this novel by the famous Romantic writer of the early nineteenth century.

6

The Expansion of Europe

Fifteenth Through Seventeenth Centuries

I Introduction

Most historical geographies provide a series of maps showing what they commonly call the "known world" at certain periods—starting usually from the known world of Homer, little more than the eastern Mediterranean and its fringes. Next come the known worlds of Alexander the Great and the Romans, centered still on the Mediterranean, hazy or blank for much of interior Europe and Africa, with only the western fringes of Asia known, and with the Americas still unsuspected. Then from late medieval explorations through the great modern discoveries, the series goes on to the full fruition of geographical knowledge, which happened only yesterday. There is a revealing symbolism in that phrase "known world," for we really mean "known to interested members of Greco-Ro-

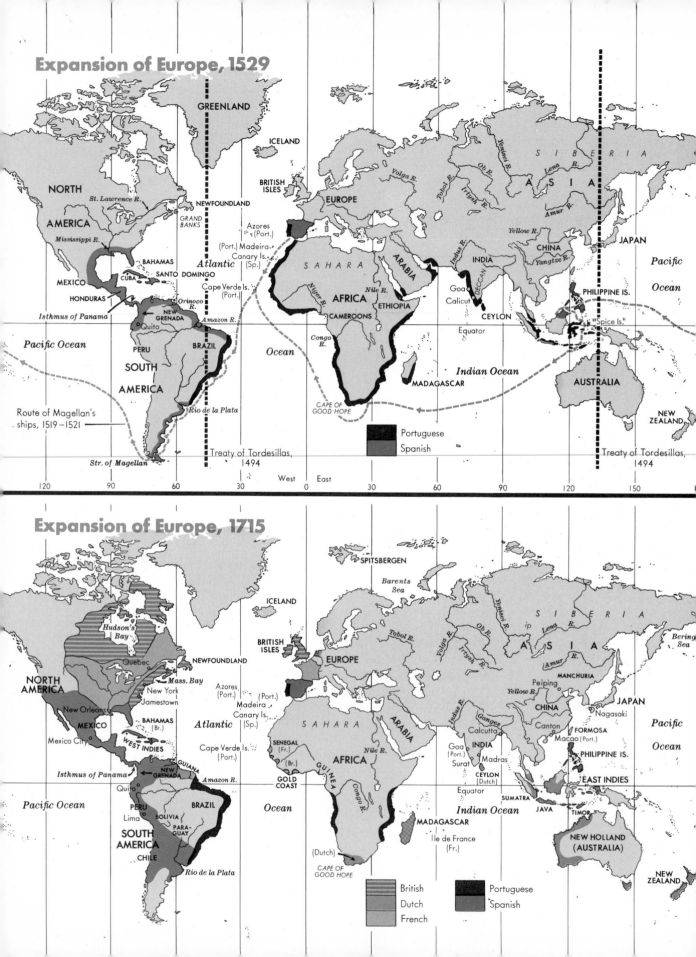

Expansion of Europe, 1529

GREENLAND

ICELAND

NORTH AMERICA

St. Lawrence R.
NEWFOUNDLAND
GRAND BANKS

Mississippi R.

BRITISH ISLES

EUROPE

Volga R.

Ob R.

Yenisei R.

Lena R.

SIBERIA

ASIA

Azores (Port.)
(Port.) Madeira
Canary Is. (Sp.)

Atlantic

SAHARA

ARABIA

Yellow R.

CHINA

INDIA

Yangtze R.

JAPAN

Pacific Ocean

BAHAMAS
CUBA
SANTO DOMINGO

MEXICO

HONDURAS
Isthmus of Panama

Cape Verde Is. (Port.)

Orinoco R.
NEW GRENADA
Quito
Amazon R.

Niger R.

AFRICA

Nile R.

ETHIOPIA

Goa
Calicut

DECCAN

PHILIPPINE IS.

CEYLON

"Spice Is."

CAMEROONS

Equator

Pacific Ocean

PERU

BRAZIL

SOUTH AMERICA

Congo R.

Ocean

Indian Ocean

MADAGASCAR

AUSTRALIA

NEW ZEALAND

Route of Magellan's ships, 1519–1521

Rio de la Plata

CAPE OF GOOD HOPE

Portuguese
Spanish

Str. of Magellan

Treaty of Tordesillas, 1494

West | East

Treaty of Tordesillas, 1494

120 | 90 | 60 | 30 | 0 | 30 | 60 | 90 | 120 | 150

Expansion of Europe, 1715

SPITSBERGEN

Barents Sea

ICELAND

NORTH AMERICA

Hudson's Bay

Quebec

Mass. Bay
New York
Jamestown

BRITISH ISLES

EUROPE

Tobol R.

Ob R.

Yenisei R.

Lena R.

SIBERIA

ASIA

Bering Sea

New Orleans
MEXICO
Mexico City

BAHAMAS (Br.)

WEST INDIES

Azores (Port.)
(Port.)
Madeira
Canary Is. (Sp.)

Atlantic

SAHARA

ARABIA

Volga R.

Irtysh R.

ip

Amur R.

MANCHURIA

Peiping

Yellow R.

CHINA

JAPAN
Nagasaki

Isthmus of Panama
Quito

Cape Verde Is. (Port.)

SENEGAL (Fr.)
(Br.)
GOLD COAST

Nile R.

AFRICA

GUINEA

Indus R.

Ganges R.

Goa (Port.)
Surat

INDIA

Calcutta

Madras

Canton

FORMOSA
Macao (Port.)

PHILIPPINE IS.

NEW GRENADA
GUIANA
Amazon R.

CEYLON (Dutch)

EAST INDIES

PERU
Lima
BOLIVIA
PARAGUAY

BRAZIL

Ocean

Congo R.

Equator

SUMATRA
JAVA

TIMOR

SOUTH AMERICA

CHILE

Rio de la Plata

(Dutch)

CAPE OF GOOD HOPE

Indian Ocean

MADAGASCAR

Ile de France (Fr.)

NEW HOLLAND (AUSTRALIA)

NEW ZEALAND

Pacific Ocean

British
Dutch
French

Portuguese
Spanish

man society and its Christian successor states of the West." The Chinese, too, had a "known world," and even the Red Indians.

Ancient and Modern Expansion Contrasted

Men have always moved about on this planet. In the prehistoric ages of movement and migration, which include such daring feats as the Polynesian settlement of the Pacific islands, the movers kept no written records and no concrete ties with their place of origins. They were not societies in expansion, but groups of individuals on the move, carrying no more than traditions, habits, and tools. The expansion of the West was a very different thing. From the very start in ancient Greece and Rome, records were kept, indeed maps were made, and the nucleus always remained in touch with its offshoots. Western society has expanded *as a society*, often as a group of states.

The modern western expansion, which began in the mid-fifteenth century, however, differed in important ways from the expansion that had carried the cultures of the ancient Near East as far as western and northern Europe. In the first place, this modern expansion was much faster and covered more ground. Although some secrets of the Arctic and the Antarctic, some details of the wilder interiors of the world, were not known to us until the twentieth century, it is broadly true that the whole world was revealed to Europeans within the two and a half or three centuries after 1450 — within four long lifetimes. In the second place, this modern expansion was the first time our western society crossed great oceans. Ancient and medieval western navigation had clung to the narrow seas and the shorelines. The ancients had even commonly drawn up their boats on land to spend the night. Now westerners crossed Atlantic and Pacific, far from the protecting land. In the third place, this expansion carried westerners well outside the orbit of relations with Byzantines and Mohammedans, who were also successors to the cultures of Socrates and Christ, into relations with a bewildering variety of races, creeds, and cultures, from naked savages to cultivated Chinese. Not since the Germanic peoples had been tamed and converted in the early Middle Ages had westerners come into close contact with primitive peoples. Finally, and of very great importance, expanding Europe possessed a margin of superior material and technological strength that lasted in some respects up to our own time, a margin that enabled western society to do what no society had ever done before — extend its influence around the world.

An important element of that margin was the possession of firearms; yet firearms could be legally or illegally acquired by non-Europeans, and very soon were. The strength by which Europeans overcame the world was not quite so simple as the possession of firearms. It was a compound of technological and economic superiority and of superior political and social organization, which in turn permitted superior military organization. This superiority was not exercised from a common western center, but rather by half a dozen competing western nations, each anxious to cut the others' throats, and quite willing to arm and organize natives against its western competitors. Frenchmen in North America armed the savages against the British and the British armed them against the French. Yet not even the Iroquois were able to maintain themselves against white society. French, British, Portuguese, Dutch, Spaniards, and later Germans and Americans all intrigued against one another in the Far East, and yet not until the mid-twentieth century did any Asian nation (save only Japan, and Japan not until about 1900) really compete successfully in war and politics with a western land. So great was western superiority that the rivalries of competing powers did not delay the process of expansion but probably stimulated and hastened it.

How far this physical superiority in the expansion of the West throughout the world was — and is — also a spiritual and moral superiority is a problem we in the West today cannot answer as firmly as did our fathers. But you will not understand the successful expansion of Europe if you do not realize that those who carried out the expansion, though moved often by greed, by love of adventure, by sheer despair over their lot at home, and by many other motives, were also moved by the conviction that they were doing God's work, the work of civilization, that they were carrying with them a better way of life. They were confident and energetic people, capable of great endurance and courage, and they have made over the face of the globe.

The Motives and Nature of Modern Expansion

Why did men living on the Atlantic coasts of Europe in the second half of the fifteenth century venture out on an ocean that ancient and medieval mariners had not seriously tried to penetrate? We cannot answer the question with finality. Indeed, though it is rather a question of fact than a question of value judgments, it is still a most difficult one. The Americas, Africa south of the Sahara, Australia, all were there for the Phoenicians or the Greeks or the Romans to find. Yet it was left for Europeans in the fifteenth and the sixteenth centuries to find them, systematically and surely.

The great explorations were part of the Renaissance, part of a general stirring of European nations, of an era of adventure and the energetic pursuit of new things. So small a thing as the magnetic compass helped make ocean voyages possible. Without the compass, earlier mariners had been helpless, except when clear weather gave them sun or stars as guides. The actual origins of the compass are obscure, but we know that by the beginning of the fifteenth century it was familiar to European sailors and was a normal part of navigation by the time of Columbus. Better instruments and better methods of determining a ship's position at sea were also fully in hand by the late fifteenth century. Shipbuilders were getting away from older types of traditional Mediterranean ships, building somewhat longer and narrower vessels that could stand the long swells of the ocean, deliberate-

ly trying to find the kind of ship that could be handled in these unknown waters. Technologically, the way was ready for the great explorations.

Politically, the blocking or at least hindering of the usual trade routes in the Near East by the new and still unsettled Turkish power turned men's minds to the search for another way to India and China. Complete denial of the importance in this respect of the fall of Constantinople to the Turks in 1453 is an example of excessive and inaccurate historical revisionism. Yet the Italians, especially the Venetians and Genoese, had installed themselves in the Near East and were making arrangements with the Turks in spite of difficulties. More important, actually, was the fact that Spain, Portugal, France, and England were all rising in political and economic activity, all on the way up that had been shown them by the Italians. Blocked in the Near East, in part by Italians, they eyed the unoccupied and for them near-by Atlantic. Those addicted to Marxist or other variants of the innocent economic interpretation of everything can answer our question readily: Renaissance men discovered new worlds because the aggressive economic drives natural to nascent capitalism sent them on their way.

Yet technology and the politics of the trade routes had to be taken advantage of by men, men in the state of mind that sent Columbus out across the unknown ocean—to see with his own eyes what was there, to test in experience a set of concepts. Columbus deliberately sought to prove his theory that because the earth is round one can travel from Europe westward and reach Asia. No sensible person would maintain that even the first voyage of Columbus can be explained entirely in such purely intellectual terms; but neither can it be explained without such terms. One of the essential characteristics of the explorations and the subsequent expansion of Europe is that this was a movement guided in part by the new spirit of empirical science, the spirit that impelled men, if for instance they heard about the existence of unicorns, to go out and try to find some. Their medieval predecessors did not need to see a unicorn to believe in its existence. This new scientific spirit, however, did not immediately banish unicorns, mermaids, and sea serpents from men's minds, and has not yet done so now that the whole world has been thoroughly explored. Indeed, the first news of these strange worlds resulted in a whole new set of wonders, some real or merely exaggerated, which the publishing of accounts of travel brought to all Europe.

Nothing makes more clear the consecutive, planned, deliberately scientific nature of these early modern explorations and settlements than the contrast with the sporadic, unplanned, and perhaps wholly mythical, earlier oceanic navigation. Tradition is full of these early voyages, and of Atlantis, a lost continent, now sunk beneath the waves, but once inhabited, which Plato and later commentators tell about. Irishmen, Norsemen, Breton fishermen, and others have all been credited with the "discovery" of America, a discovery that was never widely spread abroad in the medieval West. Of all these tales of pre-Columbian discovery, that of the Vikings' reaching the

North American continent about the end of the tenth century is most likely. There is not the slightest doubt that Norsemen reached Iceland and settled it for good, and that they had outpost settlements in Greenland. Their traditional literature, the heroic poems known as sagas, credit Leif Ericson with reaching a Wineland (or Vineland), which most experts believe to have been some part of the New England or Nova Scotian, or, given possible climate changes since then, the Newfoundland coast. It is quite possible that all during the Middle Ages, more probably toward their close, fishermen from northwest Europe fished the Grand Banks off the coast of Newfoundland. The main thing for us to understand is this: Even if hundreds of Europeans reached the New World before Columbus, they did not establish a permanent link between the two worlds; they were not explorers of the kind we are about to talk about, and they were, above all, not supported by the organized social purpose that we are about to encounter.

East by Sea to the Indies

Prince Henry and the Portuguese

There is, as the historically minded would expect, abundant medieval background for the great explorations we are about to describe. The overland voyages to China of the Venetian Marco Polo (c. 1264–1324) were widely known through manuscripts of his own account of his travels. But there were other less well-known travelers in the late Middle Ages, which were years of ferment and search for the new and the striking.

The first of the great names in modern expansion is not that of a bold explorer or *conquistador*, but that of an organizing genius who directed the work of others—in fact, in modern terms, a "planner." Prince Henry of Portugal, known as "the Navigator," lived from

1394 to 1460. He was a deeply religious man, and he may well have been moved above all by a desire to convert the populations of India and the Far East, whose existence had been well known to westerners since the travels of Marco Polo. Indeed, there was a widespread conviction in the West that these distant peoples were in fact already Christian and for true salvation needed only to be brought in direct contact with the Roman Catholic Church. One of the great medieval legends was that of Prester (that is, Priest) John, a powerful Christian ruler somewhere out in the vague East. Fragments of one of the very early heretical sects, who were called Nestorians, had indeed survived in the East, and there were Coptic Christians in Ethiopia. But Prester John was never found, and the Portuguese in India were soon disabused of their first notion that the Hindus—since they were not Mohammedans—must be Christians.

Prince Henry and his fellow workers presumably wanted to promote Portuguese commerce and national power as well as the Christian faith. They must also have felt pride in Portugal the homeland, which now appears for the first and last time as a major factor in the broad story of western civilization. They went about their work carefully, planning and sending out frequent expeditions equipped with the best technical means they could devise. Gradually, these expeditions crept southward along the harsh desert coast of Africa where the Sahara meets the Atlantic, until in 1445 Cape Verde was doubled, and the land began to grow greener and to trend hopefully eastward. Whether Henry himself believed that Africa could be circumnavigated is not absolutely certain, but according to tradition the Phoenicians had done it, and Greco-Roman geographers had believed that Africa was surrounded by the ocean.

By 1472, after Henry's death, the Portuguese reached the end of the bulge of West Africa at the Cameroons, and faced the disheartening fact that the coast was once more trending southward, not eastward. But they kept on, stimulated by royal patronage, and in the next generation two great explorers finished the job. In 1488, Bartholomew Diaz, blown far south by a great storm, turned northeast and found that he had rounded the great cape called later the Cape of Good Hope. He was followed by Vasco da Gama, who set out in 1497 with four ships to reach India. He rounded the Cape of Good Hope, thanks to the previous discoveries of Diaz, and worked northward along the east coast of Africa, coming soon to an area of Arab trading where the route to India was well known. Despite Arab jealousy of the intruder, da Gama secured a pilot and reached the Malabar coast of India at Calicut ten months and fourteen days out from Lisbon. The Portuguese now had an ocean route to the East.

On the next great voyage toward India, the Portuguese made a lucky strike that was to break the Spanish monopoly in South America and ensure that one of the great Latin-American states would be Portuguese, not Spanish, in language and culture. Pedro Cabral, in 1500, started out to repeat da Gama's voyage to India. But by now the Portuguese were used to long voyages on the open ocean, far from sight of land, and they no longer needed to creep around the coast of Africa. Cabral kept boldly southward from the bulge of Africa, and was apparently blown somewhat westward of his course so that he made a landfall on the bulge of the South American continent in what is now Brazil. He at once detached a ship and sent it home to announce his discovery. Now the voyages of Columbus were of course well known to navigators by this time, and some geographers think that in fact Cabral set out deliberately to see what he could find south of the westward route Columbus had taken. Six years previously, in 1494, Spain and Portugal had by the Treaty of Tordesillas agreed to partition these new lands along a north-south line three hundred and seventy leagues (about a thousand miles) west of the Azores, so that Brazil fell quite definitely into the Portuguese sphere.

The main Portuguese push, however, was toward India and the Far East. The explorer was succeeded by that other characteristic agent of European expansion, the trader. But the trader by no means worked alone. He was aided and protected by the power of his state, which aimed to set up for its nationals a monopoly of trade with the newly discovered lands. The great figure of early Portuguese imperialism is Alfonso de Albuquerque, governor of the Indies from 1509 to 1515, under whom the Portuguese set up a firm base in their capital at Goa in India, and from that base organized regular trade routes toward southeastern Asia and China. By 1557, the Portuguese had established a base at Macao in China near Canton, and they had begun trade with the Japanese. Portugal had assembled a colonial empire.

Africa

The two new worlds thus opened to Europeans were very different both from Europe and from each other. Africa was hot, relatively thinly populated, relatively poor by current European standards. India, China, and much of southeastern Asia were even then thickly populated, with great wealth accumulated in a few hands, with much that Europeans wanted in the way of silks, spices, and other luxury goods. Africa was in a sense by-passed, though the many coastal stations that the Europeans founded soon carried on a flourishing trade in Negro slaves. The African tribes, at least in the northern center and along the bulge of the continent westward, had not been wholly out of touch with the more efficient societies to the north. They had long been in contact overland with the Arabs, who had found them a good source of slaves, and who had brought Islam and some of the wares of civilization with them. But, for the most part, the tribes in central and southern Africa were, in terms of their command over material goods, still in the Stone Age. They were primitives, men without cities and states, men with cultures so different from those of Europe that few Europeans made any effort to understand them. Nor did the Europeans, at least in these centuries, do much to undermine these primitive cultures. Save for the enforced mass migration of Negroes as slaves, most of them to the Americas, save for some trade in ivory and other tropical goods, Africa had for years little effect on Europe, and Europe had little effect on Africa. Except for South Africa, where the Dutch began settlement in the seventeenth century, Africa was not to be subject to "colonialism" until the partitions of the nineteenth century (see Chapter 16).

India

The India that Europeans thus reached around Africa had been marginally in touch with Europe for several thousand years. Alexander the Great had actually campaigned in northern India, and throughout the Middle Ages the Arabs had served as a link in trade, and, in at least vague general knowledge, as a link between the West and India. But now a direct link was forged, never to be loosened. The link was not of course a form of union or assimilation, and especially in these early modern centuries, West and East hardly communicated at the higher levels of cultural interchange. Indeed, the Portuguese were contemptuous of the Indians, once they dis-

The Polo brothers with their caravan, about 1270.

covered that the inhabitants of India were not, as they had believed, the Christians of Prester John or some other Christian leader. Among the Dutch, French, and British who followed the Portuguese to India, this attitude of contempt became set in the conventional idea of white superiority. This feeling of European superiority among all the many agents of the West in India has probably been exaggerated both in our western literary tradition and in the minds of educated Indians quick to take offense. Still, this sense of superiority was there, perhaps most clearly reflected centuries later in Kipling's too famous

> Oh, East is East and West is West, and never the twain shall meet,
> Till Earth and Sky stand presently at God's great judgment seat. . . .*

Inescapably, this western superiority was at bottom a superiority on the battlefield. In the last analysis, and long after the initial European monopoly of firearms had ended, a European or European-trained and commanded native army or navy could always subdue a native Asiatic army or navy. In India, at least, this European domination was greatly helped by the political and military disunity of the subcontinent. The Portuguese reached India when in the north Moslem invaders were consolidating a foreign rule of the sort which, from the earliest Mesopotamian civilization, had periodically brought comparative order to these regions. This Mogul (Mongol) Empire in the north had little hold on regions of the south where the Europeans established firm footholds. Local Indian rulers, whether they were Moslem or Hindu in faith, were in intense rivalry and were a ready prey to European promises of aid. All the European powers found it easy, not merely to win Indian princes to their side, but to raise and train on their own responsibility native armies to fight under Portuguese, French, Dutch or British flags.

Perhaps the lack of political and social integration in India is the basic reason why a few handfuls of Europeans were able to dom-

*R. Kipling, *Ballad of East and West.*

inate the country until 1945. China, too, saw her armed forces beaten whenever they came into formal military conflict with European or European-trained armies or fleets; China, too, was forced to make to European nations all sorts of concessions—treaty ports, and above all extraterritoriality, that is, the right of Frenchmen or Britishers for instance, to be tried in French or British courts for offenses committed on Chinese soil. Yet China, unlike India, was never "annexed" by a European power, never lost its "sovereignty." For China preserved a fairly strong central government, and had many strands of ethical and political unity that India lacked.

Indeed, the variety and range of Indian life are extraordinary. Some of the more isolated parts of India in the Deccan or southern peninsula were inhabited by tribesmen of no higher level than many African tribesmen. Some, on the northern edges, were warrior tribesmen much like those of the highlands of Central Asia. In the great valleys of the Indus and the Ganges, and in the richer parts of the Deccan, there was a wealthy, populous society basically Hindu in culture, though when the Europeans arrived, it was dominated in many areas by Central Asiatic invaders of Moslem faith and culture. Hindu society itself was the result of an amalgamation between earlier native stocks and invaders from the north who certainly spoke a language closely related to Greek, Latin, and indeed our own, and who probably were white "Indo-Europeans" or "Aryans." The early history of India, however, is most confusing, and we cannot tell how many these invaders were, or just where they came from, though the invasion apparently had taken place between 2000 and 1200 B.C. It seems almost certain that the white invader's consciousness of differing from the natives is responsible basically for the characteristic Indian institution of *caste.*

According to the laws of caste, men and women were by the fact of birth settled for life in a closed group which pursued a given occupation and occupied a fixed position in society. When the Europeans reached India, there were apparently something over a thousand castes, including a group at the bottom without caste, the "untouchables." The ruling groups were of two main castes, the Brahmins or priests, and the Kshatriya or warriors. The great multiplicity of castes lay in the third group, the Vaisya or commonalty, and was based largely on vocation or trade. In theory, marriage between members of different castes was forbidden, as was change of caste through social mobility. In fact, in the centuries since the invasion by the "Indo-Europeans" considerable human intermixture had undoubtedly occurred. Yet even today the upper classes in most of India are of a lighter color than the lower.

The most striking thing about Indian culture was the high place occupied by the priestly caste, the Brahmins. The Brahmin faith has strains of a most other-worldly belief in the evils of the life of the flesh and the attainment of salvation by a mystic transcendence of the flesh in ascetic denial. With this is a doctrine of the transmigration of souls, in which sinful life leads to reincarnation in lower animal life, and virtuous life leads, at least in some forms of Hindu belief, to ultimate freedom from flesh or any sort and reunion with the perfect, the ineffable. But official Brahminism became a series of rigid and complicated rituals, and the religion of the common people became, or rather retained from earlier times, an elaborate polytheism lush with gods and goddesses by no means ethereal, but fleshly indeed. Against all this worldliness there rose in the sixth century B.C. a great religious leader, Gautama Buddha, himself of noble stock. Buddhism is in origin one of the great higher religions of the world. It accepts the basic Brahminical concept of the evil of this world of the flesh, but it finds salvation, the *nirvana* of peaceful release from the chain of earthly birth and rebirth, in a life ascetic but not withdrawn, a life of charity and good works. Buddhism died out in the land of its birth, but it spread to China, Japan, and southeastern Asia.

In these lands it took two forms, still existing. In the northern lands of Tibet, China, Japan, the Mahayana (Great Vehicle) continued in theology to emphasize Buddha's strong ethical desire to make salvation (*nirvana*) available to all. In southeastern Asia and Ceylon, the Hinayana (Lesser Vehicle) prevailed. In theory, the Hinayana relies more on ritual, and its monks are wholly detached from the world. In fact, the two vehicles are not in our times clearly distinguished as *popular religions.* Buddhism remains a great world religion, which has made some converts among western intellectuals. In an altered form known as Zen Buddhism, originally a kind of Japanese stoicism, it has proved popular in *avant garde* circles in the United States.

The religious thought of India has left a residue of greater other-worldliness, of greater emphasis on a mystical subduing of the flesh, on a revulsion from struggle for wealth, satisfaction of the common human appetites, worldly place and power, than has Christianity or Islam. In the practice of Indian life even before the Europeans came to India, there was plenty of violence, plenty of greed, cruelty, and self-indulgence. Except as superstition and tabu and ritual, little of the higher religions of India had seeped down to the masses. To certain types of western minds, indeed, the educated classes of India have seemed to take refuge in other-worldly doctrines as a psychological defense against the worldly superiority of the West and the poverty and superstition of their own masses. But the fact remains that for three hundred years educated Indians have insisted that they feel differently about the universe and man's place in it than do we, that theirs is a higher spirituality.

China

China, too, resisted the West, and in many ways more successfully than did India. A very old civilization that goes back several millennia before Christ, and becomes reasonably historical about 1000 B.C., was established in the valleys of the Yangtze and the Yellow rivers. Like the other civilizations peripheral to the great nomadic reservoir of the Eurasian heartland—the Mesopotamian, the Indian, the European—it was subject to periodical incursions of the Eurasian tribesmen. It was against such incursions that the famous Great Wall of

China was built in the third century B.C. On the whole, however, the Chinese protected their basic institutions against the victorious nomads, whom they absorbed after a few generations. At just about the time when the first Europeans were setting up permanent trade relations with China, the last of these "barbarian" conquests occurred. Early in the seventeenth century, Mongolian tribes established a state of their own in eastern Manchuria, to the north of China proper. In 1644, they seized the Chinese capital of Peking and established a dynasty that lasted until 1911. But the Manchus, like other outsiders before them, left Chinese institutions almost untouched.

Chinese history is by no means the uneventful record of a "frozen" and unchanging society that some westerners have thought. It is filled with the rise and fall of dynasties, with wars and plagues and famines, with the gradual spread of Chinese culture southward and eastward, to the region of Canton, to Vietnam, to Korea, to Japan. It has periods of effective governmental centralization, and periods of "feudal" disintegration. Its art and techniques were subject to periods of flourishing and decay. But there were many elements of continuity.

First of all, at the base of Chinese social life was a communal village organization, held together by very strong family ties, a cult of ancestor worship, and hard work guided by traditional agricultural techniques. The Chinese village, basically unchanged until the communist reforms of our own day, was one of the oldest socio-economic organizations in the civilized world. Second, at the top of this society was an emperor, Son of Heaven, the "natural" ruler of a great state. The Chinese were conditioned to at least formal imperial unity in somewhat the same way early medieval westerns were conditioned to the unity of Roman Catholic Christendom. Third, the business of running this vast empire was entrusted to one of the most remarkable ruling classes history has ever recorded, the *mandarins,* a bureaucracy of intellectuals, or at any rate of men who could pass literary and philosophical examinations in classics, examina-

tions that required a rigorously trained memory.

This class proved not very resilient in the face of the challenge of new ideas from Europe, and it was except at its brief best by no means free from what we know as graft and nepotism. But it had served the state for several millennia, and its existence is one of the reasons for the extraordinary stability of Chinese society. In theory, the class was one open to talents, even for the great mass of poor peasants. But for most of these centuries, the necessary education was too expensive and too hard to acquire for any but a very few gifted, lucky, and persistent poor boys.

Just as in India, there were in China an immense population at the very margin of existence, and a small upper class that enjoyed gracious living of a kind hardly available to the medieval western upper classes. The Chinese millions had their superstitions, their demons, their other-world. The earlier periods of Chinese cultural flowering show traces of mystic beliefs among the educated, traces of the eternal Platonism of the human spirit. Still, everyone who has known the Chinese, even the casual traveler who makes some effort to appreciate what is going on about him, finds in the educated Chinese a lack of mysticism, other-worldliness, "tender-mindedness"; and no great amount of sheer superstition. Or, in positive terms, he finds a sense of worldly realism, an acceptance of the universe as it appears to common sense, or at least to the "tough-minded," a concern with human relations, with politeness, decorum, and the like, and an absence of theology, sacraments, and faith in a supranatural god which we in the West expect in a higher religion.

It has been commonly said that China never had a religion, in the sense that Buddhism, Christianity, and Islam are religions with a firm doctrine of salvation in an order of existence quite different from that of our daily lives on earth. The conventional Confucianism of the upper classes is indeed a code of manners and morals, not a sacramental religion, not a religion in which the faithful undergo the miracle of sharing in something

"Sage under a Pine Tree," a Chinese painting from the Sung dynasty (960–1279).

ineffable. Confucius, a sage who flourished early in the fifth century B.C., was no mystic, no prophet, but a moralist who taught an ethical system of temperance, decorum, obedience to the wisdom of the wise and the good. This lack of commitment to an other-worldly religion, however, has hitherto by no means made the Chinese more receptive to western ideas. At least until our own times, China has resisted westernization more effectively than has any other great culture.

The Portuguese Empire

The empire that the Portuguese founded in Asia and Africa was a trading empire, not an empire of settlement. They established along the coasts of Africa, India, and China a series of posts, or "factories," over which they hoisted the Portuguese flag as a sign that they had annexed these bits of territory to the Portuguese Crown. From these posts they traded with the natives. As all the European colonial powers did later, they offered relatively cheap and relatively mass-produced articles—guns, knives, gadgets of all sorts, cheap cloth, and a great deal else. In return, they got gold and silver (when they could), spices, still essential especially for meats in those days without refrigeration, silks and other luxuries, and, finally, raw materials such as cotton and slaves, and, in the New World, tobacco and sugar.

Two guiding principles of this trade were accepted by almost all contemporaries, whether in the mother country or in the colonies, as simple facts of life. First, in this trade the mother country was the determining element, and would naturally produce manufactured goods and services while the colony produced raw materials. Second, foreigners, nationals of other European lands, were excluded from this trade; they could not deal directly with the colony or take part in the commerce between mother country and colony. The Portuguese, in sum, followed a policy of *mercantilism.*

Armed forces were essential to the establishment and maintenance of this colonial system. Relatively small land forces proved sufficient both to keep the natives under control and to ward off rival European powers

from the trading posts. A large and efficient navy was, however, necessary, for the easiest way to raid a rival's trade was to wait until its fruits were neatly concentrated in the hold of a merchant vessel, and then take it at sea as a prize. Such deeds are now known as piracy, a very common activity in these early modern centuries. Sometimes, especially in the eighteenth century, these pirates became in fact outlaws, men of no nation, willing to rob nationals of any country. In these earlier centuries, they were often openly an unofficial adjunct of a given navy, operating only against enemies or neutrals, never against their own nationals. A navy was, then, essential to protect the sea routes of a colonial power. The

A view of Macao, the Portuguese outpost in China, 1598.

AMACAO.

Portuguese fleet was not only a merchant fleet; under the command of governors like Albuquerque, it was a great military fleet that brushed aside Arab opposition and for a few decades ruled the oceans of the Old World.

The Portuguese made no serious attempt to settle large numbers of their own people either in the hot coast lands of Africa or in the already densely populated lands of India and the Far East. Nor, save in the single respect we are about to encounter, did they attempt to make over these natives into pseudo-Portuguese. There were of course useful places for Portuguese in the colonial services, both civilian and military; many of the natives were enlisted in the armed forces or used as domestic help and in subordinate posts such as clerks. These natives inevitably picked up, however imperfectly, the language and culture of the colonial power. But neither among the primitive Negro tribes of Africa nor among the Indian and Chinese masses did this process of Europeanization go very fast or far.

Nor did the Portuguese attempt to rule directly, to alter the political, social, or economic structure of native life. They left the old ruling chiefs and the old ruling classes pretty much as they had found them. In the total lives of these millions, the imported European wares played extremely little part in these early days. The native upper classes monopolized most of these wares, and Europe could not yet flood non-European markets with cheap manufactured goods made by power-driven machinery. Nothing western touched these masses of natives in the sixteenth century, nothing tempted them away from their millennial ways of life, in anything like the degree our twentieth-century West attracts and tempts the East.

There is one exception. The Portuguese and the Spanish, and even their relatively secular-minded rival nations in eastern Asiatic regions, the English, Dutch, and French, did attempt to Christianize the natives. From the very first, much sincerity, devotion, and hard work went into the Christian missionary movement. The earliest missionaries no doubt underestimated the difficulties they were to encounter. Many of them were in a sense partly converted themselves; that is, they came to be very fond of their charges, and convinced that these were in fact almost Christians already. Some of the Jesuits in China, the first European intellectuals to live in this very civilized country, seriously believed that with just a bit more effort the full reconciliation between Christianity and Confucianism could be achieved.

From the start, difficulties arose between the missionaries, anxious to protect their charges, and the traders and colonial officials, driven by their very place in the system to try to exploit the natives. Finances were always a serious problem, with so many tens of millions to convert and to tend, and with so few men, so little money, to do the work. Certainly, measured in statistical terms, the effort to convert India and the Far East to Christianity did not make a serious impression on the masses. Christianity has been part of the whole influence of the West on the East, not to be measured in terms of actual Christian church memberships in the East. Christian influence on the upper and the intellectual classes has been far greater than on the masses. Still, in the balance, the confident words of one of the pioneer Jesuits in China in the sixteenth century, Father Ricci, now sound most unrealistic:

Against this monster of Chinese idolatry . . . which has for so many thousands of years tyrannized without contradiction over so many millions of souls and sent them to the abyss of Hell, our Company of Jesus has, in conformity with its constituted purpose, arisen to make war, coming from distant lands and crossing many kingdoms and seas to deliver these unfortunate souls from eternal damnation. . . . Indeed, to the kingdom and the arms of the holy cross no force in this world or in Hell can make resistance.*

The Portuguese, though first in the field in the East, very soon had to yield to newer rivals—French, Dutch, English. A trading empire depends on naval protection and on an enterprising trading community at home, and in both these critical matters the Portuguese were unable to keep up the pace they had set.

*Quoted in Henry Bernard, *Le Père Mattheiu Ricci* (Tientsin, 1937), I, 1. Our translation.

Father Matthew Ricci, Italian missionary in China, about 1600.

ples—were not up to competition with the aggressive expanding powers of northwest Europe. After the sixteenth century, they ceased to add to their empire and their wealth, and took a decidedly secondary place in international politics. A great poem, *The Lusiads* (1572), of Camoens, is their monument.

Yet the Portuguese by no means lost their empire, which remained strong along the old trade route around Africa to Goa and other stations in India, Timor in Indonesia, and Macao in China. In Africa, it has counted nearly 800,000 square miles. It has not been a flourishing empire, but it has continued to exist. That it should have endured so long, and against such active and hungry rivals as the French, Dutch, and British, is in part evidence of the existence of a force in history difficult for modern Americans to recognize—that of inertia. It is very hard, or until the present totalitarian age it has been very hard, to destroy outright any going territorial concern. Portugal's more successful rivals took away Portuguese leadership, but left her a participant in the competition. Still, the survival of the Portuguese Empire was greatly aided by the fact that the most successful of the European imperial powers, England, remained through modern times in alliance with Portugal. The complete victory of France or the Netherlands in the colonial scramble might possibly have meant the eventual annihilation of the Portuguese Empire. At any rate, as of the mid-1960's, the Portuguese Empire was still there, almost intact, save for Goa, lost to India in 1961.

Like the Spaniards, they suffered from an inadequate, or at any rate inadequately run, home industry; their banking, their business methods, their initiative—if not their scru-

III   West by Sea to the Indies

Columbus

In the earliest days of concerted effort to explore the oceans, the Spanish government had been too busy disposing of the last

Moslem state in the peninsula, Granada, and uniting the disparate parts of Spain to patronize scientific exploration as the Portuguese had done. But individual Spanish traders were active, and Spain was growing in prosperity. As long ago as the end of the fourteenth century and the beginning of the fifteenth, Portuguese mariners had found the three groups of Atlantic islands, Azores, Madeira, and Canaries, well out in the stormy ocean, but still essentially European rather than American. By papal decree, the Canaries were assigned to the Crown of Castile, the others to Portugal. Once the marriage of Ferdinand and Isabella had united Aragon and Castile, the Spanish government wanted to catch up with the Portuguese. So it commissioned Columbus to try out his plan to reach India by going west.

Columbus (1451–1506) was an Italian, born in Genoa. He was essentially self-educated but, at least in navigation and geography, had educated himself very well. His central conception, that it would be possible to reach the Far East—"the Indies"—by sailing westward from Spain, was certainly not uniquely his. That the earth is a globe was a notion entertained by ancient Greek geographers, and revived with the renaissance of the classics. Toscanelli at Florence in 1474, Behaim at Nuremberg in the very year of Columbus' voyage, published maps that showed the earth as a globe—but without the Americas, and with the combined Atlantic and Pacific much narrower than they are in fact. To act on this notion by deliberately sailing west on the At-

lantic had become with the growth of oceanic navigation a clear possibility. But it was still a strikingly novel idea—an idea that was not acceptable to conservative minds. It took a persistent, innovating personality to get support for such an expedition.

Columbus met with many rebuffs, but finally, with the support of the wealthy Spanish trading family of Pinzon, was able to get the help of Queen Isabella. Indeed, with the sole aim of reaching the Indies he might not have been able to set out. But, as his commission shows, he was also charged to discover and secure for the Spanish Crown new islands and territories, a mission that probably reflects the importance of ancient and medieval legends about Atlantis, St. Brendan's isle, and other lands beyond the Azores. Even if he did not reach the Indies, there seemed a chance that he would reach something new.

He reached a New World. Setting out from Palos near Cadiz on August 3, 1492, in three ships so small that they could all be propped up comfortably on the deck of a modern airplane carrier, he made a landfall on a Bahaman island on October 12 of the same year, and eventually went on to discover the large islands we know as Cuba and Santo Domingo. On a second voyage, in 1493, he went out

The earliest known European illustration of the natives of South America; German woodcut, about 1505.

with seventeen ships and some fifteen hundred colonists, explored further in the Caribbean, and laid the foundations of the Spanish Empire in America. On his third voyage in 1498–1500, he reached the mouth of the Orinoco in South America but encountered difficulties among his colonists and was sent home in irons by the royal governor Bobadilla, who took over the administration of the Indies for the Crown. He was released on his return to Spain, and in 1502–1504 made a fourth and final voyage, in which he reached the mainland at Honduras. He died in comparative obscurity at Valladolid in Spain in 1506, totally unaware that he had reached, not Asia, but a new continent.

That continent was, by a freak of history, not destined to bear his name, though it is now liberally sprinkled with other place-names in his honor. News of Columbus' voyages soon spread by word of mouth in Europe. But printing was still in its infancy; there were no newspapers or geographical institutes; the international learned class—the humanists—were more interested in Greek manuscripts than in strange lands; and, from early Portuguese days on, governments had done their best to keep their discoveries as secret as possible. The most effective spreading of the work in print about the New World was done by another Italian in the Spanish service, Amerigo Vespucci, who wrote copiously about his explorations in the immediate footsteps of Columbus. Scholars still dispute whether or not Vespucci really made all the discoveries, from the southeastern United States to the tip of South America, that he claimed to have made. But his letters came to the attention of a German theoretical geographer, Martin Waldseemüller, who in 1507 published a map blocking out a land mass in the southern part of the New World which he labeled, from the latinized form of Vespucci's first name, America. The map was read and copied, and though Waldseemüller in a new map of 1531 removed it in favor of a noncommittal "Terra Incognita" (unknown land), he had successfully christened two new continents.

Later Explorers

From now on, the roster of discovery grows rapidly. Ponce de León reached Florida in 1512, and Balboa in 1513 crossed the Isthmus of Panama and saw a limitless ocean, on the other side of which the Indies did indeed lie, for it was the Pacific. Many other Spaniards and Portuguese in these first two decades of the sixteenth century explored in detail the coasts of what was to be Latin America. It was now quite clear that an immense land mass lay athwart the westward route from Europe to Asia, and that even the narrow isthmus of Panama was an obstacle not readily to be overcome by a canal. Maritime exploration was therefore turned to the problem of getting around the Americas by sea and into the Pacific. North America proved an obstacle indeed, for none of the great estuaries—Chesapeake, Delaware, Hudson—promising though they looked to the first explorers, did more than dent the great continent, the breadth of which was totally unknown. The St. Lawrence looked even better, for to its first French explorers it seemed like the sought-for strait. But even the St. Lawrence gave out, and the rapids near Montreal, which showed it was only another river after all, received the ironic name of Lachine (China) Rapids, for this was *not* the way to China. Not until the mid-nineteenth century was the usually ice-choked "Northwest Passage" discovered by the Englishman Sir John Franklin, who died in the Arctic wastes before he could return to civilization.

The "Southwest Passage" was found only a generation after Columbus, in the course of an expedition that is the most extraordinary of all the great voyages of discovery. Ferdinand Magellan, a Portuguese in the Spanish service, set out in 1519 with a royal commission bidding him to find a way westward to the Spice Islands of Asia. Skirting the coast of South America, he found and guided his ships through the difficult fogbound passage that bears his name, the Straits of Magellan, reached the Pacific, and crossed it in a voyage of incredible hardship. Scurvy alone, a disease we now know to be caused by lack of vitamin C, and a standard risk in those early days, meant that he and his men had to surmount torturing illness. After he had reached the islands now known as the Philippines, Magellan was killed in a skirmish with the natives. One of his captains, however, kept on along the known route by the Indian Ocean and the coast of Africa. On September 8, 1522, the "Victoria" and her crew of eighteen men—out of five ships and 243 men that had sailed in 1519—landed at Cadiz. For the first time, men had sailed around the world, and had proved empirically that the world is round.

What these explorations cost in terms of human suffering, what courage and resolution were needed to carry them through, is very hard for our easy-traveling generation to imagine. Here, from the bare report the sailor Pigafetta gives of Magellan's expedition, is a firsthand account of one of the crises:

Wednesday, the twenty-eighth of November, 1520, we came forth out of the said strait, and entered into the Pacific sea, where we remained three months and twenty days without taking in provisions or other refreshments, and we only ate old biscuit reduced to powder, and full of grubs, and stinking from the dirt which the rats had made on it when eating the good biscuit, and we drank water that was yellow and stinking. We also ate the ox hides which were under the main-yard. . . . Besides the above-named evils, this misfortune which I will mention was the worst, it was that the upper

Magellan passing through the Straits later named for him; late sixteenth-century engraving.

and lower gums of most of our men grew so much that they could not eat, and in this way so many suffered, that nineteen died.*

Such accounts could be multiplied for every part of the newly discovered world and for every nation taking part in the expansion of the West.

The Foundation of the Spanish Empire

As a by-product of Magellan's voyage, the Spaniards who had sent him out got a foothold in the Far East, which they had reached by sailing west. As we have seen, by the Treaty of Tordesillas in 1494 Spain and Portugal had divided the world—the world open to trade and empire—along a line that cut through the Atlantic in such a way that Brazil became Portuguese. This same line, extended round the world, cut the Pacific so that some of the islands Magellan discovered came into the Spanish half. Spain conveniently treated the Philippines as if they also came in the Spanish half of the globe, though they are just outside it, and colonized them from Mexico.

Up to now, we have concerned ourselves mostly with maritime explorations and the founding of coastal trading stations. The Spaniards in the New World, however, very soon explored by land, and acquired thousands of square miles of territory. To the explorer by sea there succeeded the *conquistador,* half explorer, half soldier and administrator, and all adventurer. Of the *conquistadores,* two, Hernando Cortés and Francisco Pizarro, have come down in history with a special aura of tough romance. With a handful of men they conquered the only two civilized regions of the New World: the Aztec empire of Mexico, conquered by Cortés in 1519, and the Inca empire of Peru, conquered by Pizarro in 1531–33. The narrative of these conquests, whether in the classic nineteenth-century histories of the American Prescott or in the nar-

*Lord Stanley of Alderly, *The First Voyage Round the World by Magellan,* translated from the accounts of Pigafetta, and other contemporary writers (London, 1874), 64–65.

ratives of actual participants, remains among the most fascinating if not among the most edifying chapters of western history. A book of this scope cannot possibly do justice to the drama of the conquerors of Mexico and Peru, nor to the many other Spaniards who in search of glory, salvation, gold, and excitement toiled up and down these strange new lands — Quesada in New Granada (later Colombia), Coronado, de Soto, and Cabeza de Vaca in the southwest of what became the United States, Mendoza in the La Plata (the lands around the River Plate), Valdivia in Chile, Alvarado in Guatemala, and many others, not least Ponce de León hunting for the fountain of eternal youth in Florida. These are the men who opened up the New World for Spain, as our own North American pioneers from Captain John Smith to Lewis and Clark and Kit Carson opened up the New World for the English-speaking peoples.

Unlike the great cultures of the Middle and Far East, the pre-Columbian cultures of the Americas went down pretty completely before the Europeans. It is certainly true that from Mexico to Bolivia and Paraguay and even to Patagonia there survive millions of men and women of Indian stock, true that for a full understanding of the Latin-American republics one needs to know something about the traditions and the folkways of many tribes and peoples. That Mexican artists and intellectuals have in our day proudly held up their Indian heritage against the Yankees, and against their own Europeanized nineteenth-century rulers, is important for us to know. But the structure of the Aztec or the Inca empire has simply not survived. The sun-god in whose name the Inca ruled, the bloody Aztec god of war, Huitzilopochtli, are no longer a part of the lives of men, as Confucius and Buddha are. Perhaps someday social scientists can tell us what part—if any—the old civilizations of Peru and Central America play in the behavior of present-day Latin Americans. But now it looks as though these old civilizations are chiefly of interest as specimens, fossils, no longer alive. At most, knowledge of them may help us establish a kind of genetics or evolutionary theory of civilization. In themselves, however,

Machu Picchu, ancient Inca city in the Andes of Peru. Corn and potatoes were grown on the terraces.

these cultures are fascinating examples of the variety of human life on this earth. And the fact that they existed at all, as organized, large territorial states, and that they made high achievements in the arts and the sciences, is further evidence against naive western notions of racial superiority.

The First True Colonial Empire

Well before the end of the sixteenth century, the work of the *conquistadores* had been done, and in Latin America the first of the true colonial empires of Europe—in contrast to the trading empires in Africa and Asia—had been founded. Nowhere, save in the region of the La Plata and in central Chile, was the native red Indian stock eliminated and replaced by a population almost entirely of old world stock —something that *has* happened in the United States and Canada, save for a tiny Indian minority almost certainly doomed to absorption. Over vast reaches of Mexico and Central and South America, a crust of Spanish or Portuguese formed at the top of society and made Spanish or Portuguese the language of culture; a class of mixed blood, the *mestizos,* was gradually formed from the union, formal or informal, of Europeans and natives; and in many regions the native Indians continued to maintain their stock and their old ways of life al-

213

most untouched. Finally, wherever, as in the Caribbean, the Indians were exterminated under the pressure of civilization, or, as in Brazil, they proved inadequate as a labor force, the importation of Negro slaves from Africa added another ingredient to the racial mixture.

Moreover, geography and the circumstances of settlement by separate groups of adventurers in each region combined to create a number of separate units of settlement tied together only by their dependence on the Crown and destined to become the independent nation-states of Latin America today. Geography alone was perhaps a fatal obstacle to any subsequent union of the colonies, such as was achieved by the English colonies that became the United States of America. Between such apparently close neighbors as the present Argentine and Chile, for instance, lay the great chain of the Andes, crossed only with great difficulty by high mountain passes. Between the colonies of the La Plata and the colonies of Peru and New Granada lay the Andes and the vast tropical rain-forests of the Amazon Basin, still essentially unconquered today. The highlands of Mexico and Central America are as much invitations to local independence as were the mountains of Hellas to the ancient Greeks. Cuba and the other Caribbean islands have the natural independence of islands. And even had the coastal

fringes of Brazil not been settled by Portuguese, men of a different language from the Spaniards, these regions have for the most part no easy land connections with the rest of Latin America. Geography alone would probably have made Brazil independent.

The Spanish used the centralized administrative institutions that were then the rule among the new monarchies of Europe. At the top of the hierarchy were two vice-royalties, that of Peru with its capital at Lima and that of New Spain with its capital at Mexico City. From Lima the viceroy ruled for the Crown over the Spanish part of South America, save for Venezuela. From Mexico City the viceroy ruled over the mainland north of Panama, the West Indies, Venezuela, and the Philippines. Each capital had an *audiencia,* a powerful body operating both as a court of law and as an advisory council, and there were *audiencias* in such major centers as Guatemala, New Granada (modern Colombia), Quito, and the Philippines.

The Balance Sheet
of Latin-American Empire

This was certainly a centralized, paternalistic system of government, which has rightly enough been contrasted with the "salutary neglect" in which the North American colo-

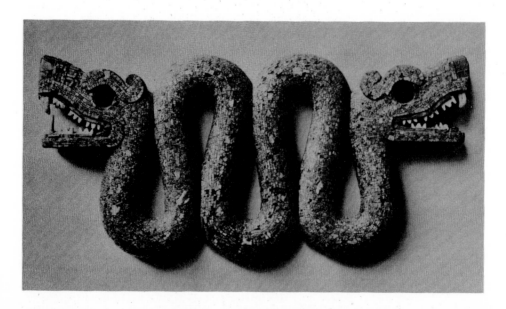

Turquoise mosaic ornament believed to be part of the Aztec treasure shipped to Spain by Cortés.

nies were generally left by the home government until the crisis that led to our American Revolution. But it was not—given the vast areas and the varied peoples under its control, it could not be—as rigid in practice as it was in theory. The rudiments of popular consultation of the Spanish colonists existed in the *cabildos abiertos* or assemblies of citizens. Moreover, as time went on the bureaucracy itself came to be filled largely with colonials, men who had never been in the home country, and who developed a sense of local patriotism and independence. Madrid and Seville were simply too far away to enforce all their decisions. Notably in the matter of trade, it proved impossible to maintain the rigid monopolies of mercantilistic theory, which sought to confine trade wholly to the mother country, and to prohibit, or severely limit, domestic industry in the colonies. Local officials connived at a smuggling trade with the English, Dutch, French, and North Americans which in the eighteenth century reached large proportions.

The hand of Spain was heaviest in the initial period of exploitation, when the rich and easily mined deposits of the precious metals in Mexico and Peru were skimmed off for the benefit both of the Spanish Crown, which always gots its *quinto*, or fifth, and of the *conquistadores* and their successors, Spaniards all. This gold and silver did the natives no good, but in the long run it did no good to Spain, since it went to finance a vain bid for European supremacy. By the seventeenth century, the Latin-American colonial economy and society had settled down in a rough equilibrium. It was not a progressive economy, but neither was it a hopelessly backward one. Colonial wares—sugar, tobacco, chocolate, cotton, hides, and much else—flowed out of Latin America in exchange for manufactured goods and for services. Creoles (American-born of pure European stock) and mestizos were the chief beneficiaries of this trade. The Indians remained at the bottom of the social pyramid, relatively untouched by the new society.

Certainly the two great Indian civilizations, the Mexican and the Peruvian, were wiped out by the Spaniards. Certainly all over Latin America the natives fell to the bottom of a caste system based on color, a system never quite so rigid as it became in North America, but still a system that damaged the native's pride and self-respect. Yet Spanish imperial policy toward the natives was in aim by no means ungenerous, and even in execution holds up well in the long and harsh record of contacts between whites and non-whites all over the globe. Especially in the Carribbean, but to a degree everywhere, the whites tried to use native labor. The first result was disastrous for the natives; new diseases, to which the natives had no immunity, decimated their ranks. Here, as with the gold and silver, some ironic spirit of history seems to have taken revenge on the whites: though the question of the origin of syphilis is still disputed, many historians of medicine believe that it was brought from the West Indies, where it was mild, to western civilization, where until very recently, it has been deadly, and where it may yet recover its virulence. The attempt to regiment native labor in a plantation system, or to put it on a semi-manorial forced-labor system, known as the *encomienda,* proved almost as disastrous. Negro slavery was an inevitable result of the shortage of native labor. Finally, the colonial whites tended toward the aggressive, the insensitive, the hard-boiled; by and large, the gentle souls stayed at home.

Yet, against all these forces making for harshness and cruelty, there were counteracting forces. The natives were regarded as wards of the Crown, and their actual enslavement was prohibited by the New Laws of 1542. The central Spanish government passed a good many laws to protect the Indians, and though these were often flouted in the colonies—a phenomenon not unknown in the English colonies—they put a limit to wholesale exploitation of the natives. Their cause was championed by men of great distinction, and notably by Bartholomew de Las Casas (1474–1566), "Father of the Indians," Bishop of Chiapas in Mexico. The kind of man he is is clear even in these brief passages from his *Short Report on the Indies* (1542):

God has created all these numberless people [Indians] to be quite the simplest, without malice or duplicity, most obedient, most faithful to their natural Lords, and to the Christians, whom they serve; the most humble, most patient, most peaceful, and calm, without strife nor tumults; not wrangling, nor querulous, as free from uproar, hate and desire of revenge, as any in the world.*

Unlike the Asian and African masses, the Indians were formally converted to Christianity. Church and State in the Spanish and Portuguese colonies in the New World worked hand in hand, undisturbed for generations by the troubles roused in Europe by the Protestant Reformation and the rise of a secular anti-Christian movement. The Jesuits in Paraguay set up among the Guarani Indians a remarkable society, a benevolent despotism, a utopia of good order, good habits, and eternal childhood for the Guarani. On the northern fringes of the Spanish world, where it was to meet the Anglo-Saxons, a long line of missions in California and the Southwest held the frontier. Everywhere save in wildest Amazo-

*Francis Augustus MacNutt, *Bartholomew de Las Casas* (New York, 1909), 314.

nia and other untamed areas the Christianity of the Roman Catholic Church brought to the natives a veneer of western tradition, made them in some sense part of this strange new society of the white men.

In the main, the Portuguese settlements in Brazil have a character much like those of the Spaniards elsewhere in Latin America. The Portuguese, perhaps because of the proximity of Brazil to European waters, had more serious trouble with rival nations than the Spanish did. Indeed, the existence of those two fragments of imperial hopes—French Guiana and Surinam just north of Brazil on today's map —is a witness to the fact that the northern maritime nations made a serious effort to settle in what became Brazil. The race mixture in Brazil came also in colonial times to be somewhat different from that in most Spanish colonies, except Cuba. A large number of Negroes were imported into tropical Brazil, and, because the white males drew no sexual color line, were thoroughly mixed with the rest of the population. But in its mercantilist economics, its close tie with the home country, its close union of Church and State, Brazil resembled the Spanish colonies.

IV The Latecomers: France, Holland, England

Early French and English Activity

Spain and Portugal enjoyed a generation's head start in exploration and one of nearly a century in founding empires of settlement. Without this head start, which they owed in part to their position as heirs of the Mediterranean trade, Spain and Portugal could scarcely have made the great mark in the world that they have made. For the northern Atlantic states soon made up for their late start. As early as 1497 the Cabots, father and son, Italians in the English service, saw something of the North American coast, and gave the English their exploration-based claims

there. Another Italian, Verrazzano, and the Frenchman Cartier gave France a claim based on exploration, claims reinforced by the early seventeenth-century detailed explorations of Champlain. Dutch claims began with the voyages of Henry Hudson, an Englishman who entered their service in 1609.

The English did not immediately follow up the work of the Cabots. Instead, they put their energies in the mid-sixteenth century into the profitable business of breaking into the Spanish trading monopoly. John Hawkins, in 1562, started the English slave trade, and his nephew, Francis Drake, penetrated to the Pacific, reached California, which he claimed for England under the name of New Albion, and returned to England by the Pacific and Indian oceans, completing the first English circumnavigation of the globe. By the end of the century, the great fishing grounds off northeastern North America had become an important prize, and under Sir Humphrey Gilbert in 1583 the English staked out a claim to Newfoundland which gave them and their later colonists a firm place in these valuable fisheries.

The Thirteen Colonies: Settlement

In 1584, Sir Walter Raleigh attempted to found a settlement on Roanoke Island (in present-day North Carolina) in a land the English named, from their Virgin Queen Elizabeth, Virginia. Neither this, nor a colony sent out in 1587, managed to survive. But early in the next century the English established two permanent footholds, at Jamestown in Virginia, 1607, and at Plymouth in New England, 1620. Both were to become colonies of settlement, regions in which the sparse native population was exterminated and replaced by men and women for the most part of British stock. But in their inception both were nearer the pattern of trading posts set by the Spanish and Portuguese. Both were established by chartered trading companies with headquarters in England; both, and especially the Virginian, cherished at first high hopes that .they would find, as the Spaniards had, great stores of precious metals. Both were disappointed in these hopes, and managed to survive the first terrible years of hardship by the skin of their teeth. Tobacco, first cultivated in 1612, and the almost legendary Captain John Smith, explorer and man of resourcefulness, saved the Virginia colony, and furs, notably beaver, codfish, and Calvinist toughness saved Plymouth. Both colonies gradually built up an agricultural economy, supplemented by trade with the mother country and interloping trade with the West Indies. Neither received more than a few tens of thousands of immigrants from abroad. Yet both these and the later colonies expanded by natural increase in a country of abundant land for the taking. The thirteen colonies by 1776 were a substantial series of settlements with almost three million inhabitants.

Before these English colonies were completed, one important and one very minor foreign group had to be pushed out. The Dutch, after their successful resistance to Spain (see Chapter 5), had entered the competition for commerce and empire. They had founded a trading colony at New Amsterdam at the mouth of the Hudson and had begun to push into the fur trade. This made them rivals of both the French and the English. They lacked an adequate home base to be a great power, however, and in a war with England in the 1660's they lost New Amsterdam, which was annexed by the English in 1664 and became New York. The Dutch, though very few in numbers, were destined to supply some important families to the future United States, as names like Stuyvesant, Schuyler, and Roosevelt suggest.

The Swedes, too, were now making a bid for greatness, and in 1638 they founded Fort Christiana on the Delaware. But New Sweden was never a serious competitor, and in 1655 Fort Christiana was taken over by the Dutch, who in turn were ousted by the English. Pennsylvania, chartered to the wealthy English Quaker, William Penn, in 1681, filled the vacuum left by the expulsion of the Swedes and the Dutch from the Delaware and was to be the keystone colony before it became the keystone state.

By the early eighteenth century, the English settlements formed a continuous string from Maine to Georgia. Each of the thirteen was founded separately. None had quite identical charters. Perhaps American popular tradition exaggerates the differences between the southern and the northern group. Massachusetts was not settled wholly by democratic plain people, "Roundheads," nor was Virginia settled wholly by great English landowners, gentlemen or "Cavaliers." Both colonies—and all the others—were settled by a varied human lot, which covered most of the range of social and economic status in the mother country, save for the very top. Dukes and earls did not emigrate. But the poorest could and did, as indentured servants or as impressed seamen who deserted ship. The middling men came, and everywhere, even in New England, witness the Winthrops, Saltonstalls, Pynchons, and others, provided a solid sprinkling of the well-to-do.

Still, it is true that New England was for the most part settled by Calvinist Independents (Congregationalists), already committed to wide local self-government and to a distrust of a landowning aristocracy; and it is true that the southern colonies, especially tidewater Virginia, were settled for the most part by Anglicans used to the existence of frank social distinctions and to large landholdings. In Virginia, the Church of England became the established church; in Massachusetts, the Puritan Congregationalists, nonconformists in the homeland, almost automatically became conformists in their new home, and set up their own variety of state church. Geography, climate, and a complex of social and economic factors drove the South to plantation monoculture of tobacco, rice, indigo, or cotton even in colonial days, and drove New England and the Middle Colonies to small farming by independent farmer-owners and to small-scale industry and commerce. Yet in the Piedmont sections of Virginia and the Carolinas, there were small farmers, Presbyterians, "Scotch-Irish," Germans from Pennsylvania, a very northern mixture. Some historians hold that the natural environment, and not any original difference of social structure and beliefs, accounts for the diverging growths of North and South and their eventual armed conflict.

The Thirteen Colonies: Institutions

To us who are their heirs, it has seemed that these English colonists brought with them the religious freedom, the government by discussion, and the democratic society of which we are so proud. So they did, though they brought the seeds, the potentialities, rather than the fully developed institutions. These colonists came from an England where the concept of freedom of religion was only beginning to emerge from the long struggles of the sects. It was quite natural for the

Virginians and the New Englanders to set up state churches. Yet, just as in contemporaneous England, these immigrants represented too many conflicting religious groups to enforce anything like the religious uniformity that prevailed to the south among the Spanish colonists and to the north among the French. Even in New England, "heresy" appeared from the start, with Baptists, Quakers, and Anglicans, these last seeping into New Hampshire and eventually even into Boston. Moreover, some of the colonies were founded by groups which from the first practiced religious freedom and separated Church and State. In Maryland, founded in part to give refuge to the most distrusted of groups at home, the Catholics; in Pennsylvania, founded by Quakers who believed firmly in the separation of Church and State; in Rhode Island, founded by Roger Williams and others unwilling to conform to the orthodoxy of Massachusetts Bay—in all these colonies there was something like the complete religious freedom that was later embodied in the Constitution of the United States, and, as the eighteenth century came on, the characteristic modern freedom not to belong to any formal religious organization at all.

The seeds of democracy, too, existed, although the early settlers, not only in Virginia but even in the North, accepted class distinctions more readily than we now do. No formal colonial nobility ever arose, however, and the early tendency to develop a privileged gentry or squirearchy in the coastal regions was balanced by the equalitarianism of the frontier and the careers open to talent in the towns. Government by discussion was firmly planted in the colonies from the start. All of them, even the so-called proprietary colonies like Pennsylvania, which were granted to a "proprietor," had some kind of colonial legislative body.

Here we come to the critical point of difference between the English and the Spanish and French governments in the New World. The Spanish and French governments were already centralized bureaucratic monarchies; their representative assemblies were no more than consultative and had no power over taxation. Royal governors in Latin America and in New France could really run their provinces, leaning on men they appointed and recalled, and raising funds by their own authority. England was indeed a monarchy, but a parliamentary monarchy, torn by two revolutions in the seventeenth century. Though the Crown was represented in most colonies by a royal governor, the English government had no such bureaucracy as the Spanish and French had. Royal governors in the English colonies had hardly even a clerical staff and met with great difficulty in raising money from their legislative assemblies. The history of the colonies is full of bickerings between governors and assemblies, in which the governor, with little local support, and with but sporadic backing from the home government, was often stalemated. Moreover, in the local units of government—towns in New England, counties in the rest of the colonies—there was the same participation of the people—the established landowners, merchants, and professional men, if not everywhere all the people—and the same absence of an authoritative bureaucracy. Finally, the settlers brought with them the common law of England, with its trial by jury, and its absence of bureaucratic administrative law.

In sum, not only the opportunities of an almost empty land—the frontier—but also English traditions and ideas and the weakness of the central government were major factors in the growth of American democracy. Frenchmen and Spaniards did not bring to their colonies what the English brought to theirs. Their "frontier" was a very different one.

New France

To the north, in the region about the Bay of Fundy and in the St. Lawrence Basin, the French built on the work of Cartier and Champlain. New France was to be for a century and a half a serious threat to the English North American colonies. The St. Lawrence and the Great Lakes gave the French easy access to the heart of the continent, in marked contrast to the Appalachians which stood between the English and the Mississippi. The French were also impelled westward by the fact that the fur trade was by all odds their major economic interest, and furs are goods of very great value and comparatively little bulk, easily carried in canoes and small boats. Moreover, led by the Jesuits, the Catholic French gave proof of a far greater missionary zeal than did the Protestant English. The priest, as well as the *coureur des bois* (trapper), led the push westward. Finally, the French in North America were guided in their expansion by a conscious imperial policy directed from the France of the Bourbon monarchs, *la grande nation* at the height of its prestige and power.

The result was that not the English but the French explored the interior of the continent. By 1712 they had built up a line of settlements—or rather, isolated trading posts, with miles of empty space between, thinly populated by Indians—which completely encircled the English colonies on the Atlantic coast. The story of these French explorers, missionaries, and traders, admirably told by the American historian Francis Parkman, is one of the most fascinating pages of history. The names of many of them—La Salle, Père Marquette, Joliet, Frontenac, Cadillac, Iberville—are a part of our American heritage. From Quebec, one line of outposts led westward, and from Mobile and New Orleans, in a colony founded at the beginning of the eighteenth century and named after Louis XIV, Louisiana, lines led northward up the Mississippi to join with those from Canada and Illinois.

Yet, impressive though this French imperial thrust looks on the map, it was far too lightly held to be equal to the task of pushing the English into the sea. It was a trading empire with military ambitions, and save in Quebec it never became a true colony of settlement. And even there it never grew in the critical eighteenth century beyond a few thousand inhabitants. Frenchmen simply did not come over in sufficient numbers, and those who did come spread themselves out over vast distances as traders and simple adventurers. Frenchmen who might have come, the Huguenots who might have settled down as did the Yankee Puritans, were excluded by a royal policy bent on maintaining the Catholic faith in New France.

The Indies, West and East

The northwestern European maritime powers intruded upon the pioneer Spanish and Portuguese both in the New World and in the Old. The French, Dutch, and English all sought to gain footholds in South America, but had to settle for the unimportant Guianas. They broke up thoroughly the Spanish hold on the Caribbean, however, and ultimately made that sea of many islands a kaleidoscope of colonial jurisdictions and a center of constant naval wars and piracy. These West Indian islands, though today for the most part a seriously depressed area with the growth of the tourist industry their main hope, were in early modern times one of the great prizes of imperialism. Here the cheap Negro slave labor that had replaced the exterminated Caribs raised for their masters on the plantations the great staple tropical crops, tobacco, fruits, coffee, and, most basic of all, subtropical cane sugar, which had as yet no rival in beet sugar, a

crop that flourishes today in northern climates.

The French, Dutch, and English began as well to raid the trading empires the Iberian powers had set up in the Old World. They also raided one another, both in times of official peace and in wartime. By 1715, the bases of their trading and colonial empires had been firmly laid in Asia and Africa.

India proved in these early modern centuries to be the richest prize, and the most ardently fought for. The Mogul Empire (see above, p. 202) was not strong enough in southern India to keep the Europeans out, but it did prove strong enough to confine them on the whole to the coastal fringes. Gradually, in the course of the seventeenth century both the French and the English established themselves in India on the heels of decaying Portuguese power and wealth. The English defeated a Portuguese fleet in 1612 and immediately thereafter got trading rights at Surat on the western coast. Although the able and active Mogul emperor, Aurangzeb, tried to revoke their rights in 1685, he soon found their naval and mercantile power too much to withstand. In 1690, the English founded in Bengal in eastern India the city they were to make famous, Calcutta. Meanwhile, the French had got footholds on the south coast near Madras, at a place called Pondichéry, and soon had established other stations. By the beginning of the eighteenth century, the stage was set in India as in North America for the decisive struggle for overseas empire between France and Britain.

Both countries operated in India, as they had initially in North America, by means of chartered trading companies, the English East India Company and the French *Compagnie des Indes Orientales*. The companies traded, and in trading were backed up by their governments when it was clear that bits of land around the trading posts had to be held, and that the whole relation with India could not be a purely commercial one. Gradually, both countries became involved in support of their companies in Indian politics and wars. But neither country made an effort to found a New England or a New France in the East.

The Dutch, too, entered vigorously into the competition. Their own East India Company, founded in 1602, succeeded in the next few

decades in pushing the Portuguese out of Ceylon. But the great Dutch effort rather bypassed India to concentrate on southeastern Asia, and especially the East Indies. Here again they pushed the Portuguese out, save for part of the island of Timor; they also discouraged English interlopers. In spite of their rapid political decline as a great power in the eighteenth century, they got so firm a hold in Java and Sumatra that their empire in the Netherlands East Indies was to last until our own day.

Africa

All three of the northern maritime powers needed to use the same basic ocean route around Africa that the Portuguese had pioneered in the fifteenth century. All three got African posts. The Dutch put themselves in a good strategic situation by occupying the southern tip of Africa, the Cape of Good Hope, in 1652. The Cape was for them essentially a fitting station for their ships on the

"Barbarian Royalty Worshiping Buddha," handscroll, color on silk, Northern Sung dynasty (960–1127).

long voyage to Indonesia and the Far East, but it was empty except for primitive tribes, and its climate was suitable for Europeans. Though immigration was never heavy, a colony of settlement did grow up, the nucleus of the Afrikaners of South Africa today. Here, notably, the French Huguenots were welcomed. In West Africa, the Dutch took from the Portuguese some posts on the Gold and Guinea coasts, and got a share of the increasingly lucrative slave trade.

The French also worked down the African coast, which was not held in the blocks of territory seen on the map today, but in separate posts which gave ample room for interlopers. In 1626, the French were in Senegal in West Africa. In the Indian Ocean they were on the island of Madagascar, formally annexed by Louis XIV in 1686, and in 1715 they took the island of Mauritius from the Dutch, rechristening it the Isle de France. The British broke into the competition by securing a foothold at the mouth of the Gambia River in West Africa (1662), later followed by other acquisitions at French and Dutch expense. Thus a map of Africa and adjacent waters in the eighteenth century shows a series of coastal stations controlled by the various European imperial powers. But the interior remained untouched, save by the slavers and native traders, and was to all intents and purposes unexplored. Only in the nineteenth century was the "Dark Continent" opened up to European expansion.

The Far East

China, long established as a great empire, was better able to withstand European pressure for territory. Somehow, even in the decay of their imperial power, the Portuguese were able to cling to Macao, and the Dutch, on their heels as always, obtained a station on Formosa in 1624. The Jesuits, bringing with them European instruments and learning that

interested the Chinese, were able in the seventeenth century to get tolerated positions in China, but they made little real headway against rooted Chinese ways of life. Indeed, the Chinese, convinced that their own land was the "Middle Kingdom" — that is, *central* in a spiritual and cultural sense — of the whole world, regarded the Europeans as ignorant barbarians who should be paying them tribute. They kept open only the slender privileged trade from Canton and Macao. This trade was indeed enough to keep Chinese and Europeans in firm contact, but the real opening of China was not yet.

In Japan, the European penetration started much as in China. In 1549, the great Jesuit missionary, St. Francis Xavier, had begun work with the Japanese. In the sixteenth century the Portuguese, and in 1609 the Dutch, won trading footholds. General trade with the Europeans was carried on from Nagasaki. But the Japanese reacted even more strongly than did the Chinese. Though Christianity did not make wholesale conversions, it did make considerable headway. The Tokugawa family, the feudal military rulers of Japan from 1600 to 1868, feared Christianity not only as a threat to national traditions but also as a threat to their own rule, because of the opportunities it might give European powers to intervene in Japanese politics and intrigue with the enemies of the Tokugawa. The Tokugawa therefore decided to close their land entirely to foreign dangers. In the early seventeenth century, they suppressed Christianity by force and literally sealed off Japan. Foreigners were refused entry, and Japanese were refused exit. Even the building of large ships capable of sailing the ocean was forbidden. The Dutch, strictly supervised, were allowed to cling to an island in Nagasaki harbor, where after 1715 they were limited to two ships a year. Not until the American Perry came to Japan in 1853 was this amazing self-blockade really broken and Japan thrown open to the rest of the world.

V The Beginnings of One World

The expansion of Europe in these early modern centuries was not restricted to the Atlantic maritime powers. Although our own American tradition naturally centers on the Columbuses, the Magellans, the Captain John Smiths, general history must find a place for the extraordinary Russian exploration and conquest of Siberia. It offers all sorts of parallels with European expansion in the New World, from the chronological (the Russians crossed the Urals from Europe into Asia in 1483) to the political, for the expanding Muscovite state of Russia was a "new" monarchy, newer in some ways than the Spain of Charles V and Philip II or the England of Elizabeth I.

By 1715, the expansion of Europe was beginning to affect almost every part of the globe. European explorers, missionaries, traders, proconsuls of empire, had spread out in all directions. Even Arctic exploration, stimulated by the hope of finding a Northwest or a Northeast Passage that would shorten the route to the Far East, had already gone a long way by the beginning of the eighteenth century. Henry Hudson had found not only the Hudson River but also Hudson's Bay in the far north. In the late seventeenth century, English adventurers and investors formed an enterprise that still flourishes in Canada today — the Hudson's Bay Company, originally set up for fur trading along the great bay to the northwest of the French settlement in Quebec. In the late sixteenth century, the Dutch under Barents had penetrated far into the European Arctic, had discovered Spitsbergen, and had ranged across the sea named after their leader, the Barents Sea. Finally, the Russians under government patronage explored most of the long Arctic coasts of their empire early in the eighteenth century.

The Black Side of the Record

The record of European expansion contains pages as grim as any in history. The African slave trade, begun by the Portuguese and entered by other peoples for its financial gains, is a series of horrors, from the rounding up of the slaves by native chieftains in Africa through their transportation across the Atlantic to their sale in the Indies. What strikes a modern most of all is the matter-of-fact acceptance of this trade, as if the Negroes were literally so much livestock. The Dutch slave trader *St. Jan* (note the irony of the saint's name) started off for Curaçao in the West Indies in 1659. Her log recorded every day or so deaths of slaves aboard, in parallel columns for men, women, children, until between June 30 and October 29 a total of 59 men, 47 women, and 4 children had died. But there were still 95 slaves aboard when disaster struck, thus simply and unmovingly recorded:

Nov. 1. Lost our ship on the Reef of Rocus, and all hands immediately took to the boat, as there was no prospect of saving the slaves, for we must abandon the ship in consequence of the heavy surf.

Nov. 4. Arrived with the boat at the island of Cuaraçao; the Hon'ble Governor Beck ordered two sloops to take the slaves off the wreck, one of which sloops with eighty four slaves on board was captured by a privateer.*

Americans need hardly be reminded of the fact that we virtually exterminated the native Indian population east of the Mississippi, and that if they massacred us when they could, we replied in kind often enough, and with supe-

Documents Illustrative of the History of the Slave Trade to America, Elizabeth Donnan, ed. (Washington, D. C., 1930), I, 143.

rior means. There were, of course, exceptions to this bloody rule. In New England, missionaries like John Eliot did set up little bands of "praying Indians," and in Pennsylvania, the record of the relations between the Quakers and the Indians was excellent. The white man's diseases, which in those days could hardly have been controlled, and the white man's alcoholic drinks, which were surely quite as hard to control, did more to exterminate the red men than did fire and sword.

The Economic Record

Seen in terms of economics, however, the expansion of Europe in early modern times was by no means the pure "exploitation" and "plundering" it sometimes appears to be in the rhetoric of anti-imperialists. There was robbery, just as there was murder or enslavement. There was, in dealing with the natives, even more giving of slight or nominal value in exchange for land and goods of great value. Just as all Americans are familiar with the slogan, "The only good Indian is a dead Indian," so they are familiar with a dozen variants of how little the Indians sold the Island of Manhattan for. Finally, the almost universally applied mercantilist policy kept money and manufacturing in the hands of the home country. It relegated the colonies to the production of raw materials, a role not so well rewarded, generally speaking, as other economic roles, and one that tended to keep even colonies of settlement in a relatively primitive and certainly economically dependent condition.

Still, with all these limitations granted, the expansion of Europe was in economic terms an expansion of the total wealth produced here on earth. Although Europeans certainly took the lion's share in these early days, the expansion added to the goods available to non-Europeans. Although few Europeans settled in India or in Africa, their wares, and especially their weapons, began gradually the process of Europeanizing, or westernizing or "modernizing" the rest of the world. By the eighteenth century this process was only beginning, and in particular few of the improvements in public health and sanitation that Europeans were to bring to the East had yet come about; nor had any greater public order come to India and Africa. But over the whole world, in the New World especially, there were signs of the material progress that was to result in the world-wide "revolution of rising expectations" of our own time.

Effects of Expansion on the West

The West has in its turn been greatly affected by its relations with other peoples. The list of items that have come into western life since Marco Polo and Columbus is long. It includes foodstuffs above all; utensils and gadgets, pipes for smoking, hammocks and pajamas; styles of architecture and painting, bungalows and Japanese prints; and much else. Some of the novelties caught on more quickly than others. Tobacco, brought into Spain in the mid-sixteenth century as a soothing drug, had established itself by the seventeenth century a essential to the peace of mind of many European males. Potatoes, on the other hand, though their calorie content is high and though they are cheaper to grow in most climates than the staple breadstuffs, did not immediately catch on in Europe. In France, where they are now a necessity of life, potatoes had to be popularized in a regular campaign which took generations to be effective. Tomatoes, the "love-apples" of our great-grandfathers, were long believed to be poisonous and were cultivated only for their looks.

Among westerners, knowledge of non-European beliefs and institutions eventually penetrated to the level of popular culture, where it is marked by a host of words—pow-wow, kowtow, tabu, totem, for instance. At the highest level of cultural interchange, that of religion and ethical ideas, however, the West took little from the new worlds opened after Columbus. The first impression of westerners, not only when they met the relatively primitive cultures of the New World, but even when they met the old cultures of the East, was that they had nothing to learn from them. Once the process of interchange had gone far enough, some individuals were impressed with the mysticism and other-worldliness of Hindu philosophy and religion, and with the high but quite this-worldly ethics of Chinese Confucianism. Others came to admire the dignity and simplicity of the lives of many primitive peoples. But for the most part what struck the Europeans—when they bothered at all to think about anything more than money-making and empire-building—was the poverty, dirt and superstition they found among the masses in India and China, the low material standards of primitive peoples everywhere, the heathenness of the heathens.

Yet certainly exposure to these very different cultures acted as a stimulus in the West and broadened our horizons. The mere accumulation of so much new information gave the western mind something new to occupy itself with. Perhaps the first effect was no more than to increase the fund of the marvelous, the incredible. The early accounts of the New World are full of giants and pygmies, El Dorados where the streets are paved with gold, fountains of eternal youth, wonderful plants and animals. All this was a great stimulus to the literary and artistic imagination. From the island of Shakespeare's *Tempest* to the Xanadu of Coleridge's *Kubla Khan* you will find in our own literature the clear mark of all these new worlds.

But science, too, was stimulated. A dip into any of the early collections of voyages, say the famous and easily available voyages edited in English by Richard Hakluyt in 1582, gives an impression more of the realistic sense and careful observation of these travelers than of their credulity and exaggerations. Here is modern geography already well on the way to maturity, and here too is the foundation of the modern social sciences of anthropology, comparative government, even of economics. Here, as well as in the work of a Bacon or a Galileo, you will find the origins of that important modern western contribution to the culture of our world, natural science. A good exam-

ple is the following attempt to report on the puzzling Hindu institution of caste. It is from the travels of Pietro della Valle, an early seventeenth-century Italian:

The whole Gentile-people of *India* is divided into many sects or parties of men, known and distinguisht by descent or pedigree, as the Tribes of the Jews sometimes were; yet they inhabit the Country promiscuously mingled together, in every City and Land several Races one with another. 'Tis reckon'd that they are in all eighty four; some say more, making a more exact and subtle division. Every one of these hath a particular name, and also a special office and Employment in the Commonwealth, from which none of the descendants of that Race ever swerve; they never rise nor fall, nor change condition: whence some are Husbandmen, others Mechanicks, as Taylers, Shoemakers and the like; others Factors or Merchants, such as they whom we call *Banians*, but they in their Language more correctly *Vania*; others, Souldiers, as the *Ragiaputi;* . . . so many Races which they reckon are reduc'd to four principal, which, if I mistake not, are the Brachmans, the Souldiers, the Merchants and the Artificers; from whom by more minute subdivision all the rest are deriv'd, in such number

A fifteenth-century European's fantastic conception of people in unknown lands.

as in the whole people there are various professions of men.*

It may well be that the intellectual effects of the great discoveries were on the whole *unsettling, disturbing*. They helped, along with the new astronomy, the new mechanics, the Protestant Reformation, and much else, to break the medieval "cake of custom." They helped, literally, to make a New World of ideas and ideals. Such changes are always hard on ordinary human beings, for they demand that men change their minds, something which most

The Travels of Pietro della Valle in India, Edward Grey, ed. (London, 1892), I, 78–79.

of us, in spite of current American belief to the contrary, find it very hard to do.

One great effect of the discoveries is quite clear, and of much importance to us. However uncertain the degree of economic change or dynamism may have been for the late Middle Ages (see Chapter 2), for the sixteenth and seventeenth centuries there can be no doubt. The great new supplies of gold and silver from the Americas set in motion a secular trend toward price rises—toward, in current terms, inflation. This inflation accompanied, perhaps indeed "caused" or at least helped, general economic expansion. In this process, which has continued with ups and downs to

The Great Wall of China: built in the third century B.C. to guarantee an isolation that proved elusive.

the present, some groups gained, and others lost. In general, the merchants, financiers, "businessmen" in the broadest sense, gained; those on fixed incomes suffered; and wage earners, peasants, and the like generally until very recent years did not receive additional income as fast as prices rose. In short, here as elsewhere, the effects of expansion were unsettling, often indeed harsh, as well as stimulating.

A distinguished contemporary American historian, the late Walter P. Webb, made a still more sweeping generalization about the effects of these extraordinary discoveries. The vast new lands of the "frontier" in the New World were, he maintained, a bonanza or windfall, and supplied the real force behind the great increase in man's power to get more out of his natural environment with less sacrifice, the real force behind the great novelty of modern western civilization—its *wealth and power.*

Here it must be noted again that the attempt to find a *single, one-way* causative factor in the great movements of history is a dangerous one. The great opportunities for expansion that the discoveries of the explorers gave to Europeans were certainly a factor in the rapid growth of productivity, population, and technical skills that characterizes the modern world. The great and easily acquired supplies of gold and silver from the New World were in the late sixteenth century a specific and useful "pump-priming" that furthered the growth of modern capitalism in northwest Europe. But the "frontier theory" of modern western capitalist society is no more to be taken as a sole explanation than, say, the Marxist theory of economic determinism or the Weber theory of the spirit of Protestant ethics. Most obviously, the roots of the discoveries themselves, like the roots of Protestantism and modern science, lie deep in the Middle Ages. Before the new worlds could be available to Europeans at all, trade, navigation, government organization—all had to arrive at the

*Walter P. Webb, *The Great Frontier* (Boston, 1952).

point where Henry the Navigator, Columbus, da Gama, and the others could proceed methodically to the discoveries and conquests that after all had been there for the Greeks, the Phoenicians, the Romans or the Vikings to make, had they been able and willing.

The One World of the Eighteenth Century

By the beginning of the eighteenth century, there were still blank spots on the map of the world, especially in the interior of Africa and in our Pacific Northwest. Yet, in spite of this and in spite of the insignificance of the impression made by Europe on China and Japan, it was already clear that only one system of international politics existed in the world. From now on, all general wars tended to be world wars. They were fought, if only by privateers, on all the Seven Seas, and, if only by savages and frontiersmen, on all the continents. Sooner or later, any considerable transfer of territory anywhere, any great accession of strength or wealth anywhere, had its effect on the precarious international equilibrium that we call the balance of power. From the eighteenth century on, there was One World.

This was certainly not One World of the spirit. There was no common authority of any kind that could reach all men. There were pockets of isolated peoples. And the masses of the world, even at its center in Europe, were ignorant enough of what really went on in the hearts and heads of men elsewhere. But already western goods penetrated almost everywhere, led by firearms, but followed by a great many other commodities, not all of them "cheap and nasty." Already an educated minority was growing up all over the world from professional geographers to journalists, diplomatists, and men of business, who had to deal with what are now for the first time quite literally the affairs of the whole world and its peoples.

Reading Suggestions on the Expansion of Europe

(Asterisk indicates paperbound edition.)

General Accounts

J. N. L. Baker, *A History of Geographical Discovery and Exploration*, rev. ed. (Barnes and Noble, 1963). A modern revision of a standard work.

P. Sykes, *A History of Exploration from the Earliest Times to the Present* (Routledge, 1934). A comprehensive treatment of the subject.

C. R. Beazley, *The Dawn of Modern Geography*, 3 vols. (John Murray, 1897–1906). An authoritative account; stops in 1420 but useful for the background of this chapter.

J. H. Parry, *The Age of Reconnaisance* (World Publishing Co., 1963). A first rate outline covering the fifteenth through the seventeenth centuries, with up-to-date bibliographies.

C. L. Sanford, *The Quest for Paradise: Europe and the American Moral Imagination* (Univ. of Illinois Press, 1961). An important study of the "Edenic myth" and American cultural development.

B. Penrose, *Travel and Discovery in the Renaissance* (Harvard Univ. Press, 1955). Very good survey of the literature, with narratives of voyages not elsewhere easily available.

C. E. Nowell, *The Great Discoveries* (Cornell Univ. Press, 1954). A handy introductory manual.

P. Herrmann, *The Great Age of Discovery*, English trans. (Harper, 1958). Covers the fifteenth and the nineteenth centuries. A highly seasoned account, too romantic for the scholar, but full of interesting material.

R. Koebner, *Empire* (Grosset and Dunlap, paperback, 1965). Deals with the British Empire from the Elizabethans to the Victorians with a suggestive mixture of semantics and history.

W. P. Webb, *The Great Frontier* (Houghton Mifflin, 1952). A daring series of generalizations about the role of the New World in western history.

J. H. Rose and others, eds., *The Cambridge History of the British Empire*, Vol. I (Cambridge Univ. Press, 1929). A convenient account of developments up to 1783.

H. I. Priestley, *France Overseas through the Old Regime* (Appleton-Century-Crofts, 1939). A rather pedestrian study, but the best available in English.

See also the reading suggestions for Chapter 16.

Special Studies: Primarily on Explorers and Navigators

G. Jones, *The Norse Atlantic Saga* (Oxford Univ. Press, 1964). A recent summary of what we know, not exaggerated.

E. Prestage, *The Portuguese Pioneers* (Black, 1933). Stresses the early Portuguese work.

E. Sanceau, *Henry the Navigator* (Norton, 1947). A good biography of the Portuguese sponsor of exploration.

S. E. Morison, *Admiral of the Ocean Sea*, 2 vols. (Little, Brown, 1942). The best book on Columbus; Professor Morison retraced Columbus' route in a small ship as part of his preparation for writing.

H. H. Hart, *Sea Road to the Indies* (Macmillan, 1950). Deals with Da Gama and other Portuguese explorers.

C. McK. Parr, *So Noble a Captain* (Crowell, 1953). A very scholarly treatment of Magellan and his circumnavigation.

J. B. Brebner, *The Explorers of North America, 1492–1806* (Macmillan, 1933; *Anchor). A good brief account.

Gustave Lanctot, *History of Canada,* 2 vols. (Harvard Univ. Press 1963–1964). English translation of work of a distinguished French Canadian scholar, from the origins to 1713.

C. Lloyd, *Pacific Horizons* (Allen & Unwin, 1946) and *Captain Cook* (Faber and Faber, 1952). These readable books give a modern review of early Pacific explorations.

<table><tr><td>Special Studies: Primarily on Asia and the East</td><td>

D. F. Lach and C. Flamenhauf, eds., *Asia on the Eve of Europe's Expansion* (Prentice-Hall, 1965).

The Cambridge History of India, 5 vols. (Macmillan, 1922–1937). A fully detailed account.

R. Grousset, *The Civilizations of the East,* 4 vols. (Knopf, 1931–34). Vol. III (China) is particularly good on Chinese culture. The other volumes deal with the Near and Middle East, India, and Japan.

J. K. Fairbank, *The United States and China* (*Viking, 1962). A most discerning general view of China past and present.

E. D. Reischauer and J. K. Fairbank, *East Asia: The Great Tradition* (Houghton Mifflin, 1960). A survey of China, Japan and Korea from the beginnings by two distinguished experts.

W. A. Fairservis, Jr., *The Origins of Oriental Civilization* (*New American Library, 1959). A good introduction to the prehistory and archaeology of China and Japan.

K. S. Latourette, *China* (Prentice-Hall, 1964), also in paperback. Probably the best single introductory volume on the subject.

G. B. Sansom, *Japan: A Short Cultural History* (Appleton-Century-Crofts, 1962, rev. ed.). Perceptive book by a distinguished British expert on the subject.

G. B. Sansom, *A History of Japan,* 3 vols. (Stanford Univ. Press, 1958–1963). A standard detailed history from the beginnings to 1867.

A. L. Basham, *The Wonder That Was India* (*Evergreen, 1959). A more sober and careful survey of Indian history and culture up to the Moslem invasions than the title would indicate.

B. H. M. Vlekke, *Nusantara: A History of Indonesia,* rev. ed. (Lorenz, 1959). Good introduction to the study of an important but often neglected area.

A. Hyma, *The Dutch in the Far East* (Wahr, 1942). Emphasizes social and economic developments.

</td></tr><tr><td>Special Studies: Primarily on the Americas</td><td>

W. H. Prescott, *The Conquest of Mexico* and *The Conquest of Peru* (many editions). Two classic accounts, written a century ago, by a famous American historian.

C. H. Haring, *The Spanish Empire in America* (Oxford Univ. Press, 1947). The best general study of the subject.

J. F. Rippy, *Latin America* (Univ. of Michigan Press, 1958). An authoritative recent survey, part of a fifteen volume series written with a focus on world, as opposed to European, history.

S. E. Morison, ed., *The Parkman Reader* (Little, Brown, 1955). A convenient selection from the celebrated multi-volumed *France and England in North America* by Francis Parkman.

G. M. Wrong, *The Rise and Fall of New France,* 2 vols. (Macmillan, 1928). Sound study by a Canadian.

A. P. Newton, *The European Nations in the West Indies, 1493–1688* (Black, 1933). The best account.

R. Hofstadter, W. Miller, D. Aaron, *The American Republic,* 2 vols. (Prentice-Hall, 1959). Vol. I of this excellent textbook summarizes the development of the thirteen English colonies.

O. T. Black, and H. T. Lefler, *Colonial America* (Macmillan, 1958). A good up-to-date American textbook.

</td></tr></table>

D. J. Boorstin, *The Americas: The Colonial Experiment* (Random House, 1958). A provocative treatment.

L. B. Wright, *Cultural Life in the American Colonies, 1607–1763* (Harper, 1957). An excellent volume in Harper's current New American Nation Series.

Historical Fiction

N. Shute, pseud., *An Old Captivity* (Morrow, 1940). On the Viking explorer, Leif Ericson.

L. Wallace, *The Fair God* (Osgood, 1873). A real thriller, unduly forgotten, on the Aztecs of Mexico; by the author of *Ben-Hur*.

S. Shellabarger, *Captain from Castile* (Little, Brown, 1945). On Cortés and the conquest of Mexico. The "cloak and bosom" school of historical fiction, but based on sound scholarship.

C. S. Forester, *To the Indies* (*Bantam). An excellent novel on Columbus.

R. Sabatini, *The Sea Hawk* (Houghton Mifflin, 1923). A good melodramatic novel of adventures on the sea in the late sixteenth century.

C. Kingsley, *Westward Ho!* (many editions). Rather juvenile in tone, but gives a good picture of the excitement of English exploration.

W. Cather, *Shadows on the Rock* (Knopf, 1931). Sensitive re-creation of life in New France by a distinguished modern American novelist.

7

Divine-Right Monarchy

— and Revolution

I International Politics: France as Aggressor

By the mid-seventeenth century, it was pretty clear that neither the Spanish nor the Austrian Habsburgs were going to break down the European state-system and set up a new form of that haunting old institution, the Roman Empire. Yet for several generations, and in spite of Spain's reputation as a decaying power, men still feared a possible Spanish aggression. The actual aggressor in the great wars of the later seventeenth and early eighteenth centuries was France, the real victor in the Thirty Years' War. Well recovered from the wounds of her own religious wars, prospering economically and politically, with a young and ambitious king, Louis XIV (1643–1715), on the throne, France was ready for expansion.

As always in attempts to describe what the

aggressor or "disturber" wanted, there is some exaggeration in attributing to Louis designs for "world conquest." He clearly wanted French culture, French taste in the arts, French social ways, to influence all Europe, which to an amazing extent they did in the late seventeenth century. Yet neither he nor his ministers can possibly have envisaged an organized world-state in which everyone was a subject of Louis XIV. In North America, however, in India, in Holland, on the Rhine, in dozens of other places, the agents of Louis were hard at work trying to increase their master's power and prestige — the latter a vague but very real and important word. Other peoples believed that France was threatening something they held dear — life, property, independence, self-respect. Under this threat, most of the European states finally united against the French aggressor, and beat him.

Before Louis XIV:
Henry IV and Sully

Other kings in other days, like Louis XI of France and Henry VII of England, had accomplished the restoration of law and order. But only Henry of Navarre (Henry IV, 1589–1610) made the restorer a genuinely popular hero. Witty, dashing, with a pronounced taste for pretty women and bawdy stories, he was the most human king the French had had for a long time, and the best-liked monarch in their whole history. His court casually included his wife, his mistresses, and his children, legitimate and otherwise. He made jokes about his financial difficulties. And, most of all, he convinced his subjects that he was really concerned for their welfare. Among ordinary Frenchmen, Henry IV is still remembered as the king who remarked that every peasant should have a chicken in his pot on Sunday.

Henry's economic experts reclaimed marshes for farm land, encouraged the luxury crafts in Paris, and planted thousands of mulberry trees to foster the culture and manufacture of silk. They extended canals and launched a program of building roads and

bridges that eventually won France the reputation of maintaining the best highways in Europe. Faced with a heavy deficit when he first took office, Henry's great minister, Sully (1559–1641) systematically lowered it until he brought government income and expenditure into balance.

In 1610, when a madman assassinated Henry IV in the prime of his career, the new king, Louis XIII (1610–1643), was only nine years old. The succession of a child presents grave difficulties in a monarchy where the king really rules; in France, the reins of government went slack during the minority of Louis XIII. The queen-mother, Marie de' Medici, attempted to rule but showed little of her famous family's political skill. Her Italian favorites and French nobles, Catholic and Huguenot both, carried on a hectic competition which threatened to undo all that Henry IV had accomplished. In the course of these troubles, the French representative body, the Estates-General, met at Blois in 1614 for what was destined to be its last meeting until 1789 on the eve of the great French Revolution. Finally, Louis XIII came of age and, though incapable himself of asserting a strong rule, in 1624 picked a minister who could.

Before Louis XIV:
Richelieu and Mazarin

The minister was Cardinal Richelieu (1585–1642), Bishop of Luçon, a sincere but not an ardent, certainly not an evangelical Catholic, efficient and ambitious, a born administrator. As the virtual ruler of France for the next eighteen years, Richelieu proved to be a good Machiavellian and a good *politique*. He subordinated religion and every nonpolitical consideration to *raison d'état* (literally, reason of state), a phrase that he probably coined himself.

Raison d'état determined Richelieu's policy toward the Huguenots. The Edict of Nantes had given them certain political privileges, notably the right to govern some hundred fortified towns located mostly in the southwestern quarter of France. To Richelieu these

Protestant towns formed a state of strong centralization; they were to him a hundred centers of potential rebellion that should be brought under control. Alarmed, the Huguenots did in fact rebel. It took the royal forces fourteen months to besiege and take their chief stronghold, the port of La Rochelle, which finally fell in 1628. Richelieu thereupon canceled the political clauses of the Edict of Nantes but left its religious provisions intact.

The siege of La Rochelle lasted fourteen months, because France scarcely possessed a navy worth the name. In the next ten years, Richelieu created a fleet of thirty-eight warships for the Atlantic and a dozen galleys, manned by slaves (an exception to the rule that white men were never enslaved in the modern Western world), for the Mediterranean. Meanwhile, he skillfully guided France through the Thirty Years' War, his eye always on the greatness of France, husbanding French resources carefully, committing them only when concrete gains for France seemed possible. Richelieu was one of the great practitioners of realistic power politics in international relations.

Raison d'état, indeed, motivated all his policies. He lived in elaborate style, accompanied on his travels by his private choir and corps of musicians, not just because he was fond of music but because he believed such a retinue befitted the chief minister of a great and splendid kingdom. In 1635, he founded the *Académie,* the famous French Academy, to compile a dictionary of the French language and to set the standards and style of the national culture. He tried to curb the factious nobles, though with only middling success, by ordering the destruction of some of their châteaux and forbidding the favorite aristocratic indulgence of private duels. More significant was his transfer of effective supervision over the local administration from the nobles to the more reliable *intendants.* These royal officials had existed earlier but had only minor functions; now they received greatly increased powers, particularly in the vital work of apportioning and collecting taxes.

Richelieu was unquestionably a great statesman, a man largely responsible for building *la grande nation* of Louis XIV. Historians have always differed in their estimates of how good for France in the long run his work was to prove. For royalists generally, his work was sound, an efficient, centralized state. For others, he built in a sense too well, made the French government so centralized, so professionally bureaucratic, that it had no place for the give and take of politics, for government by discussion, above all, no political place, save for

Richelieu, by Champaigne.

a few bureaucrats, for the new and ambitious middle classes.

Richelieu himself had picked and schooled his successor, the Italian-born Mazarin (1602–1661). Mazarin, too, was a cardinal and a past master of *raison d'état*. He, too, was careless about the finances of the French state and, unlike Richelieu, amassed an immense personal fortune during his public career. Soon after taking over, Mazarin faced the emergency of a long minority and regency. When the thirteenth royal Louis died in 1643, the fourteenth was a boy of four and a half. The feudal nobles resented being excluded from the regency by a foreigner; the judges and other high officials, who had invested heavily in government securities, particularly disliked Mazarin's casual way of borrowing money to meet war expenses and then letting the interest payments on government borrowings fall into arrears. The discontent boiled over in the uprising of the Fronde, 1648–1653, named for the slingshot used by Parisian children to hurl pellets at passers-by.

The narrative history of the Fronde is a complicated set of plots, interspersed with some very mild battles and Mazarin's repeated flights from the capital. Its upshot was to confirm Mazarin in his power and to pave the way for the personal rule of Louis XIV. The youthful king got a bad fright when the *frondeurs* actually broke into the room where he was feigning sleep, and he resolved to hold firmly to the reins of state. The Fronde failed essentially because it had no real roots in the country, not even in the rising middle classes. It was a struggle for power between Mazarin and his new bureaucracy, and two privileged groups, the old nobles and the newer official nobles of the law courts, especially the higher courts or *parlements*. Each of the noble groups distrusted the other, and in the long run Mazarin successfully applied the old Roman adage: Divide and rule.

The Successes of Louis XIV

Richelieu and Mazarin had seldom gone beyond the point of maintaining French power and prestige; they attempted little actual French expansion in Italy or in Germany and the Low Countries. Louis XIV, however, definitely did attempt to add to French territories. His main effort was no longer, as had been that of the Valois kings, toward Italy, but northeast toward Germany and the Low Countries. He sought also to secure Spain, if not quite as a direct annexation, at least as a French satellite with a French ruler. Finally, French commitments overseas in North America and in India drove him to attempt, against English and Dutch rivals, the establishment of a great French empire outside Europe.

The first actual war of Louis XIV was a minor affair, but it showed how he was going to move. When he married the daughter of Philip IV of Spain, his bride had renounced her rights of inheritance. Now Louis claimed that, since her dowry had never been paid, her renunciation was invalid. His lawyers dug up an old family rule, the *right of devolution*, which Louis claimed gave his wife lands in what is now Belgium. In the ensuing "War of Devolution" with Spain, the great French general, Turenne, won various victories, but Louis was feeling his way and did not press them. A compromise peace at Aix-la-Chapelle in 1668 settled little and left the Dutch, next door to the Spanish Netherlands, which is now Belgium, quite rightfully alarmed for the independence they had won from Spain.

In 1672, Louis began his war on the Dutch, against whom he eventually secured a fair number of allies, notably England, bought off in 1670, Sweden, and some of the German states. The Dutch, however, resisted stoutly under their strong leader, William III of Orange, a descendant of William the Silent. Even without William, Europe would probably have responded to the threat of French domination by an anti-French alliance. As it was, Spain, the Holy Roman Empire, and a still not very important German state, Brandenburg-Prussia, joined against France and her allies. The anti-French coalition was not very effective, and French diplomacy separated the allies at the treaties of Nijmegen (Nimwegen) in 1678–79. Holland was left intact at the cost of promising neutrality; Spain yielded to France the Franche Comté (County of Burgundy) and some towns in the Spanish Netherlands; Prussia, which had won a crucial battle against Sweden at Fehrbellin in 1675, was obliged by French pressure to give the Swedes back their Baltic German lands.

The French had not only succeeded to the military preponderance Spain had once enjoyed; they had improved upon it. The French armed forces were strong not only in the conventional field forces but also in artillery, engineering, and siege techniques. The French navy had expanded around the nucleus provided by Richelieu. And behind these efficient armed forces the ministries maintained an adequate service of supply. It is true, as we have noted of Spanish organization, that the fighting arms of this "absolute" French monarchy were by modern standards inefficient and loosely organized. Everything moved slowly and ponderously. There was still a great deal of leeway in the armies and civilian bureaus for semi-feudal independence; there was still nothing like the modern standardization of munitions, supplies, and channels of command. For manpower, Louis increasingly depended either on foreign mercenaries, who were expensive, or on Frenchmen drafted, not according to any broad system of universal military service, but chiefly from the poorer classes and by methods that allowed wide scope for favoritism and bribery. Leadership, however, was largely professional. At the best period of the reign, in the 1670's and 1680's, the officers were, for an old society, chosen and promoted to an extraordinary degree for ability rather than for family ties.

The power and prestige of France were now at their peak. Louis' place in Europe rested by no means solely on his armed forces. He was well served by a diplomatic corps trained in the niceties of *raison d'état*. Above all, he enjoyed to an unusual degree the position of leader and exemplar of culture and taste. Rulers all over Europe, and in particular the host of princes and princelets in the Germanies, aped the standards of Louis' court at Versailles. French manners, French language, French clothes, French dishes, French art, were all the fashion. The prestige of France was not diminished by those who hated while they envied her; France was hardly loved, but she was admired and imitated. All in all, France in 1680 enjoyed assets Spain had never enjoyed. She was now *la grande nation,* adding to material power the very great power of cultural prestige.

The Failures of Louis XIV

Yet in the last three decades of Louis' reign most of these assets were dissipated, especially the concrete ones of wealth and efficient organization. Not content with the prestige he had won in his first two wars, Louis embroiled himself with most of the western world in what looked to that world like an effort to destroy the independence of Holland and most of western Germany, and to bring the great Iberian Peninsula under a French ruler. The third of his wars, the War of the League of Augsburg, broke out in 1688 basically over the continued French nibbling at bits of territory in western Germany. Louis' assertion of a dynastic claim to most of the lands of the German Elector Palatine was the last straw. The league against him was largely put together by his old foe, William of Orange, who after 1688 shared the throne of England with his wife Mary, daughter of James II of England. Thenceforth, England was thoroughly committed to take sides against Louis. The great sea victory of the English over the French at Cape La Hogue in 1692 showed that England, not France, was to be mistress of the seas. But on land the honors were more nearly even. William was beaten in battle in the Low Countries time and again, but he was never decisively crushed. In Ireland, French attempts to intervene on behalf of the deposed English king, James II, were foiled at the Battle of the Boyne in 1690.

Louis was growing old, and perhaps for the moment he had had enough. The Peace of Ryswick, concluded in 1697, was one of those comparatively rare peaces without victory, a general agreement to keep things as they were. It lasted barely four years, for in 1701 Louis, after much personal soul-searching, took a step that led to the great world war over the Spanish succession. His brother-in-law, the Habsburg king of Spain, Charles II, died in 1700 without a direct heir. For several years the diplomatists of Europe had been striving to arrange by general consent a succession that would avoid putting on the Spanish throne either a French Bourbon or an Austrian Habsburg. They had agreed on a Bavarian prince; but he had died in 1699, and the whole question was reopened. New plans were made, partitioning the Spanish inheritance between Habsburgs and Bourbons. But Charles II of Spain made a new will, giving his lands intact to Philip of Anjou, the grandson of Louis XIV, and then died. Louis could not withstand the temptation. He accepted on behalf of Philip, despite the fact that he had signed the treaty of partition. The threat to the balance of power was neatly summarized in the remark a gloating Frenchman is supposed to have made, "There are no longer any Pyrenees" (the great mountain chain that separates France and Spain). England, Holland, the Empire, and many German states formed the Grand Alliance to preserve the Pyrenees.

In the bloody war that followed, the French were gradually worn down in defeat. Their North American possession of Acadia (Nova Scotia) was taken by the English. In four major European battles, Blenheim (1704), Ramillies (1706), Oudenarde (1708), and Malplaquet (1709), the French were beaten by the Allies under two great generals, the English John Churchill, Duke of Marlborough, ancestor of Winston Churchill, and the Savoyard Prince Eugene. But the French were not annihilated. The last of the great Allied victories, Malplaquet, had cost the Allies 20,000 casualties, and somehow, by scraping the bottom of the barrel for men and money, the French managed even after Malplaquet to keep armies in the field.

Moreover, the Grand Alliance was weakening. The English, now following their famous policy of keeping any single continental power from attaining too strong a position, were almost as anxious to prevent the union of the Austrian and Spanish inheritances under a Habsburg as to prevent the union of the French and the Spanish inheritance under a Bourbon. At home, they faced a possible disputed succession to the throne, and some of the mercantile classes were sick of a war that was injuring trade, and that seemed unlikely to bring any compensating gains. In 1710, the Tory party, inclined toward peace, won a parliamentary majority and began negotiations that culminated in a series of treaties at Utrecht in 1713.

The Utrecht Settlement

Utrecht was a typical balance-of-power peace. France was contained but by no means humiliated. She lost to England Newfoundland, Nova Scotia, and the Hudson's Bay territories, but she preserved Quebec and Louisiana, as well as her Caribbean islands. Louis gained in a sense what he had gone to war over, for Philip of Anjou was formally recognized as King Philip V of Spain and secured the Spanish lands overseas. The French and Spanish crowns were however, by specific provision, never to be held by the same person, so the Allies, too, had won a point. Furthermore, England took from Spain the Mediterranean island of Minorca, which she handed back later in the century, and the great Rock of Gibraltar guarding the Atlantic entrance to the Mediterranean. The English also gained, by what was called the Asiento, the right to supply Negro slaves to the Spanish colonies, a right that gave them a chance also at interloping trade or just plain smuggling.

The Austrian Habsburgs, denied the main Spanish succession, were compensated with the former Spanish Netherlands, modern Belgium. Holland was granted the right to maintain garrisons in certain fortified towns in these now "Austrian" Netherlands for better defense against possible French aggression. Savoy, an Italian state that had been true to the Grand Alliance, was rewarded with Sicily; though diplomatic jockeying substituted for this prize in 1720 the lesser island of Sardinia, the Duke of Savoy was able to call himself King of Sardinia and thus started the long process that united Italy under the crown of Savoy in the nineteenth century. The Elector of Brandenburg-Prussia, too, was rewarded with a royal title, King *in* Prussia (not *of*, for Prussia was outside the Holy Roman Empire).

In all the general European settlements of modern times—Westphalia, Utrecht, Vienna, Versailles—historians discern the elements, the imperfections, that led to subsequent unsettlement and another general war. Utrecht is no exception, even though of all the great modern settlements it is the one in which victors and vanquished seem closest. First of all, the rivalry between France and England for empire overseas was not at all settled. In India, as in North America, each nation was to continue after Utrecht as before the effort to oust the other from land and trade. In Europe, the Dutch were not really protected from French expansion by the right to garrison forts in the Austrian Netherlands. The Austrian Habsburg leader, now the Emperor Charles VI, never forgot that he had wanted to be "Charles III" of Spain and never quite gave up hope that somehow he could upset the decisions made at Utrecht. No one seemed to have quite what he wanted, which is one of the difficulties of working out reasonable, compromise solutions. The distribution of Italian lands satisfied nobody, Italian or outsider, and the next two decades were filled with intrigues, negotiations, and very mild wars over Italy. In short, the settlement at Utrecht, though it seemed to have been a reasonable one, not a vengeful "Carthaginian" peace, was followed by a most confusing series of diplomatic and military struggles. Indeed, John Morley, a distinguished English Victorian man of letters who had specialized in the eighteenth century, once confessed that he could never remember just who was fighting whom during its first three decades.

French Aggression in Review

In retrospect, this first period of French aggression seems one of the less violent and critical tests of the European state-system. True, these wars caused horrors enough, especially in the deliberate French devastation of the German Palatinate during the War of the League of Augsburg. Their total cost in human and in economic resources was very great. The French were sometimes hated as foreigners and aggressors. These wars were not simply struggles among professional armies directed by professional politicians; they were wars among peoples, wars that brought out feelings of patriotism and hatred for the foreigner.

Yet in comparison with the wars of religion that had preceded them, and with the wars of nationalism and revolution that were to follow, the wars of Louis XIV seem to have lacked the all-out qualities of human drives toward both good and evil. Louis set himself up as a champion of Catholicism, especially after the revocation of the Edict of Nantes in 1685, and much was made of William of Orange as a Protestant champion. In the end, however, the coalition against Louis was a complete mixture of Catholic and Protestant, in which religion played a comparatively minor role. There were of course many elements of religious concern that entered into the struggle. Both in England and in New England the French were feared and hated as Catholics. Yet in all these matters of public attitudes toward the enemy, simple dislike of the "foreigner" is conspicuous. So too the aggressor, Louis XIV, is clearly, in comparison with his predecessor in aggression, Philip II of Spain, not motivated by any hope that he can stamp out Protestantism in the Netherlands. He simply wants to control these lands, if not to annex them.

On the other hand, no lay substitute for the crusading religious spirit had yet emerged. Unlike such later aggressors as Napoleon and Hitler, Louis XIV was not the product of a revolution, a national awakening, an obvious stimulating force. He was indeed the "Sun King," a great and admired ruler, but he was the legitimate, even conventional, ruler of a land long used to prominence in Europe. The aggression of Louis XIV was thus, like the culture of his France, a moderate, measured, "classical" aggression. It lacked the heaven-storming fervor of aggressions born of revolution, aggressions that are really crusades, efforts to remake the world in the image of some exalted ideal; revolutionary nationalist, or fascist, or communist aggressions.

Europe in 1715

Brandenburg-Prussia
Austrian Habsburg Lands
Swedish possessions
Venetian possessions
Ottoman Empire

▬▬ Boundary of the Holy
Roman Empire
■ Battle sites

NORWAY

Oslo

S
W

Stock

North Sea

SCOTLAND

Edinburgh
Berwick

ULSTER

IRELAND ■

Limerick

Drogheda
Boyne R.
Dublin

DENMARK

Copenhagen

Bal

KINGDOM OF
GREAT BRITAIN

SWEDISH
POMERANIA

Hamburg

Bremen

Fehrbellin

BRANDENBURG

ENGLAND

London

Dover

UNITED
NETHERLANDS

Ryswick

Utrecht
Nimwegen

Elbe R.

Berlin

Oder R.

THE

WEST-
PHALIA

SAXONY

EMPIRE

SIL

Tor Bay

C. La Hogue

Atlantic Ocean

AUSTRIAN
NETHERLANDS

Oudenarde
Ramillies

Malplaquet

Aachen

Rhine R.

Prague

BOHEMIA

MORA

Seine R.

Paris

Verdun

Metz

Rastadt

Augsburg

AUSTRIA

45

Versailles

Toul

LORRAINE

Strasbourg

Blenheim ■

Vienna

Nantes

Blois

Orléans

ALSACE

BAVARIA

STYRIA

Loire R.

FRANCE

FRANCHE
COMTÉ

SWITZERLAND

TYROL

CARINTHIA

CARNIOLA

Bordeaux

Geneva

SAVOY

MILAN

Venice

VENETIAN REPUBLIC

Adriatic Sea

Rhône R.

Avignon
(to the Papacy)

Genoa

Po R.

Florence

PAPAL
STATES

PORTUGAL

Burgos

Marseilles

SPAIN

Ebro R.

Lisbon

Tagus R.

Madrid

CORSICA
(to Genoa)

Rome

NAPLES

Barcelona

Mediterranean Sea

BALEARIC IS.

MINORCA
(Br.)

Naples

Guadalquivir R.

Valencia

SARDINIA
(to Austria, 1714;
to Savoy, 1720)

Seville

Granada

35

Gibraltar
(Br.)

Palermo

SICILY

(to Savoy, 1
to Austria, 1

ALGERIA

TUNIS

MALTA

0   500

Miles

5   0   5   10

FINLAND

L. Onega

L. Ladoga

Nystadt

Gulf of Finland   St. Petersburg

INGRIA

Narva

ESTONIA   Novgorod

LIVONIA

Pskov

COURLAND

W. Dvina R.

Vilna

LITHUANIA

Smolensk

nigsberg

PRUSSIA

Warsaw

POLAND

Kiev

Vistula R.

Dnieper R.   Poltava

Dniester R.

TRANSYLVANIA

MOLDAVIA

NGARY

WALLACHIA

arlovitz

de   Passarovitz

Danube R.

ONTE-
NEGRO

Vardar R.

Salonika

Constantinople

Aegean Sea

Athens

RHODES

CYPRUS

CRETE

Moscow

Oka R.

Volga R.

R U S S I A

Volga R.

Don R.

CRIMEA

Black Sea

O T T O M A N

E M P I R E

Caspian Sea

Tigris R.

Euphrates R.

ENGLAND

Calais

Rhine R.

ALSACE
1648–1681

ARTOIS
1659

THE EMPIRE

Paris

LORRAINE
1766

FRANCHE COMTÉ
1678

FRANCE   1601

Rhône R.

Avignon

ROUSSILLON
1659

CORSICA
1768

Growth of France
1559-1769

——— Boundary of the Empire, 1559

II   The France of Louis XIV

Divine-Right Monarchy

The admired and imitated French state of Louis XIV can stand in many ways as the best example of divine-right monarchy, the absolute monarchy of early modern times. We have for the France of Louis' prime one of those convenient but certainly oversimplified tags that history furnishes so abundantly. Perhaps Louis never actually said *"L'Etat, c'est moi"* (I am the State), but the phrase has stuck, and it is certainly not altogether misleading as an attempt to summarize a state of mind and an ideal. In theory, Louis was for his subjects the earthly representative of God on earth—or at least, in France. He held this position by the divinely ordained workings of the principle of primogeniture; he was not elected by his subjects, nor did he acquire his throne by force of arms. He was born to a position God had planned for the legitimate male heir of the tenth-century Hugh Capet. As God's agent, his word was final, for to challenge it would be to challenge the whole structure of God's universe. Disobedience was both a political and a religious offense.

Now though Louis has been dead less than three centuries, the ideas and sentiments centered on this divine-right monarchy are so utterly alien to contemporary Americans that it takes an effort of the historical imagination not to dismiss them as nonsense. There they were, however, clearly enough believed by many sensible men of the day. Two clues may help us understand why they were held so widely and so firmly. The first clue is the survival of the characteristic medieval view that right decisions in government are not arrived at by experiment, discussion, and negotiation but by "finding" the authoritative answer provided for in God's scheme of things. In the days of Louis XIV men still believed that God

through his chosen agents directly managed the state. Men were indeed beginning to question this idea, but the full force of their questioning was not to come for another generation or two on the continent of Europe.

A second clue lies in the deliberate effort by the makers of the new French monarchy to cope with specific problems. Their central problem we have already noted: How to bring men together into those larger political units necessitated by the course of technological and economic growth, the overseas discoveries, and the pressure of a slow but steady increase of population. How to make men who were used to thinking, feeling, and behaving as Normans, Bretons, Flemings, Alsatians, Burgundians, Provençaux, Gascons, Basques—even simply as villagers or townsmen or members of a medieval "corporative" society—think, feel, and behave as *Frenchmen*. The makers of the new French monarchy could not rely on a common language, for only a minority spoke standard French; the fifteen or twenty millions who had to get along together as Frenchmen spoke several dozen mutually incomprehensible languages or at least dialects. And of course they could not rely on a common educational system, a common press, common participation in political life; all that lay in the future. They could, and did, attempt to set up at least a symbol of common Frenchness, a King of France who was king for Celtic-speaking Bretons as for Catalan-speaking southerners. That king collected taxes, raised armies, touched in a hundred ways the lives of ordinary men who had to feel somehow that the king had a right to do all this, had to feel that he was indeed doing this *for* them, rather than *to* them. A king who was, if not like the old Roman emperors a god himself, at least the agent of God, was the kind of king they could understand and accept.

Divine-right monarchy, with its corollary of

obedience on the part of subjects, is thus one phase of the growth of the modern centralized nation-state. It was an institution that appealed to very old theological ideas, such as the Biblical admonition to obey the powers that be, for "the powers that be are ordained of God."* But it was an institution that was also inspired by the newer ideas of binding men together in a productive, efficient state. In practice, naturally, the institution did not wholly correspond to theories about it. Louis XIV was not the French state, and his rule was not absolute in any full, logical sense of that word. He simply did not have the physical means for controlling in detail what his subjects did. Such control is actually much more completely possible under modern techniques of communication, propaganda, and administration than it ever was in days of "absolute" monarchy.

The early modern monarchy in France and throughout the West was subject to many limitations besides those set by the physical possibilities of supervision. Medieval survivals made for diversities of many sorts, in language, laws, customs, even in weights and measures. All stood in the way of the uniformity, the administrative neatness and exactness, that are essential to the smooth working of a chain of command. Important groups still clung to medieval privileges—that is, to rights, immunities, a status, which they felt did not depend on the king's will, which were, certainly in the minds of those who enjoyed them, legal limitations on the power of the king. Many of these groups were corporations—municipal boards, judicial boards, economic groups such as guilds—which usually possessed written charters and traditional privileges very difficult for the government to override. Two of these groups, the old nobility and the clergy, deserve special mention.

The Nobility

In all the important countries the feudal nobility maintained themselves into early modern times. The degree to which they were integrated into the new machinery of state was

*Romans 13:1

of crucial importance in the development of modern Europe. In Habsburg Spain, as indeed in the Habsburg lands of Central Europe, the old nobility generally accepted the new strength of the Crown, but maintained much of their privilege and all their old pride of status. In Prussia, they were most successfully integrated into the new order, becoming on the whole faithful servants or soldiers of the Crown, but with a social status that set them above mere bourgeois bureaucrats. In England, as we shall shortly see, the nobility achieved a unique compromise with the Crown. In France, they—the old feudal nobility, the "nobility of the sword"—were in effect shoved aside by the Crown and deprived for the most part of major political functions, but they were allowed to retain social and economic privileges and important roles as officers in the king's army.

This process of reducing the old French nobility to relative powerlessness at least in national political life had begun during the fifteenth century, and had been hastened by the religious and civil wars of the sixteenth century. An important part of the nobility, perhaps nearly half, had espoused the Protestant cause, in large part from sheer opposition to the Crown. The victory of Henry IV, purchased by his conversion to Catholicism, was a defeat for the nobility. The process was completed by the increasing use under Richelieu and Louis XIV of commoners in the task of running the government, from the great ministers of state, through the *intendants,* down to local administrators and judges. These commoners were usually elevated to a status technically noble, a status that came to be hereditary, but they were known by a special term, the *noblesse de la robe* (from the robes or gowns worn by judges and other officials). This official bureaucratic nobility did not, however, have at first the social prestige of the old nobility of the sword, the *noblesse de l'épée.* The old nobles felt a contemptuous envy toward the newcomers of the gown; they knew they were shelved. By the early eighteenth century, however, the two kinds of nobility had become much better amalgamated, giving the whole order a new lease on life.

The Clergy

In medieval times, the clergy had been a separate order, backed by the supra-national power and prestige of the papacy and possessing privileges not wholly in the control of the Crown. In the new centralized France, however, the Crown had fostered a national Gallican Church which was indeed Catholic but also under good control by the monarchy, and friendly to new ideas, political, social, and economic. Under Louis, this Gallican union of throne and altar reached a high point, and the greatest of his bishops, Bossuet (1627–1704), wrote firmly in support of royal absolutism. Yet even under Louis XIV the French clergy continued to possess important corporate privileges. They were not subject to royal taxation; they contributed of their own free will a gift of money which they voted in their own assembly.

Moreover, Louis was by no means wholly master of the religious beliefs and practices of his subjects. Whereas Richelieu had attacked only the political privileges of the Huguenots, Louis attacked their fundamental right of toleration and finally abolished it. Pressed by the clergy, he revoked the Edict of Nantes in 1685 not so much for theological as for political motives. After the revocation, fifty thousand Huguenot families fled abroad, notably to Prussia, Holland, Belgium, England, and the new colonial lands of British North America. The practical skills and intellectual gifts of these early "refugees" greatly strengthened the lands that received them. Some Huguenots also remained in France, where they continued to worship underground in spite of persecution.

Within the Catholic Church itself, Louis had to contend with two important elements that refused to accept his Gallicanism. The Quietists, a group of religious enthusiasts led by Madame Guyon, sought for a more mystical and emotional faith. The Jansenists, sometimes called the "Puritans of the Catholic Church," were a high-minded group whose most distinguished spokesman was the scientist and philosopher, Pascal. Named for Cornelius Jansen, Bishop of Ypres in the early seventeenth century, the Jansenists took an almost Calvinistic stand on the issue of predestination. They stressed the need to obey the authority of God rather than that of man, no matter how exalted the position of the particular man might be. They therefore questioned both the authority of the pope (and of his agents, the Jesuits) and that of the king. On the surface, Louis was successful in repressing both Quietists and Jansenists, but the latter in particular survived to trouble his successors in the eighteenth century.

The Royal Administration

Louis did not quite succeed in building up an administrative machine wholly under royal control. It was not for want of application that he fell short. When he began his personal rule in 1661, he was only twenty-two years old but had already impressed a seasoned observer of the court with his earnestness:

As the single desire for glory and to fulfill all the duties of a great king occupied his whole heart, by applying himself to toil he began to like it; and the eagerness he had to learn all the things that were necessary to him soon made him full of that knowledge. His great good sense and his good intentions now made visible in him the rudiments of general knowledge which had been hidden from all who did not see him in private.

. . .

He was agreeable personally, civil and easy of access to every one; but with a lofty and serious air which impressed the public with respect and awe . . . , though he was familiar and gay with ladies.*

Louis continued to be "familiar and gay" with the ladies until finally, after the death of his Spanish queen, he settled down to a proper middle-aged marriage with Madame de Maintenon, a devout Catholic who had been the governess of his illegitimate children. Mean-

*Memoirs of Madame de Motteville, K. P. Wormeley, trans. (Boston, 1902), III, 243.

while, he had provided himself a setting worthy of the Sun King by building a few miles outside Paris the celebrated Palace of Versailles, which was more than a third of a mile long and housed, counting dependents and servants of all sorts, a court of ten thousand.

At Versailles, Louis met regularly with his ministers, who headed departments essentially like those of any modern state—War, Finance, Foreign Policy, Interior. The ministers were responsible directly to him, and not to any legislative body. The Estates-General never met during his lifetime. From the top, a reasonably clear chain of command proceeded down through the *intendants,* who were now the heads of *généralités* (big administrative units roughly corresponding to the older provinces), thence through smaller units to the town or village. Even the indefatigable Louis, however, could do no more than exercise general supervision over the affairs of his large and complex kingdom. And he probably could not have achieved even partial success without the invention of printing. For the familiar government printed forms to be filled out were already in existence. And they are still there, duly filled out and filed in their hundreds of thousands in the local historical archives of France.

In practice, naturally, the royal administration was full of difficulties and contradictions. There were many superimposed and often

Aerial view of the Palace of Versailles.

conflicting jurisdictions, survivals of feudal-ism and the medieval struggle to control feu-dalism. The officials of Louis XIV, by the very fact of being nobles of the gown, possessed a privileged status which they could hand down to their heirs. They, too, tended to form a corporation, tended even as individuals to be more their own masters in their own baili-wicks than the theory of royal absolutism would allow. The key provincial administra-tors, the *intendants,* may seem to have been no more than agents of the Crown. Yet anyone who pursues in local history the detailed records of what the *intendants* actually did sees that many of them exercised considerable initiative and were by no means rubber-stamp officials. Nor was the old administrative de-vice of moving the *intendants* about from one *généralité* to another sufficient to overcome this centrifugal tendency.

Still another set of institutions gave trou-ble. These were the *parlements,* the supreme courts of appeal in the various provinces, of which one, the Parlement of Paris, enjoyed special prestige and power from its place at the capital and from the size of its territorial jurisdiction, almost half of the kingdom. The judges who staffed the courts headed the no-bility of the gown, owned their offices, and were not removable at the will of the king. In addition to the usual work of a court of ap-peals, the *parlements* claimed through their function of registering royal edicts something very close to what in American usage is called the right of judicial review. That is, they claimed to be able to refuse to register an edict if they thought it "unconstitutional," not in accord with the higher law of the land. The claim, of course, negated theoretical royal absolutism.

Actually, Louis got around the difficulty in his own lifetime. The Parlement of Paris had already lost a round in its struggle with the royal power by entering the lists against Ma-zarin in the Fronde. Now Louis successfully utilized another old institution, the *lit de jus-tice* (literally, "bed of justice"), in which he summoned the Parlement of Paris before him in a formal session and ordered the justices to register a royal edict. In this way, for instance, he enforced measures against Jansenism which was strong among the judges. But the *parle-ments,* too, were to plague his eighteenth-century successors.

Mercantilism in Theory

Just as divine-right monarchy was not pe-culiarly French, so the mercantilism identified with the France of Louis XIV was common to many other western states in the early mod-ern period. But, like divine-right rule, mer-cantilism flourished most characteristically under the Sun King. Its most famous exponent was one of Louis' greatest ministers, Colbert (1619–1683).

Mercantilism comprised a set of economic aims and practices, particularly in the field of relations between government and business. The central doctrine of mercantilism is that hard money, gold and silver, is the basic wealth, that a given state should aim to ac-quire as much hard money as possible, and that therefore it should aim always at a "fa-vorable balance of trade." It encourages ex-ports to bring in money from abroad and dis-courages imports to prevent money from being paid out; it puts high protective tariffs against imports, and perhaps even places bounties on exports. In this simple form, the doctrine can readily be made absurd. A coun-try that took in huge amounts of gold and sil-ver would thereby simply increase prices within its borders, for gold and silver are merely media of exchange. No one can eat the precious metals or even find much practical use for them.

But mercantilism was much more than an oversimple and perhaps mistaken theory of international trade. It was part and parcel of the early modern effort to construct strong, efficient, political units. The mercantilists quite frankly aimed to make a given nation as self-sustaining as possible, as independent as possible of the need to import from other na-tions, which were its rivals and its potential enemies. As a policy, it is not entirely remote from us today; indeed, there are those who maintain that the policy of most twentieth-century great nations is "neo-mercantilism."

Within a given nation, the mercantilists held that national production should provide the necessities of life for a hard-working population, and the necessities of power for a nation able to fight and win wars. These ends and the means for achieving them, they believed, demanded planning and control from above. They did not think that the old traditional ways of manor and guild, the old standard of the "just price," brought out the energies and abilities needed in an expanding economy. They were all for sweeping away these remnants of medieval controls. But they did not believe, as the free-trade economists after them were to believe, that all that was necessary was to destroy these controls and leave individual businessmen free to do whatever they thought would enrich them most as individuals. Instead, the mercantilists would channel the national economic effort by government subsidies, by grants of monopolies, by direct production in government-run industries, by encouraging scientific and technological research, fairs and expositions, and of course by protective tariffs.

At this point we come back to a phase of the expansion of Europe. Already in the seventeenth century many foodstuffs and raw materials were more easily available overseas than in Europe. The colonies could supply necessities that could not be so well produced at home, but that thanks to the existence of the colonies need not be imported from a rival. Thus the mercantilist viewed France overseas as a special part of France, a part that should be run from the homeland by a strong government, as indeed the homeland itself should be managed. Since the homeland produced industrial goods and the colonies produced raw materials, the two were mutually supplementary, and free trade between the two would give each partner what it needed. This mercantilistic attitude toward colonies was held not only by absolutist France and Spain, but by the more limited governments of England and Holland.

Mercantilism in Practice: Colbert

The great practitioner of mercantilism, Colbert, never quite attained the supremacy reached by Richelieu and Mazarin; he was the collaborator, never the master, of Louis XIV. Other great ministers, Louvois for military affairs especially, stood in the way of his supremacy. Yet Colbert was influential in all matters affecting the French economy, most interested in foreign trade and in the colonies, and therefore in the merchant marine and in the navy. His hand was in everything, in invention, in technological education, in attracting enterprising foreigners to settle in France, in designing and building ships, in founding and encouraging industries. The eight big volumes of his Letters, Instructions, and Memorials, published in the nineteenth century, gave an admirable general view of the activities of this first great modern exponent of the controlled economy—not yet by any means the "welfare state."

Whether the great prosperity France achieved in the first thirty years of Louis' reign came about because of, or in spite of, the mercantilist policies of Colbert is a question difficult to answer. The convinced adherent of laissez-faire doctrines will argue that France would have done even better had her businessmen been left alone. But this was not the seventeenth-century way, not even in England and Holland. Under the mercantilist regime, France did attain an undoubted leadership in European industry and commerce. That lead she lost, in part because the last two wars of Louis XIV were ruinously expensive, in part because from the eighteenth century on France's rival, England, took to the new methods of power machinery and concentrated on large-scale production of inexpensive goods. France remained largely true to the policies set by Colbert—relatively small-scale production of a variety of goods, often luxuries, and predominantly consumers' goods. But the difference between French and English industry was also as a difference of natural re-sources—coal, iron, and water power were more easily exploited in England than in France—and, even more, a difference in the focus of national energies. France in early modern times, like Spain before her, spent an undue proportion of her national product in the ultimately unfruitful effort to achieve the political domination of Europe and the over-seas world by force of arms.

These late seventeenth-century wars bring up a still unsolved problem: does—or at any rate, until the present, did—modern warfare act as a stimulant, or as a depressive to eco-nomic life? Did they more than balance their destructiveness by creating demand for goods, for new techniques, by giving "full employ-ment" if only to soldiers? It is pretty clear that the late seventeenth century was in general a period of economic decline or crisis in Eu-rope. But it is not clear that Louis' wars were a "cause" of these economic difficulties. Suffi-cient perhaps here for us to note is that France, in particular, carried the heavy debt burden of these wars into the eighteenth cen-tury, which, with the aid of the philosophers of the Enlightenment, was to culminate in the great French Revolution.

III   England in Revolution

The Constitutional Tradition

To the men of the seventeenth century, France seemed the home of a stable govern-ment and society, and England seemed the land of violence and change. Within the cen-tury, to the scandal of continental Europeans living under divine-right monarchies, the English cut one king's head off and drove another into exile. It is hard for us today, to whom the English seem the most orderly of people, to realize that they were once regarded as politically disorderly, as hard to govern. Yet they ushered in with considerable tur-moil an important modification of the new-model state, a modification that was to make its way with greater or less success, and greater or less deviation from the English original, all through western civilization by the end of the nineteenth century.

This modification should not yet in the seventeenth century be given the name of "democracy"; it is more safely called constitu-tional, representative or parliamentary gov-ernment. To the extent that such government used to the full the new methods of profes-sional administration developed in the fif-teenth and sixteenth centuries, it may be con-sidered just as "absolute" as any divine-right monarchy. But representative government has grown in the West under historical conditions that have provided a check on the potential absolutism it shares with divine-right monar-chy. This check is the concept of a "constitu-tion," a set of rules, written or traditional, not to be altered by the ordinary processes of government. These rules, which the Italian political scientist Mosca called rules of "juri-dicial defense," are in the modern western tradition felt to be limitations on the author-ity even of a government elected by the ma-jority of the people, a guarantee to the indi-viduals and to groups that they may do certain things even though men in governmental posts of authority do not want them to. With-out these rules and habits of constitutional-ism, or "civil rights,"—and without powerful and widespread human sentiments backing them up—the machinery of parliamentary government could be as ruthlessly absolute as the machinery of Soviet Russian government.

English-speaking people throughout the world have come to believe that England has always had a representative and constitutional government; or, put negatively, that England never went through the stage of divine-right absolute monarchy most of the continental states went through. This belief is partly correct. But it would be better stated as follows: England in the fifteenth and sixteenth centuries began, as did the continental states, to develop a new-model centralized monarchy; but the development in the seventeenth century was checked and modified by the continued growth of representative institutions at both the local and the national level. In France, for instance, cardinal-ministers and kings were able to raise money and govern without the Estates-General. In England, Parliament met in 1629 and quarreled violently with King Charles I. For eleven long years, until 1640, Charles too governed without calling Parliament. But in 1640 he felt obliged to call Parliament and, though he dismissed it at once when it proved recalcitrant, he had to call another in that same year. This was the famous Long Parliament, which sat—with changes of personnel and with interruptions—for twenty years, and which made the revolution that ended the threat of absolute divine-right monarchy in England. If we understand why Charles, unlike his French counterpart, was obliged to call Parliament, we have gone a long way toward understanding why England had a head start in modern representative government.

One very basic reason goes back to later medieval history. As we have already seen, the English Parliament diverged in one important detail of organization from continental parliaments. The House of Commons represented two different social groups not brought together in one house on the Continent, the aristocratic "knights of the shire" and the "burgesses" of the towns and cities. The strength of the Commons lay in the practical working together of both groups, which intermarried quite freely and, in spite of some economic and social tensions, tended to form a single ruling class with membership open to talented and energetic men from the lower classes (see p. 177).

The Middle Ages left another important heritage—the persistence in local government of magistrates who were not directly dependent on the Crown. We must not exaggerate: England, too, had its bureaucrats, its clerks and officials in the royal pay. But whereas in France and in other continental countries the new bureaucracy tended to take over almost all governmental business, especially financial and judicial affairs, in England the gentry and the higher nobility continued to do important local work. The Elizabethan Poor Law of 1601 put the care of the needy not under any national ministry but squarely on the smallest local units, the parishes, where decisions lay ultimately with the amateur, unpaid justices of the peace, recruited from the gentry. In short, the privileged classes were not, as in France, shelved, thrust aside by paid agents of the central government; nor did they, as in Prussia, become themselves mere agents of the Crown. Instead, they preserved a firm base in local government and an equally firm base in the House of Commons. When Charles I tried to govern without the consent of these privileged classes, when he tried to raise from them and their dependents money to run a bureaucratic government without these privileged amateurs, they had a solid institutional basis from which to resist.

The Role of the Crown

But they had to struggle. They had to fight a civil war. No matter how much emphasis the historian may put on the social and institutional side, he cannot ignore what looks like the sheer accident of human personality. The Tudors from Henry VII to Elizabeth I, with some faltering under Edward VI and Mary, had been strong personalities and had been firmly—quite as firmly as any Valois or Habsburg—convinced that they were called to absolute monarchy. They had slowly built up a very strong personal rule, handling their Parliaments skillfully, giving in occasionally in detail, but holding the reins firmly. Henry VIII and his daughter Elizabeth both commanded the kind of devotion from their subjects that can be built in time into formidable personal rule; they could hold the emotional loyalty of the English. Their successors could not. Elizabeth I was childless, and in 1603 she was succeeded by the son of her old rival and cousin, Mary Queen of Scots. James Stuart, already King of Scotland as James VI, became James I of England (1603–1625), thus bringing the two countries, still legally separate, under the same personal rule. James was a pedant by temperament, very sure of himself, and above all sure that he was as much a divine-right monarch as his French cousins. He was a Scot—that is, a foreigner—and as such an object of distrust to his English subjects. He lacked entirely the Tudor heartiness and tact, the gift of winning people to him.

His son, Charles I (1625–1649), under whom the divine-right monarchy came to an end, was by no means as unattractive a monarch and, partly because of his martyrdom, has had his ardent partisans among historians. But if he had many of the graces of a monarch, it is still true that Charles I was no man to continue the work of the Tudors. He was quite as sure as his father had been that God had called him to rule England, and he could never make the happy compromises the Tudors made. Neither father nor son had what we nowadays know as popular appeal or "charisma."

Issues between Crown and Parliament

The fundamental fact about the actual break between the first two Stuarts and their parliamentary opponents is that *both* were in a sense revolutionaries. Both were seeking to bend the line of English constitutional growth away from the Tudor compromise of a strong Crown working with and through a late medieval Parliament based on the alliance of nobility, gentry, and commercial classes. James and Charles were seeking to bend the line toward divine-right monarchy of the continental type; the parliamentarians were seeking to bend it toward something even newer in England and in the world, the establishment of a legislative body possessing the final authority in the making *and carrying out* of law and policy.

Behind this struggle lay the fact that the business of state was gradually growing in scope and therefore in money cost. Foreign relations, for instance, which had been most rudimentary in the Middle Ages, had by the end of the sixteenth century begun to take on modern forms, with a central foreign office, ambassadors, clerks, travel expenses and the like, all involving more money and personnel. The money required by Stuarts—and indeed by Bourbons, Habsburgs, and the rest of the continental monarchs—did not simply go for high living by royalty and the support of parasitic nobles. It went to run a government that was beginning to take over the many functions of the new-model state, if not yet by any means the "welfare state." Basically, James I and Charles I failed to get the money they needed because those from whom they sought it, the ruling classes, succeeded in placing the raising and spending of it in their own hands through parliamentary supremacy. The Parliament that won that supremacy was in fact a committee—a big one, but still a committee—of the ruling classes. It was not a democratic legislature.

One final fact in the background of this struggle between Crown and Parliament: Religion played a major part in welding both sides into cohesive fighting groups. The struggle for power in England was in part a struggle to impose a uniform worship on Englishmen. The royalist cause was identified with High Church Anglicanism, that is, with an episcopalian church government and a liturgy and theology that makes it a "sacramental" religion relatively free from the "liberal" or "rationalist" touches of other forms of Protestantism, and quite free from "holy rolling." The parliamentary cause, at first supported by many moderate Low Church Anglicans, also attracted a strong Puritan or Calvinist element. Later, it came under the control of the Presbyterians and then of the extreme Puritans, the Independents or Congregationalists.

The term "Puritanism" in seventeenth-century English history is a confusing one, and must remain so to those who demand simple, clear-cut definitions. For it was used as a blanket term to cover a wide variety of religious experience, from that of moderate evangelical Anglicans to that of the radical splinter sects of the 1640's and 1650's. Its core went back to Zwingli and Calvin, to the repudiation of Catholic sacramental religion and the rejection of music and the adornment of the church. It placed a positive emphasis on sermons, on simplicity in church and out, and on "purifying" the tie between the worshiper and his God of what the Puritans thought of as Catholic "superstitions" and "corruptions." Early twentieth-century historical writers were often hostile and unfair to Puritanism; and they tended also to deny the importance of religious "ideas" and to insist on the priority of economic and political motives in this English Revolution. The tide has begun to turn, however, and respectable historians once more insist that religion played a great part on both sides of the struggle.

The Reign of James I (1603-1625)

In the troubled reign of James I, we may distinguish three major threads of the struggle in which his son was to go under—money, foreign policy, and religion. In all three issues, the Crown and its opposition each tried to bend the line of constitutional development in its own direction. In raising money, James sought to make the most of revenues which he did not need to ask Parliament to grant. Parliament sought to make the most of its own control over the purse strings by insisting on the principle that any new revenue-raising had to be approved by Parliament. On the whole, James got along, though he levied some taxes without parliamentary grant. One of these, on the somewhat insignificant commodity of imported dried currants, was refused by an importer named Bate. Bate's case was decided in favor of the Crown by the Court of Exchequer, and the decision attracted much attention because the judges held the King's powers in general to be absolute. Then a royal "benevolence"—a euphemism for a direct imposition on an individual—was resisted by a certain St. John, and his appeal was sustained by the Chief Justice, Sir Edward Coke. James then summarily dismissed Coke from office and thereby once again focused the

attention of his subjects on his broad use of the royal prerogative.

Foreign affairs had been regarded by the Tudors as strictly a matter of royal prerogative. The delicate problem of marriage for Elizabeth I, for instance, had indeed concerned her Parliaments and the public. But Parliament made no attempt to dictate a marriage, and Elizabeth was most careful not to offend her subjects in her own tentative negotiations. On the other hand, when James I openly sought a princess of hated Spain as a wife for his son Charles, his subjects did more than grumble. The Commons in 1621 made public petition against the Spanish marriage. When James rebuked them for what he considered meddling, the House drew up the Great Protestation, the first of the great documents of the English Revolution, in which they used what they claimed were the *historic* liberties, franchises, privileges, and jurisdictions of Parliament to assert what was in fact a *new* claim for parliamentary control of foreign affairs. James responded by dissolving Parliament and imprisoning four of its leaders. The Spanish marriage fell through, but the betrothal of Charles in 1624 to a French princess, also a Catholic, was hardly more popular with the English people.

In religion, the policy of Elizabeth I had been broad and moderate. Though she persecuted—that is, refused to permit open religious services of—both extremes of Catholics and Puritans, she allowed much variety of actual practice within the Anglican Church. James neatly summed up his religious policy in the phrase, "No bishop, no king"—which meant that he believed the enforcement of the bishops' monarchical power in religion was essential to the maintenance of his own monarchical power. James at once took steps against what he held to be Puritan nonconformity. He called a conference at Hampton Court in 1604, at which he presided in person and used the full force of his pedantic scholarship against the Puritans. The conference dissolved with no real meeting of minds, and royal policy continued to favor the High Church, anti-Puritan party. In spite of James' failure to achieve anything like religious agreement among his subjects, his reign is a landmark in the history of Christianity among English-speaking peoples. In 1611, after seven years' labor, a committee of forty-seven ministers authorized by him achieved the English translation of the Bible that is still used among all the astounding variety of Protestant sects in the English-speaking world. The King James Version remains a masterpiece of Elizabethan prose, perhaps the most remarkable literary achievement a committee has ever made.

The Troubles of Charles I

Under Charles I, all his father's difficulties came to a head very quickly. England had been maneuvered into war against Catholic Spain, always a popular kind of war among Englishmen of the time. Though English forces were small, any war costs money; Charles found Parliament most reluctant to grant him funds, even though the members hated Spain. Meanwhile, in spite of his French queen, Charles got involved in a war against France. This he financed in part by a forced loan from his wealthier subjects and by quartering his troops in private houses at the householders' expense. Consequently, Parliament in 1628 passed the Petition of Right, in which some of the most basic rules of modern constitutional government are first explicitly stated: No taxation without the consent of Parliament; no billeting of soldiers in private houses; no martial law in time of peace; no one to be imprisoned except on a specific charge and subject to the protection of regular legal procedure. Note that all the principles set forth in this Stuart Magna Carta are limitations on the Crown.

Charles, to get money in new subsidies from Parliament, consented to the Petition of Right. But he also collected duties not authorized by Parliament. Parliament protested by resolutions, not only against his unauthorized taxes but also against his High Church policy. The King now veered from conciliation to firmness; he dissolved Parliament in 1629 and then had Sir John Eliot, mover of

the resolutions, and eight other members arrested. Eliot died in prison in the Tower of London, the first martyr on the parliamentary side.

For the next eleven years (1629–1640), Charles governed without a Parliament. He squeezed every penny he could get out of the customary royal revenues, never quite breaking with precedent by imposing a wholly new tax, but stretching precedent beyond what his opponents thought reasonable. Ship money illustrates how Charles worked. It had been levied by the Crown before, but only on coastal towns for naval expenditures in wartime; Charles now imposed ship money on inland areas, and in peacetime. A very rich gentleman named John Hampden from inland Buckinghamshire refused to pay it. In 1637, he lost his case in court by a narrow margin, but he had directed public attention to the new expedient.

In religious matters, Charles was under the sympathetic guidance of a very High Church archbishop of Canterbury, William Laud, who systematically enforced Anglican conformity and deprived even moderate Puritans of their pulpits. In civil matters, Charles made use of an opportunist conservative, Thomas Wentworth, Earl of Strafford, who had deserted the parliamentary side.

As with all modern revolutions, including our own American one of 1776, there arises this problem: just what were the tensions of this society, just who were hurt, oppressed— or felt so—what changes were being promoted by whom, resisted by whom? In other words, we face the old problem of the causes of a great successful revolution. Americans tend to seek some economic explanation, even if it is exalted into a moral issue such as "taxation without representation is tyranny." Certainly in seventeenth-century England the great changes of the sixteenth century—confiscation of monastic lands, the shift to sheep farming, enclosures, the new commerce, inflation, the legacy of the Wars of the Roses, the many "squeezes" on those with fixed possessions— all this had hurt many people, put them in a mood to blame "the government," to support parliamentary attacks on royal prerogative.

England was seething with repressed political and religious passions underneath the outward calm of these years of personal rule. Yet England was certainly prosperous, at least as prosperous as she had been under Tudor rule. The relative weight of the taxation that offended so many Englishmen was, as far as one can tell from the imperfect statistics of early modern times, less than on the Continent and certainly far less than taxation in any modern nation in the western world. The Englishmen who resisted the Crown by taking arms against it were clearly not downtrodden, poverty-stricken people revolting from despair, but hopeful, self-assertive people out to get the things they wanted—power, wealth, their own form of religious worship, their own newly conceived *rights*.

The Road to Civil War, 1638-1642

The English revolution actually began in Scotland. If Charles I had not had to contend with his fellow Scots, he could perhaps have weathered his financial difficulties for a long time. But in Scotland Laud's attempt to enforce the English High Church ritual and organization came up against the three-generations-old Scots Presbyterianism. In 1638, a Solemn League and Covenant banded the Presbyterians of the Scottish Kirk to resist Charles by force if need be. Charles marched north against the Scots but concluded a temporizing pacification in 1639. Even this mild campaign had been too much for the treasury, and Charles, facing an empty one called an English Parliament in 1640. This Short Parliament, firmly denying any money until the piled-up grievances of nearly forty years were settled, was dissolved at once. Then the Scots went to war again, and Charles, defeated in a skirmish, bought them off by promising them £850 per day until peace was made. Since he could not raise £850 a day, he had to call another Parliament, which became the famous Long Parliament of the revolution.

Holding the unpaid Scots army as a club over Charles' head, the Long Parliament put through a great series of reforms that struck at

King Charles I, by Van Dyck.

the royal power. It abolished ship money and other disputed taxes. It disbanded the unpopular royal administrative courts, like the Star Chamber (see Chapter 2), which had become symbols of Stuart absolutism. The Star Chamber, operating as it did without the safeguards for the accused afforded by common law courts, had most certainly been used by the Stuarts in ways contrary to English traditions. Up to now, Parliament had been called and dismissed at the pleasure of the Crown; the Triennial Act of 1640 made obligatory the summoning of future Parliaments every three years, even if the Crown did not wish to do so. Parliament also attacked the royal favorites, whom Charles reluctantly abandoned. Archbishop Laud was removed, and Strafford, having been declared guilty of treason, was executed in May, 1641.

Meanwhile, Strafford's unfeeling policy toward the Irish had borne fruit in a terrible rebellion that resulted in the massacre of

251

thousands of Protestants in northern Ireland. Parliament, unwilling to trust Charles with an army to put down this rebellion, drew up in 1641 the Grand Remonstrance summarizing all its complaints. Charles now made a final attempt to repeat the tactics that had worked in 1629. Early in 1642, he ordered the arrest of five of his leading opponents in the House of Commons, including Hampden of the ship-money case. The five took refuge in the privileged political sanctuary of the City of London, where the king could not reach them. Charles I left for the north and in the summer of 1642 rallied an army at Nottingham; Parliament simply took over the central government. The Civil War had begun.

Signs were already evident during these first years of political jockeying that strong groups in England and in Parliament wanted something more than a return to the Tudor balance between Crown and Parliament, and between religious conservatives and religious radicals. In politics, the Nineteen Propositions that Parliament submitted to the King in June, 1642, and that he of course rejected, would have firmly established parliamentary supremacy and left Charles a rather weak "constitutional" monarch much like the present English queen. In religion, the Root and Branch Bill, introduced in 1641 but not enacted, would have radically reformed the whole Church of England, destroying, "root and branch," the bishops and much of what had already become traditional in Anglican religious practices. The moderates in politics and religion were plainly going to have trouble defending their middle-of-the-road policies among the extremists of a nation split by civil war.

The Civil War, 1642–1649

England split along lines partly territorial, partly social and economic, and partly religious —*theological,* not "ideological." The royalist strength lay largely in the north and west, relatively less urban and less prosperous than other parts and largely controlled by country gentlemen loyal to throne and altar. Parliamentary

strength lay largely in the south and east, especially in the great city of London and in East Anglia, where even the gentry were firm Puritans (see map, p. 190). The Scots were always in the offing, distrustful of an English Parliament but quite as distrustful of a king who had sought to foist episcopacy on their kirk.

In the field, the struggle was at first indecisive. The royalists, or "cavaliers," recruited from gentlemen used to riding, had at first the important advantage of superior cavalry. What swung the balance to the side of Parliament was the development under a Puritan gentleman named Oliver Cromwell (1599–1658) of a special force, recruited from ardent Puritans of the eastern counties, and gradually forged under strict discipline into the famous "Ironsides." At Marston Moor in 1644, Cromwell won a crucial battle. The parliamentary army, now reorganized into the "New Model Army," staffed by radicals in religion and politics, stood as "Roundheads" (from their short-cropped hair something like our crewcut) against the cavaliers. At the battle of Naseby in 1645, the New Model was completely victorious over the King, and Charles in desperation took refuge with the Scots army, who turned him over to the English Parliament in return for £400,000 back pay.

Now there arose a situation that was to be repeated, with variations for time and place, in the French Revolution in 1792 and the Russian Revolution in 1917. The group of moderates who had begun the revolution and who still controlled the Long Parliament were confronted by the much more radical group who controlled the New Model Army. In religion, the moderates, seeking to retain some ecclesiastical discipline and formality, were Presbyterians or Low Church Anglicans; in politics, they were constitutional monarchists. The radicals, who were opposed to churches disciplined from a central organization were Independents or Congregationalists, and they already so distrusted Charles that they were able at least to contemplate that extraordinary possibility, an England under a republican form of government. The situation was complicated by the Scots, firmly Presbyterian and hostile to the radical Roundheads, whom they regarded as religious anarchists.

The years after 1645 are filled with difficult negotiations, during which Charles stalled for time to gain Scots help. In 1648, Cromwell beat the invading and now royalist Scots at Preston, and his army seized the King. Parliament, with the moderates still in control, now refused to do what the army wanted, to dethrone Charles. The Roundhead leaders then ordered Colonel Pride to exclude by force from the Commons ninety-six Presbyterian members. This the Colonel did in December, 1648, in true military fashion, with no pretense of legality. After "Pride's Purge" only some sixty radicals remained of the more than five hundred members originally composing the Long Parliament; they were known henceforth as the Rump Parliament. The Rump brought Charles to trial before a special high court of trustworthy radicals, who condemned him to death. On January 30, 1649, Charles I was beheaded.

Cromwell
and the Interregnum, 1649–1660

England was now a republic, under the government known as the Commonwealth. But the radicals did not dare call a free election, which would almost certainly have gone against them. A similar phenomenon is not uncommon in other revolutions, witness Lenin's arbitary dissolution in January, 1918, to dissolve the constituent assembly elected by universal suffrage (see Chapter 18). From the start, the Commonwealth was in fact the dictatorship of a radical minority come to power through the tight organization of the New Model Army. From the start, too, Cromwell was the dominating personality of the new government. He was, in a sense, an unwilling dictator. In religion an earnest and sincere Independent, but no fanatic, a patriotic Englishman, strong-minded, stubborn, but no pathological luster after power, by no means unwilling to compromise, he was nevertheless a prisoner of his position.

Cromwell faced a divided England, where the majority were no doubt royalist at heart and certainly sick of the fighting, the confiscations, the endless changes of the last decade. He faced a hostile Scotland and an even more hostile Ireland. The disorders in England had encouraged the Catholic Irish to rebel once more against the Protestant English "garrison." Finally, Cromwell faced a war with Holland, brought on largely by the Navigation Act of 1651, a typically mercantilist measure. By forbidding the importation of goods into England and the colonies except in English ships or in ships of the country producing the imported goods, the Navigation Act deliberately struck at the Dutch carrying trade.

Execution of Charles I, from a woodcut of 1649.

Charles II, eldest son of the martyred Charles I, landed in Scotland, accepted the Covenant—that is, guaranteed the Presbyterian faith as the established Scottish Kirk—and led a Scots army once more against the English. Once more the English army proved unbeatable, and at the battle of Worcester in September, 1651, the hope of the Stuarts went down for the time. Charles took refuge on the Continent, after a romantic escape in disguise. The Dutch War was almost wholly a naval one, and ended victoriously for the English in 1652.

By 1654, Cromwell had mastered all his foes. He himself went to Ireland and suppressed the rebellion with bloodshed that is still not forgotten. In the so-called "Cromwellian Settlement," he dispossessed native Irish landholders in favor of Protestants; he achieved order in Ireland, but not peace. Cromwell also waged an aggressive war against Spain, from whom the English acquired the rich Caribbean sugar island of Jamaica. Even in this time of troubles, the British Empire kept on growing.

Cromwell, however, could not master the Rump Parliament, which brushed aside his suggestions for an increase of its membership and a reform of its procedures. In April, 1653, he forced its dissolution by appearing in Parliament with a body of soldiers. In December, 1653, Cromwell took the decisive step of setting himself up as Lord Protector of the Commonwealth of England, Scotland, and Ireland, with a written constitution—the only one England has ever had—known as the Instrument of Government. Under this constitution an elected Parliament of 460 members was provided for. It was in fact chosen by Puritan sympathizers, for no royalist dared vote. Even so, the Lord Protector had constant troubles with his Parliaments and in 1656 yielded to pressure and accepted some modifications in his dictatorship. Oliver Cromwell died in 1658, and was succeeded as Lord Protector by his son Richard. But Richard Cromwell was a nonentity, and the army soon seized control. By now some army leaders saw in the restoration of the Stuarts the best hope of putting an end to the chronic political turbulence. To insure the legality of the move, General Monk, commander of the Protectorate's forces in Scotland, summoned back the Rump and readmitted the living members excluded by Pride's Purge. This partially reconstituted Long Parliament enacted the formalities of restoration, and in 1660 Charles Stuart came back from exile to reign as Charles II.

The Revolution in Review

It is no doubt misleading to say that there was a Reign of Terror in the English Revolution. Much of the bloodshed was the respectable bloodshed of formal battle between organized armies, not the revolutionary bloodshed of guillotine, lynching, and judicial murder. Still, Charles I was beheaded; Strafford, Laud, and others suffered the death penalty; royalists had their properties confiscated. Above all, the Puritans at the height of their rule in the early 1650's attempted to enforce on the whole population the difficult, austere life of the Puritan ideal. This enforcement took the familiar form of "blue laws," of prohibitions on horse-racing, gambling, cock-fighting, bear-baiting, dancing on the green, fancy dress, the theatre, on a whole host of ordinary phases of daily living.

This English Reign of Terror and Virtue, coming too early for modern techniques of propaganda and control over the masses, was in fact very different from the absolutism, say, of the communist minority in the Russian Revolution. Many an Anglican clergyman, though officially "plundered"—that is, deprived of his living—kept up his worship in private houses; many a cock fight went on in

The House of Commons, as shown on the Great Seal of England used by the Commonwealth (1651).

secluded spots. Nevertheless, the strict code was there, with earnest persons to enforce it, and with implacable enemies to oppose it. The famous remark of the historian Macaulay — that the Puritans prohibited bear-baiting, not because it gave pain to the bear, but because it gave pleasure to the spectators — is a sample of the deep hostility that still survives in England toward the reign of the Puritan "Saints." So too is the popular doggerel of the time:

> To Banbury came I, O profane one,
> Where I saw a Puritane-one,
> Hanging of his cat on Monday
> For killing of a mouse on Sunday.*

Many Englishmen have seemed rather ashamed of their great revolution, preferring to call it the "Civil War" or the "Great Rebellion," and recalling instead as their "Glorious Revolution" the decorous movement of 1688–89, to which we shall come in a moment. Yet the events of 1640–1660 are of major importance, not only in the history of England, but in the history of the West. Here for the first time the monarchy was firmly challenged in a major revolt and a constitutional and representative government was set up, based on a legislature backed by politically active private citizens. Though the Stuarts were restored, no English king ever again could hope to rule without a Parliament, or restore the Court of Star Chamber, or take ship money, benevolences, and other controversial taxes. Parliament thenceforward retained that critical weapon of the legislative body in a limited monarchy, ultimate control of the public purse by periodic grants of taxes.

Moreover, minority groups had gone much farther, and in their extraordinary fermentations had foreshadowed much modern social thought and action. One such group, the Levellers, though they never attained power, won considerable sympathy from the revolutionary army. They put forward a program later carried by emigrants to the American colonies. The Levellers anticipated much of what we now call political democracy — universal suffrage, regularly summoned Parliaments, progressive taxation, separation of Church and State, protection of the individual against arbitrary arrest, and the like. There are even hints of the "socialistic" drive toward economic equality, though in those days collectivist programs were tied up closely with Biblical ideas. The Diggers, for example, were a small sect that preached the sharing of earthly goods in a kind of communism. They actually dug up public lands in Surrey near London and began planting vegetables. They were driven off, but not before they had got their ideas into circulation. The Fifth Monarchy men, the Millennarians, and a dozen other radical sects preached the Second Coming of Christ and the achievement of some kind of utopia on earth.

Still more important, there emerged from these English struggles, even more clearly than from the religious wars on the Continent, the conception of religious toleration. The Independents, while they were in opposition, stood firmly on the right of religious groups to worship God as they wished. Though in their brief tenure of power they showed a willingness to persecute, they were never firmly enough in the saddle to make of England another seventeenth century Geneva or Boston. Moreover, many of the Puritans sincerely believed that compulsion should not be exercised to secure conformity.

At least one of the sects held to the idea and practice of religious toleration as a positive good. The Quakers, led by George Fox (1624–1691), were Puritans of the Puritans. They themselves eschewed all worldly show, finding even buttons ostentatious, the names of days and months indecently pagan, the polite form "you" in the singular a piece of social hypocrisy and legal oaths or oathtaking most impious. Hence they met for worship not on Sunday, the day of the pagan sungod, but on First Day; they addressed any man as "thee" or "thou"; and they took so seriously the basic Protestant doctrine of the priesthood of the believer that they did entirely without a formal ordained ministry. In the Religious Society of Friends, as they are properly known,

*Richard Brathwaite, *Barnabee's Journal* (London, 1774), Pt. I.

any worshiper who felt the spirit move might testify in what in other sects would be a sermon. But Quakers felt too deeply the impossibility of forcing the inner light in any man, were too sure that conversion is the work of God alone, to try to *make* men Quakers. They would abstain entirely from force, particularly from that shocking kind of force we call war, and would go their own Christian way in peace, in the hope that in God's good time men would freely come to God's way—and their way.

Still another of our basic freedoms owes much to this English experience. Freedom of speech was a fundamental tenet of the Puritans, though again at the height of their power they by no means lived up to it. The pamphlet literature of the early years of the great turmoil is a lively manifestation of free speech in practice. And it received a classic statement in the *Areopagitica* of the poet, John Milton, who was the secretary of the Commonwealth.

The Restoration, 1660—1688

The Restoration of 1660 kept Parliament essentially supreme but attempted to undo some of the work of the Revolution. Episcopacy was restored in England and Ireland, though not as a state church in Scotland. Against the "dissenters," as Protestants who would not accept the Church of England were then termed, the so-called Clarendon Code set up all sorts of civil liabilities and obstructions. For instance, by the Five-Mile Act all Protestant ministers who refused to subscribe to Anglican orthodoxy were forbidden to come within five miles of any town where they had previously preached. Yet the dissenters continued to dissent without heroic sufferings. In characteristically English fashion, the Test Act of 1672, which prescribed communion according to the Church on England on all officeholders, local as well as national, was simply got around in various ways, though it was not actually repealed until 1828. One way was "occasional conformity," by which a dissenter of not too strict conscience might worship as a Congregationalist, say, all

year, but might once or twice take Anglican communion. Another, developed in the eighteenth century, was to permit dissenters to hold office, and then pass annually a bill of indemnity legalizing their illegal acts. Dissenters remained numerous, especially among the artisans and middle-class merchants, and as time went on they grew powerful, so that the "non-conformist conscience" was a major factor in English public life. Indeed, the three century progression of names by which these non-Anglican Protestants were called is a neat summary of the growth of their power and status—the hostile term "dissenter" became "non-conformist" in the nineteenth century and "Free Churchman" in the twentieth.

The Restoration was also a revulsion against Puritan ways. The reign of Charles II (1660–1685) was a period of moral looseness, of gay court life, of the Restoration drama with its indecent wit (the Puritans in power had closed the theaters), of the public pursuit of pleasure, at least among the upper classes. But the new Stuarts had not acquired political wisdom. Charles II dissipated some of the fund of good will with which he started by following a foreign policy that seemed to patriotic Englishmen too subservient to the wicked French King Louis XIV. The cynic is tempted to point out that, if Charles's alliance with Louis in 1670 was most un-English, it did result in the final extinction of any Dutch threat to English seapower. And it sealed a very important English acquisition, that of New Amsterdam, now New York, first taken in the Anglo-Dutch War of 1664–1667.

What really undid the later Stuarts and revealed their political ineptitude was the Catholic problem. Charles II had come under Catholic influence through his French mother and very possibly embraced the Roman religion before he died in 1685. Since he left no legitimate children, the crown passed to his brother, James II (1685–1688), who was already a declared Catholic. In the hope of enlisting the support of the dissenters for the toleration of Catholics, James II issued in 1687 a "Declaration of Indulgence," granting freedom of worship to *all* denominations, Protestant dissenters as well as Catholics, in

England and Scotland. This was in the abstract an admirable step toward full religious liberty.

But to the great majority of Englishmen, Catholicism still seemed what it had seemed in the time of Elizabeth I, the great menace to the English nation. Actually, by the end of the seventeenth century the few remaining Catholics in England were glad to be left in something like the status of the dissenters and were no real danger to a country overwhelmingly Protestant. But they were an unappeased majority in Ireland, and it was always possible to stir Englishmen to an irrational pitch by an appeal to their fear and hatred of Catholicism.

The political situation, moreover, was much like that under Charles I; the Crown wanted one thing, Parliament wanted another. Although James II made no attempt to dissolve Parliament or to arrest members, he simply went over Parliament's head by issuing decrees, like the "Declaration of Indulgence" granting full religious toleration, in accordance with what he called the "power of dispensation." Early in his reign, he had made a piddling rebellion by the Duke of Monmouth, a bastard son of Charles II, the excuse for two ominous policies. First, his judges organized the "bloody assizes" which punished suspected rebel sympathizers with a severity that seemed out of all proportion to the extent of the rebellion. Second, he created a standing army of 30,000 men, part of whom he stationed near London in what appeared an attempt to intimidate the capital. To contemporaries it looked as though James were plotting to force both Catholicism and divine-right monarchy on an unwilling England. The result was the "Glorious Revolution."

The Glorious Revolution of 1688–1689

The actual revolution was in fact a *coup d'état* engineered at first by a group of James' parliamentary opponents who were called *Whigs,* in contrast to the *Tories* who tended to support at least the more moderate measures of the later Stuart monarchs. Both these names are political "slang"—Whig merely a Scots variant of "wig"; Tory apparently derived from a Gaelic word meaning "robber." Both words were originally words of contempt, as "Yankee" apparently also was; time has made them all at least neutral if not respectable. The Whigs were the direct heirs of the moderates of the Long Parliament, and they represented an alliance of the great lords and the prosperous London merchants. James II married twice. By his first marriage he had two daughters, both Protestant—Mary, who had married William of Orange, the great Dutch opponent of Louis XIV, and Anne. Then in 1688 a son was born to James and his second wife, who was Catholic, thus apparently making the passage of the crown to a Catholic heir inevitable. The Whig leaders responded with a great barrage of propaganda, including a "whispering campaign." It was rumored that the Queen had not even been pregnant, but that a new-born babe had been smuggled into her chamber in a warming pan, so that there might be a Catholic heir. Then the Whigs and some Tories negotiated with William of Orange, the son-in-law of James. William could hardly turn down a proposition that would give him the solid assets of English power in his struggle with Louis XIV. He accepted the offer of the English crown, which he was to share with his wife, the couple reigning as William III (1689–1702) and Mary II (1689–1694). On November 5, 1688, William landed at Tor Bay on the Devon coast with some 14,000 soldiers. When James heard the news, he tried to rally support, but everywhere the great lords and even the normally conservative country gentlemen were on the side of the Protestant hero. James fled from London to France in December, 1688, giving William an almost bloodless victory.

Early in 1689 Parliament formally offered the crown to William on terms that were soon enacted into law as the Bill of Rights. This famous document, summing up the constitutional practices that Parliament had been working for since the Petition of Right in 1628, is in fact almost a succinct form of written constitution. It lays down the essential principles of parliamentary supremacy—control of the purse, prohibition of dispensation power to the Crown, regular and frequent meetings of Parliament. Three major steps were necessary after 1689 to convert the British Constitution into a parliamentary democracy in which the Crown has purely symbolic functions as the focus of patriotic loyalty. These were, first, the concentration of executive direction in the hands of a committee of the party in majority in a given Parliament—that is, the Cabinet headed by a Prime Minister, the work of the eighteenth and early nineteenth centuries; second, the establishment of universal suffrage and payment of members of the Commons, the work of the nineteenth century, completed in the twentieth; and third, the abolition of the power of the House of Lords to veto legislation passed by the Commons, the work of the early twentieth century. Thus we can see that full democracy was still a long way off in 1689. William III and Mary certainly did not think of themselves as purely ornamental monarchs, without power over policy. They were indeed real rulers.

Childless, they were succeeded by Mary's younger sister Anne (1702–1714). Anne and her nonentity of a husband strove hard to leave an heir to the throne, but all their many children, perhaps merely because of the inadequacies of medical science of the day, were still-born or died in childhood. The exiled Catholic Stuarts, however, did better. The little boy born to James II in 1688, and brought up at the court of St. Germain near Paris, grew up to be known as the "Old Pretender." But in 1701 Parliament passed the Act of Settlement, which settled the crown, in default of heirs to Anne, the heir apparent to the sick William III, not on the Catholic pretender but on the Protestant Sophia of Hanover or her issue. The line to her went back to her grandfather, James I. On Anne's death in 1714, the crown therefore passed to Sophia's son, George, first king of the House of Hanover. It need hardly be pointed out that in so regulating the succession Parliament had clearly established the fact that it, and not the divinely ordained succession of the eldest male in direct descent, made the King of England.

One more act of Queen Anne's reign helped settle for good an old problem. This was the formal union of the kingdoms of England and Scotland under the name of Great Britain in 1707. Scotland was to send sixteen peers to the Lords and forty-five members to the Commons of the Parliament of the United Kingdom. One flag, the Union Jack, with the superimposed crosses of St. George for England and St. Andrew for Scotland, was henceforth to be the national flag of Great Britain. (This is the flag rejected by Canada in 1964.) The union, most necessary to insure the carrying out of the Hanoverian succession in both kingdoms, met with some opposition in both. But on the whole it went through with surprising ease, so great was Protestant fear of a possible return of the Catholic Stuarts. And, in spite of occasional sentimental outbreaks of Scottish nationalism even as late as our own day, the union has worked very well. With the whole of England and the colonies open to Scots politicians and businessmen, the nation famed for its thrifty and canny citizens achieved a prosperity it had never known before.

The Glorious Revolution did not, however, settle one other perennial problem—Ireland. The Catholic Irish rose in support of the exiled James II and were put down at the battle of the Boyne in 1690. William then attempted to apply moderation in his dealings with Ireland, but the Protestant "garrison" there soon forced him to return to the severe spirit of Cromwellian policy. Although Catholic worship was not actually forbidden, all sorts of galling restrictions were imposed on the Catholic Irish, including the prohibition of Catholic schools. Moreover, economic persecution was added to the religious, as Irish trade came under stringent mercantilist regulation. This was the Ireland whose misery inspired a great writer, Jonathan Swift, to make his bitter "modest proposal" that the impoverished Irish solve their economic problems by selling their babies as articles of food. Ireland continued to fester all through the eighteenth century.

IV The Century of Genius

In the seventeenth century the cultural, as well as the political, hegemony of Europe passed from Italy and Spain to France, England, and Holland. Especially in literature, the France of Corneille, Racine, Molière, Boileau, Bossuet, and a host of others set the imprint of a style on the West. Yet the men who achieved the abiding effect of the seventeenth century on our culture were truly international in origin and outlook, and were rather philosophers and scientists than men of letters. When the twentieth-century philosopher, Alfred Whitehead, christened the 1600's the "century of genius," he was thinking above all of men like Galileo, Harvey, Newton, Descartes, Huyghens, and Pascal.

Natural Science

The Renaissance had certainly prepared the way for modern science, first by its successful attack on the abstract, deductive, over-refined late medieval philosophy, and second by its emphasis on this world, on the life of the senses (see Chapter 3). But the seventeenth century made the great advances that established the natural sciences as part of our common heritage. The Englishman Francis Bacon (1561–1626) bore a major part in the rise of modern science. He was really no scientist; he experimented in a somewhat random and unproductive fashion. But he was the tireless proponent of one of the essentials of scientific achievement—observation of phenomena, the patient accumulation of data. If you observe enough facts, he seems to say, they will somehow make sense of themselves in a process called "induction," which he contrasts with the medieval "deduction" he was attacking:

There are and can be only two ways of searching into and discovering truth. The one [deduction] flies from the senses and particulars to the most general axioms, and from these principles, the truth of which it takes for settled and immovable, proceeds to judgment and to the discovery of middle axioms. And this way is now in fashion. The other [induction] derives axioms from the senses and particulars, rising by a gradual and unbroken ascent, so that it arrives at the most general axioms last of all. This is the true way, but as yet untried.*

Both deduction and induction are essential in science, but Bacon's emphasis on induction was a necessary corrective in his time and helped to set modern science on its way.

Progress along that way was facilitated by the invention of new instruments, by the establishment of scientific societies, and by the advance of mathematics. Both the great figures of the "century of genius" and scores of unknown or now forgotten individuals contributed to the new instruments that permitted more exact measurements and more detailed observations. For instance, Dutch glassmakers probably first put two lenses together and discovered that they could thus obtain a greater magnification. By 1610, the Italian Galileo was using the new device in the form of a telescope to observe the heavens, and by about 1680 the Dutchman Van Leeuwenhoek was using it in the form of a microscope to discover tiny creatures—protozoa—hitherto unknown. Working from a discovery made by Galileo, another Italian, Torricelli, invented the barometer. The Frenchman Pascal (1623–1662), using Torricelli's invention, proved by measuring the height of a column of mercury at the base and then at the top of a mountain that what we call air pressure diminishes with altitude, and went on to show that a vacuum is possible, in spite of the old adage "Nature abhors a vacuum."

*Bacon, *The Great Instauration*.

Two important organizations promoting scientific investigation were the English Royal Society for Improving Natural Knowledge, founded in 1662, and the French *Académie des Sciences,* founded in 1666. The one, in characteristic English fashion, was a private undertaking; the other, sponsored by Colbert for the greater glory of Louis XIV and the mercantilistic state, was a government enterprise. Both financed experiments and both published scientific articles in their "house organs," the *Philosophical Transactions* and the *Journal des Sçavans* (savants). Scoffers sometimes mocked their activities; Charles II, for example, roared with laughter at the news that the Royal Society was weighing the air. But ultimately the scientific societies exerted a strong affirmative influence, at least on the community of learned men. It would be hard even today to improve on the Royal Society's statement of purpose, in which it promised "to examine all systems, theories, principles, hypotheses, elements, histories and experiments" and "to question and canvass all opinions, adopting nor adhering to none, till by mature debate and clear arguments, chiefly such as are deduced from legitimate experiments, the truth of such experiments be demonstrated invincibly."

Meanwhile mathematics took a great leap forward. In 1585, Stevin, a Fleming, published *The Decimal, Teaching with Unheard-of Ease How to Perform All Calculations Necessary among Men by Whole Numbers without Fractions.* A generation later, Napier, a Scot, offered *The Marvelous Rule of Logarithms* (1616), which provided the principle of the slide rule and a wonderful short cut in the laborious processes of multiplying, dividing, and taking square root. Next, the Frenchman Descartes worked out analytical geometry, which brings geometry and algebra together, as in the plotting of an algebraic equation on a graph. The mathematical achievements of the century culminated in the perfection of a method of dealing with variables and probabilities. Pascal had made a beginning with his studies of games of chance, and Dutch insurance actuaries had devised tables to show the life expectancy of their clients. Then Newton and the German

Leibniz, apparently quite independently of one another, invented the calculus. The detailed description of the new invention must be left to the experts, but its practical value is indicated by the fact that without the calculus, and indeed without Cartesian (from Descartes) geometry, Newton could never have made the calculations supporting his revolutionary hypotheses in astronomy and physics.

The Englishman Isaac Newton (1642–1727), building on the work of earlier astronomers, especially Copernicus, Kepler, and Galileo made the great theoretical generalization that is now, of course in simplified form, part of every schoolboy's picture of the astronomical universe. This is the law of gravitation. The sun, the planets, and their satellites are, according to this theory, held in their orbits by the force of mutual attraction. Newton stated the formula that this force is proportional to the product of the masses of two bodies attracted one to the other, and inversely proportional to the square of the distance between them. Modified by Einstein, the law still holds.

The law of gravitation is a part of physics as well as of astronomy. Physics too came of age in the seventeenth century, and like astronomy is capped by the work of Newton. Here too Galileo is of importance, though recent research has shown that a devoted follower may have invented the story of how by dropping balls of different weights from the Leaning Tower of Pisa he disproved Aristotle's theory that objects fall with velocities proportional to their weight. Galileo's studies of projectiles, pendulums, and falling and rolling bodies helped to establish modern ideas of acceleration.

Newton also contributed to optics, using a prism to separate sunlight into the colors of the spectrum. He demonstrated that objects only appear to be colored, that their color is not intrinsic but depends on their reflection and absorption of light. Newton first hit on some of his great discoveries when he was an undergraduate at Cambridge, but published them only many years later in the *Principia Mathematica* (1687)—"The Mathematical Principles of Natural Philosophy" is the English

most influential of these philosophers, the Frenchman Descartes (1596–1650), began to put himself straight:

> I thought . . . that I ought to reject as downright false all opinions which I could imagine to be in the least degree open to doubt—my purpose being to discover whether, after so doing, there might not remain, as still calling for belief, something entirely indubitable. Thus, on the ground that our senses sometimes deceive us, I was prepared to propose that no existing thing is such as the senses make us image [*sic*] it to be; and because in respect even of the very simplest geometrical questions some men err in reasoning . . . , I therefore rejected as false (recognising myself to be no less fallible than others) all the reasonings I have previously accepted as demonstrations; and, finally, when I considered that all the thoughts we have when awake can come to us in sleep (none of the latter being then true), I resolved to feign that all the things which had entered my mind were no more true than the illusions of my dreams. But I immediately became aware that while I was thus disposed to think that all was false, it was absolutely necessary that I who thus thought should be somewhat; and noting that this truth *I think, therefore I am*, was so steadfast and so assured that the suppositions of the sceptics, to whatever extreme they might all be carried, could not avail to shake it, I concluded that I might without scruple accept it as being the first principle of the philosophy I was seeking.[*]

From this start, Descartes arrived finally at God—but a God who in his mathematical orderliness, in his remoteness from this confusing world, must seem most unreal to any believer in a personal God.

Scientist and rationalist helped greatly to establish in the minds of educated men throughout the West two complementary concepts that were to give the Enlightenment of the eighteenth century a pattern of action toward social change, a pattern still of driving force in our world. These were first, the concept of a regular "natural" order underlying the apparent irregularity and confusion of the universe as it appears to unreflecting man in his daily experience; and second, the concept

of a human faculty, best called "reason," buried and obscured in most men by their faulty traditional upbringing, but capable of being brought into effective play by good—that is, rational—upbringing. Both these concepts can be found in some form in our western tradition at least as far back as the Greeks. What gives them novelty and force at the end of the seventeenth century is their being welded into the doctrine of progress—the belief that all human beings can attain here on earth a state of happiness, of perfection, hitherto in the West thought to be possible only for Christians in a state of grace, and for them only in a heaven after death.

Two literary movements at the end of the seventeenth century are neatly symptomatic of the coming Enlightenment—the quarrel of the "ancients" and the "moderns" in France, the "battle of the books" in England. In both these literary disputes the issue was fundamentally the same. Can any "modern" write or paint or do anything better than the Greeks and Romans? Or, in terms of our own day, can we *progress* beyond those giants of old, beyond their Golden Age? It is significant that most Americans today would unhesitatingly answer that we *have* progressed far beyond the ancients. And it is significant of the turn the eighteenth century was to take that most of the educated public of the day generally considered the "moderns" to have won this battle of the books.

The Classical Spirit

Art and letters as well as science and philosophy had a part in setting the pattern of the Enlightenment. The characteristic style of the seventeenth century, which flowered in the France of Louis XIV, is often known as *l'esprit classique*. The classical spirit leans toward measure, toward discipline, toward conformity with "those rules of old discover'd, not deviz'd," toward a dignified eloquence, toward an aristocratic refinement and avoidance of the undignified that could forbid so vulgar an object as a handkerchief to the heroine in tears—that could in fact rather dislike even

---

[*]*Discourse on Method*, Pt. IV, in *Descartes' Philosophical Writings*, N. K. Smith, trans. (London, 1952), 140–141.

the tears. There seems something paradoxical in maintaining that devotees of the classical tradition could have aided in setting up attitudes that undermined the veneration paid those classics of classics, the Greeks and Romans. The paradox is heightened by the fact that the writers and artists of the Age of Louis XIV were generally pillars of the established order, supporters of authority and tradition, politically conservative.

The paradox, however, diminishes when you realize that the best writers of the age found in their classical models not a confirmation of existing standards but a better, simpler set of standards that the eighteenth century could later easily express in terms of nature and reason. Boileau (1636–1711), the chief literary critic of the day, who set the rules for writing poetry, issued the pronouncement, "Que toujours le bon sens s'accorde avec le rhyme" (Always have good sense agree with the rhyme). The great French dramatists, in particular, were trying to find in the infinite variety of men and manners something universal, something typical of all men and all times. Molière (1622–1673) made the main characters of his satirical comedies not only individuals but also social types—the miser in *L'Avare,* the hypocrite in *Tartuffe,* the boastful and ignorant newly rich man in *Le Bourgeois Gentilhomme.* Corneille (1606–1684) and Racine (1639–1699) followed the classical canons of tragedy. They took subjects from mythology and wrote in the rhymed couplets of Alexandrine verse. To observe the rigid rules governing time, place, and action—the "unities" derived from Aristotle's *Poetics*—they pruned the dramatic action of irrelevance and restricted it to one place and a time-span of twenty-four hours. But within this rigid form Corneille and Racine created moving portraits of human beings seeking exalted ideals of honor or crushed by overwhelming emotions. The French tragedies of the seventeenth century may be ranked next to the Greek tragedies of antiquity, not so much because of their classical form, but rather because of their psychological insight and emotional power.

Even in its broadest sense, the term "classical spirit" does not do justice to the full range of seventeenth-century literature. La Rochefoucauld (1613–1680) mastered an epigrammatic prose of classic simplicity but used it for devastatingly realistic—or cynical if you think that word fits better—maxims far removed from the lofty ethical decencies of the classics:

We all have enough strength to bear the misfortunes of others. . . . We generally give praise only in order to gain it for ourselves. . . . Virtue in woman is often the result of love of reputation and ease. . . . We always find something not altogether displeasing in the misfortunes of our friends.[*]

With the seventeenth century, the business of printing, as distinguished from the art of printing, began to take on some of the attributes of bigness. The number of people who could read increased all through the West, though most strikingly in northwestern Europe. From now on, there is a printed literature in all the main languages of the West, and a full history of ideas in the West would not neglect any of them. Yet seen in broad outline, German literature, though in bulk sufficient to occupy plenty of modern scholars, had not attained greatness or wide influence, and Spanish and Italian literature had passed their Renaissance peaks. The seventeenth was, as we have seen, the great century of French literary flowering. As yet, English remained a tongue peripheral to European culture, and English writers, even Shakespeare, and most certainly the Milton of *Paradise Lost,* were not generally known abroad. England by her political example, by her great contributions to natural science, and at the end of the century by her political and philosophical writers, Locke above all, had indeed entered fully into the current of the common culture of the West. But the most important work of the two great English scientists Newton and Harvey, as well as the most important theorizing of Francis Bacon, was first published in Latin.

Yet to all of us to whom English is a mother-tongue the seventeenth century pro-

[*]*The Maxims of La Rochefoucauld,* F. G. Stevens, trans. (London, 1939), 9, 49, 65, 173.

duced one of the great classics, Milton. We have already noted his famous defense of freedom of the press, the *Areopagitica*. *Paradise Lost* is the only epic written in English in the grand style that still finds readers—and it does find them, not all of them compelled by the formalities of higher education. Milton must be tagged a Christian humanist; both terms are important. His classical erudition is to a twentieth-century American staggering, and he needs copious footnoting. He was an active worker on the Puritan side in the Great Revolution and has left many incidental writings, all of which seem now to most of us in a somewhat difficult periodic prose style.

For to the historian of culture the major fact of English writing in the seventeenth century is not Milton, classic though he is, nor the brilliant, witty, and indecent comedies of the Restoration stage, but the simplification, the clarification, the modernization of English prose style that was achieved in the last half of the century. At the level of high formal culture, and perhaps above all under the influence of the poet Dryden (1631–1700), English began to model itself on French, on its straightforward word order, on its comparatively brief sentences, free from long periodic clauses, and on its polish, neatness, and clarity. But also at a level addressed to the common

Christopher Wren: St. Paul's Cathedral, London (1675–1710).

Baroque art: Bernini's Baldacchino, begun in 1624, in St. Peter's, Rome.

man, and exemplified in the prose of John Bunyan (1628–1688) of *The Pilgrim's Progress* and later, in that of Daniel Defoe (c.1660–1731) of *Robinson Crusoe,* English began to simplify itself. Even a modern American can read a piece of English prose picked at random from writings of 1700 and not feel he is reading something strange; this would hardly be true of a random choice from a mere fifty years earlier, which would seem almost another language.

The Arts

The term "classical spirit" hardly expresses the full achievement of seventeenth-century art. The France of Louis XIV did indeed produce neoclassical monuments like the balanced and columned *exterior* of Versailles or of the wings of the Louvre in Paris. But the *interior* of Versailles has acres of ceiling painted with smirking cherubs. This lavish embellishment is one aspect of Baroque, the foremost artistic style of the century.

Baroque added a profusion of detail and fantastic and theatrical effects to the basic geometrical patterns of Renaissance design. Sir Christopher Wren used a moderate Baroque style, still somewhat under classical restraints, for St. Paul's Cathedral in London, the only major church building ever designed and completed by a single architect. The dramatic qualities of Baroque are evident at

Philip IV of Spain, by Velasquez.

the seventeenth century followed, however, the secular and realistic aspects of the Renaissance tradition. A court painter, he did forty portraits of the Habsburg king, Philip IV, and in some of his best work he produced what one critic has called "optical," as opposed to "photographic," realism. Velasquez depicts what the eye sees at a glance, rather than what is actually there.

In the Low Countries, the chief centers of northern European painting, artists planted themselves thoroughly in the workaday world of business, farming, taverns, and even almshouses. The Fleming Rubens (1577–1640) not only received commissions from French and English royalty but also made a fortune from his art and established a studio with two hundred students, a veritable factory of painting. The rosy, fleshy nudes for which Rubens is famous have the exuberance of Baroque, and he himself worked on the grand scale, contributing, it has been estimated, at least in part to more than two thousand pictures. Most of the Flemish and Dutch masters of the seventeenth century, however, seem rather apart from Baroque theatricality and still farther apart from the "classical spirit." They were quite willing to paint handkerchiefs and even less dignified objects, and by their quiet realism they made the commonplace uncommonly lovely. In the hands of the greatest Dutch painter, Rembrandt (1609–1669), the commonplace—the municipal "Night Watch," the "Syndics of the Cloth Guild," even "The Anatomy Lesson of Dr. Tulp"—receives a transcendental glow that already deserves to be called "romantic." (See also Chapter 5.)

In music, the term "Baroque" conveys much of the accomplishment of the seventeenth century, though many critics find it a term better applicable to the visual arts than to music. Here Italy took the lead, following in the paths laid out by the musicians of the Renaissance (see Chapter 3). In Rome, Frescobaldi (1583–1644) released the dramatic potentialities of that most Baroque instrument, the organ, and attracted thousands to his recitals at St. Peter's. In Venice, Monteverdi (1567–1643), contending that "speech should be the master of music, not its servant,"

Rome in the vast open spaces and eye-catching colonnades of St. Peter's Square, and at Versailles in the Hall of Mirrors, the majestic Staircase of the Ambassadors, and the elaborate gardens, lagoons, and fountains. Baroque at its most fantastic produced the *baldacchino,* the twisting bronze canopy rising to a height of eight stories above the altar of St. Peter's. Though not Gothic in origin, the Baroque style yet achieved a kind of translation of Gothic decorative richness into classical terms. Some of its most interesting monuments are Mexican churches.

In painting, the late sixteenth-century master, El Greco, had achieved a thoroughly Baroque effect in his distorted and mystical canvases (see Chapter 5). Velasquez (1599–1660), the outstanding Spanish painter of backed his contention in practice by writing the first important operas. This Baroque compound of music and the theater gained immediate popularity. Venice soon had no fewer than sixteen opera houses, which were already establishing the tradition of slighting the chorus and orchestra to pay for the "stars." The star system reached its height at Naples, the operatic capital of the later 1600's. There conservatories (originally institutions for "conserving" orphans) stressed voice training; composers provided operatic vehicles that were little more than loose collections of arias; and the crowning touch of unreality came with the Neapolitan custom of having the male roles sung by women and the female by *castrati*—that is, eunuchs, permanent boy sopranos.

Seventeenth-century opera at its best rose above the level of stilted artificiality. Purcell (1658–1695), the organist of Westminster Abbey and virtually the only significant native composer of opera in English musical history, produced a masterpiece for the unpromising occasion of graduation at a girls' school. This was the beautiful and moving *Dido and Aeneas*. In France, Louis XIV realized the potentiality of opera for enhancing the resplendence of the Sun King, and from Italy imported Lully (1632–1687), musician, dancer, speculator, and politician extraordinary, who vied with Molière for the post of "cultural director" at court. Lully's operatic exercises on mythological themes are for the most part now forgotten, but the overtures and dances that he wrote for them live on as a prelude to the great eighteenth-century achievement in instrumental music.

Left: "Susanna Fourment in Hat," by Rubens. Right: Rembrandt: Self-Portrait.

Seventeenth-Century Culture
in Review

The "century of genius," then, produced a rich and complex culture, at once scientific, classical, Baroque, and much else besides. It is the complexity that must now be underscored once more. In religion, for example, the seventeenth century was not simply a preparation for the toleration and the diluted "natural religion" of the eighteenth-century Age of Prose and Reason. Against the practical toleration resulting in England from the Glorious Revolution must be set the savage persecutions still prevailing in Ireland and Louis XIV's revocation of the Edict of Nantes. Remember, too, the variety of religious sects that flourished in revolutionary England, the heaven-stormers, the Quakers, whose other-worldly beliefs were to prove so disconcertingly compatible with material success in this world, the Independents, and all the others. In France, along with a conventional Gallican like Bossuet, there flourished the Quietists and the Jansenists, groups who went well beyond orthodoxy into mystical beliefs that conformists were already damning with one of the Enlightenment's favorite words of reproach—"enthusiasm." In Germany, the spiritual descendants of the Anabaptists were laying the foundation of that evangelical appeal to human emotions which in the very midst of the Age of Prose and Reason was to flourish in German Pietism and English Methodism, and which, carried to the shores of the New World by immigrants, was to play so important a part in the early religious history of our own country.

The contrasts presented by the seventeenth century, this fecund "century of genius," come out in one of its great men, the Frenchman Pascal (1623–1662). As mathematician and physicist, Pascal has an important place in the history of science. His barometric experiment on the Puy-de-Dôme and his other experiments to prove the possibility of a vacuum we have already noted (see p. 259). And in this-worldly activity Pascal was wide-ranging and very modern. He made contributions to pure mathematics, invented and tried not very successfully to market a calculating machine, forerunner of our modern ones, and started the first bus line—horse-drawn, of course—in Paris. Yet Pascal was also a profoundly other-worldly man, who spent the last years of his life in religious meditation, defended the Jansenists against the Jesuits—incidentally in lively, epigrammatic modern French, with the skill, fervor, and one-sidedness of the born pamphleteer—and left unfinished at his death one of the most remarkable works of Christian apologetics in existence, the fragments known as the *Pensées* (thoughts). Here he could write:

Man is but a being filled with error. This error is natural, and, without grace, ineffaceable. Nothing shows him the truth: everything deceives him. These two principles of truth, reason and the senses, besides lacking sincerity, reciprocally deceive each other. The senses deceive reason by false appearances: and just as they cheat reason they are cheated by her in turn: she has her revenge. Passions of the soul trouble the senses, and give them false impressions. They emulously lie and deceive each other.*

These are hardly the words of a typical rationalist of the Enlightenment. Nor is one of his best-known aphorisms: "Cleopatra's nose: if it had been shorter, the whole face of the earth would have been changed." The "century of genius" was no mere prelude to the Enlightenment, but an age in which men were "voyaging on strange seas of thought."

The seventeenth century, and not the sixteenth, is perhaps the clearest point of time where the "modern" comes fully into existence. In this century the new science, the new technology, the new economic life finally made possible—indeed among the educated, common—a belief in progress, in steadily increasing human command over material resources, in steadily increasing and widening possibilities of happiness for most men and women right here on earth. In this century Christianity met in this new spirit of belief in progress the sternest challenge to new adapta-

*Pascal, *Thoughts, Letters, and Opuscules*, O. W. Wright, trans. (Boston, 1882). 192.

tions it had met in nearly two millennia. And yet, as we see with much of its classical literature, with much baroque art, with the new religious movements, the seventeenth century was keenly aware of mystery, of horror, of emotion, of the apparently insoluble paradoxes that face man, this "reed, but a thinking reed." Once more to quote Pascal, the seventeenth century was aware, far more than the eighteenth was to be, of *both* the *esprit de finesse* (the hunch, the immeasurable gift of measure) and the *esprit de géométrie* (mathematics, reason cold, clear, always answering to summons, always the same).

Reading Suggestions on Divine-Right Monarchy — and Revolution

(Asterisk indicates paperbound edition.)

General Accounts

D. Ogg, *Europe in the Seventeenth Century*, 6th ed. (Black, 1952); and G. N. Clark, *The Seventeenth Century*, 2nd ed. (Clarendon, 1947). Readable accounts now in paperback editions. Clark's is more useful; it is organized by topics and centers on developments in France.

C. J. Friedrich, *The Age of the Baroque, 1610–1660* (Harper, 1952); F. L. Nussbaum, *The Triumph of Science and Reason, 1660–1685* (Harper, 1953); and J. B. Wolf, *The Emergence of the Great Powers, 1685–1715* (Harper, 1951). These three volumes (also now available in paperback editions) in the "Rise of Modern Europe" series provide a treatment of the seventeenth century fully abreast of modern scholarship.

Special Studies:
Primarily Economic
and Military

E. F. Heckscher, *Mercantilism*, 2 vols., rev. ed. (Macmillan, 1955). A famous work, the subject of much scholarly controversy; indispensable for an examination of the topic.

H. Heaton, *Economic History of Europe*, rev. ed. (Harper, 1948); and S. B. Clough and C. W. Cole, *Economic History of Europe*, 3rd ed. (Heath, 1952). General economic histories.

C. Petrie, *Earlier Diplomatic History, 1492–1713* (Macmillan, 1949). A useful manual.

A. Vagts, *A History of Militarism* (Norton, 1937); E. M. Earle, ed., *Makers of Modern Strategy* (Princeton Univ. Press, 1943); J. F. C. Fuller, *Military History of the Western World* (Funk & Wagnalls, 1954–1956). All useful on seventeenth-century developments.

A. T. Mahan, *The Influence of Sea Power on History, 1660–1783* (Little, Brown, 1890; *Saga). A most celebrated book, but no longer a very reliable guide to the subject.

E. Barker, *The Development of Public Services in Western Europe, 1660–1930* (Oxford Univ. Press, 1944). Attempts to treat an important topic usually totally neglected.

F. L. Nussbaum, *A History of Economic Institutions of Modern Europe* (Crofts, 1933). An abridgment of Sombart's *Moderne Kapitalismus*, with its argument that war is economically creative.

J. U. Nef, *War and Human Progress* (Harvard Univ. Press, 1950). An answer to Sombart above, arguing that war is economically destructive.

Special Studies:
France

L. von Ranke, *Civil Wars and Monarchy in France* (Harper, 1853). This great old classic continues to be worth reading for the seventeenth century.

A. Guérard, *The Life and Death of an Ideal*, new ed. (Braziller, 1956). Perhaps the best single volume in English on the Age of Louis XIV; and does full justice to the cultural side.

G. Duby, R. Mandrou, *A History of French Civilization* (Random House, 1964). An admirable book, good for any period in French history from Charlemagne to Charles de Gaulle, but perhaps especially useful for the *grand siècle*.

C. V. Wedgwood, *Richelieu and the French Monarchy* (Macmillian, 1950), and M. P. Ashley, *Louis XIV and the Greatness of France* (Macmillan, 1947). Two good brief accounts in the "Teach Yourself History Library."

O. A. Ranum, *Richelieu and the Councillors of Louis XIII* (Oxford Univ. Press, 1963). An important, scholarly, monograph by a young American scholar.

H. B. Hill, ed., *The Political Testament of Cardinal Richelieu* (Univ. of Wisconsin Press, 1961). Good translation of a major work with critical commentary.

L. B. Packard, *The Age of Louis XIV* (Holt, 1929. A Berkshire Study). Very short and very good.

W. H. Lewis, *The Splendid Century* (Sloane, 1954; *Anchor). A well written account with emphasis on French society.

J. E. King, *Science and Rationalism in the Government of Louis XIV* (John Hopkins Univ. Press, 1949). A significant monograph.

P. R. Doolin, *The Fronde* (Harvard Univ. Press, 1935). Especially interesting, not only for the topic dealt with but for the thesis that the so-called absolute monarchy in France was really not so absolute.

C. W. Cole, *Colbert and a Century of French Mercantilism,* 2 vols. (Columbia Univ. Press, 1939). A solid, detailed study.

W. J. Stankiewicz, *Politics and Religion in Seventeenth Century France* (Univ. of California Press, 1960). A good study of political thought.

Special Studies: England

L. von Ranke, *A History of England,* 6 vols. (Clarendon, 1875). Another classic account by the great German historian.

S. R. Gardiner, *History of England, 1603–1642,* 10 vols.; *History of the Great Civil War, 1642–1649,* 4 vols.; and *History of the Commonwealth and Protectorate, 1649–1656* (Longmans, Green, 1904–1913). A really major work of detailed history.

G. Davies, *The Early Stuarts, 1603–1660,* and G. N. Clark, *The Later Stuarts, 1660–1714,* new eds. (Clarendon, 1949). These two volumes in the "Oxford History of England" provide a briefer scholarly account.

Christopher Hill, *Society and Puritanism in Pre-Revolutionary England* (Schocken Books, 1964). A recent analysis of the special form of the "protestant ethic" taken in England. The same author's *The Century of Revolution, 1603–1714* (Nelson, 1961) is a stimulating volume in a new eight volume *History of England* published by Nelson in Edinburgh.

C. H. Firth, *Oliver Cromwell and the Rule of the Puritans in England* (Putnam's, 1900). Often considered the best of the very many books on Cromwell.

C. V. Wedgwood, *The King's Peace, 1637–1641,* and *The King's War, 1641–1647* (Macmillan, 1955, 1959). The first two volumes of a detailed study of the Great Rebellion by the best contemporary specialist. Miss Wedgwood is the acknowledged expert of our generation, an excellent writer, and a conservative historian untainted by sociological learnings.

G. Davies, *The Restoration of Charles II, 1658–1660* (Huntington Library, 1955). An authoritative monograph completing the work of Gardiner and Firth.

A. Bryant, *King Charles II* (Longmans, Green, 1931). An unusually sympathetic account.

F. C. Turner, *James II* (Macmillan, 1948). A balanced treatment of a highly controversial figure.

G. M. Trevelyan, *The English Revolution, 1688–1689* (Butterworth, 1938. The Home University Library). A very good study by an historian who has written several famous works on the Stuart period.

D. L. Keir, *The Constitutional History of Modern Britain, 1485–1937,* 4th ed. (Black, 1950). A good introduction.

J. R. Tanner, *English Constitutional Conflicts of the Seventeenth Century* (Cambridge Univ. Press, 1928). A full and scholarly account.

C. Brinton, *The Anatomy of Revolution,* rev. ed. (*Vintage, 1957). Generalizations based on England's seventeenth-century revolution, France's eighteenth-century one, and Russia's twentieth-century one. Selected bibliographies for each revolution.

W. Notestein, *The English People on the Eve of Colonization, 1603–1630* (Harper, 1954). An admirable piece of social and intellectual history.

G. P. Gooch, *English Democratic Ideas in the Seventeenth Century,* H. J. Laski, ed. (Cambridge Univ. Press, 1927; *Harper Torchbook, 1959). Essential for understanding the scope of the English revolution.

E. Bernstein, *Cromwell and Communism: Socialism and Democracy in the Great English Revolution* (Allen and Unwin, 1930). The second part of the title of this significant study is the more accurate.

Everybody's Pepys, O. F. Morshead, ed. (Harcourt, Brace, 1926). A useful abridgment of the famous diary kept during the 1660's; a fascinating document of social history.

Special Studies: The Century of Genius

C. Brinton, *Ideas and Men* (Prentice-Hall, 1950); and J. H. Randall, Jr., *Making of the Modern Mind,* rev. ed. (Houghton Mifflin, 1940). Two general books on intellectual history with useful sections on the seventeenth century.

P. Smith, *A History of Modern Culture,* Vol. I (Holt, 1930). A mine of information on topics often passed over in general histories. Now a paperback.

B. Willey, *The Seventeenth Century Background* (*Anchor). Reprint of a modern classic; essays on Descartes, Hobbes, Milton, and other major figures in the intellectual and religious life of the century.

P. Hazard, *The European Mind, 1680–1715* (Hollis and Carter, 1953). A significant reëvaluation of the intellectual history of the period.

Ernest Mortimer, *Blaise Pascal* (Harper, 1959). A sympathetic study, admirably written.

F. H. Anderson, *Francis Bacon: His Career and His Thought* (Univ. of Southern California, Press, 1962). The best recent treatment.

A. R. Hall, *The Scientific Revolution 1500–1800* (*Beacon, 1965). A careful historical treatment.

L. S. Feuer, *The Scientific Intellectual; The Psychological and Sociological Origins of Modern Science* (Basic Books, 1963). A controversial book, but supplements the historical approach of A. R. Hall, above.

A. N. Whitehead, *Science and the Modern World* (*Mentor). A major essay by a great philosopher and mathematician; not easy reading.

Charles Singer and others, eds., *A History of Technology* (Oxford Univ. Press, 1954–1958). The third volume of this magnificently designed and expensive work covers this period. The authoritative work of our time on the subject.

A. Wolf, *A History of Science, Technology, and Philosophy in the Sixteenth and Seventeenth Centuries,* rev. ed. (Allen & Unwin, 1950; *Harper Torchbooks). A standard, detailed account. See also the work by H. Butterfield cited for Chapter 3.

M. R. Bukofzer, *Music in the Baroque Era* (Norton, 1947); and H. Leichtentritt, *Music, History, and Ideas* (Harvard Univ. Press, 1938). Both are useful introductions to the development of music in the period; see also the works of P. Láng and C. Gray cited in the reading suggestions for Chapter 3.

H. J. C. Grierson, *Cross-Currents in English Literature of the 17th Century* (*Harper Torchbook, 1958). Important studies in the history of ideas.

S. E. Bethell, *The Cultural Revolution of the Seventeenth Century* (Roy, 1951). Another study of the literature with fruitful suggestions for the historian of social and political ideas.

Historical Fiction

A. Dumas, *The Three Musketeers, Twenty Years After, The Vicomte de Bragelonne* (many editions). The famous "D'Artagnan" trilogy, set in seventeenth-century France; properly swashbuckling, yet based on sound research.

T. Gautier, *Captain Fracasse* (Bigelow, Smith, 1910). A good picaresque tale, based on conscientious research; set in the France of Louis XIII.

A. Manzoni, *The Betrothed,* A Colquhoun, trans. (Dutton, 1951). Milan about 1630; a famous Italian novel.

N. Hawthorne, *The Scarlet Letter* (many editions). The best introduction to the Puritan spirit through fiction.

R. Graves, *Wife to Mr. Milton* (Creative Age, 1944). A good novel, though not very kind to Milton.

W. M. Thackeray, *Henry Esmond* (many editions). A famous novel, set in England about 1700.

8

The Old Régime

and the International Balance,

1715–1789

I   Introduction:
    The Prospect in 1715

Long years of peace and quiet appeared to be in prospect for Europe in 1715. In the West, the Utrecht settlement of 1713 had ended Louis XIV's prolonged threat to the balance of power, and in the Baltic, as we shall see, the protracted Great Northern War between Russia and Sweden was nearing a settlement. The death of Louis XIV himself in 1715 gave fresh promise of international stability, for the crown of France passed to his great-grandson, Louis XV, a boy of five. During the long regency now ahead, France would probably be too preoccupied with internal matters to attempt adventures abroad. Finally, the great conflicts of Louis XIV had exhausted his own state and had also brought his victorious opponents to the edge of bankruptcy. Europe needed an extended period of convalescence.

273

Historians use the term "Old Régime" to describe the institutions prevailing in Europe, especially France, before 1789: It was the Old Régime of the eighteenth century in contrast to the "new" régime of the French Revolution. In many respects the Old Régime resembled the still older régime of the Middle Ages. Its economic foundations were agrarian, for most Europeans lived in farming villages and retained the parochial outlook of the peasant. In Western Europe—particularly in Britain, France, the Low Countries, and Germany west of the Elbe River—the great majority of peasants had long been free of the bonds of serfdom. In Eastern Europe, however—notably in Germany beyond the Elbe, and in Hungary, Poland, and Russia—the majority were still serfs.

The social foundations of the Old Régime rested firmly on the medieval division of society into the first estate of the clergy, the second estate of the nobility, and the third estate of commoners, who included the urban bourgeoisie as well as the peasantry. Within the third estate, only the men at the top exerted much political influence—well-to-do businessmen in England and Holland, French lawyers or merchants wealthy enough to purchase government office. Generally, bourgeois influence diminished as one moved eastward. Almost everywhere the titled nobles and the landed gentry of the second estate still wielded substantial power and wanted to regain some of that assumed by the "vile bourgeois," in the phrase of the aristocratic Duc de Saint-Simon. As the present chapter will show, every government in Europe tended to represent the interests of the few, whether it was an absolute monarchy, like France or Prussia, a constitutional monarchy, like Britain, or a republic, like the Dutch United Provinces.

Europe had long been oligarchical, agrarian, and parochial, and in 1715 it seemed likely to remain so forever. The Old Régime, however, did not last forever; its apparent stability was deceptive. By the middle of the eighteenth century, its social and economic foundations were beginning to crumble under the pressure of revolutionary economic changes. Leaders of the intellectual movement called the Enlightenment (see Chapter 9) were voicing the demands for institutional reform that culminated in the revolution of 1789.

The international stability promised by the Utrecht settlement also faded relatively soon. The defeat and death of Louis XIV did not end the world-wide rivalry of Britain and France, who began another round of their long conflict in 1740. Meanwhile, the rapid emergence of two new states caused shifts in the balance of power. Russia was moving out of semi-isolation to take an active and often aggressive part in international affairs, and the once-obscure German electorate of Brandenburg-Prussia was developing into a first-class military power, intent on expansion.

II The Western Powers

The changes in commerce, agriculture, and industry that helped to undermine the Old Régime were most evident in Western Europe, especially in France, the Low Countries, and, above all, Britain. They were in fact economic revolutions, though some historians shy away from the term because it may suggest a more sudden discharge of economic energy or technological inventiveness than actually occurred. The commercial, agricultural, and industrial revolutions, while slower and less dramatic than political revolutions, were in the long run perhaps even more revolutionary in their effects upon human history.

The Commercial Revolution

In the eighteenth century, the commercial revolution was more advanced than the other two. Its basic institutions had been developed before 1715, banks and insurance firms in the Renaissance, for example, and chartered trading companies in the sixteenth century. Mercantilism, the rather ill-defined set of principles determining governmental policies toward commerce, had matured in the Spain of Philip II and the France of Louis XIV and Colbert. The steady growth of trade in the eighteenth century, however, quickened the pace of the commercial revolution.

For example, it increased the demand for insurance on ships and cargoes. Early in the century the insurance brokers of London often gathered in coffee houses to discuss business, news, and politics. Specialists in marine insurance gravitated to Edward Lloyd's coffee house in Lombard Street and continued to meet there after Lloyd died in 1713. Thus was born Lloyd's of London, the firm that developed the standard form of policy for marine insurance and published *Lloyd's List*, the first detailed and accurate shipping newspaper. Another great London institution to emerge from the informal atmosphere of the coffee house was the stock exchange. As the buying and selling of shares in joint-stock companies increased, traders began to gather at Jonathan's; in 1773 the name was changed from Jonathan's to the Stock Exchange Coffee House.

Marine insurance prospered in part because improved charts and the installation of lighthouses and buoys made navigation safer. At sea, captains could determine their geographical position by using two new instruments, the sextant and the chronometer. The sextant, an elaboration of the telescope, showed the altitude of the sun at noon and thus indicated the ship's latitude. The chronometer, a clock unaffected by the motion of the ship, was kept on Greenwich Mean Time (the time at the meridian running through Greenwich near London). The two new instruments made it possible to calculate the ship's longitude, which represented the difference between Greenwich Mean Time and the local time aboard ship calculated with the sextant.

On land, the improvements in communication and transport came much more slowly. Except for the good highways of France, Euro-

pean roads were scarcely better than paths or trails. The shipment of goods overland remained slow, unsafe, and expensive until after 1750, when the construction of turnpikes and canals gradually eased the situation. The pioneer English canal, built in 1759–1761 by the Duke of Bridgewater, cut in half the cost of moving coal from the mines on his estate to the new factory town of Manchester.

Businessmen also faced the handicaps imposed by restrictive guild regulations and by the abundance of coins, weights, measures, and local tolls. Sweden, for example, minted only copper money, including a monstrosity weighing 43 pounds. Baden, one of the smaller German states, had 112 separate measures for length, 65 for dry goods, 123 for liquids, and 163 for cereals, not to mention 80 different pound weights! A German merchant who shipped timber down the Elbe from Dresden in Saxony to Hamburg had to pay so many tolls to the towns and principalities along the way that of 60 planks floated at Dresden only six would reach Hamburg. Even in France, the land where uniformity and centralization were supposedly the rule, all sorts of local taxes and other obstacles to internal trade persisted.

The survival of local vested interests showed the limitations of the power of the mercantilist state. Mercantilism required the regulation of trade on the national, rather than the local, level. But no eighteenth-century government possessed the staff of officials needed to make national regulation effective; states had to rely heavily on private companies and individuals to execute most of their policies. Thus the English and Dutch East India Companies exercised not only a trading monopoly in their colonial preserves but also virtual sovereign powers, including the right to maintain soldiers and conduct diplomacy. Inventors worked on their own, not in government laboratories, although the state occasionally offered prizes on matters of critical importance to the business community. Although the English Parliament promised £20,000 for the invention of a reliable "seagoing" clock, the inventor of the chronometer had to wait twenty-five years to collect his prize money. Private initiative, not sluggish governments, made the commercial revolution advance at a swift pace in the eighteenth century. The fact was underlined by two speculative booms that occurred early in the century —the Mississippi Bubble in France and the South Sea Bubble in England.

The Mississippi and South Sea Bubbles

In 1715, hardly a state in Europe could manage the large debts that had piled up during the recent wars. Yet all of them had to find some way of meeting at least part of the large annual interest on bonds and other obligations, or else go bankrupt. The governments of France and England chose the way of experiment. They transferred the management of state debts to joint-stock companies, which they rewarded with trading concessions. The commerce of the companies, it was hoped, would prove so lucrative that their profits would easily cover the interest charges on government bonds.

John Law (1671–1729), a Scottish mathematical wizard and an inveterate gambler, presided over the experiment in France. He studied monetary problems and banking methods in Amsterdam, at that time the commercial capital of Europe. Law was a mercantilist, but with a difference. He agreed with the doctrine that the strength of a state depended upon the quantity of money it possessed. But, he asserted, the limited supply of silver and gold made it difficult to increase the amount of specie circulating in any country and therefore difficult to promote business. Paper money, Law concluded, was the solution—paper money backed by a nation's wealth in land and in trade. The quantity of paper money in circulation could easily be raised or lowered in accordance with the needs of business. Trading companies would prosper as never before, the whole country would prosper, and, in the general prosperity, government debts would be paid off.

The death of Louis XIV gave Law the opportunity to try his "system." The regent for Louis XV, the Duke of Orléans, who was a gambling crony of Law, permitted him to set up a central bank in Paris. Whereas the value of French money had been sinking lower and lower because of the government's debasing the coinage, Law's bank, following the practice of the Bank of Amsterdam, issued paper notes of stable value. Business activity at once increased. Next, Law set up the Mississippi Company, which received a monopoly of commerce with the Louisiana colony and soon absorbed the other French colonial trading companies.

Law's system now reached to almost every corner of the French economy, and Law himself, appointed controller-general, became the economic dictator of the kingdom. His company took over the government debt and agreed to accept government bonds in partial payment for shares of Mississippi stock. Many bondholders responded enthusiastically to Law's offer, because the bonds had depreciated to 20 per cent or less of their face value. Law, however, had to sell additional shares of Mississippi stock in order to obtain sufficient working capital for his company. To attract cash purchasers, Law promoted a boom in Mississippi stock, painting the company's prospects in brightest colors. Investors, large and small, caught the fever of speculation, and by the close of 1719 Mississippi stock was selling at forty times its par value.

The Mississippi Bubble soon burst, for Law's paper money could not stand the pressure. As the price of Mississippi shares rose higher and higher, cautious investors decided to cash in. They sold their shares, received payment in banknotes, then took the notes to Law's bank and demanded their redemption in specie. The bank exhausted its reserves of gold and silver and suspended specie payments in February, 1720. Law was forced to relinquish the post of controller-general in May, 1720; he fled France shortly thereafter.

The explosion of the Mississippi Bubble had international repercussions, for within a few weeks of Law's resignation the South Sea Bubble burst in London. It might have been expected that management of the English government's debt would devolve upon the Bank of England. Founded in 1694 as a private institution (it was fully nationalized only after

World War II), the Bank of England issued banknotes and rendered other valuable services to the government during the last wars against Louis XIV. The debt, however, was taken over not by the Bank but by the new South Sea Company, which paid the government the exorbitant sum of more than seven and a half million pounds. The resources of the South Sea Company were slim, consisting largely of the right to exploit the trading concessions that Britain obtained under the Asiento agreement at the end of the War of the Spanish Succession. These privileges were limited to furnishing Spain's American colonies with 4800 slaves annually and to sending one ship a year to Panama for general trade.

The South Sea Company, like the Mississippi Company, invited government creditors to transfer their bonds into company stock. The directors of the company bought and sold shares in secret to create a more lively market for them, encouraged purchases of stock with a down payment of only 10 per cent in cash, and spread reports of forthcoming sailings by the company's ships on voyages of unparalleled promise. In short, like Law, they created a speculative boom. South Sea shares, with a par value of £100, sold for £129 in January of 1720, and for £1050 in June. Dozens of other promoters sprang into action, advertising schemes for wheels of perpetual motion, for making salt water fresh, "for carrying on an undertaking of great advantage, but nobody to know what it is." The gullibility of the investing public was remarkable, but it was not inexhaustible. South Sea shares fell to £880 in August, 1720, and to £150 in September. Parliament ordered an investigation and, to protect the company's creditors, seized the estates of its directors, who had meantime destroyed the company's books and fled the country.

The two bubbles produced some unfortunate results. The collapse of the Mississippi scheme ruined Law, whose talents, if used more discreetly, might have revitalized the French economy. In England, the South Sea fiasco long impeded the development of new stock companies, which were henceforth required to buy costly charters. It tarnished the reputations of many in high places. The mistresses

London during the South Sea Bubble. The hunchback is hiring himself out as a desk.

of George I and the King himself had been "let in on the ground floor" in return for endorsing the venture enthusiastically, and more than a hundred members of Parliament had borrowed money from the company in order to buy its shares on the installment plan.

The bubbles were by no means total misfortunes. They were an acute instance of the economic growing pains suffered as the states of Europe groped for solutions to baffling financial problems. Voltaire later correctly observed that Law's "imaginary system gave birth to a real commerce," and released French business from the torpor induced by the defeats of Louis XIV. The Mississippi Company, reorganized after 1720, consistently made a handsome profit. In England, the South Sea Bubble scarcely affected the strongest institutions. The East India Company continued to pay an annual dividend of 5 to 10 per cent. The Bank of England, no longer competing with the South Sea Company for government favors, became more than ever the financial mainstay of the realm. In the political shake-up following the Bubble, the Whig statesman, Robert Walpole (see pp. 282–283), came to power with a program of honoring the debt as a *national* debt. This was a novel concept and a great step forward in fiscal morality in an age when most states still treated their debts as the monarch's personal obligation, to be acknowledged or repudiated as he saw fit.

The Agricultural Revolution

The agricultural revolution, the second of the forces transforming the modern economy, centered on improvements that enabled fewer farmers to produce more crops. The application of technological discoveries to agriculture was an old story, as old as the irrigation ditches of ancient Mesopotamia and the improved plows and horse-collars of the Middle Ages. What was new and revolutionary in the eighteenth century was the accelerating tempo of the advance in farming techniques.

The leaders of the movement were the "improving landlords" of England, who often owed much to innovators on the Continent. Jethro Tull (1674–1741), for example, studied French truck-gardens and vineyards, where farmers obtained heavy yields from small plots by planting seeds individually and by carefully hoeing the soil around each plant and vine. Tull adapted French methods to the much larger grain fields of England. In place of the inefficient custom of scattering seed broadcast, he planted it deeply in regular rows with a horse-drawn "drilling" machine, and he cultivated his crops with a horse-drawn hoe. Viscount Townshend (1674–1738) experimented with two new crops brought in from Holland, turnips and clover. The former made it possible to feed all the livestock until the arrival of the spring pasturing season, and thus to avoid the customary slaughter of stock

at the onset of winter. Clover, by fixing nitrogen in the soil, increased the fertility of the land and curtailed the old practice of letting fields lie fallow every third year. "Turnip" Townshend's four-year rotation—planting the same field to turnips, barley, clover, and wheat, in successive years—soon became standard on many English estates.

The improvements of Tull and Townshend won enthusiastic praise from Arthur Young (1741–1820), the articulate publicist of the new agriculture, who reported at length on his frequent trips throughout the farming districts of the British Isles and part of the Continent. Young won an international following that included George III, George Washington, the Marquis de Lafayette, and Catherine the Great. Before 1789, however, the new agriculture gained the support of only the most enterprising landlords, and even in Britain it appealed chiefly to the holders of large estates.

The agricultural revolution of the eighteenth century, uneven though it was, marked an important stage in the long, gradual shift from the largely self-sufficient manor of the Middle Ages to the modern capitalist farm producing specialized crops. The improving landlords needed large amounts of capital, and they also needed large plots of land that were not subdivided into long narrow strips for individual cultivators or otherwise used in common by many individuals. Since these old ways hampered the new agriculture, there was a mounting demand that common fields be fenced off as the private lands of single proprietors. Enclosures, which in Tudor days were introduced to extend sheep pastures, were now aimed to increase crop land. The new enclosure movement reached its peak in the last decades of the eighteenth century and the first decades of the nineteenth, when Parliament passed hundreds of separate enclosure acts affecting several million acres. Rural England was assuming its modern aspect of large fields fenced by hedgerows.

Enclosures, then, created large farms well suited to the application of drill-planting, horse-hoeing, and crop rotation. They enabled Britain to feed her growing population by increasing her agricultural output. But they also created widespread social misery. In Georgian England, as in ancient Greece and Rome, the development of capitalistic estates ruined many small farmers, or yeomen, who could not get along without their rights to use common lands and who could not afford to buy tools, install fences, and become improving landlords themselves. Many of them became hired hands on big farms or sought work in the expanding towns.

The Beginnings
of the Industrial Revolution

By increasing productivity and at the same time releasing part of the agricultural labor force for jobs off the farm, the agricultural revolution was assisting the industrial revolution. Industry also required raw materials, markets for its manufactures, and capital to finance the building and equipping of factories. The raw materials and the markets were supplied in part by the colonies overseas, and the capital in part by merchants. Thus the commercial revolution, too, assisted the industrial revolution.

In textiles, the making of yarn and cloth had long been organized under the "domestic system." Spinners or weavers worked at home on simple wheels or looms; often they did not buy their own raw materials or market their finished products but worked as wage-laborers for an entrepreneur who furnished the raw materials and sold the finished yarn and cloth. In some industries, however, production was organized not under the domestic system but in primitive factories, which assembled many laborers in a large workshop, though still relying on hand processes rather than on machines. These early factories were particularly common in enterprises utilizing expen-

Eighteenth-century grinders at work, as illustrated in the *Encyclopédie*.

sive materials, like gold or silver threads for luxury cloth, or requiring close supervision for reasons of state, like cannon foundries.

The industrial revolution made the domestic system obsolete and transformed the factory system. Machines superseded simple hand tools, like the spinning-wheel and the home loom, and water or steam replaced human muscles and animal energy as the source of power. Because power-driven machines were often big, complicated, and costly, larger factories were needed to house them. By 1789, these revolutionary changes had affected only a few industries, but they were key industries — mining, metallurgy, munitions, and textiles.

Coal-mining was becoming a big business, largely because of the increased demand for coke by iron-smelters. Smelters had always used charcoal to make iron from ore, and they continued to do so in countries like Sweden that had abundant wood for charcoal. But in England, where most of the great forests had been cut down, the price of charcoal rose so high that it constituted 80 per cent of the cost of producing iron. By 1750, despite the abundant native supply of ore, the output of English smelters was declining rapidly, and the country was using more and more imported iron. Ordinary coal could not replace charcoal as smelter fuel because the chemicals in coal made the iron too brittle. Here necessity mothered invention, as the Darby family of Shropshire discovered how to remove the chemical impurities from coal by an oven process that converted it into coke, which was almost pure carbon.

In England, the Darbys and other private firms were the pioneers in metallurgy. On the Continent, governments took the lead — a significant exception to the rule about the inability of states to solve economic problems. Warfare required weapons and munitions in large quantities; France and Prussia met the demand by setting up state-financed and state-operated foundries and arms factories.

The revolution in textiles was focused on the cheaper production of cotton cloth. The "flying shuttle," a technical device first applied to the hand loom in England (1733), enabled a single weaver to do work that had previously required the services of two. Looms equipped with the flying shuttle used up the supply of hand-spun thread so rapidly that the London Society for the Encouragement of Arts, Manufactures, and Commerce offered a prize for improvement of the spinning process. James Hargreaves won the prize in 1764 with his "spinning jenny," a series of spinning wheels geared together which made eight threads simultaneously. Soon the jenny was adapted to water power, and its output was increased to a hundred or more threads at once. The eventual emancipation of industry from dependence on unreliable water power was foreshadowed in the 1760's when the Scotsman, James Watt, introduced the steam engine.

Although Britain had nearly 150 cotton mills in 1789, woolens and dozens of other basic commodities were still made by hand. Full industrial development would not take place until the canal and railroad permitted cheap transport of heavy freight and until the shortages of capital and skilled labor were overcome. A Swedish inventor of the early 1700's designed excellent machines for cutting wheels and files but could not raise the money to put them into operation. And in Britain the difficulty of making precise parts for Watt's engine delayed its production in large quantities. While the eighteenth century had taken many of the initial steps in the industrial revolution, it remained for the next century to apply them on a truly revolutionary scale (see Chapter 12).

The Assets of Britain

Leadership in the economic revolutions was making Britain the wealthiest nation in the world. British bankers, buttressed by the Bank of England and by the careful management of the national debt, extended credit to business enterprises at the relatively low interest rate of 5 per cent. The City, the square mile comprising the City of London proper and including the financial district, recovered quickly from the South Sea Bubble and challenged Amsterdam's position as the international capital of trade and finance. In the course of the eighteenth century, British merchants outdistanced their old trading rivals, the Dutch, and gradually took the lead over their new competitors, the French. Judged by the three touchstones of mercantilism—commerce, colonies, and sea power—Britain was the strongest state in Europe.

The British colonial empire, however, was not a mercantilist undertaking in the full sense. Supervision of the colonies rested with a government department, the Board of Trade, which followed an easygoing policy contrasting with the rigid controls exerted by other colonial powers over their possessions. This was the famous policy of "salutary neglect." In the long run, as the American Revolution was to show, "salutary neglect" did not satisfy the colonists, but in the short run it worked reasonably well by promoting the colonists' prosperity and self-reliance.

The Royal Navy enjoyed the assets of a superior officer corps and greater size. Future captains went to sea at the age of sixteen, or even younger, and passed through long practical training before receiving commissions. The ships they commanded in the mid-century wars were inferior in design to those of France and Spain; but there were more of them. Britain had a 2 to 1 advantage over France in number of warships, a 6 to 1 lead in merchant ships, and a 10 to 1 lead in total number of experienced seamen, merchant and naval. In wartime, the fleet could draw on the merchant marine for additional sailors and auxiliary vessels. Service in the Royal Navy had its grim aspects. Food was monotonous and unhealthy, and punishments included flogging and keel-hauling, in which the victim was dragged the length of the barnacle-encrusted keel. Since these were the common afflictions of all sailors in the eighteenth century, however, they did not put the British navy at a comparative disadvantage.

The British army, by contrast, was neither large nor impressive. Its officers were reputed to be the poorest in Europe, and its soldiers were in part mercenaries from the German state of Hesse-Cassel, the Hessians of the American Revolutionary War. Neglect of the army was a deliberate policy. The British Isles were relatively safe from invasion; moreover, statesmen feared that a standing army might become an instrument of potential absolutism, for they remembered the uses that Cromwell and James II had made of this weapon.

The Glorious Revolution, which had done so much to confirm distrust of the army, had also confirmed Britain's unique and greatest asset—the supremacy of Parliament over the King. Parliament had approved the accession of William and Mary in place of James II; when Anne, Mary's sister and the last Stuart monarch, died in 1714, Parliament had already arranged for the succession of the House of Hanover. Under the first kings of the new house—George I (1714–1727) and George II (1727–1760)—the institution that was to assure the everyday assertion of parliamentary supremacy was undergoing steady development. This was the cabinet.

Cabinet Government

Today the British cabinet is a committee of the majority party of the House of Commons, headed by the prime minister, and it remains in office as long as it can continue to enlist the support of a majority in Commons. It is "Her Majesty's Government," while the chief minority party forms "Her Majesty's Opposition," a loyal opposition whose leader receives an official salary. The cabinet rules because it controls the executive branch of the government; the monarch merely reigns.

Under the first two Hanoverian kings the cabinet was only starting to accumulate this immense authority. George I and George II by no means abdicated all the old royal prerogatives. They took a direct interest in the South Sea Bubble and other financial matters, and they intervened in the conduct of war and diplomacy to a degree that would be regarded as highly improper today. George II was the last English monarch to command troops in person on the battlefield—in 1743 during the War of the Austrian Succession. The two Georges chose their cabinet ministers from the Whig party, then in control of the Commons. They did so, however, not because they were obliged to, which would be the case to-day, but because it suited their convenience, and, even more, because they really had no choice. They thoroughly distrusted the other party, the Tories, some of whom were involved in futile Jacobite plots to restore to the throne the descendants of James II (Jacobite from Jacobus, Latin for James). The Whigs, on the other hand, had engineered the Glorious Revolution and had arranged the Hanoverian succession.

For two decades after the collapse of the South Sea Bubble, from 1721 to 1742, Robert Walpole, who led the Whigs in the Commons, headed the cabinet; he was in fact prime minister, although the title was not yet official.

The House of Commons in the eighteenth century, by Hogarth. Walpole is at the left.

Walpole was a master politician who maintained his majority in the Commons by skillful manipulation of the Whigs. The task was not easy, for party discipline of the modern kind did not exist; the terms "Whig" and "Tory" referred to informal and shifting interest groups, not to parties in our sense. In 1733, when Walpole forced the resignation of ministers opposed to his plan for radical fiscal reform, he took a major step toward establishing the principle of cabinet unanimity on a crucial issue.

Under the first two Georges the Whigs were a coalition of landed gentry and "funded" gentry; that is, of nobles and squires from the country and of businessmen from London and provincial towns. Thus the Whigs renewed a political alliance that had first appeared in the later Middle Ages when the knights of the shire had joined the burgesses to form the Commons. In the Whig parliaments the country gentlemen predominated by sheer numbers; in 1754, for instance, they outnumbered by 5 to 1 the merchants and lawyers sitting in the House of Commons. Family ties, common political aims, and a common reverence for property bound together the rural and urban Whigs. In order to consolidate the gains of the Glorious Revolution, the Whigs opposed Jacobite schemes and supported the unprepossessing Hanoverians. To protect their property, they passed legislation making death the penalty for stealing livestock, for cutting down cherry trees, and for other relatively minor offenses.

Exactly what did terms like "gentry," "gentlemen," and "squire" mean in the eighteenth century with respect to social class? Historians are still debating the question, but it is generally agreed that they referred to a class just below the titled nobility. The ranks of the gentry included the younger sons of nobles, technically not nobles themselves since the title and a seat in the House of Lords passed to the eldest son. They also included other owners of landed estates, all of whom were addressed verbally as "sir" and in writing as "Esquire," originally a shield-bearer, the lieutenant of the feudal knight. Historically, the gentry lived off the revenues of landed property, but by the eighteenth century many of them also had a stake in the commercial revolution. Indeed, successful businessmen sometimes bought country estates, set themselves up as gentlemen, and were accepted as such by the local gentry. The intermingling of country gentlemen with men of business and intermarriage of the two classes demonstrated that Britain enjoyed more social mobility than did the states of the Old Régime on the Continent.

Robert Walpole himself exemplified the Whig fusion of landed and funded elements. He inherited his manners and his tastes from his father, a country squire. A heavy drinker, and an inveterate teller of bawdy stories in mixed company, he fixed the English politician's tradition of the long country weekend in order to indulge his passion for hunting. Like many Whig squires, Walpole married into the aristocracy of trade; his wife was the daughter of a timber merchant and former Lord Mayor of London. As prime minister, Walpole, the country gentleman, promoted the interests of the City. His basic policy supported the City's program of financial stability through the gradual retirement of the national debt, and political stability through Whig cabinets.

In social and political structure, the Britain of Walpole was, of course, oligarchical rather than democratic. Only gentlemen could hope to rise in the professions, to become army and navy officers, lawyers, clergymen, and physicians. In local affairs, the landed gentry alone supplied the justices of the peace, who not only presided over courts, but also fixed wage scales, superintended the relief of the poor, provided for the maintenance of bridges and highways, and were in general the despots of the English countryside. Fanatic defenders of the propertied classes, the justices of the peace inspired the saying that "You may as well be hanged for [stealing] a sheep as a lamb."

In the main, only gentlemen had the right to vote for members of Parliament. The small number of voters in many constituencies encouraged corruption, particularly in the "rotten" or "pocket" boroughs, which had such a tiny electorate that control of their vote reposed in the pocket of some wealthy lord. Politicians often bribed voters outright or else promised them places on the government payroll. An immensely rich Whig, the Duke of Newcastle, controlled the outcome of elections in four counties and in seven pocket boroughs.

In Britain, as on the Continent, the ruling classes governed the voteless masses. But the British ruling classes, selfish and narrow-minded though they often were, had at their best a sense of *noblesse oblige*, of public spirit and civic-mindedness. Within the aristocracy of land and trade there were fewer social barriers than on the Continent, and the English gentry were on the whole more responsive than their continental counterparts to the need for changes and reform. Disraeli, the great nineteenth-century Tory, dubbed the Whig cabinets of the first two Georges a "Venetian oligarchy," by which he meant that the wealthy ran the country for their private benefit, like the merchants of Renaissance Venice. And so they did; yet the Whigs, for all their oligarchy and corruption, provided the most enlightened government in eighteenth-century Europe.

The Liabilities of France

Where Britain was strong, France was weak. In the France of Louis XV (1715–1774), barriers to social mobility were more difficult to surmount, though commoners who were rich or aggressive enough did overcome them. France suffered particularly from the rigidity of its colonial system, the inferiority of its navy, and the very mediocre abilities of most of its statesmen. The Ministry of the Navy, which ruled the overseas empire, regarded these possessions as so many warships permanently at anchor. It refused to sanction steps toward self-government and applied the same regulations to colonies as different as the sugar islands of the West Indies and the wilderness of Canada. Under these policies, the mother country prospered, but the colonies languished. Commercial activity doubled in Nantes, Bordeaux, and other ports; refineries grew up to process the raw sugar imported from the plantations of Guadeloupe and Martinique. Overseas, the plethora of controls, however, stifled the initiative of the colonists, and the French imperial system lacked the elasticity to meet the test of war.

The French navy needed greater resources and better leadership. Its warships, though admirably designed, were inadequate in number. Since Dutch and British vessels carried much of French commerce, the merchant marine was too small to supplement the fleet. French naval officers, though rigorously trained in the classroom, lacked the experience gained by British captains in a lifetime at sea. Moreover, in a fashion characteristic of the Old Régime at its worst, officers from the aristocracy devoted much of their energies to thwarting the rise of those from the middle class.

French rulers were almost bound to neglect the navy in favor of the army, since France was above all a land power, and its vulnerable northeastern frontier, lying across the Flemish plain, invited invasion. Except in size, however, the army of Louis XV scarcely lived up to the great traditions of Louis XIV. The troops were poorly trained, and the organization was top-heavy. There was one officer to fifteen men, as compared with one to thirty-five in the more efficient Prussian army. Many aristocratic officers regarded a commission simply as a convenient way of increasing their personal wealth.

Both the navy and the army underwent important reforms after 1763 and the defeats suffered by France in the Seven Years' War (see p. 308). The number of warships was increased, the officer corps of the army was cleared of much dead wood, and more aggressive military tactics were introduced. These improvements accounted in part for the excellent showing made by France in the American Revolutionary War and in the military campaigns resulting from her own revolution. They came too late, however, to save the vanishing prestige of the Old Régime.

The Old Régime was weakest at its head, the monarchy itself. There were no "sun kings" in France after the death of Louis XIV, and few ministers who approached the caliber of Richelieu or Colbert. The Duke of Orléans, the Regent from 1715 to 1723, was a gambler, drunkard, and pervert, who popularized the word "roue" by remarking that his friends deserved to be broken on the wheel (*roué* is French for wheel). The Regent, however, did attempt two important experiments. He allowed John Law to try out his "system," as we have seen, and, in place of Louis XIV's method of ruling through individual bourgeois ministers, he set up a series of ministerial councils staffed by men from the most distinguished noble families of the realm. Although the first experiment produced some beneficial results, the second failed, after a three-year trial, in part because of the endless squabbles among the noble councillors. The French second estate had outlived its usefulness. The Regency proved that the nobles were no longer able to govern; the mid-century wars proved that they were no longer able to lead French armies to victory.

Soon after the regency of Orléans, power passed to one of the few statesmen of prerevolutionary France, Cardinal Fleury, the tutor of Louis XV and the chief minister from 1726 until his death in 1743 in his ninetieth year. Without attempting basic reforms, the aged Cardinal, in the words of Voltaire, "treated the state as a powerful and robust body which could cure itself." Fleury did not remedy the chronic and deep-seated injustice and inefficiency of French fiscal methods. But he did stabilize the coinage, and he put the farming of taxes on a more businesslike basis by restricting tax-farmers to the comparatively modest profit of 7½ per cent. To make loans more readily available, he established state pawnshops in the chief cities of France. Fleury's success impressed Lady Mary Montagu, the observant wife of an English diplomat, who wrote in 1739:

France is so much improved, it is not . . . the same country we passed through twenty years ago. Everything I see speaks in praise of Cardinal Fleury; the roads are all mended . . . and such good care taken against robbers, that you may cross the country with your purse in your hand. . . . The French are more changed than their roads; instead of pale, yellow faces, wrapped up in blankets, as we saw them, the villages are filled with fresh-coloured lusty peasants, in good cloth and clean linen. It is

The Marquise de Pompadour, by Quentin de la Tour. The range of her interests is indicated by the sheet music in her hands and by the books on the table, including Montesquieu's *Spirit of the Laws* and a volume of the *Encyclopédie*.

incredible the air of plenty and content that is over the whole country.*

The administrative stability achieved by Fleury soon vanished after Louis XV began his personal rule in 1743. Intelligent but timid, lazy, and debauched, Louis XV did not have the interest or the patience to supervise the details of government in the manner of Louis XIV. He appointed and dismissed ministers on a personal whim or at the bidding of his mistresses and favorites. In thirty years he had 18 different foreign secretaries, and 14 different controllers-general (the chief fiscal officer). Each change in personnel meant a shift in policy, and Louis aggravated the instability by conspiring against his own appointees.

*Letters, Everyman ed. (New York, 1906), 271–272.

France had two conflicting foreign policies: that of the diplomatic corps; and the "King's Secret," conducted by royal agents who operated at cross purposes with the regular diplomats. Louis XV, while allowing the reins of government to go slack, yet refused to give them over to firmer hands.

Nevertheless, France remained a great power. Still the most populous country in Europe, she contained almost inexhaustible reserves of strength. Her army, though enfeebled, was the largest in the world, and her navy was the second largest. She led the world in overseas trade until Britain forged ahead of her in the last quarter of the eighteenth century. French tastes, French thought, and the French language retained the international pre-eminence won in the age of Louis XIV. The misgovernment and the other weaknesses of the Old Régime were relative rather than absolute.

The Other Western States

Spain was the only other state in western Europe with a claim to great-power status. War and its aftermath had put an end to the major international roles played by Sweden and the Dutch Republic during the seventeenth century. The Great Northern War (see pp. 295–296) ruined the Baltic empire of Sweden and killed off the flower of Swedish manhood. The Dutch, exhausted by their wars against Louis XIV, were losing their commercial leadership and could no longer afford a large navy or an independent foreign policy. Eighteenth-century Holland, in the phrase of Frederick the Great, was often a "cockboat in the tow of the English frigate."

Spain, by contrast, suffered comparatively little damage from the great war over the succession to her throne that was fought in the early 1700's. The loss of Belgium and parts of Italy at the Utrecht settlement of 1713 reduced the unwieldy Spanish domains to more manageable size. The new Bourbon kings were a marked improvement over the last Spanish Habsburgs. Philip V (1700–1746), the first of the Spanish Bourbons, infused fresh life into the country's fossilized institutions by importing French advisers schooled in the system of Louis XIV. He also enlisted the aid of two able adventurers. Alberoni and Ripperdá,

whose fantastic careers almost outdid John Law's. Alberoni, the son of an Italian gardener, was successively a cook, a diplomat, the chief minister of Spain, and a cardinal. Ripperdá, a Dutch business expert and diplomat, ultimately lost the favor of Philip, entered the service of the Sultan of Morocco, and, after a lifelong alternation between the Protestant and Catholic faiths, died a Moslem. Philip and his remarkable advisers cut down the excessive formalities and endless delays of Spanish administration. They reasserted the authority of the monarchy over the traditionally powerful nobility and clergy. They improved the tax system, encouraged textiles and other industries, built up the navy, and fortified strategic points in the Spanish empire in America.

The new dispensation, however, did not strike at the root causes of Spanish decline. The greed of governors and the restrictions of mercantilism still checked the progress of the colonies. The mother country remained impoverished, burdened with reactionary noble and clerical castes, and hampered by inadequate resources. Philip V himself was neurotic, refusing, for instance, to cut his toenails which grew so long that he limped. He was dominated by his strong-willed second wife, Elizabeth Farnese, the patroness of Alberoni. Since Philip's son by his first marriage would inherit Spain, Elizabeth was determined to find thrones for her own two sons. Her persistent attempts to secure the succession of Italian states for them repeatedly threatened the peace of Europe.

III   Italy and Germany

Disunited Italy

By 1715, the Italian states had lost much of the political and economic power they had enjoyed during the Renaissance. It is easy to see why. The opening of new worlds overseas

and the rise of Spain, England, and the other Atlantic powers had diminished the importance of the Mediterranean. In the Mediterranean itself, the Ottoman Turks and their satellites in North Africa long menaced Italian shipping and trade. Moreover, beginning with the French invasion of 1494, Italy had been threatened with conquest by one of the new national monarchies.

The Spanish Habsburgs made the conquest. For almost two centuries Spain ruled Milan, Naples, and Sicily directly, and dominated the rest of the peninsula. In the readjustment of the European balance in 1713, Italy exchanged one foreign master for another, as the Austrian Habsburgs took over the Italian possessions of their Spanish cousins. On the completion of the readjustment in 1720, the political map of the peninsula showed Austria established in Lombardy, flanked by the decaying commercial republics of Venice and Genoa. In the mountainous northwest was the small but rising state of Piedmont-Savoy, technically the Kingdom of Sardinia after its acquisition of that island in 1720. Farther down the peninsula were the Grand Duchy of Tuscany (formerly the Republic of Florence), the Papal States, and the Austrian Two Sicilies. None of these states was more than a minor power.

Yet Italy could not be written off as a negligible quantity in the eighteenth century. Rome remained the capital of Catholicism, Venice still produced fine painters, and Naples was the schoolmaster of European musicians. Lombardy, Tuscany, and Naples all contributed to the economic and intellectual advances of the century. Meantime, Italy was a major stake in balance-of-power politics, a perennial source of dissension and spoils. In 1720, to counter the ambitions of the Spanish queen, Elizabeth Farnese, the Austrian Habsburgs took over the island of Sicily, which had gone to Piedmont in the Utrecht settlement; in return, Piedmont secured Sardinia, originally assigned to Austria. In the 1730's, a series of exchanges gave the Two Sicilies to Elizabeth's elder son, "Baby Carlos," while the Austrians gained some minor bits of territory and the succession of Tuscany. In 1768, Genoa sold the island of Corsica to France. Italy was, in the old phrase, merely "a geographical expression," not a political whole but a series of parts to be shifted and exchanged by ambitious dynasts and empire-builders from outside the peninsula.

Divided Germany: The Habsburg Dominions

In some ways Germany deserved even more to be called a geographical expression, for it was divided into three hundred states, large, small, and minute. The Thirty Years' War had caused wide devastation, and the Peace of Westphalia ending the war in 1648 had enhanced the sovereign rights of the individual German states and reduced virtually to zero the authority of their nominal overlord, the Holy Roman Emperor. Unlike Italy, however, Germany did include two considerable powers, Austria and Prussia.

The Austrian Habsburgs won a series of military and diplomatic victories in the two decades before 1715. In 1699, by the peace of Karlovitz, they recovered Hungary from the Ottoman Turks, thereby advancing their own *Drang nach Osten*. In 1713, though they failed to keep the old Habsburg crown of Spain from going to the Bourbon Philip V, they received handsome compensation in Belgian and Italian territories. Yet these last acquisitions were distant from the main bloc of Habsburg lands in central Europe.

Charles VI (1711–1740), aware that his title of Holy Roman Emperor conferred little real authority, concentrated on the Habsburg family possessions. He spent much of his reign persuading his own noble subjects to ratify the Pragmatic Sanction, a constitutional agreement whereby, in the absence of sons, his daughter Maria Theresa would succeed him in all his lands. A good deal of scorn has been directed at Charles for devoting so much time and energy to a scrap of paper, but recent historians have noted that the Pragmatic Sanction did indeed establish the principle of linking together the scattered family territories. Much, however, remained to be done to consolidate Habsburg rule over an assemblage of lands which represented many different nations and could never be forged into a single national monarchy. In three key national areas

—German Austria, Czech Bohemia, and Magyar Hungary—the nobles still kept most of their medieval prerogatives and, by controlling local estates and diets, controlled grants of taxes and the appointment of officials. The financial and military weakness of the Habsburg regime is suggested by the fact that when Charles VI died, in 1740, the pay of the army and of the civil service was more than two years in arrears. Small wonder that the army fell short of its paper strength of 100,000 men as it faced the great test of strength with Prussia that came in 1740.

The Rise of Prussia

Whereas Austria enjoyed the appearances rather than the realities of great-power status, Prussia possessed few of the appearances but a great many of the realities. Its territories were scattered across North Germany from the Rhine on the west to the Vistula and beyond on the east; consisting largely of sand and swamp, these lands had meager natural resources and carried on relatively little trade. With less than three million inhabitants, Prussia ranked only twelfth among the European states in population. Her capital city, Berlin, located on the unimportant River Spree, had few of the obvious geographical advantages enjoyed by Constantinople, Paris, London, and the other great capitals. A wise prophet in 1600 might well have foreseen that Catholic Austria would never unite a Germany in which Protestantism was so strong. But he would probably have predicted that a new Germany would center in Frankfurt in the heart of the Rhine country, or in Saxon Leipzig or Dresden; he would hardly have chosen the unpromising town of Berlin and the minor house of Hohenzollern.

The Hohenzollerns had been established since the fifteenth century as Electors of Brandenburg, which lay between the Elbe and Oder rivers. A Hohenzollern was the last Master of the Teutonic Knights, a crusading order which in the thirteenth century had pushed the Germanic frontier beyond the Vistula to

a land called Prussia at the southeast corner of the Baltic Sea. In 1618, when this Prussian area fell to the Hohenzollerns, it was separated from Brandenburg by Polish territory and was still nominally a fief held from the Polish king. In western Germany, meantime (1614), the Hohenzollerns acquired Cleves, Mark, and some other parcels in the lower Rhine valley. Thus, when Frederick William, the Great Elector (1640–1688), succeeded to the Hohenzollern inheritance as the Thirty Years' War was drawing to a close, his lands consisted of a nucleus in Brandenburg with separate outlying regions to east and west. With extraordinary persistence, the rulers of Brandenburg-Prussia for the next two hundred years devoted themselves to the task of making a solid block of territory out of these bits and pieces.

The Great Elector was the first in a line of able Hohenzollern rulers. In foreign policy, he won recognition from Poland as the full sovereign of Prussia, no longer subject to Polish overlordship. He also tried, with less success, to dislodge the Swedes from the Pomeranian territories, between Brandenburg and the Baltic, which they had acquired in 1648. Though he won military renown by defeating the Swedes at Fehrbellin in 1675, he made few practical gains because of his own tortuous diplomacy. In the wars against Louis XIV, he shifted repeatedly from the French to the anti-French side and back.

In his domestic policy, he made more substantial accomplishments. He had found his domains largely ruined by war, the farms wasted, the population cut in half, the army reduced to a disorderly rabble of a few thousand men. The Great Elector repaired the damage thoroughly. To augment the population, he encouraged the immigration of Polish Jews and other refugees from religious persecution, notably 20,000 French Huguenots to whom he gave partial exemption from taxation. He built a small but efficient standing army that enabled Prussia to command large foreign subsidies for participating in the campaigns for or against Louis XIV. In peacetime, he assigned the soldiers to the construc-

Growth of Prussia, 1740 to 1795

- Prussian territory at accession of Frederick the Great, 1740
- Territory acquired 1740-1786
- Territory acquired 1786-1795
- Boundary of the Empire, 1786

SWEDEN

COURLAND

Baltic Sea

Memel

Niemen R.

DENMARK

North Sea

EAST PRUSSIA

Konigsberg

Danzig

E. FRIESLAND

(to Sweden)

POMERANIA

WEST PRUSSIA

NEW EAST PRUSSIA

Stettin

Elbe R.

BRANDENBURG

Berlin

Posen

SOUTH PRUSSIA

Warsaw

Bug R.

NETHERLANDS

MINDEN

Magdeburg

P O L A N D

CLEVES

RAVENSBERG

Weser R.

Breslau

MARK

Ems R.

S I L E S I A

AUSTRIAN NETHERLANDS

T H E   E M P I R E

Rhine R.

Elbe R.

Oder R.

Cracow

Vistula R.

BAYREUTH

BOHEMIA

MORAVIA

FRANCE

ANSBACH

Danube R.

| 0 | 100 | 200 |

Miles

---

tion of public works like the canal between the Elbe and the Oder.

In administration, the Great Elector fixed the Hohenzollern pattern of militarized absolutism, a policy in which he was assisted by an educational tradition and a Lutheran state church that taught the virtues of obedience and discipline. On his accession, he found that in all three territories—Prussia, Brandenburg, and Cleves-Mark—the authority of the ruler was limited by Estates, medieval assemblies representing the landed nobles and the townspeople. In all three territories he battled the Estates for supremacy and won, thereby delaying for two centuries the introduction of representative government into the Hohen-

zollern realm. He gradually gathered into his own hands the crucial power of levying taxes. Much of the actual work of collecting taxes and performing other administrative functions was done by the War Office and the army; even policing was executed by the military. Like Louis XIV, the Great Elector reduced the power of the aristocracy; unlike Louis, however, he relied not on bourgeois officials but on a working alliance with the landed gentry, particularly the celebrated Junkers of Prussia proper. He confirmed the Junkers' absolute authority over the serfs on their estates and their preponderance over the towns, and he encouraged them to serve the state, especially as army officers. In contrast to other mon-

289

archies, the absolutism of the Hohenzollerns rested on the co-operation of the sovereign and the aristocracy, not on their mutual antagonism.

Under the Great Elector's son, Frederick I (1688–1713), Prussia played only a minor role in the great wars that humbled Louis XIV and made few territorial gains in the Utrecht settlement. But in 1701 the Elector Frederick made a significant gain in prestige by assuming the title "King in Prussia" and insisting on international recognition of his new status as the price for his entry into the War of the Spanish Succession. Though technically Frederick was king only in Prussia proper, which lay outside the boundaries of the Holy Roman Empire, even a limited royal title conferred new dignity on the Hohenzollerns. In living up to his new eminence, however, King Frederick I nearly bankrupted his state by lavish expenditures on the trappings of monarchy. Since he thought that a suggestion of marital infidelity enhanced the majesty of a king, he maintained an official mistress with whom he took decorous afternoon promenades. Actually, he was happily married, and his talented queen enlivened the provincial Hohenzollern court by inviting intellectuals and artists to Berlin. As Frederick the Great later remarked, under Frederick I Berlin was the "Athens of the north."

Frederick William I

But as Frederick the Great also remarked, under the next king, Frederick William I (1713–1740), Berlin became the "Sparta of the north." The flirtation with luxury and the finer things of life proved to be a passing exception to the usual Hohenzollern rule of austerity. Frederick William I returned with a vengeance to the policies of the Great Elector and devoted himself entirely to economy, absolutism, and the army. As soon as he had given his father a lavish funeral, he dismissed most of the officials of the court, converted a large portion of the royal palace into offices, and reduced governmental expenses to a

One of the giant soldiers of Frederick William I of Prussia.

fraction of what they had been. He reiterated the order "*Ein Plus Machen*" (make a surplus), and he bequeathed a full treasury to his son. His frugality enabled him to undertake the occasional project that he thought really worth while. Thus he financed the immigration of 12,000 South German Protestants to open up new farm lands in eastern Prussia.

To strengthen royal control over the apparatus of state, Frederick William I instituted a small board of experts, with the wonderful German title of *Generaloberfinanzkriegsund- domänendirektorium* (General Superior Finance, War, and Domain Directory). The members of the General Directory were charged both with administering departments of the central government and with supervising the provinces. The arrangement, while cumbersome, did detach provincial administration from local interests and bring it under closer royal control. The King insisted on hard work and punctuality. He treated the counselors of the General Directory as he treated lesser officials, paying them meanly and belaboring them with his cane for slovenly performance of their duties. A late arrival at one of the daily sessions of the General Directory paid a severe fine; an unexcused absentee faced six months in jail.

Frederick William I doubled the size of the standing army, but he maintained the strength of the laboring force of his underpopulated state by furloughing troops for nine months a year to work on farms. To secure guns and uniforms, he established state factories. The army also prompted his sole extravagance—a regiment of tall grenadiers, all six feet or over, who wore special caps more than a foot high to increase the impression of size. In recruiting his beloved "giants," the king threw economy to the winds, employing scores of scouts in other German states, paying exorbitant prices, and even trading royal musicians and prize stallions for especially tall specimens. Frederick William cherished his army too much to undertake an adventurous foreign policy. His only significant military campaign was against Sweden in the last phase of the Great Northern War, whereby Prussia ob-

tained in 1720 part of Pomerania and also the important Baltic port of Stettin. Thus Frederick William advanced the Great Elector's old aim of liquidating the Swedish possessions in Germany.

Eighteenth-century observers rightly called the Prussia of Frederick William an "armed camp" and berated its army for being a "gigantic penal institution" in which minor infractions of regulations entailed the death penalty. The King himself, obsessed with military matters, showed scant concern for culture, neglected the education of his subjects, and despised everything French. He carried parsimony to the extreme of refusing pensions to soldiers' widows. The inadequate fees of judges and lawyers encouraged the corruption and lethargy that obstructed the course of justice in Prussia. Yet this régime worked and, in terms of power, worked extremely well. The Junkers, although feudal in outlook, were intensely loyal to the Hohenzollerns and made splendid officers. The army itself, though smaller than those of France, Russia, and Austria, was the best drilled and the most rigorously disciplined force in Europe. When Frederick William I died in 1740, the Prussian David was ready to fight the Austrian Goliath.

IV The Eastern Powers

The Early Years of Peter the Great

Even more spectacular than the rise of Prussia was the emergence of Russia as a major power during the era of Peter the Great (1682–1725). In 1682, at the death of Tsar Fedor Romanov, Russia was still a backward eastern European country, with few diplomatic links with the West, and very little knowledge of the outside world. Contemporaries, Russians as well as foreigners, report on the brutality, immorality, drunken-

ness, illiteracy, and filth prevalent among all classes of society. Even the clergy, most of whom could not read, set no shining example by their mode of life. It is perhaps little wonder that students familiar with conditions in Russia before the advent of Peter the Great have saluted him as the great revolutionary who altered the face of his country. Yet the changes he made were neither so numerous nor so drastic as his admirers have often claimed. Moreover, the foundations for most of them were already present in the society he inherited, and Russia would no doubt eventually have become a power of international importance without Peter, although it would have taken longer. Even if we accept all these dilutions of the usual estimate of his contribution, however, the fact remains that Peter was an awe-inspiring—and terror-inspiring—figure.

Tsar Fedor died childless in 1682, leaving a fifteen-year old brother, Ivan, who was partly blind and almost an idiot, and an ugly and capable sister, Sophia, both children of Tsar Alexis (1645–1676) by his first wife. The ten-year-old Peter was the half-brother of Ivan and Sophia, the son of Alexis by his second wife, and as bright and vigorous as Ivan was debilitated. A major court feud quickly developed between the partisans of the family of Alexis' first wife and those of the family of the second. At first the old Russian representative assembly, the *zemski sobor*, elected Peter as Tsar. But Sophia, as leader of the opposing faction, won the support of the *streltsy*, or musketeers, a special branch of the military, many of whom belonged to the conservative religious schismatics known as the Old Believers. Undisciplined, and angry with their officers, some of whom had been cheating them, the *streltsy* were a menace to orderly government.

Sophia and her supporters encouraged the *streltsy* to attack the Kremlin, and the youthful Peter saw the infuriated troops murdering some of his mother's family and racing through the palace in pursuit of the rest, stabbing the furniture with swords and spears. For good measure, they killed many of the nobles living in Moscow and pillaged the archives where the records of serfdom were kept. But, though their movement obviously had some social content, it was primarily a successful effort by Sophia to gain power. Sophia now became regent for both Ivan and Peter, who were hailed as joint Tsars.

But before her power was stabilized, she had to deal with the ungovernable *streltsy*, who terrorized the capital until threatened with open war by the regular army. Once the *streltsy* were calmed, Sophia moved to punish the Old Believers and any revolting serfs that could be captured. The first woman to govern Russia since Kievan times, Sophia was bound to face severe opposition. Even her supporters would not allow her to proclaim herself autocrat. And the maturing Peter, though out of favor and away from court, posed a threat to her position; in the end, the *streltsy* let her down. In 1689, Sophia was shut up in a convent, and Peter and Ivan ruled together until Ivan's death in 1696, although in practice Ivan never counted for anything.

The young Peter was almost seven feet tall, and extremely lively. Highly intelligent, he had learned to read and write (but never to spell) from a drunken tutor who was the only academic instructor the troubled times afforded. Even in his early years, Peter was fascinated by war and military games. He set up a play-regiment, staffed it with full-grown men, enlisted as a common soldier in its ranks (promoting himself from time to time), ordered equipment for it from the Moscow arsenals, and drilled it in war games with unflagging vigor, himself firing off cannon or pounding on a drum with equal enjoyment. He discovered a broken-down boat in a barn and unraveled the mysteries of rigging and sail with the help of Dutch sailors settled in the foreigners' suburb of Moscow. Sailing remained one of his keenest passions. Though he married at the age of sixteen, Peter neglected his wife and preferred working on his military maneuvers, sailing his boats, and relaxing with his peculiar circle of cronies.

This rowdy lot smoked huge quantities of tobacco (which horrified the conservative Muscovites, who believed that smoking was specifically forbidden by the Biblical text which says that what cometh out of the mouth defileth a man), and regularly got completely drunk. Then they would engage in obscene parodies of church services, or play elaborate and highly dangerous practical jokes on the unoffending citizenry, roaring about Moscow in winter late at night on sleighs and treating the sleeping populace to shrieking serenades. Masquerades and parties lasted for days; staid Moscow ladies, accustomed to almost harem-like seclusion, were commanded to put on low-necked evening dresses in the western style, and dance and engage in social chit-chat. They were literally forced to drink with the Tsar and his friends: If a lady refused, Peter simply held her nose, and poured the wine down her throat. Peter spent enormous sums of state revenue on this sort of party and richly endowed his boon companion Lefort, a young Swiss soldier of fortune who became Field Marshal, Grand Admiral, and "chief diplomat."

The almost frantic energy that Peter devoted to pleasure reflected only part of his appetite for new experience. Just as he served in the ranks of his own play-regiment and sailed his boats himself, so he eagerly learned any new technique that came to his attention. At various times he took up carpentry, shoe-making, cooking, clock-making, ivory-carving, etching, and—worst of all—dentistry. Once he had acquired a set of dentist's tools, nobody was safe, since Peter did not care whether the intended victim had a toothache or not; whenever he felt the need to practice, he practiced—and those were the days before anesthetics. Preferring to wear shabby work clothes, driving his own horses, neglecting formal obligations and paying little attention to court and church ceremony, Peter in his own person was a shock to the Muscovites, and not in the least in keeping with their idea of a proper tsar.

After Lefort died in 1700, Peter's favorite was Menshikov, a man of low birth, who received high offices, the title of Prince, and a huge fortune. Like many of the public servants of the period, he was an unscrupulous grafter. Peter wrote to Menshikov as "my brother," and, though he came to distrust him, he never ruined him as he did many other favorites. Meantime, Peter had his first wife shut up in a convent and made a nun. He later took on as mistress a girl from the Baltic region, who had already passed through the hands of Menshikov and others, and after some years of liaison with her, during which she gave birth to two of Peter's children, he finally married her in 1712. This was the Empress Catherine, a simple, hearty, affectionate woman, long devoted to her difficult husband, and able to control him as no other human being could. But again, one can understand the horrified reaction of the old-fashioned Russian noble.

The Western Trip

In 1695, anxious to try his hand at war, Peter led a campaign against the Turks at Azov in the area of the Black Sea. He failed, but in the next year, with the help of Dutch experts, he assembled a fleet of river-boats on the Don, sailed them downriver, and defeated the Turks at Azov. Since the Habsburgs at the time were waging a long war against the Turks, this rather surprising Russian contribution aroused much curiosity. The project of forming a league against the Turks with the states of western Europe now gave Peter the pretext for a trip outside Russia, the first undertaken by a Russian sovereign since the Kievan period.

Through ostensibly traveling incognito as a noncommissioned officer, Peter naturally failed to conceal his identity: After all, there were no other authoritarian seven-footers in the party. What fascinated him was western "know-how," especially naval. He planned to go to Holland, England, and Venice, where the best ships (in his opinion) were made, find out how they were made, and bring the knowledge back to Russia for the advancement of Russian aims. He hired several hundred technicians to work in Russia, raised money when he needed it by selling to an English peer the monopoly of tobacco sales in Russia, and visited every sort of factory or museum or printing press he could find. The huge Russian Tsar in all his vigor and crudity, emerging into the air of western Europe from his antiquated and stagnant country, made an unforgettable impression.

From this celebrated trip many well-known pictures emerge: Peter laboring as a common hand on the docks in Holland; Peter and his suite, drunk and dirty, wrecking the handsome house and garden of the English diarist, John Evelyn, near London: "There is a house full of people," wrote Evelyn's harassed servant, "and that right nasty." Less well known perhaps are the spectacles of Peter dancing with a German princess, mistaking her whalebone corsets for her ribs, and commenting loudly that German girls have devilish hard bones; of Peter receiving an honorary degree at Oxford; of Peter deep in conversation (Dutch) with William Penn about the Quaker faith; of Peter gobbling his food without benefit of knife or fork, or asleep with a dozen or so of his followers on the floor of a tiny room in a London inn with no windows open.

Before Peter could get to Venice, the western trip was interrupted by news that the *streltsy* had revolted again (1698). Peter rushed home and personally participated in the punishment of the alleged plotters; he and Menshikov rather enjoyed chopping off the heads of the victims. Though many innocent men suffered torture and death, Peter had broken the *streltsy* as a power in Russian domestic life.

From the West, Peter had returned more determined than ever to modernize his country and his countrymen. The very day of his return he summoned the court jester, and with his assistance went about with a great pair of shears, stopping his courtiers and clipping off their beards. Though this may seem a trivial joke, in fact it was an action full of symbolism. The tradition of the Orthodox Church held that God was bearded; if man was made in the image of God, man must also have a beard. Deprived of his beard, man was no longer made in God's image, and was a natural candidate for damnation. This was the way the Muscovite nobles and churchmen felt. Peter now decreed that Russian nobles must shave, or else pay a substantial tax for the privilege of wearing their beards. Bronze beard-tokens worn around the neck certified that the tax had been properly paid; without such a token a bearded man ran the risk of being clipped on sight.

Presently, Peter issued an edict commanding that all boyars, members of the gentry class, and the city population generally must abandon traditional Russian dress, which included long robes with flowing sleeves and tall bonnets, and adopt western-style costume. The manufacture of the old-fashioned clothes

was made illegal, and Peter added point to his decree by taking up his shears again and cutting off the sleeves of all the people he met wearing the forbidden robes. The enactments on the beards and on dress were regarded by the victims as an assult on precious customs and a forcible introduction of hated foreign ways.

Peter's Wars

War was Peter's greatest interest. We can understand his policies at home only after we realize how closely related they were to the virtually constant warfare of his reign, and to the ever-mounting need for money for fighting. On his way back to Russia in 1698, he discovered that the Austrians, instead of being eager to join him in a full-scale crusade against the Turks, were anxious to end their Turkish war. Irritated by the Austro-Turkish Peace of Karlovitz in 1699, which he felt to be a betrayal of Russia, Peter made a separate peace of his own with the Sultan in 1700. By this time, his plans for new aggression were already formed.

The victim was to be Sweden. Peter's allies, already signed up in 1699, were Denmark and Poland, the latter under its elected king, Augustus the Strong, who was also Elector of Saxony and who had become an intimate of Peter after their first meeting in 1698. The real engineer of the alliance and moving spirit of the war against Sweden was a nobleman named Patkul from the Baltic shore, deeply resentful of measures taken by the Swedes against the feudal proprietors of that area. Patkul went from interview to interview, holding out to Augustus and Peter the prospect that after they had defeated Sweden they might divide her Baltic territories. In 1697, the Swedish throne had descended to a youth of fifteen, King Charles XII, whom Peter, Augustus, and Patkul hoped they might easily overcome. They might have reconsidered had they seen Charles strengthening his sword-arm by beheading at a single stroke apiece whole flocks of sheep driven down his palace corridors in single file.

The fact was that Peter the Great characteristically rushed unprepared into the Great Northern War (1700–1721). Charles knocked Denmark out of the war before Russia even got in. He then frustrated Augustus' effort to take the Baltic port of Riga and completely defeated a vastly larger Russian force at Narva (1700), capturing the entire supply of modern cannon of which Peter was so proud. Instead of taking advantage of Peter's helplessness, however, and marching into Russia, Charles detoured into Poland, where he spent seven years pursuing Augustus, sponsoring his own King of Poland, a noble named Stanislas Leszczynski, and eventually forcing Augustus to abandon the Polish crown to Leszczynski and to give up the Russian alliance. Charles then seized and executed Patkul.

In the interim, Peter had been busy rebuilding the Russian armies and had conquered from the Swedes the two Baltic provinces nearest to Russia, Ingria and Livonia. In the first he founded in 1703 a new city, St. Petersburg, soon to be the capital of Russia, and from the beginning the apple of Peter's eye. In 1708, Charles made the mistake of sweeping far to the south and east into the Ukraine in an effort to join forces with the Cossacks, whose leader Mazepa was an ally. Exhausted by the severe winter, the Swedish forces were finally defeated by the Russians in the decisive battle of Poltava (June 27, 1709). Charles managed to flee safely westward across the Dniester River and onto Turkish territory.

Peter was able to reinstate Augustus as King of Poland, but he was not able to force the Turks to surrender to him the refugee King of Sweden. Charles had embarked on intrigues to bring about a war between Turkey and Peter, and thus to avenge his defeat. So Peter in some dismay found himself embroiled in war against the Turks (1710–1711). For the first time in history the Russians made an appeal to the Balkan Christian subjects of the Turks on the ground of their common Orthodox faith. Bearing banners modeled on those of Constantine, first Emperor of Byzantium, and promising liberation from the Moslems, the Russian forces entered Turkish territory by crossing the river Pruth westward into the Danubian province of Moldavia (now a part of Rumania). Here the Turkish armies trapped Peter and forced him to surrender (1711).

The Turks could have dragged Peter off in captivity to Istanbul had they wanted, but they proved unexpectedly lenient. They required the surrender of Azov and the creation of an unfortified "no-man's land" between Russian and Ottoman territory. Furious with the Turks for not taking full advantage of Peter's discomfiture, Charles worked to bring about still another Russo-Turkish war. Although he came

Russian Expansion in Europe, 1689-1796

Acquired by Peter the Great, 1689-1725
Acquired between 1730-1740
Acquired by Elizabeth, 1741-1762
Acquired by Catherine, 1762-1796

very close to success, the Turks eventually tired of their firebrand visitor and expelled him. Their own peace with Russia was secure, and Charles went sadly home (1714).

Still the Great Northern War dragged on for seven more years of diplomatic intrigue and military and naval action, involving the Prussians (see p. 291) and affecting the interests of all the western European powers. As Russian forces seized Finland, inflicted naval defeats on the Swedes in the Baltic, and occupied islands only a few miles from the Swedish coast, the Swedish empire was obviously dissolving. To the last years of the Great Northern War belong a whole series of matrimonial and other alliances between Russia and the petty German courts, bringing the Russians deep into Central Europe and embroiling them in questions in which Russia really had no national interest. From a remote and little-known state somewhere behind Poland, Russia had emerged as a major military power with enough might to affect the destiny of European states.

The death of Charles XII in 1718 cleared the way for peace negotiations, but it took a Russian landing in Sweden proper (1719) to force a decision. At Nystadt (1721), Russia received all the former possessions of Sweden along the eastern shore of the Baltic. Peter returned Finland to Sweden and agreed to pay a substantial sum for the territories acquired. These Baltic lands were Peter's famous "window on the west," putting Russia into immediate contact with Europe and ending the curious situation by which all seaborne traffic to Russia had had to sail around the northern edge of Europe and into the White Sea. Next, Peter undertook a brief campaign (1722–1723) against the Persians. At his death in 1725, Russia had been at war for almost the entirety of his thirty-five-year reign.

The Machinery
Of Peter's Government

Constant warfare requires constant supplies of men and money. Since the enlistment of volunteers provided cannon fodder but not

seasoned troops, Peter's government developed a crude form of draft system according to which a given number of households had to supply a given number of recruits. More men died of disease, hunger, and cold than at the hands of the enemy, and desertion was commonplace. But the very length of the Great Northern War meant that survivors served as a tough nucleus for a regular army. Though Peter built a Baltic fleet at the first opportunity, Russian naval tradition failed to strike deep roots. From 800 ships (mostly very small) at the moment of his death, the fleet declined to fewer than twenty a decade later. There was no merchant marine whatever. The apprehensions of the English and the Dutch that Russian emergence on the Baltic would create a new maritime nation proved unfounded.

To staff the military forces and the administration, Peter rigorously enforced the rule by which all landowners owed service to the state. He eventually decreed "civil death" for those who failed to register; this put them outside the protection of the law, and anyone could attack or kill them without fear of the consequences. State service became compulsory for life; at the age of fifteen, every male child of the service class was assigned to his future post, in the army, in the civil service, or at court. Peter often forced the gentry to do jobs they considered beneath them; he did not care whether they were interested in their work or even very much whether they had been trained for it. He filled their ranks with newcomers, who obtained grants of land, rank, and title. And he required that when a member of this class died he must leave his estate intact to one of his sons, not necessarily the eldest, so that it would not be divided anew in every generation.

Thus the class of service nobility—which now substantially included the survivors of the nobility of ancient birth, the old boyars—was brought into complete dependence upon the tsar. The system threw open the possibility of a splendid career to men with talent. A person without estates or rank who reached a certain level in any branch of the service (for example, major in the army) automatically received lands and a title of nobility. The nobility of ancient birth viewed this as a cheapening of their position and hated to see new recruits come into their own social order. But under Peter there was little they could do about it.

To raise cash, Peter tried all kinds of measures. He debased the currency; he taxed virtually everything—sales, rents, real estate, tanneries, baths, and beehives—and appointed special officials called "revenue-finders" to think up new levies. The government held a monopoly over a bewildering variety of important products, including salt and oil, coffins and caviar. The basic tax on each individual household was not producing enough revenue, partly because the number of households had declined as a result of war and misery, and partly because households were combining in order to evade payment. Peter's government therefore substituted a head tax on every male—the "soul tax," as the Russians called it—making it useless for individuals to conceal themselves in households. This innovation required a new census, which produced a most important, and unintended, social result: The census-takers now classified as serfs a large number of floaters on the edge between freedom and serfdom, who thus found themselves and their children eternally labeled as unfree. At the cost of human misery, Peter's government managed in its later years to balance the budget.

In the administration, new ministries (prikazy) were first set up to centralize the handling of funds received from various sources. A system of army districts adopted for reasons of military efficiency led to the creation of the first provinces, first eight, then nine, then twelve, embracing all Russia. Each province had its own governor, and many of the functions previously carried on inefficiently by the central government were thus decentralized. With the tsar often away from the capital, and many of the former prikazy abolished, decentralization had gone so far that Russia seemed at times to have little central government. But when Peter set out for the Pruth campaign in 1711, he created a nine-man "governing Senate" to exercise power in his absence. Later, Peter copied the Swedish system of central ministries to supersede the old prikazy and created nine "colleges" —for foreign affairs, army, navy, commerce, mines and manufactures, justice, income, expenditure, and control. Each "college" was administered not by a single minister but by a majority vote of an eleven-man board of directors or collegium. Corruption now became more difficult, because the conduct of any one member of a college could be checked by his colleagues. On the other hand, the lengthy deliberations of so many directors often delayed final decisions.

The total picture of Peter's efforts to increase the efficiency of government is one of mixed success at best. Attempts to model Russian local government on Swedish practice broke down because of the enormous difference between the two countries in literacy, size, tradition, and attitude toward civic responsibility. Corruption still continued in high places; savage punishments were inflicted on some of those who were caught, while others, like Menshikov, were apparently immune. And yet the cumbrous machinery that Peter gradually established, hit or miss, to meet the immediate needs of his wars, was superior to any that Russia had previously known.

Other Innovations of Peter the Great

Ever since 1703, Peter had been building a great city in the swamps he had seized from the Swedes. Thousands of men died in the effort to drain the marshes and create a seaport and a capital worthy of its imperial resident. Remote from the rest of Russia, St. Petersburg was frightfully expensive, because all food and building materials had to be transported great distances. It was also dangerous. When floods poured through the streets, Peter roared with laughter at the sight of furniture and household effects floating away. Wolves prowled the broad new boulevards and devoured a lady in front of Prince Menshikov's own house one fine day in June. But Peter made St. Petersburg his capital and commanded all members of the nobility to make it their home. Although palaces sprang up at the Tsar's command, the nobles complained bitterly about abandoning their beloved Moscow for this uncomfortable and costly town. Thus St. Petersburg became the symbol of Peter's war against his own gentry.

Peter also determined to disarm all possible future threats to his power from the Church. Knowing how the clergy loathed the new régime he was trying to impose, he simply failed to appoint a successor when the Patriarch of Moscow died in 1700. Eventually, in 1721, he extended the collegiate system of administration to the Church itself. He put it under an agency first called the "spiritual college," and later the Holy Directing Synod, headed by a Procurator who was a layman. Thus the Church became more than ever a department of state. Peter's own statement of his purpose is remarkably frank:

> From the collegiate government of the church there is not so much danger to the country of disturbances and troubles as may be produced by one spiritual ruler. For the common people do not understand the difference between the spiritual power and that of the autocrat; but, dazzled by the splendor and glory of the highest pastor, they think that he is a second sovereign of like power with the autocrat or with even more, and that the spiritual power is that of another and better realm. If then there should be any difference of opinion between the Patriarch and the Tsar, it might easily happen that the people, perhaps misled by designing persons, should take the part of the Patriarch, in the mistaken belief that they were fighting for God's cause.*

The educational advances of the period reflected Peter's technological and military interests. Naval, military, and artillery academies were established to educate future officers and also many civil servants. When the government tried to institute compulsory education by requiring the establishment of two schools in each province, it stressed mathematics and navigation, and the attempt failed. Part of the

*Quoted by E. Schuyler, *Peter the Great* (New York, 1884), II, 389.

difficulty came from the reluctance of parents to see their children "waste time" in school, and part from the government's inexperience and its unwillingness to begin with primary education. Primary education was left to the church schools, which were few and not very competent. At all levels, foreigners had to be summoned to provide Russia with scholars. An Academy of Sciences founded just before Peter's death began with seventeen imported fellows, and eight students, also imported. Probably the mere presence in the new capital of these exotic academies helped to stimulate the native intellectual developments that would characterize the next generation. Such tokens as the first Russian newspaper (1703) and the printing of occasional textbooks also augured well for the future.

Peter continued the practice, begun long before him, of importing foreign technicians and artisans to practice their crafts and teach them to Russians. Quite aware of the mercantilist ideas of the age, he offered such inducements as freedom from taxation and from government service, and all sorts of tariff protection, to develop manufacturing. Though sometimes employing a substantial number of laborers, industrial enterprise in Russia, chiefly textiles and iron, continued to be backward. The labor force was recruited among unwilling and badly treated serfs and criminals. Factory-owners were permitted to buy and sell serfs (otherwise a privilege restricted to the gentry), provided they were always bought or sold as a body together with the factory itself. This "possessional" industrial serfdom hardly provided much incentive for good work, and Russian produce continued inferior to comparable goods manufactured abroad. In the commercial field, Peter's heavy protective tariffs discriminated against foreign goods, encouraging smuggling and false registration of foreign agents as Russian nationals. The effort to make Russia a manufacturing nation exporting its own produce was a failure. But Peter's conquests in the Baltic did give Russia the great port of Riga, and he successfully bent every effort to make St. Petersburg into a great trading center.

Peter the Great: A Final Evaluation

The records of Peter's secret police are full of the complaints his agents heard as they moved about listening for subversive remarks. The wives and children of the peasantry found themselves deserted by their men, who were snatched away to fight on distant battlefields or to labor in the swamps to build a city that nobody but Peter wanted. The number of serfs increased with the imposition of the new soul-tax and the multiplication of land grants to service men. The tax burden was back-breaking. Service men found themselves in a kind of bondage of their own, condemned to work for the Tsar during the whole of their lives and seldom able to visit their estates. Nobles of ancient birth found themselves treated no differently from the upstarts who were flooding into their class from below. Churchmen of the conservative school were more and more convinced that Peter was the Antichrist himself, as they beheld the increase of foreigners in high places and saw the many innovations imported into the government and social life from the hated West. Rumors circulated that this was not the true Tsar at all, but a changeling somehow substituted for the real Peter by foreigners during the trip abroad, and sent back to persecute Russians and to ruin Russia.

Among the lower orders of society resistance took the usual form: peasant uprisings, punished with fantastic brutality. The usual allies of the peasant rebels, the Cossacks, suffered mass executions and sharp curtailment of their traditional independence. The leaders of the noble and clerical opposition focused their hopes on Peter's son by his first wife, the young heir to the throne, Alexis, who, they believed, would stop the expensive and (they felt) needless foreign wars, and move back to Moscow and comfortable Russian conservatism. Alexis, an alcoholic, was afraid of his father and was early estranged from him. Though not stable enough to lead a true conspiracy against Peter, he fanned the hopes of the opposition by letting them know he shared their views. Eventually he caused a scandal by fleeing abroad and asking asylum from his brother-in-law, the Austrian Emperor Charles

Peter I striding along the dikes during the building of St. Petersburg; a painting by V. A. Serov.

VI. Promising him fair treatment and forgiveness, Peter lured Alexis back to Russia and
made him the show-piece of one of those
horrible Russian investigations of nonexistent
plots. Many were tortured, killed, and exiled;
Alexis himself was tortured to death in his
father's presence.

In the early nineteenth century, when the
first self-conscious group of Russian intellectuals developed a keen interest in the past
history of their country, they made a central
figure of Peter. He had, they felt, intensified
western influences on Russian society and had
thus turned his back on Russia's peculiarly
Slavic character and her Byzantine heritage.
One group hailed these actions as necessary
to put Russia on her proper course. Its opponents damned Peter for having forced an
unnatural development upon his country, and
for having warped its social and political
life by imposing an alien pattern. But both
his friends and enemies among these later
intellectuals believed, as most scholars have
since argued, that what he did was drastic
and revolutionary.

Yet we can see that Peter simply intensified the chief characteristics of Russian
society. He made a strong autocracy even
stronger, a universal service law for service
men even more stringent, a serf more of a
serf. His trip abroad, his fondness for foreign
ways, his worship of advanced technology,
his mercantilism, his wars, all had their precedents in the period of his forerunners. The
Church, which he attacked, had already been
weakened by the schism of the Old Believers,
itself the result of western influences. Where
Peter was radical was in the field of everyday manners and behavior. The attack on the
beards, the dress, the calendar (he adopted the
western dating from the birth of Christ and
abandoned the traditional dating from a hypothetical year of the Creation), his hatred of
ceremony and fondness for manual labor—
these things were indeed new. So too were the
vigor and passion with which he acted. They
were decisive in winning a revolutionary
reputation for a monarch who in the major
aspects of his reign was carrying out policies
long since established.

Poland and Turkey

By the early eighteenth century, Russia
was the only great power in eastern Europe.
Poland and the Ottoman Empire still bulked
large on the map, but their territories included lands they were soon to lose. Both
states suffered from incompetent government,
from a backward economy, and from the presence of large national and religious minorities.
The Orthodox in Catholic Poland and Moslem
Turkey were beginning to look to Russia for
protection. In addition, the evident decay of
both states stimulated the aggressive appetites
of their stronger neighbors. Poland, consequently, was doomed to disappear as an
independent power before the end of the
century, the victim of partition by Russia,
Austria, and Prussia. Turkey held on, but
only just, and was already beginning to acquire
the perilous reputation of being the "Sick Man
of Europe."

The Polish government was a political
curiosity shop. The monarchy was elective;
each time the throne fell vacant, the Diet
chose a successor, usually the candidate who
had offered the biggest bribes, and sometimes
a foreigner. Once elected, the king was nearly
powerless, since he was obliged to transfer the
royal prerogatives to the Diet when he accepted the crown. The Diet was dominated
by the nobility and was celebrated for its
liberum veto, whereby any one of its members
could block any proposal by shouting "I do
not wish it!" and then galloping off before
his colleagues could catch up with him to
make him change his mind. The Diet was not
a parliament in the western sense of the term,
but an assembly of aristocrats, each of whom
thought of himself as a power unto himself;
unanimity was therefore necessary for all decisions. This loosely knit Polish national state
had no regular army or diplomatic corps or
central bureaucracy. Unlike the English
gentry or Prussian Junkers, the dominant
nobles had no concept of service to the Crown
or indeed any sense of loyalty except to their

own social class. They helped destroy a once-flourishing urban middle class by persecuting Jewish shopkeepers and foreign merchants. On their estates, the lot of the serfs was harsher than it was in Russia.

Compared with Poland, the Ottoman Empire was still a functioning state, yet it was falling farther and farther behind the major European powers, particularly in economics and technology. It had no Peter the Great to attack traditional ways; with few exceptions, the sultans of the eighteenth century were captives of harem intrigue and could do little to discipline such powerful groups as the Janissaries, who exploited their privileges and neglected their soldierly duties. This retrograde and corrupt government did at least govern, however, and showed considerable staying power in war. So the "Sick Man" was to linger on throughout the century, kept alive in part by the still unexhausted Ottoman reserves of vitality, and in part by the rivalry between the two would-be heirs of the Turkish inheritance, Russia and Austria.

V   War and Diplomacy, 1713–1789

Main Characteristics

From the survey just concluded of the European states in the early eighteenth century, it is evident that the international balance was both fluid and precarious. Should the strong states decide to prey upon the weak, the balance was certain to be upset. One such upset resulted from the Great Northern War, which enabled Russia to replace Sweden as the dominant power in the Baltic. The expansion of Russia continued to threaten the balance during most of the eighteenth century; the chief victims, in addition to Sweden, were Poland and Turkey. A second major threat to the balance came from the expansion of Prussia at the expense of Austria, Poland, and Sweden. A third involved the colonial and commercial rivalry between Britain and the Bourbon monarchies of France and Spain.

These were not the only international issues of the day. The old competition between Austria and France, which dated back to the Habsburg-Valois wars of the 1500's, remained very lively. It was complicated by the already noted ambitions of Elizabeth Farnese, second wife of Philip V of Spain, who won the support of France and threatened the Austrian hegemony in Italy. The Austrian Habsburgs themselves were vigorous expansionists, aiming to drive the Turks from the Danube and extend their own domains southeast to the Black Sea.

While the interplay of all these rivalries led to frequent shifts in the international balance, the idea that there should be a balance of power was generally maintained. Indeed, eighteenth-century war and diplomacy are often cited as the classic case history of balance-of-power politics in operation. The limited financial resources of the governments of the Old Régime allowed only limited warfare; nobody could as yet afford the enormous armies or navies required for total war. On the battlefield, generals were reluctant to risk losing soldiers who represented a costly investment in training; they favored sieges and other formal maneuvers executed according to conventions well understood by all belligerents. At the peace table, diplomats were reluctant to destroy an opponent; according to another well-understood convention, they generally sought to award him a bit of territory or a minor throne as compensation for a greater loss. Like "total war," "unconditional surrender" was not an eighteenth-century concept.

The manner in which the century conducted war and diplomacy has often been likened to an elaborate game. It was a serious and sometimes a bloody game, but it was governed by extensive rules generally observed by the players and designed to minimize their losses and to keep any of them from being eliminated entirely from the play. The principal players —the monarchs, diplomats, generals, admirals —were for the most part aristocrats, who accepted a uniform code of behavior. Whatever their nationality, they usually understood and respected one another far more than they understood or respected the lower social classes in their own countries.

These generalizations, we shall find, did not always apply in practice. A few of the most successful players—notably Frederick the Great of Prussia and Pitt of England—did not always play the game according to the rules. And the custom of compensation was forgotten in the case of Poland, when it was partitioned out of existence late in the century. Earlier in the century, however, Poland, along with Turkey, provided a most instructive exhibit of the balance-of-power game in operation.

The Turkish and Polish Questions, 1716–1739

The Ottoman Empire suffered heavy losses in the Austro-Turkish War of 1716–1718. By the Treaty of Passarowitz (1718), the Habsburg Emperor, Charles VI, recovered the portion of Hungary still under Ottoman rule and secured other Danubian lands that form part of present-day Rumania and Yugoslavia. A second Turkish war, 1735–1739, reversed the outcome of the first and disclosed the growing infirmity of the Habsburg army. In this second war Austria was allied with Russia, but, in a fashion foreshadowing the later struggles of the two powers for control of the Balkans, they fell to quarreling over division of the prospective spoils. In the end there was little to divide, and Charles VI had to hand back to Turkey the Danubian lands annexed at Passarowitz. During the negotiations leading to the Austro-Turkish settlement of 1739, France gave the Ottoman Empire powerful support in order to redress the balance of power. This was one of many occasions on which the French used their Turkish alliance to check Habsburg expansion.

Meantime, in the early 1730's, Bourbon and Habsburg were ranged on opposing sides in a crisis over the crown of Poland. In the early stages of the Great Northern War, as we have seen, Charles XII of Sweden had unseated the Polish king, the Saxon Augustus the Strong, and had given the crown to a Polish nobleman, Stanislas Leszczynski; then, thanks to the support of Peter the Great, Augustus recovered the Polish throne. Stanislas, however, had by no means completed his historical role, for he eventually gave his daughter, Marie, in marriage to Louis XV of France. When Augustus the Strong died in 1733, French diplomats engineered the election of Stanislas to succeed him. But both Austria and Russia disliked the prospect of a French puppet on the Polish throne, and Russia sent 30,000 troops into Poland and convoked a rump session of the Diet which elected a rival king, Augustus III, son of Augustus the Strong. The stage was set for the War of the Polish Succession, 1733–1735—Stanislas, France, and Spain versus Augustus III, Russia, and Austria.

After French and Austrian armies had fired away at each other for a while in the Rhine Valley and in northern Italy, hundreds of miles from Poland, the diplomats worked out a compromise settlement. To the satisfaction of Austria and Russia, Augustus III secured the Polish throne. From the French standpoint, Stanislas Leszczynski was well compensated for his loss. He acquired the duchy of Lorraine, on the northeastern border of France, with the provision that when he died Lorraine would go to his daughter, Marie, and thence to the French crown. France would thus move one step closer toward filling out her "natural" frontiers. To be sure, Lorraine already had a duke, Francis, husband of the Habsburg heiress, Maria Theresa, who moved to the Italian Grand Duchy of Tuscany, where the old line of rulers conveniently died out in 1737. Finally, as a by-product of the settlement, Elizabeth Farnese of Spain capped twenty years of maternal perseverance by procuring the Kingdom of Naples for "Baby

Carlos," her elder and now grown-up son.

The War of the Polish Succession may well seem futile and trivial, much ado about a kingship possessing no real power. And the postwar settlement, which affected chiefly Italy and Lorraine, may seem to be a striking case of diplomatic irrelevance. Yet the whole Polish crisis neatly illustrates the workings of dynastic politics and the balance of power. Certainly no great national issues were at stake, except for the rather nebulous ones of French, Russian, and Austrian prestige. The statesmen regarded thrones as the pawns of diplomacy, to be assigned without reference to the wishes of the populations involved. No politician of the Old Régime would have contemplated canvassing Neapolitan sentiment on Carlos or holding a referendum to see whether the Poles preferred Stanislas or Augustus.

The complicated arrangements of the 1730's preserved the balance of power by giving something to almost everybody involved. Although the diplomats could not prevent a little war over Poland, they did keep it from becoming a big one. The achievement showed the old international system at its best. Throughout the period from 1713 to 1739 the force of diplomacy operated to avert or at least to localize wars. Britain and France took the lead in the campaign to keep any one power from upsetting the international apple-cart. For example, the British sent a squadron to the Baltic during the last part of the Great Northern War so that Tsar Peter's gains would not be too great. To prevent the dismemberment of Ottoman territories in Europe, Britain intervened in the negotiations between Turkey and Austria at Passarowitz in 1718, and the French revived their Ottoman alliance in the 1730's.

The War of Jenkins' Ear

The diplomatic partnership of Britain and France in the 1720's and 1730's reflected the basic policies of Walpole and Fleury, both of whom sought stability abroad to promote economic recovery at home. The partnership, however, collapsed in the face of the competition between the two Atlantic powers for commerce and empire. Neither Walpole nor Fleury could prevent the world-wide war between Britain and the Bourbon monarchies that broke out in 1739 and that lasted, with many intervals of peace, until the final defeat of Napoleon in 1815. This "Second Hundred Years' War" had, in fact, already begun half a century before 1739, in the days of Louis XIV. The Utrecht settlement of 1713 had not fully settled the rivalry between Britain and France (and France's Bourbon partner, Spain). Thus the war of 1739 was as much the renewal of an old struggle as the onset of a new one.

The specific issue behind the crisis of 1739 was the comparatively minor question of British chagrin at the disappointing results of the Asiento privilege. As the South Sea Company discovered, the Asiento gave Britain little more than a token share in the trade of the Spanish American colonies (see p. 277). What British captains could not get legitimately they got by smuggling. Spain retaliated by establishing a coast-guard patrol in American waters to ward off smugglers. British merchants complained of the rough treatment handed out by the Spanish guards, and in 1738 they exhibited to Parliament Captain Jenkins, who claimed that Spanish brutality had cost him an ear, which he duly produced, preserved in salt and cotton batting. Asked to state his reaction on losing the ear, he replied, "I commended my soul to God and my cause to my country." Walpole retorted that the protection of British smugglers against legitimate Spanish patrols did not give the government a very strong case. But Walpole could restrain neither the anti-Spanish fever sweeping the country to which Jenkins had commended his cause, nor the bellicose faction of "Boy Patriots" that had arisen within Walpole's own Whig party.

In October, 1739, to the joyful pealing of church bells, Britain began the War of Jenkins' Ear against Spain. "They are ringing their bells now," Walpole observed tartly. "They will be wringing their hands soon." As if to vindicate his prophecy, the British fleet lost the opening campaign in the Caribbean, and France showed every sign of coming to Spain's assistance. Dynastic ties had already brought the two Bourbon monarchies into alliance during the Polish war; now French economic interests were at stake, for France supplied the bulk of the wares which Spanish galleons carried to America, and which cheaper British contraband was driving out of the Spanish colonial market.

The War of the Austrian Succession, 1740–1748

In 1740, a chain of events linked the colonial war to a great continental conflict, the War of the Austrian Succession. On the death of the Emperor Charles VI in 1740, the Habsburg domains passed to his daughter, Maria Theresa, who was only twenty-three years old. Expecting to outwit Maria Theresa because of her youth, her sex, and her political inexperience, the German princes ignored the Pragmatic Sanction guaranteeing her succession and looked forward to the possible partition of the Habsburg lands. In addition, the Elector of Bavaria, a cousin of the Habsburgs, hoped to become Holy Roman Emperor, defeating Maria Theresa's candidate, her own husband, Francis of Lorraine and Tuscany. The first of the German princes to strike, however, was Frederick the Great (1740–1786), who had just inherited the Prussian throne from Frederick William I. In December, 1740, Frederick suddenly invaded Silesia, a Habsburg province located in the upper Oder valley to the southeast of Brandenburg. Though Frederick advanced a flimsy family claim to Silesia, Europe generally regarded his invasion as an act of simple aggression.

In the ensuing War of the Austrian Succession, England and Austria were ranged against France, Spain, Prussia, and Bavaria. Frederick won an emphatic victory in the campaigns on the Continent. The Prussian army astounded Europe by its long night marches, sudden flank attacks, and other tactics of surprise quite different from the usual deliberate warfare of sieges. Frederick, however, deeply antagonized his allies by repeatedly deserting them to make secret peace arrangements with Austria. And he did little to support the imperial aspirations of the Bavarian Elector, who enjoyed only a brief tenure as "Emperor Charles VII."

The Anglo-Austrian alliance worked no better than the Franco-Prussian one. Many Englishmen felt that George II was betraying their true interests overseas by entangling them in German politics and the defense of Hanover. Nevertheless, the British preference for the Hanoverians over the Stuarts was evident when "Bonnie Prince Charles," the grandson of the deposed James II, secured French backing and landed in Britain (1745). He won significant recruits only among the chronically discontented Scottish highlanders, and in 1746 he was thoroughly defeated at Culloden. Jacobitism, never a very important political threat, was dead.

Outside Europe, the fighting of the 1740's was quite indecisive. The New England colonists took Louisburg, the French naval base on Cape Breton Island commanding the approach to the St. Lawrence. On the other side of the world, the French took the port of Madras from the English East India Company. The Treaty of Aix-la-Chapelle (1748) restored both Louisburg and Madras to their former owners, and Britain later agreed to give up the troublesome Asiento privilege. In Central Europe, on the other hand, the war was a decisive step in the rise of Prussia to the first rank of powers. The new province of Silesia brought not only a large increase in the Prussian population but also an important textile industry and large deposits of coal and iron. Maria Theresa got scant compensation for the loss of Silesia. Although her husband, Francis, won recognition as Holy Roman Emperor, she had to surrender Parma and some other territorial crumbs in northern Italy to Philip, the second son of Elizabeth Farnese.

The Uneasy Peace, 1748–1756

The peace made in 1748 lasted only eight years. Then another and greater conflict, the Seven Years' War of 1756–1763, broke out, caused partly by old issues left unsettled at

The Battle of Culloden, 1746, showing the rigid battle formations used in the eighteenth century.

Aix-la-Chapelle and partly by new grievances arising from the War of the Austrian Succession. The world struggle between Britain and the Bourbons kept right on in the undeclared warfare waged during the years of nominal peace after 1748. In Asia, the English and French East India companies fought each other once removed, so to speak, by taking sides in the rivalries of native princes in southern India. By 1751, the energetic French administrator, Dupleix, had won the initial round of this indirect fight. Then the English, led by the equally energetic Clive, seized the initiative, and in 1754 Dupleix was called back home by the directors of the French company, who were unwilling to back his aggressive policy. In North America, English colonists from the Atlantic seaboard had already staked out claims to the rich wilderness between the Appalachians and the Mississippi. But the French, equally intent

on appropriating the area, stole a march on them and established a string of forts in western Pennsylvania from Presqu'Isle (later Erie) south to Fort Duquesne (later Pittsburgh). In 1754, a force of Virginians under the youthful George Washington tried unsuccessfully to dislodge the French from Fort Duquesne.

In Europe, the dramatic shift of alliances called the Diplomatic Revolution immediately preceded the outbreak of the Seven Years' War. In the new war the fundamental antagonisms were the same as in the old — Britain versus France, Prussia versus Austria — but the powers reversed their alliances. Britain, which had joined Austria *against* Prussia in the 1740's, now paired off *with* Frederick the Great. And, in the most revolutionary move of the Diplomatic Revolution, France, which had sided *with* Frederick before, not only stood *against* him but also joined *with* her hereditary enemy, Habsburg Austria. The Diplomatic Revolution reflected the resentment of the powers at the disloyal behavior of their old partners in the War of the Austrian Succession. The French had bitter memories of Frederick's repeated desertions and secret peace arrangements. Britain deplored Austrian reluctance to defend English continental interests, which included maintaining the territorial integrity of Hanover and excluding the French from the Austrian Netherlands. Austria, in turn, regarded Hanover and Belgium as peripheral to her main concern, the recovery of Silesia.

In 1755, the British almost unwittingly touched off the Diplomatic Revolution. In order to enlist a second power in the task of defending Hanover, they concluded a treaty with Russia, which had taken a minor part in the War of the Austrian Succession as an ally of England. The Anglo-Russian treaty alarmed Frederick the Great, who feared an eventual conflict between Prussia and Russia for control of the Baltic and Poland. In January, 1756, the Prussian king concluded an alliance with Britain which detached her from Russia. The alliance between England and Prussia isolated France and gave the Austrian chancellor, Kaunitz, the opportunity he had been waiting for. What Austria needed in order to avenge herself on Frederick and to regain Silesia was an ally with a large army; what Austria needed was the alliance of France, not Britain. Using the Anglo-Prussian alliance as an argument, Kaunitz convinced Louis XV and his mistress, Madame de Pompadour, to drop the traditional Bourbon-Habsburg feud in favor of a working partnership. The last act of the Diplomatic Revolution occurred when Russia joined the Franco-Austrian alliance. The Russian Empress Elizabeth (1741–1762) hated Frederick the Great and feared his aggression all the more now that he had deprived her of her English ally.

The Seven Years' War, 1756–1763

The new war, like its predecessor, was really two separate wars—one continental, the other naval and colonial. In the European campaigns of the Seven Years' War, Frederick the Great faced a formidable test. Prussia confronted the forces of Austria, France, and Russia, whose combined population was more than fifteen times larger than her own. She had almost no allies except for Britain, which supplied financial subsidies but little actual military assistance. The Spartan traditions of the Hohenzollerns enabled Prussia to survive. The King himself set the example; in 1757, he wrote to one of his French friends:

I am assaulted from every side. Domestic trials, secret afflictions, public misfortunes, approaching calamities—such is my daily bread. But do not imagine I am weakening. If everything collapses I should calmly bury myself beneath the ruins. In these disastrous times one must fortify oneself with iron resolutions and a heart of brass. It is a time for stoicism: the disciples of Epicurus would find nothing to say. . . .*

Frederick's "iron resolution" and "heart of brass" led him to adopt any expedient to gain his ends. To fill up the depleted ranks of his army, he violated international law by impressing soldiers from Prussia's smaller neighbors, Mecklenburg and Saxony. Since British subsidies covered only a fraction of his war expenses, he seized Saxon, Polish, and Russian coins, melted them down, and kept for Prussian use a large part of their precious metallic content.

A final factor in saving Prussia, perhaps the most important one of all, was the shakiness of the apparently formidable coalition arrayed against her. Most fortunately for Frederick, his enemies were never capable of exploiting their military successes to deliver a knockout blow. Russia's generals were timid, and those of France and Austria were sometimes downright incompetent. Moreover, the French, the strongest of the allies, had to fight a two-front war, in Europe and overseas, but did not have the financial resources to do both. The grand alliance created by Kaunitz suffered to an unusual extent from the frictions, mistrust, and cross-purposes that customarily beset war-

*Quoted in G. P. Gooch, *Frederick the Great* (London, 1947), 41.

time coalitions. Indeed, the coalition did not last out the war. When Elizabeth of Russia died in January, 1762, she was succeeded by Tsar Peter III, a passionate admirer of Frederick the Great, who at once deserted Elizabeth's allies and placed Russia's forces at Frederick's disposal. Although he occupied the Russian throne for only a few months (see Chapter 9), Peter's brief rule marked a decisive turning in the Seven Years' War. In 1763 Prussia won her war, and Austria agreed to the Peace of Huber-

Fredrick the Great, after the Seven Years' War.

tusburg confirming the Hohenzollern retention of Silesia.

Meanwhile, Frederick's British partner was gaining a smashing victory abroad. During the first year and a half of the fighting, the British suffered setbacks on almost every front. At sea, they lost the important Mediterranean base of Minorca in the Balearic Islands, a disaster to which the home government contributed by sending (too late) reinforcements (too few) under Admiral Byng (a poor choice).

Byng was unfairly saddled with the whole blame and was executed — "in order to encourage the others," Voltaire observed ironically. In North America, the British lost the outpost of Oswego on Lake Ontario and fumbled an attack on Louisburg, the key to French Canada. The most dramatic of Britain's misfortunes occurred in India. In June, 1756, the Nawab of Bengal, a native ally of the French, crowded 146 British prisoners into one small room with only two windows. The result was the atrocious "Black Hole" of Calcutta, thus described by an officer of the English East India Company:

> It was the hottest season of the year, and the night uncommonly sultry. . . . The excessive pressure of their bodies against one another, and the intolerable heat which prevailed as soon as the door was shut, convinced the prisoners that it was impossible to live through the night in this horrible confinement; and violent attempts were immediately made to force the door, but without effect for it opened inward.
>
> At two o'clock not more than fifty remained alive. But even this number were too many to partake of the saving air, the contest for which and for life continued until the morn. . . .
>
> An officer, sent by the nawab, came . . . with an order to open the prison. The dead were so thronged, and the survivors had so little strength remaining, that they were employed near half an hour in removing the bodies which lay against the door before they could clear a passage to go out one at a time; when of one hundred and forty-six who went in no more than twenty-three came out alive. . . .*

William Pitt turned the tide in favor of Britain. This famous representative of the Whig oligarchy sat in Parliament for Old Sarum, a notorious "rotten" borough. The grandson of "Diamond" Pitt, a merchant prince who had made a fortune in India, he consistently supported the interests of the City. In the late 1730's he had led the Whig rebels, the "Boy Patriots" who forced Britain into the War of Jenkins' Ear, against Walpole's pacifistic policy. Now Pitt's great war ministry (1757–1761) at last ended the shilly-shallying policies of the cabinets that had held office since Wal-

*R. Orme, *A History of the Transactions of the British Nation in Indostan* (London, 1778), II, sec. 1, 74 ff.

pole's downfall in 1742. When deficits rose higher and higher, Pitt used his personal and business connections with the City to assist the successful placement of government loans. He strengthened the Anglo-Prussian alliance by sending Frederick substantial subsidies and placing English forces in Hanover under an able Prussian commander in place of the bungling Duke of Cumberland, a son of George II. Everywhere Pitt replaced blundering generals and admirals; everywhere his energetic measures transformed the character of the naval and colonial war. In 1759, the Royal Navy defeated both the Atlantic and Mediterranean squadrons of the French fleet.

Britain's command of the seas enabled her to continue trading abroad at a prosperous pace, while French overseas trade rapidly sank to one-sixth of the pre-war rate. Cut off from supplies and reinforcements from home and faced by generally superior British forces, the French colonies fell in quick succession. In Africa, Britain's capture of the chief French slaving station ruined the slavers of Nantes in the mother country. In India, Clive and others avenged the "Black Hole" by punishing the Nawab of Bengal and capturing the key French posts. In the West Indies, the French lost all their sugar islands, except for Santo Domingo. In North America, the 65,000 French, poorly supplied and poorly led, were helpless against the million British colonists, fully supported by their mother country. Fort Duquesne was taken at last, and renamed after Pitt, and the British went on to other triumphs in the war that the colonists called "French and Indian." In Canada, the English General Wolfe took Louisburg (1758) and in the next year, 1759, lost his life but won immortal fame in a great victory on the Plains of Abraham outside Quebec. When the remaining French stronghold, Montreal, fell in 1760, the doom of France's American empire was sealed.

This rain of victories led the British to expect sweeping gains in the postwar settlement; their expectation was soon disappointed. Pitt had won the war, but he did not make the peace: the accession of the obstinate and ambitious George III in 1760 led to the dismissal of the Prime Minister the next year. In the Peace of Paris, 1763, the successors of Pitt allowed the French to recover their islands in the West Indies, then highly prized as a major source of sugar. British planters in the Caribbean were much relieved, for their markets had been flooded by sugar from captured French islands during the war. But to outraged patriots it seemed as though Britain had let the grand prize slip through her fingers.

France, however, lost all her possessions on the mainland of North America. Britain secured both Canada and the vast disputed territories between the Appalachians and the

North America and the Caribbean, 1763
Situation after the Seven Years' War

British Territory:
- Held before 1763
- Acquired from France
- Acquired from Spain
- —— Proclamation Line of 1763

Mississippi. Moreover, she also obtained Florida from Spain, which had joined France in 1762 when the war was already lost. And, though the French were permitted to retain a few trading posts in India, they were not allowed to fortify them or to continue their old policy of manipulating the politics and rivalries of native states. For Britain, the Seven Years' War marked the beginning of a virtually complete ascendancy in India; for France it marked the virtual end of her "old Empire."

The International Balance in Review

The peace settlements of Hubertusburg and Paris ended the greatest international crisis that was to occur between the death of Louis XIV and the outbreak of the French Revolution. New crises were to arise soon after 1763, as the next chapter will show in detail—in 1768, a Russo-Turkish war (which Russia won); in 1772, the first partition of Poland; in 1775, the American War of Independence. The new crises in the East did not fundamentally alter the international balance; they accentuated shifts that had long been underway. And, although American independence cost Britain the thirteen colonies, the maritime and imperial supremacy she had gained in 1763 was not otherwise seriously affected.

The international balance established in 1763, then, remained largely unchanged down to 1789. In the incessant struggle for power during the eighteenth century, the victorious states were the strongest states—Britain, Prussia, and Russia. The states that were less fit—France, Spain, Austria, Turkey—survived, though they sometimes suffered serious losses. The weakest units, Poland and Italy—as a Spanish diplomat observed early in the century—were being "pared and sliced up like so many Dutch cheeses."

The Duke of Choiseul, the foreign minister of Louis XV during the Seven Years' War, remarked that the "true balance of power resides in commerce." Choiseul's remark held a large measure of truth, but not the whole truth. The world struggle between Britain and the Bourbon empires did much to justify the mercantilist view that conceived of international relations in terms of incessant competition and strife. According to the mercantilist doctrine of the fixed amount of trade, a state could enlarge its share of the existing supply only if it reduced the shares held by rival states, either through war or, in time of peace, through smuggling and retaliatory legislation. All this was borne out by the War of Jenkins' Ear and by British success, and French failure, in maintaining overseas trade during the course of the Seven Years' War. Yet the modern concept of economic warfare was only beginning to take shape. During the War of the Austrian Succession, London brokers supplied both insurance and information on naval movements to French shipowners.

Moreover, economic factors did not wholly explain all the changes in the international balance during the century. For example, efficient utilization of Prussian resources played its part in the victories of Frederick the Great. But his success depended still more on qualities that had little to do with economics—his own brilliant and ruthless leadership, and the discipline of the society that he headed. The case of Britain seemingly offers the most compelling evidence to support Choiseul's contention, as Pitt turned her formidable financial and commercial assets to practical advantage. Yet Pitt himself is not to be explained in simple economic terms. His accession as prime minister in the dark days of 1757, like that of Churchill in the dark days of 1940, was made possible by a political system that enabled the right man to come forward at the right time.

Finally, the eighteenth century, despite its wars, was an interlude of comparative calm between the age of religious strife that had preceded it and the storms of liberalism and nationalism that were to be loosed by the French Revolution. The prospect in 1715, the prospect of long years of peace and quiet, had not, after all, been wholly deceptive. The Seven Years' War of the eighteenth century, for example, did not begin to equal in destructive force the Thirty Years' War of the seventeenth. Much more was involved here than the relative shortness of the Seven Years' War. Few of the combatants had the feeling of fighting for a great cause, like Catholicism or Protestantism or national independence. The fighting itself was conducted in a more orderly fashion than it had been a hundred years before; soldiers were better disciplined, and armies were better supplied; troops lived off the land less often and no longer constituted such a menace to the lives and property of civilians. Even warfare indicated that this was the century of order and reason, the Age of the Enlightenment.

Reading Suggestions on the Old Régime and the International Balance

(*Asterisk indicates paperbound edition.)

General Accounts

The following volumes in the series, "The Rise of Modern Europe," (*Torch) provide a detailed introduction to eighteenth-century war and politics and have extensive and up-to-date bibliographies: P. Roberts, *The Quest for Security, 1715–1740*; W. L. Dorn, *Competition for Empire, 1740–1763*; and L. Gershoy, *From Despotism to Revolution, 1763–1789*.

M. S. Anderson, *Europe in the Eighteenth Century 1713–1783* (Holt, Rinehart & Winston, 1961). A very good introductory volume by a British scholar.

R. J. White, *Europe in the Eighteenth Century* (*St. Martin's). Another good introduction, at a less advanced level, by a British scholar.

The New Cambridge Modern History, Vol. VII: "The Old Regime, 1713–1763" and Vol. VIII, "The American and French Revolutions 1763–1793" (Cambridge Univ. Press, 1957, 1965). Wide-ranging essays by specialists; useful mainly for interpretations and reference.

Economics and Society

E. F. Heckscher, *Mercantilism*, 2 vols., rev. ed. (Macmillan, 1955). A famous and controversial work; a mine of information on eighteenth-century economic developments.

T. S. Ashton, *The Industrial Revolution, 1760–1830* (*Galaxy). Clear and informative introduction.

P. Mantoux, *The Industrial Revolution in the Eighteenth Century* (*Torch). Scholarly study of the factory system in England.

J. Carswell, *The South Sea Bubble* (Stanford Univ. Press, 1960). Excellent monograph.

A. Goodwin, ed., *The European Nobility in the Eighteenth Century* (Black, 1953). Very helpful essays arranged country by country.

D. Ogg, *Europe of the Ancien Régime* (*Torch). A social study, focused on Britain.

The Western Powers

W. E. H. Lecky, *A History of England in the Eighteenth Century*, 8 vols. (Longmans, Green, 1883–1890). A celebrated detailed study.

B. Williams, *The Whig Supremacy, 1714–1760*, 2nd. ed., rev. by C. H. Stuart (Clarendon, 1962). A competent modern survey.

J. H. Plumb, *England in the Eighteenth Century* (*Penguin). A good brief account by an expert. Plumb has written several other studies of the period, notably *Sir Robert Walpole*, Vol. I, "The Making of a Statesman" (Houghton, Mifflin, 1956); *The First Four Georges* (Macmillan, 1957); and *Chatham* (Macmillan, 1953), an account of the elder Pitt.

C. G. Robertson, *Chatham and the British Empire* (*Collier). Brief, popular introduction to the achievements of the elder Pitt.

L. Kronenberger, *Kings and Desperate Men* (*Vintage). Lively essays on eighteenth-century English society and personalities.

A. Cobban, *A History of Modern France,* Vol. I, 1715–1799 (*Penguin). Good recent general survey by a British scholar.

J. Lough, *An Introduction to Eighteenth-Century France* (Longmans, Green, 1960). Clear and enlightening discussion of the Old Régime.

A. M. Wilson, *French Foreign Policy during the Administration of Cardinal Fleury* (Harvard Univ. Press, 1936). A sound monograph, and one of the relatively few good books in English on the France of Louis XV.

G. P. Gooch, *Louis XV* (Longmans, Green, 1956), and Nancy Mitford, *Madame de Pompadour* (*Pyramid). Entertaining and rather old-fashioned biographical studies.

F. Ford, *Robe and Sword* (*Torch). An instructive study of the French aristocracy in the eighteenth century.

The Eastern Powers

H. Rosenberg, *Bureaucracy, Aristocracy, Autocracy* (*Beacon). A somewhat opinionated analysis of Prussian history, 1660–1815.

S. B. Fay, *The Rise of Brandenburg-Prussia to 1786,* rev. by K. Epstein (*Holt). A lucid little volume, packed with information.

F. L. Carsten, *The Origins of Prussia* (Clarendon, 1954). A monograph that carries the story through the reign of the Great Elector.

F. Schevill, *The Great Elector* (Univ. of Chicago Press, 1947). A helpful study of the founder of the Hohenzollern despotism.

R. R. Ergang, *The Potsdam Führer* (Columbia Univ. Press, 1941). A splendid study of Frederick William I of Prussia.

E. Schuyler, *Peter the Great,* 2 vols. (Scribner's, 1884). An old but excellent account by an American diplomat and scholar.

V. Klyuchevsky, *Peter the Great* (*Vintage). Translation of a famous account by a pre-revolutionary Russian scholar.

B. H. Sumner, *Peter the Great and the Emergence of Russia* (*Collier). A very good introductory account.

The International Balance

A. Sorel, *Europe Under the Old Regime* (*Torch). A famous little essay on the eighteenth-century balance by a French expert.

L. Dehio, *The Precarious Balance* (*Vintage). Reflections on the shifts in the balance of power by a German scholar.

J. F. C. Fuller, *A Military History of the Western World,* 3 vols. (Funk and Wagnalls, 1954–1956). The second volume covers the seventeenth and eighteenth centuries.

C. T. Atkinson, *A History of Germany,* 1715–1815 (Methuen, 1908). An older account, particularly full on war and diplomacy.

B. H. Sumner, *Peter the Great & the Ottoman Empire* (Blackwell, 1949). A short and meaty monograph.

H. Dodwell, *Dupleix and Clive* (Methuen, 1920). A balanced treatment of the imperial antagonists in Italy.

Sources

Arthur Young, *Tours in England and Wales* (London School of Economics and Political Science, 1932). A good selection from the reports of this prolific and perceptive agricultural expert.

Lady Mary W. Montagu, *Letters* (Everyman). Perhaps the best of the century's letter-writers; particularly valuable on the Habsburg and Ottoman empires.

G. P. Gooch, *Courts and Cabinets* (Knopf, 1946). A graceful introduction to the memoirs of some of the great personages of the era.

Historical Fiction

H. Fielding, *Tom Jones* (*several editions). The greatest of social novels on eighteenth-century England.

T. Smollett, *The Adventures of Roderick Random* (*Signet). A novel that provides a good contemporary account of life in His Majesty's Navy two centuries ago.

D. Merezhkovsky, *Peter and Alexis* (Putnam, 1905). Novel, dramatizing the conflict between the great Tsar and his son.

9

The Enlightenment

I Basic Principles and Traits

Reason, natural law, progress — these were key words in the vocabulary of the eighteenth century. It was the Age of the Enlightenment, when the belief became widespread that human reason could cure men of past ills and help them to achieve utopian governments, perpetual peace, and a perfect society. *Reason* would enable men to discover the *natural laws* regulating existence, and the *progress* of the human race would thereby be assured.

The intellectuals who professed this optimistic creed were known by the French name of *philosophes*, though some of them were not French and few of them were philosophers in the strict sense. The *philosophes* were critics, publicists, economists, political scientists, and social reformers. By no means all of them expressed their views in the naïvely simple and cheerful way formulated at the end of the last paragraph. The most famous *philosophe,* Voltaire, in his most famous tale, *Candide,* ridiculed the optimists who thought that all was for the best in the best of all possible worlds. Many intellectuals followed Voltaire in stressing the unreasonable aspects of human behavior and the unnatural character of human institutions. Nevertheless, though many pessimistic cross-currents eddied beneath the gleaming surface of the Enlightenment, the main current of the age was optimistic. Voltaire himself, for all his skepticism, carried on a life-long crusade against the unnatural and the unreasonable. On the whole, the Enlightenment relied on men's capacity to correct the errors of their ways, once they had been pointed out, and to move on to a better and brighter future. A perfect instance was the American Declaration of Independence, which listed "the pursuit of happiness" as a fundamental human right along with life and liberty. The idea that men could pursue happiness and might even attain it was indeed new and revolutionary, a profound departure from the traditional Christian belief that such joy could never be expected on earth.

The Inheritance from Locke and Newton

The *philosophes* of the eighteenth century derived their basic principles from the men of the preceding "century of genius." Their faith in natural law came from Newton and their confidence in the powers of human reason in part from Descartes, who had deduced a whole philosophy from the fact that he reasoned at all, and still more from Locke. John Locke (1632–1704) wrote a celebrated defense of England's Glorious Revolution, the *Two Treatises of Government* (1690). Men are, he contended in the *Second Treatise,* "by nature all free, equal, and independent"; they submit to government because they find it convenient to do so and not because they acknowledge any divine right on the part of the monarchy. They

make a compact or contract to be governed, which they may break by revolutionary action if the monarch does not live up to his obligations as James II had not lived up to his.

The new psychology that Locke put forward strengthened his case against absolute monarchy. Defenders of political and religious absolutism contended that the inclination to submit to authority was present in men's minds when they were born. In the *Essay concerning Human Understanding* (1690), Locke denied the existence of such innate ideas. He called the new-born mind a *tabula rasa,* a blank slate:

Let us then suppose the mind to be . . . white paper, void of all characters, without any ideas. How comes it to be furnished? . . . To this I answer, in one word, from EXPERIENCE. . . . Our observation employed either about *external sensible objects, or about the internal operations of our minds perceived and reflected on by ourselves, is that which supplies our understandings with all the materials of thinking.* These two are the fountains of knowledge, from whence all the ideas we have, or can naturally have, do spring.*

In other words, the two "fountains of knowledge" were environment, rather than heredity, and reason, rather than faith. Locke's matter-of-fact outlook and his empiricism (reliance on experience) place him among the rationalists. He believed that human reason, though unable to account for everything in the universe, explains all that men need to know. "The candle that is set up in us," he wrote, "shines bright enough for all our purposes."

Locke pointed the way to a critical examination of the Old Régime. The *philosophes* read and admired both his political writings and the *Essay concerning Human Understanding.* They submitted existing social and economic institutions to the judgment of common sense and discovered many to be unreasonable and unnecessarily complex. Locke's psychology suggested to them that teachers might improve human institutions by improving the thinking of the rising generation. The *philosophes* sought what was in effect the right kind of chalk to use on the blank slates of impress-

*Essay (New York, 1947), Bk. II, Ch. I.

ionable young minds; their search brought them to accept the view of the universe that has been aptly termed the "Newtonian world machine."

The Enlightenment seized on Newton's discoveries as revelations of ultimate truth. Newton had disclosed the natural force, gravitation, that held the universe together; he made the universe make sense. The *philosophes* believed that comparable laws could be found governing and explaining all phases of human activity. They pictured themselves as the Newtons of statecraft, justice, and economics who would reduce the most intricate institutions to formulas as neat as Sir Isaac's own mathematical laws and principles. The world, they argued, resembled a giant machine. Hitherto, men had hampered its operations because they did not understand the machinery; once they grasped the basic laws by which it ran, the "world-machine" at last would function as it should.

The optimistic implications of this credo were expressed most completely in *The Progress of the Human Mind* (1794) by the *philosophe* Condorcet and written, ironically enough, when he was in hiding as a victim of political persecution during the French revolutionary Reign of Terror. Condorcet asked:

If men can predict, with almost complete assurance, the phenomena whose laws are known to them . . ., why should it be regarded as a vain enterprise to chart, with some degree of probability, the course of the future destiny of mankind by studying the results of human history? Since the only basis of belief in the natural sciences is the idea that the general laws, known or unknown, regulating the phenomena of the universe are regular and constant, why should this principle be any less true for the development of the intellectual and moral faculties of man than for the other operations of nature?*

"Nature has placed no bounds on the perfecting of the human faculties," Condorcet concluded, "and the progress of this perfectibility is limited only by the duration of the globe on which nature has placed us."†

*Condorcet, *Esquisse d'un Tableau Historique des Progrès de l'Esprit Humain* (Paris, n.d.), 203. Our translation.
†*Ibid.,* 5.

Eighteenth-Century Science

The technological and scientific advances of the eighteenth century further buttressed the faith in natural law and progress. The *philosophes* hailed both the improvements in industry and agriculture and the rapid expansion of the pure sciences. Biology and chemistry were now beginning to assume a modern look. Linnaeus (1707–1778), a Swede, demonstrated the natural laws of family relationships in biology. He took every known plant and animal, classified it by species, then bracketed several species together in a genus—and so on up the hierarchy of classification from genus through order to class. Thus arose a practice that biologists still follow in assigning a specimen two Latin names, that of its genus and that of its species.

Modern chemical analysis started with Black and Lavoisier. Joseph Black (1728–1799), a Scottish professor, exploded the old theory that air was composed of a single element by proving the existence of several airlike substances or gases. Black's French contemporary, Lavoisier (1743–1794), continued his study of gases, invented the name "oxygen," and demonstrated that water was made up of oxygen and hydrogen. Lavoisier asserted that all substances were composed of a relatively few basic chemical elements, of which he identified twenty-three.

Meanwhile, astronomy and physics were consolidating the great advances they had made in the seventeenth century. Laplace (1749–1827), the "Newton of France," rounded out Sir Isaac's investigation of celestial mechanics and explained the movement of the solar system in a series of mathematical formulas and theorems. The versatile American, Benjamin Franklin (1706–1790), showed that electricity and lightning were really the same thing. He obtained an electrical charge in a key attached to the string of a kite flown during a thunderstorm in Philadelphia. This experiment, which aroused a lively interest across the

Atlantic, was repeated at Versailles for the French royal family.

Almost everybody who was anybody in the eighteenth century attempted experiments. Voltaire made a serious hobby of chemistry; Montesquieu studied physics; and a noble French lady reportedly kept a cadaver in her carriage so that she might employ her travels profitably in dissection and the study of anatomy. Almost every state in Europe had its *philosophes* and its royal society or learned society to promote the progress of knowledge. Intellectual life was by no means limited to the capitals and big cities; France, for example, by the middle of the eighteenth century, possessed many provincial academies, well equipped with reading rooms and lending libraries. In addition, intellectuals paid scant attention to national frontiers and, even when their countries were at war, continued to visit an enemy and correspond with its citizens. It was a striking example of the eighteenth century's disposition to keep warfare within strict limits and maintain business as usual.

French Leadership

The cosmopolitan qualities of the century appeared at their best in the Enlightenment, which had its roots in France and England and extended its branches to Scotland, Germany, Italy, Spain, and the New World. Yet the Age of Reason also marked the high point of French cultural hegemony, when, as the American *philosophe* Thomas Jefferson put it, every man had two homelands, his own and France. The French language endowed the Enlightenment with its medium of communication; the *salons* of Paris helped to set the tone of enlightened writing; the great *Encyclopédie,* edited and published in France, provided a vehicle for enlightened thought.

By the eighteenth century, French was the accepted international language. Louis XIV had raised it to supremacy in diplomacy; Racine and the other great seventeenth-century writers had made it pre-eminent in literature. There was much justice in the claim that "a dangerous work written in French is a declar-

ation of war on the whole of Europe." Almost everywhere, even in distant Russia, rulers, aristocrats, and intellectuals preferred French to their native tongues. In 1783, it was not a French society but the Academy of Berlin that conducted a competition for the best reply to the question, "What has made the French language universal?" According to the prizewinning essay, "Precise, popular, and reasonable, it is no longer just French; it is the language of humanity."

The Parisian *salons* taught writers precision, reasonableness, and the popular touch. The *salon* was the reception room of a large private home where guests assembled for an afternoon or evening of conversation under the guidance of the hostess, usually a wealthy woman from the nobility or the upper bourgeoisie. Here is a contemporary report of the way in which one of them conducted her *salon:*

. . . This circle was formed of people who were not linked together. She had taken them from here and there, but chosen so well that when they were together they harmonised like the strings of an instrument tuned by a cunning hand. . . . She played on this instrument with an art that was almost genius; she seemed to know what sound the string she was going to touch would give: I mean that so well were our characters and minds known to her, that she had only to say one word to bring them into play. Nowhere was conversation livelier, or more brilliant, or better controlled. . . . The minds she worked upon were neither shallow nor weak. . . . Her gift for throwing out an idea, and giving it to men of this type to discuss; her gift for discussing it herself, like them, with precision, and sometimes with eloquence; her gift for bringing in new ideas and varying the conversation . . .; these gifts, I say, are not those of an ordinary woman. It was not with fashionable trifles or self-conceit that, every day for four hours' conversation without weariness or emptiness, she knew how to make herself interesting to these brilliant minds.*

Although some *salons* were snobbish and superficial, most of them gave young *philosophes* the opportunity to receive a hearing —and to obtain a square meal; they welcomed

Memoirs of Marmontel, Brigit Patmore, trans. (London, 1930), 270.

and, if the need arose, protected new men and new ideas. Pressure from the *salons* determined the outcome of elections to the French Academy, which passed under the control of the *philosophes* in the 1760's.

The great organ of the *philosophes* was the *Encyclopédie,* which published the first of its many volumes in 1751. Its roster of 160 contributors included Voltaire, Montesquieu, Rousseau, Condorcet, Quesnay, and Turgot. For years the editor-in-chief, Denis Diderot (1713–1784), put in a fourteen-hour working day to advance his crusade for reason and progress. He commissioned the drawing of superb plates showing the details of the new industrial machines and even learned to operate some of the machines himself. Diderot and his colleagues did not intend to create an objective compendium of information. Their purpose was didactic: to expose the superstition and intolerance of the existing order and to instruct the public in the virtues of natural law and the wonders of science. As Diderot explained in the article on the word "encyclopedia," they aimed to assemble knowledge

. . . in order that the labors of past centuries should not prove useless for succeeding centuries; that our descendants, by becoming better informed, will at the same time *become happier and more virtuous.* . . .*

While the *Encyclopédie* antagonized many defenders of the Old Régime, it accomplished its purpose and gained enough subscribers to prove a profitable business venture. Louis XV tried to prevent its being printed or circulated, the Church condemned it for its materialism and for its skepticism, and the publishers, without consulting Diderot, ordered the printers to cut out many passages likely to cause offense. But to no avail. The indignation of Diderot, the ridicule leveled by the *philosophes* at their enemies, the loyalty of the subscribers to the *Encyclopédie,* and the help given the editors by Choiseul, the foreign minister, and Madame de Pompadour, herself an enlightened spirit—all frustrated the censors. In the small provincial city of Dijon, for example, there were sixty copies of the *Encyclopédie* in 1768.

*(Our italics.)

II   The Reform Program of the *Philosophes*

Laissez-Faire Economics

Since the *philosophes* passed severe judgments on almost every facet of the Old Régime, the major reforms they proposed encompassed economic behavior, standards of justice, and quality of education, as well as religious and political practices. Their economic program was introduced in the articles written for the *Encyclopédie* by the versatile François Quesnay (1694–1774), biologist, surgeon, and personal physician to Louis XV and Madame de Pompadour. Quesnay headed a group of thinkers and publicists who adopted the name of Physiocrats, believers in the rule of nature. The name revealed the basic outlook of the school. The Physiocrats expected that they

would, as Quesnay claimed, discover natural economic laws "susceptible of a demonstration as severe and incontestable as those of geometry and algebra." And to arrive at such laws, the "sovereign and the nation should never lose sight of the fact that the land is the only source of wealth, and that agriculture increases wealth."*

This new Physiocratic concept of natural wealth clashed with the mercantilist doctrine of equating money and wealth. "The riches which men need for their livelihood do not consist of money," Quesnay argued, "they are rather the goods necessary both for life and for the annual production of these goods." Mer-

*Quesnay, "Maximes Générales du Gouvernement Economique d'un Royaume Agricole," in E. Daire, ed., *Physiocrates* (Paris, 1846), I, 82. Our translation.

cantilist states, therefore, committed a whole series of errors by placing excessive emphasis on specie. They tried to regulate commerce, when they should have freed it from controls. They made goods more expensive by levying tariffs and other indirect taxes, Quesnay concluded, whereas they should have collected only a single, direct tax on the net income from land. *"Laissez faire, laissez passer,"* the Physiocrats urged—live and let live, let nature take its course. They repudiated the controlled economy of mercantilism and enunciated the "classical" or "liberal" doctrine of the free economy. The state ought not to interrupt the free play of natural economic forces. Most of all, it ought not to interfere with private property, so necessary for the production of agricultural wealth.

The classic formulation of laissez-faire was made by the Scotsman, Adam Smith (1727–1790), in his *Inquiry into the Nature and Causes of the Wealth of Nations* (1776). Smith, too, leveled a vigorous attack on mercantilism. It was wrong to restrict imports by tariffs for the protection of home industries:

It is the maxim of every prudent master of a family never to attempt to make at home what it will cost him more to make than to buy. The tailor does not attempt to make his own shoes, but buys them of the shoemaker. The shoemaker does not attempt to make his own clothes, but employs a tailor. . . .

What is prudence in the conduct of every private family, can scarce be folly in that of a great kingdom. If a foreign country can supply us with a commodity cheaper than we ourselves can make it, better buy it of them with some part of the produce of our industry. . . .*

Like the Physiocrats, Adam Smith attributed the wealth of nations to the production of goods; but, as befitted a citizen of Britain, the leading commercial and industrial state of the day, he took a less agrarian view of the matter. For Adam Smith, production depended less on the *soil* (the Physiocratic view) than on the *labor* of farmers, craftsmen, and millhands. Again like the Physiocrats, he minimized the role of the state, claiming that men who were freely competing to seek their own

Wealth of Nations, Bk. IV, Ch. 2.

wealth would be led to enrich their whole society as if they were being guided by "an invisible hand"—that is, by nature. Thus, Smith claimed, government should merely be a passive policeman:

According to the system of natural liberty, the sovereign has only three duties to attend to; . . . first, the duty of protecting the society from the violence and invasion of other independent societies; secondly, the duty of protecting, as far as possible, every member of the society from the injustice and oppression of every other member of it, or the duty of establishing an exact administration of justice; and thirdly, the duty of erecting and maintaining certain public works and certain public institutions, which it can never be for the interest of any individual, or small number of individuals, to erect and maintain.*

The mercantilists had raised the state over the individual and had declared a ceaseless trade warfare among nations. Adam Smith and the Physiocrats, reversing the emphasis, proclaimed both the economic liberty of the individual and free trade among nations to be natural laws. The laissez-faire program of the Enlightenment marked a revolutionary change in economic thought and was later used to justify the rugged individualism of nineteenth-century industrial pioneers (see Chapter 12). It did not, however, revolutionize the economic policies of the great powers, who long remained stubbornly mercantilist. Turgot, for instance, the chief practical exponent of Physiocratic doctrine, tried in vain to emancipate French agriculture and French business from traditional restrictions during his brief tenure as chief minister of Louis XVI in the 1770's (see Chapter 10). The Physiocrats neglected what so many *philosophes* neglected. They overlooked the difficulty of accommodating the simple and reasonable dictates of natural law to the complexity of politics and the irrationality of human nature.

Justice

The disposition to let nature take its course, so evident in laissez-faire economics, also

Ibid., Bk. IV, Ch. 9.

characterized the outlook of the *philosophes* on questions of justice. They believed that man-made legislation prevented the application of the natural laws of justice. They were horrified by the cumbersome judicial procedures of the Old Régime and by its unjust and antiquated statutes. New law-givers were needed to humanize and simplify legal codes, and a new science was needed to make the punishment of crime both humane and effective.

The new science, which laid the foundations of modern sociology, was promoted by Cesare Beccaria (1738–1794), an Italian *philosophe* and the author of the *Essay on Crimes and Punishments* (1764). Beccaria formulated three natural laws of justice, which are excellent examples of the Enlightenment's confident belief that common sense would enable men to formulate nature's truths. First, punishments should aim to

. . . prevent the criminal from doing further injury to society, and to prevent others from committing the like offence. Such punishments, therefore, . . . ought to be chosen, as will make the strongest and most lasting impressions on the minds of others, with the least torment to the body of the criminal.*

Second, justice should act speedily

. . . because the smaller the interval of time between the punishment and the crime, the stronger and more lasting will be the association of the two ideas of *Crime* and *Punishment*.†

And last:

Crimes are more effectively prevented by the *certainty* than by the *severity* of the punishment. . . . The certainty of a small punishment will make a stronger impression than the fear of one more severe. . . .**

Beccaria attacked both torture and capital punishment because they deviated so sharply from these natural laws. Torture, he claimed, falsely assumed that "pain should be the test of truth, as if truth resided in the muscles and fibres of a wretch in torture." Jail sentences, not execution, should be imposed as punishments. Like many later reformers, Beccaria asserted that punishment alone was not enough. The best method of preventing crime was to "let liberty be attended with knowledge," to "perfect the system of education."

Education

In education, too, the Old Régime failed to pass the tests of reason and natural law. The *philosophes* deplored both the almost universal ecclesiastical control of education and the heavy emphasis on theology, Greek and Latin, and ancient history. They demanded more consideration of science, modern languages, and modern history. Diderot declared:

Under the name of rhetoric, is taught the art of speaking before teaching the art of thinking; and that of good expression before the students have any ideas to express.

. . .

Under the name of physics, are wearisome disputations about the elements of matter and the terrestrial systems; but not a word about natural history nor good chemistry, very little about the motion and fall of bodies, very few experiments, still less anatomy and no geography.*

Still more drastic changes were proposed by the great nonconformist of the Enlightenment, Jean-Jacques Rousseau (1712–1778). Rousseau rebelled against the strict and disciplined society of his birthplace, Calvinist Geneva. He rebelled against the intensive bookish studies he had been forced to pursue as a young boy, and against the polite conventions he later encountered in the Paris *salons*. The result was *Emile* (1762), half treatise and half romance, a long and fervent plea for progressive education. *Emile* had two heroes —Emile, the student, and Rousseau himself, the teacher. The training that Rousseau pre-

---

Essay on Crimes and Punishments, Ch. 12.
†*Ibid.*, Ch. 19.
**Ibid.*, Ch. 27.

*Quoted in F. de la Fontainerie, *French Liberalism and Education in the Eighteenth Century* (New York, 1932), 208–209.

scribed for his pupil departed in every particular from eighteenth-century practice:

> Life is the trade I would teach him. When he
> leaves me, I grant you, he will be neither a magis-
> trate, a soldier, nor a priest; he will be a man.*

Rousseau followed a policy of laissez-faire
toward his pupil. He did not argue with Emile,
or discipline him, or force him to learn reading
at any early age. Emile observed the world of
nature from first-hand experience, not in
books. He learned geography by finding his
own way in the woods (with his tutor's help),
and agriculture by working in the fields. And
when in his teens he was finally taught to read,
his first assignment was Defoe's *Robinson
Crusoe*, "the best treatise on an education according to nature."

Rousseau's educational program had many
faults. It was impractical, for it assumed that
every child should have the undivided attention of a tutor twenty-four hours a day. And it
fostered the permanent dependence of pupil
upon teacher; when Emile married and became a father, he implored his tutor to remain at his post: "I need you more than ever
now that I am taking up the duties of manhood." And yet *Emile* was a most important
book. Rousseau returned to some of the great
ideas of the past—to the Renaissance concept
of the universal man and to the ancient Greek
ideal of the sound mind in the sound body.
His theoretical program was adapted to the
practical requirements of the classroom by the
Swiss educator, Pestalozzi (1746–1827), who
set an influential example by teaching geography, drawing, and other novelties in his
experimental school. Still more influential
was the reaction of Pestalozzi against the
barracks tradition of drilling lessons into the
pupil through a combination of endless repetition and bodily punishment. Students of the
twentieth century may thank the educational
reformers of the eighteenth for having
discovered the natural law that children
should be treated as children, not as miniature adults.

Emile, Everyman ed. (New York, 1911), 9.

Attitudes toward Religion

Attacks on clerical teaching formed part of
a vigorous and growing body of criticism
against the role of the clergy in the Old
Régime. In denouncing fanaticism and superstition, the *philosophes* singled out the Society
Jesus, the symbol and the instrument of
militant Catholicism. Pressure for the dissolution of the Jesuits gained the support of
Catholic rulers, who had long been annoyed
by Jesuit intervention in politics. In 1773,
after the Jesuits had been expelled from
several leading Catholic countries, Pope
Clement XIV dissolved the Society. It was
revived half a century later, when the political
and intellectual climate had become less
hostile.

As champions of tolerance, the *philosophes*
showed a particular affinity for the religious
attitude called deism (from the Latin *deus*,
god). Deist doctrines arose in seventeenth-
century England, the England of the civil
war and Newtonian science, where the deists
sought settlement of religious strife by the
use of reason rather than by resort to arms.
All men, they asserted, could agree on a few
broad religious principles. Since the Newtonian world-machine implied the existence
of a mechanic, the deists accepted God as the
creator of the universe; they also believed
that he would preside over the Last Judgment.
But they limited his role to the distant past
and the remote future, and they doubted that
he had any concern with day-to-day human
activities or would answer prayer and bestow
grace.

The chief exponent of deism in France was
Voltaire (1694–1778), a veritable one-man
Enlightenment who poured forth a prodigious
quantity of letters, plays, tales, epics, histories,
and essays. Clear, witty, and often bitingly
satirical, his writings were enormously
popular, not least when they were printed
under an assumed name or outside France to
evade the censorship. It was Voltaire who
made Frenchmen aware of great Englishmen

like Locke, Newton, and Shakespeare (though Shakespeare was much more representative of the Renaissance than of the Enlightenment). And it was Voltaire who broadened the writing of history to include economics and culture as well as war and politics, thus foreshadowing the "new history" and "surveys of civilization" of the twentieth century.

Voltaire coined the anticlerical watchword *Ecrasez l'infâme*—crush the infamous thing, crush bigotry, superstition, perhaps the Church itself. Also, he had experienced political intolerance at first hand. As a young man he had spent a year as a prisoner in the gloomy Paris Bastille, and three years of exile in England because he had criticized the French government and had offended a member of the privileged nobility. The religious and political freedom of Britain made an immense impression on the refugee:

If there were just one religion in England, despotism would threaten; if there were two religions, they would cut each other's throats; but there are thirty religions, and they live together peacefully and happily.*

Back home, Voltaire carried on a life-long crusade for tolerance. In 1762, a Protestant merchant of Toulouse, Jean Calas, was accused of having murdered his son to prevent his conversion to Catholicism. Calas died in agony, his body broken on the wheel. Voltaire discovered that the accusation against Calas was based on rumor and that the court condemning him had acted out of anti-Protestant hysteria. He campaigned for three years until the original verdict was reversed, and the name of Calas was cleared.

The existence of evil—of injustices like that which broke Calas—confronted the Age of Reason with a major problem. Few of the *philosophes* accepted the traditional Christian teaching that evil arose from original sin,

*Lettres Philosophiques, Letter No. 6. Our translation.

Table talk with Voltaire (hand raised); among those present are Diderot and Condorcet.

from the fall of Adam and Eve. If God were purely benevolent, they asked, why then had he created a world in which evil so often prevailed? Could a perfect God produce an imperfect creation? Alexander Pope, Voltaire's English contemporary, contended that this was the best of all possible worlds:

> All Nature is but Art, unknown to thee;
> All chance, direction which thou canst not
>   see;
> All discord, harmony not understood;
> All partial evil, universal good:
> And, spite of Pride, in erring Reason's spite,
> One truth is clear, *Whatever is, is right.*

Voltaire took his stand in *Candide*, which satirized the disasters abounding in the best of all possible worlds. A real disaster had inspired the writing of *Candide*—the great earthquake, tidal wave, and fire that engulfed the city of Lisbon on November 1, 1755, and killed upwards of 10,000 people.

Deism enabled Voltaire to effect a kind of reconciliation between a perfect God and the imperfect world. Voltaire believed that God was indeed the Creator:

> When I see a watch . . . , I conclude that an intelligent being arranged the springs of this mechanism so that the hand should tell the time. Similarly, when I see the springs of the human body, I conclude that an intelligent being has arranged these organs to be kept and nourished in the womb for nine months; that the eyes have been given for seeing, the hands for grasping, etc.*

But, Voltaire concluded, there was no way to determine whether or not God would attempt to perfect his creation. On one point Voltaire had no doubts: He never questioned the social usefulness of religion. "Man," he stated, "has always needed a brake." For the masses of people almost any religion, no matter how primitive, was better than atheism.

Baron d'Holbach (1723–1789), however, the most outspoken atheist of the Enlightenment, argued that men did not need the brake of religion; simple self-interest would suffice to make them behave morally. For

*Le Traité de Métaphysique, Ch. II. Our translation.

Holbach, organized religions were sinister institutions that thwarted the benevolent operations of reason and natural law, and God was merely a "phantom of the imagination," whose existence was denied by the evils and imperfections of the world that he was alleged to have created. A wealthy man, Holbach extended the hospitality of his *salon* to all, even to Jesuit refugees from anticlerical persecution. His tolerance impressed his contemporaries more favorably than his atheism did; most *philosophes* continued to profess deism, which was at least halfway between belief and disbelief.

Political Thought: Montesquieu

"In politics as in religion toleration is a necessity," decreed Voltaire. To him, therefore, tolerant Britain seemed utopia, and he paid the British constitution the most flattering compliment at the command of his age when he claimed that it "might have been invented by Locke, Newton, or Archimedes." Montesquieu (1689–1755), a French lawyer and *philosophe*, set out to analyze the political virtues of Britain. In his major work, *The Spirit of the Laws* (1748), Montesquieu laid down the premise that no one system of government suited all countries. Laws, he wrote,

> . . . should be in relation to the climate of each country, to the quality of its soil, to its situation and extent, to the principal occupation of the natives, whether husbandmen, huntsmen, or shepherds: they should have relation to the degree of liberty which the constitution will bear; to the religion of the inhabitants, to their inclinations, riches, numbers, commerce, manners, and customs.*

Montesquieu cautioned against supposing that old customs could simply be decreed out of existence, and he cited the telling example of Peter the Great's failure to impose western ways on Russia.

In spelling out the influence of tradition and environment upon forms of government,

*The Spirit of the Laws, Thomas Nugent, trans. (New York, 1949), Bk. I, Ch. 3.

Montesquieu concluded that republics were best suited to the small and barren countries, limited monarchies to the middle-sized and more prosperous, and despotisms to vast empires. Britain, being middle-sized and prosperous, was quite properly a monarchy limited by aristocracy. The hereditary nobility sat in the House of Lords; a kind of nobility of talent, the elected representatives, composed the Commons. All this was admirable in Montesquieu's view, for he pronounced the mass of people "extremely unfit" for government. If only the French monarchy had let the aristocracy retain their old political functions, France would never have sunk to her present low state.

Montesquieu found another key to the political superiority of Britain in the famous concept of checks and balances. In Parliament, Lords and Commons checked each other; in the government as a whole, the balance was maintained by means of *the separation of powers:*

When the legislative and executive powers are united in the same person, or in the same body of magistrates, there can be no liberty; ·because apprehensions may arise, lest the same monarch or senate should enact tyrannical laws, to execute them in a tyrannical manner.

Again, there is no liberty, if the judiciary power be not separated from the legislative and executive. Were it joined with the legislative the life and liberty of the subject would be exposed to arbitrary control; for the judge would be then the legislator. Were it joined to the executive power, the judge might behave with violence and oppression.*

Here Montesquieu failed to take into account a development that was not exactly obvious in the mid-eighteenth century, when *The Spirit of the Laws* appeared. He failed to see that the British constitution was moving, not toward the separation of powers, but toward their concentration in the House of Commons; the cabinet was becoming the instrument for the assertion of legislative supremacy over the executive.

Montesquieu likewise ran into trouble when he tried to derive specific corollaries from his general theorem about the influence

The Spirit of the Laws, Bk. XXI, Ch. 6.

of climate and geography on human institutions. Autocracy and Catholicism, he asserted, flourish in the Mediterranean states where the climate is warm and natural resources abundant. Moderate government and Protestantism, conversely, are at home in the colder and harsher environment of northern Europe. The facts did not always confirm this rule about North and South. Freedom-loving Protestant Britain and Holland behaved in good northern fashion; but if Montesquieu were correct, barren, northern, Protestant Prussia should have been a citadel of liberty, not the stronghold of Hohenzollern absolutism. By jumping to conclusions from insufficient evidence, Montesquieu committed a fault common among the *philosophes.* But, unlike some of them, he had too firm a grasp on political realities to assume that governments either were or should be the same everywhere. Later political thinkers made good use of the comparative methods introduced by *The Spirit of the Laws* and refined Montesquieu's judgments on the interrelationship of geography, religion, and politics.

Political Thought: Rousseau

From the standpoint of American history, as we shall see, Montesquieu and Locke proved to be the most influential political thinkers of the Enlightenment. From the standpoint of European history, the most important was Jean-Jacques Rousseau, who inspired the radicals of the French Revolution. Rousseau's ideas proceeded from a sweeping generalization very typical of the Enlightenment. Whereas nature dignifies man, he contended, civilization corrupts him; man would be corrupted less if civilized institutions followed nature more closely. This theme ran through many of Rousseau's principal writings. In *Emile,* it was at the heart of his program for educational reform; earlier, it was enunciated in the *Discourse on the Moral Effects of the Arts and Sciences* (1750), which won a competition set by the Academy of Dijon. The Academy asked: Has the restoration of the arts and sciences had a purifying effect upon morals? Certainly not, the prize-winner answered; it has nearly ruined them.

In a second discourse, *On the Origin of the Inequality of Mankind* (1755), Rousseau blamed the vices of civilization on private property:

The first man who, having enclosed a piece of ground, bethought himself of saying, 'This is mine,' and found people simple enough to believe him, was the real founder of civil society. From how many crimes, wars, and murders, from how many horrors and misfortunes might not any one have saved mankind, by pulling up the stakes, or filling up the ditch, and crying to his fellows: 'Beware of listening to this imposter; you are undone if you once forget that the fruits of the earth belong to us all, and the earth itself to nobody.'*

Men accepted laws and governors in order to protect their property:

. . . They had too many disputes among themselves to do without arbitrators, and too much ambition and avarice to go long without masters. All ran headlong to their chains, in hopes of securing their liberty; for they had just wit enough to perceive the advantages of political institutions, without experience enough to enable them to foresee their danger.†

Government was evil, Rousseau concluded, but a necessary evil. "What, then, is to be done? Must societies be totally abolished? . . . Must we return again to the forest to live among bears?" No, civilized men could not return to a primitive existence, could "no longer subsist on plants or acorns, or live without laws and magistrates."**

Rousseau's major political work, *The Social Contract* (1762), attempted to reconcile the liberty of the individual and the institution of government through a new and revolutionary version of the contract theory of government. Earlier theories of contract, from the Middle Ages to John Locke, had hinged on the agree-ment between the people to be governed, on the one hand, and a single governor or small group of governors, on the other. Earlier theories postulated a political contract; Rousseau's contract was social in that a whole society agreed to be ruled by its *general will:*

Each of us puts his person and all his power in common under the supreme direction of the general will, and, in our corporate capacity, we receive each member as an indivisible part of the whole.*

"Each individual," Rousseau continued, "may have a particular will contrary or dissimilar to the general will which he has as a citizen." If the individual insists on putting self-interest above community interest, he should be obliged to observe the general will. "This means nothing less than that he will be forced to be free."† Thus, the general will was moral as well as political in nature, for it represented what was *best* for the whole community, what the community *ought* to do.

Formulating the general will, Rousseau believed, was the business of the whole people. The power of legislation, he argued, could never be properly transferred to an elected body:

The deputies of the people . . . are not and cannot be its representatives; they are merely its stewards, and can carry through no definitive acts. Every law the people has not ratified in person is null and void—is, in fact, not a law. The people of England regards itself as free; but it is grossly mistaken; it is free only during the election of members of Parliament.**

Executing the general will, however, could legitimately be the business of a smaller group. Like Montesquieu, Rousseau believed that the number of governors should vary inversely with the size and resources of the state—monarchy for the wealthy, aristocracy for the state of middling size and wealth, and democracy for the small and poor. Rousseau doubted, however, that any state was ready

---

*"Discourse on the Origin of Inequality," in *The Social Contract and Discourses*, Everyman ed. (New York, 1913), 192.
†*Ibid.*, 205.
**Ibid.*, 228.

The Social Contract, Everyman ed. (New York, 1913), 13.
†*Ibid.*, 15.
**Ibid.*, 78.

for the absolute form of democracy in which the people actually execute the laws. "Were there a people of gods, their government would be democratic. So perfect a government is not for men."*

Rousseau was quite aware that *The Social Contract* was not a manual of practical politics. On another occasion, when he made suggestions for the reform of the Polish government, his counsels were decidedly more cautious. He admonished the Poles to renew their national spirit through education and patriotic festivals. While favoring the abolition of the *liberum veto* (see p. 300), he recommended that the elective monarchy be retained, that the nobles keep many of their privileges but acquire a new sense of duty, and that the serfs be liberated but only after they had been taught responsibility.

Although these suggestions were moderate enough, the influence of Rousseau has not been exerted on the side of moderation. Almost every radical political doctrine in the past two centuries has owed something to Rousseau. Socialists justify collectivism on the basis of his attacks on private property and of his insistence that "the fruits of the earth belong to us all." Patriots and nationalists hail him as an early prophet of the creed that nations do—and should—differ. Throughout his writings as well as in his advice to the Poles, he referred to "the dear love of country." *The Social Contract* concluded with a plea for the establishment of a "civil religion," which would displace the traditional faith. The moral code of early Christianity might be retained, Rousseau allowed, but the State should no longer have to compete with the Church for the allegiance of citizens.

Rousseau's concept of the general will has aroused conflicting interpretations. Because it is ethical in character, it seems to represent something more than the sum of individual wills—the whole appears to be more than the sum of its parts. Many, therefore, see in Rousseau a man who exalted the welfare of the nation over that of the citizens composing it, who indeed worshipped the state. Dictators

*The Social Contract, 56.

have justified their totalitarianism by asserting that they have a special insight into the general will; Hitler's celebrated "intuition" is an example. The police state can be justified on the grounds that it is doing its subjects a favor by "forcing them to be free."

The authoritarian interpretation indicates some of the possible consequences of Rousseau's ideas, but it overlooks both the strongly idealistic and democratic tone of his writings and his personal hostility toward the absolutism of the Old Régime. "Were there a people of gods, their government would be democratic." This declaration has moved the democratic disciples of Rousseau from the French Revolution on down to the present. The people are not gods? Then they must be trained in godliness, and Rousseau himself pointed the way. *Emile* showed how education could help, and *The Social Contract* at least implied that men might one day become so virtuous that they would follow the general will naturally and would no longer have to be "forced to be free."

Enlightened Despotism

Some *philosophes,* however, sought a short cut to utopia, a political prescription that was more practicable than the *Social Contract* and that could operate within the framework of existing monarchical insitutions. They found the answer in enlightened despotism. The Physiocrats, the chief theorists of enlightened despotism, had little sympathy with the concern of Montesquieu and Rousseau over the status of the legislative power. In the Physiocratic view, God was the legislator, nature preserved the divine legislation, and the sole duty of government was to administer these natural laws. Democracy and aristocracy alike had the fatal weakness of delegating administrative authority to individuals whose transient selfish aims clashed with the permanent welfare of the nation. By contrast, the Physiocrats explained, the personal interests of a hereditary monarch coincided with national interests through his "co-ownership" of the territories under his rule. Because the king was best qualified to work for the national interest, he should be a despot, not in any sinister sense but on the model of the tyrants of ancient Greece or the best of the Renaissance despots. Like a new Solon, the enlightened despot should unearth the natural laws decreed by God and clear away the accumulation of artificial, man-made law that was choking progress.

III   The Enlightened Despots

In the eighteenth century, self-styled "enlightened" or "benevolent" despots occupied many thrones—in Prussia, Frederick the Great; in Austria, Joseph II; in Russia, Catherine the Great; in Spain, Charles III; in Sweden, Gustavus III; and still others. The program of enlightened despotism won such wide endorsement from European monarchs because it gave them the opportunity to pose as the champions of reason and progress while pressing their age-old fight to make royal authority more absolute. Their mixture of motives made their kingdoms at best uncertain proving grounds both for the theory of enlightened despotism and for the practicality of the whole reform program of the Enlightenment.

Prussia: Frederick the Great

Of all the monarchs of eighteenth-century Europe, Frederick II, the Great, of Prussia (1740–1786), appeared best attuned to the Enlightenment. As a youth, he rebelled against the drill-sergeant methods of his father, Frederick William I (see Chapter 8). He delighted in music, and played the flute, which he took with him even on military campaigns. An attentive reader of the *philosophes,* he exchanged letters with them and brought Voltaire to live for a time as his pensioner in his palace at Potsdam near Berlin. He wrote a pamphlet, *Anti-Machiavel,* denouncing the immorality of *The Prince.* And he himself laid down the fundamental requirements for an enlightened despot:

Princes, sovereigns, kings are not clothed with supreme authority to plunge with impunity into debauchery and luxury. . . .[The prince] should often remind himself that he is a man just as the least of his subjects. If he is the first judge, the first general, the first financier, the first minister of the nation, . . . it is in order to fulfill the duties which these titles impose upon him. He is only the first servant of the state, obliged to act with fairness, wisdom, and unselfishness, as if at every instant he would have to render an account of his administration to his citizens.[*]

Frederick was indeed "the first servant of the state," shunning luxury, wearing stained and shabby clothing, and toiling long and hard at his desk. But did he also act with "fairness, wisdom, and unselfishness"? Despite his *Anti-Machiavel,* Frederick conducted foreign and military affairs in true Machiavellian style; his invasion of Silesia (see Chapter 8) would have aroused the envy of Caesar Borgia. At home, closeted in his Potsdam palace where he conducted the business of state by correspondence, he drove his subordinates like slaves. Viewed as a general, diplomat, and the master mechanic of Prussian administration, Frederick the Great was efficient and successful, but he was scarcely enlightened. His claim to be a benevolent despot must rise or fall on the record of his social and economic reforms.

No Physiocrat could have done more than Frederick to improve Prussian agriculture. From England he imported clover, crop rotation, and the iron plow, which turned up the soil more effectively than the old wooden share. He drained the swamps of the lower Oder Valley, opened up farms in Silesia and

---

[*]"Essai sur les Formes de Gouvenement et sur les Devoirs des Souverains." *Oeuvres Posthumes* (Berlin, 1788), VI, 64, 83–84. Our translation.

elsewhere, and brought in 300,000 immigrants to populate the new lands. After the ravages of the Seven Years' War, he gave the peasants tools, stock, and seed to repair their ruined farms. He nursed along the admirable German tradition of scientific forestry, then in its infancy.

Frederick, however, was hostile to the doctrine of laissez-faire and cut imports to the bone in order to save money for support of the army. His mercantilism stimulated the growth of Prussian industry, particularly the textiles and metals needed by the army. But it also placed a staggering burden of taxation on his subjects and produced several economic absurdities. For instance, Frederick tried to make Prussia grow its own tobacco, for which the climate was not suited. And, since the German taste for coffee required a large outlay of money abroad, he laid a heavy duty on imported coffee beans, and even established a special corps of French "coffee-smellers" to trap smugglers.

The religious and social policies of Frederick the Great likewise combined the Age of Reason at its most reasonable with the Old Régime at its least enlightened. A deist, Frederick prided himself on religious tolerance. He invited Jesuits to seek refuge in Prussia and protected the minority of Catholics in his predominantly Protestant kingdom, urging them to build their church steeples as high as they liked. He even boasted that he would build a mosque in Berlin if Moslems wanted to settle there. Yet the same Frederick alleged that Jews were "useless to the state," levied special heavy taxes on his Jewish subjects, and tried to exclude them from the professions and from the civil service.

Frederick rendered Prussians a great service by his judicial reforms. He reduced the use of torture; he put an end to the curious custom of taking appeals from the ordinary courts to university faculties and instituted a regular system of appellate courts. He mitigated the venal practice of bribing judges by insisting that "tips" received from litigants be placed in a common pool from which each judge should draw only his fair share.

Yet the same Frederick took a positively

Frederick the Great playing the flute in characteristically untidy surroundings.

medieval view of the merits of social caste. He did nothing to loosen the bonds of serfdom that still shackled much of the Prussian peasantry. When he gave the peasants material assistance and urged them to learn the "three r's," his aims were severely utilitarian. Peasants were to learn nothing beyond the rudiments of reading and writing; otherwise, they might become discontented with their station in life. Regarding the middle class, too, with disdain, Frederick respected only the landed nobility and gentry. And even the favored Junkers did not escape Frederick's penny-pinching. Although he appointed only Junkers as army officers, he discouraged their marrying to reduce the number of potential widows to whom the state would owe a pension.

While Frederick indulged his favorite dogs and horses, giving them special house privileges, he was temperamentally incapable of getting along with people. He despised and neglected his wife. Voltaire, that great French champion of toleration, could not tolerate the strain of prolonged daily association with Frederick. When the King requested him to edit his rather feeble French verses, Voltaire made a cutting remark about washing the dirty linen of royalty; Frederick retorted by comparing his guest to an orange, to be sucked dry and thrown away. The two men eventually renewed their friendship through the less demanding medium of correspondence.

Frederick's will directed that he be buried beside his pet dogs—"Such," remarked a French observer, "is the last mark of contempt he thought proper to cast upon mankind." The verdict has been sustained by many liberal historians, who pronounce Frederick's supposed enlightenment a mere device of propaganda, an attempt to clothe the nakedness of his absolutism with the decent intellectual garments of the age. This is, however, rather too harsh and one-sided, an attempt perhaps to fix on Frederick part of the guilt for the atrocities committed by Hitler and the Nazis almost two centuries after him. It would be fairer to argue that Frederick espoused two often conflicting philosophies—the Spartan traditions of the Hohenzollerns and the humane principles of the Enlightenment. He was an enlightened despot only so far as he could reconcile the precepts of the Age of Reason with the imperatives of Prussian kingship. He was a Hohenzollern, first and always.

Austria: Maria Theresa and Joseph II

Frederick's decisive victory in the War of the Austrian Succession (see Chapter 8) laid bare the basic weaknesses of the Habsburgs' dynastic empire. The Empress Maria Theresa (1740–1780) at once saw the need for reform and often took as her model the institutions of her hated but successful Hohenzollern rival. She and her capable ministers increased taxes, especially on the nobility, and strengthened the central government at the expense of local aristocratic assemblies, building up the still

rather sketchy departments of central administration. They obliged the non-German provinces to accept the hegemony of the German officials and German language of Vienna. Unlike Frederick the Great, Maria Theresa also took the first steps toward the abolition of serfdom. While personally very devout, she extended her policies to the Church, subjecting it to heavier taxation and confiscating some monastic property.

Maria Theresa employed both force and charm to get her way. The nobles of Hungary momentarily forgot their anti-German tradition when the beautiful and spirited empress, her infant son in her arms, personally appealed to their chivalry in the crisis of the War of the Austrian Succession. She was the first housewife of the realm as well as the first servant of the state. She was the mother of sixteen children, and she adored and respected Francis, her grasping, fickle husband. Francis' will provided a large bequest for his mistress; his widow executed its terms to the letter.

As a pious Catholic, Maria Theresa was fundamentally out of sympathy with the Age of Reason. "Lady Prayerful," as Catherine the Great called her, banned the works of Rousseau and Voltaire and even forbade the circulation of the Catholic *Index,* lest that list of forbidden books pique the curiosity of her subjects. History, therefore, has denied her the title of enlightened despot and chosen instead Joseph II, her eldest son, who became emperor after the death of Francis in 1765 and was co-regent with his mother until her death in 1780. Frederick the Great wrote Voltaire a glowing estimate of the new Emperor:

Born in a bigoted court, he has cast off its superstition; raised in magnificence, he has assumed simple manners; nourished on incense, he is modest; burning with a thirst for glory, he sacrifices his ambition to the filial duty which he executes scrupulously; and, having had only pedantic teachers, he still has enough taste to read Voltaire and to appreciate his merits.*

Frederick exaggerated only a little. Earnest,

*"Correspondance avec les Souverains," *Oeuvres Complètes de Voltaire* (Paris, 1828), LXXIV, 37. Our translation.

industrious, and puritanical in temperament, Joseph promised to make "philosophy the legislator of my empire." Thwarted and restrained by Maria Theresa during her lifetime, the impatient Emperor plunged into activity after her death. During his ten years as sole ruler (1780–1790), eleven thousand laws and six thousands decrees issued from Vienna. For the first time in the history of Catholic Austria, Calvinists, Lutherans, and Orthodox gained full toleration. And, with a generosity unparalleled in Habsburg annals, the Emperor took measures to end the ghetto existence of the Jews, exempting them from special taxes and from the requirement of wearing a yellow patch as a badge of inferiority.

Joseph intensified his mother's Catholic policies. While a faithful churchgoer, he insisted that he himself and not the Pope should be the arbiter of the Church's activities in Austria. He encouraged what he considered socially useful in Catholicism and dealt ruthlessly with what he judged superfluous and harmful. Thus he established hundreds of new churches and at the same time reduced the number of religious holidays. He called monks "the most dangerous and useless subjects in every state" and promised to convert "the monk of mere show into a useful citizen." He cut in half the number of monks and nuns and, of 2100 monasteries and nunneries, he suppressed 700, chiefly those run by the contemplative orders. Houses actively engaged in educational or charitable work were generally spared. The government sold or leased the lands of the suppressed establishments, applying the revenue to the support of the hospitals that were beginning to earn Vienna its reputation as a great medical center.

Unlike Frederick the Great, Joseph really believed in popular education and social equality. His government provided the teachers and textbooks for primary schools. More than a quarter of the school-age children in Austria actually attended school—the best record of any country in late eighteenth-century Europe. Everyone in Vienna, high and low, was invited to visit the Prater, the great public park of the capital, the entrance to which bore the inscription, "A place of pleasure for all men,

prepared for them by their friend." The new Austrian legal code followed the recommendations of Beccaria in abolishing capital punishment and most tortures and in prescribing equality before the law. Aristocratic offenders, like commoners, were sentenced to stand in the pillory and to sweep the streets of Vienna. Joseph's peasant policy marked the climax of his equalitarianism. He freed the serfs, abolished most of their obligations to manorial lords, and deprived the lords of their traditional right of administering justice to the peasantry. He also experimented with the collection of a single tax on land as recommended by the Physiocrats, a revolutionary innovation from the social as well as the economic point of view, because the estates of the aristocracy were to be taxed on the same basis as the farms of the peasantry.

Joseph's economic policies, however, often followed the traditions of mercantilism, notably in the erection of high protective tariffs and in the government's close supervision of economic life. In politics Joseph continued his mother's Germanizing program. He customarily spoke German, patronized German writers, and made the French playhouse in Vienna a German-language theater. He attempted to terminate the autonomous rights of his non-German possessions, such as Bohemia, Hungary, and Belgium.

Both Joseph's enlightened reforms and his Germanizing policies aroused mounting opposition. Devout peasants, almost oblivious of his well-meaning attempts to improve their social and economic status, keenly resented his meddling with old religious customs. The nobility clamored against his equalitarian legislation; in the case of the single-tax experiment their opposition was so violent that he had to revoke the decree a month after it was issued. Hungary and Belgium rose in open rebellion against his centralizing efforts and forced him to confirm their autonomous liberties. In foreign policy, too, his ambitious projects miscarried. By supporting Russian plans for the dismemberment of Turkey (see p. 343), Austria gained only a narrow strip of Balkan territory. Joseph also attempted to annex lands belonging to the neighboring South German state

Emperor Joseph II of Austria working a plow.

of Bavaria, where the death of the ruler opened another of those succession quarrels so common in the eighteenth century. But Frederick the Great was determined to check any advance of Habsburg power in Germany. In the half-hearted "Potato War" of the late 1770's, Austrian and Prussian troops spent most of their time foraging for food, and Joseph secured only a tiny fragment of the Bavarian inheritance.

Joseph II worked himself to death, as one of his friends observed, "by governing too much and reigning too little." Where his mother had often sought to flatter or charm her opponents out of their opposition, Joseph simply laid down the law. He defended his habit of interfering personally in almost every detail of government:

What else can I do in this country devoid of mind, without soul, without zeal, without heart in the work? I am killing myself because I cannot rouse up those whom I want to make work; but I hope I shall not die until I have so wound up the machine that others cannot put it out of order, even if they try to do so.*

*Quoted in Prince de Ligne, *His Memoirs, Letters, and Miscellaneous Papers* (Boston, 1902), II, 132.

Joseph never got the machine properly wound up; he could not implant in the Austrian bureaucracy the almost inhuman Prussian discipline that was needed to serve his purposes. Joseph II died unshaken in the conviction that he had pursued the proper course, yet believing that he had accomplished nothing. In the judgment of posterity, however, Joseph appears as the most truly enlightened despot. In ten years he attempted more than Frederick attempted in almost half a century. Though some of his major reforms, like the abolition of serfdom, were repealed soon after his death, others survived him, helping to transform the Habsburg lands into a more modern centralized state.

Other Despots

Prominent among the enlightened rulers of lesser states was Joseph's younger brother Leopold, Grand Duke of Tuscany from 1765 until he became emperor in 1790. Leopold tidied up the administration of his Italian duchy, which included the busy port of Leghorn in addition to the city of Florence. He introduced economic reforms along Physiocratic lines and judicial reforms following the recommendations of Beccaria on the abolition of torture and of the death penalty. Unlike his brother, Leopold actively enlisted the participation of his subjects in affairs of state, and, unlike any other enlightened despot, he contemplated establishing a representative assembly and studied the constitution of Virginia for guidance.

Sweden's benevolent despot, King Gustavus III (1771–1792), was the most theatrical monarch of the century. Like his uncle, Frederick the Great, Gustavus admired the French and French ideas, and, when he inherited the Swedish crown, he proclaimed in

King Charles III of Spain in hunting costume, by Goya.

ringing speeches his devotion to the Age of Reason. He also resolved not to be cramped by the oligarchical factions that had run the country since the death of the warrior king, Charles XII, early in the century. While he distracted Swedish party leaders at the opera one evening, his soldiers staged a *coup* that enabled him to revive the royal authority and to dissolve the factions. In economics and religion, his enlightenment outdistanced that of his uncle in Prussia, for he removed obstacles to both domestic and foreign trade and extended toleration to Jews as well as to the non-Lutheran Christian sects. Success, however, turned the head of Gustavus III. As he became more and more arbitrary, the nobles determined to recover their old power; in 1792, he was assassinated at a masquerade in Stockholm, and oligarchy resumed its sway.

One of the most remarkable features of enlightened despotism was its emergence in the Iberian Peninsula, so long the preserve of aristocratic and clerical influence. Its representative in Portugal was not a monarch but the Marquis of Pombal, the first minister of King Joseph I (1750–1777). Pombal secured his reputation by the speed and good taste he demonstrated in rebuilding Lisbon after the earthquake of 1755. The Portuguese economy depended heavily on income from the colonies, on the sale of port wine to Britain, and on the purchase of manufactured goods from Britain. Pombal tried to enlarge its base by fostering local industries and encouraging the growth of grain in addition to grapes. To weaken the grip of clericalism on Portuguese life, he expelled the Jesuits, advanced religious toleration, and modernized the curriculum of the national University of Coimbra. To weaken that of the nobles, he attacked their rights of inheritance. Pombal's methods were in every instance high-handed, and when he fell from power in 1777 the prisons released thousands of men whom he had confined years earlier for their alleged involvement in aristocratic plots.

The Spanish enlightened despot was Charles III (1759–1788), Elizabeth Farnese's "Baby Carlos." When he inherited the crown on the death of his half-brother, he had already been seasoned in the struggle against

feudalism and clericalism by a long and successful apprenticeship as King of Naples. With
the assistance of Italian advisers whom he
brought from Naples and of lawyers from the
lower ranks of the Spanish nobility, Charles
III energetically advanced the progressive
policies begun under his father, Philip V (see
Chapter 8). Though a pious Catholic, he objected strongly to the political activities of
the Church and expelled the Jesuits from the
native country of their founder, Loyola. He
reduced the authority of the aristocracy, extended that of the Crown, and made Spain
more nearly a centralized national state. He
curbed the privileges of the great sheep-
ranchers, whose almost unlimited grazing
rights blighted Spanish agriculture. To re-
vivify the torpid economy, he undertook irrigation projects, reclaimed waste lands, and
established new roads, canals, banks, and textile mills. The results were astonishing: Spain's
foreign commerce increased fivefold during
the reign of Charles III. His successors, however, abandoned many of his forward-looking
policies, and Spain soon began to slip back
into her old ways, though the influence of the
Enlightenment at least remained alive.

Limitations
of Enlightened Despotism

The question of succession, in fact, vitiated
the whole structure of enlightened despotism.

So long as monarchs came to the throne by the
accident of birth, there was nothing to prevent the unenlightened or incapable mediocrity from succeeding the enlightened despot.
This happened in Spain, where the well-
meaning but feeble Charles IV (1788–1808),
succeeded Charles III; it happened in Sweden,
where the weak Gustavus IV (1792–1809),
succeeded Gustavus III; and it happened in
Prussia under Frederick the Great's unenlightened nephew, Frederick William II
(1786–1797). The principal exception to the
rule occurred in Austria, where Emperor Leopold II (1790–1792), with his long experience
in Tuscany, managed to salvage some of the
reforms of Joseph II.

Even the least of the enlightened despots
deserve the credit for having improved a few
of the bad features of the Old Régime. But
not even the best of them could strike a
happy balance between enlightenment and
despotism. Joseph II was too doctrinaire, too
inflexible in his determination to apply the
full reform program of the Age of Reason.
Pombal and Gustavus III, in particular, were
too arbitrary. Frederick the Great, obsessed
with strengthening the crown, entrenched
the power of the Junkers, who were hostile
to the whole Enlightenment. Finally, in Russia,
events during the century after the death of
Peter the Great, a forerunner of the enlightened despot, furnished another lesson in
the difficulty of adjusting rational principles
to political realities.

IV   Russia, 1725–1825

The Fate of the Autocracy,
1725–1762

When Peter the Great died, he left a tangled
family situation in which nobody could truly
decide who was his legitimate successor. Over
the course of the next thirty-seven years, the
throne changed hands seven times. The suc-

cession zigzagged across the family tree of the
Romanovs: first to Peter's widow, who ruled as
Empress Catherine I (1725–1727); then to
Peter's young grandson, son of the murdered
Alexis (see p. 300), who became Peter II (1727
–1730); then to Peter's niece, who reigned as
Empress Anne (1730–1740); then to Anne's
great-nephew, Ivan VI, who was only eight
weeks old when he began his one-year reign

(1740–1741); then to Peter's own daughter by Catherine I, the Empress Elizabeth (1741–1762); then to Elizabeth's nephew, Peter III, who reigned only for six months in 1762; and finally to Peter III's brilliant young widow, who became Catherine II, the Great (1762–1796), and dominated Russia as Peter I himself had done. More important than the individuals who governed Russia between Peter and Catherine the Great were the social forces contending for power, and the social processes at work in an autocracy suddenly deprived of its autocrat and for so long unable to produce a new one. In the series of palace overturns, the guards' regiments founded by Peter exercised a decisive influence. The service nobility, no longer restrained by the tsar, now entered into its era of dominance.

On the death of Peter the Great, his immediate circle, particularly Menshikov (see Chapter 8), had every reason to fear the passage of the throne to the nine-year-old Peter, son of Alexis, and possible heir to the loyalties of the old nobility who had hated Peter the Great. Menshikov therefore strongly supported his one-time mistress, the Empress Catherine I, and succeeded in rallying to her side members of the guards who had come to like her while on campaigns. Since Catherine herself took little interest in affairs of state, Menshikov ran Russia during the two years of her reign. He tried to make himself secure by appointing a six-man "Supreme Privy Council" at the top of the administration, and to perpetuate his power he even planned to marry his daughter to the young heir, the future Peter II. On the death of Catherine I in 1727, he took the eleven-year-old boy into his house, where he proceeded to make him an alcoholic, as his father had been.

But Menshikov's arrogance had alienated even his followers. By 1728, the old boyars, led by the families of Dolgoruky and Galitsyn, had captured the throne, and Menshikov was exiled. Two Dolgoruky princes put themselves on the Supreme Privy Council, and the young Peter was engaged to a member of their family. The ascendancy of boyar families marked the return to supreme influence of a group that had been losing power ever since the days of Ivan the Terrible. Their plans were brought into crisis by the sudden death of Peter II on the very day scheduled for his coronation (January 19, 1730).

Their program can be studied in the conditions they submitted to the new candidate for the throne, Anne, the widow of the Duke of Courland. Summoning her from her petty Baltic principality, the Dolgoruky and the Galitsyns demanded that she sign these "Articles" before she take the throne. By their terms, she undertook never to marry or name an heir, and to continue the Supreme Privy Council, which by now had eight members, including four Dolgoruky and two Galitsyns. She further swore not to make peace or war, levy taxes, confer ranks in the army above that of colonel, or spend state funds without the specific consent of the Council. Moreover, the Councillors claimed for themselves supervision over the guards' regiments. This insistence on limiting the power of the new Empress reflected the outraged feelings of the old boyars, who had long been claiming the right to be consulted on all matters of state. The entire program was the most explicit constitutional destruction of all that Peter the Great had striven for. Anne signed the "Articles." Had she kept to their provisions, Russia would have embarked on an era of boyar oligarchy.

But the military-service nobility looked with horror at the prospect of taking orders indefinitely from the small group of old boyars. And the service gentry had a powerful lever in the guards' regiments. What its members wanted was an autocrat who would loosen the bonds that Peter the Great had forged for them. And so, when one of the Supreme Privy Councillors, the clever German Ostermann, convinced Anne that she need not abide by the Articles, the gentry in its armed might supported him. Anne simply tore up the Articles; thus, the attempt to create an oligarchy of the two great families failed. The gentry now had the real power in Russia.

Anne allowed her lover, the German adventurer Biren, and a flock of Germans to obtain the most influential positions in the state. The secret police, abolished after the death of Peter the Great, was now revived, and many thousands suffered torture, exile, and death at its hands. When Anne died, the German favorites fell out among themselves. Ostermann, a man of real ability, together with an excellent soldier, Marshal Münnich, brought about Biren's downfall and exile; then Ostermann forced Münnich out. Meanwhile, the tsar was the infant Ivan VI, whose mother, a German princess, acted as regent, and was so lazy that she lounged in her bedroom without the energy even to put on her clothes. Foreign intrigue produced the next shift in the imperial title. The French were anxious to terminate the power of Ostermann, who had been instrumental in cementing an alliance between Russia and France's traditional enemy, Austria. A clever French ambassador played on the patriotic feelings of the guardsmen, disgusted with the behavior of the Germans at court. In 1741 a guards' *coup* brought to the throne the daughter of Peter the Great, Elizabeth. The infant Ivan VI vanished into a prison cell with his indolent mother.

Elizabeth inherited her father's lust for life but not his brains or interest in matters of state. A succession of lovers had kept her busy all her life, and her habits did not change when she came to the throne. Though owning thousands of splendid dresses, she lived rather sluttishly in grubby palaces and enjoyed most of all a rousing peasant banquet with plenty to drink and lots of rustic music. Important state papers languished for days because the Empress could not be bothered to read them, much less sign them. Though she proclaimed her intention of restoring her father's methods of rule, she had no clear conception of what these had been. In an autocracy the autocrat has to take an interest in the affairs of state and assume responsibility for them; this Elizabeth did not do, and Russia drifted.

Soon after her accession, Elizabeth proclaimed her nephew, the half-mad Peter, heir to the throne. In 1745 he married a clever little German princess, the future Catherine II. Peter III, as he became after his succession in January, 1762, has had a bad "press"; he surely was not unusually intelligent, but was hardly the utter lunatic portrayed in the memoirs of his celebrated wife, who loathed him. The chief trouble with Peter seems to have been his great admiration for Prussia and his dislike of Russia. His effort to introduce rigid discipline on the Prussian model into the Russian army and his hatred for the influential guards' regiments cost him the friends he needed most. He could have played his wargames with his toy soldiers, held court-martials on rats whom he convicted of gnawing cardboard fortresses, and swilled his favorite English beer with impunity, and he would not have been any worse than many another tsar. But to drill the guards in the Prussian manner was unforgivable. So a new palace revolution took place, and Peter was eventually murdered by one of Catherine's lovers. The Empress' own role in his overthrow is still obscure.

Nobles and Serfs, 1730–1762

A deeply dissatisfied social group that had the power to make and unmake autocrats naturally had a program for the redress of its own grievances. Once the gentry had enabled Anne to tear up the Articles in 1730, it began strenuous efforts to emancipate itself from the servitude riveted upon it by Peter. Anne repealed the law requiring the noble to leave his estate intact to one of his sons. She founded a military school for noblemen's sons, graduation from which entitled one to a commission; no longer did young gentlemen have to start their careers in the ranks, as under Peter. Anne shortened the terms of service from life to twenty-five years, and exempted one son of every family with at least two sons, so that there would be one member of each generation able to look after the estate.

Simultaneously came a deepening of the authority of the nobles over the serfs. The proprietors became the government's agents for the collection of the poll tax. Serfs could no longer obtain their freedom by enlisting in the army and could not engage in trade or purchase land without written permission from their masters. Masters could deport their serfs to Siberia and might punish them physically in any way they wished. Moreover, under Elizabeth, a series of laws restricted the right of owning serfs to those who were already nobles. Thus the class that had been open to new recruits under Peter was closed by his daughter.

In 1762, finally, Peter III decreed that the nobles no longer need serve at all unless they wished to do so; except in the midst of a war, they might resign any time they chose. It was little wonder that some of the nobles proposed to erect a solid gold statue of Peter III. To understand the revolutionary nature of this liberation of the nobles from a duty to serve, we must remember that they had historically obtained their lands and serfs only on condition that they would serve. Now they kept their lands and serfs but had no obligations. Yet the service that had been hated when it was compulsory became fashionable now that it was optional; there was really little else for a Russian noble to do except serve the state. In contemplating all this, a great Russian historian remarked that the logic of history would have properly required that all serfs be liberated the day after the nobles were released from their duty to serve. But nothing could have been further from the thoughts of Peter III or of any other Russian leader.

In these middle decades of the eighteenth century, successive waves of foreign influence affected the Russian nobility. It was not only the influx of foreigners that brought in western habits; it was also the involvement of Russia in the European wars of the period, and the increased travel abroad by Russians. Under Elizabeth, when the hated Germans disappeared from court, the way was clear for the French to exert their influence. With the French language came the literature, and many a Russian noble bought French books by the yard for his library because it was the thing to do. The champagne business boomed (the Russians liked the sweet kind that most Frenchmen despised); French styles of dress were copied by both men and women. Francomania took its extreme form among those Russians who were ashamed of being Russian and who would not fall in love with any girl unable to speak French. Indeed, the noble and the peasant no longer spoke the same language. This deep rift between the Frenchified nobles and the Russian people was to prove of critical importance for later Russian history.

Catherine the Great (1762–1796)

With the advent of Catherine II, we come to the most arresting personality to occupy the Russian throne since the death of Peter. Brought up in a petty German court, she found herself transplanted to St. Petersburg as a mere girl, living with a husband she detested, and forced to pick her way through the intrigues that flourished around the Empress Elizabeth. She managed to steer clear of trouble only by using her keen wits. Catherine fancied herself as an intellectual; she wrote plays, edited a satirical journal, and steeped herself in the literature of the Enlightenment. Both before and after ascending the throne she maintained a goodly supply of lovers, several of whom had important roles in affairs of state.

Catherine had a truly twentieth-century feeling for the importance of public relations, and cared deeply that leading spirits in the West should think well of her and of the state of Russia under her rule. Hence her voluminous correspondence with westerners. She invited Diderot to take up in Russia the task of editing the *Encyclopédie;* then she bought his library, but he kept his books, and received a pension—very favorable publicity for Russia and the Russian Empress. Diderot himself visited Russia in 1773; though he came back entranced with Catherine, who, he said, had the soul of Brutus and the charms of Cleopatra, the visit was not entirely a success. Catherine complained that in the excitement of conversation he pinched her legs until they were black and blue. Voltaire, though he judiciously stayed away from Russia, accepted Catherine's bounty, and in return poured out the praises that she yearned for, calling her "the north star" and "the benefactress of Europe."

Catherine would perhaps have liked to reform conditions in Russia; there was something of the enlightened despot about her "style." But as a woman and a foreigner and a usurper, owing the throne to a conspiracy, she could not act upon her inclinations. Depending

Catherine the Great, about 1762.

as she did upon the good will of the nobility, she could not lay a finger on the institution of serfdom. She had to reward her supporters with vast grants of state land, inhabited by hundreds of thousands of state peasants, who once could not be sold but who now became privately owned serfs who could be sold. Even in theory, Catherine felt, Russia was so large that the only possible form of government was an autocracy. As an autocrat she was as arbitrary as any of her predecessors.

Once firmly established on the throne, however, Catherine decided to convoke a commission to codify the laws of Russia, a task that had not been accomplished since 1649. Catherine herself, with the help of advisers, spent three years composing the *Instruction* to the delegates, a long, rather windy document, full of abstract argument drawn from Montesquieu's *Spirit of the Laws* and Beccaria's *Crimes and Punishments* but altered to conform with the Empress' own beliefs. Here one can discern no intention to meddle with the fundamental institutions of Russia, but some concern for eliminating their worst abuses. The 564 dele-

gates to the commission were elected by organs of the central government and by every social class in Russia except the serf peasants. Each delegate—noble, townsman, crown peasant, Cossack—was charged to bring with him a collection of written documents from his neighbors presenting their grievances and demands for change.

Many of these survive and teach us a great deal about the state of public opinion in Catherine's Russia. Nobody seems to have been dissatisfied with the autocracy; at least we find no requests that it modify its power or consult its subjects. People did seek more rights and duties for local government and wanted their own obligations more clearly defined. Each class of representatives was eager to extend the rights of that class: The free peasants wanted to own serfs; the townsmen wanted to own serfs and be the only class allowed to engage in trade; the nobles wanted to engage in trade, and to have their exclusive right to own serfs confirmed. After 203 sessions lasting over a year and a half, devoted to inconclusive and sometimes heated debate, Catherine put an end to the labors of the commission in 1768. It had not codified the laws, but from Catherine's own point of view it had been a success; she knew that most of her subjects supported her as absolute autocrat. It is important to remember that the commission, with all its imperfections, was the last effort by the tsardom to consult the Russian people as a whole for 138 years—until revolution summoned the first duma into existence in 1906 (see Chapter 14).

Catherine turned the spadework of the legislative commission to good advantage in her later reforms, which resulted from the great rebellion of the Cossacks under the leadership of Pugachev, 1773–1775. Pugachev roused the frontiersmen to revolt against Catherine's cancellation of their special privileges. Pretending to be Tsar Peter III, and promising liberty and land to the serfs who joined his forces, Pugachev swept over a wide area of southeastern Russia and finally marched toward Moscow. Like the disturbances of the seventeenth century, Pugachev's revolt revealed the existence of bitter discontent in Russia, a discontent directed not at the supreme autocrat but at the landlords and local officials.

The ramshackle provincial administration almost collapsed under the strain of Pugachev's rebellion. Orders filtered down slowly to local officials, and the soldiers defending the government moved almost as slowly. When the rebels were finally suppressed, and Pugachev was traveling northward in an iron cage before being drawn and quartered, Catherine took action. Her reorganization of local government (1775) created fifty provinces where there had been twenty before. She thus replaced a small number of unwieldy units with a larger number of small provinces, each containing roughly 300,000 to 400,000 inhabitants. The reform of 1775 gave the nobles the lion's share of provincial offices but subjected them to the close direction of the central government, which had its own administrative, financial, and legal representatives in each province.

In the charter of 1785 the nobles received exemption from military service and taxation and secured absolute mastery over the fate of their serfs and their estates. A charter to the towns in the same year (1785) disclosed Catherine's sympathy with the tiny but growing middle class. It established the principle of municipal self-government, but the principle remained a dead letter because of the rigorous class distinctions maintained in the backward urban centers of Russia. For the serfs, needless to say, there was no charter. Indeed, besides adding almost a million to their number by the gifts of state lands to private persons, Catherine increased still further the power of the proprietors. Long accustomed to selling the serfs without their land, the landlords now received the right to make such sales legally. Serf families were broken up, violent punishments and even torture employed (one notorious lady tortured seventy-five of her own serfs to death, but she was imprisoned for it), serfs were gambled away at cards, given as presents, and mortgaged for loans. All serf-owners were not cruel any more than all slave-owners in our own slave states, but both institutions tended to degrade both master and man. As in the American South, there was a distinction in Russia between field hands and household servants. Great landowners often had hundreds of the latter, some of whom were formed into orchestras, gave dramatic performances, tutored the sons of the family, or acted as household poets and scientists.

The contrast between the climate of the Enlightenment which surrounded the court and the actual conditions in Russia was keenly felt by sensitive men. Foremost among them was a young noble, Alexander Radishchev, educated abroad and widely traveled. In his *Journey from St. Petersburg to Moscow,* Radishchev included vivid and horrifying vignettes of serfdom and the abuses of the administration. Moreover, Radishchev's poetry praised Cromwell, the regicide. It is possible that the author's truly western culture might have enabled him to get away with this in the early days of Catherine's reign. But by 1790 the French Revolution was under way, and Catherine had begun to hate the French and "their abominable bonfire" as much as she had formerly loved them. Proposing to burn the dangerous books of the Enlightenment, she could hardly overlook the subversive character of Radishchev's writings. Off he went into exile in Siberia. Similarly, the humanitarian Freemason, Nicholas Novikov, manager of the newly active Moscow University Press, editor of newspapers, and sponsor of campaigns to raise money and food for famine-stricken peasants, was also jailed on flimsy charges. Though Novikov had done nothing against the régime, it could not tolerate the continuance of any enterprise it did not dominate. The two enlightened intellectuals, Radishchev and Novikov, not only serve as an illustration of the contrast between Catherine's professed principles and her actual conduct but also provide the first real examples of thoroughly westernized individual Russians.

Paul (1796–1801)

Catherine's son Paul (who may or may not have been the son of Catherine's husband, Peter III) succeeded her in 1796 as a man of forty-two. All his life his mother had distrusted him, fearing that there might be a conspiracy to oust her and install Paul, ostensibly a legitimate Romanov. The best-educated Russian royal personage to date, active and eager to serve the state, Paul found himself given no duties, kept in the dark about the secrets of state, and even deprived of his two eldest children, Alexander and Constantine, whom Catherine insisted on educating herself. All he could do was drill a small garrison on his country estate and dress them in Prussian uniform.

Consequently, when Paul finally did succeed to the throne, he appeared to be motivated chiefly by a wish to undo his mother's work and act in every possible way contrary to the precedents she had set. He exiled some of Catherine's favorites, and released many of her prisoners, including Radishchev and Novikov. Paul believed in legality and system, and hoped to install a great deal more of both in Russia. He tried to restore more power and order to the central administration by putting the colleges (see p. 297) under single ministers in place of the former boards of directors. Paul's behavior, however, was spasmodic and eccentric. He forbade the importation of sheet-music because he feared that all music would be as revolutionary as the *Marseillaise*. He imposed a strict curfew on the capital. He issued a manifesto limiting to three the number of days per week a serf might be required to work on his master's land, but it is not clear whether this was a binding law or only a recommendation. In any case, he continued to give away state lands, and transformed some half a million state peasants into privately owned chattels.

What was probably fatal to Paul was his policy of toughness toward the nobility. A noble, he is said to have remarked, is the man I am talking to at the moment, and he ceases to be a noble when I stop talking to him. This definition could hardly be expected to appeal to the privileged masters of Russia. Paul exacted compulsory service again, and in the provinces he curtailed the powers of the nobility. Nobles found themselves forced to meet the bills for public buildings, paying new taxes on their lands, and subjected to corporal punishments for crimes. Paul, like Peter III,

wanted to Prussianize the army, and especially to inculcate in the officers a sense of responsibility for the men. In the guards' regiments such programs were detested, and a conspiracy of guardsmen ended in 1801 with Paul's murder and Alexander's succession. The forces behind the *coup* were the same as those that had engineered so many shifts of power during the preceding century. The precise degree to which Alexander was informed of the *coup* in advance is sometimes debated, but he knew at least that the conspirators intended to force his father's abdication.

Alexander I (1801–1825)

In Alexander I there came to the throne an emperor whom historians usually call "enigmatic." Educated by a liberal Swiss tutor, he absorbed so much of the new eighteenth-century doctrines that he actually blossomed out with a red-white-and-blue ribbon, the colors of revolutionary France, on hearing of the fall of the Bastille to the Paris mob. Yet the application of liberal principles in Russia would involve a direct challenge to the most powerful forces in society. So, although Alexander would occasionally say to his intimates that some day he would grant Russia a constitution and himself retire to a castle on the Rhine, in fact this was little but romantic twaddle. Tall and handsome, utterly devastating to the ladies, charming and cultivated, Alexander liked to please everybody; he vacillated, compromised, and in the end accomplished very little. Moreover, he loved power dearly, and always shied away from proposals to limit it.

The quarter-century of his reign was twice interrupted by major wars against Napoleon, in 1805–1807, and in 1812–1815 (see Chapter 10). In the first period of relative peace, 1801–1805, Alexander gathered round him a small group of young men which he called the "unofficial committee." One of the members, Stroganov, had been an active member of the Jacobin Club in Paris during the revolution; two others greatly admired the English system of government. Meeting regularly after dinner over coffee and brandy, the unofficial committee had as its self-appointed task the preparation of a constitution for Russia, after due study of all known constitutions. But its discussions were little more than the unsystematic talk of pleasant, well-born young men who had dined well. A decree sponsored by the committee did abolish the administrative colleges and created eight new ministries to take their place; but this in fact had largely been accomplished by Paul. When the committee stopped meeting in 1803, it had done nothing with regard to serfdom. The Tsar himself in these years passed two laws, whose very mildness shows how little he intended to disturb existing institutions. One of them forbade the public advertisement of sales of serfs without land, but the law was easily circumvented. The other created a new category of "free farmers," serfs who had been freed by their masters, and prescribed that if a proprietor freed an entire village of serfs he must confer their land upon them at the same time. Since this left the initiative for liberation entirely in the hands of the proprietor, fewer than 40,000 among all the millions of serfs in Russia actually received their freedom.

In the second period of peace, 1807–1811, Alexander had as his chief mentor a remarkable figure, Michael Speransky, son of a Russian priest, intelligent, well-educated, and conscientious. Utilizing Montesquieu's principle of the separation of powers, Speransky drafted for Alexander a constitutional project that would have made Russia a limited monarchy. A series of elected assemblies, beginning at the lowest level of administrative subdivision and continuing on up through district and province, would culminate in a great national assembly, the duma. A similar pyramid of courts and a new set of executive institutions was also planned. The duma would have to approve any law promulgated by the Tsar and would have been a genuine Russian parliament. It is true that the franchise Speransky proposed would have enormously favored the nobility, while the serfs of course would not have participated in government. It is also true that Speransky did not include emancipation of the serfs in his proposal. None

the less, the plan was decidedly advanced; Speransky knew that not everything could be accomplished at once. Indeed, as it turned out, Alexander balked at executing the plan that he himself had commissioned Speransky to draw up.

This is one of the most critical moments in all Russian history. Why did Speransky fail? He instituted a reform of the civil service, requiring examinations and a system of promotion by merit, which disturbed many of the almost illiterate and thoroughly incompetent men in high office. He even proposed that the nobility pay an income tax. Friends and intimates of the Tsar spread slander about Speransky, but at bottom Alexander himself was at fault and unwilling to act on his own alleged beliefs. Speransky's scheme was shelved, except for two elements that in no way diminished the power of the Tsar. A Council of State, which could advise the Tsar, was created, but he was not obliged to take its advice. Since he appointed and dismissed all members, the effect was simply to increase imperial effi-

Tsar Alexander I of Russia.

ciency, not to limit imperial authority. Further administrative efficiency was obtained through the reorganization of the ministries, whose duties were set out clearly for the first time, eliminating overlapping.

During the second war against Napoleon (1812–1815) Alexander fell under the influence of a Baltic Baroness named Madame de Krüdener, a mystical lady now repenting an ill-spent youth. She convinced the Tsar that he was a "man from the North" designed by destiny to overthrow Napoleon and institute a new order. At the Russian court an atmosphere of pious mysticism and conservatism replaced the earlier flashes of liberal views. Although the leading spirits of the new religiosity were all nominally Orthodox, its character was rather Protestant. It was based upon assiduous reading of the Bible, and it also included a mixture of elements from Freemasonry, Pietism (see p. 349), and the more eccentric Russian sects. It aimed at the union of all Christendom in one faith and thus aroused the fear and opposition of many Orthodox clerics. Its real importance lay in its impact on Alexander, who was now convinced that as the bearer of a sacred mission all he needed to do was follow the promptings of his inmost feelings.

During the last decade of Alexander's reign, 1815–1825, the most important figure at court was Count Arakcheev, a competent but brutal officer, who once bit off the ear of one of his men as a punishment. The chief innovation of the decade, accomplished under Arakcheev's direction, was the hated system of "military colonies," the drafting of the population of whole districts to serve in the regiments quartered there. When not drilling or fighting, the soldiers were to work their farms, and their entire lives were subject to the whims of their officers. Far from being model communities, the military colonies were virtual concentration camps. By the end of Alexander's reign, almost 400,000 soldiers were living in them.

Though Alexander gave Russia no important reforms, he did act on liberal principles outside Russia, in Poland and in Finland. Made King of Poland by the Vienna settlement of 1815 (see Chapter 11), Alexander gave the Poles an advanced constitution, with their own army, their own Polish officialdom, and the free use of their own language. He allowed the Finns, after their annexation by Russia in 1809, to preserve their own law codes and the system of local government introduced during the long preceding Swedish rule. But the "liberal Tsar" was liberal only outside his Russian dominions.

Russian Foreign Policy, 1725–1796

The motives of Russian foreign policy in the century between the death of Peter the Great and that of Alexander I were still the ancient ones of expansion against Sweden, Poland, and Turkey. But as a new member of the European power constellation, Russia found that pursuit of these old aims was now involving her in matters that had primary significance for western Europe. In 1726 Ostermann concluded an alliance with the Habsburg Empire which was to be a cornerstone of Russian foreign policy. Yet, especially in joint undertakings against the Turks, the Russians and Austrians found, as early as the 1730's, that they had conflicting ambitions in southeast Europe. This early conflict of interests was a cloud, still no larger than a man's hand, but destined to swell into the colossal thunderhead that exploded in the World War of 1914–1918. To the eighteenth century also belong the first regular Russian diplomatic service, the first Russian participation in international espionage and intrigue, and the first real Russian foreign ministers: Ostermann and his Russian successor Bestuzhev-Ryumin, men of enormous personal influence on the course of Russian diplomacy.

In the War of the Polish Succession (see p. 303) Russian forces took part in alliance with Austria in supporting Augustus III and helped to force the abdication of Stanislas Leszczynski. Immediately, the Russians and Austrians became allies in a new war against the Turks, 1735–1739 (see p. 302). Though Marshal Münnich successfully invaded the Crimea, Russian gains at the Treaty of Belgrade in 1739 were limited to Azov. The Austrians failed to co-operate satisfactorily in an invasion of the Danubian principalities and made it clear that they did not relish a Russian advance into the principalities and thus to the Habsburg frontiers.

At the opening of the War of the Austrian Succession in 1740, the Russians were preoccupied with the dynastic problem. We have already seen how the French ambassador worked to put Elizabeth on the throne and to bring about the downfall of the pro-Austrian Ostermann. But, since Bestuzhev-Ryumin continued Ostermann's policies, French hopes were largely disappointed. Prussian (and therefore anti-Austrian) influence manifested itself with the appearance of Peter III as heir, and with the choice of the future Catherine II as his bride. Thus, during the War of the Austrian Succession, there was a good deal of jockeying for Russian assistance. The advance of Frederick the Great along the Baltic shore alarmed the Russians, and so, as the war ended, a Russian corps was leisurely pushing westward, intending to join the fighting.

Anti-Prussian sentiment crystallized during the interval of peace before the outbreak of the Seven Years' War. Bestuzhev labored mightily to obtain an alliance with England, which he managed in 1755, the Russians accepting a large subsidy in exchange for a promise to keep troops in readiness against the Prussians. But the Diplomatic Revolution of 1756, making Prussia and England allies, negated this arrangement. The Russians thus remained loyal to Austria and fought the Prussians in the Seven Years' War. Once more Russian forces marched west, so slowly that there was suspicion of treason and the commander was removed. In 1758 the invasion of East Prussia began; and eventually in 1760 Russian forces entered Berlin. Elizabeth's death and the succession of the pro-Prussian Peter III led the Russians to change sides and join the Prussians briefly against the Austrians and French. Catherine, on her succession, withdrew the Russian forces, but

did not again attack the Prussians. Thus Russia found herself excluded from the peace conferences of 1763.

In foreign policy, Catherine the Great was as vigorous and unscrupulous as she was at home. She concentrated on the traditional anti-Polish and anti-Turkish aims of Russia. In 1763, only a year after she became Empress, the throne of Poland fell vacant, and Catherine secured the election of her protégé and former lover, a pro-Russian Pole, Stanislas Poniatowski. Frederick the Great joined with Catherine in a campaign to win rights for the persecuted Lutheran and Orthodox minorities in Catholic Poland. One party of Polish nobles, their national pride offended at foreign intervention, resisted, and secured the aid of France and Austria, which adopted the stratagem of pressing Turkey into war with Russia to distract Catherine from Poland.

In the first Russo-Turkish War (1768–1774), Catherine's forces won a series of victories. A Russian Baltic fleet, sent all the way around Europe and into the Mediterranean through the Straits of Gibraltar, destroyed the Turkish fleet in the Aegean (1770), largely owing to the superior seamanship of a few English officers who were advising the otherwise inefficient Russians. But the Russians failed to follow up their initial advantage by storming the Straits and attacking Istanbul, and operations shifted to the Crimea and the Danubian principalities. While the Russians and Turks were discussing peace terms, Frederick the Great had concluded that Russia had been too successful against the Turks and might seize most of Poland for herself unless he acted quickly.

So Frederick took the leading part in arranging the first partition of Poland (1772). Poland lost to Russia, Prussia, and Austria almost one-third of her territory and one-half of her population. Frederick's share of the loot—the lands immediately to the west of East Prussia— was the smallest but the most strategic. It included the region that had previously separated Brandenburg from East Prussia. Maria Theresa, the Empress of Austria, abandoned her Turkish and Polish allies to participate.

She did seem somewhat reluctant, yet, as Frederick the Great observed, "She wept, but she kept on taking." Russia received a substantial area of what is now known as Belorussia, or White Russia.

Two years later, the Russians imposed upon the Turks a most humiliating peace treaty, at Kutchuk Kainardji (1774). Catherine annexed much of the formerly Turkish stretch of Black Sea coast and two places in the Crimea; the rest of the Crimea was separated from the Ottoman Empire as an independent Tartar state.

She also obtained something the Russians had long coveted: freedom of navigation on the Black Sea and the right of passage through the Bosphorus and the Dardanelles. A vaguely worded clause gave her various rights to protect the Christian subjects of the sultan, thus providing a convenient excuse for Russian intervention in Turkish affairs later on.

Catherine now began to dream of expelling the Turks from Europe and reviving the Byzantine Empire under Russian protection. She saw to it that her younger grandson was christened

Partitions of Poland, 1772, 1793, 1795

SWEDEN

Baltic Sea

PRUSSIA
Berlin

EAST PRUSSIA

Danzig
Königsberg
Memel
Libau
Riga
Vilna
Minsk
Smolensk
Moscow
Volga R.
Dvina R.

RUSSIA

Posen
Warsaw
Cracow
Lemberg
GALICIA
Zhitomir
Kiev
Pripet R.
Niemen R.
Vistula R.
Bug R.
Oder R.
Elbe R.

AUSTRIA
Vienna
Danube R.
HUNGARY
Buda
Pest

Dniester R.
Pruth R.
Dnieper R.
Odessa

OTTOMAN

EMPIRE   Black Sea

0   100   200
Miles

	1772	1793	1795
To Prussia			
To Russia			
To Austria			

Constantine and imported Greek-speaking nurses to train him in the language. She also proposed to set up a kingdom of Dacia (the Roman name for the area) in the Danubian principalities to be ruled by her lover and general, Potemkin. By way of preparation, in 1783, Catherine annexed the Tartar state of the Crimea, where she built a naval base at Sebastopol. To achieve these grandiose designs, Catherine sought the consent of Austria and invited Joseph II on a famous tour by riverboat of the newly developed and annexed territories of the Russian southwest. On this tour, the Austrian Emperor was allegedly shown the famous "Potemkin villages," mere cardboard facades facing the river to look like settlements but with nothing behind them; like so many other good stories, this one is untrue. At Sebastopol, however, signs pointed across the Black Sea, saying, "This way to Byzantium." In a second Russo-Turkish war (1787–1791), Catherine's allies, the Austrians, once again provided feeble assistance and made a separate peace. Again, a conflict of interests over the European lands of the Sultan precipitated Austro-Russian disagreement. In the end, Catherine had to abandon her Greek project and content herself with annexing the remaining Turkish lands along the northern coast of the Black Sea and securing recognition of Russian sovereignty over the Crimea.

Before her death, Catherine participated in two more partitions of Poland. The second partition came as the result of a Polish constitutional movement, supported by the Prussians in opposition to Russian interest. Catherine intervened on the pretext of defending the established order in Poland and fighting the virus of revolution. In 1793, both the Russians and Prussians took large new slices of Polish territory; the Austrians did not participate in this second partition of Poland. An attempted Polish revolution against the reduction of their state to a wretched remnant dominated by foreigners was followed by the third and final partition of 1795, by which Poland disappeared from the map. This time Austria joined the other two powers and obtained Cracow; Prussia got Warsaw, and Russia secured Lithuania and other Baltic and east Polish lands.

The spectacular successes of Catherine meant the transfer to Russia of millions of human beings — Poles, Lithuanians, Belorussians — who loathed the Russians, and left a legacy of trouble. It also meant that Russia had destroyed useful buffers in the shape of the Polish and Tartar states, and now had common frontiers with her potential enemies, Prussia and Austria. The last two partitions of Poland had been made possible by the preoccupation of the western powers with their war against revolutionary France; the story of Russian foreign policy after Catherine forms part of the larger story of this great war (see Chapter 10).

V George III and the American Revolution

George III

Though Catherine the Great failed to apply the ideas of the Age of Reason, her name usually appears on lists of enlightened despots. Another name might possibly be added to the list — George III, King of Great Britain (1760–1820). Actually, "Farmer George" showed very little enlightenment beyond taking an interest in the agrarian revolution and writing articles on turnips for Arthur Young's *Annals of Agriculture.* In politics, however, he did attempt a course that may be termed a dilute form of enlightened despotism, or, more exactly, a reassertion of the monarch's authority. The first of the Hanoverian monarchs born and bred in England, George III proposed to reassert some of the royal prerogatives that had lapsed under the first two Georges. He tried to wrest control of the House of Commons from the long-dominant Whig oligarchy and retain it by the Whig devices of patronage and bribery. He endeavored to beat the Whigs at their own parliamentary game.

Virtuous as a person and devoted to his family, George as a monarch was stubborn, short-sighted, and in the long run unsuccessful. It was easy for him at first to exploit the factional strife among the Whigs, maneuver Pitt out of office in 1761, and make his friend and tutor, Lord Bute, the head of the cabinet. Bute and the King, however, found it hard to justify their failure to deprive France of the sugar-rich West Indies in the Peace of Paris, which brought the Seven Years' War to a conclusion (see Chapter 8). The Commons ratified the treaty, but George dismissed Bute to appease the critics of British diplomacy.

The harshest criticism came from John Wilkes, a member of Commons, who dubbed the Peace of Paris "the peace of God, for it passeth all understanding." Wilkes' attack on the treaty in his paper, the *North Briton*, infuriated the King; bowing to the royal anger, the Commons ordered the offending issue of the *North Briton* to be burnt. Later, Wilkes ran for Parliament three separate times, and three times the Commons, under royal pressure, threw out his election. When Wilkes finally took his seat again in 1774, he was a popular hero, and riots had occurred in defense of "Wilkes and Liberty." A wise king would have reconsidered his course, but George III did not relax his determination to manage both Parliament and cabinet. After seven years of short-lived, unstable ministries (1763–1770), George finally found a man to fill Bute's old role and do the King's bidding—Lord North, who headed the cabinet for a dozen years (1770–1782). Under North, royal intervention in politics at first stiffened, then wavered, and at length collapsed. At home, the King unwittingly prepared the way for the increase of parliamentary authority; abroad, he lost the thirteen North American colonies.

Background of the Revolution

The breach between colonies and mother country first became serious at the close of the Seven Years' War when Britain began to retreat from the old policy of "salutary neglect" and to interfere more directly and more frequently in colonial matters. But, by 1763, the colonies had acquired the habit of regulating their own affairs, though the acts of their assemblies remained subject to the veto of royally appointed governors or of the King himself. The vast territories in Canada and west of the Alleghenies acquired in 1763 brought Britain added opportunities for profitable exploitation and added responsibilities for government and defense. When an uprising of Indians under Pontiac threatened frontier posts in the area of the Ohio Valley and the Great Lakes, colonial militias failed to take effective action, and British regulars were brought in. The continuing threat from the Indians prompted the royal proclamation of October, 1763, forbidding "all our loving subjects" to settle west of a line running along the summit of the Alleghenies. To His Majesty's "loving subjects" in the seaboard colonies, however, the proclamation seemed deliberately designed to exclude them from the riches of the West.

The colonies resented still more keenly the attempt by Parliament to raise more revenue in North America. The British government had very strong arguments for increasing colonial taxes. The national debt had almost doubled during the Seven Years' War; the colonies' reluctance to recruit soldiers and raise taxes themselves had increased the cost of the war to British taxpayers; now the mother country faced continued expense in protecting the frontier. Surely the Americans would admit the reasonableness of the case for higher taxes.

That, however, was precisely what the Americans did *not* admit. The first of the new revenue measures, the Sugar Act of 1764, alarmed the merchants of the eastern seaboard because the customs officers actually undertook to collect duties on molasses, sugar, and other imports. Here was a departure from the comfortable laxity of salutary neglect. And here was a threat to the colonial economy, for the import duties had to be paid out of the colonies' meager supply of specie (metal coin). The second revenue measure, the Stamp Act of 1765, imposed levies on a wide variety of items, including legal and commercial papers, liquor licenses, playing cards, dice, newspapers, calendars, and academic degrees. These duties, too, drained the supply of specie, which sank so low that some merchants faced bankruptcy.

The revenue measures touched off a major controversy. Indignant merchants in the New World boycotted all imports rather than pay the duties, and in October, 1765, delegates from nine of the thirteen colonies met in New York City as the "Stamp Act Congress." The Congress complained that the new duties had "a manifest tendency to subvert the rights and liberties of the colonists." The Congress resolved:

That His Majesty's liege subjects in these colonies are entitled to all the inherent rights and liberties of his natural born subjects within the kingdom of Great Britain.

That it is inseparably essential to the freedom of a people, and the undoubted right of Englishmen, that no taxes be imposed on them but with their own consent, given personally or by their own representatives.

That the people of these colonies are not, and from their local circumstances cannot be, represented in the House of Commons in Great Britain.

That the only representatives of these colonies are persons chosen therein by themselves, and that no taxes ever have been, or can be constitutionally imposed on them, but by their respective legislatures.*

The Stamp Act Congress thus proclaimed the celebrated principle of no taxation without representation. Britain surrendered on the

*Documents of American History, H. S. Commager, ed. (New York, 1940), 58.

practical issue, but did not yield on the principle. The appeals of London merchants, nearly ruined by the American boycott against British goods, brought the repeal of the Stamp Act in 1765. In 1766, however, Parliament passed the Declaratory Act asserting that the King and Parliament could indeed make laws affecting the colonies.

For the next decade, Britain adhered firmly to the principles of the Declaratory Act, and colonial radicals just as firmly repeated their opposition to taxation without representation. Parliament again tried to raise revenue, this time by the Townshend duties (1767) on colonial imports of tea, paper, paint, and lead. Again the merchants of Philadelphia, New York, and Boston organized boycotts. In 1770, Lord North's cabinet withdrew the Townshend

An English commentary on the Boston Tea Party and the tarring and feathering of a royal tax collector, who is forced to drink under a liberty tree.

duties except for the three-penny tariff on a pound of tea, retained as a symbol of parliamentary authority over the colonies. Three years later, the English East India Company attempted the sale of surplus tea in North America, hoping to overcome American opposition to the hated duty by making the retail price of East India tea, duty included, far cheaper than that of Dutch tea smuggled by the colonists. The result was the Boston Tea Party. On December 16, 1773, to the cheers of spectators lining the waterfront, a group of Bostonians, who had a large financial stake in smuggled tea, disguised themselves as Indians, boarded three East India ships, and dumped into the harbor chests of tea worth thousands of pounds.

Britain answered defiance with coercion, and the colonists met coercion with resistance. The Quebec Act (1774), incorporating the lands beyond the Alleghenies into Canada, bolted the door to the westward expansion of colonial frontiers. The "Intolerable Acts" (1774) closed the port of Boston to trade and suspended elections in Massachusetts. At Lexington and Concord in April, 1775, the "embattled farmers" of Massachusetts fired the opening shots of the War of Independence. At Philadelphia on July 4, 1776, the delegates to the Continental Congress formally declared the American colonies independent of Great Britain.

Implications of the Revolution

For the mother country, the American Revolution implied more than the secession of thirteen colonies. It involved Britain in a minor world war that jeopardized her dominance abroad and weakened the power and prestige of King George III at home. The most crucial battle in North America came early in the war—the surrender at Saratoga in 1777 of the British forces under Burgoyne, who had been marching south from Montreal with the aim of driving a wedge between New England and the other rebellious colonies. Burgoyne's surrender convinced the French that support of the American colonists would give them an excellent chance to renew their world-wide struggle with Britain and avenge the humiliation of 1763. Entering the war in 1778, France soon gained the alliance of Spain and eventually secured the help, or at least the friendly neutrality, of most other European states. French intervention prepared the way for the victory of George Washington's forces and the final British surrender at Yorktown in 1781. In the peace signed at Paris in 1783, Britain recognized the independence of her former colonies. To Spain she handed back Florida, which she had taken in 1763, and the strategic Mediterranean island of Minorca. But she kept Gibraltar, which the Spanish had also hoped to recover, and she ceded only minor territories to France.

During the early years of the war, the British public had been inclined to agree with Dr. Samuel Johnson that the Americans were "a race of convicts" and "ought to be thankful for anything we allow them short of hanging." But the temper of opinion changed as the strength of American resistance became evident, as instances of British mismanagement piled up, and as most of Europe rallied to the rebellious colonies. By 1780, George III and his policies were so unpopular that the House of Commons passed a resolution declaring that "the influence of the crown has increased, is increasing, and ought to be diminished."

The influence of the Crown *was* diminished. In 1782, Lord North, who had been imploring the King for three years to accept his resignation, finally stepped down. In the next year, the post of prime minister fell to William Pitt the Younger, son of the heroic Pitt of the Seven Years' War. Though only twenty-five years old, he was a seasoned parliamentarian who was to head the cabinet for the next eighteen years. With the advent of Pitt, control of British politics shifted away from the King and back to the professional politicians. George III briefly contemplated abdication and then gradually resigned himself to the passive role of constitutional monarch. The British flirtation (it was really no more than that) with enlightened despotism had come to an end.

While American independence was a nationalist rather than a social revolution, the movement that produced it did have social implications. In the colonies, opinion was by no means unanimous in support of the revolution. Many well-to-do colonists, including southern planters and Pennsylvania Quakers, either backed the mother country or took a neutral position in the struggle; New York supplied more recruits to George III than to George Washington. Some of these "Loyalists" or "Tories" were to flee to Canada when independence became a fact. Scholars, however, now find that the traditional estimate—that only one-third of the colonists actively backed the Revolution—is too low. Revolutionary sentiment ran particularly high in Virginia and New England and among social groups who had the habit of questioning established authority—the pioneers living on the frontier, and the numerous Presbyterians, Congregationalists, and members of other strong-minded Protestant sects. Like adolescents everywhere, the colonists resented parental tutelage yet appealed to family precedent. They claimed that they were only following the example set by Englishmen in 1688 and defended by John Locke.

The ideas of Locke and Newton were as well known and as much respected in North America as they were in Europe. They underlay the Declaration of Independence:

When in the course of human events, it becomes necessary for one people to dissolve the political bands which have connected them with another, and to assume among the Powers of the earth, the separate and equal station to which the Laws of Nature and Nature's God entitle them, a decent respect to the opinions of mankind requires that they should declare the causes which impel them to the separation.

The opening paragraph of the Declaration thus expressed the concept of a world-machine ruled by the "Laws of Nature." The next paragraph applied to the colonies Locke's theory of contract and his justification of revolution:

We hold these truths to be self-evident, that all men are created equal, that they are endowed by their Creator with certain unalienable Rights, that among these are Life, Liberty and the pursuit of Happiness. That to secure these rights, Govern-

ments are instituted among Men, deriving their just power from the consent of the governed. That whenever any Form of Government becomes destructive of these ends, it is the Right of the People to alter or to abolish it, and to institute new Government. . . .

Another political idea of the Enlightenment congenial to the revolutionaries was the separation of powers proposed by Locke and by Montesquieu as a guarantee against tyranny. At the heart of the draft drawn up by the delegates to the constitutional convention at Philadelphia in 1787 was the separation of the executive, legislative, and judicial arms of government. Each of the branches had the power to check the other two. The President, for instance, could check the Congress by applying a veto; Congress could check the executive and the judiciary through impeachment and the right of confirming appointments; and one house of Congress exercised a check on the other by the requirement that both houses consent to legislation. Since these balancing devices were in part derived from Montesquieu, it may be argued that the recurrent tensions between President and Congress originated in the American adaptation of an eighteenth-century French misreading of British constitutional practice. The "Founding Fathers" of the American republic sought guidance not only from *The Spirit of the Laws* but also from the constitutions of the thirteen original states and from English precedents. The first ten amendments to the Constitution (1791), guaranteeing freedom of religion, freedom of the press, and other basic liberties, were taken mainly from the English Bill of Rights of 1689.

The Constitution abounded in compromises. It attempted a balance between states' rights and the central power of the federal government, and between the democratic principle of a directly elected House of Representatives and the aristocratic principle of an indirectly elected and conservative Senate. It was a compromise designed to win support from both rich and poor and from both the Tory opponents and the democratic supporters of the recent revolution. Like any compromise, it did not at first please all parties, but it worked well enough to make the new American republic a going concern. The "Founding Fathers" of the United States had succeeded perhaps better than any other statesmen of the century in adjusting the ideals of the *philosophes* to the realities of practical politics.

VI   The Culture of the Eighteenth Century

The Limitations of Reason

The Enlightenment, however, seldom produced such happy political results as it did in the United States. On the whole, the *philosophes* expected men to see reason when it was pointed out to them, to abandon the habits of centuries, and to revise their behavior in accordance with natural law. But men would not always see reason; as Joseph II discovered to his sorrow, they *would* cling perversely to irrational customs and unnatural traditions. The rationalism of the Enlightenment tended to omit the complexities of human nature from its calculations.

Responsibility for this major shortcoming lay partly with the "classical spirit" of the seventeenth century, inherited by the Enlightenment of the eighteenth. The writers of the Age of Louis XIV had found in their classical models, not a confirmation of existing standards, but a better, simpler set of standards that the eighteenth-century *philosophes* easily adapted to the concept of "nature's simple plan." The great writers achieve the miracle of giving life to these abstractions. But the lesser ones make only bloodless types, and encourage in their hearers and readers—the men and women who finally do work out social change—the belief that these easy mental images are somehow more real, and certainly more desirable, than the bewildering complexity of their concrete experiences. Like the "classical spirit," the spirit of natural science went too far when it was applied uncritically to problems of human relations. It gave men the illusion that what was going on in their minds would shortly go on in reality.

A minor *philosophe,* the Abbé Mably, got at this central problem when he asked: "Is society, then, a branch of physics?" Most of the *philosophes* and their followers believed that it was. They applied to the unpredictable activities of man the mathematical methods used in the physical sciences. The Physiocrats, for example, tried to reduce the complexities of human economic activities to a few simple agricultural laws. Like the stars in their courses, human beings were thought to fit neatly into the Newtonian world-machine.

A few eighteenth-century minds disagreed. David Hume (1711–1776), the skeptical Scottish philosopher, insisted on submitting principles to the test of factual observation. The *philosophes,* he said, failed to do this and thus deduced untested conclusions from two great abstract principles—faith in natural law, belief in reason. Hume made short work of the *philosophes'* appeals to nature. The laws of justice, he argued, were not absolute and inflexible natural laws:

. . . Suppose a society to fall into such want of all common necessaries, that the utmost frugality and industry cannot preserve the greater number from perishing, and the whole from extreme misery; it will readily, I believe, be admitted, that the strict laws of justice are suspended, in such a pressing emergence, and give place to the stronger motives of necessity and self-preservation. Is it any crime, after a shipwreck, to seize whatever means or instrument of safety one can lay hold of, without regard to former limitations of property?*

Nor, Hume argued, could human conduct be analyzed "in the same manner that we discover by reason the truths of geometry or algebra."

*An Enquiry concerning the Principles of Morals, L. A. Selby-Bigge, ed. (Oxford, 1902), 186.

It appears evident that the ultimate ends of human actions can never, in any case, be accounted for by *reason*, but recommend themselves entirely to the sentiments and affections of mankind, without any dependance on the intellectual faculties. Ask a man *why he uses exercise:* he will answer, *because he desires to keep his health.* If you then enquire, *why he desires health,* he will readily reply, *because sickness is painful.* If you push your enquiries farther, and desire a reason *why he hates pain*, it is impossible he can ever give any. . . .*

David Hume was among the first and most profound critics of the Age of Reason. The Romantics of the next generation would repeat his warnings against reason and his pleas on behalf of the "sentiments and affections of mankind" (see Chapter 11). In Hume's own day, Rousseau and Kant were also worried by rather similar problems. Rousseau both represented the Enlightenment and foreshadowed the revolt against it. No *philosophe* defended natural law more ardently, yet no Romantic argued more powerfully on behalf of the irrational faculties of man. "Too often does reason deceive us," Rousseau wrote in *Emile*. "We have only too good a right to doubt her; but conscience never deceives us; she is the true guide of man; . . . he who obeys his conscience is following nature and he need not fear that he will go astray."†

Immanuel Kant (1724–1804), who taught philosophy at the University of Königsberg in Prussia, raised Rousseau's argument to the level of metaphysics. While advocating many of the doctrines of the Enlightenment, Kant also believed in a higher reality reaching ultimately to God. He called the eternal verities of the higher world "noumena," in contrast to the phenomena of the material world. Knowledge of the noumenal realm, Kant believed, reached men through reason—reason, however, not as the Enlightenment used the term, not as common sense, but as intuition. The highest expression of the Kantian reason was the "categorical imperative." This was the moral law within, the conscience implanted in man by God. It was the inescapable realization by the individual that, when confronted with an ethical choice, he must choose the good and avoid the evil. Kant's redefinition of reason and his rehabilitation of conscience exemplified the philosophical reaction against the dominant rationalism of the Enlightenment. The popular reaction took the very different form of the evangelical revival, which began with the German Pietists.

The Evangelical Revival

The Pietists were the spiritual descendants of the sixteenth-century Anabaptists. Deploring alike the growing Lutheran concern with the formalities of religion and the deists' emphasis on natural law, the Pietists asserted that religion came from the heart, not the head. For the Pietists God was far more than the watchmaker, the remote creator of the world-machine. One of the chief leaders of Pietism was a German nobleman, Count Zinzendorf (1700–1760), founder of the Moravian Brethren, who set up a model community based on Christian principles. Moravian emigrants to America planted a colony at Bethlehem, Pennsylvania, helping to give the "Pennsylvania Dutch" their reputation for thrift, hard work, and strict living. In England, meanwhile, the example of Zinzendorf and other Pietists inspired Wesley.

Ordained a priest of the Church of England, John Wesley (1703–1791) at first stressed the ritualistic aspects of religion. But after the failure of his two-year ministry to the backward colony of Georgia (1736–1737), he felt his own faith evaporating: "I went to America, to convert the Indians: but Oh! who shall convert me! Who, what is he that will deliver me from this evil heart of unbelief?"* Pietism converted Wesley and taught him that he would find faith through inner conviction. For more than fifty years, Wesley labored tirelessly to share his discovery, traveling throughout the British Isles, and preaching in churches, in the fields, at the pitheads of coal mines, and even in jails. Angry crowds came to scoff but remained to pray. When Wesley died in 1791,

---

Ibid., 293.
†*Emile*, Everyman ed. (New York, 1911), 249–250.

*John Wesley, *Journal.* Everyman ed. (New York, 1907), I, 74.

his movement had already attracted more than a hundred thousand adherents. They were called Methodists, because of their methodical devotion to piety and to plain dressing and plain living. Though Wesley always considered himself a good Anglican, the Methodists eventually set up a separate organization—their nonconformist "Chapel" in contrast to the established Church of England. The new sect won its following almost entirely among the lower and middle classes, among people who sought the religious excitement and consolation that they did not find in deism or in the austere formalism of the Church of England.

Although the beliefs of the Methodists diverged entirely from those of the enlightened rationalists, both groups worked in their different ways to improve the condition of society. Where the *philosophes* advised public reform, the Methodists favored private charity; and where the *philosophes* attacked the *causes* of social evils, the Methodists accepted these evils as part of God's plan and sought to mitigate their *symptoms*. They had in full measure the Puritan conscience of the nonconformists. They began agitation against drunkenness, the trade in slaves, and the barbarous treatment of prisoners, the insane, and the sick. John Wesley established schools for coalminers' children and opened dispensaries for the poor in London and Bristol. While the Methodists' success came in part from their social activities, it also came from the magnetism of John Wesley and his talented associates. His brother Charles composed more than 6500 hymns, and in America Methodist missionaries flourished under the dynamic leadership of Francis Asbury (1745–1816). The number of colleges called Wesleyan and the number of churches and streets called Asbury testify to the significance of Methodism in American social history.

Literature

The middle-class public so strongly attracted to Methodism welcomed the novels of the Englishman, Samuel Richardson (1689–1761), who made a significant contribution to this emerging literary form. A printer by trade, Richardson turned to writing late in life and produced three gigantic novels in the form of letters by the chief characters. In *Clarissa Harlowe* (1748), for example, Richardson devoted 2400 pages of small print to the misfortunes of Clarissa, whose lover was a scoundrel, and whose relatives were a greedy pack, scheming to secure her considerable property. Whatever her plight, Clarissa never lost the capacity to pour out her miseries on paper. If anyone missed the point of the story, he had only to turn to Richardson's preface:

What will be found to be more particularly aimed at in the following work is—to warn the inconsiderate and thoughtless of one sex, against the base arts and designs of specious contrivers of the other—to caution parents against the undue exercise of their natural authority over their children in the great article of marriage—to warn against preferring a man of pleasure to a man of probity upon that dangerous but too-commonly-received notion, *that a reformed rake makes the best husband*—but above all, to investigate the highest and most important doctrines not only of morality, but of christianity, by showing them thrown into action in the conduct of the *worthy* characters; while the *unworthy*, who set these doctrines at defiance, are condignly, and, as may be said, consequentially punished.

Clarissa was read aloud at family gatherings, it is said, and whenever some new disaster overwhelmed the heroine, the members separated for a good solitary cry. In spite of Richardson's exaggerations, his descriptions of the struggles of passion and conscience carried conviction.

By no means all the masters of English fiction were as sentimental as Richardson. In *Roderick Random* (1748), Tobias Smollett drew an authentic picture of life in the navy, with all its cruelty and hardship. Henry Fielding introduced a strong leaven of satire and burlesqued the excesses of Richardson. Fielding covered a broad social scene in his masterpiece, *Tom Jones* (1749), depicting both the hard-riding country squires and the low characters of the city slums. Richardson gave the English novel emotional and moral earnestness; Smollet and Fielding gave it vigorous realism.

On the whole, the eighteenth century was an age of prose and produced few poets of stature. Its literary monuments were the novels of Richardson and Fielding, the tales and essays of Voltaire, Gibbon's *History of the Decline and Fall of the Roman Empire* (1788), and Dr. Johnson's *Dictionary* (1755). Edward Gibbon utilized history for a sustained Voltairian attack on Christian fanaticism and employed a Ciceronian prose style which, by its balance and discipline, perfectly suited the classical temper of the Enlightenment. Dr. Samuel Johnson's dictionary also expressed the "style" of the age. He declared in the preface:

When I took the first survey of my undertaking, I found our speech copious without order and energetick without rules: wherever I turned my view, there was perplexity to be disentangled, and confusion to be regulated; choice was to be made out of a boundless variety, without any established principle of selection; adulterations were to be detected, without a settled test of purity; and modes of expression to be rejected or received, without the suffrages of any writers of classical reputation or acknowledged authority.

Pedantry and prejudice sometimes overcame the autocratic doctor. His definition of a cough—"a convulsion of the lungs, vellicated by some sharp serosity"—revealed the dangers of employing little-known Latinisms. Whenever he could, he aimed a volley at his favorite target, the Scots. Thus he defined oats as "a grain, which in England is generally given to horses, but in Scotland supports the people." In the main, however, Dr. Johnson succeeded admirably in his aim of becoming a kind of Newton of the English language.

Art

The classicism of the century strongly affected its art. Gibbon's history, the researches of scholars and archaeologists, and the discovery in 1748 of the ruins of Roman Pompeii, well-preserved under lava from Vesuvius, raised the interest in antiquity to a high pitch. For the men of the Enlightenment, the balance and symmetry of Greek and Roman temples represented, in effect, the natural laws of building. Architects retreated somewhat from the theatricalism of the Baroque style and adapted classical models with great artistry and variety. We owe to them the elegance of the London town house, the monumental magnificence of the buildings flanking the Place de la Concorde in Paris, and the country-manor charm of Washington's Mount Vernon. The twentieth-century vogue of the "colonial" and the "Georgian" testifies to the lasting influence of this neoclassical architecture.

In painting, neoclassicism had an eminent spokesman in Sir Joshua Reynolds (1723–1792), the president of the Royal Academy and the artistic tsar of Georgian England. Beauty, Sir Joshua told the academy, rested "on the uniform, eternal, and immutable laws of nature," which could be "investigated by reason, and known by study." Sir Joshua and his contemporaries, though preaching a coldly reasoned aesthetic, gave warmth to the

Dr. Samuel Johnson, by Sir Joshua Reynolds.

Left: Eighteenth-century classical design: the Library at Ken Wood, near London, designed by Robert Adam.

Right: The Gothic revival in design: gallery at Horace Walpole's Strawberry Hill, near London.

portraits that they painted of wealthy English aristocrats. This was the golden age of English portraiture, the age of Reynolds, Lawrence, Gainsborough, and Romney. But it was also the age of William Hogarth (1697–1764), who cast aside the academic restraints of neoclassicism to do in art what Fielding did in the novel. Instead of catering to a few wealthy patrons, Hogarth created a mass market for the engravings that he turned out in thousands of copies, conveying with brutal frankness the vices of London—*Marriage à la Mode, The Rake's Progress, The Harlot's Progress,* and *Gin Lane.*

The realism of Hogarth was not the only exception to the prevailing neoclassicism. The fashions for the oriental, the natural, and the Gothic, which were to be so important in the Age of Romanticism were already beginning to catch on. The taste for the exotic produced Chinese wallpaper, the "Chinese" furniture of Thomas Chippendale, and the familiar Chinese pattern of "willowware" plates. Gardens were bestrewn with pagodas and minarets, and gardeners abandoned Louis XIV's geometrical landscaping for the natural English garden. Even the dominance of neoclassical architecture was challenged. At Strawberry Hill near London, Horace Walpole, the son of the great Robert, endowed his house with an abundance of Gothic "gloomth"—battlements in the medieval style, and "lean windows fattened with rich saints in painted glass."

352

The Great Musicians

Music was perhaps the queen of the arts in the eighteenth century, and music, too, transcended the boundaries of narrow classicism or rationalism. Early in the century Johann Sebastian Bach (1685–1750) brought to perfection the Baroque techniques of seventeenth-century composers. He mastered the difficult art of the fugue, an intricate version of the round in which each voice begins the theme in turn while the other voices repeat and elaborate it. Bach also composed a wealth of material for the organ, the most Baroque and the most religious of instruments. His sacred works included many cantatas, the Mass in B minor, and the two gigantic choral settings of the Passion of Christ according to St. John and St. Matthew. The religious music of Bach, dramatic and deeply felt, was a world apart from the anticlericalism of the Enlightenment.

In contrast to Bach's quiet career as composer and conductor in Germany was the stormy international experience of his contemporary, Handel (1685–1759). Born in Germany, Handel studied in Italy, then spent most of his adult years in England trying to run an opera company in the face of the intrigues, clashes of temperament, and fiscal headaches inevitable in artistic enterprise. Handel wrote more than forty operas, including *Xerxes*, famous for "Handel's Largo." He used themes from the Bible for *The Messiah* and other vigorous oratorios directed at a mass audience and arranged for large choruses. These elaborate works differed greatly from the original oratorios of seventeenth-century Italy, which had been written for the tiny prayer chapels called oratories.

While Bach and Handel composed many instrumental suites and concertos, it was not until the second half of the century that orchestral music really came to the fore. New instruments appeared, notably the piano, which greatly extended the limited range of the older keyboard instrument, the harpsichord. New forms of instrumental music also appeared, the sonata and the symphony, developed largely by Haydn (1732–1809). Haydn wrote more than fifty piano pieces in the form of the sonata, in which two contrasting themes are stated in turn, developed, interwoven, repeated, and finally resolved in a *coda* (the Italian for "tail"). Haydn then arranged the sonata for the orchestra, grafting it onto the Italian operatic overture to create the first movement of the symphony.

The operatic landmark of the early century was John Gay's *Beggar's Opera* (1728), a tuneful work caricaturing English society and politics in Hogarthian vein. Later, Gluck (1714–1787) revolutionized the technique of the tragic opera. "I have striven," he said,

> to restrict music to its true office of serving poetry by means of expression and by following the situations of the story, without interrupting the action or stifling it with a useless superfluity of ornaments. . . . I did not wish to arrest an actor in the greatest heat of dialogue . . . to hold him up in the middle of a word on a vowel favorable to his voice, nor to make display of the agility of his fine voice in some long-drawn passage, nor to wait while the orchestra gives him time to recover his breath for a cadenza.*

Accordingly, Gluck's operas were well-constructed musical dramas, not just vehicles for the display of vocal pyrotechnics. He kept to the old custom of taking heroes and heroines from classical mythology, but he tried to invest shadowy figures like Orpheus, Eurydice, and Iphigenia with new vitality.

Opera, symphony, and chamber music all reached a climax in the works of Mozart (1756–1791). As a boy, Mozart was exploited by his father, who carted him all over Europe to show off his virtuosity on the harpsichord and his amazing talent for composition. Overworked throughout his life, and in his later years overburdened with debts, Mozart died a pauper at the age of thirty-five. Yet his youthful precociousness ripened steadily into mature genius, and his facility and versatility

*Preface to *Alcestis*, as translated by Eric Blom and quoted in Curt Sachs, *Our Musical Heritage* (New York, 1948), 287.

grew ever more prodigious. He tossed off the sprightly overture to *The Marriage of Figaro* in the course of an evening. In two months during the summer of 1788, he produced the three great symphonies familiar to concert audiences as No. 39 (E flat major), No. 40 (G minor), and No. 41 ("The Jupiter"). Mozart's orchestral works also included a long list of concertos, with the solo parts sometimes for piano or violin and sometimes, just to show that it could be done, for bassoon or French horn. In chamber music, Mozart experimented with almost every possible combination of instruments.

Three of Mozart's great operas were in the comic Italian vein—the farcical *Così Fan Tutte* ("Thus Do All Women"); *The Marriage of Fi-garo* based on Beaumarchais' famous satire of the caste system of the Old Régime, in which Figaro the valet outwits and outsings his noble employers; and, finally, *Don Giovanni*, depicting the havoc wrought by Don Juan on earth before his eventual punishment in hell. Mozart composed with equal skill mournful and romantic arias for the Don's victims, elegantly seductive ballads for the Don himself, and a catalog of the Don's conquests for his valet ("A thousand and three in Spain alone"). The instruments in the pit dotted the "i's" and crossed the "t's" of the plot—scurrying violins to accompany characters dashing about the stage, portentous trombones to announce the entrance of the Devil. For the ballroom scene of *Don Giovanni*, Mozart employed three or-

Mozart singing his Requiem, a painting by Thomas W. Shields.

chestras, playing simultaneously three different tunes for three different dances — a minuet for the aristocracy, a country dance for the middle class, a waltz for the lower orders. In his last opera, *The Magic Flute*, Mozart tried to create a consciously German work; but only the vaguest political significance emerged from the fantastic libretto, which apparently sought to vindicate the enlightened ideas of Joseph II and to decry the conservatism of Maria Theresa.

The Magic Flute was a rare exception to the cosmopolitanism of eighteenth-century music. The great composers with the German names had very little national feeling. Almost all of them felt equally at home in Vienna, Prague, Milan, Paris, and London, and they gratefully accepted patrons in any country. The fortunate Haydn moved from the princely estate of the Hungarian Esterhazy family to score an equal success with the paying public of the London concert-halls. Italian music was never totally eclipsed, nor was German dominance complete. Bach patterned his concertos on Italian models, Haydn borrowed Italian operatic overtures for his symphonies, and every oper-atic composer of the century profited from the labors of his Italian predecessors. The great composers also borrowed freely from folk-tunes and ballads, the popular music of their day, and were rewarded by having their themes whistled in the streets. Mozart's operas, Haydn's symphonies, and the choral masterpieces of Bach and Handel retained the capacity to engage the listener's emotions.

Of all the arts, music probably came closest to resolving the great conflict in eighteenth-century culture, the tension beteen reason and emotion, between the abstractions of the Enlightenment and the flesh-and-blood realities of human existence. In other realms, however, as the century drew toward its close, the lines were drawn for the vigorous prosecution of the conflict. In thought, the ideas of Kant and Hume were challenging the optimistic rationalism of the *philosophes*. Romantic artists and writers were beginning to defy the defenders of classicism. And in politics, as the century ended, the European powers sought to thwart the supreme effort to realize on earth the Enlightenment's dream of reason, natural law, and progress — the French Revolution.

Reading Suggestions on the Enlightenment

(*Asterisk indicates paperbound edition.)

General Accounts

W. L. Dorn, *Competition for Empire, 1740–1763* (*Torch). Contains a meaty chapter on the Enlightenment and a full bibliography.

L. Gershoy, *From Despotism to Revolution, 1763–1789* (*Torch). A sympathetic study of the ideas of the Enlightenment, and a comprehensive and sometimes caustic analysis of the Enlightened Despots; with full bibliographies.

F. Manuel, *The Age of Reason* (*Cornell Univ. Press), and G. Bruun, *The Enlightened Despots* (Holt, 1929). Two helpful brief introductions.

R. R. Palmer, *The Age of the Democratic Revolution,* Vol. I (Princeton Univ. Press, 1959). A political history of Europe and America at the close of the Old Régime, stressing the parallel developments on the two continents.

New Cambridge Modern History, Vol. VIII: "The American and French Revolutions, 1763–1793" (Cambridge Univ. Press, 1965). Some chapters in this collaborative work are quite helpful.

Peter Gay, *The Enlightenment: The Rise of Modern Paganism* (Knopf, 1966). The first half of a projected two-volume study by a leading scholar; with a rich bibliographical essay.

The Ideas of the Enlightenment

G. R. Havens, *The Age of Ideas: From Reaction to Revolution in Eighteenth-Century France* (*Free Press). A most useful volume, fully abreast of modern research.

P. Smith, *The History of Modern Culture,* Vol. II (Holt, 1934). A mine of information on details often neglected in intellectual histories.

E. Cassirer, *The Philosophy of the Enlightenment* (*Beacon, 1955). An important study of the great principles of eighteenth-century thought.

P. Hazard, *European Thought in the Eighteenth Century* (*Meridian). A useful survey of some of the thinkers of the Enlightenment.

K. Martin, *French Liberal Thought in the 18th Century* (*Torch). A brilliant and opinionated survey of the *philosophes.*

C. Becker, *The Heavenly City of the Eighteenth-Century Philosophers* (*Yale Univ. Press). A delightful and influential essay, stressing the parallels between the medieval Age of Faith and the Age of Reason. May be coupled with R. O. Rockwood, ed., *Carl Becker's Heavenly City Revisited* (Cornell Univ. Press, 1958).

J. B. Bury, *The Idea of Progress* (*Dover, 1955). A famous old pioneering study of enlightened optimism.

L. I. Bredvold, *The Brave New World of the Enlightenment* (Univ. of Michigan Press, 1961). Controversial, basically hostile, but deserves attention.

L. G. Crocker, *An Age of Crisis: Man and World in Eighteenth Century French Thought* (Johns Hopkins Univ. Press, 1959). An informative recent study.

F. Manuel, *The Eighteenth Century Confronts the Gods* (Harvard Univ. Press, 1959); R. R. Palmer, *Catholics and Unbelievers in Eighteenth-Century France* (*Princeton Univ. Press). Informative studies on attitudes toward religion.

T. D. Kendrick, *The Lisbon Earthquake* (Lippincott, 1957). An instructive account of the social and intellectual ramifications of the catastrophe.

Some Individual Thinkers

A. Wilson, *Diderot: The Testing Years, 1713–1759* (Oxford Univ. Press, 1957). The first part of a definitive biography.

N. L. Torrey, *The Spirit of Voltaire* (Columbia Univ. Press, 1938). A thoughtful study.

Peter Gay, *Voltaire's Politics: The Poet as Realist* (*Vintage). By a leading expert on the subject.

A. Cobban, *Rousseau & the Modern State* (Allen & Unwin, 1934). A good introduction to the implications of Rousseau's thought.

J. L. Talmon, *The Origins of Totalitarian Democracy* (*Praeger). Another interpretation of Rousseau.

F. Manuel, *The Prophets of Paris* (Harvard Univ. Press, 1962). Turgot and Condorcet are among those considered.

The Arts

F. Fosca, *The Eighteenth Century* (Skira, 1953). Handsomely illustrated introduction to the painting of the era.

J. Reynolds, *Discourses on Art* (*Collier). By the great eighteenth-century champion of neoclassical painting.

M. Bukofzer, *Music in the Baroque Era* (Norton, 1947). Survey of the period before 1750.

E. M. and S. Grew, *Bach* (*Collier); A. Einstein, *Mozart: His Character, His Work* (*Galaxy); E. J. Dent, *Mozart's Operas* (*Oxford). Informative works on individual musicians.

The Enlightened Despots

G. P. Gooch, *Frederick the Great* (Knopf, 1947), and F. J. P. Veale, *Frederick the Great* (Hamish, Hamilton, 1935). Two reasonable and balanced assessments.

L. Reniers, *Frederick the Great* (Oswald Wolff, Ltd., 1960). A critical evaluation.

W. H. Bruford, *Germany in the Eighteenth Century* (*Cambridge Univ. Press). A descriptive study, stressing social and intellectual history.

C. L. Morris, *Maria Theresa, The Last Conservative* (Knopf, 1937). Informative and sympathetic.

S. K. Padover, *The Revolutionary Emperor* (Ballou, 1934). Warmly favorable account of Joseph II.

G. Scott Thomson, *Catherine the Great and the Expansion of Russia* (*Collier). A sound, brief introduction. Of the full biographies of Catherine, one of the best is K. Walizewski, *The Romance of an Empress* (Appleton, 1894); a recent one is Z. Oldenbourg, *Catherine the Great* (*Bantam).

R. Herr, *The Eighteenth-Century Revolution in Spain* (Princeton Univ. Press, 1958). A full account of the reign of Charles III and of the impact of the Enlightenment.

George III and the American Revolution

J. C. Miller, *Origins of the American Revolution* (*Stanford Univ. Press). Excellent study.

L. H. Gipson, *The Coming of the Revolution, 1763–1775* (*Torch); J. R. Alden, *The American Revolution, 1775–1783* (*Torch). Full accounts in the "New American Nation" series.

E. S. Morgan, *The Birth of the Republic, 1763–1789* (*Phoenix). Another good introductory account.

C. Becker, *The Declaration of Independence* (*Vintage). An admirable monograph, analyzing the Declaration sentence by sentence and examining its European roots.

M. Beloff, *Thomas Jefferson and American Democracy* (*Collier). A good introduction to one of the most versatile and intellectual of the Founding Fathers.

J. S. Watson, *The Reign of George III, 1760–1815* (Clarendon, 1960), Volume XII of *The Oxford History of England*. An up-to-date general account, incorporating recent scholarly reinterpretations of this important reign.

E. A. Reitan, *George III: Tyrant or Constitutional Monarch?* (*Heath). Excerpts from the diverse judgments passed on George.

L. B. Namier, *The Structure of Politics at the Accession of George III* (*St. Martin's), and *England in the Age of the American Revolution* (*St. Martin's). Detailed and controversial studies of politics in the 1760's.

G. Rudé, *Wilkes and Liberty* (*Oxford). Analysis of the unrest in Britain early in George's reign.

Sources

C. Brinton, ed., *The Portable Age of Reason Reader* (*Viking). A good cross-section of the writing of the Enlightenment.

F. Manuel, ed., *The Enlightenment* (*Spectrum), and I. Berlin, ed., *The Age of Enlightenment: the 18th-Century Philosophers* (*Mentor). Two other useful anthologies.

B. R. Redman, ed., *The Portable Voltaire* (*Viking, 1949). A well-chosen selection, prefaced by an informative introduction.

Montesquieu, *The Spirit of the Laws* (*Hafner).

Rousseau, *The First and Second Discourses* (*St. Martin's); *The Social Contract* (*Hafner).

F. de La Fontainerie, ed., *French Liberalism and Education in the Eighteenth Century* (McGraw-Hill, 1932). Proposals for educational reform by Diderot and others.

Beccaria, *On Crimes and Punishments* (*Liberal Arts).

A. Smith, *The Wealth of Nation.* (*several editions of selections).

B. Dobrée, ed., *The Letters of King George III* (Cassell, 1935).

M. Beloff, ed., *The Debate on the American Revolution, 1761–1783* (*Torch). Handy compilation of British speeches and writings for and against the rebels.

H. S. Commager, ed., *Documents of American History* (*Appleton-Century-Crofts).

W. F. Church, ed., *The Influence of the Enlightenment on the French Revolution* (*Heath). Selections from later historians, with a useful, brief, critical bibliography on the Enlightenment.

Historical Fiction

S. Richardson, *Clarissa* (*Riverside).

See also the works suggested for Chapter 8.

10

The French Revolution

and Napoleon

I   Causes of the Revolution

In France, as in the thirteen North American colonies, a financial crisis produced a revolution. There was not only a parallel but also a direct connection between the revolution of 1776 and that of 1789. French participation in the War of American Independence increased an already excessive governmental debt by more than 1,500,000,000 *livres*,* and the example of America fired the imagination of discontented Frenchmen. To them, Benjamin Franklin, the immensely popular American envoy to France, was the very

*It is impossible to set a very meaningful value on the pre-revolutionary *livre* in terms of present-day money. It has been estimated that the *livre* was worth a little over $1.00 in terms of the 1966 dollar, but the estimate is misleading because of the enormous increase in prices and the shifts in the proportionate cost of basic necessities during the two centuries since the Old Régime.

embodiment of the Enlightenment, and the new republic overseas promised to become the utopia of the *philosophes*. Yet it would be going too far to claim that the American Revolution actually caused the French Revolution; rather, it speeded up developments in France that had long been under way. The forces causing the upheaval of 1789 were almost fully matured in 1776. And, just as the reasons for revolution were more deeply rooted and more complicated in France than in America, so the revolution itself was to be more violent and more sweeping.

The *immediate* cause of the great French Revolution, then, was financial. King Louis XVI vainly tried one expedient after another to avert bankruptcy and finally summoned the Estates General, the central representative assembly that had last met 175 years earlier. Once assembled, the deputies of the nation initiated the reforms that were to destroy the Old Régime in France. The *basic* causes of the Revolution, however, reached deep into France's society and economy and into her political and intellectual history. Behind the financial crisis of the 1780's lay many decades of fiscal mismanagement; the government had been courting insolvency since the last years of Louis XIV. The nobles and clergy, jealously guarding their traditional privileges, refused to pay a fair share of the taxes. Resentment against inequitable taxation and inefficient government built up among the unprivileged —the peasantry, the workers, and, above all, the bourgeoisie. The ideas of the *philosophes* translated bourgeois resentment into a program of active reform.

The Monarchy

France, the home of the Enlightenment, was never ruled by an enlightened despot until the advent of Napoleon. King Louis XV had refused to take decisive steps to remedy the abuses of the Old Régime (see Chapter 8). What Louis XV would not do, his grandson and successor could not do. Louis XVI (1774–1792), unlike his grandfather, was earnest and pious, but he had a slow mind and

was both irresolute and stubborn. He also labored under the handicap of a politically unfortunate marriage. Marie Antionette, his wife, was frivolous and ignorant; worse still, she was a Habsburg, the daughter of Maria Theresa, a constant reminder of the ill-fated Franco-Austrian alliance during the Seven Years' War.

For want of a good mechanic, the machinery of centralized royal absolutism was gradually falling apart. The fact that it functioned at all could be credited to a relatively few capable administrators, notably the *intendants* who ran so much of provincial France. The best of the *intendants*, like the Physiocrat Turgot at Limoges, provided a welcome touch of enlightened despotism, but they could do little to stay the slow disintegration of the central government.

The whole legal and judicial system required reform. The law needed to be codified to eliminate obsolete medieval survivals and to end the overlapping of the two legal systems—Roman and feudal—that prevailed in France. The courts needed a thorough overhaul to make them swift, fair, and inexpensive. Many judges and lawyers purchased or inherited their offices and regarded them not as a public trust but as a means to private enrichment. Louis XV had permitted his ministers to attack the strongholds of these vested interests, the high courts known as Parlements which existed in Paris and in a dozen provincial centers. One of the last acts of his reign had been the suppression of the Parlements; one of the first moves taken by Louis XVI was their restoration. Many Frenchmen viewed the Parlements favorably as a constitutional check on the absolutism of the monarchy, but the Parlements were also a formidable obstacle to social and economic reform.

The First and Second Estates

Like the monarchy itself, the social and economic foundations of the Old Régime were beginning to crumble by the middle of the eighteenth century. The first estate, the clergy, occupied a position of conspicuous importance in France. Though forming less than one per cent of the total population, the clergy controlled extensive and lucrative properties and performed many functions that are normally undertaken by the state today. They ran schools, kept records of vital statistics and dispensed relief to the poor. The Gallican Church, however, was a house divided. The lower clergy came almost entirely from the third estate; humble, poorly paid, and generally hardworking, the priests resented the wealth and the arrogance of their ecclesiastical superiors. The bishops and abbots maintained the outlook of the noble class into which they had been born. Although some of them took their duties seriously, others regarded the Church as a convenient way of securing a large income. Dozens of prelates turned the administration of their bishoprics or monasteries over to subordinates, kept most of the revenue themselves, and took up residence in Paris or Versailles.

The wealth and the lax discipline of the Church aroused criticism and envy. Good Catholics deplored the dwindling number of monks and nuns and their growing tendency to stress the exploitation of their properties. Well-to-do peasants and townspeople coveted these rich ecclesiastical estates. Taxpayers hated the tithe levied by the Church, even though the full 10 per cent implied by the word "tithe" was seldom demanded. They also complained about the Church's exemption from taxation and about the meager size of the "free gift" voted by the clergy to the government in lieu of taxes. The peasants on the whole remained moderately faithful Catholics and regarded the village priest, if not the bishop, with esteem and affection. The bourgeois, however, more and more accepted the anticlerical views of the *philosophes*. They interpreted Voltaire's plea to "crush the infamous thing" as a mandate to strip the Church of wealth and power.

Like the higher clergy, the nobles of the Old Régime, the second estate, enjoyed privilege, wealth — and unpopularity. Although forming less than 2 per cent of the population, they held about 20 per cent of the land. They had virtual exemption from taxation; they monopolized army commissions and appointments to high ecclesiastical office. The French aristocracy, however, comprised not a single social unit but a series of differing groups. At the top were the hereditary nobles, a few of them descended from royalty or from feudal lords of the Middle Ages, but more from families ennobled within the past two or three centuries. These "nobles of the sword" tended to view most of their countrymen, including the lesser nobility, as vulgar upstarts. In spite of their failure during the regency of Orléans (see Chapter 8), they dreamed of the day when they might rule France again, as the feudal nobles had ruled in the Middle Ages. Many of them, clustered at Versailles, neglected their duties as the first landlords of the realm. Arthur Young, the English economic expert who made a tour of France in the late 1780's, commented on the uncultivated aristocratic lands he found:

Much of these wastes belonged to the Prince de Soubise, who would not sell any part of them. Thus it is whenever you stumble on a Grand Seigneur, even one that was worth millions, you are sure to find his property desert. The Duke of Bouillon's and this prince's are two of the greatest properties in France; and all the signs I have yet seen of their greatness, are wastes. . . . Oh! if I was the legislator of France for a day, I would make such great lords skip again!*

Below the nobility of the sword came the "nobility of the robe," including the robed justices of the Parlements and other courts and a host of other officials. The nobles of the robe, or their ancestors, had originally secured aristocratic status by buying their offices. But, since these dignities were then handed down from father to son, the mercenary origins of their status had become somewhat obscured with the passage of time. By the late eighteenth century, there was often little practical distinction between the gentry of the robe and their brethren of the sword; marriages between members of the two groups were common. On the whole, the nobles of the robe were richer than the nobles of the sword, and

*Travels in France, Constantia Maxwell, ed. (Cambridge, England, 1929), 62.

they exerted more power and influence by virtue of their firm hold on key governmental positions. The ablest and most tenacious defenders of special privilege in the dying years of the Old Régime were the rich judges of Parlement, not the elegant but ineffectual courtiers of Versailles.

Many noblemen, however, had little wealth, power, or glamor. They belonged to the lowest level of French aristocracy—the *hobereaux*, the "little falcons" or "sparrow-hawks." They vegetated on their country estates, since they could not afford the expensive pleasures of the court. In the effort to conserve at least part of their traditional status, almost all the *hobereaux* insisted on the meticulous collection of the surviving feudal and manorial dues from the peasantry. Their exhumation of old documents to justify levies sometimes long forgotten earned them the abiding hatred of the peasants and prepared the way for the document-burning that occurred during the Revolution.

Not every noble was a snobbish courtier or a selfish defender of the status quo. Some *hobereaux* drifted down the social ladder to become simple farmers. Some nobles of the robe, attracted by the opportunities for profit, took part in business ventures. Even the loftiest noble families produced enlightened spirits, like the Marquis de Lafayette, who returned from the American War of Independence to champion reform at home, or like the young bloods who applauded the ingenious valet, Figaro, when he outwitted his social superiors in Beaumarchais' satire on aristocracy, *The Marriage of Figaro,* first staged in 1784.

The Third Estate

The first two estates included only a small fraction of the French nation; 98 per cent of Frenchmen fell within the third estate in 1789. The great majority of these commoners were peasants. In some respects, the status of the peasantry was more favorable in France than it was anywhere else in Europe. Serfdom, which was still prevalent in central and eastern Europe, had disappeared almost entirely except in Lorraine and the Franche Comté (County of Burgundy). While enclosures were gradually pushing small farmers off the land in England, small peasant holdings existed by the millions in France. Three out of every four adult peasants, it is estimated, held some land. Nevertheless, the observant eye of Arthur Young noted many signs of rural misery in 1787 and 1788. In southwestern France, for example:

Pass Payrac, and meet many beggars, which we had not done before. All the country, girls and women, are without shoes or stockings; and the ploughmen at their work have neither sabots nor feet to their stockings. This is a poverty, that strikes at the root of national prosperity. . . . It reminded me of the misery of Ireland.[*]

Although the degree of agrarian distress varied greatly from province to province, the total picture was far from bright. The trouble came in part from three factors—backward methods of farming, the shortage of land, and overpopulation. The efficient techniques of the agricultural revolution made little headway in France before 1789. Vast areas were not cultivated at all or lay fallow every second or third year in accordance with medieval practice. The constantly increasing rural population simply could not find steady employment or a decent livelihood. Primitive farming required large tracts of land, but the property-holding three-quarters of the French peasantry controlled less than one-third of the land. The average holding was so small that even a propertied peasant might face starvation in poor crop years. The landless peasant turned to begging and sometimes to theft.

Rising prices and heavy taxes also oppressed the peasants. The upward trend of prices in France throughout the eighteenth century brought prosperity to many towns, but to the backward rural economy it brought the new hardship of inflation. The price of the products sold by the farmer rose less swiftly than that of the goods which the farmer had to buy. To the Church the peasants paid the

[*]*Travels in France*, 23–24.

tithe, and to the nobility they paid feudal and manorial dues. To the state they owed a land tax, an income tax, a poll tax, and a variety of other duties, of which the most widely detested was the *gabelle*, the obligatory purchase of salt from government agents, usually at an exorbitant price.

France had a long history of agrarian unrest, going back to the *jacquerie*, the savage peasant uprising during the Hundred Years' War. In the decades before 1789 there was no new *jacquerie*, but unemployment and poverty had created a revolutionary temper among the peasants. They did not want a change in the form of government; they were ignorant of the reform program of the Enlightenment. But they most emphatically wanted more land, if need be at the expense of the clergy and the nobility; they wanted an end to obsolete manorial dues; and they wanted relief from a system of taxation that bore hardest upon those who could least afford to pay.

The other members of the third estate, the urban workers and the bourgeoisie, had little reason to cherish the Old Régime. "Labor," in our modern sense of a large, self-conscious body of factory workers, hardly existed in pre-revolutionary France, where few large factories as yet existed. Almost every good-sized town, however, had its wage-earners and apprentices employed chiefly in small businesses or workshops. These urban laborers felt with particular sharpness the pinch of rising prices. They were not, however, to take the commanding role in the Revolution itself; geographically scattered, lacking in class cohesiveness, they were ready to follow the lead of the bourgeoisie.

The bourgeoisie included Frenchmen of very divergent resources and interests — rich merchants and bankers in the cities, storekeepers and lawyers in country towns and villages, doctors and other professional men, and thousands upon thousands of craftsmen running their own little businesses. Implacable hostility to the privileged estates and warm receptiveness to the propaganda of the *philosophes* cemented this sprawling middle class into a political force. The bourgeoisie suffered fewer hardships than the peasants and workers did, but they resented the abuses of the Old Régime perhaps even more keenly. Though they paid a smaller proportion of their incomes in taxes, they violently denounced the inequality of assessments. While profiting by the rise in prices, the wealthier and more enterprising businessmen complained of guild regulations and other restrictions on free commercial activity. They found it galling to be snubbed by the nobility, treated as second-class subjects by the monarchy, and excluded from posts of power in government, Church, and army.

In sum, the men of the middle class fully realized their own growing economic importance, and they wanted social and political rights to match. Because they were wealthier, better educated, and more articulate than the peasants and wage-earners, they took the leading part in formulating the grievances of the entire third estate. These grievances were compiled in statements called *cahiers* and submitted to the Estates General in 1789.

The *cahier* of the third estate of the Longuyon district in Lorraine may serve as a sample of bourgeois attitudes toward reform.* While it dealt in part with purely local problems, like the destruction of the woods to supply fuel for iron-smelters, other portions showed a sharp awareness of the great issues of the day. The *cahier* pronounced the freedom of the press the "surest means of maintaining the freedom of the nation." It deplored the harshness of the criminal laws; they should conform to "the customs and the character of the French nation, the kindest people in the universe." It recommended "a social contract or act between the sovereign and his people," to safeguard "the personal freedom of all citizens" and "prevent the recurrence of those disastrous events which at present oppress the king and the nation." While insisting upon the sanctity of private property, the third estate of Longuyon advocated a large measure of equality. It proposed that "all Frenchmen should have the right and the hope of securing

---

*The full text of this *cahier* is printed in B. F. Hyslop, *A Guide to the General Cahiers of 1789* (New York, 1936), 318–326. The quotations that follow are in our translation.

any State office, of whatever grade, and all military and ecclesiastical dignities." Existing taxes should be swept away, to be replaced by levies on "all property without distinction as to owners, and on all persons without distinction of order and rank."

The Financial Crisis

The chronic financial difficulties of the French monarchy strengthened the hand of the middle-class reformers. The government debt, already large at the accession of Louis XVI, tripled between 1774 and 1789; about half the increase resulted from French participation in the American War of Independence. In 1789, the debt stood at 4,500,000,000 *livres*. The budget for 1788, the only one computed for the Old Régime, made alarming reading:

Estimated Expenses	(In *livres*)
For debt service	318,000,000
For the court	35,000,000
For other purposes	276,000,000
Total	629,000,000
Estimated Revenues	503,000,000
Estimated Deficit	126,000,000

Especially disturbing was the very high proportion of revenues consumed by interest payments on debts already contracted.

Louis XVI, in his feeble way, tried to cope with the growing emergency. On coming to the throne in 1774, he named as chief minister Turgot, who sympathized with the Physiocrats and had made a brilliant record as *intendant* of Limoges. Turgot temporarily reduced the deficit by imposing strict economies, particularly on the expenditures of the court. To promote the welfare of the third estate, he curtailed ancient guild monopolies, lifted restrictions on internal shipments of grain, and replaced the *corvée*, the work on highways demanded of peasants, with a tax affecting nobles and commoners alike. At this the vested interests rebelled and, seconded by Marie Antoinette, secured Turgot's dismissal in 1776. The ousted minister admonished Louis XVI: "Remember, sire, that it

was weakness which brought the head of Charles I to the block."

Louis ignored Turgot's warning. The government continued to raise new loans— 653,000,000 *livres* between 1783 and 1786 alone. Then in 1786 the bankers refused to make new advances. The French government was caught between the irresistible force of the third estate's demands for tax relief and the immovable object of the other estates' refusal to yield their fiscal exemptions. The monarchy had temporized and borrowed until it could afford neither fresh delays nor new loans. Calonne, the finance minister in 1786, proposed to meet the crisis by reviving Turgot's reforms. In the hope of persuading the first two estates to consent to heavier taxation, he convoked the Assembly of Notables, which included the chief aristocratic and ecclesiastical dignitaries of the kingdom. But the Notables declined to be persuaded.

Louis XVI dissolved the Notables and dismissed Calonne. Then, with unaccustomed firmness, he decided to levy a uniform tax on all landed property without regard to the social status of the holder. The clergy replied by reducing their "free gift" for 1788 to one-sixth of what it had previously been. The Parlement of Paris declared the new tax law illegal and asserted that only the nation as a whole assembled in the Estates General could make so sweeping a change. The King retreated and in the summer of 1788 announced that the Estates General would meet the following spring.

The Estates General

In summoning the Estates General Louis XVI revived a half-forgotten institution which did not seem likely to initiate drastic social and economic reforms. The three estates, despite their immense variation in size, had customarily received equal representation and equal voting power, so that the two privileged orders could outvote the commoners. The Estates General of 1789, however, met under unique circumstances.

In the first place, its election and subsequent meeting took place during an economic crisis that heightened chronic social and financial tensions. One difficulty was the continued gravitation of unemployed peasants to the cities, especially Paris, in search of work; another difficulty was the weather. Hail and drought had reduced the wheat harvest in 1788, and the winter of 1788–1789 was so bitter that the Seine froze over at Paris, blocking shipments of grain or flour by water. Half-starved and half-frozen, Parisians huddled around bonfires provided by the municipal government. By the spring of 1789 the price of bread had almost doubled—a very serious matter in an age when bread was the mainstay of the diet. It has been estimated that the average workingman normally spent almost half his wages on bread for his family; now he was obliged to spend a higher proportion.

France had survived bad weather and poor harvests many times in the past without experiencing revolution. This time, however, the economic hardships were the last straw. Starving peasants begged, borrowed, and stole, poaching on the hunting preserves of the great lords and attacking their game wardens. The turbulence in Paris boiled over in a riot (April, 1789), witnessed by Thomas Jefferson, then the American minister to France:

. . . The Fauxbourg St. Antoine is a quarter of the city inhabited entirely by the class of daylaborers and journeymen in every line. A rumor was spread among them that a great paper manufacturer . . . had proposed . . . that their wages should be lowered to 15 sous a day [three-quarters of a *livre*]. . . . They flew to his house in vast numbers, destroyed everything in it, and in his magazines and work shops, without secreting however a pin's worth to themselves, and were continuing this work of devastation when the regular troops were called in. Admonitions being disregarded, they were of necessity fired on, and a regular action ensued, in which about 100 of them were killed, before the rest would disperse.*

These disturbances increased the sense of critical urgency pressing on the deputies to the Estates General.

*Autobiography of Thomas Jefferson, P. L. Ford, ed. (New York, 1914), 133–134.

In the second place, the methods followed in electing the deputies aided the champions of reform. The suffrage was wide, especially in rural areas, where almost all adult males met the qualifications for voting. Indeed, it is probable that more Frenchmen actually voted in 1789 than in any subsequent election or referendum during the revolutionary era. In each district of France the third estate made its choice not directly by secret ballot but indirectly by choosing at a public meeting electors who later selected a deputy. Since this procedure greatly favored bourgeois orators over inarticulate farmers, middle-class lawyers and government administrators won control of the commoners' deputation. The reforming deputies of the third estate found some sympathizers in the second estate and many more in the first estate, where the discontented clergy had a large delegation. A majority of the deputies were prepared to make drastic changes in the Old Régime.

But in all past meetings of the Estates General each estate, or order, had deliberated separately, with the consent of two estates and of the Crown required for the passage of a measure. In 1789, the King and the privileged orders favored retaining this "vote by order." The third estate, on the contrary, demanded "vote by head," with the deputies from all the orders deliberating together, each deputy having a single vote. Pamphleteers invoked Rousseau's concept of the general will. "What is the third estate?" wrote Abbé Siéyès in an influential broadside of the same name. "Everything."

. . . If votes are taken by order, five million citizens will not be able to decide anything for the general interest, because it will not please a couple of hundred thousand privileged individuals. The will of a single individual will veto and destroy the will of more than a hundred people.*

The question of procedure became crucial soon after the Estates General convened on May 5, 1789, at Versailles. Siéyès, a priest, and Mirabeau, a renegade nobleman, both of them sitting in the third estate, led the cam-

*Emmanuel Siéyès, Qu'est-ce Que le Tiers Etat?, E. Champion, ed. (Paris, 1888), 82. Our translation.

paign for vote by head. On June 17, the third estate cut the Gordian knot of procedure by accepting Siéyès' invitation to proclaim itself the "National Assembly." It also invited the deputies of the other two estates to join its sessions. A majority of the clerical deputies, chiefly parish priests, accepted; the nobility refused.

The King then barred the commoners from their usual meeting place, whereupon they assembled at an indoor tennis court on June 20 and solemnly swore never to disband until they had given France a constitution. To the "Tennis-Court Oath" Louis replied by commanding each estate to resume its separate deliberations. The third estate and some deputies of the first disobeyed. Louis, vacillating as ever, now gave in and on June 27 directed the noble and clerical deputies to join the National Assembly. The nation, through its representatives, had successfully challenged the King and the vested interests. The Estates General was dead, and in its place sat the National Assembly, pledged to reform French society and give the nation a constitution. The revolution had begun.

II   The Dissolution of the Monarchy

Popular Uprisings, July–October, 1789

The National Assembly had barely settled down to work when a new wave of rioting swept over France, undermining further the position of the King. Economic difficulties grew more severe during the summer of 1789. Unemployment increased, and bread seemed likely to remain scarce and expensive, at least until after the harvest. Meanwhile, the commoners feared that the King and the privileged orders might attempt a counter-revolution. Large concentrations of troops appeared in the Paris area early in July—to preserve order and protect the National Assembly, the King asserted. But the Parisians suspected that Louis was planning the forcible dissolution of the Assembly. Suspicion deepened into conviction after Louis dismissed Necker, the popular financier who had been serving as the chief royal adviser.

The reaction to Necker's dismissal was immediate and revolutionary. On July 12 and 13, the men who had elected the Paris deputies of the third estate formed a new municipal government and a new militia, the National Guard, both loyal to the National Assembly. Paris was forging the weapons that made it the leader of the Revolution. Crowds were roaming the streets, demanding cheaper bread and parading busts of Necker draped in black. On July 14 they broke into government buildings in search of arms. They found one arsenal in the Invalides, the great military hospital in Paris, and they hoped to find another in the Bastille, a fortress in the eastern part of the city. An armed group, several hundred strong, stormed the Bastille, killing part of the garrison and suffering many casualties themselves.

The fall of the Bastille had immense significance. While the fortress housed only 7 prisoners, all of whom deserved to be there, it frowned like a monster sentry over a teeming quarter inhabited by woodworkers, cabinetmakers, locksmiths, cobblers, and other craftsmen and their assistants. Men of this modest social and economic background formed the bulk of the force that took the Bastille and demonstrated what could be done by an aroused people. The capture and subsequent demolition of the Bastille symbolized the destruction of the Old Régime. It is no wonder the Fourteenth of July became the great national holiday of Frenchmen, their counterpart of the American Fourth of July.

Rioting spread over much of France late in July, 1789, as the provincial population responded to the news from Paris or acted on its own. In town after town, mobs attacked the local version of the Bastille. Arthur Young, who was surveying the agriculture of Alsace, witnessed the scene at Strasbourg:

. . . The Parisian spirit of commotion spreads quickly; it is here; the troops . . . are employed to keep an eye on the people who shew signs of an intended revolt. They have broken the windows of some magistrates that are no favourites; and a great mob of them is at this moment assembled, demanding clamourously to have meat at 5 *sous* a pound.*

The countryside, in the meantime, was experiencing the "Great Fear," one of the most

*Travels in France, 181.

extraordinary attacks of mass delusion on record. From village to village word spread that "brigands" were coming, aristocratic hirelings who would destroy crops and villages and force the National Assembly to preserve the status quo. There were in fact no bands of brigands, only an occasional starving farmhand trying to steal food. But the peasants in many districts went berserk, grabbing hoes and pitchforks, anything resembling a weapon. When the brigands did not materialize, they attacked chateaux and broke into other buildings that might house a hoard of grain or the hated documents justifying collection of manorial dues. Some nobles voluntarily gave the peasants what they wanted; others saw

Scene in front of the Paris City Hall, July 14, 1789. Bust of Louis XIV "witnesses the triumph of freedom."

their barns and archives burnt, and a few were lynched. The Great Fear, beginning as a psychological aberration, ended as an uprising of the peasantry against its traditional oppressors.

By the end of July, 1789, then, four distinct sets of revolutionary events had taken place in France: (1) the constitutional revolution of June, resulting in the creation of the National Assembly; (2) the Paris revolution and the taking of the Bastille; (3) the comparable outbreaks in provincial cities and towns; and (4) the Great Fear. Each of the four drove another nail into the coffin of the Old Régime. The transformation of the Estates General into the National Assembly and the creation of new local governments undermined the traditional political advantages of the first two estates. The Great Fear began the destruction of their social and economic privileges. Everywhere, legally constituted officials were turned out, taxes went unpaid, and valuable records were destroyed.

The "October Days," the last crisis of a momentous year, demonstrated anew the impotence of Louis XVI and the power of his aroused subjects. The harvest of 1789 had been good, but a drought crippled the operation of water-mills for grinding flour from the wheat. Thus, as autumn drew on, Parisians still queued for bread and still looked suspiciously at the royal troops stationed in the neighborhood of their city. Rumors of the Queen's behavior at Versailles further incensed them. Marie Antoinette made a dramatic appearance at a banquet of royal officers, clutching the Dauphin (the heir to the throne) in her arms, striking the very pose that her mother, Maria Theresa, had employed so effectively to win the support of the Hungarians in the 1740's. And, on hearing that the people had no bread, she was said to have remarked callously: "Let them eat cake." This story was false, but it echoed and re-echoed in the lively new Paris papers that delighted in denouncing *l'Autrichienne* ("the Austrian hussy").

The climax came on October 5, 1789, when an array of determined women—rough market-women and fishwives, neatly dressed milliners, even middle-class "ladies with hats"—marched the dozen miles from Paris to Versailles in the rain. They disrupted the National Assembly, extracted kisses from Louis XVI, and later penetrated the palace, perhaps endangering the lives of Louis and, especially, Marie Antoinette. Although historians have not yet discovered who planned and organized this bizarre demonstration, it had very significant political consequences. On October 6, the women marched back to Paris, escorting "the baker, the baker's wife, and the baker's boy"—in other words, the royal family—who took up residence in the Tuileries Palace. More important, the National Assembly, too, moved to Paris. The most revolutionary place in France had captured both the head of the Old Régime and the herald of the new.

The National Assembly, 1789–1791

The outlines of the new régime were already starting to take shape before the October Days. The Great Fear prompted the National Assembly to abolish in law what the peasants were destroying in fact. On the evening of August 4, 1789, the Viscount de Noailles, a liberal nobleman, addressed the deputies:

The kingdom at this moment hangs between the alternative of the destruction of society, and that of a government which will be the admiration and the exemplar of Europe.

How is this government to be established? By public tranquillity. . . . And to secure this necessary tranquillity, I propose:

(1) . . . That taxation will be paid by all the individuals of the kingdom, in proportion to their revenues;

(2) That all public expenses will in the future be borne equally by all.*

The deputies voted the proposals of Noailles. In addition, the clergy gave up its tithes, and the liberal minority of the second estate surrendered the nobility's game preserves, manorial dues, and other medieval rights. The

Archives Parlementaires, Series 1, VIII, 343. Our translation.

assembly made it a clean sweep by abolishing serfdom, forbidding the sale of justice or of judicial office, and decreeing that "all citizens, without distinction of birth, can be admitted to all ecclesiastical, civil, and military posts and dignities." When the memorable session inaugurated by Noailles' speech ended at two o'clock on the morning of August 5, the Old Régime was dead.

Three weeks later, on August 26, 1789, the National Assembly formulated the Declaration of the Rights of Man. "Men are born and remain free and equal in rights," it asserted (Article 1). "These rights are liberty, property, security and resistance to oppression" (Article 2). Property it called "an inviolable and sacred right" (Article 17), and liberty "the exercise of the natural rights of each man" within the limits "determined by law" (Article 4). "Law," the Declaration stated, "is the expression of the general will. All citizens have the right to take part, in person or by their representatives, in its formation" (Article 6). "Any society in which the guarantee of rights is not assured or the separation of powers not determined has no constitution" (Article 16).*

The Declaration of the Rights of Man mirrored the economic and political attitudes of the middle class. It insisted on the sanctity of property, and it proclaimed that "Social distinctions may be based only on usefulness," thus implying that some social distinctions were to be expected. It committed the French to the creed of constitutional liberalism already affirmed by the English in 1688–1689 and by the Americans in 1776, and it incorporated the key phrases of the *philosophes*: natural rights, general will, and separation of powers. The National Assembly made a resounding statement of the ideals of the Enlightenment. Yet, as the subsequent history of the Revolution soon demonstrated, the Assembly found no magic formula by which to translate these ideals into practice.

The economic legislation of the National Assembly provided a case in point. Belief in the theory of the equal taxation of all Frenchmen did not solve urgent financial problems.

*G. Lefebvre, *The Coming of the French Revolution* (Princeton, 1947), Appendix.

Marie Antoinette and her children.

The new and just land tax imposed by the deputies simply could not be collected. Tax-collectors had vanished in the general liquidation of the Old Régime, and naive peasants now thought that they owed the government nothing. Once again, the French state borrowed until its credit was exhausted, and then, in desperation, the National Assembly ordered the confiscation of church lands (November, 1789). "The wealth of the clergy is at the disposition of the nation," it declared, explaining that ecclesiastical lands fell outside the bounds of "inviolable" property as defined in the Declaration of the Rights of Man because they belonged to an institution and not to private individuals.

The government thus acquired an asset worth at least 2,000,000,000 *livres*. On the basis of this collateral it issued *assignats*, paper notes used to pay the government's debts. So far, so good: The *assignats* had adequate secu-

369

rity behind them and temporarily eased the financial crisis. Unfortunately, the Revolution repeated the mistake of John Law (see Chapter 8): It did not know when to stop. As the state sold parcels of confiscated land—that is, as it reduced the collateral securing its paper money—it should have destroyed *assignats* to the same amount. The temptation not to reduce the number of *assignats* proved too great to resist. Inflation resulted: The *assignats*, progressively losing their solid backing, depreciated until in 1795 they were worth less than 5 per cent of their face value.

The state sold at auction the property seized from the Church and from nobles who had emigrated from France. Well-to-do peasants profited by the opportunity to enlarge their holdings, and many bourgeois also bought up land, sometimes as a short-term speculation, sometimes as a long-term investment. The poor and landless peasants, however, gained nothing, since they did not have the money with which to buy. True to the doctrine of laissez-faire, the National Assembly made no move to help these marginal farmers. Following the same doctrine, it abolished the guilds and the irksome tariffs and tolls on trade within France. And deeming the few primitive organizations of labor unnatural restrictions on economic freedom, it abolished them too. In June, 1791, after an outbreak of strikes, it passed the Le Chapelier Law banning both strikes and labor unions.

Since the suppression of tithes and the seizure of ecclesiastical property deprived the Church of its revenue, the National Assembly agreed to finance ecclesiastical salaries. The new arrangement virtually nationalized the Gallican Church and made it subject to constant government regulation. The Assembly's decision to restrict monasteries and convents caused little difficulty; many of these establishments were already far gone in decay. But an uproar arose over the legislation altering the status of the secular hierarchy.

The Civil Constitution of the Clergy (June, 1790) redrew the ecclesiastical map of France. It reduced the number of bishoprics by more than one-third, making the remaining dioceses

correspond to the new civil administrative units known as departments (see below). It transformed bishops and priests into civil officials, paid by the state and elected by the population of the diocese or parish; both Catholics and non-Catholics (the latter usually a small minority) could vote in these elections. A new bishop was required to take an oath of loyalty to the state, and the Civil Constitution stipulated that he might not apply to the pope for confirmation, though he might write to him as the "Visible Head of the Universal Church."

These provisions stripped the "Visible Head of the Universal Church" of effective authority over the Gallican clergy and ran counter to the whole tradition of the Roman Church as an independent ecclesiastical monarchy. Naturally the pope denounced the Civil Constitution. The National Assembly then required that every member of the French clergy take a special oath supporting the Civil Constitution, but only seven bishops and fewer than half of the priests complied. Thus a breach was opened between the Revolution and a large segment of the population. Good Catholics, from Louis XVI down to humble peasants, rallied to the non-juring clergy, as those who refused the special oath were termed. The Civil Constitution of the Clergy, supplying an issue for rebellion and civil war, was the first great blunder of the Revolution.

The Constitution of 1791

The major undertaking of the National Assembly was the Constitution of 1791. The Assembly devised a neat and orderly system of local government to replace the bewildering complex of provincial units that had accumulated under the Old Régime. It divided the territory of France into eighty-three departments of approximately equal size. Each department was small enough for its chief town to be within a day's journey of the outlying towns; each bore the name of a river, a mountain range, or some other natural landmark. The departments were subdivided into *arrondissements* or districts, and the districts into communes—that is municipalities. The commune-district-department arrangement resembled, on a reduced scale, the American hierarchy of town-county-state. In the communes and departments, elected councils and officials enjoyed considerable rights of self-government. The administration of the new France, on paper anyhow, was to be far more decentralized than that of the Old Régime.

The principle of the separation of powers guided the reconstruction of the central government. The Constitution of 1791 established an independent hierarchy of courts staffed by elected judges. It vested legislative authority in a single elected chamber. Although the king still headed the executive branch, his actions now required approval by his ministers, who were responsible only to him and not to the legislature, as they generally are in a "parliamentary" or "cabinet" government. The King did receive the power of veto, but it was only a suspensive veto, which could block legislation for a maximum of four years. Louis XVI, no longer the absolute "King of France," acquired the new constitutional title, "King of the French."

The new constitution subscribed to many other principles issuing straight from the Enlightenment. It promised to give France a new law code, and it declared marriage a civil contract, not a religious sacrament. The state took over the old ecclesiastical functions of keeping records of vital statistics and providing charity and education. Indeed, the Constitution promised a system of free public education. It also promised that the foreign policy of revolutionary France would be more virtuous than that of autocratic France:

The French nation renounces the undertaking of any war with a view of making conquests, and it will never use its forces against the liberty of any people.*

The Constitution of 1791 went a long way

*J. H. Stewart, *A Documentary Survey of the French Revolution* (New York, 1951), 260.

toward instituting popular government, but it stopped well short of full democracy. It divided Frenchmen into two classes of citizens, "active" and "passive," and limited the right of voting to "active" citizens, who paid annually in taxes an amount equal to at least three days' wages for unskilled labor in the locality. The "passive" citizens, numbering about one-third of the male population, enjoyed the full protection of the law but did not receive the franchise. Moreover, the new legislature was chosen by a process of indirect election. "Active" citizens did not vote for their deputies but for a series of electors, who were required to be men of substantial wealth, and who ultimately elected the deputies. The French middle class evidently assumed that the amount of worldly goods a man possessed determined the degree of his political wisdom.

The decentralized and limited monarchy established by the Constitution of 1791 was doomed to fail. It was too radical to suit the King and most of the aristocracy, and not radical enough for the many bourgeois who were veering toward republicanism. The majority in the National Assembly supporting the Constitution suffered the fate commonly experienced by the politically moderate in a revolution: they were squeezed out by the extremists. Despite their moderate intentions, they were driven to enact some drastic legislation, notably the Civil Constitution of the Clergy, which weakened their own position. And they failed to develop an effective party organization at a time when the deputies of the radical minority were consolidating their strength.

These radicals were the Jacobins, so named because they belonged to the "Society of the Friends of the Constitution," which maintained its Paris headquarters in a former Jacobin (Dominican) monastery. The Jacobins were no true friends of the Constitution of 1791. They accepted it only as a stopgap until they might end the monarchy and set up a republic based on universal suffrage. To prepare for the millennium, the Jacobins used all the techniques of a political pressure group. They planted rabble-rousing articles in the press and manipulated the crowds of noisy and volatile spectators at the sessions of the National Assembly. Their network of political clubs extended throughout the provinces, providing the only nation-wide party organization in France. Almost everywhere, Jacobins captured control of the new department and commune councils. In local elections, as in the elections to the Estates General, an able and determined minority prevailed over a largely illiterate and politically inexperienced majority.

The defenders of the Old Régime played into the hands of the Jacobins. From the summer of 1789 on, alarmed nobles and prelates fled France, leaving behind more rich estates to be confiscated and giving Jacobin orators and editors a splendid opportunity to denounce the rats leaving a sinking ship. Many of these *émigrés* gathered in the German Rhineland to intrigue for Austrian and Russian support of a counter-revolution. The King's grave misgivings about the Civil Constitution of the Clergy prompted his disastrous attempt to join the *émigrés* on the Franco-German frontier. In June, 1791, disguised as a valet and governess, Louis and Marie Antoinette left the Tuileries. But Louis unwisely showed his face in public, and a local official along the route recognized the royal profile from the portrait on the *assignats*. The alarm was sent ahead, and at Varennes in northeastern France a detachment of troops forced the royal party to return to Paris. After the abortive flight to Varennes, the revolutionaries viewed Louis XVI as a potential traitor and kept him closely guarded in the Tuileries. The experiment in constitutional monarchy began under most unfavorable auspices.

The Legislative Assembly, October, 1791 – September, 1792

On October 1, 1791, the first and the only legislative assembly elected under the new constitution commenced its deliberations. No one faction commanded a numerical majority in the new assembly:

POLITICAL COMPLEXION OF THE
LEGISLATIVE ASSEMBLY, 1791

	Approximate No. of Seats
Right (Constitutional Monarchists)	265
Center (Plain)	345
Left (Jacobins)	130

(In the practice followed by most continental European assemblies, the Right sat to the right of the presiding officer as he faced the assembly, the Left to his left, and the Center in between.)

The balance of political power rested with the timid and irresolute deputies of the Center, who were neither strong defenders of the Constitution nor yet convinced republicans. Since they occupied the lowest seats in the assembly hall, they received the derogatory nickname of the Plain or Marsh. The capable politicians of the Left soon captured the votes of the Plain, to demonstrate anew the power of a determined minority.

Leadership of this minority came from a contingent of Jacobins known as Girondins because some of them, though by no means all, came from Bordeaux, in the Gironde department. The Girondins specialized in patriotic oratory. They pictured revolutionary France as the intended victim of a reactionary conspiracy, engineered by the *émigrés*, aided at home by the non-juring clergy and the royal family, and abetted abroad by a league of monarchs under Leopold II, the Austrian emperor and the brother of Marie Antoinette. But Louis XVI, despite the flight to Varennes, was no traitor, and Leopold II cautiously limited his aid to the *émigrés*. The sudden death of Leopold in March, 1792, and the accession of his inexperienced and less cautious son, Francis II, at once increased the Austrian threat. At the same time, belligerent Girondins secured control of French diplomacy. On April 20, 1792, the Legislative Assembly declared war on Austria. In the eyes of Frenchmen the war was defensive, not the campaign of conquest that the nation had forsworn in the fine phrases of its constitution.

Partly because the emigration of many nobles had depleted the corps of French officers, the war went badly for France at the outset. Prussia soon joined Austria, and on July 25, 1792, the Prussian commander, the Duke of Brunswick, issued a manifesto drafted by an *émigré*. The manifesto stated the war aims of the allies:

. . . To put a stop to the anarchy within France, to check the attacks delivered against throne and altar, to re-establish legal authority, to restore to the king the security and freedom of which he has been deprived, and to place him in a position where he may exercise the legitimate authority which is his due.

A threat followed. "If the Tuileries is attacked, by deed or word, if the slightest outrage or violence is perpetrated against the royal family, and if immediate measures are not taken for their safety, maintenance and liberty"—then Paris would witness "a model vengeance, never to be forgotten."*

The Duke of Brunswick's manifesto did not frighten the French, as it was intended to do. On the contrary, it stiffened the already firm determination of republicans to do away with the monarchy. All through the early summer of 1792 the Jacobins of Paris had been plotting an insurrection. They won the support of a formidable following—army recruits; mem-

*Le Moniteur Universel, August 3, 1792. Our translation.

bers of the National Guard from the provinces, who had come to Paris to celebrate the third anniversary of the fall of the Bastille; and the rank and file of Parisians, who were angered by the depreciation of the *assignats* and by the high price and short supply of food and other necessities. One by one, the forty-eight *sections* or wards into which the city was divided came under the control of Jacobins, who advertized their democratic sympathies by inviting passive citizens to take part in political activity. The climax came on the night of August 9–10, 1792, when the leaders of the *sections* ousted the regular municipal authorities from the Paris city hall and installed a new and illegal Jacobin commune.

The municipal revolution had immediate and momentous results. On the morning of August 10, the forces of the new commune attacked the Tuileries and massacred the King's Swiss guards, while the royal family took refuge with the Legislative Assembly. The uprising of August 10 sealed the doom of the monarchy and made the Assembly little more than the errand boy of the new Paris commune. With most of the deputies of the Right and the Plain absent, the Assembly voted to suspend the King from office, to imprison the royal family, and to order the election of a constitutional convention. Until this new body should meet, the government was to be run by an interim ministry staffed largely by Girondins. The birth of the First French Republic was at hand.

III   The First Republic

The September Massacres, 1792

The weeks between August 10 and the meeting of the Convention on September 21 were weeks of crisis and tension. The value of the *assignats* depreciated by 40 per cent during August alone. Rabble-rousing Jacob-

ins continually excited the populace of Paris, already stirred by the economic difficulties and by the capture of the Tuileries. Excitement mounted still higher when the news arrived that Prussian troops had invaded northeastern France. In the emergency, Danton, the interim minister of justice, won immortality by urging patriots to employ *"de*

l'audace, encore de l'audace, toujours de l'audace"
—boldness, more boldness, always boldness.

In Paris, boldness took the form of the "September massacres," lynchings of supposed traitors and enemy agents made possible by the collapse of normal police authority. For five days, beginning on September 2, bloodthirsty mobs moved from prison to prison. At each stop they held impromptu courts and summary executions. The number of victims exceeded one thousand and included ordinary criminals as well as aristocrats and non-juring priests, who were often innocent of the treason charged against them. The crowning horror was the mutilation of the Princesse de Lamballe, the Queen's maid of honor, whose severed head was paraded on a pike before the window of the royal prison so that Marie Antoinette might see "how the people take vengeance on their tyrants." The September massacres foreshadowed the terror in store for France.

Later in the month (September 20, 1792), a rather minor French victory, grandly styled "the miracle of Valmy," turned the Duke of Brunswick's forces back from the road to Paris; more solid French successes followed during the final months of 1792. Then the tide turned again, washing away the conquests of the autumn. By the summer of 1793 half-defeated France faced a hostile coalition including almost every major power in Europe. No wonder an atmosphere of perpetual emergency surrounded the Convention.

Gironde and Mountain

In theory, the election of deputies to the National Convention (August-September, 1792) marked the beginning of true political democracy in France. Both active and passive citizens were invited to the polls. Yet only 10 per cent of the potential electorate of 7,000,000 actually voted; the others abstained or were turned away from the polls by the watchdogs of the Jacobin clubs, ever on the alert against "counter-revolutionaries." The result was a landslide for the republicans:

POLITICAL COMPLEXION OF THE
CONVENTION, SEPTEMBER, 1792

	Approximate No. of Deputies
The Right (Gironde)	*165*
The Center (Plain)	*435*
The Left (Mountain)	*150*

The radicalism of the Convention was underlined by the Jacobin antecedents of both its Right and its Left. Many ties in common existed between the Gironde and the Mountain (so named because its deputies sat high up in the meeting hall). Both factions came from the middle class, both were steeped in the ideas of the *philosophes*, and both united to declare France a republic (September 21, 1792).

Bitter dissension, however, soon arose between the Gironde and the Mountain.

Danton (1759–1794), in a sketch by David.

The Girondins favored a breathing spell in revolutionary legislation, and they also defended provincial interests against possible encroachments by Paris. As one of their deputies told the Convention (and his allusion to classical antiquity was most characteristic of the Revolution):

I fear the despotism of Paris. . . . I do not want a Paris guided by intriguers to become to the French Empire what Rome was to the Roman Empire. Paris must be reduced to its proper one-eighty-third of influence, like the other departments.*

The Gironde, therefore, favored a large measure of "federalism," which meant decentralization in the Revolutionary vocabulary, and a national government limited by many checks and balances. The details were set forth in a draft constitution completed early in 1793 by the distinguished Girondin deputy, Condorcet, the prophet of human progress (see Chapter 9). In Condorcet's draft, the executive and the legislature would be independent of each other and separately elected, the results of elections would be adjusted according to proportional representation, projected laws would be submitted to a popular referendum, and voters would have the right to recall unworthy elected officials.

The leaders of the Mountain denounced federalism and advocated an all-powerful central government. Their chief spokesman was Maximilien Robespierre (1758–1794). This earnest young lawyer did not look like a revolutionary: He powdered his hair neatly and wore the light-blue coat and knee-breeches of the Old Régime. Yet Robespierre was a political fanatic whose speeches were lay sermons couched in the solemn language of a new revelation. He put his creed most forcefully in a discourse delivered in February, 1794:

What is the goal toward which we are striving? The peaceful enjoyment of liberty and equality: the rule of that eternal justice whose laws have been engraved . . . upon the hearts of men, even upon the heart of the slave who ignores them and of the tyrant who denies them.

We desire an order of things . . . where our country assures the welfare of each individual and where each individual enjoys with pride the prosperity and the glory of our country; where the souls of all grow through the constant expression of republican sentiments; where the arts are the ornament of the freedom which in turn ennobles them; and where commerce is the source of public wealth, not just of the monstrous opulence of a few houses.*

Apparently Robespierre truly believed that he could translate the ideals of Rousseau's *Social Contract* into a practical political program. Like Rousseau, he had faith in the natural goodness of humanity, in "the laws engraved upon the hearts of men." He was sure that he knew the general will, and that the general will demanded a Republic of Virtue. If Frenchmen would not be free and virtuous voluntarily, then, as Rousseau had recommended, they would be "forced to be free."

Robespierre and the Republic of Virtue triumphed. The Mountain won out over the Gironde in the competition for the votes of the relatively uncommitted deputies of the Plain in the Convention. The first step came when, after one hundred hours of continuous voting, the Convention declared "Citizen Louis Capet" guilty of treason and by a narrow margin sentenced him to the guillotine without delay. Louis XVI died bravely on January 21, 1793. Although the majority of the French population disapproved of the King's execution, the majority did not control the Convention. The Girondin deputies made the political mistake of splitting their votes on the issue. Those who voted against the death penalty took a courageous stand in defense of the humanitarian principles of the Enlightenment, but they also exposed themselves to the charge of being "counter-revolutionaries."

A combination of events at home and abroad soon destroyed the Gironde. In February, 1793, the Convention rejected Condor-

*Lasource, September 25, 1792. *Archives Parlementaires*, Series 1, LII, 130. Our translation.

Le Moniteur Universel, February 7, 1794. Our translation.

Louis XVI, a moment before his execution.

cet's draft constitution, and in the same month it declared war on Britain, Spain, and the Netherlands. France now faced a formidable coalition of opponents, since Austria and Prussia remained at war with her. In March, the army under Dumouriez, a Girondin general, suffered a series of defeats in the Low Countries, and in April Dumouriez deserted to the enemy. At home, in the face of unemployment, high prices, and food shortages, the Gironde had little to offer except laissez-faire. The *sections* of Paris demanded price controls and food requisitioning; they also pressed for the expulsion of Girondins from the Jacobin clubs and the Convention. Finally, on June 2, 1793, a vast crowd of armed men from the *sections* of Paris, following the precedent of August,

1792, invaded the Convention and forced the arrest of twenty-nine Girondin deputies. Backed by these armed Parisians, the Mountain intimidated the Plain, and the Convention consigned the arrested Girondins to the guillotine. The Reign of Terror had begun.

The Reign of Terror, June, 1793–July, 1794

How was it that the advocates of democracy now imposed a dictatorship on France? Here is Robespierre's explanation:

. . . To establish and consolidate democracy, to achieve the peaceful rule of constitutional laws,

376

we must first finish the war of liberty against tyranny. . . . We must annihilate the enemies of the republic at home and abroad, or else we shall perish. . . .

If virtue is the mainstay of a democratic government in time of peace, then in time of revolution a democratic government must rely on *virtue* and *terror*. . . . Terror is nothing but justice, swift, severe and inflexible; it is an emanation of virtue. . . . It has been said that terror is the mainstay of a despotic government. . . . The government of the revolution is the despotism of liberty against tyranny.*

The Convention duly voted a democratic constitution, drawn up by the Mountain, granting universal manhood suffrage and giving supreme power, unhampered by Girondin checks and balances, to a single legislative chamber. The Constitution of 1793 was approved by a referendum, but its operation was then postponed indefinitely. As Robespierre explained, "To establish and consolidate democracy, we must first finish the war of liberty against tyranny."

The actual government of the Terror centered on a twelve-man Committee of Public Safety, composed of Robespierre and other stalwarts from the Mountain. Though nominally responsible to the Convention, the Committee of Public Safety exercised a large measure of independent authority and acted as a kind of war cabinet. Never under the dominance of a single individual, not even Robespierre, it really functioned as a committee— "The Twelve Who Ruled" is an appropriate description. A second committee, that of Public Security, supervised police activities and turned suspected enemies of the Republic over to the new Revolutionary Tribunal. To speed the work of repression, the sixteen judges and sixty jurors of the Tribunal were eventually divided into several courts.

The Mountain scrapped much of the local self-government inaugurated under the Constitution of 1791. Local Jacobin clubs purged department and commune administrations of political unreliables, while special local courts supplemented the grim labors of the Revolutionary Tribunal. To make sure that provin-

Le Moniteur Universel, February 7, 1794. Our translation.

cial France toed the line, the Mountain sent out trusted members of the Convention as its agents, the "deputies on mission." From the standpoint of administration, the Terror marked both an anticipation of twentieth century dictatorship and a return to the age-old French principle of centralization. The deputies on mission were the successors of the *intendants* of Richelieu, the *enquêteurs* of St. Louis, and the *missi dominici* of Charlemagne. The "Twelve Who Ruled" were more effective absolutists than Louis XIV himself.

The Record of the Terror

The "swift, severe, and inflexible justice" described by Robespierre took the lives of nearly 20,000 Frenchmen. Although the Terror claimed such social outcasts as criminals and prostitutes, its main purpose was military and political—to clear France of suspected traitors, including Marie Antoinette, and to purge the Jacobins of dissidents. It fell with the greatest severity on the clergy, the aristocracy, and the Girondins. Many of its victims came from the Vendée, a strongly Catholic and royalist area in western France which had revolted against the Republic's attempts to recruit soldiers. Many prisoners from the Vendée were among the 2,000 victims of the *noyades* (drownings) at Nantes, where the accused were set adrift on the River Loire in leaky barges. Equally grisly was the repression of an uprising of Girondin sympathizers at Lyons, which also claimed 2,000 victims.

The wartime hysteria that helped to account for the excesses of the Terror also inspired a very practical patriotism. On August 23, 1793, the Convention issued a decree epitomizing the democratic nationalism of the Jacobins:

From this moment, until the time when the enemy shall have been driven from the territory of the Republic, all Frenchmen are permanently requisitioned for the service of the armies.

Young men will go into combat; married men will manufacture arms and transport supplies; women will make tents and uniforms and will serve in the hospitals; children will make old linen into bandages; old men will be carried into the public squares to arouse the courage of the soldiers, excite hatred for kings and inspire the unity of the Republic.*

In an early application of universal conscription, the army drafted all bachelors and widowers between the ages of eighteen and twenty-five. Hundreds of open-air forges were installed in Paris to manufacture weapons. Since the war prevented the importation of the saltpeter needed for gunpowder, the government sponsored a great campaign to scrape patches of saltpeter from cellars and stables.

By the close of 1793, the forces of the Republic had driven foreign troops from French soil. Credit for this new shift in the tide of battle did not rest solely with the Jacobins. The military successes of the Republic reflected in part the improvements made in the army during the dying years of the Old Régime; they resulted still more from the weaknesses of the coalition aligned against France. Yet they could scarcely have been achieved without the new democratic spirit that allowed men of the third estate to become officers and that made the French army the most determined, the most enterprising—and, perhaps, the most idealistic—in Europe.

"Total" mobilization demanded an approximate equality of economic sacrifice. To exorcise the twin devils of inflation and scarcity, the Terror issued the "*maximum*" legislation, placing ceilings on prices and wages. In theory, at least, wages were checked at a maximum 50 per cent above the wage-rate of 1790, and prices were halted at 33 per cent above the price level of 1790. The government rationed bread and meat, forbade the use of white flour, and directed all patriots to eat *pain d'égalité*—"equality bread," a loaf utilizing almost the whole of the wheat. Finally, early in 1794, the Convention passed the "Laws of Ventôse," named for a month in the new revolutionary calendar. These laws authorized seizure of the remaining properties of the *émigrés* and other opponents of the Republic and recommended their distribution to landless Frenchmen.

*Le Moniteur Universel, August 24, 1793. Our translation.

Socialist historians have sometimes found in the *maximum* and the Laws of Ventôse evidence that the Terror was moving from political to social democracy, that the Republic of Virtue was indeed beginning the socialist revolution. Actually the *maximum* regulations did not prove very effective. Attempts by the government to enforce wage ceilings made Parisian workingmen indignant. And, though the *maximum* on prices temporarily checked the depreciation of the *assignats*, many price-controlled articles were available only on the black market, which even the government had to patronize.

Moreover, the redistribution of property permitted by the Laws of Ventôse was never implemented. When the Laws were proposed, a spokesman for the Committee of Public Safety explained that no general assault on property was intended:

The revolution leads us to recognize the principle that he who has shown himself the enemy of

Robespierre, sketched during a meeting of the Convention.

Sketch of Marie Antoinette on her way to the guillotine, by David.

his country cannot own property. The properties of patriots are sacred, but the goods of conspirators are there for the unfortunate.*

To the thorough-going socialist not even the properties of patriots are sacred. The middle-class leaders of the Terror were not genuine socialists; only the emergencies of the Revolution forced them to abandon laissez-faire. They had to make food cheaper for townspeople — whence the *maximum*; and they had to promise men some hope of future well-being — whence the Laws of Ventôse.

The Terror presented its most revolutionary aspect in its drastic social and cultural reforms. The Convention abolished slavery in the French colonies; at home, according to Robespierre, "we desire to substitute all the virtues and all the miracles of the Republic for all the vices and all the nonsense of monarchy." When Robespierre said "all," he meant "all" — clothing, the arts, amusements, the calendar, religion. The Republic of Virtue could tolerate nothing that smelled of the Old Régime. Even the traditional forms of address,

*Saint-Just, February 26, 1794, in *Le Moniteur Universel*, February 27, 1794. Our translation.

"*Monsieur*" and "*Madame*," gave way to "*Citoyen*" (citizen) and "*Citoyenne*" (citizeness).

Ever since 1789, revolutionaries had discarded elaborate gowns and knee-breeches (*culottes*) as symbols of idleness and privilege. With the exception of Robespierre, good republican men were *sans-culottes* (literally, without knee-breeches), attired in the long, baggy trousers of the humble peasant or workman. Women affected simple, high-waisted dresses, copied from the costumes of the ancient Romans. Rome became the model for behavior — the virtuous Rome of the Republic, of course, not the sordid Empire. Parents named their children Brutus or Cato or Gracchus, and the theater shelved the masterpieces of Racine and Corneille for stilted dramas glorifying Roman heroes. Cabinet-makers, deserting the graceful style of Louis XV, produced sturdy neoclassical furniture decorated with Roman symbols. "The arts," said Robespierre, "are the ornament of the freedom which in turn ennobles them." Playwrights, authors, and editors who failed to ornament freedom properly experienced censorship or even the guillotine. The Jacobins reduced the lively newspapers of the early revolution to dull semi-official organs.

They also instituted a sweeping reform of the calendar (October, 1793). The first day of the Republic, September 22, 1792, was designated the initial day of Year I, Roman numerals were assigned to the years, and the months received new and more "natural" names:

THE MONTHS OF THE
REVOLUTIONARY CALENDAR

Fall: Vendémiaire (Grape-Harvest)
        Brumaire (Misty)
        Frimaire (Frosty)

Winter: Nivôse (Snowy)
        Pluviôse (Rainy)
        Ventôse (Windy)

Spring: Germinal (Sprouting)
        Floréal (Flowering)
        Prairial (Meadow)

Summer: Messidor (Wheat-Harvest)
Thermidor (Heat)
Fructidor (Ripening)

Each month had thirty days, divided into three ten-day weeks. Every tenth day was set aside for rest and for the celebration of one of the virtues so admired by Robespierre—Hatred of Tyrants and Traitors, Heroism, Frugality, Stoicism, not to mention two anticipations of Mother's Day (Filial Piety and Maternal Tenderness). The five days left over at the end of the year were dedicated to Genius, Labor, Noble Actions, Awards, and Opinion. The revolutionary calendar, for all its sanctimonious touches, was worthy of the Enlightenment. Yet it antagonized workmen, who disliked laboring nine days out of ten, instead of six out of seven. It never really took root, and Napoleon scrapped it a decade later.

The Convention had better luck with another reform close to the spirit of the Age of Reason—the metric system. A special committee, including Condorcet, Laplace, Lavoisier, and other distinguished intellectuals, devised new weights and measures based on the uniform use of the decimal system rather than on the haphazard accumulations of custom. In August, 1793, a decree made the meter the standard unit of length, and supplementary legislation in 1795 established the liter as the measure of volume and the gram as the unit of weight. Even in some Anglo-Saxon countries, which, cling to older and less rational weights and measures, scientists have adopted the metric system of revolutionary France.

By and large, however, the forces of tradition proved too strong for the Terror. Nowhere was this fact more evident than in the attempts to destroy the old religion and legislate a new one. Many churches were closed and turned into barracks or administrative offices; often their medieval glass and sculpture were destroyed. Some of the Jacobins launched a "de-Christianization" campaign to make Catholics into *philosophes* and their churches into "temples of Reason." Robespierre, however, disliked the cult of Reason; the Republic of Virtue, he believed, should acknowledge an ultimate author of morality. The Convention

therefore decreed (May, 1794) that "the French people recognize the existence of the Supreme Being and the immortality of the soul." At the festival of the Supreme Being, June 8, 1794, Robespierre set fire to figures representing Vice, Folly, and Atheism, and from the embers a statue of Wisdom emerged, but smudged with smoke because of a mechanical slip-up. The audience laughed. The deistic concept of the Supreme Being was too remote and the mechanics of the new worship too artificial to appeal to the religious emotions of Frenchmen.

The Thermidorean Reaction

Indeed, the Republic of Virtue was too abstract in ideals, and too violent in practice, to retain popular support. Like the Geneva of Calvin, the France of Robespierre demanded superhuman devotion to duty and inhuman indifference to hardships and bloodshed. During the first half of 1794, Robespierre pressed the Terror so relentlessly that even the members of the Committees of Public Safety and General Security began to fear they would be the next victims. Robespierre lost his backing in the Convention, as more and more deputies came to favor moderation. The crucial day was the ninth of Thermidor, Year II (July 27, 1794), when shouts of "Down with the Tyrant!" drowned out Robespierre's attempts to address the deputies. The Convention ordered Robespierre's arrest, and on the next day the great fanatic went to the guillotine.

The leaders of the Thermidorean Reaction, many of them former Jacobins, soon dismantled the machinery of the Terror. They disbanded the Revolutionary Tribunal, recalled the deputies on mission, and deprived the Committees of Public Safety and General Security of their independent authority. They closed the Paris Jacobin Club and invited the surviving Girondin deputies to resume their old seats in the Convention. They took the first step toward the restoration of Catholicism by permitting priests to celebrate Mass, though under state supervision and without state financial support. The press and the theater recovered their freedom, and pleasure-seekers again flocked to Paris, now liberated from the somberness of the Republic of Virtue. France was resuming a normal existence.

Normality, however, exacted a price. In southern and western France a counter-revolutionary "White Terror," equalling the great Terror in fury, claimed many lives, not only supporters of the Mountain but also purchasers of former church and noble lands. The men of Thermidor caused an acute inflation by canceling the economic legislation of the Terror. No longer checked even slightly by the *maximum*, the prices of some foods rose to a hundred times the level of 1790, and the *assignats* sank so low in value that businessmen refused to accept them. Desperate, half-starving Parisians staged several demonstrations against the Thermidoreans during 1795. Sometimes the rioters voiced their support of the discredited Mountain and its democratic Constitution of 1793, and sometimes they let themselves be used by royalist agents, but always they clamored for bread and lower prices.

The Thermidorean Reaction concluded with the passage of the Constitution of 1795, the last major act of the Convention. The men of Thermidor wanted both to retain the Republic and to assure the dominance of the propertied classes. The Constitution of 1795 therefore denied the vote to the poorest quarter of the nation and required that candidates for public office possess considerable property. It established two legislative councils, the Five Hundred and the Elders (who had to be at least forty years old and either married or widowed); both councils were to be elected piecemeal after the American practice of renewing one-third of the Senate every two years. Two-thirds of the initial members of the councils were to be drawn from the deputies of the Convention, who were therefore labelled "*les perpetuels.*" The Council of Five Hundred nominated, and the Elders chose, five directors who headed the executive. Otherwise the Directory was almost totally independent of the legislative councils.

The Constitution of 1795 marked the third great effort of the Revolution to provide France with an enduring government. It followed in part a classical example, for the two councils were patterned on the Areopagus and the Five Hundred of ancient Athens; it also followed the American precedent of 1787 and the French precedent of 1791. It embodied the separation of powers and deferred to the aristocracy of wealth, though not to that of birth. By abandoning the political democracy of the still-born Constitution of 1793 and by reverting to the restricted suffrage of 1791, it demonstrated that the most radical phase of the Revolution had passed.

The Directory, October, 1795–November, 1799

The new regime of the Directory made a vigorous attack on economic problems. It levied high protective tariffs, both as a measure of war against England and as a concession to French businessmen. Again responding to business pressure, it destroyed the plates used to print the *assignats* and in 1797 withdrew paper money from circulation. The return to hard money required stringent governmental economies. The Directory instituted these economies, and it eased the crushing burden of the national debt by simply repudiating two-thirds of it. In short, the Directory brought a semblance of order out of chronic financial chaos.

Political instability, however, plagued the Directory. It suppressed with ease the amateurish "Conspiracy of the Equals" (1796–1797) sponsored by Gracchus Babeuf, who dreamed of a more collectivist society. But it experienced more difficulty with the recurrent plots of royalists or Jacobins. Moreover, the directors and the legislative councils clashed repeatedly, each side seeking to turn the political balance in its own favor, and each, in consequence, violating the constitution. The councils sacked directors before their terms were finished; the directors refused to allow duly elected councilors to take their seats. Disgruntled politicians and apprehensive moderates, who feared that the Directory might be taken over by extremists, began to

maneuver for the help of the army. The result of their maneuvering was the *coup d'état* of Bru-

maire in 1799 and the dictatorship of a general, Napoleon Bonaparte.

IV   Napoleon and France

Edmund Burke, the British political philosopher, foresaw very early the long process that culminated in Napoleon's dominance of France and Europe. In 1790, Burke warned the French—and his own countrymen—in his *Reflections on the Revolution in France:*

Everything depends on the army in such a government as yours; for you have industriously destroyed all the opinions, . . . all the instincts which support government. Therefore the moment any difference arises between your National Assembly and any part of the nation, you must have recourse to force. Nothing else is left to you. . . .

It is besides to be considered, whether an assembly like yours . . . is fit for promoting the discipline and obedience of an army. It is known, that armies have hitherto yielded a very precarious and uncertain obedience to any senate, or popular authority. . . . The officers must totally lose the characteristic disposition of military men, if they see with perfect submission and due admiration, the dominion of pleaders; especially when they find that they have a new court to pay to an endless succession of those pleaders. . . . In the weakness of one kind of authority, and in the fluctuation of all, the officers of an army will remain for some time mutinous and full of faction, until some popular general who understands the art of conciliating the soldiery, and who possesses the true spirit of command, shall draw the eyes of all men upon himself. Armies will obey him on his personal account. There is no other way of securing military obedience in this state of things. But the moment in which that event shall happen, the person who really commands the army is your master; the master . . . of your king, the master of your assembly, the master of your whole republic.*

In 1790, however, except for Burke, no one outside France paid much heed to the French army. It was widely believed that the very in-

*Everyman ed. (New York, 1910), 215–217.

tensity of domestic problems made France incapable of a vigorous foreign policy. Catherine the Great predicted as late as 1792 that ten thousand soldiers would be sufficient to conquer France. Liberals everywhere hailed the peaceful promise of the Revolution. The capture of the Bastille delighted Charles James Fox, a leading English Whig: "How much the greatest event it is that ever happened in the world! and how much the best!"

The First Coalition, 1792–1795

The war that broke out in the spring of 1792 soon destroyed the illusions of French military weakness and French liberal purity. The war was to last continuously, save for a few intervals of peace, down to the final defeat of Napoleon. It deserves to be called the World War of 1792–1815, for almost all the European powers eventually participated, and the fighting ranged far beyond Europe. By the time the war was a year old, Austria and Prussia, the charter members of the First Coalition against France, had been joined by Holland, Spain, and Great Britain. The British had both ideological and strategic interests at stake. They regarded the attack on the Tuileries, the September massacres, and the execution of Louis XVI as outrages against human decency and the institution of monarchy. And the French invasion of the Austrian Netherlands in the fall of 1792 raised the unpleasant prospect that this Belgian "cockpit of Europe" would fall under French control. The early campaigns of the war were indecisive. Late in 1792, the French followed up their success at Valmy by invading Belgium, only to lose ground again in 1793 after the defeat and desertion of Dumouriez (see p. 376). Then in 1794 the French definitely gained the advantage, and by 1795 French troops had occupied Belgium, Holland, and Germany west of the Rhine.

One reason for French success we have already seen—the Convention's energetic mobilization of national resources. Another reason, equally important yet easy to overlook, was the weakness of the First Coalition. The partners in the coalition lacked a first-rate commander; nor did they achieve effective co-ordination of their efforts. The Duke of Brunswick's failure to take Paris in 1792 resulted as much from his own deficient generalship as from the "miracle" of Valmy. Moreover, the partitions of Poland in 1793 and 1795 greatly assisted the French by distracting Prussia, Russia, and Austria. The pick of the Prussian army was diverted to occupation duty in newly annexed Polish provinces. By 1795 things had come to such a pass that the Prussians did not dare attack the French for fear of being assaulted from the rear by their nominal Austrian ally.

Prussia was the first member of the coalition to make peace. In the Treaty of Basel (1795) she ceded to France the scattered Prussian holdings west of the Rhine on the understanding that she might seek compensation elsewhere in Germany. Spain and Holland soon deserted the coalition also. In 1795, then, France at last secured her "natural frontiers." In addition to Belgium and the Rhineland she had also annexed Savoy and Nice, thereby extending her southeastern border to the crest of the Alps. These conquests, however, belied the ideals of the Revolution. In declaring war on Austria in 1792, France had sworn to uphold the promise of the Constitution of 1791: that she would never undertake a war of conquest. This was to be "not a war of nation against nation, but the righteous defense of a free people against the unjust aggression of a king." But the conquering armies of the First Republic brought closer the day when nation would fight nation—when the European nations would invoke "the righteous defense of a free people against the unjust aggression" not of a king, but of revolutionary France.

Napoleon's Early Career

At the close of 1795, only Britain and Austria remained officially at war with France. To lead the attack against Habsburg forces in northern Italy, the Directory picked a youthful general who was something of a *philosophe* and revolutionary as well as a ruthless, ambitious adventurer. He was born Napoleone Buonaparte on Corsica in 1769, soon after the French acquisition of that Mediterranean island from Genoa. He retained throughout his life the intense family loyalty characteristic of the rather primitive society of Corsica and bestowed on the members of the Bonaparte clan all the spoils of conquest, even thrones.

As a boy, Napoleon attended military school in France and, though he now spelled his name in the French style, was snubbed as a "foreigner" by some of his fellow cadets. He immersed himself in his studies and in reading (Rousseau was his favorite) and dreamed of the day when he might liberate his native island from French control. Later, however, his zeal for Corsican independence faded in consequence of the rupture between the Bonapartes and the hero of Corsican nationalism, Paoli, who was an ally of Britain. When the Revolution broke out, the young artillery officer helped to overthrow the Old Régime at home and then went back to France to resume his military career. He defended the Convention, but more out of expediency than from conviction, and commanded the artillery in December, 1793, when the forces of the Jacobin Convention recaptured the Mediterranean port of Toulon, which had fallen to the British earlier in the year. In October, 1795, he rescued the Thermidorean Convention in the last moments before the Directory took over by mowing down royalist rioters with the famous "whiff of grapeshot." Then he married Josephine de Beauharnais, a widow six years his senior and an intimate of the ruling clique of the Directory. Josephine's connections and Napoleon's own demonstrated talent gained him the Italian command in 1796.

In the celebrated Italian campaign Napoleon cleared the Austrians out of their strongholds in the space of a year and made them sue for peace. He showed a remarkable ability to strike quickly and by surprise before his opponents could consolidate their defenses. He also showed a gift for propaganda and "public relations," as this proclamation from the early phases of the campaign will illustrate:

Soldiers! In two weeks you have won six victories; you have made 15,000 prisoners; you have killed or wounded more than 10,000 men.

Deprived of everything, you have accomplished everything. You have won battles without cannon, negotiated rivers without bridges, made forced marches without shoes, encamped without brandy, and often without bread. Only the phalanxes of the Republic, only the soldiers of Liberty, would have been capable of suffering the things that you have suffered.

You all burn to carry the glory of the French

people; to humiliate the proud kings who dared to contemplate shackling us; to go back to your villages, to say proudly: 'I was of the conquering army of Italy!'

Friends, I promise you that conquest; but there is a condition you must swear to fulfill: to respect the people whom you are delivering; to repress horrible pillaging.

Peoples of Italy, the French army comes to break your chains; greet it with confidence; your property, religion and customs will be respected.*

It was characteristic of Napoleon to promise all things to all men. He encouraged the nationalism of underpaid and underfed French soldiers; yet he appealed also to the nationalism of the Italians, promising them liberation from Austria and guaranteeing the orderly conduct of the French army. He did not, of course, tell the Italians that they might be exchanging one master for another, nor did he publicize the money that he seized from Italian governments and the art treasures that he took from Italian galleries and shipped back to France.

In the Treaty of Campoformio (1797) terminating the Italian campaign, Austria acknowledged the loss of Belgium and recognized the two puppet states that Napoleon set up in northwestern Italy, the Ligurian Republic (Genoa) and the Cisalpine Republic (the former Austrian possession of Lombardy). In return, the Habsburgs received the Italian territories of the Venetian Republic and a secret French assurance that Prussia, despite the specific promise made to her in 1795, would not be permitted to compensate for her losses in the Rhineland by taking lands elsewhere in Germany.

Only Britain remained at war with France. Napoleon decided to attack her indirectly through Egypt, then a semi-independent vassal of the Ottoman Empire. This would-be Alexander the Great, seeking new worlds to conquer, talked grandly of digging a canal at Suez, which would give French merchants the monopoly of a new short trade-route to India and exact belated retribution from Britain for Clive's victory in the Seven Years' War. Since Napoleon shared the passion of the Enlighten-

Napoleon, 1798; unfinished portrait by David.

*Abridged from *Le Moniteur Universel*, May 17, 1796. Our translation.

ment for science and antiquity, he invited archaeologists and other experts to accompany his army and thereby helped to found the study known as Egyptology. Frenchmen discovered the Rosetta Stone, later deciphered by Champollion, the first key to the translation of ancient Egyptian hieroglyphics. Napoleon's experts established in Egypt an outpost of French cultural imperialism that lasted until the twentieth century.

From the military standpoint, however, the campaign failed. Having eluded the British Mediterranean fleet commanded by Nelson, Napoleon landed in Egypt in July, 1798, and quickly routed the Mamluks, the ruling oligarchy. Then disaster struck. On August 1, 1798, Nelson discovered the French fleet moored at Abukir Bay along the Egyptian coast and destroyed it before its captains had time to weigh anchor. Nelson's victory deprived the French of supplies, of reinforcements, and even of news from home. After a year of futile campaigning in the Near East, Napoleon suddenly left Egypt in August, 1799, and returned to France.

Brumaire

Napoleon found the situation in France ripe for a decisive political stroke. The Directory was shaken by a strong revival of Jacobinism. Several hundred deputies in the legislative councils belonged to the "Society of the Friends of Liberty and Equality," essentially the old Jacobin club. Under their influence, the councils in 1799 decreed a forced loan from the rich and passed a Law of Hostages, designed to make the *émigrés* behave by threatening their relatives in France with reprisals if they engaged in activities hostile to the French Republic. Moderates feared that a new Reign of Terror would soon be unleashed.

Abroad, the Directory had established four new satellite republics with classical names— the Roman, the Parthenopean in Naples, the Batavian in Holland, and the Helvetian in Switzerland. But this new success of French imperialism upset the European balance and provoked the formation of the Second Coali-

tion, headed by Britain, Austria, and Russia. The Habsburgs resented the extension of French influence in their former Italian preserve, and Tsar Paul I (1796–1801) feared that Napoleon would damage Russia's Mediterranean interests. The eccentric Tsar was head of the Knights of Malta, a Catholic order dating back to the Crusades, whom Napoleon had expelled from their headquarters on the island of Malta. In the campaign of 1799, Russian troops fought in Italy and Switzerland, and the Russian General Suvorov, who defeated the French repeatedly, became the hero of western Europe. By August, 1799, the French had been expelled from Italy, and their puppet republics—Cisalpine, Roman, and Parthenopean—had been dismantled.

In these circumstances, Napoleon got a rousing reception on his return from Egypt. Soon he was engaged in a plot to overthrow the Directory, with the complicity of two of the five directors, Roger-Ducos and Siéyès, the old champion of the third estate. On November 9 and 10, 1799 (18 and 19 Brumaire by the revolutionary calendar), the plot was executed. The three directors not in the plot resigned, and the two legislative councils named Napoleon military commander of Paris. He was then to persuade the councils to entrust to the two remaining directors and himself the task of drafting a new constitution. The Elders agreed, but in the Five Hundred, where there were many Jacobin deputies, Bonaparte heard the ominous cry, "Down with the tyrant!," which had doomed Robespierre on the 9th Thermidor. He was jostled and fainted, but his brother Lucien, the presiding officer of the Five Hundred, saved the day until a detachment of troops loyal to Napoleon expelled the hostile deputies.

This almost comic *coup d'état* of Brumaire ended the Directory. The Bonapartist minority in the council vested full power in the victorious triumvirate of Roger-Ducos, Siéyès, and Napoleon, of whom only Napoleon really counted. It had all happened just as Edmund Burke had predicted:

In the weakness of authority, . . . some popular general shall draw the eyes of all men upon himself.

Armies will obey him on his personal account. . . .
The person who really commands the army is
your master.

Napoleonic Government

The Constitution of the Year VIII, drawn
up after Brumaire, was based on Siéyès' autocratic maxim, "Confidence from below, authority from above." It erected a very strong executive, the Consulate, named, like other bodies
set up by the constitution, after institutions
of republican Rome. Although three consuls
shared the executive, Napoleon as First Consul
left the other two only nominal power. Four
separate bodies had a hand in legislation: (1)
the Council of State proposed laws; (2) the
Tribunate debated them but did not vote; (3)
the Legislative Corps voted them but did not
debate; (4) the Senate had the right to veto
legislation. The members of all four bodies
were either appointed by the First Consul or
elected indirectly by a process so complex that
Bonaparte had ample opportunity to manipulate candidates. The core of this system was
the Council of State, staffed by Bonaparte's
hand-picked choices, which served both as a
cabinet and as the highest administrative court.
The three remaining bodies were intended
merely to go through the motions of enacting
whatever the First Consul decreed. Even so,
they were sometimes unruly, and the Tribunate
so annoyed Napoleon that he finally abolished
it in 1807.

Meantime, step by step, Napoleon increased
his own authority. In 1802, he persuaded the
legislators to drop the original ten-year limitation on his term of office and make him First
Consul for life, with the power to designate
his successor and amend the constitution at
will. France was now a monarchy in all but
name. In 1804, he took the next logical move
and prompted the Senate to declare that "the
government of the Republic is entrusted to an
Emperor." A magnificent coronation took
place at Notre Dame in Paris on December 2.
The Pope consecrated the Emperor, but, following Charlemagne's example, Napoleon
placed the crown on his own head.

Each time Napoleon revised the Constitution in a non-republican direction he made the
republican gesture of submitting the change to
the electorate. Each time, the results of the
plebiscite were overwhelmingly favorable: In
1799–1800, the vote was 3,011,107 for Napoleon and the Constitution of the Year VIII, and
1,562 against; in 1802, it was 3,568,885 for
Napoleon and the life Consulate, and 8,374
against; in 1804, 3,572,329 for Napoleon and
the Empire, and 2,579 against. Although the
voters were exposed to considerable official
pressure and the announced results were perhaps rigged a little, the majority of Frenchmen
undoubtedly supported Napoleon. His military triumphs appealed to their growing nationalism, and his policy of stability at home
insured them against further revolutionary
crises and changes. Confidence did indeed
seem to increase from below as authority increased from above.

If by any chance confidence failed to materialize below, Napoleon had the authority
to deal with the recalcitrant. He wiped out
the local self-government remaining from the
early days of the Revolution. In place of locally elected officials, he substituted those appointed by himself—prefects in departments,
sub-prefects in *arrondissements,* mayors in communes—and all were instructed to enforce
compliance with the Emperor's dictates. Napoleon brought the old French tradition of
centralization to a new peak of intensity.

Men of every political background staffed
the imperial administration. Napoleon cared
little whether his subordinates were returned
émigrés or ex-Jacobins, so long as they had ability. Besides, their varied antecedents reinforced the impression that narrow factionalism
was dead and that the Empire rested on a
broad political base. Napoleon paid officials
well and offered the additional bait of high
titles. With the establishment of the Empire
he created dukes by the dozen and counts and
barons by the hundred. He rewarded outstanding generals with the rank of Marshal and other
officers and civilian officials with the Legion of
Honor. "Aristocracy always exists," Napoleon
remarked. "Destroy it in the nobility, it re-
moves itself to the rich and powerful houses

of the middle class."* The imperial aristocracy gave the leaders of the middle class the social distinction that they felt to be rightfully theirs.

Law and Justice

Napoleon revived some of the glamor of the Old Régime but not its glaring inequalities. His series of law codes, the celebrated *Code Napoléon* (1804–1810), declared all men equal before the law without regard to their rank and wealth. It extended to all the right to follow the occupation, and embrace the religion, of their choosing. It gave France the single coherent system of law which the *philosophes* had demanded and which the revolutionary governments had been too busy to formulate.

The *Code Napoléon* did not, however, embody the full judicial reform program of the Enlightenment; it incorporated from the old Roman law some practices that strengthened the absolutism of the Empire. It favored the interests of the state over the rights of the individual, and it permitted some use of torture in trial procedure. Judges were no longer elected, as they had been under the Constitution of 1791, but appointed by the Emperor; jurors were selected by his prefects. Though Napoleon confirmed the revolutionary legislation permitting divorce by mutual consent, the code cancelled other revolutionary laws protecting wives, minors, and illegitimate children. The man of the family regained his old legal superiority. At times confirming the principles of 1789, and at times betraying them, Napoleonic law and justice offered a fair summary of the fate of the Revolution under the Empire.

A similar ambiguity clouded Napoleon's attitude toward civil liberties. He practiced religious toleration of a sort and welcomed former political heretics into his administration. But his generosity stemmed always from expediency, never from any fundamental belief in liberty. If he failed to get his way by conciliation, he used force. In the western de-

partments, where royalist uprisings had become chronic since the revolt in the Vendée, he massacred the rebels who declined his offer of amnesty in 1800. In 1804, he kidnapped the Duke of Enghien from the neutral German state of Baden because the Duke was believed to be the choice of monarchist conspirators for the throne of France. Though Napoleon immediately discovered the Duke's innocence, he had him executed none the less.

Napoleon cared little for freedom of speech. In July, 1801, for example, he directed his librarian to read all the newspapers carefully and

. . . make an abstract of everything they contain likely to affect the public point of view, especially with regard to religion, philosophy, and political opinion. He will send me this abstract between 5 and 6 o'clock every day.

Once every ten days he will send me an analysis of all the books or pamphlets which have appeared . . .

He will take pains to procure copies of all the plays which are produced, and to analyse them for me, with observations of the same character as those above mentioned. This analysis must be made, at latest, within 48 hours of the production of the plays.*

And so on through "bills, posters, advertisements, institutes, literary meetings, sermons and fashionable trials"—no segment of public opinion escaped Napoleon's manipulation. He reduced by five-sixths the number of Paris newspapers and pestered theater managers with suggestions for improving the patriotic tone of plays. When he wanted to arouse French feelings, he simply started a press campaign, as in this instance from 1807:

A great hue and cry is to be raised against the persecutions experienced by the Catholics of Ireland at the hands of the Anglican Church. . . . Bishops will be approached so that prayers will be offered entreating an end to the persecutions of the Anglican Church against the Irish Catholics. But the administration must move very delicately and make use of the newspapers without their realizing

*Quoted in H. A. L. Fisher, *Napoleon* (New York, 1913), Appendix I.

*Quoted in J. M. Thompson, ed., *Napoleon's Letters* (London, 1954), 93–94.

what the government is driving at. . . . And the term 'Anglican Church' must always be used in place of 'Protestants,' for we have Protestants in France, but no Anglican Church.*

Religion

Political considerations colored all Napoleon's decisions on religion. "I do not see in religion the mystery of the incarnation," he said, "but the mystery of the social order. It attaches to heaven an idea of equality which prevents the rich man from being massacred by the poor."† Since French Catholics loathed the anticlericalism of the Revolution, Napoleon sought to appease them by working out a reconciliation with Rome.

The Concordat negotiated with Pope Pius VII (1800–1823) in 1801 accomplished the reconciliation. It canceled only the most obnoxious features of the Civil Constitution of the Clergy. The French state, while agreeing to pay clerical salaries, also agreed to suppress the popular election of bishops and priests. The bishops were to be nominated by the government and then consecrated by the Pope; the priests were to be appointed by the bishops. At this point, Napoleon's concessions stopped. By declaring that Catholicism was the faith of the "great majority of Frenchmen," rather than the state religion, the Concordat implicitly admitted the toleration of Protestants and Jews. Also by implication the Pope accepted such important measures of the Revolution as the abolition of the tithe and the confiscation of ecclesiastical lands.

Finally, the Concordat made the activities of the Church in France subject to the "police regulations" of the state. These regulations were spelled out in the Organic Articles, which Napoleon appended to the Concordat without consulting the Pope. The French government was to supervise the publication of papal bulls, the establishment of seminaries, the nature of catechisms, and a host of other details. The Articles also reaffirmed the principle of the special autonomy enjoyed by the Gallican Church within Catholicism. Despite all this, the anticlericals opposed the Concordat, and it took all Napoleon's pressure to obtain ratification of the Concordat by the legislative bodies of the Consulate.

The Concordat, then, made the Church a ward of the French state. Though it antagonized anticlericals, it did conciliate large numbers of Catholics, and it remained in force until 1905. The Concordat, however, did not bring complete peace between France and the Vatican, for Napoleon insisted that the Pope should render to Caesar the things that were Caesar's. When Pius VII objected to Napoleon's making a French satellite of the Papal states, the new Caesar lectured him on the proper division of authority between the spiritual and temporal powers. Pius passed the last years of the Napoleonic regime as Bonaparte's prisoner, first in northern Italy and then in France.

Education

The Revolution and Napoleon cost the Church its monopoly over education. The Constitution of 1791 had promised France a system of state schools. The Convention, while doing little to apply this principle to primary education, did set up institutions for advanced training, like the famous *Ecole Polytechnique* in Paris for engineers. In each department it established a "central school" to provide secondary education of good quality at relatively low cost to students. Napoleon abolished these central schools in 1802 and replaced them with a smaller number of *lycées* open only to the relatively few pupils who could afford the tuition or who received state scholarships. The change had a political motive, for Napoleon intended the *lycées* to groom capable and loyal administrators. The students wore uniforms and marched to military drums and the curriculum, too, served the ends of patriotic indoctrination. To provide for the superintendence of all schools, lay and clerical, Napoleon founded in 1808 a body with the misleading name of the "University." He neglected primary schooling

Lettres Inédites de Napoléon (Paris, 1897), I, 93–94. Our translation.

†Quoted in H. A. L. Fisher, *Napoleon* (New York, 1913), Appendix I.

almost completely; yet building on the revolutionary base, he did advance the construction of secular schools. The educational competition of Church and State, so often a bitter issue in modern French life, dates back to the Revolution and Napoleon.

Economics

Political aims likewise governed the economic program of an emperor determined to promote national unity. The French peasants wanted to be left alone to enjoy the new freedom acquired in 1789; Napoleon did not disturb them, except to raise army recruits. The middle class wanted a balanced national budget and the end of revolutionary experiments with paper currency and a controlled economy. Napoleon continued the sound money of the Directory and, unlike the Directory, balanced the budget, thanks to the immense plunder that he gained in war. He greatly improved the efficiency and probity of tax-collectors and established the semi-official Bank of France (1800) to act as the government's financial agent. He strengthened the curbs placed on labor by the Le Chapelier Law of 1791 (see p. 370) and obliged every workman to carry a written record listing his jobs and his general reputation. Though seaports suffered from the decline of overseas trade, rich war contracts and subsidies kept employment and profits generally high. As the war went on and on, however, Napoleon found it increasingly difficult to keep the peasantry and the bourgeoisie contented. Despite the levies on conquered countries, he had to draft more soldiers from the peasantry and increase the already unpopular taxes on salt, liquor, and tobacco.

In summary, the domestic policies of Napoleon I had something in common with the methods of all the celebrated one-man rulers. Like Caesar in Rome, Napoleon rendered lip-service to the Republic while subverting republican institutions; he used prefects to impose centralized authority as Louis XIV had used *intendants*; and, like modern dictators, he scorned free speech. Yet Napoleon was also a genuine enlightened despot. His law code and some of his educational reforms would have delighted the *philosophes*. He ended civil strife without sacrificing the redistribution of land and the equality before the law gained in 1789 and the years following. Abandoning some revolutionary policies, modifying others, and completing still others, Napoleon regimented the Revolution without wholly destroying it.

V   Napoleon and Europe

To many Frenchmen, Napoleon was the Man of Destiny, the most brilliant ruler in their country's long history. To most Europeans, on the other hand, Napoleon was the sinister Man on Horseback, the enemy of national independence, the foreigner who imposed French control and French reforms. As French conquests accumulated, and as nominally free countries became French puppets, Europe grew to hate the insatiable imperialism of Napoleon. Napoleonic France succeeded in building up a vast empire, but only at the cost of arousing the implacable enmity of the other European nations.

The War, 1800–1807

Napoleon had barely launched the Consulate when he took to the field again. The Second Coalition, which had reached the peak of its success in August, 1799, was now falling to pieces. Tsar Paul of Russia alarmed Britain and Austria by his interest in Italy, and

Britain offended him by retaining Malta, the headquarters of his beloved Knights. The Tsar launched against Britain a Baltic League of Armed Neutrality linking Prussia, Sweden, and Denmark with Russia. He even contemplated joining with France to drive the British out of India; this fantastic scheme collapsed when he was murdered in 1801 and succeeded by his son, Alexander I. Meanwhile, in the spring of 1800 Napoleon crossed the Alps with much fanfare, acting as though no one had ever made the passage before. He defeated the Austrians in Italy and negotiated the Treaty of Lunéville (1801), whereby Austria recognized the reconstituted French satellites in Italy and agreed that France should have a hand in redrawing the map of Germany.

After Lunéville, as after Campoformio four years before, Britain alone remained at war with France. British taxpayers, however, wanted relief from their heavy burden; British merchants longed to resume trading with continental markets partially closed to them since 1793. Though Britain had been unable to check Napoleon's expansion in Europe, she had very nearly won the colonial and naval war by 1801. She had captured former Dutch and Spanish colonies, and Nelson's fleet had expelled the French from Egypt and Malta. The British cabinet was confident that it held a strong bargaining position and could obtain favorable terms from Napoleon. But in the Peace of Amiens (1802) the British promised to surrender part of their colonial conquests and got nothing in return. The French failed either to reopen the Continent to British exports or to relinquish Belgium, which remained, in Napoleon's phrase, "a loaded pistol aimed at the heart of Britain."

In 1803 Napoleon alarmed Austria and Prussia by promoting a major revision of the map of Germany. In that year the *Reichsdeputationshauptschluss* (a fine German word, "chief decree of the imperial deputation") abolished more than a hundred of the Germanies, chiefly city-states and small ecclesiastical principalities. The chief beneficiaries of this readjustment were the south German states of Bavaria, Württemberg, and Baden, which Na-

poleon clearly intended to form into a "third" Germany, dominated by France, as opposed to the "first" and "second" Germanies of Austria and Prussia, respectively.

Meantime, the one-sided Peace of Amiens provided only a year's truce in the world-wide struggle of France and Britain. Napoleon aroused British exporters by a more stringent tariff law (1803) and jeopardized British interests in the Caribbean by a grandiose project for a colonial empire based on the island of Haiti (Santo Domingo) and on the vast Louisiana territory that Spain had returned to France in 1801. French soldiers wrested Haiti from the able Negro chieftain, Toussaint l'Ouverture; but the continued resistance of the Haitians and an outbreak of yellow fever took a fearful toll of French troops and forced Napoleon to abandon the American project. In 1803, he sold to the United States for about $15,000,000 all of Louisiana, which later formed the whole or part of 13 states.

When the Louisiana Purchase was completed, France and Britain were again at war. Napoleon interned many of the British tourists who had flocked to Paris since the Peace of Amiens, thus striking a new note of "total" war, contrasting with the eighteenth-century custom that permitted enemy citizens to circulate relatively freely even during hostilities. From 1803 through 1805, Napoleon actively prepared to invade England. He assembled more than a hundred thousand troops and a thousand landing barges on the French side of the Straits of Dover. In 1805, he sent Admiral Villeneuve and the French fleet to the West Indies to lure the British fleet away from Europe. Then Villeneuve was to return posthaste to convoy the French invasion force across the Channel while Nelson was still vainly combing the Caribbean. Villeneuve failed to give Nelson the slip; back in European waters, he put in at a friendly Spanish port instead of heading directly for the Channel as Napoleon had ordered. Nelson engaged the combined French and Spanish fleets off Cape Trafalgar at the southwest corner of Spain (October, 1805). He lost his own life but not before he had destroyed half of his adversaries' ships without sacrificing a single one of his own. The hapless Villeneuve, long aware of French naval inferiority, committed suicide. Trafalgar gave the British undisputed control of the seas and blasted French hopes of a cross-Channel invasion.

By the time of Trafalgar, Austria and Russia had joined with Britain in the Third Coalition. Bonaparte routed his continental opponents in the most dazzling campaign of his career. At Ulm, on the upper Danube (October, 1805), he captured 30,000 Austrians who had moved westward without waiting for their Russian allies. He met the main Russian force and the balance of the Austrian army near the Moravian village of Austerlitz. The ensuing battle (December 2, 1805) fittingly celebrated

the first anniversary of Napoleon's coronation as emperor. Bringing up reinforcements secretly and with great speed, Napoleon completely surprised his opponents; their casualties were three times greater than his own. Within the month he forced the Habsburg emperor, Francis II, to sign the humiliating Treaty of Pressburg, giving the Austrian Tyrol to Bavaria and Venetia to the Napoleonic puppet kingdom of Italy.

A still harsher fate awaited the Prussians, brought back into the war for the first time since 1795 by Napoleon's repeated interventions in German affairs. The fact that the inept Duke of Brunswick was still the Prussian commander indicated how much the army had

A supposed Napoleonic scheme for the invasion of England, by sea, air, and cross-Channel tunnel; the kites are Britain's anticipation of anti-aircraft defense.

Napoleon's bivouac on the night preceding the Battle of Austerlitz, 1805.

deteriorated since the days of Frederick the Great. In October, 1806, the French pulverized the main Prussian contingents in the twin battles of Jena and Auerstädt, and occupied Berlin. Napoleon postponed a final settlement with Prussia until he had beaten his only remaining continental opponent. Russia went down at Friedland (June, 1807).

Napoleon's great string of victories against the Third Coalition resulted partly from the blunders of his enemies. The miscalculations of Austrian, Prussian, and Russian generals contributed to French successes at Austerlitz and at Jena. Furthermore, the French army was the most seasoned force in Europe. Its soldiers of every rank were well trained, and new recruits were quickly toughened by the French custom of the *amalgame*, assigning them in small batches to veteran units. Its officers were promoted because of ability rather than be-

cause of seniority or influence. Bonaparte seldom risked an engagement unless his forces were the numerical equal of the enemy's; then he staked everything on a dramatic surprise, as at Austerlitz. Yet even this French army had defects. The medical services were poor, the pay was low and irregular, and supplies were also irregular, since the French made a policy of having their soldiers live off the land to economize on time and expense. Though eventually serious in their impact, these shortcomings did not prevent Napolean's ascendancy over Europe in 1807.

The Empire at Its Height, 1807–1812

Napoleon reached the pinnacle of his career when he met Tsar Alexander I on a raft anchored in the Niemen River at Tilsit, on the frontier between East Prussia and Russia. There, in July, 1807, the two emperors drew up a treaty dividing Europe between them. Alexander acknowledged France's hegemony over central and western Europe and secured in return the recognition of eastern Europe as the Russian sphere. Napoleon pledged Russia a share in the spoils if the Ottoman Empire should be dismembered. He demanded no territory from the defeated Tsar, only a commitment to cease trade with Britain and to join the war against her. The Tilsit settlement, however, made Alexander bitterly unpopular at home, where Russian propaganda had been denouncing Napoleon as anti-Christ.

While the two emperors negotiated on the raft, Frederick William III (1797–1840), the Prussian king, nervously paced the banks of the Niemen. He had good cause to be nervous, for Tilsit cost him almost half his territory. Prussia's Polish provinces formed a new puppet state, the Grand Duchy of Warsaw, which Napoleon assigned to a French ally, the King of Saxony. Prussian territory west of the Elbe River went to Napoleon to dispose of as he wished. Napoleon also stationed occupation troops in Prussia and fixed the maximum size of its army at 42,000 men.

Under this latter-day Caesar almost all Europe could be divided into three parts. First came the French Empire, including France proper and the territories annexed since 1789. Second were the satellites, ruled in many cases by relatives of Napoleon. And third came Austria, Prussia, and Russia, forced by defeat to become the allies of France. The only powers remaining outside the Napoleonic system were Britain, Turkey, and Sweden. In 1810, Bernadotte, one of Napoleon's marshals, became Crown Prince for the childless Swedish king, but he, too, guided Swedish policy against France.

The frontiers of the French Empire at their most extensive enclosed Belgium and Holland; the sections of Germany west of the Rhine and along the North Sea; the Italian lands of Piedmont, Genoa, Tuscany, and Rome; and finally, physically detached from the rest, the "Illyrian Provinces," stretching along the Dalmatian coast of the Adriatic, taken from Austria in 1809, and named after an old Roman province. The annexed territories were usually subdivided into departments and ruled by prefects, just like the departments of France proper.

The satellites flanked the French Empire. The Kingdom of Italy, an enlarged version of the Cisalpine Republic, included Lombardy, Venetia, and the central Italian lands not directly annexed by France. Napoleon was the king, and his stepson, Eugène de Beauharnais, was viceroy. In southern Italy, Napoleon deposed the Bourbon king of Naples in 1805 and gave the crown first to his brother Joseph and then to Joachim Murat, the husband of his sister Caroline. Joseph moved from Naples to Madrid in 1808 when Napoleon deposed the Spanish Bourbons in order to force the Spaniards to remain in the war against Britain.

In Central Europe, Napoleon energetically pursued his project of a "third" Germany. He decreed a further reduction in the number of German states, and in 1806 aided the dissolution of that museum-piece, the Holy Roman Empire. Francis II, the reigning Habsburg, last of the Holy Roman Emperors, now styled himself Emperor of Austria. To replace the vanished Empire, Napoleon created the Confederation of the Rhine, which included almost every German state except Austria and Prussia. At the heart of this confederation, Napoleon carved out for his brother Jerome the Kingdom of Westphalia, which incorporated the Prussian holdings west of the Elbe seized at Tilsit. Two states completed the roster of French satellites—Switzerland and the Grand Duchy of Warsaw. Europe had not seen such an empire since the heyday of imperial Rome.

Napoleon longed to give dignity and permanence to his creations. It was not enough that his brothers and his in-laws should sit on thrones; he himself must found a dynasty, must have the heir so far denied him in fifteen years of childless marriage. He divorced Josephine, therefore, and in 1810 married Marie-Louise, the daughter of the Habsburg Francis II. In due time, Marie-Louise bore

UNITED KINGDOM
OF GREAT BRITAIN
AND IRELAND

SCOTLAND

North Sea

SWEDEN

KINGDOM OF DENMARK AND NORWAY

IRELAND

WALES

ENGLAND

London

Atlantic Ocean

Oldenburg   Hamburg

NETHERLANDS

Antwerp
Waterloo
Amiens

Paris
Varennes
Versailles   Valmy
Longuyon

LORRAINE
Luneville

ALSACE
Strasbourg
Ulm

Nantes

Loire R.

FRANCE

Gironde R.

Limoges

Bordeaux

Payrac

Rhône R.

Lyons

PIED-
MONT

Nice

Marengo
Genoa

Po R.

K. OF
WESTPHALIA

CONFEDERATION
Auerstädt   Leipzig

OF THE
Jena

RHINE

BAVARIA

SWITZERLAND

TYROL

Basel

Campoformio

Milan

Danube R.

Prague

Austerlitz

Vien

Pressburg

PRUSSIA

SAXONY

Berlin

Elbe R.

Weser R.

Meuse R.
Rhine R.
Seine R.

BADEN

Venice

Adriatic Sea

ILLYRIAN PROVINCES

KINGDOM OF ITALY

TUSCANY

ELBA

CORSICA

PAPAL STATES
Rome

SARDINIA

BALEARIC IS.

KINGDOM
OF
NAPLES

Naples

PORTUGAL

SPAIN

Madrid

Tagus R.

Ebro R.

Guadalquivir R.

CAPE
TRAFALGAR

SICILY

Palermo

MALTA
(Br.)

Napoleonic Europe, 1812

Empire of France
States under French control
Allied with France
■ Battle sites

FINLAND

Gulf of Finland

L. Ladoga

30   35   40

Volga R.

W. Dvina R.

Moscow

55

Vitebsk

Smolensk   *Oka R.*

Vilna

riedland
berg

Niemen R.

Napoleon's Route, 1815

RSAW

Varsaw

50

Kiev

R U S S I A

Dnieper R.

Don R.

Volga R.

45

Dniester R.

Pruth R.

Caspian Sea

40

E

OF

RIA

GARY

Black Sea

50

Morava R.

Danube R.

NTE-
EGRO

PERSIA

35

O   T   T   O   M   A   N   E   M   P   I   R   E

Vardar R.

Euphrates R.

Aegean Sea

Tigris R.

CYPRUS

CRETE

Mediterranean Sea

ARABIA

0   500

Miles

Abukir Bay

Alexandria

EGYPT   Cairo

20   25   35   40   45

Western Europe, 1798

GREAT
BRITAIN

P R U S S I A

BATAVIAN
REPUBLIC

GERMANY

FRANCE

AUSTRIA

SWITZ.

0   200

Miles

CISALPINE REP.

LIGURIAN REP.

OTTOMAN
EMPIRE

SPAIN

CORSICA

Western Europe, 1798
Extent of French influence

PARTHENOPEAN
REPUBLIC

a son, whom his father called "The King of Rome."

"Napoleon II," however, was never to rule in Rome or anywhere else. Throughout the new French acquisitions and the satellites Bonaparte and his relatives played the part of enlightened despots, curbing the power of the Church, abolishing serfdom, building roads, and introducing the metric system and the new French law codes. Everywhere, however, they exacted a heavy toll of tribute and subjection. In the Kingdom of Italy, for instance, Napoleon doubled the tax rate previously levied by the Austrians; half the revenues of the kingdom went to defray the expenses of the French army and the French government. Napoleon flooded his relatives with instructions on the government of their domains and brought them abruptly to heel whenever they showed signs of putting local interests above those of France. When Louis Bonaparte in Holland dared to disobey the imperial orders, his brother delivered a crushing rebuke:

In ascending the throne of Holland, Your Majesty has forgotten that he is French and has stretched all the springs of his reason and tormented his conscience in order to persuade himself that he is Dutch. Dutchmen inclining toward France have been ignored and persecuted; those serving England have been promoted. . . . I have experienced the sorrow of seeing the name of France exposed to shame in a Holland ruled by a prince of my blood.*

Louis' boldness cost him his throne; his Dutch kingdom was annexed to France in 1810.

The Continental System

Nowhere was Napoleon's imperialism more evident than in his attempt to regulate the economy of the whole Continent. The Continental System had a double aim: to build up the export trade of France and to cripple that of Britain. The collapse of Napoleon's cross-Channel invasion plans led him to expand the earlier tariff measures against

*Lettres Inédites de Napoléon (Paris, 1897), I, 382–383. Our translation.

Britain into a great campaign to bankrupt the nation of shopkeepers. The defeat of the Third Coalition gave him the opportunity to experiment with economic warfare on a continental scale and to carry mercantilism to extremes.

The Berlin Decree, issued by Napoleon in November, 1806, forbade all trade with the British Isles and all commerce in British merchandise. It ordered the arrest of all Britons on the Continent and the confiscation of their property. Britain replied by requiring that neutral vessels wishing to trade with France put in first at a British port and pay duties. This regulation enabled Britain to share in the profits of neutral shipping to France. Napoleon retaliated with the Milan decree (December, 1807), ordering the seizure of all neutral ships that complied with the new British policy. The neutrals, in effect, were damned if they did and damned if they didn't.

Napoleon's vassals and allies had to support the Continental System or suffer the consequences. Of all the "un-French" activities countenanced by Louis Bonaparte in Holland, the worst, in Napoleon's view, was his toleration of Dutch smuggling of English contraband. The Emperor likewise expected the satellites to feed French industrial prosperity. When Italians objected to the regulation of their silk exports, Napoleon lectured his viceroy, Eugène, on the facts of economic life:

All the raw silk from the Kingdom of Italy goes to England. . . . It is therefore quite natural that I should wish to divert it from this route to the advantage of my French manufacturers: otherwise my silk factories, one of the chief supports of French commerce, would suffer substantial losses. . . . My principle is: France first. . . .

It is no use for Italy to make plans that leave French prosperity out of account; she must face the fact that the interests of the two countries hang together.*

The gigantic attempt to make "France first" failed almost totally. Only a few French industries benefited from the Continental System; the cessation of sugar imports from the

*Quoted in J. M. Thompson, ed., Napoleon's Letters, 241–242.

West Indies, for example, promoted the cultivation of native sugar beets. But the decline of overseas trade depressed Bordeaux and other French Atlantic ports, and the increasing difficulty of obtaining raw materials like cotton caused widespread unemployment and produced a rash of bankruptcies. The new French markets on the Continent did not compensate for the loss of older markets overseas; the value of French exports declined by more than one-third between 1805 and 1813.

The Continental System did not ruin Britain, although it did confront the British with a severe economic crisis. Markets abroad for British exports were uncertain; food imports were reduced; and, while prices rose sharply, wages lagged behind. Both farm workers, already pinched by the enclosure movement, and factory workers suffered acutely. Yet Britain, fortified by her leadership in the economic revolutions and by the overwhelming superiority of her navy and merchant marine, rode out the storm. Every tract of land at all capable of growing food was brought under the plow. Exporters not only developed lucrative new markets in the Americas, the Ottoman Empire, and Asia but also smuggled goods to old customers on the Continent. Napoleon lacked the vast naval force to apprehend smugglers at sea, and he lacked the large staff of incorruptible customs inspectors to control contraband in the ports. Moreover, since the French army simply could not do without some items produced only in British factories, Napoleon violated his own decrees by authorizing secret purchases of British cloth and leather for uniforms.

The Continental System antagonized both the neutral powers and Napoleon's allies. French seizure of American vessels in Euro-

Gillray, "Tiddy-Dolly, the great French Gingerbread-Baker, drawing out a new Batch of Kings—his Man, Hopping-Talley, mixing up the Dough"—a British comment on Napoleon's imperialism.

pean ports under the terms of the Milan Decree put a dangerous strain on Franco-American relations. But British restrictions likewise bore heavily on the Americans. British impressment of American seamen on the pretext that they were deserters from the Royal Navy, together with the designs of American expansionists on Canada, produced the indecisive Anglo-American War of 1812–1814.

The Peninsular War

In Europe, the political and military consequences of the Continental System formed a decisive and disastrous chapter in Napoleonic history. The chapter opened in 1807 when the Emperor decided to impose the System on Britain's traditional ally, Portugal. The Portuguese expedition furnished Napoleon with an excuse for the military occupation of neighboring Spain. In 1808 he lured the Spanish royal family away from Madrid and made his brother Joseph King of Spain. But every measure taken by Napoleon—the removal of the ineffectual Bourbons, the installation of a foreign monarch, the attempted enforcement of the Continental System, and, not least, the suppression of the Inquisition and the curtailment of noble and clerical privileges —violated Spanish customs and offended Spanish nationalism. The irreconcilable Spaniards began fighting Napoleon when the population of Madrid rose in revolt on May 2, 1808.

While the rising in Madrid was soon repressed, the Peninsular War (named after the Iberian Peninsula), rapidly grew from a minor irritation to a deadly cancer on the body of the Napoleonic Empire. The Spaniards employed ambushes and poisoned wells and used other guerrilla devices. The expedition that Britain sent to assist them upset all the rules about British inferiority in military, as opposed to naval, matters. It was ably commanded by Sir Arthur Wellesley (later the Duke of Wellington), generously supplied from home, and based on Portugal and on Britain's unshakable command of the seas. Napoleon poured more than 300,000 troops into the Peninsular campaign, but his opponents gained the upper hand in 1812, when he detached part of his forces for the invasion of Russia. In 1813, King Joseph left Madrid forever, and Wellington, having liberated Spain, crossed into southern France.

German Resistance

Napoleonic imperialism also aroused a nationalistic reaction among the traditionally disunited Germans. Intellectuals launched a campaign against the French language and French culture, which had long exerted a powerful influence. Johann Grimm and his brother Wilhelm contributed not only their very popular—and very German—*Fairy Tales* (1812) but also philological researches designed to prove the innate superiority of the German language. The philosopher Fichte delivered at Berlin the highly patriotic *Addresses to the German Nation* (1807–1808), claiming that German was the *Ursprache*, the fountainhead of language. And the Germans themselves, Fichte continued, were the *Urvolk*, the oldest and the most moral of nations.

Napoleon began to feel the impact of German nationalism when Austria re-entered the war in 1809. For the first time, the Habsburg monarchy now attempted a total mobilization comparable to that decreed by the French Convention in 1793. While the new spirit enabled the Austrians to make a better showing, they were defeated by a narrow margin at Wagram (1809) and for the fourth time in a dozen years submitted to a peace dictated by Napoleon. The Treaty of Schönbrunn (1809) stripped them of the Illyrian Provinces and assigned their Polish territory of Galicia to the Grand Duchy of Warsaw. Francis II gave his daughter to Napoleon in marriage, and his defeated land became the unwilling ally of France. Leadership in the German revival passed to Prussia.

The shock of Jena and Tilsit jarred Prussia out of the lethargy that had overtaken her since the death of Frederick the Great in 1786. The new University of Berlin, founded in 1810, attracted Fichte and other prophets of German nationalism. Able generals and

Goya, "The Third of May, 1808," now in the Prado Museum, Madrid; Spaniards being executed by Napoleonic troops.

statesmen, most of them non-Prussian, came to power. General Scharnhorst headed a group of officers who abolished the inhuman discipline of the army and improved its efficiency. The ceiling of 42,000 soldiers imposed by Napoleon was evaded by the simple device of assigning recruits to the reserve after a fairly brief period of intensive training and then inducting another group of recruits. By 1813, Prussia had more than 150,000 trained men available for combat duty.

The social and administrative reorganization of the Prussian state was inspired by the energetic Stein — Baron vom und zum Stein, an enlightened aristocrat from the Rhineland. Stein conciliated the middle class by granting towns and cities some self-government. To improve the status of the peasantry, he sponsored the edict of October, 1807, at long last abolishing serfdom in Prussia. The edict, however, did not break up the large Junker estates or provide land for the liberated serfs; nor did it terminate the feudal rights of justice exercised by the Junker over his peasants. Stein and the others eliminated only the worst abuses of the Old Régime and left authority where it had traditionally rested — with the king, the army, and the Junkers. The Hohenzollern state was not so much reformed as restored to the traditions of absolutism and ef-

ficiency established by the Great Elector and Frederick the Great.

The Russian Campaign

The event that enabled a developing German nationalism to turn its force against Napoleon was the French debacle in Russia. French actions after 1807 soon convinced Tsar Alexander that Napoleon was not keeping the Tilsit bargain and was intruding on Russia's sphere in eastern Europe. When Alexander and Napoleon met again at the German town of Erfurt in 1808, they could reach no agreement, though they concealed their differences by a show of great intimacy. French acquisition of the Illyrian provinces from Austria in 1809 raised the unpleasant prospect of French domination over the Balkans, and the simultaneous transfer of Galicia from Austria to the Grand Duchy of Warsaw suggested that this Napoleonic vassal might next seek to absorb the Polish territories of Russia. Meanwhile, Napoleon's insistent efforts to make Russia enforce the Continental System increasingly incensed Alexander. French annexations in northwest Germany completed the discomfiture of the Tsar, for they wiped out the state of Oldenburg, where his uncle was the reigning duke. All these factors caused the break between the Tsar and the Emperor, and the famous invasion of Russia by the French in 1812.

For the invasion Napoleon assembled the *Grande Armée* of nearly 700,000 men. A large proportion of the Grand Army, however, were not Frenchmen but unwilling conscripts in the service of a foreign master. The supply system broke down almost immediately, and the Russian scorched-earth policy made it very hard for the soldiers to live off the land. As the Grand Army marched eastward, one of Napoleon's aides reported:

> There were no inhabitants to be found, no prisoners to be taken, not a single straggler to be picked up. We were in the heart of inhabited Russia and yet we were like a vessel without a compass in the midst of a vast ocean, knowing nothing of what was happening around us.*

Napoleon marched all the way to Moscow without ever managing to strike a knockout blow. He remained in the burning city for five weeks (September-October, 1812) in the vain hope of bringing Tsar Alexander to terms. But Russian obduracy and the shortage of supplies forced him to begin a retreat that became a nightmare. Ill-fed and inadequately clothed and sheltered, the retreating soldiers suffered horribly from Russian attacks on stragglers and from the onslaughts of "General Winter." Less than a quarter of the Grand Army survived the retreat from Moscow; the rest had been taken prisoner or had died of wounds, starvation, disease, or the cold.

The Russian leaders had feared that Napoleon would liberate the serfs and turn them against their masters. Nevertheless, the peasants, despite the ill-treatment to which they had been subject for so long, formed guerrilla bands, harassed Napoleon's forces, and proved that their patriotic sentiments outweighed their class grievances. Kutuzov, the victorious Russian commander, now wanted to allow Russia's allies to prosecute the war. But Alexander insisted on pursuing the French,

*A. A. L. de Caulaincourt, *With Napoleon in Russia* (New York, 1935), 62.

and sent Russian armies westward beyond the Russian frontiers on the track of Napoleon's forces.

The Downfall

The British had been the first to resist Napoleon successfully, at Trafalgar and on the economic battlefields of the Continental System. Then had come Spanish resistance, then Russian. Now in 1813 almost every nation in Europe joined the final coalition against the French. Napoleon raised a new army, but he could not replace so readily the equipment squandered in Russia. In October, 1813, he lost the "Battle of the Nations," fought at Leipzig in Germany, and by April, 1814, the forces of the coalition occupied Paris. Faced also with mounting unrest at home, the Emperor abdicated. After attempting suicide by poison, which turned out to have lost much of its strength since he had procured it for the Russian campaign, he went into exile as ruler of the minute island of Elba not far from the western coast of Italy.

The statesmen of the victorious coalition gathered in the Congress of Vienna to draw up the terms of peace (see Chapter 11). The Bourbons returned to France in the person of Louis XVIII, a younger brother of Louis XVI. Realizing that he could not revive the Old Régime intact, the new king issued the Charter of 1814 establishing a constitutional monarchy. The returned *émigrés*, however, showed no such good sense. They unleashed a new "White Terror" against the Revolution and all its works. Then, on March 1, 1815, Bonaparte pulled his last surprise: He landed on the Mediterranean coast of France.

For a hundred days, from March 20, 1815, when Napoleon re-entered Paris, the French Empire was reborn. Once again the Emperor rallied the French people, this time by promising a truly liberal régime, with a real parliament and genuine elections. He never had time, however, to show whether his promise was sincere, for on June 18, 1815, the British under Wellington and the Prussians under

Blücher delivered the final blow at Waterloo, near Brussels. Again Napoleon went into ex- ile, to the remote British island of St. Helena in the South Atlantic. There, in 1821, he died.

VI   The Legacy of the Revolution and Napoleon

Bonapartism did not die in 1815 or 1821, any more than the Caesarism of ancient Rome had died on the Ides of March. A Napoleonic legend arose, fostered by the Emperor himself on St. Helena. It glossed over the faults and failures of its hero, depicting him as the paladin of liberalism and patriotism, and paved the way for the advent of another Napoleon in 1848 (see Chapter 11). This legend, with its hero-worship and belligerent nationalism, was one element in the legacy bequeathed by revolutionary and Napoleonic France. A second, and still more powerful, element was the great revolutionary motto—*Liberté, Egalité, Fraternité.* The motto lived on, to inspire later generations of Jacobins in France and elsewhere. And behind the motto was the fact that Frenchmen enjoyed a larger measure of liberty, equality, and fraternity in 1815 than they had ever known before 1789.

The Revolution founded a potent new tradition of liberty. True, the Mountain's deputies on mission and Napoleon's censors and prefects gave new force to the old traditions of absolutism and centralization, the middle class had won its freedom from obsolete restraints, and Protestants, Jews, and free-thinkers had gained toleration both in France and in French-dominated countries. While French institutions in 1815 did not measure up to the liberal ideals expressed in the Declaration of the Rights of Man, the ideals had been stated, and the effort to embody them in a new regime was to form the main theme of French domestic history in the nineteenth century.

The revolutionary and Napoleonic regimes introduced a large measure of equality. They established the principle of equal liability to taxation. They provided a greater degree of economic opportunity for large numbers of the third estate by breaking up the large landholdings of the clergy and nobility and by removing obstacles to the activity of businessmen, big and little. The *Code Napoléon* buried beyond all hope of exhumation the worst legal and social inequalities of the Old Régime. There was a good deal of truth in Napoleon's boast:

Whether as First Consul or as Emperor, I have been the people's king; I have governed for the nation and in its interests, without allowing myself to be turned aside by the outcries or the private interests of certain people.*

The Revolution and Napoleon promoted fraternity in the legal sense by making all Frenchmen equal in the eyes of the law. They advanced fraternity in a broader sense by encouraging nationalism, the feeling of belonging to the great corporate body of Frenchmen who were superior to all other nations. French nationalism had existed long before 1789; Joan of Arc, Henry IV, and Louis XIV had all been nationalists in their diverse ways. But it remained for the Convention to formulate a fervent new nationalistic creed in its decree of August 23, 1793, providing for total mobilization. The Napoleonic Empire then demonstrated how easily nationalism on an unprecedented scale could lead to imperialism of unprecedented magnitude. A century ago, Alexis de Tocqueville, the great French student of democracy, wrote:

The French Revolution was . . . a political revolution, which in its operation and its aspect resem-

*Quoted in Caulaincourt, *With Napoleon in Russia,* 364.

bled a religious one. It had every peculiar and characteristic feature of a religious movement; it not only spread to foreign countries, but it was carried thither by preaching and by propaganda.

It roused passions such as the most violent political revolutions had never before excited. . . . This gave to it that aspect of a religious revolution which so terrified its contemporaries, or rather . . . it became a kind of new religion in itself—a religion, imperfect it is true, without a God, without a worship, without a future life, but which nevertheless, like Islam, poured forth its soldiers, its apostles, and its martyrs over the face of the earth.*

*A. de Tocqueville, *The Old Régime and the Revolution*, Part I, Ch. 3. (London, 1888).

Its early adherents were fanatics—Robespierre and the Jacobins. Its later exponents—the men of Thermidor and Brumaire—modified the creed in the interests of practicality and moderation. Even in the hands of Napoleon, however, the Revolution remained a kind of religion, demanding political orthodoxy and punishing heretics, as Napoleon punished King Louis Bonaparte of Holland, by political excommunication. And after 1815, as we shall see in the next chapter, the "new religion" of the Revolution continued to pour forth "its soldiers, its apostles, and its martyrs over the face of the earth."

Reading Suggestions on the French Revolution and Napoleon

(*Asterisk indicates paperbound edition.)

General Accounts

C. Brinton, *A Decade of Revolution, 1789–1799* (*Torch), and G. Bruun, *Europe & the French Imperium, 1799–1814* (*Torch). Comprehensive volumes in the "Rise of Modern Europe" series, treating the whole of the Continent; with full bibliographies.

G. Lefebvre, *The French Revolution*, 2 vols. (Columbia Univ. Press, 1962, 1964). Another comprehensive treatment, ranging beyond France itself, by an eminent French scholar.

R. R. Palmer, *The Age of the Democratic Revolution*, 2 vols. (Princeton Univ. Press, 1959, 1964). Detailed exposition of the thesis that the French Revolution was part of a general democratic revolution in the West; by a first-rate American scholar, who examines revolutionary movements both in France and elsewhere.

Jacques Godechot, *France & the Atlantic Revolution, 1770–1799* (Free Press, 1965). A ranking French scholar comes to conclusions similar to Palmer's.

P. Amann, ed. *The 18th-Century Revolution, French or Western?* (*Heath). Selections from writings both hostile and sympathetic to the Palmer-Godechot interpretation.

L. Gershoy, *The French Revolution & Napoleon* (Appleton-Century-Crofts, 1964). Lucid textbook account, stressing events in France.

G. Rudé, Revolutionary Europe, 1783–1815 (*Meridian). A brief account by one of the younger generation of historians, with bibliography.

The French Revolution

P. Farmer, *France Reviews Its Revolutionary Origins* (Octagon, 1963). A history of French historical writing about the revolution.

A. de Tocqueville, *The Old Regime & the Revolution* (*Anchor). A celebrated essay of interpretation, more than a century old, stressing continuities between the old and new régimes.

A. Mathiez, *The French Revolution* (*Universal). Narrative treatment to 1794, by an eloquent French scholar sympathetic to the Jacobins.

G. Lefebvre, *The Coming of the French Revolution* (*Vintage). Masterly short study of the causes of the revolution and of its course to October, 1789.

G. Salvemini, *The French Revolution, 1788–1792* (*Norton). Colorful narrative by an Italian scholar of warm, liberal outlook.

J. M. Thompson, *The French Revolution* (*Galaxy). Good account by a British scholar.

A. Cobban, *The Social Interpretation of the French Revolution* (Cambridge Univ. Press, 1964). A critique of attempts to view the revolution as a class struggle.

N. Hampson, *A Social History of the French Revolution* (Univ. of Toronto, 1963). Well-balanced synthesis of recent scholarly work in the field.

G. Rudé, *The Crowd in the French Revolution* (Oxford Univ. Press, 1959). Fascinating study of the great revolutionary "days" and the demonstrators who took part.

R. B. Rose, *The Enragés: Socialists of the French Revolution?* (Melbourne, Australia Univ. Press, 1964). An excellent monograph.

A. Soboul, *The Parisian Sans-Culottes & the French Revolution, 1793–1794* (Clarendon, 1964). An important monograph, based on Paris police records; by a capable Marxian scholar.

C. Brinton, *The Jacobins* (Macmillan, 1930), and M. J. Sydenham, *The Girondins* (Oxford Univ. Press, 1961). Informative analyses of major political groupings.

R. R. Palmer, *Twelve Who Ruled* (*Atheneum). Highly readable collective biography of Committee of Public Safety; sympathetic in tone.

J. M. Thompson, *Robespierre & the French Revolution* (*Collier), and G. Bruun, *Saint-Just: Apostle of the Terror* (Houghton, Mifflin, 1932). Biographical sketches of particularly significant figures.

C. H. Tilly, *The Vendée* (Harvard Univ. Press, 1964). An original treatment by a sociologist well trained in historical research.

C. Brinton, *The Anatomy of Revolution* (*Vintage). Examines the common denominators of the Puritan English, the American, the French, and the Russian revolutions.

Napoleon

J. M. Thompson, *Napoleon Bonaparte: His Rise and Fall* (Oxford Univ. Press, 1952), and F. Markham, *Napoleon* (*Mentor). Readable biographies, based on up-to-date scholarship.

H. A. L. Fisher, *Napoleon* (Oxford Univ. Press, 1945), and A. L. Guérard, *Napoleon I* (Knopf, 1956). Good, shorter biographies.

F. Markham, *Napoleon & the Awakening of Europe* (*Collier). Brief account, arguing that European nationalisms, while aroused by Napoleon, were as yet underdeveloped.

E. Heckscher, *The Continental System: an Economic Interpretation* (Clarendon, 1922), Important monograph by a Swedish economist.

P. Geyl, *Napoleon, For and Against* (*Yale). Lengthy survey of judgments passed on Napoleon by historians from his own day to the mid-twentieth century.

H. A. L. Fisher, *Studies in Napoleonic Statesmanship: Germany* (Clarendon, 1903). A detailed evaluation of the impact of French reforms on some Napoleonic satellites.

O. Connelly, *Napoleon's Satellite Kingdoms* (Free Press, 1965). Analysis of Spain, Holland, Westphalia, Naples, and Italy.

Sources

J. H. Stewart, *A Documentary Survey of the French Revolution* (Macmillan, 1951). Ably edited collection of constitutional texts and other official documents.

E. Higgins, *The French Revolution as Told by Contemporaries* (Houghton, Mifflin, 1938). Handy compendium of reports by participants and eye-witnesses.

A. Young, *Travels in France*, C. Maxwell, ed. (Cambridge Univ. Press, 1929). Spirited diary of the English agricultural expert, who journeyed over much of France on the eve and during the early days of the revolution.

E. Burke, *Reflections on the Revolution in France* (*several editions). The celebrated indictment of the revolution.

J. M. Thompson, ed., *Napoleon's Letters* (Everyman). A most interesting collection, arranged chronologically.

J. C. Herold, ed., *The Mind of Napoleon* (*Columbia Univ. Press). Another most interesting collection, from his writings and conversations, arranged topically.

A. de Caulaincourt, *With Napoleon in Russia* (*Universal), and *No Peace with Napoleon* (Morrow, 1936). Vivid memoirs of the last campaigns by one of the Emperor's chief aides.

Historical Fiction

A. France, *The Gods Are Athirst* (Roy). Excellent brief novel about a fanatical Jacobin.

C. Dickens, *A Tale of Two Cities* (*many ed.). Famous, colorful — and inaccurate.

R. Sabatini, *Scaramouche* (*Bantam). Delightful yarn set in an authentic revolutionary background.

L. Tolstoy, *War & Peace* (*several editions, often abridged). The epic novel about the Russian campaign.

11

Revolution

and Counter-Revolution,

1815–1850

I   Introduction

While the half century after Napoleon recorded no crisis so momentous as that of 1789 and produced no personality so dominant as Bonaparte, it was still crowded with major developments. Between 1815 and 1870 the industrial revolution came of age, modern doctrines of socialism were born, and Darwin's evolutionary hypothesis revolutionized the social sciences as well as biology. In politics, Great Britain and the United States moved steadily, and France more erratically, toward the practical establishment of democracy; Italy and Germany at last achieved national unification. All these developments, though they were well under way by 1850, reached a climax after the mid-century mark and will therefore be discussed later (Chapters 12–15). The present chapter focuses on the interaction of cultural and political forces, particularly in continental Europe, during the post-Napoleonic generation from 1815 to 1850.

The terms "reaction" and "counter-revolution" are often applied to this generation. By 1815, Europe was reacting strongly both against the French Revolution, which had made Napoleon possible, and against the Enlightenment, which had made the Revolution possible. The reaction against the Enlightenment took the form of the Romantic movement. Romantic writers and artists protested against the omnipotent reason of the eighteenth century and championed faith, emotion, tradition, and other values slighted by many *philosophes*. The political counter-revolution came of age at the Congress of Vienna in 1814–1815, where the leaders of the last coalition against Napoleon re-established the

European balance of power and repudiated the revolutionary principles, though not all the revolutionary achievements, that had shattered the eighteenth-century balance. Reason and natural law, in the judgment both of political leaders and of many Romantics, had led not only to progress but also to the Reign of Terror and Napoleonic imperialism.

But the spirit of 1789 did not die in 1815; revolution persisted, despite the ascendancy of counter-revolutionary forces. Liberal and nationalistic ideas and aspirations produced new outbreaks of revolution in the 1820's, in 1830, and in 1848. Although none of these revolutions proved to be as formidable as the great upheaval of 1789, all of them threatened the status quo. In addition, the revolutions of 1848 marked a critical turning point in the development of European liberalism and nationalism.

II   The Romantic Protest

The Romantic protest against reason rose to full force during the first third of the nineteenth century—the Romantic decades of 1800 to 1830 or 1840. Actually, as Chapter 9 has already shown, the reaction against the Enlightenment had set in much earlier. Before 1750, Wesley and the Pietists were challenging the deism of the *philosophes* and preaching a religion of the heart, not the head. Soon Rousseau proclaimed conscience, not reason, the "true guide of man"; Hume fastened on men's "sentiments and affections" as the mainsprings of their actions. Kant elevated intuition over the common-sense reason of the Enlightenment and restated, in very philosophical language, the Platonic belief in a noumenal realm of eternal verities beyond the world of transient phenomena. Then in 1790 Edmund Burke's *Reflections on the Revolution in France* neatly turned against the *philosophes* their favorite appeal to the simple mathematical laws of Newtonian science. Natural rights, Burke argued,

. . . entering into common life, like rays of light which pierce into a dense medium, are, by the laws of nature, refracted from their straight line. Indeed in the gross and complicated mass of human passions and concerns, the primitive rights of men undergo such a variety of refractions and reflections, that it becomes absurd to talk of them as if they continued in the simplicity of their original direction. The nature of man is intricate; the objects of society are of the greatest possible complexity. . . .*

The protest against the oversimplification of man and society, and the insistence on the intricacy and complexity of humanity, formed one common denominator of the Romantic movement. Romanticism, however, was much too complex and contradictory to be defined by a simple formula. Other common denominators will emerge from a survey of the achievements of the Romantics, beginning

---

Reflections on the Revolution in France, Everyman ed. (New York, 1910), 59.

with their most characteristic and productive realm of activity—literature.

The Revolt against Reason

Literary Romanticism may be traced back to the mid-eighteenth-century novels of sentiment and duty, like Richardson's *Clarissa.* Its immediate precursor was the German movement of the 1770's called *Sturm und Drang* ("Storm and Stress") after the title of a contemporary play. The hero of the drama, totally incapable of settling down, flees Europe to fight in the American Revolution:

Have been everything. Became a day-labourer to be something. Lived on the Alps, pastured goats, lay day and night under the boundless vault of the heavens, cooled by the winds, burning with an inner fire. Nowhere rest, nowhere repose. See, thus I am glutted by impulse and power, and work it out of me. I am going to take part in this campaign as a volunteer; there I can expand my soul, and if they do me the favour to shoot me down,—all the better.*

Yearning, frustration, and despair were also dominant emotions in the most popular work of the *Sturm und Drang* period, *The Sorrows of Young Werther*, a lugubrious short novel by the youthful Goethe (1749–1832). Even the seemingly hard-boiled Napoleon claimed to have read it seven times over, weeping copiously each time as the hero shoots himself to death because the woman he loves is already married. Self-pity, self-destruction, the sense of alienation, of being an "outsider" continued to be favorite themes of the Romantic writers. In contrast to the optimism of the *philosophes*, the Romantics sounded chords of pessimism and despair.

Goethe himself, however, whose career extended through the whole Romantic era, was no Romantic hero. In many respects he was a good eighteenth-century man of reason, interested in natural science, comfortably established at the enlightened court of a small

*Klinger, *Sturm und Drang*, quoted in Kuno Francke, *A History of German Literature as Determined by Social Forces*, 4th ed. (New York, 1931), 309.

German state at Weimar, and quite detached from the political passions sweeping Germany and Europe in the revolutionary and Napoleonic age. Yet Romantic values lie at the very heart of Goethe's greatest work—many would say the greatest work in the German language—*Faust.* Begun when he was in his twenties, and finished only when he was eighty, this long poetic drama was less a play in the conventional sense than a philosophical commentary on the main currents of European thought. According to the traditional legend, the aged Faust, weary of book learning and pining for eternal youth, sold his soul to the Devil, receiving back the enjoyment of his youth for an allotted time, and then, terror-stricken, went to the ever-lasting fires. Goethe transformed the legend. While Faust finds intellectual pursuits disillusioning and profitless and makes his infernal compact, he is ultimately saved through his realization that he must sacrifice selfish concerns to the welfare of others. A drama of man's sinning, striving, and redemption, Goethe's *Faust* is a reaffirmation of the Christian way that the Enlightenment had belittled. The return to Christian values was a striking feature of Romanticism.

By the early 1800's, Romantic writers decried what seemed to them the stilted and artificial verses of Racine and Pope and praised the color and vigor of the Bible, Homer, and Shakespeare. They called for a literary renaissance, a rebirth of imagination, feeling, and sensitivity. In consequence, the Romantic era was an age of poetry, in contrast to the eighteenth-century age of prose.

Britain produced a galaxy of Romantic poets—Byron, Shelley, Keats, Wordsworth, Coleridge, and still others. Of them all, Wordsworth (1770–1850) and Coleridge (1772–1834) perhaps pressed farthest in reaction against classicism and rationalism. In 1798, the two men published *Lyrical Ballads,* an early landmark in English Romanticism. As Coleridge later explained, their purpose was explicitly anti-classical:

In the present age the poet . . . seems to propose to himself as his main object . . . new and striking images; with incidents that interest the affections or excite the curiosity. Both his characters and his descriptions he renders, as much as possible, specific and individual, even to a degree of portraiture. In his diction and metre, on the other hand, he is comparatively careless.*

To *Lyrical Ballads* Coleridge contributed the *Rime of the Ancient Mariner,* a supernatural and very Romantic tale of the curse afflicting a sailor who slays an albatross. Among Wordsworth's contributions was *The Tables Turned,* notable less for its poetry than for its specific attack on conventional learning:

> Come forth into the light of things,
> Let Nature be your teacher.
>
> She has a world of ready wealth,
> Our minds and hearts to bless —
> Spontaneous wisdom breathed by health,
> Truth breathed by cheerfulness.
>
> One impulse from a vernal wood
> May teach you more of man,
> Of moral evil and of good,
> Than all the sages can.
>
> Sweet is the lore which Nature brings;
> Our meddling intellect
> Mis-shapes the beauteous forms of things: —
> We murder to dissect.
>
> Enough of Science and of Art;
> Close up those barren leaves;
> Come forth, and bring with you a heart
> That watches and receives.†

Wordsworth transformed the old concept of nature; nature was no longer something to be analyzed and reduced to laws but a mysterious, vitalizing force that had to be sensed and experienced. Here, from his long autobiographical *Prelude,* are two passages that express his beliefs more poetically:

> Ye Presences of Nature in the sky
> And on the earth! Ye Visions of the hills!
> And Souls of lonely places! can I think
> A vulgar hope was yours when ye
>   employed

Biographia Literaria, Everyman ed., (New York, 1908), 173.
†*The Tables Turned,* lines 15–32.

> Such ministry, when ye, through many
>   a year
> Haunting me thus among my boyish
>   sports,
> On caves and trees, upon the woods and
>   hills,
> Impressed, upon all forms, the characters
> Of danger or desire; and thus did make
> The surface of the universal earth,
> With triumph and delight, with hope
>   and fear,
> Work like a sea?

> · · ·

> Dust as we are, the immortal spirit grows
> Like harmony in music; there is a dark
> Inscrutable workmanship that reconciles
> Discordant elements, makes them cling
>   together
> In one society.*

"Presences," "Visions," "Souls," "haunting" — this is truly Romantic language. In place of the light shed by Newton's laws, Wordsworth finds "a dark inscrutable workmanship," and in place of the *philosophes'* belief in the perfectibility of man through reason he puts his faith in the "immortal spirit" of the individual. Wordsworth in fact lived in France during the early years of the Revolution and was disillusioned by the failure of rational reform.

The Return to the Past

It may seem a long leap from the almost pantheistic universe of Wordsworth to the Romantics' enthusiasm for the Middle Ages in general and for the earlier history of their own nations in particular. And yet nationalism is an irrational, almost mystical force that — so its devotees believe — "reconciles discordant elements, makes them cling together in one society." The heightened sense of nationalism evident almost everywhere in Europe by 1815 was in part a matter of political self-preservation. In the crisis of the Napoleonic wars, for example, the Spaniards became more aware of their Spanish heritage and the Germans of

The Prelude, Book I, lines 464–475, 340–344.

their Germanic one. The Romantic return to the national past, however, though intensified by French imperialism, had begun before 1789 as part of the general retreat from the Enlightenment. The pioneers of Romanticism tended to cherish what the *philosophes* detested, notably the Middle Ages and the medieval preoccupation with religion.

The German writer, Herder (1744–1803), provided intellectual justification for medieval studies with his theory of cultural nationalism. Each separate nation, he argued, like any organism, had its own distinct personality, its *Volksgeist* or "folk spirit," and its own pattern of growth. The surest measure of a nation's growth was its literature—poetry in youth, prose in maturity. Stimulated by Herder, students of medieval German literature collected popular ballads, and the brothers Grimm compiled their *Fairy Tales.* In 1782, the first complete text of the *Nibelungenlied* was published, a heroic saga of the nation's youth that had been much admired in the later Middle Ages only to be forgotten in succeeding centuries. By putting a new value on the German literature of the past, Herder helped to free the German literature of his own day from its bondage to French culture. Herder, however, was no narrow nationalist and asserted that the cultivated man should know cultures other than his own. So Herder also helped to loose the flood of translations that poured over Germany about 1800—translations of Shakespeare, of *Don Quixote,* of Spanish and Portuguese poetry, even of works in Sanskrit.

Some German Romantics, stirred by the patriotic revival after Jena and Tilsit, (see Chapter 10), carried national enthusiasm to an extreme that Herder would have deplored. Thus the Grimms claimed pre-eminence for the German language, and the dramatist Kleist (1777–1811), in his *Battle of Arminius,* boasted of the prowess of the ancient Germans in defeating the legions of Augustus, in 9 A.D. For the Romantic extremists, the mere fact of being German appeared to be a cardinal virtue. Yet many German writers struck Herder's happy balance between national and cosmopolitan interests; Goethe, for example, prided himself on being a good European, not simply a German.

Other nations, too, demonstrated that the return to the past meant veneration of the Middle Ages rather than classical antiquity. In Britain, Sir Walter Scott (1771–1832) assisted in collecting the vigorous medieval folk ballads and went on to write more than thirty historical novels, of which *Ivanhoe,* set in the days of Richard Lionheart and the Crusades, is the best known. In France, the home of the "classical spirit," the Romantic reaction gathered slowly but reached full strength after 1825 with the vivid historical dramas of Victor Hugo (1802–1885) and his famous novel of fifteenth-century France, *Notre Dame de Paris.* In Russia, to cite a third example, the poet Pushkin (1799–1837) deserted the archaic Slavonic language of the Orthodox Church to write the first major literary works in the national vernacular. He took subjects from Russia's past and introduced local color from its newly acquired provinces in the Crimea and the Caucasus. He also celebrated his own exotic grandfather, Hannibal, the African Negro slave of Peter the Great.

Music

Romantic musicians, like the poets, sought out the popular ballads and tales of the national past. They, too, were inventive and imaginative, seeking to make their compositions more dramatic and flexible, less constrained by classical rules. To achieve color and drama, composers of opera and song often turned for subjects to literature—Shakespeare's plays, Scott's novels, and the poems and tales of Goethe and Pushkin. Yet, although literature and music often took parallel paths during the Romantic era, the parallel was far from complete. Romantic musicians scarcely revolted against the great eighteenth-century composers in the way that Wordsworth and Coleridge revolted against their predecessors. Rather, Romantic music evolved peacefully out of the older classical school.

The composer who played the commanding part in this evolution was Beethoven

(1770–1827), a Fleming by ancestry and a Viennese by adoption. Whereas Coleridge had said that the Romantic artist might be careless in matters of diction and meter, Beethoven showed a classical concern for the forms and techniques that were the musical counterparts of diction and meter. Yet his experiments and innovations also enriched the great tradition that he inherited from Bach, Haydn, and Mozart. For example, where Mozart and Haydn had used the courtly minuet for the third movement in a symphony, Beethoven introduced the more plebeian and rollicking *scherzo.* Where earlier composers had indicated the tempo with a simple *allegro* (fast) or *andante* (slow), Beethoven added such designations as *appassionato* and "Strife between Head and Heart." Part of the color and passion of Beethoven's works derived from his skill in exploiting the resources of the piano, which was perfected during his lifetime. He also scored his orchestral compositions for a greater number of instruments, especially winds, percussion, and doublebasses, than had been the practice of Mozart and Haydn.

After Beethoven, orchestral works took on increasingly heroic dimensions. The French composer, Berlioz (1803–1869), projected an orchestra of 465 pieces, including 120 violins, 37 double-basses, and 30 each of pianos and harps. Although this utopian scheme remained on paper, Berlioz was virtually the first to score his compositions for the full complement of instruments, especially winds and percussion, that make up the modern orchestra. His experiments with the theatrical potentialities of orchestral music created a series of landmarks in musical history, among them the "Fantastic Symphony" (1830), based, it is said, on Goethe's *Werther.*

Music for the human voice reflected both the increased enthusiasm for instruments, particularly the piano, and the general Romantic nostalgia for the past. In composing songs and arias, Romantic musicians devoted as much skill to the accompaniment as to the voice part itself. Franz Schubert (1797–1826), Beethoven's Viennese contemporary, made a fine art of blending voice and piano in more

than six hundred sensitive *Lieder* (songs), seventy of them musical settings of poems by Goethe. Meantime, Von Weber (1786–1826) was striving to create a truly German opera, taking an old legend as the libretto for *Der Freischütz* ("The Freeshooter," 1820). Its plot ran the good Romantic gamut of an enchanted forest, a magic bullet, and an innocent maiden outwitting the Devil, and its choruses and marches employed many folk-like melodies. Weber was by no means the only serious composer to utilize national folk tunes. In Russia, Glinka (1804–1857) cast aside the Italian influences that had previously dominated the secular music of his country. He based his opera, *Russlan and Ludmilla* (1842), on a poem by Pushkin and embellished it with dances and choruses derived from the native music of Russia's Asian provinces.

The Arts

In the fine arts, the forces of Romanticism gained no such triumph as they won in literature and music. The virtual dictator of European painting during the first two decades of the nineteenth century was the French neoclassicist, David (1748–1825), who was the official painter of the French Jacobins and then of Napoleon. David's canvases formed a capsule history of the rise and decline of revolutionary fervor—before 1789, Roman republican heroes and victims of aristocratic persecution like Socrates; after 1789, dramatic moments like the Tennis Court Oath and the death of Marat; and, still later, Napoleon's crossing of the Alps and his coronation. No matter how revolutionary the subject, David employed traditional neoclassical techniques, stressing form, line, and perspective.

The works of David's Spanish contemporary, Goya (1746–1828), were much less conventional and much closer to the Romantic temper with their warmth and passion and sense of outraged patriotism. No one could have any illusions about Spanish royalty after looking at Goya's revealing portraits of the enlightened Charles III and his successors. After viewing Goya's etchings on the Peninsular War, no one could doubt the horrors of warfare (see illustration on p. 399). Goya is said to have made the sketches for these etchings in the very blood of the executed Spanish patriots whose agonies he was portraying.

Romantic painting did not acquire formal recognition until the official Paris exhibition of 1824. Although many of the pictures hung in the salon of 1824 came from the school of David, the two leaders of Romantic painting were also represented — the Englishman, Constable (1776–1837) and the Frenchman, Delacroix (1799–1863). Constable took painting out of doors, studied nature afresh, and produced a series of landscapes that stressed light and color more than classical purity of line, and paved the way for the impressionists of the later nineteenth century (see Chapter 15). Delacroix, too, championed color and light and urged young painters to study the flamboyant canvases of Rubens, whom David had banished from the ranks of orthodox artists. The purpose of art, Delacroix claimed in a good Romantic definition, was "not to imitate nature but to strike the imagination." His painting of "The Massacre of Scio," a bloody episode in the Greek War of Independence (see p. 425), was denounced at the salon of 1824 as "barbarous, drunken, delirious" — the "massacre of painting." Today, however, the work of Delacroix seems conventional enough and less experimental than that of Goya. By the 1830's, French painters were divided into opposing schools: the still influential disciples of David, and the Romantic followers of Delacroix, with the master himself finding exotic new subjects in North Africa.

In architecture, also, two schools flourished during the first half of the nineteenth century — the neoclassical, looking to Greek and Roman antiquity, and the neo-Gothic, or Gothic revival, looking to the Middle Ages. Significantly, the label "Gothic" was no longer derogatory, as it had once been when employed by rationalist haters of things medieval. While there were obvious differences between the two schools, the contrast was not total. Many architects of the early 1800's mastered both styles; moreover, they did not so much copy ancient or medieval structures

outright as adapt them to the needs and tastes of the day. Generally, the basic design was classical in its proportions, even if the external shell and decoration were medieval. The Houses of Parliament in London, rebuilt in the 1830's and '40's after a disastrous fire, seem very Gothic at first glance with their spires and towers. But a longer look shows that they also embody classical principles of balance and symmetry. Romantic architecture anticipated the eclecticism, the wide range of inspiration and style, characteristic of the later nineteenth century.

As the nineteenth century began, the Roman vogue, so firmly set by the French Revolution, reached a peak in Napoleonic Paris with the *Arc de Triomphe* and with the Church of the Madeleine, patterned on an actual Roman temple (the *Maison Carrée* or "square house" at Nîmes). In America, the versatile Thomas Jefferson, who was a gifted designer, pronounced the *Maison Carrée* a perfect example of "cubical" architecture and adapted it to secular purposes for the Virginia capitol building at Richmond. At Charlottesville, about 1820, Jefferson provided the University of Virginia with a most distinguished group of academic buildings focused on a circular library, derived from the Roman Pantheon (the perfect example of "spherical" architecture). From the library, somewhat in the manner of a large Roman villa, he extended two rows of smaller structures, each recalling a different Roman temple and interconnected by colonnades. By the second quarter of the nineteenth century, neo-Roman was yielding place to the "Greek revival," stirred in part by the wave of Philhellenic enthusiasm then sweeping the western world (see p. 425). London's British Museum and Philadelphia's Girard College are two of many splendid examples of the Greek revival.

Meantime, especially in Britain, the Gothic revival was gaining ground, stimulated by the wealth of medieval architectural lore in Scott's novels, by the revival of religion, and by buildings like Fonthill Abbey, which had been started in 1797 and boasted an immensely long and high hall. Though it cost its owner, an eccentric millionaire, £500,000, it was so shoddily built that the central tower collapsed twenty-five years later. Undeterred, British architects applied the Gothic manner to every kind of structure after 1820, to public buildings like the Houses of Parliament, to churches, to elaborate villas, and modest cottages. Excessive "gloomth" often resulted, and the fad for "medieval" furniture, bristling with spikes, prompted one critic to warn that the occupant of a neo-Gothic room would be lucky to escape being "wounded by some of its minutiae." Though the Gothic revival prompted some monstrosities, it also fostered the preservation or restoration of medieval masterpieces half ruined by neglect or by anti-clerical vandalism.

Religion and Philosophy

Neo-Gothic architecture was one sign of the Christian revival that formed part of the Romantic movement; another sign was the

Delacroix: self-portrait.

The Houses of Parliament, London.

pope's re-establishment in 1814 of the Jesuit order, whose suppression in 1773 had been one of the great victories of the Enlightenment. Most of the Romantics were horrified by the religious skepticism of the *philosophes;* an outspoken atheist like Shelley was an isolated exception. In Germany, Catholicism gained many converts among Romantic writ-

pounded in Germany. Chief among these German philosophers was Hegel (1770–1831), a follower of Kant and a professor at the University of Berlin. Like his master, Hegel attacked the tendency of the Enlightenment to see in human nature and human history only what first met the eye. The history of mankind, properly understood, was the

Monticello, the house that Jefferson designed for himself in Virginia.

ers, and in England Wordsworth and Coleridge vigorously defended the established Church. Coleridge declared:

. . . that the scheme of Christianity, as taught in the liturgy and homilies of our Church, though not discoverable by human reason, is yet in accordance with it; that link follows link by necessary consequence; that Religion passes out of the ken of Reason only where the eye of Reason has reached its own horizon; and that Faith is then but its continuation. . . .*

Coleridge introduced his countrymen to the new Romantic philosophies being ex-

Biographia Literaria, Everyman ed., 334.

history of human efforts to attain the good, and this in turn was the unfolding of God's plan for the world. For Hegel, history was a *dialectical* process—that is, a series of conflicts. The two elements in the conflict were the *thesis,* the established order of life, and the *antithesis,* the challenge to the old order. Out of the struggle of thesis and antithesis emerged the *synthesis,* no mere compromise between the two but a new and better way, another step in man's slow progression toward the best of all possible worlds. The synthesis, in turn, broke down; a new thesis and antithesis became locked in conflict; the dialectic produced another synthesis—and so on.

The death throes of the Roman Republic

afforded Hegel an illustration of the dialectic at work. The thesis was represented by the decadent republic, the antithesis by oriental despotism, and the synthesis by the Caesarism of the early Roman Empire. Hegel explained that "This important change must not be regarded as a thing of chance; it was *necessary*," a part of God's grand design. Julius Caesar himself Hegel called a "hero," one of the few "world-historical individuals" who "had an insight into the requirements of the time" and who knew "what was ripe for development." This concept of the hero as the agent of a cosmic process is another characteristic of the Romantic temper.

The dialectical philosophy of history was the most original and influential element in Hegel's thought, one antecedent, for example, of the dialectical materialism of Karl Marx (see Chapter 12). It is perhaps difficult for citizens of a twentieth-century democracy to appreciate that Hegel was once even more famous as a liberal idealist. His emphasis on duty, his choice of Alexander the Great, Caesar, and Napoleon as "world-historical" heroes, his assertion that the state "existed for its own sake"—all suggest a link with authoritarianism. Hegel himself, however, seems to have foreseen the final synthesis of the dialectic not as a brutal police state but as a liberalized version of the Prussian monarchy.

The Romantic "Style"

Thus Hegel, like the *philosophes,* believed in progress and the perfectibility of man, though he also believed that the process would require far more time and struggle than a man like Condorcet had ever imagined. Indeed, the "style" of Romanticism by no means contrasted in every particular with that of the Enlightenment. Not only a modified doctrine of progress but also eighteenth-century cosmopolitanism lived on into the nineteenth. Homer, Cervantes, Shakespeare, and Scott won appreciative readers in many countries; the giants of the age, men like Beethoven and Goethe, were not merely Austrian or German but citizens of the world.

These similarities and continuities notwithstanding, Romanticism did have a decided style of its own—imaginative, emotional, and haunted by the supernatural and by history. The Romantics could no longer view history in Gibbon's terms of a classical golden age followed by long centuries of benighted superstition. Rather history was, as Hegel and Herder had argued an organic process of growth and development, which was indebted to the Middle Ages for magnificent Gothic buildings, religious enthusiasm, folk ballads, and heroic epics. Just as the Romantics rejected the Enlightened view of the past, so they found the Newtonian world-machine an entirely inadequate interpretation of the universe. It was too static, too drab and materialistic, and in its place they put the neo-Gothic world of religious mystery, the Hegelian world of dialectic and heroes, the poetic and artistic world of feeling, color, an "impulses from the vernal wood." Perhaps the most conspicuous feature of the Romantic style was its insistence that society was more than a branch of physics and man more than a cog in a machine.

III   The Conservative Outlook and the Vienna Settlement

The usual image of the Romantic political figure is the rebel or the defender of a cause—Shelley preaching anarchism, Byron dying in the Greek War of Independence, revolutionaries protesting against the status quo. This image is, however, misleading. While it is true that Romanticism by its stress on the individual ultimately enriched the doctrines of liberalism and by its emphasis on the national community strengthened the force of nationalism, its immediate political influence was more frequently counter-revolutionary. More representative of the Romantics than Shelley and Byron were Wordsworth and Coleridge who, in their maturity, lost their youthful zeal for the French Revolution and adopted conservative views in politics as well as in religion.

Burke and Metternich

The man who set the tone of Romantic conservativism was Edmund Burke (1729 –1797). Unlike the champions of revolution, Burke could not accept simple black-and-white assumptions about the goodness of man and the unmitigated evil of the Old Régime. He revered the social and political institutions so painstakingly built up over the centuries. He, however, did not believe that these institutions were petrified; they had developed gradually in the past, they would develop gradually in the future. Political change was possible but difficult, he concluded. Reforms had to be introduced so that "the useful parts of the old establishment" might be preserved; they had to be managed slowly and "with circumspection and caution"—in a word, conservatively.

Burke approved of the American Revolution, for it was not so much a revolution as a reaffirmation of the glorious tradition of 1688. The same reasoning drove Burke to violent condemnation in his *Reflections on the Revolution in France* (1790). The men of 1789 destroyed everything, good, bad, and indifferent. Rage and frenzy, he observed, "pull down more in half an hour, than prudence, deliberation and foresight can build up in a hundred years";* thereby society itself is jeopardized. "Society is indeed a contract," Burke wrote, but he did not mean what Rousseau had meant:

The state ought not to be considered as nothing better than a partnership agreement in a trade of pepper and coffee, calico or tobacco, or some such other low concern, to be taken up for a little temporary interest, and to be dissolved by the fancy of

*Reflections, Everyman ed., 164.

the parties. It is to be looked on with other reverence, because it is not a partnership in things subservient only to the gross animal existence of a temporary and perishable nature. It is a partnership in all science; a partnership in all art; a partnership in every virtue, and in all perfection. As the ends of such a partnership cannot be obtained in many generations, it becomes a partnership not only between those who are living, but between those who are living, those who are dead, and those who are to be born.*

The force of tradition so revered by Burke bore heavily upon the politics of post-Napoleonic Europe. This was the Age of Metternich—Prince Clement Wenceslas Lothair Népomucène Metternich (1773–1859), Austrian foreign minister from 1809 to 1848 and the chief figure in European diplomacy during most of his long career. Handsome, dashing, an aristocrat through and through, Metternich retained some of the eighteenth century's belief in reform through enlightened despotism. But, he also believed, reform should proceed with Burkean caution, not at a revolutionary pace. His own family, living in the German Rhineland, had suffered directly from the French Revolution. Moreover, Metternich served a state that was particularly susceptible to injury by the liberal and nationalist energies released by the Revolution. Tradition, he knew, was the cement that held together the disparate parts of the Austrian Habsburg realm; it should be fortified as much as possible.

The Congress of Vienna

In 1814 and 1815, Metternich was host to the Congress of Vienna, which approached its task of rebuilding Europe with truly conservative deliberateness. For the larger part of a year, the diplomats indulged to the full in balls and banquets, concerts and hunting parties. "Congress dances," remarked an observer, "but it does not march." Actually, the brilliant social life distracted the lesser fry while the important diplomats settled things in private conference.

*Ibid. 93.

Four men made most of the major decisions at Vienna—Metternich, Castlereagh, Talleyrand, and Tsar Alexander I. Viscount Castlereagh, the British foreign minister, shared the conservative outlook of Metternich. He was less concerned with punishing the French for their past sins than with preventing the appearance of new Robespierres and Bonapartes. Castlereagh announced that he went to Vienna "not to collect trophies, but to bring the world back to peaceful habits." The best way to do this, he believed, was to restore the balance of power and keep any of the major states, including France, from becoming either too strong or too weak.

Talleyrand, the foreign minister of Louis XVIII of France, scored at Vienna the greatest success of his long career. Originally a worldly bishop of the Old Régime, he had in succession rallied to the Revolution in 1789, supported the Civil Constitution of the Clergy (one of the very few bishops to do so), served as Napoleon's foreign minister, and intrigued against him during the years after Tilsit. Now he was serving the restored Bourbon king, and in his old age he would take an important part in the Revolution of 1830. This supremely adaptable diplomat soon maneuvered himself into the inner circle at Vienna, and the representatives of the victorious powers accepted the emissary of defeated France as their equal. Talleyrand was particularly adept in exploiting his nuisance value—acting as the spokesman of lesser diplomats who resented being shoved aside, and making the most of the differences that divided the victors.

To these differences Alexander I contributed greatly. Metternich actually called the Tsar a Jacobin, although Alexander's reputation for enlightenment was only partially deserved (see Chapter 9). By 1814, the Tsar had acquired a thoroughly Romantic enthusiasm for religion. For hours on end, he prayed and read the Bible in the company of Madame de Krüdener and under her influence prepared a "Holy Alliance" whereby all states would regenerate their policies by following Christian teachings. In the first months at Vienna, it was not Alexander's Romantic scheme of a Holy Alliance but rather his Polish policy that nearly disrupted the Congress. He proposed a partial restoration of pre-partition Poland, with himself as its monarch. Austria and Prussia would lose the Polish lands they had grabbed late in the preceding century. Alexander won the support of Prussia by backing her demands for the annexation of Saxony, whose king had remained loyal to

Talleyrand in 1809.

The statesmen of Europe at the Congress of Vienna, 1814–1815. Metternich is standing prominently at left front, Wellington at extreme left. Talleyrand is seated at right with his arm resting on the table.

Napoleon. Metternich, however, did not want Austria's traditional Prussian rival to make such a substantial gain. Moreover, both Metternich and Castlereagh disliked the prospect of a large, Russian-dominated Poland.

The dispute over Saxony and Poland gave Talleyrand a magnificent chance to fish in troubled waters. Thus it was that in January, 1815, the representative of defeated France joined Metternich and Castlereagh in threatening both Prussia and Russia with war unless they moderated their demands. The threat produced an immediate settlement. Alexander obtained Poland but agreed to reduce its size and allow Prussia and Austria to keep part of their loot from the partitions. Prussia took about half of Saxony; the King of Saxony retained the balance.

Once the Saxon-Polish question was out of the way, the Congress achieved a fairly amicable resolution of other important dynastic and territorial questions. According to the doctrine that Talleyrand christened "the sacred principle of legitimacy," thrones and frontiers were to be re-established as they had existed in 1789. In practice, however, legitimacy was ignored almost as often as it was enforced, since the diplomats at Vienna realized that they could not undo all the changes worked by the Revolution and Napoleon. Although they restored Bourbon dynasties to the thrones of France, Spain, and Naples in the name of legitimacy, they did not attempt to resurrect the Republic of Venice or to revive all the hundreds of German states that had vanished since 1789.

In Germany, the Congress provided for thirty-nine states, loosely grouped together in a weak confederation. The German Confederation came close to reincarnating the impotent Holy Roman Empire; its chief organ, the diet, was to be a council of diplomats from sovereign states rather than a representative national assembly. Its most important members were Prussia and Austria, for the German-speaking provinces of the Habsburgs were considered an integral part of Germany. Both states obtained important new territories at Vienna. Prussia, in addition to her Saxon annexation, expanded the old scattered Hohenzollern lands in western Germany into the imposing new Rhine Province. Austria lost Belgium, which was incorporated into the Kingdom of the Netherlands in order to strenghten the northern buffer against France. But she recovered the old Habsburg territory of Lombardy in Italy, to which Venetia was now joined, and she also recovered the Illyrian Provinces along the eastern shore of the Adriatic.

In Italy, too, the Congress of Vienna confirmed the tradition of political disunity. It restored the Bourbon Kingdom of Naples in the south and the Papal States in the center. In the northwest it gave Genoa to the Kingdom of Piedmont-Sardinia. Austria was in a position to dominate Italy both by her possession of Lombardy-Venetia and by the close family ties between the Habsburgs and the ruling dynasties in the other Italian states.

Elsewhere in Europe, the Congress of Vienna restored to independence the Republic of Switzerland and enlarged it somewhat as another buffer against France. It sanctioned the transfer of Norway from the rule of Denmark, which had generally been pro-French, to Sweden. And it confirmed the earlier transfer of Finland from Sweden to Russia. Great Britain received the strategic little Mediterranean island of Malta and, outside Europe, the former Dutch colonies of Ceylon and the Cape of Good Hope plus a few insignificant French outposts.

The Quarantine of France

France at first was given her boundaries of 1792, which included the minor territorial acquisitions made during the early days of the Revolution. Then came Napoleon's escape from Elba and the Hundred Days. The final settlement reached after Waterloo assigned France the frontiers of 1790, substantially those of the Old Régime plus Avignon. In addition, the French were to return Napoleon's art plunder to its rightful owners, pay the victorious allies an indemnity of 700,-000,000 francs (roughly $140,000,000), and finance allied military occupation of 17 frontier fortresses on French soil for not more than five years.

The Vienna diplomats did not so much punish France as take measures to quarantine any possible new French aggression. Castlereagh conceived the policy of strengthening France's neighbors so that they would be able to restrain the troublemaker in the future. Thus to the north the French faced the Belgians and the Dutch combined in the single Kingdom of the Netherlands. On the northeast they encountered the Rhine Province of Prussia, and on the east the expanded states of Switzerland and Piedmont. The Quadruple Alliance, signed in November, 1815, constituted the second great measure of quarantine. The four allies—Britain, Prussia, Austria, and Russia—agreed to use force, if necessary, to preserve the Vienna settlement. At Castlereagh's insistence, the allies further decided on periodic conferences to consider the measures "most salutary for the repose and prosperity of Nations, and the maintenance of the Peace of Europe." The Quadruple Alliance was to be both a watchdog against France and an experiment in government by international conference, a modest step along the road leading to the League of Nations and United Nations of the twentieth century.

Public opinion, especially in the English-speaking countries, unfortunately confused the Quadruple Alliance with Alexander's Holy Alliance, which it identified with the blackest reaction. The Holy Alliance, signed in September, 1815, was actually a fairly harmless document dedicated to the proposition that "the policy of the powers . . . ought to be guided by the sublime truths taught by the eternal religion of God our Saviour." Although most of the major European rulers signed the Holy Alliance, only Tsar Alexander seems to have taken it seriously. Castlereagh called it "a piece of sublime mysticism and nonsense," and Britain declined to participate—the first sign of the rift that was to open between her and the continental powers. The pope, refusing an invitation to join, remarked tartly that the Vatican needed no new interpretations of Christian doctrine by the laity.

Together with Westphalia (1648), Utrecht (1713), and Versailles (1919), the Vienna settlement of 1814–1815 marked one of those rare attempts at the massive political reconstruction of Europe. Of the four, Vienna in many respects succeeded best. There was to be no major European war until the Crimean conflict of the 1850's, and none embroiling the whole of Europe until 1914. Most of the leading diplomats at Vienna could have said with Castlereagh that they acted "to bring the world back to peaceful habits." Seldom have victors treated the defeated aggressor more generously. Castlereagh, above all, deserved credit for his project of pacifying international disputes through conferences of the Quadruple Alliance. In operation, however, the Quadruple Alliance never fulfilled the noble aims of Castlereagh. Within five years of the Congress of Vienna, revolution broke out again in Europe, causing serious dissension within the Quadruple Alliance. And for these outbreaks the Congress of Vienna was itself responsible, at least in part because it attempted to stifle both liberal and nationalist aspirations.

IV   The Revolutions of the 1820's

The Revolutionary Credo

The revolutionary leaders of the early nineteenth century despised the traditions so revered by conservatives. Opposing the counter-revolutionary alliance of Throne and Altar, they stood for Liberty, Equality, and Fraternity. In the revolutionary credo, Liberty and Equality continued to signify the abolition of noble and clerical privileges in society and, with few exceptions, the application of laissez-faire to economics. They also involved the broadening of civil rights, the institution of representative assemblies, and the granting of constitutions, which would bring limited monarchy to most states but a republic to the truly advanced, like France. For these aspects of the revolutionary program, the best label is liberalism. Almost every leader of revolution proclaimed himself a liberal, although, as we shall soon see, the kind of liberalism actually practiced varied from the narrow to the sweeping.

The third word of the great revolutionary motto now came to have a more precise meaning. Fraternity, intensified by the Romantic cult of the nation, continued to evolve into the formidable doctrine of nationalism. The nationalists of the post-1815 generation dreamed of a world in which each nation would be free of domination by any other, and all nations would live together harmoniously. In terms of practical politics, this signified movements toward national unity and national independence. It meant growing pressure for the unification of Germany and Italy. And it inspired demands for freedom by peoples living under the control of a foreign power—by Belgians against their Dutch rulers, by Poles against Russians, by Greeks and Serbs against Turks, and by Italians, Hungarians, and Czechs against the Habsburgs of Vienna.

The Iberian States and Naples

The first revolutionary outbreaks after 1815 took place in Spain, Portugal and the Kingdom of the Two Sicilies. In all three states the return to legitimacy restored the Old Régime at its least enlightened. The great majority of the population responded to the restoration calmly, even enthusiastically. The aristocracy were delighted to recover their ancient privileges and the peasantry welcomed the return of familiar traditions; a small minority, drawn chiefly from the middle class, the intellectuals,

KINGDOM OF
NORWAY
AND SWEDEN

UNITED KINGDOM
OF GREAT BRITAIN
AND IRELAND

SCOTLAND

North Sea

DENMARK

IRELAND

WALES

ENGLAND

London

The Hague

Atlantic Ocean

K. OF NETHERLANDS

Brussels

Aachen

LUX.

Frankfurt

Hambach

Paris

Seine R.

Meuse R.

Rhine R.

Elbe R.

Weser R.

Oder R.

Berlin

P R U S S I A

Wartburg

SAXONY

GERMAN

Carlsbad

Prague

BOHEMIA

Tro

CONFEDERATION

Danube R.

AUSTRIA E M

A

Vienna

Loire R.

FRANCE

Garonne R.

Rhône R.

SWITZERLAND

LOMBARDY

Novara

Milan

Turin

PIEDMONT

Genoa

PARMA

MODENA

TYROL

Custozza

VENETIA

Venice

PORTUGAL

Lisbon

SPAIN

Madrid

Tagus R.

Ebro R.

Barcelona

Guadalquivir R.

Cadiz

CORSICA (Fr.)

KINGDOM OF SARDINIA

BALEARIC IS.

SARDINIA

TUSCANY

Florence

PAPAL

STATES

Rome

Naples

Adriatic Sea

KINGDOM
OF THE
TWO SICILIES

SICILY

Mediterranean Sea

MALTA
(Br.)

0   500

Miles

Europe after 1815

— Boundary of the German Confederation
■ Battle sites

FINLAND

L. Onega

L. Ladoga

Gulf of Finland

St. Petersburg

Volga R.

Moscow

W. Dvina R.

Oka R.

R U S S I A

Niemen R.

Warsaw

Don R.

Ural R.

LAND

Kiev

Volga R.

OF

OW

GALICIA

Dnieper R.

OF

Dniester R.

Odessa

Pruth R.

Caspian Sea

A

MOLDAVIA

CRIMEA

DANUBIAN
PROVINCES

WALLACHIA

Black Sea

Bucharest

Morava R.

Danube R.

ONTE-
EGRO

Vardar R.

Adrianople

O

Istanbul

T

T

O

M

A

N

E

M

P

I

R

E

Aegean Sea

Euphrates R.

Tigris R.

CHIOS

Athens

Navarino

CYPRUS

CRETE

ARABIA

and the army, dissented. In Spain and Italy, they greatly regretted the abrogation of the *Code Napoléon,* and of the anti-feudal and anti-clerical legislation introduced by the French. In all three states the discontent of the liberal minority produced the revolutionary movement of 1820.

The trouble began in Spain. During the war against Napoleon, representatives from the liberal middle class of Cadiz and other commercial towns had framed the Constitution of 1812. Based on the French revolutionary Constitution of 1791, this document limited greatly the power of the monarchy, gave wide authority to a Cortes elected on a broad suffrage, and deprived the Spanish Church of some of its lands and privileges. This liberal constitution was doubtless too liberal to be very workable in traditionalist Spain, and the Bourbon Ferdinand VII soon suspended it after he assumed the Spanish crown in 1814. Ferdinand also restored the social inequalities of the Old Régime and re-established not only the Jesuits but also the Spanish inquisition. Army officers, alienated by his high-handedness and clericalism, and merchants, facing ruin because of the revolt of Spanish colonies in the New World, joined the political clubs and masonic lodges that formed the liberal opposition.

It was Ferdinand's attempt to subdue the rebellious colonies that triggered revolution at home. The independence movement in Spanish America was caused directly by the refusal of the colonial populations either to recognize Napoleon's brother Joseph as their king or to accept the closer ties between colonies and mother country proposed by patriots in Spain. Behind the Spanish-American independence movement lay several other factors: the powerful examples of the American and French revolutions; the sympathetic interest of Great Britain, anxious to release lucrative markets from Spanish mercantilist restrictions; and the accumulated resentment of colonial peoples at the centuries of indifferent rule by Spanish governors. The colonial rebels won their initial success at Buenos Aires in 1810, and their movement spread rapidly to Spain's other American possessions.

Ferdinand now determined to crush the rebels by force; to transport troops he augmented the small Spanish fleet with three leaky hulks purchased from Russia. At the end of 1819, this motley new armada, carrying 20,000 men, was about to sail from Cadiz. It never sailed, for on January 1, 1820, a mutiny broke out at Cadiz led by the liberal Colonel Riego. Uprisings soon followed in Madrid, in Barcelona, and in other Spanish cities.

Centers of Revolution

The revolutionaries sang "Riego's Hymn," with the refrain "Swallow it, you dog" (the "it" referred to the Constitution of 1812). Ferdinand surrendered.

The liberal minorities in Portugal and Naples followed the Spanish lead. An army faction seized control of the Portuguese government in 1820, abolished the Inquisition, and set up a constitution on the Spanish model of 1812. In Naples, the revolution was the work of General Pepe, backed by the *Carbonari* (charcoal-burners). This secret society, with a membership exceeding 50,000, had been opposed to the French and to reforms in the days of Napoleon's hegemony but now sponsored a vaguely liberal program inspired by the French Revolution. King Ferdinand I of the Two Sicilies, who was the uncle of the Spanish Ferdinand VII, gave in at the first sign of opposition in 1820 and accepted a constitution of the Spanish type.

The strength of the revolutionary movement of 1820 ebbed as quickly as it had risen. The reforms introduced precipitately by the inexperienced liberal leaders in Spain and Naples alienated the bulk of the population at home and so alarmed the conservative leaders of the great powers that they sponsored counter-revolutionary intervention. The Spanish revolutionaries were further weakened by a split between *moderados,* who wanted to restore the Constitution of 1812, and *exaltados,* led by Colonel Riego, who wanted to go much farther and set up a violently anticlerical republic. Only in Portugal did the revolutionary regime survive, and only because it had British protection. Even so, there was enough confusion to enable the great Portuguese colony of Brazil to declare itself independent of the mother country (1822).

The revolutions of 1820 tested both the stability of the Vienna settlement and the solidarity of the Quadruple Alliance of Britain, Prussia, Austria, and Russia. Legitimacy was again restored in Spain and Italy, but in the process the Quadruple Alliance was split in two. While the continental allies increasingly favored armed intervention to suppress revolution, Britain inclined more and more toward the principle of non-intervention.

The split became evident at the conference of the Quadruple Alliance meeting at Troppau in Silesia late in 1820. Castlereagh, the British foreign minister, knowing that the Neapolitan revolution threatened the Habsburg hegemony in Italy, was willing to see Austria intervene in Naples, but without the backing of the Alliance. The Alliance, Castlereagh declared, was never designed "for the superintendence of the internal affairs of other states," and Britain refused to participate formally in the Troppau meeting. Metternich, supported by Alexander, pressed for a blanket commitment from the Alliance, and the result was the Troppau Protocol (November, 1820), signed by Austria, Prussia, and Russia. It declared that

States which have undergone a change of Government, due to revolution, the results of which threaten other states, *ipso facto* cease to be members of the European Alliance, and remain excluded from it until their situation gives guarantees for legal order and stability. If, owing to such alterations, immediate danger threatens other states, the Powers bind themselves, by peaceful means, or if need be by arms, to bring back the guilty state into the bosom of the Great Alliance.[*]

Under the terms of the Troppau Protocol, an Austrian army duly toppled the revolutionary government of Naples in 1821. In 1823, a French army crossed the Pyrenees and restored the absolute authority of Ferdinand VII, who proceeded to execute Colonel Riego and hundreds of his followers.

French intervention in Spain provoked the strong opposition of Great Britain and ended the Quadruple Alliance. Canning, who had succeeded Castlereagh as British Foreign Minister in 1822, suspected that the continental powers might now aid Spain to recover her former American colonies. So also did the United States, which had recognized the independence of the Latin-American republics. But America also feared both a possible Russian move southward from Alaska along the Pacific coast and an attempt by Britain to

*Quoted in W. A. Phillips, *The Confederation of Europe* (New York, 1920), 208–209.

extend her sphere of control in the Caribbean. Therefore, when Canning proposed a joint Anglo-American statement to ward off any European interference in Latin America, the government of President Monroe refused the invitation.

In a message to the American Congress in December, 1823, the President included the statement that is known to history as the Monroe Doctrine:

> In the wars of the European powers, in matters relating to themselves, we have never taken any part, nor does it comport with our policy so to do. It is only when our rights are invaded, or seriously menaced, that we resent injuries or make preparation for our defence. With the movements in this hemisphere, we are, of necessity, more immediately connected, and by causes which must be obvious to all enlightened and impartial observers. The political system of the allied powers is essentially different, in this respect, from that of Amer-

ica. . . . We owe it, therefore, to candor, and to the amicable relations existing between the United States and those powers, to declare, that we·should consider any attempt on their part to extend their system to any portion of this hemisphere, as dangerous to our peace and safety. With the existing colonies or dependencies of any European power, we have not interfered, and shall not interfere. But with the governments who have declared their independence, and maintained it, and whose independence we have, on great consideration, and on just principles, acknowledged, we could not view any interposition for the purpose of oppressing them, or controlling, in any other manner, their destiny, by an European power, in any other light than as the manifestation of an unfriendly disposition towards the United States.

Although this document marked an important assertion of policy on the part of the youthful American republic, it had little immediate international significance. The European powers were not fully committed to the project of restoring Spain's American empire. And, so far as they were deterred from that venture, they were deterred not by President Monroe but by Canning and the possible actions of the British fleet.

The Greek War of Independence

The British fleet was soon to take an important role in the Greeks' bid for national independence. The Greek revolt was part of the general movement of the Balkan nations for emancipation from their Turkish overlords. During the last quarter of the eighteenth century, the Christian peoples of the Balkan peninsula began to awaken to their national identities under the impulse from French Revolutionary and Romantic ideas. They examined their national past with new interest and affection, and they put an especially high value on their native languages. The first outbreak against the Turkish authorities came in Serbia in 1804 and was led by a well-to-do pig-raiser named Karageorge. From the first, the Serb nationalists knew they would need outside help; some turned to Russia, others to Austria, thereby fixing a pattern of conflicting

Latin America, 1828

After the Wars for Independence

interests that ultimately led to World War I. Napoleon's venture in the Illyrian provinces (see p. 393) further stimulated the south Slavic desire for independence. After Karageorge's defection in 1813, leadership of Serb nationalism passed to his rival, Milosh Obrenovich, who won Russian support and succeeded by 1830 in becoming prince of an autonomous Serbia. Although he still paid tribute to the Ottoman Emperor, and a Turkish garrison remained in the Serb capital of Belgrade, a major step toward eventual independence had been completed.

Meantime, the Greeks had launched a revolution. Leadership came from two groups — the Phanariot Greeks, named for the quarter where they lived in Istanbul, and the Island Greeks, merchants from the ports and islands of the Aegean. The Phanariots had long held positions of power and responsibility in governing the Orthodox subjects of the Ottoman Empire. The Island Greeks dominated the commerce of the Near East and had business outposts at Vienna, Marseilles, London, and Russia's Black Sea port of Odessa. The Island Greeks revived not only the old Greek trading tradition but also some of the old Greek zeal for self-government. From their home islands and from their merchant colonies abroad they poured forth a stream of patriotic exhortation. Greek nationalists sponsored a campaign to purge the modern Greek language of its Turkish and Slavic words and to return it to the classical tongue of the Age of Pericles. A revolutionary secret society was formed in Odessa, patterned after the *Carbonari* of Italy and headed by Ypsilanti, a Phanariot who was a general in the Russian army.

In 1821, Ypsilanti led an expedition into the Rumanian areas of the Ottoman Empire but failed in his aim to stir up a major revolt. The conspirators were more successful in the Morea (the ancient Peloponnesus) where they formented an uprising among the peasants. The ensuing war for independence was a ferocious conflict: the Morean peasants slaughtered every Turk they could lay their hands on; the Ottoman government retaliated by killing or selling into slavery thirty thousand Greeks from the prosperous Aegean island of Chios

(Scio), an atrocity that inspired Delacroix's famous painting. In the work of repression, the Ottoman emperor supplemented his own inadequate forces by those of his vassal, the governor of Egypt, Mehemet Ali. By 1827, it appeared likely that the Egyptian expedition would recapture the last rebel strongholds. Then Britain, France, and Russia intervened to save the Greek independence movement at its darkest hour.

The three-power action resulted from the combined pressures of public opinion and strategic interests. In Britain and France, and also in Germany and the United States, the Philhellenic (pro-Greek) movement had won legions of supporters. Philhellenic committees sent supplies and money and demanded that civilized governments intervene directly. Intervention hinged on the action of Russia, for Greek patriots had formed their secret society at Odessa, on Russian soil and with Russian backing. For a time, Metternich was able to restrain Russia by pointing out the dangers to the European balance in supporting revolution in one country and repressing it in others. Ultimately, however, Russia's Balkan aspirations won out over her concern for preserving the status quo, and she rallied openly to the Greek cause. Britain and France now felt obliged to take action because of Philhellenic pressure and, still more, because they feared to let Russia act alone lest she gain mastery over the whole Near East. A three-power intervention seemed the only course that would both rescue the Greeks and check the Russians.

Neither aim was fully achieved. In October, 1827, Russian, British, and French squadrons sank the Turkish and Egyptian vessels anchored at Navarino, on the southwest corner of the Morea, and thus destroyed the chief Ottoman base. The subsequent Treaty of Adrianople, 1829, while allowing Russia to annex outright only a little Turkish territory, arranged that the Ottoman Danubian provinces of Moldavia and Wallachia (the heart of present-day Rumania) should become a virtual Russian protectorate. After considerable wrangling, the European powers accorded formal recognition to an independent Greek

Delacroix, "The Massacre of Scio," in the Louvre, Paris.

kingdom of very modest size, which left many Greeks still within the Ottoman Empire. Neither nationalism nor liberalism had won a complete victory in the Greek war. Greek patriots now schemed for the day when they might enlarge the boundaries of their new kingdom. And Greek politicians were to threaten its stability and disillusion Philhellenists abroad by continuing the bitter feuds that had divided them even in the midst of their desperate struggle for independence.

The Decembrist Revolt in Russia

Russia, who did so much to determine the outcome of revolutions elsewhere, herself felt the revolutionary wave, but with diminished force. A brief uprising took place after the death of Tsar Alexander I (December, 1825), as the "Decembrists" vainly attempted to apply and extend the program of liberal reforms apparently promised by the Tsar but seldom implemented by him.

The last period of Alexander's reign, marked by the influence of the unpopular Arakcheev and by the establishment of the hated military colonies (see Chapter 9), had thoroughly disappointed Russian liberals. Liberal ideas, however, continued to penetrate the country. As in other European states, secret societies flourished in Russia after 1815. The introduction of Freemasonry during the eighteenth century, and the secret ritual connected with many of the lodges, had given jaded nobles a thrill and had also enabled them to meet on equal terms with men from other ranks of society. Masonry aroused humanitarian urges; it also afforded a cover of secrecy under which subversive ideas might be incubated. Moreover, the contrast between the relatively enlightened West and backward Russia made a deep impression on officers who had served in the campaigns against Napoleon. One of the future Decembrist leaders left this report of his reactions upon returning home:

From France we returned to Russia by sea. The First Division of the Guard landed at Oranienbaum and listened to the *Te Deum.* . . . During the prayer the police were mercilessly beating the people who attempted to draw nearer to the lined-up troops. . . . Finally the Emperor appeared, accompanied by the Guard, on a fine sorrel horse, with an unsheathed sword, which he was ready to lower before the Empress. But at that very moment, almost under his horse, a peasant crossed the street. The Emperor spurred his horse and rushed with the unsheathed sword toward the running peasant. The police attacked him with their clubs. We did not believe our own eyes and turned away, ashamed for our beloved Tsar.*

High-ranking officers at St. Petersburg secretly formed the Northern Society, which aimed to make Russia a limited, decentralized monarchy, with the various provinces enjoying rights somewhat like those of the states in the American republic. The serfs would receive their freedom but no land, and the whole series of reforms would be achieved by peaceful means. A second secret organization, the Southern Society, with headquarters at Kiev, included many relatively impoverished officers among its members; its leader was Colonel Pestel, a Jacobin in temperament and an admirer of Napoleon. On every main issue the program of the Southern Society went beyond that of the Petersburg group. It advocated a highly centralized republic, the granting of land to liberated serfs, and the use of violence—specifically, assassination of the

*Quoted in Anatole G. Mazour, *The First Russian Revolution* (Berkeley, Calif., 1937), 55.

Tsar—to gain its ends. Pestel himself planned to install a dictatorship, supported by secret police, as an interim government between the overthrow of the tsardom and the advent of the republic.

Both the Northern Society and the Southern Society tried to profit by the political confusion following the death of Alexander I. Since Alexander left no son, the crown would normally have passed to his younger brother, Constantine, his viceroy in Poland. Constantine, however, had relinquished his rights to a still younger brother, Nicholas, but in a document so secret that Nicholas never saw it. On the death of Alexander, Constantine declared that Nicholas was the legal tsar, and Nicholas declared that Constantine was. While the two brothers were clarifying their status, the Northern Society summoned the Petersburg garrison to revolt against Nicholas. Throughout the day of December 26, 1825, the rebels stood their ground in Russia's capital city until Nicholas subdued them. Two weeks later, the Southern Society launched a movement that was doomed from the start because its leader, Pestel, had already been placed under arrest.

The Decembrist revolt, for all its ineffectiveness, was an important episode. It thoroughly alarmed Tsar Nicholas I (1825–1855), who now resolved to follow a severely autocratic policy (for details, see Chapter 13). Although Nicholas dismissed the unpopular Arakcheev and put an end to the military colonies, he also had five of the Decembrists executed and exiled more than one hundred others to Siberia, where many of them contributed to the advance of local government and education. The Decembrists were the first in the long line of modern Russia's political martyrs, and the program of Pestel's Southern Society may now be seen as a kind of early blueprint for the revolutionary dictatorship that came to Russia as a consequence of the Bolshevik uprising of 1917 (see Chapter 18).

V   The Revolutions of 1830

France: The July Revolution

The next revolutionary wave—that of 1830—swept first over the traditional home of revolution, France. King Louis XVIII (1814–1824) had given the Bourbon restoration a fairly promising start. By personal inclination he would have preferred to be an absolute ruler, but he was sensible enough to know that a full return to the Old Régime was impractical, especially since he was declining in years and in health and suffered from the additional political handicap of having been imposed on the French by their enemies.

The middle-of-the-road policies of Louis XVIII were well exemplified by the constitutional Charter that he issued in 1814. Its preamble asserted the royal prerogative: "The authority in France resides in the person of the King." But the Charter then proceeded to grant a measure of constitutional monarchy. There was a legislature, composed of a Chamber of Peers appointed by the king, and a Chamber of Deputies elected on a very restricted suffrage that allowed fewer than 100,000 of France's thirty millions the right to vote. "In the King alone is vested the executive power," the Charter stated, and the Chambers had no formal right to confirm the King's choices as ministers. Yet since Louis tended to select ministers acceptable to majority opinion in the legislature, this was a kind of back-handed parliamentary government. The Charter confirmed many of the decisive changes instituted in France since 1789. It guaranteed religious toleration, equality before the law, and equal eligibility to civil and military office; it likewise accepted the *Code Napoléon* and, still more important, the revolutionary property settlement.

The Charter, however, greatly irritated the ultra-royalist faction, drawn from the noble and clerical *émigrés,* who had returned to France after their revolutionary exile. These "Ultras," grouped around the King's brother and heir, the Count of Artois, were determined to recover both the privileges and the property they had lost during the Revolution. Louis XVIII held the Ultras at bay for five years. When the election of 1815 gave them control of the Chamber of Deputies, he dismissed the Chamber at the insistence of the allies, and held a new election, which returned a less fanatical majority. He chose moderate ministers who worked to pay off the indemnity to the victorious allies and, in general, to put French finances in good order. Events, however, soon strengthened the Ultras' hand. Anti-revolutionary fears swept France in the wake of the Spanish uprising of 1820 and of the assassination of the Duke of Berri, the King's nephew (February, 1820), stabbed by a fanatic who hoped to extinguish the Bourbon line (the widowed duchess, however, gave birth to a son seven months later). The Ultras won control of the Chamber of Deputies, clamped controls on the press, and obliged Louis XVIII to appoint a reactionary ministry, which sent French troops to aid Ferdinand VII against the Spanish revolutionaries.

The tempo of the reaction quickened when Louis died and the Ultra leader, Artois, became King Charles X (1824–1830). A charming and graceful man, Charles had little sense of political realities. He tried to revive some of the medieval glamor of monarchy by staging an elaborate coronation ceremony—and arranged a nine-month prison term for the witty poet who called it "The Consecration of Charles the Simple." He greatly extended the influence of the Church by encouraging the activities of the Jesuits, who were still legally banned from France, and by appointing clerics as principals and administrators in the state school system. The *émigrés,* in compensation for their lost property, were granted state annuities. It was widely, though not entirely correctly, believed that the reduction of the annual interest on government obligations from 5 per cent to 3 was designed to help finance the annuities. The indemnification of the *émigrés* could be defended as a sensible political move that lifted the last threat of confiscation from those who had acquired property during the Revolution. But the reduction of interest on government obligations, together with Charles' clericalism, infuriated many influential Parisian bourgeois.

The Ultras, therefore, lost ground in the elections of 1827, and Charles for a time endeavored to put up with a moderate ministry. But he wearied of the attempt and in 1829 appointed as his chief minister the Prince of Polignac, an Ultra of Ultras, who claimed to have had visions in which the Virgin Mary promised him success. Polignac hoped to bolster the waning prestige of his monarch by scoring a resounding diplomatic victory. He therefore attacked the Dey of Algiers (a largely independent vassal of the Ottoman emperor) who was notorious for his collusion with the hated Barbary Pirates and who had insulted the French consul by striking him with a fly-whisk. The capture of Algiers (June, 1830) laid the foundation of the French empire in North Africa. Meanwhile, the liberal majority in the Chamber of Deputies had attacked Polignac's ministry as unconstitutional because it did not command the approval of the legislature. In the hope of securing a more tractable chamber, Charles X held a new election in May, 1830, but the opposition won. On July 25, 1830, without securing the legislature's approval, Charles and Polignac issued ordinances muzzling the press, dissolving the newly elected Chamber, ordering a fresh election, and introducing new voting qualifications that would have disfranchised the bourgeois who were the mainstay of the opposition. The King and his chief minister believed that public opinion, mollified by the recent victory at Algiers, would accept these July Ordinances calmly. They miscalculated utterly.

Aroused by the protests of Thiers and other liberal journalists, and encouraged by the fine summer weather, the Parisians staged a riot that became a revolution. During *les trois glorieuses* (the three glorious days of July 27, 28, and 29) they threw up barricades, captured the Paris city hall, and hoisted the tricolor atop Notre Dame. When Charles X saw the revolutionary flag through a spyglass from his suburban retreat, he arranged to abdicate on behalf of his grandson, the posthumous son of the Duke of Berri, and sailed to exile in England. Contrary to an impression often held, the July Revolution was not bloodless: some 1,800 insurgents and 200 soldiers were slain.

Contrary to another widespread impression, the revolutionaries were not the poor and the downtrodden. Although there was unemployment, as a result of bank failures, and although poor harvests created high food prices, this suffering remained in the background. The revolutionary leaders of 1830 came mainly from the parliamentary opposition to Charles X, and the revolutionary crowds from the solid working class and from the lower bourgeoisie. The men of 1830 were very much like those of 1789 or 1792. Again like the men of the great revolution, they were not agreed on the kind of regime they wanted. The radicals, who rallied around that aged revolutionary symbol, Lafayette, wanted a democratic republic based on universal suffrage. The moderates wanted a safe and sane constitutional monarchy with a fairly narrow suffrage; they wanted France's 1830 to be the counterpart of England's 1688. The moderates were headed by the young Thiers, by the elderly but still astute Talleyrand, and by the banker Laffitte. They had the money, they had the brains, and they had the support not only of the parliamentary opponents of Charles X but also of veteran Napoleonic officials, who were weary of languishing in the political wasteland. And they had the perfect candidate for the throne—Louis Philippe, the Duke of Orléans.

Louis Philippe was a symbol of revolution at its most moderate. His father had participated in the Paris demonstrations of 1789, had assumed the revolutionary name of *Philippe Egalité*, and voted for the execution of Louis XVI, only to be guillotined during the Terror.

Louis Philippe himself had fought in the revolutionary army at Valmy in 1792, then had emigrated in 1793 before the worst of the Terror. He claimed to have little use for the pomp of royalty and dressed and acted like a sober and well-to-do businessman. Having deceived the gullible Lafayette into thinking he was a republican, he accepted the crown at the invitation of the Chamber that had been elected in May, 1830.

The July Monarchy, as the new regime was termed, retained many features of the Charter of 1814. It did, however, allow the legislature more initiative, delete references to royal absolutism, and call Louis Philippe not King of France but, following the precedent of 1791, King of the French. It also substituted the revolutionary tricolor for the white flag of the Bourbons. The suffrage, though doubled in size, was still highly restricted; in 1831 only 166,000 Frenchmen had the right to vote. The July Monarchy left France a long way from democracy and did little to fulfill the radical revolutionaries' concept of Liberty, Equality, and Fraternity.

Belgium

Within a month of the July uprising in Paris, a nationalistic and liberal revolution began in Belgium. The union of Belgium and the Netherlands, decreed by the peacemakers of 1815, worked well only in economics. The commerce and colonies of Holland supplied raw materials and markets for the textile, glass, and other manufactures of Belgium, at that time the most advanced industrial area of the Continent. In the very sensitive areas of language, politics, and religion, however, King William I of the Netherlands exerted arbitrary power where he might better have made tactful concessions. He made Dutch the official language throughout his realm, including the French-speaking Walloon provinces. He denied the pleas of Belgians for more equitable representation in the States-General, where the Dutch provinces, with their two million inhabitants, and the Belgian, with their three and a half million, were given the same number of seats. He refused to grant special status to the Catholic Church in Belgium and particularly offended the faithful by insisting that the education of priests be subject to state supervision. All these grievances tended to create a Belgian nationalism and to forge common bonds between the Catholic Dutch-speaking Flemings of the provinces north of Brussels and the French-speaking Walloons of the highly industrialized southern provinces. The Flemish-Walloon partnership, however, has never been an easy one.

The revolution broke out in Brussels on August 25, 1830, at a performance of a Romantic opera which depicted a revolt in Naples. Headed by students, inspired by the example of Paris—and perhaps incited by French agents—the audience rioted against Dutch rule. By the end of September, Dutch troops had been driven out of Brussels, and Dutch rule was collapsing. The insurgents recruited their fighters chiefly from the industrial workers, many of whom complained of low pay and frequent unemployment. The better-organized middle-class liberals soon captured control of the revolutionary movement and predominated in the national Belgian congress that convened in November, 1830.

This congress proclaimed Belgium independent and made it a constitutional monarchy. The new constitution granted religious toleration, provided for wide local self-government, and put rigorous limits on the king's authority. Although it did not establish universal suffrage, the financial qualifications for voting were markedly lower in Belgium than they were in Britain or France, and the electorate was proportionately larger. The congress first chose as king the Duke of Nemours, a son of Louis Philippe. Britain protested violently, for this would have brought Belgium within the orbit of France. The congress then picked Leopold of Saxe-Coburg, a German princeling, and the widowed son-in-law of George IV of Britain. Leopold was admirably fitted for the exacting role of a constitutional monarch in a brand-new kingdom. He had already shown his political shrewdness by refusing the shaky new throne of Greece; he now demonstrated it by marrying a daughter of Louis Philippe, thus mitigating French disappointment over the aborted candidacy of the Duke of Nemours. Under his rule, the Kingdom of the Belgians became a model of laissez-faire liberal monarchy, early nineteenth-century style.

The Belgian revolution made the first permanent breach in the Vienna settlement. Although it aroused little enthusiasm among the great powers, Metternich and Tsar Nicholas were too distracted by revolutions in Italy and Poland to organize a crusade on behalf of King William. Representatives of Britain, France, Prussia, Austria, and Russia guaranteed both the independence and the neutrality of Belgium. (It was this guarantee that the German government called "a scrap of paper" when its forces invaded Belgium in 1914.) King William, stubborn as the proverbial Dutchman, tried to retake Belgium by force in 1831–1832. A French army and a British fleet successfully defended the Belgians, and negotiations finally resulted in Dutch recognition of Belgium's new status in 1839.

Poland

The course of revolution in Poland contrasted tragically with that of Belgium. In 1815, the Kingdom of Poland possessed the most liberal constitution on the Continent; twenty years later, it had become a mere colony of the Russian Empire. The constitution given to the Poles by Tsar Alexander I preserved the *Code Napoléon* and endowed the diet with limited legislative power. A hundred thousand Poles received the franchise, more than the total number of voters in the France of Louis XVIII, which had a population ten times greater. In practice, however, difficulties arose. Many of the men chosen for official posts in Poland were not acceptable to the Poles; indeed, one may doubt that any government imposed by Russia would have satisfied them. Censorship, unrest, and police intervention developed during the last years of Alexander I.

The advent of the highly conservative Nicholas I in 1825 increased political friction, although the new tsar at first abided by the Polish constitution. Meantime, Romantic doctrines of nationalism made many converts at the Universities of Warsaw and Vilna (in Lithuania). Polish nationalists demanded the transfer from Russia to Poland of provinces that had belonged to the pre-partition Polish state—Lithuania, White Russia, and the Ukraine. Secret societies on the *Carbonari* model arose in these provinces and in the Kingdom of Poland.

A secret society of army cadets in Warsaw launched a revolution in November, 1830. The rebels soon split into the two hostile camps of "Whites" and "Reds," the former representing the highly conservative aristocrats, the latter the somewhat less conservative gentry. Neither "Whites" nor "Reds" gained the support of the peasants, whom both factions had long oppressed. The misery of the Poles increased with a terrible epidemic of cholera, the first outbreak of that Asian disease in Europe. Russian forces, at first taken off guard, had mastered the situation by 1833. Nicholas I then scrapped the constitution, imposed a regime of permanent martial law, and closed the universities of Warsaw and Vilna, the chief centers of Polish nationalist propaganda. To escape the vengeance of Nicholas, Polish intellectuals fled the country by the tens of thousands and Paris became a kind of capital for Polish exile groups.

Italy and Germany

The liberals and nationalists of Italy and Germany likewise suffered defeat in the early 1830's. In 1831, *Carbonari* insurgents in north central Italy briefly controlled the little duchies of Parma and Modena and a sizable part of the Papal States, including the city of Bologna. Among the participants was the youthful Louis Napoleon Bonaparte, nephew of Napoleon I, who was later to become Emperor Napoleon III. The revolutionaries counted on French assistance, but the July Monarchy had no intention of risking war with Austria by poaching on the Habsburg preserve. Again, as in 1821, Metternich sent troops to restore legitimacy in Italy.

Metternich did not require soldiers to preserve legitimacy in Germany; whenever a crisis arose, the Diet of the German Confederation obediently followed the Austrian lead. In Prussia, King Frederick William III (1797–1840) had never fulfilled his promise to grant a constitution, though he did set up provincial diets. Only Weimar and a few south German states enjoyed liberal constitutions, on the order of the French Charter of 1814. Political agitation came almost entirely from the small minority of intellectuals who had roused national resistance to Napoleon—journalists, Romantic writers, university professors, and students.

After 1815, German university students formed a new organization, the *Burschenschaften* ("Students' Union"). In October, 1817, students of the University of Jena held a rally on the Wartburg, where Luther had worked on his German translation of the Bible, to celebrate both the tercentenary of the Ninety-Five Theses and the fourth anniversary of the battle of Leipzig (see p. 390). During the rally the *Burschenschaften* burned a diplomat's wig, a Prussian officer's corset, and books by reactionary writers. In March, 1819, a demented theological student, apparently influenced by *Burschenschaften* ideas, assassinated one of the writers, Kotzebue, who was also a Russian agent. Metternich, already alarmed by the student prank of 1817, now got the Diet of the German Confederation to approve the Carlsbad Decrees (September, 1819), which stiffened press censorship, dissolved the *Burschenschaften*, and curtailed academic freedom.

Despite the Carlsbad Decrees, mild political ferment continued in Germany, and the *Burschenschaften* reorganized underground. In 1830 and the years following, a few rulers in northern Germany, notably in Saxony and Hanover, were forced to grant constitutions. Excited by these minor successes, twenty-five thousand revolutionary sympathizers gathered in May, 1832, to toast Lafayette and demand the union of the German states under a re-public. Effective action for unification, however, was another matter. In 1833, the would-be republicans made a forlorn effort to seize Frankfurt, the seat of the Diet and capital of the German Confederation, and then relapsed into inactivity.

The Lessons of 1830

The revolutionary wave of the 1830's revealed two great facts of political life. First, it widened the split between the West and the East already evident in the wake of the Revolutions of 1820. Britain and France were committed to support mild liberalism both at home and in neighboring Belgium. On the other hand, Russia, Austria, and Prussia were more firmly committed than ever to the counter-revolutionary principles of the Troppau Protocol (see p. 423). In 1833, Tsar Nicholas I, Metternich, and King Frederick William III formally pledged their joint assistance to any sovereign threatened by revolution.

Second, revolution succeeded in 1830 only in France and Belgium, only where it enlisted the support of a large segment of the population. It failed in every country where the revolutionaries represented only a fraction of the people. In Poland, the peasantry viewed both "Whites" and "Reds" as oppressors. Italian revolutionaries still relied on their Romantic *Carbonari* tradition and on flimsy hopes of foreign aid. In Germany, revolution was a matter of student outbursts, toasts to Lafayette, and other gestures by a small minority. Liberal and nationalist intellectuals needed to make their doctrines penetrate to the grass roots of society; they needed to develop able political leaders and to mature well-laid plans for political reform. These were the tasks which they undertook after 1830; their success was to be tested in the most formidable and the most extensive chain of political uprising in the history of nineteenth-century Europe—the Revolutions of 1848.

VI   The Revolutions of 1848

Common Denominators

One of the common denominators of revolution in 1848 was nationalism. It prompted the disunited Germans and Italians to attempt political unification, and it inspired the subject peoples of the Habsburg Empire to seek political and cultural autonomy. The Romantic movement had stimulated a nationalistic renaissance among most peoples in central and eastern Europe. For the national minorities within the Habsburg Empire, as for the Christian nationalities within the Ottoman Empire, the new nationalism tended to be focused on language. The Czech language, for example, was on the verge of extinction in the later eighteenth century; the population of Bohemia increasingly used the German of their Austrian rulers. By 1848, however, a Czech linguistic and literary revival was in full swing. Patriotic histories of Bohemia and collections of Czech folk-poetry kindled a lively interest in the national past and fostered dreams of a Pan-Slavic awakening in which the Czechs would lead their brother Slavs.

The nationalists of 1848 were not necessarily generous or liberal. While some of them preached with Mazzini, the democratic Italian patriot, that each nation's "special mission" fulfilled the "general mission of humanity," others held less generous views. John Stuart Mill, the English liberal observer, deplored those who ignored the welfare "of any portion of the human species, save that which is called by the same name and speaks the same language as themselves."* There were many self-styled Chosen People in the revolutions of 1848.

Liberalism, the second common denominator of the revolutions, also encompassed a

*J. S. Mill, "The French Revolution and Its Assailants," *Westminster Review,* II (1849), 17.

wide range of programs. In central and eastern Europe, where much of the Old Régime survived, liberals demanded constitutions to limit absolute monarchy and to liquidate feudal rights and manorial dues. In France, where constitutional monarchy had already been achieved, many liberals sought to replace the July Monarchy with a democratic republic. French liberalism, in fact, shaded into socialism; the Paris radicals of 1848 demanded the guarantee of the right to work and other advanced measures.

Finally, in the Europe of 1848, as in the France of 1789, an economic crisis helped to catalyze discontent into revolution. A blight ruined the Irish potato crop in 1845 and soon spread to the Continent; the grain harvest of 1846 also failed in western Europe. The consequences were a sharp rise in the price of bread and bread riots; mass starvation occurred in Ireland, and widespread misery affected France, Germany, and Austria. The food crisis was compounded by an industrial depression, touched off in 1847 by the collapse of a boom in railroad construction. The number of unemployed mounted just as food prices were rising, thus intensifying popular suffering.

France

The economic crisis hit France with particular severity. Railroad construction almost ceased, throwing more than half a million laborers out of work; coal mines and iron foundries, in turn, laid men off. Unemployment increased the discontent of French workers already embittered by their low wages and by the still lower esteem in which they were held by the government of Louis Philippe. Under the July Monarchy, French agriculture experienced a golden age, while industrialization also began to develop. The government, however, appeared to be indifferent to the social misery that accompanied the new prosperity. In eighteen years, it took only two steps to improve the welfare of the industrial working class: an extension of state aid to primary schools in 1833, and a laxly enforced law in 1841 limiting child labor. There was a great deal of truth in the famous judgment passed by Alexis de Tocqueville, an acute political observer—that "Government in those days resembled an industrial company whose every operation is undertaken for the profits which the stockholders may gain thereby."

The "stockholders" of the July Monarchy were the Napoleonic veterans who emerged as prefects and diplomats after a wholesale overturn of official personnel, and the landowners,

Daumier, "The Fight of the Citizens of France against the Oppression of Louis-Philippe."

investors, and businessmen who had the right to vote and whose numbers never exceeded 200,000. They answered demands for liberalization of the suffrage with the curt reply of one of their leaders: *Enrichissez-vous!*—make yourself rich enough to meet the stiff fiscal qualifications for voting. The government banned labor organizations and repressed harshly the workmen of Paris and Lyons who

demonstrated in the early 1830's to demand a republic and higher wages. It imposed a censorship when the press caricatured the pear-shaped head and the inevitable umbrella of Louis Philippe.

Opposition to the July Monarchy, though stifled in the 1830's, revived rapidly during the 1840's, nourished in part by the fiasco of the French attempt to back the empire-building of the Egyptian governor, Mehemet Ali, whose ambitions alarmed both his Ottoman overlord and most of the great powers. The opposition in France, however, was far from united—a fact that does much to explain the hectic course of the revolution it set off. Heading one group was Adolphe Thiers, a principal architect of the July Monarchy, who was shelved by Louis Philippe in favor of Guizot, the chief minister from 1840 until 1848. Thiers continued to support the principle of constitutional monarchy, and cynics claim that the chief difference between him and Guizot was the fact that he was out of office while Guizot was in. The disappointed republicans of 1830 formed a second opposition group. The third, and smallest, group took in various socialists, who were to gain recruits from the economic depression of the late 1840's. Potentially more formidable than any of these, but as yet representing only a vague, unorganized sentiment, were the Bonapartists. The return of the Emperor's ashes from St. Helena to Paris in 1840 revived and renewed the legend of a glorious and warlike Napoleon, so different from the uninspiring Louis Philippe.

In the summer of 1847, constitutional monarchists of the Thiers faction joined with republicans to stage a series of political banquets throughout France calling for an extended suffrage and the resignation of Guizot. This campaign appeared comparatively harmless until a particularly huge banquet was announced for February 22, 1848, to be held in a radical quarter of Paris. When the Guizot ministry forbade the banquet, the Parisians substituted a large demonstration. On February 23, Louis Philippe dismissed Guizot and prepared to summon Thiers to the ministry. But his concessions came too late. Supported by workers, students, and the more radical republican leaders, the demonstration of February 22 turned into a riot on the 23rd. More than fifty of the rioters who attacked the residence of Guizot were killed or wounded. It has never been established who fired the first shots, but the casualties of February 23rd at once intensified the revolutionary atmosphere. On the next day, Louis Philippe abdicated.

Again, as in 1830, radicals and moderates competed to fill the political vacuum. In 1848, however, the radicals had a more pronounced working-class character, since their ranks had been swelled by laborers from new industries and their ideas had been influenced by the new doctrines of socialism. They demanded both a republic and the extensive social and economic reforms summed up in the formula, the right to work. The radicals, however, still lacked organization and hard-headed leadership; their spokesmen in 1848 were only slightly less gullible than Lafayette had been in 1830. The middle-class moderates were

ready to concede universal suffrage but were determined to protect the rights of property and to keep social and economic concessions to a minimum.

The moderates secured the direction of the provisional government formed on February 24. To calm the Parisian radicals, they promised to guarantee the right to work and authorized the establishment in Paris of National Workshops, apparently inspired by the socialist, Louis Blanc (1811–1882). Louis Blanc had long advocated "social workshops," which the workers themselves would own and run with the financial assistance of the state. The National Workshops of 1848, however, were simply a relief project organized along semimilitary lines, and enrolling more than 100,000 unemployed from Paris and the provinces. About 10,000 of the recruits received two francs (about 40 cents) a day for working on municipal improvements; the rest received a dole of one franc a day.

The moderates commanding the provision-

Daumier, "The Uprising, 1848," in the Phillips Memorial Gallery, Washington.

al government gained new strength as a result of the election of April, 1848 — the first election in European history in which almost the entire adult male population of a country voted. Eight million Frenchmen elected members of the National Assembly that was to draw up a new constitution. The conservative peasants, who still made up the bulk of the population, approved the fall of the July Monarchy but dreaded anything resembling an attack on private property. Of the almost 900 deputies elected, therefore, only a hundred or so sympathized with the Paris radicals.

The latter, however, refused to accept the decision of the country. On May 15, a huge crowd of noisy but unarmed demonstrators invaded the meeting hall of the National Assembly and proposed the dissolution of the Assembly and the formation of a new provisional government at the Paris City Hall. The moderates, now thoroughly alarmed, arrested radical leaders and decided that the National Workshops threatened law and order because they concentrated so many economically desperate men in Paris. The Assembly therefore dissolved the Workshops and gave the recruits the alternative of enlistment in the army or accepting work in the provinces. The workers of Paris resisted. From June 23 to June 26, 1848, the radical districts of the capital rose in insurrection until they were finally subdued by the troops brought in by General Cavaignac, the energetic Minister of War.

These "June Days" were a landmark in modern history, the first large-scale outbreak with very strong overtones of open class warfare. Among the insurgents were men of the new industrial age — mechanics, railroad men, stevedores — as well as wine-sellers, masons, locksmiths, cabinet-makers, and other artisans who had been prominent in the capture of the Bastille in 1789. The possibility of a social revolution terrified and consolidated the propertied classes, and Tocqueville reported that "peasants, shopkeepers, landowners, and nobles" were all pouring into Paris by the new railroads to quell the uprising. The spirit of panic accounted for the severe repression of the insurgents: nearly 1,500 were killed during the fighting; others were subsequently deported, chiefly to Algeria. All socialist clubs and newspapers were padlocked, and Louis Blanc fled to England. France became a virtual military dictatorship under General Cavaignac.

The fears of the moderates were evident in the formal constitution of the Second French Republic which the National Assembly completed in November, 1848. The Assembly declared property inviolable and rejected a motion to list the right to work among the fundamental rights of French citizens. In other respects, however, the constitution was a daring venture in representative democracy and in combining a strong president and powerful legislature. The legislature was a single chamber, to be elected by universal male suffrage every three years. The president was to be chosen by popular election every four years. The French Constitution of November, 1848, thus reflected the influence of both Montesquieu's doctrine of the separation of powers and the example of the United States. Circumstances, however, did not favor the success of the Second French Republic. The military rule exercised by Cavaignac while the Assembly was drafting the constitution was one ominous sign. Another was the outcome of the presidential election in December, 1848. Fewer than half a million votes were polled by the three genuinely republican candidates, a million and a half were cast for General Cavaignac, and some five and a half million votes and the Presidency of the Republic went to Louis Napoleon Bonaparte, the nephew of the great Napoleon. President Bonaparte was to subvert the constitution in 1851 and then to proclaim himself Emperor Napoleon III (see Chapter 13). The French Revolution of 1848, like that of 1789, had established a republic that ended in a Napoleonic empire.

Italy

In 1849, President Bonaparte sent French troops to Rome to defend the pope against Italian radicals. By then the Italian revolutions were petering out. The Italian movement was ambitious, but weak and divided; it attempted to cast off the Austrian hegemony

Joseph Mazzini (1805 – 1872).

pope in the task of freeing Italy from the control of a German emperor. The Neo-Guelf leader, the priest Gioberti, declared that the future depended on "the union of Rome and Turin" (the Piedmontese capital). The pope would head, and the army of Piedmont would defend, a federation of Italian states, each with its monarch and its cautiously liberal constitution.

The third group of liberals, "Young Italy," so named because only those under the age of forty were eligible for membership, asserted that Italy should be unified as a democratic republic. Its founder, Mazzini (1805 – 1872), hoped to create an organization more effective than the *Carbonari* but was frustrated by his own prolonged exile and by the frequent ineptitude of his lieutenants. Mazzini did, however, achieve an enduring reputation as the great democratic idealist of modern Italian politics. Here is a statement of his political credo:

> We believe, therefore, in the Holy Alliance of the Peoples as being the vastest formula of association possible in our epoch; — in the *liberty* and *equality* of the peoples, without which no true association can exist; — in *nationality*, which is the *conscience* of the peoples, and which, by assigning to them their part in the work of association, . . . constitutes their mission upon earth, that is to say, their *individuality*, without which neither liberty nor equality are possible; — in the sacred *Fatherland*, cradle of nationality; altar and workshop of the individuals of which each nation is composed.*

A good European as well as an ardent Italian nationalist, Mazzini inspired the formation of Young Germany, Young Poland, and similar movements, all joined together in a federation called "Young Europe."

Revolution struck first (January, 1848) in Sicily and Naples, and King Ferdinand II was obliged to grant the Two Sicilies a constitution on the lines of the revised French Charter of 1814. During the next two months, King Charles Albert of Piedmont, the Grand Duke

with only the slender military resources of the separate Italian states. Piedmont rejected the offer of assistance from revolutionary France in 1848 with the proud but unrealistic boast, *Italia farà da se*—Italy will do it alone.

Throughout the 1840's three schools of liberalism, none of them commanding really wide popular support, competed for leadership in Italy. The two moderate schools, while agreeing that political power in emancipated Italy should be limited to the nobility and the bourgeoisie, disagreed on the form that a united Italian nation should assume. One group of moderates, centered in the north, favored the domination of Piedmont. Among them was the eventual unifier of Italy, Count Cavour, a great admirer of British and French liberal ways, and the editor of the newspaper, *Il Risorgimento* (meaning resurgence or regeneration), which gave its name to the whole process of unification. The other moderate group called themselves "Neo-Guelfs" because, like the Guelf political faction of the Middle Ages, they hoped to engage the

---

*"Faith and the Future," in *Life and Writings of Joseph Mazzini* (London, 1905), III, 129.

Barricades in Milan, 1848.

of Tuscany, and Pope Pius IX (1846–1878) —whose mild reforms had already aroused great liberal expectations—all followed suit. Next it was the turn of Lombardy and Venetia, where Habsburg rule had been relatively mild and enlightened, but where the ideas of Young Italy had inspired a revolutionary movement. News of the Viennese revolution and the resignation of Metternich (see p. 443) touched off a successful insurrection in Milan, the capital of Lombardy (March 18–22), which produced some extraordinary barricades made of pianos, sentry boxes, and omnibuses in addition to the usual paving blocks. At the same time, Venice, the capital of Austria's other Italian province, proclaimed herself the independent Republic of St. Mark. The rapid collapse

of Habsburg rule in Lombardy-Venetia touched off a national crusade against the Austrians and brought the more moderate leaders of the Neo-Guelf cause to the fore. As Charles Albert of Piedmont assumed command of the Italian forces, Naples, Tuscany, and the Pope sent contingents. For the moment, it seemed likely that both nationalism and liberalism would win in Italy.

But only for the moment. During the spring and early summer of 1848, Piedmont annexed Lombardy and the two small North Italian duchies of Parma and Modena. The other Italian states, jealous of their particularist traditions, commenced to fear the imperialism of Piedmont more than they desired the unification of Italy. On April 29, 1848,

438

Pope Pius IX announced that his "equal affection" for all peoples obliged him to adopt a neutral position in the war with Austria and to recall his soldiers. The Pope could not be both an Italian patriot and an international spiritual leader. Moreover, Pius was alarmed by the increasingly radical political temper of the Roman population and by the threats of German bishops to create an anti-pope. The Neo-Guelf cause had received a fatal blow. In May, 1848, the King of Naples, who had scrapped his constitution, withdrew his contingents from the war. The Austrians, taking the offensive, reconquered Lombardy and crushed the forces of Charles Albert at Custozza (July, 1848). Italy had not been able to do it alone.

A few months later, the revolutionary movement got a brief second wind. Roman adherents of Young Italy, dissatisfied with the mildly liberal constitution of March, rose up in November, 1848. After Pius IX had fled to Neapolitan territory, they transformed the Papal States into a democratic Roman Republic, headed by Mazzini himself, who proved to be fairly authoritarian in a position of power. In March, 1849, radicals in Piedmont forced the reluctant Charles Albert to renew the war with Austria, but within the month Austria again overwhelmed Piedmont, at the battle of Novara. In August, 1849, the Austrians put an end to the Republic of St. Mark after a prolonged siege and bombardment of Venice, which suffered acutely from famine and cholera. Meanwhile, besieged by French troops, Mazzini's Roman Republic had surrendered (July, 1849).

Again subdivided into many sovereign states, again dominated by the Habsburgs, Italy returned almost completely to its pre-revolutionary status. Both the Neo-Guelfs and Young Italy were discredited. The only bright spot in the picture was the emergence of Piedmont as the natural leader of Italian nationalism and liberalism. Despite the defeats at Custozza and Novara, despite the loss of the territories momentarily annexed in 1848, Piedmont enjoyed the prestige of having twice defied the hated Austrians.

Germany

The course of the German revolutions in 1848 roughly paralleled that of the Italian. In Germany, too, liberalism and nationalism won initial victories and then collapsed in the face of internal dissension and Austrian resistance. The failure in Germany was the more surprising—and ominous—since the revolutionary movement had begun to recruit support among industrial workers, among craftsmen who feared industrial competition, and among peasants who wished to abolish the relics of manorialism. Liberal and nationalist agitation, however, centered in the well-to-do business and professional classes, especially university professors, who enjoyed more influence and respect in Germany than anywhere else in Europe. Except for a few republicans and socialists, the German liberals were moderates. They wanted constitutional monarchies in the various German states, the strengthening of the German Confederation, and an end to the repressive hegemony of Metternich.

The hero of German liberals was King Frederick William IV of Prussia (1840–1861). Attractive and cultivated, but unstable and infatuated with Romantic concepts of divine-right kingship, Frederick William promised much and delivered little. He promised to carry out his father's unhonored pledge to give Prussia a constitution and an elected assembly; however, the meeting of representatives from the provincial diets he convoked at last in 1847 was a great disappointment.

Not this royal knight-errant, but the architects of the *Zollverein* (customs union) constituted Prussia's most solid contribution to German unification before 1848. In 1818, Prussia had abolished internal tariffs within its scattered territories and applied a uniform tariff schedule to imports. The first states to join the *Zollverein* wee small neighbors of Prussia. Membership proved so profitable that by 1844 almost all the German states, except for Austria, had joined. The *Zollverein* liberated Germany from an oppressive burden of local tolls and taxes and cleared the way for her phenomenal economic development later in the century. Although it did not exercise a decisive influence on politics, it suggested that the state which had fostered German economic unification might naturally take the initiative in politics.

Unification seemed almost a certainty in 1848. Stimulated by the example of Paris, the revolutionaries scored their first successes in the western German states at the end of February, 1848. From there, the demands for constitutions, civil liberties, and a strengthened German Confederation fanned out rapidly. By mid-March, demonstrators were throwing up barricades in Berlin. Frederick William IV accepted some of the liberals' demands and appealed for calm among "ye inhabitants of my true and beautiful Berlin." Before his appeal could be publicized, rioting broke out with redoubled violence, and more than two hundred rioters, chiefly workingmen, were killed. The mob broke into the royal palace and forced the King to go through a grotesque ceremony of saluting the corpses of the victims. Overwrought by the humiliation to himself and by the death of his subjects, Frederick

William accepted all the demands of liberals and nationalists. He summoned an assembly to draw up a constitution, declared Prussia "merged in Germany," and proclaimed himself "King of the free regenerated German nation."

Drastic reform of the German Confederation now began. In May, 1848, a constitutional convention held its first session in the Church of St. Paul at Frankfurt, the capital of the Confederation. Its 830 members, popularly elected throughout Germany, represented the flower of the German intelligentsia—18 doctors, 33 clergymen, 49 university professors, 57 schoolteachers, 223 lawyers and judges. While some 140 deputies were businessmen, there was only one dirt farmer, and not a single laboring man. The Frankfurt Assembly lacked a broad popular base, and, as events soon demonstrated, many of its members also lacked political experience and talent for practical statesmanship.

The Frankfurt Assembly had to decide the geographical limits of Germany. The Confederation included Austria proper but excluded most of the non-German Habsburg territories. Neither did it include the eastern provinces of Prussia, notably those acquired in the partitions of Poland. The Austrian issue divided the Assembly into two camps: the "Big Ger-

Barricades in Berlin, March, 1848.

mans" who favored the inclusion of Austria and Bohemia, with its large Czech population, in the projected German state, and the "Little Germans," who opposed it. Austrian objections to a "Big Germany" insured the Assembly's adoption of the "Little Germany" proposal.

On the question of Prussian Poland, the nationalism of the Frankfurt Assembly overcame its liberalism. By a large majority it voted to include some Prussian areas in which the Poles formed the majority of the population. The arguments advanced against the Poles in the debates revealed German nationalism at its most superheated. One orator declared that the minority of Germans had a natural right to rule the Poles, who had "less cultural content":

> It is high time for us . . . to wake to a wholesome national egotism, to say the word right out for once, which in every question places the welfare and honour of the fatherland uppermost. . . . Our right is none other than the right of the stronger, the right of conquest.*

In contrast, the national constitution promulgated by the Frankfurt Assembly in March, 1849, was a decidedly liberal document, a combination of principles drawn from the American federal system and British parliamentary practice. The individual states were to surrender many of their powers to the German federal government. The federal legislature would consist of a lower house, elected by universal male suffrage, and an upper house, chosen by the governments and the legislatures of the constituent states. Ministers responsible to the legislature would form the federal executive. Over all would preside a constitutional monarch, the German emperor.

The Frankfurt constitution died a-borning. The Assembly elected the King of Prussia to be emperor, but Frederick William, ignoring his fine promises of March, 1848, and alarmed by Austrian opposition, rejected the offer. He called the Frankfurt constitution a "bastard" product:

*Quoted in J. G. Legge, *Rhyme and Revolution in Germany* (London, 1918), 397.

> The crown is no crown. The crown which a Hohenzollern could accept . . . is not one created by an Assembly born of revolutionary seed. . . . It must be a crown set with the seal of the Almighty. . . .*

Since the major candidate for the imperial office had balked, the Frankfurt Assembly soon came to an end. It had never secured recognition from foreign governments, had never raised a penny in taxes, and had never exerted real sovereignty over Germany. The couplet mocking the plethora of academic deputies had been justified:

> *Hundert fünfzig Professoren!*
> *Lieber Gott, wir sind verloren!*
> (A hundred and fifty professors!
> Good God, we're sunk!)

German liberalism had suffered a major defeat. After the initial shock of the revolutions, the comfortably situated professional and business classes began to fear the radicalism of the workers and artisans. The German princes soon either revoked or abridged the constitutions that they had granted in 1848. In Prussia, Frederick William and his conservative advisers repeatedly doctored the work of the constitutional convention summoned in 1848. The end product, the Constitution of 1850, made Prussia relatively safe for autocracy and aristocracy down to World War I (see Chapter 14).

The Habsburg Domains

The fate of German and Italian nationalism in 1848 hinged partly on the outcome of the revolutions in the Habsburg Empire. If these revolutions had immobilized the Habsburg government for a long period, then Italian and German unification might have been realized. But Austria, though buffeted by wave after wave of revolution, rode out the storm. The success of the counter-revolution in the Habsburg Empire assured its victory in Italy and Germany.

*Ibid., 516–517.

The nature and the outcome of the Habsburg revolutions depended in turn on the complex structure of nationalities within the Austrian Empire:

NATIONALITIES
UNDER HABSBURG RULE, 1848

Nationality	Percentage of Total Population
German	23
Magyar (Hungarian)	14
Czech and Slovak	19
South (Yugo-) Slav	
Slovene	4
Croat	4
Serb	5
Pole	7
Ruthenian (Little Russian)	8
Rumanian	8
Italian	8

These national groups were not always neatly segregated geographically, each in its own compartment. For instance, in the Hungarian part of the Empire, the dominant Magyars fell slightly short of a numerical majority. Hungary contained important minorities of Slovaks, Rumanians, Croats, Serbs, and Germans. Moreover, while the bulk of the population was rural, the German element, chiefly bureaucrats and tradesmen, predominated in most of the towns and cities throughout the Empire, even in the Czech capital of Prague and the Magyar capital of Budapest.

Among the component peoples of the Habsburg realm in 1848 nationalism ran strongest among the Italians of Lombardy-Venetia, the Czechs of Bohemia, and the Magyars and Croats of Hungary. Language was an important issue with the Magyars as it was with Czechs, so that the replacement of Latin by Hungarian as the official tongue of the eastern part of the Empire in 1844 marked a victory for Magyar nationalism. Since Hungary was an overwhelmingly agricultural land, nationalism, like all other aspects of political life, was dominated by nobles and country squires who monopolized the seats in the county assemblies and the central diet. One group of Magyar nationalists aimed at the gradual modernization of Hungary's culture and economy along moderate English lines. The more extreme nationalists, however, whose spokesman was the spellbinding orator, Louis Kossuth (1802–1894), regarded the linguistic reform of 1844 as but the first in a series of revolutionary projects cutting all ties with the Vienna government. Magyar nationalists bitterly opposed the satisfaction of the growing national aspirations of their Slavic subjects. The most discontented were the Croats, whose national awakening had begun when their homeland became the Illyrian province of Napoleon's empire.

The antagonism between Croats and Magyars revealed an all-important fact about the nationalistic movements within the Habsburg Empire. Some groups—Italians, Magyars, Czechs, Poles—resented the German-dominated government in Vienna. Others, notably the Croats and Rumanians, were not so much anti-German as anti-Magyar. Here was a situation where the central government in Vienna might apply the policy of "divide and conquer," pitting the anti-Magyar elements against the anti-German Magyars, and subduing both. This was substantially what happened in 1848. A similar policy had already been used in 1846 to suppress a revolt in Galicia, the province that Austria had acquired in the partitions of Poland. When the Polish landlords revolted, their exploited Ruthenian peasants rose against them and received the backing of Vienna.

Liberalism also played a significant part in the Habsburg revolutions, especially in Austria proper. The expanding middle class desired civil liberties, a voice in government, and the lifting of mercantilist restrictions on business. In Vienna, as in Paris and Berlin, some workers went farther and demanded radical democratic reforms.

From 1815 to 1848, the Habsburg government virtually ignored the grumblings and protests that arose in almost every quarter of the Empire. If Prince Metternich had had his way, he would probably have made some concessions to liberal and nationalist aspirations. But Metternich, though he enjoyed a nearly free hand in foreign affairs, did not have his way in domestic policy. He was blocked by the emperors—the bureaucratic Francis I (1792–1835) and the feeble-minded Ferdinand I (1835–1848)—and by the vested interests of the aristocracy. The Habsburg government, though buttressed by an army of censors and spies, was at best an inefficient autocracy; Austria, Metternich accurately stated, was "administered, but not ruled."

The news of the February revolution in Paris shook the Empire to its foundations. Four separate revolutions broke out almost simultaneously in March, 1848—in Milan and Venice, in Hungary, in Vienna itself, and in Bohemia. In Hungary, Kossuth and his ardent Magyar supporters forced Emperor Ferdinand to accept the "March Laws," which gave Hungary political autonomy. The March Laws instituted parliamentary government and substituted an elected legislature for the feudal Hungarian diet. They abolished serfdom and ended the immunity of nobles and gentry from taxation. But they rode roughshod over the rights of non-Magyars by making use of the Hungarian language a requirement for election as a deputy to the legislature.

Aroused by the Hungarian revolt, workers and university students in Vienna rose on March 12. On the next day, Prince Metternich resigned from the post he had held for thirty-nine years and fled to Britain. Although the imperial government repeatedly promised reforms, rioting continued in Vienna, and by May the political atmosphere was so charged that Emperor Ferdinand and his family left the capital. Pending the meeting of a constituent assembly in July, in Vienna a revolutionary council ran affairs.

Meanwhile, in Prague, Czech nationalists were demanding rights similar to those granted the Magyars in the March Laws. Discontent mounted with the news that the "Big German" faction in the Frankfurt Assembly was contemplating the inclusion of Bohemia in a German federation. In June, 1848, the Czechs organized a Pan-Slav Congress to promote the solidarity of Slavic peoples against "Big German" encroachments. The Pan-Slav Congress set off demonstrations, in the course of which the wife of Prince Windischgrätz, the commander of the Austrian garrison of Prague, was accidentally killed (June 12, 1848). Five days later, Windischgrätz, after bombarding Prague, dispersed the Czech revolutionaries and established a military régime in Bohemia. The counter-revolution was beginning.

A month later (July), the Austrian army in Italy defeated Piedmont at Custozza. In September, 1848, the Vienna Constituent Assembly, which represented all the provinces of the Empire except the Italian and Hungarian, passed a great reform measure that actually accelerated the counter-revolution. It emancipated the peasants from their last remaining servile obligations, notably the requirement to work for their landlords. The peasants, the core of the Habsburg population, had achieved their main goal; they now tended to withhold support from further revolutionary activities.

The time was ripe for the policy of "divide and conquer." In Hungary, the Germans, Slovaks, Rumanians, Serbs, and Croats, all outraged by the discrimination against them in the March Laws, had risen up against the Magyars. In September, 1848, the imperial government authorized Jellachich, the governor of Croatia, to invade central Hungary. While the hardfighting Magyars held off the forces of Jellachich, the radicals of Vienna revolted again, proclaiming their support of the Magyars and declaring Austria a democratic republic. But the armies of Jellachich and Windischgrätz crushed the Vienna revolution (October 31, 1848) and executed the radical leaders.

The counter-revolution was hitting its full stride. In November, 1848, the energetic and unscrupulous Prince Felix Schwarzenberg, the brother-in-law of Windischgrätz, became chief minister of the Habsburg government. Schwarzenberg arranged the abdication of the incapable Ferdinand I in December and the accession of Ferdinand's eighteen-year-old nephew, the Emperor Francis Joseph (1848–1916). Schwarzenberg declared that the promises made by the old emperor could not legally bind his successor and therefore shelved the projects of the Austrian Constituent Assembly. Schwarzenberg's high-handedness infuriated the Magyars, who fought on like tigers. In April, 1849, the parliament of Hungary declared the country an independent republic and named Kossuth its chief executive. Russia now offered Austria military assistance, for Tsar Nicholas I feared that the revolutionary contagion might spread to Russian Poland unless it was checked. Schwarzenberg accepted the Tsar's offer, and in August, 1849, Russian troops helped to subjugate the Hungarian republic.

The Lessons of 1848

The Tsar boasted in 1850 that Providence had assigned him "the mission of delivering Europe from constitutional governments." By 1850, almost the whole Continent was in the process of being delivered from the regimes of 1848. In France, the Second Republic faced a very uncertain future under an ambitious president and a conservative assembly, both very much concerned with preserving order against liberty. In Prussia, Frederick William IV, and in Austria and Italy, Prince Schwarzenberg, guided the triumphant course of the counter-revolution. Kossuth, Mazzini, and other revolutionaries went into exile. In the early months of 1848, enthusiastic liberals had hailed the arrival of the "peoples' springtime." It had been a false spring.

Mazzini undertook to explain why. In 1850, he wrote from London:

Why, then, has *reaction* triumphed?

Yes: the cause is in ourselves; in our want of organisation; . . . in our ceaseless distrust, in our miserable little vanities, in our absolute want of that spirit of discipline which alone can achieve great results; in the scattering and dispersing of our forces in a multitude of small centres and sects, powerful to dissolve, impotent to found.

The cause is in the gradual substitution of the worship of material interests . . . for the grand problem of education, which alone can legitimatise our efforts. . . . It is in the narrow spirit of *Nationalism* substituted for the spirit of Nationality; in the stupid presumption on the part of each people that they are capable of solving the political, social, and economical problem alone; in their forgetfulness of the great truths that the cause of the

peoples is one; that the cause of the Fatherland must lean upon Humanity. . . . The language of narrow nationalism held at Frankfort destroyed the German Revolution; as the fatal idea of aggrandisement of the House of Savoy [Piedmont] destroyed the Italian Revolution.*

The revolutionaries of 1848 had not fully learned the lessons of 1830. They relied on moral exhortation and pinned their hopes on spontaneous uprisings when they would have done better to concentrate on discipline and organization. Many of them were either too doctrinaire or too idealistic to make practical politicians. The strength of the revolutionary forces was sapped by the tensions between artisans and industrial workers, between radicals and moderates, between the followers of Mazzini and those of Gioberti, between "Big" and "Little" Germans, and between Magyars and Slavs.

"The narrow spirit of nationalism" deplored by Mazzini was to grow ever more intense after 1848. It was to haunt the Habsburg Empire for the rest of its days and eventually destory it. The failure of the liberals to unify Italy and Germany in 1848 transferred the leadership of the nationalist movements from the amateur revolutionaries to the professional politicians of Piedmont and Prussia. In the case of Italy, the transfer augured well; Piedmont, alone among the Italian states, retained the moderate constitution it had secured in 1848; in the case of Germany, the anti-liberal Bismarck was to achieve through "blood and iron" what the Frankfurt Assembly had not accomplished by peaceful means.

Equally prophetic were the first signals of class warfare, especially in the June Days in Paris. Europe was beginning to experience the challenge of the forces released by the industrial revolution, and new demands for drastic social and economic improvements were arising alongside the older demands for political liberties and constitutions. The year 1848 was not only the year of revolution but also the year when Marx and Engels published *The Communist Manifesto*.

Life and Writings of Joseph Mazzini (London, 1905), III, 76–77.

Reading Suggestions on Revolution and Counter-Revolution, 1815–1850

(Asterisk indicates paperbound edition.)

General Accounts

F. B. Artz, *Reaction & Revolution, 1814–1832* (*Torch). A painstaking survey of all aspects of Europe in the post-Napoleonic period; with very full bibliography.

The Cambridge Modern History, Vols. IX and X (Cambridge Univ. Press, 1965, 1960). Comprehensive account from 1793 to 1870; useful for reference.

A. J. May, *The Age of Metternich, 1814–1848,* rev. ed. (*Holt, Rinehart & Winston). Helpful brief introduction.

E. J. Hobsbawm, *The Age of Revolution, 1789–1848* (*Mentor). Stimulating analysis, stressing the social impact of the French Revolution and industrialism.

The Romantic Protest

J. B. Halsted, ed., *Romanticism: Problem of Definition, Explanation, Evaluation* (*Heath). Introductory exploration.

G. Brandes, *Main Currents in Nineteenth-Century Literature,* 6 vols. (Heinemann, 1901–1905). A monumental detailed study.

I. Babbitt, *Rousseau & Romanticism* (*Meridian). A hostile evaluation.

C. Brinton, *Political Ideas of the English Romanticists* (*Ann Arbor). A perceptive analysis.

G. Boas, *French Philosophies of the Romantic Period* (Johns Hopkins Univ. Press, 1934). Very helpful study.

K. Francke, *A History of German Literature as Determined by Social Forces,* 4th ed. (Holt, 1931). An older study, fully living up to the promise of the title.

A. N. Whitehead, *Science & the Modern World* (*Mentor). Includes a sympathetic and influential re-evaluation of Romanticism.

J. Bronowski and B. Mazlish, *The Western Intellectual Tradition from Leonardo to Hegel* (*Torch). Stresses the links between economics, politics, and intellectual history.

M. Raynal, *The Nineteenth Century: Goya to Gauguin* (Skira, 1951). Handsome volume.

K. Clark, *The Gothic Revival* (*Penguin). Good on the neo-Gothic vogue in England.

H. R. Hitchcock, *Architecture: Nineteenth and Twentieth Centuries* (Pelican, 1958). Encyclopaedic study, giving full attention to both Europe and America.

A. Einstein, *Music in the Romantic Era* (Norton, 1947). Helpful and suggestive survey.

J. Barzun, *Berlioz and His Century* (*Meridian). Exhaustive study of Berlioz.

Conservatism and the Vienna Settlement

E. L. Woodward, *Three Studies in European Conservatism* (Constable, 1929). Thoughtful essays on Metternich, Guizot, and the Catholic Church.

H. F. Schwarz, ed., *Metternich, the Coachman of Europe: Statesman or Evil Genius?* (*Heath). Good introduction to the variety of opinions on the man.

P. Viereck, *Conservatism Revisited* (*Free Press). Brief and sympathetic reappraisal.

H. Nicolson, *The Congress of Vienna* (*Compass). Analyzed by an expert on diplomacy.

C. Webster, *The Congress of Vienna* (*Barnes & Noble). Excellent manual.

G. Ferrero, *The Reconstruction of Europe* (*Norton). Detailed study of Talleyrand and the Congress of Vienna.

C. Brinton, *The Lives of Talleyrand* (*Norton). Sympathetic biographical study.

The Revolutions: Studies of Particular Countries

J. Lucas-Dubreton, *The Restoration & the July Monarchy* (Putnam, 1929). Perhaps the most detailed account in English; conservative in tone.

A. Cobban, *A History of Modern France* Vol. II (*Penguin). A briefer and more up-to-date account.

F. B. Artz, *France under the Bourbon Restoration, 1814–1830* (Harvard Univ. Press, 1931). Monograph written from the liberal point of view.

T. E. B. Howarth, *Citizen-King* (Eyre & Spottiswoode, 1961). Biography of Louis Philippe.

D. C. McKay, *The National Workshops* (Harvard Univ. Press, 1933). Monograph on an often-misinterpreted facet of the Paris Revolution of 1848.

G. F. H. Berkeley, *Italy in the Making*, 3 vols. (Cambridge Univ. Press, 1932–1940). Very detailed study from 1815 through 1848.

A. J. Whyte, *The Evolution of Modern Italy* (*Norton). Sound introduction.

G. Salvemini, *Mazzini* (*Collier). Sympathetic scholarly analysis.

H. Treitschke, *History of Germany in the Nineteenth Century*, 7 vols. (McBride, Nast, 1915–1919). Colorful detailed narrative; strongly Prussian and nationalistic in sympathy.

A. J. P. Taylor, *The Course of German History* (*Capricorn). A lively essay on the period since 1815; a good antidote to Treitschke.

T. S. Hamerow, *Restoration, Revolution, Reaction* (*Princeton Univ. Press). Scholarly re-evaluation of German economics and politics, 1815–1871.

P. H. Noyes, *Organization & Revolution* (Princeton Univ. Press, 1966). Enlightening study of the disunity of the German working class in 1848.

A. J. P. Taylor, *The Habsburg Monarchy, 1809–1918*, 2nd ed. (Hamish Hamilton, 1948). Spirited brief treatment.

R. J. Rath, *The Viennese Revolution of 1848* (Univ. of Texas Press, 1957). Detailed monograph.

C. M. Woodhouse, *The Greek War of Independence* (Hutchinson). Readable short account.

A. G. Mazour, *The First Russian Revolution* (*Stanford Univ. Press). Excellent monograph on the Decembrists.

The Revolutions: Other Studies

P. Robertson, *Revolutions of 1848: A Social History* (*Torch). Stresses colorful details.

R. Postgate, *Story of a Year: 1848* (Oxford Univ. Press, 1956). A lively chronicle; well-illustrated.

G. Rudé, *The Crowd in History, 1730–1848* (*Wiley). Includes a chapter analyzing the make-up of the demonstrators in the Paris Revolution of 1848.

L. B. Namier, *1848: The Revolution of the Intellectuals* (*Anchor). An influential essay castigating some of the liberals for their illiberal attitudes.

H. Ausubel, ed., *The Making of Modern Europe*, Vol. II (Dryden, 1951). Includes several useful essays on the material covered in this chapter, notably a reappraisal of the German Revolution of 1848 by F. Meinecke.

Sources

H. E. Hugo, ed., *The Romantic Reader* (*Viking, 1957). Excellent cross-section of early nineteenth-century literature, with a very helpful introduction.

I. Silone, ed., *The Living Thoughts of Mazzini* (Longmans, Green, 1939). Good selection from the prolific writings of the democratic nationalist.

J. C. Legge, ed., *Rhyme and Revolution in Germany: A Study in German History, Life, Literature, and Character, 1813–1850* (Constable, 1918). An admirable collection, doing full justice to its title.

Note: Virtually all the landmarks in Romantic literature mentioned in the text of this chapter are available in inexpensive paperbound editions.

12

The Impact

of the Economic Revolutions

I   The Industrial Revolution

On May 1, 1851, in London, Queen Victoria opened the "Great Exhibition of the Works of Industry of All Nations." The first of many "world's fairs," this international exposition displayed the latest mechanical marvels in a setting that was itself a marvel of engineering—the Crystal Palace, a structure of iron and glass stretching like a mammoth greenhouse for more than a third of a mile in Hyde Park. To the visitors who thronged the Crystal Palace it was evident that Britain was the workshop of the world. To succeeding generations the London exhibition marked the heyday of British leadership in the industrial revolution. Machines and factories had already begun to change the face of Britain in the late eighteenth century (see Chapter 8), and in the century since 1851 they have transformed

447

not only Britain and other western nations but also many other countries on the globe.

By the mid-nineteenth century revolutionary changes in technology and business organization were exerting a revolutionary impact on society and politics. Industrialism bound nations closer together by stimulating international trade and by lowering the barriers of distance through improved transport and communication. Yet it heightened international tensions by fortifying nationalism with economic appetite and by inspiring a bloodless war for markets and raw materials. Businessmen demanded that governments pursue policies that would foster economic development, and they sought the political rights that would give them a voice in determining those policies. By making goods cheaper and more plentiful, industrialism raised standards of living and enabled increasing numbers of men to enjoy the decencies and comforts of existence. Yet it created problems of unemployment, low wages, and bad living and working conditions. Laborers clamored for the right to work, the right to organize, to strike, and to vote.

The rise of industry and labor inspired divergent schools of economic and social thought. The classical economists advocated laissez-faire, preaching that the state should let the economy regulate itself, and that what was good for business was bound to be good for labor, too. If a worker wanted economic security and political status, he should win them through his own efforts, by getting rich, as Guizot had advised the citizens of the July Monarchy. Another school of liberals, however, believed that state intervention in economic life might sometimes be justified to protect or assist the working class. The prospect of moderate reform and of gradual advance toward democracy offered by these liberals satisfied some workers. Others, however, hoping for swifter achievement of their goals, favored the more drastic but still peaceful changes of the type recommended by Louis Blanc and his fellow advocates of Utopian socialism. Still others accepted revolutionary socialism, the violent and inevitable class war predicted by Marx and Engels.

The industrial revolution thus brought to the fore economic and political issues that are still very much alive today. It created a new labor problem and intensified the older farm problem. It sharpened the differences between the champions of relatively free international trade and the economic nationalists who demanded protective tariffs. It divided liberals into the opponents and the defenders of the benevolent or welfare state. It created a radical wing of the working class, soon to be split between the rival schools of Utopian and Marxian socialism. It altered the course of human history even more radically than did a great political upheaval like the French Revolution of 1789. The forces that produced these momentous changes fully deserve to be recognized by history as the industrial revolution.

Preparation and Take-off

What has made some historians shy away from the term "industrial revolution" is the fact that economic change occurred both too slowly and too peacefully to be called truly revolutionary. The American economic historian, W. W. Rostow, has suggested that three stages may be discerned in a given country's emergence into the industrial age — preparation, take-off, and the final phase when the economy is self-sustaining and self-renewing and is, so to speak, in orbit. In Britain the crucial take-off stage was reached in the latter half of the eighteenth century as a result of the steam engine, the spinning jenny, and other inventions. While the take-off came relatively abruptly, it had been preceded by a preparatory stage lasting hundreds of years. This stage has been traced all the way back to the monasteries of the early Middle Ages, which, by their insistence on discipline and on the performance of specified tasks at specified times, have been likened to a model for the organization of the laboring force in a mine or mill.

The factors that prepared Europe and America for industrialism included, obviously, the capitalism of medieval and Renaissance bankers and merchants, and the colonialism and mercantilism of the sixteenth and subsequent centuries. Less obviously, they also included most of the forces that shaped the early modern world. The rise of the competitive state system, the Protestant stress on hard work, the brushing aside of tradition by the scientists of the seventeenth century and by the *philosophes* of the eighteenth—all played their part in creating a society ready for sweeping economic changes. Although the ultimate causes of the industrial revolution involved political, religious, and intellectual activities, its immediate causes were largely economic. Four interlocking developments, beginning in the eighteenth century, directly produced the industrial revolution of the nineteenth: (1) the increasing application of power-driven machinery to the processes of production; (2) the more efficient production of coal, iron, and steel; (3) the construction of railroads and other swift methods of transport and communication; and (4) the expansion of banking and credit facilities.

In the mid-nineteenth century, cotton was the king of mechanized industries. Beginning with the spinning jenny in the 1760's, the use of machinery gradually spread to many phases of cotton manufacturing. In 1793, the American Eli Whitney devised the cotton "gin," an engine that separated the fibers of the raw cotton from the seeds and enabled a single slave to do what had previously required the hand labor of fifty slaves. Meanwhile, British inventors perfected a power-driven loom for weaving cotton thread into cloth. By 1830, Britain operated more than 50,000 power looms, and cotton goods accounted for half of her exports. The British census of 1851 listed more than half a million workers employed in cotton manufacturing alone.

Advances in mechanical engineering made this rapid expansion possible. Earlier, for instance, the difficulty of securing exactly fitting parts had hampered the use of machines like Watt's steam engine. Then British engineers studied the precision techniques used by watchmakers. They devised a lathe that turned screws of almost perfect regularity, and they developed machines for sawing, boring, and turning the pulley blocks used by British vessels in the Napoleonic Wars. Eli Whitney, meantime, was undertaking important experiments at his arms factory in Connecticut. He explained that he planned to "make the same parts of different guns, as the locks, for exam-

Power looms in a factory, about 1820.

ple, as much like each other as the successive impressions of a copperplate engraving." In other words, Whitney was utilizing the concept of standardized parts, one of the basic principles of mass production.

Many American and British manufacturers, however, ignored the revolutionary implications of Whitney's experiments. The tempo of mechanization, though quickening, was held back by the survival of handicraft techniques. Even in cotton, weaving on the hand loom long continued in districts with a large reservoir of cheap labor, like Ireland and Central Europe, where peasants could produce cloth in their cottages. In the woolen and clothing industries mechanization did not come until the 1850's, when Britain produced a machine for wool-combing and the American, Isaac Singer, popularized the sewing-machine.

Coal and Iron

Coal ranked with cotton as an industry that pioneered in the solution of technical problems. Steam engines pumped water from the mines; ventilating shafts and power fans supplied them with fresh air; and safety lamps gave miners protection against dangerous underground gases. The coal output of Britain, then the world's leading producer, rose steadily from about 16,000,000 tons in 1816, to 30,000,000 in 1836, and 65,000,000 in 1856. The increased consumption of coal resulted from its growing use as a household fuel in wood-short Britain, from its importance in producing steam power, and from its contribution to the expanding iron industry, which consumed large quantities of coal to make the coke needed in smelting.

The efficiency of smelting advanced rapidly after the development of the blast furnace (1828), in which fans provided a blast of hot air to intensify the action of the hot coke on the iron. Thanks to the blast furnace, Britain produced iron strong enough for use in bridges and in factory buildings. Yet the best grade of iron lacked the tremendous strength of steel, which is iron purified of all but a

minute fraction of carbon by a process of prolonged, intensive heating. Steel for industrial purposes could be made in the early 1800's, but only by ruinously expensive methods. Then in 1856 Bessemer, an Englishman of French extraction, invented the converter, which accelerated the removal of impurities by shooting jets of compressed air into the molten metal. A decade later, Siemens, a German living in England, devised the "open-hearth" process, which utilized scrap as well as new iron, and which handled larger amounts of metal than the converter could. The inventions of Bessemer and Siemens lowered the cost of making steel so substantially that the world output increased tenfold between 1865 and 1880.

Transport and Communication

The railroad consumed large amounts of iron and steel (on the average, 300 tons were required for a single mile of track). The revolution in transport began early in the nineteenth century with the growth of canals and hard-surfaced roads. During the century's first three decades many hundreds of miles of canals were dug in Europe and in North America, and highway construction was improved by the Scot, McAdam, who devised the durable road surface of broken stones that still bears his name. Shippers, however, also required a means to convey overland heavy items like coal and iron; the railroad furnished the solution. In the 1820's, methods of rolling rails and constructing solid roadbeds were already known, and only mechanization remained to be accomplished. Then George Stephenson and others put the steam engine on wheels and created the locomotive. In 1830, Stephenson's "Rocket" demonstrated its power by running twelve miles in fifty-three minutes on the new Liverpool and Manchester Railway, the first line to be operated entirely by steam. The railroad building boom was soon in full swing: Britain had 500 miles of track in 1838, 6,600 miles in 1850, and 15,500 in 1870.

Steam also revolutionized water transport,

though more gradually. Fulton's steamboat, the "Clermont," made a successful trip on the Hudson River in 1807, and soon paddle-wheel steamers plied the inland waterways of the United States and Europe. Ocean-going steamships, by contrast, long proved uneconomical to operate because of the inefficiency of the marine engine for long trips. When the Scot, Samuel Cunard, inaugurated the first regular transatlantic steamer service (between Liverpool and Boston in 1840), the coal required for the voyage took up almost half of the space on his vessels. Consequently, only passengers and mails went by steamship; most freight was still handled in sailing ships, like the beautiful and efficient American clippers. Finally, in the 1860's, the development of improved marine engines and the substitution of the screw propeller for the cumbersome paddle wheel forecast the eventual doom of the commercial sailing vessel. All these improvements in transport by sea and land greatly aided industry by facilitating shipments of raw materials and finished products and by opening up almost the whole world as a potential market.

Meanwhile, communications were also experiencing radical improvements. A beginning was made in 1840, when Great Britain inaugurated the penny post: to send a letter from London to Edinburgh, for instance, now cost only a penny, less than one-tenth of the old rate. More dramatic was the utilization of electricity for instantaneous communication. An impressive series of "firsts" started with the first telegraph message, from Baltimore to Washington in 1844. Then came the first submarine cable, under the English Channel in 1851; the first transatlantic cable, 1866; and the first telephone, 1876.

Banking and Capital

The exploitation of all these new inventions and discoveries required a constant flow of fresh capital. From the first, the older commercial community supported the young industrial community. The slave traders of Liverpool financed the cotton mills of Manchester and other nearby towns in Lancashire, thereby increasing the demand for American raw cotton and for slaves to grow the cotton. Tobacco merchants of Glasgow provided the funds that made their city the foremost industrial center of Scotland, and tea merchants in London and Bristol aided the ironmasters of South Wales. Bankers played such an important role that Disraeli, the British politician, listed the Barings of London and the international house of Rothschild among the great powers of Europe. In the early nineteenth century each of the five Rothschild brothers, sons of a German Jewish banker, established himself in an important economic center—London, Paris, Frankfurt, Naples, and Vienna. The Rothschilds prospered because, in an age of frequent speculation, they avoided unduly risky undertakings, and because they facilitated investment by residents of one state in the projects of other states. The Paris Rothschild, for instance, negotiated the investment of British capital in the construction of French railroads during the 1840's.

Banks further assisted economic expansion by promoting the use of checks and banknotes in place of specie. During the Napoleonic Wars the shortage of coins forced some British mill-owners to pay their workers in goods; the British government empowered local banks to issue paper notes supplementing the meager supply of coins. But whenever financial crises occurred—and they came frequently before 1850—dozens of local banks failed and their notes became valueless. Parliament therefore encouraged the absorption of small shaky banks by the larger and more solid institutions, and in 1844 it gave the Bank of England a virtual monopoly of the issuing of banknotes, thus providing a very reliable paper currency. It also applied, first to railroads and then to other companies, the principle of limited liability, indicated by the familiar "Ltd." after the names of British firms. Earlier, the shareholders in most British companies had unlimited liability: they might find their personal fortunes appropriated to satisfy the creditors of an unsuccessful company. The practice of limiting each shareholder's liability to the value of his shares encouraged investors by diminishing their risks.

The Timetable of Industrialization

The ready availability of capital was only one factor among many accounting for Britain's head start in industrial development. She possessed large and easily available deposits of coal and iron; the geographical compactness of the British Isles made shipments from mine to smelter and from mill to seaport short and cheap. Britain had a large reservoir of potential factory labor in the marginal farmers, driven off the land by the enclosure movement, and in the Irish, emigrating from their poverty-ridden and overcrowded island. The commercial and naval leadership gained by Britain in the eighteenth century and fortified by the Napoleonic Wars paved the way for her industrial leadership. It facilitated the search for raw materials and markets, and the profits from overseas trade

and the empire swelled investment in industry. The Napoleonic Wars themselves stimulated demand for metal goods and the invention of new machines. And the construction of great docks along the lower Thames during the wars entrenched London in its position as the greatest economic center in Europe.

Finally, it has also been argued, the fact that Britain did not have the rigid and elaborate centralized administrative structure found in France and other continental countries permitted more flexibility in accepting new enterprises. If, for example, a capitalist who wanted to set up a factory found himself blocked by vested interests in one locality, he simply went to another, where the local authorities were more agreeable. Thus it was that Manchester, which had the barest minimum of governmental apparatus in the eighteenth century, became the textile capital not only of Lancashire but also of the world.

In the mid-nineteenth century, the tangible signs of Britain's economic predominance were evident on every hand—in the teeming London docks, in the thriving financial houses of the City, in the exhibits at the Crystal Palace, in the mushrooming factory and mining towns of the Midlands, the North of England, and Scotland, and in other quarters of the globe as well. British capital and thousands of skilled British workers participated in the construction of French railroads. American trains ran on rails rolled in British mills and on the capital from British investors. Cotton goods made in Lancashire clothed a sizable part of the world's population, and British entrepreneurs and inventors brought the industrial revolution to Belgium and parts of Germany.

Britain, even in the heyday of her leadership, did not monopolize inventive skill. Frenchmen, for example, devised the chlorine process of bleaching cloth and the Jacquard loom for weaving intricate patterns. German technicians led the world in agricultural chemistry and in the utilization of the valuable by-products of coal. And from the United States came Eli Whitney and the cotton gin, Morse and the telegraph, Singer and the sewing machine, and Cyrus McCormick, whose

Industrial United States, 1860

Coal fields
Iron ore deposits
Principal manufacturing cities

reaper (1831) was the first of many agricultural machines developed in America.

The timetable of industrialization depended on much besides inventions; factories required raw materials, large amounts of capital and skilled labor, and a favorable political climate. The presence of all these elements made Britain the workshop of the world in the nineteenth century. But when other countries, notably the United States and Germany, began to enjoy a favorable combination of industrial requisites, Britain lost the advantage of her head start. Although the textiles of New England had been flourishing since the early 1800's, the exploitation of rich agricultural resources dominated the American economy until the time of the Civil War. Then the United States reached the stage of industrial "take-off." Germany followed suit under the stimulus of the successful completion of political unification in 1871.

Since the turn of the century the industrial revolution has continued: Japan, Russia, and others have joined the ranks of those whose economies have "taken off." Oil and electricity have ended the dominance of coal; aluminum and the alloys have challenged that of steel; rayon and other synthetic fibers have partly displaced cotton and wool; automobiles, trucks, and airplanes have partly superseded the railroad. Industry has created great corporations, which are virtually powers in their own right; it has made possible the newspaper, television, and other media of mass communication; it has devised assembly-line methods of mass production applicable to many fields of human endeavor. The full implications of industrialization, especially since 1900, will become more evident in later chapters of this book. In this chapter, we shall stress its economic and social consequences in the nineteenth century.

II   Economic and Social Consequences of Industrialization

The Agricultural Revolution

The industrial and agricultural revolutions have always been interdependent. Industry relies on a more efficient agriculture for raw materials and for additions to its labor force, recruited from surplus workers no longer needed on mechanized farms; agriculture depends on industry for the tools and short-cuts that enable fewer and fewer men to produce more and more. In the nineteenth century, factory-made implements like the steel plow and the reaper improved the cultivation of old farmlands and permitted the opening of vast new areas, like the North American prairies, that could scarcely have been touched if the pioneers had had to rely on hand labor. The mechanical cream-separator raised the dairy industry to a big business, and railroads and steamers sped the transport of produce from farm to market. The processes of canning, refrigeration, and freezing, all industrial in origin and all first applied on a wide scale during the last third of the century, permitted the preservation of many perishable commodities.

Farmers found a steadily growing market both in the industrial demand for raw materials and in the food needs of the mining and factory towns. International trade in farm products increased rapidly during the second half of the nineteenth century. The annual export of wheat from the United States and Canada rose from 22,000,000 bushels in the 1850's to 150,000,000 in 1880. Imported flour accounted for one-quarter of the bread consumed in Britain during the 1850's and for one-half in the 1870's. Denmark and the Netherlands increasingly furnished the British table with bacon, butter, eggs, and cheese; Australia supplied its mutton and Argentina its beef.

Germany now partly assumed Britain's old role as the pioneer of scientific agriculture. German experimenters, shortly after 1800, extracted sugar from beets in commercially important quantities, thus ending Europe's dependence on the cane sugar of the West Indies. In the 1840's the German chemist, Liebig, published a series of influential works on the agricultural applications of organic chemistry. Plant growth, Liebig argued, depended on three basic elements—nitrogen, potassium, and phosphorus. But the production of crops and fodder leached these elements from the soil; unless they could be returned to it, fertile lands might go the way of "the once prolific soil of Virginia, now in many parts no longer able to grow its former staple productions—wheat and tobacco." Liebig's warnings promoted the wide use of fertilizers—guano from the nesting islands of sea-birds off the west coast of South America, nitrate from Chile, and potash from European mines.

Farming progressed and prospered in the nineteenth century as never before. Yet the agricultural revolution exacted a price, sometimes a very high price. Faced with the competition of beet sugar, the sugar-cane islands of the West Indies went into a permanent depression, from which some of them have never fully recovered. In the highly industrialized countries the social and political importance of agricultural interests began to decline. Farming was no longer the principal occupation of Englishmen in the nineteenth century, and land was no longer the almost universal yardstick of wealth and power. The manufacturers and merchants of Britain scored a decisive victory over the landed gentry in the campaign to repeal the Corn Laws, the tariffs on the importation of the wheat and other cereals which the English term collectively "corn." The powerful Anti-Corn Law

League protested that the tariffs "artificially enhance the price of food," and "prevent the exchange of the products of industry for the food of other countries." Free trade was the remedy prescribed by the Anti-Corn Law League, and free trade came when Parliament repealed the Corn Laws in 1846. The decisive factor was the disastrous attack of black rot that ruined the Irish potato crop two years running and made the importation of cheap grain imperative to prevent the worsening of an already disastrous famine in Ireland, as the next chapter will show in more detail. Great Britain thus abandoned the attempt to be self-sustaining in food.

Changes in Population

As a matter of fact, the population of the British Isles was growing so rapidly that self-sufficiency was virtually impossible. Despite substantial emigration, the number of inhabitants in England and Wales more than tripled during the course of the nineteenth century, from about 9,000,000 in 1800 to 32,500,000 in 1900. Demographers tend to believe that the increase may be attributed not to an increased birth rate but to the lowered death rate resulting from the improved standard of living brought by the economic revolutions. In a predominantly agrarian country like Russia, which also experienced a steady rise in population (36,000,000 in 1800, about 100,000,000 in 1900), the experts attribute the growth also to a high birth rate.

In any event, the most important social change flowing from the industrial revolution was not the increase of the population but the alteration of its structure and balance. Wherever mines and factories were opened, towns and cities appeared. Large areas of once-rural England became urban England, and a similar transformation was beginning in the lowlands of Scotland around Glasgow, in the northern French plain around Lille, in the German Rhineland, and along the rivers of the northeastern United States. The growth of an urban population caused a rise in the numbers and influence of the two social classes that form the backbone of an industrial society. These are the businessmen and the workingmen. Industrialists, bankers, managers, and promoters of every sort joined the already established capitalists to form the modern middle class or bourgeoisie, Millhands, railwaymen, miners, clerks, and a host of other recruits swelled the ranks of wage-earning laborers.

The impact of capital and labor upon the life of industrial nations was becoming increasingly evident by the middle of the nineteenth century. Some of the signs pointed to steady material progress—the wonders of the Crystal Palace, or the conquest of space by the railroad, the steamship, and the telegraph. Other signs, however, portended serious dislocation and violent change. The repeal of the Corn Laws buried an old agrarian way of life

Conservative politicians defending the Corn Laws: The Earl of Derby says, "Now Gents, give us only a little encouragement—say a 5-shilling duty, and up goes the Quartern loaf."

"Work," by Ford Madox Brown, 1852.

in Britain. The collapse of the French railroad boom in the late 1840's suggested that in an industrial society economic slumps might have alarming consequences, for the hundreds of thousands thrown out of work aggravated the political unrest in Paris and, as we have seen, formed part of the background of the June Days of 1848.

Now it is essential for the student of history to fix his attention on both the disruptive social effects of the industrial revolution and the peaceful improvements it made possible in society. Unemployment and the other miseries of industrial labor have produced some of the most sordid pages of modern history, but they do not tell the whole story. The slums of the ugly new factory towns were often horrible indeed, yet they sometimes represented a

positive improvement over the rural slums in which the grandparents of the millhands had lived. Too often, white-washed or vine-covered country cottages concealed behind their picturesque exteriors a contaminated water supply, a total lack of sanitary facilities, and an appalling incidence of infant mortality and tuberculosis. In the cities, infant mortality dropped because of improvements in medicine and sanitation. Adults lived longer because they had better medical facilities, ate a more balanced and nourishing diet, and observed a higher standard of personal cleanliness. The economic revolutions increased the supply of fresh food and permitted the use of cheap and washable cotton clothing in place of woolens which were seldom, if ever, laundered.

The Aspirations of the Middle Class

Both the businessmen and the workingmen nourished grievances—and aspirations. A revealing view of middle-class complaints and hopes is given in a famous parable published in 1819 by the French social planner, Saint-Simon. Saint-Simon supposed that France suddenly lost fifty of her best mechanical engineers, of her finest architects, doctors, bankers —and so on through a long list comprising the three thousand leading men in business, science, and the arts. These men, Saint-Simon stated, are "the most useful to their country"; "the nation would become a lifeless corpse as soon as it lost them."

Let us pass on to another assumption. Suppose that France preserves all the men of genius that she possesses in the sciences, fine arts and professions, but has the misfortune to lose in the same day Monsieur the King's brother [and many other members of the royal family]. Suppose that France loses at the same time all the great officers of the royal household, all the ministers (with or without portfolio), all the councillors of state, all the chief magistrates, marshals, cardinals, archbishops, bishops, vicars-general, judges, and, in addition, ten thousand of the richest proprietors who live in the style of nobles.

This mischance would certainly distress the French, because they are kind-hearted, and could not see with indifference the sudden disappearance of such a large number of their compatriots. But this loss of thirty thousand individuals, considered to be the most important in the State, would only grieve them for purely sentimental reasons and would result in no political evil for the State.

These suppositions underline the most important fact of present politics: . . . that our social organization is seriously defective. . . .

The scientists, artists, and artisans, the only men whose work is of positive utility to society, and cost it practically nothing, are kept down by the princes and other rulers who are simply more or less incapable bureaucrats. Those who control honours and other national awards owe, in general, the supremacy they enjoy, to the accident of birth, to flattery, intrigue and other dubious methods. . . .

These suppositions show that society is a world which is upside down.*

To the men of the middle class, society indeed seemed upside down. In the Britain of the 1820's the new industrialists had small opportunity to mold national policy. Booming industrial cities like Manchester and Birmingham sent not a single representative to the House of Commons. A high proportion of businessmen belonged not to the Church of England but to non-Anglican Protestant chapels; nonconformists, as these dissenters were now termed, still suffered discrimination when it came to holding public office or sending their sons to Oxford or Cambridge. Even in France, despite the gains made since 1789, the bourgeois enjoyed as yet only the second-class status sketched by Saint-Simon.

The middle classes very soon won the place in the sun which they felt they deserved. In Britain, the gradual process of reform gave them substantially all they wanted. The high spot, higher even than the repeal of the Corn Laws, was the Reform Bill of 1832, which extended the suffrage to the middle class (for details, see Chapter 13). In France, as we have already seen, the bourgeois had their revolution in 1830 and got their citizen-king. In Belgium, the revolution of 1830 marked a very great advance in the power of the middle class. Elsewhere the movements of 1830 and 1848 had less favorable results, yet even at their most disappointing they represented a step forward in the political evolution of the middle class.

The Grievances of the Working Class

The grievances of workingmen were more numerous than those of their masters, and they were more difficult to satisfy. The difficulties may be illustrated by the long struggle of laborers to secure the vote and the right to organize and to carry on union activities. In Britain, substantial numbers of workers first

*Saint-Simon, *Selected Writings*, F.M.H. Markham, ed. (New York, 1952), 72–74.

secured the vote in 1867, a generation after the enfranchisement of the wealthier middle class. In France, universal male suffrage was tried for a brief period starting in 1848; it became permanent only with the establishment of the Third Republic after 1870. The unified German Empire had a democratic suffrage from its inception in 1871, but without some other institutions of democracy. Elsewhere, universal manhood suffrage came slowly — in Belgium (1893), and not until the twentieth century in Italy, Austria, Russia and, more surprisingly in the light of their subsequent reputation for progressive democracy, in Sweden, Denmark, and the Netherlands as well.

During most of the nineteenth century, labor unions and strikes were regarded as improper restraints on the free operation of natural economic laws. Hence the specific ban on such combinations, as they were termed, imposed by the British Combination Acts at the close of the eighteenth century. Continental governments imposed similar restrictions, as in the Le Chapelier Law passed by the French National Assembly in 1791. It took labor a long time to win legal recognition of union activities — until 1890 in Germany, for instance, 1867 in Austria, and 1872 in the Netherlands. In France, the July Monarchy repressed strikes with great brutality; the Le Chapelier Law was relaxed in the 1860's and finally repealed outright in 1884. In Britain, Parliament modified the Combination Acts early, in the 1820's but did not repeal them until 1876.

Labor's drive for political and legal rights, however, was only a side issue during the early days of the industrial revolution. Many workmen faced more pressing problems: they had to find jobs and to make ends meet on inadequate wages. The modern western world had long experienced the business cycle, with its alternations of full employment and substantial unemployment. The industrial revolution intensified the cycle. Boom periods became more hectic, and general depressions, like that of the late 1840's, became more frequent and more severe. Factories at first made little attempt to provide a fairly steady level of employment in both boom times and slack times. When a batch of orders came in, machines and men were worked to capacity until the orders were filled. Then the factory simply shut down to await the next batch.

A century and more ago labor sometimes got such low wages that a family man might have to put both his children and his wife to work as a matter of sheer economic necessity. Humanitarian tradition probably exaggerates the extent to which industry exploited and degraded women and children, probably tends to view the exceptional instance of extreme hardship as the average situation. Nevertheless, exploitation and degradation did occur. Here is the testimony of a factory worker, Samuel Coulson, before a British parliamentary committee in 1831–1832:

At what time in the morning, in the brisk time, did those girls go to the mills?
In the brisk time, for about six weeks, they have gone at 3 o'clock in the morning, and ended at 10, or nearly half-past, at night.

What intervals were allowed for rest or refreshment during those nineteen hours of labour?
Breakfast a quarter of an hour, and dinner half an hour, and drinking a quarter of an hour.

Was any of that time taken up in cleaning the machinery?
They generally had to do what they call dry down; sometimes this took the whole of the time at breakfast or drinking, and they were to get their dinner or breakfast as they could; if not, it was brought home.

Had you not great difficulty in awakening your children to this excessive labour?
Yes, in the early time we had them to take up asleep and shake them when we got them on the floor to dress them, before we could get them off to their work; but not so in the common hours.

What was the length of time they could be in bed during those long hours?
It was near 11 o'clock before we could get them into bed after getting a little victuals, and then at morning my mistress used to stop up all night, for fear that we could not get them ready for the time. . . .

So that they had not above four hours' sleep at this time?
No, they had not.

For how long together was it?
About six weeks it held; it was only done when the throng was very much on; it was not often that.

The common hours of labour were from 6 in the morning till half-past eight at night?
Yes.

With the same intervals for food?
Yes, just the same.

Were the children excessively fatigued by this labour?
Many times; we have cried often when we have given them the little victualling we had to give them; we had to shake them, and they have fallen to sleep with the victuals in their mouths many a time.

Did this excessive term of labour occasion much cruelty also?
Yes, with being so very much fatigued the strap was very frequently used.

. . .

What was the wages in the short hours?
Three shillings a week each.

When they wrought those very long hours what did they get?
Three shillings and sevenpence halfpenny.

For all that additional labour they had only sevenpence halfpenny a week additional?
No more.*

Excessively long hours, low pay, rigorous discipline, and subhuman working conditions were the most general grievances of early industrial workers. Many plants neglected hazards to their employees, few had safety devices to guard dangerous machinery, and cotton mills maintained both the heat and the humidity at an uncomfortable level because threads broke less often in a hot, damp atmosphere. Many workers could not afford decent housing, and if they could afford it, they could not always find it. Some of the new factory towns were reasonably well planned, with wide streets and space for yards and parks. Some even had a copious supply of good water and arrangements for disposing of sewage. But many had none of these necessities, and in rapidly growing London the Thames soon became an open sewer so foul that riverside

*Bland, Brown, and Tawney, *English Economic History: Select Documents* (London, 1915), 510–513.

Child laborers in a textile factory, about 1840.

dwellers were reluctant to open their windows. Fantastic numbers of human beings were jammed into the over-crowded slums of Lille in France and of Liverpool and Manchester in Lancashire.

Lord Shaftesbury, an English reformer of the 1840's, predicted that, unless conditions were improved, Lancashire would soon become a "province of pigmies." It was estimated that the life expectancy of a boy born to a working-class family in Manchester was only half that of one born to rural laborers. The industrial nations also threatened to remain nations of semi-literates. Until they made provisions for free public schools, during the last third of the nineteenth century, educational facilities were grossly inadequate. In England, as often as not, only the Sunday school gave the millhand's child a chance to learn his abc's. The millhand himself, if he had great ambition and fortitude, might attend one of the adult schools known as "mechanics' institutes." No wonder that in the 1840's one-third of the men and one-half of the woman married in England could not sign their names on the marriage register and simply made their mark. And no wonder that Disraeli, the Tory reformer, in his novel, *Sybil,* called Britain "two nations"—the rich and the poor.

III   The Responses of Liberalism

The Classical Economists

Faced with the widening cleavage between rich and poor, nineteenth-century liberals at first held to the doctrine of laissez-faire.

Suffering and evil are nature's admonitions; they cannot be got rid of; and the impatient attempts of benevolence to banish them from the world by legislation . . . have always been productive of more evil than good.*

Such was the argument advanced by liberals in the British Parliament against the first piece of legislation proposed to safeguard public health. The thinkers who advanced these ideas in the early nineteenth century are known to history as the classical economists; to their enemies they were the architects of the "dismal science." The most famous of them were two Englishmen, Thomas Malthus (1766–1834) and David Ricardo (1772–1823).

"Dismal science" is hardly too strong a term for the theories of Malthus. Though educated for the ministry, Malthus became perhaps the very first professional economist in history. In 1798, he published the famous *Essay on the Principles of Population,* a dramatic warning that the human species would breed itself into starvation. In the *Essay,* Malthus formulated a series of natural laws:

The power of population is indefinitely greater than the power in earth to produce subsistence for man.

Population, when unchecked, increases in a geometrical ratio. Subsistence only increases in an arithmetical ratio. . . . Through the animal and vegetable kingdoms, nature has scattered the seeds of life abroad with the most profuse and liberal hands. She has been comparatively sparing in the room and the nourishment necessary to rear them. . . . Necessity, that imperious, all-pervading law of nature, restrains them within the prescribed bounds. Among plants and animals its effects are waste of seed, sickness, and premature death. Among mankind, misery and vice.*

Misery and vice would spread, Malthus believed, because the unchecked increase in human numbers would lower the demand for labor and therefore lower the wages of labor.

When the wages of labour are hardly sufficient to maintain two children, a man marries and has

The Economist, May 13, 1848.

Essay on the Principles of Population, Bk. I, Ch. 1.

five or six. He of course finds himself miserably distressed. He accuses the insufficiency of the price of labour to maintain a family. . . . He accuses the partial and unjust institutions of society, which have awarded him an inadequate share of the produce of the earth. He accuses perhaps the dispensations of Providence, which have assigned to him a place in society so beset with unavoidable distress and dependence. In searching for objects of accusation, he never adverts to the quarter from which his misfortunes originate. The last person that he would think of accusing is himself, on whom in fact the whole of the blame lies. . . .*

The reduction of the human birth rate was the only hope that this prophet of gloom held out to suffering humanity. It was to be achieved by "moral restraint," specifically by late marriage and by "chastity till that period arrives."

Ricardo, too, was a prophet of gloom. He attributed economic activity to three main forces: there was rent, paid to the owners of great natural resources like farmland and mines; there was profit, accruing to the enterprising individuals who exploited these resources; and there were wages, paid to the workers who performed the actual labor of exploitation. Of the three, rent was in the long run the most important. Farms and mines would become depleted and exhausted, but their produce would continue in great demand. Rent, accordingly, would consume an ever larger share of the "economic pie," leaving smaller and smaller portions for profit-making capitalists and wage-earning workers.

Ricardo tempered his pessimistic forecasts with many qualifications and reservations. He did not, for instance, believe that the size of the economic pie was altogether fixed, in other words, that the total wealth of mankind was irrevocably "frozen." Still, he did sketch a picture of eventual stagnation, and of man as the exploiter, the depleter, the wastrel. Adam Smith had cheerfully predicted an increasing division of labor, accompanied by steadily rising wages. Ricardo, in contrast, brought labor and wages under the Malthusian formula:

The market price of labour is the price which is

*Ibid., Bk. IV, Ch. 3.

really paid for it, from the natural operation of the proportion of the supply to the demand; labour is dear when it is scarce, and cheap when it is plentiful. . . . It is when the market price of labour exceeds its natural price, that the condition of the labourer is flourishing and happy. . . . When, however, by the encouragement which high wages give to the increase of population, the number of labourers is increased, wages again fall to their natural price, and indeed . . . sometimes fall below it.*

Ricardo's disciples hardened this principle into the "Iron Law of Wages," which bound workmen to an everlasting cycle of high wages and large families, followed by an increase in the labor supply, a corresponding increase in the competition for jobs, and an inevitable slump in wages. Ricardo himself, however, regarded the cycle not as an "iron law" but simply as a probability. Unforeseen factors might in the future modify its course and might even permit a gradual improvement of the worker's lot.

While it is easy to see why Malthus and Ricardo were regarded as great exponents of laissez-faire, it is more difficult to understand why they were also ranked among liberals. Yet the classical economists were indeed liberals in a sense; like the *philosophes*, they did not doubt that natural laws were superior to man-made laws. What distinguished the classical economists from their eighteenth-century predecessors was their pessimism. Adherents of the "dismal science" no longer viewed nature as the creation of the beneficent God of the deists; she was at best a neutral force and at worst a sinister one. Man himself—wasteful, careless, improvident—seemed once more afflicted with a kind of original sin. The classical economists supplied a needed corrective to the naive optimism of the *philosophes*.

Yet the classical economists, too, had their naive faith. They viewed the economy as a world-machine governed by a few simple, almost unalterable laws—Malthusian laws of population, Ricardian laws of rent and wages. The history of the last century has demon-

*On the Principles of Political Economy, Ch. V, in The Works and Correspondence of David Ricardo, P. Sraffa, ed. (Cambridge, England, 1951), I, 94.

strated the inadequacy of their view. The size of the economic pie has expanded far beyond the expectations of Ricardo, and so have the portions allotted to rent, to profit, and to wages. Malthus did not foresee that scientific advances would make the output of agriculture expand at a nearly geometrical ratio. He did not foresee that the perils of increasing birthrates would sometimes be averted by the use of contraceptives, first popularized during the nineteenth century, or by recourse to emigration. Many millions of people moved from crowded Europe to lightly populated America during the nineteenth century. The exodus from overcrowded Ireland, in particular, continued so briskly after the famine of the 1840's that by 1900 the Irish population was little more than half what it had been fifty years earlier.

Although the classical economists did not take sufficient account of the immense changes being worked by the agricultural and industrial revolutions, the laissez-faire liberalism that they championed won particular approval from the new industrial magnates. The captains of industry were perhaps disturbed by Ricardo's prediction that profits would inevitably shrink; but they could take comfort from the theory that "suffering and evil" were "nature's admonitions." It was consoling to the rich to be told, in effect, that the poor deserved to be poor because they had indulged their appetites to excess, that whatever was, was right, or at any rate ordained by nature. To the working class, however, the vaunted freedom of laissez-faire often meant freedom to be undernourished, ill-housed, and alternately overworked and unemployed. The poor did not like to hear that they deserved to be poor, and they sometimes felt that whatever was, was wrong and needed to be remedied, if necessary by interference with supposedly sacred natural laws.

To sum up: in the face of positive social evils, the classical economists offered only the essentially negative policy of laissez-faire. They were often very earnest men, honestly convinced that letting nature take her course was the only thing to do. Yet they were open to the accusation of acting without heart and without conscience, and of advancing economic theories that were only rationalizations of their economic interests. It is not surprising that, as a practical and social political philosophy, strict laissez-faire liberalism today is almost extinct.

Utilitarianism: Bentham

The retreat from laissez-faire originated with a man who was himself the friend and patron of the classical economists—Jeremy Bentham (1748–1832). Bentham behaved as popular opinion expects an eccentric philosopher to behave, astonishing his guests by trotting and bobbing about the garden before dinner, or, as he put it, performing his "anteprandial circumgyrations." In death, he directed that his body be mummified and kept at the University College of London, which he had helped to found. In life, he projected dozens of schemes for the improvement of the human race, among them a model prison and reformatory which he called the "Panopticon," because guards stationed in a central block could survey the activities of all the inmates. He coined new words by the dozen, too; some of them have been happily forgotten but others have made valuable contributions to the language, like "minimize," "codify," and "international." Bentham founded his social teachings on the concept of utility, a modern form of the old Epicurean doctrine that morality should be based on the search for pleasure and the avoidance of pain:

Nature has placed mankind under the governance of two sovereign masters, *pain* and *pleasure*. It is for them alone to point out what we ought to do. . . . They govern us in all we can do, in all we say, in all we think: every effort we can make to throw off our subjection, will serve but to demonstrate and confirm it. In words a man may pretend to abjure their empire: but in reality he will remain subject to it all the while. The *principle of utility* recognizes this subjection, and assumes it for the foundation of that system, the object of which is to rear the fabric of felicity by the hands of reason and of law.

. . .

The interest of the community is one of the most general expressions that can occur in the phraseology of morals: no wonder that the meaning of it is often lost. . . . The community is a fictitious *body,* composed of the individual persons who are considered as constituting as it were its *members.* The interest of the community then is, what? — the sum of the interests of the several members who compose it.

It is in vain to talk of the interest of the community without understanding what is the interest of the individual. A thing is said to promote the interest, or to be *for* the interest of an individual, when it tends to add to the sum total of his pleasures: or, what comes to the same thing, to diminish the sum total of his pains.*

Bentham listed a dozen or so simple pleasures and pains — the pleasures of the senses and the corresponding pains, the pleasure of wealth and the pain of privation, the pleasure of skill and the pain of awkwardness, and so on. Each category was subdivided, the pleasures of the senses, for instance, into those of taste, intoxication, smelling, touch, hearing, seeing, sex, health, and novelty. And each pleasure or pain could be evaluated according to its intensity, its duration, its certainty or uncertainty, its propinquity or remoteness, its fecundity, and its purity. This "felicific calculus," as Bentham termed it, was a good example of the Enlightenment's attempts to measure the immeasurable and to apply the exact methods of natural science to the subtleties of human behavior.

Nevertheless, Bentham was no doctrinaire *philosophe* and had no patience with attempts to equate principles with nature's laws. He made short work of the French revolutionaries' Declaration of the Rights of Man: *"Natural rights* is simple nonsense: natural and imprescriptible rights, rhetorical nonsense, — nonsense upon stilts." He dismissed the eighteenth-century theory of political con-

An Introduction to the Principles of Morals and Legislation, Wilfrid Harrison, ed. (New York, 1948), Ch. I, 125–127.

tracts as a mere fiction. Ordinarily, he believed, governments could best safeguard the security of their subjects by following a hands-off policy. In social and economic matters, they should act as "passive policemen," and give private initiative a generally free hand. Hence the close and sympathetic relationship between Bentham and the classical economists. Yet Bentham realized that the state might become a more active policeman when the pursuit of self-interest by some individuals worked against the best interest of other individuals. If the pains endured by the many exceeded the pleasures enjoyed by the few, then the state should step in. In such a situation Bentham believed the state to be, in a word of his own devising, "omnicompetent," fit to undertake anything for the general welfare. Twentieth-century theories of the welfare state owe a considerable debt to his utilitarianism.

By the time of his death, Bentham was already gaining an international reputation. He had advised reformers in Portugal, Russia, Greece, and Egypt, and his writings were to exert a broad influence, particularly in France, Spain, and the Spanish-American republics. As late as 1920, his "Panopticon" provided the plan for an American prison (in Joliet, Illinois). Naturally, his most important disciples were English. The middle-class group called the Philosophic Radicals pressed for parliamentary legislation to reform and simplify court procedures and local government. Their aims, however, were sometimes so narrowly utilitarian that critics claimed they wanted to drain life of all its savor and variety. Dickens lambasted them and the laissez-faire liberals to boot in his novel, *Hard Times,* with its famous description of Coketown:

. . . .It contained several large streets all very like one another, and many small streets still more like one another, inhabited by people equally like one another, who all went in and out at the same hours, with the same sound upon the same pavements, to do the same work, and to whom every day was the same as yesterday and to-morrow, and every year the counterpart of the last and the next.

You saw nothing in Coketown but what was

severely workful. If the members of a religious persuasion built a chapel there—as the members of eighteen religious persuasions had done—they made it a pious warehouse of red brick. . . . All the public inscriptions in the town were painted alike, in severe characters of black and white. The jail might have been the infirmary, the infirmary might have been the jail, the town-hall might have been either, or both, or anything else, for anything that appeared to the contrary in the graces of their construction. Fact, fact, fact everywhere in the material aspect of the town; fact, fact, fact everywhere in the immaterial. The M'Choakumchild school was all fact, and the relations between master and man were all fact, and everything was fact between the lying-in hospital and the cemetery, and what you couldn't state in figures, or show to be purchaseable in the cheapest market and saleable in the dearest, was not, and never should be, world without end, Amen.*

Democratic Liberalism: Mill

The man who injected a new note of democracy and humanity into nineteenth-century liberal teachings was John Stuart Mill (1806–1873). Mill grew up in an atmosphere dense with the teachings of utilitarianism and classical economics. From his father, who worked closely with Bentham and was a good friend of Ricardo, he received an education almost without parallel for intensity and speed. He began the study of Greek at three, was writing history at twelve, and at sixteen organized an active "Utilitarian Society." At the age of twenty the overworked youth suffered a breakdown; as Mill relates in his *Autobiography,* he had become "a mere reasoning machine." So Mill turned for renewal to music and to the poetry of Wordsworth and Coleridge; presently he fell in love with Mrs. Taylor, a woman of warm personality, to whom he assigned the major credit for his later writings. They remained friends for twenty years until the death of Mr. Taylor at length enabled them to marry. Mill's personal history is important, for it goes far to explain why he endowed the liberal creed with the warmth

*Book I, Ch. V.

and compassion it lacked in the hands of the classical economists and utilitarians.

Mill's humane liberalism was expressed most clearly in his essay *On Liberty* (1859) and his *Autobiography* (1873). But it is evident, too, in his more technical works, notably *The Principles of Political Economy.* He first published this enormously successful textbook in 1848 and later revised it several times, each revision departing more and more from the "dismal science" of Ricardo and Malthus. The first edition of the *Principles* rejected the gloomy implications of the "iron law" of wages:

By what means, then, is poverty to be contended against? How is the evil of low wages to be remedied? If the expedients usually recommended for the purpose are not adapted to it, can no others be thought of? Is the problem incapable of solution? Can political economy do nothing, but only object to everything, and demonstrate that nothing can be done?*

*J. S. Mill, *Principles of Political Economy,* Bk. II, Ch. xiii (Boston, 1848).

John Stuart Mill (1806–1873).

Of course something could be done, and Mill proceeded to outline schemes for curbing overpopulation by promoting emigration to the colonies and by "elevating the habits of the labouring people through education."

This one example is typical of the way in which Mill's quest for positive remedies led him to modify the laissez-faire attitude so long associated with liberalism. Although he did not accept the socialistic solution of abolishing private property, he sympathized with the French "National Workshops" of 1848 (see Chapter 11) and with some of the moderate socialistic projects that we shall examine shortly. He asserted that the workers should be allowed to organize trade unions, form co-operatives, obtain higher wages, and even receive a share of profits. These changes could best be secured within the framework of private enterprise, Mill believed, and not by public intervention. But he also believed that there were some matters so pressing that the state would have to step in. He read the reports of parliamentary investigating committees, like that on child labor cited earlier in this chapter, and he was shocked by their accounts of human degradation. So he recommended legislation to protect children and to improve intolerable living and working conditions.

Whereas Bentham had accepted universal suffrage and universal education only as ultimate goals for the distant future, Mill made them immediate objectives. All men, he believed, should have the right to vote; all should be prepared for it by receiving a basic minimum of schooling, if need be at state expense. Moreover, women should have the same rights—for Mill was a pioneer in the movement for feminine emancipation, thanks in part to the influence of Mrs. Taylor. He also proposed the introduction of proportional representation in the House of Commons, so that political minorities might be sure of a voice and might not be overwhelmed by the tyranny of the majority. The proposal and the fears that actuated it are particularly characteristic of Mill. He made protection of the individual's rights the basis of his famous essay *On Liberty:*

A government cannot have too much of the kind of activity which does not impede, but aids and stimulates, individual exertion and development. The mischief begins when, instead of calling forth the activity and powers of individuals and bodies, it substitutes its own activity for theirs; when, instead of informing, advising, and, upon occasion, denouncing, it makes them work in fetters, or bids them stand aside and does their work instead of them. The worth of a State, in the long run, is the worth of the individuals composing it . . . a State which dwarfs its men, in order that they may be more docile instruments in its hands even for beneficial purposes—will find that with small men no great thing can really be accomplished. . . .*

Critics have claimed that Mill's eloquent defense of the dissenting individual had undemocratic implications, for he seemed to mistrust the opinions of the majority to favor those of the intellectual and moral élite. At any rate, Mill did not so much reject as transform the liberalism of the classical economists. He had a more tender conscience than Adam Smith, Ricardo or Bentham, and he lived at a later age, when the defects of industrialism were plainer. Therefore he found the exceptions to the rule of laissez-faire more numerous and urgent than his predecessors had ever imagined them to be. Liberalism, as we understand the term today, is the legacy not of the "dismal scientists" but of Mill and of the enlightened politicians who have shaped the western democracies over the past century.

Utilitarianism, Liberty, and Representative Government, Everyman ed. (New York, 1910), 169 f.

IV   The Socialist Response — the Utopians

In his later years, Mill referred to himself as a "socialist"; by his standard, however, most of us are socialists today. Universal suffrage for men and for women, universal free education, the curbing of laissez-faire in the interests of the general welfare, the use of the taxing power to limit the accumulation of masses of private property — all these major reforms foreseen by Mill are now widely accepted. But they are not authentically socialistic. The authentic socialist does not stop, as Mill did, with changes in the *distribution* of wealth; he goes on to propose a radical change in arrangements for the *production* of goods. The means of production are to be transferred from the control of individuals to the control of the community as a whole.

Socialism — like fascism, liberalism, democracy — is one of those words in the political vocabulary so laden with moral connotations and personal conviction that their real meaning is often obscured. Everyone uses the word, yet mostly to indicate emphatic approval or disapproval of a given policy. The historian, however, attempts to use the word neutrally, for purposes of description and not of passing judgment. Historically, socialism denotes any political or economic philosophy that advocates the vesting of production in the hands of society and not those of private individuals. In practice, it usually means that the state, acting as the trustee of the community, owns major industries like coal, railroads, and steel. Socialism in its most complete form involves public ownership of almost all the instruments of production including the land itself.

Today we tend to call this complete form "communism"; a century ago, however, the terms "socialism" and "communism" were used almost interchangeably. A hundred years of history have gone into making the distinction now usually drawn between the two, which is not simply a matter of more and less complete versions of the same thing. Especially since the Bolshevik Revolution in Russia in 1917, a communist has come to mean someone who believes that the collectivization of property can only be accomplished swiftly and violently, by revolution and outright seizure, while a socialist has come to mean someone who believes that it should be accomplished gradually and peacefully through normal political procedures and with at least some compensation for private owners. Though the ends have their similarities, the means are worlds apart. This highly significant difference started to appear long before 1917, with the development of two divergent schools of socialist thought in the mid-nineteenth century, the Utopian and the Marxian.

The Utopian socialists were essentially good sons of the Enlightenment. If only men would apply their reason to solving the problems of an industrial economy, if only they would wipe out man-made inequalities by letting the great natural law of brotherhood operate freely — then utopia would be within their grasp, and social and economic progress would come about almost automatically. This is the common belief linking together the four chief Utopians of the early nineteenth century — Saint-Simon, Fourier, Robert Owen, and Louis Blanc.

Saint-Simon and Fourier

Henri, Count of Saint-Simon (1760–1825), belonged to a French noble family so old and aristocratic that it claimed direct descent from Charlemagne. Educated by *philosophes*, Saint-Simon fought with the French army in the American War of Independence. During the

French Revolution he won a large fortune by speculating in lands expropriated from the Church and the *émigrés*, then lost most of it through the trickery of an unscrupulous partner. Despite his own reverses, he never lost his enthusiasm for the industrial age, which reached a high pitch in the parable of the old and the new leaders of France, already quoted above, p. 457.

In accord with the parable, Saint-Simon would have given supreme political authority to a Parliament of Improvements, composed of 10 industrialists and 5 each of artists, philosophers, chemists, physiologists, physicists, astronomers, and mathematicians, and presided over by one of the mathematicians. He admonished the members of the new elite: "Christianity commands you to use all your powers to increase as rapidly as possible the social welfare of the poor!"* Saint-Simon combined the Enlightenment's respect for science with Romanticism's zeal for the community. So he proclaimed the one science transcending all others to be the application of the Golden Rule. Reform should come peacefully, through "persuasion and demonstration," and it should affect particularly the idlers, the rich drones of existing society. Since all men were brothers, even men of different nations, Saint-Simon envisaged a federation of European states. It would start with a union of the most advanced countries, France and Britain, under the "Council of Newton," and would culminate in the establishment of a European parliament when all states had been "organized" to the point where they could live together in "harmony."

"Organization," "harmony," and "industry" were three of Saint-Simon's catchwords. When all three elements were co-ordinated, he believed, mankind could achieve some of the major improvements he proposed, among them great networks of highways and waterways, including inter-oceanic canals. After Saint-Simon's death, his followers focused on the strain of social Christianity in his teaching and formed a fantastic religious cult. Later followers shared his enthusiasm for public improvements. One of them combined local lines into a great trunk railroad, the Paris-Lyons-Mediterranean; another was Ferdinand de Lesseps, who built the Suez Canal and made an abortive start at digging across the Isthmus of Panama. The very vagueness of Saint-Simon's concepts, and his failure to define them precisely, permitted almost every kind of social thinker, from laissez-faire liberal to communist, to cite him with approval. What was socialistic about Saint-Simon was his goal of achieving the reorganization and harmony of society as a whole, rather than the welfare of its individual members.

Saint-Simon's compatriot and contemporary, Fourier (1772–1837), also extolled harmony, and to achieve it drew up an elaborate blueprint. At the French textile center of Lyons, Fourier was shocked by the wealth of the silk manufacturers and the misery of their workmen. At Paris, he was shocked when he found that a single apple cost a sum that would have bought a hundred apples in the countryside. Clearly, he concluded, something was amiss in a society and economy that permitted such fantastic divergences. He compared the historical importance of his apple with that of Newton, and honestly believed himself to be the Newton of the social sciences. Just as Newton had found the force holding the heavenly bodies in a state of mutual attraction, so Fourier claimed discovery of the force holding the individuals of human society in a state of mutual attraction.

This force was *l'attraction passionnelle:* human beings are drawn to one another by their passions. Fourier drew up a list of passions, rather like the list of pleasures in Bentham's "felicific calculus"—sex, companionship, food, luxury, variety, and so on, to a total of 810. Since existing society thwarted their satisfaction, Fourier proposed its remodeling into units that he called *phalanges,* "phalanxes," each containing 400 acres of land and accommodating 500 to 2,000 human beings. Volunteers would form a phalanx by setting up a community company, agreeing to split its profits three ways—five-twelfths to those who did the work, four-twelfths to those who un-

*Saint-Simon, *Selected Writings,* F.M.H. Markham, ed. (New York, 1952), 116.

dertook the management, and three-twelfths to those who supplied the capital.

Fourier's phalanx, with its relatively generous rewards to managers and capitalists, fell short of complete equality. However, it gave labor the largest share of the profits, and it foreshadowed many other features of socialist planning. Each phalanx would be nearly self-sufficient, producing on the spot most of the things required by its inhabitants. Adult workers who performed the most dangerous or unpleasant tasks would receive the highest remuneration. The inhabitants of the phalanx were to live in one large building, a sort of apartment hotel, which Fourier called a *phalanstère*. The *phalanstère* would provide the maximum opportunity for the satisfaction of man's sociable passions, and it would also make the routine of daily living more efficient by substituting one central kitchen for hundreds of separate ones. The sordid features of housekeeping could be left to little boys, who loved dirt anyway and would cheerfully form special squads to dispose of garbage and refuse.

Other details of the phalanx bore witness to Fourier's reaction against the kind of monotony pictured in Dickens' Coketown. Places of work would be made as pleasant as possible by frequent, colorful redecoration. Members of the phalanx would change their jobs eight times a day because of the human predisposition to the *passion papillonne* (butterfly passion)—"enthusiasm cannot be sustained for more than an hour and a half or two hours in the performance of one particular operation." They would work from four to five in the morning to eight or nine at night, enjoying five meals, plus snacks, needing only five hours of sleep, since the delightful variety of work would not tire them and the days would not be long enough to permit them to taste all the pleasures of life. It would all be so healthy that physicians would be superfluous and everyone would live to 140.

Fourier carried the principle of uninhibited human association to the point of advocating sexual promiscuity, and recommending marriage only for the elderly whose passions had cooled, thus identifying Utopian socialism with "free love" in the popular mind. Yet Fourier cannot be dismissed as a mere crackpot, for he made substantial contributions to socialist theory and to social psychology. Some of his recommendations, like higher pay for dangerous jobs and devices for relieving the tedium of work, have become common practice in the modern business world.

Owen

One of the greatest Utopians was a self-made British businessman, Robert Owen (1772–1858). When he was still in his twenties, Owen took over the large cotton mills at New Lanark in Scotland. Although the former owner of the mills had been accounted benevolent by the standards of the day, conditions there shook Owen to the core. A large part of the working force consisted of children who had been recruited from institutions in Edinburgh when they were between six and eight years old. Although the youngsters did get a little schooling after hours, Owen found many of them "dwarfs in body and mind." Adult laborers at New Lanark fared little better.

Owen set out to show that he could increase his profits and increase the welfare of his laborers at the same time. He made New Lanark over into a model industrial village. For the adults he provided better working conditions, a ten-and-a-half-hour day, higher pay, and cleaner and roomier housing. He restrained the traditional Scottish Saturday night brawl by closing down the worst drinking places, making good liquor available at cheap prices, and punishing offenders who made themselves a public nuisance. As for the children, he raised the minimum age for employment to ten, hoping ultimately to put it at twelve, and he gave his child laborers time for some real schooling. His educational preferences followed Rousseau; advanced bookish subjects were avoided, while crafts, nature study, and other utilitarian subjects received much attention. A properly educated nation, Owen believed, would confute the gloomy predictions of Malthus, who "has not told us how much more food an intelligent and industrious people will create from the same soil, than will be produced by one ignorant and ill-governed."*

Owen inherited much of the optimism of the *philosophes;* he also inherited some of their failures and disappointments. Despite his own success as a philanthropic capitalist, few businessmen followed his example. Disappointed but not disheartened, Owen drew up plans for an idealized version of New Lanark, very much like Fourier's phalanx. He called his utopia a "parallelogram," for the buildings were to be arranged in that geometrical pattern. It was to be a voluntary organization, relatively small in size, neatly balanced between farming and industry, and decidedly advanced in Owen's recommendation for the partial abandonment of conventional ties of marriage and the family. In the 1820's, Owen visited America to finance an abortive effort to set up a parallelogram at New Harmony, Indiana. Undaunted by this failure, he spent the rest of his career publishing and supporting projects for social reform. He advocated the association of all labor in one big union—an experiment that failed; and he sought to reduce the expenditures of workingmen by promoting the formation of consumers' cooperatives—an experiment that succeeded. He also offended many of his contemporaries by his advocacy of sexual freedom, by his Voltairean attacks on established religion, and by his enthusiasm for spiritualism.

*Robert Owen, *A New View of Society* (Glencoe, Illinois, 1948), 174–175.

Parallelogram projected by Robert Owen for New Harmony, Indiana.

The Early Utopians Appraised

Both Owen and Fourier attracted followers not only in their native lands but also in the United States, where religious sects were already launching ventures in communal living. The American Fourierists included many intellectuals, among them the crusading editor, Horace Greeley, and the poet, John Greenleaf Whittier. They sponsored more than thirty attempts to set up phalanxes; two celebrated ones were Brook Farm, near Boston, and Phalanx, in New Jersey. America also witnessed more than half a dozen Owenite experiments in addition to New Harmony. Like New Harmony itself, however, most of these utopias did not prosper very long; and the few that were firmly established returned to conventional ways of individual profit-taking and family life.

Louis Blanc (1811–1882).

Owen and Fourier relied on private initiative to build the model communities that they so hopefully expected to become widely copied examples for the reconstruction of society. Expecting some millionaire to finance his phalanxes, Fourier vainly kept a daily office hour for ten years to receive him. Saint-Simon, with his stress on "organization," presumably meant to give government a larger role; his follower, Louis Blanc, explicitly advocated intervention by the state to achieve utopia.

Author of a pioneering history of the French Revolution from the socialist standpoint, and implacable critic of the bourgeois policies of the July Monarchy, Louis Blanc (1811–1882) projected the scheme that led to the controversial national workshops of 1848. He outlined the scheme first in a pamphlet, *The Organization of Labor* (1839). "What proletarians need," he wrote, "is the instruments of labor; it is the function of government to supply these. If we were to define our conception of the state, our answer would be, that the state is the banker of the poor."* The government would finance and supervise the purchase of productive equipment and the formation of "social workshops"; it would withdraw its support and supervision once the workshops were on their feet. As the workshops gradually spread throughout France, socialistic enterprise would replace private enterprise, profits as such would vanish, and labor would be the only class in society. Much of Louis Blanc's socialism is typically Utopian; he, too, relies on the workers to make their own arrangements for communal living. The real novelty of his plan lies in the role assigned to the state. With Blanc, socialism is beginning to move away from the realm of philanthropy and into the realm of politics.

*"L'Organisation du Travail," in *The French Revolution of 1848*, J. A. R. Marriott, ed. (Oxford, 1913), I, 14. Our translation.

V   The Socialist Response — Marx

With Karl Marx (1818–1883) socialism assumed its most intense form — revolutionary communism. Whereas the early socialists had anticipated a gradual and peaceful evolution toward utopia, Marx forecast a sudden and violent proletarian uprising, by which the workers would capture governments and make them the instruments for securing proletarian welfare. Dogmatic and cocksure, Marx was certain that he alone knew the answers and that the future of mankind would develop inevitably according to the pattern which he found in human history. His self-confidence, his truculence, and the fact that he was born at Trier, in the Prussian Rhineland, have earned him the label of the "Red Prussian."

Basic Principles

Marx found three laws in the pattern of history. First, *economic determinism:* he believed that economic conditions largely determined all other human institutions — society and government, religion and art. Second, the *class struggle:* he believed that history was a dialectical process, a series of conflicts between antagonistic economic groups. In his own day the antagonists were the "haves" and the "have-nots" — the propertied bourgeois and the propertyless proletarians, who, possessing nothing but their working skills, had nothing to fall back on in bad times and were thus at the mercy of their masters. Third, the *inevitability of communism:* he believed that the class struggle was bound to produce one final upheaval that would raise the victorious proletariat over the prostrate bourgeoisie in eternal triumph.

The Marxian philosophy of history derived from many older schools of thought. Although

Marx himself was born and died in the nineteenth century, he belonged in spirit partly to the eighteenth. Both his grandfathers were rabbis, but his father was a deist and a skeptic who trained him in the rationalism of the Enlightenment. Marx early acquired the kind of faith in natural law that had characterized the *philosophes.* In his case it was faith in the natural laws of economic determinism and the class struggle, fortified by the crude materialistic teaching of Feuerbach, famous for proclaiming that *"Man ist was er isst"* (one is what one eats). From this followed the boast made by Marx and his disciples that their socialism alone was "scientific," as opposed to the Romantic doctrines of the Utopians.

The Romantic philosophy of Hegel, however, provided the intellectual scaffolding of Marxism. Although Hegel had died in 1831, his influence permeated the University of Berlin during Marx's student days (1836–1841). Marx translated the Hegelian dialectic into the language of economic determinism and the class struggle. In his own day he believed that capitalistic production and the bourgeoisie comprised the thesis; the antithesis was the proletariat; and the synthesis, issuing from the communist revolution, would be true socialism. In later years Marx summarized his relation to Hegel:

My dialectic method is not only different from the Hegelian but is its direct opposite. To Hegel, the life-process of the human brain, . . . which, under the name of 'the Idea,' he even transforms into an independent subject, is the demiurgos of the real world, and the real world is only the external, phenomenal form of 'the Idea.' With me, on the contrary, the ideal is nothing else than the material world reflected by the human mind, and translated into forms of thought.

. . .

The mystification which dialectic suffers in Hegel's hands, by no means prevents him from being the first to present its general form of working in a comprehensive and conscious manner. *With him it is standing on its head. It must be turned right again,* if you would discover the rational kernel within the mystical shell.*

By the time Marx was thirty, he had completed the outlines of his theory of scientific, revolutionary socialism. He had also become a permanent exile from his native Germany. On leaving the University of Berlin, he worked for a newspaper at Cologne in the Prussian Rhineland, then moved to Paris in 1843 after his atheistic articles had aroused the authorities against him. Exiled again, because the government of Louis Philippe feared his anti-bourgeois propaganda, he went to Brussels in 1845. Wherever he happened to be, he read widely in the economists of the past and talked with the socialists and other radicals of his own generation.

Everything Marx read and everyone he met strengthened his conviction that the capitalistic order was unjust, rotten, doomed to fall. From Adam Smith's labor theory of value he concluded that only the worker should receive the profits from the sale of a commodity, since the value of the commodity should be determined by the labor of the man who produced it. The "iron law of wages," however, confirmed Marx's belief that capitalism would never permit the worker to receive this just reward. And from reading other economists and observing the depression of the late 1840's, he concluded that economic crises were bound to occur again and again under a system that allowed capital to produce too much and labor to consume too little.

Meanwhile, Marx began his long friendship and collaboration with Friedrich Engels (1820–1895). In many ways, the two men made a striking contrast. Marx was poor and quarrelsome, a man of few friends; except for his devotion to his wife and children, he was utterly preoccupied by his economic studies.

*Preface to the second edition of *Capital,* Modern Library ed. (New York, n.d.), 25. (Italics ours).

Engels, on the other hand, was the son of a well-to-do German manufacturer and represented the family textile business in Liverpool and Manchester. He loved sports, women, and high living in general. But he also hated the iniquities of industrialism and, when he met Marx, had already written a bitter study, *The Condition of the Working Class in England.* Both Engels and Marx took an interest in the Communist League, a small international organization of radical workingmen. In 1847, the London office of the Communist League requested them to draw up a program. Engels wrote the first draft, which Marx revised from start to finish; the result, published in January, 1848, was *The Manifesto of the Communist Party.*

The Communist Manifesto

Today, more than a century after its original publication, the *Manifesto* remains the classic statement of Marxian socialism. It opens with the dramatic announcement that "A spectre is haunting Europe—the spectre of Communism." It closes with a stirring and confident appeal:

Let the ruling classes tremble at a Communist revolution. The proletarians have nothing to lose but their chains. They have a world to win.
Workingmen of all countries, unite!

In the few dozen pages of the *Manifesto,* Marx and Engels rapidly block in the main outlines of their theory. "The history of all hitherto existing society," they affirm, "is the history of class struggle." Changing economic conditions determined that the struggle should develop successively between "freeman and slave, patrician and plebeian, lord and serf, guildmaster and journeyman." The guild system gave way first to manufacture by large numbers of small capitalists and then to "the giant, modern industry."

Modern industry will inevitably destroy bourgeois society. It creates a mounting economic pressure by producing more goods than it can sell; it creates a mounting social pressure by narrowing the circle of capitalists to fewer and fewer individuals and depriving more and more people of their property and forcing them down to the proletariat. These pressures increase to the point where a revolutionary explosion occurs, a massive assault on private property. Landed property will be abolished outright; other forms of property are to be liquidated more gradually through the imposition of severe income taxes and the abolition of inherited wealth. Eventually, social classes and tensions will vanish, and "we shall have an association in which the free development of each is the condition for the free development of all."

"The free development of each is the condition for the free development of all"—the *Manifesto* provides only this vague description of the society that would exist after the revolution. Since Marx defined political authority as "the organized power of one class for oppressing another," he apparently expected that, in the famous phrase, "the state would wither away" once it had created a classless regime. He also apparently assumed that the great dialectical process of history, having achieved its final synthesis, would then cease to operate in its traditional form. But, readers of the *Manifesto* may inquire how is this possible? Will not the dialectic continue forever creating economic and political theses and antitheses? Will not the state always be with us? To these questions Marx offered no satisfactory answer beyond the implication that somehow the liquidation of bourgeois capitalism would radically alter the course of history and transform humanity.

Marx oversimplified the complexities of human nature by trying to force it into the rigid mold of economic determinism and ignoring the non-material motives and interests of men. Neither proletarians nor bourgeois have proved to be the simple economic stereotypes Marx supposed them to be. Labor has often behaved in scandalously un-Marxian fashion and assumed a markedly bourgeois outlook and mentality. Capital has put its own house in better order—and eliminated the worst injustices of the factory system. No more than Malthus did Marx foresee the notable rise in the standard of living that would take place between the mid-nineteenth and mid-twentieth centuries.

Marx never made a greater mistake than when he failed to observe the growing strength of nationalism. The *Manifesto* confidently expected the class struggle to transcend national boundaries. In social and economic warfare, nation would not be pitted against nation, nor state against state; the proletariat everywhere would fight the bourgeoisie. "Workingmen have no country" and "national differences and antagonisms are vanishing gradually from day to day." In Marx's own lifetime, however, national differences and

Friedrich Engels (1820–1895).

antagonisms were increasing rapidly from day to day. Within a few months of the publication of the *Manifesto,* the revolutions of 1848 disclosed the antagonism between Italians and Austrians, Austrians and Hungarians, Hungarians and Slavs, Slavs and Germans.

The *Communist Manifesto* anticipated the strengths as well as the weaknesses of the communist movement. First, it foreshadowed the very important role to be played by propaganda, supplying the earliest of those effective catch-phrases that have become the mark of Marxism—the constant sneering at bourgeois morality, bourgeois law, and bourgeois property, and the dramatic references to the "spectre haunting Europe" and to the proletarians who "have nothing to lose but their chains." Second, the *Manifesto* anticipated the emphasis to be placed on the role of the party in forging the proletarian revolution. The communists, Marx declared in 1848, were a spearhead, "the most advanced section of the working class parties of every country." In matters of theory, "they have over the great mass of the proletariat the advantage of clearly understanding the line of march, the conditions, and the ultimate general results of the proletarian movement."

Third, the *Manifesto* assigned the state a great role in the revolution. Among the policies recommended by Marx were "centralization of credit in the hands of the state," and "extension of factories and instruments of production owned by the state." Thus, despite the supposition that the state would wither away, the *Manifesto* faintly foreshadowed the totalitarian regime of the Soviet Union. And, finally, it clearly established the line dividing communism from the other forms of socialism. Marx's dogmatism, his philosophy of history, and his belief in the necessity for a "total" revolution made his brand of socialism a thing apart. Like a religious prophet granted a revelation, Marx expected his gospel to supplant all other. He scorned and pitied the Utopian socialists. They were about as futile, he wrote, as "organizers of charity, members of societies for the prevention of cruelty to animals, temperance fanatics, hole-and-corner reformers of every kind."

The Later Career of Marx

Age neither mellowed Marx nor greatly altered his views. From 1849 until his death in 1883, he lived in London. There, partly because of his own financial mismanagement, the Marx family experienced at first hand the misery of a proletarian existence in the slums of Soho; poverty and near-starvation caused the death of three of the Marx children. Eventually, Marx obtained a modest income from the generosity of Engels and from his own writings.

Throughout the 1850's Marx contributed a weekly article on British politics or international affairs to Horace Greeley's radical paper, *The New York Tribune.* He produced a series of pamphlets, of which the most famous was *The Eighteenth Brumaire of Louis Napoleon,* a study of the fall of the short-lived Second French Republic. Meantime, he spent his days in the British Museum, reading the reports of parliamentary investigating committees and piling up evidence of the conditions of miners and factory hands. Thus Marx accumulated the material for his full-dress economic study, *Das Kapital.* The first volume of this massive analysis of capitalism appeared in 1867; two further volumes, pieced together from his notes, were published after his death.

In *Das Kapital,* Marx elaborated, but did not substantially revise, the doctrines of the *Communist Manifesto.* He spelled out his labor theory of value, according to which the worker created the total value of the commodity that he produced yet received in the form of wages only a part of the price for the item. The difference between the sale price and the worker's wages constituted *surplus value,* something actually created by labor but appropriated by capital as profit. *Das Kapital* goes on to relate surplus value to the ultimate doom of capitalism. It is the nature of capitalism, Marx insists, to diminish its own profits by replacing human labor with machines and thus gradually choking off the source of surplus value. Hence will arise the mounting crises of overproduction and underconsumption predicted by the *Manifesto*. In a famous passage toward the close of Volume I of *Das Kapital*, Marx compared capitalism to an integument, a skin or shell, increasingly stretched and strained from within. One day these internal pressures would prove irresistible:

This integument is burst asunder. The knell of capitalist private property sounds. The expropriators are expropriated.*

In 1864, three years before the first volume of *Das Kapital* was published, Marx joined in the formation of the First International Workingmen's Association. This was an ambitious attempt to organize workers of every country and of every variety of radical belief. A loose federation rather than a coherent political party, the First International soon began to disintegrate, and expired in 1876. Increasing persecution by hostile governments helped to bring on its end; but so, too, did the internal quarrels that repeatedly engaged both its leaders and the rank and file of its members. Marx himself set the example by his intolerance of disagreement and his incapacity for practical politics.

In 1889, the Second International was organized; it lasted down to the time of World War I and the Bolshevik revolution in Russia.

Capital, Modern Library, ed., 837.

The Second International was more coherently organized and more political in character than the First International had been. It represented the Marxian socialist parties, which, as we shall see in later chapters, were becoming important forces in the major countries of continental Europe. Among its leaders were men more adept than Marx himself at the political game. Yet the old spirit of factionalism continued to weaken the International. Some of its leaders tenaciously defended laws handed down by the master and forbade any cooperation between socialists and the bourgeois political parties; these were the orthodox Marxists. Other leaders of the Second International, however, were from the orthodox standpoint heretics. They, too, called themselves disciples of Marx; yet they revised his doctrines in the direction of moderation and of harmonization with the views of the Utopians. These "revisionists" believed in co-operation between classes rather than in a struggle to the death, and they trusted that human decency and intelligence, working through the machinery of democratic government, could avert the horrors of outright class war. Though the precise connotations have varied with the shifts of the party line, "orthodox" and "heretical" communists have persisted. The factionalism that had split the First International lived on to plague the Second and its successors in twentieth-century communism.

VI   Other Responses

Socialism, both Marxian and Utopian, and liberalism, both bourgeois and democratic, were the most important responses to the economic and social problems of the nineteenth century. But they were not the only responses. As later chapters will show, nationalists gave new life to the old ideas of mercantilism, not only advocating tariffs to protect agriculture and industry but also demanding empires abroad to provide new markets for surplus products, new fields for the investment of surplus capital, and new settlements for surplus citizens. Two very different types of response came from the anarchists and the reformers known as Christian socialists or Christian democrats.

The Anarchists

An anarchist believes that the best government is no government at all. Most of the recipes for socialism contained at least a dash of anarchism: witness the withering-away of the state promised by the Marxists and the Utopians' mistrust of governments. For a few of Marx's contemporaries, however, it was not enough that the state should wither at some distant time; such an instrument of oppression should be annihilated at once. The means to this end was terrorism, especially assassination of heads of state. These terrorists provided the stereotype of the bearded, wild-eyed, bomb-carrying radical. At the turn of the century, their assassinations levied an impressive toll—the French President Carnot in 1894, King Humbert of Italy in 1900, and the American President McKinley in 1901. Otherwise the terrorists accomplished little except to drive the governments they hated to more vigorous measures of retaliation.

Though negative and destructive in practice, anarchism exerted an important doctrinal influence on the proletarian movement. The Russian scientist and thinker, Prince Peter Kropotkin (1842–1921), made the most complete statement of its theory and ideals in his book, *Mutual Aid: A Factor in Evolution* (1902). Kropotkin foresaw a revolution that would abolish the state as well as private property and that would lead to a new society of autonomous groups whereby the individual would achieve greater self-realization and would need to labor only four to five hours a day. The most famous anarchist was Kropotkin's countryman, Bakunin (1814–1876), who helped to shape the Russian revolutionary movement (see Chapter 14) and won the attention of workers from many countries by his participation in the First International. Although Bakunin drew only a vague sketch of his utopia, he made it clear that the millennium was to be achieved through an international rebellion set off by small groups of anarchist conspirators.

Bakunin contributed to the formation of the program known as *anarcho-syndicalism* (from the French word *syndicat,* which means an economic grouping, particularly a trade union). The anarcho-syndicalists disbelieved in political parties, even Marxist ones; they believed in direct action by the workers to culminate in a spontaneous general strike that would free labor from the capitalistic yoke. Meantime, workers could rehearse for the great day by forming unions and by engaging in acts of anti-capitalist sabotage. These theories received forceful expression in *Reflections on Violence* published early in the twentieth century by the French exponent of anarcho-syndicalism, Georges Sorel.

Proudhon

The writer most frequently cited by the anarcho-syndicalists was the French publicist, Proudhon (1809–1865). "What is property?" Proudhon asked in a famous pamphlet of 1840; "property is theft." Marx praised the pamphlet for its "scientific" socialism and predicted it would rank in importance with Siéyès' *What Is the Third Estate?* Within a few years Marx's praise had turned to contempt, since Proudhon refused to accept the correctness of all of his own views. A second pamphlet by Proudhon, *The Philosophy of Poverty,* therefore, elicited a Marxian rebuttal tartly entitled *The Poverty of Philosophy.* The property that Proudhon called "theft" was not all property but unearned income, the revenues that men gained from investing their wealth rather than from the sweat of their brows. Of all the forms of unearned income, the worst, in Proudhon's view, was the "leprosy of interest," and the most diabolical of capitalists was the money-lender. Under existing conditions, only those who were already rich could afford to borrow, but in the utopia envisaged by Proudhon all men would be able to secure credit. Instead of private banks and the Bank of France, there would be only a "People's Bank," lending to all without interest and issuing notes that would soon replace ordinary money. The credit provided by the People's

Bank would enable each man to become a producer on his own.

Thus, where Marx foresaw a revolution in ownership of the means of production, Proudhon foresaw a "revolution of credit," a revolution in financing production. Where Marx proposed to have the proletariat liquidate the bourgeoisie, Proudhon proposed to raise the proletarians to the level of the bourgeois by making every worker an owner. Proudhon's utopia was not collectivized or socialized; it was a loose association of middle-class individualists. Because Proudhon dreaded restraints upon the individual, he opposed the social workshops of Louis Blanc and the phalanxes of Fourier as too restrictive. He projected, instead, a society founded upon "mutualism." Economically, mutualism would take the form of associations of producers in agriculture and industry, not unlike the producers' co-operatives found among farmers today. Politically, it would take the form of "federalism" — that is, a loose federation of associations would replace the centralized state rather on the model of the Swiss confederation of local cantons.

Proudhon's doctrines exerted a strong appeal in France, with its devotion to individualism and with the legacy of "federalism" bequeathed by the Girondins of the Revolution. Tens of thousands of small businessmen in France were often denied financial credit by the bankers denounced by Proudhon, and thus always stood on the edge of being displaced from the lower fringes of the middle class to the proletariat. Proudhon's attacks on the state naturally fed the anarchist strain in anarcho-syndicalism. Yet much of his teaching contradicted the syndicalist strain. Not only did he dislike trade unions as unnatural restrictions on individual liberty; he deplored all activities suggesting class strife, including the very strikes so beloved by the syndicalists. These views, together with his expressed hostility to Jewish money-lenders, have led some modern critics to call Proudhon an incipient fascist; other critics, however, have dismissed the charge as absurd because Proudhon seemed to reject the kind of totalitarian state identified with fascism.

The Christian Socialists

Like Proudhon, the Christian socialists endeavored to mitigate class antagonisms. The name was first applied, in the mid-nineteenth century, to a small group of English reformers, drawn from the clergy of the established Church, who believed that the Church of England needed to put theological problems to one side and direct its efforts to ending social abuses. One of their best known leaders was Charles Kingsley (1819–1875), who wrote earnest social novels and a stream of pamphlets against the wickedness of laissez-faire. His didactic novel, *Alton Locke,* and his bitter tract, *Cheap Clothes and Nasty,* both published in 1850, exposed the sweating of labor in the "show shops" and "slop shops" which forced tailors and seamstresses to work long hours for meager pay, often in appallingly crowded and unsanitary surroundings.

The positive doctrine of the Christian socialists was notable for its attack on materialism and its stress on brotherly love as against un-brotherly strife, on association and co-operation as against exploitation and competition. It was notable also for its optimism: if men would only act as Christians, they might solve their social problems. Indeed the Christian socialists were far more Christian than socialist and relied more on private philanthropy than on state intervention. Kingsley himself set an example for concrete improvement when he helped to launch the Working Men's College in London and promoted other activities of the type that organizations like the YMCA have made familiar.

The Catholic Response

Catholics, too, reacted against the evils of industrialism. Essentially, their program resembled that of the Anglican Christian socialists, but they called it by the more accurate name of "Christian democracy" or "social Christianity." Christian democracy formed a central part of the Catholic response to the problems of the modern world. As we shall see in later chapters, these problems bore heavily upon the Church. Anticlerical legislation threatened its position in France, Germany, Italy, and elsewhere. The Papal States and then the city of Rome itself, after more than a thousand years of papal rule, passed to the control of the newly unified Kingdom of Italy. Science, nationalism, and the materialistic doctrines issuing from the industrial revolution were all competing for the loyalties of men. In Catholic countries the working classes especially were drifting away from the Church.

The Church first tried to take refuge in the past. Pope Pius IX (1846–1878), whose experience in the revolution of 1848 (see p. 439) had ended his earlier flirtation with liberalism, issued in 1864 the *Syllabus of Errors,* condemning many social theories and institutions not consecrated by centuries of tradition. While Pius also condemned the materialism implicit in laissez-faire, socially-minded Catholics were disturbed by his apparent hostility to trade unions and democracy and by his statement that it was an error to suppose that the pope "can and ought to reconcile and harmonize himself with progress, liberalism, and modern civilization."

The successor of Pius, Leo XIII (1878–1903), recognized that the Church could hardly continue to turn its back on progress, liberalism, and modernity without suffering serious losses. Pope Leo fully recognized the rapid changes being worked by science and technology, and as a papal nuncio, he had witnessed them at first hand in the industrial regions of Belgium, France, and Germany. He knew that Catholicism was flourishing in the supposedly hostile climate of the democratic and Protestant United States. Moreover, his studies of St. Thomas Aquinas convinced him that the Church had much to gain and little to lose by following the middle-of-the-road social and economic policies recommended by that great medieval Schoolman. Accordingly, Leo XIII issued a series of famous documents, notably the encyclical letter, *Rerum Novarum* ("concerning new things," 1891).

In *Rerum Novarum,* the Pope exposed the defects of capitalism with as much vigor as any socialist. Then he attacked with equal vigor the socialist view of property and the socialist doctrine of class war. He pronounced it a "great mistake" to believe

. . . that class is naturally hostile to class, and that the wealthy and the workingmen are intended by nature to live in mutual conflict. . . . Each needs the other: Capital cannot do without Labor, nor Labor without Capital.*

Leo therefore urged the economic man to act as a Christian man of good will:

Religion teaches the laboring man . . . to carry out honestly and fairly all equitable agreements freely entered into; never to injure the property, nor to outrage the person, of an employer; never to resort to violence . . . ; and to have nothing to do with men of evil principles, who work upon the people with artful promises, and excite foolish hopes which usually end in useless regrets, followed by insolvency. Religion teaches the wealthy owner and the employer that their work-people are not to be accounted their bondsmen; that in every man they must respect his dignity and worth as a man and as a Christian; that labor is not a thing to be ashamed of, if we lend ear to right reason and to Christian philosophy, but is an honorable calling, enabling a man to sustain his life in a way upright and creditable; and that it is shameful and inhuman to treat men like chattels to make money by, or to look upon them merely as so much muscle or physical power.†

While Leo XIII believed that the state must always remain subordinate to the interests of the individuals composing it, he did not necessarily defend laissez-faire policies. On the contrary, he repeatedly cited St. Thomas to prove that the state should take measures for the general welfare. On behalf of capital, it should discourage agitators and protect property from violence. On behalf of labor, it should work to remove "the causes which lead to conflict between employer and employed." For example, it might regulate child labor, limit the hours of work, and insist that Sun-

The Great Encyclical Letters of Pope Leo XIII (New York, 1903), 218.
†*Ibid.,* 219.

days be free for religious activity and for rest. Leo also believed that the workers must help themselves, and *Rerum Novarum* concluded with a fervent appeal for the formation of Catholic trade unions.

These Catholic unions exist today, but they are only a minority in the realm of organized labor. Neither the Christian democracy of Leo XIII nor the Christian socialism of the Anglican reformers has achieved all that the founders hoped. Yet the Christian democrats eventually came to play a central part in the politics of Germany, Italy, and other European states, particularly after World War II. And in Britain both Marxism and the Christian socialist tradition helped to attract workingmen and middle-class intellectuals to the developing Labor Party at the beginning of the twentieth century. In the perspective of history, the Anglican and Catholic reformers succeeded in attracting an influential following and in arousing the conscience of prosperous industrial nations to the human problems created by the economic revolutions.

Reading Suggestions on the Impact of the Economic Revolutions

(Asterisk indicates paperbound edition.)

General Accounts

E. J. Hobsbawm, *The Age of Revolution, 1789–1848* (*Mentor). A survey doing full justice to the social impact of industrialism.

A. Birnie, *Economic History of Europe, 1760–1939* (*Dover). Helpful introduction.

R. C. Binkley, *Realism & Nationalism, 1852–1871* (*Torch), and C. J. H. Hayes, *A Generation of Materialism, 1871–1900* (*Torch). Stimulating comprehensive surveys in the "Rise of Modern Europe" series; with full bibliographies.

T. S. Ashton, *The Industrial Revolution, 1760–1830* (*Galaxy). Lucid introduction, centering on Britain.

A. Toynbee, *The Industrial Revolution* (*Beacon). Pioneering study, first published nearly a century ago, and influenced by Christian socialist ideas.

J. L. and B. Hammond, *The Rise of Modern Industry,* 8th ed. (Methuen, 1951). Seen from a doctrinaire socialist point of view.

L. Mumford, *Technics and Civilization* (*Harbinger). A sweeping survey, now somewhat outdated but still very suggestive.

Special Studies: Mainly Economic and Social

P. Mantoux, *The Industrial Revolution in the Eighteenth Century* (*Torch). Standard account of the beginnings of the factory system in England.

J. Clapham, *An Economic History of Modern Britain,* 3 vols., rev. ed. (Cambridge Univ. Press, 1930–1938). Major scholarly study of the workshop of the world.

J. Clapham, *Economic Development of France and Germany, 1815–1914* (*Cambridge Univ. Press). An older book and a very good one.

W. O. Henderson, *The Industrial Revolution in Europe, 1815–1914* (Quadrangle, 1961). Recent survey, stressing Germany and France.

A. L. Dunham, *The Industrial Revolution in France, 1815–1848* (Exposition, 1955). Scholarly monograph.

W. W. Rostow, *The Process of Economic Growth* (*Norton). Influential analysis responsible for adding the term "take-off" stage to the economic vocabulary.

M. C. Buer, *Health, Wealth, & Population in the Early Days of the Industrial Revolution* (Routledge, 1926). A balanced appraisal of the social consequences of industrial change.

Special Studies:
Mainly Ideological
and Political

C. Brinton, *English Political Thought in the 19th Century* (*Torch). Essays on Bentham, Mill, Owen, Kingsley, and other important figures.

J. S. Schapiro, *Liberalism and the Challenge of Fascism: Social Forces in England and France, 1815 – 1870* (McGraw-Hill, 1949). Stresses ideological consequences.

E. Halévy, *The Growth of Philosophic Radicalism* (*Beacon, 1955). The standard study of Bentham and his Utilitarian followers.

H. W. Laidler, *Social-Economic Movements: An Historical and Comparative Survey of Socialism, Communism, Coöperation, Utopianism* (Crowell, 1949). An encyclopaedic introduction to the topics enumerated.

J. C. Schumpeter, *Capitalism, Socialism, and Democracy* (*Torch). A thoughtful survey, extending down to the mid-twentieth century.

E. Wilson, *To the Finland Station* (*Anchor). A sympathetic and balanced history of socialism, Utopian and Marxian.

F. E. Manuel, *The New World of Henri Saint-Simon* (*Notre Dame). Sympathetic biography and evaluation.

F. Podmore, *Robert Owen, A Biography* (Appleton, 1924). An instructive account.

I. Berlin, *Karl Marx: His Life and Environment* (*Galaxy). Short and excellent.

L. Schwarzchild, *The Red Prussian: The Life and Legend of Karl Marx* (*Universal). A hostile interpretation.

R. Fülöp-Miller, *Leo XIII and Our Times* (Longmans, Green, 1937). A warmly sympathetic account.

Sources

J. Bowditch and C. Ramsland, eds. *Voices of the Industrial Revolution* (*Ann Arbor). Selections from the liberal economists and their critics.

T. R. Malthus, *Population: the First Essay* (*Ann Arbor). The original essay of 1798, stating Malthusianism in its starkest form.

D. Ricardo, *The Principles of Political Economy & Taxation* (*Irwin).

J. S. Mill, *Autobiography* and *On Liberty* (both in several * editions).

C. H. de Saint-Simon, *Social Organization, the Science of Man, & Other Writings* (*Torch).

The Life of Robert Owen, by Himself (Knopf, 1920).

K. Marx and F. Engels, *Basic Writings on Politics & Philosophy* (*Anchor).

The Great Encyclical Letters of Pope Leo XIII (Benziger, 1903). Fundamental to the understanding of modern Catholic social thought.

Historical Fiction

C. Dickens, *Hard Times* (*several editions). The shortest of Dickens' social novels; first-rate descriptions of "Coketown" and its citizens.

Mrs. E. Gaskell, *North and South* (Dutton, 1914) and *Mary Barton* (Dutton, 1912). Most instructive social novels by a perceptive contemporary of Dickens.

E. Zola, *Germinal* (*several editions). The best French novel on industrial problems; less genteel than its English counterparts.

E. Bellamy, *Looking Backward, 2000 – 1887* (*several editions). A highly interesting adaptation of Utopian socialist views by an American of the late nineteenth century.

13

The Western Democracies
in the Nineteenth Century

We shall now trace the background history of the major self-governing western states: Great Britain, France, Italy, and the United States. These are now all democracies; and though they have all had, especially in wartime, lapses from democratic standards, they are all, as the twentieth-century world goes, "old" democracies.

The smaller nations of western and northern Europe—the Netherlands, Belgium, Switzerland, the Scandinavian countries—are also part of the North Atlantic community. All these smaller states have worked out their own national variants of liberalism and democracy. In particular, the Scandinavian countries, with their homogeneous populations, their common Lutheran religion, their common traditions, and their very high rate of literacy, have sometimes surpassed the larger states in making democracy function effectively. Visitors to Copenhagen or Stockholm are impressed not only by their tidiness but also by the absence of slums and other signs of poverty. And the co-operatives of Denmark and Sweden have received much praise as the "middle way" between welfare socialism and uncontrolled economic individualism.

Nor should the histories of these smaller states be considered uninteresting or unimportant. They too underwent most of the stresses and strains of the rest of Europe. Belgium, notably, was divided—and still is—between French-speaking and Flemish-speaking areas, often in conflict. Switzerland in the nineteenth century underwent a real if not very long and bloody war, that of the Sonderbund, between the more conservative and rural Catholic counties and liberal urban ones. Sweden and Norway, yoked together in 1815, parted company peacefully in 1907, after nearly a century of restive partnership. But we simply cannot include these histories in a work of this scope.

These smaller states have also helped to maintain the balance of international politics and to shape European opinion, a role for which they are particularly well suited by their relative detachment from ambitious na-

tionalist aspirations. They have collaborated effectively in many forms of internation activity. In many fields their citizens have contributed proportionately more heavily to our modern western culture than their numbers would suggest. To cite a few examples: Switzerland supplied the great historian of the Renaissance, Burckhardt, and Belgium the poet and playwright, Maeterlinck. From Finland came the composer Sibelius; from Norway, Ibsen and his modern social dramas; from Holland, the physicist Lorentz, winner of the Nobel Prize in 1902; and from Sweden, Nobel himself, the munitions king who endowed the Nobel prizes for peaceful achievement, and the novelist and playwright Strindberg.

Spain, too, had a varied and interesting history in the nineteenth century, swinging between conservative monarchy and radical republicanism. But Spain was now a minor power and, though especially in the novel, she had a distinguished cultural achievement, we must postpone longer consideration of Spanish history until in the Civil War of the 1930's Spain once more enters the mainstream of events. We must now turn to the states that fate, or history, has assigned the major roles in our story. Of these in the nineteenth century, Britain was unquestionably the first, the leading power.

I Britain, 1815-1914

The Process of Reform

In the years immediately after Waterloo, Britain went through a typical postwar economic crisis. Unsold goods accumulated, and the working classes experienced widespread unemployment and suffering. Although trade unions were forbidden by the Combination Acts, the workers none the less asserted themselves in strikes and in popular agitation that helped prepare the way for the parliamentary Reform Bill of 1832. But by

the 1820's, economic conditions had improved, and Britain had embarked on the first stage of those political reforms that were to make of her a democratic state.

Into this process, of course, there went economic and social drives, and the Britain of our mid-twentieth century was to be not only a very complete political democracy but also in part an economic and a social democracy. But the process of reform focused always on concrete political action. It is a process of which the British are very proud, for it was achieved without revolution and almost without vi-

Europe in the Mid - Nineteenth Century

— Boundary of the German Confederation

GREAT BRITAIN

SCOTLAND
Edinburgh
Glasgow
IRELAND
Lancaster
Liverpool
Manchester
WALES
ENGLAND
Oxford
Cambridge
London

Atlantic Ocean

North Sea

NORWAY
Oslo
SWEDEN
Stockholm
FINLAND
St. Petersburg

Copenhagen
DENMARK
SCHLESWIG
HOLSTEIN
Kiel
Hamburg
HANOVER

Baltic Sea
Memel
Königsberg
POLAND
Warsaw
United with Prussia, 1824-1878

R U S S I A
Moscow
Volga R.
Oka R.
Don R.
Dvina R.
Dnieper R.
DONETS BASIN
Kiev
Dniester R.
Odessa
Pruth R.

Volga R.

Berlin
Elbe R.
Oder R.
SAXONY
Prague
BOHEMIA
Olmütz
Vienna
AUSTRIAN EMPIRE
HUNGARY
Budapest
TYROL
Zagreb
SERBIA
Belgrade
BOSNIA-HERZEGOVINA
MONTENEGRO

Black Sea

OTTOMAN EMPIRE

Constantinople

NETH.
Brussels
BELG.
Lux.
Metz
Lille
Frankfurt
WÜRTEM-BERG
BADEN
BAVARIA
SWITZ.
RUHR

FRANCE
Paris
Seine R.
Loire R.
Bordeaux
Rhône R.
Marseilles
Rhine R.

PIEDMONT
Turin
Genoa
SARDINIA
VENETIA
LOMBARDY
Venice
Po R.
PARMA
MODENA
TUSCANY
PAPAL STATES
Rome
CORSICA

KINGDOM OF SARDINIA

Adriatic Sea

Naples
KINGDOM OF THE TWO SICILIES
SICILY
Str. of Messina

Mediterranean Sea

Aegean Sea
GREECE
Athens
CRETE
CYPRUS

SPAIN
Madrid
Ebro R.
Guadalquivir R.
BALEARIC IS.

PORTUGAL
Lisbon

MOROCCO
ALGERIA
TUNIS
TRIPOLI
Tripoli

EGYPT
Cairo
Suez
SYRIA
Tigris R.
Euphrates R.

Miles

olence or indeed any serious civil disturbance. The fruits of discussion, education, and propaganda were consolidated in a specific "reform bill," followed by another stage of preparatory work and another reform bill.

Parliamentary Reform

The process is most clearly marked in the great milestones of parliamentary reform that transformed the government of Britain from an oligarchy into a political democracy. Britain emerged from the Napoleonic Wars with its executive, a cabinet of ministers presided over by a prime minister, wholly under the control of Parliament. The Crown was now, as the nineteenth-century political writer Bagehot was to put it, largely "decorative." On that decorative post, held for most of the century (1837–1901) by Queen Victoria, who has given her name to an age and a culture, were centered the patriotic emotions of loyal British subjects. Victoria never thought of herself as a mere figurehead; she was a determined, sensible, emotional, conventional, and intellectually unsophisticated Victorian lady.

Real power lay in the legislative branch, in the early nineteenth century by no means directly representative of the masses. The House of Lords, which for all save money bills had equal power with the lower house, was composed of the small, privileged class of peers born to their seats in the Lords, with the addition of a relatively few new peers created by the Crown from time to time. The House of Commons, its members unpaid, was recruited wholly from the gentry, the professional classes, and very successful businessmen, with a sprinkling of sons of peers (who were for electoral purposes commoners) and was chosen by less than one-sixth of the adult male population. Both the working classes in town and country and the run of prosperous but not spectacularly successful middle-class people were excluded from the franchise. Moreover, the largely rural South, once the most populous area of the kingdom, now had more representatives than it deserved, including a large contingent from the "rotten boroughs," towns

of very small population, or, as in the notorious Old Sarum, once a lively medieval town, none at all. The teeming new industrial centers of the North, such as Manchester, Liverpool, Sheffield, were grossly under-represented.

Projects to begin modernizing the structure of representation came close to being adopted in the late eighteenth century. But the wars with Revolutionary and Napoleonic France made reform impossible; in wartime and in the immediate postwar years, even moderate reformers were denounced as Jacobins. In 1819, a nervous Tory government permitted the soldiery to break up a large and peaceful mass meeting assembled at St. Peter's Field near Manchester to hear speeches on parliamentary reform. Soon after this "Peterloo" with its echo of "Waterloo," however, moderation prevailed, and the peaceful campaign of agitation which produced the parliamentary reform of 1832 was resumed.

In this campaign the middle class did not hesitate to appeal to the lower classes for aid by using freely the language of popular rights, and even of universal suffrage. Many popular leaders talked as if the Reform Bill would bring political democracy to England at once. Yet much of the preparation for reform was actually the work, not of liberal agitators, but of conservatives. Guided by enlightened individuals such as Canning and Robert Peel, the Tory governments of the 1820's lifted the various restrictions on civil rights imposed during the war period and the postwar crisis. They partially repealed the Combination Acts against trade unions; reformed the antiquated criminal code, so that, for example, the theft of a sheep no longer carried with it in theory a death penalty; and began the reduction in protective tariffs that was to lead to free trade. The seventeenth-century Test Act, which, though not observed, legally excluded nonconformists from public life, was repealed. So, under the name of "Catholic emancipation," were the laws that really did exclude Catholics from public life. In international politics, Canning lined Britain up as a "liberal" power against the conservative monarchies of central and eastern Europe (see Chapter 11).

The Reform Bill itself was enacted under

the leadership of the Whig Lord Grey, backed by a full apparatus of agitation and pressure groups. Tory opponents of parliamentary reform were won over—even the very Tory Duke of Wellington was converted at the last moment—until only the Tory House of Lords blocked the measure. At this climax, Lord Grey persuaded King William IV (1830–1837) to threaten the creation by royal prerogative of enough new Whig peers to put the reform through the Lords. This threat, combined with the real, or perhaps merely widely feared danger of popular violence, put the bill through on June 4, 1832.

This First Reform Bill did not bring political democracy to England. It did diminish the great irregularities of electoral districts, wiping out more than fifty rotten boroughs and giving seats in the Commons to more than forty hitherto unrepresented industrial towns. The number of voters was increased by about 50 per cent so that virtually all the middle class got the vote, but the bill by no means enfranchised the "lower" classes in urban or rural areas.

From the new ground of the partly reformed Parliament, the agitation for a still wider suffrage went on. The middle class had won its gains, not in the name of its own admission to an oligarchy, but in the name of the right of all competent men to have the vote. With the gradual spread of literacy to the lower classes, with their gradual political awakening, the middle classes could not find very good arguments for refusing to extend the franchise; moreover, a good many of the British middle classes sincerely believed in a gradual widening of the franchise.

The Second Reform Bill came in 1867, by one of the ironies of history put through by that Tory party that traditionally stood for resistance to the widening of the suffrage. But the three decades after 1832 had produced a ground swell of agitation for more parliamentary reform, a ground swell with many cross-currents from down-right radical republicanism to a resigned belief that democracy was irresistibly the wave of the future. Disraeli (1804–1881), the Tory leader in the Commons, almost certainly thought that if one party did not put through reform the other one would. With a politician's sense of reality, he decided his party might as well get the credit. Disraeli also thought that the newly enfranchised urban working class, hostile to their middle-class employers, would vote for the Tories, who were country gentlemen, good responsible caretakers of the lower classes, not exploiters like the middle-class businessmen. He was proved wrong by the very first general election after the reform, for in 1868 the Tories were turned out of office.

The Second Reform Bill did not introduce full manhood suffrage. Like the first, it was a piecemeal change that brought the electoral districts into more uniformity and equality,

Caricature of Disraeli, 1869.

Gladstone advising Queen Victoria.

former Whigs under the leadership of Gladstone (1809–1898). Even these reforms of 1884 and 1885 did not introduce universal manhood suffrage or a neat democratic uniformity. They still tinkered with medieval forms, which were now pretty completely modernized. Lodgers and a few "floaters" (people whose specific "home" was hard to define in settled Victorian terms), and women were still without the vote; districts were not quite equalized; a few thousand voters with business property in one district and a home in another could vote twice; and graduates of Oxford and Cambridge could vote a second time for special university members; indeed, a university man with scattered property could, if he could get around to the polls fast enough, cast a dozen votes. Only in 1918, in a major Reform Act, was plural voting limited to two votes—a property and a university vote. Still, by 1885 Britain was clearly a political democracy, in which the majority of the people, through their representatives in the House of Commons, were politically "sovereign." Perhaps not quite, for the hereditary House of Lords had still a veto power over legislation that did not specifically appropriate money. This last limitation was removed in 1911, in a kind of codicil to the reforms of the nineteenth century, when the Parliament Act of that year ended the real power of the Lords, leaving them with no more than a delaying or suspensive veto.

The Two-Party System:
Liberals and Conservatives

We have outlined above the legislative landmarks in the nineteenth-century democratization of the British constitution. Now the dynamics of that process are certainly in part explicable in terms of the "class struggle." Broadly speaking, over the century the "have nots"—perhaps better, the "have littles"—gained a voice in the politics of Britain they did not have in 1815. But the central human institution of the dynamics, the *party*, clearly does not present a neat alignment of the "have littles" against the "have much." That

but left them still divided into boroughs and shires as in the Middle Ages. It about doubled the number of voters in Britain by giving the vote to householders—that is, settled men owning or paying rent on their dwellings—in the boroughs. But the Reform Bill of 1867 did not give the vote in rural areas to men without the "stake" of property—that is, men who did not own a piece of real estate or even a bank account, men who were therefore felt by many upper-class Victorians to be irresponsible, willing to vote away other people's property. It did, however, give the vote to several millions of wage-earners without other sources of income.

The next reforms in the series were, more logically, put through by the Liberal party, the should be clear even from the very summary account of the reform bills we have given. The Disraeli who took the "leap in the dark" of 1867 was a conservative, not a radical leader, and he hoped that the newly enfranchised workingmen would vote conservative, not radical. He was wrong in 1868, but in the longer run not wholly wrong, for after his death his party was returned to power triumphantly under the even wider franchise of 1885 for a whole decade, 1895–1905. Some British poor and middling men obviously still continued to vote for the party of their "betters."

The fact is that the nineteenth-century British party system was not clearly based on an opposition between a possessing class and a non-possessing class. The eighteenth-century oligarchic factions of Whigs and Tories were transformed in the course of the nineteenth century into the modern mass parties of Liberals and Conservatives, both organized on a national basis, with local committees at the bottom, and making full use of party machinery for getting out the vote. The Whigs, in broadening into the Liberals, sought an electoral base ranging from the old great families, still represented in the early and middle part of the century by men like Grey and Palmerston, to the little and big businessmen, the nonconformists, the radical white-collar men, and the politically conscious workingmen. The Tories, in broadening into Conservatives, sought a base, first under Peel and then under Disraeli, from the country gentlemen, army and navy officers, and Anglican clergymen down to the agricultural laborers, the small townspeople, and even some of the urban white-collar and working classes. Both parties frankly appealed to the "people"; and the Conservatives, with their "Primrose League" in memory of Disraeli's favorite flower, their appeal to love of Queen and country, their record of social legislation against the worst evils of the new factory system, did at least as good a job in building a party machine as did the Liberals. In the Victorian heyday, the librettist Gilbert was quite justified in having his guardsman sing in the operetta "Iolanthe":

That every boy and every gal
That's born into the world alive
Is either a little Liberal
Or else a little Conservative.

The Two-Party System:
An Explanation

The two-party system was almost wholly confined to the English-speaking lands, to Britain, the United States, and the British Commonwealth countries. On the Continent, not only in France, Italy, and pre-Hitler Germany, but also in the little democracies of Scandinavia, Switzerland, Holland, and Belgium, the multi-party system usually prevailed, and governments were generally coalitions of parties with separate organizations. English-speaking opinion probably exaggerates the defects and dangers of multi-party democracy. But it is clear that a two-party democracy does have distinct advantages in the way of stability and continuity of policy, if only because a given group can enjoy a longer, more assured tenure of power. The historian must attempt somehow to explain why the English-speaking peoples developed this unique institution. He must seek somewhat different explanations for Britain and for the United States, for though both have two-party systems, their total political situations and traditions are far from alike.

In terms of political psychology, the two-party system means that the millions of individual voters who make up each party are in greater agreement than disagreement over what the party stands for; or at least that when they vote for a candidate they feel he stands more for what they want than for what they don't want. Each voter makes some kind of compromise *within himself*, takes something less in practice than he would ideally like. This sort of compromise the French voter of the 1880's for instance did not need to make, at any rate not to anything like the same degree as the British voter. The Frenchman could choose, from among a dozen or more platforms and candidates, the one tailored closest to his desires.

We must still ask why Englishmen made these compromises, why they agreed more than they disagreed. The answer must be sought in the long working out of British history. One part of it lies in the relative security of the islands from external foes, in the long years in which British political habits of moderation and compromise could mature without the constant pressure of foreign wars. The immediate crisis of war may indeed promote a temporary unity in a threatened nation, like the France of 1792–1794. But long, steady exposure to war danger—and all continental states were so exposed—seems to promote psychological tendencies to seek final and extreme solutions.

This same relative isolation of Britain also contributed to the relatively mild form that the universal western struggle between feudalism and the new-model centralized state took there. In France, and on the Continent generally, the new model triumphed only in the seventeenth century, and in the form of divine-right monarchy. Continental states in the nineteenth century had only just gone through—or were still going through—the popular revolutionary modification of absolutism, and were still torn by major class antagonisms between a noble privileged class, backed usually by orthodox religion, and a middle class. In England, as we have seen in earlier chapters, that struggle had occurred a full century and a half earlier and had never been quite as bitter as on the Continent. It had left England in charge of a ruling class that was itself the product of a compromise between the old landed gentry and the new commercial classes, a ruling class that could develop within itself habits of moderation and compromise. The deep abyss the French Revolution had dug between nineteenth-century royalists and republicans and between "clericals" and "anticlericals" on the Continent did not exist in nineteenth-century England.

Thus, even more important than the fact that the Liberals and Conservatives each held together as parties whose members could sink differences in a common party action is the fact that both parties had a wide area of mutual agreement above and beyond party. To put it quite baldly, there wasn't much difference between the Conservatives and the Liberals. When one went out of power and the other came in, the ship of state tacked a bit, but it did not change direction. The Conservative Disraeli and the Liberal Gladstone were perhaps not quite shadowboxing in their heated parliamentary exchanges, but they clearly were not fighting to kill, nor perhaps even for the knockout.

To sum up, government by discussion, Her Majesty's Government and Her Majesty's Opposition equally loyal to established ways, under the shelter of the English Channel and the British navy, in a prosperous land without deep-seated class antagonisms or insuperable class barriers and rigidities—all this had developed in the British people habits of compromise, of law-abidingness, a sort of political sportsmanship. And these habits survive even in the mid-twentieth century, when Victorian geographical security has gone with the airplane and Victorian economic preponderance has gone with the rise of competing industrial nations. The British, who once cut off a king's head and drove another king into exile, have for nearly two centuries enjoyed remarkable political stability. Why these people, once thought hard to govern, have had so stable a government, is still by no means wholly understood.

Reforms of the Utilitarians

The Reform Bill of 1832 was soon followed by a series of major reforms that helped make over, not merely British political life, but British economic and social life as well. The inspiration of these reforms came in large part from a small but influential middle-class group, the "Philosophic Radicals" or Utilitarians (see Chapter 12). These disciples of Bentham and of the Enlightenment believed that men are, if once properly educated, impelled by rational self-interest and thus automatically do what is best for themselves and all their fellows. Under the influence of the Philosophic Radicals, English local government and the English legal system were made simpler and were cleansed of some of the impediments to efficient government action left by the long accumulation of traditional forms, now become "red-tape." Legal procedures, for instance, which had been so complicated that the Chancery Court was many years behind its backlog of cases, were gradually speeded up. In local government, though many medieval offices remained at least in name, the essential work was done by an elective council and by elective officers with supervisory powers over the professional civil servants — including now for the first time professional "policemen." Indeed, London policemen are still occasionally called "Bobbies," after Robert Peel's innovation of the late 1820's.

The middle-class radicals, however, believed firmly that that government governs best which governs least, and they sought rather to expedite that minimum of government than to add to its tasks. They believed in education, but not in compulsory public education; private initiative would in their opinion do well what the government would do poorly and tyrannically. Large-scale government reform of British popular education had therefore to wait until 1870. Meanwhile, the private initiative preached by the Utilitarians sponsored mechanics' institutes and other means of adult and "practical" education. It also sponsored all sorts of private schools, and universities in London, Manchester, and some other British cities. These universities, resembling in many ways our American urban universities, first broke into the centuries-old monopoly of Oxford and Cambridge.

The typical Utilitarian reform, the one that stirred up public opinion most thoroughly, was the New Poor Law of 1834. This bill codified, centralized, and made more coherent a complicated system of public relief that had originated in the Elizabethan Poor Law of 1601 and earlier Tudor legislation. But it did more. It shifted the base of this relief. The old methods of home relief, "outdoor relief," had gradually come to permit supplementary payments from the parishes to able-bodied poor working on low wages, supplements for children, and in general by no means generous but still easy-going "doles" direct to families in their homes. The new system would have none of this laxness, this encouragement of men in what the Utilitarian in spite of his belief in human rationality, rather feared was their "natural" laziness. Poor Law Unions united parishes for greater efficiency, permitted greater supervision by the central government in London, and supplied in formidable poorhouses in which the sexes were firmly separated, the "indoor relief" by which able-bodied paupers were made as uncomfortable as decency would allow. These pains, it was held, would encourage them to try to become self-supporting outside. The New Poor Law offended humanitarians in the upper classes, but from the point of view of middle-class business interests it had the decided merit of making poor relief both more efficient and more economical. The poor at least managed to survive in the workhouses.

Free Trade

Greatest of these Utilitarian reforms in its long-run consequences was the repeal of the Corn Laws in 1846, after a long campaign headed by the Anti-Corn-Law League (see p. 455). What these pressure-group agitators wanted, and ultimately got, was a political economy in which food and other raw materials were imported from abroad without tariffs, and the new efficiently produced manufactured goods were exported to pay for the imports. In the long run — in another century — the difficulty for Britain would lie in the fact that other parts of the world too would become industrial workshops. In the short run, in the early and middle nineteenth century, the difficulty was that protective tariffs in favor of English agriculture made importation of the cheapest possible foodstuffs from abroad impossible. To this difficulty the English industrialists addressed themselves in the campaign against the Corn Laws. Their victory was achieved in 1846 by the conversion of the Conservative leader Peel to their cause, and by the alliance of Peelites and Liberals that put the bill through. Britain was now a free-trade nation, the only major free-trade nation in a world that never quite lost its mercantilist preconceptions and habits. The repeal of the Corn Laws had, however, temporarily split the Conservative party into two groups, one the "Peelites," who accepted the repeal; the other, soon led by a brillant young man named Disraeli, who continued to support high tariffs on wheat. Within a decade the Conservatives were once more united in a single party under Disraeli's leadership.

Labor and Factory Legislation

Still another series of reforms helped make the prosperous England of Gladstone and Disraeli. These were the Factory Acts, begun in 1802 and 1819 with bills sponsored by Peel's father. Addicts of the economic interpretation of history hold that middle-class people put through reforms like those of the Poor Law and the repeal of the Corn Laws, but that the landed gentry and upper-class intellectuals, jealous of the new city wealth and outraged by the ugliness of the new industrial towns, put through reforms like those of the Factory Acts regulating hours of labor, sanitation, and the labor of women and children. It is true that many leaders of the movement to use the power of the state to regulate some part of economic life were not themselves businessmen or industrialists. They were either members of the Tory ruling class, like the Peels, or intellectuals, like Coleridge, Disraeli, Carlyle, Ruskin, and Matthew Arnold, who preached against the horrors of working-class life in prosperous Victorian England. And it is true that the formal philosophy of the British business class was laissez-faire. But the practice was a different matter. None of the Factory Acts and similar reforms of the nineteenth century could really have gone through Parliament successfully without some support from both political parties. Moreover, neither landed gentry nor industrialists and businessmen were mutually exclusive "classes" in a neat Marxist sense. Rather, they were thoroughly mingled in education, marriage, and even in economic interests, since the gentry invested in stocks and bonds and the industrialists invested in landed estates. The elder Peel, father of the Factory Acts, was a self-made industrialist.

The Factory Acts followed a sequence not unlike the sequence of acts that reformed the suffrage. The first acts were very modest indeed; they underlined the frightful conditions they were designed to remedy. That of 1819, for instance, applied only to the cotton industry, forbade night work for children, and limited day work to twelve hours. Even so, it provided for no really effective inspection, and was violated with impunity by many employers. The Act of 1833, forbidding child labor entirely below the age of nine, and restricting it to nine hours for those below thirteen, and twelve for those below eighteen, marked an important stage by setting up salaried inspectors to enforce the law.

By the end of the nineteenth century, there was on the books a whole code of labor legislation, regulating hours of labor for everyone, giving special protection to women and children, and including provisions that made the employer responsible for workmen's compensation in industrial accidents. Then in 1911 came the great National Insurance Act, which provided through combined payments from the state, from employers and from employees, compulsory health and unemployment insurance. The "welfare state" was firmly established in Britain well before the Labour party of our own day had come to power.

Education

The same story of piecemeal but cumulative reform holds true in education. The commonly held Victorian idea that education is not properly a function of the state postponed a general education act until 1870. The issue was complicated by the wrangling of Anglicans and nonconformists, for many existing schools were controlled by a private society that made instruction in the doctrines of the Church of England compulsory. But even before 1870 a government committee had been supplementing local education boards by making grants from the national treasury (in 1860 these grants reached nearly a million pounds), by providing an inspection service, and by helping to organize teacher training. School attendance, however, was not compulsory, and the average age for leaving school was eleven years. After most workingmen got the vote in 1867, worried Tories—and Liberals—began to urge the slogan, "Educate your masters." The bill of 1870, put through under Gladstone's Minister of Education, William Forster, did not quite set up compulsory national education at the elementary level. It did permit the local school boards to compel attendance, and it did extend national aid and supervision. Church schools continued to get aid from taxes levied by the central government, however—an offense to radicals who wanted complete separation of Church and State. Non-sectarian religious instruction was given even in the equivalent of our public schools supported by local taxes, but it was not compulsory.

Beginnings were made in publicly supported schools at the secondary level, though the British "public school," which in American terms is a "private school," continued until our own day to maintain a privileged position in the British social system. In comparison with the public school systems in Germany, France, and the United States, British education on the eve of World War I was administratively complex and full of anomalies. On the whole, though, it got the job done, and the general level of popular education in the British Isles was at least as high as in the other liberal democracies at the time.

Chartism

The most radical of major organized reform movements in nineteenth-century England was Chartism, which played an important part in the political excitements of the 1830's and 1840's, and greatly alarmed the conservative classes. The Chartists were the closest English equivalent of the radical parties which on the Continent carried on the Jacobin tradition of the French Revolution, mingled with the ele-

ments of nascent socialism. The Chartists had a formal program drawn up in a "People's Charter," calling for universal manhood suffrage, the secret ballot, abolition of property requirements for members of Parliament, payment of members, equal electoral districts, and annually elected Parliaments. Their strength lay in the new urban industrial proletariat, supported by many intellectuals of varied social origins, men who clearly believed that if they got the political democracy they wanted the masses would vote themselves the kind of institutions — those of the "welfare state"—that, though maintaining free enterprize, would promote greater economic equality. The movement petered out in a monster petition to Parliament which was never even considered, and in the rising prosperity of the 1850's and 1860's it was effectively stifled. Yet of the original Chartist program all but the demand for annually elected Parliaments, which soon seemed pointless even to radicals, was achieved by act of Parliament in 1918.

Foreign Policy

Nowhere does the basic unity that underlies the party strife of nineteenth-century Britain come out more clearly than in foreign relations. The strife is real enough on hundreds of concrete matters of detail; but so is the unity in the broad lines of British policy. Almost all Englishmen (an unavoidable term, which, though offensive to many of them, has to include Scottish, Welsh, and Ulstermen) were agreed on the fundamental position of Britain: maintain the European state-system in balance, preferably by diplomatic rather than military action, but seek no new territories in Europe; police the seas with the British navy; open world markets to British goods; maintain—and in Africa extend—the vast network of the British Empire, made up of self-governing, English-speaking lands and colonial "possessions" in lands inhabited by the darker-skinned peoples. It is certainly true that the Liberals verbally and emotionally sided in Europe with the liberal nationalist movements, that they sympathized with the struggling Italians, Greeks, and Poles, and that they disliked the old Metternichian powers, especially Russia. It is even true that a Liberal—or better, a belated Whig—foreign minister like Palmerston in mid-century pursued an active policy of near-intervention in behalf of oppressed nationalities, and that British benevolence was a factor in the attainment of Italian unity.

Yet the only European war in which Britain became involved between 1815 and 1914 was the Crimean War of 1854–1856, in which France and England went to war as allies against Russia to protect Turkey and their own Near Eastern interests from what they held to be Russian aggression (see Chapter 14). This was a blundering war on both sides. But it at least checked Russian advances for a time and made the ultimate disposition of the Balkan regions of the decaying Turkish Empire unavoidably a matter for joint action by all the great powers. It was, in fact, a typical balance-of-power war in which Britain played its traditional role of taking arms against a major power (Russia) that seemed about to add unduly to its lands or its "spheres of influence."

Imperial Policy

On imperial policy, it seems at first glance as though British public opinion really was deeply divided. Disraeli and Gladstone were never so gladiatorially fierce as when the Conservative defended the greatness of the Empire and the Liberal attacked imperialism at home and abroad as un-Christian, illiberal, and unprofitable. And it would be absurd to maintain that in action there was no real difference between the two. Disraeli, on the one side, bought up the financially embarrassed Khedive of Egypt's controlling shares in the French-built Suez Canal (1875), thus initiating the British control of Egypt, and triumphantly made Queen Victoria Empress of India (1876). On the other side, Gladstone, in his succeeding ministry, withdrew British troops from Afghanistan in 1880, conceded virtual independence to the Boer Republics in South

Africa by the Pretoria Convention of 1881, and in 1884–1885 neglected General Gordon surrounded by rebels in the Sudan. Yet Gladstone kept British armies on the northwest frontier of India. It was under his administration in 1882 that the British actually bombarded Alexandria and monopolized control of Egypt. Gladstone did send troops to rescue Gordon, though they arrived too late, and even in South Africa the Boer Republics were freed only under the "suzerainty" of Britain. In short, Gladstone regretted and no doubt even neglected the Empire; but he kept it (for details, see Chapter 16).

The Irish Problem

Much nearer home, a nationality problem grew more acute as the nineteenth century came to a close, and did draw something more than a verbal line between Conservatives and Liberals. This was the Irish problem, a problem that had beset the English in one form or another, now acute and now mild, ever since the Norman-English conquest of Ireland in the twelfth century. The English, and the Scots who came to settle in the north of Ireland province of Ulster in the sixteenth and seventeenth centuries, had remained as a privileged Protestant landowning group in the midst of a subject population of Catholic Irish peasants. There were indeed native Irish among the ruling classes, but many if not most of them had been Anglicized and had turned Protestant. For three centuries, religious, political, and economic problems in Ireland had remained unsolved. As the nineteenth century opened, the English attempted to solve the political problem by a formal union of the two kingdoms, with Irish members admitted to the British Parliament, in which they were of course a minority. On January 1, 1801, began the United Kingdom of Great Britain and Ireland. In the prevailing temper of nineteenth-century Britain, it was quite impossible to deny the Irish natives all political rights; and indeed, beginning with the Catholic Emancipation Act of 1829, which allowed Irish voters to elect Catholics to office, most of the various reforms we have outlined above were extended to Ireland. The Irish, led by Daniel O'Connell, the "Great Emancipator," organized politically to press for more thoroughgoing reforms and, eventually, for home rule of the kind the overseas dominions were to achieve (see Chapter 16). They sought not only for political home rule, but also for land reforms, and for disestablishment of the Anglican Church in Ireland — that is, abolition of a state church supported by taxes levied on both members and nonmembers of the church.

Irish hatred for the English was fanned by the disastrous potato famine of the 1840's, when blight ruined a crop essential to the Irish food supply. Although the beginnings of modern transportation by railway and steamship existed, the British government was not organized for prompt and efficient relief measures, nor was the kind of international organization for such relief afforded nowadays by the Red Cross yet in existence. The result was a medieval famine in the heart of modern western civilization, in which tens of thousands died of starvation, and other tens of thousands were forced to migrate, mostly to the United States. The immigrants added to British difficulties, for they carried their inevitable hatreds with them, and formed pressure groups, like the Fenian Brotherhood organized in New York in 1858 to raise funds to aid Irish resistance and to make trouble generally for the British wherever they could. Indeed, the existence of these British-hating Irish-Americans was to be for nearly a century a serious problem for those directing American foreign policy, notably in the first World War.

British governments made piecemeal reforms. The Anglican Church in Ireland was disestablished in 1869, and in the next year an Irish Land Act began a series of agrarian reforms that were designed to protect the tenant from "rack-renting" — the extraction by the landlord, often an absentee member of the British "garrison," of as high a rent as the tenants could pay. The reforms were neither far-reaching nor rapid enough to satisfy the Irish. Moreover, the emotional strength of Irish nationalism grew with the spread of elementary education and the usual literary and cultural forms of national self-consciousness. The Irish question was not just a matter of land, or of religion, but also of a peculiarly intense form of underdog awareness of cultural differences and of nationality. Then in the 1870's a brilliant Irish leader arose, Charles Parnell, himself a Protestant descendant of the "garrison," but a firm Irish patriot. Under the leadership of Parnell in the British Parliament, the Irish nationalists were welded into a firm, well-disciplined party which, though it held less than a hundred seats in the House of Commons of the now United Kingdom, could often swing the balance between Liberals and Conservatives.

The critical step came when in 1885 Gladstone was converted to Home Rule, and introduced his first Home Rule Bill. This bill provided for a separate Irish parliament with some restrictions on its sovereignty, and of course under the Crown. Gladstone's decision split his own Liberal party in something like the way Peel's conversion to Free Trade had split the Conservatives in 1846 (see p. 489). A group led by Joseph Chamberlain, who had begun political life as the reform leader of the great city of Birmingham, seceded under the name of "Liberal Unionists." In effect, they joined the Conservative party, which was often known in the next few decades, so great were the passions aroused in Great Britain by this proposed cutting loose of Ireland, simply as the "Unionist" party. Gladstone lost the election brought on by the split, and Home Rule was dropped for the moment.

Agitation continued in Ireland. It became more bitter when Parnell, involved in a divorce scandal, was dropped by the virtuous Gladstone and by some of his own, equally virtuous Irish followers. In 1892, however, Gladstone won a close election on the Irish issue — or, rather, he obtained enough English seats to get a Second Home Rule Bill through the Commons with the aid of eighty-one Irish nationalists. The bill was defeated, however, in the Conservative House of Lords, and was dropped once more. The Conservatives, when they came in for their ten-year reign in 1895, sought to "kill Home Rule by kindness," carrying several land reform bills that furthered the process of making Ireland a land of small peasant proprietors.

But Ireland was now beyond the reach of kindness, and Irish problems were no longer—if they ever had been—largely economic and administrative. Irish nationalism was now a full cult, nourished by a remarkable literary revival in English and in Gaelic which produced writers like W. B. Yeats, John Synge, and Lady Augusta Gregory. Irish men and women everywhere—including definitely the Irish-Americans—were keyed to a pitch of emotional excitement. They would be satisfied with nothing less than an independent Irish nation.

The Liberals, back in power after 1905, found they needed the votes of the Irish nationalists to carry through their proposal for ending the veto power of the Lords. After some soul-searching, the Liberals struck the bargain: Home Rule in return for the Parliament Act. They introduced in 1912 a Home Rule Bill which—the Parliament Act in 1911 having destroyed the veto power of the Lords—was placed on the books as a law. It never went into force, however, for as Home Rule seemed about to become a fact the predominantly Protestant north of Ireland, the province of Ulster, bitterly opposed to separation from Great Britain, was organized to resist by force of arms. The Home Rule Bill as passed carried the rider that it was not to go into effect until the Ulster question was settled. The outbreak of war in 1914 made such a settlement out of the question, and the stage was set for the Irish Revolution of the 1920's (see Chapter 20).

The Threat to Free Trade

As Great Britain approached the twentieth century, then, new problems arose to disturb the underlying serenity and assurance of the Victorian Age. The Boer War in South Africa (see Chapter 16), Irish troubles, the rising international tensions that were to lead to World War I (see Chapter 17), and the difficulties of securing by taxation and adjusting

the distribution of the new government income made necessary by the rise of the "welfare state," confronted the British people all at once. Though here as always in history we must avoid the temptation to seek a single underlying cause, there was undoubtedly one major factor at work. The long lead Britain had gained in the industrial revolution was being lost as other nations acquired the technical skills of large-scale production. Germany, the Low Countries, Switzerland, the United States, and in a measure all the West, were competing with Britain on the world market.

Under such conditions, it was natural that some Britishers should come to doubt the wisdom of the free trade policies that had won the day in 1846. For the Germans and others were not only underselling the British abroad; they were actually invading the British home market. Why not protect that market by a tariff system? Few Britishers were foolish enough to believe that the home islands, already by the 1880's too densely populated to feed themselves and constitute a self-sufficient economy, could surround themselves with a simple tariff wall. But the Empire was world-wide, with abundant resources, with thousands of square miles of agricultural lands. Within it the classical mercantilist interchange of manufactures for raw materials could still in theory provide a balanced economic system. Britain could still be, if not the workshop of the world, at least the workshop of the quarter of the world that composed the British Commonwealth and Empire.

The same Joseph Chamberlain who led the secession from the Liberals on the question of Home Rule for Ireland also led a secession on an issue of even more fundamental importance. He became a protectionist and imperialist. He gave special importance to the establishment of a system of imperial preference through which the whole complex of lands under the Crown would be knit together in a tariff union. Many Conservatives, never wholly reconciled to free trade, welcomed the issue, and the new Unionist party made protection a major plank in its program. Liberal opposition, however, was still much too strong, and there was opposition also in Conservative ranks. Chamberlain, reversing the aims but imitating the methods of Cobden and the Anti-Corn Law League of the 1840's, organized a Tariff Reform League. In 1903, he made in cabinet sweeping proposals that would have restored moderate duties on food-stuffs and raw materials (largely to give a basis for negotiating with the dominions, which already had tariff systems of their own) and on foreign manufactured goods. But the Conservative leader, Balfour, did not dare go so far, and Chamberlain resigned with his bill unpassed. Indeed, Chamberlain, who had already split the Liberal party on Home Rule, now split the Conservatives on tariff-reform. The new Liberal government after 1905 continued the policy of free trade. The rift Chamberlain had made in the old Liberal party was, however, never really repaired. Its right wing was driven to Toryism; its left wing to the Labour party.

The Welfare State

The Liberals were, however, committed to another policy as contrary to the classical philosophy of laissez-faire as was protectionism. This was the welfare state—social security through compulsory insurance managed by the state, and in part financed by the state, minimum-wage laws, progressive taxation on incomes and inheritances, compulsory free public education, public works and services of all kinds. The dramatic point in the working out of the program was the "People's Budget" of 1909, introduced by a new figure on the political stage, a Welshman, the Liberal Chancellor of the Exchequer, Lloyd George (1863–1945). This budget, which frankly proposed to tax the rich to finance the new welfare measures, and also the rising naval costs brought on by the aramament race with Germany (see Chapter 17), was clearly no ordinary tax measure. It was a means of altering the social and economic structure of Britain. Its opponents not unjustly called it "not a budget, but a revolution." It passed the Commons, but was thrown out by the Lords, even though it was a "money bill." The Liberals went to the country for the second time in 1910 and after a close and exciting election were able to put through the Parliament Act of 1911, which took away from the Lords all power to alter a money bill, and left them with no more than a delaying power of not more than two years over all other legislation. The Liberal program of social legislation was saved. It was saved under conditions strongly reminiscent of 1832 (see p. 485), for the new king, George V (1910–1936), had promised Prime Minister Asquith that if necessary he would create enough new peerages—which might have meant several hundred—to put the Parliament Act through the House of Lords. As in 1832, the threat was enough, and the Peers yielded.

David Lloyd George, 1898.

But was it a *Liberal* program? The dissenting Liberals who had followed Joseph Chamberlain out of the party in the 1880's thought not, and it was normal enough for Chamberlain's two sons, Austen and Neville, who played an important part in twentieth-century politics, to think of themselves as Conservatives. For what happened in the generation after 1880 was a major change in the political orientation of British parties. The Liberals, who had believed that that government governs best which governs least, and least expensively, had come to believe that the state must interfere in economic life to help the underdog, and had come to adopt Lloyd George's plan for redistributing the national wealth by social insurance financed by taxation of the rich and well-to-do. And the Conservatives, who in the mid-nineteenth century had stood for factory acts and at least mild forms of the welfare state, were now in large part committed to a laissez-faire program against government "intervention," a program astonishingly like that of the Liberals of 1850. Whatever the future verdict of historians on the "welfare state" of the twentieth century, they will note that Great Britain was the first great democratic society to institute such a state.

The Labour Party

One factor in this change had been the growth of the British Labour party, which originated in a number of groups formed in the late nineteenth century. Labour, though not yet unified, had developed by 1905 into a party able to command fifty-three seats in the Commons. The political ideas that went into the making of the British Labour Party antedate by a good deal its formal organization. Basically these are the common democratic drives and principles of the Western world, which were first clearly shaped and disseminated in the Enlightenment of the eighteenth century (see Chapter 9). It wanted the welfare state, and indeed some Labourites wanted a socialist state in which at least the major industries were nationalized. Part of the motivation for the Liberal program of social legislation was a desire to forestall Labour. Just as in 1867 the Tories had "walked away with the Whigs' clothes" and had given the workingman the vote, so in 1911 the Liberals stole Labour's clothes and gave the workingman social security. But these tactics worked no better in the twentieth century than in the nineteenth, and the workingmen on the whole stuck by the Labour party. The party could not, of course, in a country like Britain have attained national power from a base limited to workingmen. It has had from the start support from many "intellectuals" as well as from many upper and middle class people who sympathized with the cause of social justice. The Liberal party began a long decline, hastened by the upsetting effects of World War I, by the addition of many new working-class voters by the Reform Act of 1918, and no doubt by many other factors.

Not all the motivation of the Liberals in these early years of the twentieth century was, however, mere fear of Labour. In part, their conversion from laissez-faire to social security was a positive one, a sincere belief that the logic of their democratic assumptions must drive them to raise the general standard of living in Britain by state action. Something broadly analogous was happening throughout the democratic West—in France, in the smaller democracies, and, a few decades later, in the United States. An important part of the bourgeoisie in all these countries swung over, not to doctrinaire socialism, but to programs of social legislation put through by the usual machinery of change under a wide democratic suffrage. The English Chartists back in the early nineteenth century had had the apparently naive belief that universal suffrage would pave the way to greater social and economic equality. In the long run, events were to prove that the Chartists were far from being entirely wrong. The welfare state began in a democracy, although in Bismarck's Germany there was also early social legislation. (see pp. 532–533).

II   France—Second Empire and Third Republic

The Coup d'État of 1851

A century ago France seemed to many English-speaking critics, as she seems to many today, a rather uncertain member of the community of nations ruled by the democratic decencies—that is, government by discussion, peaceful alternation of "ins" and "outs" through the working of the party system, and the usual freedoms of "civil rights." The democratic revolution, so optimistically begun in 1848 (see Chapter 11), had by 1852 brought still another Bonaparte to the throne of France in the person of Napoleon III, nephew of the first Napoleon. (Note that "Napoleon II," son of the first Napoleon by Marie Louise, never really ruled, any more than did the son of Louis XVI, the "Louis XVII" who died in prison during the great French Revolution.) As President of the Second Republic, Prince Louis Napoleon had soon quarreled with the National Assembly, which refused to amend the Constitution of 1848 to allow him a second term of office. Fearful of radicals and socialists, the Assembly also whittled down the universal male suffrage of 1848 and thus enabled the Prince President to maintain that he was acting as the champion of persecuted popular democracy.

The *coup d'état* of December 2, 1851, artfully timed for the sacred Bonapartist day of the coronation of Napoleon I (December 2, 1804) and the greatest Napoleonic victory, the battle of Austerlitz (December 2, 1805), was a sterotyped affair. Controlling the army, Louis Napoleon and his fellow conspirators found it easy to purge the Assembly and make way for a popular vote on a new constitution. Even the expected street fighting on the barricades of Paris, which broke out on December 3, proved to be no wholesale bloodletting. It left victims enough as martyrs, however, and, po-litically more important, it enabled the President to pose as the champion of order against a largely imaginary socialist plot. Napoleon quickly got himself approved by a plebiscite, which by 7,500,000 votes to 640,000 gave him the right to draw up a new constitution. Napoleon III's use of his strong presidential office to destroy the Second Republic left its mark on the Third and Fourth Republics; French republicans came to fear a strong president of the American type, and devised institutions which, until De Gaulle in 1958 apparently overcame this fear in many (see Chapter 23), tended to keep the French executive weak and divided.

The plebiscite was accompanied by skillful propaganda, but it was not crudely a work of force. Though many opponents of Napoleon simply did not vote, it seems that at least a very substantial majority of Frenchmen over twenty-one really were willing to try another dictator. There were many reasons why men voted "yes." Almost all were weary of the struggles of the last three years. Many were frightened by the specter of socialism, now for the first time under that name a definite factor in western politics. For nearly three decades the full force of fashionable French literature had been at work making the Napoleonic legend and identifying the name of Napoleon with the "pooled self-esteem" of French patriotism. Many a man voted "yes" not to Louis Napoleon, nor to any approval of dictatorship for itself, but to the music of the "Marseillaise," the cannon of Austerlitz, to all the glories of France.

The Second Empire, 1852–1870: Domestic Developments

The new constitution set up a lightly veiled dictatorship very much like that of Napoleon I.

The "chief of state" (he became formally "emperor" on the sacred date, December 2, in 1852) had full authority; he was responsible only to the nation. He governed through ministers, judges, and a whole bureaucracy, in the appointment of which he had the final voice. The popularly elected assembly, the *Corps Législatif,* was filled with "official" candidates sent up by influence of the efficient appointed officials in the provinces. It had no power to initiate or amend legislation; it had only a veto, which in the first few years it rarely used. Yet Napoleon III insisted that he was no mere tool of the possessing classes, no conservative, but an agent of real reform, an emperor of the masses, a kind of continental equivalent of the "Tory democrat" that Disraeli in England was claiming to be. This claim indeed has been made by almost all our recent dictators, Communist or Fascist; they all claim to be *real* democrats, real protectors of ordinary men who in the classical western democracies, they insist, are actually victims of capitalist exploitation. Napoleon III has sometimes been seen as the first of these modern dictators, as a "proto-fascist"; and the careful student of his career can learn much that throws light on our own problems today.

Certainly by comparison with later social legislation in Germany, Britain, or Scandinavia, Napoleon's concrete achievements in direct benefit of the workers were slight. He did carry through a great program of public works, notably in Paris, where his prefect Haussmann cut through the medieval mazes of streets, those broad straight avenues which all the world knows so well, and which, incidentally, could be easily swept by gunfire and made street fighting that much more difficult. And he did help with housing and encourage workers' mutual aid societies. But the legal code of labor in France in 1860 was less "modern" than that of England. The standard of living of French labor in the growing cities was well behind that of Britain, and behind that of Germany and the smaller democracies. French labor did indeed benefit from the general prosperity that came to France in the 1850's, as it came to Great Britain, but the gains in wages were at least partly counter-balanced by

rising prices. France lagged as a welfare state.

It was the bourgeoisie that made most out of the Second Empire. Napoleon's government encouraged improvement in banking facilities, helped the great growth of French railways by state guaranties, and in general furthered the rise of industry in the two decades after 1850. That rise was, especially in large-scale heavy industries, definitely inferior to that of the British and to the already growing German industry. But it was in absolute terms a very real rise. Paris grew into a major metropolitan area, and centers like Lyons and Rouen in textiles, Clermont-Ferrand and St. Etienne in metallurgy, and many other cities came to have genuine industrial economies, with all the problems of slums, trade unions, and other signs of modernity. Yet there remained then as under later French governments an adhesion to older methods of doing business, to small firms often under family control, to luxury trades in which handicraft skills remained im-

Napoleon III (1808–1873).

portant in spite of the machine, all of which meant that in quantitative terms of actual production France fell behind the industrial West. In the '60's she lost her Continental leadership in iron and steel production to the new Germany, and was subsequently far outdistanced by the burgeoning economy of the United States. Her growth in population, too, fell well behind that of the others. At the end of the nineteenth century, she was not much more than 50 per cent more populous than at the beginning—and this with almost no emigration. Britain, in spite of a large emigration, had about tripled her population, and Germany, too, was growing rapidly. Even Italy, with slender natural resources and less industry than France, was growing in population faster than France, and was to outstrip her in our own times (in 1966 Italy about 52,000,000, France about 49,000,000). It must be confessed that the reasons for this demographic weakness of nineteenth- and early twentieth-century France remain a problem for the sociological historian. In view of the actual fecundity of the kindred French-Canadian stock, it would seem that "race" factors depending on biological inheritance must be ruled out; moreover, the striking increase in the French birth rate since 1946 took place in the same "race" that had fallen behind in the nineteenth and early twentieth centuries.

The Second Empire: Foreign Policy

Yet the France of the Second Empire was still a very great power, and the extent of her comparative decline was by no means clear to contemporaries. Although the French gained little from the Crimean War, they did at least have the satisfaction of playing host to the postwar congress at Paris in 1856. And the Paris Exposition of 1855, a counterpart of the famous London exhibition of 1851, was a great success that showed Napoleon III at the height of his power. He had pledged himself to use that power for peace, but he allowed himself, partly through a romantic interest in "oppressed nationalities," partly from age-old motives of prestige, to become involved in a war against Austria for the liberation of Italy. French armies won victories in this war of 1859; characteristically, in these modern times of "publicity," the names of the French victories of Magenta and Solferino were taken up into dressmaking, cookery, and urban real estate.

In 1860 the Italians took things into their own hands and set about organizing the whole peninsula, including papal Rome, into an Italian kingdom. Napoleon depended too much on Catholic support at home to be able to permit the extinction of papal territorial power; moreover, the too great success of his plans was threatening the European balance of power. He therefore temporized, permitting the union of most of Italy under the house of Savoy, but protecting the Pope's temporal power with a French garrison in Rome, leaving Venetia still in Austrian hands, and taking the city and region of Nice and the French-speaking part of Alpine Savoy away from Piedmont as a reward for his services. He thus managed to offend most Italians, and liberals everywhere, as well as most of his own Catholic supporters at home.

To make matters worse, in 1861 Napoleon began a wild adventure in Mexico, supporting with French arms and men an expedition to put the Austrian prince Maximilian on an imperial throne. The Europeanized Mexican upper classes were in part willing to support this venture, for like most Latin Americans of the nineteenth century, their cultural ideal was France. But from the start the Mexican people resented the foreign intruder, and Maximilian had to rely heavily on French support to penetrate to Mexico City, where he was proclaimed Emperor in June, 1863. The United States, engaged in the Civil War, could do nothing at the time against what Americans regarded as an infraction of the Monroe Doctrine. But after peace had been restored in the United States, the American government protested strongly. The rival of Maximilian, the republican leader Juarez, had no difficulty in defeating the Mexican supporters of Maximilian, once Napoleon under American pressure had abandoned them. The unfortunate Maximilian fell before a firing squad in 1867. This unsuccessful venture was the last direct attempt made by a European power to install a new government in any of the Americas in defiance of the Monroe Doctrine. Soviet support of Castro's Cuba did not quite constitute such direct interference.

The "Liberal Empire"

Napoleon had come to power, as we have seen, on a platform of national unity against the extreme demands of the social revolutionists of 1848. But in spite of the plebiscite, it became more and more clear that if France had a national unity, it was not of the monolithic, totalitarian sort, but a unity that had to be worked out in the open competition of modern western political life with parties, parliamentary debate, newspapers, in short, with government by discussion. Napoleon could not in fact be a symbolic head of state, above the struggle, nor even a final umpire. He could not be a republican; he could not be a legitimate monarchist, though much of France, and particularly the conservative France which held authoritarian views, was loyal to the legitimacy of the Bourbons, or the somewhat dubious legitimacy of the Orléanists. He could not even be a good devout Catholic, in spite of the orthodoxy of his wife, the Empress Eugénie, for his Bonapartist background was heavily tinged with the anticlericalism of the eighteenth century, and his bungling of the Italian problem had deeply offended clericals. He could only head an "official" party, relying on the manipulative skills of his bureaucrats to work the cumbersome machinery of a parliamentary system designed, like that of Napoleon I, as a disguise for dictatorship.

As the pressure of genuine party differences rose, in reflection of genuine moral, social and economic group interests, Napoleon slowly abandoned the measures of repression he had begun with and sought to establish himself in something like the position of a constitutional monarch. An act of 1860 gave the Legislative Assembly power to discuss freely a reply to the address from the throne, and throughout the 1860's these powers were extended in the

name of the "Liberal Empire." Gradually, political life in France took on a pattern of parliamentary government, with a Right, Left, and Center. As a result of the general election of 1869, the government was faced with a strong legal opposition, thirty of whom were declared republicans. On July 12, 1869, Napoleon capitulated and granted the Legislative Assembly the right to propose laws, and to criticize and vote the budget. Partial ministerial responsibility seemed just around the corner as Napoleon entrusted the government to the head of the moderates, Emile Ollivier. A plebiscite in May, 1870, overwhelmingly ratified these changes.

It is at least possible that the Second empire might thus have been converted into a constitutional monarchy. The changes had indeed been wrung from the Emperor by popular agitation, not merely political but also economic in the form of strikes. It is quite as possible that a radical republican ground swell would have gone on to submerge the Empire in any case. But the disastrous defeats of the French armies in the Franco-Prussian War into which Napoleon was maneuvered by the skill of Bismarck (see Chapter 14) put an end to the experiment of the Liberal Empire. On September 4, 1870, after the humiliating capitulation of Sedan, a Parisian mob forced a rump Legislative Assembly to decree the fall of the Empire, and at the classic center of French republicanism, the Paris City Hall, the Third Republic was proclaimed.

The Birth of the Third Republic

The government of the new Republic was too good a child of 1792 to give up the war against the national enemy. A government of national defense tried to continue the struggle, but the miracle of Valmy (see p. 374) was not to be repeated. In October, General Bazaine surrendered a large French force at Metz, and the disorganized elements of other French armies were helpless before the powerful German forces. An exhausted nation, sick of the war, chose in February a National Assembly that met at Bordeaux and sued for peace. The special circumstances of that election, however, placed on the new Republic an additional handicap. For meanwhile Paris, besieged by the Germans, had resisted desperately until starvation forced its surrender in January, 1871. Even under pressure of the siege, Parisian radicals tried to seize power and revive the old Paris Commune, or city government, of 1792. These radicals could not stomach the capitulation that the rest of the country seemed to be preparing. In the elections to the National Assembly, their intransigence helped to turn the provincial voters toward conservative candidates pledged to make peace — and to restore, not the Republic, but the old monarchy.

This new Assembly, on March 1, 1871, voted to accept a peace ceding Alsace and a substantial part of Lorraine to Germany and paying an indemnity of five billion francs (about $1,000,000,000). Then the Paris National Guard, which had not been disarmed by the Germans, went over to the radicals, and the Paris Commune was set up. Marxist legend has consecrated the Parisian Commune of 1871 as the first major socialist government. The Communards were in fact rather Jacobins, radical anticlericals and highly patriotic republicans who wanted a society of small independent shopkeepers and artisans, not the abolition of private property. In any case, they had no chance in the besieged city to introduce sweeping social reforms. But their revolutionary aspect alarmed the rest of France, and their refusal to accept the peace was a challenge the National Assembly had to meet. To the horrors of the first siege by the Germans

Barricades in Paris during the Commune, 1871.

were added the horrors of a new siege by the government of the National Assembly, which gathered its troops at Versailles and in the "Bloody Week" of May 21–28 advanced through the barricades to clear the city.

The Third French Republic was thus born in foreign and in civil war and began with a heritage of unresolved cleavages. Indeed, it was not at all clear in 1871 that there was a Third Republic at all. More than half the members of the new National Assembly were monarchists, anxious to undo the formal declaration of a republic made in republican Paris right after Sedan. But now we encounter one of those concrete events that are the despair of those who seek the clue to history in vast impersonal forces beyond the play of human personality. About half the monarchist deputies were pledged to the elder "legitimate" Bourbon line represented by the Count of Chambord, grandson of Charles X, and the other half to the younger Orléanist line that had come to the throne in 1830, represented by the Count of Paris, grandson of Louis Philippe. Chambord might have become in fact what he was to his supporters, King Henry V, had he been willing to make the slightest concession to Orléanist sentiments and accept the revolutionary blue, white, and red tricolor flag that Louis Philippe had himself accepted as the flag of France. But he insisted on the white flag and gold lilies of Bourbon, which for millions of Frenchmen meant complete repudiation of all that had happened since 1789. Chambord did not, of course, act *just* for a white flag and against a tricolor one; behind these symbols lay real motives tied up with all French history. He meant to be not just a Victorian symbol, a purely "decorative" monarch, but a real king. No one, however, could be that sort of king in France at that moment.

In the resulting stalemate, the republican minority was able to maintain itself, and slowly gather strength. Thiers, the elder statesman of the Orléanist monarchy, who had been a leader in the opposition to Napoleon III, was recognized as "President of the Republic" and carried through the final settlement with Germany. He was succeeded in 1873 by Marshal MacMahon, a soldier and a monarchist, who was elected to hold the government together while the monarchist majority sought to unite in some kind of compromise Bourbons and Orléanists. That compromise was never achieved, as Chambord continued to insist on the white flag, and in 1875 a series of constitutional measures formally established the Third Republic.

The Constitution of 1875

These laws, known collectively as the Constitution of 1875, provided for a president elected by an absolute majority of Senate and Chamber of Deputies sitting together as a National Assembly, the usual ministers, and a bicameral legislature elected by universal manhood suffrage. The Senate was chosen by indirect election, the Chamber of Deputies by direct election; all legislation had to pass both houses, though only the lower could initiate finance bills. The critical point was that of the responsibility of the ministers. Had the president been able to dismiss them, a new Napoleon III might easily have arisen to destroy the Republic. MacMahon attempted to exercise this power when on May 16, 1877, he dismissed the anticlerical premier, Jules Simon, and got the conservative Duke of Broglie to form a cabinet. But the Chamber was now really republican—or at least anti-monarchist—and voted "no confidence" in Broglie by a big majority. MacMahon was thus forced to dissolve the Chamber and call for a new national election—which he could do constitutionally. In the new elections the republicans, though losing some seats, still retained a good majority in the Chamber, and could now force the president to name a republican premier. Disgruntled, MacMahon resigned in 1879 and was succeeded by a conservative republican, Jules Grévy. This crisis of the *Seize Mai* (May 16) set a precedent for the Third Republic. No president thereafter dared to dissolve the Chamber, and the presidency became a ceremonial office, made fun of in the press and on the stage. But at any rate, nine years after its establishment in name, the Third Republic had at last become a fact.

It was in form a kind of republican transposition of constitutional monarchy, with an ornamental president instead of an ornamental king. The real executive, as in England, was the ministry, in effect a committee responsible to the legislature—indeed to the Chamber of Deputies, which soon became the focus of political action, leaving the Senate little real power. The Chamber, reflecting the political habits of the ideologically divided country, was composed not of two, but of a dozen or more parties, so that any ministry had to be supported by a coalition subject to constant shifting in the play of personalities and principles. The result was a marked instability of ministries. The "life expectancy" of a ministry under the Third Republic was hardly a year.

Yet such a figure is misleading. A French ministry under the Third Republic—and indeed under the Fourth Republic—did not usually resign and give way to a totally different ministry with totally different policies. Instead, its personnel was shifted a bit, a compromise or so was made with certain parliamentary groups, and the new ministry carried on much as did the old. For instance, Briand, the great champion of collective security (after the war of 1914–1918), headed ten different cabinets at various times between 1909 and 1926; Delcassé, the architect of France's entente with England, served as foreign minister continuously through several cabinets and seven years (1898–1905). And in our own day two individuals from the same party, Schuman and Bidault, alternated in the foreign ministry through a dozen cabinets of the Fourth Republic. Moreover, the day-to-day task of governing was carried on by a civil service, by experts in the law courts and in the educational system as well as in the executive department. This permanent personnel, or "bureaucracy" subject only to broad policy control from above, preserved a basic continuity in French political action, especially in foreign policy, which if not always successful, was at least as consistent and persistent under the Third Republic as that of any western democracy.

The system was highly democratic, for it could work only by means of constant and subtle compromises. These, the essence of democratic government, were made in France

—and in most of the democratic world outside the English-speaking countries—by the several parties in open debate and voting in the legislature *after* an election. In the English-speaking countries, these compromises are

Cartoon of 1873, illustrating the National Assembly's division into competing Bourbon, Orléanist, and Bonapartist choruses. The sculptor depicting the Republic looks down from the scaffold, and Thiers leaves the scene in despair.

made *before* an election, *within* each of the two major parties, often in the privacy of the famous smoke-filled room. Probably the English-speaking method both conceals antagonisms and encourages the habit of willing compromise more effectively than does the continental method. But neither method will work if the underlying antagonisms are really intense, beyond compromise. For example, the American two-party system obviously failed to avert the Civil War, had indeed begun in the 1850's to break down into a plural-party system.

Boulanger and Panama

Bitter antagonisms did indeed threaten the Third French Republic between 1879 and 1914, but they did not destroy it. For one thing, the Republic's opponents on the Right and on the Left could never get together. On the Right, although the royalists eventually patched up their quarrels between Bourbon and Orléanist, and although they had some support in literary circles, they could not recover the strength they had dissipated in the 1870's. Nor could the Bonapartists make serious gains in public opinion, though they survived as a political group into the twentieth century. The Catholics, though they feared the anticlerical orientation of many republicans, were after the accession of Pope Leo XIII in 1878 encouraged to develop their way of life by frank acceptance of the freedom of worship that the Constitution of the Republic offered them. Many of the out-and-out Rightist enemies of the Republic were forced to do violence to their own conservative and legitimist principles by seeking some new man who would win over the floating discontent always present in a modern industrial state and set up a dictatorship.

In the 1880's, they hoped that they had found such a man in General Boulanger, an ambitious soldier who had as minister of war catered to French desire for revenge on Germany. But the Boulangist movement was founded on a man of straw. The General cut an impressive figure in public appearances, and in by-elections to fill vacancies caused by deaths or resignations in the Chamber he showed he could command a popular following. But from the point of view of many traditional conservatives he had compromising origins and radical friends, and, as it became clear that Boulanger in power might rush the country into war, his following threatened to

desert him. In January, 1889, he swept a by-election in Paris, but his nerve failed when he was faced with the need to resort to the classic technique of the *coup d'état*. Instead of seizing power by force of arms, he sought refuge with his mistress. The government now took courage and threatened to try him for treason; Boulanger fled to Brussels and committed suicide on the grave of his beloved in 1891. The Republic had surmounted its first great crisis.

Boulanger's cause had gained strength from a scandal in republican ranks. Daniel Wilson, President Grévy's son-in-law, was implicated in the selling of posts in the Legion of Honor. The opposition press made out that the government was riddled with graft. More fuel went on the fire in the early 1890's, when there burst into publicity one of those crises of corruption, graft, and racketeering that seem endemic in modern western societies. This was the Panama scandal which was brought on by the failure of De Lesseps' attempt to duplicate in Panama his success in building the Suez Canal. It involved accusations of criminal corruption against ministers, deputies, financiers, and an unfortunate Jewish banker, Reinach, who either committed suicide or was murdered just before his trial. And indeed, as in the somewhat comparable Crédit Mobilier scandal in the United States in 1873, it was established that ministers and deputies had accepted financial reward for backing the shaky Panama company. Bad as it was, the Panama scandal was to pale before the Dreyfus affair. For with this famous affair a force that was to trouble the western world for decades to come first really attained dramatic intensity and world-wide attention. This was anti-Semitism.

The Dreyfus Case

Dreyfus, a Jew and a captain in the French army, was the almost accidental victim of an espionage intrigue and of the anti-Semitism then prevalent in France, especially in military and Catholic circles. Accused of selling military secrets to the Germans, he was railroaded into trial as a scapegoat and was convicted of treason in 1894. Colonel Picquart, an intelligence officer, became convinced that the document on which Dreyfus had been convicted was a forgery, and that the real traitor was a disreputable adventurer of Hungarian blood but of French birth, Major Esterhazy. Picquart was quietly shipped off to Africa by his superiors, who wished to let sleeping dogs lie. But the Dreyfus family, by independent investigation, arrived at the conclusion that Esterhazy was the traitor, and sought to reopen the case. Esterhazy was tried and acquitted, but the affair was now too public for such silencing. In 1898, the famous novelist Zola brought matters to a crisis by publishing his open letter, *"J'Accuse."* Zola accused the military leaders, one by one, of sacrificing an innocent man deliberately in order to save the reputation of the army.

France was now divided into Dreyfusards and Anti-Dreyfusards; the former defended in Dreyfus the Republic, the latter attacked it. Almost all the far Left, which had hitherto held aloof from the affair as just one more example of the rottenness of the bourgeois state, now rallied to the Third Republic. Dreyfus was brought back from his prison on Devil's Island in French Guiana and was retried in the midst of a frenzied campaign in the press and on the platform. The military court, faced with new evidence brought out by the suicide of Colonel Henry, the real forger of the most incriminating of the original documents used to convict Dreyfus, again found Dreyfus guilty of treason, but with the almost incredible qualification—in a treason case—of "extenuating circumstances." This attempt at face-saving saved nothing. Dreyfus was pardoned by the President of the Republic in 1899, and in 1906, after the tensions had abated, he was acquitted and restored to the army with the rank of major.

The Dreyfus affair presents a remarkably well-documented case study in social psychology. The simple juridical issue—was this man guilty or not guilty of treason—never wholly disappeared in the mass hysteria. Many Frenchmen who did not like Dreyfus or Jews or who did revere the Church, army, and the whole apparatus of the Right, none the less sought to make up their minds solely on the basis of the facts. Yet many on both sides worked themselves up to a point where the question of Dreyfus' guilt was wholly submerged in this great confronting of the "two Frances"—the France of the Republic, heir to the great revolution and the principles of 1789, on the one hand, and, on the other, the France of the monarchy, of Throne and Altar, and of the army, which had never really reconciled itself to the great revolution. For the ordinary person, the open admission of forgery by Colonel Henry and his subsequent suicide were enough; he now thought Dreyfus innocent. But for the violent Anti-Dreyfusard, Henry's act made him a hero and a martyr; he had died for his country! A paper was circulated in Paris asking for a memorial to Henry:

Colonel Henry's Devotion to his Country.
Public subscription for a monument to be raised to him.

When an officer is reduced to committing a pretended forgery in order to restore peace to his country and rid it of a traitor, that soldier is to be mourned.

If he pays for his attempt with his life, he is a martyr.

If he voluntarily takes his life,
    HE IS A HERO.*

These were months of real mass hysteria, in which both sides were swayed by emotions far too strong for reason to control.

The Republic after Dreyfus

With the victory of the Dreyfusards, the Republic moved to the Left and punished the Church for its support of the army and the Anti-Dreyfusards. The triumphant republicans in a series of measures between 1901 and 1905 destroyed the Concordat of 1801 between Napoleon I and the Pope which had established the Roman Catholic Church in a privileged position in the French state (see p. 388). The Catholic teaching orders were forced to dissolve, and some 12,000 Catholic schools, which had been formidable rivals of the state school system, had to close down. The state was

*F. C. Conybeare, *The Dreyfus Case* (London, 1898), 298.

Help Keep the City Clean
AND BE A
PUBLIC BENEFACTOR

USE ONLY
TEXAS MADE BAGGING.
MADE BY
GALVESTON BAGGING MILLS
MANUFACTURERS OF JUTE BAGGING.
BRANDS, "Texas" 2-lb Bagging.
"Star" 2¼-lb Bagging.
DEALERS IN COTTON TIES.
Write us for Prices.
GALVESTON BAGGING AND CORDAGE CO.,
GALVESTON, TEX.

GRAND OPERA HOUSE.
Nine Days, Beginning Today Matinee.
MATINEES DAILY
THE MANHATTAN STOCK CO.
25 PEOPLE—25
Band and Orchestra. Special Scenery.
Double Company—Dramatic and Vaudeville.
Matinee Prices ....10c, 20c.
Night Prices ....10c, 20c, 30c.
Today Matinee { "Lightning Rod Agent," at 2:30 p. m.
To Night { "A Chain of Evidence."
SEATS ON SALE TO-DAY.

THE TELEPHONE
Is recognized by the ADJUTANT GENERAL of Texas, as an important AID to the STATE MILITIA. Every COMPANY OFFICER, every SOLDIER and EVERYBODY ELSE should have one. CHEAP RATES. Call us up.

Southwestern Telegraph & Telephone Co.

COTTON.
We are prepared to make liberal advances on COTTON shipped to us for prompt sale or to be held, and our chances are as low as it be offered by any reputable house. If you have to get shipped cotton to us, give us a trial and you will be pleased with the results. Send and daily quotations furnished free.

GROCERIES.
Interview our traveling salesmen or send us your open orders, and note what prompt and satisfactory service and courteous treatment you will receive.

CARSON, SEWALL & CO.,
Wholesale Grocers and Cotton Factors
HOUSTON, TEX.

Bagging AND Ties
We are prepared to make prompt shipment of BAGGING and TIES.
Ask us for prices.

F. Cannon Commission Co.,
Galveston, Tex.

Prof. L. G. de la Canal,
Instructor on the Piano.
For terms apply to the Mexican Consul.
P. O. 991.

For Shipment Monday.
Fancy Colorado Cabbage,
Fancy Ben Davis Apples,
Assorted California Fruits,
Grapes, Peaches and Pears.

T. H. Thompson & Co.,
HOUSTON, - - - TEXAS.

DISTURBANCES IN RENNES

BEGUN BY THE ANTI-DREYFUSARDS, TWO MEN ENTERED THE HOTEL MODERNE AND

INSULTED LADIES IN THE GARDEN

La Dame Blanche the Special Object of Their Ire—Raised Trouble Elsewhere.

Rennes, Sept. 9.—Scenes of great excitement occurred at Rennes to-night. The anti-Dreyfusards broke loose and started a demonstration which, but for prompt and rigorous measures by the police, would undoubtedly have developed into serious disorders.

The first sign of trouble manifested itself immediately after the verdict became known. The streets leading to the Lycee were at that time filled with crowds of people awaiting news from the court room. The announcement of the sentence—the condemnation was agreeable to a majority of those, and cheers and cries of "Vive l'armee" were raised, the gendarmes and the troops looking on without making any attempt at interference. The terrace in front of the Cafe de la Paix, the leading cafe in Rennes, was filled with people taking their afternoon drinks and aperitives. When the verdict of the court was announced the customers rose to their feet and demanded that the string band should give "Die Marseillaise." The band struck up the air and the crowds, both inside and out, joined in the national song.

Colonel Jouaust passed by a little later on foot and in full uniform on his way from the Lycee to his home. The crowd, with bared heads, cheered him, crying: "Vive l'armee."

Colonel Jouaust, in reply to their cheers, saluted with his hand to his kepi.

As dinner time approached the streets became empty, but about 8 o'clock the crowds again gathered. Just then an incident occurred at the Hotel Moderne, which is known as the Dreyfusard center. Two men, notorious anti-Dreyfusards, came in at the rear garden, inside the hotel, and sat down at one of the little marble tables under the palm trees and ordered coffee. At an adjoining table sat La Dame Blanche, with a companion, while at other tables were seated MM. Bernard, Labori and Gorinteri, with other Dreyfusards. The two newcomers at once began to make offensive remarks about Dreyfus and Jews generally. One of them, turning to La Dame Blanche, said: "Oh, these dirty Jews; these dirty Dreyfusards!"

La Dame Blanche replied, telling him not to address her. The men, however, persisted and added personal insults, whereupon La Dame Blanche became greatly excited and called them cowards to insult a woman. The man retorted offensively and in a moment La Dame Blanche clutched a menu card to a heavy metal frame and threw it at the head of her insulter, narrowly missing him. The other diners, seeing the trouble, rose en masse and threatened to throw the men out of the garden. In an instant the place became a perfect Babel, every one shouting at the top of his voice, calling the men cowards and "canaille."

The ladies present hastily withdrew, Madame Lazare being carried away in a fainting condition. Just as the threatened free fight was at the point of breaking out a detachment of gendarmes arrived and after a scene of intense excitement put the men who had caused the row into the street.

This, however, was but the beginning. The men proceeded to the terrace of the Cafe de la Paix, which was now crammed with anti-Dreyfusards, and there gave their own version of the row, and in a few moments an anti-Dreyfus demonstration was in full swing.

The people sitting at the tables rose with shouts of "Down with the Jews" and "Vive l'armee" and demanding that the band play the "Marseillaise." The band was compelled to comply with the demand and the crowd howled the air at the top of their voices, altering the words to "March on, march on, against the Jews."

Bricks, canes and hats were waved and then the crowd shouted "Vive l'armee! Vive l'armee! Conspuez les Juifs!"

Finally one man waved his hat and shouted, "Let us march on the Hotel Moderne." The crowd showed a strong disposition to take this advice, and as the hotel is within a hundred yards of the cafe the situation began to look ugly. Two Englishmen who were sitting in the cafe were recognized as foreigners and the crowd hustled them out.

At this moment the cry of "Police!" was raised, and in an instant a strong body of gendarmes and police, headed by a detective, rushed into the cafe and there came a general squadron of mounted gendarmes and dragoons, with carbines slung across their backs, galloped up and threw themselves across the road leading to the Hotel Moderne. Other detachments of cavalry cordoned all the approaches to the cafe, and thus gradually closed in on the crowd, which now overflowed into the road and drove them like cattle across the bridge over the river and

into the upper part of the town, which was filled with shouts of "Vive l'armee!" and "Down with the Jews!"

A number of the most noisy of the demonstrators were arrested, and the cavalry at a quick trot broke up every group and forced the participants in the demonstration out of the center of the town, around which was formed a cordon through which no one was allowed to pass except he was provided with a pass from the police authorities.

The demonstrations dwindled from this time until this evening, when only a few noisy bands were left, parading the smaller streets, but running at the first sight of a man in blue.

Strong repressive measures, however, alone can prevent serious disturbance. The cafes in the neighborhood have been closed, some of them by the police and others through panic, and tranquillity is now practically restored, though to-night's trouble may be only the prelude to a bigger demonstration to-morrow.

Bridge Building Trust.
New York, Sept. 9.—The first steps in the consolidation of 90 per cent of the bridge building concerns of the United States under the name of the American bridge company are completed, the representatives of the thirty companies that have formed the combination having concluded their work here to-day. The capital will be in the neighborhood of $66,000,000.

Train Wrecked in Mexico.
City of Mexico, Sept. 9.—The south bound express and mail train on the Mexican National road was wrecked last night south of Acambaro. The passengers escaped unhurt, but Engineer Rafferty received severe injuries.

Lieutenant Appointed.
Washington, D. C., Sept. 9.—Among the army appointments announced to-day was that of Fred Impgley, late first lieutenant of the First Arkansas volunteers, to be a second lieutenant in the Forty-fourth regiment.

Venezuelan Revolution.
Caracas, Venezuela, Sept. 9.—(Delayed in transmission.)—The revolution under the leadership of General Castro is gaining ground. The insurgents now occupy Nirgua, three days' march from Valencia.

INDEX OF TO-DAY'S IMPORTANT NEWS

FIRST PAGE:
Disturbances in Rennes.
Reviewing the Verdict.
Views of Zangwill.

SECOND PAGE:
The Trial of Dreyfus.
Transvaal Situation—Foreign News.
Reports on Yellow Fever.

THIRD PAGE:
General War News.
Cable Letter From Berlin.
London Cable Letter.

FOURTH PAGE:
Pecos Valley Facts.
General Sporting News.
Austin News.

FIFTH PAGE:
The Houston Budget.
State Truck Farmers.
Religious News.

SIXTH PAGE:
Marine Matters.
Growing American Exports.

SEVENTH PAGE:
Canadian Pacific Railway—General Railroad News.

EIGHTH PAGE:
Galveston Military Company.
Police and Franchises.

NINTH PAGE:
New Military Sensation.
The Hero of the Railroad.

TENTH PAGE:
Confederate Veterans' Department.

ELEVENTH PAGE:
London Now Has a Borosis.

TWELFTH PAGE:
Our Splendid Artillery at Work.
Questions and Answers.
Knute to Unite.
Casey Has His Fortune Told.

THIRTEENTH PAGE:
Unique Mail Service.

FOURTEENTH PAGE:
Houston Society News.
Sons of the Confederacy.

FIFTEENTH PAGE:
Theatrical Mention.

SIXTEENTH PAGE:
Editorial.
Cost of Living Increased.

SEVENTEENTH PAGE:
New Life Discovered in Our Lakes.
The Extravagant Dressing of Canine Pets
Surpasses all Limits.
The Greatest Moving Feat Ever Accomplished.

EIGHTEENTH PAGE:
The Travelers' Protective Association.
Some Discord Up in Maine.
Classified Advertising.

NINETEENTH PAGE:
Classified Advertising.
Displayed Advertising.

TWENTIETH PAGE:
Cotton Markets.

TWENTY-FIRST PAGE:
Woman's Page.

TWENTY-SECOND PAGE:
An Object Lesson in Our Tariff System.
General Financial News.

TWENTY-THIRD PAGE:
General Markets Abroad.

TWENTY-FOURTH PAGE:
Local Society News.
Books and Magazines.

TEXANS ABROAD.

Special to The News.
New York, Sept. 9.—The following Texans are registered at New York hotels:
Earle, H. D. Detroe, St. Denis.
Dallas—J. J. Orchard, Fifth Avenue.

FINE ARTS AT THE EXPOSITION.

Juries on Painting and Sculpture to Be Announced Shortly.

New York, Sept. 9.—John B. Caldwell, director of the arts of the commission to the Paris exposition in 1900, in an interview said that the juries for painting and sculpture will be announced in about ten days. The personnel of these juries, which will be composed entirely of professional painters and sculptors, with the exception that Mr. Caldwell will probably act ex-officio on all juries, has naturally been a matter of lively speculation in art circles. The interest in fact has been so keen that Mr. Caldwell has been unaccountably blamed in some quarters for not making the appointments last summer. But he has had excellent reasons for his delay, which he does not think will cause any material inconvenience to painters, as the making of the exhibition is in one sense retrospective.

The French authorities having decided that it shall cover the period of eleven years since the exposition of 1889, most of the work to be exhibited will have been already completed; and it would be prejudicial to the interests of the exhibit that this work should be specially created with the view of appealing to any given jury. A general verdict to be passed upon the department of fine arts in a few days has been decided upon, the names of the various members of which will be associated with them at an early day.

James R. Eustis Dead.
Newport, R. I., Sept. 9.—James R. Eustis, ex-ambassador to France during the second Cleveland administration, and formerly a senator from Louisiana, died at his summer home in this city at 9 o'clock to-night of pneumonia. Mr. Eustis was taken ill on Wednesday, but the local physician, after an examination, thought the trouble to be heart failure. The patient grew worse on Thursday, developing symptoms of pneumonia, and on Friday there was a consultation of physicians, who stated that there was scarcely any hope of recovery. The end came to-night very peacefully. Mr. Eustis' son, James R. Eustis, jr., and his sister, Mrs. Cyrus, were at the bedside.

No arrangements have yet been made for the funeral, but it is thought the body will be taken to Louisiana.

The Letter Carriers.
Scranton, Pa., Sept. 9.—The letter carriers today elected the following officers: President, W. V. Farnon, New York. Re-elected vice president, Charles D. Duffy, Chicago; secretary, S. W. Cantwell, Brooklyn, re-elected; treasurer, Alex. McDonald, Grand Rapids, Mich.; executive committee, John M. McElroy, Bridgeport; A. K. Young, Cincinnati; W. J. Minor, St. Louis; H. B. Seaton, Denver; William B. Moynihan, Rochester. The various standing committees were also chosen. Detroit was selected as the place for the next convention.

RECEIVING THE VERDICT.

Imprisonment of Dreyfus for Ten Years in Corte Fortress, Corsica.

He Must Serve His Time From Day of Second Degradation.

Scenes in the Rennes Court Room When the Verdict in the Dreyfus Case

Was Delivered by the President of the Court-Martial.

CAPTAIN DREYFUS, FROM HIS LATEST PHOTOGRAPH.
(Copyright by New York Journal and Advertiser.)

Words Can Not Describe the Painful, Tremendous Shock of the Verdict.

There Was No Outbreak, No Threat, No Passion.

Reporting the Verdict to the Prisoner by the Court-Martial Usher

And Conveying the Information to Madame Dreyfus.

Special to The News.
Rennes, Sept. 9.—The judges returned at a quarter to five, the audience all standing, not sitting down. All ears were strained to catch the vital word, the president's voice being low and rapid.

Jouaust read rapidly in a low monotone till he came to the word "guilty." A strange sound rose all over the court, a general gasp, a curse, a stamp of the feet, then breathless silence. Confusion was caused by a man fainting. We was held up by his friends, who kept their eyes fixed on the judges. The end of the judgment was awaited with anxiety. All the gendarmes turned and faced the audience, expecting an outbreak. But there was no manifestation whatever. The audience filed out in good order without a word.

After judgment had been read to Dreyfus, I interviewed Conpuis, who said:

"Dreyfus showed no sign whatever of hearing his sentence."

The sentence - 'en years' imprisonment in the fortress of Corte, in Corsica. The five years he has already served do not count; he must serve ten years from the day of degradation, which must take place within fifteen days if there be no appeal to the court of revision within eight days.

The judges took one ballot on retiring—is Dreyfus guilty or not? Two judges voted no. The judges then discussed the penalty. The two judges in favor of Dreyfus pressed for a low penalty on account of his sufferings, and induced the others to fix it at ten years, which is the very lowest possible penalty for the crime of which he was found guilty. In fact the judges have lowered the penalty by two degrees less than ever known in the French army before for a conviction of this kind.

Dreyfus was waiting, with feelings which can only be imagined, in a room back of the stage.

When word was given to the audience to disperse, M. Hild, Labori's assistant, at a sign from Labori, went to tell him.

Labori sat in a chair as if paralyzed. A moment before, as the judges came in, he had been pulling the end of his beard in quiet satisfaction, confident that after Demange's speech the verdict would be four to three. The result stupefied him.

Demange sat collapsed, saddened to the last degree. It was evident in the heat and fervor and feeling of the close of his speech that his whole heart was set in securing the freedom of his client. His voice was deeply hoarse, worn down by his long speech; his face as solemn as tragedy. When the verdict came he sat silent, like a man collapsed; like a man who has just heard news of death.

Hild stepped along the corridor to the room where Dreyfus was, went in and closed the door. Dreyfus looked at him and saw from his face he had bad news. Dreyfus said:
"Tell me."
"Ten years in a French fortress."

Dreyfus turned white, sank into a chair and covered his face with his hands. He sat a long time, neither Hild nor the gendarme saying anything. Then an usher came to Dreyfus. He said:
"One moment."

He rose like a drunken man, his eyes unsteady, and passed his hand over his brow. The color was all gone out of his face, which was the color of ashes. The usher gave him a moment to pull himself together. Then he went into court to hear the decision read again. Dreyfus listened stupidly, facing Conpuis, who read it. He said nothing, went out and was taken over to prison like a man under the influence of morphine.

Words can not describe the painful, tremendous shock of the verdict. When the judges came in, their faces were eagerly scanned. They gave everybody hope. Jouaust looked gentle and genial; even Brogniart looked quietly pleased. All the court looked like men who had done a kindly act and felt better. The curse which went up from the audience was so bitter, so strange, that those who heard it will never forget it. Then men turned their heads away and took no further notice of the penalty.

Hope was gone. The audience went out absolutely quietly. Not a word was said. There was no demonstration, not even a single cry. The Dreyfusards were depressed, busy with their own thoughts. The police and gendarmes hurried everybody away from the Lycee, and absolutely barred return.

Outside the court, in the squares and cafes, there was a sharp silence. A sort of spell seemed to be upon men, over the whole city. There was no outbreak, no threat, no anger, no passion. Everybody seemed to be in a state of shock. This shows how very general was the conviction that the verdict would be at least four to three. It was fully an hour before bitterness began to manifest itself, beginning with fiery, caustic dispatches which socialists and Dreyfusards began to place on the wires.

Meanwhile, the sickening news was being conveyed to Madame Dreyfus by George Hadamard, her brother. Hadamard is a gentle-natured fellow, slender, about 35, with pale and small blonde mustache. Yesterday he rode up the Rue with confidence and joy, and left his bicycle just under the gate of the Lycee. He fully expected acquittal, as did Madame Dreyfus up to yesterday. To-day, however, he did not take his bicycle, but walked slowly up the avenue de la Gare to the house, about three blocks away. His father, unpatient, came out of the gate to meet him. When he heard the news he stopped a moment to realize it. Then both went in together. Madame Hadamard, the mother of Madame Dreyfus, was on the steps of the house crying. She did not need to be told. All went in together. George told the news to the old people, who tried to comfort their daughter.

Madame Dreyfus took it calmly, as if prepared for it. The only agony she seemed to experience was dread of the second degradation, from which she recoils in horror.

It was a time of strange, sickening suspense, that wait in the courtyard for the verdict. It seemed to affect everybody in the same way. Men would place their hands on their hearts and say, "I am ill." Two men said this in my hearing in court, five in the courtyard, when we went out to wait for the verdict. Three men were so ill they had to leave and be driven to hotels in cabs.

When the verdict was announced one man fainted, but was held erect, unconscious, by the men next to him in the packed crowd, while they looked not at him, but at the judges.

HARRY J. W. DAM.

PAPERS IN GERMANY

Lie Ready for Publication Which Will Prove Henry and Esterhazy Guilty of Treason and the Condemnation of Dreyfus a Brutal Judicial Crime.

(Copyright by the New York Journal and Advertiser.)

Special to The News.
Berlin, Sept. 9.—In the safe keeping of the military staff of the German empire all the documents, which positively and unmistakably will prove that Major Esterhazy and Colonel Henry are guilty of high treason, lie ready for publication. It is confidently expected that after the judicial outrage at Rennes to-day the kaiser will give the magic word that will reveal the truth to the whole world. These documents will brand the condemnation of Dreyfus as a brutal judicial crime. That France will be in the throes of another revolution in a short time is not doubted here.

The Kreissinger Zeitung says that the generals who secured the condemnation of Dreyfus stand condemned before the moral court of the world.

THE SENTIMENT IN WASHINGTON

Special to The News.
Washington, D. C., Sept. 9.—The news of the verdict in the Dreyfus case was received in Washington with a feeling of astonishment in official quarters, notwithstanding the general opinion that, regardless of the evidence, the court-martial would find him guilty.

The liveliest interest has been manifested in this case among army officers and others in official life. The president, himself, has watched it closely and has carefully followed the evidence adduced before the court. Mr. McKinley was in his office this afternoon when a bulletin announcing the verdict was carried to him. What the president may have said is maintained as a profound secret at the white house, but no effort was made to disguise the fact that the president was full of sympathy for the prisoner and was much depressed at the verdict of the court-martial.

Every member of the cabinet in the city discussed the case privately and expressed regret that Dreyfus should have been made the victim of circumstances that made it impossible to clear him of the charges. One member of the cabinet who has never been heard to utter an oath used a vigorous expletive when told of the verdict and denounced it as an outrage.

THE VIEWS OF ZANGWILL, THE FAMOUS JEWISH AUTHOR.

Special to The News.
New York, Sept. 9.—Israel Zangwill, the famous Jew author, speaking of the Dreyfus case in to-morrow's Journal, says:

"The idea said to be simmering in Chicago of a boycott of the Paris exposition by the Jews of America because of the conviction of Dreyfus does not seem to me entirely well advised, although I sympathize very strongly with the moral indignation that lies behind it. But this attempt to meet force by force seems to me the wrong way for the Jews to assert their place and mission in history.

"What I suggest myself is that every Jew who feels an injustice has been committed should of himself stay away from the exposition, and I fully expect that this course will be followed by thousands of Christians. Instead of a specific Jewish protest, I should prefer a protest in the name of the human brotherhood.

"Let Jews, if they will, take the lead in stimulating this protest if nobody else is found to initiate it, but for the sake of the head of humanity and civilization, not of a scattered race, a member of which has been wronged.

"Dreyfus himself places France first and Israel second. He in no way pretends to be part of a Jewish nation working for common aims. His greatest desire is to die, not for Israel, but for France. If ever ethics is to rule international relations, as it already does in private relations, then a beginning must be made somewhere, and France certainly should be made to feel that she has offended against the moral code and shocked the conscience of civilization, and, I repeat, the protest of Jews should be a protest on behalf of civilization and humanity, and not on behalf of a brother Jew—a protest on behalf of these great ideals which France was the first to express for the modern world."

ROYAL BAKING POWDER
ABSOLUTELY PURE
Makes the food more delicious and wholesome
ROYAL BAKING POWDER CO., NEW YORK.

no longer to pay the clergy, and private corporations organized by the faithful were to take over the expenses of worship and the ownership and maintenance of the churches. The Catholics refused to accept this settlement, and the churches remained technically government property.

But, though the separation had been carried out amid great bitterness, though the debates had revived the ferocious language of the 1790's, there was no recourse to the violence of the past. Catholicism was not proscribed, and somehow or other worship continued in churches that were not the full legal property of the faithful. Catholic education was indeed severely hindered, but there was no formal persecution. The separation did not really alter the fundamental social position of the Church in France. The upper classes, and the peasantry of the north, northeast and west, remained for the most part loyal Catholics; many of the urban middle and working classes, and many peasants in parts of the south, southwest, and center remained what they had become over the last few centuries, indifferent Catholics or outright and determined secularists.

The indifferent Catholics and the anti-clericals formed the backbone of the central supporting party of the Republic, the Radical Socialists, who were not socialists at all but petty bourgeois, French Jeffersonians. Indeed, the French Republic of the early twentieth century was a typically bourgeois state. It made certain concessions to demands from the workers for social security and better living conditions, but not nearly so many as the British constitutional monarchy was then making, nor indeed so many as the only partly constitutional German monarchy had made already. Trade unions in France were legal, but they had hard sledding against the reluctance of French workers to pay dues and accept union discipline. Moreover, good democrats, like Clemenceau and Briand, had no scruples about using force against strikers.

France remained fundamentally in the early

twentieth century what she had been since 1789, a land of small farm-owning peasants, very conservative in their farming methods, and of relatively small family-controlled industries, very conservative in their business methods. There were some elements of big industry by the early 1900's, and French steel production at that time was actually growing faster than that of Britain, Germany, and the United States. None the less, great industry was not typical of the French economic scene, which was backward in comparison with the achievements of the industrial giants just mentioned, but at the same time well balanced by old-fashioned standards of the nearly self-sufficient national economy. But the whole question as to why France, in 1800 their equal or superior, fell so far behind Britain, Germany, and the United States in the nineteenth and early twentieth centuries as regards general economic growth remains a puzzle to the historian. The one sure thing is that there was no single, simple cause, but a whole complex set of causes.

The Third Republic had weathered the storms of domestic differences at bottom because, though some Frenchmen disliked it intensely, and though many Frenchmen felt toward it that distrust of the "government" not unknown in the American democracy, most Frenchmen felt it somehow to be the embodiment of *la patrie*, the fatherland. Differences did arise among them, notably on questions of colonial policy. The great expansion of French power in Africa, Indo-China, and Oceania which made the world empire of France second only to Britain's was the work of a determined minority (see Chapter 17). Many Frenchmen viewed their colonies with antagonism or apathy.

France since 1870 had often seemed dangerously divided on matters of domestic and imperial concern; yet on foreign policy the Third Republic was essentially united. Disagreement on the big question of foreign policy concerned details of timing, not ultimate aims. France wanted revenge for 1870, wanted Alsace-Lorraine back. In the complex workings of international politics from 1870 to 1914, the foreign ministries of the Third

Opposite: The Dreyfus case as covered in the American press.

Republic, though shifting their top elected personnel through the workings of the multi-party system, none the less brought France to a position of strength through alliances in which revenge on Germany became possible. Democracies are sometimes held to be at a disadvantage in the conduct of foreign relations in comparison with states under strong monarchic or dictatorial control. Soon after the war with Prussia, democratic France was isolated, and imperial Germany was the center of a marvelous system of alliances; yet by 1914, democratic France was firmly allied with a powerful Britain and a Russia powerful at least for the moment; and imperial Germany, save for a weak Austro-Hungarian ally and a dubiously loyal Italian one, was essentially isolated.

III   Italy, 1848 - 1914

Italian national unity, which seemed after the events of 1848–1849 (see Chapter 11) as far away as ever, was triumphantly achieved between 1859 and 1870. The Kingdom of Italy that began to emerge after 1860 had a constitution very much like that of the Third French Republic, with an ornamental king instead of an ornamental president. The ministry was responsible to a lower house which in practice developed a multi-party system rather like that of France. At first, a property qualification severely limited the suffrage; after 1881, this qualification was low enough—a direct tax of 19 lire, or about $4.00—so that the electorate numbered over 2,000,000. What amounted to full universal manhood suffrage was not, however, introduced until 1912. But the new united Italy was clearly a democracy.

A caricature of Camillo di Cavour (1810–1861).

Cavour and the Completion of Unification

The architect of Italian unification was Cavour (1810–1861), who became the chief minister of Piedmont in 1852. Though of aristocratic origin himself, and trained for the highly conservative career of an army officer, Cavour enthusiastically supported the economic revolutions and the aspirations of the business classes. He visited France and England as a young man and was deeply influenced by their economic accomplishments and by their economic and political ideas and institutions. Back in Piedmont, he applied the newest agricultural methods to his family estates and promoted the introduction of steamboats, railroads, industries, and banks in order to prepare Piedmont for leadership in unified Italy. Cavour was a good, moderate, mid-nineteenth-century liberal.

But Cavour was also a superlatively adept practitioner of the realistic diplomacy often called *Realpolitik*. As the chief minister of Piedmont, he set about cultivating French and English support, bringing Piedmont into the Crimean War on their side against Russia. He got no immediate award, for England was unwilling to take steps that would offend Austria, possessor of Lombardy and Venetia. But, though bitterly disappointed, he put a good face on his defeat and finally persuaded Napoleon III that the Austrian hold in northern Italy was an anachronism, a flying in the face of the principle of nationality. In 1859, France and Piedmont went to war with Austria and won bloody victories at Magenta and Solferino in June. Sympathetic nationalist risings broke out in Tuscany and the Papal States. But the threat of Prussian help to Austria alarmed Napoleon, who held a conference with the Emperor of Austria, Francis Joseph, at Villafranca (July, 1859) and arranged a compromise by which Lombardy was to go to Piedmont but Venetia was to remain Austrian, and the rest of the peninsula to remain divided. Cavour resigned in bitter protest.

He had, however, already won. A wave of popular agitation in the smaller states of northern and central Italy brought almost bloodless revolutions and plebiscites demanding annexation to Piedmont. Cavour came back into office to accept the annexations and to take advantage of the promising situation developing in the Papal States and the South. For in May, 1860, a most successful expedition had set out for Naples and Sicily under the command of a radical, indeed republican, nationalist agitator, the romantic red-shirted Garibaldi. Cavour deeply distrusted Garibaldi's radicalism, which he feared might make Italy a republic and might so alarm the powers that they would intervene to undo Cavour's own annexationist achievements. For these reasons, Cavour sought first to prevent the departure of Garibaldi's expedition, and then, after this had proved impossible, to control its progress and

Giuseppe Garibaldi (1807–1882).

exploit its success in the interests of his own policy. Garibaldi and his thousand "redshirts" had relatively little trouble in overcoming the feeble opposition of the Bourbon Francis II in Sicily. Recruits swarmed to his flag. Popular opinion throughout the West, even in cautious England, was overwhelmingly on the side of this romantic adventurer. Garibaldi, who had announced his loyalty to the King of Piedmont, Victor Emmanuel, now crossed the Straits of Messina to the mainland with the approval of the British minister, Lord Palmerston, and continued his victorious march. Cavour, alarmed lest Garibaldi bring on a crisis with Napoleon by taking Rome, sent Piedmontese troops into the Papal States. They disposed of the papal forces easily, and occupied all save the area about Rome itself. King Victor Emmanuel soon joined forces with Garibaldi near Naples and assured the triumph of Cavour's policy.

Unification of Italy, 1859-1870

Kingdom of Sardinia before 1859

To Kingdom of Sardinia:
1859   1860

To Kingdom of Italy:
1866   1870

Italia Irredenta

■ Battle site

FRANCE
SWITZERLAND
AUSTRIA
SAVOY
Trent
VENETIA
Magenta
LOMBARDY
Custozza
Trieste
Novara
Milan
Verona
Po R.
Solferino
Villafranca
Venice
Turin
PIEDMONT
PARMA
Po R.
To France
1860
Genoa
MODENA
ROMAGNA
DALMATIA
NICE
"THE MARCHES"
Nice
"THE RIVIERA"
Leghorn
Florence
Adriatic Sea
CORSICA
(French)
TUSCANY
PAPAL
UMBRIA
KINGDOM
Tiber R.
Rome
STATES
KINGDOM
Bari
ALBANIA
OF SARDINIA
Naples
APULIA
SARDINIA
Taranto
Tyrrhenian Sea
TWO
CALABRIA
SICILIES
Mediterranean Sea
Palermo
Straits of Messina
SICILY
Tunis
AFRICA
(Br.)
MALTA
0   100   200
Miles

Meanwhile, in plebiscites, Naples and Sicily voted for union with the North.

The upshot of all these rapidly unrolling events was the proclamation of the Kingdom of Italy with Victor Emmanuel of Savoy at its head, and with Florence as its capital, in March, 1861. Cavour died in June, but what had seemed impossible only two short years ago at Villafranca had now been realized. Rome, under French occupation, and Venetia, still held by Austria, kept the new kingdom from the territorial completion the patriots wanted.

Venetia and Rome soon came easily into the kingdom in the play of international politics and cost Italy little in bloodshed. Venetia came as a reward for Italy's siding with Prussia in the brief war of 1866 that saw Prussia defeat Austria; Rome came when the war of 1870 with Prussia forced Napoleon III to withdraw from papal territory (see Chapter 14). On October 2, 1870, Rome was annexed to the Kingdom of Italy and became its capital. All the

510

peninsula, save for Trieste and Trent in the North, was now under one rule. These two small bits of *Italia Irredenta* (Italy unredeemed) were of no small importance, for Italian patriots remained unreconciled to Austrian possession of them and went to war against Austria and her German ally in 1915 largely to obtain them.

Assets and Liabilities of United Italy

The new kingdom started out with the asset of favorable public opinion throughout the non-Catholic segments of the western world. Italian national unity seemed a natural and desirable thing, and it had been achieved without very much bloodshed, with a mixture of Garibaldian romance and Cavourian realism. Within the kingdom the enthusiasm that had brought the *Risorgimento* (resurrection) to fruition was now in the service of united Italy. Italians were a frugal, hard-working people, and in the north they made promising beginnings in the new industry of the machine age.

Yet striking liabilities impeded the new Italy. The Italians had, like the French, a division between Catholics and anticlericals—better, anti-Catholics—difficult for a modern American to understand. Still, the division was perhaps less sharp than in France; there were in Italy more middle-of-the-roaders in practice. On the other hand, ardent Italian Catholics were embittered by the circumstances of the final drive for union, the annexation of the Papal States without the Pope's consent, the "Roman question." Italy lacked coal and iron; in terms of modern economic competition, she was a "have-not" country, a shocking discovery that the Italians made in the years following unification. Much of mountainous central Italy and all southern Italy were really marginal to nineteenth-century western civilization, with a poverty-stricken, illiterate peasantry rooted in age-old local ways utterly different from those of modern urban life, and with a small feudalistic aristocracy to whom a man like Cavour was really quite incomprehensible. Neapolitans and Sicilians resented

the new political preponderance of North Italians in the unified kingdom, much as American Southerners resented Yankee "carpetbaggers" after the Civil War. If one spoke of the "two Italies," the division would be that between the already somewhat industrialized North, especially the thoroughly "modern" Po Valley, and the rural, impoverished South, still "medieval."

Moreover, at least half of Italy lacked experience in self-government. It had no tradition of government by discussion, of law-abidingness, of comfortable middle-class compromise. Italy was not indeed the land of mixed stereotypes—sunny gaiety, dark passions, music, and *banditti*—which northern Europeans and Americans believed it to be. It was a land of deep-seated class antagonisms, regional variations, fervent localism, a whole inheritance from the past which made democratic government very difficult.

The Roman question became a chronic rather than a critical one. The Pope, who refused to accept the legality of the new kingdom, simply stayed in the Vatican Palace as a "prisoner." The Vatican remained the center of the world-wide organization of the Roman Catholic Church, and in no important sense was the Pope impeded in the exercise of his powers over the faithful throughout the world. Within Italy, the Church forbade Catholics to participate in politics and urged a Catholic boycott of the new state. Gradually, in fact, Catholics did take an increasing part in politics, but the Roman question itself remained unsettled until 1929, when Mussolini and Pope Pius XI agreed to set up the Vatican City as a sovereign state of 108 acres.

The new kingdom made appreciable economic progress. Railroads, built and managed by the state, were pushed rapidly into the backward South, where some of the seaboard area came by the twentieth century to look deceptively prosperous and modern; a brand-new merchant marine brought the new Italian flag onto the seven seas; and an army and navy gave it standing as a power. Even the national finances seemed for a time under conservative leadership to be sound. In the political field, the 1880's brought a letdown, the growth of parliamentary corruption, the beginning of a long era of unashamed political opportunism. Meantime, the industrial proletariat was small, labor inadequately organized, and the socialists were both too small and too rent by divisions to constitute a dynamic instrument of opposition and reform. Moreover, as recent economic historians insist, the very economic progress of the North, made in part at the expense of a South both exploited and neglected, increased regional differentiation and helped build up the social tensions that were to affect twentieth-century Italy very seriously indeed.

Finally, Italy was now launching itself on a career of imperial aspiration which seems a good example of the desire to keep up with the Joneses. Since France—the envied "Latin" sister—and Britain had empires, since a great power had to have an empire, and since Italy, or rather the guiding groups in Italy, wanted to be a great power, some way of territorial expansion had to be found. The Marxist or other economic explanations of the imperialist drive hardly make sense for the Italy of the 1880's and 1890's, a nation with no important exportable capital, with no need for colonial markets, and with plenty of domestic difficulties. True, Italy had a rapidly expanding population that found relatively few economic opportunities at home, especially in the South. But, since other countries had such a head start in empire-building, what was left open to Italian seizure was very little indeed. And even these leftovers were not suitable for colonial settlement by Europeans. They were the poorer parts of Africa, hardly worth the difficulty of exploitation.

Even so, the effort to take Ethiopia (then called Abyssinia) drained the resources of the government and was halted by the disastrous military defeat inflicted by the Abyssinians on the Italian expeditionary force at Adowa in 1896. This relatively unimportant battle was nevertheless an important landmark in the history of the colonial expansion of Europe which had begun some five hundred years earlier. Even the British had had to fight with the natives in many parts of the world, and had suffered temporary defeats. But they had not withdrawn from any important part of their colonial enterprises. Adowa was, however, a portent and much publicized in the newspapers of the world. The Italians had lost a pitched battle and had been obliged to give up the attempt to add Abyssinia to their colonial empire. True, under Mussolini in 1935 they temporarily succeeded in annexing Abyssinia (Ethiopia), but by that time the magic of white supremacy had ceased to impress the rest of the world.

The general depression of the 1890's, a bank scandal, and the Adowa failure cast a shadow on the last years of the century. Grave bread riots broke out in Milan in May, 1898, the "fatti di Maggio" (deeds of May), and in 1900 King Humbert was assassinated by an anarchist. The accession of a new king, Victor Emmanuel III, who was believed to have liberal leanings, gave new heart to many, and the years just before the outbreak of World War I were on the whole years of comparative quiet and prosperity, of partial reconciliation with the Church, and of the final establishment of universal suffrage. Parliamentary democracy seemed at last to be sending down solid roots. And in the years 1890–1914 the vast emigration to North and South America—the number of emigrants exceeded half a million in the peak year of 1913—almost canceled out the serious economic difficulties attendant on the high Italian birth rate and lack of new industrial employment.

Yet the men who ran Italy could never quite content themselves with a position, say like that of a Mediterranean Sweden, quite outside the competition for empire and quite outside the "great powers." Italy was not a great power, but her leaders, and millions of their followers, wanted very much to make her one. Pushed out of Abyssinia, and forced by the increasing tensions of international politics to yield to the French in Tunisia, Italy finally got from the other great powers a free hand in poverty-stricken and parched Tripoli, a fragment of the old Turkish Empire in North Africa now known as Libya. In 1911, she went to war with Turkey over Tripoli, thus stimulating the cycle of Balkan wars that were to develop into World War I.

IV   The United States

World War I was also to mark the full participation in the international balance of another relative newcomer to the family of nations, the United States. The simplest and in many ways the most important fact of her brief national history is that in a little over a century the United States secured in terms of actual power a position like that of the great states that have filled these pages for many chapters—Austria, France, England, and the rest. The United States came to be a "great power," despite words and even sentiments that placed her outside international competition, in "isolation." Two simple sets of statistics point up this fact. In 1790, the United States comprised 892,000 square miles, and in 1910 3,754,000 square miles; even more important, the population of the United States was 3,929,000 in 1790, and 91,972,000 in 1910. The 1910 population was greater than that of either of the most powerful European states, Germany and Great Britain, indeed second only to that of Russia. And, still more important, American combined industrial and agricultural capacities were already greater than those of any other single country.

The Federal Union

The land that had become so powerful in a brief century was in the late eighteenth century almost empty beyond the Alleghenies, save for a few Indians of Stone Age culture; yet millions of acres were as suited to intensive human use as any in Europe. Most interested observers knew this at the end of the American Revolution, and they expected the central parts of the North American continent to fill up eventually with white men. But most of them, including Americans like Jefferson, did not believe that the process would be as rapid as it in fact was. Moreover, all but the most san-guine felt that the developed and fully peopled continent could not possibly come under one political rule. They felt that it must be divided —as indeed the South American continent came to be—into a number of independent nations on essentially the European model. Indeed, the most pessimistic or merely hostile observers did not believe that the thirteen Atlantic seaboard colonies gathered together to fight the British could possibly maintain their own union. Here is a sample prediction from the eighteenth century:

As to the future grandeur of America, and its being a rising empire under one head, whether republican or monarchical, it is one of the idlest and most visionary notions that ever was conceived even by writers of romance. The mutual antipathies and clashing interests of the Americans, their difference of governments, habitudes, and manners, indicate that they will have no centre of union and no common interest. They never can be united into one compact empire under any species of government whatever.[*]

Yet hold together the former colonies did. Though the union was often sorely tested, once in the bloodiest war Americans have yet fought, it is a central fact of history that the United States did not go the way of the Latin American states. Why the United States held together cannot be explained by any single factor. Geography was certainly kinder to her than to the Latin Americans, for the Appalachians were no real barrier at all; the Rockies were not the barrier the Andes are; and the Mississippi Valley, unlike that of the Amazon, was a help rather than a hindrance to settlement and communications. The railroad and the telegraph arrived just in time to enable goods and ideas to move fast and far enough

[*]Josiah Tucker, Dean of Gloucester, quoted in John Fiske, *The Critical Period of American History, 1783–1789* (Boston, 1888), 57–58.

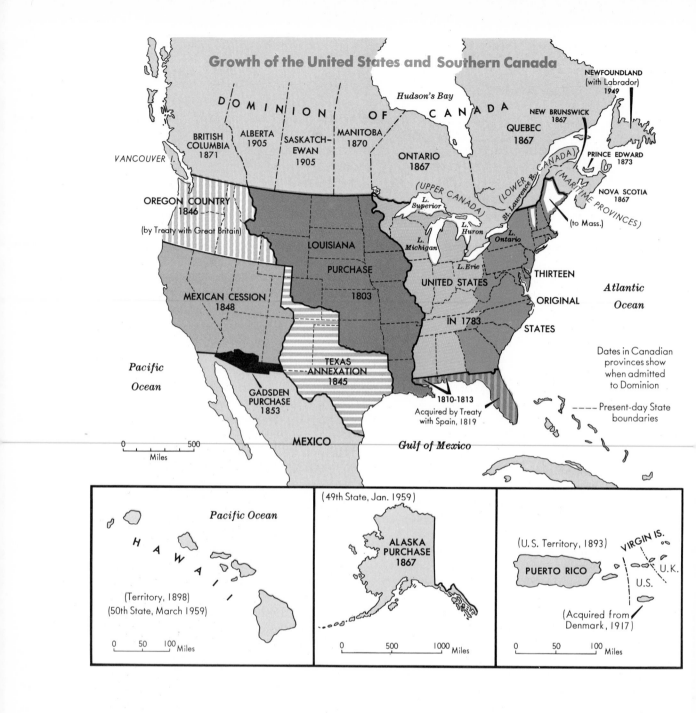

DOMINION OF CANADA

Hudson's Bay

NEWFOUNDLAND
(with Labrador)
1949

NEW BRUNSWICK
1867

QUEBEC
1867

BRITISH
COLUMBIA
1871

ALBERTA
1905

SASKATCH-
EWAN
1905

MANITOBA
1870

ONTARIO
1867

VANCOUVER I.

PRINCE EDWARD
1873

(UPPER CANADA)

(LOWER CANADA)

St. Lawrence R.

(MARITIME PROVINCES)

NOVA SCOTIA
1867

OREGON COUNTRY
1846

(by Treaty with Great Britain)

L. Superior

L. Huron

L. Michigan

L. Ontario

L. Erie

(to Mass.)

LOUISIANA

PURCHASE

1803

UNITED STATES

IN 1783

THIRTEEN

ORIGINAL

STATES

Atlantic
Ocean

MEXICAN CESSION
1848

Pacific

Ocean

Dates in Canadian
provinces show
when admitted
to Dominion

- - - - Present-day State
boundaries

TEXAS
ANNEXATION
1845

GADSDEN
PURCHASE
1853

1810-1813
Acquired by Treaty
with Spain, 1819

MEXICO

Gulf of Mexico

0   500
Miles

Pacific Ocean

HAWAII

(Territory, 1898)
(50th State, March 1959)

0   50   100 Miles

(49th State, Jan. 1959)

ALASKA
PURCHASE
1867

0   500   1000 Miles

(U.S. Territory, 1893)

VIRGIN IS.

PUERTO RICO

U.K.

U.S.

(Acquired from
Denmark, 1917)

0   50   100 Miles

to hold Americans together. The communications and transportation network already
developed by 1860 enabled the North to count
on the West in the decisive struggle of the
Civil War. The sheer size of the new republic
after the acquisition of the Mississippi-
Missouri Valley by purchase from Napoleon in
1803 seemed historically compatible with a
loosely held empire of many tongues and peoples, like those of ancient Persia or Rome, but
not with a unified nation-state. The achievements of modern technology in effect reduced
sheer size to manageable proportions. After
the first transcontinental railway was completed in 1869, Californians could get to the
federal capital at Washington more quickly
than New Yorkers could in 1801.

Yet it will not do to emphasize purely material factors in the holding together of the
United States. The resistance to Britain had

514

helped forge a genuine national patriotism. The colonists, in spite of contrasts between seventeenth-century "Puritan" New England and "Cavalier" tidewater South, in spite of Dutch and German elements in the middle colonies, brought with them one language and one law, one basic culture. Almost all the colonies had "frontiers"—in the new American sense of the word, not a guarded line with custom houses as in Europe, but free areas on their western edges where a lively population was winning new lands from the wilderness. This frontier population was a powerful force for unity, for it had little attachment to the older centers of colonial (now state) group-consciousness, and it had great confidence in its own "manifest destiny" to keep pushing westward with the blessing and patronage of, and without more than remote control by, the new federal government.

Americans gained their independence from Britain in a civil war and a social revolution that were rather mild affairs compared with the French Reign of Terror. And, after the more committed Loyalists had left for Canada or Britain, Americans took up national life without any seriously alienated minorities. They achieved at the Philadelphia convention of 1787 and in the campaign for adoption during the next two years a federal constitution that set up a central government with the essential attributes of all governments—the ability to tax individuals (not just to ask for monies as contributions from constituent states), to control armed forces, and to maintain a monopoly of foreign relations. The new constitution, in short, set up a sovereign federal state, not a mere league of sovereign states—in neat German words, a *Bundesstaat*, not a *Staatenbund*. On the whole, this result was achieved under conservative groups anxious to preserve their economic and social privileges, afraid that democracy in separate, quasi-independent states would go too far. But this conservative conclusion to the American Revolution gave the infant federal state a safer start. And the exclusively economic interpretation of the Constitution is of course hopelessly one-sided. Patriotism, moderation, even common sense played their part with other human sentiments. Finally, the threat that British control of Canada seemed to offer put a limit on domestic divisions. The United States grew up in its critical earliest years aware of the need for union against a possible foreign danger.

The new republic entered the world war of the Napoleonic period in 1812. Neither the French nor the British really tried to observe the freedom of commerce that the United States claimed as the right of a neutral, but the British, who were by 1812 masters of the sea, seemed to be infringing neutral rights more seriously than the French. Moreover, American expansionists, the "war hawks," saw a possible prize in Canada to be wrested from England, and no such prize to be got from France. The American attempt to invade Canada failed, not only from ineptness, but from the determined resistance of the Canadians. In isolated combats on the seas, the United States won victories that made up for her failures on land, and helped bolster national pride. The war on the whole was a stalemate, in which the United States experienced no important gains or losses. From the Mexican War of 1846–1848, a war in which the United States, however much harassed by a Mexican government angry at the loss of Texas to rebellious Yankee settlers, was clearly the aggressor, we gained an enormous block of territory from Texas to California.

Civil War and Reconstruction

The great test of the Federal Union was the war which broke out in 1861 after long years of sectional strife within the union between North and South. The Civil War was really an abortive nationalist revolution, the attempt of the Confederate states to set up a separate sovereign nation. The South was predominantly agricultural, with a society based on plantation slavery and on cotton and tobacco, much of which was exported abroad. The North was increasingly industrial, with a society based on free labor and on independent farm owners.

To the conflict of economic interest was

added, as almost always in human affairs, a conflict of ideals, of ways of life. That conflict was not so deep-seated, so irreconcilable, as it seemed to be to the generation that went to war in 1861—or the South, like Ireland or Poland, would presumably have tried again to free itself, something it did not attempt—or really discuss seriously—even in the integration crises of the 1950's and 1960's. The fires of conflict were fanned especially by the question of slavery, which seemed immoral to many in the North and which seemed the order of nature to many in the South. They were fanned also by writers and preachers on both sides, the Northerners thinking of themselves as heirs of the Puritans, the Southerners as heirs of the Cavaliers. With the secession of South Carolina and its sister states, antagonism reached the point of open war.

In retrospect, the victory of the North has an air of inevitability, especially since by 1861 the middle and upper Mississippi Valley was bound firmly to the North by economic and cultural ties. In population—especially since the South could not, did not dare, use the Negroes as soldiers—and in industrial resources above all, the North was greatly superior. Yet, aided by a very able corps of officers, by the advantages in morale that accrue to determined underdogs, and by the disastrous early overconfidence of the North, the South won initial victories that gave its cause great momentum. But the North thwarted the efforts of Confederate diplomats to secure British intervention and was able to improvise a naval force that gradually established a blockade, shutting off the South from importation of necessary war materials. In the long run, Northern strength in men and materials wore the Southern armies down.

The striking thing about the Civil War is not that the North won it finally in the field, but that the South accepted the verdict of battle as final, that the Union in which Americans today have grown up should be so firm and final. The "Road to Reunion" after 1865 was indeed no easy one, and in the first years of the Reconstruction period after the war it appeared to many an almost impossible one.

With the assassination of Lincoln by the fanatical Booth in 1865, the one great moderate who might have lessened the vengefulness of the Northern radicals was lost. The South was occupied by Northern soldiers, the illiterate Negroes were enfranchised, and Northern "carpetbaggers" and Southern "scalawags"—and many sincere idealists who believed they could bring liberty and equality to a "misguided" South—combined to bring what seemed a reign of terror to old Confederates.

Yet even in these early days the Civil War did not end, as such wars have often ended, in wholesale reprisals, executions, and exile. Northerners had sung during the war, "We'll hang Jeff Davis to a sour apple tree"; but after the war Jefferson Davis, President of the Confederacy, was not hanged on a sour apple tree or anywhere else. He was imprisoned for two years, and then lived quietly for another thirty, of course writing a book to justify his career. The fate of Davis measures the miracle of reunion. There were extremely few political refugees of the kind that often attend defeated causes. The soldiers of the South returned, often to devastated homes and lost fortunes, but they returned home under amnesty. Gradually the crusading fervor of the North wore off, and the Southerners, reinforced by new men, some of them immigrant Northerners, took over control in their states. Slavery, abolished by Lincoln's proclamation in 1863, was never restored, but the Negroes were in effect disenfranchised, "white supremacy" was restored, and the race question in the New South took on forms familiar to us today.

The end of the attempt to make radical reforms in the South was clear when a disputed presidential election in 1876 saw the Republican Hayes win over the Democrat Tilden after some very unprincipled political maneuvering which was certainly contrary to the spirit of the Constitution. No doubt conservative, business-conscious Northerners were anxious to get back to normal conditions, and quite willing to compromise with like-minded Southerners at the expense of race equality and other high ideals. Still, the final abandonment of idealistic reconstruction seems largely a usual, to-be-expected letdown of the energies behind a great crusade. In a sense, the crusade was renewed in 1954 with the decision of the Supreme Court against segregated public schools.

The South of the later nineteenth century was in part a "New South," which is one of the basic reasons why the region has come to accept the Civil War as ended, with due sentimental compensations in wistful feeling for the past. Slowly in the late nineteenth century, more rapidly in the twentieth, it has built up its own industries, taken steps to free itself from cotton monoculture and to integrate its economy and its society with the rest of the country. The South remained throughout this period a relatively backward area, with its own special problems of poverty, illiteracy, and race difficulties, but it was not an alien land, not an oppressed nationality eager to revolt.

The end of Reconstruction left the Democratic party in control of what came to be called the "solid South." This was a natural development, for it was the Republican party that had guided the North during the war, and that had tried to carry through Reconstruction. This fact worked to strengthen the American two-party system, since with so solid a block secure for the Democrats, the Republicans have been forced either to make compromises among themselves to preserve their own party unity, or to lose power; and the Northern Democrats have been forced to make compromises with their Southern wing.

It is possible, perhaps probable, that the renewed attempt to "reconstruct" the South in our time will mean a new party alignment. But for a century that alignment was, in spite of Populists, Progressives, New Dealers and the like, essentially the same, and, like the two-party alignment in Victorian Britain, rested on a tacit agreement not to disagree totally all down the line. The fact that the presidency, the great prize of political action, could be obtained only by securing a majority of the Electoral College meant also that a careful balancing of regional interests had to be maintained; a minority party could get nowhere in American politics.

Economic and Social Development

In 1865, the American economy was in many senses still "colonial"—that is, it produced in the main foods and other raw materials to be exchanged abroad for manufactured goods and, in financial terms, it was dependent on foreign money markets (chiefly London). But by 1914 the United States had been transformed into a great industrial nation, with its agriculture already to a high degree mechanized, and with financial resources so great that after World War I New York was to take over in part the place of London as a world financial center. This transformation could not have taken place, certainly not at the rate it did, without the existence of abundant manpower, of great and still almost untouched natural resources, and of the traditions of individual initiative and freedom of enterprise—which in part were certainly a product of the "frontier." Europe played a significant role in American economic growth by furnishing investment capital and, above all, by sending forth a steady flow of emigrants.

This great expansion in national wealth was achieved in a climate of opinion that supported overwhelmingly the view that the federal government should not interfere directly with business enterprise beyond maintaining public order, enforcing contracts, exercising some control over the actual coinage of money—and maintaining a protective tariff. Nor, of course, were the state and local governments supposed to go beyond such appropriate limits. This view we have already met in the classical economists who followed Adam Smith in Britain and in some of the continental states. It is a view that in the West has generally accompanied the first stages of the industrial revolution. But this revolution came relatively late to the United States, and for this if for no other reason a belief in free enterprise, in a minimum of government interference in economic activities, maintained itself more firmly in the twentieth century there than in the other parts of the western world.

This belief was reinforced by the Fourteenth Amendment to the Constitution, passed in 1866 and aimed to protect the freed Negroes in the South from state action to deprive them of civil rights. The Amendment contained the famous "due process" clause: "nor shall any state deprive any person of life, liberty, or property without due process of law." In the great era of free enterprise that followed the Civil War, the Supreme Court of the United States interpreted the celebrated clause to mean that state governments should not deprive businessmen—including corporations as "persons"—of property by regulating wages, prices, conditions of labor, and the like.

Immigration since the 1890's had brought in millions of aliens from eastern and southern Europe, men and women ignorant of American ways, and readily exploited by unscrupulous or merely conventional employers. These immigrants were hard to organize in labor unions; moreover, they and their children, uprooted, scorned, though they might be, readily absorbed the American beliefs that no man is a proletarian by nature, that there is always room on top. Yet even at the height of this "Gilded Age" or "Age of the Robber Barons" there was a movement toward the welfare state. Apparently there never was a time when laissez-faire was a universally accepted principle (except for the tariff), and wistful businessmen who nowadays look back to the nineteenth century in America as free from the curse of government interference are simply inventing a myth.

Much the same forces that had produced the Factory Acts in Britain gradually brought to the United States minimum-wage acts, limitation of child labor and women's labor, sanitary regulation, control of hours of labor, and workmen's compensation. Characteristically, and in spite of the Fourteenth Amendment, these measures were taken at the state rather than at the national level, and they varied greatly in the different states. The state of Wisconsin early established a reputation for advanced social legislation, but many of the older northeastern states played an important

Honest Money

Cartoon of Marcus A. Hanna, businessman adviser of President McKinley.

part in the movement. By the early twentieth century, public opinion was ready for increased participation of the national government in the regulation of economic life.

Theodore Roosevelt, a Republican, president from 1901 to 1909, promised to give labor a "square deal" and to proceed vigorously with "trust-busting," attacks on the great trusts or combinations that had come to monopolize important sectors of the American economy. Although Roosevelt did not always fulfill his promises, his administration did assail the trusts in railroads and tobacco and did press the federal regulation of great corporations. A federal prosecution of the Standard Oil Company begun in 1906 resulted in 1911 in a Supreme Court decision dissolving the great holding company. Some of the separated parts familiar today, such as Esso (Standard of New Jersey), Socony-Vacuum (Standard of New York), and Calso (Standard of California), are in fact "bigger" than was the dissolved parent company of John D. Rockefeller. Yet the work of the radicals of 1900, particularly the "muckrakers" who wrote exposés of questionable business practices for popular magazines, was clearly not in vain. American "big business" was in the 1950's bigger than it was in the days of Theodore Roosevelt. But, to put the matter nicely and in good terms, it was aware of its responsibilities to the public—or, to put it not so nicely, it was afraid of what might happen to it if it followed the advice of one of the great nineteenth-century "robber barons," Cornelius Vanderbilt: "The public be damned!" In short, big business in the United States is ultimately, as in democratic theory it must be, under the control of public opinion. This is a "realistic," not an "idealistic" statement: American public opinion is not at bottom hostile to the existence of wealthy individuals, but it does resent excessive exploitation by big corporations.

During the first administration of Woodrow Wilson (1913–1917), a Democrat, the process of regulation gained momentum. The Federal Reserve Act of 1913, for example, gave federal officials more control over banking, credit, and currency. Approval of such measures was not, of course, unanimous, since Americans differ loudly and widely about almost everything from metaphysics to sports. But, save for the Civil War, they have usually been willing in the end to differ no more than vocally, to accept varieties of belief and action where they appeared harmless or unavoidable, to conform to the law with no more than occasional violence. To outsiders, and to many native critics, American life in the decades between the Civil War and 1917 often seemed one great brawl, a more-than-Darwinian struggle for wealth and power. Yet this apparently anarchistic society achieved extraordinary material things—bridges, dams, railroads, great cities—which required the co-operation of millions of men and women disciplined to a common task. This paradox of the co-existence in the United States of "rugged individualism" and social cohesion still disturbs and puzzles many commentators on the American scene.

In spite of the more than usual dose of distrust of "government" common in western —perhaps in human—tradition, government has in the United States come to play a larger and larger part in the lives of all. Although this is true of local and state governments too, it holds more especially of the federal government. The gradually increasing importance of the federal government, and the gradually decreasing initiative of state governments, are as objectively clear in the period 1789–1917 as is the material growth of the United States in population and wealth.

The Myth of Isolation

Quite as objectively clear, though still the subject of infinite debate among Americans, is the emergence of the United States as a great international power. The United States was never literally "isolated." From the very beginning, this country had a Department of State, our senior department, and the proper apparatus of ministers, consuls, and, later, ambassadors. The United States was involved in the world war of the Napoleonic era, and by the Monroe Doctrine of the 1820's took the firm position that European powers were not to extend their existing territories in the Western Hemisphere. This was no mere negation, but an active extension of American claims to a far wider sphere of influence than the continental United States. Although Americans took no direct part in the complex nineteenth-century balance-of-power politics in Europe, they showed an increasing concern with a balance of power in the Far East, where they had long traded. After the brief war of 1898 with Spain, a war that broke out in Cuba, always a close concern of the United States, Americans found themselves directly involved with the newly annexed territories of the Philippine Islands, Hawaii, Puerto Rico—in short, with what looked to outsiders, and to many Americans, like an American empire.

Theodore Roosevelt, who owed his rapid political rise partly to his military leadership of the "Rough Riders" in the Spanish War, was a vigorous imperialist. He pressed the building of the Panama Canal, upheld the Far Eastern interests of the United States, and advocated a larger navy. This new "navalism," which also had assertive spokesmen in Britain and Germany, derived many of its doctrines from the writings of an American officer, Captain Alfred T. Mahan. Mahan's book, *The Influence of Sea Power upon History* (1890), and his later works assigned navies a place of preeminent importance in determining power status and found an influential audience both at home and abroad. Americans as individuals had long been active in work for better international organization, world peace, a world court.

Furthermore, over these many decades of expanding wealth and trade, the United States had come to take full part in international commercial relations. In these relations she had, save when the federal government was blockading the Confederacy, stood out firmly for rights to trade even though there was a war on somewhere, stood out for the "rights of neutrals." This fact alone would probably have brought the United States into the world war of 1914–1918, as it had brought her eventually into the world war of 1792–1815. But in 1917 America was, as she had not been in 1812, a great and active participant in the world state-system, though in formal alliance with no state.

Reading Suggestions on the Western Democracies in the Nineteenth Century

(Asterisk indicates paperbound edition.)

Britain

E. Halévy, *A History of the English People in the Nineteenth Century*, 2nd rev. ed., 5 vols. (P. Smith 1949–1951; *Barnes & Noble). The classic detailed study; does not cover the entire period.

E. L. Woodward, *The Age of Reform* (Clarendon, 1938), and R. C. K. Ensor, *England, 1870–1914* (Clarendon, 1936). Two full and very useful volumes in the *Oxford History of England*.

D. Thomson, *England in the Nineteenth Century* (*Penguin, 1950). Excellent account.

A. Wood, *Nineteenth Century Britain* (Longmans, Green, 1960). Excellent survey.

M. Cole, *The Story of Fabian Socialism* (Heinemann, 1961). Excellent account, important for understanding the contemporary British Labor party.

P. Magnus, *Gladstone: A Biography* (Dutton, 1955). A sound study of the great Victorian liberal.

Roy Jenkins, *Asquith* (Collins, 1964). A good biography of a main figure.

A. Briggs, *The Age of Improvements* (Longmans, Green, 1959). A general history of England, 1783–1867, which lives up to its apt, and not wholly ironical title.

M. Bruce, *The Coming of the Welfare State* (Batsford, 1961). A good general study for Britain.

R. E. Barry, *Nationalisation in British Politics: The Historical Background* (Stanford Univ. Press, 1965). A useful monograph.

David Owen, *English Philanthropy 1660–1960* (Harvard Univ. Press, 1964). A major work, important throughout its period, perhaps most so for the nineteenth century.

Note: See also titles cited for Chapter 12.

France

D. W. Brogan, *The French Nation from Napoleon to Pétain, 1814–1940* (Harper, 1957; *Colophon). A brilliant essay by a writer who knows first-hand the great Western democracies of Britain, France, and the United States. A bit severe on the Third Republic as a political structure.

G. Duby and R. Mandrou, *A History of French Civilization* (Random House, 1964). An admirable general history. See reading suggestions for Chapter 7.

G. Wright, *France in Modern Times* (Rand McNally, 1960). The best single volume on the subject, with good reading suggestions.

A. Maurois, *The Miracle of France* (Harper, 1948). A general survey by a Frenchman with great literary gifts.

Adrien Dansette, *The Religious History of Modern France*, 2 Vols. (Herder and Herder, 1961). Major study from French Revolution to the present. Well translated from the French.

A. Guérard, *Reflections on the Napoleonic Legend* (Scribner's, 1924). Interesting study of the magnetic attraction exerted by Bonaparte after his death.

F. A. Simpson, *The Rise of Louis Napoleon,* 3rd ed. (Longmans, Green, 1950), and *Louis Napoleon and the Recovery of France,* 3rd ed. (Longmans, Green, 1951). The most detailed study in English; goes only to 1856.

J. M. Thompson, *Louis Napoleon and the Second Empire* (Blackwell, 1954). A useful synthesis, based on detailed scholarly works.

A. Guérard, *Napoleon III* (Harvard Univ. Press, 1943). A spirited attempt to picture the emperor in the attractive role of "Caesarean democrat."

D. W. Brogan, *France under the Republic* (Harper, 1940). A witty, perceptive, but allusive history of the Third Republic.

D. Thomson, *Democracy in France: The Third and Fourth Republics,* 3rd ed. (Oxford Univ. Press, 1958). A brilliant essay of interpretation; assumes basic factual knowledge.

R. Soltau, *French Political Thought in the Nineteenth Century*, new ed. (Russell & Russell, 1959). A good survey, though perhaps unfair to the conservative thinkers.

G. Chapman, *The Dreyfus Case: A Re-assessment* (Viking, 1956). The most searching treatment of the "Affair" available in English; neglects the historical results of the case.

H. Goldberg, *Life of Jean Jaurès* (Univ. of Wisconsin Press, 1962). Best treatment in English. Very favorable to Jaurès.

G. Bruun, *Clemenceau* (Harvard Univ. Press, 1943). A first-rate biography of the redoubtable politician of the Third Republic.

S. B. Clough, *France: A History of National Economics, 1789–1939* (Scribner's, 1939). A valuable treatment of topics often hard to find information on; the notes are most helpful.

C. P. Kindleberger, *Economic Growth in France & Britain 1881–1950.* (Harvard Univ. Press, 1964). A stimulating study by a professional economist.

Italy

D. Mack Smith, *Italy: A Modern History* (Univ. of Michigan Press, 1959). A sound and detailed study, actually confined to "modern" history. Good reading suggestions.

A. J. B. Whyte, *The Making of Modern Italy* (Blackwell, 1944). One of the very few good accounts in English.

B. King, *A History of Italian Unity*, 2 vols., rev. ed. (Nisbet, 1924). An old account, but still informative.

R. A. Webster, *The Cross and the Fasces: Christian Democracy and Fascism in Italy* (Stanford Univ. Press, 1960). Goes back to 1870; good general study of the background of twentieth-century Italy.

R. Grew, *A Sterner Plan for Italian Unity: The Italian National Society in the Risorgimento* (Princeton Univ. Press, 1963). Good study of the important place of Italian parties, 1848-1870.

D. Mack Smith, *Garibaldi* (Knopf, 1956). Brief and up-to-date; the best biography available in English.

D. Mack Smith, *Cavour and Garibaldi, 1860: A Study in Political Conflict* (Cambridge Univ. Press, 1954). Important monograph.

B. Croce, *A History of Italy, 1871–1915* (Clarendon, 1929). By a distinguished thinker.

S. B. Clough, *The Economic History of Modern Italy* (Columbia Univ. Press, 1964). Authoritative; useful for the nineteenth and twentieth centuries.

United States

R. Hofstadter, W. Miller, D. Aaron, *The United States: The History of a Republic,* 2nd ed. (Prentice-Hall, 1967). A readable account, well illustrated.

R. B. Morris, ed., *Encyclopaedia of American History* (Harper, 1961). A standard reference work.

C. A. and M. A. Beard, *The Rise of American Civilization* (Macmillan, 1936). A famous popular account, written from the standpoint of the economic interpretation of American history.

O. Handlin, *Chance or Destiny: Turning Points in American History* (Little, Brown, 1955). Most readable general essay by a distinguished scholar.

L. Hartz, *The Liberal Tradition in America: An Interpretation of American Political Thought since the Revolution* (Harcourt, Brace, 1955). Provocative survey that has stirred up considerable controversy.

S. E. Morison, *The Oxford History of the American People,* new ed. (Oxford Univ. Press, 1965). A complete re-working of an earlier book. Most readable and authoritative.

R. Hofstadter, *The American Political Tradition* (*Vintage), and C. Rossiter, *Conservatism in America* (Knopf, 1955). Complementary studies; liberal and conservative, respectively.

The Smaller Democracies

The following is a list of brief national histories which will enable the student to go further with the history of any one of these countries.

R. Carr, *Spain, 1808–1939* (Oxford Univ. Press, 1966).

E. Bonjour and others, *A Short History of Switzerland* (Oxford Univ. Press, 1950).

H. van der Linden, *Belgium: The Making of a Nation* (Oxford Univ. Press, 1920).

G. Edmundson, *A History of Holland* (Cambridge Univ. Press, 1922).

J. Danstrup, *A History of Denmark* (Wivel, Copenhagen, 1949).

K. Larsen, *A History of Norway* (Princeton Univ. Press. 1948).

I. Andersson, *A History of Sweden* (Praeger, 1956).

J. H. Wuorinen, *A History of Finland* (Columbia Univ. Press, 1965).

Historical Fiction

B. Disraeli, *Coningsby* (Dutton, 1911, Everyman ed.). Significant for Tory democracy.

A. Trollope, *The Prime Minister* (Oxford Univ. Press, 1951, World's Classics ed.). Probably the best novel on Victorian politics.

E. Zola, *The Downfall* ("La Débacle") (Appleton, 1902). Good novel of War of 1870.

A. Bennett, *Old Wives' Tale* (Modern Library). Contains a superb account of life in Paris under the siege of 1870–1871.

A France, *Penguin Island* (A Bantam paperback, also Modern Library, 1934). A satirical history of France.

R. Martin du Gard, *Jean Barois* (Viking, 1949). Sound novel of Dreyfus affair.

W. D. Howells, *The Rise of Silas Lapham* (many editions). Typical realistic novel.

U. Sinclair, *The Jungle* (Viking, 1946). A famous exposé of the atrocious conditions in the meat-packing industry of Chicago about 1900.

M. Kantor, *Andersonville* (*Signet, 1957). Grim and realistic novel of the Civil War.

M. Mitchell, *Gone with the Wind* (Macmillan, 1936; *Pocket Permabooks).

14

Central and Eastern Europe

To the Outbreak of World War I

I Introduction

In this chapter we shall deal with Germany (1850–1914), the Habsburg Monarchy (1850–1914), and Russia (1825–1914). These three empires were partners in crime in the partitions of Poland of the late eighteenth century, and firm allies in the Metternich system of European balance after 1815. After 1850, they passed through periods of mutual affection and hatred. In 1914 all went to war, with Germany and Austria-Hungary as allies against Russia. Internally they had much in common, although each followed its own peculiar development. In contrast with the countries of western Europe, these were the lands of autocratic monarchy and relatively powerless parliaments appearing on the scene relatively late; all were still "empires," a title that only the tottering Ottoman state also claimed in Europe.

II Germany, 1850-1914

In 1914, the militarist and nationalist German Empire was a powerful, unified industrial state with a highly educated, obedient, and competent population. By supporting the Balkan policies of its ally, Austria-Hungary, it helped to plunge the entire world into the first of the twentieth century's wars of mass slaughter. Germany had emerged as a great continental power only after 1850, although for more than 1,400 years millions of Germans had been living in the heart of Europe under a variety of political regimes. The militarism, the authoritarianism, the whole social and cultural tone of the Germany of 1914, were determined by the fact that it was the Kingdom of Prussia that had achieved German unification. Characteristic Prussian attitudes had overcome other German ways of looking at society and had imposed themselves on non-Prussians. The Prussian triumph was complete by 1871.

Between 1850 and 1871, and especially after 1862, Prussia moved with ever-accelerating speed from triumph to triumph. Doubters and protesters were silenced or dazzled by the glitter of each new achievement; moral objections were regarded as unpatriotic. Otto von Bismarck, who directed policy, spoke of respect for legality and decency as "humanitarian twaddle" and proclaimed an era when "blood and iron" alone would decide. The ends seemed so desirable and were being gained so rapidly that even stern moralists could tell themselves that this time they need not examine the means. They shook their heads and voted the government new subsidies.

The creation of imperial Germany was above all the work of Bismarck (1815–1898). Brilliant, unscrupulous, ruthless, a genius at maneuver and at concealing his real intentions, Bismarck was often bewilderingly inconsistent in his policies. Sometimes he pursued two apparently contradictory policies at the same time, until the moment came when he had to make a final decision on which policy to follow. His intense loyalty to the Prussian Crown, however, did not falter during his long years in office, although after his dismissal by William II in 1890 he felt that his work was being undone, and he often tried to embarrass the Emperor and his own successors in the government. He could not endure criticism of himself. At different periods, he loathed liberals, Catholics, and socialists. And he despised his intellectual inferiors even when they belonged to his own class, the Prussian landed nobility: the Junkers, who believed firmly in their own privileges, monopolized commissions in the Prussian army, and dominated the administrative services of the Prussian state. Whatever Bismarck's policy of the moment, force lay at its roots. Influential before 1862, he towered over Prussia from 1862 to 1871, and over the German Empire thereafter until 1890. Yet his efforts could not have succeeded had they not met with general approval from the German people, who had hungered for unity since before 1848.

Prussia and the German Confederation, 1850–1859

The first major question facing the statesmen of Central Europe after the revolutions of 1848 was whether Prussia or Austria would dominate the German Confederation. A creation of the Congress of Vienna (see Chapter 11), it had been temporarily shaken and split by the developments of 1848, and now needed to be rebuilt. The "Big German" solution called for federation with Austria; the "Small German" solution called for separation from Austria or even from South Germany. The "Small German" program meant Prussian

Unification of Germany, 1866-1871

Prussia before 1866

Annexed by Prussia, 1866

Other states that joined Prussia to form North German Federation

.... Boundary of North German Federation, 1866

States joining Confederation to form German Empire

Territories annexed by Treaty of Frankfurt

—— Boundary of the German Empire, 1871   ■ Battle sites

domination of the non-Austrian German states, and therefore became Bismarck's goal.

The period after 1848 opened with a defeat for a Prussian "Small German" solution. King Frederick William IV, who had refused to accept the imperial crown "from the gutter" when it was offered by the Frankfurt Assembly (see Chapter 11), none the less cherished the hope that the German princes might offer it to him. Taking advantage of Austria's preoccupation with the remnants of the Revolution of 1848, and overriding his own Prussian conservatives, who wished simply to strengthen their own state, Frederick William IV formed the Erfurt Union of Princes, an agreement to pool military resources. This union was designed to lead to Prussian political as well as military dominance.

The Austrians managed to bring Russian pressure to bear on Prussia. The Tsar opposed the unification of the Germans no matter under whose auspices. At Olmütz, in November, 1850, the Prussians renounced the Erfurt Union and reluctantly agreed to the revival of the Confederation. This episode is known as the "humiliation" of Olmütz, a term that shows how bitterly many Prussians resented it. Yet Bismarck himself defended the treaty, and as a result was sent as Prussian representative to the Diet of the Confederation.

At the Diet Bismarck took every occasion to work against Austria, and to thwart

Austrian designs. As one facet of his policy, he favored Prussian neutrality in the Crimean War (1854–56), in which England and France fought with Turkey against Russia, and Austria harassed rather than helped the Russians (see p. 551). Realizing that Austrian behavior was alienating Russia, and that Russian friendship would be valuable later when Prussia came to grips with Austria, Bismarck frustrated those Prussians who hoped that Prussia would enter the war against Russia and thus line up with the West. He was counting on a military showdown with Austria. With this purpose in mind, he also wooed the French Emperor Napoleon III, despite the horror that many Prussians felt over dealings with a Bonaparte, whom they regarded as the heir of the French Revolution.

Both the constitutional and economic foundations of future Prussian development were laid during the 1850's. The Prussian Constitution of 1850, which lasted down to the end of World War I, provided for a bicameral legislature: a hereditary upper house including the nobles and royal appointees, and an elected lower house. But the method of electing this lower house made it certain that the popular will would be frustrated. Electors were divided into three classes, according to the amount of taxes they paid. The 4 per cent of the electorate who paid high taxes selected one-third of the representatives. The 14 per cent of middle taxpayers selected another third, and the remaining 82 per cent of low taxpayers selected the last third. The preponderant power of the wealthy is clear.

Even so, the lower house had very little to do beyond approving the budget. Policy questions were decided in the upper house, or still more often by the king and his personal circle of military and political advisers. The king appointed his ministers, could veto any bill he disapproved, and had a fixed sum of money at his disposal for expenses. He had a special "military cabinet" for army affairs that reported neither to the ministers nor to the legislature. Practically speaking, the king and the Junkers ran Prussia.

With its possessions in western Germany, including the Ruhr, Prussia had the richest coal deposits in Europe. The iron and steel industry, without which her future political and military triumphs would have been impossible, now began its phenomenal growth. Alone among the continental nations, the Prussians turned over the planning of their new railway system to the army general staff, which laid out the lines with an eye to rapid and efficient mobilization and transportation of troops and military supplies in time of war.

Bismarck Comes to Power

Indeed these military concerns led directly to the beginning of Bismarck's undisputed domination of Prussian policies. King William I, who succeeded Frederick William IV in 1861, was above all a soldier. His minister of war, Roon, a friend of Bismarck's, easily persuaded the King that an army reorganization was necessary. He wanted to increase the number of conscripts drafted each year from 40,000 to 63,000, and to lengthen the term of their service from two to three years. Roon hoped that a big conservative army might serve as counter-weight to any liberal or revolutionary tendencies in the state. A prolonged political crisis arose over these aims in 1861 and 1862, when the Prussian parliament refused to vote the budget. At the very height of the crisis, the King, convinced that Bismarck could outwit the parliament, appointed him to the key posts of prime minister of Prussia and minister of foreign affairs.

On the fallacious principle that there was a "gap" in the constitution that permitted the government to collect taxes even when the budget had not been approved by parliament, Bismarck now collected and spent revenue quite illegally. Again and again he dissolved the parliament, called new elections, faced another hostile house, and then repeated the process. He suppressed opposition newspapers in defiance of a constitutional provision that the press should be free. He indicted an opposition deputy, himself a judge and a loyal Prussian, in spite of the constitutional provision that deputies could not be indicted for anything they said on the floor of the house. Yet after four years of this illegal behavior (1862–1866), he got away with everything in the end because of the glittering successes he scored by his unorthodox daring in foreign policy.

Since Bismarck intended to overthrow the German Confederation as it was then constituted, he opposed Austrian efforts to reform it. Austria wished to create an assembly of delegates chosen by the parliaments of the member states, in addition to those named by the princes, and a directorate of six monarchs. Bismarck prevented William I from attending a congress of princes called by Austria to discuss these proposals, and thus wrecked the congress (1862). In 1863, he kept Austria out of the *Zollverein*, the German Customs Union (Chapter 11). He also consolidated his good relations with Russia during the Polish revolt (see p. 533) by concluding the Alvensleben convention, which allowed the Russians to pursue fleeing Poles onto Prussian territory and capture them there. Thus Bismarck wooed the Russians a second time, as he had during the Crimean War.

Bismarck in 1859.

The Schleswig-Holstein Question, 1863–1865

When the King of Denmark died in late 1863, the celebrated Schleswig-Holstein question gave Bismarck further opportunities. The prime minister of England once remarked that only three men had ever understood this complex problem, and that one was dead and one insane, while he himself, the third, had forgotten all about it. In brief, the duchies of Schleswig and Holstein at the southern base of the Danish peninsula had been ruled by the King of Denmark, but not as part of Denmark. A fifteenth-century guarantee assured the duchies that they could never be separated from one another. Yet Holstein to the south was a member of the German Confederation; Schleswig to the north was not. Holstein was mostly German in population; Schleswig was mixed German and Danish. In 1852, Prussia had agreed in an international conference on an heir who would succeed both to the Danish throne and to the duchies. At the same time, Prussia had joined the other powers in recommending that Denmark and the duchies should be united by a constitution. But, when the constitutional union of Denmark and the duchies was attempted, the duchies resisted, and the Danes tried to incorporate Schleswig. German patriots objected. The Prussians and Austrians wanted the duchies to have special representation inside the Danish parliament and insisted that Schleswig should *not* be incorporated into Denmark. None the less, the King of Denmark in 1863 followed a policy that supported annexation.

Into this situation Bismarck now moved to win the duchies for Prussia. He wanted both the prestige that Prussia would gain and the valuable commercial port of Kiel in Holstein. First he maneuvered Prussia and Austria together into a victorious war against Denmark (1864), although Austria had no real interest in the duchies. Then he quarreled with the Austrians over the administration of the duchies. At the Convention of Gastein,

1865, it was decided that Prussia was to administer Schleswig and that Austria was to administer Holstein. But this arrangement provided only a temporary halt in Bismarck's drive against Austria.

War with Austria, 1866

Bismarck kept nagging Vienna about Austrian behavior in Holstein. He tried and failed to tempt France into an alliance. But he did succeed in lining up the Italians, who secretly obliged themselves to go to war on the side of Prussia if Prussia fought Austria within three months. This was contrary to the constitution of the German Confederation, which forbade members to ally themselves with a foreign power against other members. So distressed was William I at this illegality that he lied flatly when the Austrian emperor asked him if such a treaty existed. Finally, Bismarck suddenly proposed that the German Confederation be reformed, and that an all-German parliament be elected by universal suffrage, which everybody knew he hated.

Bismarck probably advanced this proposal for universal suffrage in order to make it appear that his quarrel with Austria rested on a less sordid ground than the mere Schleswig-Holstein question. Yet the proposal also reflected his calculation that enfranchisement of all Germans would weaken the Progressive party, heir to the liberalism of 1848, and would produce many conservative and royalist votes from the peasantry. He had seen how Napoleon III had risen to imperial power in France on the strength of universal suffrage. And he had been influenced by conversations with Ferdinand Lassalle, a German socialist, who argued that universal suffrage would weaken the middle classes. Bismarck had hoped that the Austrians might try to throw his plan out, but the other members of the Confederation asked Prussia to propose a full plan of reform. Austria now laid the Schleswig-Holstein question before the Diet of the Confederation. Bismarck ordered Prussian troops into Holstein and declared that Austrian motions in the Diet were unconstitutional.

He succeeded in provoking war with Austria. It was an all-German civil war, since Bavaria, Württemberg, Saxony, Hanover (the four other German kingdoms), and most of the lesser German states sided with Austria.

The war lasted seven weeks and was virtually decided in less than three. The Austrians had to commit a substantial part of their forces against Italy. Skillfully using their railway network, the telegraph, and superior armaments, the Prussians quickly overran northern Germany, invaded Bohemia and defeated the Austrians at Königgrätz (Sadowa), defeated the Bavarians, and entered Frankfurt, seat of the German Confederation. The states of Hanover, Hesse-Cassel, and Nassau were all annexed to Prussia and their dynasties expelled. Schleswig-Holstein and the free city of Frankfurt were also taken over.

Bismarck successfully opposed the generals, and even his king, who wished to punish Austria severely. Except for the cession of Venetia to Italy, Austria suffered no territorial losses as a result of the Peace of Prague (1866), but she did pay a small indemnity. Most important from Bismarck's point of view, Austria had to withdraw forever from the German Confederation, which now ceased to exist. Germany north of the Main River was to join a new North German Confederation to be organized by Prussia. However, it was stipulated that the German states south of the Main were to be free to form an independent union of their own. But Bismarck had previously concluded secret treaties of alliance with the most important South German states —Bavaria, Württemberg, and Baden—who promised to put their armies at the disposal of the king of Prussia in case of war. So the proposed South German union could never come into existence. Bismarck thus broke the Peace of Prague before it had been concluded, a real piece of diplomatic skill. Bismarck's gentle treatment of Austria was not just a matter of generosity. He was convinced that Prussia would need Austrian help in the future. Now that he had expelled Austria from Germany, imposed a "Small German" solution, and elevated Prussia to the position of dominance, he had scored his point.

Now Bismarck was free to turn to the Prussian parliament, with which he had been feuding for four years. He asked for an "indemnity"—that is, a certification that all the revenue he had illegally collected and illegally spent, ever since the parliament had refused to pass the budget in 1861, had in fact been legally collected and legally spent. The deputies were so dazzled by the feats of arms against Denmark and Austria, and by the enormous new acquisitions of power and territory, that they voted the indemnity and awarded Bismarck personally a cash gift of roughly $300,000.

The North German Confederation

An assembly elected by universal manhood suffrage now debated and adopted a constitution for the new North German Confederation, of which the Prussian king was president. The draft that Bismarck submitted is eloquent testimony to his determination to "kill parliamentarism through parliament." The future parliament (*Reichstag*) was to have no power over the budget, and the ministers were not to be responsible to it. Instead, a Federal Council (*Bundesrat*), consisting of delegates from the member states and voting according to instructions from their sovereigns, would reach all key policy decisions in secret and would have veto power over any enactment of the Reichstag. A chancellor would preside over the Bundesrat, but would not have to explain or defend its decisions before the Reichstag. Since Prussia now had not only its own votes in the Bundesrat but also those of the newly annexed states, Bismarck's plan in effect made it possible for the king of Prussia to run Germany.

This plan was only slightly modified so that the future chancellor would have to sign every act undertaken by the king of Prussia as president of the Confederation. But the executive was in no way made "responsible" to the Reichstag. Bismarck's plan also specified that, beginning five years later in 1872, the size of the army would be fixed by law and that the

Reichstag would have a vote on the budget. However, Bismarck, who became chancellor, saw to it that the debate on the military budget did not take place every year, but that sums were appropriated for long periods in advance.

Showdown with France

As long as Bismarck needed the benevolent neutrality of Napoleon III, he had hinted that he might not object if Napoleon took Belgium. Now the gullible Napoleon found that Bismarck no longer remembered the matter. Hoping to be compensated for his assistance in making peace between Prussia and Austria, Napoleon III tried to acquire Luxemburg by purchase from the king of Holland. Again he was frustrated by Bismarck. Suddenly confronted with the new Germany, many members of the French public and press hoped to get "revenge for Sadowa," and became strongly anti-German. The German press responded in kind. Napoleon III tried to obtain an alliance with Austria and Italy in order to thwart further Prussian expansion. But the Austrians shied away from a true commitment, and the Italians were unable to reach an agreement with the French because of the Roman question (see Chapter 13).

When the Spaniards ousted their queen in 1868, one of the candidates for the throne was a Hohenzollern prince, whom Bismarck secretly backed by discreetly bribing influential Spaniards. Because of family dynastic practice, it was necessary to secure the consent of the reluctant King William I of Prussia, and this Bismarck finally extracted without hinting that war with France might result. Napoleon III, also deep in Spanish intrigue, feared that a Hohenzollern on the Spanish throne would expose France to a two-front attack. French diplomatic pressure was exerted directly on King William, and the Hohenzollern candidate withdrew. At this moment, Bismarck seemed to be defeated.

But the French, overstimulated by their success, now demanded that William publicly endorse the withdrawal of the candidacy, and promise never to allow it to be renewed. William, who was at Ems, courteously refused, and sent a telegram to Bismarck describing his interchange with the French ambassador. Bismarck then abridged this famous Ems telegram, and released his doctored version to the press and all the European chanceries. He made it seem that William had thoroughly snubbed the French ambassador, and that the ambassador had been "provocative" to the King. Public opinion in Germany was now inflamed, and Bismarck set out to bait the French still further by unleashing a violent campaign against them in the German press, and boasting of his prowess in editing the Ems despatch. The French reacted as Bismarck had hoped. They declared war on July 19, 1870.

Within six weeks the Germans had advanced into France, bottled up one French army inside the fortress of Metz, defeated another at Sedan, and captured Napoleon III himself. The protracted siege of Paris followed, ending in surrender early in 1871. A new French government had to sign the treaty of Frankfurt. Bismarck forced the French to pay a billion-dollar indemnity, to cede the rich province of Alsace and about two-fifths of Lorraine (which the German military wanted as a defense against possible future French attack), and to support German occupying forces until the indemnity had been paid.

The German Empire

Even before this peace had been imposed, King William of Prussia was proclaimed Emperor of Germany in the great Hall of Mirrors in Louis XIV's palace at Versailles. Bismarck had to make a few unimportant concessions to the rulers of the South German states to secure their entry into the new empire, but he never had to consult the Reichstag, which simply hastened to send its own deputation begging the King to accept the Crown. The proclamation took place in a ceremony of princes and soldiers. When a constitution for the new empire was adopted, it was simply an extension of the constitution of the North German Confederation of 1867.

As Chancellor of the German Empire from 1871 to 1890, Bismarck became the leading statesman in all Europe. He felt that Germany had no further need for territory or for war. As a nineteenth-century realist with no dream of world-empire, he felt that his limited goals had been attained. As diplomat, he henceforth worked for the preservation of Germany's gains against threats from abroad, especially the threat that haunted him most: foreign coalition against Germany (see Chapter 17). As politician, he worked for the preservation of the Prussian system against all opposing currents.

Bismarck's chancellorship falls naturally into two periods: (1) a period of free trade, co-operation with the Liberals, and opposition to the Catholics (1871–1878); and (2) a period of protective tariffs, co-operation with the Catholics, and opposition to the socialists (1878–1890).

Domestic Developments, 1871–1878

At home, a multitude of economic and legal questions arose as a result of the creation of the new empire. Working with the moderate Liberal party in the Reichstag, Bismarck put through a common coinage and a central bank, co-ordinated and unified the railroads and postal systems, and regularized the legal and judicial systems. In 1871, the Reichstag voted to maintain 1 per cent of the population under arms for three years. In 1874, Bismarck, simply by threatening to resign, forced the Reichstag to fix the size of the army at 401,000 for a seven-year period, until 1881. In 1880, a year before the period expired, he forced an increase to 427,000 for another seven years, to 1888. The privileged position of the army made a military career ever more attractive and served as a constant spur to German militarism.

But the great drama of the 1870's in Germany was furnished by Bismarck's attack on the Roman Catholic Church, the *Kulturkampf* ("battle for civilization"). The "Syllabus of Errors," published by the Vatican in 1864 (see Chapter 12), had denounced the toleration of other religions, secular education, and state participation in church affairs. Then in 1870 the Vatican Council, the first general council of the Church to meet since the Council of Trent in the Reformation period, adopted the dogma of papal infallibility. This dogma asserted that the judgments of the pope on faith and morals were infallible. To many non-Catholics, this seemed to say that no state could count on the absolute loyalty of its Catholic citizens.

In Germany, the Catholics were a large minority of the population. They had formed a political party, the Center, that quickly became the second strongest party in the Empire. The Center defended papal infallibility, and wished to restore the pope's temporal power, which had been ended by the unification of Italy. The Center not only had many sympathizers in the Catholic Polish provinces of Germany but also sponsored a labor movement of its own, which seemed to pose a social threat. Catholic peasant and workman, priest and nobleman, all opposed the Protestant urban middle class and the Prussian military predominance in the state. Bismarck identified his clerical opponents with France and Austria, the two nations he had defeated in making the new Germany.

In collaboration with the Liberals, Bismarck put through laws expelling the Jesuits from Germany, forbidding the clergy to criticize the government, and closing the schools of religious orders. In Prussia, civil marriage was now required, appropriations for the Catholic Church were stopped, and priests were forced to study at secular universities. The Pope declared these laws null and void, and summoned all good Catholics to disobey them. Catholic services stopped in towns and villages, and many Catholics were deprived of their sacraments.

Bismarck never appreciated that the Church thrives on persecution. By declaring that he would not "go to Canossa," he summoned up for Protestant Germans the picture of the German Emperor Henry IV humbling himself before the Pope in 1077. But Bismarck in the end had to go to Canossa, and repealed in the eighties most of the anti-Catholic measures he had passed in the seventies. By then he needed the support of the Center party against his former allies the Liberals, whose demands for power he found exorbitant, and against the growing menace of the Social Democrats. Moreover, the Protestant Church itself and many of the conservative Prussian nobility had grown alarmed over the excesses of the anti-Catholic campaign.

Domestic Developments, 1878–1890

Indeed, in 1877 and 1878, Bismarck had begun a gradual shift in policy, dictated in the first place by the need for more revenue. The Empire got its money in part from indirect taxes imposed by the Reichstag on tobacco, alcohol, sugar, and the like. The rest came from the individual states, which controlled all direct taxation and made contributions to the imperial budget. As military costs mounted, the government's income became insufficient, and Bismarck did not want to increase the Empire's dependence on the states by repeatedly asking them to increase their contributions. He wanted the Reichstag to vote higher indirect taxes, but its Liberal members suspected that if they acceded he might do to them what he had formerly done to the Prussian parliament: govern without them if a dispute arose, and depend on the money he would collect from the higher taxes they had granted him. Therefore they wanted some sort of guarantee before they untied Bismarck's hands.

Basically, German tariff policy had been one of free trade, with little protection for German goods. But after a financial panic in 1873, the iron and textile industries put pressure on Bismarck to shift to a policy of protection that would help them compete with England. Moreover, an agricultural crisis led conservatives to abandon their previous support of free trade, and to demand protection against cheap grain from eastern Europe. In 1879, Bismarck put through a general protective tariff on all imports, a move on which his former allies, the Liberals, were split.

In order to avoid granting the constitutional guarantees demanded by the Liberals, Bismarck gradually abandoned the *Kulturkampf.* The Catholic Center favored his protectionist policy; moreover, the lessening of the clerical threat in France and the conclusion of a firm German alliance with Austria in 1879 (see Chapter 17) removed the foreign causes for the attack on the Church. Bismarck therefore secured the support of the Center as well as that of the conservatives. Thus he was able to avoid making concessions to the Reichstag, and thus he launched Germany on an era of protection. The protectionist policy spurred still further the rapid and efficient growth of industry, especially heavy industry. Politically, the conservative Protestant agrarian forces now grew stronger, and gained many urban votes. But Bismarck never entirely trusted the Center, and strove successfully to remodel the Liberals into a stanchly conservative industrialist group.

While he was easing the *Kulturkampf* and swinging to protection in 1878–1879, Bismarck also began to proceed against the Social Democratic party. The Marxists Liebknecht and Bebel had founded this small party in 1869; in 1875, they enlarged it, much to Marx's own disgust, by accepting the followers of Lassalle, an apostle of non-violence. The German Social Democrats were not nearly so revolutionary as their own Marxist phraseology suggested, and had no doubt inherited some of Lassalle's willingness to make a deal with the existing regime. They had many supporters among intellectuals and former liberals, and a substantial trade-union following, polling half a million votes in 1877, about 10 per cent of the total electorate. They were prepared to concentrate their efforts on improving working conditions rather than on revolution. But Bismarck always needed an enemy against whom he could unify his supporters; besides, he had been deeply impressed by the Paris Commune (see Chapter 13), and believed that something similar might occur in Germany.

Using as a pretext two attempts by alleged Social Democrats to assassinate William I, Bismarck called a general election in 1878 and rammed through the Reichstag a bill making the Social Democratic party illegal, forbidding its meetings, and suppressing its newspapers. Individual socialists could even be expelled from their domiciles by the police. Abandoning their alleged principles, the Liberals supported this law, but they would not allow Bismarck to make it a permanent statute. He had to apply to the Reichstag for its renewal every two or three years; it was renewed each time, until just before Bismarck's own downfall in 1890. Interestingly enough, Social Democrats were still allowed to run for the Reichstag, and their votes increased during the years when they were suffering legal disabilities.

But Bismarck felt that "a remedy cannot be sought merely in repression of Socialist excesses — there must be simultaneously a positive advancement of the welfare of the working classes." As a result, all during the 1880's, the government put forward a series of bills in favor of the workers: in 1882 compulsory insurance against illness, and in 1884 against accidents. The sickness insurance funds were raised by contributions from both workers and employers; the accident insurance funds were contributed altogether by the employers. In 1889, old-age and invalidism insurance followed, with employers and employees contributing equally, and with an additional subsidy from the state. The German system of social security as developed initially under Bismarck did not reduce the Social Democratic vote, but it did provide much that the worker desired.

William II

Bismarck's faithful William I died at the age of ninety in 1888, and William's son, Frederick III, already mortally ill, ruled for only about three months. The next emperor was Frederick's son, William II, a young man of twenty-nine whose advent his father had greatly feared because of his immaturity, impulsiveness, and conceit. William I had allowed Bismarck to act for him, but William II was determined to act for himself. This determination underlay the subsequent controversy between him and Bismarck.

On his accession, William loudly proclaimed his sympathy with the workingman. When the anti-socialist law came up for renewal, the Emperor supported a modified version that would have taken away the power of the police to expel Social Democrats from their residences. Bismarck opposed the measure, hoping that the Social Democrats would indulge in excesses which would give him the excuse to suppress them by armed force. As a result, there was no anti-socialist law after 1890. Other differences arose between the Chancellor and the Emperor over relations with Russia, and over procedure in reaching policy decisions. Finally, in March, 1890, William commanded Bismarck to resign.

Although four chancellors succeeded him during the years before the outbreak of war in 1914, none of them can be compared with Bismarck in ability and influence. The years 1890–1914 are truly the years of William II. Energetic but unsteady, pompous and menacing but without the intention or the courage to back up his threats, emotional and vacillating, William was ill-suited to govern any country, much less the militaristic, highly industrialized, imperial Germany with its social tensions and its lack of political balance.

Domestic Tensions, 1890–1914

Party structure reflected the strains in German society. The Liberals, a party of big business, usually had little strength in the Reichstag, although many industrialists were on intimate terms with the Emperor personally. The great landowners banded together in protest against a reduction in agricultural duties which was included in a series of trade treaties concluded between Germany and other continental European countries between 1892 and 1894. In 1894, they organized the Agrarian League, which spearheaded all conservative measures and became enormously powerful

in German politics. In 1902, they forced a return to protection.

The electoral strength of the Social Democrats increased during William's reign from 1,500,000 to 4,250,000, and embraced one-third of the voting population by 1914. Freed from interference by the removal of the anti-socialist law, they organized trade unions, circulated newspapers, and successfully brought pressure on the regime for more social legislation. The party had no immediate plan for a revolution, although its radical wing expected, especially after the Russian Revolution of 1905 (see pp. 559–560), that a revolution would come. The moderate or "revisionist" wing, which expected no open conflict between capital and labor, felt that, by allying them-

Emperor William II (1859–1941).

selves with the middle class to attain a majority in the Reichstag, the Social Democrats might eventually overthrow the militarist regime. This the radical wing scornfully dismissed as mere temporizing.

As the Social Democrats became more powerful, the government allied itself more closely with the Catholic Center. Between 1895 and 1906, and again between 1909 and 1914, a coalition of conservatives and the Center formed the majority group in the Reichstag. The coalition did not wish to see any increase in the powers of parliament. Yet left-wingers within the Center party occasionally called for a liberalization of the system, and for tactical purposes would even ally themselves with the Social Democrats.

Meanwhile, issues of military, colonial, and foreign policy began to complicate the internal politics of Germany. The size of the army rose from 479,000 in 1892 to 870,000 in 1913. And for the first time Germany sought a big navy, after Admiral Tirpitz became minister of the navy in 1897. The Emperor issued a series of warlike and grandiose statements hailing Germany's "future on the waters," and he and Tirpitz planned a high-seas fleet to supersede the naval forces that had been designed for coastal defense and for the defense of commerce. The navy boom was at least partly intended to supply a market for the expanding steel industry. A Navy League, ostensibly a private organization but constantly hand in glove with the regime, spread propaganda on behalf of the new fleet. The first rather modest naval law of 1898 provided for a navy that was doubled by the second law of 1900.

But the army and navy were only the most obvious weapons of world power. Bismarck's satisfied country seemed satisfied no longer. The Colonial Society thrived, as Germany seized lands in the Far East and in Africa (see Chapter 16), despite the drain on the budget (for the colonies were never profitable), and despite scandal after scandal (for the Germans were often brutal colonial administrators). "Pan-Germans" planned the great Berlin-Baghdad railway to the Near East and cried shrilly for more and more adventure and conquest.

William's naval and colonial policies embittered Germany's relations with Great Britain. In 1896, the Emperor himself sent the Boer President Kruger a telegram congratulating him on his having repelled the Jameson Raid (Chapter 16) and hinting that Germany would have been willing to intervene on the side of the Boers against Britain. Again in 1908, he gave an interview to a London newspaper, the *Daily Telegraph*, in which, with monumental indiscretion, he protested his friendship for Britain, yet at the same time declared that the English had been ungrateful to him in not acknowledging that his own military plans, sent to them in secrecy, had enabled them to win the Boer War. Of course there was nothing in his claim.

The *Daily Telegraph* affair aroused a storm of protest against William in Germany itself, and the Emperor had to apologize and promise to do better in the future. This episode illustrates the dangerous instability of the man who was all-powerful in a mighty military state. Moreover, it also reveals the general uneasiness that underlay the apparently smooth and prosperous surface of William's Germany. The protest against the anachronistic system under which Germans lived and labored, and against the external bombast and internal insecurity of the regime, was expressed in the enormous vote of the Social Democrats in 1912.

In 1913–1914, a German army officer in the Alsatian town of Saverne (Zabern) wounded a lame shoemaker with his sword, and the commanding officer of the German garrison illegally arrested and jailed townspeople who protested. The bitter resentment of the Alastians was echoed by a tremendous number of Germans who had become resentful over the outrageous and unrestrained behavior of their military. By a vote of 293 to 54, the Reichstag passed a resolution of censure against the government. Even more interesting is the sequel, for William decorated the guilty officer, who was acquitted by a court-martial. The Saverne affair proved that the German public was still capable of feeling discomfort over the excesses of their Prussian masters, but it also proved tht even a public expression of disapproval had little effect on these masters — the Emperor, the Junkers, and the military.

III   The Habsburg Monarchy, 1850-1914

Character of the Empire

The extraordinary empire of the Habsburgs has been called ramshackle, heterogeneous, and anachronistic. And much scorn has been poured upon it for its incompetence, its smugness, its stupidity, and its failure to keep up with modern times. No doubt these charges are largely justified. But in recent years voices have been raised mourning the Empire's disappearance, and regretfully echoing a nineteenth-century Czech patriot's celebrated remark that if the Empire did not exist it would be necessary to invent it. These expressions of longing come not only from monarchists and clericals lamenting a past hopelessly beyond recovery, but from many who have experienced the far more oppressive nationalist or Fascist regimes that governed much former Habsburg territory in the 1920's and 1930's, or the Communist régimes of the period since 1945. By contrast, even the Habsburgs seem preferable.

For sixty-four mortal years from 1850 to 1914, the Emperor Francis Joseph sat on the Habsburg throne. Simple in his personal life and immensely conscientious, he worked hard at his desk, reading and signing state papers for hours every day. But he was without fire or imagination, uninterested in books dealing with current problems, or even in newspapers, devoted to the rigid court etiquette prescribed for Habsburgs, inflexibly old-fashioned and conservative. He was intensely pious. He loved to hunt. His mere longevity inspired loyalty, but it must be admitted that he was a dull fellow, in every sense of the term. His decisions usually came too late, and conceded too little. His responsibility for the course of events is large.

Political Experiments, 1850-1867

Habsburg history between 1850 and 1914 divides naturally into unequal portions at the convenient date 1867, when the Empire became the dual monarchy of Austria-Hungary. After the suppression of the Revolution of 1848, there was a decade of repression usually called the "Bach period," from the name of the Minister of the Interior, ending in 1859 with the war against Piedmont and France (see Chapter 13). Then came eight years of political experimentation, from 1859 to 1867, punctuated by the war of 1866 with Prussia.

In 1849, all parts of the Empire were for the first time unified and directly ruled from Vienna by German-speaking officials. In 1855, the state signed a concordat with the Catholic Church, giving clerics a greater influence in education and in other fields than they had enjoyed since the reforms of Joseph II. The repressive domestic policies of the Bach period required expensive armies and policemen. Instead of investing in railroads and industry, Austria went into debt by enforcing the Bach system. These expenditures left it at a disadvantage compared with Prussia. Then, during the Crimean War, instead of repaying Tsar Nicholas I for Russia's aid in subduing the Hungarian revolution, Austria "astonished the world by her ingratitude." Not only did Francis Joseph fail to assist the Russians, he actually kept them in fear of an attack by occupying the Danubian principalities (modern

Rumania). In 1857, Austria experienced a severe financial crisis partly as a result of this long mobilization.

The defeat of 1859 at the hands of the French and Italians, and the loss of Lombardy with its great city of Milan, brought about the end of the Bach system. War continued to threaten, and the nationalities inside the Empire, especially the Magyars, could not be kept in a state of smoldering discontent which would render their troops unreliable. Several solutions were now tried in an effort to create a structure that would withstand the domestic and foreign strains, but that would not jeopardize the Emperor's position. Francis Joseph made no effort to consult the people. Instead, he listened first to the nobles, who favored a loose federalism, and then to the bureaucrats, who favored a tight centralism.

The "October Diploma" (1860) set up a central legislature to deal with economic and military problems. To it the provincial assemblies (diets) throughout the Empire would send delegates. All other problems were left to the provincial diets, elected by a system that worked to disfranchise the peasants, and to benefit the rich, and (in Bohemia) the German townspeople rather than the Czech farmers. But the October Diploma did not satisfy the most important non-German province: Hungary. The Magyars continued to press for autonomy, as they had in 1848. Francis Joseph, who really preferred the Bach system, opposed Magyar wishes for special treatment, and hoped that the nobles could stave off further liberalization.

On the other hand, the German liberals and bureaucrats of Austria felt that the October Diploma went too far and gave the Magyars too much. To them it seemed that the Empire was being dismembered on behalf of the nobility, who dominated the provincial assemblies. The "February Patent" of 1861 was actually a new constitution in line with their views. It proclaimed a more centralized scheme. The imperial legislature took over most of the powers the October Diploma had reserved for the provincial assemblies or diets.

Naturally, the Magyars objected to this second solution even more than to the first, and flatly refused to participate. To the applause of the Germans in Vienna, including the liberals, Hungary was returned to authoritarian rule. Czechs and Poles also eventually withdrew from the central parliament and left only a German rump. Disturbed, the Emperor suspended the February Patent; he began to negotiate with the Magyars, who were represented by the intelligent and moderate Francis Deák, but the negotiations were interrupted by the war with Prussia in 1866. The Austrian defeat at Sadowa (see above), the expulsion of Austria from Germany, and the loss of Venetia seemed to threaten the entire Habsburg system. Francis Joseph resumed negotiations with the Magyars, with the help of the great Magyar noble, Andrássy, and of Beust, who had become Austrian foreign minister. In 1867, a formula was found which was to govern and preserve the Habsburg domains down to the World War of 1914–1918.

The Dual Monarchy, 1867

This formula was the famous *Ausgleich*, or "compromise," which created the "dual monarchy" of Austria-Hungary. The Hungarian constitution of 1848 was restored, and the entire Empire was reorganized on a strict partnership basis. Austria and Hungary were united in the person of the emperor, who was always to be a Catholic legitimate Habsburg, and who was to be crowned King of Hungary in a special ceremony in Budapest. For foreign policy, military affairs, and finance, the two states had joint ministers appointed by the emperor. A customs union subject to renewal every ten years also united them. Every ten years the quota of common expenditure to be borne by each partner was to be settled. A unique body, the "delegations," made up of sixty members from the Austrian parliament and sixty members from the Hungarian parliament, meeting alternately in Vienna and in Budapest, was to decide on the common budget. After the budget had been approved, it had to be ratified by the full

Emperor Francis Joseph (1830–1916).

parliaments of both countries, and signed by the emperor-king. The delegations also had supervisory authority over the three joint ministers, and might summon them to give an account of their activities. In practice, the delegations seldom met, and were almost never consulted on questions of policy. The system favored Hungary, which had 40 per cent of the population but never paid more than one-third of the expenses. Every ten years, when the quota of expenses and the customs union needed joint consideration, a new crisis arose.

Otherwise, Hungary and Austria were separate states. As King of Hungary, Francis Joseph appointed cabinet ministers, professors, bishops, civil servants, and other officials. He was obliged at least once a year to summon the Hungarian legislature, which had an upper house of hereditary peers and a lower house elected by an elaborate system with more than fifty types of voters. However, qualifications regarding economic status and nationality made the Hungarian lower house entirely undemocratic; the voters never totaled more than 6 per cent of the population. For its part, Austria retained the parliament and the seventeen provincial assemblies provided by the February Patent of 1861. According to the new Austrian constitution of 1867, the authority of the emperor somewhat resembled that of other constitutional monarchs, with the fundamental exception that he could legislate by himself when parliament was not in session. Since he could dissolve parliament at will, he enjoyed a very large discretion and was potentially a strong personal ruler.

The dual structure of Austria-Hungary was unique in Europe, and indeed in history. Because of it, many domestic developments in the two parts of the monarchy may be considered quite separately. Yet one overwhelmingly important and complicated problem remained common to both halves of the monarchy: the problem of the national minorities that had not received their autonomy. Some of these minorities (Czechs, Poles, Ruthenes) were largely in Austria; others (Slovaks, Rumanians) were largely in Hungary; the rest (Croats, Serbs, Slovenes, all of them south Slavs) were in both states. These nationalities were at different stages of development and of national self-consciousness. Some of them were subject to pressures from fellow-nationals living in states outside the dual monarchy.

The Austrian constitution of 1867 provided that all nationalities enjoy equal rights, and guaranteed that each might use its own language in education, administration, and public life. Even the Hungarians in 1868 abandoned on paper the fierce Magyar chauvinism of Kossuth and the superpatriots of 1848 (Chapter 11), and put on the statute books a law that allowed the minorities to conduct local government in their own language, to hold the chief posts in their counties, and to have their own schools. But in practice, neither the Austrian nor the Hungarian statute was respected. The nationalities suffered varying degrees of discrimination and even persecution. Since the nationality problem was common to Austria and to Hungary, and since it ruined the entire dual monarchy in the end, after the disastrous defeats of World War I, we must examine it in some detail.

The Czechs

After 1867, many Czechs felt that they were entitled to an *Ausgleich* on the model which the Magyars had obtained. They argued that the lands of the Crown of St. Wenceslaus (d. 929)—the provinces of Bohemia, Moravia, and Austrian Silesia—possessed rights comparable to those that the Magyars had successfully claimed for the lands of the Crown of St. Stephen (997–1038). But the Czechs never had the power or the opportunity that the Magyars had to bring pressure on the Austrians, although Czech deputies boycotted the Austrian parliament in the hope that Francis Joseph would consent to become King of Bohemia in Prague as he had become King of Hungary in Budapest.

In 1871, the Emperor did indeed offer to be crowned as King of Bohemia. The Bohemian diet, from which all Germans had withdrawn in a fury, drew up proposals that would have produced a triple instead of a dual monarchy. The rage of Austrian and Bohemian Germans, the opposition of Magyar politicians, who predicted chaos, and a Slavic uprising in southern Austria forced Francis Joseph to change his mind. Deeply disappointed, the Czech nationalist leaders returned to passive resistance.

By 1879, when the Czech deputies returned to the Vienna parliament, they were divided into moderate "old Czechs" and radical and impetuous "young Czechs." In the 1880's and 1890's, each time the Czechs won cultural or political gains, the German extremists bitterly opposed them, strengthening the Czech extremists and weakening the moderates. A statute requiring all judges in Czech lands to conduct trials in the language of the petitioner led to the development of an experienced body of Czech civil servants, since many Czechs knew German already, while Germans usually had to learn Czech. In 1890, the gov-

ernment and the old Czechs had tentatively agreed on an administrative division of Bohemia between Germans and Czechs, but the young Czechs rioted in the Bohemian diet, and Prague was put under martial law, which lasted until 1897. When a new law was passed requiring that all civil servants would have to be bilingual after 1901, the Germans in the Vienna parliament threw inkwells, blew whistles, and forced out the ministry, while Czech extremists began to talk ominously about a future Russian-led Slavic showdown with the Germans. All moderation vanished in the waves of noise and hatred. No Austrian parliament could stay in session, and the government had to be conducted by decree.

Under the stress of prolonged agitation, and influenced by the apparent triumph of constitutionalism in Russia (see p. 561), Francis Joseph finally decided to reform the franchise. In 1907, all male citizens of the Austrian lands were now enfranchised and could vote for deputies on their own nationality. Of the 516 deputies in the new parliament, 233 would be German and 107 Czech, a figure almost proportional to the census figures.

Yet in 1913 the Bohemian diet was dissolved by a *coup*, and in 1914 Czech deputies in the Austrian parliament refused to allow national business to proceed. Thus World War I began with both parliament and the Bohemian diet dissolved, and with the Emperor and ministers ruling by themselves. Perhaps chief among the many causes for this general parliamentary breakdown was the failure to give the Czech provinces the self-government they had vainly sought since 1867. Most Czechs did not wish to cut loose from the Empire and establish a separate state of their own. Amounting to about 23 per cent of the Austrian population, the Czechs formed a hard core of discontent.

Yet, from the economic and cultural points of view, the Czechs were by far the most advanced of the Slavic peoples in the dual monarchy. By 1900, the famous Skoda armament works had become the largest in the Empire, and the rival of Krupp in Germany. Porcelain and glassware, lace and beer, sugar and the tourist trade, made the Czech middle class

North Sea

NORWEGIANS

SWEDES

FINNS

SWEDES

Baltic Sea

ESTONIANS

DANES

LETTS

LITHUANIANS

GREAT RUSSIANS

FINNS

DUTCH

WHITE RUSSIANS

GERMANS

GERMANS

FLEMINGS

P O L E S

ALLOONS

LUX.

ALSATIANS

CZECHS

LITTLE RUSSIANS
(UKRAINIANS)

RENCH

SLOVAKS

RUTHENIANS

KALMUKS

SWISS

SLOVENES

MAGYARS

MAG.

R U M A N I A N S

CROATS

ITALIANS

Adriatic Sea

CROATS

S E R B S

Black Sea

GEORGIANS

GREEKS

BULGARS

GREEKS

GREEKS

ALBANIANS

ARMENIANS

TURKS

KURDS

Aegean
GREEKS
Sea

ARABS

Mediterranean Sea

GREEKS

GREEKS

**Nationalities in
Central and Eastern
Europe**

— About 1914 —

ARABS

ARABS

——————— Political boundaries, 1914

- - - - - - - Boundary between Austria
and Hungary

0   Miles   500

rich and Czech craftsmen famous. Laboring conditions were bad, however, and the Czech Social Democrats were weakened by their refusal to work with their German opposite numbers.

Czech nationalism was fostered by an active Czech-language press, by patriotic societies, by Czech schools, and by the famous *sokols* ("hawks"), a physical-training society with strong nationalist leanings. At the ancient Prague University, learned Czech scholars taught, of whom Thomas Masaryk, married to an American, became the most famous. Professor of philosophy and student of Slavic culture, but a lover of the West, Masaryk deeply influenced generations of students, and upheld democratic ideals in politics. Historians studied the heroic past of the Czechs, and poets, novelists, and musicians glorified it for the popular audience. Deprived of their national autonomy and exposed to German bias though the Czechs were, they can hardly be regarded as a persecuted minority. They had their language and their freedom to develop under Austrian domination.

Poles and Ruthenians

Of all the minorities in Austria, the Poles (18 per cent of the population) were the most satisfied, the only contented Poles in Europe. Most of them lived in Galicia, where they formed the landlord class and generally oppressed their peasants, especially the backward Ruthenians (Ukrainians). Like the Czechs, the Galician Poles asked for provincial self-government on the Magyar model, and like the Czechs, they were denied. But they had their own schools, and Polish was the language of administration and the courts. The Poles enjoyed favorable financial arrangements, and after 1871 there was a special ministry for Galicia in Vienna. Since they hated Russia, Pan-Slavism never tempted them as it did the Czechs; they were not even very much interested in a future independent Poland.

The contrast between this generous treatment and the brutality suffered by the Poles living in Prussian and Russian Poland led Poles everywhere to look to Austrian Galicia as the center of national life and culture. Polish refugees from tyranny elsewhere took refuge in the cities of Cracow and Lemberg. Here were splendid Polish universities, noble families living grandly as they always had in Poland, and opportunities to serve the Crown in the provincial administration. The universities trained generations of Poles who were available later for service in independent Poland. Polish literature and the study of Polish history flourished. Though slowly, industrialization began, and a promising petroleum industry was launched. Only the Ruthenians and the Jews suffered discrimination and hardship.

The Poles eliminated Ruthenians from the Galician diet, and until 1907 kept them from the imperial parliament. The Ruthenians themselves were divided into an older pro-Russian generation, and a younger generation of Ukrainian nationalists, often fanatical, who hated Poles and Russians alike, and who hoped for their own autonomous status within the monarchy. In 1908, a Ukrainian assassinated the Polish governor of Galicia after a horrible instance of Polish police brutality.

Other Minorities in Austria

The other minorities in Austria were far less numerous. Less than 3 per cent of the population was Italian in 1910; about $4\frac{1}{2}$ per cent was Slovene; and less than 3 per cent was Serb and Croat. The Italians of the south Tyrol and Istria, where their center was the seaport of Trieste, were far more important than their numbers warranted, however, because of the existence of the Kingdom of Italy across the monarchy's frontier. Almost all of them wanted to belong to Italy, and Italy regarded their lands as *Italia Irredenta* (see Chapter 13). Of all the Austrian minorities, the Italian steadily proved itself the most anxious to get out of the Habsburg Monarchy altogether.

Among the south Slavs in Austria proper, the Slovenes were the most contented. Scattered in six provinces, and often living at odds with their German or Italian neighbors, they usually made only local demands, like that for lecture courses in Slovene at Graz university. The Croats in Austria (mostly in Dalmatia) were fewer and less disaffected than those in Hungary, and the Serbs in Austria were far fewer and less disaffected than the Serbs in Hungary and in the separate province of Bosnia. Yet both Serbs and Croats in Austria were divided: some preferred autonomy within the Empire and others hoped one day to join a still hypothetical south Slav state.

Minorities in Hungary: Slovaks, Rumanians, South Slavs

In Hungary, minority problems were even more acute. Magyar behavior toward other national groups grew increasingly outrageous as moderate counsels vanished in the face of short-sighted demagoguery. The Slovaks, the Rumanians, and the Serbs and Croats living in Hungary proper were the worst victims of a deliberate policy of Magyarization, but even the Croatians of Croatia, whose province had its own constitutional special status, suffered. The Magyar aim was actually to destroy the national identity of the minorities, and to transform them into Magyars. The weapon used was language.

It is difficult to understand the passionate attachment felt by the backward peasant peoples of southeastern Europe for their own languages. Yet, deprived of economic opportunity and sometimes of complete religious freedom, these peoples in the nineteenth century found in the languages they talked a living proof of national identity. The Magyars too, who made up only 55 per cent of the population of their own country exclusive of Croatia, had a fanatical devotion to their own language, an Asian tongue quite unrelated to the German, Slavic, or Rumanian languages of the minorities. They tried to force it upon the subject peoples, particularly in education. All state-supported schools, from kindergartens to universities, had to give instruction in Magyar. The state postal, telegraph, and railroad services used only Magyar.

The Slovaks, numbering about 11 per cent of the population of Hungary, were perhaps the most Magyarized. Poor peasants for the most part, the more ambitious of them often became Magyars simply by adopting the Magyar language as their own. As time passed, a few Slovaks came to feel a sense of unity with the closely related but far more advanced Czechs across the border in Austria. The pro-Czechs among the Slovaks were usually liberals and Protestants. Catholic and conservative Slovaks toward the end on the century found their leader in a priest, Father Hlinka, who advocated Slovak autonomy. After Czechoslovakia had been formed in 1918, the Hlinka movement continued to be anti-Czech, and became pro-Hitler in the 1930's.

The Rumanians, who lived in Transylvania, amounted in 1910 to $16\frac{1}{2}$ per cent of the population of Hungary, and possessed a majority in Transylvania itself. For centuries they had been downtrodden by the Magyars, and had had to fight to achieve recognition of their Orthodox religion. Indeed, largely in the hope of receiving better treatment, many of them had become "Uniates," accepting the supremacy of Rome but otherwise preserving their own liturgy. Despite laws designed to eliminate the use of the Rumanian language, and a great deal of petty persecution, the Rumanians stoutly resisted assimilation. For redress of grievances, many looked to Vienna, which before the *Ausgleich* had often been a source of assistance against the Magyars, but which was now committed to give the Magyars a free hand. These Rumanians hoped that Transylvania might again be made autonomous, as it had once been in the past. They pressed for the enforcement of the liberal Hungarian nationalities law of 1868. They wanted their language and their church to have equal standing with other languages and other churches.

But when in 1892 the Rumanians petitioned Vienna on these points, their petition was returned unopened and unread. When they circulated the petition widely abroad, their leaders were tried and jailed. It was little wonder that many Transylvanian Rumanians ceased to look west to Vienna for help that never came, and began to look south and east across the Carpathians to Rumania, where their fellow-nationals had a kingdom of their own and a strong wish to annex the whole of Transylvania.

Under Magyar rule, some Serbs and Croats lived in Hungary proper and others in Croatia. In 1910, those in Hungary totaled about 600,000, of whom two-thirds were Serbs. Living in a compact mass in the southern and western frontier regions, these were the inhabitants of the old Habsburg "military frontier" against the Turks. They were transferred to Magyar rule in 1869, and they resented it. The Serbs especially disliked Hungarian administration and looked to the independent kingdom of Serbia to the south. But a far greater menace to Hungarian unity was provided by Croatia proper.

Croatia

The Croats, though connected since the eleventh century with the Crown of Hungary, had become strongly nationalistic under the impact of the Napoleonic occupation, and had fought on the side of the monarchy against the Magyar revolutionaries of 1848. None the less, Francis Joseph, as part of the *Ausgleich* settlement, handed them back to the Magyars. Croatian nationalists were deeply disappointed. Led by the Roman Catholic Bishop Strossmayer, a man of deep intelligence, high culture, and liberal views, they had hoped for an autonomous Croatia and Dalmatia inside the Empire, which would serve as a nucleus to attract all the other southern Slavs. But instead, the Magyar moderates, led by Deák, worked out in 1868 an *Ausgleich* of their own between Hungary and Croatia.

All military and economic affairs were to be handled in Budapest by a special cabinet minister for Croatian affairs. Representatives from the Croatian parliament at the Croatian capital of Zagreb would sit in Budapest whenever Croatian affairs were under discussion. Croatian delegates would be part of the Hungarian "delegation" of the dual monarchy. The Croatian language could be spoken by Croat representatives at the sessions of any body they attended, and the language of command in the Croatian territorial army would be Croatian. The Croats would control their own educational system, their church, their courts and police, but all taxes would be voted by Budapest and collected by agents of Budapest. Although the Croats were far better off than any national minority in Hungary, this "compromise" did not satisfy them.

The "Party of the Right," the ancestor of Croat extremism in our own day, wanted a completely autonomous Croatia, and scorned as inferior the Serbs and other non-Catholic south Slavs, whom Strossmayer had hoped to attract. Further problems were created in Catholic Croatia by the existence of a Serb Orthodox minority (more than a quarter of the population), which spoke the same language as the Croats, and which was racially indistinguishable from them. But the Orthodox minority worshipped in different churches, and was therefore subject to religious discrimination.

For twenty years at the close of the nineteenth century, the Hungarian-appointed governor cleverly fostered this Serb-Croat antagonism by using the Serbs for local offices. He received the support only of those Croats who had become Magyar-speaking, usually great landowners or government officials.

By 1903, Serbs and Croats were beginning to co-operate against Hungarian rule, and to spread pro-Slav propaganda in Dalmatia. In 1905, Croats asked Vienna for Dalmatia and for electoral reforms, but professed that they wanted to observe faithfully the arrangement of 1868 with Hungary. Serbians endorsed these Croatian demands, though some Serbs hoped for union with independent Serbia, and some Croats still hoped for complete independence.

In spite of these hopeful signs, the hopes of the moderates were dashed by the fearfully unpopular Railway Servants Act (1907), which forced all railroad workers to speak Magyar. Croats began to boycott Hungarian-made goods; the Croatian diet refused to collaborate with the new governor, who in 1909 arrested fifty-odd Croats and Serbs and charged them with plotting to unite Croatia and Bosnia with Serbia. The evidence was ridiculously inadequate, and the defendants, though condemned, obtained a reversal of the sentences on appeal to a higher court. But these Zagreb trials gave the Slavic press a splendid opportunity to denounce the policy of the dual monarchy.

In the same year, 1909, a celebrated Austrian historian, Friedjung, charged in the Vienna press that the Croatian and Serbian politicians in Croatia were plotting with Serbians in Serbia. Friedjung was eventually forced to admit that his documentary sources, which in all probability had been fed to him by the Vienna foreign office, were forgeries. The Zagreb trials and the Friedjung case, coming only five years before the assassination of Francis Ferdinand by a Bosnian Serb and the outbreak of war, demonstrated the incompetence of the dual monarchy in dealing with its own loyal south Slav inhabitants. In 1912, 1913, and 1914, Bosnian students tried to assassinate the Hungarian governor of Croatia. These were ominous rehearsals for the crime of June 28, 1914, which led not merely to internal crisis but to world war.

Bosnia-Herzegovina

In the dual monarchy, the region of Bosnia-Herzegovina had a special status. By the 1870's, these two provinces had been part of the Ottoman Empire for about four centuries. Although ethnically south Slavic, the population included in 1879 about half a million Moslems, half a million members of the Orthodox Church, and perhaps 150,000 Catholics. Under Turkish rule, those who accepted Islam had enjoyed economic advantages. Most of the Orthodox Christian population consisted of peasants working on the estates of Moslem landlords, and looking across the frontiers to Serbia in hope of liberation. Some of the Catholics were educated in Strossmayer's seminary, and leaned toward eventual absorption in his south-Slav state, but almost nobody wanted to join the Habsburg monarchy as it was then constituted.

The Herzegovinian uprising of 1875 against the Turks precipitated a general Balkan Slavic attack on the Turks. Russia too went to war against the Turks, but first the Austrian and Russian foreign ministers reached an agreement on the future status of the two provinces. But they later disagreed on what the agreement had been. At the Congress of Berlin in 1878 (see p. 556), the Austrians obtained the right to occupy the provinces, but not to annex them.

From 1878 to 1908, the forces of the monarchy occupied Bosnia and Herzegovina. The sovereignty of the Turkish sultan was recognized throughout this period, but in fact the provinces were ruled from Vienna, though not as part of either Austria or Hungary. Instead, they were put under the common Austro-Hungarian minister of finance.

The discontent of the Orthodox Serbs of Bosnia was fanned by propaganda from Serbia itself. Patriotic Serbs considered that the first logical step toward creating a greater Serbia would be to incorporate these provinces inside their own frontiers, and they resented the decision of the Congress of Berlin that had allowed Habsburg occupation. However, so long as the occupation was not turned into annexation, the Serbs preserved the hope that the provinces might some day become theirs, and meanwhile flooded them with agents and plotters. The Moslems, though favored by the Habsburg authorities, never reconciled themselves to the ending of Turkish rule, and the Catholics hoped to join Croatia.

Thus these provinces perpetually threatened to create an explosion. The more intelligent observers in Vienna pressed for some sort of an all-south-Slav solution, not unlike that of Strossmayer. This would have put Dalmatia, Croatia, and Bosnia-Herzegovina together into a south-Slav kingdom under Francis Joseph, with the same status as Hungary — a triple rather than a dual monarchy. The advocates of this solution, known as "trialists," met with violent Magyar opposition.

However, the Young Turk Revolution of 1908 caused the adventurous Austrian foreign minister Aehrenthal to fear that the status of the provinces might be changed. Fortified by a prior secret agreement with Russia, Aehrenthal simply annexed the two provinces in October, 1908, and announced that they would be given a diet of their own. This move precipitated a major European crisis (Chapter 17), which threatened world war, but eventually subsided, leaving the Serbs bitterly resentful. Serbian ambition to acquire the provinces now seemed permanently checked. The humiliation of Serbia, the disappointment of Russia, the solidarity of Germany with Austria-Hungary as revealed by the crisis, helped set the stage for the catastrophe of 1914. The discontent of the population of Bosnia, when added to the discontent of the Czechs and Italians in Austria, and of the Slovaks, Rumanians, Croats, and other south Slavs in Hungary, goes far to account for the wartime weaknesses and postwar disintegration of the dual monarchy.

Yet the minority question, critical though it was, does not provide the entire answer. We must now briefly consider the Austrian-German and Hungarian majorities, both in their separate development and in their critical relationship to each other. Only then can we see that even the two ruling groups were subject to divisive forces that crippled them individually and together.

Austrian Society and Politics, 1867–1914

From the earliest days of the *Ausgleich*, the Austrian liberals fought the clerical conservatives. They legalized civil marriages, secularized all but religious instruction, canceled the concordat of 1855 after the proclamation of papal infallibility in 1870, and taxed church property (1873). These measures were the Austrian counterpart of the German *Kulturkampf*, but they were much milder, since Austria was 90 per cent Catholic, and did not share the Protestant Prussian suspicion of the Vatican. The liberals were discredited by the financial crash of 1873, during which it was revealed that some of them had accepted bribes in return for voting in favor of charters for shady and unstable new companies. From this period dates the earliest political anti-Semitism in Austria, since some Jewish liberals were involved in the scandals and served as convenient scapegoats. Economic advance during the early years

of the monarchy had brought the usual increase in the working class, which after the crash turned toward socialism in both its Marxist and its milder forms.

The Austrian nobles, who often owned great estates which they ruled almost like independent potentates, were on the whole frivolous in their tastes, and took little interest in the problems of the nineteenth and twentieth centuries. They squandered their incomes on high living and gambling. Yet they supplied almost all the political leadership that the nation got. The large size of their estates was one fundamental reason for the small size of the average peasant holding, and made it necessary even for landowning peasants to try to obtain part-time employment on a noble's property. The peasants' standard of living and level of literacy were extremely low, yet the influence of the clergy kept them subservient to their masters, loyal to the dynasty, and almost contented with their lot.

The middle class of town-dwellers and men of business, so familiar in western Europe, came later and was smaller in number in Austria. The wealthier tried to imitate the aristocracy's mode of life and to buy their way into the charmed circle. Others joined the professions, which they found overcrowded and badly paid. The unemployment of intellectuals is an extremely dangerous matter politically.

Among the bourgeoisie there were many Jews. Numbering 5 per cent of the total population of Austria, the Jews (except for very few) could not be nobles, peasants, members of the clergy, bureaucrats, or army officers. So they were forced to enter trade, the professions, and the arts, where they often prospered and distinguished themselves. What we mean when we refer loosely to pre-war "Viennese" life, with its charm and gaiety, its cultivation, its music, its cafés, its high reputation in medicine and science, was the life of a society very largely Jewish or part-Jewish. Conversion, intermarriage, and assimilation were not uncommon among the upper-middle-class Jews.

Anti-Semitism, fanned by the continued migration of poorer Jews from regions of eastern Europe where oppression had rendered them squalid and uncouth, was general among the non-Jews of Austria. But we must distinguish between the social anti-Semitism of most aristocrats, which was often simply a form of snobbery, and the serious political anti-Semitism of the lower middle classes, often the unsuccessful competitors of the Jews in the world of small shop-keeping. Partly out of religious prejudice, partly out of distaste for the liberal politics usually preferred by the middle-class Jews, the clericals inveighed against them. One response among the Jews to the swelling chorus of anti-Semitism was Zionism (sponsorship of a Jewish state in Palestine), which originated in the dual monarchy.

The stresses and strains inherent in this social structure, aggravated by the problems of the national minorities, produced in the late nineteenth century two important new political movements among the Germans of Austria: Pan-Germanism and Christian Socialism. In the early 1880's, even moderate Austrian Germans wanted to hand over the Slavic lands of Austria to the Hungarians to rule, and then, stripped to the German core, to unite economically with Germany. The Pan-Germans were more radical and more violent. They opposed the Habsburg dynasty. They opposed the Catholic Church and led a noisy movement called "Away from Rome" (*Los von Rom*). They demanded that Austria become Protestant, and unite politically with Germany. They were furiously anti-Slav and anti-Semitic. They adored Bismarck and Wotan, but Bismarck did not encourage them. Their leader, Schönerer, himself a convert to Protestantism, was elected to the Austrian parliament in 1873 from the same district that later gave birth to Adolf Hitler. But the Pan-Germans never managed to become more than an extreme vocal minority.

The Christian Socialists, on the other hand, became the most important Austrian political party. Strongly Catholic and loyal to the Habsburgs, they appealed at the same time to the peasant and the small businessman by favoring social legislation and by opposing big business. They too were violently anti-Semitic. At first skeptical of the value of Christian Socialism, the clergy later made the movement its own, and especially in the country prevailed on the people to vote for its candidates. The most famous single Christian Socialist was the perennial Mayor of Vienna after 1895, Karl Lueger, the idol of the lower middle classes of the capital. For years he sponsored public ownership of city utilities, parks, playgrounds, free milk for schoolchildren, and other welfare services. Lueger always catered to his followers' hatred of Jews, Marxian socialists, and Magyars. Hitler, who saw Lueger's funeral procession in 1910, hailed him in *Mein Kampf* as the greatest statesman of his times. It is impossible to understand the doctrines of German Nazism in this century without understanding the social and racial structure of the Habsburg monarchy in which Hitler grew up, and especially the doctrines and the appeal of Pan-Germanism and Christian Socialism.

To the Pan-Germans and the Christian Socialists, the Austrian Social Democrats, founded in 1888, responded with a Marxist program calling for government ownership of the means of production and for political action organized by class rather than by nationality. But the Austrian Social Democrats were not revolutionaries, and set as their goals such political and social gains as universal suffrage, secular education, welfare legislation, and the eight-hour day. They were usually led by intellectuals, many of them Jewish, but they were followed by an ever-increasing number of workers.

On the nationality question, Social Democratic leaders strongly urged a reform in the direction of democratic federalism. Each nationality should have control of its own affairs in its own territory; in mixed territories, minorities should be protected; and a central parliament should decide matters of common interest. Cultural autonomy for the nationalities of a multi-national state was by no means an impractical or doctrinaire Marxist idea. Its practicality was later attested by the Soviet Russians, faced as they were with a similar problem and much influenced by the thinking of Austrian Social Democrats on the question. Otto Bauer, a doctrinaire Marxist, tried to explain away national antagonisms in the Empire as a manifestation of class warfare. But the program of another Social Democrat, Karl Renner, who lived to be chancellor of the Austrian Republic when it was founded in 1919 and again when it was re-created in 1945, might have averted the necessity for the foundation of any republic at all. A believer in the dual monarchy, Renner advocated treating the nationalities as if they were churches, and allowing each citizen to belong to whatever one he chose. Each of these "national associations" would have its own schools, and disagreements among them would be settled by a high court of arbitration. Who is to say that if these views had been adopted, the monarchy might not have been preserved?

Hungarian Society and Politics, 1867–1914

In Hungary, the social structure was somewhat different. The great landed nobility, owning half of Hungary in estates of hundreds of thousands of acres apiece, were a small class numerically. Loyal to the dynasty, sometimes kind to their tenants, and socially contemptuous of all beneath them, they were often intelligent and discriminating, yet more often just as frivolous and empty-headed as their Austrian counterparts. But Hungary had a much larger class of country gentlemen, the squirearchy, whose holdings were far smaller and whose social position was lower, but whose political influence as a group was even greater. After the emancipation of the serfs in 1848, and during later periods of uncertain agricultural conditions, many members of the gentry became civil servants or entered the professions. The peasantry suffered from small holdings, insufficient education, primitive methods of farming, and a low standard of living.

The Magyars were country folk, and the towns for centuries had been centers for Germans and Jews. But during the nineteenth century, the towns became steadily more Magyar, as members of the gentry and peasantry moved into them. The Jewish population grew enormously during the same period, mostly by immigration from the north and east. In Hungary, many Jews were converted and assimilated and became strongly Magyar in sentiment and be-

havior. When they grew rich enough, they bought land and titles, and became gentry. But here too they were greatly disliked, especially among the poorer city population, and in the countryside, where they were associated with money-lending and tavern-keeping, two professions that kept the peasant in their debt. Yet though anti-Semitism existed in Hungary, it never gained as many followers or became as important a political movement as in Austria.

At the bottom of the social pyramid was a small class (never more than 20 per cent of the population) of industrial workers in the cities, mostly in the textile and flourmilling industries. Wages were low, and living and working conditions were abominable, like those in Russia rather than those in the West. Yet more and more welfare measures were passed toward the end of the century. Because of its feebleness and lack of self-consciousness, this class could not be organized into an effective socialist party.

The Catholic Church was immensely powerful and rich in Hungary as in Austria, but in Hungary Catholicism was the faith only of about 60 per cent instead of 90 per cent of the population. Some Hungarian magnate families and many of the gentry had never returned to Catholicism after the Reformation. They remained Calvinists. Several hundred thousand Germans, chiefly in Transylvania, were Lutheran. And in Transylvania also there were Magyar Unitarians. Clericalism could never become in Hungary the dominant force it was in Austria.

Thus, because of its differing social and religious structure, Hungary could not produce strong parties like the Austrian Social Democrats and Christian Socialists. Austria had a relatively liberal franchise before 1907 and universal manhood suffrage thereafter. Hungary, in contrast, never really changed its law of 1874, by which only about 6 per cent of the population could vote. Moreover, Magyars of all shades were pretty well united in their determination to subjugate the national minorities in Hungary. Internal political or social issues, therefore, did little to determine Hungarian political alignments. The only real issue, and the chief source of Magyar political differences, was the question of Hungary's position in the dual monarchy.

Hungarian opponents of the *Ausgleich* were in the early days organized into two groups. The Kossuthists favored complete independence; a slightly more moderate party called the "Tigers" wished to improve the position of Hungary inside the monarchy by securing for the Hungarians control over their own army, their own diplomatic service, and their own finances, and by limiting the tie with Austria to the person of the monarch. When the great Deák passed from public life, one of the Tigers, Coloman Tisza, abandoned his opposition to the *Ausgleich,* joined the pro-*Ausgleich* Deákists, and came to power in 1875, to govern as prime minister for the next fifteen years. Thereafter, this merger of the Tigers and Deákists dominated Hungary except for the period from 1905 to 1910, and stayed in power largely by electoral manipulation. Called the Liberals, this group resisted any reform of the franchise and agrarian conditions, or of the treatment of the minorities.

Kossuthists maintained their opposition to the *Ausgleich*. They wanted Magyar used as the language of command for all Hungarian troops in the army, and agitated against Austria. In 1902, when the government refused their demands, they began to filibuster, and effectively paralyzed the Hungarian parliament. The Emperor refused to yield to pressure. Coloman Tisza's son, Stephen, became premier in 1903, and worked through the increasing storm to preserve the *Ausgleich*. When he tried to limit debate in order to permit the accomplishment of official business, the Kossuthists wrecked the parliament chamber. In 1905, Tisza was defeated by an opposition coalition including the Kossuthists, who now won a majority. When Francis Joseph refused to meet the demands of the new majority and appointed a loyal general as premier, the Kossuthists screamed military dictatorship, and urged patriots not to pay taxes or perform military service.

This struggle between the partisans of dualism and those of independence moved only the ruling caste of Magyars and bore no relation to the sentiments and needs of the larger part of the population. To mitigate the struggle, Francis Joseph had only to threaten to decree universal suffrage for Hungary, as he intended to do in Austria. This would open the gates to the discontented minorities and would encourage social and economic change. Under this threat, the opposition coalition eventually yielded (1906) and voted the necessary economic and military laws. They obtained the right to revise the franchise themselves, a task they had every interest in putting off.

In 1910, the younger Tisza won a victory in the elections by the time-honored methods of corruption and intimidation. He dropped the separatists' demands, which had been convulsing the country for more than a decade. Hungary got no bank, no separate army, and no substantial franchise reform. Kossuthists had to be removed by force from parliament, and gag-rule had to be imposed. Tisza was kept busy fighting saber duels with the Kossuthist leaders. It was in this deplorable atmosphere that Hungary received the news that Franz Ferdinand, heir to the throne, had been assassinated.

IV Russia, 1825 - 1914

Character of the Empire

The third and largest of the great eastern European empires, Russia, took far longer, as was its way, to catch up with the political and social developments elsewhere in Europe. Thus there was no parliament in Russia until after the Revolution of 1905, and even then the tsardom was able to weaken and eventually to dominate the new representative body. Serfdom did not disappear until 1861, and agrarian problems were in some ways intensified by the liberation of the peasants. Each time reform came, in the 1860's and in 1905 and 1906, it came as a direct result of military defeat abroad, which rendered reform absolutely essential. Thus the reforms of Alexander II (1855–1881) were inspired by Russia's defeat in the Crimean War (1854–1856), and the revolution of 1905 was made possible by Russia's failure in the Russo-Japanese War (1904–1905). During most of the nineteenth and early twentieth centuries, even after the reforms, the Russian Tsars claimed for themselves the same autocratic rights that Peter the Great and his Muscovite predecessors had exercised. Thus the Russian people experienced long periods of reaction: the entire reign of Nicholas I (1825–1855), and a protracted period from 1866 through 1904, including the last fifteen years of Alexander II's reign (1866–1881), the whole of Alexander III's (1881–1894), and the first ten years of Nicholas II's (1894–1917), the last of the tsars.

The failure to adjust willingly to the currents of the times and the attempt to preserve autocratic rule produced unparalleled discontent in Russia. Disillusioned and angry intellectuals in the 1830's and 1840's gave way to proponents of social change in the 1850's and early 1860's, and then to determined revolutionaries and terrorists in the late 1860's and the years that followed. Although Marxist literature was known early in Russia, and Marxist political groupings existed after 1896, the Marxists were by no means either the most numerous or the most effective of Russian revolutionaries. Native non-Marxist revolutionary parties long performed the killings and other acts of violence that convulsed the regime and won the support of large groups of Russians. It was only Lenin's transformation of the Marxist doctrines and his adaptation of Marx to the Russian scene that made it possible for his Bolsheviks to emerge as an important threat. And it was only Lenin's supreme tactical skill and boldness that enabled him to bring his Bolsheviks, still a minority, to power during the Revolution of 1917, a movement that was itself made possible by Russian losses in still another war. There was nothing inevitable about the triumph of the Bolsheviks (see Chapter 18).

Amid the official attempt to preserve sixteenth-century patterns, Russia experienced the impact of nineteenth- and twentieth-century industrialization. New resources were developed, thousands of miles of railroads were built, and factories sprang up, engaged in both heavy and light industry. A new laboring class thronged the cities, as elsewhere in Europe, but it lived and worked under conditions far worse than those in any other country. The native Russian revolutionaries looked to the peasants, in traditional Russian fashion, to provide them with their base, and they considered peasant problems paramount. The Marxists, on the other hand, true to the teachings of their master, recruited their following among this new proletariat and focused their attention on its problems. But they deliberately relied for their tightly organized leadership almost exclusively on a little body of intellectuals and theorists.

Despite censorship and an atmosphere of repression, Russia experienced during the nineteenth century an amazing literary flowering. Poets, novelists, and playwrights produced works that rank with the greatest of all time. Like a sudden blossoming of orchids on an iceberg, the Russian literary renaissance cannot easily be explained. The literary talents of the Russian people had long lain dormant, and now awoke in an expression of unparalleled vigor and beauty.

Nicholas I (1825–1855)

Coming to the throne amid the disorders of the Decembrist Revolution (see Chapter 11), Nicholas I (1825–1855) himself personally presided over the investigation of the revolutionaries and prescribed their punishment. He used their confessions as a source of information on the state of Russian opinion. Nicholas I has been more resoundingly damned by liberals, both Russian and foreign, than has any other tsar. They have portrayed him as a kind of scarecrow of an autocrat. Reactionary and autocratic though he was, literal-minded and devoted to military pursuits, he was perhaps not such an inflexible tyrant as he has been made out.

Nicholas I worked hard at the business of the state, and firmly believed that the imperial word was sacred. Although he despised all constitutions, he honored the liberal constitution which his elder brother Alexander had granted to the Poles (Chapter 11) until the Poles themselves revolted. He believed that his own autocratic power had been ordained by God; the autocrat could not, even if he wished, limit his own authority. Naturally such a man loathed the thought of revolution anywhere, and was perfectly prepared to cooperate abroad with the Metternich system. At home, he was prepared to make changes and improvements, but not to touch the fundamental institution of the autocracy. Though he was uneasy over the dangers inherent in serfdom, he was afraid to reform it in any serious way, because he feared that concessions would stimulate revolution among the peasants. Nicholas leaned heavily on the nobility as a class, referring to its members as his "benevolent police-chiefs."

So personal was Nicholas' rule that his own

Tsar Nicholas I, by Landseer.

chancery or secretariat became the most important organ of Russian government. He enlarged it by creating several sections, including a notorious "third section" for political police activity, which spread rapidly and kept Russian political life under surveillance. This enormous expansion of the Tsar's own secretariat did not result in the abolition of any of the older organs of government. Consequently, bureaucratic confusion became very great, paper work was multiplied, and much injustice was done through sheer incompetence. Although the Russian laws were collected, under the direction of Speransky for the first time since 1649 (see Chapter 9), the collection was not a true codification or modernization.

In the field of education, Nicholas favored the improvement of technical schools, but was deeply worried about the possibility that subversive foreign ideas might penetrate into the universities. After the Revolutions of 1848 in Europe, his reactionary minister of education, Uvarov, abolished the study of philosophy in the University of St. Petersburg, because, as he said, the usefulness of the subject had not been proved, and it might do harm. Uvarov formulated Nicholas' policies under the three heads of Autocracy, Orthodoxy, and Nationality: the unlimited power of the monarch, the sanctity of the Russian Church, and the adoption of policies in accordance with the "Russian national character." The result was a police-state, complete with censorship and terror, yet not nearly so efficient as a twentieth-century despotism.

We have already seen Nicholas putting down the Polish revolution of 1830 and intervening in 1849 to restore Hungary to the Habsburgs (see Chapter 11). He believed in dynastic friendships, and counted on the alliance with Prussia and Austria without realizing that conflicting national interests were more important than friendships between monarchs. Thus he failed to see that Prussia would combat his own efforts to thwart the unification of Germany, and that Austria's interests conflicted with his own in southeastern Europe. It was partly Nicholas' failure to see the weaknesses of his own system of alliances that led him into the disastrous Crimean War.

The Crimean War

Like other Russian leaders before him, Nicholas confidently expected the collapse of the Ottoman Empire. Russia wished to protect the Orthodox subjects of the sultan, and also had important economic interests at stake. The great Russian wheat-producing areas in the south were being developed in earnest, and Odessa on the Black Sea had become a great commercial port for the grain trade. Nicholas hoped to establish a Russian sphere of influence in the Balkans, and even to take possession of Istanbul itself. We have already witnessed his intervention in the Greek War of the 1820's (see Chapter 11). When the governor of Egypt, Mehemet Ali, revolted against the Ottoman Sultan in 1832 and threatened Istanbul, Nicholas landed a Russian army and got credit for saving the sultan's capital.

In 1833, the Turks paid the bill for these services by signing the Treaty of Unkiar Skelessi with Russia. Nicholas took the Ottoman Empire under his protection, and the Turks agreed to close the Straits (the Bosphorus and Dardanelles) to the warships of any nation. Alarmed at the preponderance that the treaty gave to Russia in an area of the world vital to British imperial and commercial interests, British diplomacy turned its efforts to undoing it. The next time Mehemet Ali revolted, in 1839, the British were able to put him down with their fleet before he came within distance of a Russian land force. In 1841, all the other important powers joined Russia in guaranteeing the integrity of Turkey, thus putting an end to the exclusive position obtained by Russia at Unkiar Skelessi.

During the next twelve years (1841–1853), Nicholas tried to reach an agreement with Britain on what should be done with Ottoman territory if Turkey collapsed. The British did not believe that such collapse was imminent, and they hoped to prevent Russia from doing anything to hasten it. The two parties misun-

BURSTING OF THE RUSSIAN BUBBLE.

Cartoon by Leech, 1854, indicating effect on Russia of the Crimean War.

derstood each other. By 1853, the Tsar mistakenly felt that Britain was not opposed to Russian domination of Turkey, and Britain mistakenly believed that the Tsar would not act in Turkey without consulting her.

Then a dispute arose over whether the Roman Catholics, backed by Napoleon III, or the Orthodox clergy, backed by the Tsar, should have the right to perform certain functions in the Christian "Holy Places" in Palestine, which was still part of the Ottoman dominions. This trivial dispute was the immediate cause of the Crimean War. But the underlying cause was the Tsar's wish to re-establish the exclusive Russian position of the Treaty of Unkiar Skelessi, and the British unwillingness to permit him to do so. Nicholas coupled a demand for this exclusive position with the demand that the Turks settle the dispute over the Holy Places amicably. The latter demand was possible; the former was not. When Nicholas oc-

cupied the Danubian principalities to enforce his demands, the situation became even tenser. And so, after many months of elaborate diplomatic negotiations in which all the powers strove to work out a suitable formula to avoid war, the drift toward war proved too strong to be checked.

Famous as the occasion of the charge of the Light Brigade, and of Florence Nightingale's pioneer efforts to save the lives of sick and wounded soldiers, the Crimean War consisted mostly of the English and French siege of the great Russian naval base at Sebastopol in the Crimea. Military operations on both sides were inefficiently conducted, but eventually the Russians were compelled to surrender. In the Peace of Paris of 1856, Russia was forbidden to fortify the Black Sea coast or to maintain a fleet there. This made it impossible for the Russians to defend their own shores or to conduct their shipping in security. It now became the paramount object of Russian foreign policy to alter the Black Sea clauses of the treaty. Not only had Russia lost the war, but Prussia had not helped her, and Austria had been positively hostile (see pp. 535–536). Nicholas did not live to see the total failure of his policy. He died during the war and was succeeded by his son Alexander II (1855–1881).

Alexander II and Reform

By this time a very substantial segment of Russian public opinion favored reforms, in reaction to the long period of repression at home and failure abroad. Moreover, the economic developments of the early nineteenth century had rendered the system of serfdom less and less profitable. In the south, where land was fertile and crops were produced for sale as well as for use, the serf tilled his master's land usually three days a week, but sometimes more. In the north, where the land was less fertile and could not produce a surplus, the serfs often had a special arrangement with their masters called "quit-rent." This meant that the serf paid the master annually in cash instead of in work, and usually had to labor at home as a craftsman or go to a nearby town and work as a factory hand or small shopkeeper to raise the money. It is probable that about a quarter of the serfs of all Russia paid quit-rent by 1855. Neither in the south nor in the north was serfdom efficient in agriculture. As industries grew, it became clearer and clearer to factory owners who experimented with both serf and free labor that serf labor was not productive. Yet free labor was scarce, and the growing population needed to be fed. Many estates were mortgaged to state credit institutions, because of inefficient management and the extravagance of the landlords. Serfdom had become uneconomic.

But this fact was not widely realized among Russian landowners, who knew only that something had gone wrong somewhere. They wished to keep things as they were, and they

Tsar Alexander II (1818–1881).

did not as a class feel that emancipation was the answer. Yet the serfs showed increasing unrest, and cases of revolt rose in number. Abolitionist sentiment had now spread widely among intellectuals. Conscious of the unrest, Alexander II, though almost as conservative as his father, determined to embark on reforms, preferring, as he put it, that the abolition of serfdom come from above rather than from below. Through a cumbersome arrangement in which local commissions made studies and reported their findings to members of the government, an emancipation law was eventually formulated and proclaimed early in 1861.

A general statute declared that the serfs were now free, laid down the principles of the new administrative organization of the peasantry, and prescribed the rules for the purchase of land. A whole series of local statutes governed the particular procedure to be followed in the different provinces. All peasants, crown and private, were freed, and each peasant household received its homestead and a certain amount of land, usually the amount the peasant family had cultivated for its own use in the past. The land usually became the property of the village commune, which had the power to redistribute it periodically among the households. The government bought the land from the proprietors, but the peasants had to redeem it by payments extending over a period of 49 years. The proprietor retained only the portion of his estate that had been farmed for his own purposes.

This statute, liberating more than 40 million human beings, has been called the greatest single legislative act in history. There can be no doubt that it acted as an immense moral stimulus to peasant self-respect. Yet there were grave difficulties. The peasant had to accept the allotment, and since his household became collectively responsible for the taxes and redemption payments, his mobility was not greatly increased. The commune took the place of the proprietor, and differing local conditions caused great difficulty in administering the law. Moreover, the peasants in general got too little land, and had to pay too much for it. They did not get important forest and pasture lands. The settlement, however, was on the whole surprisingly liberal, despite the problems it failed to solve and despite the agrarian crises that developed in part as a result of its inadequacies.

The end of the landlords' rights of justice and police on their estates made it necessary to reform the entire local administration. By statute, in 1864, provincial and district assemblies, or *zemstvos*, were created. Chosen by an elaborate electoral system that divided the voters into categories by class, the assemblies none the less gave substantial representation to the peasants. The assemblies dealt with local finances, education, medical care, scientific agriculture, maintenance of the roads, and similar economic and social questions. Starting from scratch in many cases, the *zemstvos* made great advances in the founding of primary schools and the improvement of public health. They brought together peasant and proprietor to work out local problems. They served as schools of citizenship for all classes, and led tens of thousands of Russians to hope that this progressive step would be crowned by the creation of a central parliament, or *duma*. Despite the pressure that such men tried to bring on the government, the duma was not granted, partly because after the first attempt on the life of the Tsar in 1866 the regime swung away from reform and toward reaction.

But before this happened, other advances had been made. The populations of the cities were given municipal assemblies, with duties much like those of the *zemstvos* in the countryside. The Russian judicial system and legal procedure, which were riddled with inequities, were reformed. For the first time, juries were introduced, cases were argued publicly and orally, all classes were made equal before the law, and the system of courts was completely overhauled. Censorship was relaxed, new schools were encouraged, the universities were freed from the restraints that Nicholas had imposed on them, and the antiquated and often brutal system of military service was modernized and rendered less severe.

Yet, despite all these remarkable advances accomplished in a relatively few years, Alex-

ander II became the target for revolutionaries in 1866, and terrorist activity continued throughout the seventies until the assassins finally killed the Tsar in 1881. It is impossible to understand these developments without taking a brief look at Russian intellectual life under Nicholas and Alexander.

Russian Intellectual Life

Early in Nicholas' reign, Russian professors and students, influenced by German philosophers, were devoting themselves to passionate discussions on art, philosophy, and religion. Many intellectuals outside the universities followed suit. These were the first groups known as the "intelligentsia," a peculiarly Russian class. By the 1830's, they were beginning to discuss Russia's place in the world, and especially its true historical relationship to the West and the proper course for it to follow in the future. Out of their debates there arose two important opposing schools of thought: the "Westerners" and the "Slavophiles" (friends of the Slavs).

The Westerners stated their case in a famous document called the "Philosophical Letter," published in 1836, though written earlier. Its author, Chaadaev, lamented the damaging effect of Byzantine Christianity and the Tartar invasions upon Russian development, and declared that Russia had made no contribution to the world. He hailed Peter the Great's efforts at westernizing Russia as a step in the right direction. He regarded the Roman Church as the source of much that was fruitful in the West of which Russia had been deprived. Nicholas I had Chaadaev certified as insane, and commanded that he be put under house arrest with a physician visiting him every day. Yet, despite scorn and censorship, the Westerners could not be silenced. They continued to declare that Russia was a society fundamentally like the West, but that history had delayed its full development. Russia should now catch up. The implication was that the time had come for Russia to emerge from a period of absolutism, and to enter upon the paths of parliamentary government and constitutional monarchy already trodden by the West.

In response, the opponents of the Westerners, the Slavophiles, vigorously argued that Russia had its own national spirit, like the *Volksgeist* that Herder (see Chapter 11) had discovered in the Germans. Russia was, they maintained, essentially different from the West. The Orthodox religion of the Slavs was not legalistic, rationalistic, and narrow like the Roman Catholicism of the West, but substantial, emotional, and broad. The Slavophiles violently attacked Peter the Great for embarking Russia on a false course. The West ought not to be imitated but opposed. The Russian upper classes should turn away from their Europeanized manners, and look for inspiration to the simple Russian peasant who lived in the truly Russian institution of the village commune. Western Europe was urban and bourgeois; Russia was rural and agrarian. Western Europe was materialistic; Russia was deeply spiritual. Like the Westerners, the Slavophiles attached fundamental importance to the national religion, and made it the center of their arguments; but they praised where the Westerners damned. The Westerners' views had democratic and constitutional political implications; the Slavophiles' views had anti-constitutional and anti-democratic implications.

It is very important, however, to realize that this does not mean that the Slavophiles embraced the "nationality" doctrine of Nicholas I, or that they approved of his regime. These were not the chauvinist nationalists who appeared later. They opposed the tyranny and the bureaucratic machine of Nicholas I as bitterly as did the Westerners. But they wanted a patriarchal, benevolent monarchy of the kind they fancied had existed before Peter the Great, instead of a constitutional regime on the western pattern. Instead of a central parliament, they looked back with longing to the feudal Muscovite assembly, the *zemski sobor*, and to other institutions of the tsardom before Peter. Extremists among them went about the streets dressed in the old boyars' robes that Peter had made illegal. Many intellectuals

shifted back and forth between the hotly debating camps, and few ever adopted in full the ideas of either side.

Alexander Herzen (1812–1870), for example, began his intellectual career as a Westerner and a devotee of French culture. The illegitimate son of a nobleman brought up in his father's house, he was charming, engaging, and highly intelligent. Like most Russians, he was not a reliable interpreter of western society, however, and was deeply fascinated with the thought that its structure might be rotten and doomed. The failure of the Paris revolution of 1848, which he saw as an eye-witness, convinced him that this was true, and he now became a revolutionary socialist. At the same time, he became convinced that the Westerners' thesis must be wrong. How could Russia in a short time pass through the stages of development which the West had taken centuries to experience but which Russia had missed? So Herzen became a Slavophile. As a revolutionary, he preached the destruction of existing institutions, and as a Slavophile he looked to Russia, with its peculiar institution of the peasant commune, the *mir*, to provide an inspiration for all Europe. Herzen became an influential publicist and issued a Russian-language paper in London which was widely read by Russian intellectuals. His memoirs provide perhaps the best picture preserved to us of the intellectual ferment of the age of Nicholas.

Michael Bakunin (1814–1876) reached roughly the same conclusions as Herzen at roughly the same time. But he was a practical anarchist tactician who loved violence, not a peaceful man of letters (see also Chapter 12). He enjoyed participating in revolutions, and had a long career in and out of jail in most of the countries of Europe. He looked forward to a great revolution spreading perhaps from Prague to Moscow and thence to the rest of Europe, followed by a tight dictatorship; beyond this he was entirely vague about the future. Atheism was a fundamental part of his program—not a casual part, as it always was to the Marxists. In his long career, Bakunin was to exert from abroad a considerable influence on Russian radicals.

Nihilism, Populism, Terrorism

In the 1860's, and especially after the emancipation in Russia, the Russian "intelligentsia," like intellectuals elsewhere in Europe, reacted against the romanticism of their predecessors. Suspecting idealism, religion, and metaphysics, they turned now to a narrowly utilitarian view of art and society. As one of these young men said, a pair of shoes to him was worth more than all the madonnas of a great Renaissainace painter. All art must have a social purpose, and the bonds holding the individual tightly to society must be smashed. Away with parental authority, with the marriage tie, with the tyranny of custom. For these people the name "nihilist" (a man who believes in nothing) quickly became fashionable. The portrait of a nihilist was drawn by the great novelist Turgenev in Bazarov, the hero of his novel *Fathers and Sons*. Rude and scornful, obstinate and arrogant, Bazarov was actually accepted as a model by intellectual leaders of youth in revolt against established ways of behavior. Yet nihilism as such was not a political movement. The nihilists enjoyed shocking their parents by calling for an end to the old moral system, advocating, for instance, the extermination of everybody in Russia over the age of 25.

In the 1860's, many of these young Russian intellectuals went to Switzerland, where the proper Swiss bourgeoisie were scandalized at the men with their hair cut long and the girls with their hair cut short, at their loud voices and insolent behavior. The standard cartoonist's picture of a Russian revolutionary dates from the first startled glimpse which the Swiss had of the nihilists, who at the time had not even begun to be interested in political revolution. Herzen himself was shocked by their behavior. He died in 1870, his intellectual leadership forfeit. But Bakunin understood them, and influenced many of them during their stay in Switzerland. Bakunin urged them to go back to Russia and preach an immediate revolution to the peasants.

Also present in Switzerland were two other important Russian revolutionary thinkers: Lavrov and Tkachev. Lavrov (1823–1900) taught his followers that as intellectuals they owed a great debt to the Russian peasant, whose labor for many generations had enabled their ancestors to enjoy leisure, and had made their own education possible. More gradual in his approach and more realistic in his estimates of the Russian peasant than Bakunin, Lavrov advised the nihilist students first to complete their education and then to return to Russia and go among the peasants, educating them and spreading among them propaganda for an eventual, not an immediate, revolution of the masses. On the other hand, Tkachev (1844–1886) taught that no revolution could ever be expected from the peasant masses, but that it would have to come from a tightly controlled small revolutionary elite, a little knot of conspirators who would seize power. Though not very influential at the time, Tkachev was important in Lenin's later thinking.

Under the impact of these teachers, especially Bakunin and Lavrov, Russian nihilism turned to a new kind of movement, which is called "populism." Young men and women, swept by idealistic fervor, decided to return to Russia and live among the peasants. When a government decree in 1872 actually summoned them back, they found that a parallel movement had already begun at home. About three thousand young people now took posts as teachers, innkeepers, or store-managers in the villages. Some tried to spread revolutionary ideas, others simply to render social service. Their romantic views of the peasantry were soon dispelled. The young populists did not know how to dress like peasants or how to talk to peasants. Suspicious of their talk, the peasants often betrayed them. The populists became conspicuous, and were easily traced by the police, who arrested them in droves. Two famous mass trials were held in the 1870's, at which the general public for the first time learned about the populist movement. After the trials, the populists who remained at large decided that they needed a determined revolutionary organization. With the formation of the "Land and Liberty" society in 1876, the childhood of the Russian revolutionary movement was over.

The revolutionaries had been stimulated by Alexander II's grant of reforms. So great had the discontent become that it is doubtful whether any Russian government could have proceeded fast enough to suit the radicals, who had come to believe in violent overturn of the régime, and were not satisfied with piecemeal and gradual reform. Stemming from John Stuart Mill and from western Utopian socialists like Fourier and Robert Owen (see Chapter 12), Russian socialism was not yet greatly influenced by Marx. In some ways it was almost Slavophile, not urban but rural, not evolutionary but revolutionary, not a mass political party but a conspiracy. Its members lived underground, and developed a conspiratorial psychology. They proposed to overthrow a bourgeois society before one ever got started. The movement became more and more radical, and in 1879 those who believed in the use of terror as a weapon separated from the others and founded the group called the *People's Will;* the anti-terrorists called themselves the *Black Partition.*

The members of the People's Will now went on a hunt for Tsar Alexander II himself. They shot at him and missed. They mined the track on which his train was traveling, and blew up the wrong train. They put dynamite under the dining room of the palace, and exploded it. But the Tsar was late for dinner that night, and eleven servants were killed instead. They rented a cheese-shop on one of the streets along which he drove, and tunneled under it. Finally they killed him (March, 1881) with a crude hand-made grenade, which blew up the assassin too. The supreme irony was that Alexander II had that day signed a document designed to summon a consultative assembly, which everybody expected to lead to further constitutional reform. His successor, the reactionary Alexander III (1881–1894), refused to confirm the document, and Russia was left to stagnate in a renewed repression. The terrorists were rounded up and punished, and their organization was smashed. Despite their occasional high-flown claims to enormous popular support, they had never numbered more than a mere handful of people, and their movement had been a failure.

Foreign Policy under Alexander II

In foreign policy, Alexander II made an uneven record. In Europe, the Russians successfully repressed the Polish uprising of 1863. They seized the opportunity provided by the Franco-Prussian War of 1870, and simply tore up the Black Sea provisions of the Treaty of Paris, declaring unilaterally that they would no longer be bound by them. This was an illegal act, to which the powers later reluctantly gave their assent. It was another illustration of the immorality in international affairs that Bismarck had made fashionable.

In 1877, the Russians went to war against Turkey on behalf of the rebellious Balkan Christians of Bosnia, Herzegovina, and Bulgaria. By the peace of San Stefano, dictated early in 1878 to the defeated Turks, Russia obtained, contrary to her previous agreements, a large independent Bulgarian state, which Russian policy-makers hoped to turn into a useful Balkan satellite. But the powers at the Congress of Berlin later in the same year reversed the judgment of San Stefano. They permitted only about one-third of the planned Bulgaria to come into existence as an autonomous state, while another third obtained autonomy separately, and the rest went back to Turkey. Russian public opinion resented the powers' depriving Russia of the gains scored in the Russo-Turkish War. Bitterness ran particularly high among those who hoped to unite all Slavs in a kind of federation, the Pan-Slavs (not to be confused with the Slavophiles).

Meanwhile, in Asia, encroachments begun under Nicholas I against the Chinese territory in the Amur River valley were regularized by treaty in 1860. Russian settlements in the "maritime province" on the Pacific Ocean continued to flourish. In Central Asia, a series of campaigns conquered the native Turkish khanates and added much productive land to the crown. Here, however, the advance toward the northwest frontier of India seemed to threaten British interests, and aroused public opinion in Britain against Russia.

The Reaction, 1881–1904

The reign of Alexander III and the first ten years of the reign of his son, Nicholas II, formed a quarter-century of consistent policies (1881–1904). Both tsars loathed liberalism as expressed in the earlier reforms, and were determined that there would never be any more of it. Yet a peasant bank set up under Alexander III made the redemption payments easier for the peasants to pay. And a few pieces of labor legislation, enacted under the influence of Bismarck's example, made working conditions a bit more tolerable—for example, hours were shortened for women workers. Offsetting these measures were the establishment of a special bank that extended credit to the impoverished nobility, the re-institution of rigorous censorship, and the institution in the countryside of so-called "rural leaders" or "land captains" in place of the elected justices of the peace of Alexander II. Election procedure for the *zemstvos* and for the city assemblies was made far less democratic. Now there began a vigorous persecution of the minority nationalities, a policy called "Russification," and quite in line with the "nationality" of Nicholas I's formula. The Finns, Poles, Ukrainians, Armenians, and Jews all suffered discrimination, varying from loss of their own institutions, which the Finns had enjoyed, to outright government-sponsored massacres in the case of the Jews. On his accession, Nicholas II referred to all hopes for a change as "senseless dreams."

These years were notable also for the steady growth of the Russian railroad network, largely built and owned by the state. The Donets coal basin was exploited for the first time; the Baku oil fields came into production; steel and cotton output soared. In 1892, there came to the Ministry of Finance a self-made railroad man, Witte, who for the next twelve years was personally responsible for the ever-mounting economic progress. Witte began the Trans-Siberian railroad, put Russia on the gold standard, attracted much foreign capital, especially French, for investment, and balanced the budget, in part through government monopoly of the sale of vodka. The railroad network doubled in length between 1894 and 1904, and the need for rails stimulated the steel industry. Correspondingly, the number of urban workers multiplied, and strikes called in protest against wretched working conditions mounted in number. In 1897, the working day was fixed by the state at eleven hours for adults, and other provisions were adopted to improve and regularize conditions. These laws, however, were difficult to enforce.

Under the circumstances, many of the young generation of revolutionaries now

Tsar Alexander III.

turned to Marxist "scientific" socialism, preaching the class struggle and predicting the inevitable downfall of capitalism. A small clandestine group of "intelligentsia," formed in 1894–1895 at St. Petersburg, proposed to overthrow the regime, working with all opponents of the class system. The members of the group included Lenin, a vigorous young intellectual of upper-middle-class origin, whose brother had been executed for an attempt on the life of Alexander III. In 1898, this group and others formed the Social Democratic party, which in 1900 began to publish its own newspaper. Within party ranks, grave dissension sprang up over the question of organization. Should the party operate under a strongly centralized directorate, or should each local group of Social Democrats be free to agitate for its own ends? In the tradition of Bakunin and Tkachev, Lenin insisted on the tightly knit little group of directors at the center. At the party congress of Brussels and London in 1903, the majority voted with him. Lenin's faction thereafter was called by the name Bolshevik, meaning majority, as against the Menshevik (minority) group, which favored a loose democratic organization for the party. Both groups remained Social Democrats, or SDs, as they were often called.

Meanwhile, the non-Marxist revolutionaries, who were the direct heirs of the People's Will tradition, also organized a political party. They were the Social Revolutionaries, or SRs, with their own clandestine newspaper. Whereas the SDs as Marxists were interested almost exclusively in the urban workers, the SRs as populists were interested in the peasantry. Their chief aim was to redistribute the land, but they continued in their terrorist ways. They assassinated several cabinet ministers, using as their slogan the cry, *We don't want reforms, we want reform.*

A third political grouping was that of the moderates and liberals, not SD or SR in orientation, but mostly veterans of the *zemstvos* and intellectuals indignant over the government's policies of repression, who favored only such measures as compulsory free private education and agrarian reform. The regime stupidly made no distinction between these men and the die-

hard terrorists or the rabid Marxists. Thus the moderates also gradually organized, and had their own clandestine paper favoring a constitution and a national parliament for Russia. In 1905, they took the name Constitutional Democrats and were thereafter usually referred to as Kadets, from the Russian initials KD. Faced by this political activity among its radical and moderate opponents, the government only tightened the reins and by 1904 had adopted the view that a short victorious war was all that would be necessary to unite the country.

The Russo-Japanese War

Trans-Siberian railway construction made it desirable for the Russians to obtain a right of way across Chinese territory in Manchuria. They took the initiative in preventing Japan from establishing herself on the Chinese mainland after her defeat of China in 1895, and then required the Chinese in exchange to allow the building of the new railroad. In 1897, they seized Port Arthur, the very port they had earlier kept out of Japanese hands. Further friction with the Japanese took place in Korea, where both powers had interests. Then, after the Boxer Rebellion of 1900 in China (see Chapter 20), the Russians kept their troops in Manchuria after the other nations had withdrawn theirs. Although the Russians promised to withdraw their forces by stages, they failed to do so, largely because Russian foreign policy fell into the hands of shady adventurers, some of whom had a lumber concession in Korea and wanted war with Japan. After it became apparent that the war party had got control in Russia, the Japanese without warning attacked units of the Russian fleet anchored at Port Arthur in February, 1904. The Russo-Japanese War had begun.

Far from their bases and taken by surprise, the Russians none the less stabilized a front on land. But their fleet, which had steamed all the way around Europe and across the Indian Ocean into the Pacific, was decisively defeated by the Japanese in the battle of Tsushima (May 27, 1904). To the Russian people, the war was a mysterious, distant political adventure of which they wanted no part. Many intellectuals opposed it, and the SRs and SDs openly hoped for a Russian defeat, which they expected would shake the government's position. Alarmed at the growing unrest at home, the Russian government was persuaded by President Theodore Roosevelt to accept his mediation, which the Japanese also actively wished.

Witte, the go-getting businessman who had opposed the war from the first, was sent to Portsmouth, New Hampshire, as Russian representative. Here he not only secured excellent terms for Russia, but also won a favorable verdict from American public opinion, which had previously been strongly pro-Japanese, and had thought of Russians as either brutal aristocrats or bomb-throwing revolutionaries. By the Treaty of Portsmouth (1905), Russia recognized the Japanese protectorate over Korea, ceded Port Arthur and the southern half of Sakhalin Island, together with fishing rights in the North Pacific, and promised to evacuate Manchuria. Russian prestige as a Far Eastern power was not deeply wounded or permanently impaired by the defeat or by the treaty. Yet the effect of the defeat in Asia was to transfer Russian attention back to Europe, where a world crisis had already begun (see Chapter 17).

The Revolution of 1905

The most important immediate result of the Russo-Japanese War was its impact on Russian domestic developments. While it was still going on, Plehve, the reactionary minister of the interior, was assassinated by an SR bomb in July, 1904. His successor was a moderate. The *zemstvo* liberals, the future Kadets, were encouraged, and held banquets throughout Russia to adopt a series of resolutions for presentation to a kind of national congress of *zemstvo* representatives. Although the congress was not allowed to meet publicly, its program—a constitution, basic civil liberties, class and minority equality, and extension of *zemstvo* responsibilities—became widely known and approved. The Tsar temporized, issued so vague a statement

that all hope for change was dimmed, and took measures to limit free discussion.

Ironically, it was a police agent of the government itself who struck the fatal spark. He had been planted in the St. Petersburg factories to combat SD efforts to organize the workers, and to substitute his own union. He organized a parade of workers to demonstrate peacefully and to petition the Tsar directly for an eight-hour day, a national assembly, civil liberties, the right to strike, and a number of other moderate demands. When the workers tried to deliver the petition, Nicholas left town and ordered the troops to fire on the peaceful demonstrators, some of whom were carrying his portrait to demonstrate their loyalty. About a thousand workers were killed on "Bloody Sunday" (January 22, 1905). The massacre made revolutionaries out of the urban workers. Strikes multiplied, the moderate opposition joined with the radical opposition, and university students and professors demanded the same reforms as wild-eyed bomb-hurlers.

Amid mounting excitement, the government at first seemed to favor the calling of a *zemski sobor*, consultative, not legislative, in the old Russian pattern rather than the western parliamentary one, but still a national assembly of sorts. But then even this project was whittled away, as the timid, vacillating, and unintelligent Nicholas II listened to his reactionary advisers. Under the impact of delays and disappointments, demonstrations and outbreaks occurred during the summer of 1905. In October, the printers struck. No newspapers appeared, and the printers, with SD aid, formed the first "soviet" or workers' council. When the railroad workers joined the strike, communications were cut off between Moscow and St. Petersburg. Soviets now multiplied. Of the one formed in St. Petersburg, Lenin declared that it was "not a workers' parliament, nor an organization of proletarian autonomy, but a combat organization pursuing definite ends."

This reflects the Bolsheviks' view of the soviet as an instrument for the pursuit of their program of armed revolt, for the establishment of a provisional government, for the proclamation of a democratic republic, and for the summoning of a constituent assembly. This pro-

Bloody Sunday (January 22, 1905): demonstrators and soldiers in Petersburg.

gram, put forth by the most "extreme" of the revolutionaries of 1905, differed relatively little from the program of the most moderate liberals, who would, however, have kept the monarchy and striven to obtain their ends by persuasion and pressure rather than by violence. At the time, and for years to come, the Bolsheviks, like other Marxists, accepted the view that it was necessary for Russia to pass through a stage of bourgeois democracy before the time for the proletarian revolution could come. They were therefore eager to help along the bourgeois revolution.

Nicholas was faced, as Witte told him, with the alternatives of imposing a military dictatorship and putting down the opposition by force, or of summoning a truly legislative assembly with veto-power over the laws. The Tsar finally

chose the latter course, and in October, 1905, issued a manifesto that promised full civil liberties at once, and a legislative assembly or *duma* to be elected by universal suffrage. In effect, this famous October Manifesto put an end to the autocracy, since the duma was to be superior to the tsar in legislation.

Yet the issuance of the October Manifesto did not meet with universal approval or even end the revolution at once. On the Right, a government-sponsored party called the "Union of the Russian people" demonstrated against the manifesto, proclaimed its undying loyalty to the autocrat, and organized its own storm troops, or "Black Hundreds," which killed more than 3,000 Jews in the first week after the issuance of the manifesto. The armies returned from the Far East, and proved to be still

560

loyal to the government. Thus the soviets of 1905, unlike those of 1917 (see Chapter 18), included only workers, and no soldiers. On the Left, the dissatisfied Bolsheviks and SRs made several attempts to launch their violent revolution, but failed, and the government was able to arrest their leaders and eventually to put them down after several days of street fighting in Moscow in December, 1905. In the Center, one group of liberals, pleased with the manifesto, urged that it be used as a rallying point for a moderate program. These were the Octobrists, so called after the month in which the manifesto had been issued. The other group, the Kadets, wished to continue to agitate by legal means for further immediate reforms. But the real fires of revolution had burned out by the opening of the year 1906.

The Dumas, 1906–1914

Suffrage for the Duma was universal, but voters chose an electoral college which then selected the 412 deputies. Although SRs and SDs boycotted the elections out of discontent over the indirect election system, many of their number were elected. The Kadets were the strongest single party. Quite against the expectation of the government, the peasants' vote was not conservative, but highly liberal. But even before the first Duma had met, Witte was able to reduce its powers. He secured a large French loan, which made the government financially independent of the Duma, and issued a set of "fundamental laws," which the Duma was not to be competent to alter. The Crown was to continue to control war and foreign policy; the minister of finance was to control loans and currency. The tsar's council of state was transformed by adding members from the clergy, nobility, the *zemstvos*, the universities, and chambers of commerce. It became a kind of upper house, which had equal legislative rights with the Duma, and could therefore submit a rival budget, for example, which the government could then adopt in preference to that of the Duma. Finally, the tsar could dissolve the Duma at will, provided he set a date for new elections. When it was not in session he could

legislate by himself, although his enactments had later to be approved by the Duma.

The first Duma, the "Duma of Popular Indignation," met between May and July, 1906. It addressed a list of grievances to the Tsar, asking for a radical land reform that would give the peasants all state and church land, and part of the land still in private hands. The government flatly refused to accept this attack on property, and after some parliamentary skirmishing the Duma was dissolved. The Kadet membership, maintaining incorrectly that the dissolution was unconstitutional, crossed the frontier into Finland, and there issued a manifesto urging the Russian people not to pay taxes or report for military service unless the Duma was recalled. Its authors were soon tried and declared ineligible for office; so future Dumas were deprived of the services of this capable Kadet group of moderates.

With the dissolution of the first Duma there came to power as chief minister the highly intelligent and conservative Peter Stolypin, who stayed in office until 1911, when he was assassinated. Together with Witte, he was the leading statesman of the last period of tsarist Russia. Stolypin put through a series of agricultural laws which enabled the peasants to free themselves from the commune. A peasant wishing to detach his property could demand that he be given a single tract, which meant that the scattered strips assigned to other families would also be consolidated so that each would obtain a single plot. This program Stolypin called the "wager on the strong and sober"; he was encouraging the initiative and enterprise of individual Russian peasants who had the will to operate on their own as successful small farmers. His program accomplished much of what he hoped for. It is estimated that about a quarter of the peasant households of European Russia (almost 9,000,000) emancipated themselves from the communes during the years between 1906 and 1917. Only war and revolution kept the process from going still further. Lenin and others who hoped for revolution were deeply suspicious and afraid of Stolypin's agrarian reforms. They rightly feared that the peasant grievances would be removed, and understood that no revolution in

Russia could in the end succeed without the peasants.

Simultaneously with his agrarian program, Stolypin carried on unremitting war against terrorists and other revolutionaries. He showed no hesitation in acting in the most unconstitutional fashion when it suited him. He did everything he could to interfere with the elections to the second Duma, but the SRs and SDs were well represented, and the Duma itself (March-June, 1907) would not work with the government. It was dissolved because it refused to suspend the parliamentary immunity of the SD deputies, whom Stolypin wanted to arrest.

After the dissolution of the second Duma, the government quite illegally altered the election laws, cutting the number of delegates from the peasants and national minorities, and increasing the number from the gentry. By this means the government got a majority, and the third Duma, (1907–1912) and the fourth (1912–1917) lived out their constitutional lives of five years apiece. Unrepresentative and limited in their powers though they were, they were still national assemblies. In their sessions the left-wingers could be heard, and could question ministers like any other members. The Dumas improved the conditions of peasant and worker and helped strengthen national defense as the World War drew closer. Their commissions, working with individual ministers, proved extremely useful in increasing the efficiency of government departments. The period of the third Duma, however, was also notable for the continuation of "Russification," and the Finns in particular lost their remaining rights (1910).

Under the fourth Duma, the government, with Stolypin dead, tended more toward reaction. The Leftists organized busily for another revolution, working in unions, cooperatives, evening classes for workmen, and a whole network of other labor organizations. A vast web of police spies challenged them at every turn. Meanwhile, the imperial family drifted into a very dangerous situation, as the fanatically religious and autocratically minded empress fell more and more under the sway of a half-mad, wholly evil, dirty, ignorant, and power-hungry monk from Siberia. This man, Rasputin, had the mysterious ability, possibly hypnotic, to stop the bleeding of the young heir to the throne, who suffered from hemophilia. Since the Empress had enormous influence on her beloved husband, Nicholas II, Rasputin became in a real sense the ruler of Russia, much to the horror of a great many loyal supporters of the imperial house, and greatly to the detriment of the rational conduct of affairs in an enormous twentieth-century state. At the moment when the World War began, Russia was in the throes of a major crisis precipitated by the government's reactionary policies, the scandal of Rasputin's influence, and the indignation of the loyal Duma. There was a threat of revolution, then, even before 1917.

V Conclusion

Parliamentary government was, as we have seen, a comparative stranger to the three eastern European empires. The King of Prussia, with Bismarck's help, used his extraordinary military system to conquer and unify Germany. He imposed on all non-Austrian Germans the Prussian system of autocracy almost undiluted by a weak and subservient parliament, and backed by the army and the Junkers. The Habsburg emperor, though faced after 1907 with an Austrian parliament elected by universal suffrage, in 1914 still made virtually all policy decisions by himself. The Hungarian parliament was never genuinely representative, and the Emperor successfully used universal suffrage as a threat to quell Magyar separatism. The tsars, forced at last by defeat in wars to grant a modified constitution in 1905, were still able to hamstring their own central legislative body, and to wield a preponderant personal influence in politics.

In all three countries, none the less, for the first time in their history, modern political parties during this period coalesced around principles. As in the West, the governments collaborated with parties or coalitions of parties, but always faced an opposition. What a party stood for was determined largely by the peculiar circumstances of the country that gave it birth. Yet certain parallels reached across national boundaries. Although no group in Russia can be compared with the German Catholic Center, the Austrian Christian Socialists do resemble it in many ways. No group in either Germany or Austria is comparable with the Russian populists (Social Revolutionaries). Yet German Liberals, Austrian Liberals, and Russian Kadets or Octobrists can perhaps be roughly equated. So can the Pan-Germans with the Pan-Slavs. The Social Democrats were Marxist in all three countries, but increasingly less revolutionary in Germany and Austria-Hungary, and increasingly more so in Russia.

All three countries during this period experienced an economic boom and an occasional depression; the industrial revolution struck them late, but with terrific impact. By the turn of the twentieth century, Germany had made such advances that its steel production surpassed that of England, and was second in the world only to that of the United States. Though far behind Germany both in resources and in technology, Austria-Hungary too was becoming rapidly industrialized. In Russia, transport and industry boomed.

Yet in all three countries, the landed nobility continued to exercise political influence quite out of proportion to their numbers. Everywhere the existence of a new and underprivileged class of urban workers stimulated intellectual leaders to form Marxist political groups, to preach the class struggle, and, except in Russia, to strive for immediate improvements in conditions rather than for the violent overthrow of the regime. Last of all the European countries, Russia emancipated her serfs in 1861 and began a new era of agrarian experiment and unrest. In Germany, protection was the great agrarian issue after the late 1870's. In Austria-Hungary, the peasants suffered with docility.

All three countries had minority problems of varying seriousness. Germany persecuted the Poles and, after 1871 and less severely, she persecuted the Alsatians and Lorrainers. More and more, Russia persecuted the Finns, Poles, Ukrainians, and Armenians. In Austria-Hungary alone, however, the minority problem proved fatal. German anti-Slav sentiment in Austria, and Magyar mistreatment of all non-Magyars in Hungary, alienated potentially loyal subjects, and finally helped explode the state from inside. In all three countries, the Jews created a special problem and suffered different degrees of discrimination and persecution.

In Germany, a combination of circumstances led first to an assault by the government on the Catholic Church, and then to an alliance between the government and the Catholic political party. In the Habsburg monarchy, a milder anticlericalism had its day, but the Church retained its hold on the population, and continued to exercise enormous political influence. In Russia, the Orthodox Church as usual played almost no role in the cultural development of the people. But one group of influential intellectuals attacked it as the source of Russia's troubles, while another group hailed the Church as the true source of Russia's strength and the fountainhead of all national virtue.

So it was that the main currents of the time flowed with uneven force over the Germans, Austrians, and Russians. Nationalism, materialism, militarism, imperialism, clericalism, constitutionalism, landlordism, and socialism were all experienced to a varying degree by all the countries. What determined each country's answer to social pressure, however, was its own peculiar past and its own peculiar character.

Reading Suggestions on Central and Eastern Europe

(Asterisk indicates paperbound edition.)

General Accounts

R. C. Binkley, *Realism and Nationalism, 1852–1871* (Harper, 1935). Though this volume, in the "Rise of Modern Europe" series, develops a somewhat implausible thesis about the possibilities of "federative polity," it provides an often illuminating discussion of the period indicated.

C. J. H. Hayes, *A Generation of Materialism, 1871–1900* (Harper, 1941). Another volume in the "Rise of Modern Europe" series, this does some penetrating probing beneath the surface on an apparently successful era, particularly in Germany.

A. J. P. Taylor, *The Struggle for Mastery in Europe, 1848–1918* (Clarendon, 1954). A volume in "The Oxford History of Modern Europe"; crisp and provocative.

Special Studies:
Germany

R. Flenley, *Modern German History* (Dutton, 1953), and K. S. Pinson, *Modern Germany, Its History and Civilization* (Macmillan, 1954). Two textbooks, of which Pinson's is the longer and Flenley's perhaps the more useful.

A. J. P. Taylor, *The Course of German History* (Coward-McCann, 1946). A lively essay on the period since 1815, with strong, but not unreasonable, anti-German overtones.

F. Meinecke, *The German Catastrophe* (Harvard Univ. Press, 1950). A useful antidote to Taylor, by a very great German historian.

T. Veblen, *Imperial Germany and the Industrial Revolution,* new ed. (Viking, 1954). An old, brilliant, and still very important analysis by a great American sociologist.

J. H. Clapham, *The Economic Development of France and Germany, 1815–1914*, 4th ed. (Cambridge Univ. Press, 1936; reprinted 1955). A somewhat out-of-date but still instructive introduction to the subject.

F. Darmstaedter, *Bismarck and the Creation of the Second Reich* (Methuen, 1948). A valuable study.

E. Eyck, *Bismarck and the German Empire* (Allen and Unwin, 1950). Translation and condensation of a large standard work in German.

A. J. P. Taylor, *Bismarck: The Man and the Statesman* (Knopf, 1955). A provocative and often hostile re-evaluation.

E. J. Passant, *A Short History of Germany, 1850–1945* (Cambridge Univ. Press, 1959). An up-to-date general survey.

H. von Treitschke, *History of Germany in the 19th Century,* 7 vols. (Humanities Press, 1915–1919), and *Origins of Prussianism,* ed. by E. and C. Paul (Humanities Press, 1942). Celebrated detailed studies emphasizing the period before 1870; strongly Prussian in tone and sympathy.

Special Studies:
The Habsburg
Monarchy

A. J. May, *The Hapsburg Monarchy, 1867–1914* (Harvard Univ. Press, 1951). Concise general account.

A. J. P. Taylor, *The Habsburg Monarchy, 1809–1918*, 2nd ed. (Hamish Hamilton, 1948). A spirited brief treatment.

R. A. Kann, *The Multinational Empire,* 2 vols. (Columbia Univ. Press, 1950). A monograph, arranged nationality by nationality, and discussing national sentiments and the government's efforts to deal with them.

O. Jászi, *The Dissolution of the Habsburg Monarchy* (Univ. of Chicago Press, 1929). From a rare point of view, that of the liberal Magyar.

R. W. Seton-Watson, *German, Slav, and Magyar* (Williams and Norgate, 1916). By the greatest British authority on southeast Europe, the author of many other valuable studies of the area.

E. Wiskemann, *Czechs and Germans* (Oxford Univ. Press, 1938). A good case history of national antagonisms.

Special Studies: Russia

H. Seton-Watson, *The Decline of Imperial Russia, 1855–1914* (Praeger, 1952). The only sound work in English covering virtually all the period dealt with in this chapter.

G. T. Robinson, *Rural Russia under the Old Regime,* 2nd ed. (Macmillan, 1949). A splendid monograph on the peasant question.

A. Herzen, *My Past and Thoughts*, 6 vols. (Chatto and Windus, 1924–1927). The classic picture of nineteenth-century Russia, by its most distinguished rebel.

Martin Malia, *Alexander Herzen and the Birth of Russian Socialism* (*Grosset and Dunlap, Universal Library, 1965). Excellent monograph on Herzen's life and thought, considered in the framework of contemporary European ideas.

N. V. Riasanovsky, *Russia and the West in the Teaching of the Slavophiles* (Harvard Univ. Press, 1953). A useful study of one side of the chief intellectual controversy of the period.

Sidney Monas, *The Third Section: Police and Society in Russia Under Nicholas I* (Harvard Univ. Press, 1961). Pioneering study of the repressive machinery and its impact.

D. Footman, *Red Prelude* (Yale Univ. Press, 1945). A good biography of Zhelyabov, populist and terrorist.

Peter Kropotkin, *Memoirs of a Revolutionist*, ed. James A. Rogers (*Anchor, 1962). A delightful anarchist's story of his own life and times.

James Joll, *The Anarchists* (*Grosset and Dunlap, Universal Library, 1964). Excellent chapters on Bakunin and Kropotkin, and a fine study of the movement.

B. Pares, *The Fall of the Russian Monarchy* (Jonathan Cape, 1939). An excellent study of the period 1905–1917; by an authority who was frequently on the spot.

S. Witte, *Memoirs* (Doubleday, 1921). The somewhat apologetic memoirs of the man who did most to industrialize imperial Russia.

B. D. Wolfe, *Three Who Made a Revolution* (Dial Press, 1948; *Beacon). A fine triple study of Lenin, Trotsky, and Stalin; with emphasis on the period before 1914.

A. Lobanov-Rostovsky, *Russia and Asia*, rev. ed. (G. Wahr, 1951). A useful introductory survey.

B. H. Sumner, *Russia and the Balkans, 1870–1880* (Clarendon, 1937). A monograph including a helpful discussion of Panslavism.

Historical Fiction

T. Mann, *Buddenbrooks* (*Pocket Books). Inexpensive reprint of a long novel about a family in imperial Germany.

G. Hauptmann, *The Weavers, Hannele, The Beaver Coat* (*Rinehart, 1951). Three plays that convey some of the flavor of nineteenth-century Germany.

R. Musil. *The Man without Qualities* (Coward-McCann, 1953). A novel steeped in the atmosphere of pre-1914 Vienna.

M. Jókai, *Eyes Like the Sea* (Putnam, 1901). Fictionalized autobiography of a romantic Hungarian novelist, the author of many novels that give insights into Magyar nationalism.

N. Gogol, *The Inspector General* (many editions), and *Dead Souls,* George Reavey trans. (Oxford Univ. Press, 1957—The World's Classics; *Rinehart Editions). Brilliant satirical play and novel.

I. Turgenev, *Fathers and Sons* (sometimes called *Fathers and Children*—many editions), and *Smoke* (Dutton, 1949; *Everyman). Superb contemporary realistic fiction reflecting Russian intellectual and political life.

F. Dostoevsky, *The Brothers Karamazov* (*Modern Library, 1937), and *Crime and Punishment* (*Modern Library, 1932). Famous novels depicting the turbulent life of Russian intellectuals in the mid-nineteenth century; more romantic in tone than Turgenev's works.

The Portable Chekhov (*Viking, 1947). A selection from the short stories and plays of A. Chekhov, a skillful portraitist of the upper classes in tsarist Russia.

L. Tolstoy, *Anna Karenina* (*Modern Library). A celebrated novel set in late nineteenth-century St. Petersburg and the countryside.

15

The Intellectual Revolution

The sources for the intellectual history of the nineteenth century—the great books and the ephemeral books, the articles, stories, advertisements, sermons, paintings, sculptures, all the accumulated symbols of culture—have been preserved in bewildering quantity. The last century seems, in our present retrospect, to have presented samples of almost all varieties of human thought and feeling, of all western "styles." A detailed catalogue of these varieties would be dull and confusing. Here we shall center on one main theme—the qualifications, emendations, even repudiations, made by the late nineteenth century in the western heritage of the Enlightenment, that heritage of optimistic faith in simple, static, reformist "reason" and a simple "natural law," largely divorced from its Roman and Christian meanings, which rules men and matter. The most striking of these emendations was made by Darwin.

I   Darwinism

The Origin of Species

Darwin's *On the Origin of Species by Means of Natural Selection* (1859) is one of the books that mark a revolution in intellectual history. Like all important revolutions, the Darwinian was no bolt from the blue. Into Darwin's work had gone long years of preparation, not merely those of Darwin's own life, but those of his predecessors and colleagues in the scientific study of what was then called natural history and is now called biology or ethology. Before him was the long record of the hundreds of thousands of years of organic life on earth. Already well established by geologists like Sir Charles Lyell and by paleontologists, this record told of the rise, development, sometimes of the disappearance, of thousands of different forms of plant and animal organisms, or *species*. The record contradicted an important part of the commonly accepted theory men of the West had about the past of organic life. The Bible in the Book of Genesis described all forms of life as begun in the space of a single week by a Creator about 6,000 years ago. And this same religious account furthermore stated explicitly that all existing men and animals were descended from single pairs of each species preserved in Noah's ark during a great universal flood that took place some time after the Creation.

Now Darwin was by no means the first to find a discrepancy between the historical and scientific record and the accepted Biblical explanation. The men of the Enlightenment had felt compelled by the facts of the record to give up the Biblical explanation. Some of them had gone so far as to conceive the record as a very long evolutionary process in which no God, at least no personal, Christian God, had a hand, but only the impersonal forces of Nature or the deist's "watchmaker God" (see Chapter 19). But they had arrived at no satisfactory explanation of how Nature or the watchmaker God had done the job; they had no satisfactory theory of how organisms had evolved. This Darwin gave the world.

Darwin's Theories

One of his clues he found in the work of the economist Malthus (see Chapter 12). In his *Essay on Population,* Malthus had maintained that organisms—including man—tended to multiply to a point where there simply was not food enough for them all. In the intense competition for food, some of these organisms did not get enough, and died. This was the germ of the conception Darwin phrased as the *struggle for existence.* He next asked himself what determined that certain individuals would survive and that others would die. Obviously the surviving ones got more food, better shelter, better living conditions of all sorts. If they were all identical organisms, the only explanation—apart from the intervention of a supernatural being or force—would have to be accidental variations in their environment. But it was clear from observation that individual organisms of a given species are not identical. Variations appear even at birth. Thus in a single litter of pigs there may be sturdy, aggressive piglets and a runt. The runt, even if a sentimental farmer tries to protect it, is likely to get shoved aside in suckling by his sturdier brothers, and starve. In the wild state, in free competition, the runt is almost certain to die. In the struggle for existence, the runt is proved "unfit."

Here is the second of Darwin's key phrases, the *survival of the fittest.* The organism best endowed in its variations to get food and shelter lives to procreate young that will tend to inherit these favorable variations. The variations are slight indeed, but over generation after generation they are cumulative; finally an organism so different from the long-distant ancestor is produced that we can speak of a new species. This new species has *evolved.* It has evolved by the working of *natural selection.* Man as a plant and animal breeder has long made use of this process and has hastened and indeed guided it for his own purposes by *artificial selection,* by breeding only the best strains—"best," of course, from a human point of view. But man has been doing this with domesticated plants and animals for but a tiny period of geological time, and with but few species. Over the eons, *natural selection* has been the working force; *and for man himself,* according to the Darwinian system, natural selection alone has been at work, since man has yet to breed his own kind as he breeds his domestic plants and animals.

Darwin held that the variations in individuals of the same species at birth are accidental, and that they are generally transmitted through inheritance. Those biologists who developed his doctrine, notably the German Weismann, did not—and this is a very important point—believe that the evidence showed that variations produced in an individual organism in the course of its life could be transmitted to its offspring. Thus, orthodox Darwinism denies the inheritance of "acquired characteristics." Obviously, a man with an amputated leg will not produce one-legged children. Experimenters have docked the tails of generations of laboratory rats, but the rats are still born with long tails. Efforts by such Russian geneticists as Lysenko to show that environmental changes can be transmitted to offspring have not yet convinced most scientists.

Today, more than a century after the publication of the *Origin of Species,* Darwin's work as a biologist is still accepted in most of its larger outlines. Later work, however, has found that variations of importance in the evolutionary process are probably not so much the numerous tiny ones Darwin emphasized, but rather bigger and much rarer ones now known as "mutations." Scientists have begun to study the effect of various forms

of radiation on such mutations. A still much-disputed geological theory holds that catastrophic crustal movements in the past have so radically altered environment as to wipe out whole species and speed up the evolution of others. Emphasis on either mutations or on extensive crustal movements tends also to be emphasis on the sudden and catastrophic rather than on the gradual. Such emphasis may well reflect the violent character of our twentieth century in contrast with the relatively peaceful nineteenth. For, though many scientists would deny this, it would seem that even science is to a degree affected by human "attitudes."

Darwin believed that what he called "sexual selection"—that is, the ability of the fittest individual to attract and mate with fittest individuals of the opposite sex and thus produce the fittest offspring—was a very important factor in natural selection. Although sexual selection is by no means wholly discarded by geneticists today, many of them do not accept Darwin's version of it. The actual mechanism of heredity we know much better than Darwin did, thanks to the work of an Austrian monk, Gregor Mendel, in the late nineteenth century, and many, many successors up to the present day.

The Effect on Theology

The *Origin of Species* stirred up a most heated theological controversy. It added fuel to a fire kindled earlier by historical and linguistic scholarship with its practice of applying the same standards to the Bible that the scholar would apply to Homer, or to the old Norse and Germanic epics. Fundamentalists, both Protestant and Catholic, simply stuck by Genesis and damned Darwin and all his work. But the Catholic Church and many Protestant bodies eventually took at least a neutral attitude toward Darwinism, which they viewed as a scientific biological hypothesis neither necessarily correct nor necessarily incorrect. The great majority of Christians tacitly or openly accepted sufficient modification of Genesis to accommodate themselves to the scientist's

An 1871 anti-Darwinian cartoon by Thomas Nast. The defrauded gorilla, pointing to Darwin at right: "That man wants to claim my pedigree. He says he is one of my descendants." Mr. Bergh (founder of the Society for the Prevention of Cruelty to Animals): "Now, Mr. Darwin, how could you insult him so?"

time-scale, and adjusted the classic theological arguments from first cause, design, and the like to a God who worked his will in accordance with organic evolution; and they accepted the assimilation of the Biblical account, at least in part, with other fallible histories. In short, they were willing to grant that the *men* who wrote the Bible were not infallible. Moreover, it was quite clear to reflective men that nothing Darwin or any other scientist or scholar could produce would give ultimate answers to the kind of problem set by the existence of God. It was quite clear to them that since God's eye is now on the sparrow, it must once have been on the dinosaur. Christians can be Darwinians: millions of them are. But Darwinism, if taken over wholesale into a philosophy of life, remains a denial of any supernatural intervention in the planning and running of the universe, remains a support for secularism.

The Effect on Social and Economic Attitudes

This theological conflict had pretty well run its course by the beginning of the twentieth century. More important in the long run was the use men made of some of Darwin's basic concepts — or at least, of his more smoothly coined phrases — in debates on matters moral, economic, and political. The blanket term, "Social Darwinism," which covers all these transfers of ideas from biology to the social sciences and human relations, takes in a very wide range of persons and ideas. Darwin himself was a biologist, not a "Social Darwinist." He did not write as a social scientist. It must be noted, however, that in a free and literate society, ideas produced by scientists invariably spread to many people not trained in science, and that such ideas are modified in the process of spreading. Not all professional scientists are reconciled to this fact.

The central idea that social and political thinkers took over from Darwin was that of competition among individuals and groups of individuals. This was of course a conception already central in their thinking, but Darwin buttressed it with the prestige of the natural sciences. The majority of these late nineteenth-century thinkers interpreted the human struggle as a struggle for the means of livelihood. There is, they were sure, among men a human "struggle for life." The variations that counted here were the variations that brought success in economic competition — the variations that produced inventors, business organizers, even perhaps political, artistic, and professional leaders. Darwin's work in natural history came to confirm the economist's doctrine of laissez-faire and the nineteenth-century liberal's doctrine of individual freedom for a man to do what his capacities permitted.

Formal economists did not indeed make much use of, or have much need for, Darwin. The classical economists had already brought the arguments for laissez-faire to their height (see Chapter 12). On the whole, for the rest of the century, the economists were to temper somewhat the rigor of the doctrine of competition among individuals. But the average successful middle-class person in the West took Darwin to heart. Here was scientific confirmation of the middle-class notions that the universe was designed to reward hard work, thrift, intelligence, and self-help and to punish laziness, waste, stupidity, and reliance on charity. Above all, the middle-class person of the time took Darwin to confirm the notion that the poor were poor because they were unfit, badly designed for living. The work of Darwin confirmed the complementary notion that attempts by private charity or by state action to take from the rich and moderately well-to-do and give to the poor were useless and quite contrary to nature, shocking efforts to reverse the course of evolution. If a man cannot earn enough to feed himself, it was argued, he had better die; lowlier organisms too incompetent to feed themselves certainly die off, to the greater good of the species. Herbert Spencer (1820–1903), an ardent British evolutionist, summed it up neatly:

Of man, as of all inferior creatures, the law by conformity to which the species is preserved, is that among adults the individuals best adapted to the conditions of their existence shall prosper most, and the individuals least adapted to the conditions of their existence shall prosper least. . . . Pervading all Nature we may see at work a stern discipline which is often a little cruel that it may be very kind. . . . The ultimate result of shielding men from folly is to fill the world with fools.*

Spencer himself, if it came to that, could not have stood by while the unemployed and their families starved to death, for he was a kindly man. But he had an almost maniacal hatred of the state, of local government as well as national; he held out even against laws requiring houseowners to connect their houses with sewers in cities. But even Spencer

could not transfer to the struggle for existence among human beings the fine ruthless freedom of the jungle, of what Tennyson called "Nature red in tooth and claw." He was against all forms of government provision for what we now call social security. But what government may not do he believed the ethically sound individual will do as charity. The rich and well-to-do will take care of the poor voluntarily—not enough to spoil them, not enough to frustrate the designs of evolution by letting them prosper and propagate their kind, but enough to prevent their starving or freezing to death.

In his *Principles of Ethics,* Spencer discovered that the softer emotions promoted by Christianity and the other higher religions —kindness, dislike of cruelty, love—were also in accord with the intentions of the laws of the universe as summed up in evolution. Mutual extermination might be the law for tigers, but not for human beings. Indeed, Spencer and many other Social Darwinists held that the altruistic moral sentiments that impel us toward charity are the highest achievement of the evolutionary process, and that a society with many altruists is thereby shown to be the fittest for survival.

Eugenics

The Social Darwinists were, then, faced with this primary difficulty. Darwin seemed to have shown that the unmitigated struggle for life within a given species, and among rival species, was the law of the universe; but human history, and human feelings, showed that men could not in practice look on with indifference while their fellow men starved to death. One way out of the dilemma was that recommended by Spencer, a sort of humanized and mitigated struggle in which the incompetent were shelved but not destroyed. Many who held this view accompanied it with a faith in what came to be called eugenics.

Eugenicists sought to encourage childbearing by the fit and to discourage ever present child-bearing by the unfit. Darwin had

*Herbert Spencer, *Principles of Ethics* (London, 1879–1893), section 257; *Social Statics* (London, 1851), p. 149; *Autobiography* (London, 1904), II, 5.

begun his *Origin of Species* with a consideration of the extraordinary success men had had with artificial selection in the breeding of plants and animals. Why not do the same thing with human beings? Since, according to strict Darwinian theory, acquired characteristics were not transmitted by heredity, no amount of manipulation of the social environment, no amount of wise planning of institutions, would alter human beings. Therefore, the only way to secure permanent improvement of the race was by deliberate mating of the fit with the fit.

The eugenicists, however, ran at once against the fact that man, though he domesticates plants and animals, is still himself in this respect a "wild" animal. The individual human being in choosing a mate is no doubt influenced by a great variety of motives, which the social scientist or even the practical man in human relations still understands only imperfectly. But no master human breeder, not even an understandable master principle or idea, decides who shall mate with whom. So far, the eugenicists have had little success with the positive side of their program. On the negative side, they have urged that the obviously unfit, the idiots, the feeble-minded, the insane, be prevented, even if necessary by compulsory sterilization, from having children. Some few American states have passed laws for such compulsory sterilization, but only a tiny handful of human beings, not enough to affect in the slightest the general course of human physical evolution, have undergone this treatment. Moreover, the eugenicists have aroused the opposition of many Christians who believe that it is wrong to tamper with God's human creations.

"Racism"

By far the commonest way out of the dilemma facing the Social Darwinists lay in the obvious notion that it is not so much among individual human beings that the struggle for existence really goes on, as it is among human beings organized in groups, as tribes, "races," or national states. The struggle that counts is not the struggle, say, among individual Englishmen to survive, but the struggle between the entity England—or Great Britain—and its rivals. The struggle for existence among men is now lifted from the biology of the individual to the politics of the group. And for the nineteenth century the group had to be the nation-state, perhaps kindred nation-states that could be organized for the struggle as one bloc of states, such as the "Nordic" or the "Latin," or perhaps at the very widest the Caucasian or white peoples in competition with the colored peoples, yellow, brown, or black. This struggle had an ultimate form: war. The group that defeated another group in war had thereby shown itself, *these* social Darwinists maintained, to be fitter than the beaten group. It had a right—indeed in evolutionary terms, which usually have moral overtones, a *duty*—to eliminate the beaten group, seize its lands, and people them with its own fitter human beings. The English imperialist Cecil Rhodes held that a world wholly and exclusively peopled with Anglo-Saxons would be the best possible world.

The idea of a Chosen People was of course not a new one in Darwin's time. But there is no doubt that Darwin's work, however little he may have meant it to be, was a most important element in the special forms that competition among organized states took in the latter half of the nineteenth century, and right on to our own day. Darwinism came too late to do more than prop up the philosophy of laissez-faire in economics. But Darwinism came at just the right time to intensify the struggle among organized human groups in international politics.

The particular groups or states that were to benefit as the elect of evolution in this special political sense varied with the aims, sympathies, and actual citizenship of the individual who was seeking to promote an ultimate evolutionary victory. Britain, Germany, the United States, the Latins, the Slavs, were all defended as the true elect of evolution. Most of the writers who preached this kind of political evolution proceeded from the assumption that at bottom the men of a given group had certain physical and therefore intellectual and spiritual traits in common, traits that gave them their superiority, and that could not possibly be transmitted to men of another group. Most of these writers, in short, were "racists" who believed that in fact *homo sapiens* had already evolved into what were really separate species. A black skin, for instance, was for them a sign of innate inferiority. The blacks would simply have to go the way of the dinosaurs, into extinction. Evolution had spoken.

There were indeed all sorts of half-way stations proposed by these writers. Few of them quite dared to preach what has in our own day been christened *genocide*—that is, the actual wholesale murder of those held to be of inferior race. We had to wait for Hitler for this. Most of them, though perhaps they held that in the long run the inferior peoples would in fact die out, were willing to see the inferiors duly subjected to the superiors, to have the less fit peoples serve as hewers of wood and drawers of water for their masters.

Indeed, some Social Darwinists applied their theories to a new form of caste organization, which came to be known as "élitism." The fit were not limited to any one race, but they were still marked out by the rigid hand of biological inheritance. They were the master group, the élite, the "supermen;" and they should everywhere band together against the dull average men, and dutifully exploit them. The German, Friedrich Nietzsche (1844–1900), who gave currency to the phrase "superman," was a subtle and difficult thinker, who disliked Darwin as a grubbing Englishman, and who was certainly no racist, no Social Darwinian. Still Nietzsche's influence among the half-educated who admired him in the late nineteenth and early twentieth centuries was to further racist and élitist causes.

Theories of the evolution-guided superiority of certain groups were not limited to Europe. In the United States, the innate, unchangeable superiority of whites to blacks was an article of faith among many whites in the North and almost universally in the South. This faith was greatly bolstered by Darwinian anthropologists and biologists. The notion that the degree of blondness, and other readily visible traits, such as long-headedness and tallness, measured suitableness for citizenship in a great democracy helped dictate the American immigration act of 1924, which encouraged immigrants from northwestern Europe, and almost barred those from southern and eastern Europe. The American, Madison Grant, in his *The Passing of the Great Race,* published in 1916, asserted that the Nordics—the tall, long-headed, light-haired peoples of northern Europe—were "a race of soldiers, sailors, adventurers and explorers, but above all, of rulers, organizers and aristocrats." Grant continued confidently and picturesquely:

Before leaving this interesting subject of the correlation of spiritual and moral traits with physical characters we may note that these influences are so deeply rooted in everyday consciousness that the modern novelist or playwright does not fail to make his hero a tall, blond, honest and somewhat stupid youth and his villain a small, dark and exceptionally intelligent individual of warped moral character.*

The title of Madison Grant's book, however, betrays an anxiety that is never far from the surface even in the most confident of these Social Darwinists. Grant feared that his "great race," gifted summit of evolution though it was, was paradoxically not going to survive. The lower races were breeding faster; democratic equalitarianism was lopping off the best and encouraging the worst. Somehow evolution was going wrong. Degeneration, not progress, was the mark of the times. Like those other "scientific" determinists, the Marxists, the Social Darwinists believed that men of good will had to set to work with pen and tongue to help along the predetermined process and keep it on the right track.

A New Historical Determinism

Darwinian science no more than Newtonian science really answered the great questions about good and evil, about the ends of human life, that men have been asking and

*Madison Grant, *The Passing of the Great Race,* 4th rev. ed. (New York, 1921), 229.

trying to answer ever since we have had historical records. Darwinian science, and indeed the physics, chemistry, and other sciences that flourished in the nineteenth century, recast for many the whole frame of reference in which these questions were asked. Make no mistake. Traditional Christianity, as well as many other transcendental and supernatural faiths, survived Darwin as they had survived Newton. Many men continued to believe that a God, or powers, not bound by the laws men discovered in laboratory experiments and in other systematic observations, guided their steps and gave meaning to their lives in this world and in the other world after death. But with the spread of popular education, especially in the West, great numbers came to believe that no such God or powers existed, that the material universe of science and common sense went on its regular ways in accordance with laws or uniformities which men might eventually understand completely, and which they were already beginning to understand quite well.

Darwin's work and that of many other scientists, in combination with the work of historians and philosophers and men of letters, worked a major change in the way men looked at their universe. It is an undue simplification to say that the Newtonian universe was static, the Darwinian dynamic, but the generalization is a good rough working approximation. The eighteenth-century Enlightenment was certainly feeling its way far more than its later Romantic critics admitted toward a view of the universe as developing, progressing, evolving. But, as one can see from the work of so typical a *philosophe* as Voltaire, the eighteenth century had no good explanation of the way change came about. This explanation Darwin provided for natural history, and the Romantic historians and their fellow workers in other fields provided it for human history.

Today we are still in the climate of opinion set for us in the late nineteenth century. We still believe, to a greater or less degree, in what has been labeled "historicism"—that is, in the doctrine that the course of history in the widest sense shows a regular, if bewildering, unfolding that has "determined" everything now existing and that will determine everything in the future. The wildest believer in this doctrine had to admit that since he could not in fact understand the whole process in the past, he could not wholly understand the present or wholly predict the future, could not "extrapolate" a curve he couldn't yet plot accurately. Still, the clue lay in the past, out of which the present has developed as the oak has developed from the acorn.

The Christian and Hebraic (and Moslem) calendar made the earth 6,000 years old, but the Darwinian calendar envisaged millions of years for organic life alone. It might seem, therefore, that historicism, especially when reinforced by the emphasis Darwin put on the immense reaches of time, would confirm conservative opposition to rapid change, or at least encourage in men a certain resignation in the face of the slow-moving process of evolution on this earth. And so it did for some men. Darwin's grandson, Sir Charles Galton Darwin, published in 1953 a book entitled *The Next Million Years.* He concluded that, since it is now held that it takes about a million years for a new species to evolve, it will be a million years before evolution produces a creature any better adapted than man; and that therefore for the next million years we shall have a history much like that of the last few thousand, with wars, revolutions, pestilence, the rise and fall of thousands of Egypts, Romes, Britains, and Americas.

But historicism in the nineteenth and twentieth centuries has had for most others a quite different consequence. It has served to convince impatient and hopeful men that they had really mastered the secrets of the universe, that they understood as their misguided predecessors had not just where the forces of history were leading. They could, then, help the process instead of hindering it, perhaps even hasten it! Marxism is the classic example of this faith in historical determinism, but nationalism, racism, and a host of others all drew nourishment from it. The extraordinary speeding-up of technological improvements lent strength to this view that moral and political improvement could also be speeded up. The doctrine of Evolution, then, though logically you can argue that it should have lessened the force of utopian faiths, did in fact increase them. People thought of the sureness of evolution and forgot its slowness.

II Literature and the Arts

The Victorian Age

It is risky to generalize about the literature and the art of the later nineteenth century. But these years do largely deserve to be called the "Victorian Age." This age has not the neatness of a single style we can find in ancient Athens or Renaissance Italy or Elizabethan England. We can evoke a Victorian drawing room, where Maud or Mélanie in ringlets and crinolines, surrounded by whatnots, bric-a-brac, plush hangings, and Landseer engravings, reads Tennyson, Longfellow, or Heine, or plays Liszt on the pianoforte. But so much went on outside that drawing room!—not only in the lives of peasants, workers, and businessmen, but even in art and letters. Maud or Mélanie might indeed have been reading Dickens or Balzac, but these writers hardly fitted the drawing room. Nor would Thoreau and Melville, Zola and Dostoevski. It is quite certain that the girls would not have been reading Marx.

For the safest thing we can say about the formal culture of the second half of the nineteenth century is that it had wide variety, that it was *eclectic*. We may also add that a great deal of this formal culture, especially its more "serious" work, was now, more clearly than ever before in western history, produced and cultivated by men and women in conscious revolt against the tastes of the politically and economically dominant class of their time—that is, the middle class. Unless Maud and Mélanie were very advanced young women indeed, they did not like much of what a hundred years later we single out as important in Victorian art and literature. If they were ordinary middle-class young women, they read sentimental novels now forgotten save by the social historian, and they lived in a culture to which the derogatory overtones that the word "Victorian" still often has for us apply well enough.

Their fathers and brothers, indeed, were often so concerned with industry and trade that they had no time for literature and the arts, which they tended to leave to their womenfolk. Or if they did have wider concerns, these concerns were rather with political and social problems, with the material betterment of their class, and—to be fair—with that of the working class too. But these middle-class men felt that the most that could be done for the workers was to raise their standard of living slowly under existing capitalist laissez-faire. They held that Church and State should join to restrain by law and by religion of an essentially puritanical cast the lack of self-restraint these middle-class men found too characteristic of their inferiors. For with these Victorians, laissez-faire "liberalism" was a strictly economic matter; in morals they believed firmly that organized institutions should interfere to restrain the populace from the drunkenness, idleness, and loose living they were supposedly inclined to. Libertarians in economics, the educated, middle-class Victorians were most certainly authoritarians in morals.

The Realistic Novel

In literature, the later nineteenth century was a great period for the novel. Here the accepted label for the novel of the time is "realism," in contrast with the Romanticism of the earlier part of the century. Yet as one usually finds in examining these sharp contrasts between the cultural attitudes of succeeding generations in the modern West, the realists are quite obviously children of the Romanticists. The Romantic of 1830, fleeing this ugly world for an idealized Middle Ages, when knighthood was in flower and there were no sooty factories, or writing of the idyllic Indian tribes of America, can indeed look very different from the realist of 1860, analyzing with fascination and disgust the men and women of the mill towns, the slums of the great cities, the unidyllic countryside of peasant labor. Yet both romantic and realist are individualists, and both are in firm revolt against middle-class respectability. Both deny the older "classical" ideals of aristocratic measure, of a "natural" law of decency and decorum. Both are obsessed with the analysis of the uniquely individual human soul. In our contemporary jargon, both "psychologize."

The Englishman Dickens (1812–1870), the Frenchman Balzac (1799–1850) and the Russian Dostoevski (1821–1881) all wrote in the period we label "Romantic." They reveled in exaggerations, poured themselves out freely in undisciplined torrents of words, achieved an effect of unreal intensity—Romantic traits, surely. Yet they were thoroughly immersed in the world of their time, and were in many ways realists. Dostoevski wrote about the Russia and the Russians he knew; but his was a dark Russia, and his Russians were tortured, possessed, unhappy seekers, no children of the Age of Reason. On the other hand, the leading French realist of the later nineteenth century, Flaubert (1821–1880), wrote one of his novels, *Salammbô*, about an ancient and, in spite of his great efforts at historical accuracy, not very real Carthage. And in his masterpiece, *Madame Bovary*, which analyzes the romantic longings of a small-town doctor's wife, Flaubert betrayed a most ambivalent feeling toward his heroine. Indeed, he once said, "I am Madame Bovary." Flaubert hated the bourgeois world he wrote about quite as much as did the escapist writers of an earlier generation.

We may perhaps, along with certain modern critics, call these middle and late nineteenth-century writers "romantic realists." These writers did eschew the remote, the Gothic, the fantastic, and chose as a rule subjects close to their own time and place. But there were also more conventional—or at least more quiet—realists. We may take as representative of these last the Englishman Trollope and the Russian Turgenev. Trollope (1815–1882) wrote dozens of novels about Victorian clergymen and politicians and country gentlemen, carefully observing the English decencies, never raising his voice or his style, but imparting understanding, sympathy, and a suitable, modest irony. Turgenev (1818–1883) wrote about his fellows with classic restraint, skirting delicately the depths of the Slavic soul (see Chapter 14). Or we may take William Dean Howells (1837–1920), who in the *Rise of Silas Lapham* and other novels sought to apply realism to the American scene. But significantly, he is nowadays labeled as a follower of the "genteel tradition."

The Naturalistic Novel: Zola

For as the twentieth century drew near the realists were confronted with a rebel generation that found them not "realistic" enough. This school rose first in France, where it took for itself the name "naturalists." The leader of the naturalists, Emile Zola (1840–1902), shows clearly the influence of the scientific revolution inspired by the work of Darwin. For Zola was not content with the realist's aim to reflect the life around him with simple accuracy; he sought to arrive at laws of human development, much as the biologist seeks for laws of organic development.

The novel was to Zola an instrument of scientific generalization. He would do for society, for men in their relations with other men, what Darwin had done for natural history. He would show what men are like, of course, but he would also show how they came to be what they are, and even what they were going to be. He called his great series of novels about a family under the Second Empire, the Rougon-Macquart, the "natural history" of a family.

Zola's work points up one of the tendencies not only of the late nineteenth-century novel, in those days the spearhead of literature, but of other forms of literature as well. The literature of the time, and to a great extent of the twentieth century too, is overwhelmingly a literature of discontent, of protest against things-as-they-are, a "problem" literature. Now it is quite true that from the ancient Greek philosophers and the Hebrew prophets on, many great thinkers have held that their times were peculiarly out of joint. They had to protest against the abuses of their age, had to stir their fellows into bettering their ways. But there are certainly periods when the intellectuals are *relatively* conformist, *relatively* well disposed to the existing government and society—the Augustan Age in Rome, the Elizabethan Age, and the Age of Louis XIV, for example. And there are ages when the intellectuals, even though they are bitterly against things-as-they-are, write with hope and confidence of what is to come—as in the eighteenth-century Enlightenment. We have already noted that the Romantic movement had its pessimistic side. With the second half of the nineteenth century there set in a strain of pessimism—at least among many leading writers—that has continued to this day. It is by no means the only strain in modern western literature, and it is by no means a strain of unrelieved pessimism. Writers on the Left, notably the socialists, are obliged by their creed to hold that somehow mankind will win through to a better society.

The Literature of Pessimism and Protest

The pessimists reacted against the eighteenth-century doctrine of the natural goodness of man. Certainly "nature" and "natural" as they figure in the work of a Zola carry very different connotations from these words as the eighteenth, and even the early nineteenth, centuries used them. Nature by the late nineteenth century apparently made most men greedy, selfish, combative, not very bright, and extremely addicted to a variety of irregular sexual relations which brought out to the full their other bad traits. Sometimes, as with the English novelist Thomas Hardy, (1840–1928), this pessimism is built up from a series of incidents in private lives into a grand cosmic irony not without its consoling side. But for the most part, these writers were concerned directly with the cruelties, stupidities, the downright insanities of ordinary people.

In France, De Maupassant (1850–1893), a master of the short story, wrote sparely and simply, after the manner of his master Flaubert, about the tragedies and comedies of ordinary life; but the tragedies, or at least the ironies, prevail. In Russia, Chekhov (1860–1904), a medical man by training, used the prose drama and the short story to show how life harasses us all. Ibsen (1828–1906) in Norway, Brieux (1858–1932) in France, and George Bernard Shaw (1856–1950) in England all helped to develop the characteristically late-nineteenth-century form of the drama, the "problem play." The problem was sometimes one of wide moral and political concern, as in Ibsen's *Enemy of the People* or Shaw's *Man and Superman,* but it was very often concerned mainly with the stupid tangles of men's private, and in particular their sex, lives. Ibsen shocked his contemporaries in his *Doll's House* by having his heroine rebel against the "doll-house" atmosphere that her husband had created for her. His *Ghosts* scandalized his contemporaries by bringing to the stage the problem of syphilis.

The problem play, the problem novel, the problem short story spread through all the literatures of the West. They spread with the usual speed to the United States, where by the end of the nineteenth century the "genteel tradition" was already scorned by the bright young men. The novelists Stephen Crane (1871–1900) and Theodore Dreiser (1871–1945) were bringing out the harsh realities of war, business, and love. It took a while for the extremes of "naturalism" to gain the United States, and it was not until our own day, and then of all places in the South of magnolia and roses, that an Erskine Caldwell and others really plumbed the depths of human perversities behind the Anglo-Saxon four-letter words they used so freely.

Most of this realistic or naturalistic writing, even when it is by no means of Marxist inspiration, is hostile to the middle classes. The bourgeois is no longer just the Philistine whom the Romantic disliked, the puritanical conformist, the stuffy enemy of sweetness and light. He is still that, but he is also the rapacious titan of industry, the jingoistic nationalist, the authoritarian browbeater of his children, the tasteless addict of "conspicuous consumption" (a phrase of the American economist, Thorstein Veblen), the hypocritical practitioner of a "double standard" of sexual morality, and worse. Flaubert, who began so much, may be said to have begun this with his unfinished *Bouvard et Pécuchet*, in which he makes his two bourgeois "heroes" run the gamut of human futility, failing ludicrously in their effort to educate themselves. In England, Samuel Butler (1835–1902) in *The Way of All Flesh* set the pattern for the novel, since followed freely, in which the writer-son blames all on the tyrannical male parent. Shaw found a simple phrase to sum up what was wrong—"middle class morality." Ibsen's *Enemy of the People* is ironically named; the real enemy of the people is the people themselves, not the misunderstood leader who would bring them better things.

Even where the writers are not embittered, even where their main concern is to balance good and evil as, one suspects, they are balanced in real life, the middle class does not often come out well. English novelists like H. G. Wells, Galsworthy, and Arnold Bennett, French novelists like Anatole France, Spanish novelists like Pio Baroja, and most writers of tsarist Russia find something wrong with the middle classes. An epitome, a bit more kindly than usual in Europe, of this attack on the middle classes is afforded by an American, who wrote in the 1920's, chronologically rather later than the period with which we are

here concerned, but quite in its "style." Sinclair Lewis' *Main Street* and *Babbitt* are realistic rather than naturalistic novels, and George Babbitt is almost a hero without ironic quotation marks. Still, Babbitt came to sum up for thousands of American intellectuals what was wrong with a naive materialistic civilization. The novels of Sinclair Lewis sold by the hundred thousands, so that it is clear that

Bernard Shaw, by Max Beerbohm. Shaw's Old Self says to the Young Self: "Strange! You strike me as frivolous, irreligious, and pert; full of ludicrous faith in mankind and in the efficacy of political propaganda; squalidly needy in circumstances, and abominably ill dressed. . . . And I used to think you quite perfect."

"George Babbitt" himself in real life, and certainly his wife and his children, must have relished, or at least read, these satires on his way of life. Indeed, since many of the writers we have been dealing with were able to sell their works in a mass market, one is forced to conclude that a good portion of the middle classes in the West were in revolt against their own shortcomings.

Not all that was written between 1850 and the outbreak of war in 1914 was a literature of scorn or protest. The daughters of the Maud or Mélanie with whom we began could about 1900 read the standard conventional fare, historical novels, novels of escape, novels of true love. They could even find in writers like Kipling men who, if not exactly convinced that this was the best of possible worlds, were at least convinced that the English middle and upper classes were the least bad of the lot. They could, in short, read for pleasure and edification and go on with the serious business of life.

Poetry

Few writers tried to make poetry "naturalistic" in Zola's sense. Nor, on the other hand, was the late nineteenth century a period in which the epic or the grand philosophical poem, like Wordsworth's *Prelude*, flourished. Poets did attempt the drama in verse, but these dramas remained poetry to be read in the study, not plays for the boards. Tennyson, who can stand very well for the more conventional Victorian poets, tried the epic in his *Idyls of the King*, based on the legends about King Arthur's court, and he tried the philosophical poem, such as *In Memoriam*, and several "closet" dramas. But he perhaps succeeded best in his shorter lyrics.

In England Tennyson, in America Longfellow and his New England colleagues, in France Victor Hugo, wrote the staple poetry the late nineteenth century liked and read a great deal. These poets deserve the tag, "household words." In form, their work differs little from the norms set by the earlier Romantic movement, and their subjects are love, death, nature, patriotism, faith, doubt, and longing, the eternal lyric repertory. And they sometimes came down into the arena to deal with politics, as in Whittier's anti-slavery poems, and in James Russell Lowell's "Biglow Papers," poems in Yankee dialect on the crisis of the Civil War. The spiritual crisis brought on by loss of Christian faith in a scientific age is evident in many poems of Matthew Arnold and Arthur Hugh Clough, as well as Tennyson. Even the horrors of the industrial revolution are apparent in Thomas Hood's "Song of the Shirt":

> With fingers weary and worn,
>   With eyelids heavy and red,
> A woman sat in unwomanly rags,
>   Plying her needle and thread —
>   Stitch! stitch! stitch!
> In poverty, hunger, and dirt,
>   And still with the voice of dolorous pitch
> She sang the 'Song of the Shirt!'*

The American poet Walt Whitman too wrote poetry exalting American democracy and the common man. He wrote in what is sometimes called "free verse," but he was no radical innovator of the *avant garde*, and the common man he celebrates has no trouble understanding his poetry.

Yet in these very same years poetry went far along the road that brought it to our times, when the serious poet usually writes difficult, private, metaphysical, psychological, or at the very least, weighty experimental verse for a handful of initiates. Poetry for the Romanticist was indeed the reflection of his own inner world, but he hoped it would not prove by any means a private world. He wanted to be read, perhaps even by the Philistines, as indeed he was. In the second half of the nineteenth century, the French Parnassians deliberately sought the seclusion of perfect form, of polished verse fit for but few, of "art for art's sake." Still later, with Symbolists like Mallarmé, they went on to very difficult verse indeed, in which the meaning had to be wrung with effort from symbols nested one within another, in which the harmonies, like those of

---

*Thomas Hood, *Poetical Works*, Epes Sargent, ed. (Boston, 1855), 147.

modern music, are by no means at once apparent to the untrained listener. Significantly, when twentieth-century poets went back for precedents to their literary "fathers" or teachers, they did not go to Tennyson, Hugo, Longfellow, or Kipling, but to late Victorian poets hardly known to their contemporaries, like the English Gerard Manley Hopkins and the American Emily Dickinson. Here is a passage from Hopkins:

> Across my foundering deck shone
> A beacon, an eternal beam. | Flesh fade,
>   and mortal trash
> Fall to the residuary worm; | world's wild-
>   fire, leave but ash:
>   In a flash, at a trumpet crash,
> I am all at once what Christ is, | since he
>   was what I am, and

>   This Jack, joke, poor potsherd, | patch,
>   matchwood, immortal diamond,
>   Is immortal diamond.*

Yet the historian must not be so interested in the origins of what becomes good literature for the few as to forget what the many read. Even as late as the early twentieth century, it was not Hopkins, not Mallarmé, not Emily Dickinson who were recited at parties, on the stage, or in formal ceremonials all over the West—it was still Hugo, Heine, Longfellow, or newer poets like A. E. Housman or even Robert Service and Edgar Guest.

Painting

In Victorian literature, then, there was a popular and conventional, but not vulgar, level of writing represented by men like Hugo and Tennyson. In painting, there was a similar level, represented by artists whose work now fills many galleries—the Fontainebleau school in France; Watts, Burne-Jones, and Rossetti in England; George Inness, and later Winslow Homer and John Singer Sargent in the United States; animal painters like Rosa Bonheur ("The Horse Fair") and Sir Edwin Landseer ("The Stag"); and many, many others throughout the West. The *avant garde*, the advanced innovators in art, the rebels, gave the paintings of these men the derogatory label "academic." Actually, the academic painters were technically very skillful, for they had the advantage of the long tradition of western painting since the Renaissance. They could mirror man and nature faithfully, in a sense more faithfully than their great rival for the patronage of the many, the camera. They were perhaps realists, but they were not naturalists in Zola's sense. They rather avoided the shambles of the industrial revolution, and to their *avant garde* opponents they seemed too much concerned with the pretty in nature and with the aristocratic or striking in portraiture.

The first great innovators in later nineteenth-century painting were the French im-

Cabaret scene by Georges Seurat, who originated pointillism, an extreme development of impressionism characterized by a technique of applying colors in tiny dots according to a rigidly systematic plan.

*Gerald Manley Hopkins, *Poems,* 3rd ed. (New York, 1948), 112.

"The Starry Night," a post-impressionist painting by Vincent van Gogh, 1889.

pressionists. This school once had to content itself with separate salons, for the academics would have none of it. But it is now safely enshrined as "classic." The impressionists, too, show one of the cross-fertilizations between science and art, but in a rather subtler way than does the naturalist movement in fiction. One of the things science does is to show us that the "real" world is not what the hasty eye finds, that things are not what they seem. The impressionists were not content with the camera eye of the academics. Light, they learned from the physicists, was not a simple thing, but a complex that the eye puts together from the prismatic reflections of nature. So they proposed to break up light into its constituent colors and then allow the viewer's eye to reassemble them. They painted landscapes for the most part, and they built up their trees and flowers and buildings and skies from thousands of little dabs of color, so that the result, when seen from a few feet away, is hardly more than a formless mesh of color, but seen

from an adequate distance does indeed take the form of a landscape, a landscape flooded in light.

The great master of the impressionist school, Claude Monet (1840–1926) was a prolific painter, whose work is well represented in public museums. Monet repeatedly painted the same subjects, notably Rouen Cathedral and the lily pond in his own garden, to show how they varied in appearance at different times of day and under changing conditions of light. Light interested many other painters, like Turner in England, who specialized in marine pictures and the Anglicized American, Whistler, who did misty scenes in London and, incidentally, was very ashamed of the fact that he had been born in Lowell, Massachusetts.

Even with the Frenchman Manet (1832–1883), who began as a realist and retained a certain harshness associated with the realistic temperament, we find another great artist breaking with the "realism" of the camera.

Manet's famous "Death of Maximilian" completely destroys the Renaissance idea of perspective, placing the firing squad almost on top of its victim, and abandons "fact" by making the executioners not Mexican soldiers (which they were) but French Zouaves. Manet uses "real" objects for his own purposes, as occasions for effects of color and composition which are *his*. These effects are, for the purposes of the artist, to be preferred as truer to the realities of the universe and nature as men *ought* to see them than is all that seems to the layman's eye, the eye of vulgar common sense, to be real, natural. To put it another way: these apparently distorted effects are truer, more real, than what the ordinary man, whose vision is science-spoiled, camera-spoiled, schoolmarm-spoiled, sees as "real" or "natural." Some such feeling that the artist sees more and more profoundly than any mechanical device, or than any person with just conventional, or just "scientific," or just "rationalistic" training is common to modern art in almost all its forms. In our twentieth century, this revolt from "representational" painting has gone on to pure "abstract" painting, an art extremely hard on the traditional portrait, for we still can hardly help seeing others somewhat as we see ourselves in a mirror.

Some of the best work of the middle of the century was done in drawing and engraving, where new methods of reproduction made prints available to all. Here again the French are at their best, severe moralists in the Voltairean tradition, as in the caricatures of Daumier (see illustrations on pp. 436 and 587) and Forain.

Toward the end of the century the *avant garde* turned to another technique, somewhat more difficult than impressionism to describe. The great figure here is another Frenchman, Cézanne (1839–1906). This painter, too, wanted to go beyond the smooth techniques of the academics, but he found impressionism too fuzzy, too obsessed with light. The impressionists had to him lost the sense of shape, lost the three dimensions of the real world

A landscape by Cézanne, "La Montagne Sainte Victoire."

—at least, of the "real" world of human binocular vision. He proposed to put them back, not with the classic, flowing perspective inherited by the academics from the Italians, but with blocks, chunks of color blended into a result that is after all realistic. From Cézanne there stemmed in a sense much of twentieth-century painting. Cubism, which is the exaggeration of Cézanne's insistence on hard three-dimensionality, is most obviously in his debt, but so too are Abstractionism and even Surrealism. Cézanne's work and that of two of his contemporaries, the Dutchman Van Gogh and the Frenchman Gauguin, were once thought wild, private, and unprofitably experimental. But they are now popular in museums and in countless inexpensive reproductions. Neither the artist nor the sociologist understands the process by which a once outrageous innovation becomes an established classic well enough to be sure whether a given contemporary work will or will not survive. Indeed, the purchase of *contemporary* art for private or public collections remains one of the most speculative of human ventures. The odds are heavily against the investor. All art connoisseurship, including that of rare books, is in terms of economics about as risky a business as there is, though as usual in speculation in our culture, the successful connoisseur and collector wins great prizes.

The Other Arts

The nineteenth century was not a great period for sculpture. An age that had mastered the industrial arts so well produced monumental statues aplenty. The most famous for Americans is the Statue of Liberty in New York harbor, the work of the French sculptor Bartholdi, a gift from the Third French Republic to the American Republic. But the statues of statesmen and warriors that adorn public places everywhere in the West are so conventionally realistic that we hardly accept them as human beings. Sculpture in the large at least would appear to be an aristocratic art, designed for the palace and the formal garden. Its nineteenth-century civic use seems at its best—or least bad—in Paris, in the decoration of the great Arc de Triomphe, a delayed memorial to the Grand Army of Napoleon I, and in the new Opéra and many other buildings. Toward the end of the century, Frenchmen like Rodin and Maillol began a break with the formal statuary of their time, simplifying, strengthening and in a sense exaggerating the contours of their men and women, treating their subjects with less academic convention and more power. It should be noted that inexpensive, small-scale copies of the great sculpture of antiquity and the Renaissance now became common, and many a Victorian drawing room in Europe and in Europe overseas boasted a plaster Venus or a bronze Mercury. Museums in various parts of the world could all afford large plaster casts. Some direct acquaintance with the great artistic achievements of the past was now available to a very wide general public.

Indeed the nineteenth century knew almost too much of the past of the arts and was too eclectic and derivative in its tastes. Certainly this eclecticism weighed heavily on the architect. Somewhere in the West in these years someone built something in almost every style that had ever been used. Western men built Chinese pagodas, Egyptian pyramids, Greek temples, and, especially in America, Gothic universities. In the United States buildings were typed for style. Banks, those solid institutions, went back to Greece and Rome, at least for their fronts; churches and universities relied on Gothic; public buildings went in for the Renaissance, duly modified by the reigning taste in the Paris École des Beaux-Arts (School of Fine Arts); private citizens went in for anything that pleased them for their own houses, modified perhaps a bit by the traditions of their region. Individual architects worked on a historic style that they adapted in their own way. Thus the American Richardson revived the Romanesque, the early medieval predecessor of Gothic, with its round arches and its solidarity, achieving certainly a style of his own.

Two broad styles may be found in the confusion of nineteenth-century architecture. One style, for public buildings, was basically Renaissance, with pediments, balconies, sometimes with domes, and with friezes and other decorations. This style varies somewhat from nation to nation. French public buildings, under the influence of the Beaux-Arts, looked at least vaguely like a chateau in Touraine; German buildings kept a touch of the huddled Middle Ages; and British buildings, much imitated in Boston, New York and Philadelphia, were simpler, more in the manner of Palladio (see above, p. 103). The other style, for private homes, was represented in Europe by the "villa," and in America by the residence, often a "mansion," that the successful businessman built for himself on Elm Street. In the United States this style was at its most flaunting in the mansions of the 1870's, the "era of General Grant." These were big houses, for families were large, domestic servants were plentiful and cheap, and building costs were relatively low. They ran to high ceilings, for the bourgeois wanted nothing to remind him of the low rooms of his past. Today they look too tall for their width, and their lines seem much too broken by little towers, porches, scrollwork, all sorts of decorative devices. But they had the latest comforts, if they were in a town large enough — gas light, bathtub and water closet, and central heating, though western Europeans came rather slowly to this last innovation.

In architecture, as in painting and sculpture, true innovation began toward the end of the century. In structural steel, men now had a way

Fifth Avenue, looking north from 65th Street, 1898.

The Auditorium Hotel and Theater in Chicago, designed by the pioneering architect, Louis Sullivan.

of emancipating themselves from the limitations that had so taxed the Gothic builders; they could now go almost as high as they pleased. They began to do so in the United States, where the first "skyscraper," the Home Insurance Building in Chicago, was put up in 1885. Although some later skyscrapers ended up in Gothic towers, abundantly decorated, the general tendency imposed by the materials was toward simplicity of line. This taste for simplicity began to spread, and with the twentieth century the way was open for modern "functional" architecture. Structural steel should remind us that some of the most satisfying work of the late nineteenth century was not primarily meant for beauty, but very often achieved it. The great bridges of the time, for example, the Firth of Forth Bridge in Scotland, and Brooklyn Bridge, are still handsome as well as impressive and useful.

In the minor arts of furniture, household decoration, and clothing, the Victorian Age seems to us now most characteristic and most ugly. Although it is hard to believe that men will ever collect "antiques" of the 1870's as

they now collect the work of earlier periods, horsehair sofas and marbletopped tables are nowadays coming into the trade in antiques. So, we return to the Victorian drawing room with which we began. It was an incredibly heavy and incredibly dark room, for the height of the windows was canceled by the dark carpets, upholstery, and hangings, and by the mahogany or walnut furniture. And it was cluttered with what were known as *objets d'art*. Our taste in interior decoration today is different from that of the Victorians in part because in our society domestic labor is scarce and expensive; the mere job of dusting the bric-a-brac of a nineteenth-century house would be too much for the modern housewife.

Yet we must as always note that qualifying "in part." Simplification of interior décor was probably helped along, but not initiated or simply "caused," by scarcity and high cost of domestic labor. Even at levels of high art as well as at those of taste and fashion, human beings — modern western human beings at least — tend to rebel against the ways of a preceding generation. Reaction against Victorian decorative arts, a movement for simplification, starts in England with William Morris (1834–1896) in full Victorian times, and is in full swing by the 1890's with Voysey and Mackintosh in England, *art nouveau* France, and the Secession in Austria. Already, the "functional" chair is in sight.

Music

One great art remains to be discussed—music. Now though in music there is no such obvious common-sense basis in "Nature" as the camera eye gives the representational arts, it is not misleading to take the established "classical" eighteenth-century tonality and forms, say from Bach through Haydn and much of Mozart, as a kind of norm or "law" which nineteenth-century composers revolted against, sought to go beyond.

Early in the century at least, this revolt deserves the old label "romantic". The composer sought to move his hearers, to tears, to rapture, to ecstasy, by startling novelties, by unique and overpowering orchestra sonorities, by "programme music" in which the sounds were deliberately tied to other parts of human experience—i.e., suggested bird songs, waterfalls, wind in the pines, a thunderstorm. The old forms—sonata, symphony, concerto—were by no means abandoned; they were, rather, exceeded, burst.

By the late nineteenth century itself, the supreme achievement in music seemed clearly to be Richard Wagner's (1813–1883). After the usual struggle of the innovating artist to get a hearing, Wagner by the 1870's had become the heir of Beethoven. He set out to make opera the supreme synthesis of the arts, with drama, music, scenery all fused in one great transcendence of this dull world of ordinary living. He gave up the routine recitative—the relatively undramatic passages "explaining" the action—interlarded with arias in which the singer or singers dropped what action there had been and advanced boldly to the front of the stage to launch into song. He sought rather to combine music and action in a realistic and dramatic whole. His character-

istic device was the *Leitmotiv*, a definite and recognizable melodic theme associated with a given character or symbolizing an element in the drama. These themes he wove together for both voices and orchestra into a continuous flow of music. He chose epic subjects: the four operas of the *Ring of the Nibelungen*, in which he drew on the Teutonic myths, by no means without thought for Teutonic greatness; *Parsifal*, on the theme of the Holy Grail; *Tristan and Isolde*, a drama of fated love and death taken from the Arthurian legends. Wagner's operas call for robust voices, which in turn call for barrelchested tenors and huge sopranos ill-suited to concepts of romantic love or indeed of heroism. In our time Wagner's popularity has suffered because of his Victorian heaviness, his inordinate lengths, and the great noise he makes. Nietzsche once implied aptly that, in contrast with Bizet's "Carmen", Wagner's music *sweats*. Moreover, he has suffered—the musical purist often thinks he has suffered unjustly—from the associations of his life and work with German nationalism, racism, even Nazism.

Yet Wagner deserves his fame as a composer. His break with the norms of the classical past, his orchestration, his chromaticism, his desperate efforts to *transcend*, to express the inexpressible, or at least the extraordinary, are a landmark in the road that leads from the *Well-Tempered Clavichord* to our contemporary atonality. Even the Frenchman Debussy (1862–1918), who found Wagner too noisy, too unbridled, too *German*, and who sought to capture in his music a French sense of quiet measure, followed Wagner in this revolt against classical tonality.

Again, as in poetry, nineteenth-century music had its popular successes, free from *avant garde* difficulties. "Popular" music in most of the West was tuneful, and inclined to nostalgia, not unpleasant tears, conventional sentiment; here the work of the American Stephen Foster (1826–1864) is a superior sample indeed. Light music flourished, in the tuneful operettas of Offenbach, like *La Belle Hélène*, based on the legend of Helen of Troy, in the waltzes of Johann Strauss and Waldteufel, and for Anglo-Saxons in the gently, never bitterly or agonizedly, satirical operas of Gilbert and Sullivan.

The Arts in Review

We shall make three broad generalizations about the arts (in their widest sense, to include literature) in the nineteenth century, ever mindful of the difficulties of the undertaking, especially for historians, who nowadays are rarely trained in the arts. Nor shall we forget that the old Latin tag, *De gustibus non est disputandum* (tastes are not to be disputed) ought really to go; there is no use disputing *except* about tastes.

First, there is, as we have already noted, an amazing range and variety in nineteenth-century arts. This is a century that did not even build its public buildings in a single style. The patron—better yet in this century of the great market, the customer—could pick from the styles of centuries. Popular magazines, inexpensive reprints of older books, serializations of new works, the beginnings, especially in the United States, of circulating libraries, inexpensive (as well as expensive) reproductions of works of art, in short, the new technical and economic resources of a society on its way to democratic equalities, meant that much was available in all the arts. The reader could shift from Dickens or Tennyson to Homer or Chaucer, go frankly common with "penny dreadfuls" or "dime novels," or turn to the difficulties of innovators like Mallarmé, or Browning, held in those days to be a difficult poet. No doubt there were individuals with tastes so broad, or so undiscriminating, as to dip into all these. There were of course standards—conventional, classical, and "academic" —of good and bad in the arts, and most of these standards were dinned in firmly in the current "classical" or "liberal" education. The nineteenth-century college student, unlike the twentieth-century one, was in his formal education carefully shielded from the contemporary, the *avant garde*, in the arts.

Second, by the end of the nineteenth century there is a very clear rift, the origins of which go back several centuries, between the tastes of the few and those of the many, or in current American terms, between the tastes of the "highbrows," or "longhairs," or intellectuals, and the tastes of the rest of the people. Now these terms must not be taken to indicate the existence of two totally different groups, two circles that never intersect. Nevertheless, it is clear that from the point of view of the sociologist of knowledge, there had come to be by the end of the nineteenth century what some have called the "alienation of the intellectuals"; to this theme we shall have to return, for it must be one of the concerns of anyone who deals with contemporary western culture.

Third, there is accentuated in the nineteenth century a tendency in a sense constant in western art: the revolt of one cultural generation against the ways of its parent generation. Again, we are not here dealing with absolutes. The rebels of the "naughty 'nineties," the members of the "lost generation" of the 'twenties

Daumier caricature: How the public feels after listening to the music of the future by Wagner.

of our own century did not think and feel in ways totally alien to the ways of their parents. Moreover, the phenomenon we are here discussing is almost wholly limited to the "highbrows," to high art, and is, save at the level of trivial changes of fashion, hardly yet noticeable in popular art. No doubt the great innovators do eventually, if they are great enough, get translated, adapted, even accepted, by a wider public. Still, the gap remains. The few are indeed, as we have just noted, innovators. Like Gerard Manley Hopkins, or Monet, Manet, or Cézanne, or Wagner or Debussy, they produce something new, strange, something that widens, changes, the possibilities of human experience. They are, in short, *avant garde*—in popular language, "moderns." For those who come to share their widened experiences, they are successful innovators, men and women who add to the great cumulative culture of mankind quite as clearly as do the great scientists and inventors; for those who do not share their experiences, they are usually wild men, beatniks, rebels against the eternal verities, the eternal beauties, morally and politically undesirables to boot, and what they are trying to do can't and shouldn't be done. We shall come again to this point in a final chapter, for the problem of "modern" art is one of the many we have inherited from the nineteenth century. It remains unsolved, and in a democracy, a serious problem.

III   Philosophy

Idealism and Realism

The art and literature of the later nineteenth century furnish samples of almost the full range of human attitudes toward the world. The formal philosophy and the less formal view of life taken by ordinary educated people varied quite as widely, and we can find as many different schools in metaphysics and ethics as we can find in literature and art. The philosophical school of idealism was born in its modern form in the Germany of Kant and Hegel (see Chapters 9 and 11). In the later nineteenth century it continued to thrive in the land of its birth; it made converts in the Oxford School of T. H. Green, Bradley, and Bosanquet, and in the American philosopher, Josiah Royce; and it even penetrated into the Latin countries. The philosophical opposite of idealism, now christened "realism," was at least as widespread. Modern realism, though as a philosophy it attempted to answer questions the scientist does not try to answer *in so far as he is a scientist*, had its roots in the same soil as modern science and the scientific rationalism of the eighteenth-century *philosophes*, and was a product of the Enlightenment.

The American philosopher, William James (1842–1910), found two terms to sum up this polar antithesis of idealism and realism that runs through western philosophical tradition. Men are, wrote James, by disposition either "tender-minded" or "tough-minded." They are either tough-mindedly convinced that the world of sense-experience is the *real* world or tender-mindedly convinced that the world of sense-experience is somehow an illusion, or at any rate an imperfect, changing, and therefore unreal copy, if not a kind of caricature, of the *real* world which is in our minds—imperfectly—and perfectly in God's mind.

One might conclude that, since the later nineteenth century was a period of great material progress, deeply concerned with this world of the senses, then on the whole the "tough-minded" would prevail over the "tender-minded." Yet this was by no means true in formal philosophy, where the tender-minded were quite numerous and articulate. Perhaps the ordinary unreflective man, at least in our western civilization, leans toward the tough-minded side, if only because common sense urges upon him the presence of the world of sense-experience, the world of "matter." But there are no reliable statistics on this point, and to the extent that Christianity forms an inescapable underpinning for the world-view of western men, not even tough common sense can altogether dispose of the world of the tender-minded, of concepts like "value-judgments," "soul," "spirit," "ideal," and "other world."

Dynamism and the Cult of the Will

Certain common denominators, however, underlay the formal philosophical thought of the later nineteenth century. Here, too, Darwinism left its mark. The thought of the period had a dynamic historical and evolutionary cast that not even the tender-minded could avoid. The idealist, following Hegel, believed that above the whirl and change of this world of the senses there was an unchanging, perfect world of the Absolute. But he also believed that this imperfect world was being slowly drawn toward that other world, developing by ways he could only incompletely understand, but developing, growing, evolving. On the other hand, the nineteenth-century realist no longer held that his reason could give him a neat, static, mathematical formula for the good life; he too thought that everything grows, that even what is made according to human plans must take account of nature's mysterious ways of growth.

A second and related note in the thought of the period is an emphasis on will, often capitalized into Will, on doing, on the life-force that makes the "struggle for existence." The word appears everywhere, even as a title— Schopenhauer's *World as Will and Idea,* Nietzsche's *Will to Power,* William James' *Will to Believe.* It appears but slightly disguised in the French philosopher Henri Bergson's "creative evolution" and "élan vital" and in Bernard Shaw's "life-force." It appears as an insistence that knowing is not a passive registering, but a creative *doing,* in the work of

the Italian Benedetto Croce. It lies behind the use of the word "myth" by the French anarcho-syndicalist, Georges Sorel, and the German Hans Vaihinger's phrase, the "philosophy of the as-if." For both these latter thinkers, the great ideas, the great abstractions of Right and Wrong, are not mere attempts of the mind to understand the world; indeed they are quite false if taken as analytically descriptive of this world. But they are, rather, the guides our desires, our wills, set up for our action. They are fictions, myths, "as-if," but all the more *real* for being such. The Italian idealist philosopher Croce summarized: true knowing is doing, making, *changing.*

The pragmatism of William James, somewhat unfairly described by its critics as the philosophy that nothing succeeds like success, is clearly one of these philosophies of the will. To James, himself "tough-minded," reality is no Absolute as in the idealist tradition; indeed, reality is nothing fixed and certain. Reality is what works for us human beings; truth is what we want to believe. James thought he had saved himself from the obvious danger of this line of thought—that is, making reality and truth purely subjective, purely a matter of the individual's judgment or faith— by granting that not everything we want is practical, that not all our desires "work." If my will to believe tells me I can make a broad jump of three hundred feet, experience, the "pragmatic" test, will prove that I cannot. But to many of James' critics, he had by no means saved himself from subjectivism. Pragmatism remained to these critics a doctrine dangerously erosive of traditional values, leading either to an exaltation of mere vulgar success, or to a silly belief in believing for the sake of believing ("fideism").

The Revolt against Reason

The cult of the will brings us to a major current in the broad stream of later nineteenth-century thought, to the center of the nineteenth-century attack on the thought of the eighteenth, an attack never universal, and more evident among the creative writers, artists, intellectuals, than among ordinary educated men and women. This was an intensification of the revolt against "reason" already initiated by the Romantics earlier in the century; it may be called "anti-intellectualism," "irrationalism," or, more exactly, "anti-rationalism." Even this last term is somewhat misleading, for it stresses negation, whereas the attitude it describes is also an affirmation. There seems, however, to be no better term for the attitude than anti-rationalism.

One further caution. This anti-rationalism is one of the "roots" of contemporary totalitarianism, and especially of fascist and Nazi totalitarianism (see Chapter 19). But it is by no means a simple synonym for totalitarianism. It is a much broader and more inclusive term. It is quite possible to have been influenced by anti-rational currents and remain a good, if not altogether orthodox, democrat and individualist. It is quite possible to be a Marxist totalitarian and reject a great deal, especially in its psychological core, of modern anti-rationalism. Indeed, the conventional Marxist is in an important sense a naive, almost an eighteenth-century, rationalist. Get the economy to work perfectly, he says, and men will behave themselves perfectly.

The basic position of anti-rationalism, and one for which it is heavily indebted to the Romantic movement, is a rejection of the eighteenth-century Enlightenment's belief that the ordinary human being is naturally reasonable. To the extent that it rejects the Enlightenment, anti-rationalism is indeed a negation, as the "anti" implies. But it has its positive side—the belief that if men can accept their true nature as human beings they can lead richer lives than any rationalist ever planned for them; but what they must accept is the radical limitation of their thinking mind, or brain, to which so much of their experience never penetrates.

The Chastened Rationalists

Broadly speaking, there are two kinds of anti-rationalism, which shade into one another:

the moderate and the extreme. Moderate anti-rationalism at bottom is trying to salvage as much as possible of the eighteenth-century belief in human rationality. Such on the whole is the attitude of modern psychology from Freud (see Chapter 24) and William James on. This psychology seeks to aid human reason by pointing out the difficulties under which it must work. Reason, these thinkers maintain, is limited by men's instincts or "drives," by their biological inheritance of animality, so much emphasized by the evolutionists, and by their sociological inheritance of custom and tradition so much emphasized by historians and by the school of Edmund Burke (see Chapter 11).

To use a metaphor from John Locke, which he in turn derived from the slogan of the Cambridge Platonists, "the mind of man is the light of God," moderate anti-rationalists regard human reason as a flickering candle, not as the great white universal light it appeared to be to *philosophes* like Condorcet. *But they do not wish to extinguish this candle.* On the contrary, they wish to keep it alive, to nurse it along into greater and greater brightness. This process, in keeping again with the views of the evolutionist, they regard as inevitably long and slow, likely to be hindered rather than helped by ambitious plans to hasten it. These moderate thinkers are not so much anti-rationalists as they are disillusioned or chastened rationalists.

The Extreme Anti-Rationalists

By contrast, the second kind of anti-rationalism would actually put out the candle of human reason. For the extreme anti-rationalists reason is not just feeble; it is bad. It is for them, so to speak, a mistake evolution has made—a wrong turning, from which the human race must somehow retrace its steps to a sounder life of pure unsullied instinct, emotion, and faith. Thomas Hardy, the English novelist, put the position clearly in the remark, "Thought is a disease of the flesh." There was a strong dose of this extreme anti-rationalism in the Nazi movement. Hitler himself distrusted reason as a degenerate French invention. Good Germans, he hoped, would come to think with their blood, with their German folk inheritance. This is the attitude reflected in the cry of a Spanish falangist general in 1936: "Down with intelligence and long live death!" Extreme anti-rationalism may also be found at the bottom of some of the wilder movements in modern art, which want to do away with all the rules of grammar or harmony or perspective, and write or compose music or paint from the heart—or the guts—without regard for "meaningless forms."

The position of these extremists is strongly rooted in the Romantic movement, with its emphasis on the heart as against the head, on fresh instinct as against stale logic, on "the desire of the moth for the star," on the impossibility of the impossible, on always wanting more, more, more (see Chapter 11).

IV   Political and Social Thought

Many of the extreme anti-rationalists turned violently against democracy, which seemed to them to rest on an altogether false estimate of what human beings were really like. The democrat believes at bottom that the ordinary man can be freed from the weight of erroneous traditions, habits, and prejudices. Once he has the real facts before him, he can attain by free discussion among his fellows a series of decisions that will be incorporated in acts and institutions under which all men can live more happily. But if you hold that most, or even many, men are by nature incapable of fair, dispassionate thinking and discussion, if you hold that men are by nature hopelessly irrational, you will at least have to revise drastically your notions of democracy, or reject them.

The extreme anti-rationalist rejected the notions of democracy. The German philosopher Nietzsche, who did most of his work in the 1880's, will do as a sample of such political thinkers in this period. Nietzsche wrote mostly in short aphoristic passages, which are hard to systematize and are often quite contradictory. But the central line of his thinking led to the concept of a new aristocracy, to the "superman",—better, perhaps because of the vulgarization of that word, the "overman"—(in German, *Uebermensch*). Nietzsche's followers, who were numerous throughout the West in the two decades before 1914, insisted that he meant a new *spiritual* aristocracy. The overmen would be above the petty materialism and national patriotism of the middle classes. Nietzsche's opponents, who were also many, held that he was just another preacher of Nordic superiority, that his overmen were, as he put it in one of his famous passages, "the blond beasts" who had so often terrorized Europe. Certainly some of his German followers held that he meant the real live Germans to be his overmen.

At any rate, Nietzsche was clearly an enemy of democracy, which he held to be second only to its child, socialism, as a society in which the weak unjustly and unnaturally ruled the strong. Here are some of his aphorisms, from which the reader can judge for himself:

Democracy represents the disbelief in all great men and in all élite societies: everybody is everybody else's equal. 'At bottom we are all herd and mob.'

I am opposed to Socialism because it dreams ingenuously of 'goodness, truth, beauty, and equal rights' (anarchy pursues the same ideal, but in a more brutal fashion).

I am opposed to parliamentary government and the power of the press, because they are the means whereby cattle become masters.[*]

Nietzsche may have hoped that the herd, the slaves, the masses would, in spite of their cross materialism, somehow recognize the true mas-

[*]Friedrich Nietzsche, *The Will to Power,* A. M. Ludovici, trans. (London, 1910), II, 206.

ters, the new enlightened despots; or he may have thought of himself as the prophet of a vast moral and religious revolution which would in his own phrase, achieve a "transvaluation of all values," a new world for a new species of man. At any rate, it is—or should be—safe to say that he was no good conventional democrat.

Nietzsche is frankly attacking, from what he thought was a fundamental position, the values associated with the democratic inheritance of the eighteenth-century Enlightenment. But even those thinkers we have already noted (see Chapters 11 and 12) as defenders of that inheritance were in the nineteenth century influenced by romantic and anti-rationalist doubts as to the natural goodness and reasonableness of ordinary men and women, as to the beneficent workings of a free market, the "invisible hand" of laissez-faire economics, and much else of conventional, established, no longer innovating liberalism. John Stuart Mill in the mid-century had worried over the "tyranny of the majority." Walter Bagehot, a good English liberal much influenced by Darwin, pointed out in his *Physics and Politics* (1872) how strong was the accumulated force of habit and tradition, which he called the "cake of custom," how hard it was to persuade men to rational action. By the end of the century, liberals throughout the West were facing the problem of revising their attitudes toward life to conform with the new emphasis on the tough network of habit, custom, and prejudice.

Already by 1914 the broad lines of the social attitudes of our own time were being laid out. One line went toward some kind of revolutionary élitism, toward the seizure of power by a minority that believes itself to have the formula whereby the gifted few can put order into a society threatened with chaos because of attempts to make decisions democratically by counting heads, no matter what is inside them. The variety of these specific formulas was, however, very great, for the late nineteenth century was in its political and ethical ideas at least as eclectic as it was in architecture. Some made race the mark of the élite, and went so far as to preach world rule for their chosen race. Others made class the mark of the

élite, and sought to achieve the "dictatorship of the proletariat." Indeed, as Marxian socialism developed in Lenin's hands, the élitist implications of Marx's thought came out openly as the doctrine often called the Leninist corollary—that the enlightened minority must seize power and rule dictatorially in the name and in the "true" interest of the proletarian masses. Others dreamed of a brand-new élite, such as Nietzsche's overmen, to be created by a kind of new religion. Others looked to eugenics to make possible the breeding of such a new élite.

A second line went toward a more flexible form of élitism, one that tried to conserve as much as possible of democratic values. On the whole, English Fabianism and continental revisionist socialism deserve this classification. The leaders of these movements wanted no violent overturns, no seizure of power. They believed in gradualness, even in the basic democratic counting of heads. But there was in all of them a strong touch of doubt as to the

Friedrich Nietzsche, 1892.

political capacity of the ordinary man. They were not for the extension of New England town-meeting democracy to the millions of the modern state. They hoped they could persuade the millions to elect legislators who would listen to the wise planners who had studied the social sciences, who could devise the wise new institutions that would make human life so much better. Above all, the planners themselves would by no means disdain what the anti-rationalists had taught them about the irrationality of ordinary men; they would make full use for good ends of what they could learn from the "practical" politician, the advertising man, the skilled professional manipulator of human beings; they would be Machiavellians, but Machiavellians on the side of the angels.

A third line sought to preserve and protect what they considered a good, or at any rate an existing, élite from democratic drives toward equality, especially in the form of state intervention in economic and social life to promote security for all. This was substantially the line followed by men like the American sociologist William Graham Sumner, by the English philosopher Herbert Spencer, and by many others throughout the West. They are not unfairly labeled conservatives, for they sought to preserve in its broad lines an established order. But they were not simply routine, unphilosophical conservatives who opposed any changes at all. They had a definite philosophy, strongly influenced by the spirit of the times, by the anti-rationalism we have here outlined. Their basic position was a distrust of the instrument of thought applied unsparingly to human

society, and in this they go back to Burke and indeed to philosophical conservatives throughout the western tradition.

But they were clearly children of their age, above all in their concrete fears of "socialism." Most of them believed in progress, and most of them prized material plenty, peace, industrial society. They held, however, that on the whole the existing middle classes, the existing leaders of a business world, the existing—or rather, the recently existing—network of Victorian habits and morals, were the best insurance that progress would continue. Above all, they feared planners and planning, at least in political positions. They distrusted the state. At bottom, they were good Darwinians, who believed that the evolutionary process depended on the struggle for life among competing individuals fettered as little as possible by planned human attempts to "rig" the struggle. They believed that social evolution could not be hastened, and that attempts to hasten it, no matter how well meant, would in fact retard it by limiting actual human variation and initiative. They are by no means altogether without sympathizers among us today, but it must be admitted that theirs has not, so far, been the "wave of the future." The Herbert Spencer who thought compulsory sewage disposal in cities was an interference with the "right" of the individual to conduct his own private struggle against typhoid fever would be even more uncomfortable in the mid-twentieth century than he was in the late nineteenth. Indeed, though there are signs of a Spencer revival, he is little read today.

V   The Century of Hope

It would, however, be a great mistake to dismiss the whole nineteenth century as something altogether outlived. On the contrary, we are all, and not merely those of us brought up in western civilization, living with problems as well as with achievements the nineteenth century brought to us, its heirs.

The achievements are obvious and we have noted them in earlier chapters. They add up above all to an extraordinary command over natural forces, a command attained by the collaboration, usually by no means wholly conscious and "planned," of pure scientists, applied scientists and engineers, businessmen—yes even those abused individuals, the bureaucrats and the politicians—right on down to ordinary men and women, who had somehow to want and work for all this material progress.

The problems are also obvious and have perhaps been dwelled on at too great length in the preceding pages. There was above all the widespread feeling, obvious especially among the intellectual classes as early as the beginning of the nineteenth century, that "something went wrong," that the promised new and better world ushered in by the American and French revolutions had proved an illusion. It is easy to point out how many nineteenth-century writers—the youthful Marx, Flaubert, Kierkegaard, Nietzsche—were "alienated" from the ways of their world. It is even easier to see how many more, indeed how most of those now studied in formal courses in literature, from genteel Victorians like Matthew Arnold and John Ruskin through stormy prophets like Carlyle, worried liberals like Mill and Tocqueville, deeply concerned critics of their own culture like all the great Russian novelists of the century, even to those supposedly optimistic children of the Enlightenment, the Americans—think of James Fenimore Cooper the bitter critic of our American democracy, Mark Twain who despaired of "the damned human race," Henry Thoreau who believed that even in gentle Concord most men led lives of quite desperation—it is easy to see how all these and many more can be labeled, if not "alienated," at least pessimistic. Yet an interesting and competent American publicist of the last generation, Everett Dean Martin, could entitle a brief survey of the cultural history of the nineteenth century "The Century of Hope."

The difficulty of reconciling Martin's title with the record of nineteenth-century intellectual history cannot be wholly—though it can be partly—solved by insisting that although many if not most of the thinkers of the century tended to pessimism about their own time, the great majority of Europeans and Americans, especially the dominant middle classes, the Babbitts if you like, the Bouvards

and Pécuchets (see p. 578), were on the contrary optimists, believers in Progress, capable of singing Pippa's song:

> The year's at the spring,
> The day's at the morn;
> Morning's at seven;
> The hill-side's dew-pearled;
> The lark's on the wing;
> The snail's on the thorn:
>   God's in his heaven—
> All's right with the world!*

The bulk of newspaper and magazine writing, the testimony of informal letters, much other evidence would indeed support the social historian in an assertion that Victorian non-intellectuals, in contrast with Victorian intellectuals, were on the whole contented, hopeful, if a bit self-righteous. The gap between the state of mind, the tastes, of the intellectuals and those of the rest of mankind continues in mid-twentieth century in a somewhat different form, as we shall see.

Yet we must not take leave of nineteenth-century culture with quite so simple a dichotomy. There is even among the serious writers and artists of the time an attitude hard to pin down, impossible to put into a fine "scientific" formula, which goes far to justify even for them that phrase "the century of hope." For almost all of them, bitter and indignant though they may have been about their times, doubtful though they were about the goodness and reasonableness of "ordinary human nature," nevertheless rarely displayed a cosmic despair, rarely whined or whimpered, but shared with their grandfathers of the eighteenth century a kind of gusto, an energy, a conviction that what they wrote and said would have results, a belief in the future, even, perhaps above all, a belief in progress. The twentieth-century French royalist Leon Daudet once wrote a book entitled *The Stupid Nineteenth-Century*. But not even Daudet, who hated the century for its democratic and egalitarian aims, would have called the nineteenth

*Browning, *Pippa Passes*, Part I

century dull, despairing, disoriented, beaten. The writers and artists we have written about in this chapter did not think and feel with T. S. Eliot's "hollow men":

> This is the way the world ends
> Not with a bang but a whimper.

They did not think it would, or ought to, end.

Reading Suggestions on the Intellectual Revolution

(Asterisk indicates paperbound edition.)

General Accounts

C. Brinton, *Ideas and Men* (Prentice-Hall, 1950). The later chapters of this general survey of intellectual history are also available in an inexpensive reprint: *The Shaping of the Modern Mind* (*Mentor).

R. C. Binkley, *Realism and Nationalism, 1852–1871* (Harper, 1935), and C. J. H. Hayes, *A Generation of Materialism, 1871–1900* (Harper, 1941). These two volumes provide fairly full coverage of the topics treated in this chapter.

J. T. Merz, *A History of European Thought in the 19th Century.* 4 vols. (Blackwood, 1912–1928). Misleadingly named, for it deals with philosophy and scientific thought only.

E. S. Marvin, *The Century of Hope,* 2nd ed. (Oxford Univ. Press, 1927). A bird's-eye view of general cultural history, somewhat old-fashioned now.

Morse Peckham, *Beyond Tragic Vision: The Quest for Identity in the Nineteenth Century* (Braziller, 1962). A very modern psychological treatment. Striking contrast with the Marvin book above.

G. H. Sabine, *A History of Political Theory,* rev. ed. (Holt, 1955). The nineteenth-century portions of this general account are the best in this field. For more on socialism in the nineteenth century, see reading suggestions for Chapter 12.

K. S. Latourette, *Christianity in a Revolutionary Age: A History of Christianity in the 19th and 20th Centuries,* 5 vols. (Harper, 1958–1962). Very detailed; covers whole world.

G. D. Charlton, *Secular Religions in France, 1815–1870* (Oxford Univ. Press, 1963). An interesting and scholarly survey of "substitute religions."

F. E. Manuel, *Prophets of Paris* (Harvard Univ. Press, 1962). From Turgot to Comte, history of ideas in the best sense.

K. Löwith, *From Hegel to Nietzsche: The Revolution in 19th Century Thought* (Holt, Rinehart and Winston, 1964). A good study with emphasis on German thought.

Melvin Richter. *The Politics of Conscience: T. H. Green and His Age* (Harvard Univ. Press, 1964). Good study of a leading British exponent of German idealism.

H. D. Aiken, *The Age of Ideology: The 19th Century Philosophers* (*Mentor, 1957). A volume of selections with introduction and interpretations in the useful series "Great Ages of Western Philosophy."

Special Studies: Darwinism

C. Darwin, *On the Origin of Species by Natural Selection* (Modern Library, 1936, *New American Library), and *Journal of Researches into the Geology and Natural History of the Various Countries Visited during the Voyage of H.M.S.* Beagle *round the World* (Dutton, 1908. Everyman ed.; *Bantam). Darwin's classic expositions.

J. Barzun, *Darwin, Marx, Wagner* (Little, Brown, 1941; *2nd ed., Anchor). An interesting study; finds common denominators in men usually catalogued as quite different.

H. Spencer, *The Man versus the State,* A. J. Nock, ed. (Caxton, 1940). A representative work by a whole-hearted Social Darwinist.

M. R. Davie, ed., *Sumner Today* (Yale Univ. Press, 1940). Selected essays by William Graham Sumner, the most famous American Social Darwinist.

W. Bagehot, *Physics and Politics* (*Beacon, 1956). An early and suggestive adaptation of Darwinism to the political realm; very good reading.

B. Kidd, *Social Evolution* (Macmillan, 1898). Typical social Darwinism.

R. Hofstadter, *Social Darwinism in American Thought* (*Beacon, 1955). Interesting study of the ultimate impact of Darwin's theories.

C. Zirkle, *Evolution, Marxian Biology, and the Social Scene* (Univ. of Pennsylvania Press, 1959). A controversial treatment of a controversial subject.

Special Studies:
Literature
and the Arts

G. M. Young, *Victorian England: Portrait of an Age* (Doubleday, 1954; *Anchor). A brilliant evocation.

E. Wilson, *Axel's Castle. A Study in the Imaginative Literature of 1870–1930* (Scribner's, 1931; *same publisher). A suggestive study.

G. Brandes, *Main Currents in Nineteenth-Century Literature,* 6 vols. (Heinemann, 1901–1905). A valuable detailed study.

J. C. Sloane, *French Painting between the Past and the Present: Artists, Critics, and Traditions from 1848 to 1870* (Princeton Univ. Press, 1951).

C. Graña, *Bohemian vs. Bourgeois: French Society and the French Man of Letters in the 19th Century* (Basic Books, 1964). Interesting socio-economic history.

W. L. Burn, *The Age of Equipoise: A Study of the Mid-Victorian Generation* (Norton, 1964). Stimulating study in British intellectual history.

M. Raynal, *The Nineteenth Century: Goya to Gauguin* (Skira, 1951). Superbly illustrated.

S. Giedion, *Mechanization Takes Command* (Oxford Univ. Press, 1948). Interesting account of the effects of industrialism on the arts.

P. H. Lang, *Music in Western Civilization* (Norton, 1941), and C. Gray, *History of Music,* 2nd ed. (Knopf, 1947). Two very different and helpful histories of music.

H. R. Hitchcock, *Architecture: Nineteenth and Twentieth Centuries* (Pelican, 1958). A massive detailed study.

Novels and Dramas

G. Flaubert, *Madame Bovary* (many editions). The classic novel of French realism.

E. Zola, *Germinal* (many editions) and *L'Assommoir* (translated under several titles). Two characteristic novels by the great French exponent of naturalism.

S. Butler, *The Way of All Flesh* (many editions). A good example of gloomy naturalism in the novel, English-style.

S. Lewis, *Babbitt* (Harcourt, Brace, 1949), and *Main Street* (Harcourt, Brace, 1950). Novels that are important documents of American social history.

E. Bellamy, *Looking Backward, 2000–1887* (*Modern Library, 1951); H. G. Wells *A Modern Utopia* (Scribner's, 1905); and W. Morris, *News from Nowhere* (Longmans, Green, 1901). Three contrasting visions of Utopia in the light of science and industrialism.

H. Ibsen, *Six Plays: A Doll's House, Ghosts, An Enemy of the People, Rosmersholm, Hedda Gabler, The Master Builder* (*Modern Library). Six pioneering dramas by a master.

E. Brieux, *Damaged Goods*, preface by G. B. Shaw (Fifield, 1914). On venereal disease.

G. B. Shaw, *Man and Superman* (*Penguin), and *Back to Methuselah* (Oxford Univ. Press, 1947. World's Classics). Plays on aspects of the modern intellectual revolution.

16

Nineteenth-Century Imperialism

I   The Movement in General

In the *Oxford English Dictionary*, which tries to find the earliest possible example of a definition, the editors can go no further back than 1881 for "imperialism: the principle of the spirit of empire; advocacy of what are held to be imperial interests." The word is new; what it stands for is in part very old indeed—as old as human war and conquest. Yet there were some important new elements in the imperialism of western peoples in the nineteenth century. Nineteenth-century imperialism was in almost every country a major part of political life, with goals, methods, and advocates known to all who were concerned with politics. And since by 1900 almost all of western and central Europe, the United States, and indeed all the outposts of European culture enjoyed high literacy and widespread public discussion, imperialism took its place with liberalism, conservatism, nationalism, socialism, and a host of other "isms" as a subject of universal debate. Perhaps no important "ism" seems to us now, a mere half-century after the heyday of this imperialism, to be quite so outdated. Indeed, we now use as a smear word the term "colonialism" rather than "imperialism."

The Economic Aspect

Carefully defined, another element, the economic, may be said to distinguish nineteenth-century imperialism from early forms of imperialism. No doubt the material, acquisitive motive runs through all forms of territorial expansion from prehistoric times to the present. It is clear in the earliest days of Spanish and Portuguese expansion in the quest for gold, silver, and profits. But, as the nineteenth century wore on, imperialist nations were responding to economic pressures in a new form. Liberal, and especially Marxist, economists and sociologists no doubt exaggerated this new element, but there is a basis of truth in their arguments.

According to these economic critics of imperialism, capitalists and industrialists in the older countries began to discover in the nineteenth century that they were unable to market at home all they could produce. But, being capitalists, they could not bring themselves to solve their difficulties by paying proportionately *less* of the total product of society in interest, dividends, and other payments to their own kind of people, the upper classes, and paying *more* in wages, pensions, bonuses, and the like to their workmen. Instead of sharing the wealth and creating at home the mass purchasing power and the mass market they needed, they preferred to turn to the non-western world, to markets abroad, to the exploitation of dependent peoples. This attempt to bolster the capitalist system meant competition among the great western industrial powers for land and peoples to exploit. Lenin, in his *Imperialism as the Latest Stage of Capitalism*

(1917), stressed the need to use the finance-capital that was rapidly accumulating, rather than the need for markets. The great bankers, according to Lenin, drove the willing politicians into the search for dependencies in which this available capital could be profitably invested, a search that marked what he termed the inevitable "last stage of capitalism."

A non-Marxist would of course call attention to the fact that the "nineteenth-century colonial" world produced raw materials and little else; the exchange of these for European and American manufactured goods was easy, "natural," and not yet held to be wicked or unfair to the colonial areas. Furthermore, as we have already seen, leading industrial powers in both America and Europe were experiencing an increasing demand for higher tariffs by the late 1800's. In the United States and Germany, and even in free-trading Britain, industrialists wanted protection against foreign competitors. This was an era of neo-mercantilism, reviving and "streamlining" the older mercantilist doctrines of Colbert and others. Colonies as well as tariffs entered into the strategy of the neo-mercantilists, as they had done in the case of the old.

The Powers Involved

The year 1870 is a convenient dividing line between the more active age of imperialism that was to come and the less active age that had preceded. The period from 1815 to 1870 saw a partial decline in imperialist fortunes, as most of Spain's American colonies gained their independence, and as Britain took the first steps leading to the virtual independence of Canada (see p. 620). In this same period, however, the French established themselves in Algeria, and the British extended their rule in India. The dividing line of 1870 does not mark a sharp break in the history of imperialism, but rather the acceleration of a movement that had never ceased.

The successful competitors in nineteenth-century imperialism, those who brought new lands under their flags, were Great Britain,

Atlantic Ocean

OTTOMAN EMPIRE

SYRIA

PERSIA

AFGHANISTAN

BALUCHISTAN

Mediterranean Sea

Casablanca
MOROCCO
ALGERIA
TUNIS

Cairo
Suez

CANARY IS.
(Sp.)

TRIPOLI

EGYPT

Nile R.

ARABIA

RIO DE ORO

Red Sea

FRENCH WEST AFRICA

GAMBIA
PORT. GUINEA
SIERRA LEONE
LIBERIA

Niger R.

NIGERIA

GOLD
COAST

TOGO

KAMERUNS

ANGLO-
EGYPTIAN
SUDAN

ERITREA

FR. SOM.
BR. SOM.

ABYSSINIA

ITALIAN
SOMALILAND

FERNANDO PO (Sp.)
PRINCIPE
(Port.)
SÃO TOMÉ
RIO MUNI

CONGO

UGANDA

BR. EAST
AFRICA

Indian Ocean

CABINDA

BELGIAN
CONGO

Congo R.

GERMAN
EAST
AFRICA

ZANZIBAR
(Br.)

Africa and the
Middle East, 1910

ANGOLA

N.E.

MOZAMBIQUE

N.W.

RHODESIA

S.

NYASALAND

MADAGASCAR

	Belgian
	British
	French
	German
	Italian
	Portuguese
	Spanish

WALVIS BAY

GERMAN
SOUTH-
WEST
AFRICA

BECHUANA-
LAND

| | British Occupation |
| | Independent |

TRANSVAAL

SWAZILAND

NATAL
BASUTOLAND

UNION OF
SOUTH AFRICA
Cape Town

CAPE
COLONY

0   500   1000
Miles

which already in 1815 had a great empire, France, Germany, Italy, and the United States. Even little Belgium, itself a "new" nation in 1830, acquired a tremendous piece of tropical Africa, the Congo, 900,000 square miles in area in comparison to the homeland's 11,775 square miles. Russia did not expand overseas, and indeed parted with her vast but thinly inhabited possession in North America when the tsarist government sold Alaska to the United States in 1867. But she began the effective settlement of the great areas east of the Urals and began to push into the borderlands of the Middle and Far East, toward Persia, India, and China.

In the process of expansion, the expanding nations inevitably rubbed up against one another in all sorts of competition, from the economic to actual shooting war. Almost every great international conflict of the nineteenth century, save for the mid-century duels between Prussia and Austria and between Prussia and France, had a direct concern in imperialist rivalries outside Europe. Imperial competition is a complicated story, then, woven into the whole fabric of international relations in the nineteenth century. We shall note briefly the major areas of inter-European rivalries and then summarize the growth of the major empires over the century.

599

The Areas Involved

The Monroe Doctrine (see Chapter 11), toward which European nations were increasingly respectful as the strength of the United States increased, helped to keep both American continents free from further actual annexation by outside powers. So, too, did the British navy, for British policy was there to support the *status quo*. Toward the fateful year 1914, the competition between Britain and Germany for markets and for fields of invest-

Chinese painting of the arrival of one of the first English steamers and her passengers at Canton, about 1840.

ment in South America grew intense and was one of the many factors that brought these powers to war. Since no state was strong enough to take from Britain her older colonies, throughout the nineteenth century British problems in both colonies of settlement and colonies of exploitation were limited to the British system itself. The Americas and the lands of the British Empire were then, on the whole, outside the scramble.

A major field of imperialist rivalry and penetration was the Near or Middle East, essentially the widespread lands under varying degrees of Turkish control, and Persia. In earlier chapters (11 and 14) we saw how the Balkans and the Straits became major issues in nineteenth-century diplomatic history. The whole "Eastern Question," as it used to be called, revolved around the problem of what was to be done with these old lands, which were peopled almost wholly by Moslems. They were backward lands by nineteenth-century western standards, mostly with poor rainfall, farm lands exhausted by centuries of primitive agriculture, and their ancient irrigation systems long since in disrepair. They were poor also in natural resources, for their great wealth in petroleum was not really known or very important until the twentieth century. England, France, and Russia were in active competition over the Near East early in the nineteenth century, and they were later joined by Italy and Germany.

Africa was the scene of the most spectacular imperial rivalry. In 1815, except for the nominally Turkish lands of North Africa, the little Dutch settlement at the Cape of Good Hope (taken over by the British in 1815), and a string of Portuguese, Spanish, French, and British "factories" or trading posts along the old Portuguese exploration route that went back to the fifteenth century, Africa was untenanted by Europeans and, in the interior, almost unexplored. It was peopled by Negro races, long subjected to the horrors of the slave trade and often living at the level of primitive tribesmen. The slave trade was almost abolished in many areas by mid-century, and exploration was well under way. Then in the latter half of the century the great powers

Asia and the Pacific, 1910

British territory
British protected States
Dutch territory
French territory
German territory
Japan and Japanese territories
United States and possessions

1 Port Arthur (Jap.)
2 Wei-hai-wei (Br.)
3 Kiaochow Bay (Ger.)

CANADA

UNITED STATES

MEXICO

ALASKA (U.S.)

San Francisco

ALEUTIAN IS. (U.S.)

Pacific Ocean

HAWAIIAN ISLANDS (U.S.)
Honolulu
JOHNSTON (U.S.)
KINGMAN REEF (U.S.)   PALMYRA

MIDWAY IS. (U.S.)

International Date Line

HOWLAND (U.S.)
BAKER (Br.)
PHOENIX IS. (Br.)

AMERICAN SAMOA (U.S.)
W. SAMOA (Ger.)

GILBERT IS. (Br.)
ELLICE IS. (Br.)
FIJI IS. (Br.)

WAKE I. (U.S.)

MARSHALL IS. (Ger.)

Equator

CAROLINE ISLANDS (Ger.)

MARIANAS IS. (Ger.)

GUAM (U.S.)

PHILIPPINE IS. (U.S.)

SOLOMON IS. (Br.)

BISMARCK ARCH. (Ger.)

NEW HEBRIDES (Br. and Fr.)

NEW CALEDONIA (Fr.)

NEW GUINEA (Ger.)
(Port.)

Brisbane

AUSTRALIA
QUEENSLAND
NEW SOUTH WALES
Sydney
Canberra
VICTORIA
Melbourne
SOUTH AUSTRALIA
NORTHERN TERRITORY
WESTERN AUSTRALIA
Perth
Adelaide
TASMANIA

Auckland
NEW ZEALAND

KAMCHATKA

KURILE IS.

SAKHALIN

JAPAN
Tokyo
Kyoto
KOREA
Seoul
Vladivostok

SIBERIA

Amur R.

RUSSIA

L. Baikal
Chita
Krasnoyarsk
Omsk
Irtysh R.
Yenisei R.
Ob R.
Lena R.

TRANS-SIBERIAN RAILROAD

Aral Sea

AFGHANISTAN

MONGOLIA
TANNU TUVA
SINKIANG
TIBET
MANCHURIA
Peking
Tientsin
Yellow R.
Nanking
Yangtze R.
CHINA
YUNNAN
Canton
Macao (Port.)
Hong Kong (Br.)
Kwangchou (Fr.)
FORMOSA
OKINAWA
Foochow
Wenchow
Shanghai

NEPAL
BHUTAN
BU
INDIA
PUNJAB
Bombay
Goa (Port.)
Diu
Daman
Chandarnagar (Fr.)
Calcutta
Madras
Pondichéry (Fr.)
Karikal (Fr.)
Yanaon (Fr.)
Mahé (Fr.)
CEYLON

BURMA
SIAM
INDO-CHINA
Saigon
Mekong R.
FED. MALAY STATES
Singapore
SUMATRA
Batavia
JAVA
DUTCH EAST INDIES
BORNEO
CELEBES
TIMOR (Port.)

Indian Ocean

Inset (top right)

PHILIPPINE ISLANDS (U.S.)

Pacific Ocean

LUZON
Manila
MINDORO
PANAY
NEGROS
PALAWAN
PANAY
SAMAR
LEYTE
MINDANAO

South China Sea

BORNEO

Miles 0 200

—Britain, France, and Germany—with Portugal, Italy, and Belgium tagging along, succeeded in blocking out in territorial units under their respective flags almost the whole of the continent. The only exceptions were the small Republic of Liberia, which had been set up by American anti-slavery groups as a land for emancipated American Negro slaves (though very few of them went there), and the mountainous and backward inland state of Abyssinia (now known as Ethiopia). Abyssinia, coveted by Italy, had a very narrow escape. In 1896, the Abyssinians, under their Emperor Menelek and with French help, defeated an Italian army at Adowa and secured a respite in independence until the Italians tried again under Mussolini in 1935.

The Far East, too, was a major scene of imperialist rivalries. European powers strengthened their hold on older colonies and acquired new ones in Southeast Asia—the mainland areas of Burma, Indo-China, and Malaya, and the island groups of Melanesia and Polynesia. But the ancient, thickly populated, highly civilized Chinese Empire was never subjected, as was Africa, to actual partition and direct annexation. China was, however, not well enough organized politically or industrially to stand up against European penetration and was by the end of the century subjected to a rough, *de facto* partitioning

among Britain, France, Germany, and Russia. Each power, operating from certain "treaty ports" as centers, was able to exercise a degree of control—basically economic—over considerable areas, typical "spheres of influence" as they were called. Rivalry among these European powers, and the rising power of the United States, which was exercised in favor of the "Open Door" policy of permitting as much free trade in China as was possible and of preserving Chinese sovereignty, served to counterbalance Chinese weakness and kept China throughout this period on the list of independent nations.

Finally, Japan kept herself isolated from the rest of the world for two centuries, from the mid-seventeenth to the mid-nineteenth. This compact island empire was closed to foreigners during the period when the European powers slowly strengthened their small holds in China. Then in 1853 the American naval officer, Perry, induced Japan to open her ports to outside trade. By adopting some western ways, particularly economic ways, Japan was able not merely to preserve her real independence during the late nineteenth century but actually to begin her own imperial expansion on the mainland of Asia after winning a brief war with China in 1894–1895 (see p. 616). Japan was thus the first modern nation-state in the Far East.

II   The British Empire

We may now move on through the imperial record, country by country. Nineteenth-century Britain retained and, with the help of emigrants from the mother country, developed the great areas that were suitable to white colonization—Canada, Australia and New Zealand, and South Africa. This section focuses on Britain's imperial possessions in Africa and Asia. The development of self-government in Canada, Australia, and New Zealand will come more appropriately at the

close of this chapter, in our survey of the results of nineteenth-century imperialism.

South Africa

In 1815, Britain had just acquired Cape Colony at the southern tip of Africa from the Netherlands. Cape Colony was inhabited by a few Dutch and French Huguenot colonists and was suited, in spite of a relatively low rainfall, to European living. As Britishers moved in, the older colonists, known in their own Dutch vernacular as Boers, grew more and more discontented. The adoption of English as the sole official language, the abolition of slavery throughout the Empire in 1834, the attempts of the government at London to protect the native blacks, and other measures of Victorian liberalism went against the grain of the patriarchal Boers, who were fundamentalist Christians for whom slavery was ordained of God and for whom liberalism was the work of the devil. Between 1835 and 1837, some ten thousand Boers moved north overland into country sparsely settled by primitive Negro tribes in the "Great Trek," a heroic folk migration that bulks even larger in contemporary nationalist South African feeling than do the comparable sagas of covered-wagon days in American tradition. After some confused three-cornered fighting among Boers, British, and native Zulus, the Boers established two virtually independent South African states — the Transvaal and the Orange Free State. Well inland, on territory suitable for grazing but not for intensive agriculture, these thinly populated states lived on for a time hardly noticed by the outside world.

The British in South Africa noticed them, of course, and many of the British wished to add these lands directly to the Empire. They settled from the sea another British province to the east, along the Indian Ocean side, known as Natal. In the course of the century, Cape Colony and Natal, which together had a black population heavily outnumbering the British and remaining Boers combined, acquired the self-governing rights that British colonies of settlement in Canada, Australia, and New Zealand were also acquiring. British South African leaders for the most part wanted to bring the Boer Republics under the British flag. But as the London home government swung between Tory and Liberal domination, it also swung between a policy of imperialist expansion and the "Little Englander" policy of leaving the Trekkers alone. In 1852, by the Sand River Convention, the British acknowledged the independence of Transvaal.

But in 1877 they reversed themselves and annexed it as a step toward the federation of all South Africa under the British Crown. The Boers revolted in 1880 and the Liberal Gladstone, then in power, lived up to his principles by making at Pretoria in 1881 a treaty with the Boers which re-established Transvaal as independent, though under the "suzerainty" of Great Britain.

The British were already filtering up through the semi-desert country to the west of the Boer Republics when the discovery of gold and the development of the diamond industry in these republics undid Gladstone's work. The Transvaal was no longer just a poor and isolated grazing country; it offered a great source of wealth that tempted quite different kinds of settlers. The region about Johannesburg, the famous Rand, filled up with adventurers and entrepreneurs of a dozen nations, all looking to Britain to protect them from the conservative Boers, to whom they were undesirable *Uitlanders* (outlanders, foreigners).

The Boer War and After

The inevitable conflict came to a head with the Jameson Raid of December 29, 1895 — midsummer in South Africa. The British in South Africa were now under the leadership of Cecil Rhodes, prime minister of Cape Colony, a determined and articulate imperialist who had made a quick fortune consolidating the chaotic diamond industry. The raid itself, under a follower of Rhodes, Dr. Jameson, was an invasion of Transvaal from British territory to the west, and was planned to coincide with a rising of Uitlanders in Johannesburg. But the rising did not take place, and the President of Transvaal, Kruger, had no trouble in defeating Jameson's handful of invaders. The famous "Kruger telegram," in which the German Kaiser congratulated the Boer President, was one of the critical steps in sharpening the Anglo-German rivalry that helped lead to world war in 1914 (see Chapter 17). Its immediate effect in South Africa was to harden Boer resistance and bring about in 1899 open war between Britain and the two Boer Republics.

The war, following the pattern of British wars in modern times, went badly at first for the British, who did not have enough troops immediately available to put down determined men who had been brought up in outdoor life and who were fighting on their own ground. Western opinion, including opinion in the United States, generally sided with the underdog Boers, and in Britain itself many Liberals and Laborites strongly opposed the war as rank imperialism. But in the long run the overwhelming strength of the British prevailed. By the middle of 1900 the British had won in the field, but they needed another eighteen months to subdue the desperate guerrilla bands into which Boer opposition dissolved. In 1902, by the Treaty of Vereeniging, the Boers accepted British rule, with the promise of ultimate self-government. This promise the British fulfilled speedily. In 1910 there came into being a Union of South Africa, uniting Cape Colony, Transvaal, Orange Free State, and Natal in a state in which the central government was stronger than the provinces. English and Afrikaans, as the South African Dutch dialect had come to be called, were set up as equally official languages.

On the eve of World War I, South Africa was among the self-governing British dominions. British and Boer seemed to be well on the way to composing their long quarrel and to be ready to collaborate in setting up a new outpost of the West. But there were ominous signs even then. The Boers had by no means been Anglicized, and they were still fundamentally opposed to their partners in empire. And the two European elements together were in a minority of one to four as

The Boer War: British advance toward Johannesburg, 1901.

compared with the non-Europeans—the native blacks, the East Indians (who had come in numbers as immigrants, especially to Natal), and the "colored" peoples of mixed blood. The seeds of the current troubles in South Africa were clearly present even in the hopeful days immediately after the establishment of the Union.

Egypt

At the opposite end of Africa, Britain during the last half of the nineteenth century took over from the French the control of Egypt, nominally a vassal state of the crumbling Ottoman Empire. French influence there, already strong in the eighteenth century, was increased by Napoleon's expedition (see Chapter 10); indeed, a degree of French cultural influence persists among the Egyptian upper classes and intellectuals to this day. Under French supervision, a private company built between 1859 and 1869 the Suez Canal, which united the Mediterranean with the Red Sea and shortened the sea trip from Europe to India and the Far East by thousands of miles. The British had bitterly opposed the building of this canal under French patronage; but now that it was finished, the canal came to be considered an essential part of the "lifeline" of the British Empire.

Accordingly, the British took over Egypt and with it Suez. They carried out this action skillfully and slowly, threatening at crucial moments to use force, but not using it on any large scale. The decisive step in the process was the purchase by the British under Disraeli of 176,000 shares of stock in the Suez Canal Company. These shares had originally been assigned to the ruler of Egypt, the Khedive, as the price of his co-operation in the canal project. The Khedive, a great and unwise spender, was heavily in debt to European financiers by 1875, and he sold his shares for a good price. The largest block of Suez stock was now in British hands.

By the eve of World War I, Britain exercised virtual sovereignty over Egypt. The

PUNCH, OR THE LONDON CHARIVARI.—December 11, 1875.

"MOSÉ IN EGITTO!!!"

Khedive and his government remained. Legally Egypt was still a separate state. But a British Resident was always at hand to exercise firm control, especially over foreign relations. Under this British regime—the word "protectorate" is the usual term—much was done to modernize Egypt. The standard of living of the masses in Egypt was by no means raised to anything like that of the European masses. But the great dam at Aswan on the Nile, finished in 1902, was the first of a series of public works that added to the total productive power of the country, improved public health, lowered the mortality rate, and strengthened the numbers and prosperity of the middle class. Modernization also meant the beginnings of a wider literacy, of an educated middle class, and indeed of an intellectual class that earned its living by the written or spoken word. Most of these people responded by hating the British and by nursing

605

a constantly growing nationalism—"Egypt for the Egyptians." We shall encounter this pattern again elsewhere.

The Rest of British Africa

In between South Africa and Egypt the British pieced out their African possessions throughout the century. At its end, they had the lion's share of the continent. They had only 4,000,000 square miles out of over 11,000,000, but they controlled 61,000,000 people out of some 100,000,000. A mere listing of these holdings would be a dull and unenlightening catalogue. They can be found, usually colored red, in any good atlas of the turn of the century and, also with British possessions colored in red, on a famous Canadian postage stamp of 1898 (see map, Chapter 23). A good sample of these colonies is Nigeria, in which the great administrator Sir Frederick (later Lord) Lugard worked out the characteristic British method of colonial government in tropical Africa that was known as "indirect rule."

The colony and protectorate of Nigeria, centering around the great river Niger, was formally put together from earlier West African colonies in 1914. Northern Nigeria was ruled by Moslem emirs of the Fulani race whose culture was superior to that of the subject and exploited Negroes; southern Nigeria was inhabited by numerous heathen tribes that had long been harassed by slave raids. The British had first to subject the Fulani by force, a process that was completed late in the nineteenth century.

They then applied, as a French statesman put it, "with method but not with system," what came to be called indirect rule. Emirs and chieftains were confirmed in their separate rules, subject to the banning of internal warfare, the abolition of slavery, and similar measures imposed from above. A British Resident supervised the rule of the leading chiefs, with district Residents (later Commissioners) to supplement the work in the local subdivisions. But native law, native religion, and native traditions, in so far as they did not conflict violently with western standards, were carefully maintained. The British staff was never large; Lugard complained that in 1903 he had only one British administrator on the average for every 400,000 natives. But somehow the handful of imperial officials were able to ensure the peace. Slowly, much too slowly for impatient idealists, railroads, roads, improved agriculture, commerce, and education—the externals at least of western civilization—began to appear in Nigeria. Early in this century the first African Negro students began to appear in British universities. By mid-century, there was already a small western-educated group of native Nigerians using English as their chief language.

Other British Spheres

In the Americas, Britain maintained her colonial dependencies in the Caribbean, in Bermuda and the Bahamas, and, on the mainland, in British Honduras and British Guiana. Limited self-government of the seventeenth-century kind, which some of them had lost in the mid-nineteenth century, was only gradually granted them in the twentieth. These were all tropical or semitropical lands, with a relatively small planter class and with large Negro or mixed lower classes. These lands suffered gradual impoverishment as a result of certain economic developments, notably the great competition offered to the staple cane sugar of the region by the growth in temperate climates of the beet-sugar industry, together with an increase in population beyond the limited resources of the region. By 1914, the British West Indies had already become a "problem area."

In the Pacific and in Southeast Asia, Britain in the nineteenth century added some red dots on the map of her empire, and especially in Malaya she developed the great industries of rubber and tin that were to be major factors in her economy after World War I. She took an important part in the process of opening China to western trade by means of treaty-port concessions and spheres of influence. Indeed, Britain took one of the great steps in breaking

German view of British imperialism in Africa.

down Chinese attempts to keep off the foreigner, for in 1841 she waged what has come to be called invidiously but not unjustly the "Opium War." This war was brought on by a Chinese attempt to control the opium trade in which British merchants had an important stake. By the Treaty of Nanking in 1842, Britain acquired Hong Kong and secured the opening of five ports, including Canton and Shanghai.

India: Political Organization

In China, however, Britain was but one, though the most important, of the Great Powers scrambling for empire in that densely peopled land. In India her victory over France in 1763, confirmed by her victory in 1815, left her in sole control over a subcontinent of Asia, for the remnants of French and Portuguese possessions there hardly counted. India was the richest of Britain's overseas possessions, the center and symbol of empire, as the imaginative Disraeli realized when in 1876 he had Queen Victoria proclaimed Empress of India.

In 1763, India was already a great and well-peopled land, but not, in the western sense, a single *nation*. It was a vast congeries of races and religions, ranging from the most cultivated and philosophic Brahmins to the most primitive tribesmen, still in the Stone Age. As the nineteenth century began, the two

main methods of British control had already become clear. The richest and most densely populated regions, centering on the cities of Calcutta, Madras, Bombay, and on the Punjab, were maintained under direct British control. The British government did not originally annex these lands; they were first administered as the property, so to speak, of the English East India Company, a chartered enterprise surviving from the great days of mercantilism in the seventeenth and eighteenth centuries. The company in its heyday, led by empire-makers like Clive and Warren Hastings, had taken on enormous territories and made treaties like a sovereign power. Hastings was prosecuted for "high crimes and misdemeanors" in a famous trial of the late eighteenth century. But what he acquired the British kept.

In the nineteenth century, the company was regarded by most economists and political thinkers as a shocking anomaly, and the India Office of the central government in London gradually took over the real control and administration of British India. The trading monopoly of the company had long since been undermined. In 1857, the company's native army of Sepoys rebelled. As usual in such major uprisings, the rebellion was brought on by a number of causes. But the basic cause was that the soldiers, Hindu, Moslem, and others, all had come to fear that British ways were being imposed on them to the destruction of their own ways. The Sepoy Rebellion was put down, but not before several massacres of Europeans had occurred, and not without a serious military effort by the British. The mutiny meant the end of the English East India Company. In 1858, the British Crown took over the company's lands and obligations, announcing that no further annexations were sought in India.

The rest of India—roughly a third of its area and a fourth or a fifth of its population—came to be known as the "feudal" or "native" states. These were left nominally under the rule of their own princes, who might be the fabulously rich Sultan of Hyderabad or the Gaekwar of Baroda, or merely a kind of local chieftain. The "native" states were actually governed by a system of British Residents somewhat like the system we have just seen in Nigeria. The India Office never hesitated to interfere with the succession, or to disallow acts of princes, who were frequently irresponsible and extravagant, or even to assume direct rule for a time when it was thought necessary. The "native" states add many picturesque notes to a detailed history of India, but in the long run the distinction between direct and indirect rule in India did not mean very much in practice.

India: "The Meeting of East and West"

The years between 1763 and 1919 in India are a fascinating record of what Arnold Toynbee, the philosopher of history, calls "contacts between civilizations." Indeed, anyone who wants to understand the great contemporary problem of relations between the West and the rest of the world—to use clear terms, between white peoples and colored peoples—will do well to learn all he can of this great meeting of East and West in the subcontinent of India.

In material terms, many phases of the British rule in India are readily measurable. In 1864, the British *Statesman's Year Book* gave the population of India as about 136,000,000, and in 1904 close to 300,000,000. Although the latter figure includes additional territories, in Burma and elsewhere, it is clear that nineteen-century India experienced a significant increase in total population. In 1901, one male out of ten could read and write, a low rate of literacy by western standards, but already a high one by contemporary Asian standards. It is characteristic of Indian society that the comparable figures for women in the same census of 1901 show that only one out of one hundred and fifty could read and write.

Such statistics are plentiful, and what they show is an India on the eve of World War I with thousands of miles of railroads, telegraph lines, universities (teaching in English), hospitals, factories, and great and busy seaports. But, in proportion to the total population, India did not have these advantages to anything like the extent that even the poorest of European countries had them. Statistics show a native ruling class sometimes fantastically rich, and an immense peasant class for the most part living as their ancestors had lived, on the edge of starvation. A middle class was just beginning to form, and, like all the middle classes formed in non-European lands under European penetration, it had proportionately far more aspirants to genteel white-collar posts in the older "liberal" professions than to posts in commerce, engineering, and industry, to say nothing of scientific research.

The total wealth of India certainly increased under British rule in this century and a half, and in 1914 it was spread more widely among the Indian populations, save for the most primitive areas, than it had been in 1763. Proportionately less and less wealth went directly from an "exploited" India to an "exploiting" Britain. The familiar Englishman of the seventeenth and eighteenth centuries, the "nabob" who made a fortune in India and retired with it to comfort, and perhaps to a peerage, in England, almost ceased to exist as the nineteenth century wore on. Anglo-Indian economic relations took on more and more the form of trade between a developed industrial and financial society in Britain and a society geared to the production of raw materials—we should now call it an "underdeveloped" society—in India. In this trade, native Indians took an increasing part if only as middlemen, and toward the end of the century native industries, notably textile manufacturing, financed for the most part with British capital, began to arise in India.

Throughout the century, of course, a large number of British—small in proportion to the total population, but numbering in the thousands—were basically supported by the Indian economy; they "lived off India." Some of them were private businessmen, but the greater number were military and civilian workers, the latter the celebrated Indian Civil Service who "ran" India. Yet natives were gradually working their way into positions of greater responsibility, into both private and public posts at the policy-making level.

Of this British ruling class in India one very important fact is now plain. It did not, like the English and Scots who went to Ireland in early modern times, really take root in India. Britain—one must be careful not to say "England," for the Scots played a conspicuous role in India as they did throughout the Empire—was always "Home," always the place where one hoped to end one's days. Though son not infrequently followed father in the Indian army or civil service, or even in business, these "Sahibs" as a whole never became fully adjusted to life in India. The spiritual climate was perhaps an even greater barrier than the physical climate. Here is a letter from an Englishwoman in Madras in 1837:

It is wonderful how little interested most of the English ladies seem by all the strange habits and ways of the natives. . . .

I asked one lady what she had seen of the country and the natives since she had been in India. 'Oh, nothing!' said she: 'thank goodness, I know nothing at all about them, nor I don't wish to: really I think the less one sees and knows of them the better!'[*]

The natives, too, often found the gap between East and West too great to be bridged. Another Englishwoman writes in 1913:

Coming home we saw a native cooking his dinner on a little charcoal fire, and as I passed he threw the contents of the pot away. Surprised, I asked why. 'Because,' I was told, 'your shadow fell on it and defiled it!'[†]

Yet the work of raising the economic basis of Indian life was in large part the work of the British. They were often overbearing, insensitive, white men at their worst in their dealings with the natives. But they were, more often than the doctrinaire liberal will admit, men devoted to the task of bettering the lot of their charges, men who made a real effort to understand them. Some of them studied with western scholarly methods the past and present of Indian culture and society, thus laying the foundations on which Indian scholars now build.

[*]Hilton Brown, ed., *The Sahibs* (London, 1948), 225.
[†]*Ibid.*, 230.

III   The Other Empires

The French: North Africa

The British victory in the "Second Hundred Years' War," capped by their defeat of Napoleon in 1815, had stripped France of all but insignificant remnants of her former empire. Yet during the nineteenth century France succeeded in building up a new colonial empire second in area only to that of the British. France, despite her frequent revolutionary changes in government, maintained an imperialist policy that added between 1824 and 1914 close to three and a half million square miles to the lands under the French flag, and some fifty million people, almost all non-European. The figures for area are indeed somewhat misleading, for a million and a half square miles are included in the Sahara Desert, which is almost uninhabited.

Little of this second French colonial empire was suitable for settlement by Europeans. The great exception was French North Africa, including Tunisia, Algeria, and Morocco. As the provinces of Africa and Mauretania, these lands were once flourishing parts of the Roman Empire; after France took them over, they reached a greater degree of material prosperity than they had enjoyed for nearly eighteen centuries. These lands, which have a typically Mediterranean climate, were inhabited chiefly by Berber and Arab peoples of Moslem faith. Though the total native population increased greatly under French rule, something over a million European colonists moved in. In majority French, but with sizable groups of Italians and Spaniards, these colonists took some land from the natives, though they added to the total arable acreage by initiating irrigation projects and other improvements. They remained, however, an alien group.

The French got a toe-hold in North Africa in 1824 through an expedition against the Algerian pirates, with whose Tripolitan counterparts, incidentally, the United States had fought in 1801. The French stayed on, increasing their control over Algeria and adding protectorates over Tunisia to the east in the 1880's and over Morocco to the west in the early twentieth century. Britain gave the French a free hand in Morocco as compensation for their exclusion from Egypt (see Chapter 17).

Especially in Algeria and Tunisia, the French promoted European settlement while trying what they thought was reasonably hard not to antagonize the natives. They called their policy one of "assimilation," in contrast with the British policy of hands off and indirect rule. They hoped, they explained, to assimilate Africans into French civilization, making them ultimately into good children of the eighteenth-century Enlightenment, good citizens of the Republic founded on the principles of 1789. They hoped to create an empire of "100,000,000 Frenchmen," more than half of them overseas, and to draw on abundant native manpower to fill up the ranks of the Republic's armies.

In the military sense, the policy of assimi-

lation worked out somewhat as the French had hoped; in the main, however, assimilation was difficult and only partially successful. The French, always desirous of spreading their culture, did indeed assimilate part of the native ruling classes. Under the Third Republic they made Algeria politically a part of France itself, organizing it into three departments and giving them representatives to the Chamber of Deputies, with a franchise open to the relatively small group of Europeanized natives as well as to colonists. In Morocco, the French took a somewhat different tack. They sought, in part successfully, to open this backward land to French business and to the international tourist trade. Their urban center of Casablanca became a great modern city. And, without quite admitting the fact, they really abandoned assimilation for something close to the British policy of indirect rule. In 1912, the very able colonial administrator, Marshal Lyautey, began to organize turbulent Morocco, applying the "splash of oil" policy—that is, he pacified certain key centers by establishing firm working relations with the natives and then let pacification spread over the surface of Morocco like a splash of oil on water. The sultan and his feudal subordinates were maintained in Morocco, relatively free to carry on many of their age-old ways, but stripped of real power. Tunisia, like Morocco, was formally a protectorate.

The French: Tropical Africa

In 1815, the British had left France her small posts in West Africa at the mouth of the Senegal River, together with the slight foothold France had obtained in the seventeenth century on the great island of Madagascar off the East African coast. By 1914, the French had been very successful in the partition of Africa, perhaps at bottom because the British preferred French to German aggrandizement, especially after 1870. By 1914, at any rate, France numbered in Africa alone nearly as many inhabitants as in her home territories (about 39,000,000).

Except in North Africa, these people were

almost all Negroes of primitive material culture who were for the most part untouched by either Islam or Christianity. Except in certain coastal towns, where their administration and business were concentrated, the French had not by 1914 achieved very much toward assimilating or westernizing these vast districts. Most of their attempts to hasten the economic development of their African lands by organized joint-stock companies failed miserably.

It is quite possible that France spent more on these African colonies than she gained from them. Indeed, one of the stock arguments of nineteenth-century anti-imperialists was that colonies did not "pay" the mother country, and the French African colonies were one of their favorite exhibits. One economist —an Englishman, to be sure, and presumably unmoved by much that moves Frenchmen —concluded that in 1892 French gains

from colonial trade were 16,000,000 francs, whereas net government expenditures for the colonies were 174,000,000 francs. For 1915, he made an even more discouraging estimate.[*] Such figures, however, seem not to have discouraged any of the great powers in their imperialist efforts. Obviously the simplest form of the economic interpretation of history, the notion that political entities are moved by simple bookkeeping concepts of governmental economic profit and loss, does not hold true for nineteenth-century imperialism. Furthermore, note that such statistics apply solely to government expenditures; many French private businessmen undoubtedly made money out of their colonial ventures.

Again, though French colonies in tropical

[*] Constant Southworth, *The French Colonial Venture* (London, 1931), 122.

Entry of the French into Algiers, July 5, 1830.

Africa had by no means been modernized even in material conditions by 1914, everywhere a beginning had been made. Everywhere the tricolor went, there also went the beginnings of medicine and hygiene, modern methods of communication, industry, and agriculture, and formal education for at least a few natives. In justifying the policy of assimilation, the French claimed for themselves, in contrast with the British, a lack of race prejudice, a willingness to accept the blacks as equals. This contrast is underlined by the English author whose figures we have just quoted:

Of course, it is true that the French also attempt to understand the native and in the main to give him freedom to produce as he pleases. The Frenchman actually tends much more to be a 'good fellow' with the natives than does the Briton, who is much more aloof. But this greater democracy does not seem to inspire a greater degree of confidence. Somehow, the Briton is more apt to succeed in instilling in the native confidence in the results of producing by the system that he recommends.*

Although there is some truth in the claim for greater French toleration, the deed is not quite up to the word. The French in Africa did not often marry Negroes; but intermarriage is in this real world an unreal test of racial equality. Negroes very rarely *commanded* white Frenchmen in military or civilian activity. Both at home and in Africa, on the other hand, once the Negroes seemed firmly under control, the French went a long way toward encouraging Negro art and folkways, in keeping with a policy very close to the ideal delineated by Lugard for Nigeria. The British, however, especially in the twentieth century, edged toward some kind of assimilation; African Negro undergraduates in British universities took on a lot more of Britishness than just their fine standard English accent. The contrast between British and French African policies was far from complete—there were many similarities.

*Ibid., 193

The French: Asia

In Asia, the French took over in the nineteenth century lands that came to be called French Indo-China. These lands included two rich rice-growing deltas (around Hanoi in the north and Saigon in the south), inhabited by peoples culturally and in part racially related to the Chinese. They also included Cambodia, culturally related to India, and the primitive mountain peoples of Laos. French experience here on the whole ran parallel to imperialist experience elsewhere in Southeast Asia, though the Anglo-Saxon fondness for nagging the French has tended to create the impression that the French did far worse in Indo-China than did the Dutch in Java or the British in Malaya. Slow but real material progress was made, though the basic problem of poverty among the masses remained unsolved. Native nationalist movements, nourished by educated natives with jobs of less dignity and authority than they believed should be theirs, rose in strength as the years went on. France also took part, from her base in Indo-China, in the struggle for control of China proper. The French sphere of influence was southern China, in particular the province of Yunnan adjoining Indo-China, and in 1898 the French got a lease on a port in Kwangchou Bay.

The Germans

We can be brief in listing the colonial acquisitions of the other powers. Germany and Italy came late to the imperial scramble, as they came late to national unity. Nevertheless, Germany was clearly a great power, and Italy aspired to be one; hence, both sought to acquire the token colonies, at least, that seemed necessary to that dignified status—the familiar policy of "keeping up with the Joneses." Germany in 1914 had three really large pieces of tropical and subtropical Africa—the Kameruns (Cameroons), German Southwest

Africa, and German East Africa—and the smaller Togoland, close to a million square miles in all, nearly four times the size of Texas. These were not rich or well-developed areas, and their total contribution to the German economy was almost negligible. The German achievement on the whole was not greatly different from that of other European powers in Africa; it was neither morally nor economically much better or much worse. In the Pacific, the Germans picked up some small islands, and a large, primitive territory on the island of New Guinea. Germany took part in the attempted partition of China; her ninety-nine-year lease was on Kiaochow Bay.

The German drive for colonies was quite self-conscious; it was well organized in a pressure group with all the fixings of modern propaganda. Bismarck himself, who cared little for the prestige of colonies, was obliged to give way and consent to African ventures. His successors went farther, and William II helped Germany to enter one of the most confused and dangerous fields of imperialist expansion, the Near East. On the eve of World War I, the German "Berlin to Baghdad" push was well under way, and the Germans had supplanted the British as patrons of the Turks.

The Italians and Belgians

Italy, condemned to the role of weakest of the great powers, got very little even out of the partition of Africa. Tunis, which she coveted, went instead to France. Italy's major effort centered on the African lands at the southern end of the Red Sea, but after her defeat by the Abyssinians under Menelek in 1896 she had to content herself with a few thousand square miles, most of it desert, in Eritrea and Somaliland. Italian efforts to add to this inadequate empire by taking Tripoli from its nominal Turkish suzerains succeeded, but these same efforts led to the Italo-Turkish war of 1911, which was in a sense the real beginning of World War I (see Chapter 17). The Italians had so little to work with it is hard to assess their success or failure.

President Theodore Roosevelt on a steam shovel in Panama during the construction of the canal.

Little Belgium, largely through the enterprise of her King Leopold II (1865–1909), managed to acquire a large piece of equatorial Africa. This project began as the Congo Free State, with all sorts of noble ideals of co-operative European civilizing missions in Africa; but it ended up in 1908 as simply the Belgian Congo. Nineteenth-century scandal about forced labor and native exploitation in the Congo called Leopold's experiment to the attention of the world and provided liberal anti-imperialists with fresh arguments. But the Belgians, who had long since moderated Leopold's policies, retained until 1960 a legal hold on a restive Congo seeking independence (see Chapter 23).

The Americans

To the horror and indignation of many Americans, to the delight of others, the United States at the very end of the century joined the great powers and acquired overseas lands. In 1898, we waged a brief and success-

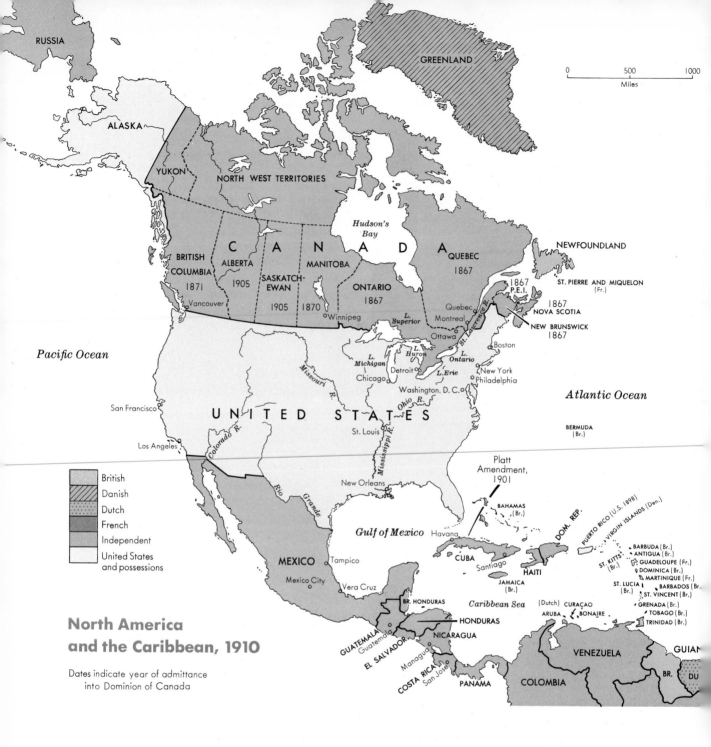

North America
and the Caribbean, 1910

Dates indicate year of admittance
into Dominion of Canada

Legend:
- British
- Danish
- Dutch
- French
- Independent
- United States and possessions

ful war with Spain, for which the immediate cause was the still mysterious sinking of the American battleship *Maine* in the harbor of Havana, Cuba. The Spanish-American War left the United States in control of the remnants of the Spanish Empire in America (the Caribbean islands of Cuba and Puerto Rico) and the large archipelago of the Philippines (about the size of Montana) off the coast of Asia. Mean-

time, the United States also acquired Hawaii (1898) and part of the Samoan Islands in the Pacific (1899). Then in 1903 American support of a revolution in Panama, then a part of Colombia, assured the independence of a new republic and direct American control of the zone of the projected Panama Canal.

The Americans withdrew from Cuba, leaving her as an independent republic, though subject under the Platt Amendment of 1901 to what in foreign eyes always seemed American "protection." The Platt Amendment, named from its proposer, Senator Orville Platt of Connecticut, limited Cuban control of its foreign policy and its national debt and gave the United States the formal right to intervene to preserve Cuban independence. It was resented bitterly by Cuban patriots as an infringement of Cuban sovereignty and was given up by the United States in 1934. The rest of her acquisitions the United States kept for the time, though in the Philippines she had to put down an armed rising by Filipinos who wanted immediate independence. American anti-imperialists attempted to upset the somewhat anomalous arrangement under which their government kept lands without strict authorization from the American Constitution. But a Supreme Court decision in the so-called "Insular Cases" (1901) held that territory might be subject to American jurisdiction without being incorporated constitutionally in the United States of America. Under this decision, Americans began the process of training the Filipinos for eventual independence. Meanwhile, the United States, too, had an empire, which on the maps was duly colored as an American "possession."

The Japanese

One more empire was being formed during the decades before World War I, the only empire to be created by a people of non-European stock—the Japanese. Even during their isolation (see Chapter 6), the Japanese had maintained an especial interest in western developments through the trading station that the Dutch were allowed at Nagasaki. When Japan was opened to the world in 1853, its basic political and economic structure had long needed overhauling. An oligarchy of the feudal type ruled, but its ineffective government made it widely unpopular. Discontent was growing, especially among two important social classes. One was the urban middle class of merchants and craftsmen. Although the industrial revolution had not yet reached Japan,

the country already had populous cities, notably Tokyo (then called Yedo or Edo). The urban middle class, somewhat like the French bourgeoisie on the eve of 1789, wanted political rights to match their increasing economic power. The other discontented class may be compared roughly with the poorer gentry and lesser nobility of Europe under the Old Régime. These were the *samurai* or feudal retainers, a military caste now threatened with impoverishment and political eclipse. The *samurai* dreaded the growth of cities and the subsequent threat to the traditional domination of agriculture and the landlords; many of them also resented the fact that they were largely excluded from positions of power by the prevailing oligarchical regime. These social pressures, more than any outside western influence, forced the modernization of Japan.

The American Commodore Perry, who "opened" Japan; Japanese woodblock print, 1853.

Economically, the transformation proceeded rapidly. By 1914, much of Japan resembled an advanced western country. She, too, had railroads, fleets of merchant vessels, a large textile industry, big cities, and big business firms. The industrialization of Japan was the more remarkable in view of her meager supplies of many essential raw materials. But she had many important assets. As a glance at the map will show, her geographical position with respect to Asia is very like that of the British Isles with respect to Europe. Japan, too, found markets for her exports on the continent nearby and used the income to pay for imports. The ambitious Japanese middle class, supplemented by recruits from the *samurai,* furnished aggressive business leadership. A great reservoir of cheap labor existed in the peasantry, a large and submissive class. The peasants, who needed to find jobs away from the overcrowded farms, were inured to a very low standard of living and were ready to work long and hard in factories for what seemed by western standards indecently low wages.

Politically, Japan appeared to undergo a major revolution in the late nineteenth century and to remodel her government along western lines. Actually, however, the change was by no means so great as it seemed. A revolution did indeed occur, beginning in 1868 when the old feudal oligarchy crumbled under the pressure of the discontented elements. Authority and prestige were restored to the position of emperor ("mikado"), a largely forgotten office whose incumbents had for years had no real power. In 1889, the emperor bestowed a constitution on his subjects, with a bicameral diet composed of a noble House of Peers and an elected House of Representatives. The architects of these changes, however,

were not democrats. They were aristocrats, ambitious young *samurai,* supported by allies from the business world and determined to make Japan over from above as they wished. The result was to substitute a new oligarchy for the old; a small group of aristocrats dominated the emperor and the state. The constitution of 1889, rather like that of the German Empire, provided only the outward appearances of liberal parliamentary government. The ministry was responsible not to the diet but to the emperor, and hence to the dominant ruling class. The diet itself was scarcely representative; the right to vote for members of its lower house was limited to a narrow electorate, including the middle class but excluding the peasants and industrial workers. As Sir George Sansom, a British expert on Japan, has observed, she had no trouble in accepting western "things" but a great deal in handling western "ideas."

Japan began her expansion by taking from China, after a brief war in 1894–1895, the island of Formosa, which she annexed, and the piece of Asiatic mainland closest to Japan, the peninsula of Korea, whose independence China was forced to recognize as a preliminary to eventual Japanese annexation. But Russia, too, had designs on Korea; the results of this rivalry were the Russo-Japanese War of 1904–1905 and a second great Japanese victory (see Chapter 14). Japan now secured unchallenged preponderance in Korea, which she annexed in 1910, special concessions in the Chinese province of Manchuria, and the cession by Russia of the southern half of the island of Sakhalin, to the north of the main Japanese islands. She had expanded in the classic European way; that is, she now had an empire.

IV   The Debate Over Imperialism

In the nineteenth century all the western countries, even monarchical states like Germany, had a wide range of free public

opinion and some kind of parliamentary government by discussion. The kind of expansion we call imperialism, therefore, had to be de-

Cecil Rhodes (1853–1902).

already begun to worry a bit. White men, this argument insisted, are simply better specimens of *homo sapiens* than are colored men; Anglo-Saxons (or Germans, or Slavs, or Latins, depending on the writer's origins) are simply better specimens than other white men.

An imperialist like Cecil Rhodes, to judge from much that he wrote and said, very likely dreamed of a world which in the fullness of time and evolution would be peopled entirely by Anglo-Saxons. Their breed would actually be improved over their ancestors of 1900, after the inferior peoples had died out—or had been killed off. But these were very distant views indeed. The prospect of ruddy Kentish farmers actually established in freeholds along the Congo simply was unrealistic. More fashionable imperialistic doctrine held that throughout the tropical world, the superior white men would put order and prosperity into the lives of colored men, would as trustees of civilization give up the comforts of Europe to rule in discomfort in the hot countries. Some imperialists thought that this benevolent rule of white men in the tropics would last indefinitely, since in their opinion non-whites were totally unable to undertake tasks of leadership and to assume moral responsibility.

fended articulately, since it was attacked articulately. The defense and attack are both important parts of the intellectual history of our times.

Pro: The Argument from Social Darwinism

One central argument for the defense borrowed heavily from the Social Darwinists (see Chapter 15). Europeans both in Europe and in their "colonies of settlement," so ran the argument, were able to beat non-Europeans in war. By this very fact they had shown that they were in terms of evolution and progress more fit to survive than were the non-Europeans. Eternal competition is the price of survival and the best always survive—or *ought* to survive, for these theorists of imperialism had

Pro: The Argument of Duty

Other European imperialists, however, took the attitude that, though the non-whites could not run their own affairs then, they could ultimately learn to do so. For the present and for a good many years to come, whites would have to educate them on the spot; someday—the length of time judged necessary varied with the temperament of the judge—these non-whites would have matured sufficiently to take over responsibilities now confined to whites. These whites will not be *owners,* merely *trustees.* Kipling put the case comfortably enough—for white men—in his famous poem:

> Take up the White Man's Burden—
>   Send forth the best ye breed—
> Go bind your sons to exile

> To serve your captives' need;
> To wait in heavy harness,
> On fluttered folk and wild—
> Your new-caught, sullen peoples,
> Half-devil and half-child.*

This argument of trusteeship was by all odds the most popular defense of imperialism, particularly among Anglo-Saxon peoples.

Yet the historian, aware of the complexities of human nature, will be wary of the notion that the ethical arguments of the imperialists were insincere. Many a European both in and out of the colonies of exploitation really believed in the trusteeship theory, and really did his best to live up to it. The Christian missionary is a major factor in the nineteenth-century expansion of the West. Indeed, Kenneth Latourette's long and thorough history of the expansion of Christianity has a final volume entitled *The Great Century* for the nineteenth century. More formal converts to Christianity were made all over the world in this century, so often labeled the century of materialism, than ever before.

The reality of the conversion of the colored peoples presents a difficult problem. In areas of primitive culture, whole tribes nominally accepted Christianity but continued many of the immemorial ways of their heathen past. In India, China, and Japan, old civilized countries with deep-rooted religious faiths of their own, Christianity did not win over anything like a majority of the people. Nevertheless, the missions did succeed in the course of the century in building up devoted native followers, of whom the most intelligent or most enterprising were often sent to Europe or the United States to complete their education.

Pro: The Defensive Argument

Finally, the imperialist philosophy of 1900 was by no means based on an unworried sense of white supremacy. Western civilization is

*"The White Man's Burden," from "The Five Nations," *Rudyard Kipling's Verse, 1885–1932* (London, 1933), 320.

one of the most worrying of all civilizations. Many publicists regarded imperialism as essentially defensive. The whites, outnumbered in a harsh world, had to organize themselves and hold the non-whites off. There was talk of the "yellow peril" and of white "race suicide." The writings and speeches of such apparently confident imperialists as Rhodes, Kipling, the German Emperor Wilhelm II, and Theodore Roosevelt sounded this curious note of fear and uncertainty. We are the best, but really we are a little too good for this world; we cannot breed fast enough.

One further aspect, or variation, of the defensive argument involved the importance of naval bases and coaling stations. Here the appetite tended to grow by eating. First, the French could argue that security of the homeland required control of North Africa, but presently the far-off holdings in Indo-China demanded a string of bases along which the navy could operate to protect the empire.

Con: Anti-Imperialist Arguments

Against imperialism, opponents marshaled a great many arguments. To the Social Darwinists the anti-imperialists replied by denying that the struggle for existence applied to human groups in the way it applied to plants and animals. It is precisely by sublimating the crude conflict of kill-or-be-killed into the higher rivalry for cultural excellence, they argued, that human societies transcend the struggle for life. Each group, each race, has something to contribute to the total of civilization, and the deliberate destruction or suppression of any group lames and lessens the others, prevents the true working out of evolution—that is, *cultural* evolution—among human beings as contrasted with mere animals. The anti-imperialists also brought forward very prominently the economic argument we have already noted (p. 611). They worked hard to show that in fact, especially in Africa, colonies did not "pay," that the imperialist appeal to self-interest in the homeland was a delusion, the dishonest work of propagandists for the privileged minority in the homeland and in the colonies who *did* profit personally from imperialist ventures.

From this point the anti-imperialists went on to maintain that support at home for colonial expansion rested therefore on the ordinary man's vicarious satisfactions from national achievements. The ordinary man liked to see his country figure in the world atlas as an imperial power. He liked to think of Britain's empire on which the sun never set; or, if he was a Frenchman, of the tangible evidence that France was still a great power, still carrying on her *mission civilisatrice;* or, if he was an Italian, that at last Italy too was a nation, and behaving as nations should. The anti-imperialists were on the whole not very successful in their attempts to use ridicule and irony against behavior that they found irrational. But their conviction that human action ought to be rational and devoted to the greatest good of the greatest number placed them firmly in the liberal tradition.

So strong was the anti-imperialists' belief that they were right—in spite of the growth of empires all about them—that in Britain the school of "Little Englanders," much influenced by laissez-faire economics, came to the comforting assurance that imperialism was impossible. The colonies, they held, must inevitably drop away from the mother country—to use their favorite stereotype—like ripe fruit from a tree. Why not then avoid getting into the futile process further by *not* taking any more of Africa or China? Why not hasten the inevitable by giving up the empire?

In fairness, we must add that much liberal opposition to imperialism was motivated by humanitarian sympathy for the colored peoples under imperial rule.

Not all the anti-imperialists were liberals or idealists. Indeed in France some of the most vehement were the extreme nationalists who wanted *revanche* (revenge) on Prussia for the French defeat in the war of 1870. These *revanchards* were not sorry for the Negroes; they opposed French colonialism because it distracted French energies from what they thought was the sole proper national business—getting ready to beat the Germans.

What sank into the mind and feelings of the ordinary westerner as a result of the anti-imperialist arguments was an uneasy awareness that somehow the practice of imperial expansion did not square with the best avowed intentions of democracy. Particularly in the United States, the feeling grew that imperialism and colonialism were contrary to the ideas of liberty and equality, even if the imperialists honestly claimed to be following the "trusteeship" principle. America took over an empire in 1898, but not without vigorous protests from numerous groups of anti-imperialists, and not without specific promises from the government that it would "free" dependents the moment they were capable of self-rule. This opposition of Americans to colonialism, especially when practiced by themselves, is one of the important factors in the world situation of the mid-twentieth century, and we shall return to it in later chapters, for it played a large part in our foreign policy.

V   The Colonies of White Settlement

Thus far our account of the nineteenth-century expansion of Europe has been limited largely to the "colonies of exploitation," the protectorates, and the spheres of influence held by Europeans. No such account is at all complete, for the most striking

thing about this expansion was that it involved an actual transplantation of Europeans to "colonies of settlement" on a scale incomparably greater than in the previous three centuries since Henry the Navigator and Columbus.

The colonies of settlement were originally

very thinly inhabited lands. Australia, indeed, was almost empty; and the whole native Red Indian population of America north of the Rio Grande was almost certainly in 1800 not over a million, perhaps less. The European settlers simply overwhelmed these primitive peoples. In Tasmania, a large island to the south of the Australian mainland, the natives were totally wiped out, and in Australia itself they were very nearly wiped out. In the United States the Red Indians were so far eliminated that many an American grew up in the later nineteenth century without ever seeing a redman except in a Wild West show.

In most of Latin America, however, the native Indian stock, far from being wiped out, persisted; the upper class, politically and economically, was drawn from European "creole" stock; and a great many people of mixed European and Indian and Negro blood filled the lower social ranks. In the far south of the continent, in the Argentine, Uruguay, and Chile, conditions resembled more nearly those in the United States, and these twentieth-century nations are now almost wholly European in stock, largely from the Iberian peninsula and Italy.

The expansion of Europe into the Americas was also an expansion of Africa. By 1850 the leading European powers had pretty generally got the slave trade under control; but the nucleus of Negroes brought into both North and South America by the trade in the earlier centuries continued to grow. Despite handicaps of race barriers, strongest in the United States, the Negroes multiplied; by 1900, for example, there were some 9,000,000 of them in the United States.

Canada: Background of Revolt

Apart from the extraordinary growth of the United States, the most important phase of the nineteenth-century movement of Europeans overseas is the growth of what is now called the British Commonwealth of Nations, or, more correctly, simply the Commonwealth. Doubtless it is an oversimplification to claim that the British learned their lesson from the American Revolution, and that consequently in Canada, Australia, and South Africa they were wise enough to abandon the policies of George III and Lord North. But the formula is fundamentally sound. The first laboratory for this experiment in a new kind of "colonialism" was Canada (see map on p. 614).

The rebellious thirteen colonies of North America had wanted to add a fourteenth, and had tried hard to win Canada. But a complex of causes all contributed to leaving Canada in British hands at the peace in 1783. The French Canadians in Quebec distrusted the new Protestant power growing up to the south; the American rebels had grave difficulties keeping up an army to cope with the British in the United States itself; America's French ally did not wish the new country to be too strong. Later, as we have seen in Chapter 14, the United States failed in the War of 1812 to reverse the verdict of 1783.

Upper Canada (Ontario), which was mainly British in stock, and Lower Canada (Quebec), which was mainly French, and the Maritime Provinces of Nova Scotia, New Brunswick, and Prince Edward Island were at first quite separate British "colonies," as the American thirteen had once been. Each had an apparatus quite like the old American one—a royal governor appointed by the Crown, a council appointed by the governor, and an elected assembly based on a more or less popular franchise. But just as in the thirteen colonies during the preceding century, the arrangement bred conflicts between the assemblies and the royal government. In 1837, revolts broke out in both Upper and Lower Canada, with popular leaders like Mackenzie and Papineau arrayed against the governor and his followers, and with essentially the same kind of constitutional and financial grievances that the thirteen colonies had had sixty years before.

Canada: Durham and a New Status

The revolt of 1837 was a military fiasco, and it is probable that public opinion in both provinces was against the rebels; there was a fear that too close an imitation of the American Revolution would lead to absorption by the United States. But the British government was alarmed and sent out as governor-in-chief of all the British North American provinces the Earl of Durham, a young lord of Whig antecedents and Utilitarian leanings. Durham, feeling that he was not properly supported from London, resigned after less than a year in Canada. But the famous report he made to the British Parliament on his return in 1839 became the cornerstone of the new British imperial structure of dominions, a constitutional document that Durham's admirers have sometimes ranked with Magna Carta.

The Durham Report proposed the union of Upper and Lower Canada and the establishment of responsible government—that is, a popularly elected legislature with ultimate authority—for both the union and each of the separate provinces. The report is still of great interest. Durham had all the average Englishman's insensitivity to things French, and it is an understatement to say that he never understood the Québecois of Lower Canada. But he was true to his principles—even these French Canadian Catholics must have their own responsible government. As he wrote, with prescience:

The maintenance of an absolute form of government on any part of the North American Continent can never continue for any long time, without exciting a general feeling in the United States against a power of which the existence is secured by means so odious to the people; and as I rate the preservation of the present general sympathy of the United States with the policy of our Government in Lower Canada as a matter of the greatest importance, I should be sorry that the feeling should be changed for one which, if prevalent among the people, must extend over the surrounding Provinces. The influence of such an opinion would not only act very strongly on the entire French population, and keep up among them a sense of injury and a determination of resistance to the Government, but would lead to just as great discontent among the English. . . .*

The actual realization of Durham's recommendations was achieved with due British slowness. The first step, the Union Act of

*Sir Reginald Coupland, *The Durham Report* (Oxford, 1954), 155–156.

1840 passed by the British Parliament, though it did unite Upper and Lower Canada, was at the very least unspecific on the critical point of responsibility—that is, on whether an administration defeated in the legislature had to resign or not. Nearly a decade later, under the governorship of Lord Elgin, the principle was quietly established in practice, never to be withdrawn. Nor was the next step unduly hurried. The British North America Act of 1867 achieved in principle the union of all the British provinces in North America, except Newfoundland, oldest of all, whose separatist tendencies were so strong that it did not join Canada until 1949. The act of 1867, itself basically due to formal Canadian initiative at a meeting of the "Fathers of Confederation" at Charlottetown, set up the Dominion of Canada by the union of Ontario, Quebec, and the Maritime Provinces, with provision for the admission of territories in the west as provinces on something like the pattern for admission of the western states in the United States. There were still many survivals of the former "colonial" status of Canada, from the bestowal of titles, especially knighthood with its unrepublican and undemocratic "Sir," to the possibility of judicial appeal from Canadian courts to the Privy Council in Westminster. Above all, the relation of Canada to Britain in terms of international affairs, armed forces, right of secession, and much else was not yet spelled out, and was not to be spelled out formally until the Statute of Westminster in 1931 (see Chapter 20).

The Extension of Dominion Status

The individual provinces of Australia had common British origins and had relatively short lives as separate territorial units—the oldest, New South Wales, dates only from 1788. But, in spite of these facts, these provinces developed their local differences and separateness, symbolized by the fact that they used differing gauges for their railroads. They gained the essentials of self-government in the Australian Colonies Government Act of 1850, but federal union of New South Wales,

Victoria, Queensland, and the others was not achieved until the Commonwealth of Australia was formed in 1901. The influence of the American example is clear in the constitution of the Commonwealth, which provides for a senate with equal membership for each of the six states, a house of representatives apportioned on the basis of population, and a supreme court with something close to the American power of judicial review. But in Australia as in the other British dominions, the parliamentary system of an executive (prime minister and cabinet) dismissible by vote of the legislative body was retained; the American "presidential" system was deliberately rejected.

Australia, like Canada, was essentially an empty country in 1800, and like Canada it filled gradually with immigrants, mostly from Britain. Perhaps the head start of the United States, with its great attraction for British and European immigration, slowed down the growth of these British dominions. But the process, though slow, was steady, and by 1914 all the dominions, including the quiet islands of New Zealand, traditionally most "English" of them all, were prosperous, democratic societies just settling down from the last of the pioneer stage. Their narrative history is most interesting, but we cannot go into it here, nor into the fascinating and illuminating subject — insufficiently pursued — of the likenesses and unlikenesses of the corporate personalities of these new countries and the United States, all offsprings of the "frontier."

The Commonwealth in Review

In the nineteenth century, Americans pushing west and Russians pushing east added millions of square miles to their respective lands as colonies of settlement. Although in both, and especially in America, this process of the "frontier" had important effects on their national character, it did not create great immediate problems concerning the "independence" of the settlers. The British, however, went thousands of miles overseas for their colonies of settlement. They found very soon that these colonies could not be treated as the long tradition since Columbus prescribed — that is, as mere outposts of the mother land with no political self-rule, held in strict mercantilist economic leading strings. Nor could they be, if only because of the separating seas, simply added as they filled up as a territorial continuation of the mother land, as Siberia was added to Russia and the territories of the American West to the federal Union. By 1914, the British at home and the citizens of their overseas colonies of settlement had worked out something new in political configurations, unprecedented in man's brief history.

Canada, Australia, New Zealand, and South Africa were indeed by 1914 wholly self-governing. They could and did even levy customs dues on imports from Britain. They had the beginnings of military forces of their own, and of course complete control of that clear attribute of "sovereignty" — their own internal police. Men were even beginning to speculate about whether they were not in possession of that other clear attribute of sovereignty — the right to conduct foreign relations, both diplomatic and military. For example, could Canada be at peace with a country with which Great Britain was at war?

The first test came in 1914. All the dominions went to war against Germany and her allies. Even the dubiously loyal Union of South Africa went to war against the sender of the Kruger telegram; we are bound to record that the always land-hungry Boers had their eyes on the German colonies in Africa, and especially on the big empty colony of German Southwest Africa, right adjacent to the Union. The government of each dominion, however, went through the formal process of declaring war, just as "sovereign" countries do. Yet the relation between Canada, for instance, and Great Britain was something different from the relation between two such sovereign countries as the Argentine and Spain. The dominions had not quite set up wholly for themselves, nor, to revert to the favorite cliché of the nineteenth-century Little Englander, had they dropped off like ripe fruit. The nature of the tie between the dominions and Britain was not clear then, and it must be admitted it is not fully clear even now. But it still exists, though greatly weakened, and to it also we shall return in a chapter on imperialism in our own day. (See Chapter 23.)

VI   The Results of Imperialism

The broad general results of this long phase of European expansion down to 1914 may now be summarized.

First and most obviously, in the nineteenth century almost the whole planet was affected by the process. The white man was almost everywhere by 1914, and white explorers not infrequently found that the tin can, that ubiquitous symbol of the West, had got there ahead of them.

Second, the expansion of Europe was accompanied by a numerical expansion of the whole human race. Between 1800 and 1900, the population of the world just about doubled, from some 800,000,000 in 1800 to some 1,600,000,000 in 1900. European white stock did indeed account for the most spectacular part of the rise, but non-whites in Asia and elsewhere also increased. We do not sufficiently understand human population growth to say flatly that the expansion of Europe *caused* the growth of population among non-European peoples in the nineteenth century. But it did bring to many areas of the world some increase of law and order, some increase in material production and improvements in transportation and distribution, health and sanitation—factors that probably contribute to population growth. And, with such exceptions as the native Australian "Blackfellows" and some North American Indians, European expansion did not usually mean the physical extermination of non-European peoples.

Third, we may say with no reservations whatever that by 1914 it was quite clear that "natives" were beginning to reject the claims of white supremacy. Among the more civilized and long-established peoples in the Near East and Asia, the educated classes were already developing a sense of nationalism. They took over from the West that particular form of group consciousness that is attached to a territorial political unit and that is shared, in principle at least, by all who live within the unit. This nationalism was a new thing outside Europe, and a very important one for us today, for it has gone on increasing and developing. In the early twentieth century, it was most evident in Japan and, to some extent, China, and in advanced "colonial" nations like Egypt and India, though there were signs of it almost everywhere.

This new phenomenon was not the same thing as simple hostility to whites, or to particular nations among the whites. It was an organized political faith—in short, modern "patriotism." Naturally, Egyptian, Indian, and Chinese patriots were first of all concerned with getting rid of their European imperial masters; their attitudes were those of oppressed nationalistic groups everywhere, even in Europe itself. After all, the most striking and most successful rebellion of early twentieth-century nationalist movements against an imperial "master" was that of very European and very white Ireland against the British. These "colonial" peoples were touchy, addicted to nursing grievances imaginary as well as real, eager to seize on any national trait that could be glorified, admiring, hating, and envying their masters. Above all, they were organized on a new principle taken from the West, a principle that is ultimately perhaps more destructive of their own traditional cultures than anything else that has come to them from the West. This is the equalitarian and leveling, if not democratic, spirit inherent in the secular religion of nationalism. In theory at least nationality transcends the dividing lines of profession, social class, and even caste. The fellah, the Egyptian peasant whose ancestry reaches back through the centuries, could claim to be as good an Egyptian as the aristocratic pasha — indeed a better one, since he was uncorrupted by European culture. People began to talk and write of "Arab" nationalism; yet the "Arabs" were not exactly a race, nor a people, nor any specific political-territorial entity — at most, "Arab" referred to a language, a culture, and to a part of those who held the Moslem faith.

Fourth, and in spite of the gloomy economic conclusions of anti-imperialists, there seems no doubt that over the century the homelands of Europe gained in total wealth from their expansion overseas. Indeed, raw materials from overseas were necessary to maintain the standard of living in thickly populated countries like Britain, Germany, Belgium, and the Netherlands. Theoretically, these raw materials could have come into European lands in free trade with free countries overseas; actually they came in part from imperial expansion. In purely empirical terms, the imperialism of the nineteenth century does seem to confirm Professor Walter P. Webb's analysis (see Chapter 6): The expansion of Europe was a great demographic and economic bonanza, a dynamic material growth never before attained by man.

Finally, imperialist rivalries, especially after 1870, exacerbated the normal rivalries among the European great powers and were thus a major factor in the complex of causes that brought on general war in 1914. This is particularly true of the Anglo-German rivalry, which, unlike that of France and England or of Austria and Russia, had no long historical background. This Anglo-German rivalry was everywhere by 1900 — among commercial travelers of both nations, trying to sell machinery in Peru; among missionaries trying to convert the heathen in Africa; among army officers, naval officers, editors, organizers, all seeking to make German influence more important than British somewhere or to keep British influence more important than German. The rivalry extended even to the academic world and to that world in the United States. There were those who regarded the Rhodes Scholarships for study at Oxford (1904) as a British attempt to counterbalance the great prestige that the German universities, and especially their degree of Ph.D., had acquired in America during the latter nineteenth century.

Reading Suggestions on Nineteenth-Century Imperialism

(Asterisk indicates paperbound edition.)

General Accounts

W. L. Langer, *The Diplomacy of Imperialism, 1890 – 1902*, 2nd ed. (Knopf, 1951). Study of a hectic period of the imperial scramble; includes a discussion of forces making for imperialism.

J. A. Hobson, *Imperialism. A Study* (Nisbet, 1902). Famous attack on imperialism.

V. I. Lenin, *Imperialism, The Highest Stage of Capitalism* (International Publishers, 1939). The classic expression of the communist interpretation of imperialism.

R. Koebner and H. D. Schmidt, *Imperialism: The Story and Significance of a Political Word, 1840 – 1960* (Cambridge Univ. Press, 1964). Important sequel to Dr. Koebner's *Empire*.

B. Kidd, *The Control of the Tropics* (Macmillan, 1898). A defense of imperialism.

J. A. Schumpeter, *Imperialism and Social Classes* (Noonday, 1955; *Meridian). A valuable essay on imperialism from the standpoint of the economist and sociologist.

D. K. Fieldhouse, *The Colonial Empires: A Comparative Survey from the Eighteenth Century* (Delacorte Press, 1967). Authoritative and complete.

K. S. Latourette, *A History of the Expansion of Christianity*, 7 vols. (Harper, 1937 – 1945). Volumes 5 and 6 concern the expansion of Christianity into the non-European world.

Special Studies: Africa

L. Woolf, *Empire and Commerce in Africa* (Allen & Unwin, 1919). A left-wing critique.

H. H. Johnston, *The Opening Up of Africa* (Holt, 1911. Home University Library). Sympathetic popular account by the author of many other works on Africa.

H. L. Hoskins, *European Imperialism in Africa* (Holt, 1930. A Berkshire Study). Handy introductory manual.

James Duffy, *Portugal in Africa* (Harvard Univ. Press, 1962). The best account.

R. L. Buell, *The Native Problem in Africa* (Macmillan, 1928), and H. A. Wieschoff, *Colonial Policies in Africa* (Univ. of Pennsylvania Press, 1944). Two solid and helpful studies.

R. Robinson and others, *Africa and the Victorians: The Climax of Imperialism in the Dark Continent* (St. Martin's Press, 1961). Excellent study from archival material.

C. W. de Kiewiet, *A History of South Africa, Social and Economic* (Clarendon, 1941), and E. A. Walker, *A History of South Africa*, 2nd ed. (Longmans, Green, 1940). Two good studies.

B. Williams, *Cecil Rhodes* (Constable, 1921). Probably the best book on the famous empire-builder. But for a different estimate, see G. S. Millin, *Cecil Rhodes* (Harper, 1933).

W. H. Hancock, *Smuts: The Sanguine Years* (Cambridge Univ. Press, 1962). A final volume is promised in this definitive biography of a major South African leader.

B. Williams, *Botha, Smuts, and South Africa* (Macmillan, 1948. Teach Yourself History series). Introduction to the period following the Boer War.

F. D. Lugard, *The Dual Mandate in British Tropical Africa,* 3rd ed. (Blackwood, 1926). Significant detailed account of British colonial policy in action.

H. R. Rudin, *Germans in the Cameroons, 1884–1914: A Case Study in Imperialism* (Yale Univ. Press, 1938). Good study of the topic indicated.

L. de Lichtervelde, *Léopold of the Belgians* (Century, 1929), and L. Bauer, *Leopold the Unloved, King of the Belgians and of Wealth* (Little, Brown, 1935). Vindicating and attacking, respectively, the great exploiter of the Congo.

Special Studies: Asia

J. T. Pratt, *The Expansion of Europe into the Far East* (Sylvan Press, 1947). Excellent introduction to the subject.

D. E. Owen, *Imperialism and Nationalism in the Far East* (Holt, 1929. A Berkshire Study). Handy brief introductory manual.

K. S. Latourette, *The Development of China,* new ed. (Houghton, Mifflin, 1956). A good survey.

A. C. Lyall, *The Rise and Expansion of British Dominion in India,* 5th ed. (Murray, 1914). Sympathetic account.

R. Coupland, *Britain and India, 1600–1941* (Longmans, Green, 1941). Very brief introduction by an authority on imperial questions.

G. Sansom, *The Western World and Japan, A Study in the Interaction of European and Asiatic Cultures* (Knopf, 1950), and *Japan, A Short Cultural History,* rev. ed. (Appleton-Century, 1943). Two indispensable works by a great authority on Japan.

S. N. Fisher, *The Middle East: A History* (Knopf, 1959). A solid detailed account, emphasizing the nineteenth and twentieth centuries.

K. S. Latourette, *A History of Modern China* (*Penguin). Sound reliable survey.

E. O. Reischauer, *Japan, Past and Present* (Knopf, 1946). Reliable introduction.

B. H. Sumner, *Tsardom and Imperialism in the Far East and Middle East, 1880–1914* (British Academy, 1944). Good short account.

R. E. M. Wheeler, *Cambridge History of India,* Vols. V and VI (Cambridge Univ. Press, 1929). A new edition of these standard detailed volumes is in preparation.

V. H. Smith, *The Oxford History of India*, 3rd ed. (Oxford Univ. Press, 1958). Brief detailed account of the history of India, edited by Percival Spear.

H. Brown, ed., *The Sahibs: The Life and Ways of the British in India as Recorded by Themselves* (Hodge, 1948). An illuminating compilation.

Special Studies: British Empire and Dominions

J. H. Rose and others, eds., *The Cambridge History of the British Empire*, 7 vols. (Macmillan, 1929–1940). Separate volumes on India, Canada, and Australia and New Zealand.

P. Knaplund, *The British Empire, 1815–1939* (Harper, 1941). An authoritative work.

C. E. Carrington, *The British Overseas: Exploits of a Nation of Shopkeepers* (Cambridge Univ. Press, 1950). An advanced and detailed study from a British point of view.

R. Anstey, *Britain and the Congo in the Nineteenth Century* (Oxford Univ. Press, 1962). A good special study.

M. Perham and M. Bull, eds., Diaries of Lord Leyard, 4 vols. (Northwestern Univ. Press, 1959–1963). Useful source material for the state of mind of a superior "imperialist."

C. P. de T. Glazebrook, *Canada: A Short History* (Oxford Univ. Press, 1950). A good brief survey.

C. F. Wittke, *A History of Canada,* 3rd ed. (Crofts, 1941). Emphasis on recent history.

R. Coupland, ed., *The Durham Report* (Clarendon, 1946). The famous document that in a sense marks the beginning of the development of the British Commonwealth.

G. Greenwood, ed., *Australia: A Social and Political History* (Praeger, 1955). Good collaborative work, with bibliographies.

M. Barnard, *A History of Australia* (Praeger, 1963). A readable brief history.

H. Belshaw, ed., *New Zealand* (Univ. of California Press, 1947). An informative volume.

J. B. Condliffe, *New Zealand in the Making,* and *The Welfare State in New Zealand* (both Macmillan, 1959). These books provide a good economic history of 1792–1957.

Special Studies: Other Subjects

S. H. Roberts, *History of French Colonial Policy, 1870–1925,* 2 vols. (King, 1929). Detailed.

M. E. Townsend, *The Rise and Fall of Germany's Colonial Empire, 1884–1918* (Macmillan, 1930). A useful account.

J. W. Pratt, *America's Colonial Experiment* (Prentice-Hall, 1950). A valuable survey.

D. Perkins, *Hands Off: A History of the Monroe Doctrine* (Little, Brown, 1941). A useful popular account by a leading specialist.

Historical Fiction

R. Kipling, *Kim* (many editions) and *Soldiers Three* (many editions). Famous works by the even more famous champion of imperialism.

N. Coward, *Cavalcade,* in *Play Parade* (Garden City Publishing, 1933). A patriotic play and a sentimental tribute to old imperial glories.

S. Cloete, *The Turning Wheels* (Houghton, Mifflin, 1937). A novel about nineteenth-century Boers.

A. Gide, *The Immoralist* (*Vintage). European hero corrupted by North Africa.

E. M. Forster, *A Passage to India* (many editions). A celebrated and astringent novel.

L. Hémon, *Maria Chapdelaine* (Macmillan, 1940; *Image). The best-known novel about rural French Canada.

Hugh McLennan, *The Precipice* (Duell, Sloan & Pearce, 1948). One of the few good psychological studies of relations between English-speaking and French-speaking Canadians.

H. H. Richardson, *The Fortunes of Richard Mahony* (Readers Club, 1941). A series of novels about modern Australia by an Australian.

H. Rider Haggard, *King Solomon's Mines* (Longmans, Green, 1926). A splendid example of the rousing novel of imperialist adventure.

17

The First World War

I Introduction

On June 28, 1914, the Habsburg Archduke Francis Ferdinand, heir to the throne of Austria-Hungary, and his wife were assassinated in the streets of Sarajevo, capital of the recently (1908) annexed provinces of Bosnia and Herzegovina, which had been occupied by Austria-Hungary since 1878 (see Chapter 14). The assassin, Princip, was a Serbian nationalist. Bosnia had long been coveted by the Serbs. The Austro-Hungarian government, alarmed by the ambitions of Serbian nationalists, took the occasion of the assassination to send a severe ultimatum to Serbia. The Serbian government's refusal to accept the ultimatum in its entirety led to an Austrian declaration of war on Serbia, on July 28. Within the week, the great states of Europe were engaged in a general war—the Central Powers (Austria-

Hungary and Germany) against the Allies (Serbia, Russia, France, and Britain). Princip's revolver shot was eventually to kill some ten million men.

This was the first general war, the first war to involve most of the members of the world state-system, since the wars of the French Revolution and Napoleon a century earlier. There had indeed been wars enough, foreign and civil, in the century between. They were, however, save for relatively minor wars like the Crimean War of 1853, wars between two parties, like the Franco-Prussian War of 1870, the bloody American war between North and South in 1861–1865, and a whole series of colonial wars against rebellious natives.

In 1914 a great many people in Europe and America felt that this sort of general war was all but impossible. These people, predominantly liberal intellectuals, had been alarmed by the series of crises we shall shortly describe, crises that showed how close a general war might be. But they had followed hopefully the movements for international peace and cooperation—the Red Cross, the international labor movements, and the Hague conferences of 1899 and 1907, which, though they failed to achieve their avowed purpose of limiting armaments, did set up a tribunal for the arbitration of international disputes, the "world court." And many intellectuals simply refused to believe that a world war, should it break out, could last more than a few months. The cost of such a war, they maintained, would be so great it would bankrupt any government. Such was the thesis of a best seller, Norman Angell's *The Great Illusion* (1910).

World War I was long, bloody, and destructive. The shock of its outbreak, vastly increased by the strains of the war itself, and above all by the failure of the postwar peace settlement, brought on in the 1920's a most extraordinary discussion of the causes of the war. This discussion was by no means limited to professional historians. It was carried on in the press and on the platforms by all the agencies that touched public opinion. Most of it was designed to "revise" the verdict of the Versailles Treaty of 1919, in which the victorious Allies declared Germany and Austria-Hungary solely responsible for precipitating the war of 1914. The beaten Germans, penalized in the peace, had obvious reasons for trying to prove themselves innocent of war guilt. But important currents in public opinion in Great Britain, the United States, and even in France also flowed into this "revisionist" movement. So far did revisionism go in the 1920's that some American historians parceled out varying portions of the guilt among the victors and the vanquished alike, with the confidence of schoolmasters handing out merits and demerits.

We cannot be so confident today. From our further perspective, the question of war guilt in 1914 fades out into a question of historical causation, and into the fact of historical tragedy. We can say with the English writer, George Meredith:

> In tragic life, God wot,
> No villain need be! Passions spin the plot.
> We are betrayed by what is false within.*

No one power or group of powers "caused" the war of 1914. Its causes lie deep in the history of the state-system of western civilization, and, more particularly, in its history since 1870. They lie deep also in that fundamental form of group-consciousness we call "nationalism" and in the very structure of the modern nation-state. The dramatic date of the assassination of Francis Ferdinand, June 28, 1914, serves as a dividing line between the ultimate, or long-term, factors and the proximate, or short-term, factors.

Modern Love, XLIII.

II Causes of the War

The Shift in the Balance of Power

In the long term, an obvious factor that made war more likely was the unification of Germany and Italy. The creation of these two new major states in the 1860's and 1870's altered the always delicate balance of power in the European state-system. The efforts of statesmen during the next forty years to adjust the system and to take account of the two new powers and their claims proved ultimately unsuccessful. The older established powers were by no means willing to give up their own claims. We have seen that ever since the modern European—or, better, the western —state-system developed out of medieval fragmentation, the separate units, the states, have tried to grow. They have tried to grow in wealth, in prestige, and, most conspicuously of all, in territory. In the second half of the nineteenth century, with the principle of national sovereignty well established, with even the smaller states like Switzerland and Sweden generally accepted as not to be swallowed, there was little territory in Europe that could be easily disposed of for the purpose of making adjustments. Unification had closed off Germany and Italy, which as recently as 1815 had been classic areas for "compensation." Only southeastern Europe, the Balkan lands of the obviously weakening Turkish Empire, remained in the late nineteenth century as possible pickings for ambitious powers. Even there, the growth of national feeling in states like Rumania, Serbia, Bulgaria, and Greece made sheer annexation difficult. Nevertheless, Russia and Austria-Hungary both had ambitions in the Balkans; behind them, aiming rather at domination of Turkey and the Near East, came Germany and Great Britain. Finally, as we have noted in Chapter 16, much of Africa, Asia, and Oceania had been partitioned among the great powers amid intense rivalry. It seemed always possible to re-do this partitioning.

Meantime, influenced by their rivalries in Europe and abroad, the great powers were also choosing sides in a series of alliances and agreements. By the early years of the twentieth century two camps existed—the Triple Alliance of Germany, Austria-Hungary, and Italy, and the Triple Entente of France, Britain, and Russia. The system, as many people at the time saw clearly, had grown so tightly organized that there was almost no free play left, and with the wisdom of hindsight we can now see that after 1900 almost any crisis might have led to war. Sarajevo was the one that did.

This state of international politics was christened by an English liberal, Lowes Dickinson, "the international anarchy." It was, however, no chaos, but a highly organized rivalry, "anarchical" only in the sense that there was no higher authority to put a stop to the rivalry. In concrete instances, two or more powers wanted the same piece of land, as a territorial addition or as a sphere of influence. France and Great Britain both wanted Egypt; France and Germany both wanted Morocco; Russia and Austria-Hungary both wanted control over the Balkans; Russia and Japan both wanted Manchuria; and so on around the map. Compromises were made, lands and spheres of influence were shared, but in the long run there simply wasn't enough to go around.

The Role of Public Opinion

We have in this outline used the shorthand of names like "Great Britain" or "Germany." But these are mere symbols, as colored blobs on a map are symbols, for millions of human beings whose desires somehow do add up into the actions of states, did add up to the war of 1914. In no state were the millions all in agreement. There were Germans who wanted no bit of Africa or any other piece of land. There were Englishmen who, far from being content with Britain's place in the world, wanted more, wanted Britain to be for the whole round world what Rome had been for the Mediterranean world in the first centuries of the Christian Era, hoped eventually to eliminate all but Englishmen (and perhaps Scotsmen) in a fine Darwinian struggle. There were everywhere in Europe at least a few absolute pacifists, men who were determined under any conditions to refuse to fight, men who once war broke out became "conscientious objectors." We must not think of the war and the events that led up to it as simply the work of a few men at the top in each nation, the professional soldiers, the villainous diplomats in frock coats and striped trousers. In all the countries, there was a spectrum that ran from militarist to pacifist, through all shades of opinion.

But the outbreak of the war saw in each belligerent nation a broad national public opinion in support of the government. In 1914, a good many men marched to war convinced that war was a beneficial thing; the bands played, the crowds shouted, and war, perhaps for the last time in our day, seemed romantic as well as necessary. Here is the account of a young German on the last train out of Switzerland before the outbreak of war:

> An elderly gentleman was sitting in our compartment. He began to talk to us at once, as if we were intimate acquaintances. On the back of his hotel bill he had added up the numerical strength of the European armies and balanced them against each other. He compared the two totals and assured my mother that the spiritual qualities of the German troops compensated for the numerical superiority of the Russians. For in this war spiritual qualities alone would decide the day, and Germany's spiritual qualities were the best in Europe. As a university professor he knew that our youth were ready for the fray, and full of ideals. At last the hour had come when our people could enter on its great world mission. . . .*

*Ernst Glaeser, *Class of 1902*, Willa and Edwin Muir, trans. (London, 1929), 171–172.

"European Balance," viewed by Daumier after 1870.

German Aspirations

The Germans were led by their Kaiser, William II, who had come to the throne in 1888. The "revisionist" historians have been able to show that in the hectic five weeks after the assassination at Sarajevo the Kaiser, contrary to world opinion at the time, did not work steadily for war, that toward the end he tried to avoid a general war. But he cannot be even partially absolved for the long-term, for the ultimate, causes of the war. In the decisive years between 1888 and 1914 he was the posturing, aggressive leader of patriotic expansion, the "White Knight" leading his people to glory (see also Chapter 14). He was perhaps more of a figurehead, less of an actual maker of policy, than the world took him to be, but still a willing and effective figurehead for expansionists and violent nationalists.

German ambitions and German fears produced an intense hatred of Britain, a hatred mixed with envy and a sense of inferiority, a hatred that focused on the English upper

630

classes, perfectly tailored, serene in effortless superiority, the favorite children of fortune. Many a German tourist, perhaps quite accidentally given an Italian hotel room inferior to that given a traveling Englishman, would come home burning with indignation at this personal evidence that Germany was being denied its place in the sun. In the German navy, in the years just before the war, there was a simple toast in the officers' mess: *Der Tag* (The Day). Everyone knew that this was the day of the declaration of war between Germany and Britain. These feelings are all condensed in the famous "Hymn of Hate" of the German poet Ernst Lissauer:

> We will never forego our hate,
> Hate by water and hate by land,
> Hate of the head and hate of the hand,
> Hate of the hammer and hate of the Crown.
> Hate of the seventy millions choking down.
> We love as one, we hate as one,
> We have one foe and one alone:
> > England!*

*Ernst Lissauer, "A Chant of Hate Against England," trans. by Barbara Henderson, in Burton E. Stevenson, comp., *The Home Book of Verse,* 3rd ed. (New York, 1918), II, 2549-2550.

British Aspirations

Few Englishmen returned this hate; the English were still on top. Yet as the years wore on, the expensive race between Britain and Germany in naval armaments continued; in incident after incident German and British diplomats took opposite sides; and—this seemed especially important to the hardheaded—German wares of all sorts undersold British wares in Europe, in North and South America, and in Asia. Englishmen began to think that someone ought to teach these ill-mannered Germans a lesson. Moreover, they had begun to worry about their own position of prosperity and leadership. In India, the greatest possession of the English, it was clear already that great concessions toward self-government would have to be made to the natives. Close at home the Irish crisis was in one of its most acute phases, with Protestant Ulster in arms against the proposed Home Rule. British officers were indeed guilty of planning actual mutiny, much as did French officers in

Soldiers leaving Berlin for the front.

1961 during the Algerian crisis. Englishmen were worried about their obsolescent industrial plants, their apparent inability to produce goods as cheaply and as efficiently as the Germans; they were self-critical about their failures as salesmen abroad, their stodgy self-satisfaction.

A great many Britishers thought of themselves as good liberals and good internationalists, anxious to preserve the peace and the decencies of international life. Many were radicals and Labor party men committed to pacifism. The coming of war in 1914 was to show how thoroughly almost all these men identified Great Britain and righteousness. As for the bulk of the conservatives, they were as nationalist as in any other great country. In Britain, their nationalism attached itself to the Empire, to the "White Man's Burden," to a whole set of symbols that the Germans found intolerable.

The Other Belligerents

In democratic France as in democratic England there was a wide spread of opinion on international politics. A numerous socialist Left was committed to pacifism and to the concept of an international general strike of workers at the threat of actual war. A more moderate group also opposed conventional patriotic aggressiveness toward the foreigner. Both among the men who conducted French foreign relations and among the general public, however, there remained right down to the eve of the Great War the embittered patriotism of the beaten. Frenchmen wanted *revanche*, revenge for the defeat of 1870. They wanted Alsace-Lorraine back. For all these years, the statue representing Strasbourg among the cities of France in the Place de la Concorde in Paris was draped in black. With the warmest patriots, the organizers of patriotic societies, the editors of patriotic journals, this feeling for revenge was an obsession.

By the opening decade of the 1900's many observers thought that the new generation was losing its desire for revenge, that Frenchmen had at last decided to accept the verdict of

1870. But French diplomatists continued to preserve and strengthen the system of alliances against Germany, and in the excited weeks of July, 1914, it was clear that the French were ready for war.

Among the other major belligerents, too, the ultimate decisions of governments won much popular support. Russians were filled with the "pooled self-esteem" of nationalism, were convinced that God and the right were on their side. Italians saw in war the chance to get *Italia Irredenta* (Trent, Trieste, and their surrounding lands) and still more territory from the Habsburg Monarchy. In the dual monarchy, as we have seen (see Chapter 14), the loyalty of subject nationalities could scarcely be counted on; but the dominant Germans of Austria and Magyars of Hungary welcomed the opportunity to put the troublesome Slavs in their place for good and all.

The Era of Bismarck, 1871–1890

The road to Sarajevo starts in 1871, at the Treaty of Frankfurt, where France was obliged to cede Alsace and Lorraine to the new German Empire. It was no straight road, but one of many twists and turnings, and few historians would now maintain that 1871 made 1914 inevitable. We cannot follow the road in detail, but we must map its main course.

For some twenty years Bismarck was its chief engineer. In fairness to the Iron Chancellor, it must be said that during his last twenty years in office he sought peace, and indeed obtained it. Powerful elements in the new empire made it impossible for him to grant to France the same kind of generous peace he had given Austria in 1866. Yet Bismarck did try to salve the wound he knew France had suffered; he encouraged her to expand her empire in North Africa by the acquisition of Tunisia in 1881, even though this offended the Italians, who also coveted Tunisia. But he feared a French attempt at revenge and sought to isolate her diplomatically by building a series of alliances from which she was excluded. Germany, he insisted, was now a "saturated" power, and wanted nothing more in Europe; and in a famous phrase he insisted that all the Balkans were not worth "the bones of a single Pomeranian grenadier." Above all, he sought to keep on good terms with *both* Austria and Russia, and, what was much more difficult, to keep both these powers on good terms with each other. Since both wanted predominance in the Balkans, Bismarck's task was formidable.

He laid the cornerstone of his diplomatic system by a defensive alliance with Austria-Hungary in 1879, an alliance that held right down to 1918. And he was able to make a not-so-secret treaty, the so-called League of the Three Emperors, which bound Germany, Russia, and Austria together. The three powers agreed to act together in dealings with Turkey and to maintain friendly neutrality should any one of them be at war with a fourth power other than Turkey. Next, working skillfully on Italian annoyance over the French expansion in Tunis, Bismarck secured an alliance among Germany, Austria-Hungary, and Italy, directed chiefly against France. This was the famous Triple Alliance of 1882, often renewed, which still existed on paper in 1914.

On this series of tightropes Bismarck maintained a precarious balance through the 1880's. Chief in his mind was the danger that the Russians, always fearful of Austrian schemes in the Balkans, would desert him and ally themselves with France, still a great power and anxious to escape from the isolation that Bismarck had designed for her. In 1887, Russia did refuse to renew the League of the Three Emperors, but Bismarck was able to repair the breach for the moment by a secret Russo-German agreement known as the Reinsurance Treaty. The two promised each other neutrality in case either was involved in a war against a third power; but this neutrality was not to hold if Germany made an "aggressive" war against France or if Russia made an "aggressive" war against Austria. Since Russian nationalist agitation continued against both Austria and Germany, Bismarck in 1888 made public as a warning to Russia the terms of the Austro-German alliance and allowed the main terms of the Triple Alliance to be known informally.

Formation of the Triple Entente, 1890–1907

Then in 1890 the young Emperor William II dismissed Bismarck. The Emperor's advisers, headed by Baron von Holstein, persuaded him not to renew the Reinsurance Treaty with Russia, in spite of Russian desire for such renewal. Shortly afterward, what Bismarck had worked so hard to prevent came about. After lengthy negotiations, Russia and France in 1894 came together in an alliance that ended French isolation. It was formally a defensive alliance, in which each was to come to the aid of the other if Germany or Austria made "aggressive" war against either, and it was accompanied by the necessary military agreements between the two general staffs. Against the Triple Alliance there now stood, quite openly, a Dual Alliance of France and Russia. Great Britain as yet remained technically uninvolved by any formal treaty with a European ally and indeed never did make a full legal commitment even with France.

The next great stage in the tightening network of alliances was to bring Great Britain in against the Central Powers, at least by informal "entente" or agreement. In the two decades after the accession of William II, Britain made a formal alliance with Japan and informal "understandings" (*ententes*) with France and Russia. What chiefly drove Britain to these actions was the naval race with Germany and the rapid worsening of Anglo-German relations, a worsening even more evident perhaps at the level of public opinion than at the level of formal diplomacy.

A good concrete instance of this rising hostility is the Kruger telegram of 1896, in which the Kaiser congratulated President Kruger of the Boer Republic of Transvaal on the defeat of the Jameson raid (see pp. 603). It may be that the Kaiser and his circle hoped at bottom that this gesture would be taken by the English government as a kind of polite and permissible diplomatic blackmail, an evidence of how great a nuisance the German government could be

Diplomatic Alignments before 1914

Dates indicate Alliances

TRIPLE ENTENTE

TRIPLE ALLIANCE

Atlantic Ocean

NORWAY

SWEDEN

IRELAND

GREAT BRITAIN

North Sea

DENMARK

London

NETH.

BELG.

LUX.

Elbe R.

Berlin

Oder R.

Vistula R.

RUSSIA

St. Petersburg

1907

1894

1887-1890

1904

Paris

FRANCE

SWITZ.

Rhine R.

Rhône R.

Loire R.

G E R M A N Y

1879-82

Vienna

AUSTRIA-HUNGARY

Dnieper R.

Dniester R.

1882

1882

ITALY

MONTE-NEGRO

RUMANIA

SERBIA

BULGARIA

Danube R.

Black Sea

PORTUGAL

SPAIN

Tagus R.

Ebro R.

CORSICA

SARDINIA

Rome

ALBANIA

GREECE

OTTOMAN EMPIRE

SICILY

Mediterranean Sea

CRETE

0   500

Miles

---

to the British if it were not on their side. But the British press took the telegram as an unbearable insult, and the German press replied angrily to British anger.

It was fear of Russia rather than fear of Germany, however, that inspired Britain to make the first break with formal isolationism, the alliance with Japan in 1902. The outbreak of war between Russia and Japan hastened negotiations between Britain and France. In the Anglo-French Entente of 1904, France gave England a free hand in Egypt, England gave France a free hand in Morocco, and various outstanding difficulties between the two in other parts of the world were ironed out. More important, the base was laid for general collaboration between the two in international affairs. Only six years previously, in 1898, there had been a grave flareup of the traditional colonial rivalry between France and England when a French column was met by a British column at Fashoda in the disputed Sudan

territory of the upper Nile Valley. Fashoda caused quite as big an outbreak of fury in the French and the British press as the Kruger telegram only two years before had caused in the German and the British press. Yet Fashoda left wounds much less deep than the Kruger telegram; the contemporary press is not always a faithful guide to the climate of public opinion, let alone to that of professional diplomacy.

The final stage in aligning the two camps came in 1907 when Russia, chastened by her defeat at the hand of Japan and encouraged by the French, came to an understanding with Great Britain. Both countries made concessions in regions where they had been imperialist rivals—Persia, Afghanistan, Tibet—and the British at last made some concessions toward the Russian desire to open up the Straits. The agreement was scarcely based on any genuine sympathy between the two peoples, for the British, notably, had been

634

Russophobic for well over a century. Nevertheless, it did round out the Triple Entente against the Triple Alliance.

A Decade of Crises, 1905–1914

The last decade before 1914 was a series of crises and local wars, any one of which might have spread into a world war. First came a deliberate theatrical gesture from the Kaiser, when in 1905 he made a ceremonial visit to Tangier in Morocco as a way of telling the world that the Germans would not accept the Anglo-French assignment of Morocco to France. The net effect of this blustering was to *tighten* the entente between France and Britain, for the British indicated clearly to the French that they would support them. Indeed at this time there began the informal military and naval conferences between the British and the French that the French, at least, believed "committed" the British to armed support if the Germans attacked. Although the French Foreign Minister, Delcassé, a partisan of firm policy toward the Germans, was forced out of office, even this partial victory did the Germans no good. French public opinion was infuriated by this intervention in their domestic politics. In the end, a general international conference at Algeciras in Spain (1906) backed up the French, who went ahead with their plans for a protectorate in Morocco. At Algeciras American diplomatic influence was used on the side of France; the United States, too, was beginning to emerge from its own variety of isolationism.

A "second Moroccan crisis" in 1911 heightened tensions and brought the possibility of a general war home to most Frenchmen. The Kaiser sent a German gunboat, the *Panther*, to the Moroccan port of Agadir as a protest against French occupation of the old city of Fez. In ensuing negotiations, well-publicized in the press, the Germans finally agreed to leave the French a free hand in Morocco, but only at a price the French considered blackmail: part of French Congo was ceded to Germany.

In the Balkans, a decisive turn of the road toward Sarajevo came in 1908. Austria formally proclaimed the annexation of the old Turkish provinces of Bosnia-Herzegovina, which she had occupied since 1878. Austria's decisive act infuriated the Serbs, who wanted to add Bosnia to their state. It also infuriated the Russians, all the more since few Russians knew that their diplomat Izvolski had in fact made an informal agreement with the Austrian minister Aehrenthal in September, 1908, to accept the annexation of Bosnia-Herzegovina in return for Austrian support of an agreement permitting Russian warships to use the Straits. In the event, Austria did the annexing, but Russia did not get her use of the Straits. This wound to Russian pride was profound.

War now broke out on the edges of Europe. In 1911, the Italians sent troops to Tripoli, the poorest part of North Africa, but at least a part that had not yet been taken from the Turks by other Europeans. Then in 1912 war spread to the Balkans. Nationalist revolutionaries called the "Young Turks" had risen successfully against the Sultan in 1908. The Young Turks wanted the modern industrial achievements of the West, they wanted its political apparatus of representative government, and they wanted above all to have Turks respected, admired, and feared as members of a thoroughly modern *nation*. Some of their intellectuals followed the nineteenth-century Romantic pattern back into the past, where they found, not the nomad Turks of history, but fine sturdy "Turanians" from the inspiring steppes of Central Asia. There was even a "Pan-Turanian" movement, strangest of the "Pan" movements, which sought to group Magyars, Turks, and the Turkish peoples of Central Asia, who were all only distantly related to each other, as children of a common destiny. No wonder the Habsburgs were alarmed! It began to look as if those who hoped to divide up Turkey had better hurry while the dividing was good. In the hurry, the world got swept into the War of 1914, the preliminary stages of which were the Balkan Wars.

In the first of these wars, in 1912, an alliance of Bulgaria, Serbia, and Greece beat the Turks, and started the process of dividing up most of European Turkey. But here Austria imposed an absolute veto on granting Serbia territories that would give her access to the Adriatic Sea. Meanwhile, the victors quarreled among themselves, and in the Second Balkan War (1913) the Greeks and Serbs, joined by the Rumanians and the all-but-beaten Turks, readily defeated the Bulgarians. Turkey got back some of her territory in Europe. But the Balkans were in a state of uncertainty and bad blood when Francis Ferdinand was assassinated; and Bulgaria was ready to ally with Austria and Germany against her former allies.

The Final Crisis, July-August, 1914

There are millions of words in print about the proximate causes of World War I in the six weeks between the assassination on June 28 and the general spread of war on August 4, when Britain came in against Germany. Thanks to the end of the rule of Hohenzollern, Habsburg, and Romanov houses as a result of the

"Disturbing the Peace," 1897: the Great Powers (France and Britain on the left) chorus "Scat!".

war, the secret archives were thrown open much sooner than would be normal. And in the pressure of debate in the 1920's over the question of war guilt, even the victorious countries, Britain, France, and the United States, opened their archives to a surprising extent. These are weeks for which documents, often telegrams, can be dated by the hour and minute. These are weeks in which messages are constantly crossing each other, confusing things hopelessly. These are weeks in which professional diplomatists and statesmen, egged on by an excited—and it must be said often *irresponsible*—press, nevertheless tried for the most part to master the crisis without recourse to war.

The diplomats and statesmen were drawn into war because almost all of them believed that they faced an alternative worse than war, a defeat or loss of face for their nation. Austria believed correctly, though without positive proof, that the Serbian government had some foreknowledge or at least suspicion of Princip's plot and should therefore have given her warning. For this reason, and also because she wished to check the Serb agitation that had long been unsettling the Yugoslav peoples living in the dual monarchy, Austria-Hungary decided to make stiff demands on Serbia after the assassination of Francis Ferdinand. Before doing so, however, she consulted her German ally, who promised to support whatever policy Austria might adopt toward Serbia. This German response has become famous as a diplomatic "blank check," duly signed by Germany in advance with the precise amount to be filled in later by Austria.

Thus encouraged, the Austrian government, on July 23, sent Serbia an ultimatum to be answered within forty-eight hours. The ultimatum made many separate demands, which added up to an insistence that Serbia and Serb propagandists keep their hands off Habsburg territories and populations, now and in the future. Most of the demands the Serbs accepted, at least in principle; but they refused to accept two of them, which would have permitted Austrian police or military men to take, on Serbian soil, an actual part in a Serbian investigation of Princip's plot. Probably Serbia

Princip, immediately after the assassination at Sarajevo, June 28, 1914.

had some assurance that Russia was willing to give her a kind of "blank check," and would assist her if the partial refusal of the ultimatum led to war. The Serbian reply, therefore, was a little less virtuously honest than it seemed to be to most of the world in July, 1914. Still, the Austrian ultimatum appears to have been couched in terms deliberately unacceptable to the Serbs, and the Serb reply seems to have been a base for more consideration than it got from the Austrians. Because the Serbs had not accepted the whole of the ultimatum, Austria declared war on July 28, after turning down as inconsistent with national honor a European conference proposed by the British foreign minister, Sir Edward Grey, on July 26.

From this declaration of war on, the German diplomatists, backed by William II and actually resisting the German military men, tried to hold back their Austrian ally. It is impossible to clear William from responsibility for the German "blank check," which had emboldened Austria and had perhaps been designed by Germany to do just that. Now, however, the Germans certainly tried to revoke the check and made a last effort to stop the spread of the war. Since Russia was beginning the full mobilization of her armies, the Kaiser, on July 29, told Tsar Nicholas II in a personal telegram of the German attempt to get the Austrians to compromise. Apparently this telegram served to get full Russian mobilization modified into partial mobilization and to get direct Austro-Russian talks resumed on July 30. For a brief moment it looked as if the crisis might be overcome.

But mobilization was not easy in Russia, a country of long distances, poor communications, and bureaucratic red tape; and the Russian military feared that their enemies would get the jump on them. In perhaps the most crucial decision of this hectic last week, the Russian government, probably against the deeper inclinations of the Tsar himself, decided to renew general mobilization. Germany at once insisted that all Russian mobilization cease, and, when it continued, ordered her own at 4:00 P.M. on August 1, and declared war on Russia at 7:00 P.M. the same day. France, meantime, had determined to stand by her Russian ally, now evidently about to be attacked, and also mobilized at 3:55 P.M. on August 1. Germany declared war on France on August 3.

Britain was still wavering. Although her entente with France did not legally bind the two nations together, it had led, as we have just seen, to the very close co-ordination of defense plans by the French and British military and naval staffs. Perhaps, then, Britain would have come into the war anyway. What made her entry certain was the German violation of the neutrality of Belgium, which both Britain and Prussia (now Germany) had joined with other powers to guarantee in 1839. The German military were determined to take decisive action in the West and to knock France out of the war before the Russians could get their vast but slow-moving armies into action. Accordingly, German plans called for a sweep through a corner of Belgium to avoid the heavily fortified and hilly terrain in northeastern France. On August 2, the Germans had notified Belgium that they intended to march through her territory, though they promised to respect her territorial integrity in the peace to come.

Belgium rejected this demand and appealed to the other guaranteeing powers. Sir Edward Grey, though opposed in the British cabinet by the Liberals, Lord Morley and John Burns, who did not believe defense of the neutrality of Belgium worth a war, seized firmly on this ground of action. On August 4 Britain declared war on Germany. The German chancellor, Bethmann-Hollweg, informed of this action, let slip the phrase that Britain had gone to war just for a "scrap of paper"—the treaty of 1839 that established Belgian neutrality. This unhappy phrase, seized upon by the press of the world, not only solidified British opinion in favor of the war but was responsible more than any other single factor for the charge of war guilt laid against Germany.

The Entry of Other Powers

By August 6, when Austria declared war on Russia, all the members of the Triple Alliance and the Triple Entente had come to blows, with the exception of Italy, who, however, had never really been a good ally of Austria because of the Irredentist issue. Italy, refusing to consider herself bound by the Triple Alliance, declared her neutrality. The Central Powers of Germany and Austria-Hungary, then, stood against the Allies—Russia, France, Britain, and Serbia. Japan came in on the side of the Allies late in August, and Turkey came in on the Austro-German side in November, 1914. After competing territorial offers from both Allies and Central Powers, Italy finally joined the Allies in May, 1915. Bulgaria came in on the side of the Central Powers in 1915, Rumania on the side of the Allies in 1916.

As the war turned into a stalemate, on both Western and Eastern fronts in the winter of 1916–1917, the Germans made the desperate decision to try to get at Great Britain by the only way that seemed available. They would use their submarines to cut off the food and raw materials that came to the British Isles from overseas, and without which their peoples would have starved. This unrestricted submarine warfare meant sinking American ships that Americans held were quite legally bringing such supplies, *not* contraband of war, to England and France. On April 6, 1917, the United States completed the roster of great powers involved in the conflict by declaring war on Germany. Lesser powers all over the world joined in, mostly against Germany, so that all told there were 53 declarations of war before the end in 1918.

Dissident Americans, then and since, have declared that the United States was enticed into the war by the wicked few—by sentimental lovers of England or France; by bankers who had lent money to the Allies and wanted to protect their investments; by silly idealists who agreed with President Wilson in wishing to "make the world safe for democracy"; and, of course, by scheming Allied diplomatists, corrupt Europeans who held a strange fascination over American "babes in the wood."

Deep-seated sentiments among many good Americans in 1916–1917 rebelled against our jeopardizing American ideals by involving ourselves in the conventional—and wicked—European struggle for power. Even today, after a second general or world war in which American participation aroused much less opposition at home (see Chapter 21), it is difficult for the historian to discuss objectively the causes of our entrance into this so-called First World War. The historian must indeed note that ever since what Americans call King

William's War and Europeans usually refer to as the War of the League of Augsburg (1688–1697) (see Chapter 7), we as colonists or as an independent nation have sooner or later been drawn into every major general war in the western state-system. In purely empirical terms, it may be argued that the normal expectation is for the United States to enter into any great world war. And in more disputable general terms, such as we have brought out in Chapter 5, the argument may be made that in the western (now world) state-system a general or world war never breaks out unless there is an aggressor nation whose activities in the opinion of their leaders threaten the independent existence of all other nations. The United States, in this view, went to war in 1917 for a very deep-seated reason indeed. The possible victory of Germany threatened our very existence as an independent, but committed and co-operating, participant in an international order.

More specifically, in 1917 the United States insisted that the existing international order gave Americans the right to travel and to trade freely with neutrals and, in dealings with belligerents, to be limited only by well-known principles of international law forbidding actual transport of munitions, or other *direct* forms of aid to belligerents. This is the doctrine of "freedom of the seas," which would indeed have allowed Germans to search American vessels, but which quite clearly did not permit German submarines to sink American vessels on sight and without notice. The German decision to undertake unrestricted submarine warfare was in western historical precedent a completely adequate and normal justification of, and explanation for, our declaration of war. But, we must repeat, behind this reason lay a widespread though by no means universal feeling among many Americans, a feeling especially strong in those persons most concerned with our foreign relations, that a German victory would mean a world order in which the kind of America we wanted could not be secure.

Jefferson had indeed in 1807 abandoned the doctrine of freedom of the seas and had in the Embargo Act simply forbidden American vessels to trade either with the French or the British side. In 1917, we should have had to put an embargo on all American shipping to most foreign ports, or else put up with German torpedoing of American ships, and the drowning of American citizens. Neither course would seem to have been acceptable to a majority of Americans in 1917.

III The Course of the War

Resources of the Belligerents

As the opposing nations lined up in 1914, the Allies (British, French, Russians, and others) had an overwhelming superiority in total population and resources. The Central Powers (Germany, Austria-Hungary and Turkey) had in their own continental lands not over 150,000,000 people; Britain, France, Russia, and Italy in their own continental lands had at least 125,000,000 more people than their enemies. Moreover, in their overseas possessions, which included the 315,000,000 people of India, the Allies had many millions more. As for material resources, the Central Powers had, especially in Germany, admirably organized industries and enough coal and iron to fight a long war. But here too the statistics were overwhelmingly in favor of the Allies. Moreover, though German submarines and, in the early days, surface raiders were able to interrupt seriously Allied lines of communication overseas, on the whole the Allies were still able to get from these overseas sources indispensable food and other supplies. And when in 1917 a beaten Russia, in the throes of a revolution, ceased to be of aid, the Allies gained the great resources of the United States.

In the long run, much as in the American Civil War, the side with the most men and materials wore down its enemies and won the war. But it was by no means the uneven struggle that the statistics of total population and material resources would indicate. Again as in our Civil War, the weaker side had initially important advantages, won great victories, seemed indeed at critical moments on the point of final victory.

Geography gave Germany and Austria the advantages of being side by side, and of having interior lines of communication, which enabled them to make rapid transfers of troops from one threatened front to another. Though the Germans and Austrians did not always see eye to eye, they did speak the same language and had for long been firmly allied. Most important of all, Germany in particular was more ready for war than were her enemies. She had an efficiently organized military machine and a good stock of munitions, her industry could be readily geared to war, her plans were complete, her people were united in support of the war, and they enjoyed the great psychological advantage of being on the offensive, of carrying the war to the enemy. Indeed, no important part of the war was ever fought on German soil; it ended, with important results for later history, with the German army still in being, with the soil of the German Fatherland still uninvaded.

By contrast, geography separated the western Allies from Russia. German control of the Baltic and Turkish control of the Straits proved throughout the war a serious obstacle to communication between Russia and her allies, who had to take roundabout and difficult routes through Archangel in Arctic waters and even through Vladivostok on the Pacific at the end of the long, slow, single-track Trans-Siberian railway. For the Allies, transfer of troops between eastern and western fronts was militarily almost impossible, even had it been politically possible. It was not, however, politically possible, and here is one of the greatest weaknesses of the Allies.

Russia, Britain, and France had only recently come together, as "friendly" powers and not as close allies. Each of them was a strongly marked nationality, having many sources of conflict with the others. They had no long tradition of mutual co-operation, no common language. France and England were democracies, and though the peoples of both rallied firmly to the national cause in 1914, they were of recent years unused to the kind of firm, centralized, political and military control that is necessary in war. As for unified military planning and administration, it was never achieved between Russia and the western Allies. Even among Britain, France, and the United States on the Western Front, it was not achieved until the French General Foch was appointed commander-in-chief in 1918, and then only imperfectly, for full merging of staffs was not achieved.

Finally, of the three great Allied powers in 1914, only France was ready with a good big land force, and France, with only 39 millions of people against Germany's 65 millions, was the weakest of the Allies in manpower. Britain was indeed prepared on the sea, and her navy was an invaluable asset; but it could not be of direct use against the German army. Russia had universal military service and an army great in numbers. But she had vast distances to overcome, an inadequate railway system, a relatively undeveloped heavy industry, an army whose morale had been shaken by the recent defeat at the hands of the Japanese, a people whose morale had been shaken by the recent abortive revolution, a military and a political organization riddled with inefficiency and corruption.

The Western Front: German Offensive

The Germans had a plan, the so-called Schlieffen plan, which they immediately put into execution. It called for a holding operation on the left, with a strong right wing that was to advance swiftly through Belgium, take Paris, and then fall on the rear of the French armies. While this great enveloping movement in the west swiftly eliminated France, relatively weaker German forces, it was planned, would hold down the slow-moving Russians. With France beaten, the Germans could turn their full force against the Russians and beat them. Then there would be only the British left, and the future would take care of them.

The German plan almost succeeded. It failed for two reasons, to which a great number of separate tactical factors contributed. In the first place, the German chief of staff, Moltke, had seriously modified the Schlieffen plan by weakening the critical right wing, partly in order to send divisions to the east, which, ironically, arrived there too late to participate in the defeat of the Russians. By the time the German right wing neared Paris, it had too few divisions to take the capital and then roll up the French army to the eastward. In the second place, the French, though at first they rashly developed the offensive eastward, shifted their armies northward and westward to meet the invading Germans. With the help of the British they exploited a gap that developed between the German First and Second armies. The Germans lost this first great battle, known as the Battle of the Marne.

The German advance, which had been almost continuous since August 2, had been stopped. In the next few weeks the opposing forces engaged in what came to be called the "race for the Channel," with the Germans trying to outflank the Allies and get the Channel ports, thus shutting the short sea passage to future British reinforcements. They failed here, too, and throughout the war the ports of Calais and Boulogne, and indeed a small southwestern corner of Belgium, were to remain in Allied hands—a valuable military advantage.

By the autumn of 1914 the Western Front was thus stabilized. For over three hundred airline miles between the Channel and the Swiss border of Alsace near Basel, hundreds of thousands of soldiers faced each other in a continuous line that was full of bends called "salients." Both sides "dug in" and formed a series of rough fortifications. The central feature of these fortifications was a series of parallel trenches deep enough to conceal a man standing upright. As time went on, these trenches were greatly improved; they were supplied with parapets, machine-gun nests, and an elaborate network of approach trenches and strong points, until the whole front became one immense fortification. Thousands of local actions in the four years of trench warfare shifted the lines here and there, and a series of partial break-throughs occurred on both sides. But on the whole the lines held, and the actual fighting in the west was confined to an extraordinarily narrow, though very long, field.

On this Western Front the ultimate decision was reached; but there were many other fronts. Some of them were disparagingly called "the side-shows" by those who advocated concentrating in the west. Yet in perspective we can now see that they all played a part in determining the final result. Since, over the long pull, the Germans had fewer men and resources, the dispersal of energies that these "side-shows" called for, and the continuous need to bolster their Austrian, Turkish, and Bulgarian allies, were major factors in their defeat. For the sake of clarity, we shall here take up these other fronts separately and briefly, but the reader must never forget that for the belligerents the war was a whole; its wide-flung theaters were mutually dependent, with each one influencing the others.

The Eastern Front

The Eastern Front, where the Russians faced both the Germans and the Austrians, was certainly no mere side-show. Millions of men were involved on both sides, and had the Russians not held out, as they did, until the end of 1917, the Allies in the west could hardly have withstood the reinforcements that the Germans and Austrians would have been able to send to France and Italy. The war in the east was more a war of movement than the war in the west. But even in the east there were long periods of stalemate, especially during the winters, periods when the opposing armies faced each other in long lines of improvised fortifications in trench warfare much like that in the west.

The Russians began well. Against the exposed Austrian salient of Galicia (Austria's share of the eighteenth-century partitions of Poland), the Russians threw in vast masses of men. They pushed the Austrians out of Lemberg (later the Polish Lwów, now the Soviet Lvov), and by the end of September, 1914, they had reached the northern ends of some of the passes leading into Hungary through the Carpathian Mountains. Against the Germans, who also had to defend in East Prussia a salient surrounded on the east and south by Russian territory, the Russians won the Battle

of Gumbinnen, in August, 1914, and so alarmed the German general staff that the Germans felt obliged to reorganize their eastern command. General von Ludendorff, under the nominal command of his senior, Von Hindenburg, and aided by a brilliant junior, Von Hoffmann, turned successfully against the two Russian armies, which were attempting a pincers movement. Late in August, at Tannenberg, the Germans decisively defeated a Russian army under Samsonov, who committed suicide. And early in September they won another decisive victory against the Russians at the Masurian lakes, thus clearing East Prussia of Russians.

The Germans' hard-pressed Austrian allies to the south were by now clamoring for help, and the Western Front was still demanding

Allied soldiers trying to keep warm, near Ypres in Flanders, 1914.

men. Hindenburg and his aides had to do their best with what they had. In a series of hard-fought battles in Poland, they succeeded in relieving the pressure on the Austrians. The end of the year 1914 found the Austrians still hanging on in Galicia and found the Germans in a good position to push eastward from East Prussian and Polish bases. In two great joint offensives in May and July, 1915, the Central Powers won substantial successes; they inflicted severe losses on the Russians from which the Russians never really recovered. At the end of the year 1915 the battle line ran roughly from near Riga, deep in the Baltic provinces of Russia, to the eastern edge of Galicia at Tarnopol and Czernowitz.

In 1916, the Russians, with a new commander, General Brusilov, undertook a great new offensive against the Austrians in the south. The Russian need to bolster their failing morale would probably have made some action necessary, but the Russians were also being pressed by the Western Allies to do something to help the Italians, who were threatened by the Austrians in the region of Trent. It seems likely that the Brusilov offensive was begun too soon, without adequate preparation. It scored a striking success at first; in places, the Russians drove the Austrians back some eighty miles, and they took large numbers of prisoners. But once more the Germans came to the rescue; with fresh troops transferred from the west, they halted Brusilov before he had won a decisive success.

It was from the backwash of this defeat that the Russian Revolution, which began early in March, 1917, was born. In the moderate phase of that uprising, before the Bolshevik revolution of November, 1917, Brusilov undertook one last desperate offensive. But he was soon checked, and the way was open for the Bolsheviks to carry out their promise to make peace. By the end of 1917, Russia was out of the war. She was forced by the Central Powers to sign the extraordinarily punitive Peace of Brest-Litovsk (March, 1918), by which she lost her Polish territories, her Baltic provinces, the entire Ukraine, Finland, and some lands in the Caucasus. The Caucasian lands went to Turkey; most of the others came under what

proved to be the temporary domination of Austria and Germany.

The Italian Front

In April, 1915, Italy concluded with Britain, France and Russia the secret Treaty of London, which promised the Italians their long-sought-for Trent and Trieste, and other lands at Austro-Hungarian and Turkish expense. In May, the Italians formally declared war on Austria-Hungary (they did not declare war on Germany until August, 1916), and a new front was added along the Austro-Italian frontier at the head of the Adriatic. Much of this front was too mountainous for effective action, and it was pretty much confined to some sixty miles along the Isonzo River. For two years there was a series of bloody but indecisive actions along this river that at least pinned down several hundred thousand Austrian troops. Then in the late autumn of 1917, with Russia already beaten, came the blow that very nearly knocked Italy out. Once again the Germans supplied the propulsive force. Ludendorff, now in supreme command, sent six German divisions to the Isonzo. The Germans and Austrians broke through at Caporetto and sent the Italians into a retreat across the Venetian plains, a retreat that was really a rout. French and British reinforcements were hastily rushed across the Alps, but what did most to stop the Austro-Germans was probably the grave difficulty, under modern conditions of warfare, of supplying mass armies of infantry in rapid advance. The Italians were finally able to hold along the line of the Piave River, almost at the Po.

The Dardanelles

One of the most important of the "sideshows," the Dardanelles campaign of 1915, not only proved in its failure to be a bad blow to the morale of the Allies, but was to have important repercussions in World War II. With the entry of Turkey into the war in November, 1914, and with the Western Front capable for the moment of being held against the Germans by the French alone, a group of British military and political leaders advanced the idea that British strength should be put into amphibious operations somewhere in the Aegean area. A steady drive could also be made overland toward Vienna and Berlin through territory where the Central Powers were not expecting an attack in force. The great exponent of this "Eastern Plan" was Winston Churchill, First Lord of the Admiralty. The British decided to try the plan. The point of attack chosen was the Dardanelles, the more westerly of the two straits that separate the Black Sea from the Aegean. The campaign is sometimes known as the "Gallipoli campaign" from the long narrow peninsula on the European side of the Straits which was one of the keys to the whole action. Here Allied victory would have had the additional advantage of opening communication with Russia via the Black Sea.

In March, 1915, the British and French fleets tried to force the Straits, but they abandoned the attempt somewhat prematurely when several ships struck mines. Later landings of British, Australian, New Zealand, and French troops at various points on both Asian and European shores of the Dardanelles were poorly co-ordinated and badly backed up. They met with fierce and effective resistance from the Turks—a junior officer named Mustafa Kemal greatly distinguishing himself —and in the end they had to be abandoned. Russia remained sealed in by the Straits all during the war. But Churchill continued to believe that the Dardanelles plan had failed, not because it was a bad plan, but because it had not been carried out with determination. And in the Second World War he was to revive, against American military opinion, something of his old plan, which became known as the plan to strike at the "soft underbelly" of the Axis.

The Balkan Fronts

Serbia's part in the crisis that produced the war meant that from the start there would be a Balkan front. In the end there were several such fronts, and no Balkan state remained uninvolved. The Austrians failed here also, and although in December, 1914, they did manage to take the Serbian capital, Belgrade, they were driven out again. Bulgaria, wooed by both sides, finally came in with the Central Powers in the autumn of 1915. The Germans sent troops and a general, von Mackensen, under whom the Serbs were finally beaten. The remnant of their armies was driven to take refuge on the island of Corfu in neutral Greece.

To counter this blow in the Balkans, the Allies had already landed a few divisions in the Greek city of Salonika and had established a front in Macedonia. The Greeks themselves were divided into two groups. One was headed by King Constantine, who at bottom was sympathetic with the Central Powers, but who for the moment was seeking only to maintain Greek neutrality. The other was a pro-Ally group headed by the able old politician Venizelos. Although the Allies rode roughshod over formal notions of Greek neutrality, Venizelos did not get firmly into the saddle until June, 1917, when Allied pressure compelled King Constantine to abdicate in favor of his second son, Alexander.

Meanwhile Rumania, whom the Russians had been trying to lure into the war, finally yielded to promises of great territorial gains at the expense of Austria-Hungary and came in on the Allied side late in August, 1916, at a time most inopportune for the Rumanians. Stiffened by German help, the Austrians swept through Rumania and by January, 1917, held most of the country. When the Russians made the separate Peace of Brest-Litovsk with the Germans in March, 1918, the Rumanians were obliged to make cessions of territory to Bulgaria, and to grant a lease of oil lands to Germany.

In spite of the formal accession of Greece to the Allied side in June 1917, the Macedonian front remained in a stalemate until the summer of 1918, when, with American troops pouring rapidly into France, the Allied military leaders decided they could afford to build up their forces in Salonika. The investment

rope
d the Near East,
14-1918

Atlantic Ocean

IRELAND

GREAT
BRITAIN

NORWAY

SWEDEN

Battle of
Jutland

North Sea

DENMARK

Baltic Sea

St. Petersburg

Volga R.

Riga

Moscow

London

NETH.

Ostend

BELG.

Elbe R.

Berlin

Königsberg

E. PRUSSIA
Tannenburg

Masurian Lakes

Niemen R.

RUSSIA

Smolensk

Seine R.

Paris

Verdun

LUX.

Rhine R.

GERMANY

Warsaw

Brest-Litovsk

Oder R.

POLAND

Vistula R.

Kiev

Dnieper R.

FRANCE

Belfort

SWITZ.

Danube R.

Prague

Cracow

Lemberg

GALICIA

Tarnopol

Czernowitz

Dniester R.

Loire R.

PORTUGAL

SPAIN

Madrid

Tagus R.

Ebro R.

Bordeaux

Rhône R.

Milan

Locarno

Isonzo R.

Vienna

Budapest

AUSTRIA-HUNGARY

TRANSYL-
VANIA

RUMANIA

Bucharest

Black Sea

Genoa

Piave R.

Caporetto

Rapallo

Leghorn

ITALY

Sava R.

BOSNIA

Sarajevo

DALMATIA

Belgrade

SERBIA

MONTENEGRO

Danube R.

BULGARIA

Sofia

Constantinople

Bosporus

The Straits

Gallipoli

Dardanelles

OTTOMAN EMPIRE

CORSICA
(Fr.)

Rome

SARDINIA

BALEARIC IS.

ALBANIA

Salonika

MACEDONIA

GREECE

Athens

Gibraltar (Br.)

SPANISH MOROCCO

CORFU

SICILY

MALTA
(Br.)

CRETE

DODECANESE
(It.)

RHODES

CYPRUS
(Br.)

MOROCCO

ALGERIA

TUNISIA

Mediterranean Sea

	Allied and Associated Powers
	Central Powers and their Allies
	Neutrals
——	Political boundaries, 1914
—·—·—	Boundary between Austria and Hungary
— — —	Greatest advance by Central Powers
·······	Greatest advance by Allies
■	Battle site

LIBYA

Suez
Canal

Cairo

EGYPT

Nile R.

0   500

Miles

The Middle East, 1914-18

Black Sea

Caspian Sea

Trebizond

Tigris R.

Euphrates R.

Baghdad

Damascus

Basra

Mediterranean Sea

Persian Gulf

Nile R.

Jerusalem

Cairo

Area of military action, 1914-18

Asia and the Pacific, 1914-15

Tsingtau

JAPAN

CHINA

INDIA

Madras

Pacific Ocean

FORMOSA

PHILIPPINE IS.

PENANG I.

YAP

CAROLINE IS.

Indian Ocean

Rabaul

Battles and other military
actions, 1914-15

AUSTRALIA

paid well, for under the leadership of the French general, Franchet d'Esperey, the Allied armies on this front were the first to break the enemy completely. The French, British, Serbs, and Greeks began a great advance on September 15, 1918, all along the line from the Adriatic to the Bulgarian frontier. They forced the Bulgarians to conclude an armistice on September 30, and by early November they had crossed the Danube in several places. The armistice in the west on November 11 found the tricolor of France, with the flags of many allies, well on its way to Vienna. This hark-back to Napoleon helped inspire in the French a somewhat unfounded confidence that they were once more the dominant nation on the continent of Europe.

The Near East and the Colonies

A whole series of fronts throughout the world was involved in what we may call the colonial "clean-up," the subduing of the German overseas empire and of the outlying parts of the Turkish Empire. The Turks, trained and in part officered by German experts, often resisted effectively. In Mesopotamia, in April, 1916, in a blow to British prestige as bad as the Dardanelles defeat, they forced the surrender of the British general, Townshend, who had landed at Basra from India in 1915 and had marched up the Tigris-Euphrates Valley. But the Turks were never able to take the Suez Canal, nor to advance far into Russian Armenia. Moreover, the British were able to play on the Arabs' dislike for their Turkish suzerains. In a series of desert campaigns the romantic Colonel T. E. Lawrence, an Englishman who knew the Arabs intimately, played a leading part. By the end of 1917, the British held Baghdad and Jerusalem. In September, 1918, a great British offensive in Palestine was so successful that on September 30 the Turks concluded an armistice which took them out of the war.

These campaigns, fought in the lands that had been the cradles of western civilization, were of great importance in making the world we live in today. For from them came not only

the independent Arab nations (Syria, Lebanon, Iraq, Jordan, Saudi Arabia, Egypt) but also the Jewish national state of Israel, to which these Arab states are so hostile. In November, 1917, in the Balfour Declaration, the British promised "the establishment in Palestine of a national home for the Jewish people." This promise bore fruit in the mandate of 1922 from the League of Nations, by which such a state was set up under British protection under the name of Palestine.

In the overseas colonies the Germans, though cut off from the homeland by the British navy, fought well. In German East Africa they actually managed to hold out to the bitter end in a series of skillful campaigns, so that they still had forces in the field in East Africa on Armistice Day, November 11, 1918. But elsewhere they were fighting from inadequate bases and with inadequate forces, so that by the end of 1914 the British, Australians, South Africans, French, and Japanese had pretty well taken over the German overseas possessions. The Allies had won the "colonial war." Only years later, however, did the most important result of that war become clear. The subject races had learned that their rulers were by no means invulnerable.

The War at Sea

This brings us to a most important front —the war at sea. In the long pull, British sea power, reinforced by the French and later by the Italian and the American navies, once more proved decisive. The Allied command of the sea made it possible to draw on the resources of the rest of the world, and in particular to transfer with surprisingly few losses large numbers of British and American troops to the crucial Western Front. Quite as important, sea power enabled the Allies to shut Germany and her allies off from overseas resources. The Allied blockade slowly but surely constricted Germany, limiting not merely military supplies for her armies, but food supplies for her civilian population. At the end of 1918, many Germans were suffering from malnutrition, an important factor in the German willingness to surrender without fighting to the bitter end.

Yet the war at sea was not easy for the Allies. The submarine proved every bit as dangerous as British alarmists before the war had feared. When the Germans launched their unrestricted submarine warfare, they made dangerous inroads on the merchant ships that were essential to the very life of Britain. By the end of 1917, some 8,000,000 tons of shipping had been sunk by the Germans, most of it by submarines. And at one point in 1917, the British had barely enough food reserves to last a month. The submarine menace was eventually overcome by a series of measures co-ordinated between the Allies and the Americans—extensive use of the convoy system, attack on the submarines by depth bombs, constant anti-submarine patrols, and development of small, fast "subchasers." But we might wonder what would have happened in 1916–1917 (and again in 1942–1943) if the Germans had contented themselves with holding actions on land and had put all their productive and fighting energies into the submarine. This they did not do in either war. Temptation for quick and obvious land success was too great.

The navy of surface vessels that the Germans had built up since the 1890's—and that, as we have seen, was so important in the growth of Anglo-German hostility—never played a really decisive part in the war itself. German surface-raiders caused severe damage in the first year, but they were finally swept off the seas. Once, however, the main German fleet threw a very bad scare into the British. This was the famous Battle of Jutland, which has been refought over and over again by naval historians. This running battle, fought in the North Sea on May 31 and June 1, 1916, resulted in the sinking of twice as much British as German tonnage, and showed how good the German navy was. But the German admiral, Scheer, was forced to run into port before the British capital ships, for which he was no match. Although Jutland was a tactical victory for the Germans, the strategic victory remained with the British, for never again did the German surface navy seriously threaten British command of the sea in European waters. At the war's end the German high command attempted to get the fleet out in a heroic last stand. It was the German sailors' refusal to take the ships out—their mutiny, in fact—that gave a critical push to the German revolution which led to the Armistice of 1918.

The Western Front: Allied Victory

This war also saw the beginnings of air warfare. German lighter-than-air machines, the Zeppelins, raided London many times in 1916–1917, and both sides made airplane bombing raids on nearby towns. But the total damage was relatively light and had no decisive effect on the final result. The airplane was of more importance in scouting, and especially in spotting for artillery; in spite of its short range in those days, it also proved useful as a means of locating submarines. The fighter plane was greatly improved during the war, and the base was laid for the development of the air forces we now know. Indeed, the airplane made greater technical strides in these four years of war than it had made since the Wrights first flew at Kitty Hawk in 1903.

Although the great new invention of the airplane did not itself alter traditional warfare, a new type of warfare was indeed developed, especially on the great Western Front, the warfare of the trenches. The machine gun, the repeating rifle, and fast-firing artillery, with the guidance of spotter planes, could pour in such deadly fire that it was almost impossible for either side to break through the opposing trench systems on a wide front. Both sides tried to break through in the two years after the Marne, and both sides suffered losses of a kind that had never been suffered before.

Two new weapons almost broke the deadlock. The first was poison gas, which was first used by the Germans in shells in October, 1914, with disappointing results. Then in April, 1915, the Germans used chlorine gas discharged from cylinders. The overwhelmed French broke in a line five miles wide, leaving the line completely undefended. But the Germans had not prepared to follow through,

Aerial combat in World War I.

and the gap was closed once the gas had dispersed. Meanwhile the experts developed a simple countermeasure, the gas mask, which became part of the equipment of every soldier on both sides. The age-old balance of attack and defense was once again reestablished.

The second new weapon came much nearer to producing decisive success. This was the tank, a sort of armored land battleship for which plans had been made back in the Renaissance by the fertile Leonardo da Vinci. But da Vinci's tank remained a mere sketch for lack of propulsive power. In the second decade of the twentieth century, however, the internal-combustion engine was ready to do what horses could not do. The tank was a British invention that had been nursed along in its infancy by the always adventurous Winston Churchill. But the new weapon was used too soon, in inadequate numbers and before adequate mechanical tests had been made, in the British Somme offensive of 1916. Even so, nine tanks led or accompanied the infantry triumphantly through the German lines to the capture of Flers. Had the tanks been withheld for a few more months and been backed up with careful planning, they might have broken

the German lines on a wide front. The Germans naturally took up the tank at once, and were soon producing their own.

The technique of attack in the west gradually developed over the years and in the end broke the defensive stalemate. Long and careful artillery preparation, known as a "barrage," literally flattened out a section of the enemy defenses and the "no man's land" in front of them and forced the enemy to retire to rear trenches. Then, accompanied or preceded by tanks, the infantry edged in while the artillery barrage was lifted and focused on the next enemy line. It was a slow and costly process which did not work on a wide scale until 1918. Then the Germans, with the Russians out of the fight, made a last and almost successful effort to break through, trying to separate the British from the French where their lines joined near Amiens. With the failure of this last German push in the summer, Foch ordered a general attack. French, British, and American armies had all broken the German lines by early autumn and were just gaining freedom of action in the open country when the Germans surrendered. The Germans later maintained that they were not beaten decisively in the

648

field. Most experts, however, now think that had the war gone on the Germans could not have stopped an Allied invasion of Germany in 1919.

Morale on the Fighting Fronts

The long narrow battle lines of the four-year trench war were the scene of a concentrated destruction hardly equaled in the war of 1939–1945, except by the atomic bomb at Hiroshima; at some points in France the top soil was blown completely away by shellfire, producing a desert that is still visible today. The war, however, was not unique, unprecedented, or unlike all other wars, as many an excited publicist at the time declared. It produced military heroes and military scapegoats, great generals and generals who failed. As with the Confederacy in the American Civil War, the defeated Germans seem to have had the most-praised generals, the Ludendorffs, the Mackensens, the Hoffmanns. The old traditional chivalrous warfare, the warfare of athletic heroes, was continued, and even heightened in the air, where the "aces" of the highly individualistic duels between planes were the Rolands of a machine age. And in many of the fronts on land, and in the war at sea, the age-old and for many males not altogether unhappy melodrama of war lost none of its reality. Lawrence in Arabia was no disgrace to the tradition of Sir Walter Scott or even, in the eyes of good patriotic Englishmen, to the tradition of Homer.

Yet especially on the Western Front, this war seemed to many of its participants an unheroic nightmare of blood and filth. Sensitive young intellectuals, who in earlier times would never have had to fight, survived to write bitterly about their experiences—in war novels like *Under Fire,* by the Frenchman Barbusse, or *All Quiet on the Western Front* by the German Remarque, and in war poems like those of Siegfried Sassoon and Wilfred Owen. But this literature cannot be trusted fully as an accurate reflection of what the millions of common soldiers who were not intellectuals felt about the war. We know simply that for

four years they bore up under it in stints in the front lines separated by rest leaves. For most of them the dullness, the discomforts, and the brief terror of battle must have tested their patriotism and worn out their sense of adventure.

The Home Fronts

These soldiers and sailors were, for the most part, not professionals; they were civilians, "drafted," lifted from civilian families unused to the ways of the military. Behind the front, on the production lines, subject to the unheroic but harassing strains of rationing and all sorts of limitations in daily living, subject also to the constant prodding of war propaganda, the families too were part of this great "total war." They too bore up under it, though in France in 1917, after the bloody failure of a great offensive under General Nivelle, civilian and military discontent, fanned by politicians, came almost to the point of breaking French morale. And in Germany, the collapse that resulted in the armistice of November 11, 1918, though it obviously had many complex causes, looks like a general failure of morale,

Allied tank going "over the top" on the Western front.

English policewomen hurrying to spread the news of an impending Zeppelin raid.

a psychological collapse under intolerable spiritual and material pressures.

For the Germans, still influenced by nineteenth-century ideas about the rights of the individual and laissez-faire economics, were slow to organize their society for total war. They failed notably to ensure the proper and equitable distribution of food supplies, so that as 1918 wore on whole sectors of the urban population began to suffer from malnutrition. Nor were finances and war production managed with that perfection of techniques that most of the world had already come to expect of the Germans. Rationing, strict control of production, price control, systematic use of the resources of conquered countries, these and many other measures were employed by the Germans, but not with the care, decisiveness, and long preparation that were to characterize them in the conflict of 1939–1945.

All countries engaged in the war, the democratic western Allies as well as the autocratic Central Powers, sooner or later felt obliged to introduce drastic wartime economic planning, which anticipated in some sense the more collectivistic economy of today. Everywhere there was compulsory military service. Even in Britain, proud of its long devotion to the rights of the individual, the famous Defense of the Realm Act—known with wry affection as DORA—clamped down severely on the Englishman's sacred right to say and do what he liked, even if he did not seem to be giving aid and comfort to the enemy. In the United States, all sorts of men, including the famous "dollar-a-year men," business executives who were working for the government for the first time, flocked to Washington and helped build up an enormous new central government, which regulated the economy as it had never been regulated before. And of course all the belligerents engaged in the war of propaganda, or, as it came to be called in the next great war, in psychological warfare.

The Allies won the battle of the production lines, in which the United States played a major if not a decisive part. We have already noted that in material resources the Allies had a marked potential superiority over the Central Powers; this superiority they were eventually able to realize to the full. Allied production was slow in getting started. There were mistakes, bottlenecks, and experiments like that of the tanks which failed at first because of undue haste. At the beginning the Allies were often at cross-purposes in production as well as in actual military strategy. Nevertheless, by the end of 1917 the Allied military machine was adequately, indeed in some ways wastefully, supplied.

650

The Role of Propaganda

The Allies also won the most critical phase of the war of propaganda. They sought to convince the neutral world, especially the neutrals of western civilization, the United States, Latin America, and the Swiss, Dutch, Scandinavians, and Spanish, that the Allies were fighting for the right and the Central Powers for the wrong. It was not a complete victory, for important groups in all these countries remained "pro-German" to the end, and Spain on the whole was probably throughout the war pro-German, or at least anti-French and anti-English. Still, it seems that a majority of the neutral West was early convinced that the cause of the Allies was just. This conviction was strengthened from the very start by the traditional liberalism of France and Britain in contrast with the traditional autocracy of the German and the Austrian empires, though the presence of the autocratic Russian Empire on the Allied side somewhat handicapped Allied propagandists. In the early days of the crisis of 1914, the intransigence of the Austrians toward the Serbs, and in particular the blundering phrase of Bethmann-Hollweg, that Britain had gone to war for a mere "scrap of paper," got the Central Powers off to a bad start in world opinion.

The sense of Allied rightness was strengthened by early Allied propaganda, which was often one-sided and unfair. Notably, it accused the Germans of frightful atrocities in Belgium. The Germans did indeed impose rigorous military controls on conquered populations, but little in their record was worse than is usual, and perhaps inevitable, in all warfare. Allied propaganda also simplified and falsified the complex chain of causation that produced the war, making it appear that the Germans and the Austrians were wholly responsible for the outbreak of the war, that the "predatory Potsdam gang" had planned the whole thing from the beginning, and that Serbs, French, Russians, and British had been wholly innocent of deed or word that might have brought on the war. This propaganda backfired shortly after the war; revulsion against its unfairness had much to do with the widespread acceptance of the extreme—and false—revisionist thesis that on the whole Germany, in particular, had been quite guiltless of starting the war.

World War I poster.

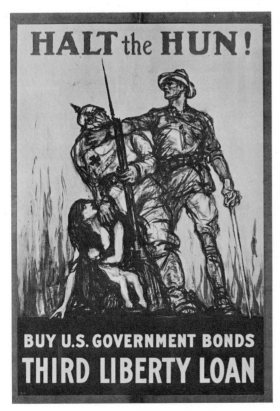

HALT the HUN!

BUY U.S. GOVERNMENT BONDS
THIRD LIBERTY LOAN

Political Repercussions

Except in Russia, the four years of war saw no major changes in political structure. The Central Empires retained until their collapse their incompletely responsible parliamentary governments, and the parliaments on the whole were reasonably submissive. And in spite of the inevitable strengthening of the executive in wartime, France, Britain, and the United States carried on their democratic institutions. In the United States the critical presidential election of 1916 came just before American entrance into the war, and resulted by a narrow margin in the return of the incumbent, Woodrow Wilson. In Britain and France the democratic process brought to power in the midst of wartime crisis two strong men — Lloyd George and Clemenceau — who carried through with great vigor the prosecution of the war, and who, though their fame was dimmed in the troubled years after the war, remain in historic memory as great national heroes of their respective countries.

In Britain the skillful but indecisive Liberal leader Asquith proved unable to master events, even though he widened his government into a coalition in May, 1915. In December of that year he was succeeded by another Liberal, Lloyd George, the architect of Britain's social insurance system (see Chapter 13), who had also proven himself an admirable organizer of war production. Under Lloyd George the coalition really worked, and his position as war leader was to remain unchallenged. We shall meet him again at the peace negotiations, as we shall meet his French counterpart, Clemenceau. The "Tiger," as Clemenceau was known to his friends and enemies alike, came to power at the end of 1917, at a time when defeatism threatened both the military and the civilian strength of France. Clemenceau took firm command of the war effort and disposed summarily of the disaffected politicians with the decisiveness — and disregard for the peacetime "rights of man" — of an old Jacobin.

IV   The Peace Settlements

As in Westphalia in 1648, at Utrecht in 1713, and at Vienna in 1815, the warring powers gathered in a great meeting to make the peace settlement. This time they met at Paris — or, rather, in suburban Paris. They met at Versailles to settle with the Germans, and at other suburban *châteaux* to settle with the rest. Peace congresses almost never meet in a world that is really at peace. There are always aftermaths, local wars and disturbances. The aftermaths of 1918–1919 were particularly numerous and acute and conditioned the whole work of the peace congresses. To them we must turn briefly before we consider the actual settlements.

The Aftermath of World War

The sorest spot was Russia, then in 1919 in the throes of civil war and foreign invasion. No sooner had the Germans been forced to withdraw from the regions they had gained at Brest-Litovsk (see p. 643) than the Allies sent detachments to various points along the rim of Russia — on the Black Sea, on the White Sea in the far north, and on the Pacific (for details see Chapter 18). The Allies still hoped to restore in Russia, if not the monarchy, at least a moderate democratic republic. Their dread of final Bolshevik success (the term "Bolshevism" was then almost universally used, instead of communism) and of the possible spread of Bolshevism westward, added to the tensions at Versailles and confirmed the conservative position Clemenceau and Lloyd George were taking.

Bolshevism was indeed spreading westward. The German revolution of November, 1918, had been carried out under socialist auspices. But all through the winter of 1918–1919 there were communist riots and uprisings, and in Bavaria in April a soviet republic was proclaimed. The government of the new republic of Germany put these communist uprisings down, but only by an appeal to the remnants of the old army and to officers thoroughly hostile to any form of republic. In the break-up of the Austro-Hungarian monarchy in the autumn of 1918, the successor states — Czechoslovakia, Austria, Hungary, Yugoslavia, Rumania—which had been formed in whole or in part out of the former Habsburg lands, were disturbed by all sorts of social and economic troubles. In Hungary, Bela Kun, who had worked with Lenin in Moscow, won power by means of a socialist-communist coalition, and then elbowed out his socialist colleagues and set up a communist dictatorship. In August, a Rumanian army that had invaded Hungary forced Bela Kun to flee. Finally, all through the Germanies groups of ex-soldiers, the *Freikorps*, were roving about, stirring up trouble, and threatening the overthrow of the German Republic (for details, see Chapter 19).

In the Near East the Allies had even worse troubles to face. Greece, which had been so hard to drag into the war, was now in full cry against the Turks. Her nationalists had revived the old hope of a restored Byzantine Empire, with the Greeks once more in command of the Straits. Her armies, not without Allied encouragement, landed at Smyrna in Asia Minor in the spring of 1919 and marched off in the track of Alexander the Great. The French and the British, to whom control over different parts of the former Turkish Empire had been assigned, began at once having trouble with their new Arab wards. The Jews were already pressing for the establishment of a national home in Palestine in accordance with the Balfour Declaration, and the Arabs were already opposing them.

In India the aftermath of war was bad indeed. The universal epidemic of influenza —actually a pandemic—in 1918 (which most public-health experts believed killed more people than were killed in battle) had been especially disastrous in India. Indians had fought well as professional soldiers during the war on the Allied side; educated Indians thought their country was ripe for much more self-rule. The disorders of 1918–1919 culminated in the Amritsar massacre of April, 1919, in which a British general, reverting to old-time methods, ordered his soldiers to fire on an unarmed crowd, killing or wounding some 1,600 people. Amritsar shocked world opinion, added to the odium the Allies were al-

ready acquiring among liberals everywhere, and knitted India more closely together in opposition to the British. In China, the weakening of Russia had been taken by the Japanese as a signal to renew their ambitious plans in the north of China, and indeed the American troops sent to Vladivostok in Siberia (see Chapter 18) were there less to oppose the Bolsheviks than to oppose the Japanese.

So the world was in turmoil and disorder when the Allies, great, small, and middle-sized, assembled in and near Paris to make the peace. The problems that faced the peacemakers were world-wide, complex, and often insoluble—insoluble in the sense that no decision on a given problem, say the disposition of the Adriatic port of Fiume which was claimed by Italians and Yugoslavs, could possibly satisfy all the major groups concerned, to say nothing of the minorities. Yet the world hoped, and indeed expected, from the peacemakers more than it had in any previous crisis. Public opinion in the eighteenth and nineteenth centuries had built up a tremendous faith in the possibility of a peaceful, just, and happy world. This war had been a war to "make the world safe for democracy," a "war to end war." It had produced in the American President Wilson a man who could phrase skillfully the hopes of men, and who as he journeyed to Paris after the Armistice appeared to be the heroic savior and hope of mankind.

These liberal dreams and expectations were, however, by no means the sole tenants of men's minds. All men were not Wilsonians. There were, inevitably, the selfish, the disillusioned, the narrow, the jingoists, and the professionals who had made promises to the Italians and the Rumanians, who had planned all sorts of compensations and adjustments. There were, more important, the plain ordinary men and women who wanted peace and security but who also wanted national glory and the punishment of the wicked Germans who, they believed, had put them through those four years of hell. There were, in short, thousands of conflicting hopes and fears, all of them embodied in living human flesh, not just the abstractions they must seem to be on the printed page.

Above: Soldiers of the American 6th Infantry Regiment celebrate the Armistice. *Below:* Paris greets the Armistice.

The Fourteen Points

The more generous of these hopes were in 1918 clearly embodied in one man and in one text. Woodrow Wilson, on January 8, 1918, in an address to the American Congress, had announced the famous Fourteen Points, which were widely accepted by people in Allied countries and even in Germany and Austria as a platform for the peace to come, but were also widely misunderstood and subject to the most divergent interpretations. Here is the whole of this most important document:

I. Open covenants of peace, openly arrived at, after which there shall be no private international understandings of any kind but diplomacy shall proceed always frankly and in the public view.

II. Absolute freedom of navigation upon the seas, outside territorial waters, alike in peace and in war, except as the seas may be closed in whole or in part by international action for the enforcement of international covenants.

III. The removal, so far as possible, of all economic barriers and the establishment of an equality of trade conditions among all the nations consenting to the peace and associating themselves for its maintenance.

IV. Adequate guarantees given and taken that national armaments will be reduced to the lowest point consistent with domestic safety.

V. A free, open-minded, and absolutely impartial adjustment of all colonial claims, based upon a strict observance of the principle that in determining all such questions of sovereignty the interests of the populations concerned must have equal weight with the equitable claims of the government whose title is to be determined.

VI. The evacuation of all Russian territory and such a settlement of all questions affecting Russia as will secure the best and freest co-operation of the other nations of the world in obtaining for her an unhampered and unembarrassed opportunity for the independent determination of her own political development and national policy and assure her of a sincere welcome into the society of free nations under institutions of her own choosing; and, more than a welcome, assistance also of every kind that she may need and may herself desire. The treatment accorded Russia by her sister nations in the months to come will be the acid test of their good will, of their comprehension of her needs as distinguished from their own interests, and of their intelligent and unselfish sympathy.

VII. Belgium, the whole world will agree, must be evacuated and restored, without any attempt to limit the sovereignty which she enjoys in common with all other free nations. No other single act will serve as this will serve to restore confidence among the nations in the laws which they have themselves set and determined for the government of their relations with one another. Without this healing act the whole structure and validity of international law is forever impaired.

VIII. All French territory should be freed and the invaded portions restored, and the wrong done to France by Prussia in 1871 in the matter of Alsace-Lorraine, which has unsettled the peace of the world for nearly fifty years, should be righted, in order that peace may once more be made secure in the interest of all.

IX. A readjustment of the frontiers of Italy should be effected along clearly recognizable lines of nationality.

X. The peoples of Austria-Hungary, whose place among the nations we wish to see safeguarded and assured, should be accorded the freest opportunity of autonomous development.

XI. Rumania, Serbia, and Montenegro should be evacuated; occupied territories restored; Serbia accorded free and secure access to the sea; and the relations of the several Balkan states to one another determined by friendly counsel along historically established lines of allegiance and nationality; and international guarantees of the political and economic independence and territorial integrity of the several Balkan states should be entered into.

XII. The Turkish portions of the present Ottoman Empire should be assured a secure sovereignty, but the other nationalities which are now under Turkish rule should be assured an undoubted security of life and an absolutely unmolested opportunity of autonomous development, and the Dardanelles should be permanently opened as a free passage to the ships and commerce of all nations under international guarantees.

XIII. An independent Polish state should be erected which should include the territories inhabited by indisputably Polish populations, which should be assured a free and secure access to the sea, and whose political and economic independence and territorial integrity should be guaranteed by international covenant.

XIV. A general association of nations must be

formed under specific covenants for the purpose of affording mutual guarantees of political independence and territorial integrity to great and small states alike.*

The fourteenth point, the germ of the League of Nations, was especially dear to Wilson.

Opposing Hopes and Promises

The hopes and promises that opposed and contradicted the Fourteen Points were not neatly embodied in a single document. We may classify them roughly in three categories: the previous diplomatic commitments made by the Allies; the immediate and widespread popular hopes fanned by Allied propaganda and confirmed at the last moment by some Allied statesmen; and—much more difficult to pin down—the long-established habits and traditions that had become part of the dominant policies and trends of each nation, big and little.

In the first category, the most difficult of the diplomatic commitments was the contradictory set of promises made to both Italy and Serbia by the original Entente, including Russia, about the disposal of Habsburg lands. And there were other commitments, especially in the Balkans, that were very difficult to sort out. In the second category were the promises, widely believed by the British and French peoples, that Germany would be made to suffer to the full for her war guilt. She would have to pay the whole cost of the war in reparations, her war criminals would be punished, she would be rendered incapable ever again of assuming the role of the aggressor. In some vague way, everything would shortly be much better for everybody. Britain, for example, would be "a land fit for heroes."

Finally, in the third category were the deeply rooted drives of the various nations —French drives for revenge against Germany, for restoration of French hegemony in Europe, and, no doubt inconsistently but very humanly,

*Woodrow Wilson, *War and Peace: Presidential Messages, Addresses, and Public Papers,* R. S. Baker and W. E. Dodd, eds. (New York, 1927), I, 159–161.

for security; the Italian Irredentist drive; the British longing for a Victorian serenity and economic leadership well armored against German commercial competition; and the nationalist aspirations of the new states of Central Europe, released at last from long frustration. And by no means the least important was the old and firmly held American tradition that Americans call "isolationism," the desire to be free from European alliances and entanglements.

The Process of Peacemaking

The Peace Conference first met formally on January 18, 1919. Nearly thirty nations involved in the war against the Central Powers sent delegates. Russia was not represented. None of the victorious great powers—Britain, France, the United States—was in a mood to invite the Bolsheviks, now in power in Moscow, to the peace table; and no Russian government-in-exile seemed to the Allies suitable for an invitation. The defeated nations took no part in the deliberations; they were simply notified of the final terms and asked to sign. The Germans, in particular, were given but the slightest chance to comment on or criticize the terms offered them. Very soon the German publicists coined a term for the treaty—"*Diktat,*" the imposed, the dictated peace. The Germans' anger over this failure of the Allies to negotiate with their new and virtuous republic was to play a large part in the ultimate rise of Hitler.

Although a few western liberals were from the first disillusioned by the exclusion of Communist Russia and the Central Powers from the Peace Conference, the conference did get off to a good start. Wilson's reception in Europe had been extremely enthusiastic. People everywhere were still rejoicing over the end of the nightmare. The Fourteen Points seemed already a realized peace; and for the future, it was held, the proposed association of nations, working together in the freedom of parliamentary discussion, would soon eliminate the costly burdens of armament. Wilson's hopeful phrases sounded in press and pulpit, and none more loudly than his "open covenants openly arrived at." To many a liberal these words meant that the peace would be made in a sort of big, idealized New England town meeting, in which the representatives of all the powers, big and little, would have their free say in public, in which decisions would ultimately be taken by majority vote, in which the caucus, the smoke-filled room, the backstairs intrigues would all be missing.

These liberals were almost at once disillusioned, for the conference soon fell into the familiar pattern of centuries. The small nations were excluded from the real negotiations; the business of the conference was carried on in private among the political chiefs of the victorious great powers—the Big Four of Wilson, Lloyd George, Clemenceau, and Orlando (it was really a Big Three, for Italy was not strong enough to impose her Orlando, who was a much less striking character than his colleagues). Decisions were made in the traditional way of diplomacy, with all the pressures, chicanery, intrigues, compromises, and plain horse-trading that go on when leaders get together in private. Public opinion was consulted only indirectly, as each statesman sought to make sure that he had at least a majority of the politically important elements of his own nation behind him in his demands.

The hopeful members of the general public were by no means the only ones who grew disillusioned as the Paris Conference went the way of the Vienna Congress a hundred years before. The professional diplomatists of the little and middle-sized powers had probably never really expected that they would be treated on equal terms, but the completeness of their exclusion from the real work of the conference annoyed them, and angered their people back home. More important, all the major powers had brought with them large staffs of experts, economists, political scientists, historians, career men in many fields. These bright young men were sure they knew better than their elders how to solve the problems of human relations, were confident that they would do the real work and make the really important decisions. They drew up report after report, some of which went up through devious channels to Clemenceau or Lloyd George or Wilson. But they did not make policy. The disillusion of the young experts was great and long-lived, and since many

The Big Four at Paris, 1919
—Lloyd George, Orlando, Clemenceau, and Wilson.

of them were quite articulate they did much to discredit the work of the conference, especially among liberal intellectuals everywhere.

Wilson and his experts were gradually badgered into accepting harsher peace terms. The reparations bill against Germany was lengthened; Poland, Italy, and Japan made claims to lands that clearly would not be theirs by self-determination of their peoples; the victors more and more openly showed that they proposed to behave as victors in war habitually have behaved. Wilson gave way or compromised on a dozen points and then chose to stand fast against the weakest of the Allies. He would not let the Italians have the Adriatic seaport of Fiume, which had once been the sole seaport of Hungary. They might have neighboring Trieste and their coveted Trentino, where they could rule over German or Slavic-speaking minorities, indeed, in some areas, majorities; but Fiume they might not have. Fiume was indeed a difficult case. It was Italian-speaking and historically was linked with the great past of Venice; but it had never been part of modern Italy, and it had *not* been promised to Italy in the secret treaties of 1915. The Italian delegation left the conference in anger, but Wilson was immovable. The fate of Fiume was not settled at the conference; only in 1924, by treaty with Yugoslavia, did the city go to Italy in return for Susak, a port right next door that served the Yugoslavs quite adequately for the next two decades.

But Wilson did get his new international organization, the cornerstone of his plans for a better world. The covenant of the League of Nations was an integral part of the Treaty of Versailles. The League was no true supranational state, but a kind of permanent consultative system composed of the victors and a few neutrals. The way was left open for the Germans and the Russians to join the League, as they later did. But in 1919–1920, Wilson's League looked to many liberals a lot like Metternich's and Castlereagh's old Congress system of 1815, by no means worth the sacrifices Wilson had made to obtain it. The League had an assembly in which each member-state had one vote, and a council in which the five great powers (Britain, France, Italy, the United States, and Japan) had permanent seats, and to which four other member-states were chosen by the assembly for specific terms. A permanent secretariat, to be located at Geneva, was charged with administering the affairs of the League. In its working out, as we shall see (Chapter 21), the League never fulfilled the hopes of the liberals. It did not achieve disarmament, nor did its machinery of peacemaking prove capable of preventing aggression. The great powers simply went on their usual ways, using the League only as their policy-makers —their heads of state rather than their diplomatists—saw fit.

The Territorial Settlement

Central to all the work in Paris was the problem of territorial changes. Here, peacemakers were confronted not merely, as at most peace conferences in our western society, with the claims of the victorious Allies but also with the claims of the new nations that had sprung up from the disintegrating Austrian, Russian, and Turkish empires. They had to try to satisfy the eternal land hunger of those who run nations, without violating too obviously the great Wilsonian principle of "self-determination of peoples." This principle was hard indeed to apply in much of Central Europe, where peoples of different language and national self-consciousness were mixed together in an incredible mosaic of unassimilated minorities (see map on p. 659). The result was to multiply the number of "sovereign" nations in this world. Nationalism, which some hopeful people had thought was on the wane, was now fanned to intense new life in a dozen states.

France received Alsace-Lorraine back from Germany. Clemenceau also hoped both to annex the small but coal-rich Saar Basin of Germany as compensation for French coal mines destroyed by the Germans during the war, and to detach from Germany the territory on the left (or west) bank of the Rhine, thereby strengthening French security and setting up a Rhineland republic that might become a French satellite. Both French hopes, opposed

Territorial Settlements in Europe, 1919-1926

Areas lost:
by Germany
by Austria-Hungary
by Russia
by Bulgaria

········· Boundaries of 1914 ——— Boundaries of 1926
Demilitarized areas (Rhineland, "The Straits")
Allied Occupation Zone (Rhineland)

by Wilson and Lloyd George, went unrealized. The Saar was to be separated from Germany for fifteen years as an international ward supervised by the League of Nations. At the end of the fifteen-year period a plebiscite would determine its future status; meanwhile, its coal output was to go to France. The Rhineland remained part of the German Republic, though it was to be demilitarized and occupied for a time by Allied soldiers.

Belgium was given some small towns on her German border. Italy gained her Irredenta of Trent and Trieste, indeed in generous measure, for thousands of German and Slavic-speaking peoples were included within her new boundaries. Poland, erased from the map as an independent state in 1795, was now restored and given lands that she had had before the partitions of the eighteenth century and that contained important minorities of Germans and other non-Polish peoples. The old Habsburg Empire was entirely dismembered. The heart of its German-speaking area was constituted as the truncated Republic of Austria, which was forbidden to join itself to Germany, and the heart of its Magyar-speaking area became a diminished Kingdom of Hungary. The Czech-inhabited lands of Bohemia and Moravia were joined with Slovakia and the Ruthenian lands of the Carpatho-Ukraine further east in the brand-new "succession state" of Czechoslovakia. This new state faced the problem of a large and discontented Sudeten German minority.

Another "succession state" was Yugoslavia, officially the Kingdom of Serbs, Croats, and Slovenes, which, as its full name suggests, represented a great expansion of pre-war Serbia to include the south Slav territories of the Habsburgs. Rumania, too, profited by the break-up of the old dual monarchy by receiving the former Hungarian lands of Transylvania. Rewarded also with Bessarabia, a Russian province that the Bolsheviks could not defend, Rumania emerged with doubled territory, and some restive non-Rumanian minorities. In the southern Balkan Peninsula, Greece received all of Thrace, at the expense of Turkey and Bulgaria.

Out of the former tsarist domains held at the end of the war by the Germans there were set up, in addition to Poland, the "Baltic republics" of Estonia, Latvia, and Lithuania. Once Europe had settled down, plebiscites were provided for to determine certain other territorial adjustments, notably whether certain parts of East Prussia and Silesia should go to Poland or remain German. The new Polish state had been granted access to the Baltic Sea through the so-called "Polish corridor," a narrow strip of land which had once been Polish, and which terminated in the almost wholly German city and port of Danzig. The Poles wanted Danzig, but the Allies compromised by setting up a Free City of Danzig and by giving the Poles free trade with the city. Even so, the Polish corridor now separated East Prussia from the rest of Germany, and Germans had to cross it in sealed trains.

Outside Europe, the Near East presented the most acute problems. By the Treaty of Sèvres the Turks were left in Europe with no more than Constantinople and a small strip of land around it, and in Asia with only their homeland of Anatolia. Mesopotamia and Palestine were given as mandates—a term we shall shortly explain—to Britain, while Syria and Lebanon were given as mandates to France. The Greeks were to hold Smyrna and nearby regions in Asia Minor for five years and then submit to a plebiscite. But the Treaty of Sèvres never went into effect, though it was duly signed by the Sultan. In Anatolia a group of army officers led by Mustafa Kemal revolted against the government at Constantinople and galvanized the Turkish people into a new national life. The Turks drove the Greek army out of their country and set up a Turkish republic with its capital not at Constantinople but at Ankara in the heart of Anatolia. With this new government the Allies were finally obliged to conclude the Treaty of Lausanne in 1923. The new peace transferred the Smyrna area and eastern Thrace from Greek to Turkish control and was in general more advantageous to the Turks than the Treaty of Sèvres had been.

The treaty of Lausanne embodied in dramatic form a principle new in part in the West —the formal transfer of populations. True, peoples had been evicted by conquers before; witness among other instances the eviction of the French Acadians from Nova Scotia by the British in the eighteenth century, or the settling of our Indians in Indian Territory, now part of the state of Oklahoma. But here was an almost complete exchange: Greeks in Turkey were moved to Greece. Turks in Greece were moved to Turkey. No very significant discontented national minorities were left. Each government was to take care of the transferred populations, and though much hardship occurred, on the whole the plan worked. There was no such exchange of populations in the then British-held island of Cyprus, on which mutually hostile Greek and Turkish towns and villages continued to exist.

The Mandates

For the rest of the world the old straightforward policy of annexing overseas territories of defeated powers, as practiced in 1713, 1763, and 1815, seemed no longer possible in 1919. Liberal opinion both in Europe and in America had already been offended to the bursting point, and Wilson himself would never have permitted outright annexations. The consequence was the mandate system, whereby control over a given territory was assigned to a particular power by the League of Nations, which undertook periodic inspections to see that the terms of the mandate were being fulfilled. This system was designed by its proponents as a means of educating colonial peoples, leading them into the ways of democratic self-government, and preparing them for eventual independence. Under it the former German overseas territories and the non-Turkish parts of the Ottoman Empire were now distributed. Of Germany's African possessions East Africa (rechristened Tanganyika, and in 1964 merged with Zanzibar as independent Tanzania) went to Britain; Southwest Africa went to the Union of South Africa; and both the Cameroons and Togoland were divided between Britain and France. In the Pacific, the German portion of New Guinea was given to Australia, western Samoa to New Zealand, and the Caroline, Marshall, and Mariana island groups to Japan. In the Near East, as we have seen, France thus secured Syria and Lebanon, while Britain took Palestine and Mesopotamia.

The mandate system may seem to have been a way of disguising annexation, the hypocritical tribute of reactionary vice to progressive virtue. And so to a man like Clemenceau it probably was. The Japanese quite openly annexed and fortified their new Pacific islands in defiance of the terms of their mandate. But to many of the men who put through the idea of mandates the system really was what it professed to be, a nursery for eventual nationhood. For the most part the mandatory powers did make some show at least of treating mandated territories in a way that would prepare them for eventual freedom. Most of them are now indeed "free," or at least independent, nations.

The Punishment of Germany

After land transfers, the most important business of the Peace Conference was reparations, which were imposed on Austria, Hungary, Bulgaria, and Turkey as well as on Germany. It was, however, the German reparations that so long disturbed the peace and the

economy of the world. The Germans were made to promise to pay for all the damage done to civilian property during the war, and to pay at the rate of five billion dollars a year until 1921, when the final bill would be presented to them. They would then be given thirty years in which to pay the full amount. The amount was left indefinite at Versailles, for the Allies could not agree on a figure. But the totals suggested were astronomical. It was clear from the first that the payments would ultimately have to be in goods—German goods in competition with the goods of the Allies. A Germany prosperous enough to pay reparations could not be the weak and divided nation that men like Clemenceau really wanted. Thus from the very start the "realists" at Versailles—Lloyd George and Clemenceau—cherished quite inconsistent hopes for the future.

The Versailles settlement also required Germany to hand over many of her merchant ships to the Allies and to make large deliveries of coal to France, Italy, and Belgium for a ten-year period. Furthermore, a whole miscellany of articles in the treaty was directed toward the disarmament of Germany on land, on sea, and in the air. The German army was to be limited in size to 100,000 men, and the western frontier zone, extending to a line 50 kilometers (about 30 miles) east of the Rhine, was to be completely "demilitarized"—that is, to contain neither fortifications nor soldiers. In addition, the Allies could maintain armies of occupation on the left bank of the Rhine for fifteen years, and perhaps longer. The treaty forbade Germany to have either submarines or military planes and severely limited the number and size of surface vessels in her navy.

Last, and by no means least important, Article 231 of the Treaty of Versailles obliged Germany to admit that the Central Powers bore sole responsibility for starting the war in 1914. Here is the article that was to cause so much history to be written—and made:

The Allied and Associated Governments affirm, and Germany accepts, the responsibility of Germany and her allies for causing all the loss and damage to which the Allied and Associated Governments and their nationals have been subjected as a conse-

The Balkans and the Middle East 1878

quence of the war imposed upon them by the aggression of Germany and her allies.

The Settlement Evaluated

To the Germans, Versailles was of course a cruel and humiliating peace, the *Diktat*, the great national grievance on which Hitler was to play so skillfully. To liberals of the time and later it seemed an unsound, revengeful peace, above all disastrous in its unrealistic reparations policy. In our present world of cold and hot wars, Versailles almost arouses nostalgia. It was at least a settlement, and one that in the best moments of the 1920's seemed a basis for slow improvement in international relations (see Chapter 21).

The League it set up was potentially a means by which a new generation of international administrators might mitigate the old rivalries of nations. The reparations could be, and indeed were, scaled down to something more reasonable. The new succession states were based on a modern popular national consciousness that had been developing for at least a hundred years. Though the theorist might protest at the "Balkanization of Europe," the creation of more weak and discontented little states like those in the Balkans, the fact remains that it would have been hard to deny national independence, or at least autonomy, to the Czechs, the Poles, the Baltic peoples, and the south Slavs. Germany, though she certainly was not treated generously, was at least not wiped off the map, as Poland had been in

The Balkans and the Middle East
1921

the eighteenth century. She was not even actually demoted to a second-rate position in the world. She remained, as she was shortly to prove, a first-rate power. In the long series of settlements under our modern western state-system, which goes back to the Italian wars of the fifteenth century, Versailles looks nowadays like neither the worst nor the best, but like a typical compromise peace.

It was, however, too much for the American people, who were not used to the harsh needs of international compromise. But it is an oversimplification to argue that this was solely a matter of American idealism turning away in disgust from a settlement that was all too spotted with unpleasant realities. The final American refusal to ratify the Treaty of Versailles, like all great collective decisions, was

the result of many forces. Politics certainly played an important part, for the Republicans had won control of both the Senate and the House of Representatives in the congressional elections of November, 1918. The President of course was still Wilson, a Democrat, and Wilson made no concessions to the Republicans either by taking a bipartisan delegation of Democrats and Republicans to Paris with him or by accepting modifications in the treaty which would have satisfied some of his Republican opponents. The Senate thereupon refused to ratify the treaty.

It is, however, extremely unlikely that even a much more pliable and diplomatic American president than Wilson could have secured from the Senate ratification of another important treaty involved in the proposed settlement.

This was the project of a defensive alliance among France, Britain, and the United States into which Wilson had been pushed as part of the price of getting France to give up her proposals for a separate Rhineland republic and for annexation of the Saar. With the United States out, Britain refused a mere dual alliance with France against a German attack. France, still seeking to bolster her security, patched up a series of alliances with the new nations to the east and south of Germany — Poland, and the "Little Entente" of Yugoslavia, Czechoslovakia, and Rumania, a rather unsatisfactory substitute for Britain and the United States as allies.

The peace thus left France with an uneasy hegemony in Europe, a hegemony dependent on the continued disarmament and economic weakening of Germany, on the continued isolation of Russia, and on the uncertain support of her new allies. Moreover, France had been disastrously weakened by the human and material losses of the war, and her position of leadership, though it alarmed the British with their long memories of French rivalry in the past, was an unreal thing. In reality, Germany was the strongest nation in Europe, and the Great War had checked, but not halted, her attempt to dominate the Continent and indeed the world. The next German attempt was to draw both Britain and America back from the isolation into which they attempted to withdraw after the collapse of the system planned at Paris in 1919.

A most important matter, however, was not directly touched by the Versailles settlement: Russia, or the Union of Soviet Socialist Republics (U.S.S.R.), the formal name of the new communist state, did not figure in the great treaties. Yet in many senses the most important result of World War I was the emergence of this new-old Russia, her strength and capabilities in the long run increased by the stimulus of successful revolution.

Reading Suggestions on the First World War

(Asterisk indicates paperbound edition.)

The Background: General Accounts

A. J. P. Taylor, *The Struggle for Mastery in Europe, 1848–1918* (Clarendon, 1954). A crisp and suggestive survey.

S. B. Fay, *The Origins of the World War,* 2nd ed. (Macmillan, 1932). A fully documented account by an American scholar; somewhat sympathetic to Germany.

B. E. Schmitt, *The Coming of the War, 1914,* 2 vols. (Scribner's, 1930). Another well-documented scholarly account; somewhat sympathetic to Britain.

H. E. Barnes, *The Genesis of the World War: An Introduction to the Problem of War Guilt* (Knopf, 1926). An extreme statement on the "revisionist" position on war guilt.

M. von Montgelas, *The Case for the Central Powers, An Impeachment of the Versailles Verdict* (Knopf, 1925). Representative of the German "revisionist" school.

L. Albertini, *The Origins of the War of 1914,* 2 vols. (Oxford Univ. Press, 1952–1953). By an Italian scholar; stresses the role of Italy.

N. Mansergh, *The Coming of the First World War* (Longmans, Green, 1949). A brief popular survey from 1878 to 1914.

Barbara Tuchman, *The Proud Tower* (Macmillan, 1966). A very good and most readable account of the European society out of which the "Great War" came.

The Background: Special Studies

W. L. Langer, *European Alliances and Alignments, 1871–1890.* 2nd ed. (Knopf, 1950). A detailed scholarly survey, favorable to Bismarckian diplomacy.

W. L. Langer, *The Diplomacy of Imperialism, 1890–1902,* 2nd ed. (Knopf, 1951). Includes much material pertaining to the shifting alliances of the European powers.

L. C. B. Seaman, *From Vienna to Versailles* (Coward-McCann, 1956). Interesting essay in interpretation by a young British scholar.

E. M. Carroll, *French Public Opinion and Foreign Affairs, 1870 – 1914* (Century, 1931), and *Germany and the Great Powers, 1866 – 1914: A Study in Public Opinion and Foreign Policy* (Prentice-Hall, 1938). Scholarly studies in a significant area of research.

R. J. S. Hoffman, *Great Britain and the German Trade Rivalry, 1875 – 1914* (Univ. of Pennsylvania Press, 1933). A helpful monograph.

E. L. Woodward, *Great Britain and the German Navy* (Clarendon, 1935); A. J. Marder, *The Anatomy of British Sea Power* (Knopf, 1940); and B. Brodie, *Sea Power in the Machine Age* (Princeton Univ. Press, 1943). Three useful studies of the important question of naval power.

E. N. Anderson, *The First Moroccan Crisis, 1904 – 1906* (Univ. of Chicago Press, 1930), and I. C. Barlow, *The Agadir Crisis* (Univ. of North Carolina Press, 1940). Two useful monographs on the issue of Morocco in pre-war diplomacy.

E. M. Earle, *Turkey, The Great Powers, and the Bagdad Railway* (Macmillan, 1923). Scholarly account of another major issue of pre-war diplomacy.

A. F. Pribram, *Austrian Foreign Policy, 1908 – 1918* (Allen & Unwin, 1923). Balanced statement from the Austrian standpoint.

P. Renouvin, *The Immediate Origins of the War* (Yale Univ. Press, 1928). Scholarly account from the French point of view.

G. P. Gooch and H. Temperley, eds., *British Documents on the Origins of the War, 1898 – 1914,* 12 vols. (His Majesty's Stationery Office, 1926 – 1938). Representative of the great collections of diplomatic documents published by the governments of the major belligerents after World War I.

Outbreak of the World War: German Documents Collected by Karl Kautsky (Oxford Univ. Press, 1924), and *German Diplomatic Documents, 1871 – 1914,* 4 vols. (Methuen, 1928 – 1931). English translations of some of the vast number of German diplomatic documents.

The Background of the War: American Policy

T. A. Bailey, *A Diplomatic History of the American People,* 4th ed. (Appleton-Century-Crofts, 1950), and S. F. Bemis, *A Diplomatic History of the United States,* 3rd ed. (Holt, 1950). Two standard surveys.

W. Millis, *The Road to War: America, 1914 – 1917* (Houghton, Mifflin, 1935). Readable journalistic account, highly critical of Wilson's policy.

C. C. Tansill, *America Goes to War* (Little, Brown, 1938). Scholarly treatment, also critical of Wilson's policy.

C. Seymour, *American Diplomacy during the World War,* 2nd ed. (Johns Hopkins Univ. Press, 1942). Sympathetic toward Wilson's policy.

The War

W. S. Churchill, *The World Crisis,* 6 vols. (Scribner's, 1923 – 1931). Detailed survey by the famous British statesman.

C. R. M. Cruttwell, *History of the Great War,* 2nd ed. (Oxford Univ. Press, 1936), and B. H. Liddell Hart, *The Real War, 1914 – 1918.* Remain the best single-volume histories. The Liddell Hart book was re-issued as a paperback (*Atlantic; Little, Brown, 1964).

H. W. Baldwin, *World War I: An Outline History* (Harper, 1962), also paperback. Most recent survey by a good military historian.

J. E. Edmonds, *A Short History of World War I* (Oxford Univ. Press, 1951). A brief account by an official British military historian.

Barbara Tuchman, *The Guns of August* (Macmillan, 1962; *Dell). A fascinating account of the immediate background and the first critical month of the war.

Alan Moorhead, *Gallipoli* (Harper, 1956), also a paperback. By a skillful writer and trained historian.

A. Horne, *The Price of Glory: Verdun 1916* (St. Martin's Press, 1964), also a paperback. An excellent narrative of a most important battle.

Note: There are many detailed military histories of World War I. The problems that arose on the home front have been the subject of a large number of special studies published under the auspices of the Carnegie Endowment for International Peace. Some idea of their scope may be had by consulting *Economic and Social History of the World War: Outline of Plan, European Series* (Carnegie Endowment for International Peace, 1924). Another useful collection of special studies has been published by the Hoover Institute of War, Revolution, and Peace at Stanford University.

The Peace

H. R. Rudin, *Armistice, 1918* (Yale Univ. Press, 1944). The standard monograph.

H. W. V. Temperley, *A History of the Peace Conference of Paris,* 6 vols. (Frowde, Hodder and Stoughton, 1920–1924). The standard detailed account; by a British scholar.

H. G. Nicolson, *Peacemaking, 1919* (Constable, 1933). A good shorter account; by a British expert on diplomacy.

P. Birdsall, *Versailles Twenty Years After* (Reynal & Hitchcock, 1941). Balanced reappraisal by an American scholar.

T. A. Bailey, *Wilson and the Peacemakers* (Macmillan, 1947). Sound study of America's role.

J. M. Keynes, *The Economic Consequences of the Peace* (Harcourt, Brace, 1920), and E. Mantoux, *The Carthaginian Peace; or, the Economic Consequences of Mr. Keynes* (Scribner's, 1952). Respectively, the most famous attack on the Versailles settlement and a thoughtful study of the results of that attack.

Historical Fiction

E. Childers, *The Riddle of the Sands* (Nelson, 1913), and H. H. Munro ("Saki"), *When William Came* (Lane, 1914). Two unusual novels, written before the outbreak of the war and predicting what it might be like. Childers' is a story of intrigue and adventure, and "Saki's" is a forecast of the German occupation of Britain.

J. Romains, *Verdun* (Knopf, 1939). Excellent and balanced novel about French troops on the western front, 1914–1916.

H. Barbusse, *Under Fire* (Dutton, 1917), and E. M. Remarque, *All Quiet on the Western Front* (Lion Books). Two famous novels, by a Frenchman and a German, respectively, reflect the horror aroused in intellectuals by trench warfare.

J. Dos Passos, *Three Soldiers* (Modern Library, 1941), and E. Hemingway, *A Farewell to Arms* (many editions). Two American novels about the war, indicative of the post-war disillusionment of the "lost generation."

E. E. Cummings, *The Enormous Room* (Modern Library, 1941), and A. Zweig, *The Case of Sergeant Grischa* (Viking, 1928). Novels about prisoners of war and the eastern front, respectively.

C. S. Forester, *The General* (Little, Brown, 1947). Astringent novel about the "brass" in World War I.

J. Buchan, *Greenmantle* (Nelson, many eds.). A novel of espionage indicating that the war contained its ingredient of high adventure in addition to blood and guts.

What Price Glory? in M. Anderson and L. Stallings, *Three American Plays* (Harcourt, Brace, 1926). A famous play showing that the war had its rowdy side.

18

Communist Russia, 1917–1941

I Introduction

On June 22, 1941, Adolf Hitler's German armies poured over the frontier of his Russian ally and began a rapid advance toward Moscow, toward the major Russian industrial centers, and toward the most productive Russian agricultural centers. The Russia Hitler invaded was no longer the Russia into which Napoleon had sent the *grande armée* a hundred and twenty-nine years before, or the Russia whose millions of embattled soldiers had perished in the First World War against the Germany of William II and his Habsburg allies. It was no longer the Russia of the tsars. Since 1917 it had been the Russia of the Bolsheviks. Yet it was still Russia.

Along with the tsars, the nobility and the bourgeoisie had gone down to ruin after the communist revolution of 1917, and the clergy as a class had suffered almost as much. A small, tightly knit, conspiratorial group of fanatical Marxist revolutionaries had seized power and for the next twenty-four years had striven to make Russia over. Drawn mostly from the peculiarly Russian class of the intelligentsia, and declaring themselves to be the representatives of the industrial proletariat, the Bolsheviks had worked gigantic changes, especially in the years after 1928. Industry, proceeding under forced draft, had expanded enormously, and the proportion of the population employed in industry had risen to almost 50 per cent; the proportion engaged in agriculture had fallen correspondingly.

The peasant had been a victim of serfdom until 1861, had been subject to the initiative-destroying domination of the commune until 1906, and had then been encouraged by Stolypin to make himself a free farmer (see Chapter 14). Now, under the Bolsheviks, he found himself subjected to new and grievous pressure. Agriculture had been collectivized, and the age-old longing of the peasant for private property in land had been ruthlessly suppressed.

These staggering social and economic changes had not been accomplished without internal friction. Inside the government, personal rivalries, plots, counter-plots, fake plots, and charges of plots had produced repeated purges extending down through the ranks of the population. The choking conspiratorial atmosphere which the Bolshevik rulers had breathed during their long years of underground preparation for a seizure of power now enveloped the citadels of power. Personal rivalries for domination of the machinery of the state were cloaked beneath the Byzantine theological language of doctrinal controversy over fine points in the sacred writings of Marx and Lenin. Yet the controversies had immediate significance in the formulation and choice of government policies. The Communist party, the secret police, and the army had become the interlocking agencies which ran the state at the bidding of the dictator. The dictator himself, Stalin, had made his own career possible chiefly through the ruthless use of his position as Secretary of the Communist party.

The foreign policy of the communist state had passed through a brief period in which ideological considerations had seemed occasionally to outweigh national interest in the old sense. It had then returned to the pursuit of traditional Russian ends, coupled with the objective of promoting eventual world-revolution. But in furthering Russian aims abroad, the Bolshevik leaders were now in possession of an instrument more flexible than any the tsars had ever commanded. This was the Communist International, or Comintern, a federation of the Communist parties in the individual countries of the world. These parties could often be used as promoters of purely Russian ends rather than strictly communist ends. With the shifting stresses and strains of international politics during the late 1920's and 1930's, the "line" of the Comintern shifted often and bewilderingly, but always in accordance with the aims of the Soviet foreign office. Usually the majority of communists elsewhere in the world fell meekly into position and loudly proclaimed when necessary the opposite of what they had proclaimed the day before.

Yet the changes during the first twenty-four years of the Soviet period, vast though they were, could not conceal the continuities between the new Russian system and the old. The dictator of 1941, the revered leader of his people, for whom his followers made increasingly grandiose claims, was not unlike the tsar of 1917 in his assumption of autocratic power. The individual Russian of 1941, despite his sufferings under the new system, had remained deeply patriotic, ready to sacrifice himself for his country, even under a government he hated. The peasant of 1941 still yearned hopelessly for his land; the worker struggled for economic advancement and social security. Bureaucrats, managers, intellectuals, and artists, all in the service of the state, formed in 1941 a new élite which replaced but did not differ greatly from the old privileged class. A police force superior in efficiency to those of Ivan the Terrible, Peter the

Great, and Nicholas I, but not different in kind, in 1941 exercised thought control over all citizens and terrorized even prominent members of the system itself.

More and more, Stalinist communism had taken on the trappings of a religion, with its sacred books, its heresies, its places of pilgrimage, its doctrinal quarrels. Thus the old Russian orthodoxy had by 1941 not been replaced but rather modified. Russian nationalism, too, asserted itself ever more insistently and crudely, until finally, in the war that Hitler began, the government encouraged the cult of traditional heroes of earlier times, and even glorified Ivan the Terrible himself, a symbol no longer of "feudal" domination but of the Russian national spirit. The early revolutionary departures from accepted standards in Russian marriage, family life, and education, had by 1941 all been abandoned in favor of a return to conventional bourgeois behavior. This chapter will trace in some detail the series of vast changes here summarized and will attempt to demonstrate the continued survival of the old Russia beneath the veneer of the new.

II   The Russian Revolution of 1917

The Immediate Background

Ridden by domestic crisis though Russia was in 1914 (see Chapter 14), the country greeted the outbreak of World War I with demonstrations of national patriotism. The Duma supported the war and did yeoman service in organizing Red Cross activities. The left-wing parties—the radical agrarian SR's (Social Revolutionaries) and the Marxist SD's (Social Democrats)—abstained from voting war credits, but offered to assist the national defense. By 1917, more than 15,000,000 Russians had been drafted into the armies. Losses in battle were staggering from the first; the Russians suffered more than 3,800,000 casualties during the first year of war. On the home front, criticism was aroused by the inadequate handling of the supply of munitions, and by mid-1915 the Center and Left groups in the Duma were urging moderate reforms, such as the end of discrimination against minority nationalities and an increase in the powers of the zemstvos, the local assemblies. The Empress Alexandra took the lead in opposing all such measures, and kept urging her weak husband, Tsar Nicholas II, to act more autocratically. When Nicholas took personal command of the armies in the field and prorogued the Duma (autumn, 1915), she became virtually supreme at home. The supremacy of the Empress meant also the supremacy of her favorite, the unscrupulous adventurer Rasputin.

With the Empress and Rasputin in control, a gang of shady adventurers, blackmailers, and profiteers bought and sold offices, speculated in military supplies, put in their own puppets as ministers, and created a series of shocking scandals. Confusion, strikes, and defeatism mounted at home during 1916, while the armies slowly bled to death at the front. Even the conservatives began to denounce Rasputin publicly, and in December, 1916, he was poisoned, shot several times, and ultimately drowned, all in one nightmare evening, by a group of conspirators closely related to the imperial family. Despite repeated warnings from moderates in the Duma that the government itself was preparing a revolution by its failure to create a responsible ministry and to clean up the mess, the Tsar remained apathetic. Relatives of the imperial family and members of the Duma began independently to plot for his abdication. In the early months of 1917, all conditions favored a revolution, but the revolutionaries were not prepared.

The March Revolution

On March 8, strikes and bread-riots broke out in the capital, and four days later Romanov rule, which had governed Russia since 1613, was doomed. Yet this revolution of March, 1917, has been well called leaderless, spontaneous, and anonymous. SR's and both Bolshevik and Menshevik factions of SD's (Chapter 14) were genuinely surprised at what happened. Indeed, the Bolshevik leaders were either abroad in exile, or under arrest in Siberia. The determining factor in the overthrow of the Tsar was the disloyalty of the garrison of Petrograd (the new Russian name given to St. Petersburg during the war). Inefficiency had led to a food shortage in the capital, though actual starvation had not set in. When the Tsar ordered troops to fire on striking workers, only a few obeyed, and on March 12, in revulsion against the order, the troops joined the strikers, broke into the arsenals,

Rasputin (1871?–1916).

and began to hunt the police, who quickly disappeared from the scene. The Duma lagged behind the revolting troops and workers in estimating the situation, and the Tsar lagged behind the Duma. By March 14, when the Tsar had finally decided to appoint a responsible ministry, it was too late; the cabinet had vanished. Troops ordered to put down the revolt simply melted away and joined the rebels.

Leftists, released from prison by the mobs, formed a Soviet of workers and soldiers, modeled on the 1905 Soviet of workers (Chapter 14), but now including soldiers as well. The Soviet proceeded to organize a workers' militia, to create a food-supply commission, and to issue newspapers. Its fifteen-man executive committee became the policy-makers of the revolution. The Soviet located its headquarters across the hall from the Duma, which did not obey the Tsar's order to dissolve, but remained in session.

The Marxists among the Soviet leaders still believed in the necessity of a preliminary bourgeois revolution, and did not yet regard the Soviet itself as an organ of power. They favored the creation of a provisional government, in which they would not participate, but to which they would offer limited support. They put themselves at the disposition of the Duma, and asked that it temporarily run the country. Thus the Duma, a limited assembly elected by a restricted franchise, was literally forced by the Soviet into the position of leading the revolution.

Negotiations between the Soviet and a Duma committee brought a provisional government into existence. Despite the widely differing social and economic aims of Soviet and Duma, both agreed to grant political liberties immediately, and to summon a constituent assembly, which was to establish the future form of government by giving Russia a constitution. The provisional government was composed mainly of Kadets (Constitutional Democrats) and other moderates, and was headed by the liberal Prince Lvov, chairman of the union of *zemstvos* and of the Red Cross. It included also one radical member of the Soviet, Alexander Kerensky, Minister of Jus-

Soldier delegates to the Petrograd Soviet meeting in the Duma building.

tice, a clever labor lawyer and member of the Duma also, who accepted office despite the understanding that members of the Soviet would not do so.

After some abortive efforts to save the dynasty in the person of the Tsar's brother, Nicholas finally abdicated, and his brother refused the throne because of the popular hatred of the family. Under pressure from the Soviet, the provisional government arrested Nicholas II and the Empress on March 20. The Duma had thus accepted the mandate given it by the revolutionaries. Had it accepted instead its dismissal at the hands of the Tsar and gone home, it seems probable that the monarchy would have been preserved at the cost of some liberal concessions. But moderate reformers were now in power, and Russia embarked on the troubled months between March and October, 1917.

The Provisional Government

The provisional government is usually regarded as having been a total failure. Measured by the final results, such a view is perhaps justified. But the judgment of history must take into consideration the dreadful difficulties that faced the provisional government. These were not only immediate and specific, but general and underlying. Russian moderates had had no experience of authority. They were separated by a great cultural gulf from the lower classes. Their opportunity to rule now came to them in the midst of a fearful war, which they felt they had to pursue while reconstructing and democratizing the enormous and unwieldy Russian Empire.

Moreover, the Soviet possessed many of the instruments of power, yet refused to accept any responsibility. Workers and soldiers in the capital supported the Soviet, while in the provinces the new governors appointed by the provisional government had no weapon except persuasion to employ against the local peasant-elected soviets, which multiplied rapidly. Present-day critics of the provisional government often denounce its failure to suppress its revolutionary opponents, but they overlook the fact that the provisional government did not possess the tools of suppression. The Petrograd garrison, for instance, by agreement with the Soviet, could not be removed or disarmed. The support given by the Soviet to the provisional government has been compared to the kind of support that is given by a hangman's noose.

The two great specific issues facing the provisional government were agrarian discontent and the continuation of the war. The peasants wanted land, and they wanted it immediately. The provisional government, however, made up as it was of responsible liberals, believed in acting with deliberation and according to law. It refused to sanction peasant seizure of land, despite increasing disorder in the countryside. Instead, it appointed a commission to collect material on which future agrarian legislation was to be based—an act totally inadequate to the emergency.

As to the war, the members of the government felt in honor bound to their allies not to make a separate peace. Moreover, most of them still unrealistically hoped that Russia might win, and gain the territories which the Allies had promised. But the Soviet subverted discipline in the armies at the front by issuing a "declaration of the rights of soldiers," which virtually put an end to the authority of officers over enlisted men. Although the Soviet made it as hard as possible for the government to pursue the war, it did not sponsor a separate peace. Even the Bolshevik members of the Soviet, who now began to return from exile, demanded only that Russia participate in general peace negotiations, which, they urged, should begin at once.

Lenin and Bolshevism

The most important of the returning Bolshevik exiles was Lenin. His real name was Valdimir Ilyich Ulianov, but in his writings he used the pen-name Lenin, to which he sometimes prefixed the initial N., a Russian abbreviation for "nobody," in order to tell his readers that he was using a pseudonym. This "N." has given rise to the mistaken but still widely held idea that Lenin's first name was Nikolai (Nicholas). Son of a provincial official and intellectual, Lenin became a revolutionary in the late 1880's and, as we have seen (Chapter 14), took a chief role in the early years of the SD's as the leader of the party's Bolshevik

wing. He had returned to Russia from abroad for the Revolution of 1905, but he left Russia once more in 1908, and stayed abroad until 1917.

When the news of the March Revolution reached Lenin in Switzerland, he made desperate efforts to get back home. Finally, through the Swiss Social Democrats, he made contact with the German general staff, which felt that it would be a good investment to see that Lenin reached Russia, where he might disrupt the Russian war effort against Germany. Thus it was that the German military transported Lenin across Germany from Switzerland to the Baltic in the famous sealed railroad car. He arrived at the Finland Station in Petrograd on April 16, 1917, a little more than a month after the March Revolution.

Most Russian Social Democrats had long regarded a bourgeois parliamentary republic as a necessary preliminary to an eventual socialist revolution and socialist society. For this reason, they were prepared to help in transforming Russia into a capitalist society, though not without grave doubts that the bourgeois capitalists might be as bad as the tsar and the landlords, or that the masses might be "deluded" into accepting the new system. They favored the creation of a democratic republic, at the same time believing that complete political freedom was absolutely essential for their own future rise to power. Despite the Marxist emphasis upon the industrial laboring class as the only proper vehicle for revolution, Lenin early realized that in Russia, where the "proletariat" embraced only about 1 per cent of the population, the SD's must seek other allies. At the time of the Revolution of 1905, he began to preach the need for limited alliances for tactical purposes between the Bolsheviks and the SR's, who commanded the support of the peasantry. When the alliance had served its purpose, the SD's were to turn on their allies and destroy them. Then would come the socialist triumph.

Instead of a preliminary bourgeois democratic republic, Lenin called in 1905 and later for an immediate "revolutionary-democratic dictatorship of the proletariat and the peasantry," a concept that seems to us self-contradictory and is surely vague. Lenin's view, however, was not adopted by most Bolsheviks. Together with the Mensheviks, they continued to believe and urge that a bourgeois revolution and a parliamentary democracy were necessary first steps.

Because Lenin did not trust the masses to make a revolution (by themselves, he felt, they were capable only of "trade-union consciousness"), he favored a dictatorship of the Bolshevik party over the working class. Because he did not trust the rank and file of Bolshevik party workers, he favored a dictatorship of a small élite over the Bolshevik party. And in the end, because he really trusted nobody's views but his own, he favored, though never explicitly, his own dictatorship over this élite. Another future Russian leader, the brilliant intellectual Leon Trotsky, early warned that in Lenin's views one-man dictatorship was implicit.

Trotsky, for his part, voiced an opinion of his own, held by neither Mensheviks nor Bolsheviks. The bourgeoisie in Russia, he argued, was so weak that the working class could telescope the bourgeois and socialist revolutions into one continuous movement. After the proletariat had helped the bourgeoisie achieve its revolution, he felt that the workers could move immediately to power. They could nationalize industry and collectivize agriculture, and, although foreign intervention and civil war were doubtless to be expected, the Russian proletariat would soon be joined by the proletariats of other countries, which would make their own revolutions. Except for this last point, Trotsky's analysis accurately forecast the course of events. Between 1905 and 1917, Lenin himself accepted Trotsky's view from time to time, but warned that it endangered political democracy.

Lenin had been deeply depressed by the failure of 1905, and by the threat posed by Stolypin's agrarian reforms. He almost despaired when the socialist parties of Europe went along with their governments in 1914 and supported the war. To him this meant the end of the second socialist International, for the Social Democrats had failed to recognize the war as the "bourgeois-imperialist" venture that it appeared to Lenin to be. He preached defeatism as the only possible view for a Russian SD to follow.

Lenin's greatest talent was not as an original thinker but as a skillful tactician. He often seemed able to judge with accuracy just what was politically possible in a given situation, and he was not afraid to gamble. Thus, even before he returned to Russia in April, 1917, he had assessed some of the difficulties facing the provisional government and decided that the masses could take over at once. Immediately upon his arrival, he hailed the worldwide revolution, proclaiming that the end of imperialism, "the last stage of capitalism," was at hand. Ignoring the positions previously taken by Bolsheviks and Mensheviks alike, he demanded now that all power immediately be given to the soviets. His speeches sounded to the SD's themselves like the ravings of a madman.

Almost nobody but Lenin felt that the losely organized soviets could govern the country, or that the war would bring down the capitalist world in chaos. In April 1917, Lenin called not only for the abandonment of the provisional government and the establishment of a republic of soviets but for the confiscation of estates, the nationalization of land, and the abolition of the army, of government officials, and of the police. He was offering land at once to the impatient peasants, peace at once to the war-weary populace. This program fitted the mood of the people far better than the cautious and well-meant efforts of the provisional government to bring about reform by legal means. Dogmatic, furiously impatient of compromise, entirely convinced that he alone had the truth, Lenin galvanized the Bolsheviks into a truly revolutionary group waiting only the moment to seize power.

The Coming
of the November Revolution

The months from March to November, 1917, before the Bolsheviks came to power, can be divided into a period between March and July, during which revolution deepened, a feeble reaction from July to September, and a new quickening of the revolutionary current from September to the final uprising in November. In the first period, the government faced a crisis, because the Kadet ministers wished to maintain the Russian war aim of annexing the Straits, while the Soviet wanted a peace "without annexations or indemnities." Out of the crisis Kerensky, now war minister, emerged as the dominant leader. He failed to realize that it was no longer possible to restore the morale of the armies, which were dissolving under the impact of Bolshevik propaganda. A new offensive ordered on July 1 collapsed, as soldiers refused to obey orders, deserted their units, and rushed home to their native villages, eager to seize the land. Ukrainian separatism also plagued the officials of the government. The soviets became gradually more and more Bolshevik, as Lenin and Trotsky worked tirelessly at recruitment and organization. Although the June congress of soviets in Petrograd was less than 10 per cent Bolshevik in make-up, the Bolshevik slogans of peace, bread, and freedom won overwhelming support.

Yet an armed outbreak by troops who had accepted the Bolshevik slogans found the Petrograd Soviet unwilling and unable to assume power. While the mob roared outside, the Soviet voted to discuss the matter two weeks later, and meanwhile to keep the provisional government in power. A regiment loyal to the Soviet protected it against the working class! The government declared that Lenin was a German agent, and, as his supporters wavered, raided the newspaper offices of *Pravda* ("Truth," the Bolshevik paper); Lenin had to go into hiding to avoid arrest. This episode of mid-July is what is known among Bolsheviks as "playing at insurrection." Though shots had been exchanged and overt action had been embarked upon, there had been no revolutionary follow-through. Power had not been seized, probably because Lenin felt that the Bolsheviks did not have enough support in the provinces.

Now Kerensky became premier. The government hardened its attitude toward the Ukrainians, but could not come to a popular decision on either land or peace. General Kornilov, chosen by Kerensky as the new commander-in-chief of the armies, quickly became the white hope of all conservative groups, and in August plotted a *coup*, intended to disperse the Soviet. His attitude toward the provisional government was uncertain, but, had he succeeded, he would probably have demanded a purge of its more radical elements. The plot, however, was a failure, because railroad and telegraph workers sabotaged Kornilov's movements, and because his troops simply would not obey him. The Bolsheviks, adopting the slogan "We will fight against Kornilov, but will not support Kerensky," threw themselves into preparations for the defense of Petrograd, which proved to be unnecessary. By September 14, Kornilov had been arrested, and the affair ended without bloodshed. The threat from the Right helped the Bolsheviks greatly, and sentiment in the Petrograd and Moscow soviets now for the first time became predominantly Bolshevik.

The Kornilov affair turned the army mutiny into a widespread revolt. Instances of violence multiplied. No longer satisfied with merely disobeying their officers, more and more soldiers murdered them instead. No longer satisfied with merely refusing to pay their rent or pasturing their animals on their landlords' land, more and more peasants burned the manor house and killed the owner. It was true that the nobility owned only a quarter as much land as the peasants, but the peasants no longer listened to statistics or to arguments that rash action retarded progress. As disorder mounted in the countryside, the Bolsheviks tightened their hold over the soviets in the cities.

Lenin returned to Petrograd on October 20. Soon thereafter the Bolsheviks got control over a Military Revolutionary Committee, originally chosen to help defend Petrograd against the advancing Germans, and now transformed, under the guidance of Trotsky, into a general staff for the revolution. Beginning on November 4, huge demonstrations and mass meetings were addressed by Trotsky, and on November 7 the insurrection broke out.

In Petrograd, the revolution had been well prepared, and proceeded with little bloodshed. Kerensky escaped in a car belonging to the American Embassy. The Military Revolutionary Committee, as an organ of the Petrograd Soviet, simply took over. The Bolsheviks called a second congress of soviets, and when the Mensheviks and right-wing SR's walked out, Trotsky called them the refuse that would be swept into the garbage-can of history. Co-operating with the left-wing SR's, and adopting their land program, Lenin abolished all property rights of landlords, and transferred the land thus affected to local land committees and soviets of peasant deputies. Though Lenin did not in the least approve of the system of individual small-holdings which this decree put into effect, he recognized the psychological advantage which the adoption of the SR program would gain him. He also urged an immediate peace without annexations or indemnities, and appealed to the workers of Germany, France, and England to support him in this demand. Finally, a new cabinet, called a

"Under the snug wing of Kerensky," a cartoon attacking Kerensky's alleged affection for the generals.

Council of People's Commissars, was chosen, with Lenin as President, and Trotsky as Foreign Commissar.

As Commissar of Nationalities the Bolsheviks installed a younger man, a Georgian, named Joseph Djugashvili, who had been a successful organizer of bank robberies in the days when the party treasury was filled in this way, but whose role had otherwise been relatively obscure. He had taken the name Stalin, which suggests a steel-like hardness. Under

Moscow at the time of the November revolution, 1917.

Lenin's coaching, Stalin had also become the party authority on questions of minority nationalities, and had published a pamphlet on the subject in 1913.

Outside Petrograd, the revolution moved more slowly. In Moscow there was a week of street-fighting between Bolshevik Reds and Whites, as anti-Bolshevik forces were already known. Elsewhere in factory towns, the Bolsheviks usually won speedily; in non-industrial centers it took them longer. Most of Siberia and of Central Asia came over, but Tiflis, the capital of Georgia, went Menshevik, and passed resolutions calling for a constituent assembly and the continuation of the war. The reason for the rapid and smooth success of the Bolsheviks was that the provincial garrisons opposed the war, and willingly allied themselves with the workers. Local Military Revolutionary Committees were created in most places, and held elections for new local soviets. Naturally there was much confusion at first, but surprisingly little resistance to the consolidation of the authority of the new regime. Gradually the town of Rostov-on-Don, near the Sea of Azov, became the main center of resistance, as Kornilov and other generals, together with a number of the leading politicians of the Duma, made their way there.

This initial triumph of the revolution did not mean that the population of Russia had been converted to Bolshevism. By cleverly sensing the mood of the people, Lenin had opportunistically given the Bolsheviks a set of slogans around which the people could rally, although some of the slogans did not at all correspond with the true Bolshevik views. As we shall shortly see, the Russian people were in fact strongly anti-Bolshevik. But the Bolsheviks had triumphed, and the democratic hopes for freedom of the press and other freedoms were now doomed to disappointment.

Deprived of competent civil servants, the new regime worried along through an atmosphere of continued crisis. Late in November, 1917, an agreement was reached with the Left-Wing SR's, three of whom entered the government, and peace negotiations were begun with the Germans. The revolution proper was over. Lenin was in power.

The Constituent Assembly

It is of great interest to record that the Bolsheviks now permitted elections for a constituent assembly. Lenin had no use for this sort of democratically chosen parliament, which he considered "inferior" to the soviet. Yet, probably because he had so long taunted the provisional government with delaying the elections, he seems to have felt compelled to hold them. The Russian people for the first and last time in their history had a completely free election, under universal suffrage. Lenin himself accepted as accurate figures showing that the Bolsheviks polled about one-quarter of the vote. The other socialist parties, chiefly the SR's, polled 62 per cent. As was to be expected, the Bolshevik vote was heaviest in the cities, especially Moscow and Petrograd, while the SR vote was largely rural.

Disregarding the majority cast for his opponents, Lenin maintained that "the most advanced" elements had voted for him. It was of course only his opinion that made those who had voted Bolshevik more "advanced" than those who had voted SR or Kadet. The constituent assembly met only once, on January 18, 1918. Lenin dissolved it the next day by decree, and sent guards with rifles to prevent its ever meeting again. The anti-Bolshevik majority was naturally deeply indignant at this pure act of force against the popular will, but there was no public outburst, and the delegates disbanded. In part, this was because the Bolsheviks had already taken action on the things that interested the people most — peace and land — and in part because of the lack of a democratic parliamentary tradition among the masses of the Russian people.

In spite of the many years of agitation by intellectuals and liberals for just such a popular assembly, Russia did not have the large middle class, the widespread literacy, the tradition of debate, and the respect for the rights of the individual which seem to be an essential part of constitutionalism. Yet it is surely extreme to decide that there was no chance for constitutional government in Russia in 1917–1918. Was the constituent assembly "an attempt to transplant an alien concept of government to a soil where it could never flourish"? Or was it "a noble experiment incorporating a sound principle but doomed by the crisis into which it was born"? The fact that Lenin had the rifles to prevent the constituent assembly from fulfilling the function which the popular will had assigned to it does not answer the question either way.

III War Communism and NEP, 1917–1928

War Communism

The first period of Soviet history, which runs from the end of 1917 to the end of 1920, is usually called the period of "war communism," or "military communism." The term itself of course implies that the main features of the period were determined by military events. Civil war raged, and foreign powers intervened on Russian soil. But the term is also somewhat misleading. This was a period of militant as well as military communism, symbolized early in 1918 by the change of the party's name from Bolshevik to Communist. At the same time, the capital was shifted from Petrograd, with its exposed location on the western fringe of Russia, to the greater security of Moscow, in the heart of the country.

Flushed with victory in Russia, the Bolsheviks firmly believed that world revolution was about to begin, probably first in Germany, but surely spreading to Britain and even to the United States. This view led the Bolsheviks to hasten the construction of a socialist state in Russia and to take a casual attitude toward their international affairs, since they expected that relations with capitalist states would be very temporary. Although the actions of the Russian government during this period were later described almost apologetically as emergency measures, this is only partly true. Many of the decisions that were taken in part under the spur of military pressure were also regarded as leading to a new society.

A supreme economic council directed the gradual nationalization of industry. Sugar and petroleum came first, and then in June, 1918, a large group including mines, metallurgy, and textiles. By 1920, the state had taken over all enterprises employing more than ten workers (more than five, if motor power was used). The state organized a system of barter, which replaced the free market. Internal trade was illegal; only the government food commissary could buy and sell; money disappeared, as the state took over distribution as well as production. It expropriated the banks, repudiated the tsarist foreign debt, and in effect wiped out savings. Church and State were separated by decree, and judges were removed from office and replaced by appointees of the local soviets.

The government subjected the peasantry to ever more arbitrary and severe requisitioning. It mobilized the poorer peasants against those who were better off, called *kulaks* (from the word meaning "fist" and used to apply to usurers, as if to say "hardfisted"). By calling for a union of the hungry against the well-fed, the regime deliberately, and not for the last time, sowed class hatred in the villages, and stimulated civil war in the countryside. It should be remembered that by western European standards even a Russian *kulak* was often wretchedly poor. The decree forming the first secret police, the "Cheka" (from the initials of the words meaning "extraordinary commission"), was issued in December, 1917, only a few weeks after the revolution and long before any intervention from abroad. Terror became a weapon in the civil war.

Before the communist government could function at all, peace was necessary, as the army had virtually ceased to exist. Negotiations between the Russians and the Germans and Austro-Hungarians at Brest-Litovsk dragged on into 1918, the Russians hoping that revolution would break out in Germany, and the Germans demanding enormous territorial cessions, which they increased as the Russians delayed. Finally, on March 3, 1918, the Russians signed the Peace of Brest-Litovsk, which deprived them of the entire Ukraine, the Baltic provinces, Finland, and some Caucasian lands. It cost Russia one-third of its population, 80 per cent of its iron, and 90 per cent of its coal. Many communists resigned rather than accept the peace, and the Left SR's quit the government. The Germans overran the Ukraine and the Crimea and installed a highly authoritarian regime, against which the communists continued to agitate. The Whites, with German help, put down the Reds in Finland.

Civil War

During the months following Brest-Litovsk, disorder in the countryside as a result of requisitioning and class warfare was swelled by the outbreak of open civil strife. During the war, a brigade had been formed inside Russia of Czechs resident in the country and of deserters from the Habsburg armies. When Russia withdrew from the war, it was decided to send the Czech brigade east across Siberia by rail, and then by ship across the Pacific, through the Panama Canal, and finally west across the Atlantic to France, to fight the Germans there. On the rail trip across Siberia, the Czechs got into a brawl with a trainload of Hungarian prisoners, and one of the Hungarians was killed. This obscure quarrel on a Siberian railway siding between members of the unfriendly races of the Habsburg Empire touched off civil war in Russia. When the Soviet government tried to take reprisals against the Czechs, who numbered fewer than 35,000 men, the Czechs seized a number of towns in western Siberia. The local Soviets were un-

prepared, and the SR's were sympathetic to the Czechs. Local anti-Bolshevik armies came into being. It was under threat from one of them in July, 1918, that a local soviet decided to execute the Tsar and his entire family rather than lose possession of them. All were murdered.

By late June, 1918, the Allies had decided to intervene in Russia on behalf of the opponents of Bolshevism. The withdrawal of Russia from the war had been a heavy blow to them, and they now hoped to re-create a second front against the Germans in the east. The idea of a capitalist "crusade" against Bolshevism, later popularized by Soviet and pro-Soviet historians as the sole motive for the intervention, was in fact much less significant. Yet the Allies had been at war a long time, and their populations were war-weary. So they naturally were apprehensive at the communist efforts to stimulate revolution in all the capitalist nations of the world.

Out at the eastern end of the Trans-Siberian Railroad in Vladivostok, the Czechs overthrew the local soviet in June, 1918, and by early August British, French, Japanese, and American forces had landed. The assignment of the Americans was to occupy Vladivostok and to safeguard railroad communications in the rear of the Czechs. Of the Allies, only the Japanese had long-range territorial ambitions in the area. In effect, the Bolshevik regime had now been displaced in Siberia; the SR's disbanded the soviets and re-established the *zemstvos*, calling for "all power to the constituent assembly." There were three anti-Red governments of varying complexions in three different Siberian centers. Elsewhere, in August, 1918, a small British and American force landed at the White Sea port of Archangel. An SR assassin killed the chief of the Petrograd Cheka, and Lenin himself was wounded.

The regime now sped its military preparations. As Minister of War, Trotsky imposed conscription, and, by a mixture of cajolery and threats of reprisals against their families, secured the services of about 50,000 tsarist officers. The Red Army, which was Trotsky's creation, grew to over 3,000,000 strong by 1920. Its recapture of Kazan and Samara on the Volga in the autumn of 1918 temporarily

Russia in Revolution, 1917-1921

Russian territorial losses, Brest-Litovsk, 1918
Boundaries as of 1914
Curzon Line
Boundary between Poland and the U.S.S.R., 1920-1939

turned the tide in the crisis that seemed about to engulf the Soviet state.

The German collapse on the Western Front permitted the Bolsheviks to repudiate the Treaty of Brest-Litovsk, and to move back into parts of the Ukraine, where they faced the opposition of a variety of local forces. Elsewhere, the opposition consisted of three main armies. General Denikin led an army of Whites, which moved from Rostov-on-Don south across the Caucasus, and received French and British aid. Admiral Kolchak's forces in

679

Trotsky and his staff in Red Square, Moscow.

western Siberia overthrew the SR regime in Omsk, and Kolchak became a virtual dictator. General Yudenich's army, including many former members of the German forces, operated in the Baltic region and threatened Petrograd from the west. Allied unwillingness to negotiate with the Bolsheviks was heightened by the successful Red *coup* of Bela Kun in Hungary (see Chapter 19), which seemed to foreshadow the further spread of revolution.

In the spring of 1919, the Reds defeated Kolchak, and by winter took Omsk. In 1920, the Admiral was arrested and executed. Though the Reds also reconquered the Ukraine, mutinies in their own forces prevented them from consolidating their victories and from moving, as they had hoped to do, across the Russian frontiers and linking up with Bela

Lenin addressing a throng in Moscow's Red Square, 1919.

Kun in Hungary. In the summer of 1919, Denikin took Kiev and struck north, advancing to within two hundred and fifty miles of Moscow itself. But his position was weakened by the repressive character of the regime he brought with him and by his recognition of Kolchak as his superior officer, together with the poor discipline of his troops and his own rivalry with one of his generals, Baron Wrangel. Yudenich advanced to the suburbs of Petrograd, but the Reds by the end of 1919 were able to defeat the White threat everywhere, though Wrangel retained an army in the Crimea. Trotsky now called for the militarization of labor to reconstruct the ravaged country; labor battalions were formed, but recovery was long delayed.

Even after the defeat of the Whites, the Reds in 1920 had to face a new war with the Poles, who hoped to keep Russia weak, and to create an independent Ukraine. After an initial retreat, the Red armies nearly took Warsaw, failing only because the French chief of staff, General Weygand, assisted the Poles. The Reds, eager to finish off the Whites, and persuaded that there was after all no hope for the establishment of a communist regime in Poland, concluded peace in October, 1920. The Poles obtained a large area of territory in White Russia and the western Ukraine. This area was not inhabited by Poles, but had been controlled by Poland down to the eighteenth-century partitions. It lay far to the east of the "Curzon line," the ethnic frontier earlier proposed by the British foreign minister, Lord Curzon. The Reds then turned on Wrangel, who had marched northward from the Crimea and had established a moderate regime in the territory he occupied. He was forced to evacuate, assisted by a French fleet, in November, 1920. The White movement had virtually come to an end.

Why the Counter-Revolution Failed

Many factors accounted for the Whites' failure and the Reds' victory. The Whites could not get together on any political program beyond the mere overthrow of the Reds. They adopted a policy of "non-anticipation," which meant that some future constituent assembly would settle the governmental structure of Russia. Their numbers included everybody from tsarists to SR's, and they disagreed so violently on the proper course for Russia to follow that they could agree only to postpone discussion of these critical problems.

Moreover, their movement was located on the geographical periphery of Russia—in Siberia, in the Crimea, in the Ukraine, in the Caucasus, and in the Baltic. But the Whites never reached an understanding with the non-Russian minorities who lived in these regions. Thus they ignored the highly developed separatist sentiments of the Ukrainians and others, to which the Bolsheviks were temporarily willing to cater.

Furthermore, the Whites could not command the support of the peasantry. Instead of guaranteeing the results of the land division already carried out with Bolshevik sanction, the Whites often restored the landlords and undid the land division. During the civil war, the peasantry on the whole grew sick of both sides. This attitude explains the appearance of anarchist bands, especially in the south. Then too, the Whites simply did not command as much military strength as the Reds, who outnumbered them in manpower, and who had inherited much of the equipment manufactured for the tsarist armies. Holding the central position, the Reds had a unified and skillful command, which could use the railroad network to shift troops rapidly. The Whites, moving in from the periphery, were divided into at least four main groups, and were denied effective use of the railroads.

Finally, the intervention of the Allies on the side of the Whites was ineffectual and amateurish. It may even have harmed the White cause, since the Reds could pose as the national defenders of the country, and could portray the Whites as the hirelings of foreigners. In the light of hindsight, it seems safe to say that either the Allies should have mounted a full-fledged military operation against the Reds, or, if this was impossible (as it probably was, in view of the condition of their own armies after the end of the First World War), they should have stayed out of Russia and allowed the civil war to burn itself out. It is still sometimes argued, however, that, although the Reds won the civil war, the Allied intervention helped keep them so heavily engaged inside Russia that they could not sponsor successful revolutions in other countries. This point of view may well have some justification.

NEP ("The New Economic Policy")

Since 1914, Russia had been deeply involved in fighting and turmoil. By early 1921, with the end of the civil war, famine was raging and sanitation had broken down. Family ties were disrupted, human beings brutalized, and class hatreds released on an unparalleled scale. Industry was producing at a level of about one-eighth of its pre-war output, and agricultural output had decreased by at least 30 per cent. Distribution approached a breakdown. The communist regime appeared to be facing its most serious trial of all: the loss of support in Russia.

A large-scale anarchist peasant revolt broke out in early 1921 and lasted until mid-1922. Lenin remarked that this revolt frightened him more than all the Whites' resistance. But the decisive factor in bringing about a change in policy was the mutiny at the Kronstadt naval base near Petrograd in March, 1921. Formerly a stronghold of Bolshevism, Kronstadt now produced a movement of rebellious anarchists who called for "soviets without communists" to be chosen by universal suffrage and secret ballot, for free speech and free assembly, for the liberation of political prisoners, and for the abolition of requisitioning. Except for the last item and for the phraseology of the first, the program was ironically similar to that of all liberals and socialists in tsarist Russia. The Kronstadt movement seems to have expressed the sentiments of most Russian workers and peasants. Had the government been conciliatory, there might have been no bloodshed; but Trotsky went to war against the rebels, and defeated them after a bloody fight.

This episode led directly to the adoption of the "New Economic Policy," always referred to by its initials as NEP. But the underlying reason for the shift was the need for reconstruction, which seemed attainable only if militant communism were at least temporarily abandoned. Lenin himself referred to "premature" attempts at socialization. It was also necessary to appease the peasants and to ward off any further major uprisings. Finally, the expected world revolution had not come off, and the resources of capitalist states were badly needed to assist Russian reconstruction. The adoption of NEP coincided with the conclusion of an Anglo-Russian trade treaty. Abroad, NEP was hailed as the beginning of a Russian "Thermidor," a return to normality like that following the end of the Terror in the French Revolution (see Chapter 10).

Under NEP the government stopped requisitioning the whole of the peasant's crop above a minimum necessary for subsistence. The peasant had still to pay a very heavy tax in kind, but he was allowed to sell the remainder of his crop and keep the money. The peasant could sell his surplus to the state if he wished, but he could also choose to sell it to a private purchaser. Peasant agriculture became in essence capitalist once more, and the profit motive had reappeared. Lenin imitated Stolypin by guaranteeing the peasant permanency of tenure. The whole system tended to help the *kulak* grow richer and to transform the poor peasant into a hired, landless laborer.

Elsewhere in the economy, under NEP the state retained what Lenin called "the commanding heights"—heavy industry, banking, transportation, and foreign trade. In domestic trade and in light industry, however, private enterprise was once more permitted. This was the so-called "private capital sector" of the economy, in which workers could be paid according to their output, and factory managers could swap some of their products in return for raw materials.

Lenin himself described NEP as a partial return to capitalism, and urged the communists to become good businessmen. Yet NEP was never intended as more than a temporary expedient. Lenin believed that it would take a couple of decades before the Russian peasant could be convinced that co-operative agriculture would be the most efficient. He also argued that a temporary relaxation of government intervention would increase industrial production and give the Russians a useful lesson in entrepreneurship.

Economic recovery was indeed obtained. By 1926–1927, industrial production was back at pre-war levels, although agriculture had not kept pace. But NEP was bitterly disliked by leading communists, who were shocked at the reversal of all the doctrines they believed in. By 1924, private business accounted for 40 per cent of Russian domestic trade, but thereafter the figure fell off. Those who took advantage of the opportunities presented by the NEP were known as NEPmen. They were often persecuted in a petty way by hostile officials, who tried to limit their profits, tax them heavily, and drag them into court on charges of speculation. The *kulak* had essentially the same experience. Thus the government often seemed to be encouraging private enterprise for economic reasons and simultaneously to be discouraging it for political reasons.

Within the Communist party, one group favored the increase of the private sector and the extension of NEP, as a new road toward the socialist goal. These were the so-called "Right deviationists." Their opponents favored the ending of concessions, the liquidation of NEPmen and *kulaks*, and a return to Marxist principles at home and the fostering of world revolution abroad—in short, the pressing of the "socialist offensive." These were the "Left deviationists," who included Trotsky. In the Center stood men who attacked both deviations, the Right as an abandonment of communism, the Left as likely to lead to a disruption of the worker-peasant alliance.

The Struggle for Power: Stalin versus Trotsky

But the NEP question was not the only one to agitate the communist leaders in the early twenties. Lenin suffered two strokes in 1922,

and another in 1923, and finally died in January, 1924. During the last two years of his life, he played an ever-lessening role. Involved in the controversy over NEP and the other controversies was the question of the successor to Lenin. Thus an individual communist's answer to the question of how to organize industry, what role to give organized labor, and what relations to maintain with the capitalist world depended not only upon his estimate of the actual situation but also upon his guess as to what answer was likely to be politically advantageous. From this maneuvering the Secretary of the Communist party, Joseph Stalin, was to emerge victorious by 1928.

The years between 1922 and 1928, especially after Lenin's death, were years of a desperate struggle for power between Stalin and Trotsky. Lenin foresaw this struggle with great anxiety. He felt that Trotsky was abler, but feared that he was overconfident, and inclined to make decisions on his own. He felt that Stalin had concentrated enormous power in his hands, in his role as party secretary, and feared that he did not know how to use it. When he learned that Stalin had gone counter to his orders in smashing the Menshevik Republic of Georgia instead of reaching an accommodation with its leaders, he wrote angrily in his testament that Stalin was too rude, and that his fellows should remove him from his post as general secretary. At the moment of his death, Lenin had published a scathing attack on Stalin, had broken off relations with him, and was about to try to relegate him to the scrapheap. Trotsky's suggestion that Stalin poisoned Lenin is not based on any evidence, but it is clear that Lenin's death rescued Stalin's career, and that, far from being the chosen heir, as he later claimed, he did not enjoy Lenin's confidence at the end.

During these years, Trotsky argued for a more highly trained managerial force in industry, and for economic planning as an instrument that the state could use to control and direct social change. He favored the mechanization of agriculture and the weakening of peasant individualism by encouraging rural co-operatives, with even a hint of the collective farms where groups of peasants, in theory, would own everything collectively, rather than individually. As Trotsky progressively lost power, he championed the right of individual communists to criticize the regime. He referred to the policies of Stalin and his other increasingly powerful enemies as "bureaucratic degeneration," and came to the conclusion that only through the outbreak of revolutions in other countries could the Russian socialist revolution be carried to its proper conclusion. Only if the industrial output and technical skills of the advanced western countries could be put at the disposal of communism could Russia hope to achieve its own socialist revolution. This is the famous theory that socialism cannot succeed within the boundaries of one country. Either world revolution must break out, or Russian socialism is doomed to inevitable failure.

The opponents of Trotsky's "left deviation" found their chief spokesman in Nikolai Bukharin. A man who never held such responsible administrative posts as Lenin or Trotsky or Stalin, and who had often shifted his position on major questions, Bukharin none the less took a consistent line during these years; as editor of *Pravda*, he was extremely influential. A strong defender of NEP, Bukharin softened the rigorous Marxist doctrine of the class struggle by arguing that, since the proletarian state controlled the commanding heights of big capital, socialism was sure of success. This view is not unlike the "gradualist" position taken by western European Social Democrats. Bukharin did not believe in an ambitious program of rapid industrialization; he favored co-operatives, but opposed collectives. In foreign affairs he was eager to co-operate abroad with non-communist groups who might be useful to Russia. Thus he sponsored Soviet collaboration with Chiang Kai-shek in China and with the German Social Democrats.

In his rise to power, Stalin used Bukharin's arguments to discredit Trotsky and to eliminate him. Then, partly because Bukharin's policies were failing, Stalin adopted many of Trotsky's policies, and eliminated Bukharin. Original Stalinist ideas, however, developed during this process. Stalin was not basically an intellectual or a theoretician; he

was a party organization stalwart. He adopted theoretical positions partly because they seemed to him the ones most likely to work, and partly because he was charting his own course to supreme power. He came to favor rapid industrialization, and to understand that this meant an unprecedentedly heavy capital investment. At the end of 1927, he suddenly shifted from his previous position on the peasantry, and openly sponsored collectivization. This shift arose because of his concern that agricultural production was not keeping pace with industry. He declared that the balance could be redressed only if agriculture, like industry, was transformed into a series of large-scale unified enterprises.

In answer to Trotsky's argument that socialism in one country was impossible, Stalin maintained that an independent socialist state could exist. This view did not at all imply the abandonment of the goal of world revolution, as has often been thought. Stalin always maintained that the socialist state (Russia) should be the center of inspiration and assistance to

Lenin and Stalin in 1923.

communist movements everywhere; Russia would help them and they would help Russia. But, in his view, during the interim period before the communists had won elsewhere, it was perfectly possible for Russia to exist as the only socialist state, and indeed to grow more socialist all the time. In international relations, this doctrine of Stalin made it possible for the Soviet Union to pursue either a policy of "peaceful coexistence" with capitalist states, when that seemed most profitable, or a policy of militant support of communist revolution everywhere, when that seemed most profitable. Stalin's "socialism in one country" also struck a responsive chord in the rank and file of Russian communists, who were disappointed in the failure of revolutions elsewhere. It also meant that Russia, not the West, was to be the center of the new society. Stalin's doctrine reflected his own Russian nationalism rather than the more cosmopolitan and more western views of Trotsky.

The Struggle for Power: Stalin's Victory

Analysis of the rival theories competing for acceptance in Russia in the twenties helps explain the alternatives before the communist leadership. It does not explain how Stalin won. To understand this, we must move from the realm of theory and political platforms to the realm of practice and political power. At the end of the civil war, Stalin was Commissar of Nationalities. In this post, he dealt with the affairs of 65,000,000 of the 140,000,000 inhabitants of the new Russian Soviet Republic. He managed the destiny of the Asians, whom he, as one of them, understood. Their local Bolshevik leaders became his men; where they did not, as in his native Georgia, he ruthlessly crushed them. Though a Georgian, he identified himself with Russian nationalism in the interests of a centralized Bolshevik state.

It was Stalin who took charge of creating the new Asian "republics," which enjoyed the appearance of local self-government, programs of economic and educational improvement,

and a chance to use their local languages and develop their own cultures. It was he who in 1922 proposed and guided the adoption of a new Union of Socialist Soviet Republics as a substitute for the existing federation of republics. In the U.S.S.R., Moscow would control war, foreign policy, trade, and transport, and would co-ordinate finance, economy, food, and labor. And on paper it would leave to the republics home affairs, justice, education, and agriculture. A Council of Nationalities, with an equal number of delegates from each ethnic group, would join the Supreme Soviet as a second chamber, thus forming the Central Executive Committee, which would appoint the Council of People's Commissars — the Government. Stalin regarded this reform as an achievement equal to Trotsky's military organizational work during the civil war.

Stalin was also Commissar of the Workers' and Peasants' Inspectorate. Here his duties were to eliminate inefficiency and corruption from every branch of the civil service, and to train a new corps of civil servants. His teams moved freely through all the offices of the government, observing and recommending changes, inspecting and criticizing. In creating this post, Lenin had hoped to clean house, but the ignorance and the lack of tradition that rendered the tsarist and Bolshevik civil service incompetent and corrupt operated in Stalin's Inspectorate as well. Although the Inspectorate could not do what it was established to do, it did perform another role. It gave Stalin control over the machinery of government. Lenin attacked Stalin's work in the Inspectorate just before he died, but by then it was too late.

Stalin was also a member of the Politbureau, the tight little group of party bosses elected by the Central Committee, which included only five men throughout the civil war. Here his job was day-to-day management of the party. He was the only permanent liaison officer between the Politbureau and the Orgbureau, which allocated party personnel to their various duties, in factory, office, or army unit. In addition to these posts, Stalin became general secretary of the party's Central Committee in 1922. Here he prepared the agenda

The exiled Trotsky and his wife arriving in Mexico, 1937.

for Politbureau meetings, supplied the documentation for points under debate, and passed the decisions down to the lower levels. He controlled party patronage—that is to say, all party appointments, promotions, and demotions. He saw to it that local trade unions, co-operatives, and army units were put under communist bosses responsible to him. He had files on the loyalty and achievement of all managers of industry and other party members. In 1921, a Central Control Commission, which could expel party members for unsatisfactory conduct, was created; Stalin, as liaison between this commission and the Central Committee, now virtually controlled the purges, which were designed to keep the party pure.

In a centralized one-party state, a man of Stalin's ambitions who held so many key positions had an enormous advantage in the struggle for power. Yet the state was so new, the positions were so much less conspicuous and so much more humdrum than the Ministry of War, for instance, held by Trotsky, and Stalin's manner was so generally conciliatory, that the likelihood of Stalin's success did not become evident until it was too late to stop him. Inside the Politbureau he formed a

three-man team with two other prominent Bolshevik leaders, the demagogue, Zinoviev, and the expert on doctrine, Kamenev. Zinoviev was chairman of the Petrograd Soviet and boss of the Communist International; Kamenev was Lenin's deputy and president of the Moscow Soviet. All three were old Bolsheviks, in contrast to Trotsky, who had been a Menshevik and an independent member of the intelligentsia.

The combination of Stalin, Zinoviev, and Kamenev proved unbeatable. The three put down all real and imagined plots against them by the use of the secret police. They resisted Trotsky's demands for "reform," which would have democratized the party to some degree, and would have strengthened his position while weakening Stalin's. They initiated the cult of Lenin immediately before his death, and kept it burning fiercely thereafter, so that any suggestion for change coming from Trotsky seemed almost an act of impiety. They dispersed Trotsky's followers by sending them to posts abroad. They prevented the publication of Lenin's "testament," so that the rank and file of the party would not know about Lenin's doubts concerning Stalin. They publicized all Trotsky's earlier statements in opposition to Lenin, and did not hesitate to "revise" history in order to belittle Trotsky. They were confident, and rightly so, that Trotsky was too good a communist to rally around him such anti-Bolshevik groups as old Mensheviks, SR's, and NEPmen.

Early in 1925, Stalin and his allies were able to force the resignation of Trotsky as Minister of War. Soon thereafter the three-man team dissolved; Stalin moved into alliance with Bukharin and other right-wing members of the Politbureau, to which he began to appoint some of his own followers. Using all his accumulated power, he beat his former allies on all questions of policy, and in 1926 they moved into a new but powerless alliance with Trotsky. Stalin now (1926) deposed Zinoviev from the Politbureau, charging him with intriguing in the army. Trotsky was the next one to be expelled from the Politbureau, and Zinoviev was ousted as president of the Comintern.

In 1927, differences of opinion over Stalin's foreign policy in England and in China (see p. 699) led to public protests by the opposition. And these in turn led to the expulsion of the opposition from the party itself. Refusing to renounce his views, Trotsky was deported to Siberia, the first stage in a long exile that took him to Turkey, Norway, and Mexico, where he died in 1940 at the hands of an assassin armed with an ice-axe. The others recanted and obtained a new lease on life. Stalin's victory was virtually complete.

IV Stalin's Supremacy: Russian Internal Affairs, 1928–1941

The Communist party congress that expelled Trotsky in December, 1927, also brought NEP to an end, and proclaimed that the new "socialist offensive" would begin in 1928. The thirteen years between 1928 and 1941 were to see almost incredible changes in the domestic life of Russia—collectivized agriculture, speedy industrialization, forced labor, the great purges and the extermination of all political opposition, the building of an authoritarian state apparatus, and a "retreat" to bourgeois standards in almost every department of social and intellectual life.

Collectivized Agriculture

In 1928, the failure of the peasants to deliver to the cities as much grain as had been required seemed to underline the dangers inherent in the land divisions of 1917 and in the concessions of NEP. Farm productivity on the small individual holdings was not high enough to feed the city population. Food prices for the workers were high, yet the kulaks wanted further concessions. Grain was hoarded. Stalin had often inveighed against "fanning the class struggle in the countryside," and had denied the intention of collectivizing agriculture rapidly or on a mass scale. The government economic plan issued during 1928 set a figure of 20 per cent of Russian farms as the *maximum* to be collectivized by 1933. Yet during 1929, Stalin embarked on immediate full-scale collectivization, declared war on the *kulaks*, and virtually put an end to individual farming in Russia.

The government did not have the money or the credit to import food. Furthermore, no governmental machinery is adequate to force peasants to disgorge crops that they are hiding. Therefore, the government enlisted on its side the small peasants; in exchange for their assistance in locating and turning over the *kulaks'* crops, they promised them a place on a collective farm, to be made up of the *kulaks'* land and equipped with the *kulaks'* implements. Probably a good many of the subsistence farmers (about 20 per cent of the number of private farms, possibly 5,000,000 households) more or less welcomed this opportunity. Initial encouraging reports led Stalin to go full speed ahead. The *kulaks,* he declared in late 1929, were to be liquidated as a class. There were about 2,000,000 households of them, perhaps as many as 10,000,000 people in all. They were now to be totally expropriated, and at the same time barred from the new collectives. Since no provision was made for them, this move turned collectivization into a nightmare.

Peasants now were machine-gunned into submission; *kulaks* were deported to forced labor camps or to desolate regions in Siberia. In desperate revolt against the command to join collectives, the peasants burned crops, broke plows, and killed their cattle rather than turn them over to the state. More than half the horses in all Russia, 45 per cent of the cattle, and two-thirds of the sheep and goats were slaughtered. Russian livestock has never since caught up with the losses it suffered because of the excesses of collectivization. Land lay uncultivated, and over the next few years famine took a toll of millions of lives. As early as March, 1930, Stalin showed that he was aware of the ghastly mistakes he had made. In a famous statement on "dizziness with success," he put the blame on local officials who had been too eager to rush through the program. By contradicting his own orders of a few months before, he managed to escape some of the hatred that would otherwise have been directed at him. As usual, many Russian peasants disliked the man they could see, the local official, and were willing to exculpate the "little father" in the capital.

Fifty per cent of Russian farms had been hastily thrown together into collectives during this frightful year. Only an additional 10 per cent were added during the next three years, so that by 1933 60 per cent in all had been collectivized. The number rose again later in the 1930's, until by 1939 more than 96 per cent of Russian farms were collectivized. In 1941, there were 250,000 collectives, 900,000,000 acres in extent, supporting 19,000,000 families. Yet the excesses of the early "dizziness with success" were never repeated.

The 1930's also brought a modification of the original rules governing collectives. Originally, collectives had been of two main types: the *sovkhoz*, or soviet farm, not strictly a collective at all but a state-owned enterprise, operated by the government and worked by hired laborers who were government employees; and the *kolkhoz*, or collective farm proper. The *sovkhozes* were designed as centers of government research and development in agriculture, and were often very large in size. But they were mostly brought to an end by Stalin in the 1930's, when he ordered some forty million acres originally allotted to them to be distributed among the *kolkhozes*. As of 1941, the *sovkhozes* occupied no significant area of land.

The *kolkhoz* itself was also originally of two types: the commune, in which all the resources of the members without exception were owned together, and the *artel*, or co-operative, in which a certain amount of private property was permitted to the members. After Stalin's modifications of the system in the thirties, the *artel* became the overwhelmingly predominant

form of collective farm. In an *artel*, each family owned its homestead, some livestock, and minor implements; these could be left by will to the owner's descendants. But most of the work was done on the collectively operated land. Each collective had its own managing board, responsible to the government, which supervised the work of the peasants, who were organized in brigades, each under a brigadier. Like factory laborers paid on a "piece-work" basis, peasants were remunerated according to their output, which was measured by the artificial unit of the "labor day." One day's work in managing a farm might be, for example, assessed at three labor days, while one day's work weeding a vegetable patch might be assessed at only half a labor day.

Each *kolkhoz* turned over to the government a fixed amount of produce at fixed rates, and the total of all these amounts was designed to guarantee the feeding of the urban population, especially workers in heavy industry and members of the Red Army. In addition, the *kolkhoz* paid further taxes to cover government expenses for local construction and education. Any surplus might be sold by the peasant directly to the consumer, without the participation of any middleman. Private resale was regarded as speculation, and was subject to punishment. After 1934, the government obtained at least two-thirds of its revenue by the resale on the markets at a large profit of farm produce bought at low fixed prices from the *kolkhoz*. This government profit was known as the "turnover tax."

The government assisted and controlled the *kolkhoz* through the supply of mechanical equipment furnished by the Machine Tractor Stations. The collectives could not own their own tractors, but rented them from the stations, paying in exchange a fee ranging up to perhaps 20 per cent of the crop. The stations became important centers for political surveillance. By the decision when and to whom to allot tractors, and how many tractors to allot, administrators of the Machine Tractor Stations could directly affect the success of a collective; their good will was therefore of the utmost importance to the management.

In general, the aim of collectivization was to reorganize farming so as to ensure food for the industrial labor force, which was being increased by recruitment from the farms themselves. Collectivization certainly increased the total food supplies at the disposal of the government, and released farmers for work in industry. But it seems certain that the over-all rise in agricultural production was small, and that in many cases the yield per unit decreased.

Industrialization

Intimately related to the drive in agriculture was the drive in industry. Here, too, Stalin originally had viewed with scorn the grandiose plans of the "superindustrializers," and as late as 1927 had proposed an annual increase rate in industrial production of only 15 per cent. But just as he shifted to the frantic pace of col-

lectivizing agriculture, so he first gradually, then suddenly, shifted to forced draft in industry also.

In 1928 began the era of the Five-Year Plans, each setting ambitious goals for production over the next five years. In 1929 and 1930, Stalin appropriated ever higher sums for capital investment, and in June, 1930, he declared that industrial production must rise by 50 per cent in the current year, a fantastic and impossible figure. Under the First Five-Year Plan, adopted in 1928, annual pig-iron production was scheduled to rise from 3,500,000 tons to 10,000,000 tons by 1932, but in that year Stalin demanded 17,000,000 tons instead. It was not forthcoming, of course, but Stalin's demand for it was symptomatic of the pace at which he was striving to transform Russia from an agricultural to an industrial country.

Part of the reason for this rapid pace lay precisely in the collectivization drive itself.

Charcoal-burning or wood-burning tractors at a Machine Tractor Station, 1939.

Large-scale farming, to which Stalin was committing Russia, must be mechanized farming. Yet there were only 7,000 tractors in all Russia at the end of 1928. Stalin secured 30,000 more during 1929, but this was nowhere near a beginning. Industry had to produce millions of machines, and the gasoline to run them. Since the countryside had to be electrified, power stations were needed by the thousands. And literally millions and millions of peasants had to be taught how to handle machinery. But there was nobody to teach them, and no factories to produce the machinery. The output of raw materials was inadequate, and the plants to process them were not there.

Another part of the reason for the drive to industrialize lay in the tenets of Marxism itself. Russia had defied all Marx's predictions by staging a proletarian revolution in a country almost without a proletariat. Yet despite the communists' initial political successes, Stalin felt that "capitalism had a firmer basis than communism in Russia, so long as it remained a country of small peasants." The communists felt that the world proletariat expected them to industrialize Russia, but even more they were determined to create as a support for themselves the massive Russian proletariat which as yet did not exist. Furthermore, Stalin was determined to make Russia as nearly self-sufficient as possible, in line with his theory of socialism in one country. Underlying this was a motive at least as intense as any dictated by Marxist doctrine—Russian nationalism.

The strength of this motive is revealed in a speech that Stalin made in 1931:

To slacken the pace means to lag behind, and those who lag behind are beaten. We do not want to be beaten. No, we don't want to. . . . Old Russia . . . was ceaselessly beaten for her backwardness. She was beaten by the Mongol Khans, she was beaten by Turkish Beys, she was beaten by Swedish feudal lords, she was beaten by Polish-Lithuanian gentry, she was beaten by Anglo-French capitalists, she was beaten by Japanese barons; she was beaten by all—for her backwardness. For military backwardness, for cultural backwardness, for political backwardness, for industrial backwardness, for agricultural backwardness. She was beaten because to

beat her was profitable and went unpunished. . . . We are fifty or a hundred years behind the advanced countries. We must make good this lag in ten years. Either we do it or they crush us.[*]

Whatever one may think of this quotation as history (and it omits all Russia's *victorious* wars), it reveals that Russian national self-interest as interpreted by Stalin required the most rapid possible industrialization. And it is of interest that ten years afterward the Germans did attack, something Stalin could of course not have predicted so accurately, but something that he seems to have sensed.

Stalin seems also to have felt that he had only to keep a fierce pressure on the management of industry, and the desired commodities and finished goods would be forthcoming in the desired quantities. The goals of the First Five-Year Plan were not attained, although fulfillment was announced in 1932. Immediately, the second plan, prepared by the state planning commission, went into effect, and ran until 1937; the third was interrupted only by Hitler's invasion. Each time the emphasis was on the elements of heavy industry—steel, electric power, cement, coal, oil. Between 1928 and 1940, steel production was multiplied by four and one-half, electric power by eight, cement by more than two, coal by four, and oil by almost three. Similar developments took place in chemicals and in machine production. Railroad construction was greatly increased, and the volume of freight carried quadrupled with the production of new rolling stock.

By 1940, Russian output was approaching that of Germany, although Russian efficiency and the Russian standard of living were far lower. What the rest of Europe had done in about seventy-five years Russia had done in about twelve. Enthusiasm was artificially whipped up by wide publicizing of the high output of individual workers called "Stakhanovites," after a coal miner who had set production records. "Stakhanovites" and "heroes of labor" were richly rewarded, and

[*]Quoted in Isaac Deutscher, *Stalin* (New York, 1950), 328.

the others were urged to imitate them in "socialist competition."

All this was achieved at the expense of dreadful hardships, yet eyewitnesses report that many of the workers were as enthusiastic as if they had been soldiers in battle, as indeed in a sense they were. Valuable machinery was often damaged or destroyed by inexperienced workers right off the farm. The problems of repair, of replacement, of achieving balance between the output and consumption of raw materials, of housing workers in the new centers, of moving entire industries thousands of miles into the Ural region and Siberia, were unending and cost untold numbers of lives. An American eyewitness estimates that Russia's "battle of ferrous metallurgy alone involved more casualties than the battle of the Marne."

Administratively, the Russian economy was directly run by the state. The Gosplan, or state planning commission, drew up the Five-Year Plans and supervised their fulfillment at the management level. The Gosbank, or state bank, regulated the investment of capital. An economic council administered the work of various agencies. Its major divisions were metallurgy and chemistry (iron and steel, nonferrous metals, chemicals, rubber, alcohol); defense (aviation, armaments, munitions, tanks, ships); machinery (heavy machines, medium machines, machine tools, electrical industry); fuel and power (coal, oil, electric power); agriculture and procurement; and consumer's goods (grain, meat and dairy products, fisheries, textiles, light industry). Under iron and steel, for example, there functioned the production trusts controlling their own mines as well as blast furnaces and rolling mills. These were the so-called "combinats," or great production complexes like that at Magnitogorsk in the Urals. In each plant, as in each collective, the manager was responsible for producing the quota set for him within the maximum cost allowed him. He was consulted on production targets, and had considerable leeway in selecting his staff and allocating labor and raw materials. He was bound to render a rigid accounting to the government, which of course fixed the price he must pay for his raw materials.

The Social Impact

The social effects of the economic program were dramatic. Urban population rose from about 18 per cent in 1926 to about 33 per cent in 1940. The number of cities with a population between 50,000 and 100,000 doubled, and the number of cities with a population exceeding 100,000 more than quadrupled. The largest cities, Moscow and Leningrad (the new name for Petersburg-Petrograd after the death of Lenin), almost doubled in size, and among smaller cities, to take just one example, Alma Ata in Siberia grew from 45,000 to 230,000 between 1928 and 1939. The entire social picture was radically altered.

The relative freedom to choose one's job which had characterized the NEP period disappeared. Individual industrial enterprises signed labor contracts with the *kolkhozes* by which the *kolkhoz* was obliged to send a given number of farm workers to the factories, often against their will. Peasants who had resisted collectivization were drafted into labor camps. In the factories, the trade unions became simply another organ of the state. The chief role of the unions was to achieve maximum production and efficiency, to discourage absenteeism and poor work. Trade unions might not strike, or engage in conflict with management. All they could do was administer the social insurance laws and seek improvements in workers' living conditions by negotiation.

Thus in the U.S.S.R. the old privileged classes of noble landlords, already weak at the time of the revolution, ceased to exist. The industrial, commercial, and financial bourgeoisie, which was just coming into its own at the time of the revolution, was destroyed after 1928, despite the temporary reprieve it had experienced under NEP. Most of the old intelligentsia, who had favored a revolution, could not in the end stomach Stalin's dictatorship, and many of them emigrated. Of the million and a half émigrés from Russia after the revolution, only a very small number (contrary to the general view in the West) were cousins of the Tsar. Those of the old intelligentsia who remained were forced into line with the new Soviet intelligentsia, which Stalin felt to be a very important class. All were compelled to accept the new Stalinist dogma and to drop their interest in the outside world. The new intelligentsia was expected to concentrate on technical advance, and on new administrative devices for speeding up the transformation of the country.

Although the effect of these social changes would presumably have been to level all ranks, Stalin set himself against the old Bolshevik principles of equality. The Marxist slogan, "From each according to his capacity, to each according to his needs," was shelved in favor of a new one, "From each according to his capacity, to each according to his work." Where Lenin had allowed none of the members of the government to earn more than a skilled laborer, Stalin set up a new system of incentives. A small minority of bureaucrats and skilled laborers, factory managers, and successful *kolkhoz* bosses earned vastly more than the great majority of unskilled laborers and peasants. Together with the writers, artists, musicians, and entertainers who were willing to lend their talents to the services of the régime, these men became a new élite, separated by a wide economic and social gulf from the toiling masses. They had a vested interest in furthering a regime to which they owed everything, and without which they would be nothing.

Soviet propagandists declared that this was a temporary situation. They described the present society in the Soviet Union as "socialist," while regarding "communism," not yet achieved, as the goal toward which the U.S.S.R. was still moving. Yet, just as the "withering away" of the state, which the Marxists predicted, was instead replaced under Stalin by the enormous swelling of state power and state machinery, so the equality predicted by the Marxists was replaced by a new caste system. The means of production were publicly owned in the Soviet Union, as the Marxists had urged. But the power of the state, the birth of a new élite, the brutalization of millions of human beings, and the ruthless use of force after the revolution had been achieved were all the contributions of Stalin.

The Purge Trials

Stalin's program was not achieved without opposition. The crisis of 1931 and 1932, when industrial goals were not being met, and starvation swept the countryside, created discontent inside the regime as well as outside. A small number of officials circulated memoranda advocating Stalin's deposition as General Secretary, an act which the party had every right to perform. Stalin jailed them for conspiracy, and one leading Bolshevik committed suicide. It is widely believed that Stalin's own wife reproached him at this time with the ravages that the terror was working, and that she too committed suicide. At one moment, but only at one, we are told, Stalin's self-confidence wavered and he offered to resign, but nobody in the Politbureau dared accept the offer, and the moment quickly passed. His attack against those he believed to be his enemies took the form of the famous purges, which began in 1934 and continued at intervals until 1938.

These purges remain the most mysterious episode in Soviet history. They are often compared with the Jacobin Terror of the French Revolution, when the revolution "devoured its children." But, in contrast to the rapid appearance of the Terror in France, the purges did not begin for seventeen years after the Russian Revolution. Members of the opposition had been demoted, expelled from the party, and even exiled, as in the case of Trotsky, but nobody had been executed. There is an entirely credible story that the Bolshevik leaders had agreed among themselves early in their career never to start guillotining each other. Yet, when the terror began in Russia, it was even more drastic than it had been in France. Moreover, unlike Robespierre, Stalin managed to survive.

From exile, Trotsky continued to attack Stalin in a journal called *The Bulletin of the Opposition*. Clever as always, he scored telling points against Stalin, and his words were carefully read by Soviet officials. Yet the older generation of communists, though they may have hated Stalin, made no move against him. A younger group, however, seemingly more restless and convinced that Stalin had abandoned Lenin's program, found the model for conspiracy in the heroes of the terrorist movement who had assassinated Alexander II (see Chapter 14). They were apparently prepared to use terrorism against Stalin and his henchmen. Even within the Politbureau men loyal to Stalin grew restless at his ruthlessness, and urged him to relax the pressure; Sergei Kirov, boss of Leningrad, took the lead.

Stalin at times seemed to yield to this urging, as when he ordered more gentle treatment for rebellious *kulaks* in June, 1932, and limited the powers of the political police. But at other times he seemed to be taking the opposite course, as when he issued a decree making an entire family responsible for the treason of any of its members. On the whole, however, tension relaxed during 1932–1934. Kirov proclaimed a new era of lenience at a party conference, and former leaders of the opposition, including Bukharin, were appointed to help draft a new and liberal constitution.

Then on December 1, 1934, Kirov was assassinated by a young terrorist communist in Leningrad. Although the story that Stalin himself had plotted the assassination cannot be confirmed, it is clear that Stalin now determined to strike at the opposition. The assassin was executed. Accused of complicity, Zinoviev and Kamenev were jailed, and forced to admit that they had plotted to restore capitalism. Yet the drafting of the new "democratic" constitution went on. Stalin became ever more withdrawn, ever more autocratic, ever more resolved to destroy the old Bolsheviks, as Ivan the Terrible had destroyed the old nobility. After an interlude during 1935 and early 1936, during which Stalin said that "life had become more joyous," the purges proper began.

The official story was that Trotskyite agitation abroad was linked with the murder of Kirov, and with the alleged plans for the murder of Stalin. A series of public political trials took place. In the first (1936), Zinoviev, Kamenev, and fourteen others admitted these charges and were executed. In the second (1937), seventeen other leading Bolsheviks declared that they had knowledge of a conspiracy between Trotsky and the German and Japanese intelligence service, by which Russian territory was to be transferred to Germany and Japan. All were executed. Then (June 1937) came the secret liquidation of the top commanders in the Red Army, who were ac-

Factory workers listening to an engineer read the charge made by Vishinsky against the "Anti-Soviet right-Trotskyist bloc" during the purge trials of 1937.

cused of conspiring with "an unfriendly foreign power" (Germany) with a view to sabotage. All were executed after an announcement that they had confessed. The last of the public trials took place in March, 1938, as twenty-one leading Bolsheviks, including Bukharin, confessed to similar charges and were executed.

But these public trials and the secret trial of the generals give only a faint idea of the extent of the purge. Every member of Lenin's Politbureau except Stalin and Trotsky was either killed or committed suicide to avoid execution. Two vice-commissars of foreign affairs and most of the ambassadors of the diplomatic corps, fifty of the seventy-one members of the Central Committee of the Communist party, almost all the military judges who had sat in judgment and had condemned the generals, two successive heads of the secret police, themselves the leaders in the previous purges, the prime ministers and chief officials of all the non-Russian Soviet Republics—all were killed or vanished. A list of those who disappeared reads like a "who's who" of high officialdom in state and party throughout the twenties and thirties. Literally thousands were executed or disappeared without a trace. The public trials probably included only those who were willing to confess, whether guilty or not. The rest were condemned privately and quite without due process of law.

Although it is clear that many of those who were executed opposed Stalin, the charges against them were certainly not true. Had they been true, the great conspiracy involving almost everybody but Stalin himself would surely have accomplished more than the assassination of Kirov. It is altogether unlikely that any of the top communists conspired with Hitler, little though they loved Stalin. Some who confessed may have felt so great a loyalty to the cause of communism, however perverted, that they sacrificed themselves for Stalin's soviet state. Some doubtless hoped to save their families, or even themselves, and a few leaders were spared the death penalty to encourage confessions from the others. Many may have hoped that the confessions were so ridiculous that nobody could believe them.

What Stalin apparently wanted was to destroy utterly all possibility of future conspiracies. So he trumped up charges against anybody who conceivably could become a member of a regime that might replace his own. Despite the enormous upheaval of the purges, no breakdown took place in the state. New bureaucrats were found to take the places of the old. The new Stalin-trained officials, uncultivated but competent, now manned all top-level positions.

The Authoritarian State

In the midst of the purges, in 1936, Stalin proclaimed the new constitution, the "most democratic in the world." By its provisions nobody was disfranchised, as priests and members of the former nobility and bourgeoisie had previously been. Civil liberties were extended, but even on paper these were never more than a sham, since the constitution provided that they could be modified in the "interest of the toilers." The fact that the U.S.S.R. was a one-party state prevented elections from being anything but an expression of unanimity. The right to nominate candidates for the Supreme Soviet belonged to Communist party organizations, trade unions, co-operatives, youth groups, and cultural societies; but all were completely dominated by the party. The party picked the candidates, and no more than one for each post was ever presented to the voters. The party controlled the soviets, and the party hierarchy and government hierarchy overlapped and interlocked.

Every citizen was eligible for membership in the party on application to a local branch, which voted on his application after a year of trial. Communist children's organizations fed the youth groups, which in turn fed the party. The party was organized both territorially and functionally in pyramidal form, with organizations at the bottom level in factory, farm, and government office. These were grouped together by rural or urban local units, and these in turn by regional and territorial conferences and congresses. The party organizations elected the All-Union party congress, which selected the Central Committee of the party, and which was in theory the highest policy-making organ, though actually no party congress was held between 1939 and 1954. The Central Committee selected the Politbureau. At each level of the party pyramid there were organizations for agitation and propaganda, for organization and instruction, for military and political training. The party exercised full control over the government, which simply enacted formally what the party had decided upon. The Five-Year Plans, for example, were party programs that went into effect even before they were formally adopted by the government.

The highest organ of the government was the Supreme Soviet, made up of two houses — a Soviet of the Union, based on population, and a Soviet of Nationalities, elected according to national administrative divisions. In theory, the Supreme Soviet was elected for a term of four years. The Supreme Soviet itself did little; it appointed a presidium which issued the decrees and carried on the work of the Supreme Soviet between sessions. It also appointed the Council of Ministers (long called the Council of People's Commissars). This cabinet, rather than the Supreme Soviet or its presidium, enacted most of the legislation, and was thus the legislative as well as the executive organ of the Russian state. The chairmanship of the Council of People's Commissars, the chairmanship of the Politbureau, and the General Secretariat of the Communist party were all posts held by Stalin, who in addition served as Commissar of Defense, chief of the State Defense Council, which ran the country during wartime, and Generalissimo. Similar overlapping of party and government posts was the regular practice.

In 1924, Stalin's constitutional reform had created the new Union of Soviet Socialist Republics, including the enormously large Russian Federative Republic, the Ukraine, White Russia, Georgia, Armenia, and Azerbaidjan, and three central Asian Soviet Socialist republics: Uzbekistan, Turkmenistan, and Tadjikistan. In 1936, Kazakh and Kirghiz republics were added, making a total of eleven. As a result of the annexations of the Baltic states and

of Finnish and Rumanian territory in 1940, five more republics were created: Lithuania, Latvia, Estonia, Karelia, and Moldavia. These sixteen "Union" republics differed widely in population. Within the huge Russian republic were sixteen "autonomous" republics, and numerous other subdivisions, all called "autonomous." The larger SSR's had similar subdivisions.

Each of the Union republics and autonomous republics had a government patterned exactly on that of the Soviet Union, except that the supreme soviet of each republic was unicameral and not bicameral, since it lacked a chamber of nationalities. Many complaints have been heard in recent years about the way in which "Great-Russian chauvinism" has permeated official policy toward the individual minority republics. Although this soviet descendant of tsarist Russification policy has always been a menace, it is widely believed that in the years before World War II, the chief objective was not to try to Russify the nationalities but to communize them. With this end in view, the party permitted and encouraged local nationalities to revive their culture, study their past traditions, and use their own language. Like every other cultural manifestation permitted in the U.S.S.R., these national cultural achievements were "managed." Not only was it impossible for anti-Soviet or anticommunist material to appear in print or in any of the plastic arts, but, as everywhere, all artistic effort was closely supervised and had to serve the regime positively. The value of "cultural autonomy" under these circumstances is of course highly debatable.

Although the Stalin constitution specifically gave each republic the right to secede, this provision was pure window-dressing. The central government was overpoweringly stronger than the government of any one republic, which in any case was often not even made up of natives. Although each of the sixteen republics was in 1944 given its own foreign office by an amendment to the constitution, this amendment was never intended to give them autonomy in this critically important field. Actually, it seems simply to have been a device for securing representation of the Ukraine and White Russia in the United Nations. The representatives of these two republics to the United Nations have never been anything but extra Soviet delegates; the first Ukrainian delegate to the U.N. was not even a Ukrainian, but a Russian who was once Soviet ambassador to the independent Ukraine of the revolutionary era.

The Russian Thermidor?

The period between 1934 and 1941, notable for the purges and for the constitutional development of Stalin's one-party state, is also called by many shrewd observers of revolutions the true Russian "Thermidor," as distinct from NEP. The term "Thermidor" has come to mean a period in which a revolution has burnt itself out, and the prevailing mood shifts from messianic enthusiasm to one of desire for normality. In revolutionary France, the shift was signalized by the fall of Robespierre and the Jacobin régime, and the advent of the Directory, a different government with different objectives, policies, and personnel, which was in turn succeeded by Napoleon's dictatorship (see Chapter 10). In the U.S.S.R., the striking fact was that Stalin stayed in office throughout. He was in effect the Russian Robespierre, Directory, and Napoleon all rolled into one. If we accept the parallel, the Russian Thermidor was a managed and manipulated Thermidor, involving no real liberalization of the regime or relaxation of controls. Yet perhaps the parallel is not entirely valid, since Stalin resembled Napoleon far more than he did the weak Directory.

In any case, the period of the late 1930's saw a wholesale retreat from many ideas of the revolution. Simultaneously with the purges and the new constitution, the bread ration was raised; the *kolkhoz* was reformed to permit the individual farmer to own his homestead; new medals and titles were awarded to leading workers in plants, and to scientists, engineers, and military men. In the Red Army, traditional tsarist distinctions between officers and men were restored, and marshals were named for the first time. Thus, without relaxing political control, Stalin introduced an element of relaxation into the daily life of the rank and file, at the very height of his Terror. The standard of living went up, as the production of consumer's goods was encouraged, and as workers were invited to spend their earnings on little luxuries previously unavailable.

Simultaneously, the state rediscovered Russia's great past. The standard communist teaching had been that proletarians have no fatherland; the very name of Russia had almost been abandoned. Now, in contrast, officially controlled organs of opinion editorialized that one should love one's own country, and hailed the heroes of the tsarist era. Alexander Nevsky, who had defeated the Teutonic knights; Dmitri Donskoi, who had defeated the Tartars; Peter the Great; Kutuzov, who had defeated Napoleon; even Ivan the Terrible—all were praised to the skies. The reputations of the great literary figures of the nineteenth century underwent a similar rehabilitation. This retreat to Russian nationalism reached its climax during World War II, when the Marxist *Internationale* itself was dropped as the national anthem.

The old Bolsheviks had attacked the family as the backbone of the old order, had made marriage difficult and divorce easy, had drawn no distinction between legitimate and illegitimate children, and had encouraged promiscuity and abortions. Stalin's state now rehabilitated the sanctity of marriage, denounced the seducer, made divorces very hard to get, declared the family essential to the state, and encouraged children to obey their parents. Doubtless the shift came in part as a result of the falling birthrate and increasing juvenile delinquency, but it was none the less part of the abandonment of radicalism.

The early Bolsheviks had destroyed the old school system, abolished homework and examinations, and allowed children to administer the schools collectively with their teachers. Attendance fell off, the schools became revolutionary clubs of youngsters, and the training of teachers was neglected. The universities deteriorated, since anybody aged sixteen could enroll in them. Degrees were abolished, and technical training was stressed to the exclusion of other subjects. Under NEP, this chaotic situation was modified, and the basic problem of increasing literacy was seriously tackled. But the subjects of ordinary school curricula were replaced by the so-called "project" system with heavy emphasis on labor problems and Marxist theory. The teachers had little to do except memorize texts, and quiz the children to test their mastery of them. The Communist party itself took over the universities, purged the faculties, and compelled the students to spend one week in three at work in factories—a system that helped neither the student nor the university, and cannot have increased industrial production by very much.

The "thermidorean reaction," as might have been expected, changed this system drastically. Training of teachers improved, their salaries were raised, and regular ranks in the civil service were established for them. The old pre-revolutionary system of admissions and degrees in the universities was restored, as was the pre-revolutionary school curriculum. Examinations and homework re-appeared; discipline was enforced on school children. The emphasis on political education was reduced, and co-education was abandoned. Fees for tuition were restored for secondary schools, the Russian counterpart of the American high school or the French *lycée*. These tuition fees made higher education difficult to obtain except for children of the new élite or unusually talented students who were able to win state scholarships. Literacy rose to about 90 per cent, if we may believe Soviet figures.

The educational reforms certainly made books, theaters, museums, and libraries available to many more Russians than ever before. Newspapers and periodicals multiplied, and the régime's respect for science and learning was genuine. But the régime's attitude was narrowly utilitarian and thoroughly intolerant. All cultural activities were measured by their positive contribution to the state. Education became indoctrination. Systems of ideas that might rival communism were not allowed to compete, since the government could always

silence those who might be their spokesmen. In this respect the Soviet régime was even more authoritarian than that of a ruler like Tsar Nicholas I (see Chapter 14).

Under Nicholas I, censorship prevented the writer from saying certain things, but it did not positively prescribe what he must say. It was a negative, not a positive censorship, and it left a margin of personal freedom that permitted some of the greatest works of all literature to be written in Russia. The Soviet censorship, on the other hand, was positive, and required of all artists that they constantly praise the new system and devote their talents to publicizing its merits. The party line extended into all cultural fields, even music, where talented composers had to apologize abjectly for failing to produce communist symphonies, whatever they may be. The creative artist, the scientist, the scholar did not know from day to day whether his efforts would win him a Stalin prize or a sentence to a Siberian labor camp.

The Russian Thermidor came last of all, and doubtless very reluctantly, to modify the traditional communist position on religion. Here militant atheism had been the policy of the early Bolsheviks. They jailed and sometimes executed bishops and priests; they sponsored an atheist society and a museum of anti-religious propaganda. Behind this attitude lay more than the standard Marxist feeling that religion was the opium of the masses; in Russia, the Orthodox Church had always been a pillar of tsarism, and had held back the intellectual advance of the country. Many years of attacks on religion, however, failed to eradicate Orthodoxy from among the people. When in 1937 Hitler built a Russian church in Berlin, and took every occasion to speak kindly of the Orthodox Church, Stalin moved in the religious field also. Declaring that Christianity had contributed to past Russian progress, the government called off its anti-religious propaganda and enlisted its own atheist society to rehabilitate the Church. Church-going became respectable once more, although members of the party were not encouraged to profess religion. As a result, when war came, the leading church dignitaries supported the régime enthusiastically, although Hitler won a number of Ukrainian clerics to his side. In 1943, Stalin received high churchmen; the government lowered taxes on church property, lifted the curfew for Easter, and appointed a new Patriarch, on whose subservience the regime could count.

Viewed together, the changes of the Thermidor period seem to have had a double purpose. They were designed in part to retain popular loyalty during a period when the party itself was being disrupted by the purges. But they were also designed in part to strengthen the country to meet an expected attack from Germany. However far the return to old and popular forms and ideas was carried, it was always the regime that took the lead. And never at any moment did Stalin relax his firm control over all departments of national public and private life.

V   Soviet Foreign Policy, 1918–1941

Foreign Office and Comintern, 1918–1928

During the period of "war communism," the Bolsheviks had a chance to reflect upon their previously firm conviction that the world revolution was to be expected in the immediate future. The communist states in Bavaria and in Hungary proved to be short-lived (see Chapter 19); everywhere the moderates triumphed. As the civil war drew to a close, Lenin and his followers realized that to rebuild a shattered Russia it would be necessary to deal with the capitalist world. In the Foreign Office they had two competent men: Chicherin, a learned aristocrat turned Bolshevik, and Litvinov, his shrewd and able chief assistant. These two and their staff now became diplomats in the service of the Soviet state, like diplomats in the service of other states.

But the idea of world revolution was of course not abandoned. Lenin in 1919 founded the Third International, known thereafter as the Comintern. It issued what amounted almost to a new Communist Manifesto, summoning communists all over the world to unite against the "bourgeois cannibals" of capitalism. Zinoviev was put in charge, and his chief assistants were also Russians. Labor, socialist, and anarchist parties in Bulgaria, Norway, Italy, and Spain began to adhere to the new organization, although many withdrew in disgust when it became clear that the Bolsheviks were establishing a dictatorship in Russia with secret police and an army. Yet the Comintern continued to operate side by side with the Foreign Office, and during the next few years often in seeming contradiction to it. This duality gave Russian foreign policy a unique aspect. The maintenance of the Comintern aroused suspicion abroad and made capitalist states reluctant even to recognize the new Russia.

The Foreign Office concluded a trade treaty with England in 1921, at the beginning of the NEP period, which bound Russia not to stir up the peoples of the British Empire by any means, and re-opened trade between the two countries. Similar treaties were concluded between Russia and Poland, the Baltic States, Scandinavia, Germany, and Italy. A truce had been arranged between the communist and capitalist worlds. In 1922, the Russians were invited to an international economic conference at Genoa. The British and French were convinced that NEP meant a return to capitalism and had worked out a scheme for investment in Russia as part of a program for the postwar economic reconstruction of Europe. Not only did the Russians reject this plan, but they signed with defeated Germany the Treaty of Rapallo (April, 1922), which provided for the renunciation of all claims for reparations, and implied a German willingness to recognize Bolshevik nationalizations. This recognition the other powers, especially France, were unwilling to grant because of the large amounts of capital they had invested in Russia before the revolution. Rapallo relieved Russian isolation, and brought German technical knowledge to the service of the Bolsheviks. They permitted the Germans to build and operate armament and aircraft factories on Russian soil in defiance of the Treaty of Versailles.

In 1923, at Lausanne, Russia lost a dispute with Britain over international regulation of the Straits, and further friction with Britain arose over Afghanistan. But Britain recognized the Soviet regime in 1924, despite Trotsky's description of the mild Laborite Ramsay MacDonald as a "Christian Menshevik" whose country was full of cockroaches—a comment that illustrates some of Russia's difficulty in getting along with the rest of the world. Later in the same year, 1924, the so-called "Zinoviev letter" was published in England. It purported to instruct the British Communist party in the techniques of revolution, and it was almost certainly a forgery; but the "Zinoviev letter" influenced the British voters to return a Conservative government, which denounced the treaties with Russia. In 1927, a raid on the offices of a Russian firm doing business in London produced further evidence of communist agitation in England, and the British government now broke relations with Russia altogether. The Anglo-Russian council of trade unions set up by the communists collapsed when the Russians criticized British moderation in the general strike of 1926. Meantime, the United States had no diplomatic relations with the Soviet regime, and did not recognize it until 1933.

During the years 1918–1927, the Comintern compiled a record of failure. First, the Russians failed to keep in line the leaders of the Italian Left in a conference at Leghorn in 1921, and thus contributed handsomely to the success of Mussolini in the next year. They failed in Bulgaria to collaborate with a liberal agrarian regime, and allowed the triumph of a right-wing group in 1923. Most important, they failed in Germany, where a revolution actually threatened during 1923 as a result of French occupation of the Ruhr (for details

of these events, see Chapter 19). After Lenin's death, the feud between Stalin and Trotsky was reflected in the Communist parties of other countries, and cost the Comintern heavily.

The Russians failed in Poland, where they helped Pilsudski to dictatorial power in 1926, after which he turned against them. They failed in the Moslem and colonial world. But their greatest failure came in China (see also Chapter 20), where in 1923 the Chinese nationalist revolutionary leader, Sun Yat-sen, agreed to take communist advice and received one of the Comintern's best men, Borodin. Borodin helped Sun re-organize his political party, the Kuomintang, and admitted communists to it, although this alienated the right-wing supporters of the national party. In March, 1926, Sun having died, his brother-in-law Chiang Kai-shek led a *coup* against the government, and began to arrest communists. It is often argued that, had Stalin at that moment broken with Chiang and proceeded to sponsor a Chinese communist revolution, he might well have won China. Indeed Trotsky analyzed the situation that way at the time. But Stalin in his own analysis went back to a theory that the Bolsheviks had not espoused since Lenin's return to Russia in April, 1917: the theory that a bourgeois revolution must precede a socialist revolution, and that all the communists could and should do in China was to help Chiang achieve this first revolution. The eventual result was a series of massacres of Chinese communists by Chiang, and a loss of prestige for Stalin and for Russia.

Indeed Stalin had apparently never really believed in the effectiveness of the Comintern as an instrument of world revolution. When he came to sole power, he could not abandon it, however, because of the criticism he would have aroused, and because he sought to dilute and eventually to eradicate the largely Trotskyite sentiments of communists in other countries. He therefore applied to the Comintern the same techniques he had used against the party at home and established full control over it through use of the Russian delegation. This delegation was responsible to the Politbureau, and as the representative of the only successful revolutionary country it enjoyed great prestige. Successively, the Comintern was influenced to denounce the enemies of Stalin: Trotsky and the Left in 1924, Bukharin and the Right in 1928. Thereafter there was no divergence between the Comintern and the Foreign Office.

Stalin and the West, 1928– 1939

Simultaneously with the adoption of the "new socialist offensive" at home, Stalin swung the Comintern leftward into a new period of militant revolutionary activity. The Social Democrats of western countries were denounced now as "social fascists" and as the most dangerous enemies of communism. The communists were going to bring about revolutions by themselves. Yet Stalin's personal belief in the possibility of revolution elsewhere seems to have been small. "One Soviet tractor is worth more than ten good foreign communists" is a remark quoted as typical of the views of Stalin's entourage in the days of the First Five-Year Plan; it reflects his real contempt for the rest of the world and his deep-rooted Russian nationalism.

This lack of real interest in the behavior of communists abroad and the failure to understand the true play of forces inside other countries led directly to the triumph of Hitler in Germany in 1933 (see Chapter 19). The communists in Germany, who had been instructed by the Comintern that the Social Democrats and not the Nazis were their worst enemies, fought the Nazis in the streets, but allied themselves with them in the Reichstag. They believed that a Nazi triumph would very soon be followed by a communist revolution. Thus even after Hitler came to power, the Russians renewed their nonaggression pact with Germany.

Yet the shock of realization that Hitler had meant precisely what he said about liquidating communists, and the fear that the U.S.S.R. itself might be in danger, soon led Stalin to modify Russian policy in the direction of collective security. After Hitler had refused to guarantee the Baltic states jointly

with Stalin, Russia entered the League of Nations in September, 1934. The Soviet delegate, Litvinov, now became the most eloquent defender of universal disarmament and of punishment for aggressors. Soon afterward, the Russians began to negotiate for an "eastern Locarno" security pact to balance the agreement reached by the western European nations at Locarno in 1925 (see p. 727). Although no such structure could be created because of Polish and German hostility to the U.S.S.R., Russia did sign pacts with France and Czechoslovakia in 1935 providing for consultation, under the terms of the League, in the event of aggression, and for mutual aid, if the League certified that aggression had occurred. Soviet aid to Czechoslovakia, if the Czechs became victims of aggression, was to be delivered only if the French, who were bound to the Czechs by a long-standing alliance, honored their obligations first.

In view of the shift in Soviet foreign policy, the Comintern also shifted its line. In 1935, their recent deadly enemies, the Social Democrats and bourgeois liberals of the West, were suddenly embraced as allies against the fascist menace. Communists were to take the lead in forming "popular fronts" against fascism, and might properly welcome anybody, no matter how conservative in other ways, who would stand together with them on this principle. Revolutionary propaganda and anti-capitalist agitation were to be soft-pedaled. The communists in all the countries of the world led the fight for the defense budgets that they had previously sabotaged. Georgi Dimitrov, the Bulgarian communist, hero of the Reichstag fire trial (Chapter 19) and a symbol of antifascist courage and wit, was made boss of the Comintern. Inside the Soviet Union, the adoption of the "popular front" strategy was probably not unrelated to the purges, since the "Right deviationists" were anxious to reach an accommodation with the fascist states, and the "Left deviationists" insisted on the steady pursuit of world revolution.

This was the period when popular front governments came to power in France and Spain, and when some people in the West naively accepted the communists as their true brothers in arms against the menace of Hitler. However effective the "popular front" may have been as a tactic with western individuals, the purges inside Russia disillusioned western governments. A state that had to exterminate its top civil and military personnel for the crime of collaborating with the enemy did not make an attractive ally. If one believed the purge charges, one regarded a Soviet alliance as of doubtful value; if one did not believe them, how could one trust Stalin? On Stalin's side, western appeasement of Hitler and Mussolini (see Chapter 21) doubtless increased his disillusionment with the West.

Russia and the western European bloc each assumed that the chief purpose of the other was to turn the full force of Hitler's forthcoming attack away from itself and in the opposite direction. That Hitler intended to attack nobody could doubt. On September 12, 1936, in a speech at Nuremberg, he specifically declared once more that

if I had the Ural mountains with their incalculable store of treasures in raw materials, Siberia with its vast forests, and the Ukraine with its tremendous wheatfields, Germany under National Socialist leadership would swim in plenty.*

There was, then, much reason for the West to hope that the attack would be directed against the U.S.S.R.; this Stalin was determined to avert.

Soviet intervention in the Spanish Civil War (see Chapter 19) is an interesting demonstration of Stalin's real position. General Francisco Franco, who led an army revolt against the republican government of Spain in 1936, soon obtained aid from Mussolini and Hitler. The Russians, though reluctant to intervene in Spain at all because of their anxiety to prove their respectability to the western powers, realized that a failure to help the Spanish republic would cost them support all over the world. But their aid was too little and came too late, and consisted largely of police agents who devoted themselves to fighting Spanish anarchists and Trotskyites. The Russians hoped

*A Hitler, *My New Order*, R. de Sales, ed. (New York, 1941), 400.

that the western powers would intervene also, feeling that if they did so they would be irrevocably committed to continue the fight against Hitler on other battlefields. But western neutrality in Spain helped convince Stalin that a western alliance could not be counted upon.

A still more important factor here was the western appeasement of Hitler, which reached its climax in the Munich agreement of Britain, France, Germany, and Italy in September, 1938 (see also Chapter 21). From the Russian point of view, the Munich cession of Czech lands to Hitler, and the French failure to support Czechoslovakia and thus make operative the Russo-Czech alliance, could have only one purpose—to drive Hitler east. Stalin was apparently ready to support the Czechs if the French did too; when they did not, he seems to have decided that he had better sound out Hitler for an understanding. Thus a truly operative alliance between Stalin and the West proved impossible between 1935 and 1939.

When the British and French realized that appeasement had failed to stop Hitler, they sought reluctantly for a firmer alliance with the U.S.S.R. From March to August, 1939, Stalin kept open both his negotiations with the West and his slowly ripening negotiations with the Germans, which at first seemed to be concerned only with a trade agreement. The British and French mission, when it finally arrived in Moscow, was not composed of sufficiently high-ranking men to inspire Russian confidence. Moreover, the western powers naturally refused to turn over to Stalin the territories that he wanted as a bulwark against Germany—Finland and the Baltic republics of Estonia, Latvia, and Lithuania.

The growing eagerness of the Germans to secure a nonaggression pact gave Stalin the opportunity he sought to divert the war from Russia. In May, 1939, Litvinov was dismissed as foreign minister because he was Jewish and could therefore not negotiate with Germans; he was replaced by Molotov. In the pact Molotov eventually reached with Hitler late in August, 1939, each power undertook to remain neutral toward the other in the event of war. A secret additional protocol provided for a division between Germany and Russia of Poland, which Hitler was about to attack. At worst, this put Russia's frontier farther west in the event of a subsequent German attack. The Russians lived up to the economic clauses of the agreement to the letter, although the Germans did not. The publication of the Hitler-Stalin pact necessitated an abrupt shift in the world communist line, which had remained staunchly "popular front." Now it was once more necessary for puzzled communists to denounce liberals and Social Democrats as enemies. They had to call the war that Hitler launched against Poland within a few days an "imperialist war," in which there was no difference between the two sides and in which communists should not get involved.

Stalin
and the Second World War

Stalin overrated the military power of the Poles to resist Hitler, and thus miscalculated the course of the first weeks of war. Faced with the complete collapse of Poland, he marched into the eastern portion. Disturbed by the lull ("the phony war") on the western fronts, he probably feared that Hitler would turn against him at once. This might well have happened

had Hitler been able to secure peace with France and England, as he strove to do. During the lull, in December, 1939, came Stalin's attack on Finland, which, unlike the Baltic states, had refused to grant him strategic bases. The attack on the Finns by Stalin aroused a storm of anti-Russian sentiment in the West. Both Britain and France supported the recruitment of armies of volunteers, and considered air raids against Russian targets in support of the Finns. The League of Nations expelled Russia. Despite severe setbacks to the Russian troops, the war against the Finns was won by the spring of 1940, before the western allies had been able to give them effective aid.

And in the spring of 1940, Stalin's second major calculation went awry. Like many observers, he apparently expected France to hold out a long time, and believed that, even if Hitler eventually defeated the French, Germany would be greatly weakened. Now instead came the lightning German operations in the west, and the war on the Continent seemed to be over. Only the British held out (see Chapter 21). Preoccupied with the security of his western frontiers, Stalin simply seized the three Baltic republics, and staged rigged plebiscites in which the Latvians, Estonians, and Lithuanians asked to be included in the Soviet Union. He demanded of Rumania in June, 1940, the

Rendezvous. Hitler-Stalin pact, August, 1939.

province of Bessarabia, whose loss after World War I the U.S.S.R. had never recognized, and also northern Bukovina, which had formerly been Habsburg, not Russian, territory, but which had a large Ukrainian population and was strategically valuable. Parts of these territories were annexed to existing SSR's and parts were incorporated into the new Moldavian SSR. The Germans had expected Russian seizure of Bessarabia, but not of northern Bukovina; they permitted the seizure, however, telling the Rumanians that they could expect no help from Hitler. But that was as far as Hitler's co-operation with Stalin in eastern Europe went. The re-annexation of Bessarabia had given the U.S.S.R. the mouths of the Danube, controlling an important artery. The Russians seemed to be moving into southeast Europe, a region in which the Germans were not prepared to let them operate alone.

Only a few weeks after the Russian seizure of Rumanian territory, Hitler asserted his own southeastern interests by forcing the Rumanians to cede territory to Hungary (August, 1940) and then guaranteeing the new Rumanian frontiers, a guarantee that could apply only against the U.S.S.R. Soon afterward, German troops appeared in Finland, "to reinforce the German armies in Norway," Hitler explained. And in the autumn of 1940, German troops entered Rumania proper, "to guard the Rumanian oil-fields against British sabotage." These maneuvers on his new frontiers deeply disquieted Stalin, as well they might have.

In October, 1940, Italy attacked Greece, and open war had spread to the Balkans. In November, when Molotov went to Berlin, Hitler tried to dazzle him with grandiose offers of an enormous future Soviet sphere of influence extending through Persia to the Persian Gulf and Indian Ocean, and including India, after the British Empire was destroyed. Each time this luscious bait was held out, Molotov tried to bring the discussion back to southeast Europe and Finland, and to establish Russia's sole rights in this sphere. This the Germans would not allow. After the failure of the conversations, Hitler ordered preparations for an attack on the U.S.S.R.

In the spring of 1941, the Germans had to rescue the Italians from the Greek campaign, which had bogged down in Albania. This rescue was preceded by the movement of German troops into Bulgaria, which the U.S.S.R. regarded as essential to its own defense. Then came an unsuccessful German effort to win Yugoslavia without war, and swift victorious German campaigns in Yugoslavia and Greece (March-May, 1941). Germany alone ruled supreme in the Balkan region, and, though the Yugoslav and Greek resistance had delayed the German timetable, Hitler was able to launch the invasion of the U.S.S.R. on June 22, 1941. Stalin must have known it was coming; indeed the western powers had warned him. But he seems to have hoped against hope to the end. A few weeks before it came, Stalin, proudly calling himself an Asiatic, had secured a neutrality pact with Japan, Hitler's ally. The Japanese, deeply engaged in China, and intending to go to war with the United States, wished as much as did the Russians for insurance against a war on two fronts.

VI Conclusion

Karl Marx, who scorned and disliked Russia, would have been utterly dumbfounded had he lived to see that backward agricultural land, almost without a proletariat, produce the only successful European communist revolution. Although much ink has been spilled in an effort to discover why a Marxist revolution took place in the country where, in theory, the conditions were least favorable, the problem is not really so difficult. Two possible general solutions suggest themselves. Either Marx was wrong, or what happened in Russia was not a Marxist revolution at all. Or perhaps both these answers are partly right. It seems clear that Marx did not correctly estimate the revolutionary force latent in the Russian peasantry; since Marx died in 1883, he could not foresee the full inadequacy of the tsarist regime, the extent of the tensions created by World War I, or the feebleness of the provisional government of 1917. But it also seems clear that to bring the Bolsheviks to power it took Lenin's appreciation of the importance of the peasantry, his grasp of the immediate situation, his willingness to risk everything, and his luck at being in the right place at the right time with the right weapons.

On the other hand, the revolution was not wholly Marxist. Once the Bolsheviks were in power, of course, it was inevitable that the succession of real situations they faced should modify their Marxist-Leninist theories. Thus civil war and foreign intervention brought chaos, from which NEP provided a necessary respite. And in Stalin there came to power an amalgam of Marxist, Russian nationalist, and power-hungry politician such as nobody could

have foreseen. Moved by a combination of motives, Stalin proceeded hastily and brutally to make over Russia in a decade. Although he fell short of his goal, his program had created an industrial state not totally unprepared for the blows that Hitler was to deal it. Slaves of the state though they were, collectivized by force, industrialized by force, purged, terrorized, and struggling by the million to exist in forced labor camps, the Russians in World War II succeeded, with much help from the United States, in defeating Hitler and his allies.

How much the loyalty of Russians to Stalin was due to the failure of the German invaders to treat them well, and how far Hitler with a different policy might have won their support are questions with which we cannot deal here. The Russians were facing a coalition of fascist states — Germany, Hungary, Rumania, and others grouped together in an alliance called "the Axis powers" (from the German-Italian "Axis"), a coalition pledged to the utter destruction of communism. We turn now to the history of these powers and of the fascist form of totalitarian doctrine they embraced.

Reading Suggestions on Communist Russia, 1917-1941

(Asterisk indicates paperbound edition.)

General Accounts

E. H. Carr, *A History of Soviet Russia*. Eight volumes of this work, still in progress, have so far appeared (Macmillan, 1950–1964). The only attempt at a complete history of the Soviet Union from original sources; Carr is a somewhat uncritical admirer of Lenin, and his work must be used with care.

B. Moore, Jr., *Soviet Politics: The Dilemma of Power* (Harvard Univ. Press, 1950). An illuminating analysis of the relationship between the communist ideology and Soviet practice.

R. N. Carew Hunt, *The Theory and Practice of Communism* (Macmillan, 1951). An excellent introduction to the subject.

M. Fainsod, *How Russia Is Ruled* (Harvard Univ. Press, 1953). An analysis of the Soviet system in 1953, firmly rooted in the historical background. Second edition, up to date, 1963.

W. W. Rostow and others, *The Dynamics of Soviet Society* (*Mentor, 1954). Attempt by a group of scholars to determine why the Russians behave as they do.

Robert V. Daniels, *The Nature of Communism* (*Vintage). A valuable study of total-itarianism.

Special Studies

W. H. Chamberlin, *The Russian Revolution, 1917–1921,* 2 vols. (*Grosset's Universal Library). Still the standard work on the subject.

L. Trotsky, *The History of the Russian Revolution*, 3 vols. (Simon and Schuster, 1932). A brilliant but biased study by one of the leading participants.

B. D. Wolfe, *Three Who Made a Revolution* (Dial, 1948; *Beacon). Excellent triple study of the careers of Lenin, Trotsky, and Stalin down to 1914.

D. Shub, *Lenin* (Doubleday, 1948; *abridgment available, Mentor). The best biography of Lenin in English.

I. Deutscher, *The Prophet Armed, The Prophet Unarmed, The Prophet Outcast* (Oxford Univ. Press, 1954, 1959, 1963; *Vintage). Biography of Trotsky, written by an admirer of the man.

I. Deutscher, *Stalin: A Political Biography* (Oxford Univ. Press, 1949). The most complete account in English.

J. Maynard, *Russia in Flux* (Macmillan, 1948). Enlightening though sometimes far-fetched attempts to show basic continuities between the old and new régimes in Russia, written by a British civil servant stationed in India who made the study of Russia his avocation.

C. Brinton, *The Anatomy of Revolution,* 2nd ed. (Prentice-Hall, 1952; *Vintage). Comparison of the Russian revolution with the French revolution of 1789 and the English seventeenth-century revolution.

M. Fainsod, *Smolensk Under Soviet Rule* (Harvard Univ. Press, 1959). A uniquely important study, based on a huge collection of captured documents, of the actual workings of the communist system in Smolensk in the 1930's.

R. C. Tucker and S. F. Cohen, eds. *The Great Purge Trials* (*Grosset's Universal Library). A translation of the major portion of the actual text of the 1938 trial.

H. Schwartz, *Russia's Soviet Economy,* 2nd ed. (Prentice-Hall, 1954). Good introduction to the subject.

N. Timasheff, *The Great Retreat* (Dutton, 1946). An account of the "Russian Thermidor."

R. Pipes, *The Formation of the Soviet Union* (Harvard Univ. Press, 1954). Excellent monograph on the question of national minorities in Russia, 1917–1923.

J. L. Wheeler-Bennett, *Brest-Litovsk, The Forgotten Peace* (Macmillan, 1938). Excellent monograph.

L. Fischer, *The Soviets in World Affairs,* 2nd ed. (Princeton Univ. Press, 1951). The only study of Soviet foreign policies up to 1929.

M. Beloff, *The Foreign Policy of Soviet Russia,* 2 vols. (Oxford Univ. Press, 1947, 1952). A solid study covering the years 1929–1941.

E. Lyons, *Assignment in Utopia* (Harcourt, Brace, 1937). An American journalist records his disillusionment with Soviet communism.

R. H. Crossman, ed., *The God That Failed* (Harper, 1959). Brief statements by Arthur Koestler, Stephen Spender, Ignazio Silone, and other intellectuals recording their disenchantment with communism.

V. A. Kravchenko, *I Chose Freedom* (Scribner's, 1946). The most celebrated of many works written by ex-Soviet officials and citizens who preferred life in the West to the U.S.S.R.

Historical Fiction

A. Koestler, *Darkness at Noon* (Modern Library, 1956; *New American Library). A famous novel, presenting in fictional form a keen analysis of the attitudes of the Old Bolsheviks whom Stalin purged.

V. Serge, *The Case of Comrade Tulayev* (Doubleday, 1950). Another excellent novel of the purges.

G. Blunden, *The Room on the Route* (Lippincott, 1947). Perhaps the most vivid fictional portrayal of the impact of terror on the ordinary person.

A. Tolstoy, *Road to Calvary* (Knopf, 1946). Translation of a Stalin Prize Novel about the revolution and civil war.

The Rise of Fascism, 1918-1939

I Introduction

In this chapter we shall deal with the rise of fascism in Europe in the period between the two great wars. By 1939, authoritarian governments of the Right had taken firm control of Italy, Germany, Spain, and all the countries of eastern and southeastern Europe except Russia. The process by which these regimes came to power differed widely from country to country, as did some of the external features of the regimes. At first glance, fascism is more complex and more difficult to understand than communism, whose development as a doctrine can be traced from Marx through Lenin before its followers were able to put it, or something like it, into practice in Russia. Unlike communism, fascism has no such line of theoretical development. Its proponents often seem to have acted first and worried about doctrine later, devising theories to meet the needs of the moment.

Fascism has been called the revolution of the classes of order. Political parties on the Continent have often represented the interests of the various social classes; when those interests have seemed to be about evenly balanced in a parliamentary state, a long and indecisive political tug-of-war has often ensued. For example, let us assume that a revolution from the Left threatens or can be made to seem to threaten. Then the middle classes, so the theory runs, seize power and take refuge in their own form of extremism—fascism, that is, nationalism tricked out with a few radical phrases to win mass support, and draped in mystical garments. This formula can be applied to Mussolini's rise to power in Italy in 1922, to Hitler's rise to power in Germany in 1933, to Franco's rise to power in Spain in 1936–1939, and to many of the eastern European dictators. Yet the formula takes us only so far. Only a study of the different circumstances in each of the different countries can give it body and meaning.

Economic depressions played a role in the rise of almost every dictator—in Italy the postwar depression, and elsewhere the world-wide depression of 1929 and later. We notice, moreover, a certain similarity in the externals of fascism everywhere—colored shirts, private armies, mass hypnotism, special salutes, special war cries and ceremonies, mystical glorification of the nation, and a vast program of conquest. The dictator justifies his program by references to "have" and "have-not" nations; his own nation is always a "have-not," always oppressed.

Fascism is just as violent in its hatred of democracy, liberalism, and parliamentary institutions as in its professed dislike of communism. Indeed fascism shares communism's abhorrence of constitutional procedure, its disregard of the individual human being, and its insistence that the state is supreme. Fascism persecutes its enemies, both real and fancied, with the same ruthlessness we have observed in Stalin's Russia. Censorship, political police, concentration camps, the rule of the bludgeon, the end of legal protection—all these practices are common to both fascism and communism.

When Mussolini ruled in Rome, public buildings everywhere carried the admonition to loyal Italians, "Believe, fight, obey" (*Credere, combattere, obbedire*). Presumably this was intended to be inspiring. Yet all it really means is: Believe (what Mussolini tells you), fight (for Mussolini and his backers), obey (Mussolini). When put this way, the formula is seen to subvert all religion and all human decency. Yet, under the stress of the unbearable pressures on individuals generated by the tension of the years between the wars many an idealist was taken in, surrendering his right to think and to make his own decisions.

II   Italy and Fascism

The Setting

Although Italy was a member of the victorious Allied coalition, she finished the First World War with a sense of defeat. Six hundred and fifty thousand of her men had been killed and one million wounded. Industry slumped immediately after the war, and within a few months 10 per cent of the industrial workers were unemployed. Prices rose rapidly, and wages failed to keep up. The promised pensions for wounded veterans and families of the killed were long delayed. Strikes and disorders became frequent. Many of the young men released from the armies with no trade but war and no job to go to drifted restlessly and discontentedly, fit prey for leaders with glittering promises.

Perhaps most important, the Italian government itself, hoping to influence the peace negotiations, began to spread propaganda among the Italian people to the effect that their wartime allies were robbing them of the Slavic lands in Dalmatia, across the Adriatic, promised to Italy by the secret Treaty of London (see Chapter 17) in exchange for Italy's entrance into the war. This arrangement the United States had never agreed to, and now would not accept. Although the Allied leaders at the Paris Peace Conference remained unaffected by the storms of protest arising from Italy, the Italian people did come to believe that they had shed their blood in vain. Popular sentiment in Italy, especially in the army, swung toward extremists of one sort or another.

Some Italians hysterically supported Gabriele d'Annunzio, a short, bald nationalist poet and romantic novelist who formed a band of volunteers. They seized the city of Fiume, the Adriatic seaport over which Croatians and Hungarians had long disagreed (Chapter 17). Referring to the "stench of peace," and denouncing Woodrow Wilson, d'Annunzio declared that the time for heroic individual action was at hand. Fiume had actually not been awarded to Italy even by the Secret Treaty of London, but d'Annunzio felt that Italy must have it, and that was enough. He ran his own government in Fiume until the end of 1920.

D'Annunzio patterned his régime there upon that of an imaginary medieval commune in a poem by Italy's romantic poet Carducci (1835–1907). Modeling himself consciously upon the governor of the commune in the poem, d'Annunzio would appear on the balcony of the city hall, address an inspirational harangue to the crowd, and ask for its unanimous consent for whatever he wished to do. This his listeners would grant, raising their right hands high, as the imaginary citizens of Carducci's commune had done. Some of d'Annunzio's followers wore black shirts. When d'Annunzio asked them to whom Fiume belonged they would shout *A noi,* "to us," and when he asked them to whom Italy belonged, they would give the same answer. Indeed, he planned to lead his followers from Fiume to Rome, and thence out into the world to conquer it, presumably with daggers, which he

preferred to mechanized weapons. He drafted the Statutes of Fiume, a constitution in which he made a conscious attempt to organize society along the lines he imagined to have existed in the guilds and artisans' corporations of the Middle Ages.

In November, 1920, the Italian government signed the Treaty of Rapallo with Yugoslavia, by which Fiume was to become a free city. Italian forces drove d'Annunzio out, and into retirement in a villa on the Italian lakes. But the techniques of force, the haranguing of the mob from the balcony, the straight-arm salute, the black shirts, the rhythmic cries, the plans for conquest, and the "corporative" scheme of the Statutes of Fiume served as precedent and inspiration for Benito Mussolini, founder of Italian fascism.

In the first four years after the end of the war, Mussolini created and brought to power a new political force in Italy. In October, 1922, he was summoned to office by King Victor

Gabriele D'Annunzio.

Emmanuel III (1900–1947); from then on he gradually created a totalitarian state of which he was the sole, undisputed ruler. Suppressing all opposition at home, and threatening the peace abroad, the fascist state in Italy served in some degree as model for the Nazis in Germany, for the Falangists in Spain, and for totalitarian regimes in virtually all the European successor states of the Habsburg and Ottoman empires. Eventually, Mussolini was forced, largely by his own propaganda, into an alliance with Hitler. In 1940, this alliance took Italy into World War II, and in 1945 it brought Mussolini himself to an ignominious death, upside down on a communist partisan gallows, with his mistress beside him.

Mussolini: Early Career

Mussolini was born in 1883, in the Romagna, a province of central Italy famous for its political extremists, and for the violence with which they express themselves. His father was an ardent socialist who had begun his career as an anarchist under the influence of Bakunin (Chapter 14). Trained as an elementary-school teacher, Mussolini was already a passionate socialist by the time he was eighteen. He spent some time as an agitator among Italian emigrant laborers in Switzerland (1902–1904) and in Austria (1909) but was expelled by the police. Back in Italy, he was imprisoned for opposing the war against Turkey over Tripoli (1911). In 1912, he became editor of the most important Italian socialist newspaper, *Forward (Avanti)*.

When World War I began, Mussolini at first vigorously opposed Italy's entry. But then, during 1914, he changed his mind. First he favored "relative neutrality," meaning that socialists should leave themselves free to support Italian entry if such a course seemed likely to prove favorable to them. When the Italian Socialist party refused to follow this idea, he resigned as editor of *Avanti*. Soon afterward (November, 1914), he founded his own newspaper, *The People of Italy (Il Popolo d'Italia)*, in Milan, and began to advocate an immediate Italian declaration of war on the side of the Al-

lies. For this the Socialist party expelled him.

But these bare bones of a biography reveal only the externals. As a socialist, Mussolini before 1914 was a passionate left-winger. He was an apostle of violent social revolution and a bitter opponent of milder evolutionary and reformist doctrine. He urged that a small, well-knit armed minority should seize power and establish a dictatorship. He loathed militarism, was himself a draft-dodger, and urged soldiers to desert the army. He hated monarchy, and savagely attacked in his writings all the crowned heads of Europe, especially the Italian House of Savoy. He was a vigorous atheist, urged workers to stay away from church, and scorned the teachings of Christ. As an international revolutionary, he opposed nationalism, and even referred to the Italian flag as "a rag to be planted on a dunghill."

Yet he was to repudiate almost all these positions, and as fascist chieftain to substitute almost the exact opposites. As a fascist, he attacked bolshevism and all left-wing movements; he made his peace with the monarchy and the Church; he became a militant nationalist, a mystic patriot, and a rabid militarist. The repudiation of the views he had held so long and advocated so skillfully is not nearly so astonishing as it seems. From the first, Mussolini did not much care for programs; what he wanted was to rule.

A complete opportunist, he could shift his line on any question at a moment's notice if it seemed advantageous. For example, after the war, though he was now a fascist, he at first supported a radical program of social change, indistinguishable from the program he would have advocated had he still been a socialist. He favored the action of the Italian workers in the fall of 1920 when they occupied the factories in a kind of sit-down strike. Yet, within a year, he was using the fears which this strike had aroused in the middle classes to argue that he was the only possible bulwark against "bolshevism." About certain matters, however, he was consistent. He always hated parliaments and he always loved violence.

Mussolini's switch from isolationism to interventionism in the war in 1914 was the first of his important shifts. After his expulsion from the Socialist party, he agitated furiously for war, speaking to groups of similarly minded young men called *fasci* or groups (the image is of a bundle of rods, a symbol of office in the Roman Republic of antiquity). Soon after Italy did enter the war in 1915, Mussolini was conscripted and sent to the front. He was wounded in 1917 by an Italian mortar shell that exploded during practice. When he got out of the hospital, he continued to edit his newspaper, spewing forth a mixture of extreme revolutionary and extreme nationalist propaganda.

Mussolini: Rise to Power

In March, 1919, Mussolini founded the first *fasci di combattimento* ("groups for combat"). There was no sign as yet to indicate that by October, 1922, the leader of this small movement would become the most powerful man in Italy. In 1919, he called for every kind of revolutionary violence—seizure of the land, attacks on the factories, shooting of storekeepers who charged high prices, expropriation of mines and transports, and war by the vanquished "proletarian" nations against the victorious capitalists who had kept Italy from annexing Dalmatia. He now maintained that socialism was too conservative; his movement, far from setting itself against a revolution, was in the vanguard of those who were crying for one.

Yet in Italy a revolution along Bolshevik patterns was most unlikely, if not impossible. The peasants were not very revolutionary, for they already held much of the land except in the extreme south. And the industrial workers, though often discontented, knew that a revolution could be starved out because the country needed to import most of its raw materials. The Socialist party was overwhelmingly in the hands of moderates, and in 1919 Catholics founded the Popular party *(Partito Populare Italiano)*, designed to compete with the Socialists for the votes of the lower classes, who now had universal suffrage.

In the postwar disorders the peasants seized without consent of the landowners less than one-tenth of 1 per cent of the arable land in Italy. The leaders of the Socialist party and the General Confederation of Labor voted down the proposals of anarchist and communist extremists to turn the workers' occupation of the factories into a revolution. The government waited for the workers to grow tired. This they did in less than a month (September, 1920); then they left the occupied factories and went home.

Yet, although the danger of revolution was small, the fear of revolution was great. During 1920 and 1921, the industrialists and landowners, squeezed by taxation and inflation, became bitter. Shopkeepers and tradesmen wanted street disorders to end, food prices to be regulated, and the co-operative food stores of the Socialist and Catholic parties to be put out of business as competitors. Professional men and others with fixed incomes suffered as prices and wages went up and salaries lagged behind. The police grew tired of suppressing local disorders and of being repaid with insults. Ex-servicemen, insulted by anarchists and communists for their war records, naturally grew more patriotic.

All these groups identified the forces they did not like as Bolshevik, and accepted as an article of faith the myth of an impending Bolshevik revolution. After a series of fascist-socialists street fights and riots, these "anti-Bolsheviks" began to look to Mussolini's fascist bands as the defenders of their interests. D'Annunzio's defeat left Mussolini as his natural heir. The Left opposition to Mussolini was weakened when the communists split off from the Socialist party in 1921. The *fasci* grew enormously, from 30,000 in May, 1920, to 100,000 in February, 1921, to more than 300,000 at the time of the "March on Rome" in October, 1922. No longer were they merely squads of discontented and idle youths with vaguely revolutionary and nationalist ideas. Now, says one fascist of the period, "the sons and hangers-on of the bigwigs" poured into the organization.

They had come into the Fascio for their own ends. . . . If they met men in working clothes, they fell on them and began beating them. Their mentality was on a par with that of the Communists, who had beaten and murdered anybody who was decently dressed. One saw . . . the well-known surly and rapacious faces of war profiteers . . . and we were obliged to accept their money because we needed it to stifle an evil worse than they.[*]

The liberal parliamentary leaders of Italy felt that the fascist bands were teaching the Left a useful lesson. They encouraged the commanding officers of the army to issue rifles and army trucks and gasoline to the fascists, and even assigned army officers to command their operations. The police were encouraged to look the other way during disorders started by the fascists, and local judges were urged to help by releasing arrested fascists. Mussolini's newspaper was circulated free to the soldiers in the army as a "patriotic" sheet.

A campaign of terror now began against the socialists and Christian Democrats, as the fascist squadrons cruised around Italy in trucks, burning down labor-union offices, newspaper offices, and local Socialist party headquarters, and beating up and sometimes murdering labor leaders or local anti-fascist politicians. The *fasci* forced duly elected officials to resign. The torch, the cudgel, and the famous castor-oil treatment were all characteristic weapons. It is estimated that 2,000 people, anti-fascist and fascist, policemen and innocent bystanders, died by violence between October, 1920, and October, 1922.

The "March" on Rome

In the elections of May, 1921, Mussolini and thirty-four other fascists were elected to Parliament, along with ten Nationalists, their political allies. The momentum of the fascist movement was now too great to be slowed down. Mussolini abandoned his anti-monarchical views, and fascism became a political party (November, 1921) as a necessary step in the drive for power. Too late, the government became alarmed, and tried to take measures against the fascists, but the squads

were too strong, the police too accustomed to collaborating with them, and the politicians themselves as yet unaware that a tightly directed armed mob could really take over the state. Inside the royal family, the King's cousin, the Duke of Aosta, had become a fascist sympathizer, as had many army generals, the entire Nationalist party, and the leading industrialists.

In the fall of 1922, it was clear that the army would not resist a fascist *coup* in Rome itself. When a decree of martial law was presented to the King, he refused to sign it, probably influenced by his knowledge that the army would not fight the fascists, and that the Duke of Aosta would gladly take his crown. The refusal of the King to declare martial law greatly heartened the fascists. Now, as the fascists "marched" on Rome, mostly by storming railroad trains and stealing free rides, the King (October 29, 1922) telegraphed Mussolini in Milan to come to Rome and form a cabinet. Mussolini arrived by sleeping-car the next morning.

Fascism, which had begun as a patriotic anti-Bolshevik movement, and had then turned into an anti-labor movement in the service of the industrialists and landowners, had finally come to power as a conspiracy against parliamentary government in the service of a military clique. Just before taking office, Mussolini announced:

Our program is simple: we wish to govern Italy. They ask us for programs, but there are already too many. It is not programs that are wanting for the salvation of Italy but men and will-power.[*]

The Fascist Dictatorship

Mussolini now moved gradually to turn his premiership into a dictatorship. A month after coming to office, he obtained dictatorial powers that were to last only until the end of 1923. Although the constitution theoretically remained in force, Mussolini proceeded to take over the administration. He created a Fascist Militia almost 200,000 strong, which owed complete allegiance to him. He en-

[*]Umberto Banchelli, *Memorie di un Fascista,* quoted by G. Salvemini in *The Fascist Dictatorship* (New York, 1927), 67–68.

[*]Quoted by H. Finer, *Mussolini's Italy* (New York, 1935), 152.

larged the regular army, and required its members to take an oath of personal loyalty to him. Before his dictatorial powers expired, he secured from Parliament by pressure a new electoral law. This law provided that the political party which received the largest number of votes in a general election, if that number amounted to at least one-quarter of the vote, should automatically receive two-thirds of the seats in Parliament. The rest of the seats would be divided proportionately. This law made certain the fascists' domination of future parliaments. Indeed, in the election of April, 1924, the fascists actually polled 65 per cent of the vote cast; but this figure reflects a widespread use of intimidation and terrorism at the polls. The first all-fascist cabinet was now appointed. Meanwhile, local administration was made secure by the appointment of fascist prefects and subprefects in the provinces; these officials pursued the enemies of fascism with the same weapons of murder and mayhem that had been used before Mussolini's March on Rome.

Early in 1924, the leader of the opposition to Mussolini, the socialist Giacomo Matteotti, published a book called *The Fascists Exposed,* in which he detailed many of the outrages the fascists had committed on their way to power. It seemed probable that further revelations were in store, exposing some of Mussolini's cabinet members as corrupt. On June 10, 1924, Matteotti was "taken for a ride" in true gangster style and murdered. The crime was traced to members of Mussolini's immediate circle. This scandal rocked Italy, and for a moment it even seemed possible that Mussolini would fall. But he dismissed from office those who were involved, and pledged himself to restore law and order. Actually, he delayed trying the guilty men until March, 1926, and even then they all got off lightly.

What really helped Mussolini over the crisis, ironically enough, was the departure of most of the opposition deputies from Parliament. They declared that they would not return until the Matteotti murder had been solved and the government had been shown to be innocent. Far from making things harder for Mussolini, as they had intended, their departure actually made things easier. Mussolini denied his own guilt, imposed a rigid press censorship, and forbade the opposition to meet. Most of the deputies never did return to Parliament, and in 1926 their seats were declared forfeit.

Mussolini during the fascist "March" on Rome, 1922.

Next, a series of laws called the "most fascist laws" (*legge fascistissime*) tightened control over the press, abolished secret societies like the Freemasons, whom Mussolini had loathed ever since his socialist youth, and replaced all elected local officials by men appointed from Rome. Opponents of the regime were arrested and exiled to desolate islands off the Italian coast. Early in 1926, Mussolini was empowered to govern by decree. Three attempts on his life led to a new law providing the death penalty for action against the King, the Queen, or Mussolini. All opposition political parties were abolished in the same year, and the Fascist party was left as the only legal political party in Italy.

More and more the Italian state and the Fascist party were brought into co-ordination. Mussolini was both the *Duce* (leader) of the fascists and the *capo di governo*, the chief of state. At one moment he also held eight cabinet posts simultaneously. The members of the Fascist Grand Council, a "politbureau" numbering roughly twenty of the highest party functionaries, all appointed by Mussolini, held all the important posts in the administration not held by Mussolini himself. In 1928, the Grand Council was given important constitutional duties: preparing the lists of candidates for election of the Chamber, advising Mussolini, and proposing changes in the constitution or the succession to the throne. The Grand Council thus became a kind of third house, above the other two houses of Parliament, the Senate and the Chamber.

The Corporative State

Mussolini believed that the interests of labor and capital could and must be made to harmonize with the over-riding interests of the state. Instead of a political system as we understand it, he accepted the idea that representation should be based on economic interests organized in "syndicates." Such an idea was not new: the French syndicalist, Georges Sorel (Chapter 12), had already argued in this vein. But Sorel believed in class warfare, and in government by syndicates of workers only.

Mussolini, following the Italian nationalist syndicalist, Rossoni, believed in capitalism, class-collaboration, and producers' syndicates as well as workers' syndicates.

In 1925, fascist labor unions were recognized by employers as having the sole right to negotiate labor contracts. Then, in April, 1926, the state officially recognized producers' and workers' syndicates in each of six areas — industry, agriculture, commerce, sea and air transport, land and inland waterway transport, and banking — plus a syndicate of intellectuals, making thirteen syndicates in all. Each syndicate could bargain and reach contracts and could assess dues upon everyone engaged in its own economic field, irrespective of membership in the syndicate. Strikes and lockouts were both forbidden. When labor conditions did not improve, a "charter of labor," promising insurance and other benefits, was issued in 1927. In 1926, the syndicates were put under the control of a special Ministry of Corporations; Mussolini was the minister.

In 1928, the system of parliamentary representation was changed in accordance with fascist syndicalism. A new electoral law provided for a new Chamber of Deputies (400 instead of 560 members). The national councils of the thirteen syndicates could nominate a total of 800 candidates. Each syndicate had a quota, half to be selected by the employers and half by the employees. Cultural and charitable foundations could nominate 200 more candidates. When the total list of 1,000 was completed, the Fascist Grand Council could either select 400 of them, or strike out names and add names of its own, or even substitute an entire new list. The voters would then vote in answer to the question: "Do you approve of the list of deputies selected by the Fascist Grand Council?" They could vote "Yes" or "No" on the entire list, but they could not choose from among the candidates. If a majority voted "Yes," the list was elected; if not, the procedure was to be repeated. Despite the highly touted role of the syndicate, all the power obviously lay with the Fascist Grand Council. Universal suffrage was abolished even for this very limited form of election. Payment of a minimum tax or dues to a syndicate was required of each voter; women could not vote. In 1929, the elections under this system produced a "yes" vote of 8,519,559 and a "no" vote of 137,761.

Between 1930 and 1938, several constitutional steps were taken which seemed to move the syndicates into the center of the stage. Representatives from the syndicates and the government were now formed into a Council of Corporations, which was to act as a coordinating committee, settle disputes between syndicates, assist production, and establish the fascist corporations themselves, which had not yet been created. The Council was divided into seven sections corresponding to the seven syndicate areas, and in 1931 each of these sections of the Council was simply declared to be a corporation. In 1933, it was announced that the whole corporate system would be revised; and in 1934 the new elections (which of course returned the Fascist Grand Council's list of candidates) produced a "suicide" Chamber of Deputies, which was expected eventually to put an end to its own existence. Its replacement was to be a new "revolutionary assembly," which Mussolini called into existence in the fall of 1934. The assembly, also called the Central Committee of Corporations, contained 824 members, representing twenty-two newly created corporations. The Fascist party, as well as employers and employees, was represented on each corporation.

Finally, in 1938 the "suicide chamber" replaced itself with the Central Committee of Corporations, now called the Chamber of Fasces and Corporations. Nothing remained of the old parliamentary constitution that had been set up by Cavour except the Senate, nominally appointed by the King but actually subservient to Mussolini, who on one occasion had the King appoint forty fascist senators all at once. This new structure, the corporative state, was influenced by d'Annunzio's strange medieval ideas, and by Mussolini's own wish to produce new political and economic forms. But in spite of much oratory by fascist sympathizers about the corporative state and its virtues, it does not appear that the new bodies ever had very much to do with running the economic or political life of Italy, which remained firmly under the direction of the fascist bureaucracy.

Other Fascist Domestic Policies

During the thirties, the fascist version of the planned economy made its appearance in Italy. The government issued or withheld permits for factory construction. In agriculture, a concerted effort was launched to make Italy more nearly self-sufficient. This effort was dramatized with the "Battle of Wheat," in which the Italians were treated to contests, prizes, and personal appearances by Mussolini. In 1932, official figures reported that wheat production had risen to a point where it could supply 92 per cent of the nation's normal needs, and the drive was enlarged to include other cereal products. The government subsidized steamship and air lines, encouraged the tourist trade, and protected Italian industries by means of high tariffs on foreign products. Marshes were drained and land was reclaimed; the incidence of malaria was reduced. Enormous sums were spent on public works, and great strides were made in the development of hydroelectric power. The trains, at least so thousands of tourists reported, ran on time; many argued that "there must be something in this man Mussolini." Yet Italy's weakness in essential raw materials proved to be insuperable.

The state reached into the life of the individual at almost every point. Though Italy was overpopulated, and had for decades relieved the situation only by mass emigration, Mussolini made emigration a crime. He encouraged people to marry and have the largest possible families. He reduced their taxes, extended special loans, taxed bachelors, and extended legal equality to illegitimate children. He hoped in this way to swell the ranks of his armies, and to strengthen his claim that Italy must expand abroad. Children, the future party members, were enrolled in a series of youth movements, beginning at the age of six. The textbooks in the schools, the books in the libraries, the professors in the universities, the plays on the stage and the movies on the screen were all made vehicles of fascist propaganda. The secret police, OVRA (from the initials of the Italian words for "Vigilance Organization against Anti-Fascist Crimes"), endeavored to discover and suppress all opposition movements.

In 1929, Mussolini settled the Roman question (see Chapter 13) by entering into the Lateran Treaty with the papacy. This treaty recognized the independent state of Vatican City, and thus restored the temporal power of the pope, though on a greatly reduced scale. Mussolini also recognized Catholicism as the state religion, and promised to halt anti-papal propaganda. He gave up the right to tax contributions to the Church or the salaries of the clergy, and paid $105,000,000 to compensate the papacy for the Italian occupation of papal territories since 1870. A further concordat legalized religious marriages and extended religious instruction in the schools. The Church agreed not to engage in politics in its newspapers and periodicals.

Yet, despite the fact that many church officials viewed the fascist movement sympathetically, difficulties arose after these agreements had been concluded. In an encyclical, Pope Pius XI (1922–1939) indicated his disapproval of Mussolini's "relentless" economic policies and of the corporations as "serving special political aims rather than contributing to the initiation of a better social order." Mussolini now charged that the Church's "Catholic Action" clubs were engaged in politics, and dissolved them. The Pope denied the charges and denounced the Fascist party's practice of monopolizing the time and education of the young. In 1931, however, a further agreement was reached, and the clubs were re-opened.

Fascist Foreign Policy and Its Consequences

Since Mussolini's foreign policies form an integral part of the international relations leading up to World War II, we shall discuss them more fully in Chapter 21. Here we may simply point out that his extreme nationalism, his love of panoply and parades, and his militarism were the logical extensions of his domestic ideas and accomplishments. Mussolini's wish to re-create the glories of ancient Rome impelled him to undertake a policy of adventure in the Mediterranean, which he called *Mare Nostrum* (Latin for "our sea") as a sign that he was the heir to the Caesars. This policy began in 1923, when five Italians working for the League of Nations were assassinated as they marked out the new frontier between Albania and Greece. Mussolini bombarded and occupied the Greek island of Corfu and refused to recognize the League's right to intervene. Only British pressure led to a settlement of the matter.

Later, Mussolini's policy of adventure led him to military aggression in Ethiopia, in Spain, and in Albania (which he dominated during the 1920's and occupied in April, 1939). It drove him into an alliance with his fellow-fascist, Hitler, and led him to voice loud claims against the French for Corsica, Tunisia, Nice, and Savoy. And it alienated Italy from her natural allies, France and Britain. Thus, Mussolini's grandiose fascist ideology first spurred Italy to win self-sufficiency, to rebuild her seaports, and to create a merchant fleet and navy. But the same ideology ultimately separated her from the only powers who might have saved her from the disaster toward which Mussolini was driving.

The German alliance was also responsible for a striking new departure in fascist domestic policy. This was the official adoption of anti-Semitism, which took place in 1938. With only 70,000 Jews, most of whom had long been resident, Italy had no "Jewish problem." Italian Jews were entirely Italian in their language and sentiments, and could be distinguished from other Italians only by their religion. Many of them were prominent in the fascist movement, and many were anti-fascist. There was no widespread sympathy in Italy for the government's adoption of Hitler's racial policies. Yet Hitler's dominating influence led Mussolini to expel Jews from the Fascist party, and to forbit them to teach or attend school, to intermarry with non-Jews, and to obtain new licenses to conduct businesses.

In summing up Mussolini's career, we may turn to a quotation from an article that he himself wrote in 1920 to denounce Lenin. In reading it, substitute Italy for Russia and Mussolini for Lenin, and you will have a clear idea of fascism:

Russia is a state . . . composed of men who exercise power, imposing an iron discipline upon individuals and groups and practicing 'reaction' whenever necessary. . . . In the Russia of Lenin there is only one authority: his authority. There is only one liberty: his liberty. There is only one opinion: his opinion. There is only one law: his law. One might either submit or perish. . . . Russia . . . swallows up and crushes the individual and governs his entire life. . . . Whoever says state necessarily says the army, the police, the judiciary, and the bureaucracy. The Russian state is the state *par excellence.* . . . It has *statized* economic life . . . and formed a huge army of bureaucrats. At the base of the pyramid, . . . there is the proletariat which, as in the old bourgeois regimes, obeys, works, and eats little or allows itself to be massacred. . . .*

*Mussolini on Lenin in 1920, quoted by G. Megaro, *Mussolini in the Making* (Boston, 1938), 325–326.

III   Germany and the Weimar Republic, 1918-1933

Whereas Mussolini took over in Italy less than four years after World War I ended, the Germans experimented with democracy for fifteen years before succumbing to Adolf Hitler. Two days before the armistice of November 11, 1918, the German Social Democrats proclaimed a republic. On July 31, 1919, this republic adopted a constitution drawn up by a national assembly at Weimar; it is therefore known as the "Weimar Republic." The Weimar Constitution was never formally abandoned, but after Hitler became chancellor on January 30, 1933, Germany was in fact a dictatorship.

The history of the Weimar Republic divides itself naturally into three periods: a period of political threats from Left and Right and of mounting economic chaos, from 1918 to the end of 1923; a period of political stability, fulfillment of the Versailles Treaty requirements, and seeming economic prosperity, from 1924 to late 1929; and a period of economic depression and mounting right-wing power, from late 1929 to January, 1933.

The Impact of Defeat

For the overwhelming majority of the German people, defeat in 1918 came as a great shock. The military authorities who ran the German Empire during the last years of the war had failed to report to the public German reverses on the battlefield. No fighting had ever taken place on German soil, and the Germans had got used to thinking of their armies as in firm possession of the foreign territories they had overrun. Now these armies came home. It is often argued that the Allies committed a grave blunder by their failure to march to Berlin and demonstrate to the German people that they had actually been defeated. Schooled in reverence for their military forces, the Germans could not grasp the fact that their armies had lost the war. Moreover, the Allies, under the leadership of Wilson, simply refused to deal with the Supreme Command of the German armies. Field Marshal von Hindenburg, as supreme commander, was never required to hand over his sword to Marshal Foch, or to sign the armistice. Rather, it was the civilian politicians who had to bear the odium. In this way, the Allies unintentionally did the German military caste a great favor.

Before the ink was dry on the armistice agreement, the generals, led by Hindenburg himself, were explaining that the German armies had never really been defeated. This was exactly what the public wanted to believe, and the harsh facts — that Ludendorff and Hindenburg had insisted on surrender because the armies could no longer fight — were never effectively publicized. So the legend that Germany had somehow been "stabbed in the back" by civilians, by liberals, socialists, communists, and Jews, took deep root, and became almost an article of faith among many Germans. This legend was widely disseminated by politicians, especially by those who had a stake in the old Prussian system — the monarchists, agrarians, industrialists, and militarists. All through the period of the Weimar Republic, these groups remained hostile toward it; their hostility ranged from political opposition to conspiracies to overthow the government.

The Allies added another error by including the celebrated "war-guilt" clause in the Treaty of Versailles. The German signatories were obliged to acknowledge what none of them believed, and what subsequent historians would disprove: that Germany alone had been responsible for the outbreak of the war. The war-guilt clause made it harder for the German public to acknowledge defeat and the evils of the past system, to sweep away the militarists, and to bend to the task of creating a virile republic. Instead, it led many Germans to dissipate their energies in denying war-guilt, in hating the enemies who had saddled them with the charge, in bewailing the sell-out of their generals, and in waiting for a chance to show by force that they had been right all the time.

Postwar Political Alignments and Activities

Threats to stability from the Left further strengthened the anti-republican forces of the Right. Responsibility for launching the republic and for preventing disorder fell upon the "majority socialists," made up of Social Democrats and right-wing Independent Socialists, and led by the Social Democrat, Ebert. The Social Democrats were a moderate group. They made no attack on agrarian property, and they allowed the Junkers to maintain intact their estates and the social and political position that went with them. True to their reformist tradition, the Social Democrats concluded with the industrialists collective bargaining agreements that guaranteed the eight-hour day, rather than trying to launch a serious movement for nationalizing German industry.

But to the left of the Social Democrats the left wing of the Independent Socialists and the communist "Spartacists" (named for Spartacus, the leader of a slave revolt in ancient Rome) agitated for a proletarian revolution on the Russian pattern. Unable to operate effectively through soviets, the Left tried to stage a revolution in the winter of 1918–1919, but Ebert called in the army to stop it. The generals used not only regular units but also newly formed volunteer units, or "Free Corps," made up mostly of professional soldiers, who were embittered by Germany's recent military defeat and were violently opposed to democracy.

Now the right wing of the Independent Socialists withdrew from the government, and sole responsibility thenceforth rested with the Social Democrats, who put their man, Noske, into the war ministry. As the civil strife continued, the communists attempted a *coup*, which Ebert, Noske, and the troops put down. Cavalry officers murdered the two chief leaders of the communists after peace had been restored, at the cost of more than a thousand casualties. Meanwhile, in Catholic Bavaria, disorders led to the brief emergence of a Soviet republic, which was liquidated in May, leaving Bavaria the home of a sort of permanent red-scare. The Bavarian local authorities, throughout the entire life of the Weimar Republic, encouraged the intrigues of monarchists, militarists, and nationalists. It was in Bavaria that Free Corps assassinations were planned, and it was there that Hitler got his start.

In this way the forces of the German Right, ostensibly crushed by the war, were given a powerful new lease on life by the Allies. Meantime, Germany still had an army, the *Reichswehr,* limited in size to 100,000 men, consisting chiefly of officer cadres, magnificently trained and able to take over the command of far larger numbers if and when troops became available.

The political constellation of the new Germany did not consist solely of Social Democrats and extremists of Right and Left. The old parties of imperial Germany (see Chapter 14) reappeared, often with new labels. The right wing of the old Liberals now emerged as the People's party, including the more moderate industrialists, with a platform of private property and opposition to socialism. Its leader was Gustav Stresemann. Former Progressives and left-wing Liberals now formed the new Democratic party, a genuine middle-class republican and democratic group, including many of Germany's most distinguished intellectuals. The Catholic Center party reemerged with its name and program unchanged. It accepted the Republic, rejected socialism, and favored social legislation under pressure from its left wing of trade-union members, but it opposed far-reaching reform under pressure from its right wing of aristocrats and industrialists. The Social Democrats, the Democrats, the Center, and the People's party represented those groups which, though not all enthusiastic, were willing to try to make the new state work. On the Right, the former Conservatives reemerged as the National People's party or Nationalists, dominated by the Junkers as before. The Nationalists had the support of some great industrialists, of most of the bureaucrats, and of a substantial section of the lower middle class, which hoped to return to the good old days of the monarchy. The Nationalists did not accept the Republic.

The Weimar Constitution, 1919

When the Germans voted for a national constituent assembly in January, 1919, the parties supporting the Republic won more than 75 per cent of the seats (see table below), with the Social Democrats alone obtaining nearly 40 per cent. The assembly met in Weimar, elected Ebert President of Germany, and formed a government that reluctantly signed the Treaty of Versailles after a delay of some months. The assembly then adopted the new constitution. The new Germany was still a federative state, but the central government had great authority to legislate for the entire country. The president might use armed force to coerce any of the states that failed to obey the constitution or national laws. The cabinet was responsible to the lower house, or *Reichstag,* which was to be chosen by universal suffrage of all citizens (including women) over twenty.

The president, who was to be elected every seven years by the entire people, was given considerable authority. He was empowered to make treaties, appoint and remove the cabinet, command the armed forces and appoint or remove all officers, dissolve the Reichstag, and

German Elections to the Weimar Assembly and Reichstag, 1919–1933

(Number of seats obtained by the major parties, arranged with the Left at the top, the Right at the bottom)

	Jan. 1919	June 1920	May 1924	Dec. 1924	May 1928	Sept. 1930	July 1932	Nov. 1932	Mar. 1933
Communists	—[a]	2	62	45	54	77	89	100	81
Independent Socialists	22	81	—[b]						
Social Democrats	163	112	100	131	152	143	133	121	125
Democrats	74	45	28	32	25	14	4	2	5
Center	71	68	65	69	61	68	75	70	74
People's party	22	62	44	51	45	30	7	11	2
Nationalists	42	66	96	103	78	41	40	51	52
Nazis			38	20	12	107	230	196	288

[a]The Communist party boycotted the elections to the Weimar constituent assembly.
[b]In these and succeeding elections the Independent Socialists had merged with the Social Democrats.

call new elections. Furthermore, he could take any measure he deemed necessary to restore order when it was threatened, and might temporarily suspend the civil liberties that the constitution granted. Yet the Reichstag could order such measures repealed. Inside the cabinet, the chancellor was a real prime minister, with responsibility for planning policy. The constitution also provided for popular initiative. One-tenth of the electorate could bring in a bill or propose an amendment to the constitution. On the economic side, the constitution provided that the government might socialize suitable enterprises, but guaranteed private property and the right of inheritance.

Several other contradictions reflected the conflict of interest between the Social Democrats and the middle-class parties. But the powers of the president and the introduction of proportional representation were perhaps the two chief weaknesses. The powers of the president made dictatorship a real possibility. Proportional representation required that votes be cast for entire party lists of candidates, and thus prevented independent voters from "splitting the ticket," and independent politicians from obtaining office. This system encouraged small splinter parties to multiply.

Right and Left Extremism, 1920–1922

In 1920, pressure from the Right loomed as the most serious threat to the Republic. In March, 1920, a *coup* (in German, *putsch*) drove the government from Berlin for several days. The commander of the Berlin military district, supported by Ludendorff and the Free Corps leaders, hoped to bring to power an East Prussian reactionary official named Kapp. Ebert managed to defeat this "Kapp *putsch*" by calling a general strike that paralyzed Germany. Because the old monarchical judicial system still existed, the men arrested and tried for the Kapp *putsch* all got off with extremely light sentences, whereas left-wingers brought before the courts were very harshly punished.

As an immediate outgrowth of the strike called by the government, a communist revolt took place in the Ruhr. In pursuit of the communists, German troops entered the area, which had been demilitarized by the Versailles Treaty; this action in turn led to French military intervention and a brief occupation of the Ruhr and Frankfurt (April-May, 1920). In the elections of June, 1920, the electorate began to support the extremists of Right and Left. The Democrats and Social Democrats lost strength.

In April, 1921, when the Allies presented the bill for reparations, which totaled 132 billion gold marks, the politicians of the Right favored simple rejection of the terms, while the Weimar parties realistically decided that the threat of invasion made this course impossible. Again, the moderates had to take responsibility for a necessary decision that was sure to prove unpopular, and that they themselves did not approve. The minister for reconstruction, Walter Rathenau, a Democrat and a successful industrialist, hoped that a policy of "fulfillment" might convince the Allies that Germany was acting in good faith, and might in the long run lead to concessions. An intensely patriotic German, Rathenau was also a Jew, and drew the particular venom of the anti-Semitic nationalist orators.

The secret terrorist groups of the Right began a campaign of assassination. They began (August, 1921) by murdering Matthias Erzberger, the Catholic Center politician who had signed the armistice, and a leading moderate. His assassins escaped through Bavaria. When one of them was caught, the courts acquitted him. When the League of Nations awarded to Poland a substantial area of the rich province of Upper Silesia, containing many German inhabitants, the Right grew still angrier. Rathenau was killed in June, 1922, by men who believed in the "stab-in-the-back" theory, and thought that by murdering a Jew they could avenge the "betrayal" of the German army.

Hitler: Early Career

During the months between the assassinations of Erzberger and Rathenau, a new and ominous element had emerged among the wel-

Officer addressing a Berlin crowd during the Kapp *Putsch* of 1920.

ter of right-wing organizations in Bavaria. This was the "National Socialist Party of the German Workers" (called "Nazi" as an abbreviation of the word *National*) led by Adolf Hitler, the son of an obscure, illegitimate Austrian customs official, whose real name had been Schicklgruber. Born in 1889, Hitler early quarreled with his father, and seems always to have felt bitter and frustrated. In 1907, he was rejected by the Vienna Academy of Fine Arts, where he wished to study painting. He became an odd-job man, selling an occasional watercolor, but always hovering on the edge of starvation. It was during these years that his hatred of the Jews began. As we know (see Chapter 14), lower-middle-class Vienna at the time was deeply devoted to its anti-Semitic Mayor Lueger, whom Hitler admired. Because Karl Marx himself had been of Jewish origin and because many Viennese Jews were socialists, Hitler associated socialism with the Jews and lumped both together as somehow responsible for his own personal troubles and for the ills of the world.

Hitler drew support for his anti-Semitism from several nineteenth-century theorists. The French Count Joseph Arthur de Gobineau (1816–1882) had laid the pseudo-scientific foundation for modern theories of "Nordic" and "Aryan" supremacy. One of Gobineau's most influential readers was the great German composer, Richard Wagner (see Chapter 15).

Wagner's son-in-law, the Englishman Houston Stewart Chamberlain (1855–1927), wrote a long and turgid book called *The Foundations of the Nineteenth Century,* which glorified the Germans and assailed the Jews; one section was devoted to a "demonstration" that Christ had not been of Jewish origin. Chamberlain furiously opposed democratic government and, interestingly enough, capitalism. Thus he provided Hitler with a congenial mixture of racism, nationalism, anti-democratic thought, and radicalism.

Hitler came to hate Vienna as a cosmopolitan and Jewish community, and moved to Munich in 1913. In 1914, he enlisted in the German army, and fought through the war as a corporal. He won the iron cross for bravery, but was regarded by his commanding officer as too "hysterical" to deserve a commission. After the war, he went back to Munich, where, as might have been expected, he loathed the new republic and the "Bolsheviks," admired the Free Corps, and decided to become a politician.

Ludendorff had moved to Munich, and had become the center of the reaction. Hitler was employed as a political education officer for the troops. While engaged in this work, he discovered a small political group that called itself the "German Workers' Party." This group combined nationalism and militarism with a generous amount of radicalism. Hitler joined

Watercolor and pencil drawing of a church in Vienna by the young Hitler.

he strengthened himself by founding the SA (*Sturmabteilung,* or storm-troops), brown-shirted units largely recruited from the Free Corps. The storm-troopers wore arm-bands with the swastika emblem, patrolled mass meetings, and performed other services for the leader. Their commander was a notorious pervert, Captain Roehm, who was also political adviser to the commander of the infantry stationed in Bavaria. So the Nazis, like the Italian fascists, could use their sym-pathizers in the army to obtain illegal access to government supplies of arms.

Besides Roehm, Hitler's closest collabo-rators included Hermann Goering, a war-time aviator who had shot down twenty Allied planes, but who found himself restless in peacetime, and took on the job of giving the SA a military polish; Rudolf Hess, his Egyptian-born lieutenant and private sec-retary; and Alfred Rosenberg, a Baltic German distinguished for fanatical hatred of Jews and Bolsheviks, and first editor of the party newspaper.

Hitler and his Nazis were still a very minor political force in 1922 when the middle-of-the-road parties attempted to strengthen the Re-public. After the assassination of Rathenau, Stresemann's People's party moved away from the Nationalists, who were now tainted by mur-der, and entered into a collaboration with Center and Democrats. So tense was the politi-cal situation that the scheduled presidential elections were postponed to 1925.

The Inflation, 1922–1923

Political maneuvers to meet the increasing threat from the Right, however, were largely nullified by the increasing economic problem posed by steadily growing inflation, which in 1922 and 1923 reached unheard-of extremes. Inflation is a complicated economic phenom-enon, and no mere list or description of its causes can really tell the full story. But the single chief cause for the runaway inflation in Germany after 1921 was probably the failure of the German government to levy taxes with which to pay the expenses of the war. The im-

the party in 1919 and soon proved himself to be a far abler politician than any of his col-leagues. He urged intensive propaganda for the union of all Germans in a greater Ger-many, for the elimination of all Jews from political life, a state guarantee of full employ-ment, the confiscation of war profits, the na-tionalization of trusts, the encouragement of small business, and a land-grant to the peas-antry. The seemingly radical character of his program caused many Germans otherwise sympathetic to hesitate before giving Hitler money. As early as 1920, he began to re-assure them by saying he opposed not "in-dustrial capital" but only "Jewish international loan capital."

Hitler was an extremely successful orator, with almost hypnotic gifts of capturing a crowd. By 1921, he had made himself the absolute leader, the *Führer* (compare with *duce*) of the Nazi party, and in the same year perial regime had expected to win, and to make the losers pay Germany's expenses by imposing huge indemnities. So it paid for only about 4 per cent of the war costs by means of taxation. As defeat neared, the government borrowed more and more money from the banks. When the loans came due, the government repaid them with paper money that was not backed by gold. Each time this happened, more paper money was put into circulation, and prices rose; each rise in prices naturally led to a demand for a rise in wages, which had to be paid with more paper money. The inflationary spiral was under way. Instead of cutting purchasing power by imposing heavy taxes, the government permitted buyers to compete with each other for goods in short supply, thus speeding up the whole process of inflation.

Many other forces helped inflation along. For several reasons, Germany lacked gold to back its currency. Germany had to pay in gold for goods bought abroad during the war; the rich sent great sums out of Germany for fear that the government would attach them to pay reparations. Raw materials were in short supply; industry was disorganized; and credit was curtailed. The armies of occupation had to be maintained at German expense, and reparation payments had to be made. Nationalist Germans maintained that these expenses, especially reparations, were the cause of inflation; but, though reparations certainly helped the process, they were by no means solely responsible for it. The total sums involved in reparations were never great enough to affect the German currency until long after the inflation was under way. Indeed, the inflation was partly due to the industrialists' wish to avoid paying reparations, and to clear their own indebtedness by letting the currency become worthless.

The following timetable shows how bad the situation had become by the end of 1922. When the war was over, the mark, normally valued at 4.2 to a dollar, had fallen to 8.4. In January, 1921, it was 45; by December, 160. By September, 1922, it was 1,303, and at the end of the year it was 7,000. In these months, the government begged for a moratorium on reparations payments and for a foreign loan.

But the French were unwilling. They had already paid billions for the rebuilding of areas that the Germans had devastated during the war, and they wanted the Germans to pay the bill. As a guarantee, the French demanded the vitally important German industrial region of the Ruhr. Despite British opposition, the French occupied the Ruhr in January, 1923, after the Germans had defaulted on their reparations payments. The French intended to run the mines and factories for their own benefit, and thus make up for the German failure to pay reparations.

The Germans could not resist with force, but they declared the occupation of the Ruhr illegal, and ordered the inhabitants to embark on passive resistance—to refuse to work the mines and factories or to deliver goods to the French. This order the people of the Ruhr obeyed. Local tension in the occupied area became serious when the French took measures against German police and workers, and when German Free Corps members undertook guerrilla operations against the French.

But the most striking result of the French occupation of the Ruhr was its effect upon the already desperate German economy. Not only

German inflation: a baker uses a cigar box to take home his week's wages, December, 1922.

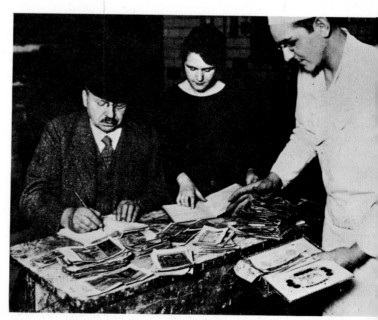

was the rest of Germany cut off from badly needed goods from the occupied area, but the Ruhr inhabitants were idle at the order of the German government, and had to be supported at government expense. The printing press struck off ever-increasing amounts of ever-more-worthless marks. Now the exchange rate went from thousands of marks to the dollar to millions, to billions, and, by December, 1923, well up into the trillions.

The Consequences of Inflation

Such astronomical figures are meaningless except in terms of the personal and social consequences. A student set off one afternoon for the university with his father's check in his pocket to cover a year's tuition, room, board, and entertainment. When he arrived the next morning after an overnight journey, he discovered that the money he got for the check would pay for one short streetcar ride! Lifetime savings were rendered valueless; people trundled wheelbarrows full of marks through the street in an effort to buy a loaf of bread. Those who lived on fixed incomes were utterly ruined, and the savings of the investing middle classes were wiped out. Real property took on fantastic value. The story is told of two brothers, one frugal and the other spendthrift, who had shared equally in a fortune inherited from their father. The frugal one had invested his money; the spendthrift had bought a fine wine-cellar, which he had proceeded to drink up. When inflation came, all the frugal brother's investments would not buy him a haircut, but the spendthrift found that the empty bottles in his cellar were worth billions on billions of marks apiece, and that he was rich again. Under such circumstances, speculation in real estate flourished and skillful speculators made immense fortunes.

For the German worker, inflation did not mean the liquidation of his savings, because he usually had none. It did mean a great drop in the purchasing power of his wages, so great that he could no longer afford the necessities of life. His family suffered from hunger and cold. Since the financial position of the labor unions was destroyed, they were no longer able to help the workers, who gave up their membership in droves. The great industrialists, however, gained from the inflation, in part just because it did cripple the labor unions, but still more because it wiped out their own indebtedness, and enabled them to absorb small competitors and build giant business combines.

Politically, inflation greatly strengthened the extremists of both Right and Left. The middle classes, although pushed down to the economic level of the proletariat, still possessed the middle-class psychology. In status-conscious Germany, they would not adhere to the working-class parties of Social Democrats or Communists. Disillusioned, they would not adhere to the moderate parties that supported the Republic—the People's party, the Center, and the Democrats. So the Nationalists, and Hitler's Nazis above all, reaped a rich harvest. The hardships of the working class led many workers to turn away from the Social Democrats to the Communists. But Soviet Russian restraint on the leaders of the German party prevented any concerted revolutionary drive until the fall of 1923, by which time poor organization and strong governmental repressive measures had doomed their efforts.

With the country seething in crisis, Stresemann as chancellor in the fall of 1923 proclaimed that because of the economic dislocation Germany could not keep up passive resistance in Ruhr. He ordered work to be resumed and reparations to be delivered once again. Political troubles multiplied when the Right refused to accept the new policy. At the height of the agitation in Bavaria, Hitler in early November, 1923, broke into a right-wing political meeting in a Munich beer-hall and announced that the "national revolution" had begun. At gun-point he tried to get other local leaders to support him in a march on Berlin. They agreed, but let him down when they learned that the national government was prepared to put down the Nazis. Although Ludendorff himself joined the Nazi demonstration in Munich, as he had joined the Kapp *putsch* of 1920, troops broke up the demonstration with only a few casualties.

The trials of Ludendorff and Hitler have become famous as the most striking example of the Weimar judicial system's partiality for men of the Right. Ludendorff was respectfully acquitted. Hitler was allowed to use the dock as a propaganda platform for his ideas and was sentenced to the minimum term for high treason: five years. He actually spent eight months in comfortable confinement, during which time he wrote large portions of *Mein Kampf* (*My Battle*), the famous bible of the Nazis.

The End of Inflation, 1923–1924

Communist disorders and the Nazi beer-hall *putsch* marked the last phase of the infla-

tion period. A couple of weeks before Hitler's effort, the government had given extraordinary financial powers to Hans Luther, minister of finance, and Hjalmar Schacht, banker and fiscal expert. All printing of the old currency was stopped. A new bank was opened to issue new marks, which were simply assigned the value of the pre-war mark (4.2 to the dollar). The new currency was backed not by gold but by an imaginary "mortgage" on all Germany's agricultural and industrial wealth, a psychological gesture that won public confidence. It took one trillion of the old marks to equal one of the new. Simultaneously, rigorous economy was put into effect in every branch of the government, and taxes were increased. The public protested loudly, but the measures remained in force until they had accomplished the intended effect. The cure for inflation produced serious hardships too. Prices fell, and

Ludendorff (center) and Hitler at their trial for involvement in the beer-hall putsch of 1923; second from the right is Captain Roehm, head of the S.A. and casualty of the blood purge of 1934 (see p. 731).

over-expanded businesses collapsed. Unemployment rose sharply, wages stayed low, and workers labored long hours.

During 1924, the Allies contributed to the ending of the crisis in Germany by formulating the Dawes Plan, named for Charles G. Dawes, the American financier and later vice-president under Calvin Coolidge. The plan recommended the evacuation of the Ruhr by the French, the establishment of a special bank to receive reparations payments, gradually rising annual payments for the first five years, and an international loan to finance the German deliveries in the first year. The Nationalists violently attacked the proposals as a sinister scheme to enslave Germany to foreign masters. In the Reichstag elections of May, 1924, the Nationalists scored impressive gains, as did the Nazis and the Communists, while the moderate parties all suffered (see table on p. 719). But a coalition managed to win acceptance of the Dawes Plan in August, 1924, by the device of promising the Nationalists representation in the cabinet. When new elections were held in December, the Nazis and Communists suffered losses, and the Social Democrats and moderates gained. A Center-People's party-Nationalist coalition took office early in 1925 and governed Germany. One wing of the Nationalists, however, led by the enormously rich industrial press and film magnate, Alfred Hugenberg, who had made a fortune during the inflation, opposed all cooperation with the Republic. Though Germany had moved appreciably to the Right, foreign policy remained in the conciliatory hands of Stresemann, who remained foreign minister through all governments between November, 1923, and his death in October, 1929.

Recovery at Home, 1924–1929

During these less-troubled middle years of the Weimar Republic, economic recovery proceeded steadily, until, in 1929, German industrial output exceeded that of 1913. First-rate German equipment, coupled with superb technical skill and a systematic adoption of American methods of mass production, created a highly efficient industrial machine. This "rationalization" of industry increased production, but brought with it over-borrowing and some unemployment. "Vertical trusts," which brought together in one great corporation all the parts of an industrial process from coal- and iron-mining to the output of the finished product; and cartels, associations of independent enterprises that controlled sales and prices for their own benefit, were characteristic of the German system. The emphasis was always on heavy industry, which meant that continued prosperity would depend upon a big armaments program.

All through this period, reparations were paid faithfully, with no damage to the German economy. Indeed, more money flowed into Germany from foreign, especially American, investment than flowed out from reparations. Dependence on foreign capital, however, which would cease to flow in time of depression, made German prosperity artificial.

In 1925, after President Ebert died, a presidential election was held in which three candidates competed. The Catholic Center, the Democrats, and the Social Democrats supported the Center leader, Wilhelm Marx. The Nationalists, People's party, and other right-wingers joined in support of Field Marshal Hindenburg, then seventy-seven years old. The Communists ran their own candidate, and thus contributed to the election of Hindenburg, who won by a small plurality. Abroad, the choice of a man so intimately connected with imperial militarist Germany created dismay; but until 1930 Hindenburg acted entirely in accordance with the constitution, to the distress of most of the nationalist groups. The domestic issues of this period all aroused great heat, but were settled by democratic process. In the elections of 1928, the Social Democrats were returned to power, and the Nationalists and Nazis were hard hit (see table on p. 719). All in all, prosperity encouraged moderation and a return to support of the republic.

'Fulfillment" Abroad, 1925–1930

In foreign affairs, this middle period of the Weimar Republic was one of gradually increasing German participation in the system of collective security. Thus in 1925 Germany signed the Locarno treaties, which took the French armies out of the Rhineland, substituted a neutral zone and a frontier guaranteed by Britain and Italy, and set up machinery for the arbitration of disputes between Germany and her neighbors. These treaties did not, however, guarantee to Poland and Czechoslovakia the eastern frontiers of Germany. In 1926, Germany was admitted to the League of Nations, with a permanent seat on the League's Council. In 1929, Germany accepted the Kellogg-Briand Pact, which outlawed aggressive war (see Chapter 21).

In 1929, a new reparations plan named after the American, Owen D. Young, chairman of the committee that drew it up, substantially reduced the total originally demanded by the Allies. The Young Plan also established lower rates of payments that those under the Dawes Plan, and allowed the Germans a greater part in their collection. Before June, 1930, the Rhineland was evacuated by the Allies, four years ahead of the date set by the Treaty of Versailles. Many of these gains for Germany were accomplished only with so much preliminary difficulty that they were robbed of their sweetness, and the German Nationalists, Nazis, and Communists thoroughly opposed them all. Yet German foreign policy was generally calculated to reassure the rest of the world.

The Impact
of the Depression, 1929–1931

But even before the last achievements of this "period of fulfillment," the depression had begun to knock the foundations out from under prosperity and moderation. Unemploy-ment rose during 1929. After the American stock-market crash in October, foreign credits, on which prosperity had so largely depended, were no longer available to Germany. Short-term loans were not renewed, or else were recalled. Tariff barriers were hurting foreign trade. Hunger and want reappeared.

Although unemployment insurance cushioned the first shock for the workers, the lower middle classes, painfully recovering from the inflation, had no such barrier between them and destitution. Their desperation helped Hitler, whose fortunes during the years of fulfillment had fallen very low, although he had attracted a number of new followers who were later to be important in his movement.

Paul Joseph Goebbels, publicist and journalist, proved to be a master of mob psychology and an effective orator. Heinrich Himmler, a mild-mannered but ruthless chicken-farmer, took charge of the élite black-shirted SS (Schutzstaffel defense corps), which was formed as a special guard of honor. The SS, with a higher standing than the SA, and with special membership requirements of "racial purity," was later to become the nucleus for the Gestapo, or secret police. Hitler also recruited Joachim von Ribbentrop, champagne salesman and party ambassador to the German upper classes.

The government fell in 1930 over a disagreement on a question of unemployment insurance benefits. Hindenburg appointed to the chancellorship Heinrich Bruening, a member of the Catholic Center party. Bruening would have liked to support parliamentary institutions and to continue Stresemann's policies of fulfillment, but he was to find it impossible to do either. President Hindenburg, now eighty-two, had fallen more and more under the influence of General Kurt von Schleicher, an ambitious political soldier who had intrigued himself into the President's favor.

Hindenburg was now itching to rule by decree, as the constitution authorized him to do in an emergency. By failing to pass Bruening's economic program, the Reichstag gave

Hindenburg the opportunity he wanted. Bruening agreed, partly because he felt that a genuine emergency existed, but partly because he was determined to keep his bitter political rivals, the Social Democrats, from replacing him in office.

A presidential decree proclaimed the new budget. When the Reichstag protested, Hindenburg dissolved it and called new elections (September, 1930). Nazis and Communists fought in the streets, but both gained greatly at the expense of the moderates (see table on p. 719). The Nazis' Reichstag representation rose from 12 to 107, and the Communists' from 54 to 77. Bruening had to carry on against the wishes of the electorate; supported only by Hindenburg, he too now turned authoritarian.

In order to avoid a new government in which Nazis would participate, the Social Democrats decided to support Bruening. When the Reichstag met, Nazis and Communists created disorder on the floor, but voted together in opposition to government measures. These measures passed only because the Social Democrats voted for them. In 1931, Bruening made an effort to arrange an Austro-German customs union which would coordinate the tariff policies of the two countries, and help them both fight the depression without affecting their political sovereignty. Whether such an arrangement between two countries that were both suffering from unemployment would actually have succeeded cannot be decided; nor can we be sure whether the impulse for Germany and Austria to unite politically might not have proved overpoweringly strong. At any rate, the whole project raised in the minds of the Allies, especially the French, the specter of a "greater Germany," and the scheme was vetoed by the World Court.

The collapse of the great Austrian bank, the *Kredit-Anstalt*, further deepened the depression, despite a British loan to Austria in 1931, and despite the one-year moratorium on reparations payments procured for Germany by the American President, Herbert Hoover.

The Republic in Danger, 1931–1932

Now Nazis, Nationalists, the veterans organization of the Steel Helmets (*Stahlhelm*), the Junkers' Agrarian League, industrialists, and representatives of the former princely houses formed a coalition against Bruening. This coalition had great financial resources and a mass backing, chiefly Nazi. It had its private armies in the SA, in the *Stahlhelm*, and in other semi-military organizations. Because the Left was split, and the Communists in effect acted as political allies of the Right, nothing stood between this new right-wing coalition and a political victory except the person of Hindenburg, who controlled the army, and by virtue of the Weimar Constitution was able to keep Bruening in office. Early in 1932, the great industrialist, Fritz Thyssen, invited Hitler to address a meeting of coal and steel magnates. Hitler won their financial support by convincing them that if he came to power he would be their man. Though some of Hitler's followers were now impatient for a new *putsch*, he curbed them, believing that the Nazis could come to power legally.

In the presidential elections of March, 1932, Hitler ran as the candidate of the Nazis, and Hindenburg as the candidate of the Center, Social Democrats, and other moderate parties. The Nationalists nominated a *Stahlhelm* man, and the Communists of course ran their own candidate. Hitler polled 11,338,571 votes, and Hindenburg polled 18,661,736, only four-tenths of 1 per cent short of the required majority. In the run-off election, the Nationalists backed Hitler, whose total rose to 13,400,000 as against Hindenburg's 19,-360,000. The eighty-four-year-old Marshal, re-elected as the candidate of the moderates, was, however, no longer a moderate himself, but the tool of the Junkers and the military.

Although the government now ordered the Nazi SA and SS disbanded, the decree was not enforced. In April, 1932, the Nazis scored impressive victories in local elections, especially in all-important Prussia. Bruening was unable to procure in time either an Allied promise to extend the moratorium on reparations payments or permission for Germany to have equality in armaments with France. Schleicher, who was now deeply involved in intrigue against Bruening, worked on Hindenburg to demand Bruening's resignation. This Hindenburg did on May 29, 1932, the first time a president had dismissed a chancellor simply because he had lost personal confidence in him. Bruening's successor was Franz von Papen, a rich Catholic nobleman and a member of the extreme right wing of the Center, who installed a cabinet composed of nobles. Papen was Schleicher's man—or so Schleicher thought.

The Center disavowed Papen, who had the real support of no political party or group, but whom the Nazis temporarily tolerated because he agreed to remove the ban on the SA and SS. In foreign policy, Papen succeeded where Bruening had failed, for the Allies scrapped the Young Plan and required Germany to pay only three billion gold marks into a fund earmarked for general European reconstruction. Instead of being bound for many decades to pay reparations, Germany was now freed from all such obligations.

On July 31, 1932, new elections for the Reichstag took place, called by Papen on the theory that the Nazis had passed their peak, that their vote would decrease, and that they would then be chastened and would cooperate in the government. But the Nazis won 230 seats and became the biggest single party in the Reichstag; the Communists gained also, chiefly at the expense of the Social Democrats. The Democrats and the People's party almost disappeared, while the Nationalists suffered, and the Center scored a slight gain (see table on p. 719). Papen had failed. He now wanted to take some Nazis into the government, but the Nazis demanded the chancellorship, which Hindenburg was determined not to hand over to Hitler. Papen now planned to dissolve the Reichstag and to call new elections. By repeating this process, he hoped to wear down Hitler's strength each time, until he brought

Hitler to support him and accept a subordinate place. As Papen put pressure on the industrialists who had been supporting Hitler, the Nazi funds began to dry up, leaving Hitler seriously embarrassed. The elections of November 6, 1932, bore out Papen's expections. The Nazis fell off from 230 seats to 196; and, although the Communists gained substantially and ominously, Papen too won some support (see table on p. 719). Now the Nazis were really desperate. Goebbels wrote in his diary:

Received a report on the financial situation of the Berlin organization. It is hopeless. Nothing but debts and obligations, together with the complete impossibility of obtaining any reasonable sum of money after this defeat.[*]

[*]Quoted by S. William Halperin, *Germany Tried Democracy* (New York, 1946), 511–512.

Berliners hailing Hitler on his being named Chancellor, January 30, 1933.

Hitler:
Rise to Power, 1932–1933

Had Papen been permitted to continue his tactics, it is possible that Hitler might have been kept from power. But Papen resigned as a matter of form because he could not count on majority support in the Reichstag. Angry with Schleicher and sorry to lose Papen, Hindenburg forced Schleicher himself to take the office on December 3, 1932. Now the back-stairs general was chancellor, but he had no political support whatever, and had alienated even Hindenburg. He lasted in office only about eight weeks before Hitler was appointed chancellor.

Schleicher did score a great diplomatic success by winning a five-power declaration that recognized in principle Germany's right to parity in armaments. At home, he made every effort to appeal to all shades of opinion, except the extreme Left. But this attempt in itself alienated the implacably anti-labor industrialists and the Junkers. The tortuous Papen, eager for revenge, intrigued with these enemies of Schleicher. Early in January, 1933,

Papen met Hitler at the house of the Cologne banker, Baron Kurt von Schroeder. The industrialists, who had temporarily abandoned Hitler, now agreed to pay the Nazis' debts. Hitler, in turn, no longer insisted on the chancellorship for himself, thus leading Papen to hope that he would come back into office with Hitler's backing. Hindenburg, too, was enlisted. When the President refused to give Schleicher the authority to dissolve the Reichstag at its first new session, which would surely have voted him down, Schleicher had no choice; he was forced to resign (January, 28, 1933).

But Hitler had now raised the ante, and demanded the chancellorship for himself. Papen consented, provided Hitler undertook to govern in strict accordance with parliamentary procedure. Papen was to be vice-chancellor, and still thought he could dominate the government, since only three of its eleven ministers would be Nazis. He therefore persuaded Hindenburg to accept Hitler as chancellor. But Papen underestimated Hitler. Though Hitler swore to Hindenburg that he would maintain the constitution, he had no intention of keeping his oath. The Weimer Republic was doomed from the moment Hitler came to the chancellor's office on January 30, 1933.

IV   Germany under Hitler, 1933 — 1939

The Nazi Dictatorship

Hitler's first weeks in power were devoted to transforming his chancellorship into a dictatorship. He dissolved the Reichstag and called for new elections. During the campaign, opponents of the Nazis were intimidated by violence and threats, and were denied radio time and free use of the press. Yet a Nazi victory in the election still did not seem sure. On February 27, 1933, fire opportunely broke out in the Reichstag building. Hitler pointed to it as a sample of the disor-

ders that the Communists were likely to instigate. Hindenburg issued emergency decrees suspending free speech and the free press, and thus made it even easier for the storm-troops to use terror against their political opponents. It is now generally supposed that the Nazis themselves set the Reichstag fire, but they convicted and condemned to death a Dutch communist named Vanderlubbe, who apparently was mentally deficient.

Despite their campaign, the Nazis won only 44 per cent of the votes, which gave them 288 seats in the Reichstag (see table on p. 719). Using the SA as a constant threat, Hitler bul-lied the Reichstag. Except for 94 Social Democrats (the Communists were denied their seats), all members voted for the famous Enabling Act (March 23, 1933). This act conferred dictatorial powers upon the government, and suspended the constitution. The act was renewed in 1937 by a subservient Reichstag, and again in 1943.

Now Hitler could act as he chose, unimpeded by the laws. He instituted a Ministry of Propaganda under Goebbels. He stripped the state governments of the powers they had had under Weimar, and made Germany a strongly centralized state (April, 1933) by appointing governors from Berlin who had the power to override the state legislatures. When President Hindenburg died in August, 1934, at the age of eighty-seven, Hitler assumed the office of president as well as that of chancellor, but he preferred to use the title *Der Führer* (the leader) to describe himself. This new move was approved by a plebiscite, in which Hitler obtained 88 per cent of the votes cast.

Political parties which opposed Hitler were forced to dissolve. The government banned Communists and Socialists (May, 1933); the Nationalists dissolved themselves (June, 1933); the government put an end to the Catholic parties (July, 1933), and all monarchist groups (February, 1934). The *Stahlhelm* was incorporated into the Nazi party (June, 1933) and was deprived of its identity (November, 1935). As early as July, 1933, the Nazis were declared to be the only legal political party in Germany.

The appeal of the Nazis to the German people lay in part in their denunciation and repudiation of the "disorderly" parliamentary system. A strong man who got things done struck a responsive chord in the public. In the last elections, November, 1933, there were no opposition candidates, 92 per cent of the electorate voted Nazi, and there were only two non-Nazi deputies in the chamber of 661. As in fascist Italy and communist Russia, youth groups fed the party, which soon had a powerful regional organization all over Germany and among Germans abroad.

Within the Nazi party itself, however, a difficult situation was created by those who had believed Hitler's more radical pronouncements on social and economic questions. Many of these Nazis were concentrated in the SA, whose members, most of them from the lower classes, were also distressed by the way in which Hitler had treated their organization. The SA had made possible his rise to power, but now it was rather an embarrassment to him, no longer quite respectable, and certainly not in favor, as were the SS and especially the army.

On June 30, 1934, Hitler ordered and personally participated in the celebrated "blood purge," or, as he himself called it, "the night of the long knives." Roehm himself, founder and leader of the SA, was shot, and so were, by Hitler's own admission, seventy-three others, including Schleicher and his wife. Other estimates of the casualties run as high as 1,000. In any case, after June, 1934, there was no further opposition to Hitler.

Racism and Political Theory

Within a few days after the passage of the enabling law, Hitler struck the first of his many blows against the Jews, whom he had so long denounced. In a country of approximately 60,000,000 people, the Jews counted less than 1 per cent of the population (something under 600,000), not including part-Jewish Germans. The Jews had become leading members of the professions and the arts, and had made outstanding contributions to German culture. Since most Jews were assimilated and patriotic Germans, many of them would probably have become Nazis if they had been permitted. They would have supported Hitler in everything but anti-Semitism. Instead, anti-Semitic doctrines required their ruthless elimination.

The businesses and professions of the Jews were boycotted; they were forbidden to hold office (April, 1933), although a temporary exception was made for veterans of World War I. In the "Nuremberg laws" of September 15, 1935, a Jew was defined as any person with one Jewish grandparent. All such persons were deprived of German citizenship. Inter-marriage between Jews and non-Jews was forbidden as "racial pollution." Jews might not fly the national flag, write or publish, act on stage or screen, teach in any educational institution, work in a bank, exhibit paintings or give concerts, work in a hospital, enter any of the government's labor or professional bodies, or sell books or antiques. They were not eligible for unemployment insurance or charity; and the names of Jews who had died for Germany in World War I were erased from war memorials. Many towns and villages, under the spur of government-sponsored propaganda, refused to permit Jews to live inside their precincts.

In November, 1938, a Jewish boy of seventeen, driven to desperation by the persecution of his parents, shot and killed a secretary of the German embassy in Paris. Two days later, organized German mobs looted and pillaged Jewish shops all over Germany, burned and dynamited synagogues, and invaded Jewish homes to beat up the occupants and steal their

"Jews not wanted in this place"—sign in a German town, 1935.

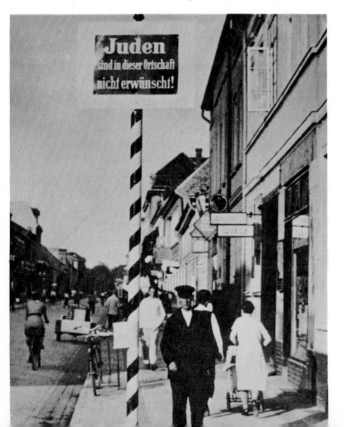

possessions. The state then compelled the Jews to restore the damaged properties and to pay an enormous fine. Jews were forced to take special names, to wear yellow stars of David, and to belong to a Reich "Union of Jews." Although some Jews managed to leave Germany, it was usually at the cost of abandoning all their possessions; yet they were the lucky ones. All these measures and many others (for example, "cows purchased from Jews may not be serviced by the communal bull") designed to drive the Jews into ghettos and starvation were but the prelude to the physical extermination in gas-ovens to which they were to be subjected by the Nazis during World War II. What distressed many horrified western observers almost more than the actions themselves was the failure of any substantial number of highly educated and "civilized" non-Jewish Germans to register any form of protest.

Enthusiasm for "racial purity" had its positive as well as its negative side. The blond, blue-eyed ideal "Nordic types" were urged to mate with each other early and to have many children. German motherhood was made the object of paeans of praise. And, to keep the race pure, sterilization was introduced, supposedly for the prevention of the inheritance of disease. The functioning of such a law depended upon the condition of the medical and legal professions, which soon fell into the hands of charlatans. Medical experimentation of horrifying cruelty and of no conceivable scientific value was practiced during the war on human beings of "inferior" races—Jews, Poles and other Slavs, and gypsies. These practices were the direct outcome of Nazi pseudo-scientific "eugenic" legislation.

The Bases of Foreign Policy

In the field of foreign affairs, German racism justified the incorporation of all territory inhabited by Germans, including Austria, the western borderlands (Sudetenland) of Czechoslovakia, Danzig, the Polish corridor, and other less important places. And the doctrine of "living-space" (Lebensraum) justified the incorporation of non-German areas—the rest of Czechoslovakia, Poland, and all southeastern Europe, as well as large areas of Russia. Hitler felt that what the Germans needed, they were entitled to take, since they were a superior people.

Some German intellectuals looked back with longing upon the Holy Roman Empire of the Middle Ages, the first *Reich*. Now that the war had ended the second *Reich* of William II, they hoped to behold a third one, incorporating the old territories, no matter who now lived in them. This is the meaning of Hitler's use of the term "Third Reich," to describe the Nazi state, which he proclaimed would last a thousand years. A "scientific" basis for the *Lebensraum* theory was supplied by the teachers of "geopolitics," chief among whom was Karl Haushofer, professor of geography, retired major-general, and teacher of Hitler's close friend, Rudolf Hess. Haushofer declared that Britain and France were decadent, that small powers must disappear (except for Switzerland and the Vatican City), that Germany, preserving its master-race pure, must possess the will to power, and expand ruthlessly, occupying the "heart land" of Eurasia, from which the world could be dominated.

Another school of thought in Germany argued that Germany's future lay in an alliance with Russia in which Russia's inexhaustible manpower would be joined with Germany's industrial output and military techniques for purposes of conquest. This notion had been strong in German army circles in tsarist days and continued to exist after the Bolshevik Revolution, especially after the Treaty of Rapallo (Chapter 18) concluded between Germany and the Soviet Union in 1922. Outside the army, other German nationalists, who were just as anti-liberal and anti-parliamentarian as Stalin, retained the Bismarckian attitudes of hostility to the West and to Poland and of friendship toward Russia, whatever the color of her regime. Moreover, many German Marxists were highly nationalistic. Indeed, Hitler's "national socialism" succeeded in part because he knew how to use old Marxist clichés in presenting an essentially nationalist program.

Legal and Economic Policies

Hitler entirely revamped the judicial system of Germany, abandoning traditional legal principles and substituting "folk" justice, which, Hitler said, subordinated the individual totally to the people (*volk*). So mystic a doctrine meant in practice that whatever Hitler wanted was German law. People's Courts (May, 1934) were established to try all cases of treason, a crime that was now extended to include a wide variety of lesser offenses, such as circulating banned newspapers. Hitler appointed all the judges of the People's Courts. Concentration camps were established for enemies of the regime, who could be immured or executed by the headsman's axe, without appeal. In fact, they could not even have defense counsel of their choice, but had to accept counsel approved by the courts. The Gestapo (*Geheime Staatspolizei,* Secret State Police) was established in April, 1933, in Prussia, and a year later was extended to all of Germany. It had a free hand in opening private correspondence, tapping wires, and spying on individual citizens.

All economic life was brought under the regime. In agriculture, the Nazis aimed at the largest possible measure of self-sufficiency, and, of course, at political control over the peasantry. The Junkers were protected, and no effort was made to divide their vast estates. In 1933, a special law protected farms of less than 312 acres against forced sale and attachment for debt, an act that won the small farmer to Hitler. But the government determined the production required of farms, and fixed farm prices and wages, and fees for distributing farm products. Unused land was put under cultivation, and private citizens were required to grow vegetables in greenhouses. This was part of Hitler's preparation for war. By 1937, Germany was 83 per cent self-sufficient in agriculture, a rise of 8 per cent since the Nazis had come to power. Fats and coffee were perhaps the two most important deficiencies remaining.

In industry, taking a leaf out of Stalin's book, Hitler proclaimed a Four-Year Plan in 1933 and a second one in 1936. The first was aimed chiefly at economic recovery and at ending unemployment. Labor camps for men and women helped decrease unemployment, as did rearmament and a program of public works. By 1936, unemployment had dropped from about 7,000,000 to less than 1,500,000. The second plan was designed to prepare for war, and especially to make Germany blockade-proof. Output of raw materials was increased and the materials were distributed first and foremost to armament and other war industries; labor was allocated with similar ends in view; and prices and foreign exchange were controlled. Goering was made boss of the plan.

Under his direction fell the new Goering Iron Works, designed to make up for the loss of the rich iron resources of Alsace-Lorraine, which had yielded three quarters of Germany's supply. To this end, low-content ores were worked, and the government absorbed the higher costs. Output went up in two years more than 50 per cent. Germany's gifted scientists were enlisted to make up for other deficiencies by devising successful but expensive synthetic products. Important in this field were the distillation of motor fuel from coal, and the production of synthetic rubber. The state also built strategic highways, the *Autobahnen*, excellent modern expressways.

The Nazis abolished all labor unions in 1933, and employers' associations in 1934. To replace them, a "Labor Front" was established under Dr. Robert Ley, including all wage-earners, salaried persons, professionals, and employers. Strikes and lockouts had been forbidden. Workers were assured of jobs so long as they quietly accepted the entire system. The Labor Front in one of its aspects was a huge spy organization constantly on the alert for anti-Nazis in the factories; it could reduce their pay, fire them, or put them in jail. An adjunct to the Labor Front was the "Strength through Joy" organization, which provided paid vacation trips for German workers to resorts or tourist centers, and which sponsored concerts and other entertainments.

As the second Four-Year Plan went into effect, the worker found himself increasingly immobile. He had a work-book, detailing his past training and positions held, and he could not get a new job unless the state decided it would be more suitable for him. All graduates of secondary schools had to register with the employment authorities. Men and women of working age were liable to conscription for labor. Just before the war, all agricultural and mining and certain industrial workers were frozen in their jobs. On the side of capital, the big cartel became the all-pervasive feature of German industrial organization—a system of profitable monopoly under state control. The interlocking directorate made the system even tighter than it looked. Six industrialists, for example, held among them one hundred and twenty-seven directorates in the largest corporations, were presidents of thirty-two, and all held government posts besides. The Minister of Economics sat at the top of the economic pyramid, authorizing plant expansion, controlling imports and exports, fixing prices, establishing costs, and allocating raw materials.

Religion and Culture

The Christian churches, both Protestant and Catholic, posed a problem for the Nazis. Extremists among Hitler's followers had always been in favor of a return to paganism and the old German gods celebrated by Wagner's operas. Hitler himself, born a Catholic, had once declared that Germany was his only God. Yet office brought sobering second thoughts, since Germany was after all nominally a Christian country. In the hope of avoiding state domination, the Lutheran ministry in 1933 organized a national synod, which the Nazis almost immediately took over by appointing their own bishop. The efforts of extreme Nazis to purge the Bible and to abandon the crucifix led to discontent. The dissidents, led by Pastor Martin Niemoeller, objected to Nazi theology and efforts at control. But Niemoeller also pledged his loyalty to Hitler, made no objections to Nazi racism, and went to a con-

Franco inspecting trenches on the Madrid front in the Spanish Civil War, 1937.

partly by the failure to solve grievous economic problems, especially after the great worldwide depression of 1929; and partly by a popular fear of Bolshevism, sometimes quite out of proportion to any serious threat, but skillfully played upon by unscrupulous leaders. Perhaps as important as all the other factors put together was the initial impression created by the successes of Mussolini and Hitler. The way to get ahead in the world, at least after 1935, seemed to be to put on a uniform, proclaim a doctrine of extreme nationalism, and launch a war of nerves against your neighbors by loudly voicing your claims, and by threatening to make them good by violence.

After the depression, the economic pressures exerted by Germany, whose industrial economy complemented the agrarian economy of these states, enabled her to dominate their foreign trade, especially in the Balkan area. To show how these factors operated, we shall now examine three case-histories—Austria, Hungary, and Yugoslavia.

Austria

The Austria that was left at the end of World War I had an almost purely German population of about 8,000,000, about 2,000,000 of whom lived in the former imperial capital of Vienna. Long the great market for an enormous hinterland and the supplier of industrial finished goods to the agricultural provinces, Vienna was now cut off from its former territories by political boundaries and tariff walls. Between 1922 and 1925, Austrian finances were under direct League of Nations supervision; a League loan and reconstruction policies brought a measure of recovery. But what might have represented one road to economic salvation—union of Austria with Germany—though voted by the assembly of the new Austrian republic in March, 1919, was forbidden on political grounds by the Allies in the Treaty of St. Germain (September, 1919). These two problems, economic survival and union with Germany, were complicated by the continuation in even more violent form of the basic political struggle of imperial Austria: Social Democrats against Christian Socialists (see Chapter 14). The Social Democrats were a gradualist reformist, but Marxist, party with strong urban support, especially in Vienna itself. The Christian Socialists were a conservative clerical party with a mass following in the countryside and among the urban lower middle classes, and counted many priests among their leaders.

In the mid-twenties, the two hostile parties, usually almost evenly balanced in the parliament, organized private armies: the Christian Socialists, the *Heimwehr* (home guard), and the Social Democrats, the *Schutzbund* (defense league). The Social Democrats governed Vienna, introducing measures for relief and for workers' housing, paid for by taxes on the rich: a program the Christian Socialists opposed. After 1930, when a treaty was signed with Italy, Mussolini more or less overtly supported the Christian Socialists, who grew more and more fascistic in their outlook. The failure of Bruening's plan for a customs union with Germany and the related collapse of the Vienna *Kredit-Anstalt* bank (see p. 728) increased tension in 1931, and in September, 1931, the *Heimwehr* tried its first fascist *coup,* which failed. Efforts in 1932 to organize a Danubian economic co-operation scheme—an alternative to Austrian union with Germany, and favored by France—were rendered futile by Italian and German opposition. After Hitler came to power in early 1933, many Christian Socialists became openly Nazi.

The Christian Socialist chancellor, Engelbert Dollfuss, however, strove to curb the Nazis. To this end he suspended parliamentary government in March, 1933, and in effect ended parliamentary democracy. He forbade the wearing of uniforms by political groups, and tried to expel Nazi agitators. In retaliation, Hitler made it prohibitively expensive for German tourists to visit Austria, and thus destroyed one of the most lucrative sources of Austrian income. In the face of Nazi-inspired disorder, Dollfuss banned the Nazi party (June, 1933). But, instead of burying the hatchet and uniting with the Social Democrats against Hitler, Dollfuss pursued them too. He banned all parties except his own "Fatherland Front," a union of all right-wing groups except the Nazis, and raided Social Democratic headquarters, precipitating a workers' riot. The government then bombarded with artillery the workers' new apartment houses, in which the Social Democratic leaders had taken refuge (February, 1934), breaking the Social Democratic Party, but alienating the workmen of Vienna, and uniting them in opposition to the regime. Dollfuss had to depend more and more upon Italy

to support him against the threat from Hitler. He established himself as a fascist dictator (April 30, 1934), but the Nazis assassinated him in July. Only Italian troop concentrations on the frontier prevented Hitler from taking Austria.

Dollfuss' successor, Schuschnigg, was committed to the same policies. But Mussolini now needed Hitler's support for Italian aggression in the Mediterranean. Schuschnigg made plans looking toward a Habsburg restoration, tried to concentrate armed power in his own hands rather than those of the *Heimwehr,* and strove to come to an understanding with France and her allies to replace the one with Italy. But he failed in the face of German aggression. In February and March, 1938, Hitler increased the pressure on Schuschnigg, who was subjected to the first of the famous

Poster of Chancellor Dollfuss and representative Austrians defaced by Nazis, 1933.

series of grim interviews between Hitler and statesmen of smaller countries. The Fuehrer demanded and obtained privileges for the Nazis in Austria. When the predictable Nazi disorders broke out, Schuschnigg desperately tried to win working-class support, but it was too late.

When Schuschnigg announced that he intended to hold a plebiscite on the question of Austrian independence, Hitler marched in, installed a Nazi chancellor, put Schuschnigg in jail, and began the extension of the Nazi system to Austria. In April, 1938, he held a plebiscite on the question of Austrian union with Germany and obtained a 99.75 per cent vote of *ja*. Mussolini had to bow in 1938 to what he had prevented in 1934, and Austria, increasingly fascist since 1930, became a mere province of Nazi Germany.

Hungary

On October 31, 1918, eleven days before the Armistice, Count Michael Karolyi became prime minister of Hungary, after the country had already severed its ties with Austria. One of the richest of the great magnates, Karolyi was also a democrat, and imbued with Wilsonian ideas. He proved his own sincerity as a social reformer by handing over the 50,000 acres of his own estate to be divided among the peasants, and by preparing a land-reform law. He made every effort to reach a compromise with the national minorities, but understandably enough they would no longer trust any Magyar. The French commander of the Allied armies did not assist Karolyi, and demanded that the Hungarians withdraw from Slovakia. In March, 1919, Karolyi resigned, in protest over the loss of Transylvania.

Thwarted nationalism now combined with a growing radicalism, stimulated by the news of Bolshevik activities in Russia brought by returning Hungarian prisoners of war. A left-wing government took over, more and more dominated by Bela Kun, Lenin's agent, a Hungarian-born Jew. He put through revolutionary nationalization decrees, and installed a soviet political system by bloody-handed ter-

rorist methods, especially in the countryside, where the peasants resented the delay in giving them the land. The Allies could not tolerate a Bolshevik régime in Hungary. The Rumanians invaded and drove Kun out; during 1919 and part of 1920 they occupied the country, and stripped it of everything they could move. Meanwhile, under French protection, a counter-revolutionary government was formed, and returned to Budapest, where Admiral Horthy, a member of the gentry, became regent and chief of state (March 1, 1920). Hungary was now a kingdom without a king, Horthy an admiral without a fleet. Twice the Habsburg King Charles tried to regain the throne, but was frustrated largely because Hungary's neighbors objected. The new counter-revolution gave free rein to a "White Terror" directed largely against the Jews but also against Magyar workers and peasants.

The Treaty of Trianon (June, 1920) confirmed Hungary's losses: a small strip of land to Austria, Transylvania to Rumania, Slovakia to Czechoslovakia, and Croatia and other Serb and Croat territories to Yugoslavia. Thereafter in Hungary the most important political issue for the ruling groups was "revisionism," the effort to revise the treaty and get these lands back. No tourist who visited Budapest could escape the huge statue of Hungary mourning the lost provinces, north, east, south, and west, or the great map laid out in flowerbeds in the public park showing in different-colored blossoms the far-flung territories relinquished but still claimed by the Magyars. The national motto was now *"Nem, nem, soha"* (No, no, never).

The rank and file of Hungarians, however, who had never cared much about the nationalist questions that had agitated the upper classes, cared relatively little about revisionism. Hungary had no land reform; the great estates remained intact; and magnates and gentry retained their dominant position. Behind a thin screen of parliamentary government, an authoritarian dictatorship governed the country on behalf of the old ruling groups. It was helped by a swollen bureaucracy, and it became more and more fascist in character as the years went by.

For ten years (1921-1931), Count Bethlen as prime minister ran the country as if nothing had changed since 1914. The peasants were effectively disfranchised as they had always been; the Social Democrats were tolerated as a trade-union party; and the upper house of magnates was re-established. The League of Nations helped economic recovery by a loan and a reconstruction plan (1923-1926), and in 1927 a treaty with Italy began an intimate relationship between Hungary and Mussolini. The depression and the financial crisis of 1931 drove Bethlen from office. His successor, the strongly nationalist and fascist-minded Gömbös, was pro-German as well as pro-Italian, and permitted the first Nazi-like organizations to form. Of these the Arrow Cross was the strongest, but it remained on the fringes of power until almost the end of World War II, largely because Hitler got what he wanted in Hungary without it.

After Gömbös died in 1936, his successors were all men of the same stripe. The Italians supplied arms to the Hungarians; Hitler favored their revisionism along with his own. After Austria had fallen to Hitler, he had Hungary in his pocket, and when he broke up Czechoslovakia in March, 1939, the Hungarians seized the extreme eastern portion, Ruthenia, and a small part of Slovakia. To pursue revisionism, the Hungarians had to follow Hitler, since he alone offered the opportunity to re-draw the map as they felt it should be drawn. So, before war broke out, they had withdrawn from the League, and had enacted anti-Semitic laws in the Nazi pattern. But because Hitler needed Rumania too, he would not give the Magyars all of Transylvania. Ironically enough, the price they paid for espousal of revisionism between the wars was the Soviet-dominated régime installed in Hungary after World War II.

Yugoslavia

In the new "Kingdom of the Serbs, Croats, and Slovenes," proclaimed in December, 1918, there came together for the first time in one state the former south-Slav subjects of Austria and Hungary and those of the former independent Kingdom of Serbia. This was in most respects a satisfied state from the territorial point of view; revisionism therefore was not an issue. But, as the name of the new state shows, it faced the serious problem of creating a governmental system that would satisfy the aspirations of each of its nationality groups. Over this problem democracy broke down and a dictatorship was established. The dictatorship was not of the fascist type, although, as German power waxed, important politicians in the country became convinced that the future lay in Hitler's hands, and responded accordingly. The rank and file of the population, by and large, were peasants deeply devoted to freedom, although unskilled in western forms of parliamentarism. They opposed fascism, and, when they got the chance, ousted the politicians who sought to align them with it.

Serbian political ambitions had helped to start the war. The Serbs were more numerous than Croats and Slovenes together (approximately six million to three and a quarter million Croats and a few over one million Slovenes in 1931). Many Serbs felt that the new kingdom, which their Serbian king ruled from his Serbian capital of Belgrade, should be that "greater Serbia" of which they had so long dreamed. Orthodox in religion, using the Cyrillic alphabet, and having experienced and overthrown Ottoman domination, many Serbs tended to look upon the Croats as effete subjects of the Habsburgs who were lucky to get the chance to live in the same state with them. Roman Catholic in religion, using the Latin alphabet, and having opposed Germans and Magyars for centuries, many Croats felt that the Serbs were crude easterners who ought to give them a full measure of autonomy within the new state. Thus the issue was posed: Serb-sponsored centralism against Croat-sponsored federalism. The Slovenes, more conciliatory and less numerous, sometimes acted as a balance wheel to keep the political machinery moving. But the Serbs forced the acceptance of their answer to the constitutional question. This brought about dictatorship, alienated large numbers of Croats, bred extremism among them, and contributed greatly to the benefit of the country's enemies and to its own sufferings during the second war.

The Croats, under their peasant leader Radich, boycotted the constituent assembly of 1920, and the Serbs put through a constitution providing for a strongly centralized state. In the 1920's, both sides generally refused to compromise, although occasionally temporary understandings were reached. When a Serb deputy shot Radich dead on the floor of parliament in June, 1928, a crisis arose that terminated only when King Alexander proclaimed a dictatorship in January, 1929. Alexander made every effort to settle the problem by wiping out all vestiges of old provincial loyalties. There was to be no more Serbia or Croatia, but new artificially created administrative units named after the chief rivers that ran through them. The whole country was renamed Yugoslavia, as a sign that there were to be no more Serbs and Croats. But it was still a Serbian government, and the Croats could not be made to forget it. Elections were rigged by the government, and all political parties were dissolved. Croat leaders spent much time in jails, which, like most Balkan jails, were highly uncomfortable. This dictatorship of King Alexander passed no racial laws, elevated no one political party to exclusive power, and had no colored shirts, special

songs, or other fascist paraphernalia. But it was unmistakably authoritarian and antidemocratic.

One result was the strengthening of Croat extremists, who had wanted an independent Croatia in the days of the Habsburgs, and who now combined this program with terrorism, supported from abroad by the enemies of Yugoslavia—Italy and Hungary. The Croat extremists were called *Ustashi* (rebels), and their leader, Ante Pavelich, was subsidized by Mussolini. He was deeply involved in the assassination of Alexander at Marseilles in October, 1934. Under the regency of Prince Paul (Alexander's cousin) the dictatorship continued. As German economic power in the Balkans grew, leading politicians grew enamored of Germany, and some efforts were made to bring Yugoslav policies into line with those of the Axis. But these policies met with such unconcealed popular opposition that they were never pursued very far. In the summer of 1939, on the very eve of war in Europe, an agreement was finally reached with the Croats that established an autonomous Croatia. But by then it was too late, since the Croats were not satisfied with the boundaries of their new province.

Though the Yugoslavs in 1941 bravely resisted German invasion, they did not have the military power to hold Hitler's armies back. When the conquering Germans and Italians

King Alexander of Yugoslavia talking with Croats loyal to him.

split the country up, they turned Croatia over to the extremist Croat Pavelich, head of the Ustashi, who carried out horrifying massacres of Serbs and Jews. The innocent men, women, and children suffering death and torture at the hands of Pavelich's forces owed some of their anguish to the short-sightedness of Serbian politicians who had failed to solve the problem of Croat autonomy within a peaceful Yugoslavia, and who had thus stimulated the extremists.

Other Authoritarian Régimes

The case-histories we have been considering are unique in detail, yet they furnish interesting parallels to developments elsewhere in eastern Europe. Thus in Poland, Pilsudski led a military *coup* against the democratic government in 1926, and exercised a military dictatorship that became ever more authoritarian, especially after the depression. This *coup* was made possible largely because of the government's failure to grant concessions to Lithuanians and other national minorities, and to deal with the economic problems left by the years of war and occupation. Tension was heightened when Germany denounced a trade treaty and precipitated a crisis in the Polish coal industry. The violent hatreds that divided the political parties made it even easier. Once he had won power, Pilsudski turned to the great landowners and

King Carol II of Rumania (1893–1953).

big industrialists and built his government on their support and on that of his military clique.

In Rumania, it was the deep entrenchment of corruption in political life that initially jeopardized the parliamentary system, as the party in power usually rigged elections without shame. In addition, there was widespread anti-Semitism, which was adopted as the chief program of the "Iron Guard," a Rumanian Nazi party. Green-shirted and wearing bags of Rumanian soil around their necks, the Guard began a program of assassinating moderate politicians early in the 1930's. Economic dislocation and peasant misery brought about by the worldwide agricultural depression strengthened the Guard and other fascist groups. To head off a Guardist *coup,* King Carol of Rumania installed his own fascist dictatorship in 1938. Although the Guardist leaders were "shot while trying to escape," Rumania could not avoid German pressure. After Hitler had acceded to Russian seizure of Bessarabia and Northern Bukovina, and had given Hungary northern Transylvania (August, 1940), Carol had to leave the country, and Hitler's man, Marshal Antonescu, took over, with Iron Guard support.

In Bulgaria, always a strongly pro-Russian country, the genuine threat of communism was a serious problem. Moreover, Bulgaria, like Hungary, was revisionist because of her failure to gain the Macedonian territory given by the peace treaties to Yugoslavia and Greece. The issue was exacerbated by the presence in the country of thousands of Macedonian refugees, who tended to join revolutionary terrorist societies. Bulgaria, an egalitarian country with no minorities problem, no rich landowners, no aristocracy, and no great industries, none the less produced political hostilities even more violent than those in countries where economic inequality prevailed. Unparalleled ferocity has marked its political life. In the early twenties, a peasant politician, Stamboliisky, gave the country a period (1920–1923) of reasonably popular government. But even he curbed the press as he fought both Macedonian terrorists and communists. His imposition of high income

General John Metaxas of Greece.

taxes alienated the bourgeoisie, and his conciliatory policies toward Yugoslavia infuriated the army. In 1923, right-wingers murdered him, and installed a strongly authoritarian régime. From then on, communist plots and bomb outrages and Macedonian terrorist strife racked the country. After 1930, the Italian marriage of King Boris led to a rapprochement with Mussolini. In 1934, a military *coup* brought a group of army officers to power; they dissolved the political parties and tried their hands at a dictatorship of their own. But this development was successfully countered in 1936 by King Boris himself, who, like Alexander of Yugoslavia and Carol of Rumania, imposed a royal dictatorship, which lasted from then until his mysterious death during World War II.

In Greece between the wars, the main issues were whether the country should be a monarchy or a republic, and how to overcome the economic difficulties consequent on the transfer of 1,250,000 Greeks from Turkey. On the constitutional question, the population wavered, voting for a monarchy in 1920, for a

745

republic in 1924, and for a monarchy again in 1935, always by enormous majorities. Economic dislocation brought strength to communism among the refugees and in labor groups. The political exuberance for which Greece is celebrated made the regular conduct of parliamentary government impossible. The inter-war period was punctuated by a whole series of *coups* by generals, some republican, some monarchist, all more or less authoritarian, but most of them ineffective and none especially bloodthirsty. The last of these was the most fascist, General John Metaxas, who became dictator in August, 1936. Metaxas abolished political parties, instituted censorship and political persecution of his opponents, launched a program of public works, and imitated the Nazis in other ways. But when the Italian invasion came from Albania in October, 1940, Metaxas ordered resistance, which was the beginning of Greece's heroic showing in World War II.

Fascism in Review

None of these regimes in eastern Europe was fascist in the full sense of the term. In Italy and Germany the regimes rested, at least initially, upon the popular support of a substantial proportion of the people, even though that support was kept alive by the technique of artificial stimulation. In eastern Europe, on the other hand, the dictatorships rested on the police, the bureaucracy, and the army, and not on the support of the peasant masses. To an eastern European politician of almost any complexion, an election was an occasion for bribery, intimidation, and promises that he had no intention of trying to fulfill. The hope placed by some western liberals in peasant parties proved in the end illusory.

Thus the growth of anti-democratic governments of the Right in Europe during the period between the wars strikingly reveals the difficulties in the way of moderate parliamentary regimes in countries without parliamentary traditions. This does not mean that the western liberal tradition cannot be exported. But a liberal constitution on paper and a liberal franchise are in themselves no guarantee that a regime on western models can become stabilized. The postwar economic agony had scarcely disappeared before the depression of the late twenties and early thirties struck. Under these circumstances, men turned to extremists of the Left and Right. But the fear of communism, combined with the seductive nationalist propaganda of the Right, brought about fascist victories in Italy and Germany. Mussolini's and Hitler's successes helped to tip the scale: the triumph of the Right elsewhere was assured, and a new world war was inevitable.

Reading Suggestions on the Rise of Fascism

(Asterisk indicates paperbound edition.)

The Roots of Fascism

A. Cobban, *Dictatorship: Its History and Theory* (Scribner's, 1939). Highly suggestive survey, reaching well back into history.

P. Viereck, *Metapolitics: From the Romantics to Hitler* (Knopf, 1941). A survey of the background in German political thought.

C. J. Hayes, *A Generation of Materialism, 1871–1900* (Harper, 1941). Contains a concise and corrosive section on the seedtime of fascism.

Note: The titles listed above present differing views on the origins of fascism, a subject still much debated by historians. Further titles bearing on the subject may be found in the reading suggestions for Chapter 15.

Italy

G. Magaro, *Mussolini in the Making* (Houghton Mifflin, 1938). An unequaled study of Mussolini's early career.

H. Finer, *Mussolini's Italy* (Holt, 1935), and H. A. Steiner, *Government in Fascist Italy* (McGraw-Hill, 1938). Two very solid studies by expert political scientists.

G. A. Borgese, *Goliath: The March of Fascism* (Viking, 1938), and G. Salvemini, *Under the Axe of Fascism* (Viking, 1936). Lively works by important anti-fascist Italians.

G. Salvemini, *Prelude to World War II* (Doubleday, 1954). A survey of Mussolini's foreign policy, by one of his most implacable enemies.

Germany

A. Hitler, *Mein Kampf* (Reynal and Hitchcock, 1939). A complete English translation of the Nazi bible, the basic work to be read for an understanding of the movement.

A. Hitler, *My New Order,* R. de Sales, ed. (Reynal and Hitchcock, 1941). Speeches after the Führer's coming to power.

A. L. C. Bullock, *Hitler: A Study in Tyranny* (Oxham's, 1952; *abridgment, Bantam). The best biography.

S. W. Halperin, *Germany Tried Democracy* (Crowell, 1946). A reliable history of the Weimar Republic, 1918–1933.

R. G. L. Waite, *Vanguard of Nazism* (Harvard Univ. Press, 1952). A good study of the "Free Corps" movement.

J. W. Wheeler-Bennett, *Wooden Titan* (Morrow, 1936), and *Nemesis of Power* (St. Martin's Press, 1954). Two first-rate studies, the first dealing with Hindenburg, and the second with the role of the German army in politics from 1918 to 1945.

F. L. Neumann, *Behemoth: The Structure and Practice of National Socialism* (Oxford Univ. Press, 1944). The best work on the subject.

K. Heiden, *History of National Socialism* (Knopf, 1935), and S. H. Roberts, *The House That Hitler Built* (Harper, 1938). Two older and still useful studies of the Nazis.

F. von Papen, *Memoirs* (Dutton, 1953). An apologetic autobiography by the scheming right-wing politician.

E. Wiskemann, *The Rome-Berlin Axis* (Oxford Univ. Press, 1949). A study of the formation and history of the Hitler-Mussolini partnership.

R. Fischer, *Stalin and German Communism* (Harvard Univ. Press, 1948). A study of the role played by the communist movement in the history of Germany between the wars.

Note: Some of the titles listed under the reading suggestions for Chapter 20 deal with international relations during the inter-war period and will illuminate Nazi foreign policy.

Other Countries

G. Brenan, *The Spanish Labyrinth* (Macmillan, 1943). A useful study of the Spanish Civil War against its historical and economic background.

C. Bowers, *My Mission to Spain* (Simon & Schuster, 1954); C. J. Hayes, *Wartime Mission to Spain, 1942–1945* (Macmillan, 1945); and Lord Templewood (Sir Samuel Hoare), *Complacent Dictator* (Knopf, 1947). Three differing views of Franco and the Spanish problem, by three ambassadors, the first two American, the last British.

Hugh Thomas, *The Spanish Civil War* (Harper, 1961; rev. ed., *Penguin, 1965). The best single work on the subject.

G. E. R. Gedye, *Betrayal in Central Europe* (Harper, 1939). A careful journalist's account of Austria and Czechoslovakia.

H. Seton-Watson, *Eastern Europe between the Wars, 1918–1941* (Cambridge Univ. Press, 1946). A useful account dealing with all the eastern European countries except Greece and Albania.

R. L. Buell, *Poland: Key to Europe* (Knopf, 1939). A helpful survey.

R. West, *Black Lamb and Grey Falcon* (Viking, 1941). A highly subjective account of Yugoslavia, loaded with political bias, but fascinating and informative reading.

Historical Fiction

I. Silone, *Bread and Wine* (*Penguin, 1946; *New American Library), and *Fontamara* (Smith and Haas, 1934). Two good novels on rural Italy under fascism; by a distinguished anti-fascist writer.

C. Levi, *Christ Stopped at Eboli* (Farrar, Straus, 1947; *Universal Library). An anti-fascist Italian doctor and painter writes movingly of his exile in a remote and poverty-striken southern Italian village.

H. Fallada, *Little Man What Now?* (Simon & Schuster, 1933; *Ungar), and E. Remarque, *Three Comrades* (Little, Brown, 1937; *Popular Library). Two touching novels of depression-ridden Germany.

E. von Salomon, *"Der Fragebogen" (The Questionnaire)* (Doubleday, 1955). One of the plotters against Rathenau, a strong sympathizer with authoritarian movements, tells his life story satirically, against the background of American military government in post-1945 Germany.

E. Hemingway, *For Whom the Bell Tolls* (Scribner's, 1940). A characteristic Hemingway novel, set in the Spain of the Civil War.

20

The Democracies

and the Colonial World

Domestic and Imperial Problems, 1919–1939

I Introduction

The central fact—or irony—of politics between the two world wars is that the war "to make the world safe for democracy" seemed to have made it in effect a difficult and dangerous place for democracy. Idealists like President Wilson had expected that the collapse of the old Romanov, Habsburg, and Hohenzollern empires would automatically ensure an increase in the number of democratic states. But instead, as we have just seen, much of Europe came under régimes that were hostile to liberal democracy. Even Italy, which had appeared to be evolving toward a democratic constitutional monarchy, turned fascist. In the 1920's and 1930's, then, the core of democracy remained in the great North Atlantic powers—Britain, France, and the United States—and in the smaller states of the Low Countries, Switzerland, and Scandinavia.

The upsurge of communism and fascism created grave problems in international relations for the three great democracies. At times in the 1920's it looked as if they might successfully overcome these problems and bring the world back to peaceful habits. But in the 1930's the great world-wide depression, the advent of Hitler, and the aggressions of fascist states in the West and of an expansionist Japan in the Far East rapidly darkened the international scene. With the outbreak of another general war in 1939, it was clear that the two decades since 1919 had been at best a twenty year's truce, a truce broken with increasing frequency by international troublemakers.

Certainly the totalitarian aggressors bore the major responsibility for the unleashing of a second world war. Yet a far from minor factor in the deterioriation of the twenty years' truce was the failure of the peaceful democracies to present a unified front against those who threatened world peace. In the 1920's Britain, France, and the United States became preoccupied with their own domestic problems. In the early 1930's their preoccupation increased as a result of the urgent crisis of the depression. But this was the very time when international problems demanded equally urgent attention. International trade was steadily shrinking in the face of the depression and of mounting tariff barriers; the prospects for peace were steadily fading before the saber-rattling and actual saber-wielding of the enemies of democracy. Faced with two equally urgent sets of problems, the democracies turned first to the domestic ones and then discovered that the international situation was rapidly moving toward war.

Nor was this all. During the twenty years' truce, the democracies faced a third set of problems, not as yet so urgent as the other two, but of very great potential importance. This third set involved imperial issues — the relationship between the great democracies and the non-western peoples, many of whom were still under colonial rule or some other form of control by democratic mother countries. Particularly in Asia and the Middle East, the non-western peoples were beginning to assert their nationalism and to demand the loosening of old imperial ties. This formidable political movement did not reach full intensity until the years following World War II when a long procession of former colonies, protectorates, and mandates began to join the ranks of independent states (see Chapter 23). But the nationalist movements that have brought these newcomers into the family of nations since 1945 grew steadily in the 1920's and 1930's.

The three sets of problems — domestic, foreign, and imperial — faced by the democracies during the twenty years' truce were interconnected and interrelated in countless ways. We shall underline some of these interrelations, as we have shown the links between the internal and external policies of the communist and fascist states. But, in order to point up the main issues, we shall also separate national, international, and colonial problems in a fashion that must oversimplify the complexities of real life. Our survey emphasizes first the chief domestic problems of the democracies in the inter-war years and then considers the growing conflict between their colonialism and the nationalism of the non-western world; in Chapter 21 we shall analyze their foreign policies, as distinguished from their imperial policies. We begin here with an examination of the crisis confronting Britain on the home front after November, 1918.

II   Great Britain

The Postwar Depression

Save for trifling losses from German Zeppelin raids and coastal bombardments, the British Isles suffered no direct material damage in World War I. But the British armed forces lost about seven hundred and fifty thousand men killed in action, and about a million and a half wounded. The casualties of the Empire and the Commonwealth as a whole came to nearly a million killed and over two million wounded. The economic losses of the mother country had been grave indeed—the almost incalculable difference between the actual cost of destructive war and what might otherwise have been productive effort.

The national debt after the war was ten times that of 1914. Many British investments abroad, returns on which had been a major factor in Victorian prosperity, had had to be liquidated to get purchasing power abroad for food and war materials. Forty per cent of the great British merchant fleet, the income from which had helped to balance Britain's international accounts and pay for her imports, had been destroyed by enemy action. The whole fabric of international trade on which Britain depended was torn in a thousand places in 1918 and could not be rapidly restored in the unsettled conditions that prevailed in the postwar world. And, finally, to supplement the war production of Britain and France, the industrial plants of the United States, of Canada, and even of India had been called on, and had received a stimulus that made them in peacetime more effective competitors of the British. In the 1920's, the industrial plant of the Germans, nourished in part by loans from America, once more took up the rivalry that had so alarmed the British before the war.

In short, victorious Britain faced in an ag-gravated form the basic economic difficulty that we analyzed in Chapter 13. The country that had been in Victorian days the "workshop of the world" had now lost its head start and could no longer give full employment to its millions of workers. And yet those workers were in no mood to accept a lower standard of living. They had made great gains in social security before the war, and they had fought the war in the hope of still better things to come. They had been promised that the defeated enemy would through reparations pay the costs of the war and give Britain a new start.

This hope was very early disappointed. No substantial reparations came through, economic difficulties soon began to accumulate, and by 1921 there were already almost a million unemployed. In that same year the British government, faced with the rising cost of living, increased the very meager unemployment payments. These payments, soon given the derogatory name of the "dole," were strictly speaking not old-fashioned poor relief, but payments on unemployment insurance policies that had been part of Lloyd George's social legislation of prewar days. However, large-scale unemployment continued, and some young workers never acquired employment status. Unemployment insurance could not be maintained on a sound actuarial basis, and the payments became in fact a form of poor relief.

The Great Britain of the 1920's experienced no equivalent of the "Coolidge prosperity" that the United States was to enjoy. We must not exaggerate: The British economic decline was not catastrophic. London, Manchester, and Liverpool did not become ghost cities, though some of the gravely depressed areas, like the coal-mining regions of South Wales, did begin to show real signs of decay. What happened was rather a *relative* decline, the comparative slowing up of an economy geared to dynamic growth, with a working population conditioned psychologically to a slowly rising standard of living and a middle class similarly conditioned to traditional comforts. Moreover, this was the twentieth century, the century of the newspaper, the movie, the radio. The British were well aware, for instance, that Americans had automobiles, radios, and a lot else; they, too, wanted those things.

Britain was, then, suffering from ills characteristic of economic old age. The coal industry is a good concrete illustration of these ills. There was still a lot of coal in Britain; but much of it was costly to mine, since the most easily and cheaply worked seams were being exhausted. The industry was badly organized, with many small and inefficient mines running at a loss, and with machinery and methods that were antiquated in comparison with American and the best continental standards. Productivity per man-hour over the whole industry was low. Worst of all, perhaps, the 1920's saw the rapid rise all over the industrialized world of major competitors of coal—oil, and electricity based on water power—and the consequent decline of British coal exports. Since the British Isles had no petroleum, and no very great potential in hydroelectric power, coal, the historic basis of British industrial power, simply had to be mined. The workers were unionized and were in no mood to accept cuts in wages; the owners did not want to run their business at a loss. A strike in March, 1921, after the government had rejected Labor party proposals for making permanent the wartime nationalization of the industry, focused national attention on this critical problem. The strike was settled in July, but only by the government's consenting to pay subsidies to cover increased wages.

The Conservative and Labor Programs

Against the background of economic depression, British domestic politics during the twenty years' truce displayed a fairly clear class basis. The Conservatives, still often called Tories, tended to get the support of aristocrats and of middle-class people who wanted to attack new problems with traditional methods and with a minimum of government intervention. The Labor party tended to get the support of trade unionists and of intellectuals from all classes who demanded that the government intervene more vigorously in the economic field. We must not oversimplify, however; not every reformer necessarily voted Labor nor every stand-patter Tory. Yet economic issues did sharpen the differences between the two major British parties.

The first casualty in the struggle between Labor and the Conservatives was the old Liberal party, which was ground to a mere husk between the two contending groups. The Conservatives, who had won the lion's share of seats in the election of 1918, held immediately after the armistice, and known as the "khaki election," decided in 1922 to withdraw their support from the coalition government headed by the Liberal Lloyd George. In the ensuing elections the Conservatives won, and the Liberals, split between the followers of Lloyd George and those of the more orthodox Asquith, lost heavily. Labor won 142 seats—more than the Liberals did—and became for the first time His Majesty's Opposition.

Both Conservatives and Labor realized the underlying difficulties of Britain's position. Both were fully aware that twentieth-century Britain had to sell enough goods and services abroad—enough manufactured goods and shipping, insurance, banking, and tourist services—so that the income from them would buy food for her people and much of the raw materials for her factories. But the parties were not agreed on how to achieve this necessary task. Broadly speaking, the Conservatives wanted to retain private industry, with government and other technical experts helping to make it efficient. But they were thwarted by high tariffs in the United States and elsewhere, by the drive to economic self-sufficiency all over the world, and by the difficulties of trade with communist Russia.

The state of world trade drove the Conservatives more and more to the solution Joseph Chamberlain (see Chapter 13) had advocated earlier: protective tariffs against competing foreign goods, and the knitting of the Empire and Commonwealth, with their vast variety of resources, into a largely self-sufficient trade area by "imperial preference" agreements. Such agreements would give raw materials from the colonies and dominions preferred treatment in the British market in return for preferred treatment of British manufactures in the colonial and dominion markets. In theory, at least, the scheme could have worked, for the Commonwealth and Empire of the nineteen-twenties—one-quarter of the world's land and people—had the requisite natural resources and offered a potential market capable of supporting the British Isles in the style to which they were accustomed. In practice, however, the great snag was the unwillingness of the constituent parts of the Empire and Commonwealth to accept for themselves the role of producers of raw materials in exchange for British manufactured goods and British services. The self-governing dominions, loyal though they had been during the war, were in no mood to assume a role essentially like that of colonies in the old mercantilistic days. They were looking toward independent nationhood, and they wanted what seems to go with nationhood in our world—their own industries. This was also true of what was potentially the richest unit in the Empire, India.

The Labor solution was nationalization—that is, government purchase and operation of key industries with just compensation to their private owners, rather than seizure without compensation as in Soviet Russia. The key industries were transportation, power, coal, steel, perhaps even textiles, cutlery, pottery, machine tools—all the industries that seem to thrive best on large-scale organization. A good many Laborites wanted nationalization simply because, as socialists, they believed that profits, rent, and interest paid to "capitalist" private owners were forms of worker-exploitation, and that under nationalization these forms of exploitation would cease. But many of their leaders knew that even nationalized

industries would still face the fundamental problem of selling enough goods abroad to keep the economy going. They argued, therefore, that nationalization would enable British industries to produce more cheaply and efficiently. It would do away with wasteful competition and with the inefficient firms so conspicuous in the coal industry, for instance. It would, they fondly believed, force into productive work both unnecessary managerial and selling staffs, and stockholders and other investors who lived without working.

Moreover, Labor supporters believed that, once nationalization had been achieved, the British workmen would take a new attitude toward their work. Knowing that they were now the *real* owners of their own industries, they would put their hearts into their work, abstain from feather-bedding, absenteeism, and similar practices, and raise production to a point where the goods of Britain could undersell those of her capitalist rivals in world markets. This belief was reinforced by the somewhat paradoxical faith in free trade that the Labor party had inherited from the Liberals, and by its high hopes for improved international relations. Consequently, Labor was hostile to the Conservative policies of protective tariffs and imperial preference.

Postwar Politics

In the twenty years between the wars, neither the Tories nor the Laborites were able to carry out their full platforms. Labor itself, though it came to power briefly in 1924 and in 1929, with its leader Ramsay MacDonald as prime minister, never had a parliamentary position firm enough to nationalize any industry. The Conservatives, by no means unanimous on the degree of economic self-sufficiency they wanted for the Empire, were decisively held up by the refusal of the Commonwealth countries to go much further than to accept certain limited imperial preferences.

Despite the wider cleavage between the two parties, British politics still retained many of the amenities of Victorian parlia-

Emergency transport conveying London office workers during the general strike of 1926.

mentary life. The House of Commons, even though it now included workingmen and others who by no means spoke with an upper-class "Oxford accent," was still one of the best clubs in the world. For a few weeks in 1926 some 2,500,000 trade-union members attempted a general strike in support of the coal-miners, who were already on strike in protest against a cut in their wages. The general strike failed, but during its brief course fundamental British attitudes were revealed. Thousands of men from the middle and upper classes volunteered to keep essential services operating, and in Plymouth a soccer team of strikers played a team of police. Britain, despite mounting tensions, remained a land of general law-abidingness, where the class struggle that the Marxists talked so much about seemed to have come thoroughly under the control of the parliamentary decencies.

In 1928, almost unnoticed, the last step was taken in the *political* democratization of Britain that had begun in 1832. In 1918, in preparation for the "khaki election," the government had put through a reform bill which eliminated all the old exceptions to universal male suffrage and gave the vote to all men over twenty-one. Culminating a long and spectacular campaign in which "suffragettes" had demonstrated, marched, orated, and even chained themselves to lamp posts, destroyed property, and gone to jail in behalf of women's rights, the bill also gave the vote to women. But, with almost a caricature of British caution, it set the voting age for women at thirty years, thus insuring that there would always be more male than female voters. The distinction was too irrational to stand up, especially after experience had demonstrated—as it also did in the United States—that women divide politically about the way men do. In 1928, a measure known irreverently as the "bill for flapper suffrage" gave women the vote at twenty-one.

Although the dole, depressed industries, and other signs of economic ill-health persisted, Britain did experience a measure of recovery in the late 1920's. But then the great depression, the signal for which was given by the New York stockmarket crash in October, 1929, began its spread around the world. Britain, already weakened, was one of the first to be engulfed. Faced by a serious deficit, and unwilling to try to meet it by cutting the dole and other social services, the second Labor government of Ramsay MacDonald resigned in August, 1931.

It gave way to a coalition of Conservatives, Liberals, and right-wing Laborites headed by the same MacDonald. This coalition cabinet put through reductions in the dole and the social services. Late in 1931, it took the decisive step, a hard one in view of Britain's traditional financial leadership and devotion to the gold standard, of going off the gold standard and letting the pound fall in value. In 1932, it made the first move away from free trade by enacting protective tariffs, and in the same year Britain ceased payment on her war

De Valera taking the salute
of the Irish Republic Army,
Western Division, in County
Clare, autumn, 1921.

debts to the United States, except for a few "token" payments. These measures did little to help the unemployed or to strike at the roots of British economic troubles. But they did stem the depression sufficiently to enable the coalition to win two general elections in 1931 and 1935.

Yet the coalition government was in fact dominated by Conservatives, and after the 1935 election the Conservative leader, Stanley Baldwin, took over the post of prime minister. Gradually the British economy pulled out of the worst of the depression, although—some economic theorists might say *because*—Baldwin did nothing beyond keeping the budget in balance. By 1936, however, Mussolini's and Hitler's aggressions were beginning to demand British attention. The economic question and the social question, by no means solved, faded before the threat of another war.

Settlement of the Irish Question

The years between the wars were of great importance for Ireland. The outbreak of war in 1914 put off the threatened revolt against Home Rule in Ulster (see Chapter 13), but the Irish were hardly reliable partners in the war. In 1916, the faction furthest removed

from the Ulster rebels, the Irish nationalists, got some German help in guns and ammunition and staged an armed rising in Dublin. The British put down this "Easter rebellion," but not before they had created a fresh and effective set of Irish political martyrs. The British government did not dare extend conscription to Ireland until April, 1918, and the attempt made then led the Irish nationalists to boycott the British Parliament and to cease attending its sessions.

By 1919, Home Rule as decreed in 1914 was not enough for the nationalists of Ireland. The Home Rulers of prewar days had yielded to more extreme rebels, the Sinn Fein (meaning in Gaelic, "ourselves alone"), who wanted complete independence. The years 1919–1921 were filled with violence, ambushes, arson, and guerrilla warfare, as the Irish, who now had their own illegal parliament, the Dail Ereann, moved into full revolution. The British, tired from their long war, were not in a state of mind to use force effectively; the Irish, on the other hand, were admirably organized and full of fight.

Yet the immediate upshot of the violent phase of the revolution was a compromise, for the Sinn Fein split in two. A moderate wing, led by Arthur Griffith and Michael Collins, was willing to accept a compromise in which Protestant Ulster would remain under direct British rule and the Catholic counties would be given dominion status. A radical wing, led by Eamon De Valera—exceedingly Irish in spite of his Spanish surname—insisted that the whole island achieve complete independence as a unified republic. The moderates negotiated with the British, and in 1921 obtained for the twenty-six counties of southern Ireland dominion status under the name of the Irish Free State. The Free State had its own parliament, the Dail, and was completely self-governing with its own army and its own diplomatic services; it merely accepted the British Crown as symbolic head. The six Protestant counties of Ulster maintained their old relationship with Britain, which now became officially the United Kingdom of Great Britain and Northern Ireland. Ulster had, however, its own parliament at Belfast, and considerable local autonomy.

This settlement was unacceptable to De Valera and the more extreme revolutionaries, and the Irish revolution now became a civil war between partisans of the Free State and partisans of a republic, with the old round of burning, ambush, and murder. But the Irish, too, were beginning to tire of violence. When the moderate leader, Michael Collins, a man much closer to earth than De Valera, was assassinated by a republican, public opinion turned away from the extremists. Meantime the Free State was gradually settling down. De Valera, after refusing to sit in the Dail because he would have had to take an oath of loyalty to the king, changed his mind and decided to bring his fellow republicans into the national parliament in 1927.

From then on, almost in the manner of illogical and compromise-loving England, the Irish Free State gradually and peacefully got what the extremists had been killing and burning for. De Valera's party won a plurality in the Dail in 1932, and a majority in 1933; thereupon it proceeded to abolish the oath of loyalty to the Crown and to cut most of the slender threads that still tied the Free State to England. In 1939, Catholic Ireland was so free from British domination that she could declare and maintain her neutrality throughout World War II. In 1949, the final step was taken when Britain recognized her as the fully independent Republic of Eire (Gaelic for "Ireland").

The Commonwealth of Nations

No such secession took place elsewhere among the British possessions in the years between the two world wars. On the contrary, definite constitutional recognition of the essential independence of the dominions seemed to make them more loyal, though at the cost of any central British authority over their economic policies, and, at least in law, over their foreign policies. The capstone of a long process that had begun with the Durham Report nearly a century before (see Chapter 16) was the Statute of Westminster of 1931. This spelled out the new relations between the dominions and the mother country that had been negotiated in an imperial conference five years earlier. The preparatory report of 1926 anticipated the gist of the Statute of Westminster by declaring that Britain and the dominions

. . . are autonomous communities within the British Empire, equal in status, in no way subordinate one to another in any aspect of their domestic or external affairs, though united by a common allegiance to the crown and freely associated as members of the British Commonwealth of Nations.

That phrase "freely associated" means also "able freely to choose to be dis-associated." In other words, the right of a state to secede, which Americans fought a great civil war to decide is *not* a part of the United States Constitution, *is* a part of the constitution of the British Commonwealth of Nations. And the twenty-six counties of Southern Ireland in effect took advantage of this right to set up their republic quite outside the Commonwealth. South Africa dis-associated itself in 1961 and became an independent republic, and in 1965 the Rhodesian government made a unilateral declaration of independence (for details see Chapter 23).

The new status acquired by the dominions in 1931 was symbolized by a change in terminology. Henceforward they were no longer to be considered parts of the British Empire but free members of the British Commonwealth of Nations. In this new relationship, Britain would have to *negotiate* with Canada or Australia about tariffs, trade conditions, immigration, and the like, just as if they were foreign countries. Although Britain was unable to build a self-sufficient economic unity out of her dominions, still in 1939, as in 1914, the dominions all came into the war on Britain's side. They made this decision even though they had the legal right to follow the example of Ireland and remain neutral.

III France

The Impact of the War

In France, both World War I and the post-war difficulties caused more serious dislocation than they did in Britain. In the war itself, France lost proportionately more in human lives and in material damage than did any other major belligerent. Two million Frenchmen in the prime of life were either killed or so seriously mutilated as to be incapable of normal living. In a land of only 39,000,000, and with an already low birth rate, it is likely that this human loss impaired the French potentiality for achievement in all phases of civilization. Many of the men who would have been statesmen, industrialists, scientists, and artists in the 1930's were killed off in 1914–1918. Three hundred thousand houses and twenty thousand factories or shops were destroyed. In a land of conservative economic organization, where work was done slowly and for the most part without large-scale automatic machinery, this material setback would be long felt. Psychologically, the feeling of victory by no means compensated for the traumatic losses of the four years of struggle.

France set as her goal the laming of her re-

Wartime devastation in Verdun's business center.

cent enemy, Germany, in every possible way. She tried to extract reparations to the last possible sum, undeterred by the arguments of economic theorists that Germany could not pay. But she insisted even more on keeping Germany down, isolated in international relations, and without the physical means of fighting. In a pinch, most Frenchmen would probably have been willing to forego reparations in order to deprive Germany of the economic plant necessary for modern war. They would have preferred this to collecting reparations from a rich and productive Germany.

In the postwar years, however, French statesmen attempted to follow both policies simultaneously and of course failed. The culmination came in January, 1923, under the premiership of the conservative Raymond Poincaré, when French and Belgian troops occupied the great German industrial region of the Ruhr in an effort to make Germany pay full reparations. The Germans replied by passive resistance (see Chapter 19). By 1925, it was clear that the Ruhr occupation had brought no gains to France, and the new French government, chosen after the failure of Poincaré's policy, withdrew the troops.

Meanwhile, the French were undergoing inflation. The inflation resulted in part from the cost of rebuilding the devastated areas—a cost that drained government finances and that was only partly covered by German payments. It resulted also from the high cost of maintaining armed forces—for the French dared not disarm, from the general disorder of international trade, and from the staggering debts piled up during the war by the French government, which, like the imperial German government, had preferred loans to taxes. By the mid-1920's, the franc had slipped from its prewar value of 20 cents to a dangerous low of about 2 cents. In the crisis, Poincaré was recalled to power to "save the franc." In 1926, he initiated new taxes and stern measures of economy which, together with the gradual restoration of normal international trade after the French withdrawal from the Ruhr, stemmed the decline of the franc. In 1928, it was officially revalued at 3.92 cents.

The French inflation, though mild compared with the German, nevertheless caused economic and social dislocation. Frenchmen who had lent their government francs worth 20 cents now found themselves deprived of four-fifths of their loans. This very considerable repudiation fell with particular severity on the middle class, especially the lower middle class, the *petite bourgeoisie*. The greatest sufferers were those living on their savings or on relatively fixed incomes—on pensions, for example, or on the return from bonds, or even on the contents of the wool sock in which the suspicious French peasant traditionally hoarded his cash. Bourgeois people naturally fear pauperization, fear being pushed down into the ranks of the proletariat, and the French were no exceptions. Inflation thus weakened a social class that had long been a mainstay of republicanism in France and added to the social tensions that form the central theme of French domestic history in the period between the two world wars.

Social and Political Tensions

During World War I, the French had temporarily put aside the great political and social conflict they had inherited from 1789. After the war, the "sacred union" of political parties that had carried France through the struggle soon dissolved, and the traditional conflict was resumed. This is sometimes termed the conflict between the "two Frances"—the republican France of the Left, and the royalist, or authoritarian France of the Right. The conflict was not quite a simple Marxian class struggle between rich and poor, capitalist and proletarian, though it was certainly in part such a struggle. On the Right were the wealthier classes, many of them openly hostile to the very existence of the parliamentary state. They were reinforced by conservative peasants and by small businessmen and investors, who were not hostile to the Third Republic as such but who were determined to resist any attempt to extend the social services of the "welfare state." As a result of this right-wing resistance,

France lagged behind Britain, Germany, Sweden, and other European states in providing measures of social security.

On the Left were the champions of the welfare state, the Socialists and the Communists, backed by the more radical workers, by many white-collar people, especially in the government service, and by some intellectuals. The effectiveness of the Left was hampered by the postwar split between the Communists, who followed the Moscow line, and the Socialists, who did not, and by a comparable schism within the major trade-union organization, the C.G.T. (*Confédération Générale du Travail*—General Confederation of Labor). Still nominally part of the Left, but actually in the political middle and not anxious to go far toward the welfare state, was the misleadingly named Radical-Socialist Party, long the political bulwark of the Third Republic. The Radicals were strong among the peasants of southern France, and among white-collar workers and smaller professional men.

Religious difficulties further embittered French politics. French Leftists, including the Radicals, were anticlerical by tradition. After the war they rashly attempted to introduce anticlerical measures into strongly Catholic Alsace. Alsace had not been affected by the separation of Church and State carried through in France after the Dreyfus crisis (see Chapter 13), since it had then belonged to Germany. In the long run, the government was obliged to make compromises on the Alsatian question and on other clerical issues. After bitter public debate, it finally decided in the mid-1920's to resume diplomatic relations with the Vatican, which had been broken off at the time of the separation.

In the late 1920's, the years of increased prosperity that followed the revaluation of the franc, the Third Republic seemed to be getting the better of its internal difficulties. Indeed, the world economic crisis that began in 1929 was late in striking France, and for a while in 1930 it looked as though the French economy, less devoted to large-scale industry than that of the United States, Britain, or Germany, might weather the crisis much more easily. But France, too, depended on international trade, particularly on the export of perfumes, wines and brandies, Paris gowns, and other luxuries. By 1932, the depression had struck, and the government was in serious economic and political difficulties.

The Stavisky Case and the Popular Front

The political crisis came to a head in February, 1934, as a result of the Stavisky case, a financial scandal reminiscent of the Panama scandal of the 1890's (see p. 504). Stavisky, a shady promoter and swindler who had all sorts of connections with important public figures of the Third Republic, was caught at last in a fraudulent bond issue of the municipal pawnshop of Bayonne. The full details have never emerged, but Stavisky's suicide—or murder—in December, 1933, rocked France. On the extreme Right, royalists, enjoying the freedom of a democratic society, had long been organized, notably in a pressure group known as the *Action Française*, and were gaining recruits among upper-class youth. The *Camelots du Roi* ("The King's Henchmen"), strong-armed squads of the *Action Française*, went about beating up Communists, who in turn responded with violence. Less fascist in character, yet also supporting the Right, was a veterans' organization, the *Croix de Feu* ("cross of fire"—the reference is to war), organized by Colonel de la Rocque. During the agitation following the Stavisky case, the *Camelots du Roi* and the *Croix de Feu* took part in riots against the government that broke out in Paris in February, 1934. The Left countered with a brief general strike; France seemed to be on the eve of revolution.

Once more, however, as in the time of Dreyfus, the republican forces rallied to meet the threat, and once more after the crisis had been surmounted France moved to the Left. The February crisis itself was overcome by a coalition of all parties save royalists, Socialists, and Communists. But the franc was again falling in value. The conservative premier,

Demonstrators in the Stavisky riots, Paris, February, 1934.

Flandin, attempted to cut back government expenditures by measures similar to those that had worked a decade earlier under Poincaré; this time they did not work. The forces of the Left responded by forming the so-called Popular Front, made up of the Radical-Socialist, Socialist, and Communist parties, and backed by the C.G.T., which had temporarily healed the schism between Communists and non-Communists. Their victory in a general election in May, 1936, led to the formation of a Popular Front ministry under the leadership of the Socialist Léon Blum.

The Popular Front came to power in part as a kind of French equivalent of the American New Deal. The workers, the white-collar men, the government employees, even many of the peasants and shopkeepers, were now convinced that the classical formulas of economic retrenchment were not the remedy for the ills of France. They wanted a direct attack on the stronghold of retrenchment, the Bank of France, still a private institution dominated by the "two hundred families" alleged to control the French economy. They wanted more equal distribution of wealth by government spending; in short, they wanted the "welfare state."

Other factors entered into the victory of the Popular Front. Mussolini had begun his Ethiopian adventure, and Hitler his rearmament; many a Frenchman in 1936 voted Left as a protest against the compromises that French politicians had been making with the dictators. Finally, these were the years when Russia, just admitted to the League of Nations, seemed to be pursuing a course of collaboration with the West against the threat of Nazi Germany. Moscow therefore urged the French Communists to give up their old policy of constant opposition and to co-operate with their hated enemies, the Socialists.

It was a bad time for a French New Deal. The nation was bitterly divided between partisans and enemies of the Popular Front; business and farming classes were traditionally reluctant to pay income taxes, which would have to be raised to meet the costs of social services; the economy was not geared to labor-saving devices. The Blum cabinet had an ambitious program—a maximum work week of 40 hours; paid vacations and the like; partial nationalization of the Bank of France, the railroads, and the munitions industry; compulsory arbitration of labor disputes; and other measures of social welfare. Although Blum achieved most of this program on paper, everything conspired to block its successful execution. The Communists did not really co-operate, for they refused to participate in the Blum cabinet and sniped at it from the sidelines in the Chamber and in the press. Businessmen took fright at the mushrooming membership of the C.G.T. and at the "sitdown" or "stay-in" strikes of French industrial workers in June, 1936.

Moreover, as the anti-democratic régimes in Germany, Italy, and Spain went on to new victories, France was driven to expensive rearmament. Capital, however, was rapidly leaving the country to be invested or deposited abroad, and the monied class would not subscribe to the huge defense loans that were essential if the French armed forces were to be put in shape to face the war that began to seem inevitable. Blum was obliged to call a halt in March, 1937. The Popular Front now disintegrated, and the C.G.T. lost millions of its newly recruited members and suffered a new schism between Communists and anti-Communists.

Divided France

The morale of the French sagged badly after the collapse of the Popular Front. Under the mounting tensions of 1938 and 1939, the Radical-Socialist premier, Daladier, kept France on the side of Britain in opposition to the Rome-Berlin axis, and various measures of retrenchment — including virtual abandonment of the 40-hour week — kept the French economy from collapse. But the workers took very badly the failure of the Popular Front, and as late as November, 1938, a general strike almost came off, and was combated by putting the railway workers under military orders. The "have" classes, on the other hand, were outraged by the fact that Blum's experiment had been made at all; many of them were convinced that their salvation lay in a French totalitarian state — "better Hitler than Blum,"

as their despairing slogan went. The France that was confronted with war in 1939 was not only inadequately prepared in terms of materials; it was psychologically and spiritually divided, uncertain of what it was fighting for.

Many Frenchmen before 1940 relied on their great empire to restore the flagging morale and material capabilities of the mother country. Colonial troops, particularly from Senegal and North Africa, had helped to replenish the diminished ranks of the army during World War I. Enthusiasts spoke of France as a nation not of just the 40,000,000 at home but of 100,000,000 Frenchmen, including the population of the colonial territories. But this was stretching the facts too far. Economically, the Empire as a whole did advance in the 1920's and 1930's, yet only small native elite groups — only a relative handful of Indo-Chinese or Senegalese or Algerian Arabs, for instance — were assimilated as Frenchmen or desired such assimilation. What the colonial populations were beginning to desire was some sort of home rule or independence. Although some leaders of the French Left urged concessions to native aspirations, little was in fact conceded, and French imperial policy in the 1920's, and 1930's continued along traditional lines. Perhaps no policy pursued then could have prevented the disintegration of the French Empire that occurred after World War II, but the old-fashioned policy that prevailed did nothing to reconcile native nationalists to the French overlords.

Yet we must not here give way to the American fondness for lecturing the French on their weaknesses, and especially on their social and political divisions. The fact remains that in the years between the two World Wars France did not take the totalitarian path, did not go the way of Italy, Germany or Russia. She remained a democracy, with a parliamentary government, and the essential freedoms of speech, press and association.

IV   The United States

Neither the human nor the material losses of the United States in World War I were at all comparable with those of Britain and France. American casualties were 115,000 dead and 206,000 wounded; the comparable French figures were 1,385,000 dead and 3,044,000 wounded *in a population one-third as large.* Moreover, in purely material terms, the United States probably gained from the war. Heavy industries were greatly stimulated by Allied war orders; the war put the growing financial center of New York at least on equal terms with that of London; the dollar had begun to dethrone the monarch of the nineteenth century, the pound sterling. The Allies had borrowed from the American government, but until 1933 some interest came in on these loans. Moreover, the stimulation of American industry resulting from these loans exceeded the loss from the final repudiation of war debts in the early 1930's. The United States, then, came out of the war almost unscathed, victorious, and prosperous.

Isolationism

Yet in some ways the American revulsion against the war in 1919 and the years following was as marked as that of Britain, France, and defeated Germany. On the level of party politics, that revulsion helped to unseat the Democrats, who, under President Wilson, had controlled the federal government since 1913. The Republicans won the presidential elections of 1920, 1924, and 1928. Three successive Republicans occupied the White House — Harding (1921–1923), Coolidge (1923–1929), and Herbert Hoover (1929–1933). The elections were uneventful and not very close; the election of 1928 was, however, notable for the bitterness aroused in many quarters by the unsuccessful candidacy of the Democrat Alfred E. Smith, a Roman Catholic. Many sound observers felt that Smith's religion had been largely instrumental in his defeat and that the American people simply would not elect a Roman Catholic to the highest office of state.

On the level of policy and public attitudes, American revulsion against war took the form of *isolationism,* the desire to withdraw from international politics. This isolationism was by no means universal among Americans. Some historians feel that the drives and attitudes of millions of men had already made isolationism certain in 1919. Others feel that a slight shift in the words and deeds of men in high places could have changed the final decision and could at least have brought America into the League of Nations. If, as we have already seen, the Democratic President Wilson had been willing to meet Republican opposition in the Senate by a few concessions, then perhaps the Treaty of Versailles, League of Nations and all, might have achieved the two-thirds majority in the Senate the Constitution requires for treaties. Or if someone on the Republican side, with skill and prestige, had been able to put through the notion of a bipartisan foreign policy, then with patience and good will the United States might have been brought into the League. Public opinion, say those who take this view, was not against our carrying on the task we had begun in 1917; only a noisy minority in the country as a whole, and the little group of obstinate senators at the top, wanted us to withdraw.

Yet those who remember the years right after 1918 find it hard to deny that the country was swept by a wave of desire to get back to "normalcy," as President Harding later termed it. A great many Americans felt that they had done all they needed to do in beating the Germans and that further direct participation in the complexities of European politics would simply involve American innocence and virtue that much more disastrously in European sophistication and vice. The not uncommon American reaction against its "strong" presidents took the form of repudiating all of Wilson's work at Paris as un-American. Furthermore, as the months of negotiation went on with no final decisions reached, Americans, always an impatient people, began to feel that sheer withdrawal was about the only effective action they could take.

The Treaty of Versailles, containing at Wilson's insistence the League of Nations, was finally rejected in the Senate on March 19, 1920. The United States remained technically at war with Germany until July, 1921, when a resolution making a separate peace was passed by Congress and signed under the presidency of Harding. American isolationism was expressed in these years in other concrete measures. The Fordney-McCumber Tariff of 1922 and the Smoot-Hawley Tariff of 1930 set successively higher duties on foreign goods and emphasized America's belief that her high wage scales needed to be protected from cheap foreign labor.

Yet the United States continued all through the 1920's to insist that the debts owed to her by the Allied powers be repaid. It is true that these were refunded in a series of agreements, and that in the closely related problem of German reparations Americans on the whole cast their weight on the side of a general scaling-down of German obligations. But Congress paid little heed to the argument, so convincing to most economists, that European nations could not repay save through dollars gained by sales of their goods in the American market, and that American tariffs continued to make such repayment impossible. Congressmen tended to reduce the complexities of international debts to President Coolidge's simple dictum: "They hired the money, didn't they?"

The spirit of isolationism also lay behind the immigration restrictions of the 1920's, which reversed the former American policy of almost free immigration. The act of 1924 set an annual quota limit for each country of 2

per cent of the number of nationals from that country resident in the United States in 1890. Since the heavy immigration from eastern and southern Europe had come after 1890, the choice of that date reduced the flow from these areas to a mere trickle. Northern countries like Britain, Germany, and Scandinavia, on the other hand did not use up their quotas.

The Road to Internationalism

Yet during this era of partial isolationism the United States by no means withdrew entirely from international politics. Rather, as an independent without formal alliances, she continued to pursue policies that seemed to most Americans traditional, but that in their totality gradually lined her up against the chief perturbing nations of the years between the two world wars. Even before the drift of her commitments against Germany, Italy, and Japan became clear in the 1930's, Americans had in fact engaged themselves. In 1928, the Republican Secretary of State Kellogg submitted to the great European powers a proposal for a renunciation of war. Incorporated with similar proposals from the French Foreign Minister Briand, it was formally adopted in August of that year as the Pact of Paris, commonly known as the Kellogg-Briand Pact. It was eventually signed by twenty-three nations, including the United States. It is now the fashion to decry the Pact as futile, and it is certainly true that it did not prevent World War II. Yet by this action the United States expressed a concrete concern over the peace of the world.

In a hundred ways the United States was at work laying the foundations for the position of world leadership it reached after World War II. American businessmen were everywhere; American loans were making possible the revival of German industrial greatness; American motors, refrigerators, typewriters, telephones, and other products of the assembly line were being sold the world over. In the Far East, the United States as early as 1922 took the lead in the Nine-Power Treaty that committed her and the other great powers, including Japan, to respect the sovereignty and integrity of China. If President Roosevelt in 1941 resisted the Japanese attempt to swallow China and other Far Eastern territory, he was simply following a line laid down under President Harding.

Boom—and Bust

In domestic affairs, the Coolidge era (1923–1929) has now become legendary. These were years of frantic prosperity; nearly everybody played the stock market and the market value of stocks rose to fantastic heights. They were the years of "prohibition," the ban on the manufacture and sale of alcoholic beverages, enforced, in theory, by the Volstead Act of 1919 under the Eighteenth Amendment to the Constitution. And so they were also the years of the speakeasy and the bootlegger. They were the years of the short skirt (it was not nearly as short as the skirt of 1966), of sex appeal (abbreviated as "SA"), the Charleston, and other forms of "sin." They were years which, like the "naughty nineties" of the nineteenth century, we look back on with a sort of reproving envy, years that now look colorful and romantic.

But the Coolidge era was by no means completely summed up in novels of the jazz age, like *The Great Gatsby* of F. Scott Fitzgerald, or even in Sinclair Lewis' half-satirical *Babbitt* and *Main Street.* It was an era of marked industrial progress, of solid advancement of the national plant and productive capabilities. It was an era of the steady spreading in the United States of standards of living heretofore limited to the relatively few, standards of living that seemed to intellectuals vulgar and inadequate, but that were nevertheless a new thing in the world. These were the years when, if you had a servant, you could no longer take her for granted, but had to take some pains to keep her satisfied. They were years for which, at their best, the right symbol is no Hollywood character, no intellectual, no great pioneer of industry, nor even a gangster, but rather President Coolidge himself, sober, plodding, insensitive, who said that "the business of America is business."

At its most glamorous, the era ended with the onset of the great depression in the autumn of 1929. During the preceding year, Wall Street had enjoyed an unprecedented boom. Speculators by the millions were playing the market in the hope of quick resale of stocks at huge profits; they bought shares "on margin," paying only a fraction of their cost in cash, and often borrowing the money to pay that small fraction. Not only stocks but many other purchases were financed on borrowed money. Credit had swollen to the point where it was no longer on a sound basis in a largely unregulated economy. Eventually, shrewd investors began to sell their holdings in the belief that the bubble soon would burst. The result was a disastrous drop in stock values, beginning in October, 1929, and continuing almost without let-up to 1933. Both the speculators and the lenders from whom they had borrowed money were ruined.

The immediate cause of the depression, then, was the stock-market crash. About the more deep-seated causes the economic physicians are not even today wholly agreed. Some of them believe that a capitalist society inevitably produces business cycles oscillating from the highs of prosperity to the lows of depression; that these cycles are of various lengths, short, medium, and long; and that an unusual number of cyclical lows coincided in the late 1920's to make the depression particularly serious. Others, not uninfluenced by Marx, hold that under American capitalism the troughs of a depression are bound to be deeper each time, if only because of the great scale of the American economy.

This much seems certain: Coolidge prosperity was very unevenly distributed among the various parts of the American economy and American society. Agriculture, notably, suffered a kind of permanent depression throughout the 1920's. At the close of World War I, farmers commanded very high prices for their produce and enjoyed an apparently insatiable market at home and abroad. They expanded their production—and borrowed to finance the expansion—often at a reckless rate. Then, as "normalcy" returned in the early 1920's, the foreign market dried up, the home market shrank, farm prices fell rapidly, and the inevitable foreclosure of farm mortgages began. Wage-earning workers, though not hard hit like the farmers, gained comparatively little increase in their purchasing power during the 1920's. The worker did often raise his standard of living, by purchasing a house or a car, but he did it on credit, by assuming the burden of a heavy mortgage or by financing a purchase on installments to be paid over a long period. The "big money" of the Coolidge era went chiefly to business, above all to big business.

The great depression was very severe in many countries throughout the world, but nowhere was it worse than in the United States. Its effects may be measured by the round figure of 16,000,000 Americans unemployed at the low point in the early 1930's—something like one-third of the national labor force. In terms of what economists call the "gross national product" (GNP), the United States Department of Commerce sets for 1929 the figure of $103,828,000,000; for 1933, however, the same department sets a figure of only $55,760,000,000.

The most remarkable thing about this grave crisis in the American economy is that it produced almost no organized movements of revolt, no threat of revolution. The intellectuals of the 1930's did indeed turn to "social consciousness," and Marxism made some converts among writers and artists. But the bulk of the population showed no serious signs of abandoning their fundamental belief that the way out lay through the legal means provided by existing American institutions. Even before the election of Franklin D. Roosevelt in 1932, local authorities and private charities, helped out by the establishment early in 1932 of the federal R.F.C. (Reconstruction Finance Corporation) to release frozen assets, did a good deal to soften the worst sufferings of the unemployed. The Republican administration of President Hoover, however, was generally committed to the philosophy of laissez-faire;

aside from the R.F.C., it did little to cushion the effects of the depression. People who wanted a more vigorous attack on economic problems voted for the Democrats in 1932; most significantly, they did not vote in very important numbers for the socialist or communist presidential candidates. In the crisis of a great depression, the American two-party system evidently continued to meet basic political needs.

The New Deal

The victory of the Democrats in 1932 seemed to give them a clear mandate to marshal all the resources of the federal government against the depression. The Democratic president, Franklin Roosevelt (1933–1945), took office on March 4, 1933, in the midst of a financial crisis that had closed the banks all over the country. He at once summoned Congress to an emergency session and declared a bank holiday. Gradually the sound banks reopened, and the New Deal began. Subsequently, under improving economic conditions, the American business community mostly turned with great bitterness against Roosevelt and all his works. But in those early months of 1933 the mere fact that a national administration was trying to do something about the situation was a powerful restorative to national morale. The nation emerged from the bank holiday with a new confidence, echoing the phrase from Roosevelt's inaugural address that there was nothing to fear "but fear itself."

The New Deal was in part a series of measures aimed at immediate difficulties and in part a series of measures aimed at permanent changes in the structure of American society. The distinction between its short-term and its long-term measures is in a sense arbitrary, for the men who carried both through were never quite clear in their own minds exactly what they were trying to do. What must chiefly interest us is the implications of their work. In the perspective of western history, the New Deal was the coming to the United States, under the special pressures of

VANITY FAIR

Cartoon on a magazine cover, 1934: the blue eagle was the symbol of the NRA, an ambitious effort by the New Deal to bolster the industrial recovery and the welfare of labor; the Supreme Court declared it unconstitutional in 1935.

the great depression, of those measures — "socialist" to some of their opponents — that we have already seen in European countries like Great Britain and imperial Germany. They are best summed up in that value-charged term, the "welfare state."

The short-term measures of the New Deal aimed by releasing the dollar from its tie with gold to lower the price of American goods in a world that was abandoning the gold standard. They aimed to thaw out credit by extending the activities of the R.F.C. and by creating such new governmental lending agencies as the Home Owners' Loan Corporation. They aimed to relieve unemployment by public works on a large scale, to safeguard bank deposits by the Federal Deposit Insurance Corporation, and to regulate speculation and other stockmarket activities by the Securities

and Exchange Commission. The historical significance of many of these innovations rested in the fact that they were undertaken not by private business or by state or local authorities but by the federal government. There was one exception to the rule of widening federal activity. The Twenty-first Amendment to the Constitution repealed the Eighteenth and abandoned the increasingly unsuccessful federal efforts to enforce prohibition.

The long-term measures of the New Deal were, of course, more important. The Social Security Act of 1935 introduced to the United States on a national scale the unemployment insurance, old-age pensions, and other benefits of the kind that Lloyd George had brought into Britain. Somewhat more equal distribution of the national wealth resulted from increased federal taxation, especially taxes on individual and corporate incomes. Congress passed a whole series of acts on labor relations, the net effect of which has been to strengthen and extend the role of organized labor in American economic life. A series of acts on agriculture, though leaving the business of farming still in the hands of several million individual farmers producing for sale in a cash market, nevertheless regulated crops and prices to a degree that would have been incomprehensible to a nineteenth-century farmer. And finally — the showpiece of the New Deal — a great regional planning board, the Tennessee Valley Authority, used government power to make over the economic and social life of a relatively backward area by checking the erosion of farmlands, by instituting flood control, and by providing cheap electric power generated at government-built dams.

Nearly thirty-five years after the bank holiday of 1933, Americans were still debating the New Deal. It unquestionably left the United States a society very different from that pictured by the classical economists. No real society has ever quite corresponded to the theoretical extreme of free enterprise, in which every man sells and buys what he wants — or can — and in which the man who cannot "earn" a living quite simply dies. But in the sense in which the United States of, say, 1870 was close to such a society, the United

States of the New Deal and after has been quite far from such a society. The rush of free competition has been tempered by government regulation, because it has become clear that in such competition much that men prize would in fact be competed out of existence. Most Americans have come to see the need for government regulation in the conservation of natural resources. Even here, however, when it comes to the overgrazing of pasture lands or the farming methods that lead to soil erosion, some Americans are still reluctant to have the government interfere with their "rights."

When the question at stake is the distribution of wealth, rather than its actual exhaustion, Americans are often unwilling to accept limitations on free enterprise. On this issue, even after the New Deal, the champions of government regulation and private initiative still do battle. The Marxist indictment of a competitive society, that under it the rich tend to become richer and the poor to become poorer, is not wholly true. But the last two hundred years of western history suggest that without some government regulation the modern scramble for wealth tends to produce a society pyramidal in structure. With a few men of great wealth at the top, the pyramid spreads out through the well-to-do to a broad base of human beings just able to scrape along. In our western society, however, the political power democracy gives to that numerous broad base has over the years been used to alter the very shape of the social pyramid. "Soak-the-rich" taxation and government aid to the poor have flattened it out, cutting it down at the top and pushing it up from the bottom. Indeed, the figure is almost certainly no longer a pyramid, but somewhere approaching a diamond shape, widest in the middle. It is not yet in any human society a straight line, representing absolute social and economic equality.

There is, then, in modern America a leveling, both up and down. The great baronial mansions of the Hudson Valley, of Newport, even of California, are too expensive to maintain, and are being turned into museums or put to institutional use. There are still a number of very rich men, but they no longer build themselves palaces, and in general they try to lead inconspicuous lives. The worst of the urban slums are being slowly demolished to make way for modern housing projects. The number of the very poor is diminishing. Meanwhile, the total national product has increased. It is not merely that a fixed national income is being more evenly distributed; despite the complaints of conservatives that the leveling process is destroying incentives to hard work and invention, the gross national product has increased greatly since the depth of the depression in 1932–1933. There is more to be shared.

It must be noted that the American society that emerged from the New Deal can by no means be accurately described as "socialistic." The United States of the mid-twentieth century is rather a "mixed economy," in which individual economic activity—that of the worker as well as that of the entrepreneur or manager—is indeed regulated and restricted, but not entirely controlled, by government. The United States still displays an extraordinary range of economic activity, from the "socialistic" Post Office to enormous private industries that are themselves societies, almost governments, with administrative problems and bureaucracies of their own, and on down to small independent businessmen, who are often the best examples of almost pure free enterprise.

Confident America

Although Americans still argue about the New Deal, it seems evident that the measures taken by the Roosevelt administration, combined with the strength of American institutions and culture, pulled the United States at least part way out of the depression. These measures also restored a high degree of confidence to Americans. The intellectuals, whose role in modern America has generally been in opposition to the men of business, in the 1920's had found the United States a hopelessly crass and vulgar society. But in the 1930's, though some intellectuals flirted with

Marxism, many of them turned to support the new American way marked out by the New Deal.

The onset of war in Europe found Americans, as we shall see in the next chapter, anxious not to jeopardize in war their still precarious prosperity, anxious to remain neutral if Europe should persist in going to war. Roosevelt and his Republican opponents had been for some time exchanging insults: the "economic royalists" fought back at "that man in the White House." Yet in the pinch of the international crisis of 1939–1941 it became clear that, although the nation was not completely united, at any rate it was not pathologically divided. As so often in American history, the violence of verbal politics masked a very basic unity. When the war came to the United States in 1941, Americans were largely ready for it psychologically and—what is really remarkable in a western democracy —not too unready for it militarily.

When the war came, moreover, the United States had already made many efforts to enlist the support of the Latin-American states. In 1930, before the so-called "Roosevelt Revolution" in American diplomacy, President Hoover's State Department issued the Clark Memorandum, specifically stating that the Monroe Doctrine does not concern itself with inter-American relations but is directed against outside intervention in the affairs of the Western Hemisphere. The United States was no longer to land the Marines in some Central American republic at the drop of a hat but was trying to strengthen hemispheric solidarity. And so, on the foundations of the Clark Memorandum, President Roosevelt built his celebrated "Good Neighbor" policy toward the other American nations (for details on Latin America, see Chapter 23).

Meantime, what may be called American imperial policy was likewise undergoing some liberalization, notably with respect to the Philippines. When the United States had annexed the islands at the close of the Spanish-American War (see Chapter 16), a stubborn Filipino insurrection broke out in protest, and it took American forces three years (1899–1902) to subdue the rebels. Filipino nationalists, though partially disarmed by the conciliatory measures taken by the United States after the suppression of the rebellion, none the less continued to advocate eventual freedom. In the 1930's, American officials negotiated with Filipino leaders with the aim at first of bestowing a rather dilute kind of dominion status on the islands. But by the outbreak of World War II the negotiations had advanced to the point where it was evident that the Philippines would soon gain at least nominal independence.

V   The Loosening of Imperial Ties

The Filipino insurrection of 1899 was a portent. Even before 1914, there were signs that many of the more advanced "colonial" peoples were already chafing under imperialism. Native nationalist movements were creating trouble for the British in Egypt and India, for the French in Morocco and Algeria, and for all the imperial powers in China. The First World War itself speeded up the process of rousing national consciousness among the "natives" of the various empires, and at its end there was no doubt that the hold of the West had been loosened. Psychologically, the experience of the war gave a lift to non-western peoples; they had often rendered important services to their white masters, and their leaders had widened their knowledge of the West. The Arab peoples of the old Ottoman Empire had raised armies of their own and had fought with European aid for their own freedom from Turkish rule. French colonial troops and British India troops had taken part in the conflict, sometimes in Europe itself.

The very spectacle of the masters quarreling among themselves did something to lower the prestige of the West among subject peoples. Moreover, the Allies had fought the war in the name of democratic ideals of self-determination for all peoples, and in their propaganda against the Central Powers they had stressed their opposition to imperialism. The fifth of Wilson's Fourteen Points asserted that in disputed claims to colonial territories "the interests of the populations concerned must have equal weight" with the interests of the colonial powers. It is true that the Allies did not give up any of their territories in 1919, and did indeed add to them under the mandate system (see Chapter 17). To many of the subject races, as to liberals in the West itself, the mandate was simply a disguise for the old imperialism; but it is surely significant that a disguise seemed necessary to the imperialist powers. The West now appeared to be committed to a process of at least gradual emancipation of the colonial dependencies.

It was in the Far East that old imperial ties were most clearly loosened during the interwar years. China, as we shall soon see in more detail, was engaged in a great struggle to free herself from the tutelage of the western colonial powers. The conflict in China, however, was much more than a simple conflict between oriental nationalists and occidental imperialists. Almost from the start it was complicated by two additional elements—increasing communist intervention in Chinese politics, and the increasing threat to Chinese independence from an expansionist Japan. It is scarcely an exaggeration to say that China faced the prospect of simply exchanging one set of imperial overlords for another.

Japan

Alone among non-western peoples, the Japanese experienced the industrial revolution and were able to maintain themselves as a fully independent major political entity during the great age of imperialism (see Chapter 16). More than that, as the twentieth century opened, Japan was clearly a great power, a full but somewhat unwelcome participant in the struggle for imperial position. As we have seen, the Japanese made these impressive accomplishments without radically altering their traditional oligarchical and absolutist political structure.

In the decade after World War I, it looked as though Japan might achieve a gradual liberalization of her political institutions. The cabinets of the 1920's included many men from the business class who favored vigorous expansion abroad but who also granted some measures of cautious liberalism at home. The suffrage was gradually extended, and in 1925 all men received the right to vote. For the first time, political parties, western-style, began to put down roots, especially in the urban population, and seemed likely to give new vitality to the Diet, the not very powerful central representative assembly of Japan. Trade unions also took shape and began to win a following.

Japan, however, did not evolve into a parliamentary democracy on the western model during the twenty years' truce. By the early 1930's, political power was falling more and more into the hands of army and navy officers, many of whom were descended from the feudal *samurai* class (see p. 615). This officer clique hated the prospect of liberal civilian government and envied and mistrusted the business class. They found a potent political weapon in the institution of the emperor, who was supposed to possess the kind of political infallibility that westerners associate with a divine-right monarch. Putting their own words into the emperor's mouth, the admirals and generals used his pronouncements to further their own ends. And, to make doubly sure, they assassinated or terrorized the chief spokesmen of nascent Japanese liberalism.

The consequence was the progressive clamping of a military dictatorship on Japan during the 1930's. Although popular elections continued to be held, their results were disregarded, and the Diet lost its recently acquired vitality. Businessmen supported the new régime out of fear or out of anticipation of the huge profits to be secured from its adventures abroad. A cult of emperor-worship, known as state Shinto, was concocted out of a rather innocuous traditional Japanese religion to focus popular loyalties on the divine mission of the emperor and to insure popular submission to the will of the men who ruled in his name. A corps of ruthless agents, picturesquely named "thought police," hounded anyone suspected of harboring "dangerous thoughts." In short, Japan now had a government that exploited many uniquely Japanese traditions but in its operations also bore a striking resemblance to the totalitarian governments of Europe.

Nowhere was the parallel with European totalitarianism more marked than in the foreign policy of Japan between the two world wars. Like Hitler's Germans or Mussolini's Italians, the Japanese claimed to be a "have-not" nation. They, too, pointed to their steadily growing population—and did all they could to encourage its further growth. They, too, harped on the over-crowding of the homeland, its inadequate resources, and its restricted markets. Behind these arguments lay real economic problems of sustaining the Japanese economy in the face of the depression and the world-wide disruption of international trade, problems of providing food and work for the 60,000,000 Japanese in 1930. In seeking to solve these problems by imperial expansion, the militarists of the 1930's were following a pattern that had already been set by the West. And they were also following the path marked out by the Japanese officers and politicians who had secured Formosa in 1895 and annexed Korea in 1910. During World War I, Japan had tried in vain to subjugate China; by World War II, she had apparently almost succeeded in doing so. To follow the course of this Japanese imperialism we must turn to the history of its chief victim, China.

"Rule, Japannia. Very nice, yes!—so long as honourable foreign ladies continue to sit apart." Cartoonist Low comments on Japan's profiting by British and American failure to pursue a coordinated Far Eastern policy during the 1930's.

Chinese prisoners taken by foreign troops suppressing the Boxer rebellion.

hina: The Revolution of 1911–1912

By 1900, the Chinese Empire was far gone in political decay. Nominally independent under the rule of its Manchu dynasty, it had lost much of its effective sovereignty through concessions of naval bases and economic and political privileges to the European powers and Japan. Following China's defeat by Japan in 1895, European imperialists engaged in a hectic scramble for further concessions. The Germans leased Kiaochow, the French Kwangchou Bay, the Russians Port Arthur, and the British Wei-hai-wei (see also Chapter 16). In 1899, the American Secretary of State, John Hay, sought to end the scramble by getting the powers to accept the principle of the "Open Door," whereby all foreign goods could be marketed in China on equal terms, with no special favors to any one power. Although the interested states subscribed to Hay's policy in principle, the Open Door meant little in practice.

Meantime, a formidable reaction to the outburst of imperialist activity was gathering within China itself. The hard-pressed Manchu government encouraged the formation of an anti-foreign nationalist secret society called the Boxers. The result was the Boxer Rebellion of 1900, in which more than 200 foreigners, mainly missionaries, were slain. The foreign powers, including the United States, used troops to protect their nationals and property against the Boxers. In 1901, they obliged the Manchu government to pay an enormous indemnity and to grant them further rights that, of course, further impaired Chinese sovereignty.

The next Chinese rebellion, the revolution of 1911, was directed against the Manchu régime that had proved so incapable of resisting the encroachments of imperialism. In this revolution, a factor operated that may often be found in the whole process of national self-assertion by non-western peoples. The movement is directed against the West—against westerners themselves or against native governors who seem to be the agents of the West. But it is a movement inspired at least in part by Western ideas and examples, led by often thoroughly "westernized" natives, a movement that could scarcely have come into being without the influence of the West.

771

The Chinese revolution of 1911 was comparatively bloodless in its early stages. It was sealed by the abdication on February 12, 1912, of the six-year-old Manchu Emperor, Pu-yi. From the start, the two chief revolutionary groups displayed conflicting ideas about the nature of the new society that would replace the discarded Manchu régime. One group soon formed the Nationalist party, the Kuomintang, led by Sun Yat-sen and many young intellectuals who had studied and traveled in the West. Its leaders wanted a democratic parliamentary republic of China modeled on the western political system, though preserving as far as possible the basic Chinese family and village structure, on which western industrial society was to be grafted. The other group, whose leader was Yuan Shih-k'ai, wanted a strong central government basically authoritarian in structure, with authority not in the hands of an emperor and the traditional and highly conservative Chinese mandarin bureaucracy, but in the hands of strong men capable of achieving the modernization of China from above.

A struggle for power broke out between the assembly elected after 1911 and Yuan Shih-k'-ai. The party of Sun Yat-sen was defeated, and by 1914, after a "purge" of the Kuomintang members of the assembly, Yuan Shih-k'ai issued a constitutional compact that put him in the presidential office for ten years. Sun Yat-sen and his followers had failed to turn China into a western parliamentary democracy. Sun was, however, a gifted leader, and the ideas for which he stood, though they never were firmly rooted in China, have never quite disappeared. Sun remains somewhat paradoxically the great hero of the Chinese revolution of 1911.

Yuan's subsequent career bears some resemblance to that of another military reformer, Oliver Cromwell. Faced with continuing opposition, not only from the republicans of the Kuomintang but also from the monarchists, Yuan decided to follow the age-old Chinese pattern and set himself up as the first of a new dynasty of emperors to follow the Manchus. A revolt caused him to revoke his plans, and early in 1916 he reorganized the republic with a military cabinet. He died on June 6, 1916, leaving the new republic enmeshed in another age-old Chinese political pattern — the dissolution of all but the shadow of central control and the assumption of real power by regional strong men. A new era of provincial "war-lords" had begun.

In the years of crisis following 1911, China also faced the aggressive attempts of Japan to take over the Far Eastern imperial interests of European powers now at war among themselves. Early in 1915, the Japanese presented in secrecy to the Chinese government the "Twenty-One Demands," which amounted to a demand for something close to a protectorate over China and for all sorts of concrete concessions. The Chinese republic, now at the nadir of its strength, countered by declaring war against the Central Powers, thus securing at least the nominal protection of two of the Allies, Britain and France. The Japanese did not feel able to defy western objections, and so contented themselves with taking over Kiaochow and other German concessions in the Shantung peninsula. At the end of the war, the victorious Allies, with the United States in the lead, acted to check the ambitions of their recent military partner, Japan. At the Washington Conference of 1922 (see also Chapter 21), Japan was forced to sign the Nine-Power Treaty guaranteeing the independence of China. This rebuff to Japan was one of the first events in the long chain that aggravated the hostility of Japan toward the United States, and ended, two decades later, in the attack on Pearl Harbor.

China between the World Wars

The details of Chinese history between the two world wars are extraordinarily complex. The main elements during this twenty-year period were the Kuomintang, the Communists, and the Japanese invaders. The Kuomintang, after the death of Sun Yat-sen in 1925, came under the leadership of Chiang Kai-shek, an army officer trained in Japan and the brother-in-law of Sun Yat-sen. The Nationalists of the Kuomintang were engaged in a constant and often very unsuccessful struggle to set up an effective central government against the power of provincial "war-lords." They were also often locked in battle with the Communists and the Japanese.

All three of the main forces fought in word and deed for the allegiance—or at any rate for the passive acceptance—of nearly five hundred million Chinese, for the most part peasants, and for the most part illiterate. For the most part, too, the masses of China were so far from sharing western attitudes toward the state that it is hardly an exaggeration to say that they felt toward politics as we westerners feel toward the weather—that it is something beyond human control. In transforming the Chinese into a nation in the western sense, the indispensable step was something more than building railroads and factories or promoting the study of modern science instead of the Chinese classics. It was getting the Chinese peasant to regard himself as an individual Chinese citizen.

This indispensable process was beginning in the 1920's and 1930's. It goes far to explain why the Japanese, when they renewed their aggression in 1931, were virtually beaten from the start in the attempt to become the true masters of China. In an earlier age one can readily imagine the Japanese as military conquerors in China setting up a new dynasty, foreign in origin, but very soon thoroughly absorbed by the Chinese. That this age-old pattern was not followed in the 1930's shows that China herself was changing, that here too the modern expansion of the West, the spread of western ways and ideas, was altering her traditional way of life.

The Japanese attack came in September, 1931, on Manchuria, an outlying northern province of China that was a particularly tempting target for Japanese aggression. Manchuria had good resources of coal and iron; it adjoined Korea, already a Japanese possession; and it had never been fully integrated into the structure of Chinese government and looked, therefore, as though it could easily be pried loose. Moreover, the Japanese regarded themselves as the natural successors of the Russians, whom they had driven from Manchuria in the Russo-Japanese War of 1904–1905. By 1932, the Japanese were strong enough in Manchuria to proclaim it an "independent" state, which they called Manchukuo, under a puppet ruler, Pu-yi, who as a boy had been the last emperor of old China.

The Chinese responded to Japan's aggression in Manchuria by a very effective boycott of Japanese goods; the Japanese countered by carrying the war to the great Chinese port of Shanghai. Given the weakness of the Kuomintang government, effective Chinese resistance would have required full support from stronger outside powers. Neither the western powers nor the League of Nations gave China more than verbal support (for details, see Chapter 21); the Chinese had to give up their boycott of Japanese goods, and the Japanese remained in Manchuria. Tension between China and Japan persisted, however, and the Japanese soon decided to attempt the absorption of all the rest of China. Their invasion came in July, 1937, without a formal declaration of war.

In a purely military way the Japanese did very well. By October, when the key southern Chinese city of Canton fell, they had taken the strategic points of the coastal area and the thickly peopled lower river valleys. Chiang Kai-shek took refuge with his army and his fellow politicians of the Kuomintang in the interior province of Szechwan. There he set up his capital at Chungking; and there, protected by distance and a ring of mountains, receiving western aid through India by the Burma Road and, when that was closed, by air, the Nationalist government held out until the end of World War II and the collapse of Japanese imperialism.

Yet the Japanese, even at the height of their success, had achieved no more than the stretching across China of a string of garrisons, and the control of great cities like Shanghai and Peiping. They held the railroads, subject to guerilla attack, but away from the relatively sparse lines of modern communication they were helpless. Many a Chinese village in the area nominally Japanese never changed its ways during the occupation. Nowhere did the Japanese win over the acquiescence, to say nothing of the loyalty, of the Chinese people.

The Nationalists of the Kuomintang led the resistance to the Japanese from the beginning, yet they, too, ultimately failed to win the full loyalty of the Chinese people. This was partly a military matter. Chiang's armies were never able to stand on equal terms with the Japanese. They lacked a good modern industrial base, and, as the Japanese early seized the few industrial cities of China, Chiang was always relatively badly off in terms of logistics. In the long exile in Szechwan, moreover, the morale of the Nationalists decayed. The ordeal, far from purifying and strengthening them, emphasized their alienation from the masses of the Chinese, their corruption and intrigue, their inability to live up to the early promise of Sun Yat-sen and the Kuomintang. For it was not the Nationalists, but the Communists, who succeeded in capturing and harnessing the human emotions and aspirations, the binding power that will hold men together in society with the tightness modern material culture demands. It was the Communists, not the Nationalists, who apparently came to stand to most Chinese for what made them Chinese; the Communists came to embody Chinese "nationalism."

The Chinese Communists

The Chinese Communist movement began in the early 1920's. It was inspired by direct contacts with the Comintern in Moscow, guided by Soviet agents, and encouraged at first by leaders of the Kuomintang. Sun Yat-sen hoped that the example and advice of the successful Russian party might help to strengthen his own faltering party organization. For a time, the Chinese Communists were no more than the left wing of the Kuomintang. Soon, however, the inevitable breach occurred between them and the more conservative elements among the Nationalists, led by Chiang Kai-shek.

The Communists lost out badly in this early struggle for power. In 1926, Chiang's forces began a campaign of persecution and assassination against them; in 1927, they were ex-

pelled from the Kuomintang. An important reason for this setback was the failure of the Chinese Communists to get effective support or help from Moscow. The years 1926 and 1927 were the years of the Trotsky-Stalin feud in Russia, and the conflict between these two titans was intensified by their differences over the "correct" Chinese policy for the Soviet Union to follow. Stalin, who was rapidly gaining the ascendancy, believed that China was not ripe for a proletarian revolution; therefore, he did nothing to succor his Chinese comrades.

During the next two decades, down to the end of World War II, the relative strength of Communists and Nationalists underwent a gradual and decisive shift. Both parties, it should be noted, were in a sense totalitarian. Both were organized on the one-party pattern, which left no place for an opposition; neither of them was geared to the give-and-take of western party politics. The Communists, driven about over much of China during the 1930's, ended up with a base in the region of Yenan in the north; their strategic position somewhat resembled that of Chiang in his southern base of Szechwan. But there was an important difference. In the long years of Japanese occupation, Chiang remained in Chungking with his army and his bureaucracy. The Communists, on the other hand, managed to string their network of organized armies and local councils in and around the Japanese in the north; they extended their apparatus right down to the sea and up through Manchuria. By 1945, the Communists were ready for a successful conflict with the Kuomintang (see Chapter 23).

Southeast Asia

The great turning point in the recent history of the Far East has been World War II, with its aftermath of Communist victory in China, of French withdrawal from Indo-China, British from Burma, Dutch from the East Indies, and American from the Philippines. Before World War II there were few clear signs of the spectacular changes to come in Southeast Asia, that part of the Far East stretching east from India and south from China through the islands of Indonesia. But informed observers during the twenty years' truce noted the slow growth of nationalist opposition to imperial rule, particularly in Indo-China and the Netherlands East Indies. They saw that the British-controlled Malay peninsula, with its characteristic colonial economy of rubber and tin production, was peculiarly dependent on the economic health of the West and peculiarly vulnerable in a major depression.

India

In India, by contrast, World War I marked a crucial turning point. India made important contributions to the British armies, particularly to their victory over the Turks. Indians, educated in the western tradition, growing in numbers and long exposed to the kind of ideas we call liberal, received the full impact of Allied propaganda in favor of the war to save the world for democracy. Monetary inflation and other war dislocations favored the growing agitation for self-government. Already in the war period the British Viceroy, Lord Chelmsford, and his experts, both British and Indian, were working toward a plan of reform. Public opinion not only in India but throughout the world was sharpened in favor of the Indians by what seemed to be a throwback to the crude days of imperial force when, in April, 1919, British troops fired on demonstrators at Amritsar (see p. 653).

The Amritsar massacre, however, was an exception. One basic fact about India after World War I was the still relatively serene British rule with its slow but steady acclimatization of Indians to western material things like railroads and hospitals and to western ideas like equality and freedom. A second basic fact, growing out of the first, was the growing Indian demand for the termination of British colonial rule. A third basic fact, conditioning the second, was the existence of tension between Hindus and Moslems, which we must now examine in some detail.

A large Moslem minority, about a quarter of the total population, had grown up in the seven hundred years since the first invasion of India by Moslem peoples. In the Indus Basin and part of the Punjab in the northwest, and in part of Bengal in the east, the Moslems were actually a majority; elsewhere they lived scattered among the Hindus and other non-Moslems. Though some of the Moslems belonged to the aristocratic classes, the bulk were peasants, and on the whole the Moslem community was outstripped financially, industrially, and culturally by the Hindu community. Although some Moslems, especially in the upper classes, were proud descendants of conquering tribes, for the most part the Moslems and the Hindus were roughly of the same racial mixtures, both really native Indians.

Yet Moslems and Hindus felt—and feel —toward each other (we are talking in terms of average members of the two communities) in a way exceedingly difficult for most westerners to understand. A friendly British observer has summed it up in this manner:

What are the things which keep Muslims and Hindus apart, which make them feel that they are different races and nations, which keep them permanently potentially on edge with each other? The first perhaps is the doctrinal issue of idolatry. The Muslim has borrowed from the Semitic races both his passionate rejection of polytheism and his passionate hatred of idolatry. . . . The worship of many gods, the portrayal of the divine in human form, is something to him which is less than human, the mark of the beast. It has, I think, no counterpart in the West; for it is far stronger than our ideas of good form or fair play or the behaviour of a gentleman. . . . The ramifications of these emotions are widespread through the whole realm of Hindu-Muslim relations because of the ubiquitous working of the Hindu doctrine of incarnation. So much in Hinduism is divine. The Muslim does not mind a Hindu not eating beef, for example, but he does object to his worshipping the cow. In times of irritation there is consequently a strong urge to kill a cow out of sheer bravado. . . .

But the mental anguish of mutual relations is not all on the Muslim side. Hindus suffer acutely in the ceremonial sphere. Hindu feelings about the cow are as untranslatable into Western terms as are Muslim feelings about idolatry, and they are no less strong. A Hindu may literally turn sick at the sight or smell of beef. Muslim practice in the matter of food seems to the typical Hindu to be impure, dirty, and degraded, something beneath the level of man. He cannot understand, on the other hand, what he calls Muslim fanaticism on the subject of idolatry. Orthodox Hindu and Muslim individuals can be, and often are, very good friends, but they usually take good care that their intercourse avoids these danger areas.*

It is not surprising, therefore, that after serious attempts to bring Hindu and Moslem into a unified resistance movement against the British, two separate bodies grew up in the twentieth century—the Indian National Congress and the All-India Moslem League. Immediately after World War I, the two bodies did often succeed in presenting a common front against the British, but as time went on their mutual opposition, indeed their irreconcilability, tended to increase rather than diminish.

In spite of these difficulties, the Indian drive for self-government and independence went on steadily from the end of World War I. For the Hindus, the Congress party was held together effectively and given extrarodinary influence over the masses by one of the great leaders of the twentieth century, Mahatma Gandhi (1869–1948). Gandhi was not a Brahmin (a member of the highest Hindu caste) but a member of the *bania* or shopkeeping caste. Educated as a lawyer at Oxford and therefore familiar with the West, trained during his youth in politics in South Africa with its Indian minority, Gandhi was admirably equipped to deal with both British and Hindus. Among his own people he appealed by his simple and austere personal life, his fasts, and his exiguous native costume. He worked out the technique of insurrection called "non-violent non-co-operation," which appealed to the fundamental Hindu belief that force is illusory and therefore ineffective. Characteristic measures sponsored by Gandhi were the organized Indian boycott of British goods and the Mahatma's own resistance through hunger-strikes.

*Percival Spear, *India, Pakistan, and the West* (London, 1949), 89–91.

Other Congress leaders, especially at the local level, were willing to use more clearly western methods of agitation, propaganda, and, it must be admitted, rather violent non-violence. Concession after concession was wrung from the British, and as the Indians gained political experience in provincial self-government and in the civil service, dominion status appeared to be just around the corner. This was the situation at the outbreak of World War II. By the time the war was over, however, it was evident that the mutual antagonism of Hindus and Moslems might well require the formation not of a single unified India but of two separate states (see Chapter 22).

Gandhi at 10 Downing Street, London, 1931.

he Middle East

The European powers had a long history of attempts to secure an imperial stake in the Near East—or Middle East, to use the roughly equivalent term that gained currency in World War II. The Middle East refers essentially to Persia and to the Asian and African lands that were still nominally part of the decaying Ottoman Empire at the opening of the twentieth century. At that time, the Middle East was still a poverty-stricken region. But by 1914 the first discoveries of petroleum had been made, discoveries that have gone on and on until today the Middle East contains the largest proved reserves of oil in the world. The whole of the area was not to share in this new wealth. The major fields were found in southwestern Persia, in the river valleys of Iraq (ancient Mesopotamia), and along the Persian Gulf.

The new-found riches of the Middle East did not lessen the interest of the European powers in the region during the twenty years' truce. And in the 1930's, as American experts began to worry about the depletion of oil reserves in the Western Hemisphere, the United States entered the Middle East in something more than its older roles of Protestant missionary and benevolent educator at the American colleges in Beirut (Lebanon) and Istanbul. American oil companies joined with British, Dutch, and French companies in developing and marketing Middle Eastern petroleum.

In the inter-war years, then, the Middle East was an area of increased economic imperialism. It was not, however, an area of the cruder sort of political imperialism, although the western powers maintained sufficient control to insure the orderly exploitation of oil resources. As we have seen in Chapter 17, at the close of World War I the Arab territories of the old Ottoman Empire were administered as western mandates, not annexed as western colonies. The French got the mandates for Syria and for Syria's half-Christian neighbor,

Lebanon. The British, who already held a protectorate over Egypt, got the mandates for Palestine and Iraq. The only Arab state of significance enjoying anything like full independence was Saudi Arabia, which occupied the bulk of the desert Arabian peninsula. It was an essentially medieval state, the personal creation of a remarkable tribal chieftain, a latter-day feudal warrior, Ibn Saud (1880–1953).

The postwar arrangements, which brought so much of the Arab world under a dilute form of imperial control, did not satisfy the aspirations of Arab nationalists. In these nationalist movements the usual ingredients —western education, hatred of westerners, desire to emulate them—were mixed with a common adherence to Islam, and a vague but real feeling of belonging to some kind of common Arab "nation." Arab nationalism was already being focused on the special problem of Palestine, for by the Balfour Declaration of 1917 the British had promised to open this largely Arab-populated territory as a "national home for the Jewish people." The immigration of Jews into Palestine during the years between the wars caused repeated clashes between Arab nationalists and Jewish nationalists or Zionists. The seeds were being sown for the Palestine problem of our own day (see Chapter 22).

The French made few concessions to Arab nationalism; in fact, they infuriated the Syrians by bombarding their capital of Damascus in the course of quelling an insurrection in 1925 and 1926. The British attempted a more conciliatory policy by granting some of their wards nominal independence and substituting the ties of alliance for the older imperial ties. In 1922, Egypt was proclaimed an independent state under King Fuad, though the British retained the right to station troops in the country and insisted that westerners resident there continue to enjoy special privileges. In 1936, an Anglo-Egyptian agreement provided for the eventual termination of foreigners' privileges and for the eventual withdrawal of British troops; Egypt, however, continued to be closely allied with Great Britain. Meantime, the British were following rather similar policies in Iraq and in Transjordan, the half-desert area east of Palestine. Until World War II, it looked as though Britain might have found a way of leading the Arabs gradually to independence and retaining their friendship. But the exacerbation of the Palestine problem after the war and the rapid intensification of Arab nationalism were to blast any hope that the Arabs would remain grateful and loyal "old boys" of the British imperial school.

In the meantime, Turkey was undergoing a political renaissance. The losses suffered by Turkey as a result of World War I reduced her territory for the first time to a cohesive national unit, the largely Turkish-populated lands of Anatolia (or Asia Minor). To defend this Anatolian core against threatened additional losses to the Greeks and to the victorious Allies, the Turks at once launched an ardent nationalist revival extending considerably the reforms begun by the Young Turks before 1914 (see p. 635). The leader of this new political revolution was a highly gifted army officer, Mustafa Kemal (1881–1938), who forced the expulsion of the Greek forces from Anatolia and negotiated more favorable terms with the Allies at Lausanne in 1923 (see p. 660). Under his guidance, the old Ottoman Empire was abolished in 1922, and in its stead the Republic of Turkey was proclaimed, with a constitution modeled on western parliamentary lines. To point up the new orientation of the republic, Kemal moved its capital from cosmopolitan Istanbul, on the western edge of Turkish territory, to Ankara in the heart of Anatolia.

Kemal also imposed rapid, wholesale, and sometimes ruthless measures of westernization. Women received the vote and, at least in theory, were emancipated from traditional Moslem restraints, including the wearing of a veil in public. The whole fabric of social and political life was removed from the highly conservative influence of Islam, again in theory at least. An advanced European law code was introduced; Sunday, not the Moslem Friday, was made the weekly day of rest; even the Turkish language was drastically reformed by the requirement that it employ a western alphabet—a move of major importance, for

only a fraction of the Turkish people had ever been able to master the old Ottoman Turkish, with its heavy content of Persian and Arabic words, and with its difficult Arabic script. All Turks were now required to take surnames in the western manner, and Kemal himself appropriately took that of Atatürk, "Father of the Turks." By the time of his death in 1938, Atatürk had indeed revolutionized his country, even though westernization was only just beginning to trickle down to the grass roots of Turkish society. And he had insured its independence of the West as Turkish neutrality during World War II was soon to demonstrate.

The example of Turkey was followed, though less sweepingly and less effectively, by the other traditionally independent major state of the Middle East—Persia, or, as it has been officially styled since 1935, Iran ("Land of the Aryans"). The Iranian revolution began in 1906 in response to the imperialist encroachments by Britain and Russia that were making Persia a kind of Middle Eastern China. The political structure inherited from the Middle Ages was gradually altered in the direction of limited monarchy, with an elected parliament and with the Shah as a constitutional ruler. Since the political transition was far from smooth, the Iranian revolution proved to be an arrested or abortive one. The country, with its highly powerful class of wealthy landlords and its millions of poor peasants and restless tribesmen, did not adapt itself readily to modern western political institutions. The nearest Iranian equivalent of Atatürk was Reza Shah, an able army officer and a feverish but erratic modernizer who lacked Kemal's sense of the possible. Reza Shah seized the Iranian throne after World War I and lost it in 1941 when his pro-Nazi sympathies led Britain and Russia to send in troops and force his abdication. The fate of Reza Shah served as a reminder that the British and the Russians still kept some of their old interests in Iran, where they had often competed for concessions and for spheres of influence in the past. It also showed that some of the seemingly sovereign states of the non-western world were not yet strong enough to maintain their independence against the might of the great powers. By the time of World War II, imperial ties had been loosened, but they were by no means severed or dissolved; the revolution against imperialism was yet to come (see Chapters 22 and 23).

Reading Suggestions on the Democracies, 1919–1939: Domestic and Imperial Problems

(Asterisk indicates paperbound edition.)

Britain and France

R. Graves and A. Hodge, *The Long Weekend* (Faber & Faber, 1940). A lively social history of Britain during the inter-war years.

G. E. Elton, *The Life of James Ramsay MacDonald* (Collins, 1939); G. M. Young, *Stanley Baldwin* (Hart-Davis, 1952); and K. Feiling, *The Life of Neville Chamberlain* (Macmillan, 1946). Biographies of three important British statesmen.

A. Bullock, *Life and Loves of Ernest Bevin, Vol I. 1881–1940* (Heinemann, 1960). A second volume is promised of this major work.

J. P. Mackintosh, *The British Cabinet* (Univ. of Toronto Press, 1962). From Charles II to the present, an important study of a key institution.

Richard W. Lyman, *The First Labour Government, 1924* (Dresser, Chapman & Grimes, 1957). An important monograph.

C. R. Attlee, *The Labour Party in Perspective,* 2nd ed. (Gollancz, 1949). A review of the inter-war period in Britain by the Labor leader.

E. Weber, *Action Francaise: Royalism and Reaction in 20th Century France* (Stanford Univ. Press, 1962). Covers the period 1898 to 1939; thorough, readable.

R. Albrecht-Carré, *France, Europe and the Two World Wars* (Harper, 1961). An admirable account of French difficulties in these years.

D. Brogan, *France under the Republic* (Harper, 1940). Still one of the most informative introductions to French history in the 1920's and 1930's. See also Brogan's *The French Nation: From Napoleon to Pétain, 1814–1940* (Harper, 1958).

D. Thomson, *Democracy in France,* 3rd ed. (Oxford Univ. Press, 1958). A most stimulating essay in interpretation for those already acquainted with the basic facts.

E. J. Knapton, *France since Versailles* (*Holt, 1952, A Berkshire Study). Handy little manual.

A. Werth, *The Twilight of France, 1933–1940* (Harper, 1942). Condensation of several longer studies by an able foreign correspondent.

The United States

Four volumes in the "Chronicles of America Series" (Yale Univ. Press) provide good coverage of the period: H. U. Faulkner, *From Versailles to the New Deal* (1950); D. Brogan, *The Era of Franklin D. Roosevelt* (1951); A. Nevins, *The United States in a Chaotic World* (1950); and A. Nevins, *The New Deal and World Affairs* (1950).

D. Perkins, *The New Age of Franklin Roosevelt, 1932–1945* (Univ. of Chicago Press, 1957). A sympathetic but by no means uncritical survey.

F. L. Allen, *Only Yesterday* (*Bantam Books), and *Since Yesterday* (Harper, 1940). Lively social histories of the 1920's and 1930's, respectively.

F. Perkins, *The Roosevelt I Knew* (Viking, 1946), and R. E. Sherwood, *Roosevelt and Hopkins,* 2 vols. (*Bantam Books). Perhaps the best of the books about Franklin Roosevelt by the people who worked with him.

F. Freidel, *Franklin D. Roosevelt* (Little, Brown, 1952–1956), 3 vols. A detailed and careful biographical study.

A. M. Schlesinger, Jr., *The Crisis of the Old Order, 1919–1933,* and *The Coming of the New Deal* (Houghton Mifflin, 1957, 1959). The first two volumes in "The Age of Roosevelt" by an historian favorable to the New deal but objective in his judgments.

J. M. Burns, *Roosevelt: The Lion and the Fox* (Harcourt, Brace, 1956). A stimulating though rather limited estimate of Roosevelt the politician.

Economic Developments

J. K. Galbraith, *The Great Crash, 1929* (Houghton Mifflin, 1955; *Sentry). A well-written study of the Wall Street slump by a prominent American economist.

P. Einzig, *The World Economic Crisis, 1929–1932* (Macmillan, 1932); H. V. Hodson, *Slump and Recovery, 1929–1937* (Oxford Univ. Press, 1938); H. W. Arndt, *The Economic Lessons of the Nineteen-Thirties* (Oxford Univ. Press, 1944). Other useful books on the great depression.

J. Schumpeter, *Capitalism, Socialism, and Democracy,* 3rd ed. (Harper, 1950; *Torchbooks); J. M. Keynes, *The End of Laissez-Faire* (Woolf, 1926). Incisive essays by economists.

D. A. Shannon, ed., *The Great Depression* (*Spectrum). A useful collection of source readings, stressing the social consequences of economic ills in the United States.

Other Topics

E. Fischer, *The Passing of the European Age* (Harvard Univ. Press, 1943). Defense of the thesis that leadership in western civilization has passed from Europe to other continents.

E. O. Reischauer, *Japan, Past and Present,* 2nd ed., rev. (Knopf, 1956). An excellent introductory account. See also Reischauer's *United States and Japan,* 3rd ed. (Harvard Univ. Press, 1965).

L. Fischer, *Gandhi* (*New American Library, 1954). A sympathetic biography.

P. Spear, *India, Pakistan, and the West,* 3rd ed. (Oxford Univ. Press, 1958). Illuminating.

W. N. Brown, *The United States and India and Pakistan,* rev. ed. (Harvard Univ. Press, 1963). An excellent introduction. This edition has a very good reading list.

J. K. Fairbank, *The United States and China,* rev. ed. (Harvard Univ. Press, 1958). Reliable, informative introduction to the controversial subject of recent Chinese history.

K. S. Latourette, *A History of Modern China* (*Penguin). A good brief account.

S. N. Fisher, *The Middle East: A History* (Knopf, 1959). Well-balanced survey.

G. L. Lewis, *Turkey* (Praeger, 1955). Summary and results of Atatürk revolution.

Sir Harry Luke, *The Old Turkey and the New* (Bles, 1955). Perceptive essay on the contrasts between the Ottoman Empire and the Turkey of Atatürk.

S. H. Longrigg, *Syria and Lebanon under French Mandate* (Oxford Univ. Press, 1958). Detailed study of the very mixed record of French rule in the Levant.

Note: Many titles useful for the history of the non-western world during the twenty years' truce will also be found in the reading suggestions for Chapter 22; for background and more information on the twenty years, see also some of the titles in Chapter 16.

Fiction

E. Waugh, *A Handful of Dust* (New Directions, 1945). Corrosive novel satirizing English society in the inter-war years.

H. Spring, *Fame Is the Spur* (Viking, 1940). A politician is corrupted by ambition; largely parallels the career of Ramsay MacDonald.

W. Holtby, *South Riding* (Macmillan, 1936). Good social novel of industrial England.

A. Gide, *The Counterfeiters* (Knopf, 1927). Mordant study of the French middle class by an eminent novelist.

21

The Second World War

General or world wars in our state-system are usually born of a previous war, or, perhaps better, of a previous peace settlement that fails to solve certain important problems. We have already been obliged in seeking the origins of the First World War to go back to 1870, to Bismarck, to the "rape of Alsace-Lorraine" and the consequent rise of the spirit of revenge among Frenchmen. We shall now have to go back to 1919 and the grave difficulties that arose in the attempt to carry out the settlement of Versailles. So troubled were international relations for the twenty years after 1919, so closely in time did the Second World War follow on the First, that the interval between the two has been christened the "twenty years' truce." And it is not impossible that historians in the future will actually consider the two wars really one war, as they now consider the wars of the French Revolution and Napoleon essentially one war. Though, to the purist historian the first world wars were perhaps those of Louis XIV, if not those of Charles V and Philip II, for the present we must use the accepted terms, World War I (1914–1918) and World War II (1939–1945). Such usage has at least the advantage of pointing up by the use of roman numerals the close relationship of these two wars. In both wars Germany appears as the perturber.

I   International Politics, 1919–1932

During the first part of the twenty years' truce, international leadership of the democratic world rested with Britain and France. Though supported in principle and often in practice by the United States, they were increasingly unable to stem the rise of powers hostile to liberal democracy—Italy, Germany, Spain, Russia, Japan. In the end, the beaten perturber of 1918, Germany, waged aggressive warfare against the major Allies of 1918. This time Germany allied with two of its former enemies, Italy and Japan, each disappointed with its share of the spoils of victory in 1918.

Why was the peace settlement of 1919 followed in twenty years by a second great war? Why was it so unlike the last great settlement, that of 1815 following the Napoleonic wars, which had inaugurated a long period of general peace, interrupted only by localized wars? Nazi Germany maintained that the second war was the direct and inevitable result of the *Diktat,* the dictated peace of Versailles that ended the first war. Supported by most Germans and many German sympathizers, the Nazis claimed that Germany was humiliated by the war-guilt clause, stripped of territories and colonies that were rightfully hers, saddled with an astronomical and unpayable reparations bill, denied the normal rights of a sovereign state in armaments—in short, so badly treated that simple human dignity made revolt against the *Dikat* and its makers a necessity. Now this is partly true. The settlement of Versailles did saddle the new German Republic with a heavy burden in part dictated by revenge and fear. A wiser Allied policy would perhaps have tried to start the new government off without too great a burden, as the Allies in 1815 did with the France of Louis XVIII (see Chapter 11).

The "Era of Fulfillment"

But the *Diktat* thesis is very far from containing the whole truth. What breaks down the argument that the iniquities of Versailles alone explain the second war is the "era of fulfillment." In spite of the Treaty of Versailles, the Germans and their former enemies did manage to come together in the 1920's.

The great landmark of the "era of fulfillment" was a general treaty negotiated in October, 1925, at Locarno in Switzerland. Germany there agreed with France and Belgium on a mutual guarantee of their common frontiers; Britain and Italy agreed to act as guarantors—that is, to provide military aid against the violator if a violation of the frontiers occurred. Germany affirmed her acceptance of the western frontier drawn for her at Versailles, and France, for her part, affirmed the new moderate direction that her German policy had taken since the failure of her occupation of the Ruhr.

The "Locarno spirit" of reconciliation endured for the next several years. It was nourished by the general prosperity of both the French and the Germans and by the constructive policies of their respective foreign ministers, Briand and Stresemann. In 1926, Germany was admitted to the League of Nations, an event that seemed to signify not only

Signing of the Locarno Pact,
October, 1925.

the restoration of Germany to international respectability but also German acceptance of the peaceful purposes and duties of League membership. These hopeful impressions received confirmation when Germany signed the Kellogg-Briand Peace Pact of 1928 (see p. 763). In 1929, the French consented to withdraw the last of their occupation troops from the Rhineland during the forthcoming year, thus ending the Allied occupation of Germany at a date considerably in advance of the one stipulated in the Versailles Treaty.

Meantime, other international developments were bolstering the "Locarno spirit." The great world-wide organization planned by Wilson, the League of Nations, began its operations in 1920. We shall soon see that the League was never able to impose its will on a determined and defiant aggressor. Yet the record of the League during the 1920's was by no means one of unmitigated failure. In the first place, the League became a going concern. Its Council, dominated by the great powers, and its Assembly, representing all its members, met regularly at the League's "capital," the Swiss city of Geneva. Second, the League played a direct part in the peaceful resolution of two crises that, had they not been resolved, might well have led to little wars — in 1920 a dispute between Sweden and Finland over some Baltic islands, and in 1925 a frontier incident in the Balkans involving Greece and Bulgaria.

The United States, though not a member of the League, took a leading part in furthering one of the League's chief objectives — disarmament. Soon after the first war, the United States invited the other principal sea powers to consider the limitation of naval armaments. Meeting in Washington during the winter of 1921–1922, the naval conference achieved an agreement establishing a ten-year "holiday" in the construction of capital ships (battleships and heavy cruisers). The agreement also set the allowed tonnages of capital ships at a ratio of 5 for the United States, 5 for Britain, 3 for Japan, and 1.67 each for France and Italy.

A conference at London in 1930, however, had less success in limiting "non-capital" ships, including submarines. The partial failure of the London naval conference was a portent. Two years later, after long preparation, the League itself convoked a meeting to address the still more pressing problem of limiting military armaments. Not only the League members, but also the United States and the Soviet Union, sent representatives to Geneva. The Geneva disarmament conference of 1932, however, accomplished nothing. It was wrecked above all by a renewal of Franco-German antagonism, by the German demand for equality in armaments with France, and by the French refusal to grant the demand.

The Failure of "Fulfillment"

In 1932, then, the "Locarno spirit" was dead, and the "era of fulfillment" had ended. There is one very obvious factor in any explanation for the failure of the hopes aroused in the 1920's — the world depression that began in 1929. In Germany itself the depression was a last straw, a decisive factor in putting Hitler in power. In the democracies, too, it had heavy consequences for the peace of the world, for the depression sapped their morale and made them less confident. But the great world-wide depression is no more in itself a *sole* explanation of World War II than is the *Diktat* of Versailles.

Another factor that was unsettling to international politics was Soviet Russia. In the eyes of the western nations, Russia was a revolutionary power that could not really be trusted, that could not be fully integrated into the international state-system. The Soviet Union was the center of a revolutionary faith hated and distrusted by the politicians of the West, who feared, by no means without justification, communist agitation among their own peoples. Westerners simply could not trust a Marxist government which was based on the belief that all western "capitalist" democracies were destined to collapse and become communist after a violent class war.

Still another basic factor that led to the second war was the continuing failure of the three great western democracies, Britain, France, and the United States, to present anything like a united front. Americans of internationalist sympathies have probably exaggerated the results of the sudden American withdrawal into isolationism in 1919. It is hard to believe, especially in light of the rivalry and cross-purposes that Britain and France displayed *within* the League of Nations, that formal American membership in the League would have helped the situation greatly. Still, the isolation of the United States undoubtedly exacerbated French fears and the French sense of weakness, and pushed France toward the sort of intransigence that was illustrated by her disastrous intervention in the Ruhr in the mid-1920's (see p. 758).

More serious was the failure of France and Britain to work together effectively. France, exhausted and in this decade with a declining population, endeavoring to play the part of a first-rate power but supported only by second-rate resources, lived in perpetual fear of a revived Germany. She sought not only to carry out to the full the economic and political measures of the Versailles Treaty that aimed at weakening Germany and keeping Germany weak, but also to make up for Russia's defection as her eastern ally against Germany. This she did by making alliances, beginning in 1921, with the smaller states to the east of Germany—Poland, Czechoslovakia, Rumania, and Yugoslavia. All of them wanted French protection against the possible restoration of the Habsburg Empire, from which they had gained so much territory, and all of them except Poland were informally linked together as the "Little Entente."

To a Britain whose statesmen knew well the long story of Anglo-French conflicts from the Hundred Years' War to Napoleon, the France of the 1920's seemed once more aiming at European supremacy, seemed once more an active threat to the traditional British policy of preventing any such supremacy. Although it is now plain that the French were animated rather by fear than by ambition, and that they could never again be major aggressors, it is true enough that many of their statesmen seemed to be falling into old ways, or at least old words, of aggression. The mistaken British diagnosis was at least understandable.

Finally, something of the old British isolationism had survived the war, and made the British—and especially their dominions—unwilling to commit themselves firmly to guarantees to intervene with force in continental Europe. Britain did indeed accept Locarno, but in the previous year the dominions had played a large part in her rejection of the more sweeping "Geneva protocol" urged upon her by France, which would have committed its signatories to compulsory arbitration of international disputes.

The difficulties of the Anglo-French partnership also go far to explain the weakness of the League of Nations. The effectiveness of any piece of machinery is bound to hinge on the skill and co-ordination of the mechanics who operate it. The League lacked a means of enforcing its decisions. And it was somewhat top-heavy, since the fully representative Assembly counted for less than did the smaller

Council, where Britain and France took a preponderant role. When these two mechanics disagreed, therefore, the machinery scarcely operated at all. One example of the way in which the grand purposes of the League suffered from Anglo-French friction is the rejection of the Geneva protocol. Another is the Corfu incident of 1923, when Mussolini for a time defied the League and set a sinister precedent for the later use of gangster tactics by the dictators (see Chapter 19). In the midst of the Corfu crisis, the League was crippled by Anglo-French discord over the Ruhr policy of France.

The Aggressors

The Corfu incident underlines the presence of one more element, the most important of all, in the rapid deterioration of the twenty years' truce. This, of course, was the fact of aggressions by Italy, Germany, and Japan. In Chapter 19, we saw how the ruthlessly ambitious programs of fascism and Nazism steadily led Mussolini and Hitler to a foreign policy of adventure and aggression. In Chapter 20, we saw how the somewhat similar totalitarian policies of the Japanese militarists led them to begin the seizure of China by their occupation of Manchuria in 1931. With this background of underlying tensions—the punitive features of the Versailles settlement, the disastrous effects of the depression on the Locarno spirit, the continuance of the revolutionary focus in Russia, the defensive attitude of the western democracies and their mutual mistrust, the new aggressive faiths of fascism and Nazism, and the rise of imperialist Japan—we may now proceed to turn our attention to the actual steps taken by the nations along the road to a second world war.

II   The Road to War, 1931-1939

The First Step: Manchuria, 1931

It is now clear that the first step along the road to war was the Japanese seizure of Manchuria in 1931. Stimson, President Hoover's Secretary of State, responded to the seizure by announcing that the United States would recognize no gains made by armed force. Stimson hoped that Britain and the other democracies might follow this American lead, but his hopes were largely disappointed. The League of Nations did send out a commission headed by the British Earl of Lytton, and the subsequent Lytton Report condemned the Japanese act as aggression. Neither the United States nor the League, however, fortified verbal protests by effective action; force was not met by force. Japan, refusing to accept the Lytton Report, withdrew from the League of Nations in March, 1933, making the first formal breach in the League's structure.

The Second Step: German Rearmament, 1935–1936

The next breach in the League's structure, and the next step toward war, was made by Germany. In October, 1933, Hitler withdrew from the League, thereby virtually serving notice on the world of his aggressive intentions. On March 16, 1935, he denounced the clauses of the Treaty of Versailles that limited German armaments and set about the open rebuilding of the German armed forces.

The response to this unilateral and hence illegal act set the pattern for the next few years. On April 17, 1935, the League of Nations formally condemned Germany's repudiation of treaty obligations—and Germany continued to rearm. In May, 1935, France hastily concluded with the Soviet Union a treaty of alliance against German aggression—and Germany continued to rearm. In June, 1935, the British, realistically and short-sightedly

Emperor Haile Selassie protesting to the League of Nations (1935) after the Italian invasion of Ethiopia.

—for their action seemed like desertion to the French—signed with rearming Germany a naval agreement limiting the German navy to one-third the size of the British, and German submarines to 60 per cent of those of Britain.

It is hardly surprising that Hitler's next act drew no more than the customary protests from the signatories of Locarno. This was the "reoccupation" of the Rhineland in March, 1936—that is, the sending of German troops into the western German zone that had been demilitarized by the Treaty of Versailles. Britain and France once more did nothing, although many military critics thought then—and still think—that united British-French military action in 1936 could have nipped Hitler's career of aggression in the bud. Such action would have been fully legal in terms of existing treaties and might well have succeeded, for German re-armament was far from complete.

The Third Step: Ethiopia, 1935

Meanwhile the Italians struck in Ethiopia. In that pocket of old Africa an independent state had precariously maintained itself, largely because its imperial neighbors, Britain, France, and Italy, would neither agree to divide it nor let any one of the three swallow it whole. The Italians, who wanted it most, had lost the disastrous battle of Adowa to the native Ethiopians in 1896. This humiliation rankled with the fascists, who felt they had to show the world that there was more than rhetoric in their talk about a revived Roman Empire.

In 1934, a frontier incident at Ualual, a desert post in Italian Somaliland—or in Ethiopia, for both sides claimed the place—put the matter before the international politicians. France and Britain were characteristically quite ready for appeasement of Italy, partly because they hoped to align Mussolini with them against Hitler. They offered him almost everything in Ethiopia, including those concrete economic concessions naive people think are the essence of imperialism—and wars, and indeed everything in human events. But since Ethiopia was a member of the League, the French and the British insisted that its formal independence be observed. This Mussolini would not accept, and in October, 1935, his troops began the invasion of Ethiopia. Airplanes, artillery, and tanks made the difference between 1896 and 1935. This time the underdog was not the winner. Poison gas finished the task early in 1936, and the King of Italy acquired the coveted title of Emperor of Ethiopia. Once more there was an emperor—of sorts—in Rome!

The League of Nations had already formally condemned the Japanese aggression in Manchuria and the German denunciation of the disarmament clauses of the Treaty of Versailles. In 1935, it at once declared that Italy, by invading Ethiopia, a League member, had violated her obligations under the Covenant of the League. Now the League made the momentous decision to test its power to move from words to deeds. This action had the accord of most of its members, and was urged on by the British, less vocally by the French, and strongly by Haile Selassie, the rightful Emperor of Ethiopia. On October 11, 1935, fifty-one member nations of the League voted to invoke against Italy the famous Article 16 of the League Covenant, which provided for economic sanctions against a member resorting to war in disregard of its covenants.

The sanctions thus invoked failed. There were loopholes; oil, for instance, was not included in the list of articles barred from commerce with Italy, which had only meager stockpiles of this vital war material. There was much mutual recrimination among members of the League over what articles should be placed on the prohibited list and over the fact that Britain and France did nothing to check Italian movements of troops and munitions through the Suez Canal, which Britain then in fact controlled. Germany was no longer in the League, and was wholly unbound by its decision. No major power applied these sanctions rigorously. To that extent, it is true that the method of economic sanctions was not really tried.

The Ethiopian fiasco was a disastrous blow to the League, which from now on was helpless in high international politics. Its special services as a group of trained international civil servants, its "functional groups," dealing with labor problems, international police matters like the drug traffic and prostitution, and much else, persisted, however, to be absorbed after World War II by the United Nations. But for the rest of the 1930's, the League was hardly even a formal factor in the increasing tensions. No one was surprised or greatly concerned when Italy, copying Japan and Germany, withdrew from the League in December, 1937.

The Fourth Step:
The Spanish Civil War, 1936–1939

The next step after Ethiopia on the road to war is of great psychological and moral interest. No doubt the later direct aggressions of Hitler in Czechoslovakia and Poland were the politically decisive steps. But the Spanish Civil War (for details, see Chapter 19), which broke out in July, 1936, was the emotional catalyst that divided millions of men and women all over the western world. It is still, in spite of the passing of years, a kind of great collective Dreyfus case, a test of conscience and loyalty for our time.

The Spanish Civil War was fought between a Right and a Left. On the Right were fascists, monarchists, and just plain conservatives; on the Left were socialists, communists, anarchists, and a few liberals or just plain democrats. As in most great civil wars, there was really no Center. It was a quasi-religious war, waged with the great violence and with the consecrated devotion that mark wars of principle. No one can say for sure how the struggle would have ended if it had remained a purely Spanish one, as the American Civil War had remained a purely American one. Certainly the Loyalists of the Left would have been in a much stronger position if the democratic powers had followed the usual practice in international law of sending arms to the *de jure* government of Spain. Such speculation, however, is useless. Almost from the very start the Spanish Civil War engaged, not merely the vicarious emotional participation of the West, not merely individual foreign enlistments, but the active though never wholly open intervention of other nations. This intervention was decisive and effective on the part of the fascist powers, Italy and Germany; it was less determined and effective on the part of communist Russia; and feeblest of all on the part of Britain and France. Early in 1939, with the fall of Barcelona, the Civil War was in effect over. Once more a fascist group had won.

Meantime, dizzy with success, Mussolini was going on to other adventures. In October, 1936, he signed a pact with Hitler, thereby formally establishing the Rome-Berlin "Axis" and committing fascist Italy to alliance with Nazi Germany. Mussolini gave strong support to Franco's rebellion in Spain. And, late in 1938, he orchestrated a public outcry in Italy for the French to hand over certain territories. He wanted not only Nice and Savoy, which had been ceded to Napoleon III during Italian unification negotiations almost a century earlier (see Chapter 13, p. 509), but also the Mediterranean island of Corsica, which had been French since the days of Louis XV in the eighteenth century, and Tunisia, which had never been under Italian rule and had been a French protectorate since 1881. These demands came to nothing, but they did not exactly improve relations between France and Italy. Finally, on Good Friday (April 7), 1939, Mussolini attacked Albania, long coveted by the Italians, and quickly subjugated this backward little Balkan state. For a few years, Victor Emmanuel was to be King of Albania as well as Emperor of Ethiopia.

The Fifth Step: "Anschluss," 1938

The immediate origins of World War II lie, however, neither in Italian nor in Spanish fascist aggression, but in the mounting series of German aggressions. Hitler had begun the open rebuilding of German armed forces in 1935. Three years later, he felt strong enough to undertake the first enterprise of expansion, an enterprise which, like all he undertook, he insisted was no more than a restoration to Germany of what the *Diktat* of Versailles had deprived her. Austria, German in language

and tradition, had been left a mere fragment by the disruption of the Habsburg Empire. Ever since 1918 there had been a strong movement among Austrians for annexation ("*Anschluss*") to Germany proper. This movement had been strenuously opposed by the victors of the first war, and especially by France, but agitation for *Anschluss* kept on, nourished by Nazi propaganda and, in 1934, an attempted *Putsch*.

Hitler carefully laid the ground for the success of the next Nazi attempt. The pact with Italy that formally established the Rome-Berlin "Axis" (October, 1936) disarmed Mussolini's opposition to *Anschluss*. Early in 1938 Hitler began what turned out to be his standard technique of softening his victims for the final blow. He unleashed a violent propaganda campaign by press, radio, and platform against the alleged misdeeds of the government of independent Austria. In February, 1938, he summoned the Austrian Chancellor Schuschnigg to his Bavarian retreat at Berchtesgaden. There he let loose a bullying

"Honest, Mister, there's nobody here but us Spaniards."—Franco's explanation to Chamberlain and Daladier.

tirade against the hapless Schuschnigg. In March, he moved his troops into Austria and made *Anschluss* a fact.

Hitler now had six million more German-speaking nationals in the fold; and in the union of Austria and Germany he had achieved something that no Habsburg and no Hohenzollern had been able to do in modern times. But he showed no signs at all of being content with what he had gained. Almost at once he went to work on the acquisition of the Sudeten Germans of Czechoslovakia.

The Sixth Step: Czechoslovakia Dismembered, 1938–1939

The Czechoslovak republic was the only state in central or eastern Europe where parliamentary democracy had achieved a real success after World War I. The republic faced a difficult problem of national minorities, but it had the good fortune to inherit some of the most highly developed industrial regions of the old Habsburg Empire. Its economy, consequently, was far better balanced between industry and agriculture than was that of the other states of eastern Europe. This healthy economy was mirrored in the social structure, where a working balance was maintained among peasants, middle classes, and industrial workers. The period immediately after the war, as well as the great depression of the 1930's, times of great suffering elsewhere, affected Czechoslovakia very lightly. Yet these advantages could hardly have preserved democracy in the republic had it not been for the enlightened policies of Thomas Masaryk, liberator and president of his country until his resignation at the age of 85 in 1935.

Even the enlightened Czech regime, however, could not keep the country from ultimately being smashed by outside pressures working on its sensitive minorities. The Sudeten German minority of 3¼ millions, feeling, as Germans, superior to Slavs, resisted the new republic at every turn, even when the Prague government made concessions to satisfy their just grievances. Sudeten extremists early turned to Hitler, but even moderates and socialists among the Sudetens were more or less pan-German in their views. From 1933 on, Nazi agitation, supported by Hitler with men and money, became increasingly serious in Czechoslovakia. Early in 1938, having secured Austria, Hitler decided to push the Czech affair next. Henlein, his Sudeten agent, made demands on the Prague government for what amounted to complete Sudeten autonomy. The summer of 1938 was spent in negotiations and in mutual propaganda blasts. The Czechs relied heavily on their French allies and on the friendly, though not formally allied, British. But by the spring of 1938, it seems clear now, Britain and France had agreed not to defend the territorial integrity of Czechoslovakia.

By the autumn of 1938, Hitler was ready for action. On September 12 he made a violent speech at Nuremberg, insisting on self-determination for the Sudeten Germans. This was the signal for widespread disorders in Czechoslovakia and for the proclamation of martial law by its government. The situation was now a full-fledged European crisis that called for the personal intervention of heads of state. The British Prime Minister, Neville Chamberlain, made two preliminary visits to Hitler in Germany in an effort to moderate German demands, and finally—with the help of Mussolini—persuaded Hitler to call a full conference of the four great western powers. This conference—Hitler, Mussolini, Chamberlain, with Daladier for France—met in Munich on September 29, 1938. Russia was not invited; her exclusion was to complete her abandonment of the "Popular Front" policy (see Chapter 18).

Munich was a sweeping victory for Hitler. Czechoslovakia was partially dismembered; her Sudeten rim-lands were turned over to Germany; the Czechs were obliged to hand over Teschen and certain other areas to the Poles; the whole economy and transportation system were lamed; the defense of her frontiers was made impossible by the loss of the border mountains and their fortifications; and Slovakia was given autonomy within a federal state, emphasized by the official change in spelling from Czechoslovakia to Czecho-Slovakia. The Czech leaders had felt it impossible to resist the Germans without the aid of the French and British; their people acquiesced bitterly in the settlement of Munich. The Germans had played fully on the differences between the more industrialized Czechs and the still largely agricultural Slovaks. But even had the country been strongly united, the laming blow of Munich would have ruined its morale. Hitler acted quickly. In the very next spring, before the final lines of demarcation set at Munich had actually been drawn, he summoned the Czech President, Hacha, to Germany for another of those ghastly interviews, in which he announced that the fate of the Czech people "must be placed trustingly in the hands of the *Fuhrer.*" In March, 1939, Hitler sent his army into the remaining fragments of Czechoslovakia, meeting no real resistance.

The most respectable defense that can be made of Munich and "appeasement" rests on the argument that the West was buying time to prepare for a war which it knew to be inevitable but for which it was not yet ready.

Chamberlain and Hitler during the negotiations preceding the Munich agreement of 1938.

Chamberlain may have thought so; but Winston Churchill and others have pointed out most cogently that the democracies were in a stronger military position relative to that of Germany in September, 1938, than in September, 1939. It also seems likely that Chamberlain and Daladier, as well as millions all over the world, believed or hoped that the acquisition of Sudeten Germans would satisfy Hitler, that after Munich he would behave as Bismarck had behaved after Sedan, and that he would settle down and try to preserve the balance of power. Some westerners even hoped that Hitler would perhaps ally with them against communist Russia or obligingly get himself so entangled in eastern Europe that he would bring on a Russo-German war. Hitler's words and deeds, however, had given no real foundation for the belief that he would now "play ball" with the West. And we now know that he had as early as November 5, 1937, announced to his close advisers his unalterable intention of destroying Czechoslovakia and moving on into Poland and the Ukraine.

The actual destruction of old Czechoslovakia in March, 1939, seems not to have surprised anyone. Indeed the curious mixture of resignation, condemnation, and resolution with which this action was greeted in the West marks a turning point. The days of appeasement were over. Munich had proved to be an epoch-making event, a catalyst for both professional western diplomatists and statesmen and for western opinion generally. Hitler's next aggression would not lead to a Munich. We can never be quite sure whether Hitler and his aides thought they could take their next step without bringing on a general war. In public and semi-public, Hitler, Goering, and the other leaders made no secret of their feeling that the British and French were decadent, spineless, inefficient societies, quite unable to summon the courage needed to resist an inspired and rejuvenated Germany. Yet there is good evidence that Hitler expected at least a local war with Poland this time, and that he was quite prepared to face involvement with the French and the British. "Whom the gods would destroy, they first make mad."

The Final Step: Poland, 1939

Poland was inexorably Hitler's next victim. The Polish corridor dividing East Prussia from the rest of Germany was an affront to great-power psychology. So, too, was the separation from Germany of the Free City of Danzig, on the edge of the Polish corridor. Danzig was thoroughly German in language and tradition. Germans, even quite enlightened Germans, thought of the Poles, as indeed of all Slavs, as inferior people who would benefit from capable German supervision. Hitler began his Baltic adventure in March, 1939, when he took the port town of Memel from Poland's northern neighbor, Lithuania.

The critical issue in the tense half-year that led up to the outbreak of war on September 1, 1939, was not at all the possibility that Poland, unsupported by Britain and France, would undergo the same fate as Czechoslovakia. The British government publicly supported Poland by signing a pact of mutual assistance with her in April. Indeed, in the midst of the final week of crisis, Chamberlain's foreign minister, Lord Halifax, sent a telegram to Hitler himself in which he made a pathetic appeal to the lessons of history:

It has been alleged that if His Majesty's Government had made their position more clear in 1914 the great catastrophe would have been avoided. Whether or not there is any force in that allegation, His Majesty's Government are resolved that on this occasion there shall be no such tragic misunderstanding. If the need should arise, they are resolved and prepared to employ without delay all the forces at their command. . . . I trust that Your Excellency will weigh with the utmost deliberation the considerations which I have put before you.*

The real critical point at issue was the attitude of Russia. Hitler had a for once sensible fear of a war on two fronts, a war against major powers to the east and to the west of the kind

*Documents on British Foreign Policy, 1919-1939, E. L. Woodward and R. Butler, eds. (London, 1954), 3rd series, Vol. II, No. 145.

on which Germany had embarked in 1914. He was in fact to be drawn within two years into just such a war. Even if he had been faced in 1939 by the united front of Britain, France, and Russia in support of Poland, it is perfectly possible that he could not have restrained himself and his followers. One is tempted to see the Nazi top command as driven on by some abnormal and obsessive motivation and quite oblivious to ordinary considerations of self-interest. Hitler perhaps could no more keep his hands off Poland than an alcoholic can keep his hands off liquor. But, as events developed, Hitler was able to seize Poland without fear of Russian intervention. Indeed, he was able to arrange with Stalin a partition of Poland quite recognizably on the model of the eighteenth-century partitions.

Why did the Russians make their about-face? They had been deeply hurt by their exclusion from the negotiations over the Czechoslovakian crisis of the year before, an exclusion that they blamed primarily on the British and the French. From the failure of the western powers to stand up to German violations of the Versailles Treaty ever since 1934, the Russians had drawn conclusions at least as disparaging to the western will to fight as those drawn by Hitler. In particular, they deeply distrusted the British Tories under Neville Chamberlain, for they believed that in many ways Tory Britain was more fundamentally hostile to communist Russia than even Nazi Germany was.

The Russians' mistrust of the West was not dispelled by the diplomatic mission that Britain and France sent, belatedly and grudgingly, to negotiate with Russia in this critical summer of 1939. The western powers proposed a mutual assistance pact, but the efforts of their negotiators were inept and halfhearted. Moreover, Chamberlain's government made a tactless choice of negotiators. One of them, Ironside, had been involved in the British intervention against the Reds at Archangel in the early beleaguered days of the Bolshevik state — he had, indeed, been made a peer under the title "Baron of Archangel and of Ironside"; another was a mere functionary of the Foreign Office. The Russians like to

Europe on the Eve,
August 1939

Neutral countries

0   300
    Miles

The Axis Powers
Areas annexed by Germany, 1935-39
Areas made "protectorates" of Germany, 1939
Annexed by Italy, 1939

deal with top people; they like to be made to feel important. Significantly, Hitler, who was also negotiating with Russia at the time, put Foreign Minister Ribbentrop himself on the job. So the Anglo-French overture to Moscow came to nothing. The Russian leaders had apparently reached the conclusion that the West was a broken reed, that if they themselves did not come to terms with Hitler he would attack them anyway.

Finally, the Russians were quite as distrustful of the Polish government as of anyone else. The western, especially the French, policy of encouraging the smaller powers of eastern Europe to act as counterweights to *both* Germany and Russia now bore its natural fruit. The Polish government would not accept Russia as protector; it would not, in these hectic months of negotiations, consent to the passage through Polish territory of Russian troops in case of war with Germany. The Russians were tempted by the opportunity to recover lands in eastern Poland that they had lost in World War I and its aftermath. To the horror of the West, they signed at Moscow on August 23, 1939, a nonaggression pact with Germany, the "Hitler-Stalin" or "Ribbentrop-Molotov pact," a cynical about-face of two supposedly irreconcilable ideological enemies (see the Low cartoon, p. 702). A week later, the German army marched into Poland. On September 3, Britain and France honored their obligations and declared war on Germany. The twenty years' truce was at an end.

Democratic Policy in Review

It is not really difficult to understand why the democracies behaved as they did in these years. Britain, France, and the United States were the victors of 1918, and by the very fact of their victory they were on the defensive. Wisdom and luck might have made their defense more effective than it was, but nothing could have altered the fact that they were on the defensive. In the long past of our state system, the defensive has always proved a difficult position, has always been — perhaps from the very nature of western culture with its drives toward change — at a disadvantage against aggression. This disadvantage seems by no means associated with democracies as such. Absolute monarchies have suffered quite as much from the difficulties of the defensive, as the failure of Metternich shows (see Chapter 11).

In the years between the two world wars, the normal tendency of the victors to relax was no doubt increased by some of the facts of democratic life. The western democracies were committed to an effort to secure for every citizen some minimum of material comforts; they were committed to the pursuit of happiness. Their normal tendency was to produce butter rather than guns. Their totalitarian opponents may well have been quite as "materialistic" as they, but for them the butter was to be attained in the future, and by means of the guns. In short, the German, Japanese, and Italian governments were able to get their societies to tighten their belts in order to make military preparation possible. On the other hand, it was exceedingly difficult for democratic governments to get such sacrifices from their citizens until war actually broke out.

III   The Nature of the War

The first world war of our century had, in its main theater, the Western Front, been one long siege. Since the military experts tended to fight it over and over again in their planning, both France and Germany in the 1930's built two confronting lines of fortifications on their common frontier. The Maginot Line, on the French side, and the Siegfried Line, on the German, were far more formidable than the improvised trenches of the war of 1914–1918. So it is not surprising that on the outbreak of hostilities in September, 1939, most people expected first, that the war would be decided primarily in the area between France and Germany, and second, that it would be a closely confined war of siege in the West, with at most diversional activity in other parts of the world.

But the war itself showed once more the perils of prediction in great human affairs. As Germany was joined by her Axis partners, Italy and Japan, and as the United States entered it, this second world war became much more truly a world war than the first had been. It was decided in Russia, in the Pacific, even in the Mediterranean, quite as much as in the West. And it turned out to be one of the most extraordinarily open wars of movement in history. Indeed, the armies of the British Montgomery and the German Rommel in

North Africa moved through the desert with the freedom of nomad hordes of old; but the gasoline engine had replaced the horse and camel.

It was also a war in which for the first time the airplane played a major role, a role foreshadowed in the fighting waged in Ethiopia and Spain during the 1930's. Over the water, the airplane, both land-based and carrier-based, soon established itself as a central factor in naval warfare; in the opinion of many experts, it had made the great warship obsolete. Over the land, the airplane soon established itself as an essential arm of the fire power of land armies, an arm that needed and in the end got careful integration with the ground forces. But even in this war the airplane did not live up to the advanced billing given it by its more imaginative proponents; it did not become the *sole* means of warfare, superseding all others. Air power by itself alone proved inadequate in the great test of 1940, when the Germans tried to reduce Britain from the air.

Aerial bombardment—toward the end of the war carried on by German pilotless aircraft and rocket missiles—did indeed bring the horrors of warfare back to the civilians of the cities. Military experts had been inclined to believe that civilians could not possibly stand aerial bombardment, and that any country whose cities were subject to a few such bombardments would be obliged to sue for peace. Yet European and Asian civilian populations proved able to stand up to months of bombardment. German civilian deaths from air bombardment have been estimated at about 500,000. Organized systems of shelter, partial dispersal of populations, the obvious but not previously noted fact that much of the space of modern cities is made up of streets, parks, gardens, churches, and other public buildings not used at night (when much of the bombing was done)—all combined to make it possible for the people of heavily bombed cities like Berlin and Tokyo to endure what were in effect front-line conditions.

Yet at the very end of the war a technical innovation was introduced that may have altered radically the character of war, may indeed make any future war so unendurably destructive that it will at least be brief. This was the atomic bomb, developed in secrecy by American, Canadian, and British experts, and first used on the Japanese city of Hiroshima on August 6, 1945. A single bomb destroyed something over half the city. Somewhat less material damage was done by a second and somewhat different bomb dropped on Nagsaki, a hilly city, three days later. But over a hundred thousand people were killed in the two cities by the two bombs, an incidence of death that seems to justify fully the fears that the atomic bomb and its still more frightful hydrogen bomb successors have aroused in our own generation.

IV   Early Successes of the Axis

Polish and Finnish Campaigns

The first campaign of World War II reached a by no means unexpected conclusion. No one had seriously supposed that isolated Poland could possibly stand up for long against the German armed forces, or that Britain and France could possibly get into action rapidly enough to help their Polish ally decisively. Yet the speed of the German conquest surprised almost everyone. The German air force, the *Luftwaffe*, soon gained absolute command of the air, and used it to disrupt Polish communications and to spread terror with its dive bombers. Special German task forces, fully motorized, swept through and around the more primitively armed Poles. This was what the Germans called a *Blitzkrieg*, or lightning war. The German word was later simplified by the English into "blitz," and was used by them to apply to the German air bombardment of Britain in the years 1940–1941.

Anxious to get his share of Poland, Hitler's new collaborator, Stalin, hastened to push the Russian armies in from the east on the hapless Poles. He also established Russian military bases in the Baltic republics of Estonia, Latvia, and Lithuania, which had been created out of Russian provinces at the close of World War I. "Mutual assistance" pacts between giant Russia and the tiny Baltic states were to be the entering wedge for their full occupation by Russia in 1940 and their amalgamation, as constituent republics, into the Union of Soviet Socialist Republics—a title officially without the word "Russia."

Fear of Germany, or an imperialistic desire to expand, or both, also drove the Russian leaders into a war with neighboring Finland for bases in the Baltic (November, 1939). The Russians, who had perhaps miscalculated the strength of their little opponent, did rather badly at first. By March, 1940, however, they had worn down the Finns; they secured their bases and annexed Finnish lands very close to the great Russian city of Leningrad. It seems quite possible that this "winter war" with Finland had a major effect in encouraging Hitler to his fateful decision of 1941 to make war on Russia. The German military experts drew from Russian difficulties in this war conclusions extremely disparaging to Russian capabilities.

"Phony War" and Blitzkrieg in the West

Meanwhile in the West what the British called the "phony war" was pursuing its uneventful course. The French and the British duly mobilized as in 1914, and as in 1914 the British sent a few divisions to the Continent. But the Germans refused to repeat the pattern of 1914. Occupied in Poland, they did nothing in the West. Occasionally a French patrol from the Maginot Line would exchange shots with a German patrol, but for the most part the troops exercised, ate, slept, and went on leave as though they were merely in training.

The Germans, however, had no intention of sitting out a defensive war in the West. But not even modern warfare is wholly emancipated from the weather. The German general staff was not prepared to begin a decisive campaign in the West with the winter ahead. They waited until spring, and in April they made sure of their northern flank, as they had not in 1914, by making without declaration of war a sea and air invasion of neutral Denmark and Norway. Denmark, totally unprepared, was occupied almost without resistance. Norway, also unprepared, made a brave showing. But neither the British nor the French were able to help her with more than token forces, and by the end of April important Norwegian resistance was broken. The Germans now had admirable bases for air and submarine action against the British.

The great blow was struck, without warning, on May 10, 1940, when the German armies, brilliantly supported in the air, invaded the Low Countries. Holland, spared in 1914, was this time invaded so that the Germans might make doubly sure of their northern flank. A carefully planned attack on the key Belgian fort of Eben Emael, an attack that had been rehearsed on a dummy of the fort set up inside Germany, was at once successful, and opened the way into the Low Countries.

In the era of weakness among western democracies in the 1930's, both the Belgians and the Dutch had been extremely anxious to avoid compromising themselves by planning for joint resistance with Britain and France against a possible German attack. They were now to suffer the full consequences of their own policy of attempting to appease Hitler. For the crucial failure to hold the Germans in actual battle was in the Low Countries. We cannot be sure that a carefully co-ordinated plan among French, British, Belgians, and Dutch would have stopped Hitler. But clearly the lack of such co-ordination was a major factor in the German success. Indeed, though much has since been written against the "Maginot mentality," it is a fact that the Germans did not take the French Maginot Line by frontal assault, but outflanked it at the critical

SYRIA

TRANS-
JORDAN

PALESTINE

Suez Canal

Cairo

TURKEY

CYPRUS

Ankara

Istanbul

Black Sea

Sevastopol

Yalta

RUSSIA

1943

1942

Stalingrad

Don R.

Moscow

Volga R.

1944

Kiev

Dnieper R.

1944

RUMANIA

Bucharest

Danube R.

BULGARIA

Sofia

Athens

GREECE

CRETE

Mediterranean Sea

MALTA

El Alamein

1942

Tobruk

1942

1943

LENINGRAD

1943

FINLAND

Helsinki

ESTONIA

LATVIA

LITHUANIA

EAST PRUSSIA

1943

Königsberg

Danzig

Baltic Sea

SWEDEN

Stockholm

Oslo

NORWAY

Warsaw

POLAND

Vistula R.

1945

Oder R.

Prague

CZECHOSLOVAKIA

Budapest

1944

HUNGARY

Vienna

AUSTRIA

YUGOSLAVIA

Belgrade

Trieste

ALBANIA

Adriatic Sea

Po R.

ITALY

1944

Monte Cassino

Naples

Rome

Anzio

Salerno

Palermo

SICILY

1943

1943

TUNISIA

Tunis

Bizerte

Bone

1943

1942

Algiers

Oran

ALGERIA

DENMARK

Hamburg

Elbe R.

RUHR

Berlin

Potsdam

Torgau

GERMANY

Cologne

Frankfurt

Berchtesgaden

Munich

Stuttgart

Rhine

SWITZ.

1945

1945

Bastogne

Trier

Maginot Line

Rheims

Seine R.

Paris

FRANCE

Vichy

Border of Vichy France

1944

Nice

Marseilles

CORSICA

SARDINIA

BALEARIC IS.

Ebro R.

Bordeaux

Loire R.

NORMANDY

Dieppe

Dunkirk

London

Coventry

Dublin

IRELAND

GREAT BRITAIN

North Sea

NETH.

BELG.

English Channel

1944

Atlantic Ocean

★ Sinking of the "Bismarck"

0   500
Miles

PORTUGAL

Lisbon

SPAIN

Madrid

Gibraltar

Tangier

Casablanca

Oran

1942

FRENCH MOROCCO

Axis Countries

Greatest military expansion by Axis

Allies

point where it tapered off along the Franco-Belgian border in the hilly region of the Ardennes.

Through the Ardennes the Germans poured their best motorized troops into France. In a blitzkrieg that once more capitalized on the "lessons of 1914," the Germans resisted the temptation to turn at once on the prize of Paris, but instead drove straight through northern France to the Channel, where the port of Boulogne fell on May 26, a little over two weeks after the start of the campaign. By this stroke the Germans separated the British, Belgian, and part of the French troops from the bulk of the French armies to the south. Shortly afterward the French replaced General Gamelin with General Weygand as commander-in-chief. Meanwhile in Britain Neville Chamberlain had resigned after an adverse vote in the Commons on May 8 as a result of failure in Norway. He was succeeded as prime minister by Winston Churchill. The British act was of major importance, comparable to the replacing of Asquith by Lloyd George in World War I. Chamberlain was neither a man of action nor an appealing or heroic figure; Churchill was to prove himself all this and more. Under him the British made a united front in the crisis.

The new leaders, in a desperate last moment, attempted to work out a plan for pinching off the adventurous German motorized thrust by a concerted attack from north and south. But the Belgians, badly disorganized, decided to capitulate, and neither the French nor the British could rally themselves to carry out the movement. In the last days of May and the first days of June the British did indeed achieve the miracle of the successful withdrawal of some 215,000 British and 120,000 French soldiers by sea from the beaches around Dunkirk at the northern tip of France. With useful protection from the Royal Air Force, an extraordinary flotilla of all sorts of vessels, including private yachts and motorboats, got the men off, though almost all their equipment had to be abandoned. Dunkirk was a courageous action, and one that did much to help British morale. But from German documents that fell to the Allies after the final defeat of Germany it is pretty clear (though the point is still controversial) that the miracle of Dunkirk was possible largely because Hitler himself decided not to press home the destruction of the British forces penned on the coast, on the ground that Britain was no longer a real threat. At the last moment, Hitler too gave in to the lure of Paris, and decided to push the attack on the French homeland at once. Here he was wholly and rapidly successful. The French under Weygand could not rally, and the Germans marched southward almost unopposed. The clear signal to the world that the rally of 1914 at the Marne would not be repeated was given on June 13, when the French declared Paris an "open city" and evacuated it without fighting.

"The Fall of France"

The battle of France was thus decided by mid-June. But the French might yet try to defend the south, or, failing that, use their navy and merchant marine to get as many men as possible across the Mediterranean into French North Africa. There, based on their great empire overseas, they might have continued with British aid the fight against the Germans. Some of the French leaders wished to do this, and in the crisis Winston Churchill made to the French the extraordinary offer of a complete governmental union of the two countries to continue the struggle. His offer was not accepted.

On June 16, Reynaud was supplanted by Marshal Pétain as prime minister, in what amounted to a kind of *coup d'état*. Pétain and his colleagues were determined on peace at any price, and this they got. On June 22, 1940, an armistice was signed at Compiègne at the spot where the armistice of November 11, 1918 had been signed. By this armistice, the French withdrew from the war, handed over three-fifths of France, including the whole Atlantic and Channel coasts, to German occupation, and retained under strict German supervision no more than the central and Mediterranean regions. This "unoccupied France" was ruled from the little resort city of

Civilians in Marseilles watching historic French battle flags being evacuated from the country, 1940.

Vichy, where Pétain set up a French form of authoritarian, anti-democratic state of which he was "chief." History has labeled his government simply "Vichy France." To most Frenchmen it was a German-imposed rule.

Some few of Pétain's collaborators were pro-German, convinced that totalitarianism was inevitable. But it is now clear that for most of them, even for men like the "collaborator" Laval, a dominant figure at Vichy, and indeed for Pétain himself, the important motive in those bewildering June days of 1940 was simply a desire to make terms with the inevitable. They were absolutely sure that Hitler had won the war. They did not believe that Britain had any chance of successfully resisting the German war machine that had crushed France. In this belief they were followed at first by the great majority of Frenchmen.

The new Vichy government attempted to remake France along conservative, indeed monarchist, lines that had not been practical politics since the *Seize Mai* of 1877 (see Chapter 13). Symbolic of why the Vichy régime failed is its attempt to substitute for the great slogan "Liberty, Equality, Fraternity" a new trinity of "Labor, Family, Fatherland." Even an outsider can see that the new slogan lacked fire. More concretely, the Vichy régime from the start was compromised by its association with the hated Germans; born of defeat, it could do little in the few years it had to live before it died in the Allied victory.

Even in the dark days of June, 1940, a few Frenchmen, led by General Charles de Gaulle, who was flown out to London at the last moment, refused to give up the fight. De Gaulle, with British aid, set up a French National Committee with headquarters in London. A nucleus of French soldiers taken off the beach at Dunkirk, and a stream of refugees who came out of France by all sorts of means in the next few years, made up the "Free French" or "Fighting French." At home in France the "Resistance movement" gradually formed underground to prepare for eventual liberation. North Africa, strongest of the French colonies, remained under the control of Vichy. But some parts of the colonies rallied to the Free French from the start. Notably in Equatorial Africa, under the leadership of the great Negro governor, Félix Eboué, a most useful base for Allied operations was secured from the first. Weak as these fighting French groups were in the early days, they were at least a rallying point. They were able to set up an effective radio center in England from which they conducted a skillful propaganda campaign against Vichy and the Germans, beamed across the Channel to the homeland, where, we now know, it achieved a large audience.

On June 10, Hitler's ally Mussolini had brought the Italians into the war against France and Britain, too late to affect the outcome of the battle of France. But this "stab in the back" as Franklin Roosevelt called it, further outraged American opinion, already alarmed by the Nazi successes. And Italy was now irrevocably engaged in the struggle, anxious to secure some kind of success that would offset the great gains of her German ally. The war, up to this time confined to northern and western Europe, now spread to the Mediterranean.

The Battle of Britain

The Germans, for all their miracles of planning and execution, had not really worked out a way to deal with Britain. Hitler seems to have believed that with France out of the war Britain would see the light and make a separate peace, a peace of compromise in which Germany would dominate the continent of Europe and Britain would continue satisfied with her overseas empire. This division of the spoils, Hitler reiterated in public and private, should be eminently satisfactory; he did not threaten the British Empire. Yet for over four centuries Britain had gone to war rather than accept the kind of one-power domination over western and central Europe that Hitler exercised after the fall of France. The British, therefore, paid no attention at all to his peace feelers.

Hitler was counting heavily on the possibility that German submarines could eventually cut off British supplies of food and raw materials from overseas, and thus starve her into submission. But at best this must take a long time. Hitler and his colleagues were impatient. The obvious thing to do was to attempt a landing in England. But the Germans had made no real preparation for amphibious warfare; they had no specially designed landing craft. Moreover, the German air force and the German navy were at odds over the best way of combining for an invasion across the Channel. A hastily assembled flotilla of miscellaneous vessels was badly damaged by British aircraft, and early in August, 1940, Hitler and Goering, his air marshal, made the fateful decision to try to do the job solely with air power.

The Battle of Britain that followed had two main phases. First, in August and September the Luftwaffe attempted in daylight bombing attacks to wipe out British airports and fighter planes. The Royal Air Force, admirably organized and directed, and using the new detection apparatus called radar to spot the attackers early, proved just barely strong enough to check the Germans. In the critical actions of September 15–21, German official records now available show 120 planes lost (the British at the time claimed 268). This was, however, a rate of loss Goering, head of the Luftwaffe, felt the Germans could not stand. This phase of the blitz was called off. In one of his imperishable phrases, Churchill said of the small group of British fighter pilots who had saved Britain, "Never . . . was so much owed by so many to so few."

The second phase began in the autumn of 1940. The Germans sought by night bombing of major British industrial centers to destroy British production and to terrify the civilian population so that the government would be obliged to sue for peace. Neither aim was successful. Even at Coventry, an important center of the automotive industry, though

Collapse of a building near St. Paul's during the London "blitz."

grave damage was done, the industry was by no means knocked out. Indeed, more damage was done to the cathedral and other buildings in the center of the city than to the great factories on the outskirts. As for civilian morale, it is clear that these bombings strengthened the British will to resist. Civilian defense measures proved adequate to protect both persons and property from that extreme of destruction which might indeed have broken the will to resist. By winter, when the weather gave the British some respite, the Battle of Britain had been won.

Mediterranean and Balkan Campaigns

Hitler now faced the possibility of a long stalemate, something that conquerors like Napoleon in the past have rarely been able to face. Like Napoleon turning to Egypt in 1798, Hitler turned at first to the obvious strategy of getting at Britain through her Mediterranean lifeline to India and the East. His ally Mussolini, already itching to expand in the Mediterranean, invaded Greece from Albania in October, 1940, with no success. The Greeks held on valiantly and even pushed the Italians back. But, just as the Germans came in the first world war to the rescue of their Austrian ally, so they now came successfully to the rescue of Mussolini.

Just how far Hitler himself wanted to invest in action in this theater is not clear. Certainly he toyed with the idea of a campaign against the British fortress of Gibraltar through Spain, to be co-ordinated with Axis attacks in the eastern Mediterranean to clear that sea of the British. But the Spanish dictator Franco wanted too high a price from the French for his consent to a German march through Spain, and Hitler was unwilling to risk driving Vichy France, which still controlled French North Africa, too far. In the upshot, the Germans had to be content with backing up Mussolini in Greece and with an attack on Egypt from the Italian colony of Libya. Efforts to rouse native action against the British and French in the Near East were sup-

pressed without grave difficulty by British and Free French action, and Turkey stood obstinately neutral.

Nevertheless, the German commitment to help the Italians in Greece took valuable German divisions away from another task in the spring of 1941, and as the Germans attempted to move overland through Yugoslavia they were involved in a costly guerrilla war. The British did their best to back up their Greek allies, but once more they were not strong enough. German air power crippled British naval power in the waters around Crete, and by June the Axis had conquered the Greek mainland and the islands.

The Invasion of Russia

The other task for which the German forces were to be used in the spring of 1941 was the conquest of Russia. Hitler had firmly resolved not to repeat what he thought was the fateful mistake of Germany in 1914; he would not engage in a war on two fronts. Yet by his invasion of Russia in June, 1941 — an invasion delayed for a perhaps decisive two months by the Balkan adventure — he committed himself to just such a war. Russia was indeed a tempting goal. The Nazi plan had always looked to the fertile areas of Poland and South Russia as the natural goal of German expansion, the *Lebensraum* (see p. 732) of German destiny. With the precedents of successful blitzkrieg in Poland, western Europe, and now Greece, Hitler and his military experts believed that they could beat the Russians in a single campaign before winter set in. It was quite clear that neither Britain nor the United States — even though the latter should enter the war — could land armies in Europe in 1941. An attack on Russia, then, Hitler seems to have told himself, would not *really* create two fronts. Indeed, once Russia was conquered, as in Hitler's mind it was sure to be, the Germans would have no trouble disposing of Britain, and, if necessary, the United States.

Russia was not conquered in 1941. But it was very close, closer perhaps than the Battle of Britain. Hitler's plan almost worked. There really was a successful blitzkrieg. Within two months the Germans were at the gates of Leningrad, and in the south they had conquered the Ukraine by the end of October. Hundreds of thousands of Russian troops had been killed or taken prisoner. In sheer distance, the German armies had pushed more than twice as far as they had in France.

Yet, as the Russian winter closed in, the Germans had taken neither Moscow nor Leningrad. Russian heavy industry had been in part transferred to the remote Urals, and existing plants there and in Siberia had been strengthened. The United States was beginning to send in supplies. The vast resources of Russian manpower were still adequate for Russian needs. The government had not collapsed, and national spirit was high. Moreover, the Germans had shown once more, as they had in the Battle of Britain, that their boasted planning was far from perfect. Their troops were not sufficiently equipped to stand the rigors of a Russian winter. Confident that one summer and autumn would be enough to finish the business, the German planners had left the winter to take care of itself. Indeed, in winter fighting between December, 1941, and May, 1942, the Russians regained much useful ground.

American Policy

Meanwhile, the Germans had fallen into a second fatal involvement. Impressed with what he thought were the disastrous failures of German policy in World War I, Hitler had sought to keep out of war with the United States. Although the United States had a strong isolationist element and even a handful of Axis sympathizers, American opinion had from the very beginning of the attack on Poland in 1939 been far more nearly unanimous against the Germans and Italians than it had been against the Central Powers in 1914. With the fall of France in 1940, anti-Axis sentiment grew stronger, reinforced by a feeling that if Hitler had his way in Europe the United States would be marked out as his next victim.

Between June, 1940 and December, 1941, the Roosevelt administration, with the consent of the Congress and with the general —though not unanimous—backing of American public opinion, took a series of steps "short of war" in aid of Britain and later Russia. By conventional nineteenth-century standards of international relations, these steps were far from being in accord with America's technical status as a neutral; they would have given Hitler ample legal justification for declaring war against the United States. The American government transferred to the British fifty "over-age" destroyers in exchange for Atlantic naval bases in British colonies, supplied the British with all sorts of arms, and used the American navy to help get these supplies across the Atlantic. Above all, in March, 1941, by the so-called "Lend-Lease Act," the United States agreed to supply materials needed for defense, including foodstuffs, to "any country whose defense the President deems vital to the defense of the United States." Supplies at once began rolling into England, and later to other allies in the struggle against the Axis, without the unfortunate complications produced by the war-debt methods employed during World War I.

This help went, as we have just noted, even to communist Russia, The "cold war" of the 1950's between Russia and the United States produced currents of opinion in this country which held that we should never have helped Russia in 1942–1945. But the historian knows that in great wars of coalition the wise rule is: help your allies even if you don't like them, even, indeed, if you don't trust them. Strict adherence to this doctrine by Roosevelt and Churchill clearly helped prevent among Britain, the United States, Russia, and the Free French the kind of actual back-stabbing and desertion that characterized the failure of Europe to defeat, or even contain, the revolutionary French and Napoleon between 1792 and 1812 (see Chapter 10).

Yet Hitler still did not let himself get involved in war against the United States. He had, however, firm commitments to aid Japan. And Japan, controlled by a militarist group, had taken advantage of the fall of France and

Part of the destruction at Pearl Harbor, December 7, 1941.

the Netherlands and the weakness of Britain to speed up vastly the policy of expansion in Asia that she had begun in Manchuria as far back as 1931. She early took advantage of the fall of France to penetrate into French Indo-China. She continued to press her campaign on the mainland of China. The American government, which had never in the days of technical peace in the 1930's been willing to accept Japanese conquests in China, did not now abandon its policy of opposition to what it considered Japanese aggression. It is indeed highly likely that had the American government been willing to allow Japan a free hand to do what she liked in the Far East there would have been no Pearl Harbor. But short of such complete abandonment of the previous American policy in the Far East, it is unlikely that the United States could have kept out of war with Japan.

Pearl Harbor and After

In the summer and autumn of 1941, the American government took steps to freeze Japanese credits in the United States, to close Japanese access to raw materials, and to get the Japanese to withdraw from China and Indo-China. Negotiations toward these ends were going on between the Japanese and the Americans when on December 7, 1941, the Japanese without warning struck with carrier-based airplanes at the American naval base at Pearl Harbor in Hawaii. Grave damage was done to ships and installations, but American power in the Pacific was by no means destroyed. Moreover, the psychological effect of the "day of infamy" on American public opinion was to produce in a nation of many millions an almost unanimous support for war against Japan. And the consequence was the immediate declaration of war against Japan by the United States. Germany and Italy honored their obligations to their Axis partner by declaring war against the United States on December 11. As the year 1942 began, the war was literally and fully a world war.

Although the United States was incomparably better prepared than she had been in 1917, she was still at a disadvantage. Against Germany she could for the moment do no more than continue, indeed increase, aid to Britain and Russia by Lend-Lease and take full part in the struggle against the German submarines. Against Japan she was almost as powerless. Her Pacific outposts of Guam, Wake Island, and the Philippines fell in rapid succession to Japanese arms. Nor could the British and the exiled Dutch governments protect their colonies in Southeast Asia. By the spring of 1942, the Japanese had taken Malaya from the British and Indonesia from the Dutch, and had virtual control of Siam (Thailand) and Burma. They seemed poised for an attack on Australia.

V The Victory of the United Nations

The Turning Points

There were several turning points in the struggle. The earliest was a series of naval actions in which Japanese expansion was stopped. In these actions, carrier-based airplanes played a decisive role. On May 7, 1942, in the battle of the Coral Sea in the southwest Pacific, Allied sea and air power halted a possible Japanese invasion of Australia and its protecting islands. In June, American sea and air power dispersed a Japanese fleet that was aiming at the conquest of Midway Island. Although the Japanese landed on American territory in the Aleutians, they never seriously threatened Hawaii or mainland Alaska.

In the West, the Americans and the British were as yet unwilling to respond to Russian pressure for a "second front" on the European mainland. But they were able in November, 1942, to effect a series of landings in French North Africa. Secret negotiations with anti-Axis elements among the French in North Africa were not completely successful, and the landings in Morocco were sharply though briefly resisted by the Vichy French. None the less, the Allies were rapidly established in force in Morocco and Algeria.

The Libyan segment of the long North African coast had been held by the Germans and their Italian allies since the beginning of the war in the Mediterranean, and there had been seesaw campaigns in these desert areas, campaigns that recaptured some of the adventure, even romance, of wars of old. At the time of the North African landings, the British under General Montgomery were holding a defensive line inside the Egyptian frontier; but on October 23, 1942, the British started on an offensive which was planned to co-ordinate with that of General Eisenhower, commander of the Allied forces in French North Africa, in the classic maneuver of catching the enemy in a vise. The Germans responded quickly to the threat, and succeeded in reinforcing their African armies through Tunis, which was delivered to them by the Vichy authorities. The planned expulsion of the Germans and Italians from North Africa was thus delayed, but the vise closed slowly. In May, 1943, Free French, British, and American troops took the last Axis strongholds of Tunis and Bizerte, and accepted the surrender of some three hundred thousand Axis troops.

The North African campaign had clearly been a turning point. The Allies had successfully made large-scale amphibious landings, and they had annihilated one of the most renowned of Axis forces, commanded by one of the few German generals in this war to strike the imagination of the world, Rommel, the "desert fox." North Africa was by no means a great central operation, but it was nevertheless a major campaign in which the Allies gained confidence and prestige.

The great turning point on land was, however, the successful Russian defense of Stalingrad, (now Volgograd), a defense that turned into an attack in the same month (November, 1942) that saw the Allied landing in North Africa. After their check in the winter of 1941–1942, the Germans had turned their Russian summer offensive of 1942 away from Leningrad and Moscow and toward the oil-rich regions of southeastern European Russia. The Germans were already beginning to suffer oil shortages, partly because of Allied bombing, but even more because, though they held the oil fields of Rumania, they simply did not have oil enough for the ravenous demands of mechanical warfare. This push toward the Russian oil fields carried the Germans a prodigious distance inside Russia, over a thousand miles from their original starting point. But again it failed, falling just short of the really rich oil fields of Grozny and Baku. Russian distance and Russian manpower, and the Russian ability to take punishment, were too much for these overextended Germans. Their armies were pinched off at Stalingrad, and early in 1943 the Russians started the long march that was to take them to Berlin two years later.

The Battle of Supply

A much less spectacular turning point than the engagements in the Coral Sea, in North Africa, and at Stalingrad was the Allied victory in the battle of supply. Yet this victory was of even greater importance, since naval and military successes ultimately depend on supplies. Even for Russia, an important source of supplies was the United States. But the United States was separated from its allies —and its enemies—by water, and all but the most precious and least bulky supplies, which could go by air, had to move across the seas. If the Germans could stop this movement, or even reduce it greatly, they might still be able to win in spite of the overwhelming resources of the Allies. They made important improvements in their submarines, notably the schnorkel, a device that enabled submarines to travel submerged for great distances. Submarine crews and commanders were well trained and resourceful. But there were not enough submarines, and the countermeasures of the Allies—radar, co-ordination of naval vessels and aircraft, the convoy system, and others —slowly reduced the proportion of sinkings.

Early in 1942, after Pearl Harbor, the rate of sinkings had been really dangerous, and German submarines had operated close to the Atlantic coast of the United States. But by the end of 1942, the statistics showed a turn of the tide, and in the summer of 1943 the Allies were confident enough to announce publicly that the number of sinkings from U-boat action in the first half of 1943 was only a quarter of what it had been in the first half of 1942.

The Axis on the Defensive

In the last two years of the war, the Axis powers were on the defensive. Both in Europe and in Asia the Allies attacked with land forces along definite lines of march; these were "campaigns" of the traditional kind. But the way for these armies was made easier by two new factors in warfare, air power and modern propaganda, or "psychological warfare." These new methods did not "win" the war by themselves, but they were useful adjuncts, and they undoubtedly hastened the process. Air bombardment, at least until the atomic bomb at Hiroshima, was never quite the perfect annihilation that the prophets of air power had preached. The Germans put some of their key production underground. Allied "precision" bombing rarely reached perfection. But as the superior Allied air power grew, as it was used systematically to destroy enemy capabilities in critical materials like ball bearings, machine tools, and oil, and as American airplanes dropped incendiary bombs on the relatively flimsy Japanese cities, it did much to destroy the Axis will and power to resist.

On Germany and Italy, the attack by land was pressed in three directions—by the Russians from the east, and by the British, French, Americans, and the other Allies from the south and from the west. In the south, the Allies moved over to Sicily in a successful amphibious operation (July, 1943) within two months of their final victory in North Africa, and from Sicily they moved in another six weeks across the Straits of Messina to the mainland of Italy. Yet the Italian campaign was never quite the great success the Allies hoped it would be in these earlier days. The Allied victories of the summer of 1943 were, however, sufficient to put Italy itself for the most part out of the war. High officers of the Italian army and others close to the king, helped by dissident fascist leaders, engineered a *coup* in July which brought about the fall and imprisonment of Mussolini and the beginnings of negotiations between the Allies and the new government headed by Marshal Badoglio.

But the Germans were quite unwilling to abandon the peninsula, perhaps as much for reasons of prestige as for military reasons. A detachment of German troops rescued Mussolini from his Apennine prison (September, 1943), and set him up as the head of a "Fascist Republic." The former *Duce* continued in this post until he was executed by partisans in April, 1945. Meantime, Italy had a civil as well as a foreign war on her hands. The majority of the Italian people, never really taken in by Mussolini's posturing as an imperial Roman, had never liked the war and were now heartily sick of it. Still, many were politically active in Italy in 1943–1945, and of these the fascist-Axis group was far less strong than the pro-Allied group. Italy came naturally enough into the United Nations. The war in Italy went on. In June, 1944, the Allies succeeded,

after particularly severe fighting around Cassino, in breaking through to Rome, and by August they were in Florence. They did not really penetrate any farther until the final collapse of the Germans in the early months of 1945.

The Defeat of Germany

The great Allied push in the west, it was finally decided at the Teheran conference of Churchill, Roosevelt, and Stalin (December, 1943), would be in France. After meticulous preparation, the long-awaited landings in France began on June 6, 1944. The Allies had chosen the Norman coast at the base of the Cotentin (Cherbourg) peninsula, and seem thereby to have gained some initial advantage of surprise, for the German high command believed the landings would come farther north and east along the Channel coast. The Germans had in their four years of occupancy fortified the French coastline with great thoroughness. But the Allies had also had those four years for study, invention, and planning. In the test, Allied landing craft, amphibious

American troops landing in Normandy, June, 1944.

trucks, called "ducks," naval and air support — by now the Luftwaffe had almost been driven from the skies — artificial harbors, and a well-organized supply system proved sufficient to gain a beachhead for the land forces. From this beachhead, a little over a month after "D-Day," they were able to break out at Avranches and sweep the Germans back across the Seine in a great flanking movement led by the American General Patton's Third Army.

A long-planned auxiliary landing on the French Mediterranean coast and a march north up the Rhone-Saône valleys was launched on August 15, 1944, and met very little resistance. Everywhere the French, by now well organized for resistance, welcomed the liberating forces, some of whom were French and French colonials fighting as heirs of the Free French of 1940. Paris, a symbol rather than a mere place, was liberated toward the end of August after its inhabitants had staged an uprising, barricades and all, in the style of 1848, against the German garrison.

The Germans were beaten, but not disorganized. In July, 1944, an attempt to assassinate Hitler and to pave the way for negotiations was made by conservative elements, both military and civilian. But Hitler survived the bomb intended for him, and the Nazis retained their firm grip on the German state. The Allies were encouraged by their rapid successes in July and August to try to destroy the German armies before winter, or to cut them off from their homeland. Patton's mechanized troops, however, ran out of fuel; the new German pilotless planes and rocked-propelled missiles delayed the full use of Antwerp as a port of supply; and by late autumn it was clear that the Germans had retired in good order to their own Siegfried Line.

From the east, the Russians had been pushing on relentlessly ever since the turning of the tide at Stalingrad. In the campaign of 1943, while the western Allies were busy in Italy, the Russians won back most of their own territories that had been lost in 1941 and 1942. They kept up the pressure during the winter and started an early spring campaign in the south. By the autumn of 1944, the Russians had been able to sweep through half-

hearted resistance from Hitler's Balkan satellite governments to a juncture with the Yugoslav communist guerrillas under Tito, and were ready for the attack on Hungary. In the center and north, they had recovered all their own territory and were ready to attack Germany itself from the east.

This year 1945 saw the rapid conclusion of the Battle of Germany. The Russians had not stopped for winter, but had pressed on through Poland to menace Berlin early in March. The western Allies broke through the Siegfried Line in February, crossed the Rhine, and entered the heart of Germany. Early in February, 1945, the leaders of the three great Allied powers, Stalin, Churchill, and Roosevelt, met at Yalta in the Crimea and confirmed final plans for the conquest of Germany. It was plain that the Germans, whose key industries had been so riddled from the air that they no longer could support their armies adequately, and whose manpower had been reduced to the very bottom, could not hold out for long. But the Allied planners were anxious to prevent, or at least to check, the race to be the first to arrive in Berlin, and they wanted to arrange peacefully for demarcations between the parts of Germany that each ally was to occupy. The decision to give the Russians the honor of taking Berlin is one that, with many other decisions reached in the conference at Yalta, has since been severely criticized in the West. At the time, however, it seemed a natural decision, a legitimate recognition of the fact that during the two years of successful offensive against the Germans the Russians had worn down many more German divisions than had the western Allies.

The Russians fought their way into a Berlin already pulverized by the air power of the western Allies. Hitler went down to his death, as he had long promised, in a Germanic funeral pyre at his Berlin headquarters.

The Allied advance into Germany revealed for the first time the full ghastliness of Nazi treatment of slave laborers from conquered lands, of political opponents and of Jews, Poles, and other German-styled "inferior" peoples. One after another, the concentration camps were liberated — Auschwitz, Belsen,

Buchenwald, Dachau, Nordhausen, and others. And the world was appalled at the gas ovens that had claimed so many victims, at the piles of emaciated corpses not yet cremated, and at the pitiful state of the prisoners who had survived. This was one of the horrors of war whose reality exceeded the grimmest expectations of Allied opinion.

By May 8, 1945, Churchill and Truman (who had become the American president on Roosevelt's death in April) were able to announce the end of German resistance, the day of victory in Europe, V-E Day. It was symbolic of difficulties to come that Stalin was offended because the western Allies had accepted from some of the German army leaders a formal surrender at Rheims in France. He chose to announce separately, on Russia's part, the final victory over Germany, and not until the next day.

The Defeat of Japan

V-J Day, the day of victory in Japan, was now the great goal of Allied effort. Russia had carefully refrained from adding Japan to its formal enemies as long as Germany was still a threat. Britain and the United States, on the other hand, were anxious to win Russia as a formal fighting ally against the Japanese. This natural desire—natural in the sense of historical precedent, for coalitions in the past have usually sought to rally as many allies as possi-

Corpses of Gestapo victims, Nordhausen concentration camp, 1945.

ble—was responsible for many of the concessions made to Russia in the last months of the German war.

The two years of Allied successes against Germany had also been two years of Allied successes against Japan. The attack on Japan had been pressed home in three main directions. First, in a process that the American press soon christened "island-hopping," the American navy drove straight toward Japan from the central Pacific. One after another, the small island bases that stood in the way were reduced by American naval forces, which used both air support and the amphibious methods that were being worked out simultaneously in Europe and North Africa. The names of these islands are now a part of the litany of American arms—Tarawa, Eniwetok, Kwajalein, Iwo Jima, Okinawa.

Second, in a series of operations calling for the close co-operation of air, sea, and land forces, the Americans and Australians, with help from other Commonwealth elements, worked their way up the southwest Pacific through the much larger islands of the Solomons, New Guinea, and the Philippines. The base for this campaign, which was under the command of the American General MacArthur, was Australia and such outlying islands as New Caledonia and the New Hebrides. The start of the campaign goes back to the first major offensive step in the Far East, the dramatic and difficult seizure of Guadalcanal in the Solomons by the United States Marines on August 7, 1942. These campaigns involved jungle fighting of the hardest sort, slow and painful work. But by October, 1944, the sea forces had won the great battle of the Philippine Sea and had made possible the successful landing of MacArthur's troops on Leyte and the reconquest of the Philippine Islands themselves from the Japanese.

The third attack on the "Greater East Asia Co-Prosperity Sphere" as the Japanese, imitating the West, as propagandists, called their conquered land, came from the south, in the "CBI"—the China-Burma-India Theater. No brief narrative can do justice to the complex interweaving of events in this theater, where the main effort of the Allies was to get ma-

terial support to Chiang Kai-shek and the Chinese Nationalists at Chungking (see Chapter 22) and, if possible, to damage the Japanese position in Burma, Thailand, and Indo-China. After Pearl Harbor, when the Japanese seized and shut the famous "Burma Road," the only way for the Allies to communicate with Chiang's Nationalists was by air. It is perhaps true that the western Allies did not invest an overwhelming proportion of their resources in this CBI Theater, but they did help keep the Chinese formally in the fight. And, as the final campaign of 1945 drew on, the British, with Chinese and American aid, were holding down three Japanese field armies in this CBI Theater.

The end came in Japan with a suddenness that the Allied peoples, perhaps even the Allied governments, hardly expected. From Pacific island bases, American airplanes inflicted crippling damage on Japanese industry in the spring and summer of 1945; the Japanese fleet had been almost destroyed; submarine warfare had brought the Japanese economy near to strangulation; and there was impressive evidence of the declining morale of Japanese soldiers. None the less, American decision-makers were convinced that only the use of their recently invented atomic bomb could bring a quick decision and avert the very heavy casualties likely in the proposed amphibious invasion of the Japanese home islands. The result was the dropping of the first atomic bomb, on Hiroshima, August 6, 1945. On August 8, the Russians, who had agreed to come into the war against Japan once Germany was beaten, began an invasion of Manchuria in full force. Faced with what they felt was certain defeat, the Japanese government, unlike the German, decided not to make a last-ditch stand in their own country. On September 2, after brief negotiations, the Japanese made formal surrender at Tokyo. Japan gave up its conquests abroad and submitted to American military occupation. Contrary to the desires of part of Allied opinion, however, the Emperor of Japan was not dethroned. Purged of most of its militarists, the Japanese government continued to rule under Allied—actually American—supervision.

Asian and Pacific Theaters, 1941-45

Area under Japanese domination, Aug. 1942
("Greater East Asia Co-Prosperity Sphere")

Island hopping U.S. – Australian joint drive

Pacific Ocean

HAWAIIAN IS. (U.S.)
Pearl Harbor

KINGMAN REEF
PALMYRA I. (U.S.)

JARVIS I.

L I N E   I S.

PHOENIX IS.

HOWLAND I.
BAKER I.

SAMOA (U.S.)

JOHNSTON I.

MIDWAY IS. (U.S.)

1943

1943

GILBERT IS.

ELLICE IS.

FIJI IS.

NEW HEBRIDES (Br. and Fr.)

NEW CALEDONIA (Fr.)
Nouméa

WAKE I. (U.S.)

BIKINI

MARSHALL IS.

ENIWETOK

KWAJALEIN

1942

GUADALCANAL

Coral   Sea

MARCUS I.

TRUK

CAROLINE ISLANDS

BISMARCK ARCH.

SOLOMON IS.

ADMIRALTY IS.

MARIANAS IS.

BONIN IS.

IWO JIMA

1945

GUAM (U.S.)

YAP

PALAU

Hollandia

NEW GUINEA

Lae

KURILE IS.

SAKHALIN

JAPAN

Tokyo

ATOM BOMB – Aug. 6, 1945
ATOM BOMB – Aug. 9, 1945

KOREA

Hiroshima
Nagasaki

Shanghai

RYUKYU IS.

OKINAWA 1945

FORMOSA

Philippine Sea
1944

LEYTE

MINDANAO

CELEBES

NETHERLANDS   INDIES

Darwin

AUSTRALIA

Vladivostok

Russian land army
1945

MANCHURIA

1945

Kirin

Peiping

Yenan

CHINA

Chungking

SZECHWAN

YUNNAN
Kunming
BURMA ROAD

Chinese land Army

Hong Kong

HAINAN

LUZON
Manila

PHILIPPINE IS. (U.S.)

CORREGIDOR

BR. N. BORNEO

SARAWAK

BORNEO

JAVA

SUMATRA

MALAYA
Singapore

INDOCHINA
Saigon

FR.

Hanoi

THAILAND (SIAM)

BURMA

Lashio

British land army

NDIA

TIBET

MONGOLIA

Russian land army

Yellow R.

Yangtze R.

1945

MOLIA

Indian Ocean

45

30

15

0

15

165

180

165

105

The Allied Coalition

The "Grand Alliance," as the historian Churchill liked to call it, but mostly known in its last years as the "United Nations," had mustered overpowering strength against Germany, Japan, Italy, and such collaborators as the Axis powers could secure in the Balkans, Southeast Asia, and western Europe. Britain, Russia, and the United States were the heart of the Allied coalition. But Nationalist China, for all its inefficiencies, had occupied the attention of hundreds of thousands of Japanese soldiers, and the resources of the French Empire and the French resistance movements at home and abroad had been most useful. The United Nations had been able to count on the resources of Latin America, and Brazil had been an active member of the alliance. In this truly global war, Brazilian troops had fought in Italy, which at the end had been the most cosmopolitan of theaters. There American (including Japanese-American, or Nisei), French imperial, British imperial, pro-Allied Italian,

Polish, and other troops had fought, in addition to the Brazilians. At the very end of the war, even Argentina was brought into the United Nations coalition, when she declared war on Germany and Japan on March 27, 1945.

The instruments of continuing Allied union were the conferences of the "Big Three"—Churchill, Roosevelt, and Stalin—with their political and military advisers and experts, and the more frequent Anglo-American conferences. Even before the United States entered the shooting war, Roosevelt and Churchill met off Newfoundland and issued the Atlantic Charter, on August 14, 1941, in which they declared for the freedom of the seas, equality of access to economic opportunity, abandonment of aggression, and the restoration of rights to conquered peoples. The Atlantic Charter had been attacked as no more than another empty assertion of impossible ideals, but the true realist sees in it an important step in rallying world opinion against the Axis. Later, formal conferences—between Roosevelt and Churchill at Casablanca (January, 1943) and Quebec (August, 1943), and among the "Big Three" at Teheran (December, 1943) and Yalta (February,

Scene in Hiroshima a few hours after the bomb hit, August 6, 1945.

1945)—brought to a head consultations that had been steadily carried on at lower political and military levels. From July 17 to August 17, 1945, a final great conference at Potsdam near conquered Berlin brought Britain, Russia, and the United States, with two new figures, President Truman and Prime Minister Attlee, together to confirm in general the Yalta decisions.

There were always grave military and political matters to be ironed out. It was not easy to maintain even the Anglo-American collaboration, which was perhaps the closest military collaboration between two major sovereign powers ever achieved. For the actual direction of operations in the field, the British and Americans decided to set up, not just the sort of supreme command the Allies painfully achieved late in World War I under Foch (Chapter 17), but a complete intermeshing of staffs. All down the line, an American in command always had a Britisher as his second, and a Britisher in command always had an American as his second. In the pinch, and in spite of normal national jealousies, the arrangement worked. An anecdote about General Eisenhower from North African days relates that he sent an American officer home, not because he called his immediate superior a so-and-so, but because he called him an *English* so-and-so. At the highest level, the Combined Chiefs of Staff, in close touch with top American and British government officials, did the over-all planning. The Russians were never brought into such close military co-operation, and in the field the Russians always fought on their own.

Political Issues

A political issue that bulked large at the time with liberals seems not to have seriously divided the Allies during the war itself. This was the issue of "unconditional surrender." Here recent history had an overpowering influence on the policy adopted. Hitler had simply followed widespread German opinion in insisting that in World War I Germany had not really been defeated in the field but had

Giraud, Roosevelt, de Gaulle, and Churchill at Casablanca, January, 1943.

been betrayed by the false promises of Wilson's Fourteen Points into surrendering while still undefeated. This time the Allied leaders were determined to give the Germans no excuse for a future rallying point of this sort. The Germans must be beaten unmistakably, and Allied troops must enter Berlin as conquerors. There must be no political negotiation at all, simply unconditional military surrender. There was some opposition to this policy during the war, at least in lands of free political expression like Britain and the United States. This opposition rested partly on humanitarian grounds, but also on the belief that the prospect of unconditional surrender would inevitably stiffen the German will to resist, and would unite the nation behind Hitler instead of allowing Allied psychological warfare its full effect by promising anti-Nazi elements some reward for deserting the Nazi cause. In retrospect, it does not seem that Hitler would ever have negotiated with the Allies; and after the failure of the attempt to kill him with a bomb in July, 1944, there was little chance that the Germans themselves would overthrow the Nazi government.

Another political problem made a much clearer rift between the British and the Americans. The underlying issue was just how far anti-German elements in France, Italy, and other occupied lands must go in proving that they were good honest democrats in order to secure the backing of the democratic western powers. Here the difference in the underlying tone of American and British policies was evident in the views of Roosevelt and Churchill. Roosevelt was convinced that if the Allies did not interfere to support scheming conservatives and reactionaries in the occupied lands, but instead allowed their peoples to choose their form of government freely, then they would choose democracy. Churchill was much less idealistic. He was eager to use any elements that were hostile to the Germans, even if their hostility was quite recent, and he had little faith in the capacity or desire of peoples like the Italians for Anglo-Saxon democracy. Therefore he was quite willing to back Badoglio and the monarchists in Italy; Roosevelt kept insisting that the Italians wanted and needed a republic. Yet the opposition between American support of democratic or Leftist elements and British support of conservative, monarchist, Rightist elements was not a clear one. We were hard on Badoglio and soft on Vichy; the British were hard on Vichy, soft on Badoglio.

In French politics the issue was further complicated by Roosevelt's suspicions of de Gaulle, whose firm resistance in June, 1940, had made him the inevitable leader of the French movement for liberation. To Roosevelt, de Gaulle seemed a potential man on horseback, no better than Boulanger or Napoleon III. To Churchill, de Gaulle seemed indeed difficult, a man obsessed with the need to restore the greatness of France, but an indispensable ally. As it turned out, the Gaullists, in collaboration with the organized French resistance in the homeland, did take over the civilian administration of French territory as it was liberated, and France by free popular vote restored in the Fourth Republic a form of government essentially like that of the Third. In Italy, the liberated people voted the establishment of a republic. What had threatened at one time to be a serious difficulty between American policy and British policy was resolved by the action of the liberated people themselves.

The anger aroused in de Gaulle himself, and in many other French leaders, by Roosevelt's policy of refusing solid support to de Gaulle and the Fighting French has embittered Franco-American relations to this day. In particular, Roosevelt's intention to "occupy" France under AMGOT (Allied Military Government in Occupied Territory) wounded the French, who thought of themselves as allies, not enemies, of the democracies.

But the political issue that has bulked largest since World War II was by no means so clear an issue during the war itself. This is the problem of Russian domination in eastern and southeastern Europe. It is easy to say that at Yalta the western powers took much too soft a line with the Russians, allowed them to push their armies much too far westward, and relied foolishly on Russian promises to permit free elections in Poland, Hungary, Czechoslovakia, and the Balkans. This criticism may be supplemented by the old British motif of the "soft under-belly," by maintaining that the western powers should have struck as soon as possible, perhaps in 1943, from the Mediterranean into the Danube Valley in order to get there ahead of the Russians. Proponents of these criticisms present us with an Iron Curtain that would then have been drawn far to the east of where it now is, with an eastern and a southeastern Europe that would now be democratic and on the side of the West rather than on the side of the Russians.

The chief trouble with this argument is that it fails to take into account two basic facts. First, most of the small eastern European countries had no real tradition of western-style democracy; most of them had moved toward fascist totalitarianism before World War II (see Chapter 19). Their transition to communist totalitarianism was easy. Second, during the war itself it was by no means clear to western leaders, or to western public opinion, that the Germans and the Japanese would be beaten so readily. Even leaders like Churchill, who seems never really to have trusted the Russians and who was to coin the phrase "the Iron Curtain" soon after the war, did not dare risk losing the aid of Russian manpower and material resources during the war itself. Even in 1945, at Yalta, with Japan still very much in the fight, appeasement of the Russians seemed absolutely essential, not only to Roosevelt, who hoped the Russians would collaborate with us in the post-war world, but also to Churchill, who seems to have had little if any hope of such collaboration from the Russians.

In the Far East, political problems seemed less serious—at least in wartime. There was general agreement that the Chinese Nationalists, however corrupt and inefficient their government was, had to be supported against the Japanese. Nor did the final decision to accept the continuance on the throne of the Japanese emperor arouse serious opposition in the West. The critical decisions on the Far East were rather the work of the troubled period after V-E and V-J days, when to the bitter disappointment of most western peoples it became clear that the peace was likely for some time to be no more than a continuation of war. Indeed, there was no peace, and these years deserve a term that was soon coined, the years of "cold war." The once "colonial" peoples throughout the world were now roused against "imperialism."

In sum, as we all know now, and as we shall see in more detail in the next three chapters, the great war of 1939–1945 ended indeed, but there was no peace. From our own western point of view, and in plain language, the defeat of the perturbers, the aggressors, the villains, Germany and Japan, was *almost immedi-* *ately* followed by the rise of a new perturber, a new villain, Russia, which had already given clear indications of its perturbing power. And indeed, it is easy to go on to the conclusion that just because the Germans and Japanese were beaten in the way they actually were, the present menace of Russia—pretty clearly a greater menace than the old German menace—was helped, was in fact made possible, by that defeat; from there it is a fatally easy step to the dangerous conclusion that Russia, not Germany, was our enemy all along.

Yet the wise student of history will not readily jump to the conclusion that any other Allied policy, and in particular a different American policy at Yalta and Potsdam, could have either prevented the rise of Russia, or produced a virtuous, co-operative, democratic Russia. We are still far too close to World War II to understand its many ramifications. The historian who sticks to his last can do no more than conclude that in the perspective of modern western history the sorely tried western statesmen at Yalta and Potsdam, in the midst of a hot war, were using time-honored methods to win that war as quickly and as decisively as possible: and in particular, with the long record of failures of coalitions in the past before them, they were determined to hold together their extraordinary and by no means "natural" coalition, known hopefully as the United Nations, until *both* the mainstay powers of the Axis coalition were beaten. This they did.

Reading Suggestions on the Second World War

(Asterisk indicates paperbound edition.)

eneral Accounts   W. S. Churchill, *The Second World War,* 6 vols. (Houghton Mifflin, 1948–1953). Magisterial account by a chief architect of Allied victory; the first volume reviews international affairs between the wars.

E. H. Carr, *The Twenty Years' Crisis* (Macmillan, 1946). A stimulating review of interwar diplomacy by a capable and opinionated Englishman. Now a Beacon paperback.

F. L. Snyder, *The War: A Concise History 1939–1945* (Messner, 1960), and K. S. Davis, *Experience of War: The U. S. in World War II* (Doubleday, 1965). These two books with notes and bibliography are good guides to the already enormous literature of the war.

J. F. C. Fuller, *The Second World War* (Duell, Sloane, and Pearce, 1949), and C. Falls, *The Second World War,* 2nd ed. (Methuen, 1948). Two succinct and very useful military accounts. Both are written from a British viewpoint.

D. Flower and J. Reeves, eds., *The Taste of Courage: The War, 1939–1945* (Harper, 1960). A good anthology of "war pieces."

F. Pratt, *War for the World: A Chronicle of our Fighting Forces in World War II* (Yale Univ. Press, 1950). A good succinct American account.

United States Army in World War II (Dept. of the Army, 1947). The official history, in many detailed volumes, to be found in library catalogues under the general title above, or under "United States: Department of the Army."

S. E. Morison, *History of United States Naval Operations in World War II* (Little, Brown, 1947–1962). 15 vols. Official but detached and professional history, with full attention to political and diplomatic problems, and to the work of other branches of the armed forces.

C. Wilmot, *The Struggle for Europe* (Harper, 1952). Highly controversial study, critical of the American high command.

Special Studies

F. Gilbert and G. A. Craig, eds., *The Diplomats, 1919–1939* (Princeton Univ. Press, 1953). A helpful symposium.

A. Wolfers, *Britain and France between Two Wars* (Harcourt, Brace, 1940). A solid analysis of the foreign policies of the two powers.

S. R. Smith, *The Manchurian Crisis, 1931–1932* (Columbia Univ. Press, 1948). Monograph on the crisis that marked the watershed between post-war and pre-war periods.

J. W. Wheeler-Bennett, *Munich: Prologue to Tragedy* (Macmillan, 1948), and L. B. Namier, *Diplomatic Prelude, 1938–1939* (Macmillan, 1948). Good studies of the last international crises before World War II.

W. L. Langer and S. E. Gleason, *The Challenge to Isolation, 1937–1940* (Harper, 1952), and *The Undeclared War, 1940–1941* (Harper, 1953). Solid studies of America's role.

C. C. Tansill, *Back Door to War: The Roosevelt Foreign Policy* (Regnery, 1952). Representative work of the "new revisionists," a school of writers who castigate Roosevelt for allegedly pushing America into war.

H. F. Armstrong, *Chronology of Failure* (Macmillan, 1940); "Pertinax" (André Géraud), *The Gravediggers of France* (Doubleday, 1944); M. Bloch, *Strange Defeat* (Oxford Univ. Press, 1949). Three perceptive studies of the French defeat in 1940.

A. J. Liebling, ed., *The Republic of Silence* (Harcourt, Brace, 1947). Excellent collection of materials pertaining to the French resistance movement.

L. Collins and D. LaPierre, *Is Paris Burning?* (Simon and Schuster, 1965). Deservedly best-selling account of the liberation of Paris.

R. Wohlstetter, *Pearl Harbor: Warning and Decision* (Stanford Univ. Press, 1962). First-rate monograph.

A. Weber, *Farewell to European History; or, the Conquest of Nihilism* (Kegan Paul, Trench, Trubner, 1947). A German sociologist reviews—and regrets—his country's part in the crises of World War II.

D. L. Gordon and R. Dangerfield, *The Hidden Weapon: The Story of Economic Warfare* (Harper, 1947). A very good popular account by trained experts.

H. Feis, *Churchill, Roosevelt, Stalin* (Princeton Univ. Press, 1957). A fascinating and very fair-minded account of the relations among these three leaders during the war.

There are many memoirs of actors in this great war. The following make a good beginning: D. D. Eisenhower, *Crusade in Europe* (Doubleday, 1948); H. Truman, *Memoirs,* 2 Vols. (Doubleday, 1958); B. L. Montgomery, *Memoirs* (World, 1958); C. de Gaulle, *War Memories,* English translation, 3 Vols. in one (Simon and Schuster, 1964).

22

The Post-War World, 1945-1953

I The Cold War

During World War II, most people expected that when the shooting stopped there would be a general peace conference, as there had been after all the major general wars of modern times. As we have abundantly seen, even a general peace conference (Westphalia, Utrecht, Vienna, Versailles) leaves many problems unsolved or solves them in a way that proves unsatisfactory. As it turned out, however, the tensions that arose between the Soviet Union and its western Allies during the war itself made it impossible to plan for, much less convoke, a Peace Conference. So World War II bequeathed to mankind a legacy of problems to be solved one by one if at all.

The damage done by World War II greatly exceeded even that done by World War I. The total number of human deaths resulting from the war has been estimated at 22 million, more than half of them civilians, who died by mass executions in concentration camps, or in air attacks, or by starvation or disease. Material damages have been estimated at more than $2,000 billion. Despite a sharply rising birth rate and vast programs of economic reconstruction, such losses could never be fully repaired, and it took the first decade after the war to launch effectively the necessary programs of modernization.

Atomic Weapons

After the defeat of the Axis powers, new and terrifying problems faced the statesmen of the world. Atomic weapons—before very long, hydrogen bombs, the possibility— and soon the development—of guided missiles, made concrete and plausible the threat that a new general war might wipe out the human race or so terribly shatter the physical and moral bases of modern civilization as to reduce what was left of mankind to something like another Stone Age. At the same time, the war had so limited the war-making potential of all other states that the United States and the Soviet Union emerged as super-powers, the only powers capable of initiating or pursuing the new warfare. Given the ideology of the U.S.S.R. and the suspicious and vengeful character of its supreme dictator, Stalin, it was inevitable that the Russians would regard the Americans as their rivals for control of the world, and that the Americans should quickly have been forced to accept the same estimate of the situation. The post-war history of international politics became in large part a history of Soviet-American rivalry.

In 1945 enemy attack and occupation had caused incalculable devastation inside the Russian borders, and left millions of survivors destitute, while Russia's capitalist ally, the United States, had invented and used a weapon so decisive as to make war against its possessor impossible for any power that did not possess it. Stalin, who liked nothing so much as the destruction of an enemy, and who regarded the whole capitalist world as his enemy, knew that if he had been the sole possessor of the atomic bomb, he would have used it. He attributed to his rival the strategy that he himself would have pursued. It seemed to him that all the technological advance of the Soviet period, undertaken precisely to bring the U.S.S.R. up to the industrialized West, had now been wiped out by the American development of the atomic bomb. It took Stalin four years (1945–1949) to catch up once again, by making his own atomic bomb. No doubt scientific information given the Russians by agents and spies made some contribution to this achievement, but only the high level of Russian science and technology and the Soviet capacity to concentrate their investments made it possible at all.

A Divided World: Germany and China

Even before the U.S.S.R. could join the United States as an atomic power in 1949, the two had engaged in a series of tests of will, in Europe and in Asia, that determined where the increasingly clear boundary between a Russian sphere of influence and an American sphere of influence would run. And the confrontation continued after 1949. In Iran, in Greece, in Berlin, in Korea the lines were drawn, tested, and re-drawn, sometimes after bloodshed. Though the Soviet Union and its former western allies were able to reach agreement on peace treaties with Italy and with three of the Axis powers' former European satellites—Hungary, Rumania, and Bulgaria—no such treaty could ever be concluded with Germany itself or with Japan.

But whereas the American occupation of Japan rendered a Russian presence there impossible, defeated Germany was divided into four zones—American, British, French, and Russian. The U.S.S.R. obtained the eastern regions of Germany, bordering on Poland, but extending considerably west of Berlin, which as the former capital, was also divided into four occupation zones. This arrangement, designed for temporary military occupation, continued in effect because no treaty could be reached. It proved dangerous in the extreme, since it left Berlin as an island surrounded by Soviet-dominated territory, yet an island including zones to which the western allies were entitled to access. The failure to reach any settlement over Germany left the most serious problem in Europe without a solution.

As time passed, the three western powers allowed their zones to unite in the "Federal Republic of Germany" (1949), called West Germany, with its capital at Bonn, and the Russians responded by creating the "German Democratic Republic"—East Germany—with its capital at Pankow outside Berlin. Many if not most West Germans were naturally eager for reunion with their fellow-Germans in the Soviet zone. Yet a reunion of Germany under western capitalist auspices was precisely what the Russians feared the most, believing that it would portend a revival of aggression, while an all-communist Germany was equally intolerable to the western powers. Indeed, few Frenchmen or Englishmen looked with any enthusiasm upon the idea of a reunified Germany, and if there were more Americans who sympathized with reunion as an ultimate goal, there were no responsible men in high places who failed to understand the dangers of trying to bring it about unilaterally. The German question would no doubt have baffled any hypothetical peace conference that had been convoked to find a solution; in the absence of any such international conference, it continued to baffle everybody.

In Asia—with Japan under American occupation—the most grievous problem remained that of China. The communists, who had challenged Chiang Kai-shek's ruling Kuomintang (nationalist) party for power in a struggle which had developed into a virtual civil war by the late 1930's, kept their forces in being during the years of Japanese occupation. The United States, having backed Chiang during the war, tried in 1946 to bring about an agreement between Chinese nationalists and Chinese communists that would end the civil war and leave China a democratic state, in which the communists, though a legal party, as in Italy or France, would not dominate the country. The American negotiator, General George C. Marshall, failed to bring the two parties into a working agreement, and after he returned to the United States early in 1947, the civil war in China continued.

Supported by Soviet aid, including former Japanese war material in Manchuria that had been surrendered to the U.S.S.R. by Japan, the communists were able by 1949 to expel the forces of Chiang Kai-shek, who took refuge on the off-shore island of Formosa (Taiwan), where the communists could not follow because they lacked the naval strength. In the last years of the struggle, Chiang had lost his hold over the Chinese people; the morale of his own forces was low, and an ever-mounting inflation ravaged the economy, already ruined by the long Japanese occupation. By 1950, mainland China had gone communist, and formed part of the Soviet bloc. Only Chiang's government in Taiwan, where it ruled ruthlessly and absolutely, remained a part of the American bloc. American foreign policy had suffered a major defeat. Though some Americans were quick to blame the failure on a conspiracy by a few evil men, the magnitude of the change, the huge numbers of Chinese involved, rendered this answer unsatisfactory.

As the case of China shows, the Soviet Union pursued its goal of turning the whole world communist through the agencies of individual Communist parties. In virtually every country a Communist party existed, sometimes strong—as in France or Italy—sometimes weak—as in Britain or the United States—often varying in its precise degree of subservience to the Communist party of the Soviet Union (CPSU) and the Soviet government, but virtually always prepared to act as the domestic agent for Soviet interests and policies. The United States in most of the world had no such disciplined and reliable supporters; it could not give orders and expect French or Italian politicians to follow them; it had to conduct its rivalry with the U.S.S.R. on other terms. Often the existence of a local

Communist party gave the Soviet Union an advantage in the Cold War.

The Two Coalitions

The situation, then, after World War II, though familiar enough in one way (after a war the victorious allies had found themselves unable to agree on a settlement and had become rivals) contained many brand new elements. There were only two super-powers. Neither of them had ever in history taken one of the leading roles in international affairs, although of course Russia since Peter the Great had played an important part in both Europe and Asia, and the United States had in the twentieth century made the decisive contribution to the Allied victory in World War I, but had then withdrawn into relative isolation. Yet at no time did the United States and the Soviet Union, taken together, possess as much productive capacity as the rest of the world combined, or more than an eighth of the population of the globe. The Cold War consisted in part of a great competition between the two for the allegiance and support of the rest of the world. And each became the leader of a great coalition, whose members were attached more or less tightly by bonds of self-interest to the senior partner.

The members of the loose American coalition, often in these years called the "free world," included in 1945 Japan, the Philippines, Australia and New Zealand, the Western Hemisphere, Great Britain, and western Europe. The Soviet coalition included the countries of eastern Europe, and by 1949 China. The border between the two coalitions in Europe—called the "Iron Curtain" for the first time by Winston Churchill in 1946—ran along a north-south line extending from Stettin on the Baltic (formerly German and now Polish) to Trieste on the Adriatic. Yugoslavia lay in the Soviet sphere, and the frontier resumed again with the border between northern Greece and the three Soviet satellites of Albania, Yugoslavia, and Bulgaria. Turkey belonged to the western coalition, and portions of the Middle East and of Southeast Asia

were linked to it by a network of pacts, often impressive chiefly on paper. India remained neutral. The dividing line between North and South Korea, with the U.S.S.R. occupying the north, and the United States the south, represented a kind of Asian extension of the long frontier between the two coalitions. Along the frontier came the aggressive Soviet probing operations that led to crises and in several cases to wars.

Repeatedly the United States sought in vain to ease the relationships between the two coalitions. In 1946, Stalin refused to join in a United Nations atomic energy commission, or to have anything to do with international control of atomic weapons. In 1947, the United States proposed an international plan of massive American economic aid to accelerate recovery from the ruin of the war, the Marshall Plan, so-called for George C. Marshall, then Secretary of State. The Soviet Union refused to accept the aid for itself, and would not let its satellites participate. The Marshall Plan nations subsequently formed the nucleus of the North Atlantic Treaty Organization (NATO: 1949). The Soviet coalition founded the Cominform ("Communist Information Bureau") in 1947, as a successor to the former Comintern, "abolished" during the war (see Chapter 18), and created the Warsaw Pact (1955), binding eastern Europe together, as an answer to NATO.

Within every country attached to either coalition there were many individuals who preferred the leader of the other coalition: thus there were pro-Soviet Frenchmen, not necessarily communists, and pro-American Bulgarians. But in addition, a good many individual human beings in the West disliked both powers, regarding them as aggressive, as vulgarly materialistic. We shall meet these alienated intellectuals again (see Chapter 24). Needless to say, many individuals neither knew nor cared about power politics at all. Others, remembering the time when their own countries (France, Britain, Germany) had shared more largely in the leadership of the world, scorned the United States and the U.S.S.R. as newcomers. But these individual neutrals did not, between 1945 and 1953, anywhere command a share of public opinion sufficiently strong to weaken their countries' memberships in one of the great coalitions.

Outside the coalitions remained the neutral nations. Some, like Switzerland or Sweden, were simply maintaining their traditional legal policies of not aligning themselves with any grouping of powers. But most belonged to the new nations that were now emerging as independent, having discarded their former colonial status. During the years between 1945 and 1953, India under Nehru (Chapter 23) was the most influential. Nehru certainly hoped by taking a lofty position above the battle to retain the confidence of both sides and to act as mediator if necessary; he also took from both the assistance that India so badly needed. As economic aid became an instrument in the Cold War, neutral nations tried, often with success, to play the Americans off against the Russians, raising the not too subtle threat that if Washington saw fit to deprive them of something they wanted, they might regretfully have to go communist. It was not until the 1960's that the United States learned to regard neutrality as often positively helpful to its interests.

The United Nations

Through the years of Cold War, and the occasional outbreaks of something hotter, the United Nations—formed during World War II from among the opponents of the Axis and chartered in 1945 at San Francisco—served as an international organization where members of both coalitions and neutrals alike could meet in peaceful discussion. As direct successor to the League of Nations, it inherited the League's duty of keeping the peace, but like the League it lacked independent sovereignty or authority over its members. Its charter created a Security Council, to deal with threats to the peace, with eleven member-states, five of which—the United States, the Soviet Union, Great Britain, France, and Nationalist China—held permanent memberships. The other six were elected to rotating two-year terms by the General Assembly. In the General Assembly,

to which all member states belonged, each had an equal voice. The Secretary General, elected by the Security Council, could exert great personal influence in international affairs. But each of the five permanent members of the Security Council had a veto over any substantive question. All five had to be unanimous before action could go forward. Both the U.S.S.R. and the United States insisted on this provision in the Charter. As a result, the Security Council often found itself unable to act because of a veto: of the eighty vetoes cast between 1945 and 1955 the U.S.S.R. cast seventy-seven.

Looking beyond the strict chronological limits of this chapter, we should note that in the mid-fifties new nations joined the U.N.: some pro-western, like Austria and Italy (both former Axis states and so originally excluded), some pro-Soviet like Albania, Bulgaria, and the other former Axis satellites in eastern Europe, and some neutral and mostly former colonies, like Ceylon or Libya. Japan joined in 1956. As former colonies obtained their independence during the late fifties and early sixties, each joined the United Nations, where the "Afro-Asian bloc" commanded a majority in the General Assembly (Chapter 23). Germany remained outside the U.N., but both East and West Germany had their observers there. The United States resisted all efforts of the Chinese communists to join, which left the permanent Chinese seat on the Security Council in the possession of Chiang Kai-shek's representative, although as we have seen, Chiang now governed only Taiwan (Formosa). Chinese aggression in Korea and elsewhere had hardened American policy against any attempt of the Chinese communists to "shoot their way into the U.N.," while by the mid-sixties, the Chinese communists often denounced the body, and seemed no longer much interested in membership.

The three successive Secretaries-General, Trygve Lie of Norway, Dag Hammarskjöld of Sweden, and U Thant of Burma, commanded universal international respect as men who served the cause of world peace. Though the U.N. could not "settle" the Cold War, or bring about the international control of atomic

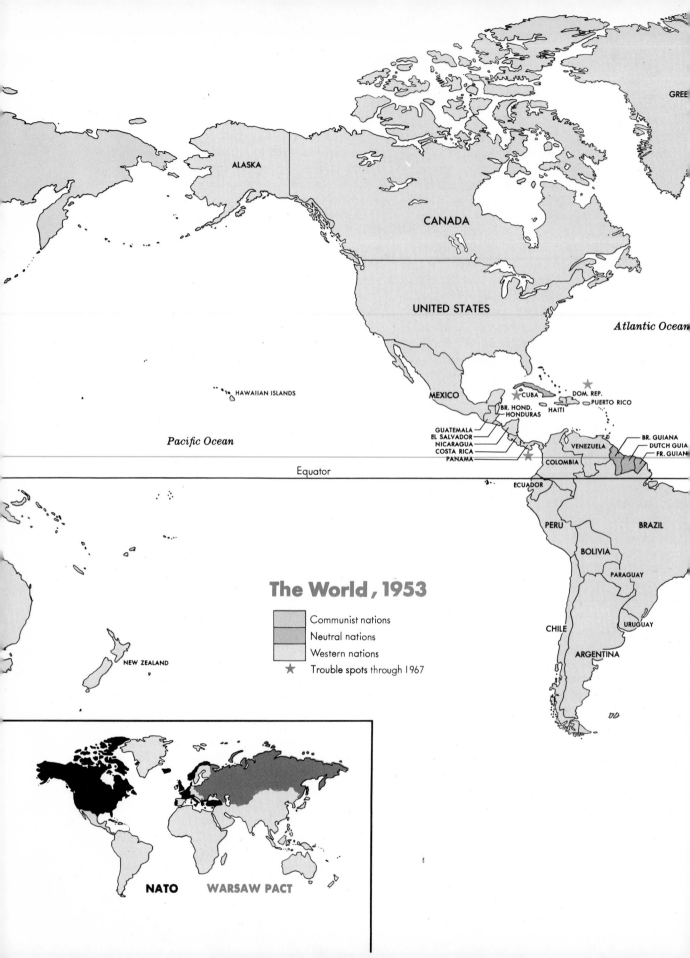

The World, 1953

Communist nations
Neutral nations
Western nations
★ Trouble spots through 1967

ALASKA

CANADA

UNITED STATES

Atlantic Ocean

MEXICO

HAWAIIAN ISLANDS

Pacific Ocean

CUBA
DOM. REP.
PUERTO RICO
HAITI
BR. HOND.
HONDURAS
GUATEMALA
EL SALVADOR
NICARAGUA
COSTA RICA
PANAMA

VENEZUELA
BR. GUIANA
DUTCH GUIA
FR. GUIAN

COLOMBIA

Equator

ECUADOR

PERU

BRAZIL

BOLIVIA

PARAGUAY

CHILE

URUGUAY

ARGENTINA

NEW ZEALAND

GREE

NATO   WARSAW PACT

ICELAND

NORWAY
SWEDEN
FINLAND

UNITED
KINGDOM

DEN.
NETH.
E.
GER.
POLAND
EIRE
BEL.
W.
L.
GER.
CZECH.
FRANCE
SW.
AUST.
HUN.
RUM.
YUG.
ITALY
BUL.
PORTUGAL
SPAIN
ALB.
TURKEY
GREECE
LEBANON
SYRIA
IRAQ
MOROCCO
TUNISIA
ISRAEL
JORDAN
IFNI
ALGERIA
LIBYA
EGYPT
SAUDI
ARABIA
OMAN
YEMEN

U.S.S.R.

MONGOLIA

KASHMIR
AFGHAN.
W. PAKISTAN
IRAN
TIBET
BHUTAN
NEPAL
KOREA
JAPAN
CHINA
FORMOSA
INDIA
E. PAK.
BURMA
THAI.
FR.
INDO-
CHINA
PHILIPPINE IS.

FRENCH WEST AFRICA
SUDAN
FR.
SOM.
NIGERIA
FR.
EQUAT.
AFRICA
ETHIOPIA
BR. SOMALILAND
LIBERIA
RIO MUNI
CAM.
SOMALIA
CEYLON
TOGO
GOLD COAST
CABINDA
UGANDA
KENYA
BELGIAN
CONGO
ZANZIBAR
RUANDA-
URUNDI
TANGANYIKA
NYASALAND
ANGOLA
NO.
RHOD.
MOZAMBIQUE
SO.
RHOD.
MADAGASCAR
SOUTH-
WEST
AFRICA
BECH.
SWAZILAND
UNION OF
SOUTH AFRICA
BASUTOLAND

BRUNEI
SARAWAK
MALAYA
BR. N. BORNEO
NORTHEAST
NEW GUINEA
NETH.
NEW GUINEA
INDONESIA
PAPUA

Indian Ocean

Atlantic Ocean

AUSTRALIA

67
OAS   **CENTO**
(Incl. U.S.)

1967
SEATO   **ARAB LEAGUE**

weapons, it did repeatedly manage to prevent small wars from becoming big ones: in Palestine, in Korea (where, because of the absence of the Soviet representative from the Security Council, the Russians failed to veto the Council's decision to intervene, and the American army fought under the sponsorship of the U.N.), and in other parts of the world (see Chapter 23).

Through its functional councils and special agencies—for example, the Economic and Social Council, the Educational, Scientific, and Cultural Organization (UNESCO), the World Health Organization, the Food and Agricultural Organization, and the World Bank—the U.N. advanced loans to governments to initiate new development plans, controlled epidemics, and provided experts on modern farming techniques. The U.N.'s international civil servants deserved well of mankind by promoting "social progress and better standards of living" as its Charter undertook to do. Occasional critics leveled their shafts at its striking new buildings in New York and wished that it had never left Switzerland because it might now be mistakenly taken for an instrument of American imperialism. Occasional isolationist Americans demanded that "the U.S. get out of the U.N. and the U.N. out of the U.S.," while their opposites could be heard asking that the U.N. be given more "teeth" and that the nations abandon more of their sovereignty to it. Yet with its successes and its faults it reflected both the diversity and the elements of unity in the world of which it was the spokesman, and perhaps it would have been unreasonable to demand more of it than that.

II   The Major Free-World States: 1945 - 1953

The United States

The most obvious fact about the post-war United States was its prosperity. But perhaps the most important, and to some observers the most surprising, development was the way in which the American people proved willing to assume the responsibilities that came their way in international politics. At the end of World War I we had cut ourselves as free of "foreign entanglements" as we could, and some of our European allies feared at the end of World War II that we might do so once more. But on the contrary we continued, after a rather abrupt cutting off of Lend-Lease in 1945, to render substantial economic aid to our allies. And when we joined NATO, we became a party to what was basically an old-fashioned alliance. In 1919 we had refused to join the League of Nations; in 1945 we were the heart and soul, the organizers, of its successor, the United Nations. Isolationists still existed and commanded great newspapers and a solid representation in Congress. But they were now a minority that was unable to block a single measure of foreign policy.

A major step in realizing this new American foreign policy was announced by General George Marshall, then Secretary of State, in a Harvard commencement address in 1947. The "Marshall Plan," of course the work of many hands in our government, promised American economic and technological help to war-stricken nations. The promise was carried out over the last two decades in many ways, commonly lumped together as "foreign aid," and was most strikingly successful in its original purpose of starting the remarkable economic recovery and indeed "boom" in western Europe during these years. Help was later extended to many neutral nations, and in particular to the "emerging" nations of the old colonial world. Some of it was direct military aid, but most of it was aid for economic development. Stalin's Russia and its allied states refused from the very start to accept the aid the Marshall Plan offered them. The Marshall Plan was in part an instrument of traditional international power politics; that is, like the subventions dominant powers in a coalition —France under Richelieu, Britain under Pitt —have extended to needy allies. But it had many new elements, notably that it was meant to be used, and to a large degree was used, to promote the material prosperity of the peoples of those states to which it was given, and not merely to add to our own military capabilities.

A well-organized movement against any of our numerous treaty commitments from the Marshall Plan of 1947 on to the present, *if it had had the majority of the American people behind it*, could have succeeded in spite of the fact that since the end of World War II official Republican and Democratic party policies were on the whole in "bipartisan" agreement on the role we were playing in international politics.

Indeed, the political history of the United

The first Marshall Plan shipment for Greece being loaded, May, 1948.

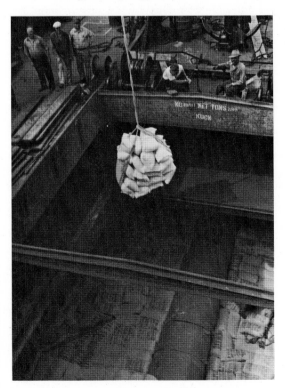

States since 1945 provided another illustration of what we have already said about the basic agreement that must be shared by both parties in the two-party system that prevails in the English-speaking countries (see Chapter 13). Harry Truman, Democrat, who as Vice-President had succeeded to the office on the death of Franklin Roosevelt in 1945, was elected over the Republican Thomas Dewey in 1948 in an election that caught the experts by surprise, for the advance polls indicated the opposite result. In 1952, however, General Eisenhower, Republican, with his immense personal popularity, was elected president over the Democratic candidate, Adlai Stevenson, and carried his party to a majority in Congress. Now by tradition the Republicans were (comparatively) conservative, the party of business and the solid prosperous farmers; and the Democrats were (comparatively) liberal or radical, the party of the working man, the "little fellow." Those parentheses were important. In fact, the victorious Republicans after 1952 left intact the essentials of Democratic legislation since Franklin Roosevelt's victory in 1932: the system of social security, which the Republicans actually extended; the Tennessee Valley Authority; and a whole complex set of federal agencies, the main task of which was to "intervene" in the economic life of the nation, as for instance, the federal purchase of farm surpluses to keep up the income of farmers. The Republicans did this, even though their official philosophy stressed free enterprise and condemned government regulation. And they also retained the great armed forces that we had had to build up since 1940, and the foreign policy we have already outlined.

The economy of the United States, which had proved more than equal to the task of carrying on the Second World War, continued its upward course in the years after 1945. There were mild "recessions" in 1948 and 1953, but nothing the most pessimistic commentator could call a real depression. Indeed, by the mid-fifties even a few Marxists were beginning to express their doubts about the inevitable "bust" their theories told them must always follow a capitalist "boom." And on the other side, orthodox western economists were beginning to assert that the United States had in fact licked the problem of the business cycle, that we had so many "built-in safe-guards" in our social insurance, our banking and corporation laws, our ability—and willingness—to undertake public works at the first sign of depression, that though we should have recessions, we should never have a depression like that of the thirties.

Socially, the American drive toward some very concrete forms of equality continued after the Second World War. It was not quite true that in the traditional sense of the word there were no "classes" in the United States in the mid-twentieth century, but it was almost true. In the polls, the overwhelming majority of Americans refused to call themselves "upper class" or "lower" or "working class"; forced to use a label, something like 90 per cent chose "middle class." In terms of sheer income, we had some very rich men in spite of graduated income taxes and inheritance taxes. And we still had, in part but not wholly because of the low economic status of many Negroes, some very poor, who were not well fed or well housed. Indeed, in terms of actual average real income, some nations of western Europe were closer to rough equality than we. And yet both in terms of the career open to talents—the absence of barriers to social mobility—and in terms of what we may loosely call the social atmosphere, the United States remained the land where the social ideals of democracy were most nearly realized. The Negroes were indeed an exception, though not wholly so; in the arts, in the fields of entertainment and sports, and within their own community in all fields, the gifted Negro could and did rise.

The most common complaint against the atmosphere, the "style" set by mid-twentieth-century democracy in the United States, was foreshadowed in the fears of men like Alexis de Tocqueville and J. S. Mill (see Chapter 12) concerning the "tyranny of the majority." Americans, so it is claimed, tended to be conformists instead of equals; they tended to eat the same frozen and packaged foods,

to look at the same television programs, ride in the same cars, and live in the same ranch houses. French or English travelers could write that if you had seen one American city you had seen them all. Americans, the argument continued, tried to keep down individuals and groups who did not conform to the general standards of mediocrity, and American society might become a kind of democratic totalitarianism of equal, average, conforming individuals. In response, the historian, trying to be objective, could point to the rich and varied group life in contemporary America. The very intellectuals who so disliked the "average" American were wholly free to attack him, wholly free to avoid him—with a little effort, perhaps—wholly free to eat their own unfrozen foods, and read their own "little magazines," attend their own "little theaters," and never look at television.

The historian must also record in the 1950's one of the occasional periods when America temporarily gave way to fear in crisis, and partly repressed civil rights. The Cold War had inevitably made difficult the existence of believers in communism in the United States. Under the leadership of the late Senator Joseph McCarthy of Wisconsin, what opponents of the process called "witch-hunts," and proponents called "security measures," were undertaken often on the flimsiest evidence, or none at all, against individuals in responsible positions, especially in education, defense industries, and government, who might be pro-communist—that is, pro-Russian. The fact that some genuine American pro-communists actually had obtained posts in positions where they could and did pass valuable information to Russian agents clouded the issue and helped make McCarthy's performances possible.

When the gifted and irresponsible English publicist Bertrand Russell wrote of a "reign of terror" in the United States in the early 1950's he was grossly exaggerating, despite the grave injustices done to many individuals. McCarthy himself was an unscrupulous demagogue. But if one compares the French reign of terror in 1792–1794 or the Russian "purge" trials of the 1930's, one is struck with the really enormous differences. No blood was shed, the prisons were not filled, and the ordinary citizen went on his way just as he always had. The beginning of the end of McCarthy's influence was his formal condemnation in the Senate in 1954, 67 to 22, for misuse of his investigative powers. Public opinion was much influenced, in one of the earliest proofs of the power of television, by the televised spectacle of McCarthy's bullying of witnesses. Even many who had thought him right were disgusted by seeing him in action. Americans did not like a bully even in a "patriotic cause."

Canada

As in the First World War, Canadian troops fought in the Second World War from the start, and proved a most important factor in the great coalition against the Axis. After 1945, Canada enjoyed an economic growth and prosperity proportionately even greater than that of the United States. A great deal of capital from the United States poured in, and much was raised at home and in Britain. Canada, though still producing vast amounts of raw materials from farm, mine, and forest, came now to be a great industrial nation, exploiting her remarkable hydroelectric resources and her oil and mineral wealth. In the mid-fifties Canada took the lead in carrying out a long-discussed plan for a canal from the Great Lakes to the lower St. Lawrence, a canal deep enough to accommodate ocean-going ships, and producing in addition important hydroelectric power. In the United States, vested interests along the Atlantic seaboard, foreseeing competition from the new seaway in the lucrative Midwest trade, had long succeeded by typical pressure-group lobbying methods in preventing American participation in the scheme. It is indicative of Canada's independent nationhood that she was able to announce her intention of going ahead with the scheme — which could be done, though imperfectly, entirely on Canadian territory — without the United States if necessary.

Faced with this prospect, the United States joined Canada in a collaborative development; work began in 1954, and the canal was opened in 1959.

Politically, post-war Canada was one of the stablest of western nations. Although in the provinces other parties at times held power, in the federal government the Liberals, first under Mackenzie King, who died in 1948, and then under Louis St. Laurent, remained in power from 1935 to 1957. The Liberals depended for their support on an effective collaboration between the English-speaking provinces and the French-speaking province of Quebec. Already in the mid-fifties there were signs that Quebec might desert the Liberals, as strong French-Canadian nationalist sentiments, accompanied by no doubt exaggerated threats of secession, had begun to manifest themselves.

The Dominion conformed to the general western pattern; it preserved freedom of the press, the "career open to talents," and a "mixed economy," in which private enterprise was perhaps somewhat stronger than government participation and regulation. Many Canadians in the immediate post-war world had begun to worry over what they felt was undue cultural and economic dependence on the United States. But relations of all sorts continued to tie the two countries closely together, and the three-thousand-mile frontier without a fort remained wholly peaceful.

Western Europe

The Cold War turned the old geographical term "western Europe" into a political, indeed a cultural, term for those nations of Europe outside Russian domination. Some of these, like Greece and Turkey, were certainly not geographically part of western Europe.

The nations of "western Europe" preserved the form of the "sovereign" state, and many of the sentiments we call "nationalism" or "patriotism," but after 1945 made real attempts to transcend the limitations of narrow nationalism to organize a "free Europe" on a level above and beyond that of the national state. The first step was the successful establishment of the European Coal and Steel Community (1952), named for the man who did much to organize it as the "Schuman Plan." (Schuman, appropriately enough, was a Frenchman with a German name). Under this plan France, West Germany, Italy, Belgium, the Netherlands, and Luxembourg ("Benelux") created for their coal and iron industries a free market area of all six nations in which a joint administrative body could make certain final and binding decisions without the participation of any government officials of any one of the six nations—and of course, without their veto power. This Coal and Iron Union meant that each nation give up some part of its "sovereignty." In spite of some pessimistic predictions, the plan was a success, and paved the way for the creation of the "Common Market" (see Chapter 23).

In military affairs, the North Atlantic Treaty Organization included the United States and indeed was led by the United States. But it was also an attempt to organize western European military capabilities more tightly than in the old-fashioned alliance system. In economic affairs the Organization for European Economic Cooperation (OEEC), also under American patronage, but none the less manned by Europeans, put into effect the American Marshal Plan for recovery. In general European politics, the Council for Europe (1949), had indeed no "teeth," no binding powers over the separate nations making it up, but acted as a kind of semi-official federal consultative parliament for western Europe, to which governments sent official representatives. It met in Strasbourg, a city delicately poised between France and Germany.

Started as they were in the immediate post-war years in a Europe keenly aware of the danger from the Soviets, and also of the need for economic cooperation in the work of restoring war damages, these attempts to organize Europe on a scale beyond its nation-states were bound to run into difficulties once the crisis that gave impetus to them was past (see Chapter 23).

Great Britain

In the United Kingdom of Great Britain and Northern Ireland (no longer "Ireland," for the South had gained its independence of the Crown) a general election held in July, 1945, after war had ended in Europe gave results opposite to those of the famous "khaki election" of 1918 (see Chapter 20). Though Churchill was even more of a national hero than Lloyd George had been in 1918, a nation clearly determined to make radical changes, not just to congratulate itself on winning the war, threw out Churchill and his Conservative party, and returned a Labour party pleged to a measure of social reform. For the first time in its half-century of existence the Labour party now secured an absolute majority of the House of Commons, 393 out of 640 seats. The Liberal party was practically extinguished; former Liberal voters had for the most part voted Labour. The new Prime Minister was Clement Attlee, himself no laboring man, (and certainly no revolutionist or communist), but a middle-class British gentleman and high-minded social worker. Under the Labour cabinet, the government proceeded to take over, with due compensation to the owners, the coal industry, the railroads, and some parts of commercial road transportation, and began to nationalize the steel industry. Britain already had a well-developed system of various social insurances; this was now capped by a system of socialized medical care for all who wished it, a system strongly opposed at first by the medical profession. The educational system was partly reformed in an effort to make education more democratic, and to lengthen the required period of compulsory education. In accordance with Labour party philosophy, various parts of the old empire were given independence, like Burma, and others were granted dominion status—that is, national independence within the extraordinary British multi-national system.

Yet the nature and extent of this British "revolution by consent" were greatly misunderstood, especially by American conservatives. We can now see clearly that the new Britain was more like than unlike the old one and the rest of the free West. What came out of the changes after the Labour party victory of 1945 was an economy pushed a little more toward collectivism than before, but still very much indeed a "mixed" economy. Coal and railroads, nationalized, did not become great state trusts run by bureaucrats on the Russian model, but rather public corporations with a structure not unlike that of great private industries in the West, run by a board not by any means wholly under either bureaucratic or political thumbs. Great sectors of the economy remained in private hands, under no more than the kind of government regulation common even in the United States, which itself had a "mixed economy."

Proof of the essential moderation of this British revolution is afforded by the conduct of the Conservatives, who with Churchill still at their head were returned to power once more in 1951. The nationalization of steel, which had begun, was indeed stopped; but otherwise the victorious Conservatives kept intact the "socialism" of their opponents, including the national health scheme of socialized medicine, to which most of the medical profession had become reconciled.

In American—and, it must be added, in German—eyes, the British were not in the post-war years resilient enough to keep up with the extraordinary pace of economic improvements through technological innovation. A symptom: the British motor-car industry, which immediately after the war was in a good position to gain a big share of the world market, in the 1950's saw its lead reduced, until the Germans, especially with their inexpensive, standardized light car, the *Volkswagen,* took over the lead. In all the various indices of production, the British were definitely behind the Germans and the Americans. But they were still a great industrial people, suffering from the fact that just because they were the *first* to industrialize in the modern manner their plant tended toward obsolescence (see p. 494) and, more important, their ways tended to be set, hard to change rapidly.

The British, for instance, were usually, in the opinion of Americans who are used to high-pressure methods, ineffective salesmen. But it must be admitted that by the mid-fifties the British economy had begun to improve, had in fact statistically outstripped its pre-war totals.

The British were the last of the major western nations to feel themselves able to give up rationing and other belt-tightening measures the war had made necessary. Britain, more than any other great nation, had completely outgrown its ability to raise enough food to supply its inhabitants. The British had to export manufactured goods to get money to import the food they needed; but they also had to limit those imports, to raise all they possibly could on home lands. The British people therefore put up with many restrictions in what they rather mildly called an "austerity program." By the mid-fifties most of these restrictions had been lifted, and the British consumer could buy whatever he could afford.

To all these troubles was added a widespread awareness of the fact that Britain, which only a long lifetime ago was the leading nation of the world, now saw herself stripped of most of her empire, with the rest uncertain, playing what American editorial writers liked to call "second fiddle" to her former colonial possession, the United States. No wonder the British felt they were suffering undeservedly, and had what a witty commentator called a "Job complex." British leaders could hardly forget their former supremacy, and still, quite naturally, could not readily adjust to their new position of comparative inferiority. Yet in spite of all these real difficulties, both material and psychological, the British remained true, often under much strain, to the American alliance. No doubt they were a "practical" people, less worried than others over prestige and "grandeur."

France

On the French the war years inflicted what the psychologists call a trauma. Complete defeat by the Germans; occupation by the hated

ICELAND
Reykjavik
Keflavik

SHETLAND IS.
0
60
10

NORWAY
Bergen
Oslo

SWED

Inverness
SCOTLAND
NO. IRELAND
Edinburgh
UNITED
KINGDOM

Skagerrak
Göteborg

North Sea

DENMARK
Copenhagen

Belfast
IRELAND
Dublin
Liverpool
Limerick

20

WALES
ENGLAND
London
Southampton

NETHER-
LANDS
Amsterdam
The Hague

Hamburg

GERMAN

Szczecin

B

50

British Zone
Bremen

DEM.
Berlin
REPUBLIC

(joint occup

Oder R.

SIL

Atlantic Ocean

CHANNEL (Br.)
IS.
Brest
Cherbourg

Brussels
BELGIUM
Rhine R.
Bonn
GERMAN

(EAST
GERMANY)

Elbe R.

Prague
CZEC

Seine R.
Paris
LUXEMBOURG
SAAR
Frankfurt
FED.

REPUBLIC
(WEST GERMANY)

Nantes

Loire R.
Nancy

Amer. Zone
Danube R.

Munich
Linz
Vienna

FRANCE
French Zone

Bay of
Biscay
Bordeaux

Bern
SWITZERLAND

AUSTRIA

Zagreb

40

Oporto
PORTUGAL

Garonne R.
Bayonne
Toulouse

ANDORRA

Geneva
Lyon

Turin
Milan
Venice
Trieste

Split

Rhône R.

Po R.

Adriatic Sea

Lisbon
Tagus R.
Madrid

Ebro R.

Marseilles
RIVIERA
Nice

Genoa

Florence
ITALY

SPAIN

Barcelona

CORSICA
(Fr.)

Rome

Guadalquivir R.
Valencia

Granada

BALEARIC IS.

SARDINIA

Naples
CAPRI

Cadiz
Gibraltar
(Br.)

Palermo

SP. MOROCCO
Oran
Algiers

Bizerte
SICILY
MT. ETN
Catania

Casablanca
Rabat

Tunis

MOROCCO
(Fr.)

ALGERIA
(Fr.)

TUNISIA
(Fr.)

MALTA
(Br.)

Europe, 1953

IFNI (Sp.)

■ NATO countries (North Atlantic Treaty
Organization)

□ Communist bloc

◉ Capital cities

Tripoli

LIBYA

FINLAND

L. Onega

L. Ladoga

Helsinki
Porkkala
Tallinn
(Reval)
ESTONIA

Leningrad

Novgorod

Gorki

Kuibyshev

Riga
LATVIA

Volga R.

Moscow

Oka R.

LITHUANIA

Smolensk

Orel

Saratov

Ural R.

Minsk

Niemen R.

UNION OF SOVIET SOCIALIST REPUBLICS

Dnieper R.

Kharkov

Stalingrad

Volga R.

Miles

500

BERLIN

French Zone
British Zone
Russian Zone
American Zone

sraw

stula R.

D

Dniester R.

BESSARABIA

Pruth R.

UKRAINE

Kiev

Dnepropetrovsk

Rostov

Don R.

Astrakhan

Caspian Sea

Cluj

Odessa

Sea of Azov

CRIMEA

40

RUMANIA

IRON GATE

Bucharest

Sevastopol

Yalta

Black Sea

Batum

Baku

50

Danube R.

BULGARIA

Sofia

Bosporus

Istanbul

C A U C A S U S

Tiflis

Yerevan

Teheran

AZERBAIJAN

Tabriz

L. Urmia

Salonika

THRACE

MACEDONIA

GREECE

Ankara

L. Van

IRAN

Aegean Sea

Dardanelles

Izmir

TURKEY

Mosul

Athens

Adana

Aleppo

Tigris R.

RHODES

SYRIA

Baghdad

Persian Gulf

CYPRUS
(Br.)

Beirut

Damascus

IRAQ

CRETE

LEBANON

Euphrates R.

Basra

Mediterranean Sea

30

ISRAEL
Tel Aviv

Amman

KUWAIT

enghazi

Jerusalem

Dead Sea

SAUDI ARABIA

Nile R.

JORDAN

NEUTRAL ZONES

Alexandria

SUEZ CANAL

EGYPT

Cairo

foe; economic exploitation by the Germans to the point where the French government was almost bankrupt; liberation which, in spite of the admirable part played in it by the Fighting French and the French Resistance movement, was still clearly the work of American and British and indirectly, of Russian arms; the grave post-war difficulties of trying to hold together an empire whose peoples were in revolt — all these were elements in a picture of drastic decline. To complete the picture must be added the fact that France had not since the early nineteenth century kept pace with the leading industrial nations in production, in finance, above all in population.

The French government in exile, led by General de Gaulle, very easily re-established in 1944 in liberated France the old republican forms of government. Frenchmen called this state the Fourth Republic; but after de Gaulle, disappointed by his failure to attain real power in a state still ruled by unstable parliamentary coalitions of "splinter parties," retired from politics in 1946, the Fourth Republic began to look exactly like the Third. Cabinets lasted on an average only a few months; to the old splinter parties was added a Communist party of renewed strength, openly dedicated to revolutionary change; the problems of the old empire, now known as the French Union, seemed insoluble. Indo-China was lost in 1954 in a great defeat at Dienbienphu at the hands of the Vietnamese rebels under the Communist Ho Chi Minh. In the same year an active rebellion against the French began in Algeria.

Thus to many, post-war France seemed sunk in a slough of despond at least as deep as that in which Britain was mired. But one fact, little noted at the time, hardly jibed with this analysis. The French birth rate began to rise. Already lower than that of France's competitors in the nineteenth century, it had by the 1930's sunk to the point where, without the immigration from neighboring countries which actually did take place, the total French population would have declined. In France in 1942 the "net reproduction rate" for 100 women had sunk to 85 — that is, fifteen less than the figure needed to maintain without immigration the existing population; by 1949 it had risen to 133 — that is, 33 above mere stability. The rate continued at 124 or higher through 1955. In a land where birth-control methods were in spite of legal restrictions fully understood and fully available to all classes of the population, this could mean only that hundreds of thousands of French men and women deliberately decided to have children, a clear sign of the recovery, the optimism, that lay just ahead.

West Germany

West Germany was in many ways the success story of the post-war world. Strengthened by refugees from the East, its population of some 50 million was nearly three times that of East Germany. The great material destruction of much of Germany's industrial plant paradoxically soon proved beneficial: the new plant was built with the latest technological equipment. The Allied High Commission, never very severe, gradually abolished controls over German industry, save for atomic energy and a few other military restrictions. They advanced economic aid, and scaled down pre-war German debts. By the early 1950's West Germany had a favorable balance of trade and was achieving industrial growth as high as 10 per cent a year. To a degree, this prosperity was shared even by the working classes, though in the first crucial years there was much plowing back into capital goods used for further production.

Politically, the independent West German state proved a workable democracy. It was endowed with a constitution providing for a bicameral legislature, with a lower house representing the people directly and an upper house representing the states (Länder), and a president elected by a special assembly for a five-year term, in practice largely a ceremonial figure. Real executive leadership was vested in a chancellor, a prime minister dependent on a parliamentary majority. One obvious fact of German political stability was soon established: the old splinter-party system, though it was not replaced by a neat two-party one, did not return to plague the new republic. Under the leadership of Konrad Adenauer, the Christian Democrats, distant heirs of the old Centrist party (see Chapter 19), maintained in the post-war decade a sufficient majority to insure steady rule. The chief opposition came from the Social Democrats. These "gradualist" socialists, firmly anti-communist, were strong in the industrial cities, and in free Berlin, but were unable to attain federal power.

"De-nazification" was of course on the Allied program, and at the Nuremberg trials in 1946 seventy-four top Nazi leaders indicted in the autumn of 1945 were convicted of war crimes. Ten were hanged, after two had committed suicide; one was sentenced to life imprisonment, others to shorter terms; and three were acquitted. Such trials were an innovation in international law and practice; as such they were condemned by many conscientious conservatives in the West as mere revenge, as punishment for "crimes" not established as such and therefore wholly *ex post facto*. But most of the free world, and perhaps most West Germans, approved the innovation.

To have dismissed all civil servants who had held posts under the Nazi regime would have dismantled German administration altogether. A moderate weeding-out of the most compromised Nazis was achieved, though not sufficiently to satisfy many western anti-Nazis. The new republic had its nationalist groups, but in the first decade after the war they were not very vocal. Skeptics remained doubtful about the extent of German conversion to the habits of democracy as practiced in the West, and there were sporadic outbreaks of antisemitism in West Germany, where, however, there were only a few thousand Jews left alive.

The Other Western Countries

In Italy a plebiscite in 1946 showed 54.3 per cent of the voters in favor of a republic. In spite of the comparative narrowness of the margin by which it was established, the new Italian republic proved a viable state. There were monarchists who regretted the forced departure of the House of Savoy, and there were even those who regretted the end of the fascist régime. But neither group was able to influence greatly parliamentary politics. A strong Christian Democratic party under an able leader, Alcide de Gasperi, with support from other centrist and right centrist groups, was able to hold power for seven years. The Christian Democratic party was a Catholic party with a relatively liberal reform program. It took positive measures to break up the large landed estates in the South with a view to redistributing the land. But Italian politics still were splinter-party politics; the necessary coalitions were assembled without much difficulty. Indeed in the post-war decade there was an approximation to two-party politics, with de Gasperi in power challenged chiefly by a very strong Communist party, the most numerous in the West, with whom the larger faction of the Socialists—that led by Pietro Nenni—was allied. The firmly anti-communist socialist faction led by Guisppe Saragat, participated in the government.

Italy shared in the post-war economic resurgence. Economic growth was strongest in the northern and central areas, but, as mentioned, the efforts to improve the conditions in the backward South were seriously undertaken and some progress was made. Italy enjoyed a cultural upswing, especially marked in the novel and in motion pictures, and Italian names like Silone, Moravia, de Sica, Rossellini were familiar throughout the West. Notably for those Americans who felt the need for a European love, Italy often supplanted France as an object of affection. Certainly among American and British intellectuals there was a sharp turn away from Paris toward Rome and Florence and Venice. Most Italians seem relieved that they no longer had to aspire to imperial greatness.

III   The Communist Bloc, 1945 to 1953

Soviet Government and the Economy

Alone among the leaders of the "Big Three" throughout the war years, Stalin remained in power after the war, the British elections having ousted Churchill, and Roosevelt having died in April, 1945. Facing the devastation caused by the war, and what he regarded as the immediate threat of American atomic weapons, Stalin felt obliged to decree a continuation of austerity into the post-war years, at just the moment when the Russian people most yearned for new housing and a few creature comforts. The party, still his docile instrument, and experiencing regular purges to prevent any relaxation, dominated political life with the constant assistance of the secret police; while the army, still mobilized at high strength and performing a variety of occupation duties abroad, remained the third Soviet institution with power of its own. Elections, held in 1946 and 1950, returned the usual government-and-party-sponsored lists of candidates to office.

Few important administrative changes took place: the "people's commissariats" became ministries (1946), and not long before he died Stalin in 1952 abolished both Politburo and Orgburo, and combined them into a new Presidium. This he planned as a larger body than the Politburo, to include the ten Politburo members and fifteen additional high-ranking Soviet officials. But he did not live to announce the membership of the new body or to summon a meeting of it. After his death, the new "Presidium" remained at ten members, and simply replaced the old Politburo. Krushchev later declared that, in enlarging the membership and changing the name of the Politburo, Stalin had been taking the first step toward the complete purge and liquida-

tion of its ten existing members; so it is perhaps no wonder that, having survived this first step, they declined to take a second.

The fourth Five-Year Plan (1946–50) and its successor the fifth (1951–55) continued to emphasize investment in heavy industry at the expense of consumer goods. Though Stalin promised that the U.S.S.R. would now soon overtake America, sheer economic statistics made this a vain dream: the United States would have had to stand still industrially for twenty years to enable the Russians to come near to realizing such an ambition. Financial measures: the raising of prices, the wiping out of savings by the establishment of a new currency, kept the severest sort of economic pressure on the population. Reparations exacted from Germany and industrial loot from the eastern European countries gave massive stimulus to Soviet reconstruction. The fourth Five-Year Plan saw the first Soviet atomic bomb completed; the fifth saw further advances in armaments and the building of the Volga-Don canal. In agriculture, the regime embarked on a policy of reducing the number and increasing the size of collective farms. In 1951, Nikita Khrushchev, now appearing as a leading party agricultural expert, proposed a plan to create great agricultural cities (*agrogoroda*), in order to concentrate farm labor, and abolish rural backwardness.

Soviet Intellectual Life

The cultural policy of the régime was in keeping with the bleak austerity and terror of these years. In the first years after the war the authoritarian Andrei Zhdanov, boss of the Leningrad party organization and a leading member of the Politburo, made the arts his special concern. Maintaining that Soviet literature had to take an active role in the "engineering" of human souls, and that the official school of "socialist realism" was the only permissible line for a writer to follow, Zhdanov denounced in particular Mikhail Zoshchenko, writer of witty and satirical short stories, whose *Adventures of a Monkey* accidentally set free by a bomb suggested strongly that life in a cage in a zoo was more agreeable than life at large among the Soviet people; and Anna Akhmatova, a sensitive lyric poet, who had had the unpatriotic ill-judgment to lament in verse her feeling of loneliness, which no proper Soviet citizen would do. Both were expelled from the Union of Soviet Writers and thus silenced. Though Zhdanov died suddenly in 1948, his principles continued to reign. Violent anti-western propaganda filled Soviet books and resounded from the Soviet stage, as in the play called *The Unfortunate Haberdasher,* in which President Truman was cast as Hitler.

With the attack on the western nations went a constant drumbeat of new (and sometimes comic) claims for Soviet, or at least Russian "firsts" in every field of intellectual and artistic endeavor. No scholar could safely investigate a topic in the social sciences or humanities without denigrating the achievements of any non-Russian predecessors in the field or without paying respects to the supreme authorities on everything: Marx, Lenin, and, chiefly, Stalin. Archaeologists, historians, students of literature began their work with a compulsory quotation from Stalin, and a genuflection before him as the great teacher, the "Choryphaeus of the sciences."

Stalin emerged as an authority on biology, when the régime supported the geneticist Trofim Lysenko, who maintained—contrary to all accepted biological doctrine—that acquired characteristics were hereditary, strongly implying that "new Soviet man" would emerge as a biological phenomenon, and giving support to the political argument that communism would change the human species. Lysenko also denounced traditional western genetics, and the leading rival Soviet biologists, whose careers were now destroyed. In linguistics too, Stalin personally intervened in 1950 to denounce the prevailing theories originated by Nikolai Marr, then sixteen years dead, who had implied that the world's languages corresponded to the degree of social development reached by their speakers, and so had at first attracted Soviet scholars. In the case of Lysenko, Stalin supported quackery (not finally denounced as mad until early 1966); in the case of Marr, Stalin supported common sense. Neither biologist nor linguist, Stalin fearlessly laid down the law for both. In the U.S.S.R. in these years, it was prudent to withhold one's views on any subject until Stalin had pronounced on it first.

As Stalin grew older, the secrecy, censorship, and conspiratorial miasma at the top of the Soviet state and society all intensified. Catering to ancient prejudices and violating Leninist precepts, Stalin now, in his fear of the West, moved against that group of Soviet citizens who had the closest contacts with the western world, the Jews. The press began to denounce long lists of "rootless, homeless cosmopolitans," who always proved to have Jewish names, thus fanning the strong traditional anti-Semitism of the Russians and Ukrainians. The government closed Jewish cultural organizations, and stopped publications in Yiddish, imposed religious restrictions, and eventually began a series of arrests and purges and deportations of prominent Jews, often those who had been active in the régime itself. Government service, the army, the professions, the universities, all experienced purges. Propaganda reached its peak with the publicity given an alleged "Doctors' Plot," in which Jewish doctors were accused of plotting to poison Stalin. When Stalin died, the stage seemed set for a full-scale anti-Semitic drive reminiscent of Hitler. Fear of the West, and detestation of Zionism—many Soviet Jews wanted to live in Israel—did not alone explain Soviet anti-Semitism. Despite their long years of preaching cultural autonomy for nationalities, many Soviet leaders were anti-Semitic, and recognized that the population at large could be expected to welcome anti-Semitism at a moment when there

The Soviet Union, 1967

Arctic Ocean

Bering Sea

Pacific Ocean

Arctic Ocean

Barents Sea

Kara Sea

NOVAYA ZEMLYA

ALEUTIAN IS. (U.S.)

SAKHALIN I.

Sea of Okhotsk

KAMCHATKA

Petropavlovsk

KURILE IS.

Anadyr

Kolyma R.

Tiksi

Khatanga

Magadan

Aldan R.

Yakutsk

Lena R.

Khabarovsk

Blagoveshchensk

Amur R.

MANCHURIA

Vladivostok

JAPAN

NORTH KOREA

SOUTH KOREA

Chita

L. Baikal

MONGOLIA

Irkutsk

Krasnoyarsk

Tunguska R.

Lena R.

Dudinka

Igarka

Yenisei R.

Novosibirsk

Novokuznetsk

KUZNETSK

Barnaul

CHINA

SINKIANG

TAIWAN (FORMOSA)

PHILIPPINE IS.

NORTH VIETNAM

SOUTH VIETNAM

LAOS

THAILAND

CAMB.

BURMA

E. PAK.

BHUTAN

NEPAL

INDIA

KASHMIR

W. PAKISTAN

AFGHANISTAN

Alma Ata

Frunze

L. Balkhash

Aral Sea

Tashkent

Dushanbe

Karaganda

Omsk

Irtysh R.

Ob R.

URAL MTS.

Vorkuta

Pechora R.

Molotov (Perm)

Sverdlovsk

Magnitogorsk

Kuibyshev

Volga R.

Gorki

Moscow

Smolensk

Leningrad (Petrograd)

Murmansk

Archangel

NORWAY

SWEDEN

FINLAND

POLAND

E. GER.

WEST GERMANY

CZECH.

AUST.

YUGOSLAVIA

ALB.

GREECE

ITALY

BULGARIA

CARPATHO-UKRAINE

Kiev

Kharkov

DONBAS

Dnepropetrovsk

Rostov

Don R.

Volgograd

CRIMEA

Black Sea

TURKEY

Tiflis

Baku

Caspian Sea

IRAN

IRAQ

SYRIA

LEBANON

ISRAEL

JORDAN

SAUDI ARABIA

Mediterranean Sea

AFRICA

1 2 3 4 5 6 7 8 9 10 11 12 13 14 15

Areas annexed since 1940

Other Communist countries

Industrial areas (in U.S.S.R.)

SOVIET SOCIALIST REPUBLICS

1. Russian Soviet Federated Socialist Republic
2. White Russia
3. Ukraine
4. Georgia
5. Armenia
6. Azerbaidjan
7. Turkmenistan
8. Uzbekistan
9. Tadjikistan
10. Kirghiz Republic
11. Kazakh Republic
12. Estonia
13. Latvia
14. Lithuania
15. Moldavia

was little else in the government's policies that they could endorse.

Soviet Foreign Policy: Europe

When the war ended, the Soviet Union did not immediately terminate all forms of co-operation with its allies. The joint plan for dividing and ruling Germany went through. The four occupying powers together tried the chief surviving Nazi leaders at Nuremberg in 1946. In February, 1947, came the peace treaties with Italy, Rumania, Bulgaria, Hungary, and (for the U.S.S.R.) Finland. These confirmed Soviet territorial gains: from Rumania, Bessarabia and northern Bukovina; from Finland, portions of Karelia and a long lease on the naval base at Porkkala. In addition, the U.S.S.R. annexed part of former East Prussia, including the capital, Königsberg, home of the great philosopher, Kant, which the Russians renamed Kaliningrad after a high Soviet official. They also annexed the extreme easternmost portion of Czechoslovakia, inhabited largely by the Ukrainian-speaking Ruthenian people (see Chapter 14), who had not, however, for almost a thousand years been subject to any Russian state.

Elsewhere in eastern Europe—in Poland, Czechoslovakia, Rumania, Hungary, and Bulgaria—the U.S.S.R. sponsored the creation of new "people's republics" under communist governments, while Yugoslavia organized its own communist state, and had Albania as its own satellite. Soviet troops formally occupied about one-third of Germany, roughly between the Elbe and the Oder rivers, where they organized a satellite communist-ruled East Germany. The parts of Germany lying east of the line formed by the Oder and Neisse rivers, save for the sections of East Prussia directly annexed to the U.S.S.R., the Russians handed over to their Polish satellite. Here a wholesale transfer of population removed the Germans, and replaced them with Poles. Finland became part of the Russian security system, but enjoyed distinctly more autonomy than the satellites, and retained its pre-war political institutions. The four Allied powers detached Austria from Germany, thus undoing Hitler's *Anschluss* of 1938; and divided it, like Germany, into four occupation zones. The presence of Soviet troops in Hungary and Rumania was specifically guaranteed, in order to "protect" the communication lines between the Soviet Union and its occupying forces in Austria.

The presence of the Red Army alone made it possible for the U.S.S.R. to install satellite régimes in Poland, Hungary, Rumania, and Bulgaria. Following slightly different time tables in each country, the Russians none the less used the same methods: the elimination of all political groups that could be claimed to have collaborated with the Germans; the formation of "progressive" coalitions of parties; the destruction of all non-communist elements in these coalitions by splitting off from each of the component political parties a small fragment that would collaborate unquestioningly with the communists; and the denunciation and persecution of the remainder. Elections, despite the promises at Yalta, were accompanied by intimidation and atrocity. Western protest uniformly failed. Most disturbing of all was the communist take-over in Czechoslovakia, delayed until 1948, and directed against the government of Edward Beneš, brave enemy of Hitler in 1938 (see Chapter 21), betrayed now for a second time. Within each satellite the communists aped Soviet policies, moving with all speed to collectivize agriculture, impose forced-draft industrialization, control religious and cultural life, and govern by police terror.

As early as 1946 the U.S.S.R. refused to withdraw its forces from northwest Iran, and yielded only to pressure from the United Nations. But a more alarming probe of the Soviet perimeter came in Greece. Here, during World War II, a communist-dominated guerrilla movement had already once (December 1944–February 1945) attempted to seize control, and had been thwarted only by British troops and Winston Churchill's determination not to allow Greece to go communist. In 1946, the Greek communists tried again, backed this time by the Soviet-dominated governments of their northern Balkan neigh-

Blockaded Berliners watch the arrival of airlift supplies, July, 1948.

bors. Simultaneously, Stalin exerted pressure on the Turks for concessions in the Straits area. Now President Truman proclaimed that countries facing the threat of communist aggression could count on help from the United States. Under this "Truman Doctrine," he sent American military aid to Greece and Turkey. The threat to the Turks evaporated, and by 1949, after severe fighting, the Greeks had put down the communist rebellion with the help of American advisers.

In Germany, on April 1, 1948, the Russians began one of the most bitter phases of the Cold War. By shutting off the land routes from the West into Berlin, they attempted to force the western Allies to turn Berlin wholly over to them. The Allies stood firm, however, and achieved the almost incredible feat of supplying a great metropolitan area wholly by air. In the six months of the blockade, Allied aircraft flew over 2,300,000 tons of coal, food, and other necessities into west Berlin. They also set up their own counter-blockade of Russian-occupied east Berlin. On September 1, the Russians gave up, and Berlin returned to its sufficiently abnormal status of joint occupation. But Soviet determination to oust the western powers from Berlin remained unaltered, and would be reiterated in 1958–1961 (see Chapter 23).

The Yugoslav Rebellion

In addition to their defeats in Greece and Berlin, the Russians found themselves, in 1948, faced with rebellion from a country that had seemed the most loyal of all their newly acquired European satellites; and this rebellion, Stalin felt, threatened their whole European position. Yugoslavia, which had overthrown a pro-German government in 1941, had remained throughout World War II a theater of intense guerrilla action against the Germans and Italians. There were two main groups of guerrillas, the Chetniks, led by General Mikhailovich, representing the Serb royalist domination over the south Slav kingdom, and the Partisans, led by the communist Joseph Broz, better known by his underground nickname, Tito. As the war continued, the communist-dominated Partisans gained ground against the Chetniks, who preferred to compromise with the German and Italian occupying forces rather than continue a war in alliance with communists. By 1943, Britain and the United States, with their eyes fixed on the paramount need to beat Hitler, decided to support Tito with supplies. When the Russians entered Belgrade in October 1944, they helped put their fellow-communist Tito in control.

Once in power, Tito installed his own communist government, abolished the Yugoslav monarchy, and in governing Yugoslavia and remaking its economy followed standard Soviet policies even more slavishly than any of the Russians' subordinates in satellite Europe. Yet in June, 1948, the world learned with surprise that the U.S.S.R. had quarreled with Yugoslavia, and expelled Tito's régime from the Cominform (see p. 835). The Soviet satellites swung into line, including Yugoslavia's own special puppet, Albania. All these east-European communist states broke their economic agreement with Yugoslavia, unloosed great barrages of anti-Tito propaganda, and stirred up border incidents. The Yugoslavs published the secret correspondence with Moscow that had led to the break, from which we learn that Soviet arrogance and insistence on penetrating the Yugoslav army and security organizations had aroused Yugoslav national feeling, never very far below the surface. Stalin, for his part, suffered from the misapprehension that he could bully the Yugoslovs into submission. "I will shake my little finger," he said, "and there will be no more Tito."

But Tito remained in power, accepting the aid that was quickly offered him by the United States. Washington saw that a communist régime hostile to Stalin was a new phenomenon that could not help embarrassing the Russians. Gradually Yugoslav communism evolved a modified ideology of its own, declaring that Stalin was a heretic and Tito and his followers the only true Leninists. Tito decentralized the economy, beginning in the factories, where workers' committees now began to participate actively in the planning. From the economy, decentralization spread to the local government apparatus, then to the central government, and finally to the Yugoslav Communist party, now rechristened "League of Yugoslav Communists." Though the régime admitted its past outrageous excesses, the police continued to be a powerful force. Tito gradually abandoned agricultural collectivization, which, as always, was most unpopular with the peasants.

The Yugoslav régime, however, remained a communist régime, suspicious of the western capitalists who were helping it, and including many men who hoped for an eventual reconciliation with the U.S.S.R. So long as Stalin lived, that proved impossible. In their fear of the spread of the new "national" communism to the other satellites, the Soviets directed the other east-European régimes in a series of ferocious purges, executing leading communists for "Titoism," and thus terrorizing anyone who might hope to establish any sort of autonomy within the communist bloc. When Stalin died in 1953, his heirs gave high priority to healing the breach with Yugoslavia, and eliminating the weakness it had created in their European position (see Chapter 23).

Soviet Foreign Policy: Asia

When balked in Europe, Tsarist Russian governments had often turned to Asia in pursuit of expansionist policies. Similarly, the Soviet Union, after the failures in Greece and Berlin, kept the pressure on its former allies by new adventures in Asia. Here, communists had tried and failed to win power in Indone-

Tito (right) and fellow partisans in a mountain retreat during World War II.

American infantrymen entering an evacuated Korean town, February, 1951.

sia, Burma, Malaya, and the Philippines, and had succeeded in China. The Korean War, which broke out in June, 1950, was in some measure a Soviet-sponsored operation, although the Russians themselves limited their contribution to support and sympathy, and allowed their Chinese ally to take the military lead. Korea, a peninsula at the eastern extremity of Asia, bordering on Manchuria and Siberia and close to Japan had been a target of Russian interest in the late-nineteenth and early-twentieth centuries, but the Japanese defeat of the Russians in 1905 (see Chapter 14) had led instead to Japanese annexation in 1910. In 1945, at the close of World War II, Russian troops occupied the northern part of Korea, and American troops occupied the southern part. The country was divided in the middle by a line along the 38th parallel of latitude; a communist-inspired North Korean People's Republic was set up on one side, and an American-inspired South Korean Republic on the other. When all American forces except for a few specialists were withdrawn from South Korea, the North Koreans marched South to unite the nation under communist control.

It is probable that the communists thought the operation was safe, since American pronouncements had stated that Korea was outside the American "defense perimeter." But when the invasion began, the United States —with U.N. approval, as the vote was taken in the absence of the Russians—at once moved troops into Korea. They got there barely soon enough to halt the North Korean drive, and then to push the enemy back well north of the 38th parallel, almost to the Yalu River, the frontier of China. At this point, Communist China entered the war, and Chinese troops joined the North Koreans in pushing the Americans southward again. By 1951, the line of battle had been stabilized roughly along the old boundary between North and South Korea. After prolonged negotiations, an armistice was finally concluded in July, 1953.

The United States carried on its defense of South Korea in the name of the United Nations and received small but valuable detachments of troops from some of its allies. Although President Truman and his advisers in Washington wanted to limit the war to the defense of South Korea, the United Nations commander on the spot, the American General, MacArthur, wanted to press the war into Communist China. American officials, and in particular America's allies, feared that such a step would bring Russia actively in on the Chinese side and might precipitate World War III. President Truman therefore recalled General MacArthur in April, 1951.

The Korean settlement by no means ended the tension between Communist China and the United States. The American government continued its refusal to recognize Red China, and serious friction developed over Formosa and the smaller off-shore islands, Quemoy and Matsu, now in the hands of Chiang Kai-shek, which the communists seemed determined to

capture and the United States seemed equally determined to keep out of communist hands. The Korean settlement of course brought understanding between the U.S.S.R. and the United States no closer. It was at best a compromise: after all the bloody fighting, the United States had managed to hang on to the devastated southern portion of the country, and the communists had been driven back to the north, which they governed undisturbed. Neither side could call it a victory. By the time it was reached, Stalin had been dead for more than three months. He had remained to the end the suspicious, ruthless dictator that he had been since the late 1920's, but his paranoia had grown so mightily over the years that his closest aides lived in constant fear of their lives. Now a transfer of power had to be made; any change seemed likely to be an improvement for the Russians and for the world at large.

IV The Revolt against Imperialism

The First World War had brought a gradual loosening of the imperial ties binding non-western peoples to the great colonial powers of the West. The Second World War greatly accelerated and intensified this process. Not only were the empires of vanquished Italy and Japan dismantled after 1945; the imperial possessions of the victors and the nominal victors—the British, Americans, French, Belgians, and Dutch—experienced major amputations. Moreover, states like China, Iran, and Egypt, that had long been sovereign in name but that in practice were often subject to political or economic tutelage by the imperial powers, vigorously asserted their independence. The nationalism of the non-western world was coming of age. It scored its first victories, in the immediate post-war years, chiefly in areas of Asia and the Middle East where anti-colonial sentiments and movements had been developing before 1939. Later, after 1953, as the next chapter

will show, it spread to Africa and within a few years revolutionized the political status of the continent that had long been dominated by European empire-builders.

Causes of the Revolt

The immediate reasons for the anti-imperialist revolution may be found in the Second World War itself. In this war, as in World War I, the western democracies often relied on colonial troops, with a consequent boost to the self-esteem of the peoples providing the troops. In both wars the propaganda of the democracies to show the justness of their cause fostered ambitions for the basic democratic rights of self-government and self-determination. In both wars inflation and other economic dislocations such as shortages, conscription of labor, and the enjoyment of war profits by the few rather than the many, heightened these ambitions and swelled the sense of grievance.

The second war, unlike the first, destroyed the magic invulnerability of the West, for the western possessions in the Far East fell before the attacks of non-western conquerors, the Japanese. The final defeat of Japan apparently did little to offset the immense damage done to western prestige. Moreover, two of the great imperial powers, the French and the Dutch, were only by courtesy numbered among the victors of World War II, with almost fatal consequences for their prestige. Nationalist leaders in the non-western world also knew that British power had been seriously weakened by the tremendous drain of the war, and that the defeat of the resolutely imperialist Conservatives by the rather anti-imperial Labour Party in the election of 1945 promised liberalization of British policy. Nationalist leaders further knew that the real victors in the war were the United States and the Soviet Union, each in its very different way outspokenly anti-colonial.

While the Second World War touched off the colonial revolt, the deeper causes of the revolt must be sought in the five-hundred-year record of western expansion, and in the western tradition itself. The mainsprings of western culture—Christianity and the secular faiths of progress, democracy, and nationalism—provided little nourishment for imperialist policies. The West could not conceal from the educated natives its own great ethical and political writings. Indeed, it often laid before them with pride the Christian Bible, the American Declaration of Independence, the French Declaration of the Rights of Man, even the Communist Manifesto. It was hardly possible to keep on insisting that "all men are created equal" really meant that "white men are created the superiors of colored men." In terms of ideals and ideology, western imperialism carried within itself the seeds of its own failure—or, more positively, its own transfiguration into self-determination for all peoples.

The great instrument for the spread of western ideas was the education, both formal and informal, provided to non-western peoples by the West itself. In the nineteenth cen-

tury, this education owed a great deal to the efforts of Christian missions, though toward the end of the century it became more secular as a result of increasing participation by the governing powers themselves. Almost everywhere formal education was limited to a comparatively small number of natives. From India, the sons of rajahs went to Oxford, and so too did bright boys from the slowly rising middle classes; by the twentieth century western education in India itself was beginning to assume the western form of "careers open to talents." Some non-Europeans turned against this western education and took refuge in a reaffirmation of the values of their traditional culture, of Hinduism or Islam, for example. But for the most part, the educated natives came to feel that independence could be won only by imitating the West, by learning its industrial, technological, and military skills.

The educated classes throughout the world of western imperialism emphatically wanted independence. Many were by the twentieth century revolutionaries; some became great admirers of the Bolshevik revolution in Russia, and a few received training in the techniques of revolution in Moscow itself. A great many westerners made the mistake of assuming that these nationalist revolutionaries were an unrepresentative minority of the native populations, and that the great colonial masses, illiterate and poor, did not really follow their own native educated class but asked nothing better than to be ruled by the kindly whites. Of course the subject races have always had their share of "Uncle Toms" (a term used in scorn by American Negroes for their fellows who appear too submissive toward the whites). But the "Uncle Toms" have not given their stamp to non-western populations. The urban masses, and then, more gradually, the peasant masses, began to share the feelings of nationalism and to demand that the foreigner must go.

The imperialist powers themselves followed policies that greatly aided the ripening of nationalism. Almost everywhere they penetrated they brought enough sanitary engineering, enough medicine, enough law and order to lower the death rate and to enable the native population to grow as it had never grown before. But that very growth made more mouths to feed, and the fact of population pressure became increasingly obvious to the educated and uneducated alike. Furthermore, education gave the natives some of the white man's special magic, his control over material things and over the elaborate machines of the modern world; the natives began to acquire scientific knowledge and engineering skills. Thereby, they came to feel more and more the white man's equal, less and less willing to accept a subordinate social and political position now that, in material things, they seemed to be drawing even.

The Far East

The Second World War produced a major shift in the balance of power in the Far East. While China turned communist and grew increasingly antagonistic to the West, as we have already seen, Japan went down to defeat. The Japanese, who were the first non-western people to be recognized as equals by the West, had conquered an empire rivaling those of the West. Their "Greater East Asia Co-Prosperity Sphere" showed at its peak many obvious analogies with Napoleon's system of satellite states, and even more with that of Hitler. The Japanese employed methods of rule that were directly patterned on western precedent; they relied chiefly on the time-honored device of setting up puppet native governments, and exploiting for their own benefit the economic resources of the conquered lands. Their empire disintegrated in the atomic blast over Hiroshima, for it had never been cemented by the loyalty of its component parts.

Yet the Japanese started with at least one very great asset: they were an Asian people, a colored people, not westerners with the burden of white supremacy to carry. They could come as the emancipators of Asians and Pacific islanders, and their propaganda sounded this note most vigorously. Yet, Asians though they were, they did not endear themselves to their fellow Asians. Their armies looted and

committed atrocities; the Japanese abroad behaved like any other master race, and did not conceal their feelings of superiority over the natives. Time might have taught the Japanese a lesson in social psychology, and they might have been able with time to consolidate their grandiloquently named "co-prosperity sphere"; but time they did not have.

The end of World War II saw Japan reduced to her own islands, stripped of her overseas possessions. The overwhelming part played by the United States in the defeat of Japan insured that the military occupation and the subsequent peace of 1952, whereby Japan regained formal independence, would be almost wholly an American concern. Though there was a strong current in American opinion that demanded the deposition of the Emperor, he was left on his throne, deprived of his divine status, and subjected to the close control of General MacArthur and the forces of occupation. Americans found to their astonishment that on the surface at least the Japanese people, far from taking the occupation with hostility, seemed almost to admire their occupiers. They seemed not to understand what democracy meant—apart from baseball and some other American folkways—but they appeared very anxious to learn. Their behavior roused a good deal of speculation about national psychology; some scholars called attention to the rigorous early toilet-training of Japanese children in order to explain the national willingness to obey a master.

In the past, the Japanese had not had a democratic society or a democratic political organization. It was by no means certain at the time of the peace treaty in 1952 that they would firmly establish a democracy of the western type, although they had made a promising start since 1945. If a well-developed industrial economy is an indispensable base for the development of democracy, the Japanese already had a great advantage over all other non-western peoples. It remained to be seen whether Japan, because she took over industrialism from the West, would automatically become thoroughly westernized. It also remained to be seen whether the Japanese would be able to secure the markets abroad that their export-centered industry required.

Southeast Asia

In Southeast Asia, too, the Second World War upset the traditional balance of power, and set off a really major political explosion. The Japanese conquest and occupation destroyed belief in the invincibility of the white nations, and in 1945 the western powers were by no means able to pick up where they had left off. Moreover, the United States was in the process of granting independence to its own imperial wards, the Filipinos. In 1949, consequently, the Dutch abandoned the attempt to retain a stake in their former colony, the Netherlands East Indies, and recognized its independence as the Republic of Indonesia. Britain gave Burma independence outside the Commonwealth (1948) and the Federation of Malaya independence within the Commonwealth (1957); the great port of Singapore at the tip of Malaya, with its largely Chinese population, secured a special autonomous status (1958). When Malaya joined with the former British protectorates on the great island of Borneo in the Federation of Malaysia (1963), Singapore at first participated, then withdrew (1965).

France, meanwhile, made rather more limited concessions to the component states of Indo-China—Vietnam, which included the populous and fairly prosperous coastal areas, and Cambodia and Laos in the more primitive hinterland. But the French did not go far enough or fast enough to prevent their involvement in a lengthy war (1945–1954), during which Indo-Chinese communist rebels called the Viet Minh received support from Communist China. Increasingly hard-pressed, the French agreed in 1954 to partition Vietnam into a communist north and a south under a rather weak anti-communist government. The sequel was the outbreak of communist guerrilla activity in South Vietnam and more prolonged warfare.

In the Philippine Republic and Malaya the communists had already launched stubborn guerrilla campaigns, which were finally checked in the late 1950's. To counter the threat of communist penetration, the West sponsored the Southeast Asia Treaty Organization (SEATO) in 1954, but only two states in the area—the Philippines and Thailand (Siam)—joined with Pakistan and the western powers in participating. By the 1960's, as we shall find in the next chapter, the communist threat was focused on South Vietnam and on Indonesia, the most populous state in Southeast Asia, and perhaps the most unstable. The whole area, moreover, faced formidable economic problems. Southeast Asia, so long cast in the colonial role of producing rice, spices, rubber, tin, and other raw materials, found it hard to achieve economic independence without western assistance. Many of its peoples regarded with suspicion the aid offered by their former masters; yet, if they did not take it, they might drift into economic chaos and possibly into the communist orbit.

India and Pakistan

At the end of World War II, the victory of the British Labour party, pledged to grant India self-government, made Indian emancipation a certainty. But the deep-seated tension between Moslems and Hindus now assumed critical importance. When the Hindus' Congress party and the All-India Moslem League faced the need to make a working constitution for India, they found themselves in complete disagreement. The Moslems had long been working for a partition into separate Hindu and Moslem states, and this was in the end reluctantly accepted by the Hindus. In 1947, Hindu India and Moslem Pakistan were set up as self-governing dominions within the British Commonwealth.

Pakistan ("land of the pure," a name coined by Moslem students in Britain in the 1930's) is a state divided into two parts, widely separated by intervening Indian territory—the larger, West Pakistan, in the northwest, and the smaller and more densely populated, East Pakistan, in East Bengal. The rest of the former British Indian Empire and four-fifths of its inhabitants became the Republic of India by virtue of its constitution of 1950. Pakistan, with its smaller population and its relatively poorly developed industry, was weaker than India and at first kept closer political ties with the British Commonwealth.

The partition was not achieved without violence. In view of the way races and religions are geographically mingled in the subcontinent, it could not result in a complete separation of Hindus in one state and Moslems in another. The line of partition between India and West Pakistan evoked bitter fighting between members of the two communities, and many thousands of lives were lost. It resulted in a wholesale transfer of populations as Hindus moved from Pakistani territory into India and Moslems moved from Indian territory into Pakistan. A particular source of trouble was the mountainous region of Kashmir, an important tourist center. Though mainly Moslem in population, it was at the time of partition ruled by a Hindu princely house which turned it over to India. India has continued to occupy most of Kashmir, to the great economic disadvantage of Pakistan. The United Nations sought to determine the fate of Kashmir by arranging a plebiscite, but failed to secure the needed approval of both parties. Generally, however, despite the passions aroused by Kashmir and despite periodic rioting between Hindus and Moslems, both India and Pakistan came to accept partition as a normal state of affairs.

In domestic politics the two states went through sharply contrasting experiences. The chief architect of Pakistani independence, Mohammed Ali Jinnah, (head of the Moslem League), died in 1948. Deprived of its leader, the young state floundered in its attempts to make parliamentary government work and to attack pressing economic difficulties. Newly emancipated India also suffered a grievous loss when Gandhi was assassinated by an anti-Moslem Hindu fanatic in 1948. But Nehru, Gandhi's "younger brother," as he was termed, at once assumed full leadership. Under the guidance of Nehru, who was already a seasoned politician, and aided also by the long experience of British administration, India accomplished a feat almost without precedent in the non-western world. It successfully inaugurated a genuine parliamentary democracy of the western type and conducted free and hotly fought elections, based on universal suffrage, among voters who were in the main illiterate and rural. Understandably, Indians have been very proud of their accomplishment.

Both countries had to cope with formidable economic problems—Pakistan with poverty and lack of industry, and India with poverty and lack of sufficient agricultural output to sustain her enormous population. India has faced in an acute form the population pressure that bears so heavily on many other non-western countries. By the 1950's there were over 400,000,000 people in the Republic of India, with approximately 8,000,000 added annually, and the threat of famine and actual death through starvation was always present. In 1950, the government launched the first in a series of Five-Year Plans for economic development. While permitting the expansion of private industry, the Five-Year Plans stressed government projects. Irrigation and flood control works were started, transport and communications improved, and a beginning made

Nehru, as Prime Minister, receiving symbolic golden mace on the eve of Indian independence.

on the enormously difficult and significant task of educating hundreds of millions of peasants in new and more efficient ways of working the land. The West helped by furnishing technical experts, money, and the surplus grain needed to avert the threat of famine. Experts estimated, however, that even with a modernized economy India would find it hard to support a population growing so rapidly. Although birth control is abhorrent to the traditional ways of Hinduism, the government sponsored a campaign for its practice.

The traditions of Hinduism have exerted manifold influences on the Republic of India, throwing much light on the whole problem of the essential differences between East and West. Hinduism is an immensely complex and ancient way of life for which the word "religion," in its western connotation, is not adequate. It has no church organization in the Christian sense, no clear-cut theology, no established Bible. Of the three major developed cultures that the West has encountered in expanding over the world, Hinduism is farthest from ours. In comparison, Islam is actually a relative of Christianity, and Chinese society, in spite of its traditional un-western family structure, has affinities with the utilitarian or worldly strain in the West.

For Hinduism, this world of sense-experience is an illusion, but an illusion that has somehow to be overcome. Death is essential to the overcoming, but death is not enough. Each living man, indeed each living thing, is a soul alienated by the very fact of living from the ultimate, universal soul which is peace, absence of struggle and desire, ineffable non-being. The holiest of men by turning away entirely from the world, by living without desire—but not by any such simple solution as suicide—can perhaps attain this nonbeing in the end. But most human beings are now living out in this world the consequences of a sinful life as another personality in the past. Indeed, the most sinful of men who have lived in the past have been punished by reincarnation as animals or even as insects (which is why the most orthodox of Hindus will harm no living thing, even wearing gauze masks so that no minute insect can be breathed in or swallowed inadvertently).

Among men, their sins in past incarnations are reflected by their status, their *caste.* The poor, the humblest, are such because their sins have been greater; they cannot improve their lot in the western sense, for they can only slowly in subsequent incarnations redeem their wickedness by living as holy a life as possible. The lowest Hindu group, actually below and outside the caste system, were called "untouchables," because even their shadow would corrupt a caste-Hindu. Yet no one can keep untouchable in a railroad car, and the Indian Constitution of 1950 abolished the outcast status of the untouchables as undemocratic. The legal change, however, penetrated Indian custom only very slowly.

Hindu society, then, with its caste system, its innumerable tabus, and its lack of any basis for belief in material progress, found grave difficulties in the way of adopting western culture. That the Hindus adopted as much as they did was testimony to the penetrating power of the West. Many Hindu intellectuals were so far westernized that they had no real basis for calling themselves Hindus. But even for them, and much more for the uneducated, the long accumulation of habits, feelings, and ingrained attitudes could not be quickly altered.

The Middle East: Three Crises

In the Middle East, the mandates obtained by France and Britain after World War I collapsed after World War II. Syria and Lebanon won their full independence from the French, and the British withdrew from Palestine. The new state of Israel took over western Palestine, and the eastern part was annexed by Transjordan, which now styled itself, after its ruling dynasty, the Hashimite Kingdom of Jordan. Still other imperial ties were severed after World War II, notably those linking Egypt and Iran to Britain.

The first major crisis in the Middle East after World War II arose over the question of

Palestine. For half a century, Zionism, with its goal of creating a new Jewish state on the site of the ancient Jewish homeland, had been attracting support among Jews, especially in the often-persecuted Jewish communities of Russia and eastern Europe. Zionist hopes of creating a new state on the site of the ancient Jewish homeland received a great lift from the Balfour Declaration of 1917 and the subsequent British policy of admitting Jewish immigrants into Palestine. Hitler's persecutions and World War II made the problem of increased immigration to Palestine critical. At the same time, Britain, the mandatory power, wished to protect its great interest in the Middle East by cultivating the friendship of the Arabs. But in Palestine itself the flooding Jewish tide was submerging the Arabs, who had long been settled there and felt that this was *their* homeland.

Worn out after a decade of fruitless efforts to secure a compromise between Arabs and Jews, the British turned the problem over to the General Assembly of the United Nations, which proposed to partition the country into an Arab state and a Jewish state. When the British withdrew their forces from Palestine in 1948, the Jews at once proclaimed their state of Israel and secured its recognition by the U.N.; the Arabs declared the proclamation illegal and at once invaded the new state. In the ensuing war, the total resources in manpower of the Arab states were far greater than those of Israel, but the dissensions among the various Arab states, their military inefficiency, and the better technical equipment and morale of the Israelis resulted in a victory for the Jews. A truce, but not a formal peace, was patched up under the auspices of the United Nations (1949). Israel secured more of Palestine than had been allotted to her under the U.N. partition plan, and took over the western part of Jerusalem, the spiritual capital of Judaism, a city which the U.N. had proposed to neutralize. The "old city" of Jerusalem, however, including the Wailing Wall and the site of Solomon's temple, remained in the hands of Jordan and thus under the control of the Arab enemy.

In the course of the Arab-Israeli struggle, most of the Palestinian Arabs, numbering nearly a million, fled from Israel to the surrounding Arab states. The United Nations organized a special agency to extend relief to the refugees and to arrange for their permanent resettlement. The Arab states, however, were either unable or unwilling to absorb them, and many refugees insisted on remaining in depressing camps, for they viewed resettlement as an abandonment of their cherished conviction that the Israelis would soon "be pushed into the sea" and that they themselves would return to their old homes. This acute problem of the Palestinian refugees sharpened the hostility between Arab and Israeli and made the truce of 1948 a most uneasy affair, frequently broken in frontier incidents by both sides.

The new state of Israel faced not only a grave problem in external relations but also grave internal problems. It could not trust its Arab minority, numbering about 200,000, approximately one-tenth of the population. It continued to admit as many Jewish immigrants as possible, some of them of advanced western culture, but others, from North Africa and Yemen, still largely living in the Middle Ages. The welding of these disparate human elements into a single nationality was a formidable task. Immigration also swelled the total population of Israel, which soon contained about a million more people than Palestine had before World War II, and in an area not much bigger than Connecticut. Much of that area is mountainous, with a thin rocky soil and inadequate rainfall, and some of it is sheer desert. The Israelis applied talents and training derived from the West to make the best use of their limited resources, but they depended on outside aid, especially from their many sympathizers in the United States.

The dependence of Israel on western support, indeed the very existence of Israel, profoundly affected relations between the Arabs and the West. To most Arabs Israel appeared to be a new outpost of western imperialism, set up in their midst to spite them. They claimed that American policy had been unduly influenced by Jewish financiers, Jewish journalists, and Jewish voters. In such an atmosphere it was difficult for the United States and other western nations to retain cordial relations with the Arabs, who were in any case very sensitive nationalists.

A second major post-war crisis in the Middle East concerned Iranian oil. The oil was extracted, refined, and marketed by the Anglo-Iranian Oil Company, in which the British government had a large stake. Since the 1930's the Iranian government had been pressing the company to make larger royalty payments, and the issue became acute after World War II when Aramco (the Arabian-American Oil Company) set a new and more generous pattern for royalty agreements by making a 50:50 split with the monarchy of Saudi Arabia. More than economics was involved here, for Iranian nationalists resented Anglo-Iranian's policy of reserving managerial and technical posts for westerners, who lived almost entirely segregated lives in the company's towns in Iran, with their own clubs, schools, and cinemas. Memories of Britain's military occupation of parts of Iran during both world wars further embittered the nationalists.

In 1951, therefore, after a campaign led by the ardent nationalist politician, Mossadeq, the Iranian legislature nationalized the properties of Anglo-Iranian. Mossadeq, who now became Prime Minister, at first won wide support among his countrymen for his bold defiance of the West in highly emotional speeches at home and at the United Nations. But a world-wide boycott of nationalized Iranian oil caused a disastrous drop in the revenues of the Iranian government and a severe economic crisis. The issue was finally resolved after a *coup* in Tehran, the Iranian capital, in which United States intelligence agents were said to be involved, had driven Mossadeq from office and into jail (1953). Although Iranian oil remained nationalized, the government now paid western companies, including the successor to Anglo-Iranian, to assist in exploiting and marketing the oil.

The third major Middle Eastern crisis was the revolution that broke out in Egypt in 1952, directed both against the British and against the traditional ruling groups among the Egyptians themselves. Although Britain had taken real steps toward freeing Egypt from her tutelage before World War II (see Chapter 20), she did not move fast enough to satisfy Egyptian nationalists. During the war, furthermore, she offended them deeply by mobilizing tanks to force King Farouk to dismiss a pro-Axis cabinet. After the war, Farouk, once a very popular monarch, lost prestige both because of his well-publicized appetite for high living and because of his involvement in a scandal concerning the provision of defective supplies to the Egyptian army in the Palestinian War. From Farouk and his palace clique the odor of corruption and scandal spread through the upper levels of the government.

The virtually bloodless revolution of July 23, 1952, was the work of a group of young army officers, who were greatly chagrined by Israel's defeat of Egypt. In some policies the new government of Egypt's strong man, Gamal Abdul Nasser, followed a path paralleling that marked out by Turkey's strong man, Atatürk, a generation earlier. (see Chapter 20). It abolished the monarchy and drew up a republican constitution. It encouraged the emancipation of women and pared down the traditionally large role of the conservative courts of religious law without, however, making the kind of frontal assault on Islam that Atatürk had attempted. In practice, the régime was rather markedly dictatorial: only one party was tolerated, elections were closely supervised, and press campaigns were orchestrated by the Ministry of National Guidance. Nasser justified this absolutism in this way:

Before July 23rd, I had imagined that the whole nation was ready and prepared, waiting for nothing but a vanguard to lead the charge against the battlements, whereupon it would fall in behind in serried ranks, ready for the sacred advance towards the great objective. And I had imagined that our role was to be this commando vanguard.

Then suddenly came reality after July 23rd. The vanguard performed its task and charged the battlements of tyranny. It threw out Farouk and then paused, waiting for the serried ranks to come up. . . .

For a long time it waited. Crowds did eventually come, and they came in endless droves—but how different is reality from the dream! The masses that came were disunited, divided groups of stragglers. . . . At this moment I felt, with sorrow and bitterness, that the task of the vanguard, far from being complete, had only begun.

We needed order, but we found nothing but chaos. We needed unity, but we found nothing behind us but dissension. We needed work but we found behind us only indolence and sloth. . . .

In addition to all this, there was a confirmed individual egotism. The word "I" was on every tongue. It was the solution to every difficulty, the cure for every ill. I had many times met eminent men—or so they were called by the press—of every political tendency and color, but when I would ask any of them about a problem in the hope he could supply a solution, I would never hear anything but "I."

Economic problems? He alone could understand them; as for the others, their knowledge on the subject was that of a crawling infant. Political issues? He alone was expert. No one else had gotten beyond the a-b-c's of politics. After meeting one of these people, I would go back in sorrow to my comrades and say, "It is no use. . . ."*

This passage nevertheless reveals much about the difficulty of establishing stable and responsible régimes in the new world of non-western nationalism. Nasser's pressing domestic problems and his need for economic and military assistance led him into further adventures after 1953 (see Chapter 23).

Latin America

At first glance it may seem odd to include parts of the Western Hemisphere in a survey of the revolution against imperialism. While remnants of old colonial empires lingered in the Caribbean after World War II, most of the Latin American republics had already enjoyed independence for a century or more and re-

*Gamal Abdul Nasser, *Egypt's Liberation* (Washington: Public Affairs Press, 1955), 32–36.

tained close bonds of language, religion, and culture with the great nations of western Europe. Populated by a mixture of Indian, Negro, and white Creole stock, many of them had advanced substantially toward the establishment of multi-racial societies. Yet a second look shows that the peoples of Latin America and the Caribbean have long been struggling with the kinds of problems we have found in Asia and the Middle East. Especially since 1945, they have been trying to go beyond their traditional and essentially colonial role as suppliers of such foodstuffs as bananas, sugar, coffee, and beef, and such raw materials as oil, nitrates, and minerals. They have sought to end their almost total dependence on commodities that fluctuate widely in price on the world market, and to lay a more stable economic base on which to raise the standard of living of their still impoverished masses. Politically, the parallels with the non-western world are often striking. There have been the same denunciations of western colonialism (in this case usually "Yankee imperialism"), the same emergence of military dictators, the same round of *coups* and revolutions, the same promises of utopia so easy to make and so hard to fulfill.

Many Latin American revolutions have actually been no more than shifts of power from one ruling strong man or clique to another; in a book of this kind we cannot survey them all, and must be content with a sample. Immediately after World War II, for example, democracy seemed to be making notable progress in several Latin American states, only to lose ground after 1948, so that by 1955, eleven of the twenty republics were ruled by dictators, most of them military men. We shall consider two case histories—those of Mexico and of Argentina.

In Mexico the overthrow of Napoleon III's puppet emperor, Maximilian, in 1867 (see Chapter 13) marked an apparent victory not only for the Monroe Doctrine but also for Mexican nationalism and liberalism. In 1876, however, power was seized by Porfirio Díaz, a leading specimen of the *caudillo* or military hero, who dominated the country for the next thirty-five years. Díaz enforced law and order, punctually met payments on foreign debts (non-payment of which had occasioned the venture of Napoleon III), won high respect abroad, and attracted the investment of much foreign capital in his country. But he also catered almost exclusively to the interests of foreign investors and the large Mexican landowners; agitation by laborers for redress of legitimate grievances was suppressed; many peasants lost their stake in the land and were reduced to being peons, hardly better than serfs, on large agricultural estates.

Popular discontent with the Díaz régime finally boiled over in 1910, and the dictator fled abroad in the next year. The acute phase of the revolution thus begun continued for thirty years, marked by intermittent violence and insurrection, by revolutionary reformers who turned into wealthy dictators, and by radical social and economic experimentation. The Catholic Church, long regarded by many Mexicans as opposed to economic and political reform and indifferent to the welfare of the masses, was the target of extreme anticlerical measures. The foreign oil companies, American and British, suffered expropriation of valuable concessions. All this did not make for harmonious relations with the United States, and at one point early in the revolution (1916) President Wilson sent troops into Mexico to retaliate for a Mexican incursion into the American state of New Mexico. The revolutionary governments gave labor unions extensive privileges and power, expropriated great estates to emancipate the peons, and began a vigorous program of educating the large and neglected population of native Indians. A remarkable cultural awakening took place, based on native traditions and crafts, and Mexican painters like Rivera and Orozco won international fame.

The Mexican revolution, however, stopped short of installing a fully socialistic régime, and by World War II seemed to be entering the Thermidorean stage. The course of Mexican history after 1945 confirmed this impression. Like many revolutions, the Mexican appeared to have lost much of its extremism, its radical dogmatism, its determination to realize for all the promises of Liberty, Equality, and Fraternity. Post-revolutionary Mexico was in part at least reconciled to the need for foreign capital, for the good opinion of North Americans, and above all for patience in the long task of raising the standards of her masses.

At the other extremity of Latin America, the Argentine Republic has not faced Mexico's problem of a large and backward Indian population, since it is peopled almost entirely by European immigrants and their descendants. Although independent for over 150 years (since 1810), Argentina had until the middle of the twentieth century a typical colonial economy, exporting beef and grain and other raw materials to Europe and importing manufactured goods. The economy was based on a social system that gave power to a small landlord class. The beginnings of industrialization, and especially the growth of the Argentine capital, Buenos Aires, into a great metropolis of nearly 5 million increased the numbers of working-class and middle-class people and increased also popular dissatisfaction with the aristocratic régime. Mussolini and Hitler won admirers in many circles in Argentina; democratic elements generally looked to France and to the radical French republican tradition. The United States, to phrase it mildly, was rather envied than admired. Argentina sat out World War II, coming in on the Allied side only at the very end.

After the war, in the national election of 1946, a newcomer to Argentine politics rose to prominence, Colonel Juan Perón. Perón became a dictator on the fascist European model — that is, he contrived to hold power by the kind of appeal and by the methods that we have analyzed for Mussolini, Hitler, and Franco. Perón, however, never established himself quite as firmly as did his European counterparts, and in 1955 he went down before a characteristic Latin-American military *coup d'état*. Many factors accounted for his fall. In searching for support, Perón was driven more and more to appeal to the poorer masses, the *descamisados* ("shirtless ones"), and thus lost much of his following in the conservative upper classes. Moreover, after the death of his actress wife Eva, who seems to have been much brighter than her husband, he quarreled with the Roman Catholic Church and put through anticlerical measures that cost him further support. Finally, Perón never solved the grave economic and financial problems arising out of his country's essentially colonial position; indeed, his extravagant spending on public works and welfare projects virtually bankrupted Argentina. Although it is hazardous to generalize on the basis of Latin-American experience, his fall suggests two tentative conclusions. First, a great weakness of the Nazi-fascist formula was its attempt to solve social problems by a modern form of the old Roman "bread and circuses," which simply would not work in the twentieth century. Second, the overthrow of Perón without outside interference showed that dictators could be unseated from within, even in modern times of mass propaganda, if they lost the support of the military. We shall encounter other examples in the next chapter.

Reading Suggestions on the Post-War World, 1945–1953

(Asterisk indicates paperbound edition.)

The Democracies

S. P. Graubard, ed., *A New Europe?* (Houghton Mifflin, 1964). Stimulating essays by specialists, analytical rather than narrative.

S. Kuznets, *Post War Economic Growth* (Harvard Univ. Press, 1964). Good analytical study of this important phase of recent history.

C. E. Black, *Dynamics of Modernization* (Harper and Row, 1966). An important essay in comparative contemporary history.

J. Freymond, *Western Europe since the War* (Praeger, 1964). Good brief manual.

A. M. Schlesinger, Jr., *A Thousand Days* (Houghton Mifflin, 1965). Fascinating account of the Kennedy years by a member of his team.

I. F. Stone, *The Haunted Fifties* (Random House, 1963). Selections from his Washington newsletter; most readable.

A. Sampson, *Anatomy of Britain Today* (Harper and Row, 1965). Lively and readable.

F. Boyd, *British Politics in Transition, 1945–1963* (Praeger, 1964). A good up-to-date account.

F. S. Northedge, *British Foreign Policy: The Process of Readjustment, 1945–1961* (Praeger, 1962). A similar up-to-date manual of foreign policy.

H. S. Hughes, *The United States and Italy,* rev. ed. (Harvard Univ. Press, 1965). This revised edition has an excellent chapter on current history and a bibliography brought up to date.

E. McInnis, *Shaping of Postwar Germany* (Praeger, 1961). A good brief survey.

D. M. Pickles, *The Fifth French Republic,* 3rd ed. (Praeger, 1966). A well-known treatment.

R. Aron, *France Steadfast and Changing* (Harvard Univ. Press, 1960). Thoughtful study by a very fair-minded Frenchman.

R. M. and J. Brace, *Ordeal in Algeria* (Van Nostrand, 1960). Objective study by two Americans.

Communism and the Cold War

D. J. Dallin, *The New Soviet Empire* (Yale Univ. Press, 1951). An anti-Soviet survey.

G. A. Almond, ed., *The Appeals of Communism* (Princeton Univ. Press, 1954). An interesting symposium.

W. Leonhard, *Child of the Revolution* (Regnery, 1958; *Gateway). Revealing account by a defecting East German Communist official.

M. Einaudi and others, *Communism in Western Europe* (Cornell Univ. Press, 1951). A very illuminating examination of French and Italian communists.

R. L. Wolff, *The Balkans in Our Time* (Harvard Univ. Press, 1956). An informed account.

H. L. Roberts, *Russia and America: Dangers and Prospects* (Harper, 1956; *New American Library). A valuable summary.

C. J. Friedrich and Z. K. Brzezinski, *Totalitarian Dictatorship and Autocracy* (Harvard Univ. Press, 1956). Systematic examination of totalitarian institutions.

W. Z. Laqueur, *The Soviet Union and the Middle East* (Praeger, 1959). A pioneering investigation of a new and important subject.

R. Walker, *China Under Communism* (Yale Univ. Press, 1955). See also books recommended in Chapters 18 and 23.

The Revolt against Imperialism

S. C. Easton, *Rise and Fall of Modern Colonialism* (Praeger, 1962). Informative survey.

V. M. Dean, *The Nature of the Non-Western World* (*Mentor). Sympathetic general appraisal.

J. Strachey, *The End of Empire* (*Praeger), Viewed by a British leftist.

F. S. C. Northrop, *The Meeting of East and West* (*Collier); B. Ward, *The Interplay of East & West* (*Norton). Two general interpretations of the confrontations of cultures.

B. Rowland, *Art in East and West* (*Beacon). A valuable comparative study.

E. O. Reischauer, *The United States & Japan* (*Compass). Admirable survey by a leading authority on Japan.

C. Dubois, *Social Forces in Southeast Asia* (Harvard Univ. Press, 1959). Valuable analysis of a basic aspect of non-Western culture.

P. Spear, *History of India*, Vol. II (*Penguin), and *India, Pakistan, and the West* (*Galaxy). Useful introductions by an expert.

W. N. Brown, *The United States and India and Pakistan*, rev. ed. (Harvard Univ. Press, 1963). Another good introduction.

W. C. Smith, *Islam in Modern History* (*Mentor). Instructive discussion of a difficult topic.

G. Lenczowski, *The Middle East in World Affairs*, 3rd ed. (Cornell Univ. Press, 1962), and *Oil and State in the Middle East* (Cornell Univ. Press, 1960). Respectively, a general review emphasizing the diplomatic aspects, and a particular study, stressing the impact of oil on the host countries.

W. R. Polk and others, *Backdrop to Tragedy: The Struggle for Palestine* (Taplinger, 1959), and D. Peretz, *Israel and the Palestine Arabs* (Middle East Institute, 1958), Balanced accounts of the controversial Arab-Israeli conflict.

D. N. Wilber, *Contemporary Iran* (Praeger, 1963), and P. Avery, *Modern Iran* (Praeger, 1965). Informative introductions to a fascinating and bewildering country.

T. Little, *Egypt* (Praeger, 1958); C. Issawi, *Egypt in Revolution* (Oxford Univ. Press, 1963); G. G. Stevens, *Egypt Yesterday & Today* (*Holt). Three helpful surveys; Issawi's is the most scholarly, Stevens' the most popular.

A. P. Whitaker, *Argentina* (*Spectrum). General introduction by a leading expert on Latin America.

H. F. Cline, *Mexico* (*Oxford). Broad survey by a specialist.

Novels

See titles listed in Chapter 23.

23

The Contemporary World

since 1953

In this chapter we are dealing largely with what most historians would consider "current events," questions on which we cannot pass even temporary judgments because time has not permitted us to view them in proper perspective. Yet we must and do try to reach tentative conclusions about them in the pages of this book, as we do in our daily lives. Two important points deserve consideration here.

In recent years, the world has seemed increasingly to divide itself into a bloc generally pro-communist, a bloc generally pro-western, and a bloc generally uncommitted. Yet at the same time it has become harder and harder to deal with any event in any one of the three blocs without discussing its impact on the other two. The Soviet Union's policies in India have implications for the United States;

a domestic Algerian or Indonesian upheaval affects both Peking and Washington; the death of Mao Tse-tung, when it occurs, will have repercussions in Tanzania and in London. Although this chapter includes sections on each of the three blocs, each section intimately involves members of all three.

Second, the murder of President Kennedy has led to the publication for the Kennedy years, 1960–1963, of a mass of detailed information of the kind ordinarily kept confidential for many years. To fail to take advantage of this information would be absurd. But to use it no doubt creates inevitable distortions: we simply do not know anything like as much about the way American decisions were reached or what other powers said before 1960 or after 1963.

I　The Communist World since the Death of Stalin: The U.S.S.R. at Home

The Soviet Succession

As Josef Stalin grew older, it had become a favorite occupation in the West to speculate on his succession, and on the forces that would be released at the moment of his death. Would it be the Communist party, or the secret police, or the army—the three agencies in the U.S.S.R. that had power of their own—that would emerge supreme? Would it be some combination of two of these against the third? Was this or that member of the Politburo identified with one or another of these three chief agencies? Would the world see ensue a bitter personal rivalry comparable to the struggle between Stalin and Trotsky for the succession to Lenin? If so, would the resulting instability go so far as to disrupt the machinery of Soviet government?

When the moment actually came, in March, 1953, there was at first no evidence of disunity or personal rivalry within the Presidium. Georgi Malenkov, personally close to Stalin, succeeded him as Premier, but surrendered his Communist party secretaryship to Nikita Khrushchev. It was thus clear from the beginning that nobody would immediately inherit all of Stalin's power, and the fact that it would be shared was underlined almost at once by the pronouncements that came from the régime, denouncing the "cult of personality"

(i.e., Stalin's former one-man rule), and proclaiming a "collegial" system (i.e., government by committee). But before the end of 1953 there came the official announcement that the dreaded chief of the secret police, and Presidium-member, Beria, always regarded as a potential heir of Stalin, had been executed for treason. The observer might interpret this move, so reminiscent of the purges of Stalin's own era, as an indication that the members of the Presidium were circling around each other with their knives out, or that the Communist party and the army had indeed united to thwart a bid for power on the part of the secret police. The emergence of the war hero, Marshal Zhukov, into positions of some political importance gave color to this view as, perhaps, did the rise to even higher eminence of the "political" general, Bulganin.

But all expectation that a "free-for-all" among the remaining members of the inner circle would ensue, or that the régime might be shaken by personal rivalries, was in error. True, Malenkov vanished from the top post of Premier, to be succeeded by Bulganin; but Malenkov, though he admitted grievous errors, was at first simply demoted to a lower cabinet post, and remained in the Presidium. Some indication of the real locus of power might perhaps be found in the fact that the errors confessed by Malenkov (especially the effort to concentrate collective farms into enormous *agrogorods* or agricultural towns, see p. 832, which had indeed failed) were actually Khrushchev's errors, for which Malenkov now had to take responsibility. Yet, though Khrushchev was certainly very powerful, his fellow-members on the Politburo had great influence, and showed no outward signs of fearing him as all had feared Stalin. On the whole, it appeared that the transfer of power had actually gone quite smoothly in the U.S.S.R. and that among the rulers, in the happy phrase from George Orwell's *Animal Farm* "all were equal, but some were more equal than others."

The Denunciation of Stalin and its Consequences

At a Party Congress, held early in 1956, Khrushchev made a speech in which he not only carried the attack on the "cult of personality" to new heights, but openly denounced Stalin by name, emotionally detailing the ghastly acts of personal cruelty to which the psychopathically suspicious nature of the late dictator had given rise. Khrushchev thus echoed what western observers of the U.S.S.R. had been saying for years. As the details of the speech were leaked out to the Soviet public, there was of course some distress at the smashing of the idol they had worshiped so long; but a good many of them no doubt had all along suspected that Stalin was something less than god-like. So the widespread disorders that some observers were predicting failed to materialize.

But outside the U.S.S.R., the sudden deflation of Stalin and the admission of so many past injustices proved far too strong a brew for the citizens of some of the European satellites to swallow. Anti-communist riots by workers— supposedly the pillars of any communist state—in Poznan, Poland, in June, 1956, were followed by severe strikes, demonstrations, and upheavals in the rest of Poland a few months later. Polish national sentiment was declaring itself, but the uprising remained within the grip of one wing of the Communist party, that led by Wladislaw Gomulka, who

had been purged for alleged Titoism in 1951. Not even the presence in Warsaw of Khrushchev himself and other members of the Soviet Presidium prevented the rise of Gomulka to power, although at one moment the Russians seem to have contemplated using their army to impose their will by force. Yet because the new government in Poland was, after all, a communist government, they allowed it to remain in power.

In Hungary, however, the movement went farther. Starting, like the Polish uprising, as a movement within the Communist party, and spurred by the outspoken writings of many communists who loathed the restraints of Stalinism, the Hungarian movement brought Imre Nagy, a communist like Gomulka, into office as Premier. But then the popular hatred for communism and for the Russians got out of hand, and heroic young men and women flew to arms in Budapest in the hope of ousting the communists and of taking Hungary altogether out of the Soviet sphere. They even denounced the Warsaw Pact, the Russian alliance of eastern European satellites set up by Moscow to oppose NATO. It was then that Khrushchev ordered full-fledged military action. In November, 1956, Soviet tanks and troops, violating an armistice, swept back into Budapest and put down the revolution in blood and fire. A puppet government led by

The Hungarian Revolt: head of the statue of Stalin toppled in downtown Budapest.

Janos Kadar was installed. More than 150,000 Hungarian refugees fled to Austria, to be re-settled in various western countries. Despite the Soviet charges that the uprising had been trumped up by the western "imperialists" and "fascists," the West in fact had played no part at all, not daring to help the Hungarians for fear of starting the world war that everybody knew must be avoided.

These momentous events of 1956 in eastern Europe gave Khrushchev's opponents at home an opportunity to unite against his policies. Within the Presidium they had a majority. But Khrushchev was able to rally to his support the larger body of which the Presidium was the inner core, the Central Committee of the Communist Party of the U.S.S.R. A veteran party worker, he had installed his own loyal supporters in all key party posts, repeating Stalin's performance after the death of Lenin (see above, Chapter 18), and emerged from this greatest test not only unscathed, but with his powers immeasurably enhanced (June, 1957). Now the Soviet press denounced the "anti-party group" of Malenkov, Molotov, and Kaganovich, three of the members of Stalin's own entourage. In Stalin's own day, this would have led them to the execution-block, or would have been reported only after they were safely dead. Khrushchev, however, acted differently. All three were expelled from the Presidium and removed from their high posts, but all three were given minor positions at a safe distance from Moscow. Molotov, for example, became ambassador to Outer Mongolia.

Late in 1957, Marshal Zhukov, who had helped Khrushchev win his struggle, and had in return received what looked like valuable concessions limiting the role of party representatives in army affairs, found himself ousted from all his political posts as a "politically deficient figure." During 1958, Bulganin followed him into the discard: he had sided against Khrushchev, and took the consequences. Men of Khrushchev's own choosing replaced them at the top level of the hierarchy. Khrushchev's succession to Stalin's position of undisputed power seemed complete.

The Khrushchev Era: The Bureaucratic Problems

Yet there were certain differences. Already in his sixties, Khrushchev could hardly hope for a quarter century of dictatorship such as Stalin had had. Moreover, in the very course of making himself supreme, he had deprived himself of some of the instruments available to Stalin. After 1953 he had released millions of captives from prisons and slave-labor camps. Almost everybody in Russia had a relative or friend now freed. These men and women now took jobs, some of them even government jobs. Within a year or two Soviet society at every level except at the very top of the bureaucracy had absorbed these sufferers from tyranny, who would be the first to oppose its reimposition. Khrushchev's own government had severely curbed the secret police. Beria, its chief, was the only major figure to have been executed after Stalin's death. It no longer enjoyed a power almost independent in the state, such as might challenge the party or the army. It no longer was the largest single "employer of labor." Khrushchev himself had emotionally denounced its terror. Though it was still possible to prosecute and even persecute individuals by terrorist means, Stalin's mass terror as a system of government had disappeared. Khrushchev's denunciation of the "cult of personality" required him to protest against the adulatory references to him that came from the Party Congress in 1959, if only because they sounded too much like the old lavish hymns of praise for Stalin.

Instead of terror, Khrushchev embarked on a series of bureaucratic changes within government and party, especially in the organs that controlled the economy. By creating for the Russian Republic, by far the largest and most populous of the republics, a special branch of the Central Committee Secretariat and a set of bureaucratic departments parallel to those that existed for the U.S.S.R. as a whole, he gave this large territory virtually a separate administration, and took complete control of its personnel. In 1963 he took parallel measures for Central Asia and the Transcaucasus. He began a whole series of moves to decentralize party activity; but in 1962, when these were considered to have failed, he re-centralized once more, and then reorganized the party on a production basis: all regional parties at every level below the republic were to be divided into industrial and agricultural wings, receiving coordination only at the level of the republic and the All-Union Central Committees. These efforts within the party were more easily understood in the light of developments within the Soviet economy during these years.

With his eye always upon production, Khrushchev wrestled with the problems of efficiency, output, and morale. Under Stalin, centralization had reached an intolerable tightness. But how far could one decentralize so huge an operation as the Soviet economy and still retain control over local operations? How far could one centralize and still obtain local co-operation, loyalty, and, especially production? Between 1953 and 1957, responsibility for many heavy industries was transferred from the ministries of the central government to those of the individual republics. In May, 1957, a decree abolished many central ministries, and transferred their duties to 105 newly created regional economic councils (sovnarkhoz), in the hope of giving full play to informed on-the-spot decisions, of improving the use of local resources, of consolidating overlapping services, and of reassigning experts from the central government to the grass-roots. Though many regarded the change as an improvement, some factory managers still complained of being bound in a strait-jacket imposed by bureaucrats closer to home than before but still bureaucrats; and many experts lamented or evaded the need to move from the capital to the provinces. "Regionalism"—devotion to regional interests as against national ones—replaced what might be called devotion to one industry ahead of others. But patriots for Armenian industry (to the detriment of other regions) were no more helpful to the national economy than patriots for the cement industry (to the detriment of other industries).

By 1960 a process of re-centralizing had begun, as republic-level councils appeared in the Russian Republic and two of the other major republics; and in 1961 nineteen new large "natural" regions, cutting across republic lines, were set up to ensure integrated economic development for each region. By the end of 1962, the *sovnarkhozes* were reduced from 105 to about 40, and new state committees appeared to oversee their work. These committees greatly resembled the old ministries, and were before long reorganized as ministries. The pendulum had swung back almost the entire distance. It was then that all lower levels of the party were reorganized along agricultural-industrial lines, in the apparent effort to make the political functionaries serve the economy more efficiently.

The Khrushchev Era and Beyond: Industry and Agriculture

Khrushchev faced the same problem that had faced all Soviet leaders: how much emphasis could be put on consumer goods, and how much still must be devoted to heavy industry? Though temperamentally more interested in providing consumer goods than Stalin or Malenkov, Khrushchev, who acceded to power during the Fifth Five-Year Plan (1951–1955), made the same choice as they: continued emphasis on the means of production. The sixth plan (1956–1960), setting more ambitious goals than ever before, aimed specifically at catching up with the United States. But the huge expenses involved in the Polish and Hungarian outbreaks ($1 billion worth of credits to eastern Europe alone) forced the Soviet government to shelve the plan. By the end of 1958 they announced a new Seven Year Plan, to run until 1965. Starting from base figures of 500 million tons of coal, 55 million tons of steel, and 113 million tons of oil, output by 1964 had reached 554 million tons of coal, 85 million tons of

Crisscross sowing of wheat on virgin land in the Altai Territory, U.S.S.R.

steel, and 224 million tons of oil. A return to the system of Five-Year Plans was announced for 1966.

Most spectacular were the successes achieved in the field of rocketry and space. It was the U.S.S.R. that successfully launched the first earth-satellite (Sputnik—1957) and that first reached the moon with a rocket (1959). Heavy payloads soared aloft before American engineers could get their lighter ones off the ground. Though inter-continental missiles were apparently more readily available to Moscow earlier than to Washington, American bases in Europe and Africa made our own shorter-range weapons equally dangerous to the U.S.S.R. Each power had enough nuclear weapons and means of delivering them to destroy the other and itself at the same time. Spurred to some degree by the Soviet technical advance, the United States itself embarked in the late fifties on an intensive program of research and development in space. Though the U.S.S.R. got the first man into space, and for some time held the lead in technical

achievements, by the mid-sixties the United States had logged more hours of flight by spaceships with one-man and two-man crews, and had virtually solved the problem of rendezvous in space, while the successful Mars-probe operation of 1965 overshadowed comparable Soviet exploration of the solar system.

Agriculture continued to present the Soviet planners with some of its seemingly most insoluble problems. In 1953 Khrushchev embarked on the "virgin lands" scheme, a crash program to plow under more than 100,000, acres of prairie in the Urals region, Kazakhstan, and Siberia. Although weather favored the operation during its first few years, drought and poor planning and performance led to a clear failure by 1963. Khrushchev then called for an all-out crash program for the production of chemical fertilizers. After the death of Stalin, the régime had continued to amalgamate collective farms. By 1964, their number was down to about 40,000 from an original quarter of a million; and the average size of the new units was far larger, perhaps about 5,000 acres. By 1965, the government recognized that many collectives were now too big.

To increase incentives, the regime in 1958 abolished compulsory deliveries of farm products, the most onerous of the peasant's burdens, and raised agricultural prices. Simultaneously, the government decreed the gradual abolition of the MTS (Machine Tractor Stations, see p. 688) and the sale of the tractors to the individual collective, which the government undertook to subsidize in part. In 1964, for the first time, the government extended its system of old-age and disability pensions to agricultural laborers: men might claim them at age sixty-five after twenty-five years of labor, and women at age sixty after twenty years of labor, in amounts calculated according to earnings. In 1964, the régime removed the ceilings on the size of the private allotment of land allowed to the individual peasant in a collective and on the number of cattle that he might own privately. Yet yields continued low; each year the U.S.S.R. had to buy many millions of tons of grain abroad; animal husbandry in particular caused grave concern, and the régime's agencies thundered against inefficiency and "fascination with administration by fiat."

In the two years after Khrushchev's fall from power in 1964, the Soviet authorities engaged in an open debate about the best way to revise the statutes governing the collective farm (*artel*) in view of the immense changes since they were used in 1936. Late in 1966 the new statute had not yet been promulgated. But the party and the government ordered the collective farms to guarantee the individual farmers a monthly sum in cash for their work, and to pay in addition for the produce actually received. The state bank would advance the farms the credit where necessary. Some economists were arguing for the introduction of a free market economy; others vigorously defended centralized planning (with improvements). It seemed improbable that the Soviet authorities would abandon their centralized control over the farms to any great degree, but it was clear that they also were recognizing the importance of incentives and of the individual in the field of agriculture as in many others. Fighting a wordy rear-guard defense of traditional communist economic practices, they were quietly retreating toward certain tested principles associated with capitalism. The Minister of Agriculture in 1966 proclaimed his hope that by constantly raising rural standards of life and education, the new Five-Year Plan would greatly diminish the "intrinsic differences between town and countryside."

Education and the Arts

In 1958 Khrushchev introduced an important change in the Soviet educational system: "polytechnization," which emphasized vocational training and on-the-job experience. This represented in some respects a reversion to the immediate post-revolutionary educational experiments of 1919 and later (see Chapter 18), and a retreat from the 1931 program setting a goal of a ten-year general educational program for all. The régime wanted to avoid producing a "white-handed elite"—young men and young women who had had no practical labor experience, and whose schooling made them feel entitled to continue their education in universities in the hope of pursuing professional careers. Since the universities could accept roughly only one-fifth of school graduates, the remainder found themselves unable to continue, and yet without experience in labor or training in technology, were unwilling to become workers. Khrushchev ordered the universities now to favor applicants who had had practical experience, and also intended to make available evening and extension classes for those whose formal education had stopped.

By the mid-sixties, almost all children in the U.S.S.R. finished the first four years of school (ages seven to eleven), and illiteracy had virtually disappeared. Almost as many finished the second four years (ages eleven to fifteen), which was now combined with "polytechnization." In August, 1964, the conventional next course of three-years (ages fifteen to eighteen) usually taken by only about 40 per cent of Soviet youth, was reduced to two years, and the heavy proportion of time now given to outside industrial work — from one third to one half — was somewhat reduced. Students received pay for their work, which was assigned them in accordance with the requirements of their native region. Soviet universities regularly reserved 20 per cent of their places for the ablest graduates of secondary schools; and the four "physicomathematical" high schools conducted a nation-wide "Olympiad" or talent contest to discover the most promising candidates in these fields.

Khrushchev extended to the field of arts and letters the same partial relaxation that accompanied de-Stalinization in other fields. It took Soviet writers some time to accustom themselves to the idea that it might now be possible to voice dissent: too many had vanished forever at Stalin's whim to make the risk an attractive one. Moreover, convinced Stalinists or party hacks who had grown up under Stalinism lay in wait to attack the innovator. They regarded as heresy all literary experiment or deviation from the old rules of "socialist realism." Khrushchev himself, though eager to destroy the cult of Stalin's personality, was himself opinionated and autocratic, declaring on one occasion that an exhibition of abstract art — entirely forbidden under Stalin — must have been painted by donkey's tails, and keeping artists and writers in constant uncertainty lest new purges break forth. The dangers of self-expression continued great indeed.

In a few individual books and authors we may find indices of the new policies. Ilya Ehrenburg, veteran propagandist for the régime, in *The Thaw* (1955) hailed the relaxation of coercive measures over artists. Vladimir Dudintsev's novel, *Not By Bread Alone* (1956), had as its hero a competent and enthusiastic engineer, whose invention of a new pipe-casting machine was thwarted at every turn by the entrenched bureaucrats. Government-controlled writers' agencies denounced Dudintsev, who retracted his views, and for six or seven years was forced to

earn his living by translation only. Boris Pasternak's *Dr. Zhivago* (1958) became a *cause célèbre* throughout the world. Pasternak, a brilliant poet, who had for years confined himself to translating Shakespeare, took advantage of the "thaw" to offer for publication his novel about a doctor who, through all the agonies of the first World War and the Russian Revolution, affirms the freedom of the human soul. Accepted for publication in the U.S.S.R., the novel was sent to Italy to be published. Then the Soviet censors changed their minds, and forced Pasternak to ask that the manuscript in Italy be returned to him. The Italian publisher refused, and versions in Russian, Italian, English, and other languages appeared abroad, and aroused great admiration. In 1958 the Nobel Prize Committee selected Pasternak as the winner of the prize for literature. He accepted. But then the Khrushchev régime reverted to Stalinism: Pasternak's fellow-writers reviled him as a pig and a traitor, and the government threatened him with exile if he accepted the prize. As a patriotic Russian he then declined it.

In the same week that a Soviet physicist accepted the Nobel prize for physics, the régime called the Nobel prize for literature a capitalist invention. And a few years later, Michael Sholokhov, author of the famous Cossack trilogy, *The Quiet Don,* and a personal friend of Khrushchev, accepted the Nobel prize in literature. Pasternak's persecution revealed the limits of the thaw as of 1958. His Jewish origins, his intellectualism, his proclamation of individualism touched hostile chords in Khrushchev himself and in other Soviet officials and writers that made it impossible to publish *Dr. Zhivago* in the U.S.S.R.

But the spirit of individualism, slow to express itself even when liberated in the older generation, found in the 1960's new and more vigorous expression among the younger poets and novelists who had grown up since the Second World War, and for whom the heroic age of the revolution and the early Bolshevik struggles were ancient history. The young Ukrainian poet, Yevtushenko, bitterly denounced Soviet anti-Semitism in his *Babi Yar* (the name of the ravine near Kiev in which the Nazis had massacred thousands of Jews), and declared his identity with the murdered human beings. In another poem he begged the government to double and triple the guard over Stalin's tomb

"So that Stalin may not rise
And, with Stalin
the past.
. . . the ignoring of the people's welfare
The calumnies
The arrests of the innocent."

Former supporters of Stalin, he went on,

"Do not like these times
When the camps are empty
And the halls where people listen to poetry
Are crowded."*

When Yevtushenko recited his verse, the halls were indeed always crowded with eager excited contentious young people, claiming the right to think for themselves. "We've found out," said another young poet, "what it leads to when somebody else does our thinking for us." Often in trouble with the régime, leading a stormy life recorded in an autobiography published first in France without permission, Yevtushenko hailed Fidel Castro and all true Leninists, but constantly needled the Soviet

*Pravda, Oct. 21, 1962.

authorities. Severely disciplined in 1963, he was publicly on the attack again in 1965.

Yevtushenko's mention of "the camps" suggests another new phenomenon in the Soviet writing of the early sixties, the deep interest in the terrible days of Stalin's labor camps and in the suffering of their inmates, reflected in the novel by Solzhenitsyn, *A Day in the Life of Ivan Denisov;* in the sensational memoirs of a Soviet General, Gorbatov, who described the horrible tortures to which he, like many others, had been subjected on mere suspicion; and in the songs of the camps that the students at the universities had begun now to sing to their guitars—bitter, mocking, cynical, and often deeply moving. Khrushchev viewed with some apprehension the flood of fiction about the camps that came pouring into the publishing houses, and only a few novels and stories were published, but even these marked an astonishing new trend. Often the anxious Khrushchev would try to remind the younger generation of the glorious revolutionary past through which their elders had triumphantly lived. He declared—as if in answer to their demands for full freedom—that even under full communism it would not be possible to give complete liberty to the individual, who would continue "like a bee in a hive" to make his contribution to society.

After Khrushchev's ouster in October, 1964 (see p. 872), his successors denounced him for

Left: Yevgeny Yevtushenko photographed at his home in Moscow; *right:* Andrei Sinyavsky (foreground) and Yuli Daniel at their trial in Moscow, February, 1966.

interfering in intellectual life, but here, as elsewhere, they did not depart very far from his policies. Writers of the Stalinist type kept on the offensive; for example, a novel called *The Plant Louse* violently denounced modern painters and painting. It received a harsh review from a critic named Andrei Sinyavsky. And in September, 1965, Sinyavsky was arrested along with another writer named Yuli Daniel. Sinyavsky, said the government, had written under the pseudonym of Abram Tertz and smuggled abroad for publication anti-Soviet fiction and an essay that had been creating a sensation for over a year; and Daniel, under the pseudonym of Nikolai Arzhak, had committed the same crime.

Indeed, Tertz's *The Trial Begins*, dealing with the purges, gave a candid and revolting picture of the life of the Soviet leaders under Stalin; his novel *Lyubimov* (translated into English as *The Makepeace Experiment*) dealt with a one-man revolt against communism in a small Russian town; and his essay *On Socialist Realism* damned what was still the official literary doctrine of the régime. Arzhak's *Moscow Calling* was a fantasy in which the Soviet government set aside one day on which murder was allowed. Foreign readers, who had been hailing Tertz for his irony, subtlety, and love of freedom had been wondering who he could be. It came as a surprise that Sinyavsky, not a Jew, but descendant of a family of Old Be-

lievers (Chapter 2, p. 70), had chosen a Jewish pseudonym. But this too was explained in January, 1966, when an American periodical, *The New Leader*, published an English translation of a popular Russian song about a thief named Abram Tertz and his girl Sonka, a prostitute. From this ballad, apparently, Sinyavsky had chosen the name. In 1966 Sinyavsky and Daniel went on trial. Soviet officialdom railed at them for publishing abroad, for suggesting the prevalence of anti-Semitism in the U.S.S.R., and for their frankness in treating sexual matters, which ran counter to the prevailing Soviet literary prudery. Their sentences served as a warning to other Soviet writers, and aroused much protest inside the U.S.S.R. and out.

When students demonstrated on behalf of the arrested writers, the régime reverted to a practice sometimes followed by Tsar Nicholas I (Chapter 14), who had confined rebellious intellectuals to insane asylums on the pretext that they must be crazy. It was clear that the "intelligentsia," now about 20 per cent of the Soviet working population, posed for its masters a continuing problem whose dimensions, during the continued thaw and occasional light freeze, grew clearer than ever. To an American observer, Soviet youth in 1967 — the "new right" in the U.S.S.R. — showed signs of resembling its American opposite numbers, the "new left" in the United States.

II   Soviet Confrontation with the West

Stalin's heirs inherited formidable powers, but they also inherited formidable problems. Any attack that threatened the vital interests of the United States, with its thermonuclear arsenal and its superior industrial resources, might well touch off the ultimate disaster. A policy of probing to see just which interests the United States considered vital had already led to the Korean War. Continued tension between the two super-powers required the U.S.S.R. to continue to devote its

resources to guns rather than to butter. To relax the tension would theoretically have meant more butter, but would in turn raise the danger that the U.S.S.R. would lose its position as leader of the world communist movement. China, with its determination to seize Taiwan and to expand in Asia, might seize the leadership of revolutionary forces at least in Asia, and would represent the Russians as old and tired, no longer true Leninists. In the end it proved to be impossible for Krushchev to hold all these threats in balance, and the choices he eventually was forced to make led to a major split in the communist world.

In the years immediately following Stalin's death, Soviet foreign policy continued along Stalinist lines. The Russians moved into the Middle East with new vigor. Here they had the advantage of being able to deal with Gamal Abdel Nasser, the new ruler of Egypt and an inveterate enemy of the West, which he associated not only with past colonialism but with support for Israel. Czechoslovak and Russian arms flowed to Egypt, and Russian technicians followed. Perhaps the high point of Soviet influence was reached during the Suez affair in 1956 (Section IV). When the United States joined the U.S.S.R. in denouncing the British and French attack, however, it became impossible for Nasser to lump all the western powers together. Soon Nasser began to learn that Russian influence usually followed Russian favors. He experienced some disillusion during the summer of 1958, when revolution broke out in Iraq, where Soviet-sponsored communists were opposing Nasser's own pan-Arab aims. Prompt American intervention in Lebanon and British intervention in Jordan in 1958 may have temporarily countered the threat of the spread of Soviet influence beyond Iraq. It was the Russians who provided the aid that made possible the high dam at Aswan and much armament for the Egyptian armies, but Nasser remained unaligned with either major bloc. In the Middle East and in other "undeveloped" areas, notably Africa, the U.S.S.R. had begun to challenge the West as the supplier of economic and technological aid. A new chapter in the Cold War had opened.

In eastern Europe, Soviet influence continued stable until Khrushchev's policies of de-Stalinization at home touched off the Polish and Hungarian uprisings (see p. 853). But even before this, Khrushchev had departed from Stalinism by making a great effort to heal the breach with Tito. In May, 1955, he went in person to Belgrade, and not only publicly apologized for the quarrel, taking the blame upon the U.S.S.R., but openly agreed that "differences in the concrete forms of de-veloping socialism are exclusively matters for the people of the country concerned," which seemed to echo Tito's own views. Relations between Tito and Moscow were temporarily improved, although the Yugoslavs never abandoned their ties to the West. Khrushchev even went so far as to declare that many prominent victims of the "Titoist" purges had been executed wrongly, and abolished the Cominform, the body that ostensibly had started the qurrel with Tito. But in making these admissions and healing the quarrel Stalin had started, Khrushchev had opened the door to the Polish and Hungarian troubles that soon began; Soviet military intervention in Hungary showed Tito and the rest of the world how limited was Khrushchev's willingness and ability to permit free choices to other communist states. Tito denounced the Soviet intervention against Nagy, though he was frightened by the wholly anti-communist character that the Hungarian revolt subsequently took on, and failed to oppose the decisive Soviet operations that put an end to the uprising.

For a second time, relations between Moscow and Tito were strained. They were patched up again in the summer of 1957; the Soviets once more hoped that Tito would again accept Moscow's leadership of the world communist movement. But when in November the Russians invited representatives of all the world's Communist parties to Moscow to celebrate the fortieth anniversary of the Russian Revolution, and produced a declaration of twelve Communist parties denouncing "revisionism" — as Tito's views had come to be known — Tito flatly refused to sign. Indeed he published his own counter-program declaring that each communist nation should make its own decisions freely. The old quarrel was renewed for the third time. Tito would not reenter a world communist union led by Russia. Khrushchev's efforts had failed. Moreover, the Poles signed the declaration with obvious reluctance, and Gomulka continued to insist on autonomy for his government in internal and party affairs.

The harshness of the onslaught against revisionism and Khrushchev's acceptance of defeat in his efforts to win the Yugoslavs by softness reflected Chinese influence. After the Polish and Hungarian revolts, the Chinese communist leaders had been invited to visit those countries, and lay down the line; they now appeared very eager to play a role in formulating world communist ideology, and displayed a strong preference (probably for internal reasons) for Stalinist orthodoxy and repression. By the spring of 1958, the Chinese and Khrushchev himself had declared that Stalin's original denunciation of the Yugoslavs back in 1948 has been correct after all. In June, 1958, the Soviet government underlined this decision in grim fashion when it announced the executions of Imre Nagy and other leaders of the Hungarian uprising, in violation of solemn promises of safe-conduct. The executions probably were intended also to serve as a warning to Gomulka not to try to push Polish independence too far. Soon afterward, Gomulka did denounce revisionism, and criticized both Nagy and the Yugoslavs, but in a tone far milder than that employed by the Russians and Chinese.

All the eastern European satellites were bound together in the "Council for Mutual Economic Aid" (Comecon) established in 1949, which took measures to standardize machinery and coordinate economic policies, and issued blasts against western European efforts at cooperation like the Common Market and Euratom. The Asian communist régimes also collaborated. Yugoslavia never was a member, and after 1958 was no longer invited to send observers. Khrushchev had not solved a problem that indeed seemed essentially insoluble: how to maintain totalitarian authority over the European satellites while simultaneously trying to relax Stalinist methods.

Berlin

But the central concern of Soviet foreign policy in Europe remained Germany. In East Germany (DDR, *Deutsche Demokratische Republik*) it had created its most industrially productive European satellite, now fully geared into the Comecon, and expected to make a long-term contribution to the development of the communist world. Except for a brief but violent workers' riot in East Berlin in 1953, the German communist puppets had succeeded in repressing the population's aversion to Soviet and communist rule. Moreover, strategically the DDR was of great importance to the U.S.S.R.: control over East Germany enabled the Russians to keep Poland surrounded, and helpless to achieve more than a token autonomy. Yet full domination over this important satellite was impeded by the fact that the United States, Britain, and France each retained a zone of occupation in Berlin, deep in the heart of the DDR, and accessible by subway from East Berlin. Every year, thousands of East Germans showed how they felt about communism by escaping into West Berlin. The East German population actually declined by 2,000,000 between 1949 and 1961. For those who stayed behind in the DDR, West Berlin provided an example of prosperity and free democratic government that acted more effectively on their minds than any mere propaganda.

This situation accounted for Khrushchev's determination to get the western powers out of Berlin. The method he proposed in 1958 and later years was thoroughly Stalinist: he threatened to sign a peace treaty with the puppet government of East Germany, never recognized by the West; to turn over to it the communications to Berlin; and to support it in any effort it might then make to cut these communications and force the western powers out. Western refusal to accept this high-handed and unilateral abrogation of agreements concluded during World War II led to a prolonged diplomatic crisis during 1959, in which the U.S.S.R. several times postponed a final date of decision, but made no real concession to the western view.

All the powers had come to realize that no problem was more critical. The West could hardly permit the U.S.S.R. to recreate the conditions it had fought during the airlift of 1948 (see Chapter 22). Nor could it accept the suggestion that, once western troops were removed, Berlin would be a "free city." Defenseless and surrounded by communist territory, Berlin and its 2,000,000 "free" citizens, it feared, would soon be swallowed up. Moreover, the negotiations proposed by the U.S.S.R., whereby the DDR would thereafter "confederate" with the West German Federal Republic, aroused the gravest doubts. How could a state that was a full member of the western system of NATO federate with one that belonged to the Soviet system's Warsaw Pact? How could a state that stood for free capitalist development federate with one completely communized? How could a parliamentary state responsibly governed by a multi-party system with checks and balances federate with a communist totalitarian state? It seemed probable that Khrushchev did not believe in the possibility of the confederation he was proposing, and hoped instead that any possible union of the Germanies would be discredited, and that the DDR, with full control over Berlin, would emerge as a permanent Soviet satellite. But even a Soviet success in Berlin short of this complete victory would have meant that the West had in some measure at least recognized East Germany, which in turn would have severely disturbed West German stability, and disrupted NATO.

U-2, The Wall, Testing, Cuba

While the Berlin threat persisted, exchanges continued between Moscow and Washington. Khrushchev's two deputies, Mikoyan and Kozlov, visited the United States, and Vice-President Nixon visited the U.S.S.R., where he and Khrushchev had a famous confrontation in a model kitchen that was part of an American exhibit. President Eisenhower and Khrushchev agreed to exchange visits, and Khrushchev actually made a dramatic, unprecedented, and highly publicized tour of the United States. When the leaders of the great powers met at the "Summit" in Paris (May 1960), tensions, however, were once again inflamed by the U-2 incident: a Soviet missile brought down a light-weight extremely fast American plane which had been taking high altitude photographs of Soviet territory, and the Russians had captured the pilot unharmed.

After an initial denial, President Eisenhower found himself obliged to acknowledge the truth of the charge and to accept responsibility for the episode; and this ended both the summit meeting and the plans for his own visit to the U.S.S.R.

Khrushchev's next move against Berlin came early in the administration of Eisenhower's successor, John F. Kennedy. In June, 1961, when the two leaders met in Vienna, Kennedy found Khrushchev adamant in insisting that the U.S.S.R. would unilaterally abrogate the agreements on Berlin and sign the treaty with East Germany before the end of the year. As the tension mounted during the summer, with Kennedy and Khrushchev both unyielding on the basic position, the number of refugees fleeing East Berlin rose to a thousand a day. On August 13, East German forces cut the communications between East and West Berlin and began to build a barrier—the Berlin Wall—to prevent further departures. Taken by surprise, the United States yet realized that it could not legitimately resort to arms to prevent the closing of the East Germans' own border, and confined its response to protests, to a military build-up, and to the mission of Vice-President Lyndon Johnson to Berlin, where he reassured the West Berliners of America's unshaken resolve to preserve their status unchanged. The wall itself became the symbol of repression, of a government that had to imprison its own people to keep them at home. Occasional hair-raising escapes and poignant recaptures or shootings continued to take place along the wall's length. But the crisis proved to be over. Khrushchev had backed away from unilateral abrogation of the Berlin treaty.

As if to warn the world not to underestimate Soviet belligerence, however, Khrushchev announced on August 30, 1961, that the U.S.S.R. would resume atomic testing in the atmosphere, which had been stopped by both powers in 1958. In the two months that followed, the Russians exploded 30 huge bombs, whose total force considerably exceeded all previous American, British, and French explosions. After months of agonizing scientific and political review of the problem,

President Kennedy decided that the United States too had to conduct a new round of tests, unless Khrushchev would agree to a treaty banning all tests. When Khrushchev refused, the new American tests began late in April, 1962. All during the months that followed, conversations on disarmament, including of course arrangements for the banning of future tests, continued with the Russians at Geneva.

During the summer of 1962, Khrushchev also decided to place Soviet missiles with nuclear warheads in Cuba, where American foreign policy had failed dismally in the Bay of Pigs fiasco of the year before. The increasingly pro-communist Castro Cuban government may not have asked for them, but in any case accepted them. Soviet officers were to retain control over their use. Their installation would effectively have doubled the Soviet capacity to strike directly at the United States, but the chief threat was political: when known, the mere presence of these weapons ninety miles from Florida would shake the confidence of all other nations in the American capacity to protect even the United States. It would enable Khrushchev to blackmail America on the question of Berlin. American military intelligence discovered the sites and photographed them from the air. Khrushchev tried to deceive Kennedy into thinking the Soviet pur-

pose was simply to help the Cubans resist a new invasion from the United States, which he professed to believe threatened.

Once he knew certainly that the missiles were in Cuba, Kennedy could not allow their installation to continue. The only course of action at first seemed an air strike, which might well have touched off the world war that both sides wished to avert but that Khrushchev seemed to be courting. Kennedy instead found a measure that would prevent the further delivery of missiles: a sea blockade ("quarantine") of the island, and combined it with the demand that the missiles already in Cuba be removed. He thus gave Khrushchev a way to avoid world war, and a chance to save face. Adlai Stevenson at the United Nations put the American case impressively. The President ordered that troops be massed in Florida ready to invade Cuba if necessary, but continued to correspond with Khrushchev, emphasizing the American eagerness for a peaceful solution. After several days of almost unbearable tension, Khrushchev backed down, agreed to halt work on the missile sites in Cuba and to remove the offensive weapons there, while reaffirming the Soviet wish to continue discussions about disarmament. Soviet ships at sea with new missiles turned back to home ports.

Berlin: the historic Brandenburg gate behind the new wall.

he Test-Ban Treaty

President Kennedy did not crow or allow American officials to crow. Khrushchev had moved aggressively in an area close to the United States, where Soviet national security was not threatened. By lying about the missiles, he had destroyed whatever case he might otherwise have had in world opinion. Kennedy did not misread the event by concluding that the U.S.S.R. would back down if Soviet vital interests were affected or if the U.S.S.R. had what it regarded as a good case. He made the American victory as little painful as possible by exploiting it only to push for a further relaxation in tensions. In November, 1962, only a month after the Cuban crisis, Khrushchev in Moscow called for a return to concentration on Soviet domestic economic problems.

Months of preparatory and often discouraging interchanges led in July, 1963, to the signing by the United States, the U.S.S.R., and Great Britain of a treaty banning nuclear weapons tests in the atmosphere, in outer space, or under water. Ratified by the Senate in September, the treaty subsequently received the adherence of more than seventy nations, though France and China—a fledgeling and a prospective nuclear power—would not sign it. Hailed as a "first step" toward reducing the likelihood of a new world war, the treaty none the less aroused the unhappiness of the West Germans: the East Germans would surely adhere to it, and the very presence of their official signature on the same document seemed to Bonn to be elevating the prestige of East Germany.

As a next step toward peace Khrushchev proposed a non-aggression pact to be signed between NATO and the Warsaw Pact nations. This would have effectively put an end to the American plan for a Multilateral Force (MLF), a naval force armed with nuclear weapons and manned by mixed crews from the NATO countries, which in turn meant that, however international the force, some Ger-

man officers and men would have obtained access to nuclear weapons. The plan appealed to the Germans, and frightened the Russians. A non-aggression pact would also have tended to weaken NATO and enabled the U.S.S.R. to hope that the French and Italian Communist parties might emerge once more to neutralize western Europe. West German apprehension at the possibility of a non-aggression pact no doubt contributed to the failure of that Soviet plan, while Soviet apprehension at the possibility of MLF no doubt contributed to the eventual failure (1965) of that American plan.

The installation of the "hot line" communications system between the White House and the Kremlin so that the leaders of the two countries might talk to each other in case of need, the sale of surplus American wheat to the Russians, and President Kennedy's proposal that the United States and the U.S.S.R. might combine their efforts for a moon-shot, which was not accepted, marked the final few months of the Kennedy administration. Despite these limited gains, Khrushchev in this period was proclaiming that "peaceful coexistence" would be impossible in the field of ideology: i.e., that the communists expected to continue their campaign against the capitalist world by words at least, and by aiding "progressive" revolutionary forces everywhere. The assassination of President Kennedy in November, 1963, by a psychopathic young American who had lived in the U.S.S.R., married a Russian, and flirted with Castroism, certainly alarmed the Soviet authorities, who took great pains to assist the American agencies investigating the murder; the act proved to be that of an individual madman and not a plot.

Rumania Disengages

In the years between 1959 and 1964, while Khrushchev was failing to win the struggle over Berlin or to redeem his failure there by blackmail in Cuba, his policies had also led to new trouble within his own eastern European bloc. In 1958–1959, Comecon called for a "specialization" plan, in accordance with which the more developed countries would concentrate on heavy industry, and Rumania in particular on the production of raw materials (chiefly food and oil). The Rumanian government, communist though it was, protested, pointing to its already considerable achievements in heavy industry, and in December, 1961, openly refused to accept the "principles" of the "international socialist division of labor," issued at the twenty-second Congress of the CPSU. All through 1962 the disagreement persisted, with Khrushchev trying and failing to force the Rumanians into line. Emphasizing the need for equal treatment and for the observance of national sovereignty, the Rumanians assumed an independent position within the communist bloc. They increased their trade with the non-communist world, and they remained neutral in the Soviet-Chinese quarrel (see p. 867). In July, 1963, the Russians gave in on the economic question, and sanctioned Rumania's continued efforts to build a steel industry, while postponing the economic integration of the bloc until 1966, by which time Rumania would be entitled to the same status as Czechoslovakia and Poland.

Though the disagreement arose in the field of economic planning, it eventually extended much farther. Soviet propaganda called for integrating the lower Danube region—which would have meant taking territory from Rumania—and denied that the Rumanians had contributed to the Allied cause in World War II. The Rumanians claimed full credit for their own "liberation from fascism," and —most important—even dared to demand the return to Rumania of the provinces of Bessarabia and northern Bukovina, annexed by the U.S.S.R. in 1940 (Chapter 18). Yugoslav-Rumanian co-operation became an important part of Rumanian policy. The signs that old-fashioned territorial nationalism still throve in Rumania raised the possibility that Hungary might one day revive against the Rumanians its old demands for Transylvania.

The "Bloc" in 1966

Rumanian "disengagement" provided certainly the most dramatic episodes in eastern Europe in the early 1960's, but it was accompanied almost everywhere else by a liberalizing trend. In Hungary a milder criminal code (1961) and a general amnesty for political prisoners (1963) preceeded acts (1963 and 1964), enabling those who had fled from the country between 1945 and 1963 to return to Hungary to visit, and to realize money on property they had had to leave behind. Increased tourism, wider trade with the West, better living conditions, even a notable success with agricultural collectivization, a new agreement with the Vatican concerning the Hungarian Church, and improved education all spoke of a combination of relaxed terror and general improvement under Premier Kadar, in 1956 a Soviet puppet but by 1966 apparently a genuinely popular figure.

In Czechoslovakia, most Stalinist of the satellites except for East Germany, the winds of change began to blow in 1963–1964, largely because of economic failure and discontent. Economic decentralization and liberalization were the first steps, despite considerable entrenched opposition. In Poland, however, which had after Gomulka's success in 1957 enjoyed more freedom of discussion and contact with the West than any other communist country, the trend was reversed. In economic planning, in agriculture, in education, in religious policies, the government tightened the strings somewhat, probably to appease hardliners within the party.

Yugoslavia, on the other hand, freed from Stalinist control five years before Stalin died, continued (in the Constitution of 1963) to give more powers of decision to local organizations of workers and producers, strengthening the judiciary, limiting the terms of office of each of the new specialized five chambers (!) of the federal assembly, and providing that the successor of Tito, (President for life but 73 years old in 1966) should serve no more than two consecutive four year terms. The Communist party (League of Yugoslav Communists) retained its hold on all branches of the national life, but life in Yugoslavia was freeer than anywhere else in the communist world. A sensational purge of the secret police in 1966, in which Aleksandar Ranković, widely regarded as Tito's most probable heir, fell from power, opened what would probably be a new period of serious further reform and of increased efforts to arrange a succession agreeable to Tito before Tito himself should actually die.

III   The U.S.S.R., China, and America in Asia

During the years between Stalin's death in 1953 and Khrushchev's denunciation of Stalin in 1956, Chinese-Soviet relations were basically amicable, and Chinese influence rose in the communist world. The Russians returned Port Arthur and Dairen to China in 1955. But when Khrushchev denounced Stalin without consulting Mao, the Chinese disapproved of the new emphasis on peaceful co-existence. They also wanted far more economic aid than the U.S.S.R. had been able or willing to provide, and especially aid in developing nuclear weapons. In 1957 Mao experimented briefly with a liberated public opinion ("let one hundred flowers bloom"), but soon returned to, and remained on, a thoroughly "leftist" and militant course at home and abroad.

Chinese intervention in eastern Europe in 1956 and 1957, though indecisive, gave them their first role in European communist affairs. They continued to denounce Tito and the Yugoslavs as "revisionists," and to try to block Khrushchev's reconciliation with them. At home, doubtful of increased Soviet aid, they embarked on forced-draft industrialization, the "great leap forward," with its backyard blast-furnaces, and its mass collectivization of the "people's communes," with disastrous results to both industry and agriculture. The Russians disapproved of their policies, and the latent disagreement between the two communist giants now began to emerge.

While the Chinese communists strove to win influence within the Communist parties of the world and to use it against the U.S.S.R., Khrushchev in 1959 told Peking that the U.S.S.R would not furnish China with atomic weapons, and launched what proved to be an unsuccessful intrigue against Mao with some dissident members of the Chinese communist leadership. The Chinese bombardment of Quemoy and Matsu (1958), the savage conquest of Tibet, and—as a result—the first invasion of Indian territory in Ladakh (September, 1959) were apparently undertaken without consultation between China and the U.S.S.R.; and the Russians publicly declared themselves to be neutral as between the Chinese and the Indians. Though the Chinese-Russian quarrel was not yet completely out in the open, and though the Chinese tactic was to avoid a complete and public rupture, western observers had already begun to take note of it, but many wondered whether it might not be a deceptive tactic of some sort.

It was not. In a series of articles ("Long Live Leninism") in April, 1960, the Chinese attacked the Russian ideological position. Khrushchev replied at a secret session of the Rumanian Party Congress (June), and withdrew all Soviet technicians from China. In November, 1960, the quarrel grew worse (privately) at the Congress of eighty-one Communist parties held in Moscow. The Chinese refused to call a halt to their efforts to take over other parties, and the Russians refused to allow the Chinese to share in the leadership of the world communist movement.

Along the way, the Chinese picked up a European satellite: Albania, smallest and poorest of the Balkan countries, with a population well under two million people, and a long historic tradition of heroism, but suffering from all forms of backwardness in a modern industrialized world. The Albanian Communist party, trained and marshaled by emissaries of Tito during World War II into a guerrilla movement, had taken power in the country after the war, and had thrown off Yugoslav domination after Tito's rebellion from Stalin in 1948. More than anything else the Albanian communists feared a renewed subjection to the Yugoslavs. When Khrushchev made his repeated efforts to conciliate Tito, the Albanians looked for a counterweight to the U.S.S.R., and found it in the Chinese. Though Khrushchev apparently tried to instigate a coup against the Albanian government, he failed, and from 1960 on, Albania belonged to the Chinese camp, and took the lead in praising Stalin's memory and denouncing Khrushchev at every turn. By the end of 1961 Khrushchev broke relations with the Albanian régime. The Chinese Foreign Minister, in Moscow, countered by defending Albania and placing a wreath on Stalin's tomb. Though to have Albania as a satellite was an economic liability, the Chinese could rejoice in having subtracted a European communist state from the Russian orbit. As Tito continued to play the role, for the Chinese, of chief traitor to the communist cause, Khrushchev's own relations with Tito grew correspondingly warmer.

In the very midst of the 1962 crisis over Soviet missiles in Cuba, the Chinese chose to attack India. At the time, it was difficult to interpret this move as anything but brutal opportunism designed to show the world that the Chinese were supreme in Asia. In retrospect it seems to have been intended as a limited operation undertaken chiefly to enable the Chinese to seize the border regions in Ladakh, including important road communications. The Chinese had long maintained that the Indian frontier in this area actually included territory that belonged to them. After smashing through the Indian defenses, the Chinese withdrew when they had what they wanted; but the U.S.S.R., though ostensibly neutral, was clearly, like the United States, pro-Indian.

By 1963, pro-Soviet delegates at communist congresses were publicly shouting down Chinese speeches. The Chinese intensified their disruptive activities within world communist bodies; built up their own organizations in Africa and Asia; and began to make threatening remarks about their boundary with the U.S.S.R. When the test-ban treaty was signed (see p. 865), the Chinese called the Russians traitors to the international communist movement. Though Khrushchev tried to arrange for a general public excommunication of the Chinese by other communist parties, he was unable to bring it off, because the Rumanian, Polish, and Italian Communist parties refused to go along, not so much because they were pro-Chinese—they were not—as because they feared the precedent: if the Soviet Union could rally the communist parties of the world to discipline the Chinese in 1963, might they not in some later year try in the same way to discipline Rumanians, Poles, or Italians? During 1964, Mao not only called for Khrushchev's removal, but accused the Russians of illegally occupying eastern European and Japanese territory. By the time of Khrushchev's fall in October, 1964, the breach between China and the U.S.S.R. seemed irreparable.

The Soviet-Chinese Quarrel: Ideology

Behind the series of incidents that revealed the mounting quarrel to the world there lay profound theoretical disagreements between the Russian and the Chinese communist leaders about the best way to impose communist control over the peoples of Africa, Asia, and Latin America. The Chinese favored direct sponsorship of local communist revolutionary movements, the Russians "peaceful" economic competition with the capitalist world for the loyalty and admiration of the emerging peoples. Khrushchev believed that undeveloped countries would be attracted by the magnitude of Soviet economic achievement, and that the Russians could then support indigenous revolutionary movements, in which the communists might at first, play a subordinate role, but could then be helped to take over. He argued that the existence of nuclear weapons and the fear of general war would inhibit the "imperialists" from resisting these efforts. The communists would win the competition without world war, while helping along local wars of national liberation—i.e., revolutions at least partly under communist control. The

Chinese refused to grant that nuclear weapons had changed war or imperialism, and regarded war as inevitable. "The bourgeoisie," they maintained, "will never step down from the stage of history of its own accord."

The disagreement, then, centered not on ends but on means. Khrushchev maintained that the U.S.S.R. would continue to support any Communist party that had decided the time was ripe for war; but he emphasized the need for correct analysis of all situations and the dangers of premature wars. He also argued that the neutralist countries were actually an asset for communism: they deprived the imperialists of support they would otherwise have had. Soviet help to their economies struck new blows at imperialism: though Nasser was no communist, Soviet aid to him in building the Aswan dam would outlast Nasser and redound to the advantage of communism by showing the Egyptian masses what it could do. Khrushchev compared the economic competition between the U.S.S.R. and the United States to an "international class struggle." The December, 1960, conference of 81 Communist parties issued a Soviet-sponsored statement recognizing the existence of "national democracies," an intermediate form of society between capitalism and socialism, a society which has already had its "anti-feudal bourgeois democratic revolution," but not yet its proletarian revolution. No state had by 1966 yet earned the classification of a national democracy, although Indonesia, Guinea, Ghana, and Mali were considered prime prospects. Castro's Cuba declined the title.

The Chinese insisted that communists alone must take charge of all revolutionary movements from the beginning, and claimed that aid to non communist countries was a delusion. They particularly objected to Soviet aid to India, their own enemy. They opposed disarmament. They had expected Khrushchev to freeze Soviet living standards at a low level and to invest the savings in helping the Chinese catch up, but of course Khrushchev preferred to let his own people enjoy some of the fruits of their own labors. Remembering their own success as a guerrilla operation that first came to control the countryside and then moved in on the cities, Chinese theoreticians extended this lesson to the whole globe, regarding Asia, Africa, and Latin America—the underdeveloped areas—as the countryside, and Europe and North America as the cities. From the massed peoples of the backward continents the communists would mount an offensive against the peoples of the developed industrial world and conquer them. How seriously even the authors of this startling theory believed what they said we cannot know.

One additional factor, seldom mentioned, but extremely important in the Chinese-Russian quarrel, was simply that of race. The Russians—though they would deny the charge—disliked and feared the Chinese, the yellow peril on their borders. The huge masses of Chinese—soon inexorably to number one billion people—crowded into territory adjacent to the vast sparsely populated regions of the U.S.S.R., to some of which they were already laying claim—would frighten any reasonable government even if the threat came from fellow whites; but since it came from yellow men, the fear increased. Despite their protestations to the contrary, the Russians were extremely race-conscious, as the experiences of many African students in Moscow testified, and they reserved for the Chinese the deepest dislike of all. The Chinese used race openly as a weapon in their efforts to win support among other Asians, Africans, and Latin Americans, lumping the Soviet Union with the United States as symbols of the evil white intention to continue dominating the world. Convinced of their own superiority to the rest of mankind, the Chinese were racists too.

Southeast Asia: Vietnam and Laos

A special problem for the Chinese, Russians, and Americans arose in Southeast Asia as the result of the revolt of the Viet Minh communist forces against France that broke out in French Indo-China with the end of World War II in 1945 (Chapter 22). During the Korean War, the United States, fearing that the Chinese communists would strike across the border into northern Indo-China, gave substantial assistance to the French, but the French did not permit any American share in political and military policy-making. In 1954, with the French defeated after the fall of their stronghold of Dienbienphu, a conference of powers at Geneva gave independence to the Indochinese provinces of Cambodia and Laos. Vietnam, the third and largest portion of the former French colony, was divided along the seventeenth parallel into a northern section with its capital at Hanoi under the government of the Communist Viet Minh party, whose leader was the veteran communist Ho Chi Minh, and a southern portion with its capital at Saigon under a nationalist leader, Ngo Dinh Diem, who was a Catholic. The Geneva agreements guaranteed free elections. The United States did not sign the agreements, but endorsed their purport, and retained the hope that the area, in which it had already invested more than four billion dollars, might not fall to the communists.

Between 1954 and 1959 Ngo Dinh Diem struggled with problems of fantastic difficulty: creating the bureaucratic machinery for a new régime, restoring order in territory that had long been held by communist guerrillas and was now held by dissident sects, providing for almost a million refugees from the communist north, resettling in the countryside millions of peasants who had fled to the cities. After the departure of the French in 1956, the Americans assumed the responsibility for assisting in the solution of these problems with financial aid and technical advice. Diem put down the dissident sects. New agencies accomplished much in dealing with the refugees, and in building new railroads, increasing rice, rubber, and electric-power production, and distributing land to 300,000 peasant families. American aid helped triple the number of trained teachers and quadruple the number of children enrolled in the schools, while drastically reducing malaria.

But Diem failed politically. He and his immediate family governed despotically and could not command widespread political support. He cancelled the scheduled elections.

In 1958 and 1959, communist-led guerrilla activity broke out again. Now known as the Viet Cong, the guerrillas set up a National Liberation Front. In September, 1960, Ho Chi Minh, no doubt convinced that Diem's economic successes had rendered South Vietnam secure except from war, endorsed the Viet Cong movement, which he was already supplying with arms and training. Using terror in the villages as a weapon, the guerrillas by 1961 were moving almost at will in South Vietnam, overrunning much of the countryside, murdering, looting, and burning.

Meanwhile, in neighboring Laos, strategically important but nationally a mere collection of unwarlike Buddhist tribes, where traditionally a small clique of families alone indulged in politics, one faction, communist-oriented, supported by Ho Chi Minh, and calling itself Pathet Lao, seized the northeastern portion of the country in 1953. The United States tried with massive financial and military aid to build a national Laotian army and establish a firm régime, but succeeded largely in creating corruption and factionalism. The head of the government, Souvanna Phouma (who was the brother-in-law of the head of the Pathet Lao), reached agreement with him in 1957 to set up a coalition government and neutralize the country, absorbing the Pathet Lao into the army. This the United States resisted, ousting Souvanna, and introducing the right-wing Phoumi Nousavan. By 1960, Souvanna was working with the Russians, and a portion of the army under the neutralist Kong Le (not a communist) was working with the Pathet Lao. Soviet airlifts of supplies to their side enhanced the possibility that the little country would be lost to the communists, and that Thailand and Burma—to say nothing of South Vietnam—would be endangered also.

President Kennedy sought for ways to neutralize Laos, and to convince the U.S.S.R. that if his efforts failed, American military intervention would follow. In April, 1961, the U.S.S.R. agreed to neutralization, but fighting in Laos itself between Soviet-backed and American-backed forces continued until mid-May, when Khrushchev apparently realized the full implications of American intentions to send marines from Okinawa to Laos. A conference at Geneva followed the cease-fire, but before an agreement was reached in July, 1962, Kennedy had to send marines to Thailand in order to stop the Pathet Lao from continuing to violate the truce. And when the decision to neutralize the country was reached—many years too late—the Pathet Lao, now a strong force armed with Russian weapons and still supported by Ho Chi Minh, withdrew from the coalition and maintained control over its own portion of the country, which bordered on South Vietnam, and included the "Ho Chi Minh trail," a road down which came supplies from Hanoi for the Viet Cong guerrillas. But a form of stability had been created in Laos itself. Souvanna and Kong Le, who had all along been neutralist, were now no longer pro-communist but anti-communist, since it now was the Pathet Lao, (and not Phoumi —who had fled the country—or the United States—which now helped Souvanna) that was keeping Laos divided and in turmoil.

Incomplete and unsatisfactory as the Laos solution was, it far surpassed any arrangement that could be reached for South Vietnam. There guerrilla warfare continued. Effective opposition required political reform as well as counter-guerrilla activity. But American efforts—including those of Vice-President Johnson—to get Ngo Dinh Diem moving politically—all failed. All that emerged was the "strategic hamlet" plan: a program to create fortified villages and "relocate" peasants in them in the hope that this would provide protection against the guerrillas and make the enemy campaigns first expensive and then impossible. More American forces arrived, and in late 1962 and early 1963 optimism rose in Washington, but was not shared by American reporters in Saigon. In May, 1963, when Diem's troops fired on a crowd of Buddhists in the city of Hue, protesting against Diem's edict that they might not display flags in honor of Buddha's birthday, riots followed, and several Buddhists soaked themselves in gasoline and set themselves afire. Though the United States tried to persuade Diem to abandon his course, in August he staged a mass arrest of Buddhists, and in November he and his brother were ousted and murdered in a coup led by dissident generals.

Between the end of 1963 and the beginning of 1966, the South Vietnamese government changed hands several times, each time by military coup. The latest and longest-lived régime, that of General Cao Ky, had more stability than its predecessors, and successfully conducted elections in September 1966. But between 1963 and 1965, the hamlet program was a failure; insurgency increased: North Vietnamese regular troops appeared in South Vietnam in support of the guerrillas; more than half a million peasant families were made refugees once more by floods and by terrorism. During 1965 and 1966, the United States stepped up the number of its troops from fewer than a single division to almost 400,000, and initiated a policy of bombing certain selected North Vietnamese installations, sparing Hanoi and other cities, but hitting transport and some industrial targets, as well as missile sites supplied by the Russians. Fleets of heavy bombers based as far away as Guam bombed the jungle refuges of the Viet Cong in South Vietnam.

Massive American intervention made it impossible for the Viet Cong to conquer the entire country, and assured the United States of certain bases along the coast; but by October, 1966, it had not induced Hanoi to negotiate the issues involved, which was what America wanted. It led to ever fiercer denunciations of the United States by Communist China, which were designed as a warning that the Chinese might intervene, as they had in Korea, something the North Vietnamese wished as little as anybody. It elicited repeated denunciations also, though in a somewhat milder key, from the U.S.S.R., pledged to support Ho Chi Minh. On this issue the communist rivals agreed, though the Russians accused the Chinese of delaying in China munitions sent from Russia to North Vietnam, in order to arouse North Vietnamese suspicions of the good faith or efficiency of their Soviet allies.

Having increased the American commitment to such a level that none could doubt his earnestness, President Johnson then began a thoroughgoing world-wide exploration of ways to bring Ho Chi Minh to the conference table. In early 1966, before such talks had begun, he was ready to assure the enemy that the United States had no long-range intention of remaining in the country, and sought no military bases there. To lend point to his overture he suspended the bombing. When this failed, he undertook many other approaches, culminating in a Conference at Manila in October, 1966, in which Asian nations participated. But while this conference sat, the enemy was still insisting that there could be no negotiations until all American troops had left the country. And the very act of offering to negotiate with the North aroused uneasiness in the South.

Much articulate public opinion in the United States itself disliked the war or professed not to understand it. Opposing public opinion urged that it be intensified and "won." Its prospective costs perhaps endangered the President's widely-hailed domestic programs. On the one hand, continued intensification ("escalation," as it was lamentably called) threatened a land-war in Asia of unprecedented difficulty and unpredictable length and severity. On the other hand, withdrawal threatened loss of the aims for which the United States had fought the Asian portion of World War II: the Chinese communists of the 1960's, like the Japanese militarists of the 1940's, would dominate the entire Asian continent in a spirit of intense hostility to the United States. In 1967, the Vietnam War presented the United States with its most grievous immediate problems.

Khrushchev's Fall:
Kosygin and Brezhnev

In mid-October, 1964, the world learned to its astonishment that Khrushchev had been removed from power, and succeeded by two members of the Presidium. L. I. Brezhnev replaced him as First Secretary of the Central Committee of the Communist party, and A. N. Kosygin as Premier (Chairman of the U.S.S.R. Council of Ministers). Both were "Khrushchev

men": Brezhnev, aged 58, a metallurgist by training, had held posts in the Ukrainian, Moldavian, and Kazakhstan Communist parties, entering the Presidium in 1957; Kosygin, aged 50, an engineer, Commissar of the Textile Industry in 1938, Premier of the Russian Republic throughout World War II, member of the Politburo from 1949 to 1952 and Minister for Light Industry, went into eclipse shortly before Stalin died and re-emerged as a member of the Presidium only in 1957. The published communiqués spoke of Khrushchev's ill health and advanced age, but it was clear that he had not acquiesced in his own removal. How had Brezhnev and Kosygin managed it? And why? And what did they stand for?

Khrushchev had grown overconfident. He made frequent trips away from Moscow, and did not practice the kind of constant vigilance over his associates that alone could have ensured him security in office. The plotters acted in his absence, and took careful steps to line up the members of the Central Committee in support of their action so that Khrushchev could not appeal to the Central Committee over the head of the Presidium as he had done in 1957 (see p. 832). It was soon clear that Khrushchev had been disgraced but not punished. He continued to live in retirement in Moscow and in his country house. No large-scale purge followed his removal, though some officials close to him personally, including his son-in-law, who was editor of one of the two official newspapers, lost their jobs.

Khrushchev was responsible for major failures, at home and abroad. Corn had refused to grow above the Arctic Circle at his bidding, the western powers remained in Berlin, and the missiles he had sneaked into Cuba he had to withdraw in the full glare of world publicity, while the Chinese were compiling an astonishing record of success in the face of his opposition. Yet he had relaxed the terror, and his rockets had greater thrust than anybody else's. Probably he might have continued in office had it not been for his personality and style of rule. He was rough, tough, and nasty, pounding the table with his shoe, not only before the world in the United Nations but no doubt with even more earthy emphasis when laying down the law to his colleagues and subordinates. The very communiqué that announced his replacement referred to his *prozhekterstvo* ("hare-brained scheming"), no doubt in reference to the virgin lands fiasco, and to "half-baked conclusions and hasty decisions and actions, divorced from reality; bragging and bluster; attraction to rule by fiat (literally 'commandism')." Caustic and crude, Khrushchev had apparently tried his former supporters too far.

Unprepared, the Communist parties of many other countries protested against the manner of the ouster. Startled, the West wondered whether perhaps a "pro-Chinese" faction had taken over the U.S.S.R. and what might happen next. But, during the first two years of the new administration, it seemed that only the boss had changed, and that bossism—now divided between two men—perhaps had been diluted. No major changes took place on the domestic scene. Foreign policy also followed the same course: there was no reconciliation with the Chinese, who continued to pose for the U.S.S.R. a problem that had come to equal in importance their confrontation with the United States.

Implacably hostile to America, the Chinese did not seem to mind having the U.S.S.R. as an enemy at the same time. By the time of Khrushchev's ouster in October, 1964, they had won the support of the North Korean and North Vietnamese Communist parties, and enjoyed a special position of strength in Indonesia and Algeria. In Europe, Albania continued as a Chinese satellite. In Africa the Chinese had established a predominant influence in the former French colony of the Congo (Brazzaville), and in the former French colony of Burundi, and took the lead in sponsoring a major rebellion in the tormented former Belgian Congo (Leopoldville) that bordered on both. In South America they had supported Castroites within the pro-Soviet Latin-American parties in the hope of starting active revolutionary movements. In the United States, Chinese propagandists won the support of some American Negroes. They had defeated India. They had exploded an atomic bomb. They were actively supporting, as were the Russians, the communist efforts in South Vietnam.

Brezhnev and Kosygin took the problem in hand. Kosygin visited North Korea and North Vietnam. The U.S.S.R. successfully countered Chinese efforts to subvert the pro-Soviet régime in Outer Mongolia. Events elsewhere also contributed notably to Chinese setbacks during 1965. A congress scheduled for Algiers, in which they had expected to condemn the Russians, had been canceled, in part because of the Algerian coup against Premier Ben Bella; the Congo revolt had been put down, and the Chinese actually expelled from Burundi. An attempted communist *coup* in Indonesia had failed after the assassination of numerous leading army officers, and the army had virtually taken power and revenged itself heavily, with the help of the Moslem population, upon the Chinese minority and upon the native communists, of whom 250,000 or more were reported killed.

The Chinese threat to renew the attack on India during the Indian-Pakistan conflict of 1965 evaporated as the United States and the U.S.S.R. tacitly co-operated in the United Nations to force a temporary cease-fire. Early in 1966, Premier Kosygin at Tashkent acted as mediator between India and Pakistan, achieving an agreement to seek a peaceful solution, and thus depriving the Chinese of a pretext for intervention, while reasserting Soviet influence in Asia. It was no accident that simultaneously Brezhnev went to Outer Mongolia and strengthened the bonds between that state and Moscow, while Alexander Shelepin, former chief of the secret police (KGB) and present member of the Presidium, visited Hanoi and reiterated past declarations of Soviet support for the North Vietnamese.

Perhaps in part as the result of successive setbacks abroad, the Chinese in 1966 began to behave at home in ways suggesting that the régime was undergoing almost unbearable tensions. Denunciations and removals of important figures at the top of the government and party were accompanied by a new wave of adulation for Chairman Mao, who—as if to disprove rumors about his ill-health—plunged

A young Red Guardsman shouts his support of "Maoism" during a demonstration in a Peking Street.

sometimes killing older people whose loyalty they professed to suspect, destroying works of art and other memorials of China's pre-communist past, and rioting against foreigners and foreign influences. It seemed possible that the Chinese leadership was trying to solve its succession-crisis while Mao was still alive, and to cow the population and the party so completely that when Mao, in his seventies, should actually die, the transfer of power to the leaders of his choice might proceed smoothly. When his government in October, 1966, successfully fired a guided missile with a nuclear warhead—the third Chinese nuclear explosion in two years—it served further notice that the political turmoil was not interfering with unbelievably rapid progress in military hardware.

The U.S.S.R. could not publicly let down the cause of the Vietnamese communist revolution and the North Vietnamese communist government. But the mood of the Chinese, and the Soviet quarrel with China, indicated that the continuation of the Vietnamese war held dangers for the Soviet Union as well as for the West. As 1966 wore on, and Foreign Minister Gromyko conferred with President Johnson, some observers thought that the Russians would be as relieved as anyone if the American efforts to negotiate the issues at stake in Vietnam should meet with success.

into the Yangtze River for refreshment, and —to believe the Chinese press—set a new world's record for a nine-mile swim. One of his military entourage, who dived in to emulate the leader, later reported that the water had acquired a heavenly new taste. Youngsters in their teens, the "Red Guards," erupted into the streets of the cities of China, beating and

IV   The Emerging Nations

The Asian and African states which thus became the arena for the competition of the western powers and the rival communist giants form part of the former colonial preserve of the West. It had taken the great imperialist nations four centuries to assemble the world-wide possessions over which they presided on the eve of World War I. It took only the two decades following World War II to liquidate the empires of Britain, France, Belgium, and the Netherlands, none of which

retained more than small outposts by the mid–1960's. By then only Portugal still held on to its major possessions overseas—Angola, on the west coast of Africa, and Mozambique, on the east coast. Though the smallest and weakest of the empire-building nations, Portugal was able to hang on largely because it was a conservative dictatorship which would not yield to the kinds of political pressures by native peoples that had often influenced the other imperial powers. The Portuguese bowed only to force, when India, for example, used its army to dislodge them from Goa in 1962.

Britain, to be sure, continued to head her Commonwealth of Nations, whose membership now included some of the new non-white nations as well as the older white-controlled dominions. Economically, the Commonwealth continued to have great significance as an association of trading partners, the nucleus of the "sterling bloc." Politically, however, the importance of the Commonwealth began to fade, in part because of the conflicting interests of its western and non-western members and in part because of the further loosening of the ties between the white dominions and the mother country. Indeed, South Africa severed its bonds with the Commonwealth in 1961 and declared itself a wholly independent republic. Australia and New Zealand, while still calling Britain "home," looked more and more to the United States as the potential defender of their security.

Altogether, then, by the 1960's it seemed old-fashioned to speak of the revolt or revolution against imperialism, as had seemed natural enough in the 1950's (see Chapter 22). With the revolt an accomplished fact, states that achieved effective independence only after 1944 now constitute about half the membership of the United Nations. It seems appropriate therefore to look to the future, not the past, and speak of the "emerging nations." We use the rubric in this chapter to cover not only the new states of the Middle East, Asia, and Africa but also the older independent states in those areas together with those in Latin America. Many of the South and Central American republics, though their independence dates back a hundred years or more, face problems not unlike those confronting the newer states on other continents. They, too, have their political life chronically punctuated by military *coups* and are still in search of stable governmental institutions. They, too, feel the pressure of a rapidly increasing population, with the consequent movement of many peasants to the squalid shantytowns of overcrowded cities. They, too, want to end their semi-colonial status of suppliers of food and raw materials to the advanced industrial powers and hope to reach the "take-off" stage of economic growth (see Chapter 12). Other common denominators will become evident in the course of this rapid survey of the emerging nations, beginning with East and Southeast Asia.

East Asia

In the Far East—East Asia and Southeast Asia, according to the more exact contemporary terminology—the headline events after 1953 were, as we have seen earlier in the chapter, the increasingly bitter war in Vietnam and the increasingly bitter rivalry between Communist China and Communist Russia. Almost equally significant was the continued recovery of Japan. The Japanese economy grew so rapidly in the late 1950's and the 1960's that experts began to predict that it would soon overtake France and West Germany and rank third among the world's industrial powers, after the U.S.A. and the U.S.S.R. Despite the strained relations between Japan and Communist China, fears that the Japanese would be unable to find adequate markets for their products proved unfounded, as sales of Japanese goods in other quarters of the world continued to mount, and as the domestic market underwent a phenomenal expansion. Signs of change and of affluence multiplied. The birth rate dropped, to become one of the lowest in the world; peasants emigrated to the cities, especially to Tokyo, which surpassed London and New York to rank as the most populous city in the world; Tokyo and Osaka, Japan's second city, were linked by a new high-speed rail line, the fastest in the world, while weekend traffic jams resulted from the rush of Tokyo residents to the beaches in the summer and the ski slopes in winter. As of the late 1960's, inflation appeared to be the main threat to Japan's continued prosperity and to her social and economic westernization.

Politically, Japanese developments were perhaps less promising. The democratic parliamentary institutions so carefully fostered by

Asia, 1967

Communist bloc nations

the American occupation forces flourished under the perennial cabinets of the essentially conservative Liberal Democratic Party. The left-wing opposition, including both socialists and communists, objected to the mutual security pact binding Japan and the United States following the official restoration of full Japanese sovereignty in 1952. The opposition staged demonstrations, which caused the last-minute cancellation of President Eisenhower's planned visit to Japan in 1960. Anti-Americanism, though not the dominant force in Japanese politics, was nurtured by resentment over the continued United States occupation of Okinawa, to the south of the main Japanese islands, by the residue of bitterness left by the defeat of 1945 and the atomic blasts over Hiroshima and Nagasaki, and by mistrust of American policy and aims in Vietnam. In addition, despite the claim of the Japanese to have the highest rate of literacy in the world, the extreme insularity of many Japanese and their ignorance of the world outside their islands combined to make Japan seem at times more nationalist and neutralist than pro-western. The cautious historian is bound to suggest that it may take more than two decades to cure the Japanese of the aggressive expansionism of the recent past or to give up their deference to traditional authority which makes it hard for them to accept the give-and-take of democracy.

The Republic of Korea, in the southern half of the former Japanese imperial possession on the Asian mainland, also attempted constitutional government in the western manner but ran into serious difficulties. Following the long and disruptive Korean War of the early 1950's, the government of Syngman Rhee, the perennial South Korean president, came under mounting criticism for its corruption and its arbitrary actions. In 1960, massive protests by students forced the 85-year-old Rhee out of office and inaugurated a hectic period of several years, marked by the political intervention of the army and then by another attempt at constitutional rule. Meantime, the political future of the Republic of Korea continued to be clouded by its ailing economy, which depended heavily on American assistance.

Southeast Asia

In Southeast Asia, too, mixed results flowed from the efforts to transplant western political institutions. The Republic of the Philippines achieved some success with a congressional-presidential régime of the American type, and the component states of the Federation of Malaysia did likewise with a constitutional monarchy fashioned on the British model. The largest state of the area, however, the Republic of Indonesia, with a population of about 100,000,000, furnished a spectacular case history of transplantation that failed.

The former Netherlands East Indies were scarcely prepared at all for eventual self-government by their former Dutch rulers —another common denominator of the difficulties facing emerging nations—for Holland was not the only imperial power to neglect the political education of its subjects. Nevertheless, the Indonesians attempted to run their government along the lines of a parliamentary democracy. Almost everything went wrong. The economy was crippled by inflation and shortages, by administrative corruption and the black market, and by the expulsion of experienced Dutch businessmen. The Moslems, who comprised the bulk of the population, were unable to form coherent, responsible political parties. The outlying islands of the archipelago, resentful of domination by the island of Java, which contained the capital (Djakarta, the former Batavia) and two-thirds of the population, rebelled against the central government. As the high expectations raised by the achievement of independence were disappointed, President Soekarno, the hero of the Indonesian struggle for independence, began to speak of the need for "guided democracy" and for the operation of indigenous rather than borrowed political institutions.

In 1959 and 1960, Soekarno suspended the ineffectual parliamentary regime and vested authority in himself and in the army and an appointive council. In practice, "guided democracy" created still more turmoil. Inflation ran wild, necessities vanished from the market, pretentious new government buildings were left unfinished for lack of funds, and all foreign enterprises were confiscated. In external policy, Indonesia pursued an increasingly hysterical course. Soekarno denounced the new Federation of Malaysia as a lackey of the western imperialists and initiated an alternating hot and cold war with Malaysia for control of the large island of Borneo, where both states had territory. When the United Nations recognized Malaysia, Soekarno withdrew Indonesia from membership early in 1965; he also told the United States "to go to hell with their aid" and provoked a series of violent anti-American demonstrations in Djakarta and other centers. Meantime, Indonesia was being propelled rapidly into the communist orbit, as it received aid from the Soviet Union and also drew closer and closer to Red China.

As we have already seen (above, p. 873), however, a *coup* planned by Indonesian communists misfired at the last moment in the autumn of 1965, and the result was a wholesale slaughter of local communists. The anti-communist forces who came to power included Moslem leaders, members of the army, and students. They appeared to resent the mounting influence of the Chinese Communists, particularly as Chinese, a people identified by the Indonesians with an often grasping minority of traders and storekeepers. Since President Soekarno still commanded a wide loyalty, especially among the people of Java, the new regime allowed him to remain in office but reduced his authority, brought some of his pro-communist associates to trial, and reversed his policies by reaching a settlement with Malaysia and rejoining the United Nations. As of early 1967, it was still problematical whether the new régime would be able to establish viable institutions in a country exceptionally hard to govern because of its geographical and political fragmentation and because of the desperate overcrowding of the island of Java, where 65,000,000 people live in an area about the same as that of New York State, with its 17,000,000.

South Asia

In South Asia—the Indian sub-continent—the building of the new nations of India and Pakistan has continued to battle against the handicaps of economic underdevelopment, population pressure, and the residues of religious hostility. In the Republic of India the democratic régime negotiated with ease two crises in leadership—when its "founding

President Soekarno (center) and his Cabinet, October, 1965.

father," Prime Minister Nehru, died suddenly in 1964, and again, early in 1966, when his successor, Shastri, fell victim to a heart attack. In both instances the new prime minister was chosen by due constitutional process; the choice in 1966 devolved upon Nehru's daughter, Mrs. Indira Gandhi. The Congress Party, long the spearhead of Hindu nationalism, continued to dominate the parliament and to provide a fairly effective rule, although its policies provoked a good deal of grumbling and occasional violent protests.

One center of political controversy was the question of language, for India contains ten major linguistic regions, each with its own distinctive tongue. Believing that a common language would be essential to a common sense of national identity, the government promoted a new national language, Hindi, to which it gave official status in 1965. It also recognized English as an associate language, though ardent nationalists deplore this "ignoble concession" to colonialism. In fact, English is indispensable both because of its modern scientific and technical vocabulary, which Hindi cannot provide, and also because it is the only common language of educated Indians, who cannot understand one another's native tongues. The elevation of Hindi to official status aroused strong opposition in some regions as an instrument of Hindu persecution of religious minorities and likewise as an instrument of the central government's hostility to regional or provincial pride in language and political home rule. The government met the problem by making some concessions to regional sensibilities, but without abandoning its aim of promoting national loyalties in every possible way. No doubt it will take a long time to forge the disparate peoples of India into a nation, as the West understands the term, but the Republic of India, in its first two decades of existence, made a notable beginning on this formidable undertaking.

Some observers believe that India's preoccupation with national political goals has created a disposition to make concessions which has weakened the government's attack on urgent economic problems by fostering compromise where bold new initiatives are required. Expert opinion also holds that India, in her planning, has put too much stress on industrial growth and invested too little in the agricultural sector. India's capacity to "take off" economically may well hinge on her ability to provide more and more of the food needed by her enormous population, which increases by about 15,000,000 annually and, at the end of 1966, was estimated to total about 500,000,000. Whenever, as frequently happens, the monsoon rains fail, India must import huge amounts of wheat from abroad, especially from the United States, to avert a famine that would cause many thousands of deaths from starvation. Paying for this wheat reduces investment in more constructive projects.

What can India do in the face of this discouraging situation? Hindu tradition does not look favorably on birth control or on measures to reduce the number of sacred cattle competing with humans for food. The government has made a modest start on the staggering task of educating the population in the benefits of contraception; as of 1966, any proposals for curbing cattle touched off storms of protest by the devout. On the other hand, western agricultural technicians believe that the low yields on much of India's crop land could be improved if the government invests more in fertilizers, promotes small local irrigation projects to supplement the showy large ones, encourages the use of modern tools and equipment, and in general convinces the Indian peasant of the desirability of changing inefficient ways of doing things.

One other major problem facing India is the question of relations with the Moslems, especially with the Islamic Republic of Pakistan. Ever since the partition of the sub-continent after World War II, sporadic outbreaks of religious persecution have taken place, especially near the line dividing overcrowded Bengal between India and East Pakistan. Deeply troubling the frontier between India and West Pakistan is the still unresolved question of Kashmir (see Chapter 22). Pakistanis have found it hard to accept permanent Indian control of Kashmir because the majority of the

Moslem refugees, driven out of India-held Kashmir during the fighting between India and Pakistan, seek shelter in refugee camps.

population is Moslem, while Indian nationalists believe that giving up Kashmir would be a deadly blow to national pride and to a lucrative income from tourists. In 1965 war seemed likely to break out over the issue until the Soviet Union invited leaders of both countries to a conference, where they agreed on a mutual withdrawal of troops from their common frontier but not to a permanent settlement. Unsolved and seemingly insoluble problems like Kashmir, where intensely felt religious or nationalist convictions are at stake, furnish yet another common denominator in the non-western world.

Pakistan itself had a full roster of domestic problems, resulting in part from the untimely death of its "founding father," Jinnah, in 1948, and in part from the division of the country into two widely separated regions, the large but arid West and the small, fertile, but over-populated East. Even more than India, Pakistan has depended on American wheat and aid to overcome the inadequacies of its own economy. The inability of the government to cope with economic problems was a major reason for the liquidation of the parliamentary régime by a coup d'état in 1958. The Army commander, Ayub Khan, took full powers, attacked administrative corruption and the black market, and instituted a program of "basic democracies" to train the population in self-government at the local level and thence gradually upward through a pyramid of advisory councils. Ayub's "basic democracies" proved more workable than Soekarno's "guided democracy" and led to the proclamation of a new constitution in 1962, which provided for a national assembly and also for a strengthened president, an office that Ayub continued to fill.

The Middle East

Despite the vagueness about the geographical limits of the Middle East, the alternative label of Southwest Asia, to match up with East, Southeast, and South Asia, has never caught on. This area also exemplifies the oscillation between democratic and authoritarian régimes and between western and indigenous political institutions. Other guideposts to follow through the jungle of Middle Eastern developments after 1953 are the continued hostility between Israel and the Arab states, the continued frustration of Arab yearnings for political togetherness, and continued world concern over Middle Eastern oil, which reached a peak during the Suez crisis of 1956.

After World War II, the Republic of Turkey, fortified against Russian designs on her eastern provinces or the Straits, settled down to work out the full consequences of the revolution launched by Atatürk in the 1920's (see Chapter 20). The Republican People's Party, the only political formation allowed in Atatürk's day, permitted the activities of an opposition, and in the election of 1950 went down to defeat at the hands of the young Democrat party. Western opinion saluted this peaceful shift of power as the coming of age of Turkish parliamentary democracy. The Democrat government of Prime Minister Menderes proceeded to promote both state and private industry, to build roads and schools, and in other ways to bring the spirit of modernization to the villages, which had been neglected in

Atatürk's day but contained three-quarters of the population. To propitiate Moslem opinion, some of Atatürk's secularist policies were moderated, religious instruction was restored in the schools, and the call to prayer sounded once more in Arabic from the minarets (sometimes on amplified tape-recordings made in Mecca).

As the 1950's wore on, Menderes' régime became increasingly arbitrary, muzzling the press, persecuting the Republican opposition both in and out of the Grand National Assembly, and restricting more and more the free conduct of elections. In May, 1960, student riots following the precedent set in South Korea a few weeks earlier, touched off a *coup* by the Turkish army, which overthrew the government, outlawed the Democrat party, and brought Menderes to trial and execution. A new constitution, in 1961, sought to avert a repetition of the experience with Menderes by strengthening the legislature and judiciary against the executive. The victory for parliamentary democracy was at best a precarious one, since the army continued to exert ultimate control, and since the new Justice party, to which followers of Menderes gravitated, soon established itself as the most popular political formation, winning a majority of the seats in the parliamentary election of 1965. Thus tensions persisted between the urban champions of secularization and westernization, represented by army leaders and by Atatürk's old Republican People's party, and the defenders of the conservative Moslem way of life in Turkish towns and villages, who tended to support the Justice party.

Meantime, low wages and the lack of employment opportunities at home were impelling tens of thousands of Turks to take jobs abroad, especially in West Germany, and the marginal quality of much Anatolian farmland, with its thin soil and scanty rainfall, promoted an even greater exodus from the villages to the towns and cities. Turkey appeared to be suffering a sharp attack of social and economic growing pains. Its hopes for achieving a quick "take off" were thwarted by the country's meager resources, by its chronic difficulty in paying for needed imports, especially oil, and by the government's slowness in fashioning an effective organization for economic planning.

The most developed and the most westernized country in the Middle East is the young State of Israel. Though without a formal constitution, it functions in practice as a multiparty parliamentary democracy on the European model. By employing compromise and tact, the Israeli government has eased, though it has not solved, the problems of absorbing large numbers of immigrants, of accommodating western ways to tradition-bound "oriental" Jews from other parts of the non-western world, and of conciliating the clashing views of orthodox Jews and secular Israelis on such issues as strict observance of the sabbath and of dietary laws. The two difficulties that Israel had scarcely begun to resolve by 1967 were its continued dependence on outside aid to subsidize its economic growth and its chronic cold war with the Arabs. Tension along Israeli frontiers reached a peak in the months before and during the Suez crisis of 1956 and mounted again in the mid–1960's, as Israel began to siphon off more water from the River Jordon for irrigation, and the Arabs retaliated by threatening to divert the Jordan tributaries rising in Syria and Lebanon; also, a militant organization of Palestinian Arab refugees stepped up its terrorist campaign in Israel, and Israel retaliated by an armed raid into the Kingdom of Jordan, which brought a censure from the United Nations late in 1966.

Israeli nervousness over Egyptian command of a possible Arab attack, the intensification of Egyptian nationalism under Nasser's leadership after the revolution of 1952 (see Chapter 22), and the determination of Britain and France to teach Nasser a forceful lesson in the old imperialist manner combined to produce the crisis over Suez in 1956. In June of that year, by prior agreement, the last British soldiers withdrew from the Suez Canal zone. In July, Nasser was told by Eisenhower's Secretary of State, John Foster Dulles, that American aid and contingent help from Britain and the United Nations would not be available to assist the building of the showpiece of Egyptian revolutionary planning—the High Dam at Aswan to impound more of the Nile's water

The Middle East, 1967

Oil Fields
Pipelines
Arab League

for irrigation. Nasser countered almost at once by announcing that the dam would be financed by the revenues received as a result of nationalizing the Suez Canal, until that moment operated by a Franco-British company. The new Egyptian management kept canal traffic moving smoothly, thus refuting western predictions that the "wogs" could never manage to operate a facility which required constant dredging and expert piloting.

In the autumn, a major international crisis resulted, made to seem still more critical because it took place at the time of the revolt in communist Hungary (pp. 853–854). Israel invaded Egyptian territory in the Sinai Peninsula, to the east of the canal, and Britain and

France began to land troops in the zone of the canal itself. As Egypt seemed to face certain defeat, the war was nipped in the bud when the Soviet Union threatened to send "volunteers" to defend Egypt, and when both the United States and a majority of United Nations members vigorously disapproved the invasion. In due course, a United Nations Emergency Force was established and moved into the troubled areas, the canal was reopened after it was cleared of sunken vessels and wrecked bridges, and the canal company accepted Egypt's offer of a financial settlement.

In 1958 Nasser pulled another surprise by proclaiming the merger of Egypt and Syria into the United Arab Republic. The two components of the U.A.R. were separated by territories of Israel, Lebanon, and Jordan; their rather unlikely union seems to have been dictated by the fear, both on Nasser's part and on that of moderate Syrian leaders, that the chronic instability of Syrian politics might precipitate a *coup* by Communists or fellow travelers. Nasser soon regretted his experiment in trying to govern the almost ungovernable Syrians, and when they revolted in 1961 announced that he could never fire on "brother Arabs" and permitted them to regain their independence as the Syrian Arab Republic. Yet after the secession, Egypt continued to style itself the U.A.R.—an ironic commentary on the difficulties of translating into action the Arabs' devotion to the ideal of Pan-Arab unity. The Arab League, a loose association of the Arabic-speaking states of the Middle East and North Africa, has often proved to be little more than a forum for expressing the conflicts of views and personalities that keep the Arab world disunited.

After the Suez crisis, Nasser continued to act the role of the leader of a "vanguard" waiting for the nation to "fall in behind in serried ranks" (see above, p. 847). Only very slowly did the Egyptians fall in, and Nasser tried one experiment after another to create a party and other institutions that would gain support for his régime at the grass roots. His economic policy has been governed by the grim struggle to support a fast-growing population (the birth-rate in Egypt is double that in the United States) in a country that is 95 per cent desert. In addition to building the High Dam, the revolutionary government undertook programs to reclaim land from the desert by exploiting underground water, and to limit the size of an individual's landholdings, so that the surplus might be redistributed to land-short peasants. To provide more jobs—and to bolster national pride—it also accelerated the pace of industrialization, often at very high cost. Following the example of the Suez Canal Company, most foreign enterprises were nationalized. As of 1966, most Egyptians seemed to accept their revolutionary government as a permanent régime, although with a good deal of grumbling over its high-handed methods and the sacrifices and shortages that its policies entailed.

Two other Arab states presently acquired revolutionary regimes—Iraq and Yemen. After World War II, the tough Iraqi politician, Nuri Sa'id, brought his country into close alignment with the West, particularly Britain, and initiated a development program of dams, oil refineries, and other public works, financed

Nasser receiving the plaudits of fellow Egyptians after announcing the nationalization of the Suez Canal, 1956.

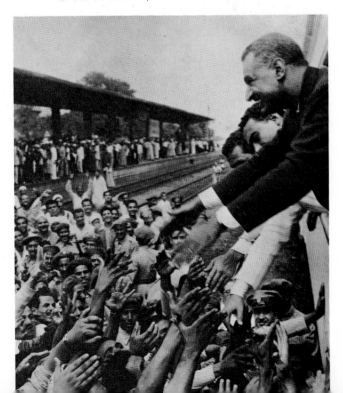

by royalties from the western-controlled Iraq Petroleum Company. Iraqi nationalists agitated against Nuri's pro-Western policies and his harsh repression of political opponents. On July 14, 1958, a conspiracy of nationalistic officers overthrew the régime, and executed both Nuri and the inoffensive young king. The revolutionary government of Iraq has had a much more hectic time than its Egyptian counterpart. Beset by the factionalism of pro-Nasser and anti-Nasser nationalists and of fellow-travelers and anti-communists, shaken by repeated *coups* and abortive *coups*, and distracted by a stubborn rebellion of the fierce non-Arab Kurdish tribes in the mountainous north, the administration did little more than tread water in the eight years following the revolution.

In remote Yemen, in the highlands of southwestern Arabia, republican rebels overthrew the very old-fashioned monarchy of the Imam in 1962. A civil war with international ramifications ensued, as Nasser sent Egyptian troops to help the republicans, and Saudi Arabia, Yemen's northern neighbor, aided forces loyal to the deposed Imam. The situation in Yemen's southern neighbor—the British colony and protectorate of Aden, from which Britain was scheduled to withdraw in 1968—apparently involved conflicting Egyptian and Saudi aspirations for an eventual sphere of influence and contributed to the failure of the cease fire arranged for Yemen in 1965.

Involved in almost all the strategic issues affecting the Middle East is the question of oil. The Middle East is the second largest oil-producing area in the world (North America is first), its reserves of petroleum are the largest, and costs of production are very low because of the immense size of individual pools and the presence of natural gas to pump the oil. The main fields are in the southeastern quadrant of the Middle East—in Iraq, in the adjacent region of southwestern Iran, and along the Persian Gulf in Saudi Arabia and Kuwait. They have been prospected and developed by European and American companies, which have not simply taken the oil, as the Spaniards took

the precious metals of the New World, but have paid for it with mounting royalty payments to the Middle Eastern states. Dissatisfaction over the amount of royalties and related issues was one of the problems accompanying the mushrooming expansion of Middle Eastern oil after World War II; it caused an acute crisis in Iran (see Chapter 22), and under the threat of possible nationalization the oil companies have granted the other Middle Eastern producing states more generous terms. A second problem was the dependence of non-communist Europe on the Middle East to supply its fast-growing demand for cheap crude. Whence the alarm of Britain and France, during the Suez crisis, over Syrian sabotage of the pipeline from Iraq to the Mediterranean and the temporary blocking of the canal to the passage of tankers. Whence also the interest of the West in alternative cheap sources of supply, especially in Libya and the Algerian Sahara, which emerged as significant competitors of the Middle East in the 1960's.

A third problem has centered on the utilization of oil revenues by the producing countries and the pressures exerted on them by their less fortunate neighbors to share their wealth. At one extreme is Saudi Arabia, where much of the income went to support conspicuous consumption on the part of the very large royal family until more moderate reforming members of the family gained the upper hand in the 1960's. At the other is Kuwait, where the ruler has used his immense wealth to make his little country a welfare state, with elaborate facilities for free education and medical care, and has also made large sums available for development projects in other Arab states. In Iran, after the fall of Mossadeq and the resumption of oil payments, the Shah and his advisers used some of the revenue to assist much-needed land reform and promote an overall economic renewal of the oil-producing province of Khuzistan on the model of the American Tennessee Valley Authority. As the Iraqi revolution of 1958 demonstrated, however, oil-financed development schemes did not necessarily insure the popularity of a government.

Africa

When the revolution against imperialism reached Africa, in the 1950's, it moved with astonishing speed. In the space of a dozen years some three dozen European colonies, protectorates, and mandates became sovereign states, a process made the more bewildering because countries with names that were barely familiar in the West took new names that were totally unfamiliar. The Gold Coast became Ghana; the French Sudan became the Republic of Mali; Tanganyika merged with Zanzibar to become Tanzania; Nyassaland became Malawi; Northern Rhodesia, Zambia; Urundi, Burundi; Basutoland, Lesotho—and so on and on. It seemed almost as if there were not enough names to go around, for the world outside had to distinguish between the Federation of Nigeria, formerly part of the British Empire, and its northern neighbor, the Republic of Niger, formerly part of the French, and also between the Democratic Republic of the Congo, the former Belgian Congo, and its neighbor, the Republic of the Congo, the former French Congo. By the close of 1966, the tradition of white domination over Negro majorities persisted only in the southern quarter of the continent—in the Portuguese territories of Angola and Mozambique, in the Republic of South Africa, and in adjacent Southern Rhodesia.

In a book like this it is impossible to list all the separate steps leading to the liberation of the African states and all the many crises that have beset their struggles to make themselves viable nations. We can, however, suggest both the causes and some of the results of a revolution that has swept over more than three-quarters of a continent. The explanation of Africa's sudden leap forward may be found in the operation of forces that we have encountered elsewhere in the non-western world. The white rulers brought with them at least a little sanitation, engineering, law and order, and economic development. Above

Sekou Touré of Guinea addresses the United Nations, October, 1960.

all, they brought the schooling which kindled in the minority of educated natives the inevitable aspirations for self-rule. Some of the future leaders of African states received their training in the West itself—Habib Bourguiba of Tunisia at the Sorbonne, Julius Nyerere of Tanzania at the University of Edinburgh, Kwame Nkrumah of Ghana at Lincoln University in Pennsylvania. The explanation may also be found in the rigors of tropical life, for only a relative handful of Europeans settled in the vast steaming areas which include most of the western half of the continent and some of the eastern. It has been easier for the colonial powers to drop their imperial reins in tropical Africa than in areas of more temperate climate, where the white man came in larger numbers, put down deeper roots, and acquired more vested interests.

A case in point is South Africa, where, beginning with the Boers' great trek of the 1830's (see Chapter 16), the Europeans began to push north from the Cape of Good Hope, establishing themselves as farmers, grazers, businessmen, and professional men, much as their contemporaries were doing in North America and in Australia. But there was one great difference. The South African whites did not push aside a relatively small group of Red Indians or Australian Blackfellows; on the contrary, they have remained a minority, dependent on the Negro Bantus for laborers on their farms and mines and for domestic servants. The consequence is that today, for every European South African, there are more than three non-Europeans—mainly Bantus but also including Asians (chiefly Indian shopkeepers) and Coloreds, the designation for those of mixed European and Negro blood. The whites, too, are divided, between the English-speaking "British" and the larger group of "Afrikaners" (the new name for the Boers), who speak a dialect of Dutch.

During World War II the Afrikaners, who often sympathized with Hitler and the Nazis, came close to preventing their country's fighting at Britain's side. In 1948, they won a national election, and ever since they have shaped South Africa's policies along lines that have produced increasing tension with Great Britain, the United Nations, and the other African states. In 1949, under Afrikaner influence, South Africa annexed the former German colony of Southwest Africa in defiance of the United Nations, which wanted South Africa to change its mandate under the League of Nations for a U.N. trusteeship. Above all, South Africa enacted increasingly stringent measures to ensure white supremacy, cutting down the rights of the Colored, and all but liquidating those of the Bantu. This was the policy called *Apartheid*, which involved a separation of the races more rigorous than that applied in the United States during the heyday of segregation. The Bantu must use separate post offices, must live where they are ordered to—in slummy "townships" outside the cities, on the poorest farmland, or in barracks near the mines, where the laborers are usually at a great distance from their families. They must not expect to advance much beyond an elementary education, and must carry passbooks to permit the police to enforce these and all other requirements of *Apartheid*.

How has it been possible for the bonds of *Apartheid* to tighten in South Africa, just as those of segregation have been loosened in the United States, and most of the rest of Africa has cast off white control? In the first place, the Afrikaners, who are mainly Calvinists, have very strong convictions that the total separation of the races is the will of God. The "British" South Africans at first often opposed very strongly the extremes of *Apartheid*, but many of them rallied to support the Afrikaners as a result of the fears aroused by the chaos in the Congo and by the uncertain future of Rhodesia. The Afrikaners met criticism from the British Commonwealth by seceding in 1961 and proclaiming the Union of South Africa an independent republic, though one that remained part of Britain's sterling bloc. At home they have silenced critics and potential opponents by censorship, internment, violent repression of demonstrations, and other acts suggesting a police state. Ultimately, the Afrikaners must rely on force, but, since they continue to rely on Bantu manpower to maintain their booming economy, the oppressed Negroes have the potential weapon of the strike at their command, if they can find a way to use it. The "if" is a very big one, for as of 1967 the Bantus were kept largely without leadership, since potential leaders were all interned.

In neighboring Rhodesia (the "Southern" was dropped when Northern Rhodesia became independent Zambia) the whites, many of them immigrants from South Africa, also seemed determined to fight on in the cause of white supremacy until some more-than-Wagnerian twilight of the gods. Though outnumbered by the Negroes by more than 10:1, they rejected the condition for independence laid down by Britain—that some step must be taken to insure the natives' participation in politics—and declared their independence unilaterally in 1965. Supplied through South Africa and Mozambique, the rebel Rhodesian régime appeared to be weathering a boycott imposed by Britain, though facing another imposed by the United Nations early in 1967. In the face of these developments at the southern end of the continent, one can understand the intensely hostile reaction of other Africans, and their determination to liquidate the last outposts of

Africa, 1967

Atlantic
Ocean

Mediterranean Sea

MOROCCO
1956

TUNISIA
1956

(Sp.)
IFNI

ALGERIA
1962

LIBYA
1951

U.A.R.
(EGYPT)
1958

SPANISH
SAHARA

Red Sea

MAURITANIA
1960

MALI
1960

NIGER
1960

CHAD
1960

SUDAN
1956

ERITREA

FRENCH
SOMALILAND

SENEGAL
1960

GAMBIA
1965

PORTUGUESE
GUINEA

GUINEA
1958

UPPER
VOLTA
1960

NIGERIA
1960

CENTRAL AFRICAN
REPUBLIC

ETHIOPIA

SOMALI
REPUBLIC
1960

SIERRA LEONE
1961

IVORY
COAST
1960

1957
GHANA

CAMEROON
1960

1960

UGANDA
1962

KENYA
1963

LIBERIA

TOGO 1960
DAHOMEY 1960

EQUATORIAL
GUINEA
(Sp.)

RÍO MUNI
(Sp.)

1960
GABON

REP. OF CONGO

THE CONGO
1960

RWANDA
1962

BURUNDI
1962

TANZANIA
1964

ZANZIBAR
(Tanzania)

CABINDA
(Ang.-Port.)

ANGOLA

ZAMBIA
1964

MALAWI
1964

MOZAMBIQUE

MALAGASAY
REPUBLIC

1960

SOUTH-WEST
AFRICA

(South Africa)

BOTSWANA

RHODESIA
1965

1966

LESOTHO
1966

SWAZILAND
(Br.)

REPUBLIC OF
SOUTH AFRICA

0   500   1000
Miles

Independent
British
French
Portuguese
Spanish

Member countries of the
British Commonwealth

Member countries of the
French Community

Dates indicate year of independence

Eritrea: united with Ethiopia in 1952

colonialism and white supremacy. This is one of the major pieces of unfinished business left by the African revolution.

For a time, in the 1950's, it looked as though the Europeans might try to hold on at all costs in two other areas. One was Algeria, where *colons* (as the settlers were called) were attracted to the pleasant regions near the Mediterranean and came to number more than a million, over ten per cent of the population. Algerian nationalists, who were not Negroes but Berbers and Arabs, had to stage a war of rebellion for eight bloody years before France gave in and granted Algeria independence in

1962. The other area was Kenya, in East Africa, lying across the Equator but with high, rolling plateaus suitable for Europeans. White settlers came and developed large farms, which used native labor, on the five million acres of Kenya reserved for white settlement. But the native tribe, the Kikuyu, living in the highland areas adjacent to the white preserve and growing in numbers, felt the pinch of land hunger and unemployment. Within the tribe a secret society was formed, the Mau Mau, which aimed at the extermination or expulsion of the whites and spread terror by murdering isolated white farmers and also the more peaceful Kikuyu.

Police disperse African women after a demonstration in Durban, South Africa, June, 1959.

The Mau Mau gained particular notoriety for the method they used to safeguard the secrecy of their operations—a solemn oath forced on reluctant tribesmen, and backed by the tribal fear of gods who would take vengeance on any backsliders and their families. After eight years of civil war (1952-1960) the British authorities finally broke the power of the Mau Mau, yet they also gave up the struggle to keep the highlands for the whites and granted Kenya independence in 1963. The whole Mau Mau experience, which had terrified westerners all over Africa, was a dramatic example of the power of pagan customs and tribal folkways.

It is a power which may be found elsewhere in the emerging nations—in the voodoo of Haiti, for example—and it is another item in the unfinished business of the African revolution. Primitive customs can assume a particularly savage aspect when they survive in a large country, populated by mutually hostile tribes, ruled after a fashion by rival political leaders, and virtually devoid of experience in self-government. The country is the former Belgian Congo, which Belgium emancipated in 1960, with no prior effort to train native administrators to take over from Europeans. The attempt to transplant into the heart of tropical

Nationalist terrorist suspects in Algerian prison compound, December, 1956.

Africa a western political structure, with parliament, president, and prime minister, at once produced a situation to which the over-worked words "anarchy" and "chaos" really do apply. The army mutinied; prominent politicians were assassinated; major provinces rebelled and for a time seceded, notably copper-rich Katanga; thousands of whites were held as hostages by rebels, and many were slain; many thousands of Congolese also died. Outside powers—Belgium, India, Ghana, Communist China, South Africa, among others—took sides in the Congolese free-for-all and actively assisted their favorites. By the mid-1960's, after prolonged assistance by the United Nations, a central government emerged which began to restore a minimum of law and order and bring mutineers and rebels under control.

Perhaps more ominous than the difficulties of the Congo were those of Nigeria, in West Africa, the most populous state on the continent (one out of every five or six Africans is a Nigerian). Endowed with diverse economic resources, carefully groomed for independence by its British overlords, and made into a federation of semi-autonomous regions to ease the tensions among its various peoples, Nigeria was widely expected to serve as a model for the smaller and less favored states of Africa. Yet it soon became doubtful whether the Nigerian Federation could survive at all because of the mounting tensions between the conservative Moslems of the inland northern region and the more aggressive peoples of the coastal regions. In 1966, attempts to end Moslem domination of the federation government precipitated the assassination of the federal prime minister, a takeover by the army, and a massacre of non-Moslems living in the Moslem northern region.

The years 1965 and 1966 were marked by political upheavals in many other young African states, with *coups* by the military occurring at an average of nearly one per month. One celebrated victim was the President of Algeria, Ahmed Ben Bella, ousted in 1965 in part because of his growing flirtation with the

A student from the Cameroon speaks at a protest meeting in Moscow against foreign interference in the Congo, November, 1964.

Chinese communists. Another was Kwame Nkrumah, the pioneer of post-war African emancipation, who had headed the government of Ghana since 1957. He had become increasingly high-handed (to put it mildly) at home, increasingly erratic in economic policy, and increasingly obsessed by schemes for a Pan African union dominated by himself. He was in China courting communist support when he learned of his ouster in 1966.

Here, then, are more matters of unfinished business for Africans. They need to find ways of engaging the loyalty of the masses, for in many states only a tiny educated elite have an allegiance to an entity transcending the tribe. They need to work out their own forms of government, not carbon copies of western models, and if the military strong man becomes the characteristic African leader, it is well to remember that historically such men have sometimes proved to be enlightened despots. The Africans also need to replace, or recall, the European experts, political, technical, and economic, who often vanished at the time of emancipation, and not only from the Congo. In the West African Republic of Guinea, for instance, the utilities ceased to function when the French withdrew abruptly in 1958 out of pique at Guinea's opting for immediate independence, and in Algeria, the precipitate departure of three-fourths of the *colons* in 1962 crippled the economy. The dismantling of empire has often proved a harsh experience.

Perhaps the most inhibiting legacy of colonialism has been the Balkanization of Africa, its division into dozens of political units, large, small, and minute. Whereas the several Balkan states of Europe before 1914 had an ethnic or religious justification for their separateness, no such rationale exists for many African entities, which are the accidental end-product of the piecemeal partitioning of the continent over the centuries by the European powers. Most experts feel that the African states must form larger entities if they are to achieve the political and economic advances they seek. A few beginnings have been made. Most of the former French colonies in Equatorial and West Africa have agreed to operate a joint airline and to co-ordinate their postal

and telecommunications services; the United Nations has a single Economic Commission for Africa, based in Ethiopia; also based in Ethiopia is the Organization of African Unity, formed in 1963 and including nearly all the African states, which had little to show, however, for its first years beyond the fact of its existence.

In 1966 one of the most moderate and successful leaders of the new Africa, President Bourguiba of Tunisia, concluded that:

African unity will be a long, hard pull. It took more than twenty years to cement the ranks of the Tunisian people. What can one expect, then, from a whole continent, as diverse, balkanized and so long subservient as Africa?*

It is very difficult, Bourguiba continued, to bring together even the three former French North African possessions of the Maghreb (Arabic for "West") — Tunisia, Algeria, and Morocco:

. . . .This region constitutes a distinct geographical bloc; we speak the same language, have the same beliefs, the same culture, and the same past. Ethnically we are homogeneous; the frontiers separating us are artificial. In spite of all this, we step gingerly. Why? Simply because we must take into account that newly independent countries are still very jealous of their sovereignty. . . .Even in purely economic matters the pace is still very slow.†

As for the rest of Africa, Bourguiba recommended:

. . . .It will be necessary for the poor countries to rid themselves of demagogues, of verbalism and the sterile conflicts engendered by power complexes or the will to dominate. Let them recognize their true problems, which are essentially domestic and, more precisely, economic.**

The achievement of a greater degree of political realism and stability may well be the essential precondition for economic growth, and thus the topmost item on Africa's agenda of unfinished business.

*Habib Bourguiba, "The Tunisian Way," *Foreign Affairs,* Vol. 44 (1966), 487.
†*Ibid.*
**Ibid.,* 488.

Latin America and the West Indies

In the Western Hemisphere, too, colonialism has left its residue of Balkanization. After World War II, Great Britain hoped to foster a federation of her separate island colonies in the West Indies as a stepping stone to their independence. But, after a brief trial demonstrated the incompatibility of the members, Britain decided to emancipate the most important islands one by one. In Latin America, the legacy of Spanish rule coupled with the geographical barriers of high mountains and tropical jungle goes far to explain its fragmentation into twenty separate republics. In the 1960's the little states of Central America, following European precedent, sought to counter the economic effects of Balkanization by joining together in a common market. A more ambitious project sponsored by the United States to help the Latin Americans to help themselves toward social and economic advance—the Alliance for Progress—has run into difficulties, because of the widely differing views on reform taken by the various Latin American régimes and also because of the wide-spread mistrust of "Yankee imperialism."

This mistrust increased because of the Dominican crisis of 1965. For thirty one years, 1930-1961, the Dominican Republic was ruled by General Trujillo, a particularly unsavory representative of the *caudillo,* the Latin military hero or dictator. After his assassination, the first freely elected government in a generation took office in Santo Domingo, but increasing tension between conservative and reforming elements led to military *coups* and finally to a civil war in 1965. Fearing that communist elements supporting the reformers might soon take over, the United States sent in troops, then tried to internationalize the intervention by appealing to the Organization of American States, the inter-American grouping for collective security formed after World War II. By a narrow margin, the OAS responded, and five of its member states, all with conservative military régimes, sent troops to join the Americans. The Dominican Republic was pacified sufficiently for constitutional

Caribbean America, 1967

elections to be held in 1966; a moderate, who had once been a lieutenant of Trujillo, became President. The oscillation between the *caudillo* and the constitutional president is a very characteristic Latin American political rhythm.

By 1966 the threat of communist penetration appeared to be subsiding not only in Santo Domingo but in many other parts of Latin America. Even in Cuba itself the dictatorship of Fidel Castro seemed to be developing more according to the usual Latin pattern of the *caudillo* and his personal following rather than along the lines of a carefully structured Marxist party and state, although Castro himself in a New Year's day speech in 1967, condemned such a trend. Castro had seized power in Havana on New Year's Day, 1959, overthrowing a particularly corrupt dictatorship after a long guerrilla struggle. Castro promised that the sweeping reforms he initiated would release the Cuban economy from its traditional—and in the eyes of patriots, humiliating—dependence on the United States and would also raise the standard of living, especially for the poor. In fact, the Cuban economy soon depended on sales of sugar to the communist world, and its productivity declined because of inept administration and because Cuban machines could not function without spare parts from the United States. After the missile crisis of 1962 (see p. 864), moreover, even the communist world seemed to weary of Castro's interminable speeches and his endless requests for assistance.

On the Latin American mainland the chief target of Castro's hopes for successful communist penetration was Venezuela, endowed with rich oil deposits but also with a very high cost of living and a social structure that permitted little of the revenues from the oil to trickle down to the average Venezuelan. In 1959, however, the last in a line of Venezuelan *caudillos* was supplanted by a constitutional President, Betancourt, who headed a moderate reforming government of civilians. Betancourt's firmness defeated a long campaign of intimidation and violence by Castro's sympathizers, who hoped to disrupt the presidential elections of 1963. In Chile, the presidential election of 1964 brought defeat to the popular Marxist candidate and victory to Eduardo Frei, a Christian Democrat committed to a program of vigorous but constitutional reform. Also in 1964, the Brazilian army turned out an erratic president, Goulart, who was unable or unwilling to check either the country's runaway inflation or the alleged penetration of its administration by pro-communists. In British Guiana, meantime, a very tense situation had developed between the two main elements in the population—the East Indians, led by the communist Cheddi Jagan, and the Negroes. The British postponed the scheduled emancipation of the colony until an effective anti-communist coalition government was in office, and in 1966 the state of Guyana joined the ranks of free nations.

Containing communism is only one element in shaping the future of Latin America; the really crucial factor is the success of other states in advancing the kind of social and political revolution begun by Mexico in the 1910's (see Chapter 22). Will Mexico's sister republics be able to equal her record in achieving a reasonably stable and democratic government, promoting a healthy economic growth, and curbing the privileges of the few, notably the landowners and the Catholic Church, for the benefit of the many? As of 1966, the answer was far from clear, and we may take as a representative sample of Latin American problems and prospects the situation in the "ABC powers"—Argentina, Brazil, and Chile.

During the eleven years after Perón's overthrow in 1955 (see Chapter 22), Argentina was still struggling to recover from the experience of his dictatorship. The economy floundered, Perónist sentiment continued strong among workers and some other groups, and on two occasions (1962 and 1966) a weak, elected government was overthrown by a military *coup*. The army régime installed in 1966 promised to purge Argentina of corruption but aroused much opposition by its pro-Catholic policies and by its repression of academic freedom. In Brazil the military régime that ousted President Goulart in 1964 seemed to dig in for a long tenure of power. It endeavored with some success to curb inflation, but it also

Caribbean Sea

PANAMA
CANAL   Cartagena

Caracas

TRINIDAD AND TOBAGO

VENEZUELA

Medellín   Orinoco R.   GUYANA   SURINAM

Bogotá   Georgetown   Paramaribo   DEVIL'S ISLAND
COLOMBIA   Cayenne

GUIANAS

ECUADOR   Quito   (1966)   (1954)   (1626)
Guayaquil   Negro R.   FRENCH GUIANA

Iquitos   Amazon R.   Belem
                          Amazon R.   Manaos   (Pará)
                                                                                    Fortaleza
                    Purus   R.   Madeira R.   Tapajos R.   Natal

PERU   B   R   A   Z   I   L   Recife
                                                                                (Pernambuco)
Callao   Cuzco
        Lima   Salvador
Arequipa   L. Titicaca   São Francisco R.   (Bahia)
              La Paz
Tacna   BOLIVIA   FEDERAL
Arica   Sucre   DISTRICT   Brasília
                                                                    Belo
                              C   Paraná R.   Horizonte
Pacific Ocean   H
                              A   São Paulo   Rio de Janeiro
        Antofagasta   C   PARAGUAY   Santos
                              O
                    G   Asunción
              Tucuman   R
                    A   N   Pôrto Alegre
                        Paraná R.   Atlantic Ocean
              Cordoba

CHILE   URUGUAY
Valparaiso   Mendoza
Santiago   Buenos Aires   Montevideo
                              Rio de la Plata
        ARGENTINA

                                                            0   500
        Colorado R.   Bahia Blanca   Miles

                                                            ⊙ Capital cities

                    FALKLAND IS.
                    (Br.)

                                                            South America, 1967

        Str. of Magellan
Punta Arenas
(Magallanes)
                CAPE HORN

strengthened the executive arm of the government at the expense of elective institutions. Brazil was one of two South American states (the other was Paraguay, a dictatorship) to send a contingent to Santo Domingo under the OAS mandate in 1965. In Chile, on the other hand, the duly elected Christian Democratic government of Eduardo Frei made good on its campaign promises by enacting a bold program of land reform, expanding oppor-

tunities for the unemployed, and in general trying to modernize and democratize a society described as composed 20 per cent of "haves" and 80 per cent of "have nots." The Latin American states, then, like their counterparts all over the world, exemplify the political uncertainties accompanying the quest of the emerging nations for the kinds of economic and social progress achieved by the western powers half a century and more ago.

V   The Free World System

It was a peculiarity of the years between 1953 and 1966 that the efforts of the nations of the free world were designed essentially to *prevent* a take-over by the communists of further territory and human beings. Accompanying and supporting this generally negative major aim, of course, were many policies and many more actions wholly positive in character: to assist in the development of the emerging nations, to strengthen and spread prosperity and contentment within the borders of the free world itself, to control the weapons of mass destruction. Yet the free world was not aggressively striving to take over territories and people already in the hands of the other side. It is hard to judge the successes of an essentially preventive policy, since these successes depend on one's worst fears *not* being realized, on Armageddon *not* happening; and who can say at any given moment that Armageddon is now beyond the bounds of possibility? Yet in 1967 one could say at least that it had not yet happened, and to this degree—a very high degree indeed—the policies of the free world had so far been successful.

NATO and the other American Alliance-Systems

To accomplish these ends, the United States had already helped to form a series of international coalitions.

The North Atlantic Treaty Organization (NATO) formed in 1949 (see Chapter 22) was the keystone. Somewhat similar treaty arrangements were formed in the Middle East, the Far East, and Latin America. Most of these arrangements survived in the mid-sixties, though all of them underwent stresses and strains. NATO in particular encountered hard sledding, since it alone was designed as a tight military force with inter-leaved staffs from various nationalities: to some degree at least a supra-national organization. Past coalitions have usually fallen apart when their members have ceased to feel immediately threatened. And the fear of Russia felt to be acute while Stalin was alive, gradually but surely diminished among Europeans after 1953. Perhaps the real marvel was not that NATO continued to have its troubles, but that nearly two decades after its foundation it continued to exist.

As the German Federal Republic formally achieved independence, the question of its future armies posed a problem for NATO. The French first proposed and then in 1954 refused to accept a plan that would have tightly integrated the new German forces in a European Defense Community (EDC). But in 1955 the West Germans became full-fledged members of NATO. Within the alliance, the Suez crisis of 1956—in which the British and French acted without informing the United States in advance—created less strain than might have been expected. But the quarrel between the Greek majority (80 per cent) and the Turkish minority (20 per cent) on the island of Cyprus severely strained the relations between Greece and Turkey, both members of NATO, especially after the island became independent of Great Britain in 1960. Its constitution made provison for representation of the Turkish minority, but the struggle over its application led to open warfare between the two peoples. The United Nations sent a force which was still present on the island in 1967.

The continuing liquidation of the British and French colonial empires, a process which American opinion and to a degree American governmental policy applauded, certainly angered many in both France and England, but in itself proved no serious challenge to NATO. Perhaps this American attitude, and the memories of American quarrels with de Gaulle during the war, sharpened official French intransigence toward the tight supranational organization of NATO. At any rate, from about 1960 on, de Gaulle, now firmly in power, began to insist that NATO be turned more and more into an old-fashioned alliance system, in which each partner had, subject to actual war needs, complete independence, with no more interleaving of staffs, no more "foreigners" commanding French soldiers and sailors. France achieved, though on a small scale, her own atomic bomb in an explosion in the Sahara desert in 1960, thus whetting the desires of other powers to join the "atomic club."

The United States and Britain, charter members of the club, sought by a variety of means to prevent the spread of atomic weapons: the chief device was the plan for the joint Multilateral (nuclear) Force in which the Germans would participate. The French rejected MLF, and in 1966 the whole problem — a grave one indeed — remained unsolved. In February, 1966, de Gaulle gave notice that at the expiration in 1969 of the treaty establishing NATO he would not renew it in its present form. By the end of 1966, NATO was planning to move its headquarters to Belgium. Despite the manifold difficulties the alliance had encountered, it was very much in being, and even de Gaulle, whatever he might say, in

fact depended for French security upon its continuance.

In the Near East, the Baghdad Pact and its successor, the Central Treaty Organization (CENTO), proved no more than a series of agreements among the United States, Britain, Turkey, Iran, and Pakistan. With the withdrawal of Iraq from the Baghdad Pact in 1959, no direct alliances linked the Arab world with the West. In the Far East, SEATO still existed (see p. 842) and the United States could count solidly on Australia and New Zealand. Despite the presence in South Korea and the Philippines of elements who disapproved of the ties with the United States, both governments helped us actively in the Vietnam war, while Thailand supplied the base for many American troops. President Johnson's trip to the area in October, 1966, helped to strengthen these ties.

The United Nations

The United Nations Organization, twenty-two years old in 1967, had already outlived the League of Nations (1919–1939). More important, the United Nations had shown possibilities of adapting to changed conditions in ways the old League never did. Yet it made little progress toward the supranational state that world-government enthusiasts aimed at. It was still no more than a league of "sovereign" states not subject to any "laws" enforceable by the agents of the United Nations. Moreover, it encountered serious opposition; it experienced financial difficulties which it could not have survived without American aid; and it probably grew too fast. Numbering 76 in 1956, its membership rose rapidly to 122 in 1966. The problem of the Chinese Nationalists' permanent seat and the exclusion of the Chinese Communists (see Chapter 22) continued to arise at every session of the Assembly.

In the old League of Nations, and almost certainly in the intention of *both* the U.S. and the U.S.S.R. in the Charter of the United Nations, a council of great powers was supposed to have sole power in important matters, such as admission of members: and in this Security Council each of the permanent members (U.S., U.S.S.R., Britain, France, Nationalist China) had a veto on all save merely procedural problems. There was a still untested provision that a permanent member of the Security Council that was party to an actual dispute being adjudicated must simply abstain from voting on that dispute. The Assembly of the U.N. in which each of the member states, big or little has one vote, played a far more important role in elections for membership than the Assembly of the old League had ever played. Moreover, the United Nations put its own military forces in the field in Israel, in Korea, in the Congo, and in Cyprus, something the old League never came close to attempting. Even though Russia and France refused to pay their assessments for the cost of the Congo operation, the organization managed to keep its head above water financially. Finally, the various social, economic, and cultural services performed by agencies of the U.N., noted earlier in Chapter 22 (see p. 822), continued to grow in scope and effectiveness. If the U.N. remained essentially a great international debating center, a place for open propaganda, it also made some real progress toward true governmental power, especially in the development of an international civil service devoted to the practical affairs of administration.

Between 1953 and 1967 the very great material progress of the free world continued apace. If we take the number 100 to represent industrial production in the year 1958, the figure for such production five years later, in 1963, is as follows:*

France	127
Italy	165
West Germany	137
United Kingdom	119
(Great Britain)	
United States	133

*Figures from the *Statistical Yearbook* of the United Nations for 1964 (New York, 1965). The high figure for Italy is to be explained partly by the comparatively low base from which her industrial production started. Similarly, the low figure for Britain is in part a reflection of her long head start in industry.

Though experience with the so-called "business cycle" made many Europeans and Americans feel that perhaps this prosperity could not last forever, nevertheless, as of 1967 we must record that in the midst of all kinds of real difficulties, from general welfare to juvenile delinquency that justifiably worried almost everyone everywhere, the "advanced" areas of the world were still enjoying material prosperity.

The United States

The year 1954, which saw Senator McCarthy condemned by his colleagues in the Senate, also saw one of those critical decisions of the Supreme Court which mark a turning point in our history. The existence of compulsory separate public schools for whites and Negroes was declared unconstitutional by a unanimous decision of the nine judges, led by Chief Justice Earl Warren of California. Notably in the District of Columbia, in Maryland, Kentucky, Missouri, and in a few districts elsewhere, steps were taken at once to implement this decision. In the rest of the South, the decision evoked serious opposition. Not even the bitterest southern opponent of desegregation talked about secession; but there was much talk about what amounted to nullification (the right claimed by South Carolina in 1832, when it declared unconstitutional the tariff acts of Congress). The majority of southerners were clearly determined to "get around" the decision somehow or other. Thirteen years after the original decision of the Supreme Court, there was at least "token" desegregation in the public schools of all fifty states. In the border states and in some of the states of the old Confederacy, and some of the big cities of the Deep South, such as Atlanta, fairly large numbers of Negro children were being taught in classes with white children. But in most of the south only a few Negro children were so taught. In both North and South, in fact more particularly in the big cities of the North, the existence of Negro "ghettos" and the deliberate policy of school committees and administrators in drawing district lines, meant that thousands of Negro schoolchildren were still segregated.

The decision of the Supreme Court on school desegregation was merely the starting point for a whole series of efforts to elevate the American Negro to the status of full citizenship, a movement known commonly as the "civil rights" movement. In this movement predominantly Negro organizations such as the National Association for the Advancement of Colored People (N.A.A.C.P.) as well as many with mixed white and Negro membership made use of the whole gamut of methods permissible in a modern western democracy, from propaganda in the various mass media to boycott, street demonstrations, "freedom marches," and pressure-group work at local, state, and federal levels.

There was indeed violence. But as such movements go, this was certainly a comparatively peaceful one, exemplified by such Negro leaders as Martin Luther King, who insisted on the "non-violent" character of their movement. By the mid-sixties some more intransigent Negro groups were angrily calling for "Black Power," and urging that the Negroes alone take control of the movement.

Pressure began with efforts to do away with "Jim Crow," the relegation of Negroes to separate and usually inferior treatment by law and custom in public accommodations of all sorts, in transportation, railroad and bus stations, airports, restaurants, hotels, golf courses, swimming pools, and churches. It is symbolic of the relative ease of changing new and modern habits and of urban as contrasted with rural ways that in general airports were the earliest and easiest to desegregate. Custom proved firmer than most Americans imagined; though the symbolism is subtler, it is a fact that churches were among the most difficult to desegregate. Even the legal changes at the heart of the movement—registration of Negro voters in particular—ran up against firm opposition. Equal employment opportunity, and its essential condition, equal educational opportunity, found hard going, and by no means solely in the South. With the passage of a fed-

eral Civil Rights Bill in 1965, the capstone of legal enactments had been placed. There remained for the future a long process of realizing in actual political and social life for Negroes the equality Jefferson held in his Declaration of Independence to be self-evident for all men.

Relatively unnoticed, another innovation took place in the structure of the American political society. The United States, regretting its experiment in "imperialism" after the Spanish-American War of 1898, had taken up a firm position in foreign policy in favor of the emancipation of dependent peoples. We ourselves freed the Philippines, which on July 4, 1946, became a sovereign state, though still clearly in the American orbit. Our relatively small Pacific island possessions we could justify on the grounds of military necessity. Alaska in 1958 and Hawaii in 1959 became full-fledged states, raising the number of states to fifty.

There remained the large and populous island of Puerto Rico, which was in fact a colonial dependency, in a singularly anomalous relation to the United States. Only a minority

Dr. Martin Luther King leads parade of civil rights marchers in Washington, D.C., August, 1965.

of its inhabitants really wanted independence on the Philippine model, because the economic advantages of free trade with and free immigration to the United States were so great for the island, which had a very high birth rate. We arrived at a compromise that probably owed something to British precedents in their Commonwealth. Puerto Rico in 1952 became an *Estado Libre Asociado,* or *Commonwealth,* with its own constitution, its own self-government, but still a part of, or "associated with," the United States. Puerto Rican emigration to the mainland raised its own problems of assimilation, notably in New York City, which had over 600,000 Puerto Ricans in 1966.

As a by-product of the presidential election of 1960, another customary barrier fell. The successful Democratic candidate, John Fitzgerald Kennedy, was the first Roman Catholic to be elected to the presidency, ending the prejudice, evident as recently as 1928 (see Chapter 20, p. 762), against a Roman Catholic in the president's office. Kennedy's presidency marked a renewed push toward the welfare state. Under his "New Frontier," plans were made, and in some cases bills were introduced in Congress, to provide hospital and medical aid for older people ("Medicare"), tax reform, civil rights, and measures against unemployment and poverty. For all his great personal charm, Kennedy had a good deal of trouble with Congress, and the actual achievement in formal legislation of most of the program of the New Frontier was the work of his Vice-President and successor, Lyndon Johnson, former Democratic leader in the Senate, and a man with rare skills in handling his fellow congressmen.

Kennedy's assassination at the hands of Lee Harvey Oswald in Dallas on November 22, 1963, shook the United States and indeed the world. The assassin was himself shot by a night-club proprietor two days later in the confusion of a public arraignment. A later inquiry headed by Chief Justice Warren concluded that Oswald was an unbalanced person, who had been involved in communist causes, but perhaps at bottom was chiefly motivated

by an insane desire to attract public attention and go down in history. Though the Warren Commission Report was later attacked by certain students both sober and sensational, it seemed unlikely that the murders involved a conspiracy of any sort.

Lyndon Johnson, who was at once sworn into office as president, made no break with Kennedy's basic policies. In 1964 he was elected president by a sweeping majority over the conservative Republican candidate Barry Goldwater, Senator from Arizona. With a comfortable Democratic majority in both houses, Johnson set about carrying out many of Kennedy's projects and others of his own, such as a national campaign to eliminate poverty and a renewed national effort to conserve our natural resources. Johnson's "Great Society" thus took its place as a democratic slogan in the long line begun with Woodrow Wilson's "New Freedom." The worsening of the international situation in 1966, however, and in particular the Vietnam war, seemed to threaten the financial underpinning of Johnson's domestic program.

The fundamental basis of American foreign policy,—containment of communist expansion—did not alter substantially under three presidents of very different personality, the Republican Dwight Eisenhower, and the Democrats John Kennedy and Lyndon Johnson. Substantially successful and substantially supported by American public opinion, many specific phases of this policy met with opposition at home and among our many allies and sympathizers in the free world. Perhaps the strongest single current in such opposition, strong among "intellectuals" here and abroad, insisted that in our opposition to communism we had in many parts of the world allowed ourselves to be maneuvered into a position of supporting the ruling classes, often a small minority of wealthy people, against all attempts to achieve a better distribution of wealth. It may well be that history will ultimately decide that this accusation was unfair. Certainly the United States sought to take firmly a position against "colonialism" and in support of the new nations of Africa and Asia in their drive to attain freedom and prosperity; and it continued to give economic aid to many of them.

Canada

A prosperous Canada, subject to occasional mild recessions and specific difficulties in world market prices for her agricultural and mineral production, changed between 1953 and 1967 for chiefly political and psychological reasons. In 1958 John Diefenbaker, a Conservative, won a close victory, ending a twenty-two year Liberal tenure of power. In 1959 a new election gave the Conservatives a landslide majority. In 1963, the Liberals returned to power, but with only 130 seats, which meant that they had to govern as the principal party in a coalition. Still another election in 1965 failed to give the Liberals a solid majority. In addition to Conservatives and Liberals there were minority parties—New Democrats, definitely to the left; Social Credit, based on some unorthodox economic ideas, not however, socialist; and a French-Canadian

variant of this last. It seemed possible that Canada was beginning to develop a splinter-party system like those of many European democracies.

One reason for this, though by no means the only one, was the rise of French-Canadian nationalist feeling in the province of Quebec and the French-speaking regions of adjoining provinces. The few thousands of French left in Canada in 1763 had multiplied by the 1960's to some seven million. Since World War II they had for the first time enjoyed a vigorous economic growth and increasingly high standards of living, after lagging for decades, in this respect, behind the rest of Canada. Their unrest was not therefore due to absolute economic deprivation, though in part it was a demand for a greater share in the Canadian managerial and financial worlds. It was also a demand for greater cultural participation in Dominion life, and especially for true bilingualism after the Swiss pattern. Many people in the rest of Canada, who long felt culturally superior to the French, resisted their demands. By 1967, the French extremists who actually proposed to secede and set up an in-

President John F. Kennedy addresses officers and civilians at NATO headquarters outside Paris, June 2, 1961.

dependent nation, were probably no more than a noisy few young people addicted to violent rejection of any kind of "establishment." A federal commission on biculturalism was set up, and Canadians were at least well alerted to the problem. Any tolerable solution they might reach would be useful for the rest of a world troubled in many regions by problems of minorities.

Western Europe

In 1957, after careful preparation, France, West Germany, Italy, Belgium, the Netherlands, Luxembourg—the six countries of the Coal and Steel Community—set up, by the Treaty of Rome, the European Economic Community (EEC), better known as the Common Market, or sometimes as just "the Six." This was the beginning of true economic union under a central administration composed of delegates from each partner nation; its administration had certain rights independent of any member government. The treaty also provided for increasing powers over trade, production, immigration, and other matters for the Common Market, according to a carefully worked-out schedule. By the 1970's, it was planned that there would be in effect one common trading and producing society, a single market free from internal tariffs, and a population of some 180 million or more, substantially equal to that of the United States and equipped with equal economic skills and experience, and with similar "mixed" economies —free enterprise under government regulation.

The decade 1956–1966 saw substantial progress toward this goal. The tourist by car or rail, who remembered pre-war travel in the six countries and the delays at frontiers, was atonished to be able to pass from one country to another almost as easily as he crossed state lines in the United States, and quite as easily as he crossed the Canadian-American frontier. Yet difficulties arose in the orderly carrying out of the schedule. In 1963, for example, France vetoed Britain's proposed entry, and insisted on specific provisions favoring French farmers in the Common Market. But the dif-

ficulty about a British part in any European supra-national arrangement was real. Many of the British regard themselves as primarily part of the Commonwealth and not as Europeans. The British set up in 1959 the European Free Trade Association, often called the "Outer Seven," with Britain, Sweden, Norway, Denmark, Austria, Switzerland, and Portugal as members. This was a much looser arrangement than the Common Market, an arrangement which allowed each member to set its own external tariffs as it wished, thus protecting British "imperial preference" in favor of Commonwealth countries.

The Council for Europe (Chapter 22, p. 826) on the whole marked time between 1953 and 1966. Yet the Council, the Common Market, the Outer Seven, and the U.N. all helped preserve the idea of supra-national grouping in Europe. There were even those who dreamed of a United States of Europe that would ultimately include Russia and her present satellites. A united Europe would not necessarily be favorable to American leadership in world politics and might indeed set itself up as definitely a rival of ours. It is perhaps a tribute to American unwillingness to look at international politics with Machiavellian eyes that, on the whole, American opinion since World War II—including the opinion of men very high in our government —generally favored movements for greater European unity.

Great Britain

During the period 1953–1967 Great Britain enjoyed virtually full employment. Her growth rate was considerably greater than in the decades between 1919 and 1939, but not equal to those of her continental neighbors. She continued as leader of the "sterling-bloc" to be a financial power in the world. An American traveler in Britain who remembered the "austerity" of the immediate postwar years was bound to be struck on his return in the 1960's by the evidence of renewed prosperity—traffic jams, new housing, modern factories, especially in the area of Greater

London, attractive window displays in the stores, even the return of "the roast beef of old England."

Yet even in purely economic terms, there was always a threat to this prosperity. The pound, a currency still used as standard along with the dollar in the "free world," was always in danger. Its exchange value, already reduced from its nineteenth-century stable equivalence to $5.00, had after 1949 been pegged at $2.80. But continued pressure on the pound in the 1960's repeatedly required help from Britain's allies in the form of rather complex financial measures to maintain this value. This weakness of the pound signaled an unfavorable "balance of trade": the British people were buying more from the rest of the world than they could sell to it.

Behind this imbalance lay a condition evident even before World War I: Britain, the first nation to industrialize, was, in part as a result of the very size of her early industrial plant, suffering from its inefficiency and its obsolescence, in comparison with that of the United States, Germany, and Japan. Observers felt that Britain's managers lacked enterprise, were unwilling to adapt new ways, or to invest sufficiently in research; and found her workers suspicious of any change in methods, regarding management as the perpetual enemy, more interested in the tea-break than in the quality of the product. Many of Britain's distinguished scientists and engineers left home to migrate to the United States, Canada, or Australia. This was what the British called the "brain drain." Finally, the loss of much of the nineteenth-century empire meant that Britain had to pay more *relatively* for the raw materials she had to import for her food and her industrial use than she did in the nineteenth century; and also, that she certainly had to face even in her old "colonies" the competition of new and more efficient industries as well as new tariff barriers. These old "colonies" now were making some of the things they had had to buy in England in the old days.

This fundamental economic difficulty, thoroughly aired in press, radio, and television, was not reflected in any threat of political instability. Certainly the Britain of the mid-1960's showed no signs of intense class or ideological warfare. The basic two-party state prevailed. The Conservatives in the general election of 1964 gave way to the Labor party, which had only a tiny majority of three in a House of Commons of 630 members. The new Prime Minister, Harold Wilson, skillfully held on until a new election in 1966, when he emerged with a greatly increased majority. Thus strengthened, he proposed in the late summer of 1966 measures to cope with the by-then menacing danger to the pound. These measures were essentially old-fashioned economic orthodoxy: a freeze of wages and prices in an effort to restore the balance between what British workmen—and managers—spent and what they produced. Put in moral rather than in economic terms, Wilson was proposing to the British that they tighten their belts, give up some of their recently acquired good things of life, and work harder for less cash return.

Wilson insisted that this renewed "austerity" would apply to everybody—managers, businessmen, upper and middle classes generally, as well as to the working classes. But his proposals threatened to split his own party down the middle, with the more radical half insisting that what he was doing was playing the capitalists' game, exploiting the poor to support the rich. At the critical Trades Union Congress of September, 1966, he won a precarious victory. The future, however, remained most uncertain. A new general election might bring in a Conservative government. But the Conservatives were no more willing than Labor to take drastic measures. The two great British parties continued not very different in fundamentals: Tories have not proposed real laissez-faire or "capitalism," and Liberals or Laborites have not proposed real "socialism," let alone totalitarian communism.

Britain, again under both Conservative and Labor party governments, remained a firm if at times somewhat critical, ally of the United States. In the difficulties encountered by NATO (see p. 894) she consistently supported American policy, though much English public opinion opposed the war in Vietnam. Anti-Americanism was a reality in many quarters in

Britain: on the left, which regarded us as too rich; on the right, which regarded us as too pushing; and among "intellectuals," who found us too immature for our power. Much of this was sheer jealousy. Prime Minister Wilson largely disregarded it, and consistently sought to play the honest broker, and to bring about a settlement at the conference table.

Thus Britain in 1967 was in real trouble. Part of that trouble was the marginal costs of preserving something of her great past as a world power; costs of relatively large armed forces; costs of her "presence east of Suez," which we very much wished her to continue; costs of an elaborate diplomatic and intelligence network; costs of a whole way of life. Perhaps the British could solve their basic problem if they accepted a small-power status somewhat like that of Sweden today; perhaps they could solve it by membership in a more united European community, or even in the existing Common Market.

West Germany

The central fact about Germany in 1967 was that there was still no Germany, but two separate Germanies. The Federal Republic of Germany (West Germany) and the German Democratic Republic had no formal diplomatic relations, neither recognizing the other as legitimate. After long years, during which East Germans attracted by better West German living conditions both material and spiritual simply crossed the border, the East German government in August, 1961, began building the "wall of infamy" between the two parts of the city (see p. 863). This wall still stood in 1967, though on special holidays, families in West Berlin were allowed to cross into East Berlin briefly to visit relatives and friends. As European tensions relaxed somewhat, West and East German teams were both entering general sports competitions, such as the World Cup in soccer, though they did not directly compete against each other. The press in West Germany and, less freely in East Germany, now at least occasionally hinted at possible improvements in relations between the two.

In West Germany, gross national product (GNP) rose from $23 billion in 1950 to $103 billion in 1964, with no serious monetary inflation. As elsewhere in the western world, this prosperity was to a large degree well spread through all classes of society. The working man in West Germany had begun to enjoy the kind of things—even a car of his own—that his opposite number in the United States had had for some time. New buildings, not by any means just replacements for those damaged by Allied air attacks, rose everywhere. Notably in the Ruhr and the Rhineland, the divided superhighways Hitler built for largely military purposes were now fearfully overcrowded, and were gradually being widened and extended.

To this economic prosperity was added an apparent political stability surprising in a society that had undergone three revolutionary changes of régime between 1918 and 1945. West Germany from 1949 to 1961 was governed federally by the moderate Christian Democrats under Konrad Adenauer (see Chapter 22) and, after he retired late in his 80's, by his successor, Ludwig Erhard. This long continuance in office was one supported by the voters, not the result of one-party totalitarian politics. West Germany seemed to be approaching two-party democratic politics, with the Christian Democrats challenged chiefly by the Social Democrats, roughly similar to the British Labor party. The Social Democrats held power in some of the states and cities of the federal union, and notably in West Berlin, whose popular mayor, Willy Brandt, ran unsuccessfully for the federal chancellorship against Erhard in 1964. A neo-Nazi minority existed in West Germany, but by 1966 it had achieved no very alarming successes at the polls, and was conspicuous largely in newspaper accounts of occasional antisemitic activities. Militant organizations of war veterans and of refugees from the "lost" eastern territories now included in Poland, the U.S.S.R., or Czechoslovakia, perhaps posed more of a possible threat to stability.

West Germany of course owed its present

position in part to the Cold War. It was allowed to re-arm early in the 1950's and to join NATO. Military conscription was introduced in 1957, and in 1967 West Germany had a relatively large and very modern army, navy, and air force. Government and people supported the armed forces as a necessity, but the old Wilhelmine and Nazi militarism did not revive among the people at large. In the autumn of 1966 a crisis arose between the military top brass and the civilian administration, in which the civilians apparently won. Access to the atom bomb was not included in this re-armament, but German public opinion apparently was not greatly exercised over this exclusion, though there were occasional ominous rumbles of discontent.

Between 1953 and 1967 the German Federal Republic maintained good relations with its hereditary foe, France, in part a product of the friendship between Adenauer and de Gaulle, both moderate conservatives, both good Catholics. Without such Franco-German cooperation, the successes of the Common Market could hardly have been achieved. In the mid-sixties a number of difficulties arose between the two. Adenauer's successor, Ehrhard — a Protestant and much disliked by Adenauer himself — got on much less well with de Gaulle than Adenauer had. Within the Common Market, difficulties arose over agricultural tariffs. Within NATO, de Gaulle's break with the closely knit military alliance confronted the West Germans with what seemed to many of them a choice between the United States and France, a choice they did not wish to make but which mere prudence dictated should be in favor of the United States. Nevertheless, Franco-German relations, diplomatic, commercial and above all, cultural, continued better than they had been for centuries.

In the late autumn of 1966 there arose in West Germany a political crisis which could perhaps indicate that her long political stability was threatened. Neither the Christian Democrats nor the Social Democrats had a secure majority in the Reichstag. Chancellor Erhard was governing in coalition with a small right-wing party, the Free Democrats, basically

non-Nazi conservatives opposed to "socialism". Mounting difficulties with some of the high command in the armed forces, diplomatic difficulties of trying to support American policies in Europe and yet not breaking entirely with France, and no doubt some underlying fears that the clear slowing down of West German economic growth in 1966 might presage a real recession, all contributed to Erhard's political difficulties. In November 1966, the Free Democrats brought his government down by refusing to support his proposals for higher taxes. But the Christian Democrats came forward with Christian Georg Kiesinger, a Catholic, who succeeded in forming a "grand coalition" with the Social Democrats. Willy Brandt became Vice-Chancellor and Foreign Minister. Though some members of both parties disapproved, and though Kiesinger's past membership in the Nazi Party aroused some alarm abroad, the new coalition, if stable, would command overwhelming popular support. It was designed to last until the next scheduled elections in 1969.

A prosperous West Germany seemed, as 1967 began, to have lived down its past as an aggressor, as a perturbing factor in the world, as a totalitarian society capable of the genocide of the 1940's (see Chapter 21). Yet the twenty-year postwar prosperity, particularly great in West Germany, might not, in spite of the optimism of many economists, prove to be depression-proof. Anything like the worldwide depression of the 1930's might well destroy the social stability on which West German democracy rests. Moreover, the separation of West from East Germany was unprecedented, yet after two decades there were no signs that a United Germany was possible. Then too, the loss of much of pre-war Germany to the Slavic powers of Poland and Russia (see Chapter 22, p. 835) was traumatic for German nationalists. If German nationalism should in the future prove anything like as strong a collective emotion as it clearly has been in the past, the unfortunate division of Germany might confront the next generation with a grave potential source of that next world war that mankind knows must not take place.

France

In France, the year 1958 saw the Fifth Republic replace the Fourth, as General de Gaulle took power in the midst of a crisis provoked largely by the revolt in Algeria. Governmental financial instability, inflation resulting from war costs in Indo-China, and a rising popular disgust with the "politicians" combined to bring about the fall of the Fourth Republic in 1958. A military and rightist *coup d'état* in Algeria, headed by General Massu, a tough veteran, took place on May 13, 1958. On May 15, de Gaulle, who must have known what was brewing, but who was in no sense part of a conspiracy, announced that he was willing to come out of retirement and take power. The army officers in revolt and their supporters wrongly assumed that he would carry out their policies for keeping Algeria French.

The change was in France itself accompanied by comparatively little violence, was confirmed by a plebiscite, and all in all looked more like a *coup d'état* than a revolution. The Constitution of 1958 substituted for *parliamentary* government of the British type, *presidential* government of something approximating the American type. The president was, after an amendment of 1962, elected for a seven-year term by direct popular vote rather than by an electoral college. An absolute majority was required, and if not achieved in a first election, was to be obtained in a run-off between the two candidates with the greatest number of votes. In the general election of 1965, de Gaulle, running for re-election, in the first round got only a plurality among four major candidates, but won in the final election against the leftist Mitterand. The president appointed the premier, who could dissolve the legislature and order new elections any time after the first year of the life of the legislature. Thus the new Constitution gave the executive more power, the legislature much less. Those who disliked the new constitution complained that it made the legislature a mere rubber stamp.

But France had still a basically democratic and not a totalitarian constitution. De Gaulle's enemies called him a dictator, and likened him to Napoleon III. Cartoonists everywhere enjoyed drawing him as Louis XIV, the *roi soleil,* with wig and silk stockings, the personification of French haughtiness and superiority. He was certainly an obstinate, opinionated man, by no means a Jeffersonian democrat; but though a general and personally authoritarian, he was no Boulanger or Pétain. He used convincingly and with conviction the vocabulary of conventional middle-class democracy. During a decade in power he never once gave even a hint of dropping that sacred word *république*; a century earlier the elected "Prince-president" Louis Napoleon had become within two years the Emperor Napoleon III.

Between 1953 and 1967 France did undergo a revolution in the daily life of the ordinary Frenchman. Once addicted to hoarding money in a sock under the mattress, he now bought cars, televisions sets, and hi-fi sets on the installment plan. Once reluctant to travel abroad, explaining that France itself had everything, he now flocked in droves to Spain, Italy, Germany, to Britain, that land of barbarous *cuisine*, and even, at bargain off-season airplane rates, to the United States. Once insistent on freshly-baked bread twice a day from the bakery around the corner, he now tentatively experimented with bread produced on a large scale, wrapped in waxed-paper, and kept—incredibly—for several days, and in a refrigerator at that. Most French intellectuals objected vainly to this "Americanization."

All this was based upon, and in turn sustained, economic growth in a thoroughly modern, large-scale industrial society. In France, the economic growth of the period was particularly striking because, unlike Britain, Germany, and the United States, it had hitherto preserved much of the older, small-scale, conservative individualistic economy. A few statistics of September 1966: growth rate, about 6 per cent annually, slightly greater than that of West Germany at the time, and well ahead of that of Britain; index of industrial production, 123, with a 1962 base of 100; consumer price level, 114 on a 1962 base of 100.* This last meant an "inflation" of a little over 3 per cent annually, which is about that of the American economy at present, a rate which many economists think is probably inevitable in a free society enjoying economic growth. The ordinary Frenchman, like the ordinary American, was having a "love affair with the automobile." It is true that relatively many more Frenchmen than Americans could not yet really express that love, but at least they could roll along on some vehicle, if only a *motovélo* (very light motorcycle) run by an internal combustion engine. One result, even in provincial cities, was a parking problem worse, if possible, than our own; another was the steadily increasing rate of fatal accidents on the roads; still another, the virtual disappearance of the peasant's horse or ox in favor of the tractor.

All these socio-economic changes in their beginnings antedated the accession of de Gaulle to power in 1958. They had their beginnings in American Marshall Plan aid in 1947, and their critical initial growth, the "take-off," came during the last years of the much maligned Fourth Republic. Yet the continuance and increase of economic growth no doubt owed much to the political stability achieved so far under the Fifth Republic. France in 1967 still enjoyed freedom of speech, of the press, of public assembly. French journalists could and did say as nasty things about their president as American journalists could and did say about ours. A best-selling phonograph record was a hilarious and most irreverent parody of de Gaulle's pontifical style of oratory. The cartoonists had great fun with his height (6' 3") and his prominent nose. The régime did control radio and television (though not the newspaper and magazine press) and monopolized these important organs of opinion between 1958 and 1965. But in the general election of 1965 it

*See the French news weekly, *L'Express,* No. 794, 5–11 September, 1966, pp. 10–11.

yielded to the pressure of public opinion, and consented to give de Gaulle's opposition candidates some time if not quite "equal time" on the air. One of the candidates, the centrist Lecanuet, proved to have the sort of TV appeal associated with J. F. Kennedy, and de Gaulle's failure to obtain an absolute majority in the first election was usually attributed to this fact.

In foreign policy de Gaulle was certainly a deeply committed French nationalist. His insistence on developing a French atomic bomb and the *force de frappe* (striking force) needed to deliver it reflected his determination to make France capable of making its own international decisions. In order to do this, he refused to sign the Test-Ban Treaty, and France continued in 1966 to test atomic weapons in the atmosphere, much to the distress of the United States, which indeed found de Gaulle's policies in general illogical, dangerous, irritating, and hard to understand. Yet it was not at all clear that he was an aggressive, romantic nationalist, intent on achieving an impossible French world leadership. He did oppose any attempt to achieve a United States of Europe, or even a closely integrated supra-national NATO; instead, he wanted what he called a *Europe des patries,* the Europe of the Fatherlands. He held that for Europe federal union was impossible, and preferred an old-fashioned "balance of power." Striking predominance of *either* American or Russian power in Europe, he argued, upset the balance of power; Russia was the danger in 1947, the United States in 1967.

De Gaulle succeeded, against his upbringing and traditions, in the task of liquidating the French colonial empire. The French, or at least the French ruling classes, believed that their colonial subjects wanted, or at least could be persuaded to want, to become real Frenchmen, the empire to become a true federal union. This feeling was strongest as regards Algeria, which was politically a part of France, organized in *départements* and represented in the legislature at Paris. But most of the Moslem nine-tenths of the Algerian population disagreed. De Gaulle had come to power in 1958 with conservative support during a series of disorders between extremists who wanted the Algerians suppressed and extremists who wanted the French to get out of Algeria at any cost. He it was who in 1962 worked out the compromises of Algerian independence, leaving France some "influence," and some rights over Saharan oil. For this "treason" the rightists never forgave him. Most of the leftists on the other hand never gave him even grudging credit for it. He remained a leader supported mostly by the moderates.

Indeed the "new France" appeared to be politically moderate. The communists on the far left were far stronger than what was left of the old rightists, who hardly any longer even claimed to be royalists. This, and not de Gaulle's claims for French "grandeur," was the striking thing about recent French history. But could this new political stability and apparent lessening of class conflict withstand a serious depression? What would happen when the aging de Gaulle died or retired? Would France revert to splinter parties, frequent cabinet changes, and *coups d'état?* These were the large unanswerable questions.

Italy

Italy's economic growth, between 1953 and 1966, was so remarkable that the Italians themselves refer to it as their *"miracolo economico."* As in France, this was achieved with some government ownership, and with much government regulation and planning. Italy was a "mixed" economy, but a free society. Milan, long a busy and active city, began to look like another Chicago. Rome had perhaps the most desperate traffic problem of any great city in the world. Membership in the Common Market, and freedom from the troubles of imperial liquidation, gave Italian enterprise opportunities it had never had before.

Politically, Italy was surprisingly stable, and that without any "strong man" like de Gaulle. Since World War II, three Christian Democrats, Alcide de Gasperi, Amintore Fan-

fani, and Aldo Moro, have somehow managed most of the time to command adequate parliamentary majorities in a multi-party state. The Italian Communist party was the strongest in the free world, and communists governed a number of important cities. But they have never attained national power. In a series of complicated negotiations in the 1960's the major political group, the Christian Democrats, in themselves a complex and by no means united group, with its own right and left, began a process the Italians called the "apertura a sinistra," the opening to the left. In this process they won over some Socialist support without altogether losing rightist support. Thus, although in the elections of 1963 the Christian Democrats had only 41 per cent of the Chamber of Deputies and 38 per cent of the popular vote (communists, 26 per cent of the Chamber, 25 per cent of the popular vote) they were able to govern by coalition with other groups without marked difficulties. A further weakening of the extreme left was achieved in 1966, when the Socialists—long split between an anti-communist wing and a wing that often collaborated with the communists—reunited as one party.

The grave problems of the "mezzogiorno," the southern part of the peninsula, and the islands of Sardinia and Sicily, were attacked by programs of investments, by providing jobs in the north or in Germany or Switzerland for the surplus workers of the south, and by old-age pensions. Italy had in the last decade made extremely effective use of one of her major assets, her natural beauty and her historic and artistic heritage. In her balance of payments, an income of about $1 billion annually from tourists brought in a useful item on the "export" side.

Among the smaller states of "free" Europe, all of which shared in the general economic prosperity, Spain—still in Franco's control almost thirty years after the Civil War—had taken major steps toward modernization and a few mild measures to relax political tyranny. In Belgium, which enjoyed great material well-being, the chronic difficulties between the French-speaking Walloons and the

Dutch-speaking Flemish continued to worsen and to threaten the stability of the country.

In 1967, a pessimist could argue that we were no nearer to a peaceful world than we were in 1946. Yet even a pessimist would have to admit that the United States, most of Europe, the former British self-governing colonies, Japan, and the Soviet Union have had plenty if not peace; that Asia, Africa, and Latin America have gained—if unevenly—in material wealth; and even that the civil wars, guerrilla wars, revolutions, and other disturbances of our day were in no way comparable to the holocausts of World War I and World War II. As the simple confrontation of the late 1940's between the American coalition and the Soviet coalition grew more complicated and more dispersed, and as Communist China rose in power and menace, the Russians lost some of their earlier fervor to make the formerly colonial world communist immediately and by force, and the sharpest edges of the tensions between the two super-powers, the United States and the Soviet Union, seemed to grow duller. Though the mid-sixties could rightly be regarded as a "Time of Troubles," the worst was not happening: the world continued to exist, to progress rapidly in material terms, and to grow in population. Here indeed, perhaps, lay the best excuse for pessimism: in the likelihood that mankind was breeding faster than its food supplies could be increased, despite the miracles in agricultural science, and the possibilities of exploiting the food supplies till hidden in the ocean depths. Compared with this threat, the continued lack of concord in international politics seemed almost bearable.

Reading Suggestions for the Contemporary World since 1953

(Asterisk indicates paperbound edition.)

Note: For the most recent materials in this chapter, the only sources are current newspapers and periodicals, both domestic and foreign.

General

Arthur M. Schlesinger, Jr., *A Thousand Days, John F. Kennedy in the White House* (Houghton, Mifflin, 1965), and Theodore C. Sorensen, *Kennedy* (Harper & Row, 1965). Extraordinarily full accounts of American foreign relations during the Kennedy era by close confidants of the President.

Dwight D. Eisenhower, *The White House Years,* 2 vols. (Doubleday, 1963–1965). Former President Eisenhower's account of his years in office, 1952–1960.

D. Donnelly, *Struggle for the World: The Cold War, 1917–1965* (St. Martin's Press, 1965. Good general account.

C. Quigley, *Tragedy and Hope: A History of the World in Our Time* (Macmillan, 1966). A long, thoughtful attempt to understand what we can learn from recent history.

U.S.S.R.

Leonard Schapiro, *The Government and Politics of the Soviet Union* (Hutchinson, 1965). Excellent short treatment by a leading authority.

Alfred G. Meyer, *The Soviet Political System. An Interpretation* (Random House, 1965). Sound recent study by a political scientist.

Randolph L. Braham, ed., *Soviet Politics and Government: A Reader* (*Knopf). Useful collection of source materials and scholarly short studies.

Donald S. Zagoria, *The Sino-Soviet Conflict, 1956–1961* (Atheneum, 1964), and William E. Griffith, *Albania and the Sino-Soviet Rift* (M.I.T. Press, 1963), and his *The Sino-Soviet Rift, Analysed and Documented* (M.I.T. Press, 1964). Three useful studies on the quarrel between the U.S.S.R. and China.

Zbigniew K. Brzezinski, *The Soviet Bloc: Unity and Conflict* (Harvard Univ. Press, 1960). A solid study by a leading political scientist.

Emerging Nations

Note: the following are all supplemental to those cited for the Revolution against Imperialism (p. 850).

V. M. Dean and H. Harootunian, *West and Non-West: New Perspectives* (*Holt). An anthology covering many aspects of the relations between the developed and the emerging nations.

E. Demig, *Modern Japan* (Praeger, 1961). Helpful general view; in the series, "Nations of the Modern world."

P. Langer, *Japan Yesterday & Today* (*Holt). Popular introduction; in the series, "Contemporary Civilizations."

K. S. Latourette, *China;* O. D. Corpuz, *The Philippines;* J. D. Legge, *Indonesia;* S. Wolpert, *India.* Informative volumes in the series, "Modern Nations in Historical Perspective" (*Spectrum).

D. N. Wilber, *Pakistan Yesterday & Today* (*Holt). Excellent popular introduction; in the "Contemporary Civilizations" series.

H. Tinker, *India & Pakistan* (*Praeger). Useful political analysis.

G. Lewis, *Turkey,* 3rd ed. (Praeger, 1965). Competent general introduction; in the series, "Nations of the Modern World."

P. Stirling, *Turkish Village* (*Wiley). Valuable insights into an essential aspect of emerging societies.

N. Safran, *The United States & Israel* (Harvard Univ. Press, 1963); W. R. Polk, *The United States & the Arab World* (Harvard Univ. Press, 1965). Detailed volumes, stressing the background of the Middle Eastern nations; in the series, "American Foreign Policy Library."

H. B. Sharabi, *Nationalism and Revolution in the Arab World* (*Van Nostrand). Valuable reflections by an expert on the subject.

J. Hatch, *A History of Postwar Africa* (Praeger, 1965). Clear and helpful guide to a complex subject.

B. Ward, *Africa in the Making* (Norton, 1966). Discussion by a well-informed publicist.

G. M. Carter, *National Unity and Regionalism in Eight African States* (Cornell Univ. Press, 1966), and G. M. Carter, ed., *Politics in Africa: Seven Cases* (*Harcourt, Brace & World). Two recent works by a ranking expert on Africa.

J. Cope, *South Africa* (Praeger, 1965). General survey; in the series, "Nations of the Modern World."

J. F. Gallagher, *The United States and North Africa* (Harvard Univ., 1963). Valuable introduction to Morocco, Algeria, and Tunisia.

J. E. Flint, *Nigeria and Ghana* (*Spectrum). Study of two states that have made more than their share of recent history; in the series, "Modern Nations in Historical Perspective."

R. J. Alexander, *Today's Latin America* (*Anchor), and T. Szulc, *Latin America* (*Atheneum). Suggestive general introductions.

M. Rodriguez, *Central America A Divided Land:* (*Spectrum, 1965); J. E. Fagg, *Cuba, Haiti and the Dominican Republic* (*Spectrum, 965).

H. Bernstein, *Venezuela & Colombia.* Handy volumes in the series, "Modern Nations in Historical Perspective" (*Spectrum).

K. Silvert, *Chile Yesterday & Today* (*Holt). In the informative popular series, "Contemporary Civilizations."

Western Democracies

S. R. Graubard, ed., *A New Europe?* (Houghton Mifflin, 1964). Essays, mostly analytical, by various hands. Stimulating.

S. Kuznets, *Postwar Economic Growth* (Harvard Univ. Prss, 1964). An important synthesis of a major topic, by a distinguished economist.

T. H. White, *The Making of the President, 1960* (*Pocket Books), and *The Making of the President, 1964* (Atheneum, 1965). Two most readable books illuminating many phases of our recent history.

D. E. Butler and A. King, *The British General Election of 1964* (St. Martin's Press, 1965). Fine example of current political scientific studies.

J. Lacouture, *De Gaulle* (*New American Library, 1966). The best short life, somewhat too allusive for American consumption.

S. Hoffmann and others, *In Search of France* (Harvard Univ. Press, 1963). Fine analytical studies of various phases of contemporary France.

L. Wylie, *Village in the Vaucluse* (*Harper Colophon), and L. Wylie, ed., *Chanzeaux* (Harvard Univ. Press, 1966). Two complementary studies of French villages today, based on field work.

M. Salvadori, *Italy* (*Spectrum). A valuable final chapter on contemporary Italy.

A. Grosser, *The Federal Republic of Germany,* (Praeger, 1964; *Praeger). Best short account.

Germany Reports, 4th ed., (Press and Information Office, West Germany, 1966). A mine of information, to be used with knowledge; it is an official government publication.

Bernard B. Fall, *The Two Viet-Nams: a Political and Military Analysis,* rev. ed. (Praeger, 1965), and Robert Shaplen, *The Lost Revolution; the U.S. in Vietnam, 1946–1966,* rev. ed. (Harper & Row, 1966). Two interesting studies of the Vietnam war.

Fiction

Note: The following books are all discussed in the text.

Ilya Ehrenburg, *The Thaw,* trans. Manya Harari (Harvil, 1955).

V. Dudintsev, *Not by Bread Alone,* trans. E. Bone (Dutton, 1957).

B. Pasternak, *Dr. Zhivago,* trans. Max Hayward and Manya Harari (Pantheon, 1958; *Signet).

Michael Sholokhov, *And Quiet Flows the Don,* trans., S. Garry (L. Putnam, 1953; *Vintage, 1966), *The Don Flows Home to the Sea,* trans. S. Garry (*Vintage, 1966), and *Harvest on the Don* (*Signet).

A. I. Solzhenitsyn, *A Day in the Life of Ivan Denisovitch,* trans., Max Hayward and R. Hingley (Praeger, 1963; *Bantam, 1963).

Abram Tertz, pseud., *The Makepeace Experiment,* trans., Manya Harari (Pantheon, 1965); and, in one volume, his *Socialist Realism,* trans., G. Dennis, and *The Trial Begins,* trans. Max Hayward (*Vintage, 1965).

Yevgeny Yevtushenko, *A Precocious Autobiography,* trans., A. R. MacAndrew (*Dutton, 1963), and his *Selected Poetry,* trans. Robin Milner-Gulland and Peter Levi (*Penguin, 1962).

24

Man's Fate

in the Twentieth Century

I The Intellectual Revolution Continues

The old truism about the difficulty of seeing the whole forest when attention is fixed on the separate trees holds especially for contemporary intellectual history. Among the countless "ideas" that come to our attention through the printed or the spoken word, through symbols, diagrams, pictures, even through musical sounds, it is almost impossible to distinguish those ideas which are characteristic of our age, which give it its flavor or style, which establish its "climate of opinion." Indeed, it is tempting to conclude that this very *variety* of ideas, spread abroad among countless millions through all the channels of mass communications, is the distinguishing mark of our time. There is, moreover, a further difficulty confronting the historian of contemporary thought and feeling. As we shall note later in this chapter, the gap between the culture of the few, the "highbrows," and the culture of the many, who are not necessarily "lowbrows," just not highbrows — this gap seems nowadays especially wide and deep. The historian who relied wholly on evidence from the work of "serious" modern poets or artists would come to quite different conclusions from one who rested on evidence from "comic" strips, popular music, conventional artists and illustrators, and what goes out over the air on television and radio.

Yet a historian writing in the twenty-first century and using only the evidence from "popular" culture would see and sense great differences from the popular culture of Victorian days. Our hot jazz would not sound to him much like a Viennese waltz, the violent and sexy "whodunits" would not be to him much like the Sherlock Holmes stories, the picture magazines would not remind him of Currier and Ives prints, and even in the so-called comic strips the frustrations, the inferiority complexes, and pathetic illusions, even the horrors that fill many strips would seem worlds apart from the naive buffoonery of the first such strips of about 1900, "Happy Hooligan," for instance, or "Buster Brown," or the "Yellow Kid."

Nor were such a twenty-first-century historian to concentrate on the high culture would he be any less struck with the great changes since 1890, perhaps in fact he would be more struck with the changes. It is true that he would readily see in the *avant garde* writers and artists and in the "anti-intellectual" philosophers of the late nineteenth century (see Chapter 15) precursors of twentieth-century philosophical and artistic movements. Yet he would surely be struck by the way the twentieth century has gone beyond its precursors. He would not confuse contemporary abstractionists with Monet or Cézanne, nor atonal music, let alone "concrete" music, with the music of Brahms, nor James Joyce's *Ulysses,* let alone some modern French "anti-novels," with the novels of Henry James or even Sinclair Lewis.

We shall slowly return to some of these specific representatives of contemporary high culture. Here let us note that our hypothetical twenty-first century historian, though he would have to note the differences between the highbrow and the popular culture of our time, would not conclude that they were wholly separate and wholly different cultures. He would see that they have much in common, that both have strong elements of contrast with the culture of the nineteenth century. We cannot of course begin to guess how he would feel toward us and our culture, nor with what terms he would try and tell his readers about us. But he would surely have to call attention to the notes of violence and despair, the unprecedented frankness with which the Anglo-Saxon four-letter words are printed as well as uttered, the repudiation of conventional representational art, the preoccupation with such psychological difficulties as are indicated by "alienation," "identity-crisis," "committment," the great premium set upon originality, novelty, youth against age, the rise of a popular slick urban cynicism, the doubts about even so ingrained a belief, in the United States at least, as the belief in inevitable progress with a capital P. We shall in conclusion consider how far all this is in fact a repudiation of, a resistance to, our democratic inheritance from the eighteenth-century Enlightenment. Meanwhile, we must essay some more specific analysis of the attitudes, the tastes, the "ideas" of our confused and confusing age. We shall not attempt a detailed "coverage," but rather attempt by concentrating on representative figures to illustrate the characteristics of our "high" culture and how it differs from that of the nineteenth century.

Psychology: Freud

Following leads from the biological sciences, the nineteenth century came to put particular emphasis on *process,* on the dynamics of change in time. The twentieth century, taking its cue from psychology, has come to put particular emphasis on the role of the unconscious in human thought and action, on the irrationality — or at least non-rationality — of much human behavior. Foremost among the

Freud, as interpreted by Cocteau, the French surrealist.

thinkers responsible for this emphasis was Sigmund Freud (1856–1939). Freud was a physician, trained in Vienna in the rationalist medical tradition of the late nineteenth century. His interest was early drawn to mental illness, where he soon found cases in which patients exhibited symptoms of very real organic disturbances, but for which no obvious organic causes could be found. Under analysis, as Freud's therapeutic treatment came to be called, the patient, relaxed on a couch, is urged to pour out what he can remember of his earliest childhood, or indeed infancy. After many such treatments the analyst can hope to find what is disturbing the patient, and by making him aware of what that is, hope to help him.

Had Freud merely contented himself with this kind of therapy, few of us would have heard of him. But from all this clinical expe-

rience he worked out a system of psychology that has had a very great influence, not only on psychiatry and psychology, but on some of our basic conceptions of human relations. Freud starts with the concept of a set of "drives" with which each person is born. These drives, which arise in the unconscious, are expressions of the "id." Freud never tried to locate the id physiologically; he used the term, which in Latin means "this [thing]," to avoid the moralistic overtones in words like "desires." These drives try to get satisfaction and pleasure, to express themselves in action. The infant, notably, is "uninhibited"—that is, his drives well up into action from the id without restraint from his conscious mind. But by no means without restraint from his parents or nurse—and there's the difficulty. The infant finds himself frustrated. As he grows, as his mind is formed, he comes to be conscious of the fact that some of the things he wants to do are objectionable to those closest to him, and on whom he is so dependent. He himself therefore begins to repress these drives from his id.

With his dawning consciousness of the world outside himself, the child has in fact developed another part of his psyche, which Freud at first called the "censor," and later divided into two phases which he called the "ego" and the "superego." The ego is the individual's private censor, his awareness that in accordance with what Freudians call the "reality principle" certain drives from his id simply cannot succeed. The superego in a way is what common language calls "conscience"; it is the individual's response as part of a social system in which certain actions are proper and certain actions improper. Now these drives of the id, and indeed in most of its phases the dictates of the superego, are for Freud a sort of great reservoir of which the individual is not normally aware—that is, they are part of his "unconscious." In a mentally healthy individual, enough of the drives of the id succeed so that he feels contented. But even the healthiest of individuals has had to repress a great deal of his drives from the id. This successful repression the Freudians account for in part at least by a process they call "sublimation." They think that the healthy individual somehow finds for a drive suppressed by ego or superego, or by both working together, a new and socially approved outlet or expression. Thus a drive toward sexual relations not approved in one's circle might be sublimated into the writing of poetry or music or even into athletics.

With the neurotic person, however, Freud held that drives, having been suppressed, driven back down into the unconscious, find no suitable other outlet or sublimation, and continue, so to speak, festering in the id, trying to find some outlet. They find all sorts of outlets of an abnormal sort, symptoms of illness in great variety. They display themselves in all sorts of neuroses and phobias, which have in common a failure to conform to the "reality principle." The neurotic individual is "maladjusted." And if the failure to meet the reality principle is really complete, the individual is insane, "psychotic," and lives in an utterly unreal private world of his own.

Freud's therapy rested on the belief that if the individual neurotic could come to understand why he behaved as he did he could frequently make a proper adjustment and lead a normal life. But here Freud parted company with the rationalist tradition of the eighteenth century. He held that there was no use preaching at the individual, reasoning simply with him, telling him the error of his ways, pointing out what was unreasonable in his behavior. Reason could not get directly at the unconscious, where the source of his trouble lay. Only by the long slow process of psychoanalysis, in which the individual day after day sought in memories of his earliest childhood for concrete details, could the listening analyst pick from this stream of consciousness the significant details that pointed to the hidden repression, the "blocking" that came out in neurotic behavior. Freud gave special importance to the dreams of the patient, which he must patiently describe to the analyst; for in dreams, Freud thought, the unconscious wells up out of control, or but partly controlled, by the ego. Once the patient, however, got beneath the surface of his conscious life, and became aware of what had gone wrong

with his hitherto unconscious life, he might then adjust himself to society.

The Implications of Freudianism

What is important for us in the wider implications of Freud's work, his part in the broad current of contemporary modifications of eighteenth-century rationalism, is first this concept of the very great role of the unconscious drives—that is, the unthinking, the non-rational, in our lives. Ordinary reflective thinking is for the Freudian a very small part of our existence. We are back at the metaphor of reason as a flickering candle, or to use another well-worn metaphor, of reason as simply the small part of the iceberg that shows above the water, while submerged down below is the great mass of the unconscious. Much even of our conscious thinking is, according to the Freudian, what psychologists call "rationalization," thinking dictated, not by an awareness of the reality principle, but by the desires of our id. One can get a good measure of the difference between eighteenth-century rationalism and Freudian psychology by contrasting the older belief in the innocence and natural goodness of the child, Wordsworth's "mighty prophet, seer blest," with the Freudian view of the child as a bundle of unsocial or antisocial drives, as in fact a little untamed savage.

But second, and most important, note that the Freudians do not wish to blow out the candle of human reason. They are moderate, not extreme, anti-rationalists; they are chastened rationalists. Their whole therapy is based on the concept, which has Christian as well as eighteenth-century roots, that "ye shall know the truth, and the truth shall make you free." Only, for the Freudian, truth is not easily found, cannot be distilled into a few simple rules of conduct which all men, being reasonable and good, can use as guides to individual and collective happiness. It is on the contrary very hard to establish, and can be reached only by a long and precarious struggle. Many will not reach it, and will have to put up with all sorts of maladjustments and frustrations. The Freudian is at bottom a pessimist, in that he does not believe in the perfectibility of man. Indeed, there are those who see in the Freudian concept of human nature something like a return to the Christian concept of original sin. They continue the parallel, which many others find absurd or offensive, by maintaining that for the Freudian too there is, though difficult to find, a way out, a form of salvation, in the full self-knowledge that comes from successful psychoanalysis.

Freud, to whom religion was an "illusion," was himself a cult-leader. His faithful disciples still form an orthodox nucleus of strict Freudian psychoanalysts. Other disciples parted with the master, notably the Swiss Jung (1875–1961) who did believe in religion, and whose great popular phrase was the "collective unconscious," and the Austrian Adler (1870–1937) who rejected the master's emphasis on the sexual, and coined the familiar phrase, "inferiority complex."

Full psychoanalysis remains an extremely expensive process limited to those who can afford it or can receive it through charity. There are, however, modified forms of analytical therapy, such as "group therapy" and the like, which are much less expensive. The Freudian influence on imaginative writing, indeed on philosophy and the arts generally, was and remains very great indeed, though usually dispersed, vague, indirect, and very hard to summarize. Negatively, the life work of this nineteenth-century-trained scientist went in these "humanistic" fields to reinforce the reaction against nineteenth-century scientific and rationalistic materialism; positively, Freud's work helped all sorts of modernisms, strengthened the revival of intuition, "hunch," sensibility, and, perhaps paradoxically, a Stoic or existentialist rejection of bourgeois optimism.

Psychology: Behaviorism

It need hardly be said that in this multanimous century of ours the Freudians hold no monopoly of the field of psychology. Indeed, the eighteenth-century tendency to regard human nature, if not as wholly rational, at

Pavlov watching an experiment with a dog.

least as wholly malleable by those who could manipulate the human and non-human environment, still had representatives in the mid-twentieth century. Yet at least one of these "behaviorist" tendencies in psychology had its own flareback to reinforce pessimism over the possibilities of immediate reform of the human condition. The Russian psychologist Pavlov (1849–1936), Nobel prize-winner in 1904, has given us the now familiar term "conditioned reflex." Pavlov's laboratory dogs, after being fed at a given signal, came to water at the mouth at this signal, though no food was within sight or smell. The "natural"—that is, inborn—response of watering at the mouth would ordinarily come only when the dog's senses showed him actual food; Pavlov got the same response artificially by a signal that certainly did not smell or look like food to the dog. The upshot was clear evidence that training or conditioning can produce automatic responses in the animal that are essentially similar to the kind of automatic responses the animal is born with.

Pavlov's experiments had important implications for the social scientist. They confirmed eighteenth-century notions about the power of environment, of training and education, in the sense that environment can be manipulated to produce specific responses from organisms.

915

But—and this is a bitter blow to eighteenth-century optimism—they suggested that once such training has taken hold, the organism has, so to speak, incorporated the results almost as if they had been the product of heredity, not environment, and further change becomes very difficult, in some instances impossible. Pavlov, after having trained some of his dogs, tried mixing his signals, frustrating and confusing the dogs by withholding food at the signal that had always produced food for them. He succeeded in producing symptoms of a kind close to what in human beings would be neurosis.

Still another lead, this time from biologists interested not in the most fashionable "microbiology" but rather in the behavior of individuals (the old-fashioned name for it was natural history), came from such scientists as the Austrian Konrad Lorenz (1903–   ) and the Dutchman Nikolaas Tinbergen (1907–   ), founders of what is called "ethology." Their key phrase is "species-specific behavior." This behavior does indeed depend on hereditary constitutional features of the organism, but especially at key moments when development of the organism must be triggered by specific normal features of the environment. Thus, for instance, newly hatched goslings normally see first and attach themselves to the mother goose; but if she is removed before they hatch, they will attach themselves to a foster mother, even to a human being. Modern ethology thus *reinforces* the notion that neither heredity nor environment alone "determine" behavior, including human behavior, but rather a complex and subtle interaction of the two. There is room for accident, and even for "will," if not quite free will.

Socio-political Thought

We have in the foregoing already edged over naturally enough from psychology to the wider field of man's behavior as a political animal. In what are sometimes optimistically called the social or behavioral sciences, the twentieth century has continued to develop the critique of our eighteenth-century inheri-

tance of belief in the basic reasonableness and goodness of "human nature." In fact, the very term "human nature" seems to some social scientists to be so all-embracing as to make no sense. Once more, let us re-emphasize, first, that this "revolt against reason" is better and more fully to be described as a revolt against reason as exemplified in popular concepts of what science is and does. Second, that many thinkers in this revolt did not attack scientific reason as such in its own fields of established sciences, but simply urged that there are other valuable ways of using the human mind. And third, that though many of these thinkers were anti-rationalists, and almost always "élitists," fascists, racists, reactionaries hostile to the democratic tradition, others were what we have called "chastened rationalists," thinkers who wished to salvage what they could of the eighteenth-century basis of the democratic tradition (see Chapter 15).

The specific programs, the emotional allegiances, the "values" of twentieth-century thinkers in this broad field we may hesitantly call "sociological" were varied indeed. And yet most of them, certainly the great ones, do have in common a sense of the subtlety, the complexities, the delicacy—and the toughness and durability—of the ties that bind human beings together—and hold them apart—in society. Indeed, that last sentence of ours, with its coupling of opposites in tension, is typical of this twentieth-century approach to problems of man in society; compare an incidental and therefore significant remark tossed off by Arthur Koestler, "for we are moving here through strata that are held together by the cement of contradiction."* Or, as the Swiss writer Denis de Rougemont puts the same kind of challenge to our conventional notions of what makes sense, tensions between two terms that are *"true, contradictory, and essential."*† The distinguished American sociologist, Talcott Parsons, in his *The Structure of Social Action* (1937) finds in the work of many different thinkers, such

---

*A. Koestler, *The Invisible Writing* (Boston, 1954), 349.

†D. de Rougemont, *Man's Western Quest* (New York, 1957), 116.

as the German Max Weber, the Frenchman Durkheim, the Englishman Alfred Marshal, the Italian Pareto, and others, a common aim to put the study of man in society on a basis that takes full account of the difficulties of "objectivity" in such study, and gives full place to our contemporary awareness of the place of the subjective and non-rational in human life.

Pareto

We may here speak for a moment about Pareto (1848–1923), not because he was the greatest or the most influential thinker, for he was not, but because the work of this scientifically trained engineer is such a clear example of the difficulties of thinking about men as we think about things. Pareto tried hard to establish a genuine *science* of sociology; but it was a sociology very different from that of his only slightly older contemporary Herbert Spencer (see Chapter 15). Pareto in his *The Mind and Society* (original Italian edition, 1916) is concerned chiefly with the problem of separating in human actions the rational from the non-rational. What interests Pareto is the kind of action that is expressed in words, ritual, symbolism of some kind. Buying wool socks for cold weather is one such action. If they are bought deliberately to get the best socks at a price the buyer can afford, this is rational action in accord with the doer's interests; it is the kind of action the economist can study statistically. If, however, they are bought because the buyer thinks wool is "natural" (as compared with synthetic fibers) or because he finds snob value in improved English socks, or because he wants to help bring sheep-raising back to Vermont, we are in a field less "rational" than price. The practical economist will still study marketing and consumer demand, but he will have to cope with many complex psychological variables.

It is these that Pareto studies under the name of "derivations," which are close to what most of us know as rationalizations. These are the explanations and accompanying ritualistic acts associated with our religion, our patriot-ism, our feelings for groups of all kinds. Prayer, for instance, is for Pareto a derivation; he was, like so many of this period, a materialist, at bottom hostile to Christianity, though he approved of it as means of social concord, and was fascinated by its hold over men. It is irrational, or non-rational, to pray for rain, because we know as meteorologists that rain has purely material causes quite beyond the reach of prayer. These derivations are indeed a factor in human social life, but they do not really move men to social action.

What does move men in society, and keeps them together in society, says Pareto, are the *residues*. These are expressions of relatively permanent, abiding sentiments in men, expressions that usually have to be separated from the part that is actually a derivation, which may change greatly and even quickly. Pagan Greek sailors sacrificed to Poseidon, god of the sea, before setting out on a voyage; a few centuries later, Christian Greek sailors prayed, lighted candles, and made vows to the Virgin Mary just before sailing. The derivations are the explanations of what Poseidon and the Virgin respectively do. They vary. The believer in the Virgin thinks his pagan predecessor was dead wrong. The residues are the needs to secure divine aid and comfort in a difficult undertaking, and to perform certain ritual acts that give the performer assurance of such aid and comfort. The residues are nearly the same for our two sets of sailors. Both the pagans and the Christians have the same social and psychological needs and satisfy them in much the same ways, though with very different "explanations" of what they are doing.

Two of the major classes of "residues" Pareto distinguishes stand out, and help form his philosophy of history. These are first the "residues" of persistent aggregates, the sentiments that mark men who like regular ways, solid discipline, tradition and habit, men like the Spartans, the Prussians, or any rigorously disciplined military class. Second, there are the residues of the instinct for combinations, the sentiments that mark men who like novelty and adventure, who invent new ways of doing things, who like to cut loose from the old and the tried, men not easily shocked, men who hate discipline, men like most intellectuals and inventors—and many entrepreneurs and businessmen. In societies of many individual members, men influenced largely by one or the other of these major residues tend to predominate and to characterize that society. Like most philosophers of history, Pareto is far from clear on just how a conservative society where the residues of persistent aggregates predominate changes into another kind of society. But he does have this conception of a pendulum swing, even a struggle of thesis and antithesis.

The nineteenth century in the West was in Pareto's mind a society in which the residues of instinct for combinations played perhaps the greatest role of which they are capable in a human society. The nineteenth century was a century of competition among individuals full of new ideas, inventions, enterprises, convinced that the old ways were bad, that novelty was the great thing to strive for at the expense of everything else. It was a society notably out of equilibrium. It had to run toward the other kind of residues, toward the persistent aggregates, toward a society with more security and less competition, more discipline and less freedom, more equality and less inequality, more uniformity and less variety. It had to go the way some writers hold that we are going in the twentieth century, toward the welfare state, even toward the totalitarian state.

The Planners and Persuaders

Yet the abiding influence of the newer psychological and sociological approach to the study of man in society has by no means been in the Paretan and conservative direction. Those who want to influence human behavior, all the way from the microcosmic field of personal consumer-choices to the macrocosmic field of international relations, have been willing to make use of the new psychological insights. From the latest piece of "motivational research" to show the cigarette manufacturer how to overcome the effects on his customers

of recent medical research on the causes of lung cancer to the high-minded efforts of proponents of world-government to devise some symbol, visual, musical, concrete, that will supplant nationalist symbols, such as patriotic hymns, flags, and the like, hard-working planners are busily engaged in trying, often successfully, to change our habits, even our prejudices. To use Pareto's now little-used terminology, they are seeking, not to change our behavior by appealing to our "reason" in the plain sense of that word; they are trying to "activate" certain of our sentiments, our residues, or "de-activate" others, or both.

In the field of serious political and social thought, this characteristic twentieth-century emphasis on the psychology of motivation has been appealed to not only by conservatives or "reactionaries" like Pareto and others, including both Mussolini and Hitler, who had pretensions to philosophy, but also by many who were democrats, or at least "progressives," at heart. An early example of this latter type of political thinker is Graham Wallas, a British leftist, whose *Human Nature in Politics* (1908) was a most influential book. Wallas, campaigning as a Progressive for a seat in the London County Council, discovered by experience that the voters he canvassed were more pleased and influenced by little tricks of baby-kissing, chit-chat, and personal flattery than by appeals to reason or even to self-interest. Something of the same emphasis on the need to go beyond abstractions to practical psychology in politics appears in the earlier writings of the American Walter Lippmann, whose *Preface to Politics* appeared in 1913. It has, of course, always been known to politicians.

There remains, especially among American intellectuals, a strong current of thought-feeling that refuses to descend into Machiavellian strategy, even—indeed most of all—in a righteous cause. It still seems to these good children of the eighteenth-century Enlightenment that reason and high ethical principles must and will prevail together, and that to appeal to the "lower" elements in nature so emphasized by modern psychology is no way to rise above the evils of existing society. Such opinions are by no means commonly held, or, at any rate, not commonly put into practice, by active politicians, and one of the many gaps that seem in our society to widen rather than to narrow in these days is the old gap between the idealistic "theorist" and the "practical man" who wants to get things done.

Yet the intellectual leaders of mid-twentieth century progressive political thought are increasingly forced to the conclusion that more has to be done in the way of planning. Notably, they urge, we must plan in the whole sector of our economy which deals with such essentials as education, social service, housing, hospital care, scientific research, public transportation, and the means of preservation of fast-vanishing natural resources, especially our scenic wildernesses, as well as means for the prevention of air- and water-pollution. All these are expensive. The planners know that in a democracy plans cannot simply be imposed on those planned for, as to a great degree they can in a totalitarian state like Russia. They are paying great attention to the problems, on which modern thinking in the field of the social sciences does throw some light, of how to get the many to want and ask for—and pay for—what the planners think the people really need, and *ought* to want. A representative writer who is concerned with such matters is the persuasive American economist J. K. Galbraith (1908–), author of *The Affluent Society.*

Philosophy

In the field of formal—which nowadays tends to mean also university-supported—philosophy the mid-twentieth century displays once more its variety. It is safe to say that in the West at least there are today representatives of almost every philosophical system, from extreme idealism to extreme materialism and complete skepticism, that has ever existed; and even in the communist countries, one suspects that there are lurking idealists ready to come out in the open if official Marxist materialist metaphysics are ever relaxed. The currents of voluntarism, pragmatism, and psychologism we noted earlier (see Chapter 15) still flow, no doubt a bit diminished.

From such nineteenth-century sources as Nietzsche and the gravely disturbed and disturbing Danish theologian, Kierkegaard (1813–1885), there has developed a philosophy known as "existentialism." The existentialists can be described as somewhat harried Stoics who find this existing reality of mid-twentieth century all there is, and pretty depressing, but are determined to face this reality as heroically as possible. They are sometimes divided into Christian existentialists, who retain a concept of God, and free-thinking or atheistic existentialists. The central theme of existentialism has been stated by the French writer Sartre (1905–) as "existence precedes essence." This cryptic pronouncement seems to mean that human awareness of living, of being, precedes in time, and is therefore somehow more important than our thinking, or than our mental ticketing of "reality" by means of words. Clearly existentialism does at bottom belong in the current of anti-intellectualism of our time.

We have certainly not done the existentialists justice in this brief description. They are sensitive artists and intellectuals, by no means simple anti-intellectuals who want us to "think with our blood"—or our hormones. They respect the instrument of thought, and use it themselves. But they do not quite trust it, and they do not trust its chief representatives in our time, the conventional scientists. Their noblest representative, though not formally one of the existentialist group, the French novelist and philosopher, Albert Camus (1913–1960) is perhaps destined to be remembered as a classic of our age. Finally, formal philosophical idealism, which a generation ago seemed, save for Croce, to be languishing everywhere, has proved of recent years to have considerable vitality, perhaps basically in forms we may call Neo-Kantian, as with the late German philosopher, Ernst Cassirer (1874–1945).

The most original, and in a sense most typical and vital, philosophic movement of our century bears clearly and paradoxically the stamp of the "revolt against reason." It looks to an outsider as if the movement called variously logical analysis, logical positivism, the linguistic philosophy, and, in one of its phases, symbolic logic, accepted most of the strictures the new psychology made on old-fashioned rationalism and then went ahead to insist that, although only a tiny bit of human experience could be brought under rubrics of rational thought, that tiny bit was indeed to be protected and explored carefully. This somewhat varied school can be considered as beginning early in the twentieth century in Vienna, the city of Freud. But such distinguished pioneers of the school as Ludwig Wittgenstein (1889–1951) and Rudolf Carnap (1891–   ) emigrated, the first to England, the second to the United States. Logical analysis could hardly flourish in Hitler's Germany or in Stalin's Russia. It is skeptical of too much to flourish in any but a very free and many-minded society.

The American physicist, P. W. Bridgman, put one of the school's basic positions clearly in various writings. Where, on the pattern of scientific practice, a problem can be answered by the performance of an "operation" and the answer validated by logical and empirical tests or observations, knowledge can be achieved; where, however, as in such problems as whether democracy is the best form of government, whether a lie is ever justifiable, or whether a given poem is a good one or a bad one—in short, almost all the great questions of philosophy, art, literature, history—no such "operation" is possible, the problem is *for the logician* "meaningless."

Most of these logical positivists would admit that non-logical or pseudo-logical methods for getting at such problems, though they could not result in the kind of finally accepted answers the scientists expect to get, are nonetheless for normal human living, useful and indeed necessary. Some of the *popularizers* of this philosophy, however, pretty explicitly held that all mental activity save logical analysis and empirical verification is at best inferior mental activity, or more likely, nonsense,

a waste of time, or worse. A distinguished American popularizer, Stuart Chase, in his *Tyranny of Words* (1938) proposed to clarify our thinking by substituting "blah-blah" for terms that have no such good logical or "operational" clearance. Thus the famous French revolutionary slogan, "Liberty, equality, fraternity" would come out simply as "Blah-blah, blah-blah, blah-blah." Approaching their problems very differently from the way Freud and Pareto did, these logical analysts nevertheless came to a similar conclusion about the reasoning capacity of most human beings. Most human beings, they conclude, are at present incapable of thorough, persistent, successful logical thinking, and they cannot be taught to do this kind of thinking in any foreseeable future. Of course, just as there are radical Freudians who hold that if everybody could be psychoanalyzed all would be well, there are radical positivists, usually labeled "semanticists" who hold that semantics, the study of meaning, if available to everyone would cure all our troubles. The leading expert of this rather naive semantic therapy was the Polish-American scientist Alfred Korzybski (1879–1950), author of *Science and Sanity* (1933).

Once more we encounter the sharp tensions of modern intellectual life. Since these logical analysts seemed to set up the practices of science, as they understood them, as the sole right way of thinking, many of those devoted to the arts and the humanistic studies generally turned in revenge to the denunciation of science as a narrowing, dangerous, use of the mind. Anti-scientism is as characteristic of our age as scientism.

Probably the most widespread philosophical movement of our century developed outside of, or on the margin of, formal professional philosophy. This movement may be called "historicism," the attempt to find in history an answer to those ultimate questions of the structure of the universe and of man's fate the philosopher has always asked. At bottom, the transfer of Darwinian concepts of organic evolution from biology to this great, sweeping field of philosophical questions contains the essence of twentieth-century historicism. Once the traditional Judaeo-Christian concepts of a single creation in time, a God above nature, and the rest of the traditional world-view were abandoned, men in search of answers to their questions about these ultimates had to fall back on the historical record. Man is not made by God, but by nature, which amounts to saying that *man makes himself* in the course of history. We get our only clues as to man's capacities here on earth, clues as to how he ought to behave, clues as to that future that so concerns him, from the record of the past.

But "clues" is a modest and misleading word here. Many of the thinkers who appealed to history found much more than indications of what *might* be, much more than the always tentative, never dogmatic or absolute "theories" the scientist produces in answer to the less-than-ultimate questions he asks. Many of these philosophers of history, to simplify a bit, found in what they held to be the course of history a substitute for the concepts of God or Providence. They found in the record of the past substantially the equivalent of what Christians found in revelation—the explanation of man's nature and destiny, his *end* in the sense of a teleology or an eschatology. Paradoxically, they found in history something quite outside and beyond history, a substitute for a theology.

Of these historicisms, the most important and the most obviously a substitute for Christianity is of course Marxism, which we have dealt with elsewhere (see Chapter 14). The theological parallels are plain, and have been frequently noted by non-Marxists: for God, absolute and omnipotent, the Marxist substitutes the absolutely determined course of Dialectical Materialism; for the Bible, he substitutes the canonical writings of Marx-Engels, with the addition, for the orthodox of the Soviet Union and its satellites, of those of Lenin; for the Church, the Party; for the Christian eschatology of divine judgment and heaven or hell, the revolution and the "classless society."

But Marxism, if the most rigorous, is only one of the historicisms of our time. The German, Oswald Spengler (1880–1936), produced in his *Decline of the West*, published just at the end of World War I, a characteristic specimen. Spengler found from the historical record that societies or civilizations have, like human beings, an average life-span, a thousand years or so for a civilization being the equivalent of seventy years or so for the individual human being. He traced several non-western civilizations, but in the West he found three main ones, a Hellenic from 1000 B.C. to about the birth of Christ, a Levantine or Middle Eastern from the birth of Christ to about 1000 A.D., and our own modern western, which began (according to him) about 1000 A.D. and was, therefore, due to end about 2000 A.D. We cannot here analyze his work at length. Spengler had real insights, but his work as a whole, most historians would say, is simply not history—it is metaphysics, or if you like a coined word, meta-history. There are critics who explain Spengler simply; he saw Germany was about to be defeated, and he therefore consoled himself by believing western civilization was about to end.

Better known nowadays than Spengler's is the work of the English historian, Arnold Toynbee (1889–   ), whose many-volumed *Study of History* (1934–1954) has been neatly condensed by D. C. Somervell into two manageable volumes. Toynbee is worth studying as a symptom of the intellectual difficulties of historicism and of our age. He has a Christian background, a careful training in historical scholarship, and a strong family tradition of kindly humanitarian social service. World War I marked him with a great hatred for war, and a conviction that nationalism, which he once declared to be the real if unavowed religion of our western society, is the villain of the piece. His great system is an attempt to trace the causes of the rise and fall of societies in the past, and owes a good deal to Spengler. But Toynbee is a gentle English Christian humanist, not a German romantic racist brought up on what is no doubt a perversion of Nietzsche. He does, like the majority of contemporary philosophers of history, conclude that our western society is facing a very serious challenge, that in terms of the cyclical rise and fall of societies he has traced it looks as if we were about to give ourselves the "knockout blow." But he refuses to abandon hope. The facts of historical development may, he holds, indicate destruction for us; but we may transcend history, and under the influence of a revived, or new, or Buddhist-influenced Christianity of gentleness and love, pull ourselves out of the hole.

Historicism has, again quite characteristically in our culture, given rise to bitter protests and to its opposite. Almost all professional historians, in the West nowadays mostly conventionally democratic in their values, simply give these philosophers of history the cold shoulder. Independent existentialists like Camus (who did not consider himself an existentialist) are firm in their contention that, though we may not neglect history as a record of human experience, we must find in ourselves something—salvation, perhaps—quite beyond history. And as for the logical analysts, history is far too lacking in precise data to make it a subject worth their while.

The Sciences

No general history can readily deal substantively with the history of science and technology in the twentieth century. Each science, each branch of each science, has continued in this century its cumulative course. The co-operation (not without rivalry) among "pure" scientists, applied scientists, engineers, bankers, businessmen, and government officials has produced in all phases of human control over material things the kind of exponential increases that send the lines of our graphs quite off the paper. Man's attained rate of travel is no doubt an extreme example, one not achieved in the same degree for instance in such fields as those of medicine and genetics. But in 1820 the fastest rate was still 12 to 15 miles an hour; railroads made it 100 miles or so by 1880; piston-engined airplanes made it 300 miles or so by 1940; jet planes broke the sound barrier only yesterday in 1947, making speeds of close to 1,000 miles per hour possible; and now in the 1960's rockets have propelled living men in space free of our

atmosphere at speeds of thousands of miles an hour.

Each science is of course highly specialized, and the active scientist usually is supreme master of only part of a given science. Indeed, one of the great worries of our numerous contemporary worriers is well expressed in the old tag that has modern specialists knowing more and more about less and less. But the tag really is an old one—and, like most such tags, partly true and worth our attention, yet not quite borne out by any catastrophic break in our culture. For the fact is that at a broad, non-specialist's level of understanding many educated men in the West have a very good idea of what modern science is trying to do, and how it does it.

The wider implications of modern science as its ways of work and its general concepts affect our world-views is a subject no general history can neglect. In the broadest sense, there can be no doubt that, though many practicing scientists are good Christians, scientific attitudes toward nature and natural laws, and scientific skepticism toward the supernatural, have added powerfully to the modern drive toward rationalism, positivism, materialism. Science continues to promote the world-view we have seen arising in early modern times, and culminating in the Enlightenment of the eighteenth century (see Chapter 9). Indeed, many scientists have managed to make of the pursuit of scientific knowledge itself a kind of religion.

More particularly, the great event of the twentieth century has been the revolution in physics symbolized for the public in the figure of Albert Einstein (1879–1955). The concepts of relativity, a space-time continuum, and quantum mechanics freed physics from the "Newtonian world-machine" and helped the very great modern innovations in the field, innovations that worked together with the late nineteenth-century discoveries of the phenomena of radiation (X-rays, the researches of the Curies, Roentgen, and others) to make possible our contemporary developments in fields like electronics. Einstein's theories on the equivalence of mass and mechanical energy, his concept of time as the fourth dimension and the representation of gravitation as a field (compare "magnetic field") rather than a force secured wide public attention, if not always comprehension. From all this a few laymen came to the conclusion that since the apparently rigid world of mechanical causation of classic physics had broken down, since there was associated with the name of the distinguished German physicist Werner Heisenberg an "indeterminacy principle" familiar to practicing scientists, the common-sense law of cause-and-effect had in fact been repealed, and the universe was once more a fine free space in which anything could happen. This of course is not true, and the work of Newton has not been so much contradicted by modern physics as supplemented. Heisenberg's principle resulted from close work on the particle called an electron. An *individual* electron observably can jump from one orbit to another without evident and predictable sequence. Yet *statistically* the behavior of many, many electrons together is predictable, as predictable as it was in Newton's day. It is quite likely that misunderstood doctrines of "relativity" in physics, misapplied to ethics and aesthetics, did have a part in the fashionable doctrines of moral and aesthetic relativism of only yesterday.

The development of astronomy has been largely influenced by that of physics. To the layman, such modern astronomical concepts as that of a finite but expanding universe, of curved space, and perhaps above all the almost inconceivable distances and quantities, light years, galaxies, and the like, have made astronomy the most romantic of sciences. And these distances and quantities *are* almost inconceivable. A light year is the distance traversed by light in one year, or roughly 5,880,000,000,000 miles; our own Milky Way Galaxy has some thirty thousand million stars and nebulae, in the form of a disk with a diameter of about 100,000 light years. Recent developments in rocketry have made our moon seem attainable by actual human flight instead of merely by flight of the science-fiction imagination. Chemistry, on the other hand, in

spite of the marvels of synthesis it produces, has less attraction for the imagination. Yet in our daily living it is surely the science of chemistry that touches us most closely, in our foods, our medicines, our clothing, almost all the material objects we use.

Chemistry has also aided the very great gains that have been made in the twentieth century in the biological sciences and in their applications to medicine and public health as well. Not only in the United States and the rest of the West, but all over the world, infant mortality, many contagious diseases, even undernourishment, have been so far conquered that the average expectancy of life at birth has gone up as much as twenty years in advanced nations since 1900. In the economically backward areas of the globe, more children are born and more live, so that the population problem has become acute, and is still unsolved. Yet even in this matter of food supply, astonishing achievements by plant-breeders, as with hybrid corn (maize), the development of fertilizers, the use of irrigation, the possibilities of food from the sea opened up by marine biology and other scientific advances promise some considerable alleviation in a foreseeable future. It is significant, however, that the actual extreme limits of the human life span have not yet been significantly affected. It does not seem that a limit of something like 110 to 120 years for human life, historically known to have prevailed for centuries, has yet been exceeded.

There remains one more major problem which the progress of twentieth-century science has sharpened, a problem closely related to that of specialization in science and learning. There is in some senses a widening gap today between those who pursue what we call "humanistic" studies and those who pursue scientific studies. It is by no means difficult philosophically to reconcile these two pursuits; the poet and the physicist have, as creative human beings, more in common than we others usually can see. But the fact remains that from the point of view of the sociologist the two groups in our cultural life do clash, the scientists finding the humanists fuzzy-minded, sloppy intellectually, and clearly inferior, the humanists finding the scientists limited, pedestrian, cold, inhuman, and quite unable to manage the Frankenstein monster of modern technology they have created. Fortunately, there are good men who are at work mediating between these two sides, men who incline to the belief that the opposition is by no means one rooted in the facts of life and human nature, but merely in present-cultural fashion.

In sum, the very great achievements of modern science and technology have raised many problems for our western democracy: the overriding problem presented by the fact that hydrogen bombs, missiles, and biological warfare have made the destruction of the human race no mere bit of rhetoric, nor a theological doctrine like that of Judgment Day, but a possible situation confronting even common sense; the problem of humanizing science; the problem of overpopulation; the problems of educating scientists and endowing scientific research; and many other problems. Yet the fact remains that science and technology seem to be the deciding factors that have raised the masses far enough beyond misery and near-starvation to make possible what we Americans call democracy. And perhaps even more important, the continuing very great vitality of western civilization—a vitality as real in the arts as in the sciences—is at its clearest in the magnificent achievements of modern science. Modern science rightly worries the worriers, but it should also console them, for it shows man still in a light reflected long ago by the Greek Sophocles:

> What a thing is man! Among all wonders
> The wonder of the world is man himself
>
>   . . .
>
> Man the Contriver! Man the Master-mind.*

Literature and the Arts

In the field of imaginative literature, music, painting, the fine arts, and the arts generally,

*Sophocles, *Antigone,* John Jay Chapman, trans. (Boston, 1930), lines 332–340.

we invent new styles and attitudes yet by no means wholly destroy what the past has left us. Here, as for all our culture, the contemporary historian has to note the great variety of tastes and standards that have piled up. But he must also note that there appears in mid-twentieth century with special sharpness another characteristic of our time on which we have already briefly touched, the wide and deep gap between the art—in the broad sense of "art" to include letters, music, architecture—of the few, or "highbrow" art, and the art of the many, or popular art. Bridges between the two there are, usually built on highbrow initiative from the highbrow side toward the lowbrow side. A good example is the fashion among the cultivated few for some phases, at least, of American popular music, or jazz. For many French intellectuals, as difficult, as refined, as remote from the masses as any intellectuals have ever been, "le jazz hot" is the only cultural achievement of the United States. Every now and then, if only briefly, some contributor to that most popular form of popular art, the American comic strip, gains a following among the highbrows or, at least, among undergraduates.

High Art: Literature

Once more, imaginative writing in the twentieth century makes no striking break with that of the late nineteenth. Poetry and literary criticism remain, as they had begun to be in the 1890's or even earlier (see Chapter 15), difficult, cerebral, and addressed to a very small, if fit, audience. An occasional poet, like the American, Robert Frost, breaks from the privacy of the little magazines and the limited editions to wide popularity and a place enshrined in old-fashioned anthologies. But Frost is no more esoteric in form or substance than Wordsworth. More remarkable and more symptomatic, there are signs that T. S. Eliot, born in St. Louis, but as an adult wholly Anglicized, an abstruse and allusive poet, an intellectual of intellectuals, is also attaining a wider audience. The figure of speech with which he began "The Love Song of J. Alfred

Prufrock" in 1917, which once seemed strange, "advanced," is now tame enough for any anthology:

Let us go then, you and I
When the evening is spread out against the sky
Like a patient etherised upon a table.*

The novel remains the most important form of contemporary imaginative writing. Critics have long bemoaned its exhaustion as an art-form, and the French have even invented what they call the "anti-novel," but the novel does not die. It is quite impossible here for us to give even a thumb-nail sketch of the contemporary novel. It is not even wise of us to attempt to indicate writers likely to be read in the twenty-first century. It may be that a social novelist like the American, J. P. Marquand (1893–1960), disliked by the pure highbrow because he wrote best sellers, will survive better than such a favorite of the pure as William Faulkner (1897–1962), who wrote existentialist novels about darkest Mississippi. The late Thomas Mann (1875–1945) seems already enshrined as a classic; but Mann, who began with a traditionally realistic novel of life in his birthplace, the old Hanseatic town of Lübeck, never really belonged to the *avant garde.* He is typical of the sensitive, worrying, class-conscious (his class was that of the artist-intellectual, no mere Marxist class) artist of the age of psychology.

More useful for us here, since it illustrates one of the problems of all contemporary art, is the career of the Irishman, James Joyce (1882–1941). Joyce began with a subtle, out-spoken, but formally conventional series of sketches of life in the Dublin of his youth, *Dubliners* (1914), and the novelist's inevitable, and with Joyce undisguised, autobiography, *Portrait of the Artist as a Young Man* (1916). Then, mostly in exile on the Continent, he wrote what may well prove a classic, the experimental novel *Ulysses* (1922). This novel is an account, rather than a narrative, of twenty-four hours in the life of Leopold Bloom, a Dublin Jew. It is full of difficult allusions,

*T. S. Eliot, *Complete Poems & Plays* (New York, 1952), 3.

parallels with Homer, puns, rapidly shifting scenes and episodes, and is written without regard for the conventional notions of plot and orderly development. Above all, it makes full use of the then recently developed psychologies of the unconscious as displayed in an individual's "stream of consciousness." The last chapter, printed entirely without punctuation marks, is the record of what went on in the mind of Bloom's Irish wife as she lay in bed waiting for him to come home. What went on in her mind was in large part too shocking for the early century, and *Ulysses,* published in Paris, long had to be smuggled into English-speaking countries. It is now freely available everywhere.

Ulysses, though it took attentive reading, and even for those most fully abreast of the *avant garde* culture was often puzzling, is still a novel in English. Joyce's final big work, long known as simply "Work in Progress," but finally published as *Finnegans Wake* (1939), is

James Joyce (1882–1941).

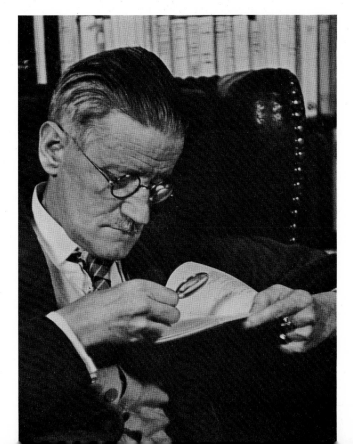

one of those works of radical experimentation about which, like many modern paintings, the ordinary educated layman simply has to say that it means nothing, or very little, to him. The continuities and conventions of narration and "plain English," not wholly flouted in *Ulysses,* are here quite abandoned. There are words, and even sentences; but *meaning* has to be quarried out by the reader and may when quarried turn out to be quite different from what Joyce intended. But there are keys to *Finnegans Wake*—we cite one in our reading list for this chapter—and the reader who wants to try to get at this interesting experiment in modern art can get his start there. Here is the beginning and ending of *Finnegans Wake:*

> rivverrun, past Eve and Adam's, from swerve of shore to bend of bay, brings us by a commodius vicus of recirculation back to Howth Castle and Environs.

> . . . A gull. Gulls. Far calls. Coming, far! End here. Us then. Finn, again! Take. Bussoftlhee, mememormee! Till thousendsthee. Lps. The keys to. Given! A way a lone a last a loved a long the*

Note once more: such writing may well be a blind alley, but the traditions of western invention—we use that word in a very broad sense—insist that it may not be declared a blind alley until it has been well explored.

High Art: The Fine Arts

It is, however, the fine arts, painting perhaps in first rank, but with sculpture, architecture, and the minor decorative arts all included, that confront the ordinary cultivated westerner with the problem of "modernism" in its most clear form. The process of getting beyond the camera eye and Renaissance ideas of perspective—in general, "realism"—which we began to trace in Chapter 15 has gone on right to this day. Indeed, painting done today can be almost—not quite—sharply divided into two groups: that done traditionally,

*J. Joyce, *Finnegans Wake* (New York, 1959), 3, 628.

academically, representational painting of the kind that surprises and puzzles no one though it still pleases many; and the many kinds of experimental or non-representational, or simply "modern," painting. The variety of these experiments is great indeed. Most of them have been made by the great figure of contemporary painting, Pablo Picasso (1880–   ).

A native Spaniard, and an adopted Frenchman, Picasso has in his long life painted in many "styles" or "periods." The paintings of his "Blue Period," for instance, executed in the first years of our century, exemplify Expressionism, the attempt to express in art such highly subjective emotional states as grief and despair. These pictures are said to have been influenced by the work of El Greco, the sixteenth-century master (see Chapter 7, p. 266); certainly, both artists convey a sense of concentrated emotion by exaggerating human proportions. Around 1905, Picasso, stimulated in part by primitive art, turned to more daring innovations, striving, as Cézanne had striven (see p. 582), to transfer to the two dimensions of a picture the three dimensions of the real world but, so to speak, their dimensions *in motion.* Sometimes he used the techniques of Abstractionism, the reduction of figures to a kind of plane geometry, all angles and lines. Sometimes he used those of Cubism, the reduction of figures to a kind of solid geometry, all cubes, spheres, and cones. Sometimes he even glued onto a picture bits of real objects—paper or the caning from a chair—in the process called *collage* ("paste-up"). In the range and inventiveness of his work Picasso calls to mind the masters of the Renaissance. On the one hand, he has done many portraits that are almost classical in style, as in the work of his "White Period" following World War I. On the other hand, he has continued radical experimentation not only on canvas but also in sculpture, in ceramics, and in "constructions" of wood and other materials that might be called the sculptor's counterpart of *collage.* Most disturbing to the ordinary viewer, perhaps, are Picasso's recurrent efforts, stemming from Cubism, to show the human figure from two or more angles simultaneously—whence the apparently misplaced eyes and the anatomical distortions and rearrangements in many of Picasso's pictures.

Most remote from this world of sense experience as organized by common sense is the work of various kinds of abstract painters, paintings which are sometimes elaborate patterns of lines and colors, sometimes geometrical, sometimes apparently mere random daubs. It all means something, if only to the painter; but that meaning cannot be seized by the uninitiated.

The conservative worried by modern art can perhaps take some comfort in the fact that the most extreme manifestation of this art is now nearly fifty years past, and has never been quite equaled in its extraordinary defiance of all conventions, all rules, all forms. This extreme manifestation, perhaps more important sociologically than artistically, was the protest made by a very alienated group of intellectuals, the Dadaists, the "angry young men" of World War I and its aftermath. They reacted against a world so much sillier than their Dada that it could slaughter millions in warfare. Here are some characteristic passages from an account of Dada written by a sympathetic observer:

In Berlin as elsewhere we notice the persistent desire to destroy art, the deliberate intent to wipe out existing notions of beauty, the insistence upon the greatest possible obliteration of individuality. Heartfield works under the direction of Grosz while Max Ernst and Arp sign each other's paintings at random.

. . .

In the first New York Independents' exhibition, 1917, he [Marcel Duchamp] entered a procelain urinal with the title *Fontaine* and signed it R. Mutt to test the impartiality of the executive committee of which he himself was a member. By this symbol Duchamp wished to signify his disgust for art and his admiration for ready-made objects.

. . .

At an exhibition in Paris among the most remarkable entries sent by the poets was a mirror of Soupault's entitled *Portrait of an unknown.* . . . Certain paintings by Duchamp supposed to be in this exhibition were replaced by sheets of paper marked with numbers which corresponded to the Duchamp entries in the catalog. Duchamp, who had

been asked to take part in the exhibition, had just cabled from New York: "Nuts."*

Again we must repeat what we have said before: it is perfectly possible that in the long run of history the directions taken in the contemporary fine arts by those we now think of as leaders, pioneers, will prove stale and unprofitable. But no one who has not made an effort to understand these arts is justified in condemning them out of hand. And one hostile position the disgruntled conservatives in these fields often take seems quite untenable: this is the labeling of such modern art as "pedantic," "decadent," as a sign of exhaustion, death, lack of creative power. Quite the contrary, this art is alive, inventive, dynamic, an attempt to extend the confines of human experience, an attempt quite as remarkable, though in its results not so readily assessed, as that of modern science and technology. The historian must note that the extreme traditionalists, doing exactly what their forefathers have done, are much more vulnerable to the accusation that their work is a sign of exhaustion and decay.

*Georges Huguet in *Fantastic Art, Dada, Surrealism,* A. H. Barr, Jr., ed. (New York, 1936), 23, 19, 33.

"Op" Art: "Current," by Bridget Riley.

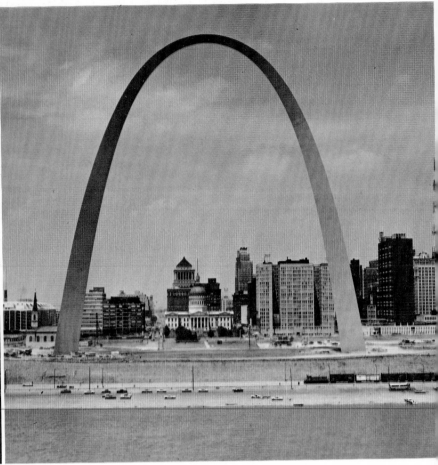

The arch in design: the IBM Building in Seattle and the Gateway Arch in St. Louis.

This remark holds even more strikingly true in architecture. The twentieth century has seen the growth of the first truly original style in architecture since the end of the eighteenth century. "Modern" or "functional" architecture is no revival of a past style, no pastiche of elements of such past styles, no living museum of eclectic choice, like most of nineteenth-century architecture. It prides itself on its honest use of modern materials, its adaptation to modern living, its dislike of waste space and over-display. There is in modern architecture a certain touch of austerity, even puritanism, that should confound those who think that our age is sunk in lush sensuality. In the long run, mid-century modern architecture will probably seem to have carried its dislike for ornamentation, especially external ornamentation, rather too far. There are already signs that architects are beginning to tire of vast expanses of plain glass and steel.

"Modern" music, unlike "modern" painting or architecture, has never quite crystallized into a distinctive style. The twentieth century has produced a great many attempts to get beyond classical music and its rules of harmony—by using scales other than the conventional one, by stressing dissonance and discord, by borrowing the insistent rhythms of popular jazz, and in extreme forms, by abolishing any formal notation and allowing the performer to bang away at will, even on pipes or tin pans. A generation ago, the general public came to identify musical innovation most closely with the Russian, Igor Stravinsky (1882–   ), who on the eve of World War I composed two ballet scores, *Petrouchka* and *The Rite of Spring,* that were far removed from the polite and formalized ballet of tradition. Stravinsky may prove to be the musical coun-

928

An unsentimental approach to design: the Central Technical School, Toronto, Canada.

terpart of the successful artistic pioneer Picasso; significantly, however, although Stravinsky has continued experimental compositions, none of his later works has equaled his great ballets in impact or popularity, and in fact, one of his phases was a return to the eighteenth century.

In sum: all the "creative" modern arts are complex and difficult, and as of this moment far from being "understanded of the people." The very evident gulf between the tastes of the many and the tastes of the few may be an indication of a dangerous side of our democratic society. Certainly this is a subject on which no one is justified in taking an attitude of "holier than thou." But here the complete prevalence of the popular side, the elimination of the art of the few, seems most unlikely.

Left: Alexander Calder: an untitled stabile-mobile of painted aluminum. Henry Moore: "Family Group," a bronze sculpture.

It would seem that contrasting sets of standards and tastes, and the consequent great variety of works of art of all kinds, are one of the marks of our democratic society.

For it is fact that the two great attempts to put across a really totalitarian society in this century, that of Stalin in Russia and that of Hitler in Germany, were marked by very successful efforts to suppress highbrow culture, especially in art and in philosophy. Science, as we now know, flourished in Nazi Germany, and continues to flourish in a Russia which bans Boris Pasternak's novel, *Dr. Zhivago*, and in 1966 sends to prison for literary "treason" two writers, Andrei Sinyavsky and Yuli Daniel, who had smuggled out of Russia mildly "modern" works under the pseudonyms of "Abram Tertz" and "Nikolai Arzhak". Russia was in most ways the most extreme example. This great socio-economic experiment, it may seem somewhat paradoxically, banned experiment in the arts and in the whole range of humanistic culture, at least after the accession of Stalin to power. Soviet architecture was even more atrociously monumental than the worst of nineteenth-century commercial architecture. Until Pasternak's novel, sent out of Russia in manuscript for translation into Italian under communist patronage, came in 1958 to widespread attention, no piece of Soviet writing really struck the imagination of the West. This failure cannot justly be laid to western censorship or banning; it is simply that the crude propaganda literature of Communist Russia did not greatly interest even fellow-traveling western highbrows. Things got worse under Stalin, when such promising beginnings as Soviet movies—those of Eisenstein, for instance—and the more daring music of Russian composers like Shostakovich, came under what one has to call censorship by bourgeois taste. For it is quite clear from the Russian experience that when the proletariat gets power, it wants, and in the arts at least gets, about what the conventional bourgeois of an earlier generation thought desirable and lovely. The Nazis, too, were all against any of the kinds of art and literature we have discussed in this chapter, all in favor of popular art in the taste of a century ago.

II   The Temper of Our Times

Modern western man is acutely conscious of what may be called, a trifle imprecisely, the spirit of the age, the temper of the time, the climate of opinion. In the United States we incline to believe that each recent decade has had a character of its own, from the naughty 'nineties to the fearful 'fifties. For the present, and the immediate past, we have a number of popular phrases—The Age of Anxiety, The Aspirin Age, The Age of Longing, The Age of Conformity, The Age of Suspicion, even The Age of Tranquilizers.

These phrases all have in common a tone of pessimism, mildly seasoned with the shrug-it-off, laugh-that-we-may-not-weep, not very profound cynicism which is a mark of our urban democratic culture. And it surely is also a mark of our age that its serious, its highbrow, culture is to an extraordinary degree pessimistic about the present state of man, gloomy and fearsome about the future, though by no means in agreement either on diagnosis of what is wrong with our culture or in prognosis of its development. Here is a dignified and eloquent sample from the late Albert Camus' speech of acceptance of his Nobel Prize in 1958:

. . . As the heir of a corrupt history that blends blighted revolutions, misguided techniques, dead gods, and worn out ideologies, in which second-rate powers can destroy everything today, but are unable to win anyone over; in which intelligence has stooped to becoming the servant of hatred and oppression, that generation [Camus' own], starting from nothing but its own negations, has had to re-establish both within and without itself a little of what constitutes the dignity of life and death. Faced with a world threatened with disintegration, in which our grand inquisitors may set up once and for all the kingdoms of death, that generation knows that, in a sort of mad race against time, it ought to re-establish among nations a peace not based on slavery, to reconcile labor and culture again, and to reconstruct with all men an Ark of the Covenant. Perhaps it can never accomplish that vast undertaking, but most certainly throughout the world it has already accepted the double challenge of truth and liberty, and, on occasion, has shown that it can lay down its life without hatred. That generation deserves to be acclaimed wherever it happens to be, and especially wherever it is sacrificing itself.*

This is not, of course, sheer pessimism, but it is a kind of unhappy faith, a Stoic determination to fight against the way things are.

Let us note that, although from Plato, even from Ikhnaton on, our serious literary and artistic culture has always shown a strain of pessimism, our own intellectual leaders are, first, more than usually apprehensive and censorious and second, more than usually aware of the gulf between their way of living, their standards of value, and those of their fellow citizens. Just one sample—here in a recent work is a well-known American writer complaining that most Americans confuse "normal" with "average," and suggesting that we need a genuine synonym for "average":

Fortunately, such a genuine and familiar synonym does exist. That which is "average" is also properly described as "mediocre." And if we were accustomed to call the average man, not "the common man" or still less "the normal man," but "the mediocre man" we should not be so easily hypnotized into believing that mediocrity is an ideal to be aimed at.†

This passage is hardly fair to American democratic beliefs; we Americans do not aim at mediocrity as an ideal, but on the contrary

admire greatly the record-breaker, the outstanding personality. But, unlike Mr. Krutch, we are not indignant over the failure of everybody to measure up to highbrow standards and we do not think "common" a synonym of "mediocre."

Now the historian, in attempting by comparative study of similar phenomena in different times and places to arrive at workable generalizations, has great difficulty with this problem of what is the "normal" or "usual" relation between intellectual classes—the writers, artists, scholars, teachers, preachers, and their followers—and other classes, even within our western culture. Such study simply isn't well enough developed to permit measurement, graphs, quantitative generalization. Qualitatively, we may risk the assertion that the gravity and extent of the gap between the way American intellectuals, and to a degree western intellectuals generally, think and feel and the way the rest of western society thinks and feels—the phenomenon we may call in shorthand "the alienation of the intellectuals"—this phenomenon may well be a grave symptom of weakness in our society.

Yet the degree of alienation of the intellectuals is hard to measure, and we may have exaggerated it in the passage above. American intellectuals complain bitterly about the impossibility of the good life in the machine age, but they for the most part use the machines with apparent satisfaction. They find fault with our business civilization, but a great many of them do a very good business in it, and the rank-and-file are not in terms of income as badly off as they think they are. They often regard themselves as a scorned and victimized minority in a hostile society of Babbitts, but a distinguished American sociologist has recently argued that they are in fact well regarded:

While he [the American intellectual] may feel himself neglected and scorned, his work poorly valued by the community, the community places him fairly high when polled on the relative status of occupations. In one such study of the ranks of ninety-six occupations, conducted in 1947 by the National Opinion Research Center of the Univer-

---

*Reprinted with the permission of Alfred A. Knopf, Inc., from Albert Camus' Speech of Acceptance upon the award of the Nobel Prize for Literature, December 10th, 1957, translated by Justin O'Brien. Copyright © 1958 by Alfred A. Knopf, Inc.

†J. W. Krutch, *Human Nature and the Human Condition* (Random House, (New York, 1959), 93.

sity of Chicago, college professors ranked above every non-political position except that of physician; artists, musicians in a symphony orchestra, and authors ranked almost as high. . . . [In another poll in 1950] professors came out fourth among twenty-four categories, and thirty-eight per cent of those polled placed them definitely in the "upper class."*

At any rate, it is clear that the great majority of Americans, and even the great majority of Europeans, are not as cosmically worried, not as pessimistic about man's fate, as are the intellectuals. Indeed, it seems likely that the many in western society still adhere basically to the eighteenth-century belief in progress, moral as well as material. A recent candidate for the American presidency could say in a campaign speech, which by its very nature must be what hearers want to hear, "It is an article of the democratic faith that progress is a basic law of life."† In fact, one of the reproaches the intellectuals make to the many in the West is that the many appear on the whole quite contented with their material prosperity, their gadgets, their amusements, their American-style "classless society," a society where one man can be said to be as good as another, where all have a high level of consumption, but where there are inequalities, "status seekers", failures, tragedies, not the Utopian, theoretical Marxist heaven of an unrealized "classless society."

Yet the pessimism of the intellectuals is understandable. The almost-Utopia which many of the thinkers of the Enlightenment believed was just around the corner in the eighteenth century is not here yet. Let us, in conclusion, briefly review that eighteenth-century basis of our western democratic faith, and see what our intellectual guides are making of that faith now, two hundred years later.

The Optimism
of the Enlightenment

As we have pointed out (Chapters 9, 12 and 15), there grew up among western men

*S. M. Lipset, *Political Man* (New York, 1960).
†Adlai Stevenson, quoted in C. A. Chambers, "Belief in Progress in Twentieth Century America," *Journal of the History of Ideas* (April, 1958), 221.

in the early modern centuries, and there came to full bloom in the eighteenth and nineteenth centuries, a view of man's fate here on earth which was essentially new. This is the view that all men may rightly expect to be happy here on earth. As St. Just, the youthful colleague of Robespierre in the French Revolution, put it, "Happiness is a new idea in Europe"; or as Jefferson, with his gift for phrasing, put it, one of the unalienable rights of man is the "pursuit of happiness." Of course men have presumably always sought happiness here on earth. In historic Christianity, however, they did not really expect it here on earth, but only in an afterlife in heaven; indeed, Christianity had an overtone of belief that happiness in heaven was in part at least a reward for suffering here on earth.

The *philosophes,* the eighteenth-century thinkers who set the broad terms of this modern optimistic world-view, meant by happiness a condition or state in which each man had at any given moment what he wanted, a state in which each man—each woman, and, incredibly, even each baby—was not aware of being thwarted, frustrated. To the inner state of this happiness there would conform an outer state of material plenty in which everyone would have what he wanted to eat, would be well housed, would have a satisfactory sex life, and would of course enjoy good health, both mental and physical. The matter may indeed be put in terms of modern psychology. Man can rightfully expect in this world, certainly before very long, a society in which everyone would have a life of perfect adjustment, a life without conflict, aggression, insecurity.

Broadly speaking, the *philosophes* held that such perfect happiness had not yet been attained on earth—an obvious fact—because there had grown up a whole set of institutions, habits, and beliefs that had brought evil into human life. Men in 1750, the *philosophes* believed, were not following the natural laws that would make them happy, but the unnatural laws that made them unhappy. The formulators of the new idea of happiness believed that the unhappy state of the world could be traced to a combination of the privileges unnaturally acquired over the centuries by the few rich and powerful (the leaders in church and state), together with the unnatural ignorance and prejudices these few had imposed on the many. They therefore concluded that the solution lay first in depriving the few of their unnatural privileges and, second, in disclosing to the many by a natural system of education and government the key to their own happiness. In short, they believed that men are *by nature* good not evil, reasonable not foolish, intelligent not stupid, certainly improvable. Though it is perhaps unfair to say that they believed in the "natural goodness of man," at a very minimum most of the philosophers held that men as they are now, but under the rule of "cultural engineers," "engineers of the soul," instead of under their present rulers, could all be happy, certainly again at a minimum, much, much happier. Something close to Utopia was to them just around the corner.

This, then, though put oversimply, is the essence of what may be called the democratic dream of the eighteenth-century *philosophes,* the dream of a heavenly city here on earth. But two hundred years later the dream has not come true. Some men still persist in it, holding that we have not yet conquered the privileged classes, not yet opened men's minds, not yet really tried full democracy or not yet allowed free play to the kindly cultural engineers. We must insist: many are now alive who think and feel about man's destiny in essentially eighteenth-century ways. Marxism, for example, in its simplest outline, is the eighteenth-century formula all over again: the bad institutional environment under which men cannot help being miserable is capitalism; the good institutional environment under which men cannot help being happy is socialism. In fact, it seems that Stalin invented that phrase "engineer of the soul." It is, however, quite unfair to limit these believers in what is essentially eighteenth-century rationalist empiricism to the Marxists. There are many respected and influential Americans—and a few such Europeans—who preserve intact a belief in the "principles of 1776 and 1789." They may concede that some men are irrational, but they hold that man is rational. Needless to

say, the Soviet Russian experiment has not yet brought this kind of socialism to earth.

But the failure of the dream has caused many more men, at least in the free world, to question its very basis, the doctrine of the basic rationality of man, or at least to question man's complete pliability to the best-intentioned cultural engineering. Such men hold that something profoundly rooted in human nature, and not merely in man's institutions, or in his environment, makes a measure of unhappiness the natural lot of mankind. The modern western world, in consequence, has witnessed a process of reaction and adjustment to the contrast between the high hopes of the Enlightenment and the continuing evils of the world. We may distinguish three broad classifications of these reactions and adjustments, which we may compare with the reactions and adjustments that faced early Christianity once the promise of an *immediate* Second Coming of Christ had to be abandoned.

Repudiation or Revision of the Enlightenment

First, there is the reaction of complete repudiation of all the Enlightenment stood for. This reaction takes many forms. One of them, limited largely to some emotional intellectuals, is the sense of doom we have just discussed, the feeling that in trying to make this earth a heaven man has in fact made it a hell. More commonly, this reaction takes the form of denying all the premises of democracy. It is maintained that most men are wicked or stupid or foolish, or at any rate not up to the burden a democratic society sets on them, that they need to be ruled by their betters, who are always few in number, and that therefore we must return to divine-right monarchy or to the feudal-clerical aristocracy of the Middle Ages, or follow the "new conservatism," or devise some new authoritarianism of the Right or Left. Such views are not commonly held, or at any rate not commonly expressed in the United States. Not even our extreme Rightists quite repudiate the *language* of Jefferson, however much at bottom they disagree with his democratic ideals.

Second, there is the Christian view that men must return to the basic Christian concept of an unavoidable mixture of good and evil in humanity. In this view, life on earth must always demonstrate the conflict between the divine and the animal in man, a conflict tragic and profound, not mean, vile, and hopeless as the mere pessimist sees it, and, above all, not for the individual a ceaseless "existentialist" conflict, but a conflict that has an end in heaven or hell, and that takes place in a universe dominated by *purpose,* not by *accident* or the *merely natural.* For some of these Christians, the desirable earthly society is indeed rather an aristocracy than a democracy. But many of them, like the American theologian and moralist, Reinhold Niebuhr, may be described as moderate democrats. Though they believe that the democratic dream in its radical eighteenth-century form is impious nonsense, they none the less hold that a balanced democratic society is the best way of attaining justice on earth, that such a society is the best, or least bad, earthly reflection of man's dual nature.

Third, there are those who accept the aims of the *philosophes* and even in part the eighteenth-century estimate of human nature. But they find that the Enlightenment of the eighteenth century went wrong in its time-sense, wrong in its hope that its claims could be attained in a generation or two. These thinkers are essentially chastened children of the Enlightenment. They share the view that men are made to be happy, but are convinced by the events of the last two generations that wickedness and unreason are not, as the *philosophes* believed, rooted shallowly in a few bad institutions. On the contrary, they believe that evil, prejudice, and stupidity are deeply rooted in very complex institutions, in tradition, and perhaps even in man as a biological organism.

These thinkers have been greatly influenced by the emphasis that modern psychology has put on the irrational character of the human personality, on the subconscious and the unconscious, and on the consequent difficulty of the actual task of "enlightenment." They now think the task of making the world better will be long and difficult. But it is a task they believe can and must be continued. And they differ basically from the Christians in that they refuse to accept the Christian tension between this world and the next one, or any other one. They do not subscribe necessarily to naive scientific "reductionism" which holds that all productive thinking will end up by accepting simple scientific materialism—or in the popular language of the cliché, that "it's all physics or chemistry." But they do hold that man is a product of nature, that the supernatural does not exist, and that individual immortality is impossible.

The important thing for us to note at the end of this long historic record is that between the second and the third groups we have been discussing, between the Christians and the chastened children of the Enlightenment, a practical accord is possible, and necessary. It is indeed being worked out in the West. In this accord lies the possibility that the men of the first group, the enemies of democracy, may be defeated, and that democracy may live on to give the lie to the prophets of doom. In such an accord we may preserve the willingness to put up with restraints, with imperfections, with frustration, and with suffering without losing the hope, the dream, that is still alive for us in "liberty, equality, fraternity," in "life, liberty, and the pursuit of happiness," in the "principles of 1776 and 1789." Perhaps, above all, those of us called to intellectual pursuits can re-learn the great Christian lesson of humility, can cease in our pride to berate our fellow men as mediocre men. We may thus avoid the illusions and retain the ideals of our historic heritage.

Reading Suggestions on Man's Fate in the Twentieth Century

(Asterisk indicates paperbound edition.)

General

There is not yet a good full intellectual history of the twentieth century; but the chapters dealing with ideas in H. Stuart Hughes, *Contemporary Europe,* 2nd ed. (Prentice-Hall, 1966) are an admirable survey.

Philosophy and Psychology

E. Jones, *The Life and Work of Freud,* 3 vols. (Basic Books, 1953–1957). The standard work.

R. L. Schoenwald, *Freud: The Man and His Mind* (Knopf, 1956), and P. Rieff, *Freud: The Mind of the Moralist* (Viking, 1959). Two good modern studies emphasizing Freud's place in our contemporary culture.

B. F. Skinner, *Science and Human Behavior* (Macmillan, 1956). A clear and extreme statement of contemporary behavioristic psychology.

M. G. White, *The Age of Analysis: Twentieth-Century Philosophers* (*Mentor, 1955). Excerpts and comments, very well chosen.

M. G. White, *Foundations of Historical Knowledge* (Harper & Row, 1965). A difficult but rewarding book which seeks to rescue historical knowledge from the skeptical position some modern analytical philosophers take toward the subject.

R. Harper, *Existentialism: A Theory of Man* (Harvard Univ. Press, 1949). A sympathetic introduction to a "movement" not quite philosophically respectable but still very fashionable.

W. Kaufman, ed., *Existentialism from Dostoevsky to Sartre* (*Meridian, 1956). Instructive selections from the existentialists, together with helpful critical comment.

P. W. Bridgman, *The Way Things Are* (Harvard Univ. Press, 1959). A distinguished physicist sets down a chastened statement of a contemporary positivist's point of view.

Politics and Sociology

H. S. Hughes, *Consciousness and Society: The Reorientation of European Social Thought, 1890–1930* (Knopf, 1958). A superb and unique study of the intellectual history of the early twentieth century, broader than its title might indicate.

T. Parsons, *The Structure of Social Action,* 2nd ed. (Free Press, 1949). A landmark in American sociological thinking.

R. D. Humphrey, *Georges Sorel: Prophet Without Honor* (Harvard Univ. Press, 1951). A suggestive study of an anti-intellectual.

V. Pareto, *The Mind and Society,* 4 vols. (Harcourt, Brace, 1935). A major work in general sociology, hardly to be read quickly. A good though difficult brief exposition of Pareto's thought is L. J. Henderson, *Pareto's General Sociology* (Harvard Univ. Press, 1937).

J. H. Meisel, *The Myth of the Ruling Class: Gaetano Mosca and the 'Elite'* (Univ. of Michigan Press, 1958). An illuminating study of an important thinker too little known in this country.

G. Wallas, *Human Nature in Politics* (Constable, 1908; *Bison). A pioneer study in political psychology. See also his *The Great Society* (Macmillan, 1915, and later editions).

K. R. Popper, *The Open Society and Its Enemies* (Princeton Univ. Press, 1950). A major work on the problems of modern democracy.

K. E. Boulding, *The Meaning of The Twentieth Century: The Great Tradition* (Harper & Row, 1964). A discerning study. See also Professor Boulding's *Social Justice* (*Spectrum).

Sciences and Arts

I. Asimov, *The New Intelligent Man's Guide to Science* (Basic Books, 1965). A good survey, with a fine bibliography, pp. 815–823).

C. T. Chase, *The Evolution of Modern Physics* (Van Nostrand, 1947), and L. Barnett, *The Universe and Dr. Einstein* (*Mentor, 1952). Two useful popular accounts of a difficult and important subject.

E. C. Berkeley, *Giant Brains* (Wiley, 1949), and N. Wiener, *Cybernetics; or Control and Communication in the Animal and the Machine,* new ed. (Wiley, 1957). Two by no means easy studies of another important related aspect of our world.

Editors of the "Scientific American," *Atomic Power* and ten other volumes covering various fields of science (Simon and Schuster, 1953–1957). These paperback volumes are admirable examples of sophisticated scientific popularization. The parent magazine, *Scientific American,* gives a fine running account of the whole range of contemporary science, including the more "scientific" of the behavioral or social sciences.

B. Barber, *Science and the Social Order* (Free Press, 1952). A suggestive study in a little-cultivated field.

M. McLuhan, *Understanding Media* (*McGraw-Hill). Controversial appraisal of communications in the present-day world.

L. Mumford and others, *The Arts in Renewal* (Univ. of Pennsylvania Press, 1951), and R. Richman, *The Arts at Mid-Century* (Horizon Press, 1954). Two wide-ranging collections of essays by Americans, touching critically on all the arts.

C. Mauriac, *The New Literature* (Braziller, 1959). Interesting essays translated from the French, mostly but not wholly dealing with French writers.

E. Wilson, *Axel's Castle: A Study in the Imaginative Literature of 1870–1930* (*Scribners, 1957). Already a classic of criticism, ranging in subject matter from French nineteenth-century symbolism to Joyce and Gertrude Stein.

F. J. Hoffmann, *Freudianism and the Literary Mind,* 2nd ed. (Louisiana State Univ. Press, 1957; *Evergreen Books). A suggestive study. See also the somewhat wider treatment of "moderns" in H. Slochower, *Literature and Philosophy between Two World Wars: No Voice Is Wholly Lost* (*Citadel).

W. P. Jones, *James Joyce and The Common Reader* (Univ. of Oklahoma Press, 1955). The simplest introduction, with good bibliographies leading to more advanced critical work.

A. H. Barr, Jr. *What Is Modern Painting?* (*Museum of Modern Art—Doubleday). Good, brief introduction, with helpful bibliography.

J. Canaday, *Embattled Critic: Views on Modern Art* (*Noonday). By the respected art critic of the *New York Times.*

T. H. Robsjohn-Gibbings, *Mona Lisa's Mustache: A Dissection of Modern Art* (Knopf, 1947). Amusing debunking.

A. H. Barr, Jr., ed., *Picasso: 75th Anniversary Exhibition* (*Museum of Modern Art-Doubleday). Illustrated review of the productions of the best-known modern artist.

D. Herzka, *Pop Art* (*George Wittenborn). Introduction to one of the most recent and most baffling *genres* of modern art.

Frank Lloyd Wright on Architecture, F. Guttheim, ed. (*Universal). Views of a great pioneer in modern architecture.

A. Copland, *Our New Music* (McGraw-Hill, 1941). A good introduction by a leading modern American composer.

P. H. Lang, ed., *Stravinsky: A New Appraisal of His Music* (*Norton). Evaluations of a characteristic modern composer.

Our Present
Discontents:
Hopes and Fears
for the Future

D. Riesman and others, *The Lonely Crowd,* abridged ed. (Doubleday, 1953; *Anchor). One of the outstanding current books in the behavioral sciences field.

W. H. Whyte, *The Organization Man* (Doubleday, 1957; *Anchor) and V. O. Packard,

The Status Seekers (McKay, 1959). Two recent best sellers of popular sociology, interesting as indications of problems we are very aware of.

L. Mumford, *Technics and Civilization* (Harcourt, Brace, 1934). A still influential work by a leading intellectual of the just-past generation.

F. E. Manuel, ed., *Utopias and Utopian Thought* (Houghton, Mifflin, 1966). An interesting symposium on an eternal theme of man's fate.

R. Williams, *Culture and Society, 1780–1950* (Columbia Univ. Press, 1958). An important book that sets in historical background the problem we here call "the alienation of the intellectuals." For other contemporary aspects of this problem, consult C. Brinton, "Reflections on the Alienation of the Intellectuals" in A. V. Riasanovsky and B. Riznik, eds., *Generalizations in Historical Writing* (Univ. of Penn. Press, 1963), with bibliographical footnotes; Lewis A. Coser, *Men of Ideas* (Free Press, 1965); G. B. de Huszar, *The Intellectuals: A Controversial Portrait* (Free Press, 1960); the older classic, J. Benda, *The Betrayal of the Intellectuals,* translated from the French, *La Trahison des Clercs* (*Beacon); and R. Hofstadter, *Anti-Intellectualism in American Life* (Knopf, 1963).

L. Mumford, *The Transformations of Man* (Harper, 1956), C. G. Darwin, *The Next Million Years* (Doubleday, 1953), R. Seidenberg, *Post-historic Man* (Univ. of North Carolina Press, 1950; *Beacon), H. Brown, *The Challenge of Man's Future* (*Viking, 1956). Four brief, diverse attempts to chart the future of the human race. For guidance in this important contemporary literature of "Whither Mankind" consult also C. Brinton, *The Fate of Man* (Braziller, 1961), with bibliography.

R. Niebuhr, *The Structure of Nations and Empires* (Scribner's, 1959). A wise book that uses history as servant, not master.

A. J. Toynbee, *A Study of History,* abridged ed. by D. C. Somervell, 2 vols. (Oxford Univ. Press, 1947–1957). A faithful condensation of a ten-volume work.

I. Berlin, *Historical Inevitability* (Oxford Univ. Press, 1954). A brief, difficult book attacking historicism. For a wide range of critics of Toynbee in particular, see M. F. Ashley-Montagu, *Toynbee and History* (Porter Sargent, 1956); and for good leads into many phases of the problem of history today, see P. Zagorin, "Historical Knowledge: A Review Article on the Philosophy of History," *Journal of Modern History,* Sept. 1959, Vol. XXXI, No. 3, pp. 243–255.

F. E. Manuel, *The Shapes of Philosophical History* (Stanford Univ. Press, 1965). An admirable summing up of western thought on history as a guide to present and future.

A. H. Leighton, *The Governing of Men,* new ed. (Princeton Univ. Press, 1955), and C. Kluckhohn, *Mirror for Man* (McGraw-Hill, 1949; *Premier Books). Two good examples of the uses of the newer concepts in the social sciences.

J. Barzun, *The House of Intellect* (Harper, 1959). A brilliant American intellectual on the present state of our intellectual life.

A. C. Valentine, *The Age of Conformity* (Regnery, 1954). A good example of the criticism of modern American democracy from the worried conservative standpoint.

C. Frankel, *The Case for Modern Man* (Harper, 1956; *Beacon). An admirable restatement of hopeful belief in democracy; antidote to the prophets of gloom.

R. L. Heilbroner, *The Future as History* (Harper, 1960). Interesting "revisionism" applied to the traditions of democratic optimism.

R. Niebuhr, *The Children of Light and the Children of Darkness* (Scribner's, 1944), and *The Irony of American History* (Scribner's, 1952). An important American theologian argues that Christian pessimism offers a good working basis for democracy.

P. Geyl, "The Vitality of Western Civilization," *Delta: A Review of Life and Thought in the Netherlands,* Spring, 1959, pp. 5–19. A splendid reply to the prophets of doom, by an esteemed intellectual.

Illustrations

Reindeer from Font-de-Gaume, *The American Museum of Natural History,* 3

Head of Nefertiti, *Formerly State Museum, Berlin,* 8

Greek statue of maiden, 11

Acropolis, *Ewing Galloway,* 12

Pont du Gard, *French Embassy Press and Information Division,* 16

Virgin and saints in Coptic monastery, 17

Charlemagne, *The Bettmann Archive,* 21

Plan of medieval manor, 28

St. Sernin (nave), *Jean Roubier, Paris,* 31

Louis XI, by Fouquet, *The Bettmann Archive,* 35

Henry VII, from a silver groat, *The Granger Collection,* 37

Lorenzo de' Medici, *The Granger Collection,* 45

Hanseatic merchants, *The Bettmann Archive,* 49

Venice, c.1500, *The Bettmann Archive,* 51

Ivan the Terrible, *Nationalmuseum, Copenhagen,* 61

St. Basil Cathedral, *Ewing Galloway,* 65

Mosque of Emperor Suleiman, *The Turkish Information Office,* 71

Dante, by Giotto, 85

Erasmus, by Durer, 91

"Joachim Returning to the Sheepfold," by Giotto, 94

"Expulsion of Adam and Eve from Eden," by Masaccio, 96

Head of Christ, by da Vinci, 97

Sistine Chapel ceiling, 99

Flemish proverbs, Breughel, 100

Mary Magdalen, by Donatello, 102

Moses, by Michelangelo, 103

St. Peter's Basilica, *ENIT,* 104

Palazzo Chiericati, 105

Sketch for a parachute, by da Vinci, *The Granger Collection,* 107

Martin Luther, by Cranach, *The Granger Collection,* 119

Anti-papal German woodcut, *The Museum of Modern Art,* 123

Rebelling German peasants, *The Bettmann Archive,* 125

Zwingli, *The Granger Collection,* 127

Henry VIII, by Holbein, *British Information Services,* 129

Anabaptists at May-dance, *The New York Public Library Picture Collection,* 131

Title page from Luther's *To the Christian Nobility of the German Nation, The Bettmann Archive,* 135

Sketches of Calvin, *New York Public Library,* 136

Ignatius Loyola, by Coello, *The Bettmann Archive,* 141

Execution of English Protestants, *The Bettmann Archive,* 142

Hanging of thieves during the Thirty Years' War, *The Granger Collection,* 156

Francis I, by Clouet, 159

Philip II, *The Metropolitan Museum of Art,* 163

Battle between the English fleet and the Spanish Armada, *Trustees of the British Museum,* 165

Escorial, *Ewing Galloway,* 167

Chateau de Chambord, 172

Henry IV, *The Granger Collection,* 174

Elizabeth I, *The Granger Collection,* 179

Mary Stuart, by Clouet, *The Granger Collection,* 180

Hatfield House, *British Travel Association,* 181

Siege of Magdeburg, *The Granger Collection,* 187

Polo brothers, *The Bettmann Archive,* 201

"Sage under a Pine Tree" (Sung dynasty), *The Metropolitan Museum of Art,* 205

Macao, *The Granger Collection,* 206

Father Matthew Ricci, *The Bettmann Archive,* 208

Earliest illustration of South American natives, *The Granger Collection,* 209

Magellan passing through the Straits (engraving), *The Granger Collection,* 211

Machu Picchu, *Ewing Galloway,* 213

Aztec ornament, *The Granger Collection,* 214

"Barbarian Royalty Worshiping Buddha" (Northern Sung Dynasty), 221

Fifteenth-century conception of people in unknown lands, *New York Public Library, Prints Division,* 225

Great Wall of China, *Ewing Galloway,* 226

Richelieu, by Champaigne, 233

Palace of Versailles, *French Government Tourist Office,* 243

Charles I, by Van Dyck, 251

Execution of Charles I, *The Granger Collection,* 253

House of Commons (1651), *The Granger Collection,* 254

Descartes, by Hals, *The Metropolitan Museum Reference Collection,* 261

St. Paul's Cathedral, *British Travel Association,* 264

Baldacchino in St. Peter's Cathedral, *Ewing Galloway,* 265

Philip IV, by Velasquez, 266

"Susanna Fourment in Hat," by Rubens, 267

"Self-Portrait," by Rembrandt, © *London County Council,* 267

London during South Sea Bubble, *The Bettmann Archive,* 277

Eighteenth-century grinders. *The Bettmann Archive,* 279

House of Commons, by Hogarth, *The New York Public Library,* 282

Marquise de Pompadour, by de la Tour, 286

Giant soldier of Prussia, *The Granger Collection,* 291

Peter I, by Serov, 299

Battle of Culloden, *The Bettmann Archive,* 305

Frederick the Great, *The Granger Collection,* 307

Table talk with Voltaire, *The Granger Collection,* 321

Frederick the Great playing the flute, *The Bettmann Archive,* 327

Joseph II, *Austrian Information Center,* 330

Charles III, *The Metropolitan Museum Reference Collection,* 331

Catherine the Great, *The Granger Collection,* 336

Alexander I, *The Granger Collection,* 339

English commentary on Boston Tea Party, *The Metropolitan Museum of Art,* 345

Samuel Johnson, by Reynolds, *The Granger Collection,* 351

Library at Ken Wood, London, 352

Gallery at Strawberry Hill, 352

Mozart, *The Granger Collection,* 354

Paris City Hall, July 14, 1789, *French Cultural Services,* 367

Marie Antoinette and children, 369

Danton, by David, *The Bettmann Archive,* 374

Louis XVI, *The Granger Collection,* 376

Robespierre, *The Granger Collection,* 378

Marie Antoinette on way to guillotine, by David, *The New York Public Library Picture Collection,* 379

Napoleon, by David, 384

Napoleonic scheme for invasion of England, *The Bettmann Archive,* 391

Napoleon's bivouac preceding Battle of Austerlitz, *The Granger Collection,* 392

Gillray, British comment on Napoleon's imperialism, *The Granger Collection,* 397

"The Third of May," by Goya, *Prado, Madrid,* 399

Delacroix, self-portrait, *French Cultural Services,* 412

Houses of Parliament, *British Travel Association,* 412

Monticello, *The Granger Collection,* 413

Talleyrand, *French Embassy Press and Information Service,* 416

Statesmen at Congress of Vienna, *The Bettmann Archive,* 417

"The Massacre of Scio," by Delacroix, 426

"The Fight of the Citizens of France against the Oppression of Louis-Philippe," by Daumier, *The Bettmann Archive,* 434

"The Uprising, 1848," by Daumier, *Phillips Memorial Gallery,* 436

Joseph Mazzini, *Istituto Italiano di Cultura,* 437

Barricades in Milan, 1848, *The Granger Collection,* 438

Barricades in Berlin, 1848, *The Granger Collection,* 440

Power looms, about 1820, *The Bettmann Archive,* 449

Corn Laws, *The Bettmann Archive,* 455

"Work," by Ford Madox Brown, 456

Child laborers, about 1840, *The Bettmann Archive,* 459

John Stuart Mill, *The Bettmann Archive,* 464

Parallelogram for New Harmony, *The Bettmann Archive,* 469

Louis Blanc, *French Embassy Press and Information Division,* 470

Friedrich Engels, *The Bettmann Archive,* 473

Disraeli, *The Granger Collection,* 485

Gladstone advising Queen Victoria, *The Bettmann Archive,* 486

David Lloyd George, *The Granger Collection,* 495

Napoleon III, *The Bettmann Archive,* 498

Barricades in Paris, *The Bettmann Archive,* 501

Division into choruses of France's National Assembly, cartoon, *The Bettmann Archive,* 503

Dreyfus case, covered by American press, *The Bettmann Archive,* 506

Cavour, *The Bettmann Archive,* 508

Garibaldi, *Istituto Italiano di Cultura,* 509

Marcus A. Hanna, *The Granger Collection,* 518

Bismarck, *The Bettmann Archive,* 527

William II, *The Granger Collection,* 533

Francis Joseph, *The Granger Collection,* 537

Nicholas I, by Landseer, *The Bettmann Archive,* 549

Bursting of the Russian Bubble, *The Bettmann Archive,* 551

Alexander II, *The Granger Collection,* 552

Alexander III, *Brown Brothers,* 557

"Bloody Sunday," *Sovfoto,* 560

Anti-Darwinian cartoon, by Nast, *The Granger Collection,* 570

Bernard Shaw, by Beerbohm, *The Bettmann Archive,* 578

Cabaret scene, by Seurat, *Otterloo Museum,* 580

"The Starry Night," by van Gogh, *The Art Institute of Chicago,* 581

"La Montagne Sainte Victoire," by Cézanne, *The Home House Trustees, London,* 582

Fifth Avenue, in 1898, *The Granger Collection,* 584

Auditorium Hotel and Theater, Chicago, *The Bettmann Archive,* 585

The public and music by Wagner, Daumier caricature, *The Bettmann Archive,* 587

Friedrich Nietzsche, *The Bettmann Archive,* 592

Arrival of one of the first English steamers, *The Bettmann Archive,* 600

British advance toward Johannesburg, *The Bettmann Archive,* 604

"Mosé in Egitto!", *The Granger Collection,* 605

British imperialism in Africa, German view, *The Bettmann Archive*, 607

Entry of French into Algiers, *The Bettmann Archive*, 611

Theodore Roosevelt in Panama, *The Granger Collection*, 613

Commodore Perry, *The Granger Collection*, 615

Cecil Rhodes, *The Granger Collection*, 617

"European Balance," by Daumier, *The Bettmann Archive*, 630

Soldiers leaving Berlin for front, *Wide World Photos*, 631

"Disturbing the Peace," *The Bettmann Archive*, 636

Princip, after assassination, *The Granger Collection*, 637

Allied soldiers keeping warm, *Wide World Photos*, 642

Aerial combat, World War I, *The Granger Collection*, 648

Allied tank on Western front, *Wide World Photos*, 649

English policewoman spreading news of Zeppelin raid, *The Bettmann Archive*. 650

Halt the Hun!, *Brown Brothers*, 651

American soldiers celebrate Armistice, *The Granger Collection*, 654

Paris greets Armistice, *The Granger Collection*, 654

The Big Four at Paris, 1919, *The Bettmann Archive*, 657

Rasputin, *The Granger Collection*. 670

Soldier delegates to Petrograd Soviet meeting, *Sovfoto*, 671

"Under the snug wing of Kerensky," *The Bettmann Archive*. 675

Moscow, 1917, *Sovfoto*, 675

Trotsky and staff, *The Bettmann Archive*, 680

Lenin addressing a throng, *Brown Brothers*, 680

Lenin and Stalin, *The Granger Collection*, 684

Trotsky and wife, *Wide World Photos*, 686

Tractors at a Machine-Tractor Station, *Sovfoto*, 689

Factory workers listening to charge made by Vishinsky, *Sovfoto*, 693

"Rendezvous," *The London Express*, 702

D'Annunzio, *Brown Brothers*, 709

Mussolini during "March" on Rome, *Brown Brothers*, 713

Officer addressing crowd during Kapp *putsch*, *The Granger Collection*, 721

Hitler watercolor and pencil drawing, *Wide World Photos*, 722

German inflation, *Wide World Photos*, 723

Ludendorff and Hitler, *The Bettmann Archive*, 725

Berliners hailing Hitler, *The Granger Collection*, 729

"Jews not wanted in this place," *Wide World Photos*, 732

Franco inspecting trenches during Spanish Civil War, *Brown Brothers*, 739

Dollfuss poster, *United Press International*, 740

King Alexander and loyal Croats, *Wide World Photos*, 743

King Carol II, *United Press International*, 744

Premier John Metaxas, *United Press International*, 745

Emergency transport carrying London office workers, *Wide World Photos*, 754

De Valera taking salute of Irish Republican army, *Brown Brothers*, 755

Wartime devastation in Verdun, *The Bettmann Archive*, 757

Demonstrators in Stavisky riots, *United Press International*, 760

NRA cartoon, *The Granger Collection*, 766

"Rule, Japannia," cartoon by Low, *The London Express*, 770

Chinese prisoners during Boxer rebellion, *The Bettmann Archive*, 771

Gandhi, *Wide World Photos*, 776

Signing of Locarno Pact, *Wide World Photos*, 783

Haile Selassie protesting to League of Nations, *The Granger Collection*, 786

"Honest, Mister, there's nobody here but us Spaniards," cartoon by Low, *The London Express*, 788

Chamberlain and Hitler, *Wide World Photos*, 790

Civilians in Marseilles watching flags being evacuated, *United Press International*, 798

Collapse of building during London "blitz," *Brown Brothers*, 799

Pearl Harbor, *United Press International* 802

American troops landing in Normandy, *Wide World Photos*, 805

Corpses of Gestapo victims, *United Press International*, 807

Hiroshima after the bomb hit, *Wide World Photos*, 810

Casablanca conference, *United Press International*, 811

Marshall Plan operation, *Wide World Photos*, 823

Berliners watching airlift during Berlin Blockade, *The Granger Collection*, 836

Tito and fellow partisans, *The Granger Collection*, 837

American infantrymen in evacuated Korean town, *Wide World Photos*, 838

Nehru receiving golden mace, *Wide World Photos*, 843

Stalin statue toppled in Budapest, *Wide World Photos*, 853

Crisscross sowing of wheat, U.S.S.R., *Sovfoto*, 856

Yevgeny Yevtushenko, *Sovfoto*, 859

Syniavsky and Daniel trial, *Sovfoto*, 859

Brandenburg gate, *Wide World Photos*, 864

Red Guardsman shouting support of Maoism, *Wide World Photos*, 874

President Soekarno and Cabinet, *Wide World Photos*, 878

Moslem refugees, *Wide World Photos*, 880

Nasser receiving plaudits, *Wide World Photos*, 883

Sekou Touré, *United Nations*, 885

Police dispersing demonstrating African women, *Wide World Photos*, 888

Nationalist terrorist suspects, *Wide World Photos*, 888

Student from the Cameroon speaking at Moscow protest meeting, *Wide World Photos*, 889

Dr. Martin Luther King, *Wide World Photos*, 897

President John F. Kennedy at NATO headquarters, *Wide World Photos*, 899

Freud, by Cocteau, *The Bettmann Archive*, 913

Pavlov watching experiment, *Sovfoto*, 915

James Joyce, *Monkmeyer Press Photo Service*, 925

"Current," by Bridget Riley, *The Museum of Modern Art*, 927

IBM Building, Seattle, *University Properties, Inc.*. 928

Gateway Arch, St. Louis, *Arteaga Photos, St. Louis*, 928

Central Technical School, Toronto, *Panda Associates*, 929

Untitled stabile-mobile, by Calder, *The Museum of Modern Art*, 929

"Family Group," by Moore, *The Museum of Modern Art*, 929

Acknowledgments

Grateful acknowledgment is made to the following publishers for granting permission to use the material quoted on the pages indicated: Allen & Unwin, Ltd., 150; Doubleday & Company, Inc., 892; E. P. Dutton & Company, Inc., 188, 285, 314, 320, 324, 325, 349, 356, 406, 407, 408, 413, 415, 460, 465; Faber & Faber, Ltd., 925; Hafner Publishing Company, 322, 323; Harcourt, Brace & World, 97, 925; William Heinemann, Ltd., 188; William Hodge & Company, Ltd., 609; Houghton Mifflin Company, 396, 717; The Macmillan Company, 457, 467; The Museum of Modern Art, 927; W. W. Norton, 109; Oxford University Press (London), 120, 121, 122, 140, 144, 579, 776; Oxford University Press (New York), 690; Penguin Books, Ltd., 85; Princeton University Press, 91; Random House, 472, 475, 931; St. Martin's Press, Inc., 262; Charles Scribner's Sons, 573; The Society of Authors, 926; University Books, Inc., 202; University of Chicago Press, 86, 87; Viking Press, Inc., 171, 926; Yale University Press, 89, 112.

"The White Man's Burden" on page 618 is from "The Five Nations" by Rudyard Kipling. Copyright 1903 by Rudyard Kipling, reprinted by permission of Mrs. George Bambridge, Doubleday & Company, Inc., and Methuen & Company, Ltd.

Index

A

Aachen, 19
Abelard, Peter, 26
Absolutism: age of, 166-175; Spanish, 166-168
Abstractionism, 926
Abukir Bay, battle of, 385
Académie, 233
Act of Settlement, 258
Act of Supremacy of *1534*, 129
Action Française, 759
Acton, Lord, 123
Adages and Colloquies, 91
Adam, Robert, *illus.*, 352
Addresses to the German Nation (Fichte), 398
Aden, 884
Adenauer, Konrad, 831, 902, 903
Adler, Alfred, 915
Adowa, battle of, 512, 786
Adrianople, Treaty of, 425
Adventures of a Monkey (Zoshchenko), 833
Aehrenthal, Count Aloys von, 543, 635
Affluent Society, The (Galbraith), 919
Afghanistan, 492, 634
Africa *(see also individual countries):* European expansion, 200-201, 221-222; imperialism in, 600-601, 606, 609-613; independence problems, 885-890; *1900, map*, 599; *1967, map*, 887
Agricola, 108
Agriculture: Canadian, 454; French, 274, 278, 362-363, 365, 433, 507; German, 454, 733; Irish land reforms, 493-494; medieval, 18-19, 23; Prussian, 326-327; Roman, 14; Russian tsarist, 551-553, 561-562; Russian Soviet, 683, 687-689, 696,

832, 852, 855-857; scientific advances in, 278-279, 454-455; Spanish, 332; U.S., 454, 764-766; Yugoslavian, 837
Aix-la-Chapelle, Peace of, 234
Aix-la-Chapelle, Treaty of, 304-305
Akhmatova, Anna, 833
Alaska, 423, 599, 897
Alba, Duke of, 164
Albania, 703; Chinese satellite, 867, 873; Italian conquest, 716, 788; U.S.S.R. satellite, 818, 837
Alberoni, Cardinal Giulio, 285
Albertus Magnus, 26
Albuquerque, Alfonso de, 200
Aldus Manutius, 108
Alexander (Greece), 644
Alexander (Yugoslavia), 743; *illus.*, 743
Alexander I (Russia), 338-340, 390, 392-393, 399-400, 416, 418, 423, 426-427, 431
Alexander II (Russia), 551-553, 556; *illus.*, 552
Alexander III (Russia), 556-557
Alexander VI, Pope, 43, 112
Alexander the Great (Macedon), 10
Alexandra, Empress (Russia), 669, 671
Alexis (son of Peter the Great), 332-333
Alexis, Tsar (father of Peter the Great), 63
Alexius Romanov, Tsar, 64
Alfonso V, the Magnanimous (Aragon and Sicily), 38, 42
Alfonso XIII (Spain), 736-737
Algeciras Conference, *1906*, 635
Algeria, 598, 610, 873, 890, 904
All Quiet on the Western Front (Remarque), 649
Alphabet, invention of, 6
Alsace-Lorraine, 35, 501, 507, 530, 534, 632, 655, 658, 759

Alton Locke (Kingsley), 477
Amenhotep IV (*see* Ikhnaton)
Amenophis IV (*see* Ikhnaton)
America (*see also* United States): Northmen, 6; thirteen colonies, 217-219; Viking discovery of, 199
American War of Independence, 364; background, 344-346; political implications, 346-348
Amiens, Peace of, 390
Amritsar massacre, 653, 775
Anabaptists, 130-132, 138-139
Anarchism, 476-477, 736-738
Anarcho-syndicalism, 476, 736
Anatomy, 108-109
Andrassy, Count Gyula, 536
Anglican church, 133-134, 243
Angola, 885
Annals of Agriculture (Young), 343
Anne, Empress (Russia), 332-334
Anne, Queen (England), 258
Anschluss, 740-741, 788-789
Anticlericalism: Austria, 329, 544; France, 321-322, 361, 370, 388, 505, 507, 759; Mexico, 848; Portugal, 331; Spain, 332, 422-423
Anti-Corn Law League, 454-455, 489
Anti-Machiavel (Frederick the Great), 326
Anti-semitism: Austria, 329, 544-545; Dreyfus case, 504-505; Germany, 731-732, 806-807; Hungary, 546, 741; Italy, 716; Prussia, 327; Rumania, 744; Russia, 557, 560, 833, 835; theorists, 835; Yugoslavia, 744
Antonescu, Marshal Ion, 744
Apartheid, 886
Appeal to the Christian Nobility of the German Nation, The, 121, 122
Aquinas, St. Thomas, 26
Arab League, 881
Aragon, 38-39
Arakcheev, Count Aleksei, 340, 426-427

Architecture: Baroque, 265-266; Chinese, *illus.*, 226; eclectic, 583-584, *illus.*, 584-585; English, *illus.*, 264; French, *illus.*, 172; French, Louis XIV, *illus.*, 243; Gothic, 30-32; Gothic revival, 411-412, *illus.*, 352, 412; Greek, *illus.*, 12; Incan, *illus.*, 213; Islamic, *illus.*, 71; medieval, 30-32; modern, 584-585, 928, *illus.*, 928-929; neoclassic, 351, *illus.*, 352; Renaissance, 102-104, *illus.*, 104, 105; Roman, *illus.*, 16; Romanesque, 30-31, *illus.*, 31; Russian, *illus.*, 65; Spanish, *illus.*, 167; Tudor, *illus.*, 181

Areopagitica, 256

Argentina, 454, 848-849, 892

Aristotle, 26, 86, 87

Armada, Spanish, 165; *illus.*, 165

Armenia, 695

Arminianism, 138

Arminius (*see* Herman)

Arminius, James, 138

Army, growth of modern, 155-157

Arnold, Matthew, 490, 579, 594

Arp, Jean, 927

Arsenal, of Venice, 51-52

Art (*see also* Architecture, Painting, Sculpture): Aztec, *illus.*, 214; Baroque, 265-266, *illus.*, 265; early Christian, *illus.*, 17; Coptic, *illus.*, 17; Dutch, 183; Egyptian, *illus.*, 8; Greek, *illus.*, 11; early medieval, *illus.*, 21; medieval, 29-32; prehistoric, 5, 6; Renaissance, 101-106, *illus.*, 45

Art of War, The, 47

Artois, Count of (*see* Charles X)

Arzhak, Nikolai (*see* Daniel, Yuli)

Asbury, Francis, 350

Asia (*see also individual countries*): in Cold War, 867-874; imperialism in, 602, 607-609, 612-616; *1900, map*, 601; *1967, map*, 876

Asiento privilege, 277, 303-304

Asquith, Herbert H., 495, 652, 752

Assignats, 369-370, 373, 378, 381

Astronomy, Renaissance contributions, 109-110

Asturias uprising, 737-738

Aswan Dam, 881

Atatürk (*see* Kemal, Mustafa)

Athens, 10-11

Atlantic Charter, 810

Atomic weapons: China, 865, 874; France, 895, 905; test ban agreement, 865; U.S., 794, 808; U.S.S.R., 816, 818, 822

Attlee, Clement, 811, 826

Audiencia, 214

Auerstädt, battle of, 392

Augsburg, 52-53; Fugger family and, 52-53

Augsburg, Peace of, 162

Augustus (Octavian) (Rome), 14

Augustus II, the Strong (Poland), 294-295, 302

Augustus III (Poland), 302, 340

Austerlitz, battle of, 391-392; *illus.*, 392

Australia, 454, 620-622, 818, 895

Australian Colonies Government Act, 621-622

Austria, 301, 340, 343, 458, 499, 550-551, 653, 900; *Anschluss*, 788-789; anti-clericalism, 329, 544; anti-semitism, 544-545; Charles VI, 287-288; Congress of Vienna, 415-419; dual monarchy, 537-538; economy, 329, 331, 739; education, 329; European revolutions, 423, 431, 436-439; fascism in, 739-741; French Revolution, 372, 376, 382-383; under Habsburgs, 40; Italy and, 287, 436-439, 509-511; Maria Theresa, 328-329; minorities in, 538-541, 545-546, *map*, 539; Napoleonic Wars, 384-385, 389-393, 398-399; occupation status, 835; politics, *1867-1914*, 544-546; politics, inter-war, 739-741; "Potato War," 330; pre-*Ausgleich*, 535-536; Prussian war, 528-529; revolution of *1848*, 441-444; social classes, 544-545; Troppau Protocol, 423; Turkish wars, 302-303; Versailles settlement, 655, 659; War of Austrian Succession, 304, 341; War of Polish Succession, 302-303; World War I, 627-629, 632-633, 635-638, 640-644

Austrian Succession, War of the, 281, 304, 328, 341

Austrian Netherlands, 189

Autobiography (Mill), 464

Aviation: in World War I, 647; in World War II, 794-795, 799-800, 804-806

Avignon, 42

Ayub Khan, 880

Azaña, Manuel, 738

Azerbaidjan, 695

Azov, 341

Aztecs, 212

B

Babbitt (Lewis), 578, 764

Babeuf, Gracchus, 381

Babi Yar (Yevtushenko), 858

Babylonian Captivity, of papacy, 42

Bach, Johann Sebastian, 353, 355, 410

Bach system (Austria), 535-536

Bacon, Francis, 182

Bacon, Roger, 259

Baden, 275, 390, 528

Badoglio, Marshal Pietro, 805, 812

Bagehot, Walter, 484, 592

Baghdad Pact, 895

Bahamas, 606

Bakunin, Michael, 476, 554-555, 710, 736

Baldwin, Stanley, 755

Balearic Islands, 307

Balfour Declaration, 646, 653, 777, 845

Balkans, 302-303, 329; in World War I, 629, 633, 635-636, 644-646

Baltic provinces, 285, 294-296

Balzac, Honoré de, 576

Bank of England, 276-278, 451

Bank of France, 389, 760

Banking, 275-278, 364, 389, 760; and Industrial Revolution, 451; late medieval, 44, 52-53; Russian Gosbank, 691

Barbary pirates, 429

Barbusse, Henri, 649

Barings of London, 451

Baroja, Pio, 578

Basel, Treaty of, 383

Bastille, fall of, 366-368

Battle of Arminius (Kleist), 409

Battle of Britain, 799-801

"Battle of the Nations," 400

Bavaria, 304, 330, 390, 528, 652, 718

Bazaine, General Achille François, 500

Beauharnais, Eugène de, 396

Beauharnais, Josephine de, 382, 393

Beaumarchais, Pierre, 362

Bebel, August, 532

Beccaria, Cesare, 319, 329, 331, 336

Beerbohm, Max, *illus.*, 578

Beethoven, Ludwig van, 409-410

"Beggars," Dutch, 163, 164

Beggar's Opera (Gay), 353

Behaviorism, 915-916

Belgium, 189, 481-482, 719; Austrian control, 285, 287, 306, 329; colonies, 599, 613, 873, 888-889; European union and, 900; Locarno treaty, 782; Napoleonic Wars, 382-384, 390, 393; Netherlands control, 418; revolution of *1830*, 430-431, 457; suffrage, 458; World War I, 638, 640, 655, 659; World War II, 795, 797

Belgrade, fortress of, 73, 74

Belgrade, Treaty of, 340

Belorussia, 342-343

Ben Bella, Ahmed, 873, 889-890

Benefice, 22

Beneš, Edward, 835

Bennett, Arnold, 578

Bentham, Jeremy, 462-465

Bergson, Henri, 589

Beowulf, 29

Beria, Lavrentia, 852, 854

Berlin, 288, 290, 817; blockade, 836; *illus.*, 836; in Cold War, 862-863; Wall, 863, 902

Berlin, Congress of, 556

Berlin Decree, 396

Berlin, University of, 398

Berlioz, Louis Hector, 410

Bermuda, 606

Bernadotte, Crown Prince, 393

Bernard, St., 26

Berri, Duke of, 428

Bessarabia, 660, 703, 744, 835, 866

Bessemer, Sir Henry, 450

Bestuzhev-Ryumin, Mikhail, 340-341

Betancourt, Romulo, 866

Bethlen, Count István, 742

Bethmann-Hollweg, Theobald von, 638 651

Beust, Friedrich Ferdinand, 536

Bible: Christianity and, 16; Erasmus and, 92; King James version, 250; origin of man and, 3; Tindal's translation, 129; Vulgate, 92

Bidault, Georges, 503

"Biglow Papers" (Lowell), 579

Bill of Rights: English, 257, 347; U.S., 347

Biology: Darwinian eugenicists, 571-572; evolutionary, 568-569; Linnaeus' contributions, 315; U.S.S.R., 833, 915-916

Bismarck, Otto von, 444; Austrian

war, 528-529; colonial policy, 613; domestic policies, 526, 530-533; foreign policies, 527-530, 613, 632-633; Franco-Prussian war, 529-530; German Confederation, 524-526; League of the Three Emperors, 633; North German Confederation, 529; Pan-Germans and, 545; Roman Catholic Church, 530-532; Triple Alliance, 633; welfare measures, 532; *illus.*, 527
Black Death, 48-49, 53
Black, Joseph, 315
Black Partition (Russia), 556
Black Sea, 342-343, 551, 556
Blanc, Louis, 435, 448, 470, 477
Blücher, Gebhard Leberecht von, 401
Blum, Leon, 760-761
Boccaccio, Giovanni, 87-88
Bodin, Jean, 175
Boer War, 534, 603-604; *illus.*, 604
Bohemia (*see also* Czechoslovakia), 288, 329, 441-442, 538, 659; Thirty Years' War and, 184-185
Bolsheviks, 558-561, 670, 673-676
Bonaparte, Jerome, 393
Bonaparte, Joseph (Naples), 393, 422
Bonaparte, Louis (Holland), 396, 402
Bonaparte, Louis Napoleon (*see* Napoleon III)
Bonaparte, Lucien, 385
Bonaparte, Napoleon (*see* Napoleon Bonaparte)
Bonapartists, in *1848* revolution, 434, 436
Booth, John Wilkes, 516
Boris, King (Bulgaria), 744
Borodin, Mikhail, 699
Bosanquet, Bradley, 588
Bosnia-Herzogovina, 543-544, 556, 645
Boston Tea Party, 346; *illus.*, 345
Borgia, Cesare, 43
Boris Godunov, 62
Bosworth Field, battle of, 37
Botticelli, 95-96
Boulanger, General Georges, 504
Boyars, 59, 61
Bourgeoisie (*see* Classes, social; Middle Classes)
Bouvard et Pécuchet (Flaubert), 578
Boxer Rebellion, 558, 771
Boyars, 333
Boyne, battle of, 235
Bradley, Henry, 588
Brandenburg, 288
Brazil, 200, 423, 892
Brest-Litovsk, Peace of, 643, 652, 678-679
Brethren of the Common Life, 112
Breughel, Pieter, the Elder, 100, 101; *illus.*, 100
Brezhnev, L. I., 872-873
Briand, Aristide, 503, 782-783
Bridgewater, Duke of, 275
Bridgman, P. W., 920
Brieux, Eugene, 577
Britannia, 19
British Commonwealth of Nations, 756-757, 842-843, 875, 886
British Guiana, 606, 892
British Honduras, 606
Brittany, Duchy of, 35
Broglie, Duke of, 502

Bronze Age, 5
Browne, Robert, 179
Brownists, 179
Broz, Joseph (*see* Tito)
Bruening, Heinrich, 727, 729, 740
Brunswick, Duke of, 373-374, 383
Brusilov, General Aleksei Alekseevich, 643
Buddhism, 203
Bukharin, Nikolai, 684, 686, 693-694, 700
Bukovina, 705, 835, 866
Bulganin, Nikolai, 852, 853, 854
Bulgaria, 556, 699, 744-745; in Soviet bloc, 818, 835; in World War I, 638, 644, 646; in World War II, 703
Bulletin of the Opposition, The (Trotsky), 692
Bunyan, John, 139
Burckhardt, 482
Burgoyne, General John, 346
Burgundy, 34-35, 158
Burke, Edmund, 382, 385-386, 406, 415
Burma, 803, 826, 838, 870
Burne-Jones, Sir Edward, 580
Burns, John, 638
Burns, Robert, 136
Burundi, 873
Business (*see* Economy; Industry; Industrial Revolution)
Bute, Lord, 344
Butler, Samuel, 578
Byng, Admiral, 307
Byron, Lord, 407
Byzantine Empire, *map*, 55; fall of, 57; history of, 55-56
Byzantium, 14; capture of, in *1453*, 33

C

Caballero, Largo, 738
Cabral, Pedro, 200
Caesar, Julius, 14
Cashiers, 363
Calas, Jean, 321
Calcutta, 221
Calder, Alexander, *illus.*, 929
Caldwell, Erskine, 578
Calonne, Charles Alexander de, 364
Calvin, John, 127-128; *illus.*, 136
Calvinism, 135-138, 329, 546; and capitalism, 147-148
Cambodia, 870
Camelots du Roi, 759
Cameroon (Kamerun) 612, 661
Camoens, 208
Campoformio, Treaty of, 384
Camus, Albert, 919, 922, 930-931
Canada, 283, 308, 344, 346, 454, 515, 598, 620-621, 825, 899-900
Candide (Voltaire), 314, 322
Canning, George, 423-424, 484
Canterbury Tales, 89
Cape Breton Island, 304
Cape Colony, 602-604
Cape of Good Hope, 418
Capet, Hugh, 27
Capetian dynasty, in France, 27, 28
Capitalism: growth of, 50-51; Protestantism and, 146-148

Carbonari, 423, 431
Caribbean, British imperialism in, 606-607
Carlism (Spain), 736, 738
Carlsbad Decrees, 432
Carlyle, Thomas, 490, 594
Carnap, Rudolf, 920
Carol, King (Rumania), 744
Carolingians: decay of empire, 21; empire of, *map*, 20
Carthage, Rome and, 13
Casablanca Conference, 810; *illus.*, 811
Casa de Contratación, 169
Cassirer, Ernst, 919
Caste system, 202-203
Castiglione, 106, 113-114
Castile, 38-39; Council of, 39
Castlereagh, Viscount, 416-419, 423
Castrati, 267
Castro, Fidel, 859, 864, 872
Cateau-Cambrésis, Treaty of, 159
Catherine of Aragon, 128, 129
Catherine I (Russia), 293, 332-333
Catherine II, the Great (Russia), 278, 333-337, 341-343
Catholic Center party (Germany), 531-532, 534, 719, 727, 729, 731
Catholic Church (*see* Roman Catholic Church)
Catholic Reformation, 139-144; Council of Trent and, 142-144; Inquisition and, 141-142; Jesuits and, 140-141
Cavaignac, General, 435-436
Cavour, Count Camillo Benso di, 437, 508-510; *illus.*, 508
Central Treaty Organization (CENTO), 898
Cervantes, Miguel de, 170-171
Ceylon, 418
Cézanne, Paul, 582-583; *illus.*, 582
Chaadaev, 553
Chamberlain, Austen, 496
Chamberlain, Houston Stewart, 721
Chamberlain, Joseph, 493-494, 496, 752-753
Chamberlain, Neville, 496, 789-790, 797; *illus.*, 790
Chanson de Roland, 29
Charlemagne, 19-21, 29; *illus.*, 21; *map*, 20
Charles I (England), 248-253; *illus.*, 251
Charles II (England), 253-254, 256
Charles III (Spain), 331-332; *illus.*, 331
Charles V, Emperor (Spain), 35, 123-124, 158-162
Charles VI (Austria), 287-288, 299-300, 302, 304
Charles VII (Bavaria), 304
Charles VIII (France), 157-158
Charles X (France), 428-429
Charles XII (Sweden), 294-296, 302, 331
Charles Albert (Piedmont), 437-439
Charter of *1814* (France), 400
Chartism, 491
Chase, Stuart, 920
Chaucer, Geoffrey, 89
Cheap Clothes and Nasty (Kingsley), 477
Chekhov, Anton Pavlovich, 577
Chemistry, 315, 923

Chetniks (Yugoslavia), 836
Chiang Kai-shek, 684, 699, 772-774, 808, 817, 819, 839
Chiaroscuro, 93, 95
Chile, 892-894
China (see also Manchuria), 558, 616, 653, 699; Africa and, 889-890; atomic weapons, 874; Boxer Rebellion, 558, 771; Civil War, 772-774, 817; civilization, 203-204; Communist party, 817, 819, 862; European expansion, 203-205, 222; Great Wall, illus., 226; imperialism in, 602, 606-607, 612; India invasion, 868; Indonesia and, 877-878; industry, 867; Japanese occupation, 772-774; Korean War, 838-839; Mao's succession, 873-874; Nine Power Treaty, 763-764; Revolution of 1911, 771-772; Russia and, 68; U.N. representation, 895; U.S.S.R. split, 862, 867-869, 873; Vietnam War, 871; World War II, 808
Chios, 425
Chippendale, Thomas, 352
Chivalry, 29-30
Choiseul, Duke of, 309-317
Christ (see Jesus Christ)
Christian IV (Denmark), 187
Christian Democratic party: Germany, 831, 902-903; Italy, 712, 906
Christian Nobility of the German Nation, The, 121-122; illus., 135
Christian Socialist party (Austria), 545, 739-740
Christianity (see also Religion; Roman Catholic Church): adaptability of, 17; Bible and, 16; Machiavelli and, 47-48; origin of, 16
Chronometer, 275
Chrysoloras, Manuel, 88
Church of England, 349, 493
Churchill, John, 236
Churchill, Winston, 644, 648, 790, 797, 799, 801, 805-806, 810, 812, 818, 826-827, 835; illus., 811
Cid, the, 171
Cisalpine Republic (Napoleonic), 384-385
Cities: city-states of Greece, 10-11; establishment of, 5-6
Civil Constitution of the Clergy, 370, 388
Civil liberties (see also Law; Religion; Suffrage); Austria-Hungary, 537; France, nineteenth century, 387-388, 401-402, 428-429; Great Britain, nineteenth century, 484; Italy, fascist, 714-715; Japan, imperial, 769; Poland, nineteenth century, 431; Prussia, nineteenth century, 432, 441; Revolution of 1820, 419; Russia, 559-560, 694-695; Spain, nineteenth century, 422; Turkey, 778; U.S. desegregation laws, 897
Civil Rights Bill of 1965 (United States), 897
Civil War (England), 251-253
Civil War (United States), 513-516
Civilization: in ancient Near East, 5-8; map, 7; Greece and, 10-13; Rome and, 13-16
Clarissa Harlowe (Richardson), 350, 407
Classes, social (see also Labor; Middle

Classes); anarchist theory, 476-477; Austrian, 544-545; British, 484-486, 495, 496, 752-754; French, 360-366, 369, 434-435, 444, 758-761; Indian, 608, 844; Industrial Revolution, 457-460; Japanese, 615-616; Marxist theory, 471-475; Russian, 336-339, 551-552; Social Darwinists' theory, 571, 573; United States, 824
Clemenceau, Georges, 652, 661; illus., 657
Clement VII, Pope, 158
Clement XIV, Pope, 320
Clergy: regular, 24; secular, 24
Cleves-Mark, 288-289
Clive, Robert, 305, 308, 607
Clough, Arthur Hugh, 579
Coal, 280, 450, 452, 526
Cocteau, Jean, illus., 913
Code Napoléon, 387, 422, 428
Code of Hammurabi, 6
Coke, Sir Edward, 249
Colbert, Jean, 244-245
Colbert, Jean Baptiste, 275, 284
Cold War: atomic weapons, 816; Berlin, 862-863; Cuban crisis, 863, 892; defensive alliances, 894; "hot line," 865; Multilateral Force, 865; in Southeast Asia, 816-817, 836, 839, 870-874; test ban agreement, 863-865; U-2 incident, 863; U.S.S.R.-China split, 867-868
Coleridge, Samuel Taylor, 407-408, 410
Coligny, Gaspard, 173
Collins, Michael, 755-756
Colombia, 614
Colonial Society (Germany), 534
Colonies (see also European expansion; Imperialism): American War of Independence, 344-348; British, 281, 305-309, 492; French, 283-284, 429, 507, 761; French Union, 830; German, 534, 612-613, 661; nationalism in, 768-769, 839-847; North African, 429; Portuguese, 423, 885; Seven Years' War, 305-309; Spanish, 422; thirteen American, 217-219
Columbus, Christopher, 208-210
Combination Acts (England), 458, 484
Cominform, 818, 837
Comintern, 668, 698-700, 818
Committee of General Security (France), 380
Committee of Public Safety (France), 377-378, 380
Common Market, 826, 900
Commons, House of, 29
Communications and the Industrial Revolution, 451
Communism: definition of, 466; Karl Marx, 471-475; revisionism, 861; U.S.S.R.-China split, 867-868
Communist League, 472
Communist parties; Chinese, 774, 862 (see also China); England, 699; French, 759-761; German, 718-719, 724-726, 728-729, 731; Italian, 906; Korean, North, 873; Pathet Lao, 870; Soviet bloc, 853, 861, 866; Spanish, 736, 738; U.S.S.R., 685-686, 852-855

Compagnie des Indes Orientals, 221
Comuneros, 167
Conciliar Movement, 42
Concordat of Bologna, 128, 173
Condition of the Working Class in England, The (Engels), 472
Condorcet, Marie Jean, 315, 317, 325, 376, 380; illus., 321
Confederation of the Rhine, 393
"Confession of Golias," 30
Confucianism, 204-205
Congo, Belgium, 599, 873, 888
Congo, French, 635, 885
Congress party (India), 776, 879
Conservative party (Canada), 899
Conservative party (England), 487-488, 492-493, 495-496, 752-755, 901
"Conspiracy of the Equals," 381
Constable de Bourbon, 158
Constable, John, 411
Constantine, King (Greece), 644
Constantine (brother of Alexander I), 427
Constantine I, Emperor, 14; conversion of, 16
Constantine XI, Emperor, 59
Constantinople, 14, 16; fall of, in 1453, 33, 57
Constitutional Democrats (Russia), 558-559, 561, 670, 674, 676
Consubstantiation, 127
Continental System, 396-398
Coolidge, Calvin, 762-764
Cooper, James Fenimore, 594
Copernicus, Nicholas, 109-110
Coral Sea, battle of the, 803
Corfu, 716, 785
Corinth, 10
Corn Laws, 454-455, 457, 489-490
Corsica, 383, 787
Cortes, 38-39
Cortés, Hernando, 212
Così Fan Tutte (Mozart), 354
Cossacks, 65-66; Tartars and, 66
Cotton and Industrial Revolution, 449-452
Coulson, Samuel, 458
Council for Europe, 826-900
Council for Mutual Economic Aid (Comecon), 862, 865
Council of Castile, 39
Council of Ferrara-Florence, 57
Council of Seventy, 44
Council of Ten, 46
Council of Trent, 142-144
Council of Troubles, 164
Counter-Reformation (see Catholic Reformation)
Courtier, The, 113-114
Courts, under Henry VII (England), 37
Crane, Stephen, 577
Cranmer, Archbishop, 178
Crete, 10; capture of, by Turks, 76
Crimea, 342-343
Crimean War, 74, 492, 499, 509, 526, 550-551
Croatia, 614-615, 865, 892
Croce, Benedetto, 589
Cromwell, Oliver, 252-254, 337, 772
Cuba, 614-615, 865, 892
Cubism, 926-927
Culloden, battle of, 304; illus., 305

Culture: European eighteenth century, 348-355; French, 379; German Nazi, 735; Prussian, 291; in review, 932-934; Russian Soviet, 697, 832-833; Russian tsarist, 291, 298, 300; twentieth century, 911-912, 924, 930-932; U.S. postwar, 824; Victorian, 575, 587-588, 593-595
Cumberland, Duke of, 308
Cunard, Samuel, 451
Curzon, Samuel, 451
Cyprus; 660, 895; capture of, by Turks, 76
Czechoslovakia: German take-over, 742, 789-790; "Little Entente," 784; U.S.S.R. treaty, 700; Versailles settlement, 652-653, 659-660, 664; satellite status, 835, 866

D

Dacia, Kingdom of, 343
Dadaism, 927
Daily Telegraph Affair, 534
Daladier, Edouard, 761, 789-790
Danegeld, 28
Daniel, Yuli, 860
D'Annunzio, Gabriele, 709, 711
Dante Alighieri, 85-86; illus., 85
Danton, Georges Jacques, 373; illus., 374
Danubian principalities (see also Moldavia; Rumania; Wallachia), 343, 535-536, 551
Danzig, 660, 791
Darby family, 280
Dardanelles, 342, 550, 643-644, 655
Dark Ages, 18-19
Darwin, Charles, 568-575
Darwinism: and eugenics, 571-572; and historicism, 573-575; philosophic effect, 589; and political thought, 592-593; and racism, 572-573; Social Darwinism, 570-571; theological effect, 569-570
Das Kapital (Marx), 474-475
Daudet, Leon, 594
Daumier, Honoré, 582; illus., 434
David, Jacques Louis, 410-411
Davis, Jefferson, 534
Dawes, Charles G., 716
Dawes Plan, 726
Day in the Life of Ivan Denisov, A (Solzhenitsyn), 859
Day of the Barricades, 174
Deák, Francis, 542-543, 547
Debussy, Claude, 586
Decameron, 87
Decembrist Revolution, 426-427, 549
Declaration of Independence (United States), 314, 347
Declaration of Indulgence, 256, 257
Declaration of the Rights of Man, 369
Declaratory Act, 345
Decline of the West (Spengler), 921
"Defenestration of Prague," 184-185
Defense of the Realm Act, 650
Defoe, Daniel, 320
De Gasperi, Alcide, 831, 906
De Gaulle, Charles, 798, 812, 830; Fifth Republic, 895, 903-906; illus., 811

De Humanis Corporis Fabrica, 109
Deism, 320-322, 327
Delacroix, Eugène, 411; illus., 412, 426
Delcassé, Théophile, 626
De Maupassant, Guy, 577
Democracy, in Greece, 11
Democrat party (Turkey), 881
Democratic party (Germany), 719
Deniken, General Anton Ivanovich, 679, 681
Denmark, 294-295, 390, 418, 458, 527, 529, 795, 900
Denmark, Thirty Years' War and, 185
Derby, Earl of, illus., 455
De Re Metallica, 108
De Revolutionibus Orbium Coelestium, 109
Der Freischütz (Von Weber), 410
Descartes, René, 262, 314; illus., 261
De Sica, Vittorio, 831
D'Esperey, Franchet, 646
De Valera, Eamon, 756
Devshirme, 71, 72
Dewey, Thomas E., 823
Díaz, Bartholomew, 200
Díaz, Porfirio, 848
Dickens, Charles, 463, 576
Dickinson, Emily, 580
Dickinson, Lowes, 629
Diderot, Denis, 317, 335; illus., 321
Diefenbaker, John, 899
Diem, Ngo Dinh, 869-870
Dienbienphu, 870
Diggers, 255
Diplomacy: European developments in, 77, 154-155; under Ottoman state, 74-75
Directory (France), 381-382, 385-386
Discourse on the Moral Effects of the Arts and Sciences (Rousseau), 323, 324
Discourses on the First Ten Books of Titus Livius, 47-48
Disraeli, Benjamin, 283, 460, 487-488, 490, 492, 605, 607
Divine Comedy (Dante), 85
Divine right of kings, 240-241
Dr. Zhivago (Pasternak), 858, 930
Doge, of Venice, 45, 46
Dolguruky family (Russia), 333
Dollfuss, Engelbert, 737, 740; illus., 740
Doll's House (Ibsen), 577
Dominican Republic, 891
Donatello, 101, 102; illus., 102
Donation of Constantine, 89
Don Giovanni (Mozart), 354
Don Quixote (Cervantes), 171
Dostoevski, Fëdor, 576
Drama: first Russian, 69; Shakespearean, 182
Dreiser, Theodore, 377
Dreyfus, Alfred, 504-506
Dubliners, The (Joyce), 925
Duchamp, Marcel, 927
Dudintsev, Vladimir, 858
Dulles, John Foster, 881
Duma (Russia), 339, 560-562, 669, 671
Dumouriez, Charles François, 376
Dunkirk, 797-798
Dupleix, Marquis Joseph François, 305
Dürer, Albrecht, 99-101

Durham, Earl of, 621
Durham Report, 621, 756
Durkheim, Emile, 917
Dutch republic, 183-184
Dutch revolt, 163-164

E

East (see Byzantium; Crusades; Ottoman state)
East India Company (British), 221, 278, 304-305, 307, 346, 607-608
East India Company (French), 305
East Indies, 220-221
Eastern Orthodox Church, 56
Ebert, Friedrich, 718-719, 726
Eboué, Felix, 798
Economic theory: classical, 460-462; Christian Socialist, 477; Marxian, 471-475; mercantilist, 317-318; J. S. Mill, 464-465; Proudhon, 476-477; Roman Catholic Church, 477-479; utilitarianism, 462-464; utopian, 466-470
Economics: European expansion and, 224; late medieval, 53-54
Economy (see also Agriculture; Industry): agricultural revolution, 454-455; Argentina, 848-849; Austria, 329, 331, 739; England, 495-496, 751, 827, 896, 900-902; Egypt, 881-883; France, 378-379, 381, 389, 396-398, 429, 433, 498-499, 507, 757-760, 830, 896, 904-905; France, Old Régime, 274, 359-366, 369-370; German, 722-728; German Nazi, 733-734; German postwar, 830-896; German Zollverein, 439-440; imperialism and, 598, 611, 618-619; India, 879; Industrial Revolution and, 447-453; Italy, 708 831, 896, 906; Italy, fascist, 714-715; Japan, 770, 875-877; mercantilism, 274-276, 317-318; Prussia, 327; Russia, tsarist, 548, 557; Russia, Soviet, 677, 682-683, 691, 832; Spain, 168-169, 332, 906; Sweden, 331; Turkey, 880-881; United States, 517-519, 764-768, 823-824, 896-897; U.S.S.R. satellites, 862-866; World War I European, 650
Edict of Nantes, 175; revocation of, 237, 242
Edict of Restitution, 185
Education: Austrian, 329; British, 460, 489-491, 826; British colonial, 606, 608-609, 612, 840; French, 361, 388-389, 505, 507; French colonial, 612; Italian fascist, 715; medieval, 24-27; J. S. Mill on, 465; Ottoman court, 72; R. Owen on, 468-469; philosophes' attitude, 319-320; Rousseau on, 319-320, 323, 325, 349; Russian tsarist, 298, 550; Russian Soviet, 696-697, 857-858; U.S. school desegregation, 897
Edward VI (England), 178
Egypt, 434, 629, 634; art, illus., 8; British protectorate, 492, 605-606, 777; Napoleonic campaign, 384-385; Nasser, 846-847, 861, 881-883
Ehrenberg, Ilya, 858

Eighteenth Brumaire of Louis Napoleon, The (Marx), 474
Einstein, Albert, 922
Eisenhower, General Dwight D., 803, 811, 823, 863, 877
Eisenstein, Serge, 930
Elba, island of, 400, 418
Elgin, Lord Victor Alexander, 621
Eliot, T. S., 595
Elizabeth, Empress (Russia), 306-307, 333-335, 341
Elizabeth I (England), 178-180, *illus.,* 179
Elizabethan age, 180-182
Emigration: from Europe, *1880s,* 455, 462; from Ireland, 493; from Italy, 512, 715
Emigrés, 373, 378, 385-386, 400, 428-429
Emile (Rousseau), 319-320, 323, 325, 349
Ems telegram, 530
Enabling Act (Germany), 731
Enclosure movement, 278-279
Encomienda, 215
Encyclopédie, 316-317, 335
Enemy of the People (Ibsen), 577-578
Engels, Frederick, 448, 472; *illus.,* 473
Enghien, Duke of, 387
England to 1707 (see Great Britain *for references after 1707; see also* Anglo-Saxons): under Charles I, 248-253; Civil War in, 251-253; under Cromwell, 253-254; under Elizabeth, 178-182; Glorious Revolution, 257-258; under Henry VII, 35-38; under Henry VIII, 128-130, 176; during Hundred Years' War, *map,* 36; Ireland and, 180, 258; under James I, 249-250; monarchy and, 28-29; Norman conquest of, 28; Reformation and, 128-130; the Restoration, 256-257; role of Crown, 247-248; under Tudors, 176-180; Wars of the Roses, 29, 37
Eniwetok, 808
Enlightenment, Age of: art, 351-352; Catherine the Great, 335-337; economic theories, 317-318; education, 319-320; enlightened despots, 326-332; French leadership, 316-317; law, 318-319; limitations of reason, 348-349; literature, 350-351; music, 353-355; political thought, 322-326; religion, 406-414; Romantic protest, 406-414; science, 315-316
Eoliths, 5
Equatorial Africa (French), 798
Erasmus, Desiderius, 91-92
Erastian, 134, 135
Erfurt, meeting, 399
Erfurt Union of Provinces, 525
Erhard, Ludwig, 902-903
Ericson, Leif, 6
Erikson, Eric, 119
Ernst, Max, 927
Erzberger, Matthias, 720
Escorial, palace of, *illus.,* 167
Essay Concerning Human Understanding (Locke), 314
Essay on Crimes and Punishments (Beccaria), 319, 336
Essay on the Principles of Population (Malthus), 460, 568

Essex, Earl of, 180
Estates General, 360, 364-366
Esterhazy, Major, 505
Estonia, 660, 695, 701-702, 795
Ethics Mathematically Demonstrated (Spinoza), 183
Eugénie, Empress (France), 500
Europe *(see also individual countries):* in *1648, map,* 190-191; in *1715, map,* 238-239; *1812* Napoleonic, *map,* 394-395; *1815, map,* 420-421; *1850, map,* 483; *1914-1918, map,* 644-645; *1953, map,* 828-829; Coal and Steel Community, 826, 900; Council for Europe, 826, 900; dynastic and religious wars, 151-192; European Defense Community, 894; late medieval period, 33-77; mid-sixteenth century, *map,* 160-161; Organization for European Economic Cooperation, 826; Ottoman empire and, 74, 76-77
European Coal and Steel Community, 826
European expansion, 195-227; atrocities of, 223-227; effects on West, 224-227; *map,* 196
European Free Trade Association, 900
Evelyn, John, 293
Existentialism, 919
Exploration: Columbus, 208-210; Dutch, 216, 220-222; English, 216-219; French, 216, 219-222; later explorers, 210-211; Portuguese, 199-211

F

Factory Acts (England), 490
Faerie Queene (Spenser), 182
Falange (Spain), 738
Fanfani, Amintore, 906
Far East, European expansion in, 222
Farnese, Elizabeth, 286-287, 301-302, 304, 331
Farouk, King (Egypt), 846
Fascism: in Austria, 739-741; definition, 707-708; in eastern Europe, 742-745; in Hungary, 742; in Italy, 707-717, 745
Fascists Exposed, The (Matteotti), 713
Fashoda incident, 634
Fathers and Sons (Turgenev), 555
Faulhaber, Cardinal, 735
Faulkner, William, 925
Faust (Goethe), 407
February Patent (Austria), 536
Federal Deposit Insurance Corporation, 766
Federal Reserve Act (*1913*), 519
Fedor Romanov, Tsar, 63
Fehrbellin, battle of, 288
Fenian Brotherhood, 493
Ferdinand I (Austria), 443
Ferdinand I (Two Sicilies), 423
Ferdinand II (Austria), 185
Ferdinand II (Two Sicilies), 437
Ferdinand V, the Catholic, 38-40, 157
Ferdinand VII (Spain), 422, 428
Ferrara-Florence, Council of, 57
Feudalism: early, 21-23; *illus.,* 28

Feuerbach, Ludwig Andreas, 471
Fichte, Johann Gottlieb, 398
Ficino, Marsilio, 90
Fief, 22
"Field of the Cloth of Gold," 176
Fielding, Henry, 350-351
Filaret, 62, 63
Finance *(see also* Banking, Economy): European, eighteenth century, 276-278, 280, 284, 359, 364; and Industrial Revolution, 451-452
Fine arts *(see* Architecture; Culture; Music; Painting; Sculpture)
Finland, 340; Brest-Litovsk Treaty, 409; Great Northern War, 296; Russian domination, 418, 643, 795; World War II, 702-703, 835
Finnegans Wake (Joyce), 925-926
First International, 476
First International Workingmen's Association, 475
Fiume, 658, 709
Five-Mile Act, 256
Flandin, Pierre, 760
Flaubert, Gustave, 576, 578
Fleury, Cardinal, 284-285, 303
Florence, Republic of, 43-44
"Flying shuttle," 280
Foch, Marshal Ferdinand, 640, 648
Forain, Jean Louis, 582
Fordney-McCumber Tariff, 763
Formosa, 616, 770, 817, 839
Forster, William, 491
Fort Duquesne, 305, 308
Foster, Stephen, 586
Foundations of the Nineteenth Century, The (Chamberlain), 721
Fourier, François M. C., 467-470, 556
Fourteen Points, 655-657
Forward, 710
France *(see also* Enlightenment, French Revolution, *Philosophes),* 273-284, 286, 288, 301-304, 343, 457, 526; as aggressor, 231-239; agriculture, 274, 278, 362-363, 365, 433, 507; Algeria and, 887, 905-906; American War of Independence, 346; Ancien Régime, 240-246; anticlericalism, 321-322, 361, 370, 388, 505, 507, 759; atomic weapons, 905; Boulanger threat, 504; under Charles VIII, 157-158; civil liberties, 369, 371, 377, 381, 387-388, 401-402, 422, 428-429; Congress of Vienna, 416-418; Continental system, 396-398; Crimean War, 492; Declaration of the Rights of Man, 369; Directory, 381, 383-385; Dreyfus case, 504-505; economy, nineteenth century, 389, 396-397; economy, twentieth century, 757-761, 830, 896, 905; education, 371, 388-389; Ethiopian crisis, 786-787; Fashoda incident, 634; Fifth Republic, 900, 904, 905; First Republic, 370-382; Fourth Republic, 827, 830; Greek War of Independence, 425; under Henry IV, 232; Hundred Years War, *map,* 36; imperialism, 283-284, 507, 598-599, 609-612, 761, 777, 830, 842; Industrial Revolution, 452; July monarchy, 428-430; Little Entente, 664, 784; Locarno treaty, 789-790; under Louis XI, 34-35; under Louis

XIV, 234-236, 240-246; monarchy of, 27-28, 171-173; Moroccan crisis, 635; Munich agreement, 789-790; Napoleon I, 382-402; Napoleon III, 497-500; Napoleonic Europe, *map.* 394-395; in North America, 219-220; Ottoman Empire and, 74; painting, 580-583; Popular Front, 760-761; Prussian War, 529-530; Reign of Terror, 376-380; Revolution of *1848,* 433-436; revolutions, nineteenth century European, 423, 430-432, 509-510; *map.* 422; Rhineland, 783, 786; Richelieu, 232-234; Ruhr, 723, 784-785; Russian relations, 334, 679, 681, 700, 785; Seven Years War, 305-309; social classes, 758-760; Stavisky case, 758; suffrage, 371, 377, 381; Third Republic, 500-508, 757-761; Thirty Years War, 187-188; Triple Entente, 633-635; Versailles treaty, 657-658; wars of religion, 173-174; World War I, 628-629, 632, 638, 640-641, 644, 646-648; World War II, 791-798, 811-812

France, Anatole, 578
Franche Comté, 34, 35
Francis I (Austria), 443
Francis I (France), 158-162, 171-173; *illus.,* 159
Francis II (Austria), 372, 391, 393, 398
Francis II (Sicily), 509
Francis Ferdinand, Archduke (Austria), 627-628, 636
Francis Joseph, Emperor (Austria), 443, 509, 535-536, 538, 542-543, 547
Franco, Francisco, 701, 737-738, 787, 800; *illus.,* 739
Frankfurt, Treaty of, 630, 632
Frankfurt Assembly, 440-441, 443-444
Franklin, Benjamin, 315, 359
Franklin, Sir John, 210
Frederick II, the Great (Prussia), 302, 304-307, 309, 326-328, 330, 332, 341-342; *illus.,* 307, 327
Frederick III (Germany), 532
Frederick III, the Wise (Saxony), 121, 122
Frederick William, the Great Elector, 288-290
Frederick William I (Prussia), 290-291
Frederick William II (Prussia), 332
Frederick William III (Prussia), 393, 431
Frederick William IV (Prussia), 439-441, 444, 525
Free Democratic party (Germany), 903
Free French, 798, 800, 806, 812
Free will, 135-136
Freemasonry, 340, 426
Frei, Eduardo, 892
French Academy, 233, 317
French Revolution: causes, 359-366; Civil Constitution of the Clergy, 370; civil liberties, 369, 371; Constitution of *1791,* 370-371; Constitution of *1793,* 377; Constitution of *1795,* 381; Declaration of the Rights of Man, 369; Directory, 381,

383-385; Estates General, 364-366; European war, 382-383; Laws of Ventôse, 378-379; Legislative Assembly, 372-373; Louis XVI, 360, 364-366, 368, 370-373, 375; National Assembly, 368-372; National Convention, 374-376; Reign of Terror, 376-380; Roman Catholic Church, 360-361, 369-371; 380; September massacres, 373-374; suffrage, 371, 377, 381; Thermidorean Reaction, 380-381
Freud, Sigmund, 590, 912-915; *illus.,* 913
Friedjung, Heinrich, 543
Friedland, battle of, 392
Fronde, the, 234
Frost, Robert, 924
Fuad I (Egypt), 777
Fugger family (Germany), 52, 54
Fulton, James, 451
Fyrd, 28

G

Gabelle, 363
Gainsborough, Sir Thomas, 352
Galbraith, John Kenneth, 919
Galen, 107, 109
Galicia, 398-399, 442, 540, 642-643
Galileo, 259, 260
Galitsyn family (Russia), 333
Gallia, 19
Gallicanism, 242
Gallipoli campaign, 643-644
Galsworthy, John, 578
Gama, Vasco da, 200
Gamelin, General Maurice, 797
Gandhi, Indira, 879
Gandhi, Mahatma, 776, 843; *illus.,* 776
Garibaldi, Giuseppe, 510; *illus.,* 510
Gas, poison, in World War I, 647-648
Gastein, Convention of, 527-528
Gauguin, Paul, 583
Gay, John, 353
General Confederation of Labor (France), 759-761
General Confederation of Labor (Italy), 711
Généralité, 243-244
Geneva, Switzerland, 127, 128, 136, 138
Geneva disarmament conference (*1932*), 783
George I (England), 258, 281-282
George II (England), 281-282, 304
George III (England), 278, 308, 343-344, 620
George V (England), 495
German East Africa, 613
German Southwest Africa, 612-613, 661
German tribes, 14, 15, 19, 22
Germany (*see also* Holy Roman Empire), 287-291, 383; agriculture, 454, 733; *Anschluss,* 740-741, 788-789; anti-semitism, 731-732, 806-807; Battle of Britain, 799-800; Bismarck era, 524, 526-533, 632-633; Boer War, 633-634; Confeder-

ation, *1850-1859,* 524-526; Congress of Vienna, 417-418; Czechoslovakia take-over, 789-790; denazification, 831; divided East and West, 816-817, 819, 831, 835-836, 862-864, 894, 900, 902-903; domestic policies, *1870-1914,* 530-535; domestic policies, Hitler, 730-735; economy, nineteenth century, 498-499; economy, twentieth century, 722-728, 733-734, 831; economy, West, 896, 902; education under Nazis, 735; Franco-Prussian War, *1871,* 500-502; Greek War of Independence, 425; Hanseatic League, 49-50; Hitler's Balkan policy, 742-744; imperialism, 534, 599, 612-613, 661; Industrial Revolution, 452-453; late medieval, 40; *map,* 41; League of Nations, 658, 782-783, 785; Locarno Pact, 727, 782; monarchy in, 29; Moroccan crisis, 635; Munich agreement, 789-790; Napoleonic Wars, 390, 393, 398; Polish invasion, *1939,* 791-793; religion, 530-532; reparations, 720-723, 726-729, 758; revolutions, nineteenth century, 431-432, 439-441; revolution, *1918,* 652; Rhineland occupation, 786; Romantic movement, 407, 409; suffrage, 458; Thirty Years' War, 184-192; Treaty of Rapallo, 698-699; unification, *map,* 525; Versailles treaty, 656-664; Weimar Republic, 717-730; World War I, 628-631, 636-649, 717-718; World War II, 795-797, 799-801, 803-807
Gestapo, 733
Ghana (Gold Coast), 885, 890
Ghosts (Ibsen), 577
Gibbon, Edward, 351
Gibraltar, 346, 800
Gioberti, Vincenzo, 437
Giotto, 93-96; *illus.,* 94
Giraud, Henri Honoré, *illus.,* 811
Girondins, 372, 374-377, 380
Gladstone, William, 486, 488, 490-493, 503; *illus.,* 486
Glinka, Fëdor N., 410
Glorious Revolution, 281-282
Gluck, Christoph, 353
Gobineau, Count Joseph de, 721
Goebbels, Paul Joseph, 727, 729, 731
Goering, Hermann, 722, 734, 799
Goethe, Johann Wolfgang von, 407, 409-410
Gold Coast, 761
Golden Book, of Venice, 46
Goldwater, Barry, 898
Goliard poets, 30
Gömbös, Gyula, 742
Gomulka, Wladislaw, 853, 862, 866
Gothic architecture, 30-32
Gothic revival, 411-412
Goulart, Juan, 892
Government: ancient Near East, 7-8; under Charlemagne, 21; feudal system, 21-23; Greek, 10-11; Italian despotism, 42; under Louis XIV, 242-244; medieval church, 27; monarchy, 27-29; Roman, 14-15; Venetian, 45-46
Goya y Lucientes, Francisco de, 410-411

Grand Remonstrance, 252
Grant, Madison, 573
Great Britain, 303-304, 341, 376, 422; agriculture, 278-279; 454-455; American War of Independence, 344-347; Boer War, 534, 603-604; Chartism, 491; classes, social, 282-283, 484-486, 495-496, 752-754; Cold War policies, 816-817, 842, 895; colonies, liquidation, 884-890; Common Market, 900; Commonwealth, 620-623, 756-757, 842-843, 875; Corn Laws, 489-490; Crimean War, 550-551; economy, 275-278, 751-755, 826-827, 896, 900-901; education, 460, 489-491, 826; education, colonial, 606, 608-609, 612; Ethiopian crisis, 786-787; Factory Acts, 490; Fashoda incident, 334; George III, 343-344; Great Northern War, 303; Greek War of Independence, 424-425; imperialism, 491-492; 602-609, 768, 776, 842, 844, 884; industry, 279-280, 447-452; Irish question, 492-494, 755-756; law, 488-489; literature, 407, 409, 576-580; Locarno treaties, 727; mercantilism, 275-276; Monroe Doctrine, 424; Moroccan crisis, 635; Munich agreement, 789-790; Napoleonic Wars, 384-385; Parliament, 281-283, 484-486; political parties, 486-488, 496; Poor Laws, 489; revolutions, European, 423, 430-432; Russian relations, 679, 698-699; Seven Years' War, 305-309; South Sea Company, 276-278; suffrage, 283, 484-486, 491, 754; test ban agreement, 865; trade policies, 396-398, 489-490, 494-495, 754-755; Triple Entente, 633-635; welfare legislation, 489-490 495-496; World War I, 628-629, 631-632, 637-641, 643-644, 646-648; World War II, 784-797, 800, 803-807, 810-813
Great Century, The (Latourette), 618
Great Council, of Venice, 46
Great Gatsby, The (Fitzgerald), 764
Great Northern War, 273, 285, 291, 294-296
Great Schism, 42
Great Wall of China, illus., 226
Greco, El, 170, 266
Greece, 653, 716; architecture, illus., 12; Balkan wars, 635-636; city-states, 10-11; Civil War, 835-836; civilization, 10-13; Cyprus question, 895; government, 10-11; independence, 424-426; Metaxas' dictatorship, 745; science and technology, 11, 13; Treaty of Lausanne, 660; Versailles settlement, 660; in World War I, 644, 646; in World War II, 703, 800
Greeley, Horace, 470, 474
Green, T. H., 588
Greenland, 199
Gregorian chant, 32
Gregory, Lady Augusta, 494
Gregory VII, Pope, 29
Grévy, Jules, 502, 504
Grey, Lady Jane, 178
Grey, Sir Edward, 637-638

Griffith, Arthur, 755
Grimm, Johann, 398, 409
Grimm, Wilhelm, 398, 409
Gromyko, Andrei, 874
Guadeloupe, 283
Guam, 802
Guelf-Ghibelline feud, 42, 43, 44
Guest, Edgar, 580
Guianea, 763
Guizot, François, 434-435, 448
Gumbinnen, battle of, 642
Gunpowder, introduction of, 108
Gustavus II (Gustavus Adolphus) (Sweden), 185-188
Gustavus III (Sweden), 331-332
Gutenberg, Johann, 108
Guyana (British Guiana), 892

H

Habsburgs, 40; Ottoman Empire and, 74, 76; Thirty Years' War and, 184-192
Habsburg-Valois Wars, 157-166, 301
Hacha, Emil, 790
Haile Selassie, 516; illus., 786
Haiti, 390
Hakluyt, Richard, 225
Halifax, Lord Edward, 791
Hamlet, 182
Hammarskjöld, Dag, 819
Hammurabi, Code of, 6
Handel, George Frederick, 353, 355
Hanover, 306, 528
Hanseatic League, 49-50
Hargreaves, James, 280
Hard Times (Dickens), 463
Harding, Warren G., 762, 764
Hardy, Thomas, 577, 590
Hastings, Warren, 607
Haushofer, Karl, 733
Hawaii, 519, 614, 802-803, 897
Hay, John, 771
Haydn, Joseph, 353, 355, 410
Hayes, Rutherford B., 516
Hegel, George W. F., 413-414, 471-472, 588-589
Heimwehr (Austria), 740
Heine, Heinrich, 580
Heisenberg, Werner, 923
Henlein, Konrad, 789
Henry IV (France and Navarre), 174-175, 232; illus., 174
Henry VII (England), 35-38
Henry VIII (England), 128-130; illus., 129
Henry the Navigator, 199-200
Herder, Johann Gottfried von, 409
Herzegovina, 556, 627
Herzen, Alexander, 554-555
Hess, Rudolf, 733
Hesse-Cassel, 528
Hidalgos, 169
Hildebrand (see Gregory VII, Pope)
Himmler, Heinrich, 727
Hindenburg, Paul von, 642-643, 717-718, 726, 728-731

Hinduism, 202-203, 775-776, 842-844
Hippocrates, 13
Historicism, 920-922
History, uses of, 2-4
History of the Decline and Fall of the Roman Empire (Gibbon), 351
History of Florence, The, 47
Hitler, Adolf, 700-701, 785, 918; Anschluss, 740-741, 788-789; anti-semitism, 545, 721-722, 731-732; Battle of Britain, 799; Czechoslovakia take-over, 789-790; dictatorial powers, 730-731; economic policy, 733-734; educational views, 735; Lebensraum theory, 732-733; legal policies, 733; Munich agreement, 789-790; Nazi party leader, 720-722, 724-725, 727-730; Poland invasion, 791-793; racist views, 731-732; Roman Catholic Church, 734-735; Rome-Berlin Axis, 787-788; Russian Campaign, 800-801; World War II, 806
Hlinka, Father, 541
Ho Chi Minh, 870-871
Hoffman, General Max von, 642
Hogarth, William, 352
Hohenzollern, House of, 288-291
Holbach, Baron d', 322
Holbein, Hans, 99, 100
Holland (see also Netherlands), 183-184, 234
Holstein, 527-528
Holstein, Baron Friedrich von, 633
Holy Alliance, 416, 418
Holy League of the Papacy, 157
Holy Roman Empire, 19, 21, 29, 189, 393, 417
Home Owners' Loan Corporation, 766
Homer, Winslow, 580
Hong Kong, 607
Hood, Thomas, 579
Hooker, Richard, 134
Hoover, Herbert, 728, 762, 765
Hopkins, Gerald Manley, 580
Horthy, Admiral, 741
House of Commons, 29, 177
House of Lords, 29, 177
Household Management, 64
Housman, A. E., 580
Howells, William Dean, 576
Hubertusberg, Peace of, 307, 309
Hugenberg, Alfred, 726
Hugo, Victor, 409, 579
Huguenots, 128, 173, 174, 175, 242
Humanism, 84-85
Human Nature in Politics (Wallas), 918
Humbert I (Italy), 476, 512
Hume, David, 348-349
Hundred Years' War, 28, 29; map, 36
Hungary, 287, 328-329, 442, 546-547, 550, 653, 744, 835; anti-semitism, 546, 741; civil liberties, 537; classes, social, 546; dual monarchy, 537-538; fascism, 741-742; minorities, 541-544; revolt, 1956, 853, 861; revolution of 1848, 442-444; revolution of 1918, 680-681; satellite status, 866; Versailles settlement, 659
Huygens, Christian, 183

I

Ibn Saud, 777
Ibsen, Henrik, 577-578
Iceland, 199
Idyls of the King (Tennyson), 579
Ikons, 65
"Il Moro" (Ludovico Sforza), 43
Il Risorgimento, 437
Ile de France, 27
Illyrian provinces, 393, 398-399, 418, 425, 442
Immigration: to Australia, 622; to Palestine, 777; Social Darwinist view, 573; to U.S., 518; U.S. restrictions, 763
Imperialism (*see also* Colonies): in Africa, 491-492, 600-606, 609-613, 768, *map*, 599; in Asia, 607-609, 612, 614-616, *map*, 601; Belgian, 613; British, 491-492, 602-609, 768, 842, 844; in the Caribbean, 606; consequences of, 623-624; definition of, 597-598; economics of, 598-624; in the Far East, 602, 841, *map*, 601; Fourteen Points, 769; French, 609-612, 768, 844; German, 612-613; India and, 307-309, 492, 842, 844; Italian, 613; Japanese, 615-616; in Latin America, 847-849; Marxist view, 598; in Middle East, 600, 844-846, *map*, 599; pro and con views, 616-619; Social Darwinist view, 617; U.S., 613-615, 768; in Western Hemisphere, *map*, 614
Imperialism as the Latest Stage of Capitalism (Lenin), 598
Incas, 212
Independent Socialists (Germany), 718
Index, of prohibited books, 144
India: Amritsar massacre, 653, 775; British control, 492, 557, 607-609, 631, 753; caste system, 202-203, 844; China attack, 873; economy, 843-844, 879; education, 840; European expansion, 201-202; Hindu-Moslem conflict, 775-776; Hinduism, 844; independence drive, 776, 842-843; Kashmir question, 863, 879-880; languages, 879; neutralism, 818-819; population, 879; Seven Years' War, 307-309
Indian: North American, 223-224; South American, 213, 215-216
Indies, 220-221
Indo-China, 612, 802, 842
Indo-European languages, 10
Indonesia, 803, 837-838, 842, 873, 877-878
Indulgences, 119-120
Industrial Revolution, 279-280, 447-453; economic and social consequences, 454-460; *illus.*, 452-453
Industry (*see also* Agriculture; Economy): in France, 433, 498-499, 507; in Germany, 532, 726, 830; in Great Britain, 752, 827; in Japan, 616; in Prussia, 526; in Russia, 298, 668, 682-683, 689-691
Influence of Sea Power Upon History, The (Mahan), 520

Ingria, 295
In Memoriam (Tennyson), 579
Inquiry into the Nature and Causes of the Wealth of Nations (Smith), 318
Inquisition, 141-142, 423; in Spain, 39
Institutes of the Christian Religion, 128
Instrument of Government, 254
Insular Cases decision, 615
Intellectual Revolution: architecture, 583-585; Darwinism's effect, 568-575; literature, 575-580, 587-588; music, 586-587; painting, 580-583, 588; philosophy, 588-591; politics and social thought, 591-593
Intendants, 243-244
International politics, 152-157
"Intolerable Acts," 346
Invasions, Germanic, 14, 15
Inventions (*see also* Science): ancient Near East and, 6; early medieval, 18-19; Leonardo da Vinci and, 157; neolithic, 5; prehistoric, 4-5; printing, 107-108
Investiture Controversy, 29
Iran, 778, 835, 846, 895
Iraq, 777-778, 861, 883-884
Ireland: Cromwell in, 254; in Elizabethan age, 180; England and, 258; Free State, 755-756; Home Rule agitation, 492-494, 631; potato famine, 455, 493
Irish Land Act, 493
Iron, and Industrial Revolution, 450, 452
"Iron Law of Wages," 461
Isabella the Catholic, 38-40
Islam, 56-57; Charlemagne and, 19; and Ottoman empire, 73
Israel (*see also* Palestine), 844-846, 881
Italy, 285-287, 302-303, 458, 499, 528-529, 536; *Anschluss* and, 740-741; anticlericalism, 511; anti-semitism, 716; Communist party, 906; Congress of Vienna, 417-418; economy, 511-512, 831, 896, 906-907, emigration from, 512; Ethiopia and, 512, 786; European union, 900; fascism in, 707-717; imperialism, 512, 599, 613, 635; late medieval, 42-43; Lateran Treaty, 716; Locarno treaties, 727; Munich agreement, 789; Napoleonic Wars, 384-385, 389-390, 393, 396; political parties, postwar, 831, 906-907; Renaissance, 43-48, revolutions, nineteenth century, 431, 436-439; Rome-Berlin Axis, 787; as "school of Europe," 46-48; social classes, 511; Spanish civil war, 787; Treaty of London, 643; Treaty of Rapallo, 709; Triple Alliance, 633; unification, 508-511, *map*, 510; Vatican City, 511, 716; Versailles conference, 655, 657-659; World War I, 629, 632, 638, 642-643; World War II, 703, 800, 803-805, 835
Ivan III, Tsar, 59, 69
Ivan IV, the Terrible, Tsar, 59, 61-62, *illus.*, 61
Ivan VI (Russia), 332-334
Ivanhoe (Scott), 409

Ivry, battle of, 174
Iwo Jima, 808
Izvolski, Aleksandr Petrovich, 635

J

J'Accuse (Zola), 505
Jacobins, 371-376, 381
Jacquerie, 363
Jagan, Cheddi, 892
James I (England), 69, 181, 248, 249-250
James II (England), 256-257, 281-282, 304, 314
James, William, 588-590
Jameson Raid, 603, 633
Jameson, Sir Leander Starr, 603
Janissaries, 72, 301
Jansenists, 242
Japan: British alliance, 633; China and, 772-774; in Cold War, 818, 877; economy, 769-770, 875-877; European expansion and, 222; imperialism, 602, 615-616, 679; Korea and, 770, 838; League withdrawal, 785; Manchuria and, 629, 773, 785; mandate islands, 661; Nine-Power Treaty, 772; occupation status, 816-817, 841-842; Russo-Japanese War, 558-559; Shintoism, 770; World War I, 638; World War II, 703, 803, 807-808
Java, 612
Jefferson, Thomas, 316, 365, 411
Jellachich, Joseph, 443
Jena, battle of, 392, 398
Jenkins' Ear, War of, 303-304, 307
Jesuits (*see also* Society of Jesus), 140-141; in China, 207; in New France, 219; in Paraguay, 216
Jesus Christ, 16
Jews (*see also* Anti-semitism): in Austria, 329; in Austro-Hungarian empire, 540, 544-546; Dreyfus case, 504-505; in fascist Italy, 716; Hitler's Aryan theories, 721; medieval banking, 52; in Nazi Germany, 731-732, 806-807; in Ottoman Empire, 70; in Poland, 66; in Prussia, 327; religion, 8; in Russia, 557, 833, 835; in Spain, 39; in Sweden, 331
Joan of Arc, 28
John, Don, of Austria, 166
John I (England), 28
John of Leyden, 138
Johnson, Lyndon Baines, 863, 871-872, 874, 895, 898
Johnson, Dr. Samuel, 346, 351, *illus.*, 351
Jordan, 881
Jordan River, 881
Joseph I (Portugal), 331
Joseph II (Austria), 328-330, 332, 343, 348, 355
Journey from St. Petersburg to Moscow (Radishchev), 337
Joyce, James, 925-926, *illus.*, 925
Judaism, 8
Julius II, Pope, 43
July Ordinances, 429

Jung, Carl, 915
Junkers, 289, 291, 327, 332, 399, 526; Weimar era, 718-719, 728, 730; in Nazi Germany, 833
Justice party (Turkey), 881
Jutland, battle of, 647

K

Kadar, Janos, 854
Kadets (see Constitutional Democrats)
Kaganovich, Lazar, 692
Kamenev, Lev Borisovich, 686, 693
Kant, Immanuel, 349, 355, 588
Kapp, Wolfgang, 720
Karageorge, 424-425
Karelia, 695
Karlovitz, Congress of, 76-77
Karlovitz, Peace of, 287, 294
Karolyi, Count Michael, 741
Kaunitz, Chancellor Anton von, 306
Kazakh Republic, 695
Kazakhs, 65
Kazan Tartars, 68
Keats, John, 407
Kellogg-Briand Pact, 727, 763, 783
Kemal, Mustafa, 644, 660, 778, 881
Kennedy, John F., 870-871, 898, assassination, 865; Cuban crisis, 864; and Khrushchev, 863
Kenya, 886
Kerensky, Alexander, 670-671, 674-675
Khmelnitsky, 66
Khrushchev, Nikita: atomic weapons, 863-864; Berlin policy, 862; China split, 867-869; Communist party and, 853-855; Cuban crisis, 864; educational policies, 857; removal, 872-873; rise to power, 852-853; satellite revolts, 853-854, 861-862, 865-866; Southeast Asia policy, 870-871; U-2 incident, 863; U.S. contacts, 863-864
Kiel, 527
Kierkegaard, Soren, 919
King, Mackenzie, 825
King, Martin Luther, 897
Kingsley, Charles, 477
Kipling, Rudyard, 202, 580, 617-618
Kirghiz Republic, 695
Kirov, Sergei, 693-694
Kleist, Paul von, 409
Knights (see Military orders)
Knights of Malta, 385, 390
Knox, John, 179
Koestler, Arthur, 916
Kolchak, Admiral Aleksandr, 679-681
Kong Le, 870
Köprülüs, 76
Koran, 56
Korea, 616, 770, 818-819, 822, 838-839, 873, 876, 895
Korean War, 838-839
Kornilov, General Lavr, 674, 676
Korzybski, Alfred, 920
Kossuth, Louis, 442-444, 537, 547
Kosygin, A. N., 872-873
Kozlov, Frol, 863
Kredit-Anstalt, 728, 740
Kremlin Palace, 59

Kronstadt Movement, 682
Kropotkin, Prince Peter, 476
Krüdener, Madame de, 340, 416
Kruger, Stephanus, 534, 603, 633-634
Kruger telegram, 603, 633-634
Kubla Khan (Coleridge), 225
Kullar, 70
Kun, Bela, 653, 680-681, 741
Kuomintang, 699, 772, 774, 808, 810, 813, 817
Kurbsky, Prince, 59
Kutchuk Kainardji, treaty of, 342
Kutuzov, Prince Mikhail, 400
Kuwait, 884
Kwajalein, 808
Kwangchow Bay, 612, 771
Ky, General Cao, 871

L

La Belle Hélène (Offenbach), 586
Labor (see also Classes, social): and enclosure movement, 278-279; France, 363, 365, 370, 389, 498; Germany, 532, 724, 734; Great Britain, 434, 490, 495-496, 754; grievances, nineteenth century, 457-460; Hungary, 546; Industrial Revolution, 279; 448; J. S. Mill on, 465; Mussolini's syndicates, 714; National Workshops, 1848, 435; Russia, tsarist, 298, 557; utopian socialist views on, 466-470
Labor Front (Germany), 734
Labour party (England), 495-496, 826-827, 842, 901
Lafayette, Marquis de, 278, 362, 429-430, 432, 435
Laffitte, Jacques, 429
Lamballe, Princesse de, 374
Lancaster, House of, 37
"Land and Liberty" society (Russia), 555
Language: of ancient Near East, 6; Arabic, 57, 70; and Austro-Hungarian minorities, 442-443, 537-538, 540-542, 547; Greek, 10; Indo-European, 10; Latin, 15-16, 30, 88; Old Church Slavonic, 65; prehistoric man and, 4; Spanish, 39; Turkish, 70; vernacular, 83-84
Langue d'oc, 83-84
Language d'oil, 83-84
Laos, 869-871
Laplace, Pierre Simon, 315, 380
Las Casas, Bartholomew de, 215
Lassalle, Ferdinand, 528, 532
Lateran Treaty, 716
Latin America (see also individual countries) 212-216; 1828, map, 424; "Good Neighbor" policy, 768; Monroe Doctrine, 423-424
Latin language, 15-16, 30
Latium, 13
Latourette, Kenneth, 618
Latvia, 660, 695, 701-702, 795
Laud, William, 250
Lausanne, Treaty of, 660
Laval, Pierre, 798
Lavoisier, Antoine, 315, 380
Lavrov, Petr Lavrovich, 555
Law (see also Civil liberties): Austria,

329; Beccaria's essay, 319, 336; Code of Hammurabi, 6; Code Napoléon, 387, 422, 428; fascist Italy, 714; France, 360, 371, 377, 387, 428; Great Britain, 488-489; under Henry VII (England), 37; Nazi Germany, 733; Norman England, 28; Ottoman Empire, 73; philosophes' views, 318-319; Prussia, 327; Roman contributions, 15; Russia, 336, 550, 553
Law, John, 276-277, 284-285
Law of Hostages, 385
"Law of Lübeck," 49
Laws of Ecclesiastical Policy, The, 134
Laws of Ventôse, 378-379
Lawrence, Sir Thomas, 352
Lawrence, T. E., 646, 655-656
League of Cambray, 157
League of Cognac, 158
League of Nations, 658, 762-763; and Austrian recovery, 739; Ethiopian crisis, 786-787; Germany and, 727, 782-783; Hungary and, 742; Italy and, 787; Manchurian War, 773, 785; mandate system, 660-661; Poland and Upper Silesia question, 720; U.S.S.R. and, 700, 702; U.S. and, 762-763; weaknesses, 784-785, 787
League of Torgau, 159
League of the Three Emperors, 633
Lebanon, 660-661, 777, 844, 880
Lecanuet, Jacques, 905
Le Chapelier Law, 370, 389, 458
Leeuwenhoek, Anton von, 183
Lefort, Field Marshal, 293
Leipzig, battle of, 400
Lend-Lease, 801-802
Lenin, 548, 558-559, 561, 598, 672-674, 676-677, 679-680. 682-683, 685-686, 698; illus., 680, 684
Leo X, Pope, 120, 123, 140
Leo XIII, Pope, 478-479
Leon, Ponce de, 210
Leopold of Saxe-Coburg (Belgium), 430-431
Leopold II (Austria), 330-332, 372
Leopold II (Belgium), 613
Lepanto, battle of, 76, 166
Lesotho (Basutoland), 885
Lesseps, Ferdinand de, 467, 504
Leszczynski, Stainislas, 295, 302. 340
Letters of Eminent Men, The, 111
Letters of Obscure Men, The, 111
Levellers, 255
Lewis, Sinclair, 578, 764
Ley, Dr. Robert, 734
l'Hospital, Michel de, 175
Libel of English Policy, 48
Liberal party (Canada), 825, 899
Liberal party (England), 486, 488, 491-496, 752, 826
Liberal party (Germany), 530-533
"Liberal Unionists" (England), 493
Liberia, 602
Liberum veto, 66
Lie, Trygve, 819
Liebknecht, Wilhelm, 532
Liege lord, 22
Ligurian Republic, 384
Lincoln, Abraham, 516
Linnaeus, Carlous, 315
Lippmann, Walter, 918
Lissauer, Ernst, 631

Literature (*see also specific forms, e.g., Drama*) 263-265; ancient, preservation of, 88-89; Enlightenment era, 350-351; Elizabethan, 181-182; European expansion and, 225; Freudian influences, 915, 925; Irish nationalistic, 494; medieval period, 29-32; modern, 924-926; Renaissance and, 83-92; Romantic period, 407-409; Russian, 64-65, 69; U.S.S.R., 833, 858-860; Victorian era, 575-580
Lithuania, 58, 59, 343, 431, 660, 695, 701-702, 791, 795
Little Entente, 664
Litvinov, Maxim, 698, 700-701
Lloyd, Edward, 275
Lloyd George, David, 495-496, 652, 659, 661, 751-752, 826; *illus.*, 495, 657
Lloyd's of London, 275
Locarno pact, 700, 727, 782
Locke, John, 314-315, 323-324, 347
"Lombard" bankers, 52
Lombardy, 287, 418, 438-439, 442, 509, 536
London Society for the Encouragement of Arts, Manufacturers, and Commerce, 280
London, Treaty of, 643, 709
Longfellow, Henry Wadsworth, 579-580
Lords, House of, 29
Lorentz, Hendrik Antoon, 482
Lorenz, Konrad, 916
Lorraine, 302, 530 (*see also* Alsace-Lorraine)
Louis IX (St. Louis) (France), 28
Louis XI (France), 28, 34-35; *illus.*, 35
Louis XII (France), 157-158
Louis XIII (France), 232
Louis XIV (France), 234-236, 273, 274, 276, 284-285, 288
Louis XV (France), 273, 276, 283, 285, 302, 306, 317, 360
Louis XVI (France), 318, 360, 366, 368, 370-373, 375, 429
Louis XVII (France), 368
Louis XVIII (France), 400, 416, 428
Louis Napoleon (*see* Napoleon III)
Louis Philippe, Citizen King, 429-430, 434-435, 472
Louisburg, 304, 307-308
Louisiana Territory, 390
L'Ouverture, Toussaint, 390
Lowell, James Russell, 579
Loyola, Ignatius, 140; *illus.*, 141, 332
Lübeck, Law of, 49
Lübeck, Treaty of, 185
Ludendorff, General Erich von, 642-643, 718, 720; in Weimar era, 720-721, 724-725; *illus.*, 725
Lueger, Karl, 545
Luftwaffe, 794-795, 799-800
Lugard, Lord Frederick, 606, 613
Lunéville, Treaty of, 390
Lusiads, The, 208
Luther, Hans, 725
Luther, Martin, 118-126; *illus.*, 119; Ninety-five theses, 119-120; opposition to, 123-124; revolt of, 120-121
Lutheran Church, 118, 124-126, 134-135, 329
Lützen, battle of, 186
Luxembourg, 529, 900

Lvov, Prince Georgi, 670
Lyautey, Marshal Louis Hubert, 610
Lyell, Sir Charles, 568
Lyrical Ballads (Wordsworth), 407-408
Lysenko, Trofim, 569, 833
Lytton Report, 785

M

Mably, Abbé, 348
McAdam, John Loudon, 450
Macao, *illus.*, 206
MacArthur, General Douglas, 808, 839, 841
McCarthy, Joseph, 824-825
McCormick, Cyrus, 452
MacDonald, Ramsay, 699, 753-754
Machiavelli, Niccoló, 44, 46-48; Christianity and, 47-48
Mackensen, General von, 644
Mackenzie, William Lyon, 620
McKinley, William, 476
Mackintosh, Charles Rennie, 586
MacMahon, Marshal Marie, 502
Madame Bovary (Flaubert), 576
Madras, 304
Maeterlinck, Maurice, 482
Magdeburg, siege of, 186; *illus.*, 187
Magellan, Ferdinand, 210-212; *illus.*, 211
Magenta, battle of, 509
Magic Flute, The (Mozart), 355
Maginot Line, 793, 795-797
Magna Carta, 28
Magyars (*see also* Hungary), 442, 444, 536, 538, 541
Mahan, Captain Alfred T., 520
Maillol, Aristide, 583
Main Street (Lewis), 578, 764
Maine (battleship), 614
Makepeace Experiment, The (Tertz), 860
Malawi (Nyassaland), 885
Malaya, 606, 612, 803, 838, 842
Malaysia, 842, 878
Malenkov, Georgi, 852-853
Mali (French Sudan), 885
Mallarmé, Stéphane, 579
Malta, 385, 390, 418
Malthus, Thomas, 460-462, 464, 568
Mamluks, 73
Man: origin of, 3; prehistoric, 3-5
Man and Superman (Shaw), 577
Manchu Dynasty, 771
Manchuria, 68, 558-559, 616, 629; Japanese designs, 773, 785; Russian invasion, 808
Mandarins, 204
Mandate System, 660-661
Manet, Edouard, 581-582
Manifesto of the Communist Party (Engels and Marx), 472-475
Manila Conference, 1966, 872
Mann, Thomas, 925
Mao Tse-tung, 867-868, 873-874
March Laws (Hungary), 443
March on Rome, 711-712; *illus.*, 713
Maria Theresa (Austria), 287, 302, 304; as enlightened despot, 328-330
Marie Antoinette, Queen, 360, 364, 368, 372, 374, 377; *illus.*, 369

Marie-Louise (wife of Napoleon), 395-396
Mark Antony (*see* Antony)
Marlborough, Duke of, 236
Marne, first battle of the, 641
Marquand, J. P., 925
Marr, Nikolai, 833
Marriage of Figaro, The (Mozart), 354
Marshal, Alfred, 917
Marshall, General George C., 817-818, 822
Marshall Plan, 822-823, 905
Marston Moor, battle of, 252
Martin, Everett Dean, 594
Martinique, 283-284
Marx, Karl, 414, 448, 471-475, 703
Marx, Wilhelm, 726
Marxism (*see also* Communism); and historicism, 921; and philosophy, 933
Marxist Socialist party (Spain), 736
Mary II, Queen, 257
Mary of Burgundy, 40
Mary Stuart, Queen of Scots, 178, 179-180; *illus.*, 180
Mary Tudor, Queen, 178
Masaccio, 95-96; *illus.*, 96
Masaryk, Thomas, 540, 789
Massu, General Jacques, 904
Masurian Lakes, battle of, 642
Mathematics: Egyptians and, 6; Greeks and, 12
Matsu, 839, 867
Matteotti, Giacomo, 713
Mau Mau, 887
Mavrocordato, Alexander, 77
Maximilian I, Emperor, 40
Maximilian of Habsburg, 35
Maximilian, Prince, 499-500
Mazarin, Cardinal, 234
Mazepa, 295
Mazzini, Giuseppe, 433, 437, 439, 444
Mecca, 56
Mecklenburg, 306
Medici, Catherine de', 174
Medici, Cosimo de', 44, 88
Medici family, 44; banking and, 52
Medici, Lorenzo de', 44; *illus.*, 45
Medici, Marie de, 232
Medicine: Greeks and, 13; Renaissance, 108-109
Medieval civilization: arts, 29-32; economic change, 53-54; education, 24-27; feudalism, 21-23; learning, 25-27; literature, 29-32; monarchy, 27-29; towns, 23-24
Mehemet Ali, 425, 434, 550
Mein Kampf (Hitler), 725
Melanchthon, 123
Mendel, Gregor, 569
Menderes, Adnan, 881
Menelek, 613
Mensheviks, 558, 670, 673; 675-676
Menshikov, Prince, 293-294, 297, 333
Mercantilism, 169, 206, 244-246, 275, 285, 309, 317-318, 327, 329; in practice, 245-246; theory of, 244-245
Meredith, George, 628
Mesopotamia, 660-661
Messiah, The (Handel), 353
Mesta, 38, 39, 53
Mestizos, 213
Metaxas, General John, 745

Methodism, 349-350

Metric system, 380

Metternich, Prince Clement, 415-417, 423, 425, 431-432, 439, 442-443

Metz, battle of, 530

Mexico, 499-500, 847-848

Michael Romanov, 63

Michelangelo, 98, 101-102; *illus.*, 99, 103

Middle classes (*see also* Classes, social); Austro-Hungarian, 544-546; French, 363-365; German, 724; Industrial Revolution and, 457; Japanese, 615-616; and nineteenth-century literature, 578-579; Prussian, 327; Russian tsarist, 337

Middle East (*see also individual countries*): imperialism in, 600 777-778, 844-846, *map*, 599, 662-663; oil in, 777, 846, 883-884

Mikhailovich, General, 736

Mikoyan, Anastas, 863

Milan Decrees, 396-397

Milan, Duchy of, 43

Mill, John Stuart, 433, 464-465, 556, 592, 594, 824; *illus.*, 464

Millet, 57

Milton, John, 256, 264

Minin, Kuzma, 63

Minoan civilization, 10

Minorca, 307, 346

Minorities: in Austria-Hungary, 536-546, *map*, 539; in Russia, 557, 669, 675-676, 685, 695

Mirabeau, Comte Honoré Gabriel de, 365-366

Mirandola, Pico della, 90

Mississippi Company, 276-277

Mitterand, François, 904

Modena, Duchy of, 431, 438

Mohács, battle of, 74

Mohammed, 56

Mohammed Ali Jinnah, 843

Moldavia, 295, 425, 695, 703

Moldavian Republic, 703

Molotov, Vyacheslav, 701, 703, 854

Moltke, Helmuth von, 641

Monarchy: divine right and, 240-241; in England, 28-29; in France, 17-28, 171-173; in Germany, 29; medieval, 27-29, 34-40

Monasticism, medieval, 24

Monet, Claude, 581

Money: European eighteenth century, 275-277; and Industrial Revolution 451; in Weimar Germany, 723-725

Monk, General, 254

Monotheism, 8

Monroe Doctrine, 500, 600

Mont-St.-Michel, 31

Montagu, Lady Mary, 284

Montenegro, 73, 655

Montesquieu, Baron de, 317, 322-325, 336, 347, 436

Montgomery, Field Marshal Bernard, 803

Monticello, *illus.*, 413

Montreal, 308

Moore, Henry, *illus.*, 929

Moravia, 538

Moravia, Alberto, 831

Moravian Brethren, 349

More, Thomas, 130

Morea, 425

Morley, Lord, 638

Morocco, 610, 629, 634-635, 803, 890

Morris, William, 586

Morse, Samuel, 452

Morton, John, Archbishop of Canterbury, 37

Moscow, 58-59; German suburb of, 69; princes of, 58-59; as "third Rome," 60; under early Romanovs, 69

Moscow Calling (Azhak), 860

Moslems, 543, 775, 842-843, 879, 889; in India, 202; in Spain, 38, 39

Mossadeq, Mohammed, 846

Mountain, and French Revolution, 374-377, 381

Mozambique, 885-886

Mozart, Wolfgang Amadeus, 353-355, 410; *illus.*, 354

Muftis, 73

Multilateral Force (MLF), 895

Münnich, Marshal, 334, 340-341

Murad IV, Sultan, 76

Murat, Joachim, 393

Music: Baroque, 266-267; eighteenth century, 353-355; medieval, 32; modern, 928-929; nineteenth century, 586-587; Renaissance, 105-106; Romantic period, 409-410

Mussolini Benito, 511, 701, 709, 785, 918; Albania invasion, 788; and *Anschluss,* 740-741; corporative state, 714-715; death, 805; domestic policies, 715-716; early career, 710-711; Ethiopian conquest, 786; fascist dictatorship, 712-714; foreign policy, 716-717, 787-788; Greece invasion, 800; Rome-Berlin Axis, 787; *illus.,* 713

Mutual Aid: A Factor in Evolution (Kropotkin), 476

Mythology, Greek, 12

N

Nagy, Imre, 853, 861-862

Nanking, Treaty of, 607

Nantes, Edict of, 175; revocation of, 237, 242

Naples, 267, 287, 302, 418, 423, 437-438, 509-510; Kingdom of, 42

Napoleon I, 21, 340, 416-418, 425; Continental system, 396-398; *coup d'état*, 385-386; early career, 383-385; domestic rule, 386-389; European wars, 389-402; Napoleonic Europe, *illus.,* 394-395; Russian campaign, 399-400; *illus.,* 384

Napoleon II (King of Rome), 396

Napoleon III, 436, 510, 526; *coup d'état,* 497; domestic policy, 498-499; foreign policy, 499-500, 529-530; *illus.,* 498

Napoleonic Wars, 384-386

Narva, battle of, 528

Nasser, Gamal Abdel, 861, 881-884

Natal, 603,604

National Association for the Advancement of Colored People, 897

National Insurance Act (England), 490

National Liberation Front (Vietnam), 870

National People's party (Germany), 719, 722, 726

National Workshops, 435, 465, 470

Nationalism: Arab, 777-778; Balkan, 635-636; colonial revolts, 623-624, 839-847; European revolutions, 424-425, 430-431, 433, 437-444, 509-511; Industrial Revolution, 448; Irish Home Rule, 493-494; Machiavelli, 48; Marxian theory, 473-474; Mussolini's use of, 716; Napoleon's impetus to, 384, 398, 401-420, 415; Protestantism, 148-149; Romantic protest, 408-409; in World War I, 630-632

Nationalist party, Chinese (*see* Kuomintang)

Nationalists, Germany (*see* National People's Party)

Navarino, battle of, 425

Navigation, Renaissance and, 108

Navigation Act of *1651,* 250

Navy: French, 233; growth of modern, 156-157; Portuguese, 206-207

Nazi party (Austria), 740-741

Nazi party (Germany) (*see also* Hitler, Adolf), 700, 721-722, 726-731

Neanderthal man (*see Homo neandertalensis*)

Near East: early civilization in, 5-8

Necker, Jacques, 366

Nefertiti, Queen, 7; *illus.,* 8

Negroes (*see also* Slavery), 620, 824, 885-886, 896-897

Nehru, Pandit, 819, 843, 879; *illus.,* 843

Nelson, Horatio, 385, 390

Nemours, Duke of, 430-431

Neo-Guelfs, 437-439

Neolithic age, 5

Neolithic revolution, 5

Nestorians, 199

Netherlands (*see also* Holland), 274, 285, 306, 376, 382-383, 393, 396, 418, 430-431, 454, 458, 481, 842, 900; Austrian, 189; revolt of, 163-164; Spanish, 189; united, 183

Neutrality: and Cold War, 818-819; Napoleon's Continental System, 396-397; World War I violations, 638-639

New Amsterdam, 217-256

New Deal, 765-768

New Economic Policy (NEP), 682-683, 686-687

New England, 218

New France, 219-220

New Guinea, 661, 808

New Harmony, 469; *illus.,* 469

New Hebrides, 808

New Lanark, 468-469

"New Model Army," 252

New Stone Age, 5

New Testament (*see* Bible)

New York, 217, 256

New Zealand, 622, 818, 895

Newcastle, Duke of, 283

Newfoundland, 199, 621

Newton, Sir Isaac, 260-261, 314-315 347

Next Million Years, The (Darwin), 574

Nibelungenlied, 409

Nicholas I (Russia), 427, 431, 444,

535, 549-551, 553-554, 556; *illus.,* 549
Nicholas II (Russia), 557, 559-560, 562, 637, 669-671
Nicholas V, Pope, 42
Niebuhr, Reinhold, 934
Niemoeller, Martin, 734
Nietzsche, Friedrich, 573, 589, 591, 919; *illus.,* 592
Niger, 885
Nigeria, 606, 889
Nightingale, Florence, 551
Nihilism, 555
Nikon, Patriarch, 64, 69
Nile Valley, 6-8
Nine-Power Treaty, 763-764, 772
Nirvana, 203
Nivelle, General Robert Georges, 649
Nixon, Richard, 863
Nkrumah, Kwame, 885-890
Noailles, Viscount of, 368-369
Nobel, Alfred, 482
Nobility: French, 361-366, 368-369; Russian, 334-335, 337-339
Nobles, in reign of Louis XIV 241
Noblesse de la robe, 241
Noblesse de l'épée, 241
Nominalism, 25-26
Normandy landings, 805-806
Normans: conquest of England, 28; in Sicily, 29
North America Act of *1867,* 621
North Africa, in World War II, 797-798, 803-804
North Atlantic Treaty Organization (NATO), 700, 818, 822, 826, 863, 894-895
North Briton, 344
North, Lord Frederick, 344-346, 620
Northern Society (Russia), 427
Northmen, 199; and Carolingian empire, 21; and Danegeld, 28; invasions of, 21; in North America, 6, 21
Norway, 418, 482, 795, 900
Noske, Gustav, 718
Not By Bread Alone (Dudintsev), 858
Notre Dame de Paris (Hugo), 409
Novgorod, 58
Novikov, Nicholas, 337-338
Noyades, 377
Nuri Sa'id, 883
Nyerere, Julius, 885
Nystadt, Treaty of, 296

O

Obrenovich, Milosh, 425
O'Connell, Daniel, 493
Octavian (*see* Augustus)
October Diploma (Austria), 536
October Manifesto (Russia), 560
Octobrists (Russia), 561
Odessa, 425
Offenbach, Jacques, 586
Oil, Middle Eastern, 777, 846, 883-884
Okinawa, 808, 877
Old Believers, 70, 292, 300
Old Church Slavonic, 65
"Old Pretender," 258

Old Stone Age, 5
Old Testament (*see* Bible)
Oldenburg, state of, 399-400
Ollivier, Emile, 500
Olmütz, humiliation of, 525
O'Neill, Hugh, 180
On Liberty (Mill), 464-465
On the Origin of Species by Means of Natural Selection (Darwin), 568-569, 572
On the Origin of the Inequality of Mankind (Rousseau), 324
"Open hearth," process, 450
Opium War, 607
Oprichniks, 62
Oprichnina, 62
Orange, House of, 183
Oration on the Dignity of Man, 90
Oratory of Divine Love, 140
Ordonnances, 28
Organization for European Economic Cooperation (OEEC), 826
Organization of American States, 891-894
Organization of Labor, The (Blanc), 470
Orgburo, 832
Orlando, Vittorio Emanuele, *illus.,* 657
Orleans, Duke of, 276, 284
Orozco, José, 848
Orthodox Church, 294, 329, 541-543, 554, 697
Osmanlis, 56-57
Ostermann, Count Andrei Ivanovich, 333-334, 340-341
Otto I (Germany), 21
Ottoman Empire (*see also* Turkey), 300-303, 393, 424-466, 543, 550-551
Ottoman state, 70-77; *map,* 75; Christians in, 70, 71, 74; decline of, 76; expansion of, 73-74; government of, 70-73; and Russia, 76-77
Ottoman Turks, 33, 56, 58
Outer Mongolia, 873
OVRA ("Vigilance Organization against Anti-Fascist Crimes"), 716
Owen, Robert, 468-470, 556
Owen, Wilfred, 649
Oxenstierna, Chancellor, 187

P

Painting (*see also* Art): Chinese, *illus.,* 205, 221; Coptic, *illus.,* 17; Dutch, *illus.,* 261; Italian Renaissance, 97; medieval, 32, *illus.,* 49; modern, 926-927, *illus.,* 927; nineteenth century, 580-583; northern Renaissance, 99-101; prehistoric, *illus.,* 3; Romantic era, 410-411, *illus.,* 412; Russian, 65
Pakistan, 842-843, 879-880, 895
Palazzo, 103, 104
Paleolithic Age, 4-5
Palestine, 646, 653, 660-661, 777-778, 822
Palladio, 103; *illus.,* 105
Palmerston, Lord, 492-509
Panama, 614
Panama Canal, 519, 614
Panama scandal, 504
Pan-German movement, 545

"Panopticon," 462-463
Pan-Slavism, 443, 540
Paoli, Pasquale, 383
Papacy: Babylonian Captivity of, 42; early history, 16; Great Schism, 42; Machiavelli, 47-48; late medieval, 42-43
Papal States, 42, 287, 418, 439, 478, 499, 511
Papen, Franz von, 729-730
Papineau, Louis Joseph, 620
Paradise Lost (Milton) 264
Paraguay, 894
Pareto, Vilfredo, 917-918
Paris: Commune of *1871,* 501-502; in French Revolution, 366-368; in revolution of *1848,* 435; in World War II , 797, 806
Paris, Peace of, *1763,* 308-309, 344
Paris, Peace of, *1856,* 551
Parlement of Paris, 364
Parliament, 244; development of, 27, 28-29; and James I, 249; Long, 251; after Restoration, 255; Rump, 253, 254; Tudor, 176-177
Parliament Act of *1911,* 486
Parliament Act of *1918,* 491
Parma, Duchy of, 431, 438
Parma, Duke of, 164
Parnell, Charles, 493
Parsons, Talcott, 916
Parthenopean Republic, 385
Particularism, 29: in Germany, 40; in Italy, 42
Partisans (Yugoslavia), in World War II, 836
Pascal, Blaise, 242, 268
Passarowitz, Treaty of, 302-303
Passing of the Great Race. The (Grant), 573
Pasternak, Boris, 858, 930
Pathet Lao, 871
Patkul, 294-295
Patton, General George, 806
Paul (Russia), 337-339, 385, 389-390
Paul, Prince (Yugoslavia), 743
Pavelich, Ante, 743-744
Pavia, battle of, 158
Pavlov, Ivan, 915-916; *illus.,* 915
Peace of Augsburg, 162
Peace of Ryswick, 235
Peace of Westphalia, 189, 192
Peasants (*see also* Serfs): in Austria, 329, 443; in China, 773; in France, 361-368, 435; in Hungary, 546; in Prussia, 289, 327; in Russia, tsarist, 336, 338, 557, 561-562; in Russia, Soviet, 668, 672, 677, 681-683, 687-689
Peel, Robert, 484, 487, 489-490
Penn, William, 217, 294
Pensées, 268
People's party (Germany), 719, 722, 726
People's Will (Russia), 556, 558
Perry, Commodore Matthew, 602; *illus.,* 615
Perón, Eva, 849
Perón, Juan, 849, 892
Persia (*see also* Iran), 634
Pestalozzi, Johann. 320
Pestel, Colonel, 327
Pétain, Marshal Philippe, 797-798
Peter I, the Great (Russia), 291-300, 302-303

Peter II (Russia), 332-333
Peter III (Russia), 307, 333-335, 341
Petrarch, Francesco, 86-87
Petrouchka (Stravinsky), 928
Philhellenic movement, 425-426
Philip II of Macedon, 10
Philip II (Spain), 162-166; *illus.,* 163; 275
Philip IV (Spain), *illus.,* 266
Philip IV, the Fair (France), 28
Philip V (Spain), 285-287, 301, 332
Philip the Good, Duke of Burgundy, 35
Philip of Hesse, 122
Philippine Islands, 212, 519, 614-615, 768, 802, 818, 838, 842, 877, 895, 897
Philippine Sea, battle of, 808
Philosophes, 313, 326, 348-349, 363, 369, 406-409, 461, 471, 932-934
"Philosophic Radicals" (*see* Utilitarians)
Philosophy (*see also specific schools, e.g.,* Stoicism): Descartes and, 261-262; eighteenth-century social, 348-349; existentialist, 919; Greeks and, 12-13; historical review, 932-934; medieval, 25-27; modern, 919-922, 930-932; nineteenth century, 588-591; of Romantic era, 413-414; Social Darwinist, 570-575
Philosophy of Poverty, The (Proudhon), 476
Physics, 315-316, 922-923
Physics and Politics (Bagehot), 592
Physiocrats, 317-318, 325-326, 329, 331, 348
Picasso, Pablo, 926-927
Piedmont, 393, 418, 437, 439, 443-444, 499, 508-509, 535
Pietism, 340, 349-350, 406
Pilgrim's Progress (Bunyan), 139
Pilsudski, Jozef, 699, 744
Pitt, William, 302, 307-309, 344
Pitt, William the Younger, 346
Pius II Pope, 42
Pius V, Pope, 144
Pius VII, Pope, 388
Pius IX, Pope, 438-439, 478
Pius XI, Pope, 511, 716
Pizarro, Francisco, 212
Plains of Abraham, battle of, 308
Plato, Renaissance revival of, 90
Platonic Academy, of Florence, 54
Platt Amendment, 615
Plehve, Vyacheslev, 559
Poincaré, Raymond, 758
Poland, 58, 59, 288, 300-303, 325, 440, 444, 527, 549-550; Congress of Vienna, 416-417; Fourteen Points, 655; Great Northern War, 294-295; Jews in, 66; Little Entente, 784; partitions of, 340-343, 383, 681; Pilsudski, *coup,* 699, 744; revolt of *1956,* 853, 861; revolution of *1830,* 431; Russia and, 66; satellite status, 835, 853, 861, 866; serfs in, 66; Upper Silesia, 720; Versailles settlement, 658-660; World War II, 702, 791-795
Police: in French Revolution, 377; in fascist Italy, 716; in Nazi Germany, 733; in U.S.S.R., 668-669, 677
Polignac, Prince of, 429

Polis, 10, 11
Polish Succession, War of the, 302-303, 340-341
Political thought: anarchist, 476-477; and American Revolution, 347-348; Burke, 415; élitist and anti-rationalist theories, 591-603; Enlightenment and, 322-326; Hegel's influence, 413-414; historical determinism, 573-575; and Industrial Revolution, 457; Locke, 314; Marxian, 473-475; J. S. Mill, 464-465; Mussolini, 714-715; nihilism, 555; Pareto, 917-918; racism, 572-573; Social Darwinist, 570-571; socialist utopian, 466-470; utilitarian ("Philosophic Radical"), 463
Politiques, 175
Polo, Marco, 6, 199, *illus.,* 201
Polytheism, 8
Pombal, Marquis of, 331-332
Pomerania, 291
Pomestie, 60
Pompadour, Madame de, 306, 317; *illus.,* 284
Poniatowski, Stanislas, 341
Pope, Alexander, 322
Popolo d'Italia, Il, 710
Popular Front, 760-761
Popular party (Italy), 711
Population (*see also* Emigration; Immigration): Austrian Empire, 442; France, 362, 499; India, 879; Industrial Revolution and, 455; Malthusian theory, 460-462; nineteenth-century world, 623; Prussia, 288, 327; Russia, 555-556
Port Arthur, 558-559
Portrait of the Artist as a Young Man (Joyce), 925
Portsmouth, Treaty of, 559
Portugal, 38, 331, 423, 874, 900; empire of, 205, 208; explorations of, 199-202
Positivists, 920
Potato War, 330
Potemkin villages, 343
Potsdam conference, 811
Pozharsky, Dmitri, 63
Pragmatic Sanction, 287, 304
Pragmatic sanction of Bourges of *1438,* 173
Prague, Peace of, 528
Praise of Folly, 91
Pravda, 674, 684
Predestination, 135-136
Preface to Politics (Lippmann), 918
Prehistoric man, 3-5; *illus.,* 3
Pressburg, Treaty of, 391
Prester John, 199
Pretoria Convention, 492
Prez, Josquin des, 105
Pride, Colonel, 253
"Pride's Purge," 253
Prikazy, 64, 68
"Primrose League," 487
Prince, The (Machiavelli), 46, 47, 326
Principles of Ethics (Spencer), 571
Principles of Political Economy, The (Mill), 464
Printing, invention of, 107-108
Professio Fidei Tridentina, 143
Progress of the Human Mind, The (Condorcet), 315

Proudhon, Pierre, 476-477
Protestantism (*see also* Protestant Reformation): capitalism and, 146-148; common beliefs, 132-133; in France, 173-174; Lutheranism, 118, 124-126; nationalism and, 148-149; place in history, 144-149
Protestant Reformation (*see also* Luther, Martin), 117-149; Peasants' Rebellion, 125-126
Prussia (*see also* Bismarck; Germany), 274, 288-291, 304, 341, 398-399, 510, 550-551; *1740-1795, map,* 289; Congress of Vienna, 416-417; European revolution, 431; Frederick the Great, 326-328; and French Revolution, 373, 376, 382-383; Napoleonic Wars, 384, 390-393; Potato War, 330; Revolution of *1848,* 439-441, 444
Psychology, 912-916, 925
Puerto Rico, 519, 614, 897-898
Pugachev, Emelyan Ivanovich, 336-337
Punic Wars, 13
Puritanism, 134, 136-137, 254
Puritans, 178-179, 248-249
Pushkin, Aleksandr Sergeyvich, 409
Pu-yi, Emperor, 772-773

Q

Quadrivium, 24
Quadruple Alliance, 418-419, 423
Quakers (*see also* Society of Friends), 347
Quebec Act, 346
Quemoy, 839, 867
Quesnay, François, 317
Quiet Don, The (Sholokov), 858

R

Rabelais, François, 89-90
Racine, Jean Baptiste, 316
Racism: in Nazi Germany, 731-732; Nietzsche and, 591-592; Social Darwinist view, 572-573
Radical-Socialists (France), 759-760
Radich, 743
Radischev, Alexander, 337-338
Railway Servants Act (Hungary), 542
Raleigh, Sir Walter, 217
Ranković, Aleksandr, 866
Rapallo, Treaty of, 698-699, 709
Rasputin, Gregory, 562, 669; *illus.,* 670
Rathenau, Walter, 720, 722
Raya, 70
Razin, Stenka, 64
Realism, 25-26
Reconstruction Finance Corporation 765-766
"Red Sunday," 599
Reflections on the Revolution in France (Burke), 382, 406, 415
Reflections on Violence (Sorel), 476

Reform Act of *1918,* 486
Reform Bill of *1832,* 484-485
Reform Bill of *1867,* 485-486
Reformation (*see* Protestant Reformation
Reign of Terror, 376-380
Reinach, Joseph, 504
Reinsurance Treaty, 633
Religion (*see also individual denominations*): ancient Near East, 7-8; Austria, 329; Austro-Hungarian minorities, 541-543; Bismarck and the Church, 530- 532; Darwinism 569-570; Deism, 320-322; evangelism, eighteenth century, 349-350; France, 380, 387-388, 428-429; Greece, 12; Great Britain 492; historicism, 920-922; imperialism and, 618; and Irish Home Rule, 492-493; Jews, 8; Nazi Germany, 734-735; *philosophes* and, 320-322; and philosophy, 934; prehistoric, 5; Prussia, 327; Renaissance, 110-113; Romantic movement, 407, 412-413; Russia, 292, 294, 340, 697
Religious Society of Friends (Quakers), 255-256
Remarque, Erich Maria, 649
Rembrandt, 183, 266; *illus.,* 267
Renaissance, 81-114; arts and, 92-106; in England, 181-182; in Italy, 43-48; literature of, 83-92; Platonic revival during, 90; science and, 106-110
Renner, Karl, 545-546
Reparations (German), 720, 723, 726-729, 758, 763
Republic of St. Mark, 45
Republican People's party (Turkey), 880
Rerum Novarum, 478-479
Resistance movement (French), 798, 812, 830
Restoration, English, 256-257
Reuchlin, John, 111
Reynaud, Paul, 797
Reynolds, Sir Joshua, 351-352; *illus.,* 351
Rhee, Syngman, 876
Rhineland, 659, 727, 780, 782
Rhodes, Cecil, 572, 603, 617-618; *illus.,* 617
Rhodes, fortress of, 73, 74
Rhodesia, 886
Ribbentrop, Joachim von, 727, 792
Ricardo, David, 460-462, 464-465
Ricci, Father Matthew, 207; *illus.,* 208
Richard III (England), 37
Richardson, Samuel, 350-351, 407.
Richelieu, Cardinal, 232-234, 284; *illus.,* 233
Riego, Colonel, 422-423
Riley, Bridget, *illus.,* 927
Rime of the Ancient Mariner (Coleridge), 408
Ring of the Nibelungen (Wagner), 586
Ripperda, 285
Rise of Silas Lapham (Howells), 576
Rite of Spring, The (Stravinsky), 928
Rivera, Diego, 578
Rivera, General Primo de, 736-737
Robespierre, Maximilien, 375-377, 379-380; *illus.,* 378

Robinson Crusoe (Defoe), 320
Robles, Gil, 737-738
Rockefeller, John D., 518
Roderick Random (Smollett), 350
Rodin, Auguste, 583
Roehm, Captain Ernst, 722, 731; *illus.,* 725
Roger-Ducos, 385
Roman Catholic Church, 19; Austria, 328-329, 535, 544-545; Belgium, 430; Bismarck and, 530-532; Darwinism and, 569; Dreyfus case, 505, 507; Eastern Orthodox, 57; education, 24-27; France, 360-361, 388, 759; French Revolution, 368-371, 380; Great Britain, 484, 492; Hungary, 546; Industrial Revolution, 477-479; Italy, 511, 716; Lateran Treaty, 716; Latin language, 15-16; Louis XIV, 242; medieval secularism, 54; Montesquieu on, 323; nation-state and, 27; Nazi Germany, 734; Ottoman Empire, 74; *philosophes'* attacks on, 320-322; Portugal, 331; Protestant Reformation, 117-149; Reformation in, 139-144; regular clergy, 24; Renaissance, 110-113; Renaissance reform proposals, 112-113; secular clergy, 24; Spain, 332, 422, 735-737
Roman Empire, 13-16; *map,* 15; basis of, 13-14; collapse of, 18-19; description of, 14
Roman Republic: Carthage and, 13; founding of, 13
Roman Republic (French), 385
Romanesque architecture, 30-31; *illus.,* 31
Romanov dynasty, 63
Romanov, Fedor, 291-292
Romanov, Ivan, 292
Romanov, Sophia, 292
Romanticism: in the fine arts, 410-412; in literature, 407-409; in music, 409-410; in philosophy, 413-414; in religion, 412-413; Romantic "style," 414
Rome, 287, 393, 510; civilization, 13-16; founding, 13; law, 15; Moscow as successor to, 60; sack of, in *1527,* 158; style of, 11-13
Rome, Treaty of, 900
Rommel, Field Marshal Erwin, 803
Romney, George, 352
Roon, Albrecht von, 526
Roosevelt, Franklin D., 765-768, 798, 801, 805-806, 810, 812-813; *illus.,* 811
Roosevelt, Theodore, 518-519; 559, 618; *illus.,* 613
Root and Branch Bill, 232
Rosenberg, Alfred, 722
Rosetta Stone, 385
Rossellini, Roberto, 831
Rossoni, 714
Rostow, W. W., 448
Rothschild, House of, 451
Rougemont, Denis de, 916
"Roundheads," 232
Rousseau, Jean Jacques, 317, 319-320, 323-325, 328, 349, 365, 375, 383, 406
Royal Academy (England), 351
Royal Society for Improving Natural Knowledge, 260

Royce, Josiah, 588
Rubens, Paul, 266
Ruhr, 720, 723-724, 726, 758, 784-785
Rumania (*see also* Moldavia; Wallachia), 541-542, 636, 638, 644, 653, 655, 660, 664, 702-703, 742, 744, 784, 804, 835, 866
Ruskin, John, 490, 594
Russell, Bertrand, 824
Russia (*after 1917 see* Union of Soviet Socialist Republics), 535-536, 543; agriculture, 551-553, 561-562; Alexander II's reforms, 551-553; anti-semitism, 557, 560; and Belgian independence, 431; Church, 64-65; civil liberties, 559-560; Congress of Vienna, 416-419; culture, 291, 298, 300; Crimean War, 492, 526, 550-551; Decembrist revolt, 426-427; development of Muscovite state, 58-70; domestic policies, *1881-1914,* 557-558; Dumas, *1906-1914,* 561-562; economy, 548, 557; education, 298, 550; eighteenth century, 273, 274, 291-300, 302-303, 306, 332-343; Enlightenment, 335-337; expansion, 65-69; expansion, in Siberia, 68; foreign policy, nineteenth century, 556-557; Greek independence, 424-425; and Hungarian *1848* revolt, 444; Imperial China and, 68; imperialism, 599; intellectual activity, 553-554; under Ivan the Terrible, 61-62; Kievan, 58-59; law, 336, 550, 553; literature, 576-577; medieval and early modern, *map,* 67; Napoleonic Wars, 385, 388-393, 399-400; Nicholas I, 549, 551; nobles, 60-61; Ottoman Empire, 76-77; and Poland, 66, 383, 431, 527; Quadruple Alliance. 423; revolution of *1905,* 559-561; revolutionary thought, 555-558; Russo-Japanese War, 558-559; serfs in, 60-61; Tartars and, 58-59; Time of Troubles, 63-63; Troppau Protocol, 423; Versailles settlement, 655-656, 658, 664; and West, 69-70; World War I, 628-629, 632-635, 637, 640-643; *zemski sobor* and, 63-64
Russian Orthodox Church, 57; schism in, 69-70
Russlan and Ludmilla (Glinka), 410
Russo-Japanese War, 558-559, 616, 634
Russo-Turkish Wars, 341, 343
Ruthenia, 660, 742
Ryswick, Peace of, 235

S

Saar Basin, 658-659
Sadowa, battle of, 528
St. Albertus Magnus, 26
St. Bartholomew's Day, 173
St. Basil Cathedral, Moscow, *illus.,* 65
St. Bernard, 26
St. Francis Xavier, 222
St. Germain, Treaty of, 739

St. Helena, 401
St. Joan of Arc, 28
St. John of the Cross, 170
St. Louis (see Louis IX)
St. Mark, Republic of, 45
St. Paul, 144-145, 146, 155, 158
St. Paul's Cathedral, London, *illus.,* 264
St. Peter's Basilica, Rome, 102-103, *illus.,* 104
St. Petersburg, 295, 297-298
Saint Simon, Count Claude Henri de, 457, 466-467, 470
St. Theresa of Avila, 170
St. Thomas Aquinas, 26
St. Thomas More, 130
Sakhalin Island, 559, 616
Salammbô (Flaubert), 576
Samoa, 614, 661
Samsonov, General, 642
Sand River Convention, 603
Sansom, Sir George, 616
San Stefano, Treaty of, 556
Santo Domingo, 390
Saragat, Giuseppe, 831
Saratoga, battle of, 346
Sardinia, 287, 906
Sargent, John Singer, 580
Sartre, Jean Paul, 919
Sassoon, Siegfried, 649
Saudi Arabia, 777, 846, 884
Savonarola, 112-113
Savoy, 787
Saxony, 306, 416-417, 528
Schacht, Hjalmar, 725
Scharnhorst, General Gerhard Johann David von, 399
Schleicher, General Kurt von, 727, 729-731
Schleswig-Holstein, 527-528
Schlieffen Plan, 640-641
Schönbrunn, Treaty of, 398
Schopenhauer, Arthur, 589
Schubert, Franz. 410
Schuman Plan, 826
Schuman, Robert, 503, 826
Schuschnigg, Chancellor, 740-741, 788
Schutzbund (Austria), 740
Schwarzenberg, Prince Felix, 443-444
Schroeder, Baron Kurt von, 730
Science (see also Inventions), 315, 316, 856, 922-924; ancient Near East and, 6; Dutch contributions, 183; Greece and, 11, 13; rediscovery of ancient, 26; Renaissance, 106-110; seventeenth century and, 259-262
Science and Sanity (Korzybski), 920
Scott, Sir Walter, 409
Sculpture: Egyptian, *illus.,* 8; Greek, *illus.,* 11; medieval, 30-32, *illus.,* 21; modern, *illus.,* 929; nineteenth century, 583; Renaissance, 101-102, *illus.,* 45, 102, 103
Sebastopol, 343, 551
Second International, 475
Securities and Exchange Commission, 766
Sedan, battle of, 500-501, 530
Selim I, Sultan, 73, 74
Sepoy Rebellion (India), 607-608
"September massacres," 374
Serbia: Balkan wars, 635-636; independence movement, 424-425;

World War I, 627-628, 635-637, 644, 646, 655; Yugoslavia, 742-743
Serfdom (see also Peasantry), 23; in Austria, 328-330, 443; Black Death and, 53; Decembrist revolt, 427; end of, 53; in France, 362; French abolition, 369; in Poland, 66, 325; in Prussia, 289; Prussian abolition, 399; in Russia, 60-61, 64, 297-299, 334-336, 338-339, 427, 548; Russian abolition, 551-553
Servetus, 132
Service, Robert W., 580
Seurat, Georges, *illus.,* 580
Seventy, Council of, 44
Seven Years' War, 284, 304-309, 341 344
Sèvres, Treaty of, 660
Sewing machine, 450-452
Sforza family, 43
Sforza, Ludovico, Il Moro, 43, 94, 95
Shaftesbury, Lord, 460
Shakespeare, William 182
Shastri, Lal Bahadur, 879
Shaw, George Bernard, 577, 589; *illus.,* 578
Sheik-ul-Islam, 73, 74
Shelepin, Alexander, 873
Shelley, Percy B., 407, 413
Shintoism, 770
Shipping, late medieval, 50-52
Sholokov, Michael, 858
Shostakovich, Dmitri, 930
Shuisky, 62, 63
Siam (see Thailand)
Siberia, 334, 679; Russian expansion in, 68
Sic et Non (Abelard), 26
Sicily, 437, 509-510, 804, 906
Siegfried Line, 793, 796
Siemens, Sir William, 450
Siéyès, Abbé Emmanuel, 365-366, 385-386
Silesia, 304, 306, 326, 538
Silone, Ignazio, 831
Simon, Jules, 502
Simplicissimus, 188
Singapore, 842
Singer, Isaac, 450
Sinn Fein, 755
Sinyavsky, Andrei, 860
Sixtus IV, Pope, 42
Skoda armament works, 538
Slavery 201, 223; Asiento agreement, 277; in British colonies, 606; French abolition, 379; under Ottoman Empire, 70-72; U.S. Civil War, 516
Slovakia, 660, 742
Slovenia, 660
Smith, Adam, 318, 461, 465
Smith, Alfred E., 762
Smith, John, 217
Smollett, Tobias, 350-351
Smoot-Hawley Tariff, 763
Social classes: growth of bourgeoisie, 54; late medieval, 53-54; Protestant Reformation and, 127-128; Rome and, 14; in Russia, 60-61
Social Contract, The (Rousseau), 324-325, 375
Social Credit party (Canada), 899
Social Darwinism, 570-575, 617
Social Democratic party (Austria), 545-546, 739-740

Social Democratic party (Germany), 532-534, 700, 718-719, 726, 831, 902-903
Social Democratic party (Hungary), 742
Social Democrats (Russia), 558-559, 561-562, 669-670, 672-673
Social Revolutionaries (Russia), 558, 561-562, 669-670, 672, 675-676, 679-681
Social Security Act of *1935* (U.S.), 766
Socialism: Austrian Social Democrats, 545; British Labor party platform, 753; British welfare measures, 495-496; and French *1848* revolution, 433-435; French movement, Third Republic, 758-759; German Social Democrats, 532-534; and Industrial Revolution, 448; Marxian, 471-475; Paris Commune of *1871,* 501-502; in Republican Spain, 736-737; Russian nineteenth century movement, 556, 558; utopian, 466-470
Socialist party (Italy), 710-712, 906
Socialist party (France), 759-760
Socialist Realism, On (Tertz), 860
Society of Friends, 255-256
Society of Jesus, 140-141, 320, 322, 327, 331-332, 413, 422, 428
Socinus, 132
Sociology, 916-918
Soekarno, President, 877-878
Solferino, battle of, 509
Solomon Islands, 808
Solzhenitsyn, 859
Sorel, Georges, 476, 589, 714
Sorrows of Young Werther (Goethe), 407, 410
Soubise, Prince de, 361
South America, 212-216
South Sea Bubble, 276-278, 281-282
Southeast Asia Treaty Organization (SEATO), 842, 895
Southern Society (Russia), 427
Southwest Africa (German), 761
Souvanna Phouma, 870
Soviets: *1905* revolution, 559-561; *1917* revolution, 670-674
Spahis, 72
Spain, 482, 529, 716; absolutism and, 166-168; under Charles V, 158-162; Civil War, 701, 736-738, 787; economy, present day, 906; economy in Renaissance, 168-169; in eighteenth century, 275, 285-287, 303-304, 309, 331, 346; empire of, 212-216; expansion of, 208-216; under Ferdinand and Isabella, 38-40; and French Revolution, 376, 382-383; Monroe Doctrine, 423-424; and Napoleonic Wars, 393; style of, 38, 170-171; wars of Philip II, 162-166; revolution of *1820,* 422-423; Spanish-American War, 613-614
Spanish Armada, 165; *illus.,* 165
Spanish Inquisition. 39
Spanish Netherlands (see Netherlands)
Spanish Succession, War of the, 236, 277, 290
Sparta, 10
Spencer, Herbert, 277, 290

Spengler, Oswald, 921
Spenser, Edmund, 182
Speransky, Michael, 339, 550
"Spinning jenny," 280, 448-449
Spinoza, Baruch, 183
Spirit of the Laws, The (Montesquieu), 322-323, 336, 347
Spiritual Exercises, 140
Stained glass, 32
Stalin, Joseph: and China, 774, 816; Cold War policies, 816; and comintern, 699-700; death and succession, 839, 852-853; domestic policies, 696-698; intellectual life under, 832-833; Poland partition, 795; purges, 692-694; Trotsky and, 675-676, 683-687; World War II, 805-806; Yugoslav revisionism, 836-837; *illus.,* 684
Stalingrad (Volgograd), 803-804
Stamboliisky, Aleksandr, 744
Stamp Act of *1765,* 345
Star Chamber, 37
Statute of Westminster, 621, 756-757
Stavisky case, 759; *illus.,* 760
Steam engine, 280, 448
Steel, Bessemer process, 450
Stein, Baron vom und zum, 399
Stephenson, George, 450
Stevenson, Adlai E., 823, 864
Stimson, Henry L., 785
Stolypin, Peter, 561-562
Strauss, Johann, 586
Stravinsky, Igor, 928-929
Streltsy, 292, 294
Stresemann, Gustav, 719, 726, 782
Strike, right to, 458 (*see also* Le Chapelier Law)
Stroganov family, 68
Stroganov, Michael, 338
Strossmayer, Bishop, 542-543
Study of History, A (Toynbee), 921
Stupid Nineteenth Century, The (Daudet), 594
Sturm und Drang, 407
Style, *defined,* 11
Subinfeudation, 22
Sudan, 492
Suez Canal, 384, 467, 492, 605
Suez crisis, 881-883
Suffrage: in Austro-Hungarian Empire, 538, 546-547; British Reform Bills, 457-458, 484-486, 754; Chartism, 492; in France, 386, 428-430, 434-435; and French Revolution, 365, 371, 374-376, 381; in Germany, 440, 526, 528-529, 719; in Italy, 508, 714-715; in Japan, Imperial, 616; in Poland, *1815,* 431; in Russia, 553, 560-562; Russian Constitution of *1936,* 694; Spanish Constitution of *1812,* 422
Sugar Act of *1764,* 344-345
Suleiman the Magnificent, 74
Summa contra Gentiles, 26
Summa Theologica, 26
Sumner, William Graham, 593
Sun Yat-sen, 699, 772, 774
Suvorov, General Aleksandr, 385
Suzerain, 22
Swammerdam, Jan, 183
Sweden, 273, 285, 288, 291, 294-296, 331, 393, 418, 458, 482, 819, 900; expansion of, 217; Thirty Years' War and, 185-188

Switzerland, 35, 385, 393, 418, 481-482, 819, 900
Syllabus of Errors, 478, 530
Synge, John, 494
Syria, 660-661, 777, 844, 881-883

T

Table Talk, 123
Tables Turned, The (Wordsworth), 408
Tadjikistan, 695
Taiwan, 817, 819
Talleyrand, 416-417, 429
Tamerlane, 57
Tanganyika, 661 (*see also* German East Africa)
Tannenberg, battle of, 642
Tarawa, 808
Tartars, 56, 58, 59; Cossacks and, 66; Kazan, 68
Tashkent Conference, 873
Tasmania, 620
Teheran Conference, 805, 810
Tempest, 225
Ten, Council of, 46
Tennessee Valley Authority, 766
"Tennis-Court Oath," 366
Tennyson, Alfred, 579-580
Tertz, Abram (*see* Sinyavsky, Andrei)
Test Act, 484
Test Act of *1672,* 256
Tetzel, J., 119, 120
Thailand, 803, 842, 871, 895
Thaw, The (Ehrenberg), 758
Thebes, 10
Theocracy, 138
Theotokopouli, Domenico, 170
Thiers, Adolphe, 429, 434, 502
Thirty-Nine Articles, 134, 178
Thirty Years' War, 76, 184-192, 288; *illus.,* 156 187
Thyssen, Fritz, 728
Tibet, 634, 867
Tilden, Samuel J., 516
Tilsit agreement, 393, 399, 416
Tigris-Euphrates valley, 6
Tilly, Johann, Count of, 185, 186
Titian, 98-99
Timars, 72
Tinbergen, Nikolaas, 916
Tirpitz, Admiral Afred von, 534
Tisza, Coloman, 547
Tisza, Stephen, 547
Tito, 806, 836-837, 861, 867, 868; *illus.,* 837
Tocqueville, Alexis de, 401-402, 434-435, 594, 824
Togoland, 613, 661
Tokugawa family, 222
Tom Jones (Fielding), 350
Tools, early human, 4-5
Tordesillas, Treaty of, 200, 212
Tories, 257
Towns, medieval, 23-24
Townshend, Viscount, 278
Townshend duties, 345-346
Toynbee, Arnold, 921-922
Trade: British Commonwealth, 753; British Corn Laws, 489-490, 494-495; eighteenth-century European, 275, 281, 303-304, 308; German nineteenth century, 531, 533;

Hanseatic League and, 49-50; late medieval, 48-49; medieval, 24; and Napoleonic Wars, 390, 396-398; wool, 48, 50-51
Trafalgar, battle of, 390-391, 400
Transjordan, 778
Trans-Siberian railway, 557-558, 640
Transubstantiation, 127
Transvaal, 603-604, 633
Transylvania, 660, 741-742, 744, 866
Treaty of Cateau-Cambrésis, 159
Treaty of Lübeck, 185
Treaty of Tordesillas, 200 212
Treaty of Vervins, 175
Trent, 511, 632, 658-659
Trent, Council of, 142-145
Trial Begins, The (Tertz), 860
Trianon, Treaty of, 741
Trieste, 511, 658-659
Triple Alliance, 629, 633
Triple Entente, 629, 633-635
Tripoli, 512, 613, 635
Tristan and Isolde (Wagner), 586
Trivium, 24, 25
Troilus and Criseyde (Chaucer), 89
Trollope, Anthony, 576
Troppau Protocol, 423
Trotsky, Leon, 674, 699-700; civil war actions, 679, 681; exile; 692-693; NEP, 682-683; during revolution. 674-675; and Stalin, 683-687; *illus.,* 680, 686
Trujillo, Rafael, 891-892
Truman, Harry S., 807, 823, 839
Truman Doctrine, 836
Tsushima, battle of, 558
"Tudor absolutism," 37
Tudor, House of, 37
Tull, Jethro, 278
Tunisia, 610, 632, 787-788, 890
Turgenev, Ivan, 555, 576
Turgot, Anne Robert, 317-318, 360, 364
Turkey (*see also* Ottoman Empire), 329, 340-342, 393, 512, 526, 556, 633; Atatürk, 778; CENTO. 895; Cyprus question, 895; Great Northern War, 293-296; Menderes crisis, 880-881; Truman Doctrine, 836; World War I, 635-636, 638, 646, 655, 660
Turkmenistan, 695
Turner, Joseph Mallord, 581
Tuscany, 44, 287, 302, 330, 393, 438, 509
Twain, Mark, 594
Two Sicilies, Kingdom of, 423
Two Treatises of Government, The (Locke), 314
Tyranny of Words (Chase), 920

U

U-2 incident, 863
U Thant, 819
Ukraine, 66, 431, 643, 678-679, 695-696; during civil war, 679-681
Ulema, 73
Ulm, battle of, 391
Ulysses (Joyce), 925-926
Under Fire (Barbusse), 649

Uniates, 541
Union Act of *1840* (Canada), 621
Union of South Africa, 622, 661, 756, 875, 885-886
Union of Soviet Socialist Republics (*see also* Russia for *pre-1917*): agriculture, 832, 856-857; anti-semitism, 697, 833; atomic weapons, 863-864; bloc relations, 835-837, 853, 861-862, 866-867; Brest-Litovsk, 678-679; China split, 817, 867-869, 873-874; civil war 679-682; Cold War policies, 816-819, 835-836; collectivization and industrialization, 687-691; Constitution of *1936,* 694-696; Cuban crisis, 865; culture, 832-833, 858-860; economy, 677-679, 682, 832, 855-857; education, 696-697, 857-858; and Egypt, 861; Finland conquest, 795; Franco-Russian alliance, *1935,* 785; Germany and, 816-817, 836, 862-863; Greek civil war, 835; Korean War, 838-839; Marxism and, 703-704; Molotov-Ribbentrop pact, 701-702; nationalizations, 677; NEP, 682-683; *1953, map,* 834; Poland partition, 791-793, 795; purge trials, 692-694; religion, 697-698; revolution of *1917,* 669-677; *map,* 679; science in, 856; Southeast Asia policies, 837-839, 870-873; Stalin-Trotsky struggle, 683-687; Stalin's successors, 852-853; test ban agreement, 865; war communism, 677-679; in World War II, 701-703, 800-801, 803-804, 806-808, 810-813
Union of Utrecht, 164
Unionist party (England), 493-494
Unitarianism, 132
Unitarians, 546
United Arab Republic, 883
United Nations: China representation, 895; and Congo, 888-889; Cyprus crisis, 894; Indonesia and, 878; Israel-Arab conflict, 845, 881; and Iran, 835; Kashmir issue, 879-880; Korean War, 838-839; powers of, 818-819, 822, 896; and Union of South Africa, 885-886
United States: agricultural revolution, 454; Alliance for Progress, 891; China policy, 817, 895; civil rights, 896-897; Civil War, 513-516; Cold War policies, 816, 818-819, 863-864, 895; and Dominican Republic crisis, 764; economy, 517-519, 764-768, 895; Germany occupation, 816-817, 862-863; and Greek independence, 425; imperialism, 599, 613-615; Industrial Revolution, 449-452; isolationism, 762-763, 784-785; Japan occupation, 841; Kellogg-Briand pact, 763; Korean War, 838-839; Lend-Lease, 801; literature, 577-580; Louisiana Purchase, 390; Marshall Plan, 822-823; McCarthyism, 824-825; Mexico and, 499-500; Monroe Doctrine, 423-424, 519; Napoleonic Wars, 398; New Deal, 764-768; Nine Power Treaty, 763-764; "Open Door" policy, 602; Russian civil war, 679; Southeast Asia policy,

869-870, 878; Spanish-American War, 519-520; test ban agreement, 865; Truman Doctrine, 836; U-2 incident; 836; Versailles treaty, 664; Vietnam War, 870-872, War of Independence, 344-348; World War I, 638-639, 650; World War II, 801-808, 810-813
Universals, problem of, 25-26
Universities, development of, 25
Unkiar Skelessi, Treaty of, 550-551
Ustashi (Yugoslavia), 743-744
Usury, 24
Utilitarianism, 462-464, 488-489
Utraquists, 184
Utrecht: peace of, 273, 274, 285, 287, 290, 303; treaties of, 236-237; Union of, 164
Uzbekistan, 695

Vaihinger, Hans, 589
Valla, Lorenzo, 88-89
Valois, House of, 157-166
Van Gogh, Vincent, 583; *illus.,* 581
Vanderbilt, Cornelius, 519
Vanderlubbe, 730
Varennes, Louis XVI's flight, 372
Vassal, 22
Vatican City, 511; Lateran Treaty, 716
Vatican Council, *1870,* 531
Venetia, 438, 442, 509-510, 528
Venezuela, 892
Venice: diplomatic service, 155; *illus.,* 51; late medieval, 45-46; trade and, 50
Venizelos, 644
Vereeniging, Treaty of, 604
Vernacular languages, 83-84
Versailles, palace of, 243, *illus.,* 243; Diktat thesis, 782, 784; settlement, *map,* 659; Treaty of, 652-664, 718, 762-763
Vervins, Treaty of, 175
Vesalius, 108-109
Vespucci, Amerigo, 210
Vichy France, 797-798
Victor Emmanuel II (Italy), 509-510
Victor Emmanuel III (Italy), 512, 709-710, 712, 788
Victoria, Queen, 447, 484, 492, 607; *illus.,* 486
Vienna: siege of *1529,* 74; siege of *1683,* 76
Vienna, Congress of, 400, 415-419
Vienna Constituent Assembly, 443
Viet Cong, 870-871
Viet Minh, 842, 870
Vietnam, 842; Vietnam War, 869-874
Vikings (*see* Northmen)
Villeneuve, Admiral Pierre, 390-391
Vinci, Leonardo da, 42, 96-98, 107, *illus.,* 97, 107
Visconti family, 43
Vochina, 60
Volstead Act, 764, 766
Voltaire, 277, 284, 307, 317, 320-322, 326, 328, 335, 341; *illus.,* 321
Von Weber, Carl, 410
Voting (*see* Suffrage)
Vulgate, 92

W

Wagner, Richard, 586, 721
Wagram, battle of, 398
Wake Island, 802
Waldseemüller, Martin, 210
Waldteufel, Emil, 586
Wallachia, 425
Wallas, Graham, 918
Wallenstein, Albrecht Eusebius von, 185-187
Walpole, Horace, 352
Walpole, Robert, 278, 282, 303-304, 307-308
War of Devolution, 234
War of the Spanish Succession, 236
War of the Three Henries, 174
Warfare: early medieval, 19; feudalism and, 22-23; Renaissance developments, 108
Warren Commission Report, 898
Warren, Earl, 896, 898
Wars of the Roses, 29, 37
Warsaw, Grand Duchy of, 343, 393, 398-399
Warsaw Pact, 818, 853
Washington, George, 278, 305, 347
Waterloo, battle of, 401
Watt, James, 280
Watts, George Frederick, 580
Way of All Flesh, The (Butler), 578
Webb, Walter P., 227
Weber, Max, 146, 917
Wei-hai-wei, 771
Weisman, August, 569
Welf (*see* Guelf)
Wellington, Duke of, 400, 485
Wells, H G , 578
Wesley, Charles, 350
Wesley, John, 349-350, 406
West Indies, 220-221, 283, 297, 308, 390, 454, 606
Westphalia, Kingdom of (Napoleonic), 393
Westphalia, Peace of, 189, 192, 287
Weygand, General Maxim, 681, 797
Whig party (England), 257, 281-283, 303, 307-308, 486-487
Whistler, James M., 581
White Mountain, battle of, 185
White Terror, 381, 400
Whitman, Walt, 579
Whitney, Eli, 449-450, 452
Whittier, John Greenleaf, 470, 579
Wilkes, John, 344
William I, the Conqueror (England), 21, 28
William I (Netherlands), 430-431
William I (Prussia), 526-527, 529-530, 532
William II (Germany), 532-534, 613, 618, 630, 633, 635, 637
William III, of Orange (England), 234, 235
William IV (England), 485
William and Mary (England), 257-258
William the Silent, Prince of Orange, 164
Williams, Roger, 218
Wilson, Daniel, 504
Wilson, Harold, 901-902
Wilson, Woodrow, 519, 652, 655-656, 658-660, 664, 709, 762-763, 848; *illus.,* 657

Windischgrätz, Prince, 443
Witte, Count Sergei, 557-558, 559-561
Wittgenstein, Ludwig, 920
Wolsey, Cardinal, 129
Wool trade: enclosure and, 53; late medieval, 48, 50-51
Worcester, battle of, 250
Wordsworth, William, 407-408, 413, 464, 579
Working classes (*see* Classes, social; Labor)
World Court, 728
World War I: *map,* 645; Balkan front, 644-646; causes, 629-639; and colonies, 646; Dardanelles campaign, 643-644; eastern front, 641-643; German defeat, 717-718; Italian front, 643; morale, 649-650; naval battles, 646-647; peace settlement, 652-664; propaganda in, 651; Russia and, 669, 674-679; technological innovations, 647-649; western front, 640-641
World War II: Allied coalition, 810-813; Axis defeats, 803-807; Battle of Britain, 799-800; casualties, 815-816, European theaters, *map,* 796; fall of France, 797-798; Finnish campaign, 795; Greek campaign, 800; Japan conquests, 802-803; Lend-Lease, 802; Pacific theaters,

map, 809; "phony war" and blitzkrieg, 795-797; Polish campaign, 794-795; Russian invasion, 800-801; supply problems, 804; technological innovations, 794; unconditional surrender policy, 811; Yalta Conference, 806
Wrangel, Baron Peter N., 681
Wren, Christopher, 265
Writing, invention of, 5
Württemberg, 390, 528

Ximenes, Cardinal, 39

Yahweh, 8
Yalta Conference, 806, 812-813, 835
Yeats, W. B., 494
Yemen, 845, 883
Yeni cheri, 72
Yermak, Cossack leader, 69
Yevtushenko, Yevgeny, 858-859
York, House of, 37
Young, Arthur, 278, 343, 367

Young Man Luther (Erikson), 119
Young, Owen D., 727
Young Plan, 727, 729
Young Turks, 543
Ypsilanti, General, 425
Yuan Shih-k'ai, 772
Yudenich, General Nikolai, 680-681
Yugoslavia, 302, 653; Constitution of 1963, 866; economy, 837; revisionism, 861; Serb and Croat extremists, 742-744; Treaty of Rapallo, 709; Tito, 818, 836-837, 861-862, 867; Versailles settlement, 660-664; World War II, 703, 800

Z

Zambia (Northern Rhodesia), 885
Zashchenko, Mikhail, 833
Zemski sobor, 61, 63-64, 292
Zen Buddhism, 203
Zhdanov, Andrei, 832-833
Zhukov, Marshal Georgi, 852. 854
Ziamets, 72
Zinoviev, Grigori, 686, 693 698-699
Zinzendorf, Count, 349
Zionism (*see also* Israel), 545, 845
Zola, Emile, 505, 576-577
Zollverein, 439-440, 527

1867	British North America Act: Canada a dominion
	Ausgleich: Habsburg Empire reorganized as Dual Monarchy
1870	Franco-Prussian War: leading to completion of German and Italian unification and to Third French Republic
1882	Triple Alliance: Germany, Austria-Hungary, Italy
1891	*Rerum Novarum,* by Pope Leo XIII: basis of modern Catholic social philosophy
1898	*J'Accuse,* by Zola: agitation over Dreyfus in France
	Spanish-American War: United States emerging as world power
1899	Boer War in South Africa
1904	*Entente Cordiale* of Britain and France: Triple Entente in formation
1905	Japan victorious in Russo-Japanese War; partly successful revolution in Russia
1909	"Soak-the-rich" budget in Britain: step toward the welfare state
1911	Onset of prolonged revolution in China and Mexico
1914	(June 28) Assassination of Archduke Francis Ferdinand at Sarajevo: outbreak of First World War
1917	(March 8) Riots in Petrograd: beginning of Russian Revolution
1919	Postwar peace conference at Paris: Treaty of Versailles
1922	(October 30) Fascist "March" on Rome: Mussolini in power
1923	Turkey declared a republic: landmark in Atatürk's revolution
1925	Locarno agreements: brief era of "fulfillment" in Europe
1929	(October) "Crash" in Wall Street: beginning of Great Depression
1931	Japanese aggression in Manchuria: first step on road to World War II
	Statute of Westminster: "constitution" of British Commonwealth
1933	Hitler Chancellor of Germany: Nazi dictatorship
	Franklin D. Roosevelt President of United States: the New Deal
1936	Outbreak of Civil War in Spain